3301524564

STREET ATLAS

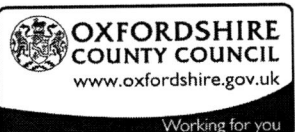

OXFORDSHIRE
COUNTY COUNCIL
www.oxfordshire.gov.uk

Working for you

GW00763801

Not For Loan

y, Dover,

nbridge Wells

www.philips-maps.co.uk
First published in 1989 by
Philip's, a division of
Octopus Publishing Group Ltd
www.octopusbooks.co.uk
2–4 Heron Quays, London E14 4JP
An Hachette UK Company
www.hachettelivre.co.uk

Second edition 2010
First impression 2010
KENBA

ISBN 978-1-84907-022-5 (spiral)

© Philip's 2010

Ordnance Survey®

This product includes mapping data licensed from Ordnance Survey® with the permission of the Controller of Her Majesty's Stationery Office. © Crown copyright 2010. All rights reserved. Licence number 100011710.

Speed camera data provided by **PocketGPSWorld.com Ltd**

Post Office is a trade mark of Post Office Ltd in the UK and other countries.

Printed by Toppan, China

X	Major administrative and Postcode boundaries
1	**Street maps** at 3½ inches to 1 mile
381	**Index** of towns, villages, streets, hospitals, industrial estates, railway stations, schools, shopping centres, universities and places of interest

Digital Data

The exceptionally high-quality mapping found in this atlas is available as digital data in TIFF format, which is easily convertible to other bitmapped (raster) image formats.

The index is also available in digital form as a standard database table. It contains all the details found in the printed index together with the National Grid reference for the map square in which each entry is named.

For further information and to discuss your requirements, please contact victoria.dawbarn@philips-maps.co.uk

Mobile safety cameras

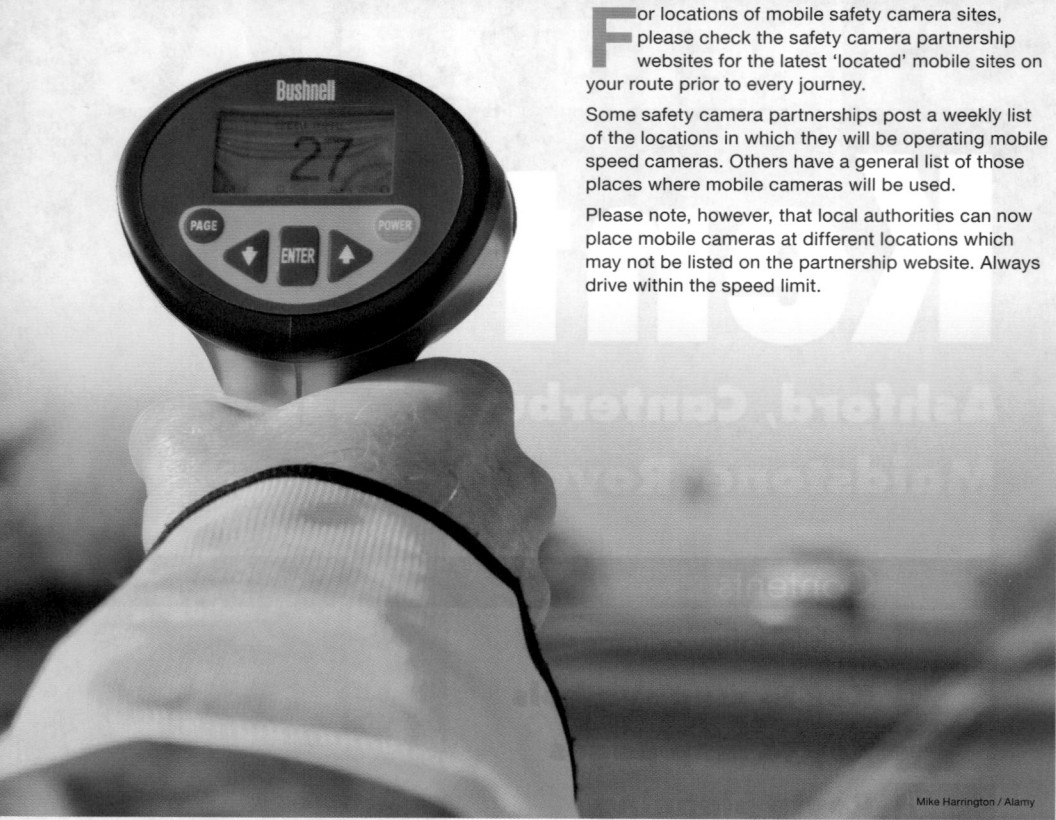

For locations of mobile safety camera sites, please check the safety camera partnership websites for the latest 'located' mobile sites on your route prior to every journey.

Some safety camera partnerships post a weekly list of the locations in which they will be operating mobile speed cameras. Others have a general list of those places where mobile cameras will be used.

Please note, however, that local authorities can now place mobile cameras at different locations which may not be listed on the partnership website. Always drive within the speed limit.

Mike Harrington / Alamy

Useful websites

Kent and Medway Safety Camera Partnership
www.kmscp.org

London Safety Camera Partnership
www.lscp.org.uk

Surrey Safety Camera Partnership
www.surrey-safecam.org

Sussex Safer Roads Partnership
www.sussexsaferroads.gov.uk

Further information
www.dvla.gov.uk
www.thinkroadsafety.gov.uk
www.dft.gov.uk
www.road-safe.org

Key to map symbols

Motorway with junction number (22)	
Primary route – dual/single carriageway	
A road – dual/single carriageway	
B road – dual/single carriageway	
Minor road – dual/single carriageway	
Other minor road – dual/single carriageway	
Road under construction	
Tunnel, covered road	
Speed cameras – single, multiple	
Rural track, private road or narrow road in urban area	
Gate or obstruction to traffic – restrictions may not apply at all times or to all vehicles	
Path, bridleway, byway open to all traffic, restricted byway	
Pedestrianised area	
BS22 Postcode boundaries	
County or unitary authority boundaries	
Railway with station	
Tunnel	
Railway under construction	
Metro station	
Private railway station	
Miniature railway	
Tramway, tramway under construction	
Tram stop, tram stop under construction	
Bus, coach station	

◆	Ambulance station
◆	Coastguard station
◆	Fire station
◆	Police station
✚	Accident and Emergency entrance to hospital
H	Hospital
+	Place of worship
i	Information centre – open all year
🛒 P	Shopping centre, parking
P&R PO	Park and Ride, Post Office
Ⓧ 🚐	Camping site, caravan site
▶ ✕	Golf course, picnic site
Church ROMAN FORT	Non-Roman antiquity, Roman antiquity
Univ	Important buildings, schools, colleges, universities and hospitals
	Woods, built-up area
River Medway	Water name
	River, weir
	Stream
	Canal, lock, tunnel
	Water
	Tidal water
58 ◀ 87 246	Adjoining page indicators and overlap bands – the colour of the arrow and band indicates the scale of the adjoining or overlapping page (see scale below)
	The dark grey border on the inside edge of some pages indicates that the mapping does not continue onto the adjacent page
	The small numbers around the edges of the maps identify the 1-kilometre National Grid lines

Abbreviations

Acad	Academy	Meml	Memorial
Allot Gdns	Allotments	Mon	Monument
Cemy	Cemetery	Mus	Museum
C Ctr	Civic centre	Obsy	Observatory
CH	Club house	Pal	Royal palace
Coll	College	PH	Public house
Crem	Crematorium	Recn Gd	Recreation ground
Ent	Enterprise		
Ex H	Exhibition hall	Resr	Reservoir
Ind Est	Industrial Estate	Ret Pk	Retail park
IRB Sta	Inshore rescue boat station	Sch	School
		Sh Ctr	Shopping centre
Inst	Institute	TH	Town hall / house
Ct	Law court	Trad Est	Trading estate
L Ctr	Leisure centre	Univ	University
LC	Level crossing	W Twr	Water tower
Liby	Library	Wks	Works
Mkt	Market	YH	Youth hostel

The map scale on the pages numbered in blue is 3½ inches to 1 mile
5.52 cm to 1 km • 1 : 18 103

0	¼ mile	½ mile	¾ mile	1 mile
0	250m	500m	750m	1km

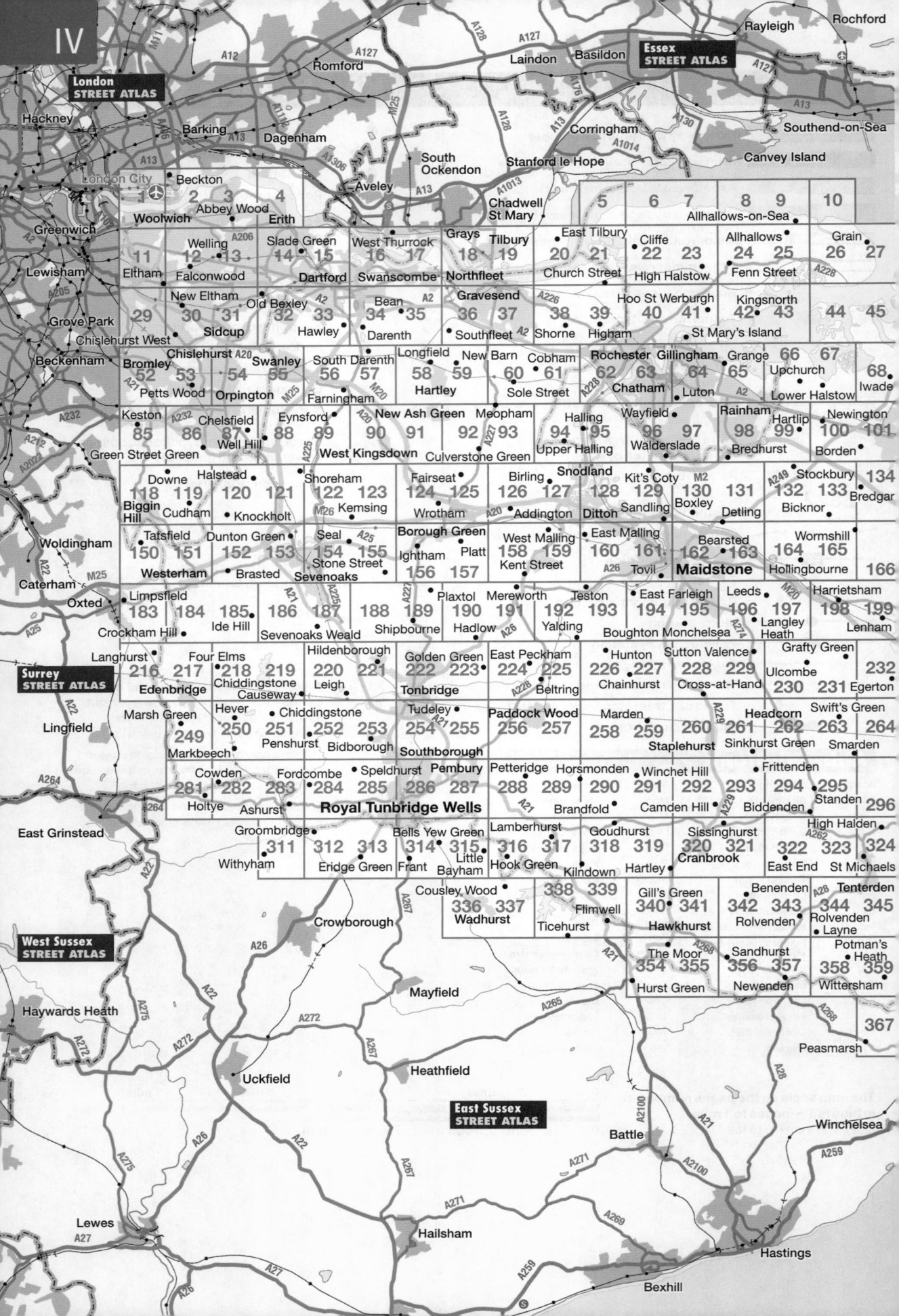

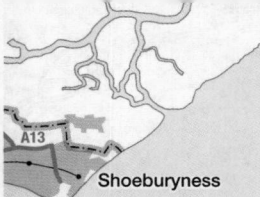

Shoeburyness

28

Sheerness

Minster
46 47 48 49 Warden
Rushenden Eastchurch Leysdown-on-Sea

Isle of Sheppey
69 70 71 72 73
Kemsley

Sittingbourne
102 103 104 105 106 107 108 109
Teynham Oare Graveney
Yorkletts

Herne Bay
74 75 76 77 78 79 80 81
Whitstable Broomfield
Seasalter South Street
Herne Common
110 111 112 113
Calcott Hersden Upstreet

Reculver
Birchington
St Nicholas at Wade Kent International
Sarre
Monkton Minster
114 115

Westgate-on-Sea Margate
50 51
Kingsgate
St Peter's
82 83 84
Manston Broadstairs
Ramsgate
116 117

135 Lynsted
136 137 Faversham
138 139 Hernhill
140 141 Blean 142 Sturry 143 Stodmarsh
144 145 Preston
146 147 148 149
Painter's Forstal Boughton Street Upper Harbledown Fordwich Wickhambreaux Ash Great Stonar
Sandwich

Doddington Eastling Sheldwich Selling
167 168 169 170 171 172 173 Canterbury
174 175 176 177 178 179 180 181 182
Throwley Old Wives Lees Nackington Littlebourne Staple Worth
Chartham Bridge Goodnestone Eastry

Warren Street
200 201 202 203 204 205 Chilham 206 207 Garlinge Green 208 209 Lower Hardres 210 211 Aylesham 212 213 Betteshanger 214 215 Deal
Molash Godmersham Petham Kingston Woolage Village Elvington Great Mongeham
Challock

Charing
233 234 235 Bilting 236 237 Crundale 240 241 Bossingham 242 243 Barham 244 245 Eythorne 246 247 Ringwould 248 Kingsdown
Westwell Wye 238 239 Waltham Stelling Minnis Denton Shepherdswell West Langdon
West Cliffe

Pluckley Hothfield Naccolt
265 266 267 268 269 Brook 270 271 Hastingleigh 272 273 North Elham 274 Selsted 275 276 277 Whitfield 278 279 West Cliffe 280 St Margaret's at Cliffe
Chambers' Green Ashford Lymbridge Green Elham Alkham Kearsney

Bethersden Daniel's Water
297 298 299 Willesborough 300 301 Brabourne Lees 302 303 Lyminge 304 305 Hawkinge Farthingloe 308 309 Dover 310
Stubb's Cross Mersham Sellindge Paddlesworth 306 307 Capel-le-Ferne
Kingsnorth Postling

Bromley Green Bliby
325 326 327 328 329 Aldington 330 331 Westenhanger 332 333 Folkestone 334 335
Woodchurch Bilsington Lympne Hythe Sandgate

Brook Street
346 347 Hamstreet Palmarsh
Appledore 348 349 350 351 352 353
Heath Wareharne Newchurch Burmarsh

Appledore Snargate Dymchurch
360 361 362 363 364 365 366
The Stocks Brenzett Ivychurch St Mary's Bay

Brookland New Romney
368 369 370 371 372 373
Iden Old Romney Greatstone-on-Sea

Rye
374 375 Lydd 376 Lade 377
Camber Lydd-on-Sea
378 379 380 Dungeness

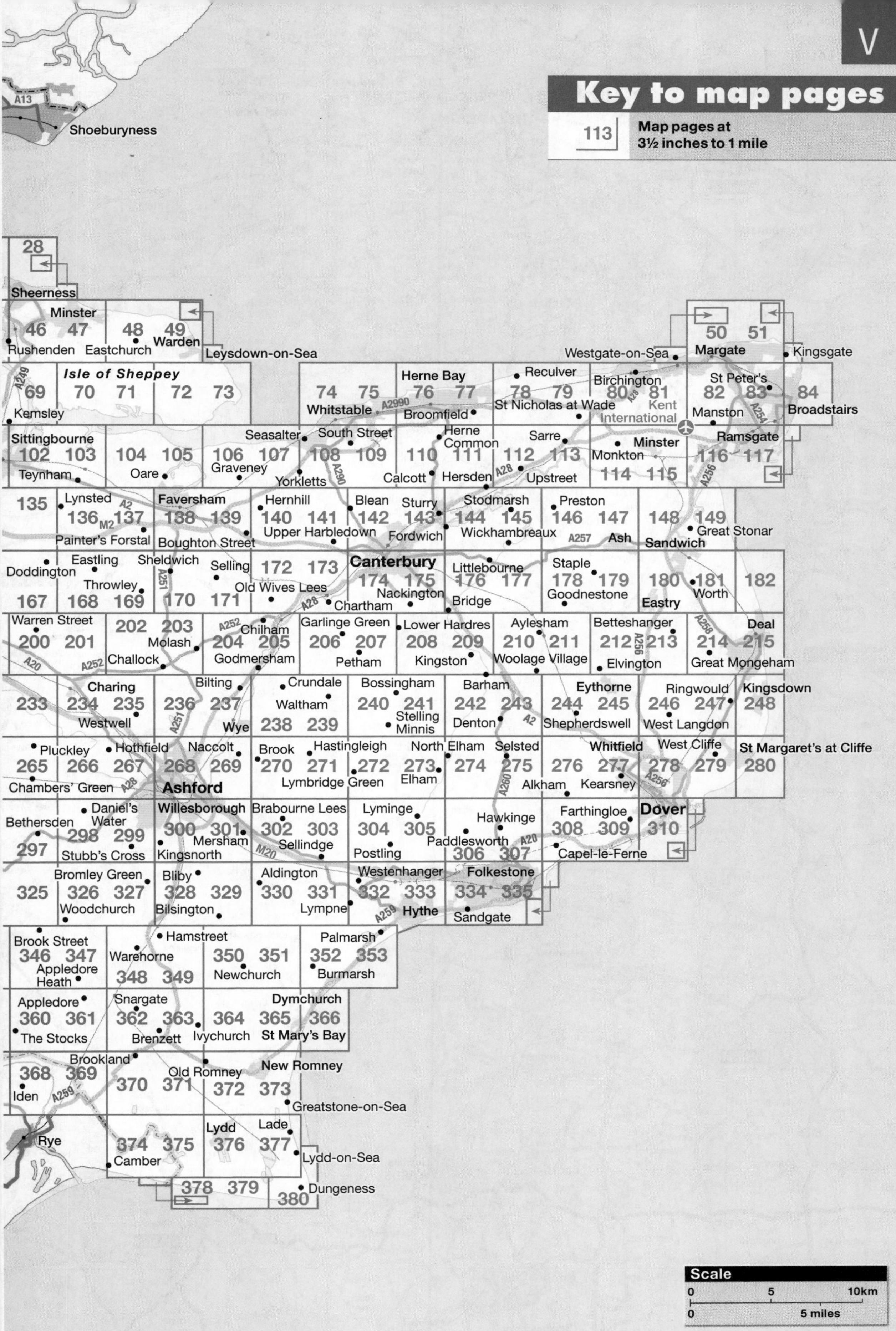

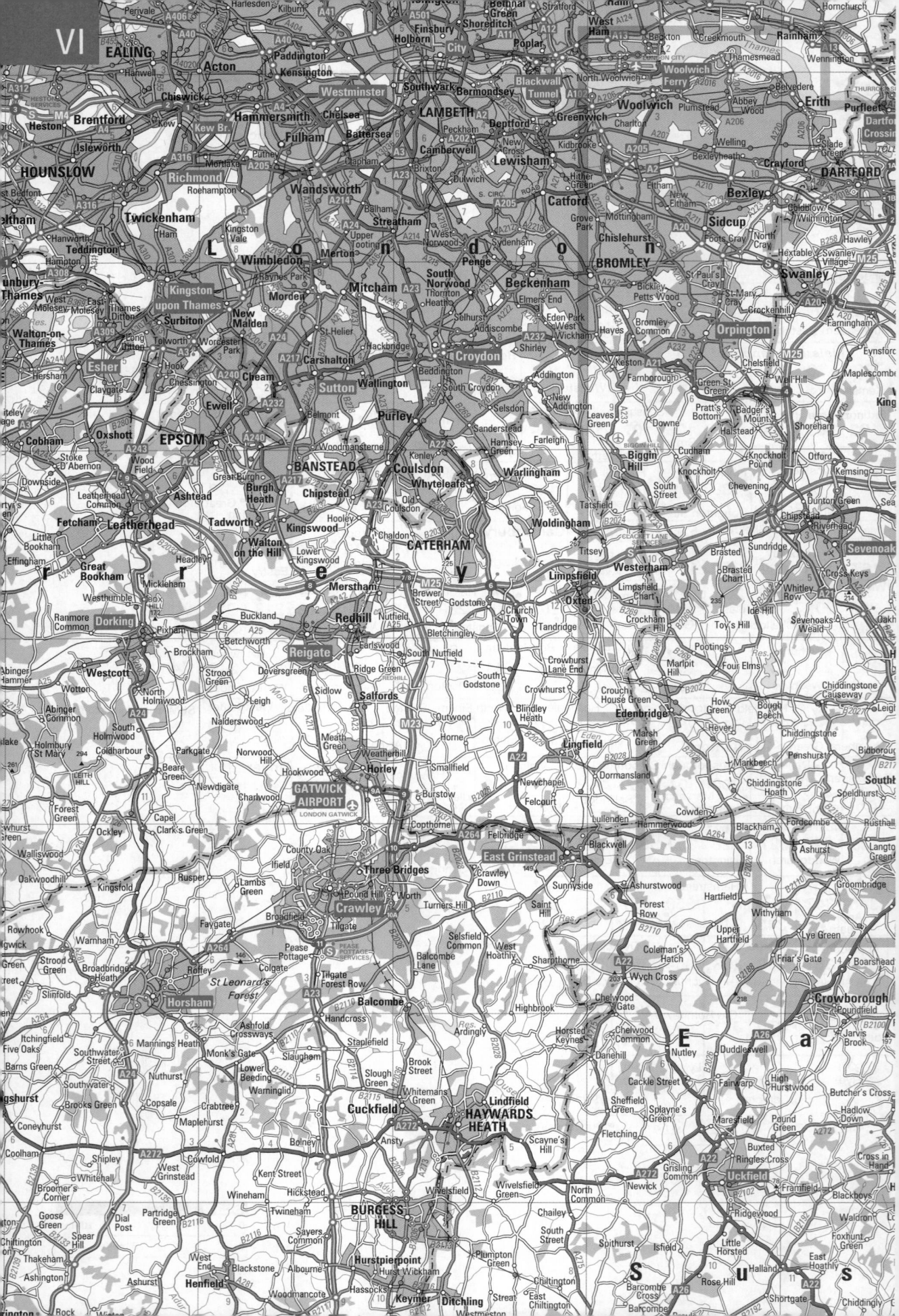

Scale

| 0 | 5 | 10km |
| 0 | | 5 miles |

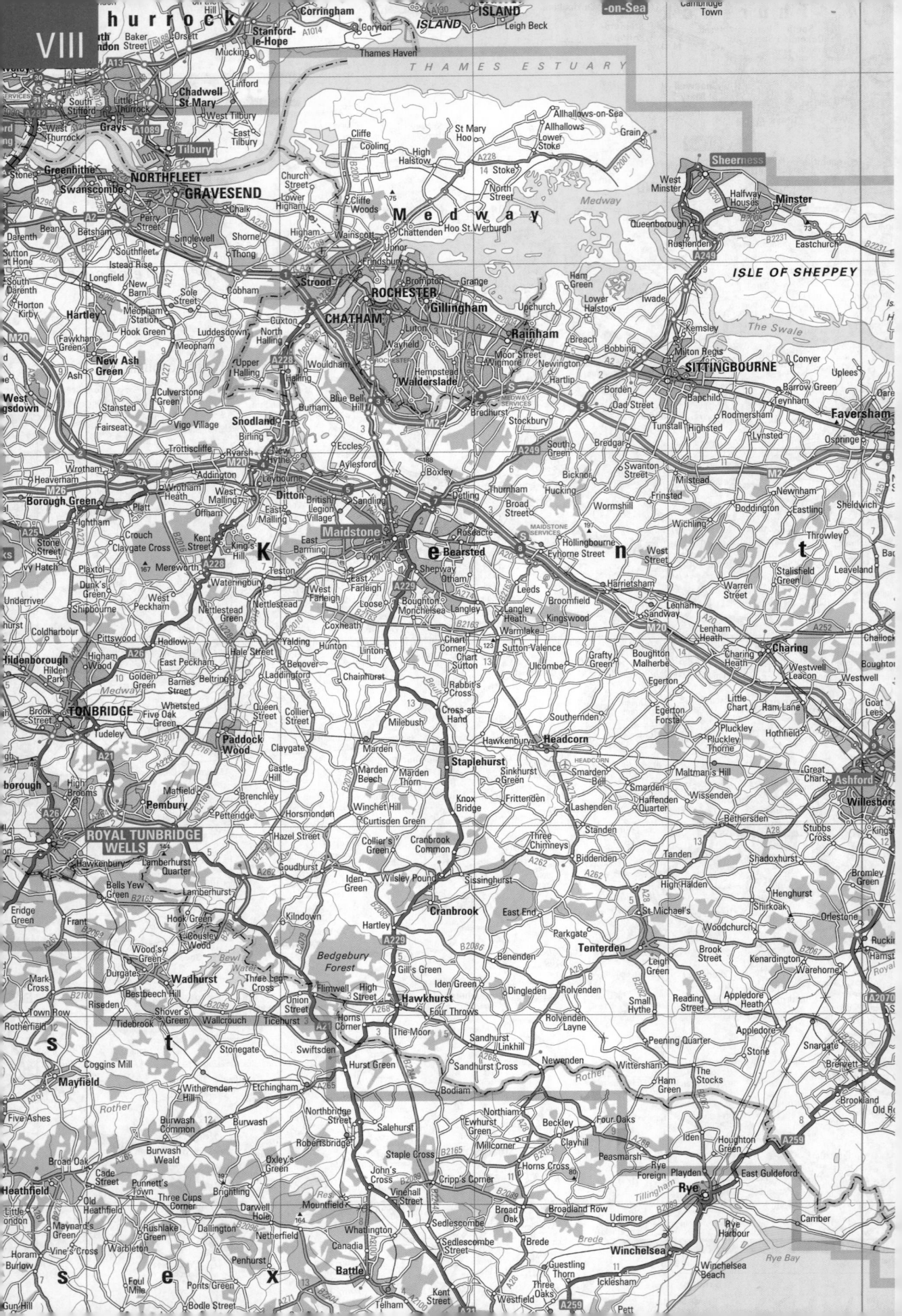

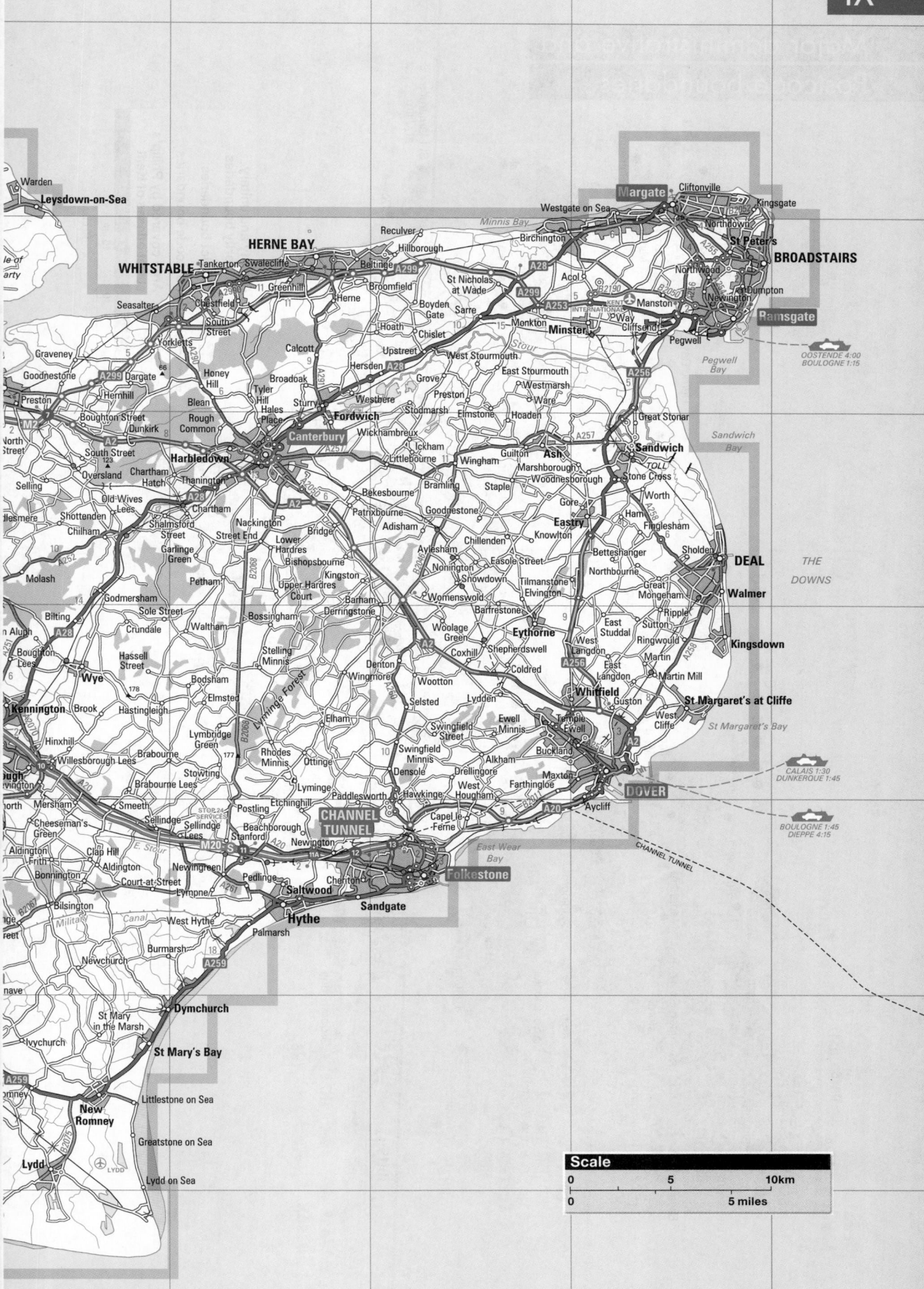

Major administrative and Postcode boundaries

Scale

0 5 10 15 km
0   5   10 miles

County and unitary authority boundaries
District boundaries
Postcode boundaries
Area covered by Philip's street atlases of Kent

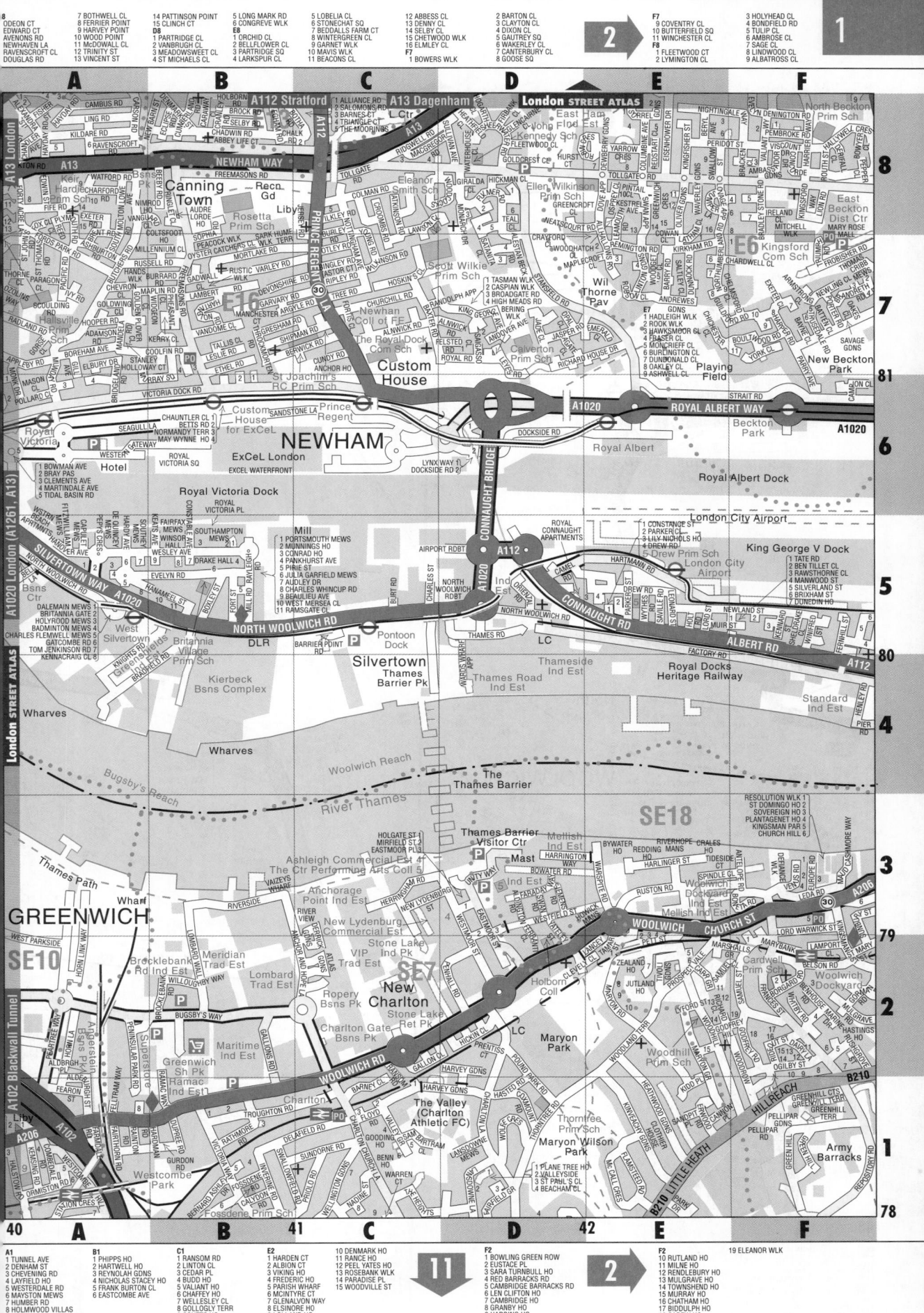

1

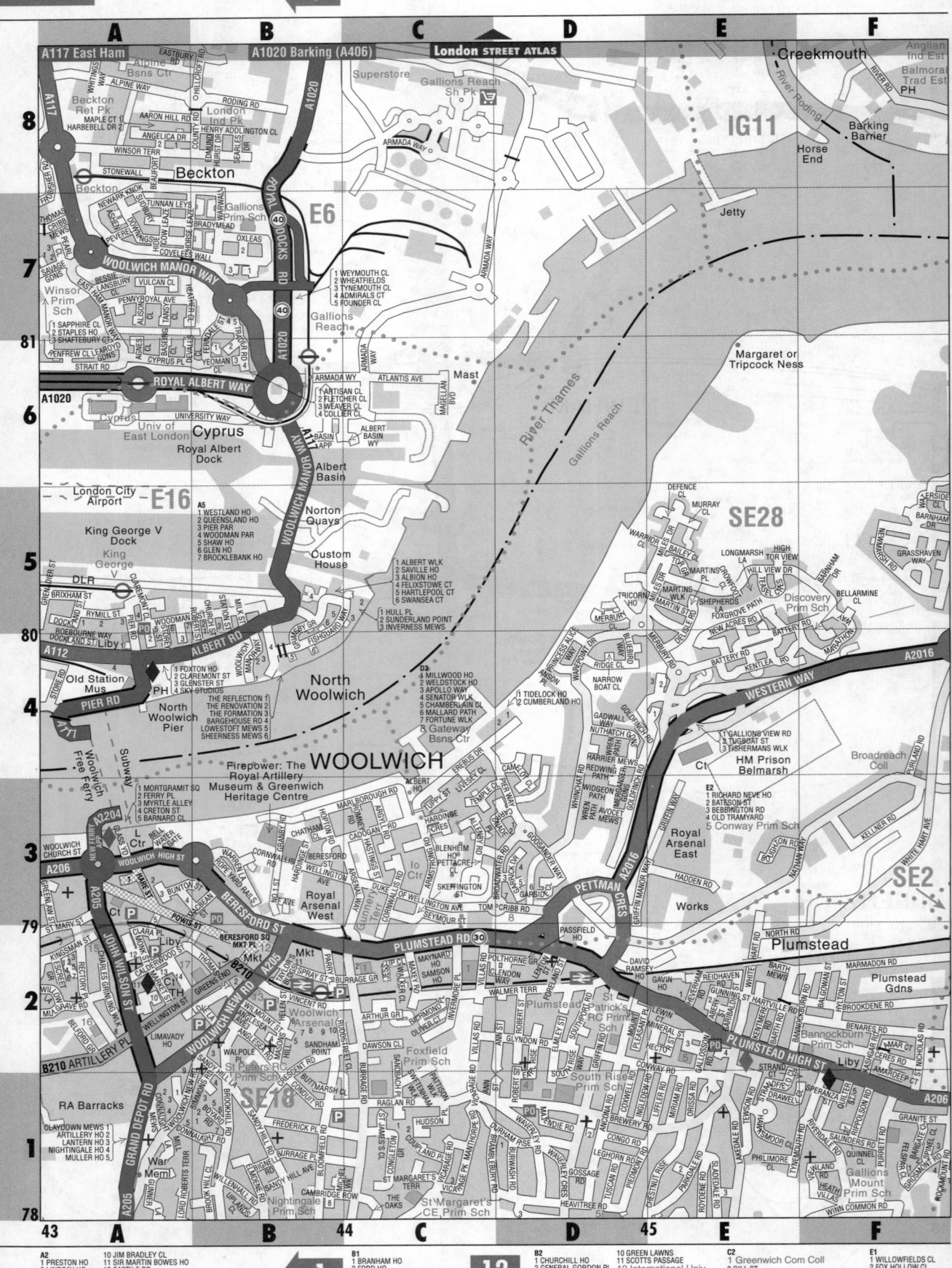

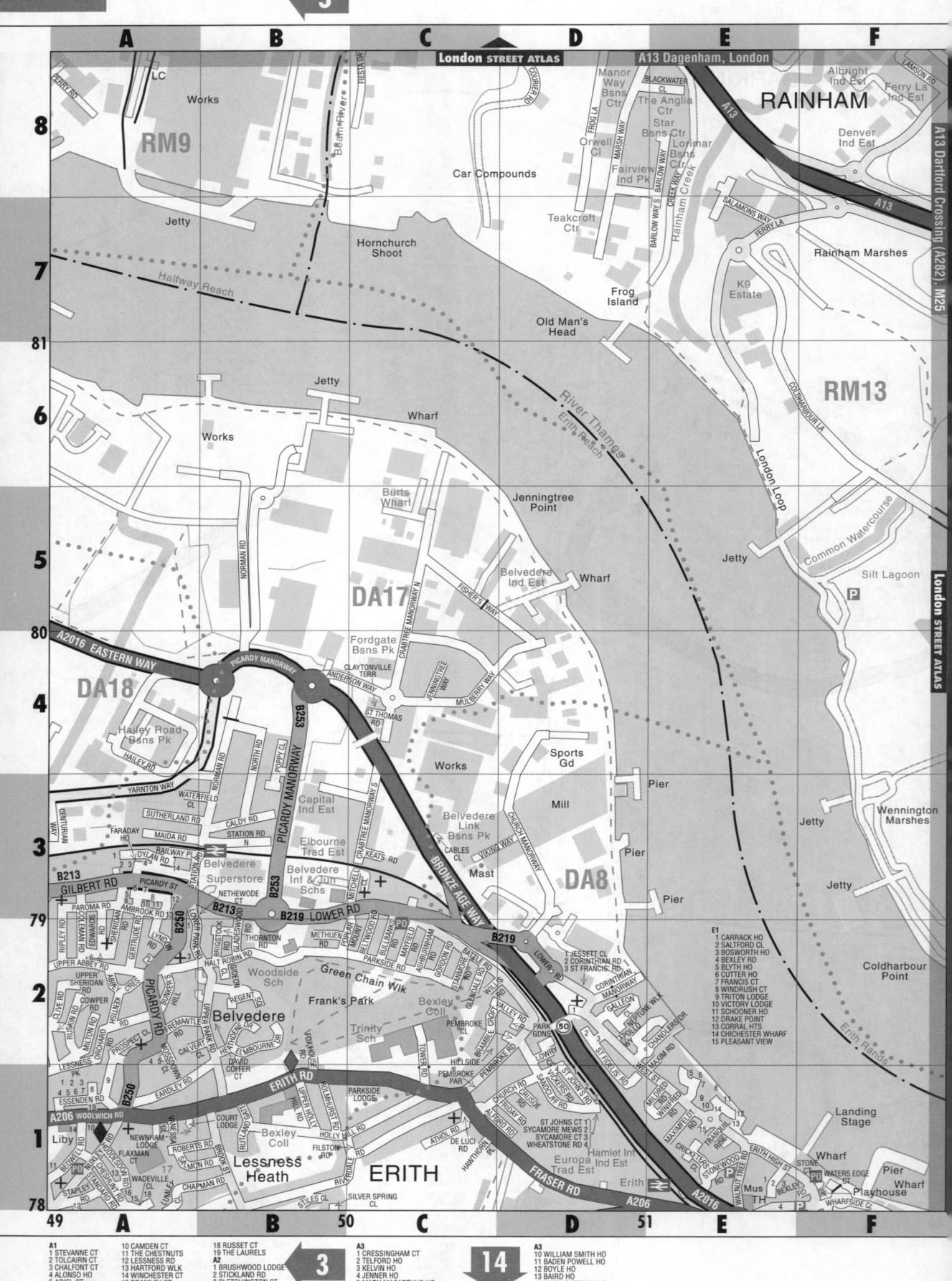

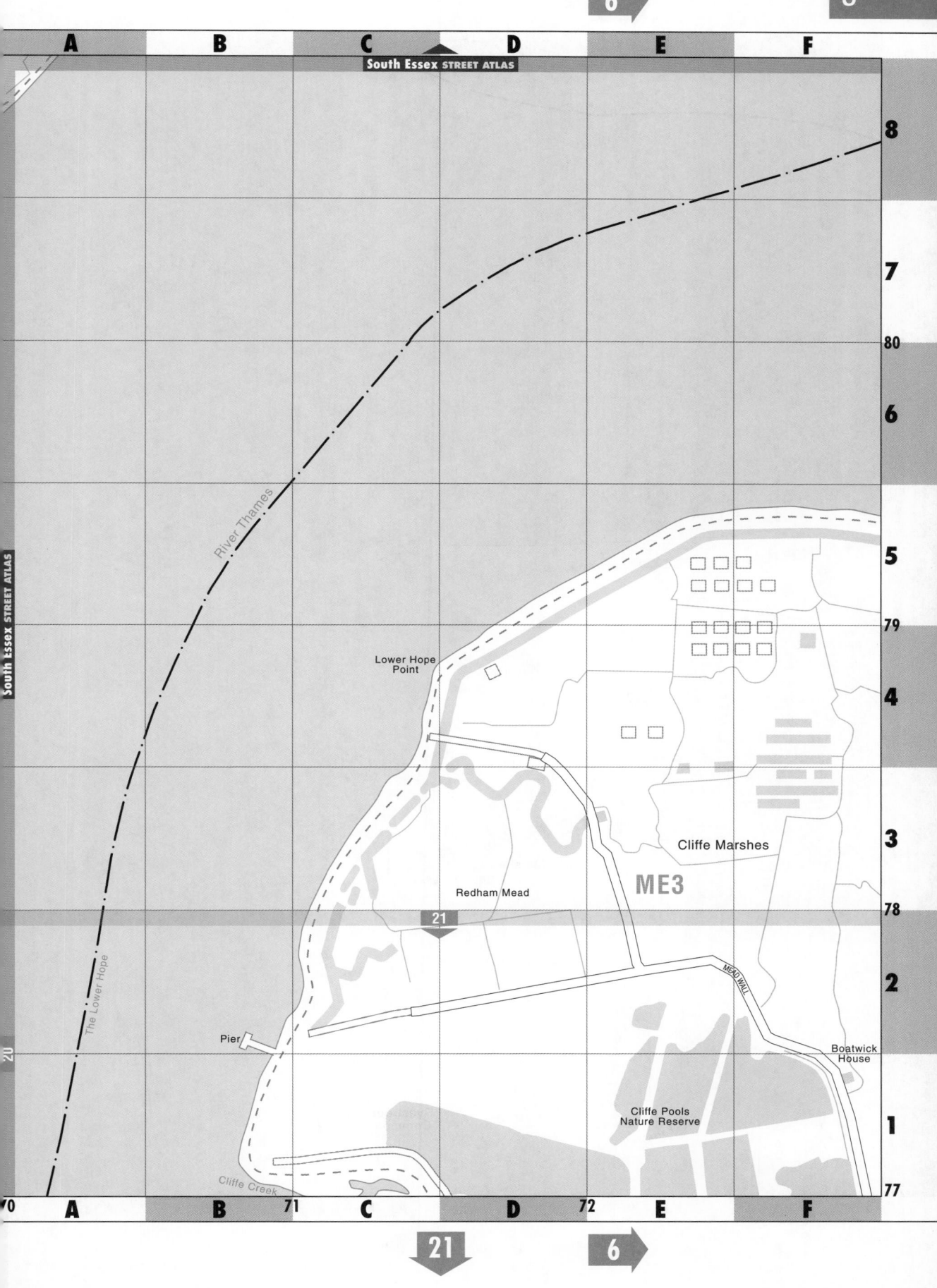

South Essex STREET ATLAS

South Essex STREET ATLAS

River Thames

Lower Hope
Point

The Lower Hope

Cliffe Marshes

ME3

Redham Mead

21

MEAD WALL

Boatwick
House

Pier

Cliffe Pools
Nature Reserve

Cliffe Creek

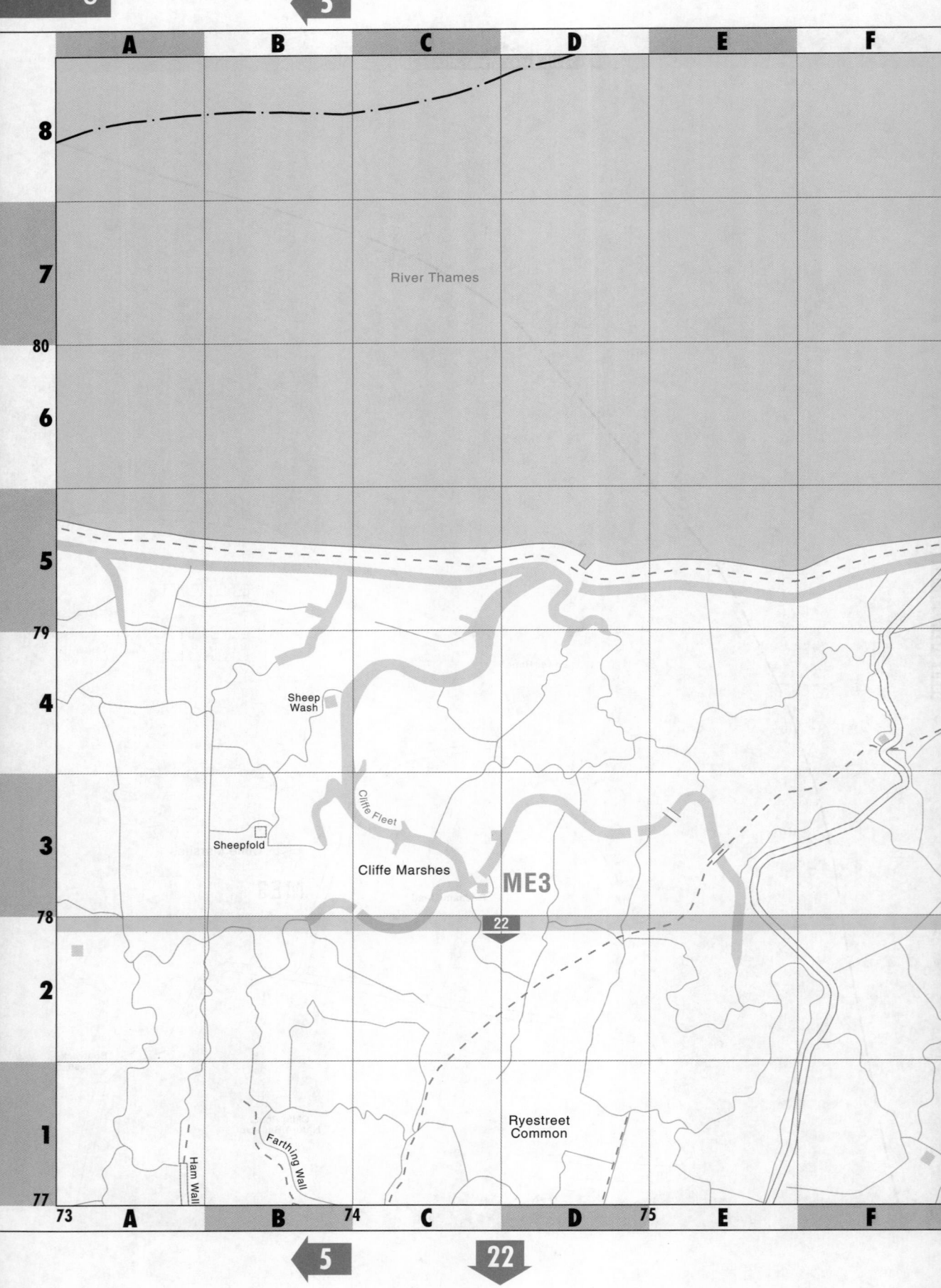

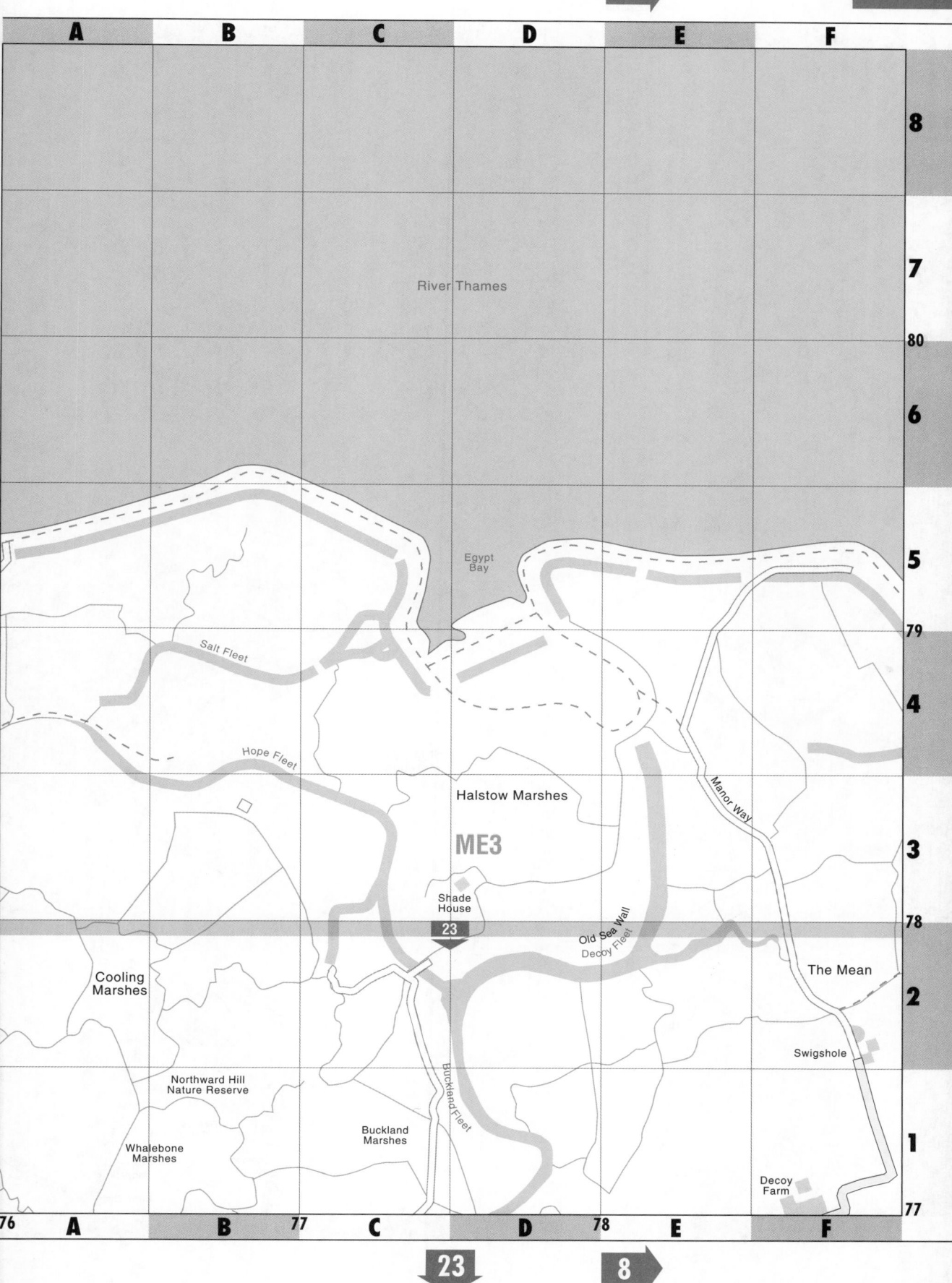

A   B   C   D   E   F

River Thames

8

7

80

6

Egypt
Bay

Salt Fleet

5

79

Hope Fleet

4

Halstow Marshes

Manor Way

ME3

3

Shade
House

Old Sea Wall
Decoy Fleet

78

The Mean

Cooling
Marshes

2

Swigshole

Northward Hill
Nature Reserve

Buckland
Marshes

Buckland Fleet

Whalebone
Marshes

1

Decoy
Farm

77

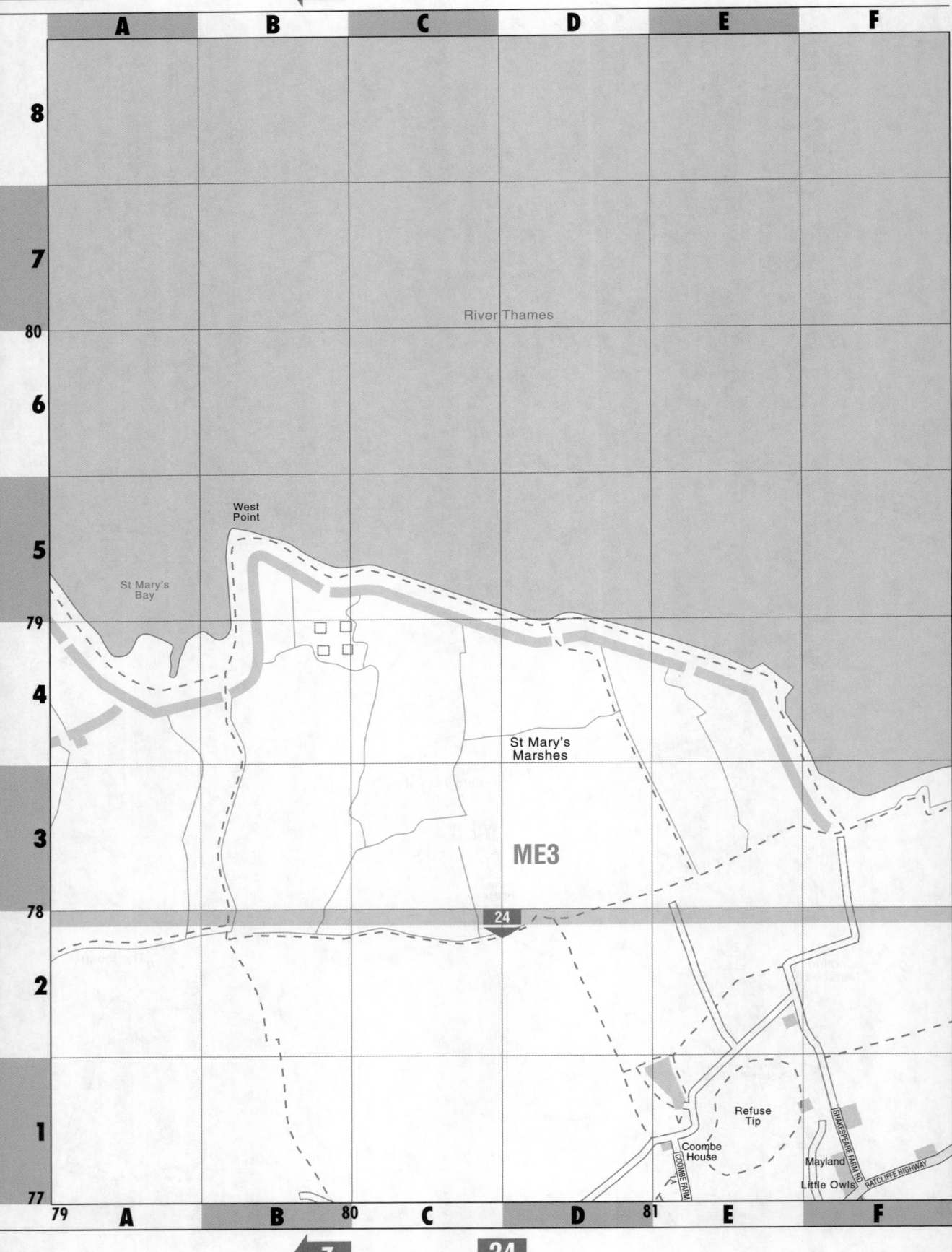

River Thames

West Point

St Mary's Bay

St Mary's Marshes

ME3

Refuse Tip

Coombe House

COOMBE FARM

SHAKESPEARE FARM RD

Mayland

Little Owls

RATCLIFFE HIGHWAY

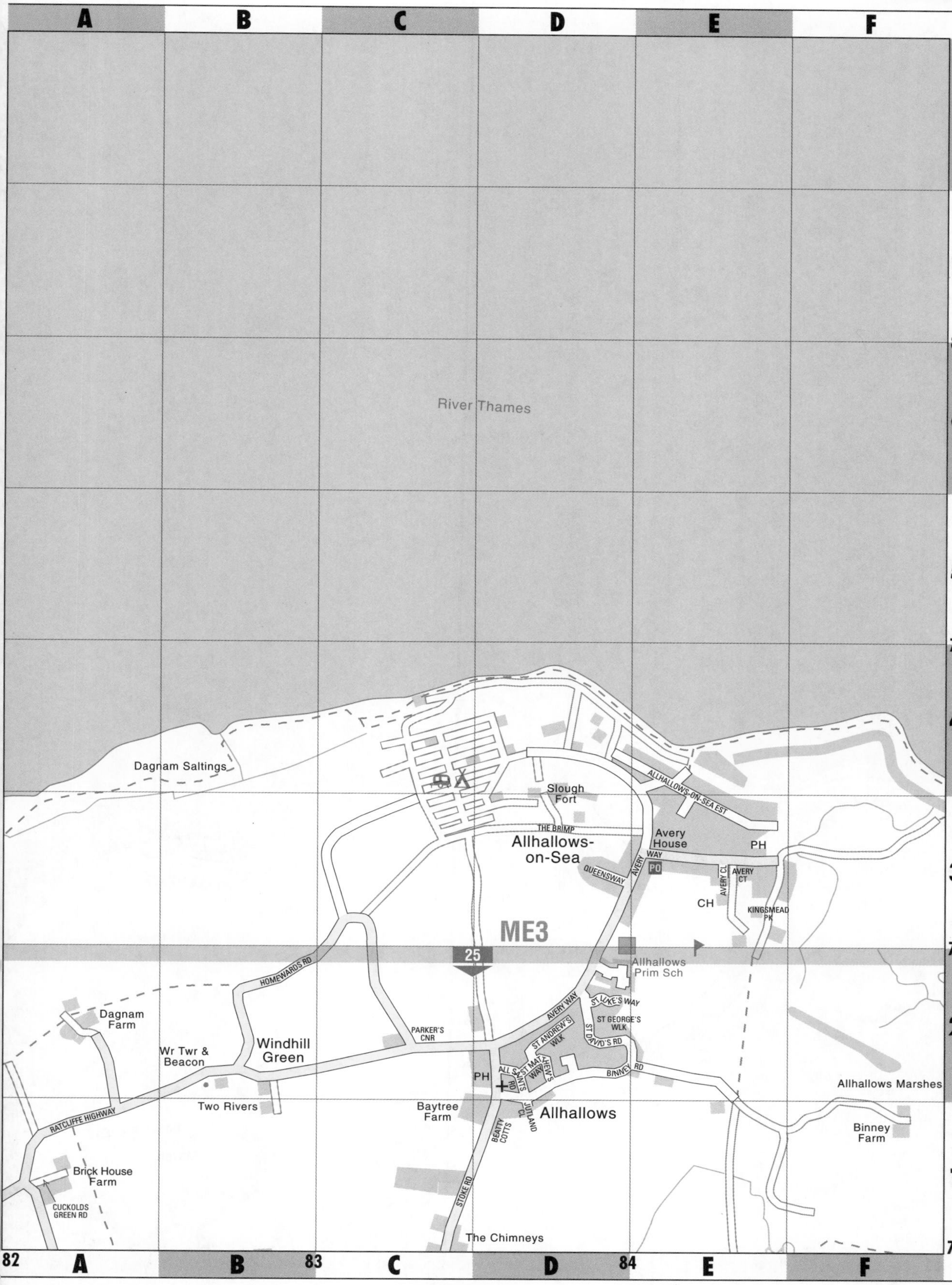

A B C D E F

8

7

80

River Thames

6

5

79

4

Dagnam Saltings

Slough Fort

THE BRIMP

Allhallows-
on-Sea

ALLHALLOWS-ON-SEA EST

Avery
House

PH

QUEENSWAY

AVERY WAY

PO

AVERY CL

AVERY CT

CH

KINGSMEAD PK

3

ME3

78

Allhallows
Prim Sch

25

HOMEWARDS RD

Dagnam
Farm

Wr Twr &
Beacon

Windhill
Green

PARKER'S
CNR

AVERY WAY

ST ANDREW'S WLK

ST LUKE'S WAY

ST GEORGE'S WLK

ST DAVID'S RD

2

Allhallows Marshes

ALL SAINTS RD

ST MARY'S WAY

AVERY'S WAY

BINNEY RD

Two Rivers

RATCLIFFE HIGHWAY

PH

Baytree
Farm

BEATTY COTTS

JUTLAND

Allhallows

Binney
Farm

Brick House
Farm

CUCKOLDS
GREEN RD

STOKE RD

The Chimneys

1

82 A B 83 C 84 D E F 77

A   B   C   D   E   F

8

7

80

6

River Thames

5

79

4

DANGER AREA

London Stone   Yantlet Beach

Cockleshell
Beach

3

North Level

DANGER AREA

Lees Marshes

78

26

ME3

2

Yantlet Creek

Buck's
Pounds

Allhallows
Marshes

DANGER AREA
Grain
Marsh

1

Wharf

WEST
LA

77

85   A   B   86   C   D   87   E   F

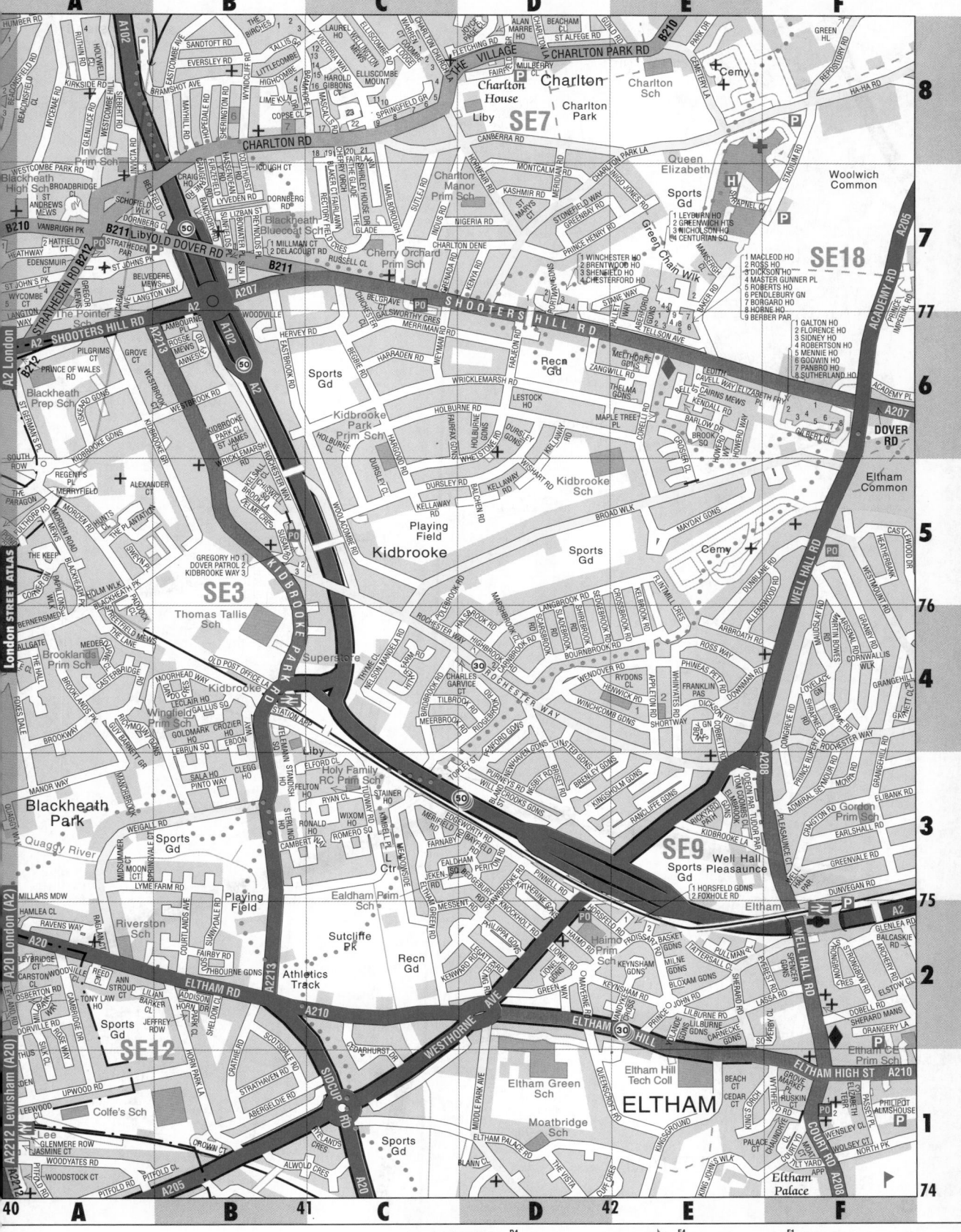

A7
1 MANDEVILLE CL
2 MARY LAWRENSON PL
3 WENTWORTH HO
4 BRADBURY CT
5 DUNSTABLE CT

A8
1 COLERAINE RD
2 HARDY RD
3 INGLESIDE GR
4 NETHERCOMBE HO

B8
1 CAPELLA HO
2 DUNCAN HO
3 COLLINGTON HO
4 JACKSON HO
5 TURNER HO

6 Sherington Prim Sch
7 Our Lady of Grace
RC Prim Sch

C8
1 WARREN WLK
2 THE WARREN
3 WILSON HO
4 PRIORY HO
5 MAR HO
6 LANGHORNE HO

1

12

7 GAMES HO
8 ERSKINE HO
9 DUCIE HO
10 DOWNE HO
11 BAYEUX HO
12 FELMA HO
13 MATTHEWS HO

14 NORRIS HO
15 KELLY HO
16 BRAMHOPE HO
17 EAST MASCALLS
18 BIRCH TREE HO
19 CHERRY TREE CT
20 ELM TREE CT

C8
21 CEDAR CT
22 LEILA PARNELL PL
23 MASCALLS CT

11

29

D4
1 ANNESMERE GDNS
2 CARNBROOK MS

12

E4
1 Henwick Prim Sch
2 St Thomas More
RC Prim Sch

F1
1 WEATHERSFIELD CT
2 PHILPOT PATH
3 Belcanto Theatre Acad

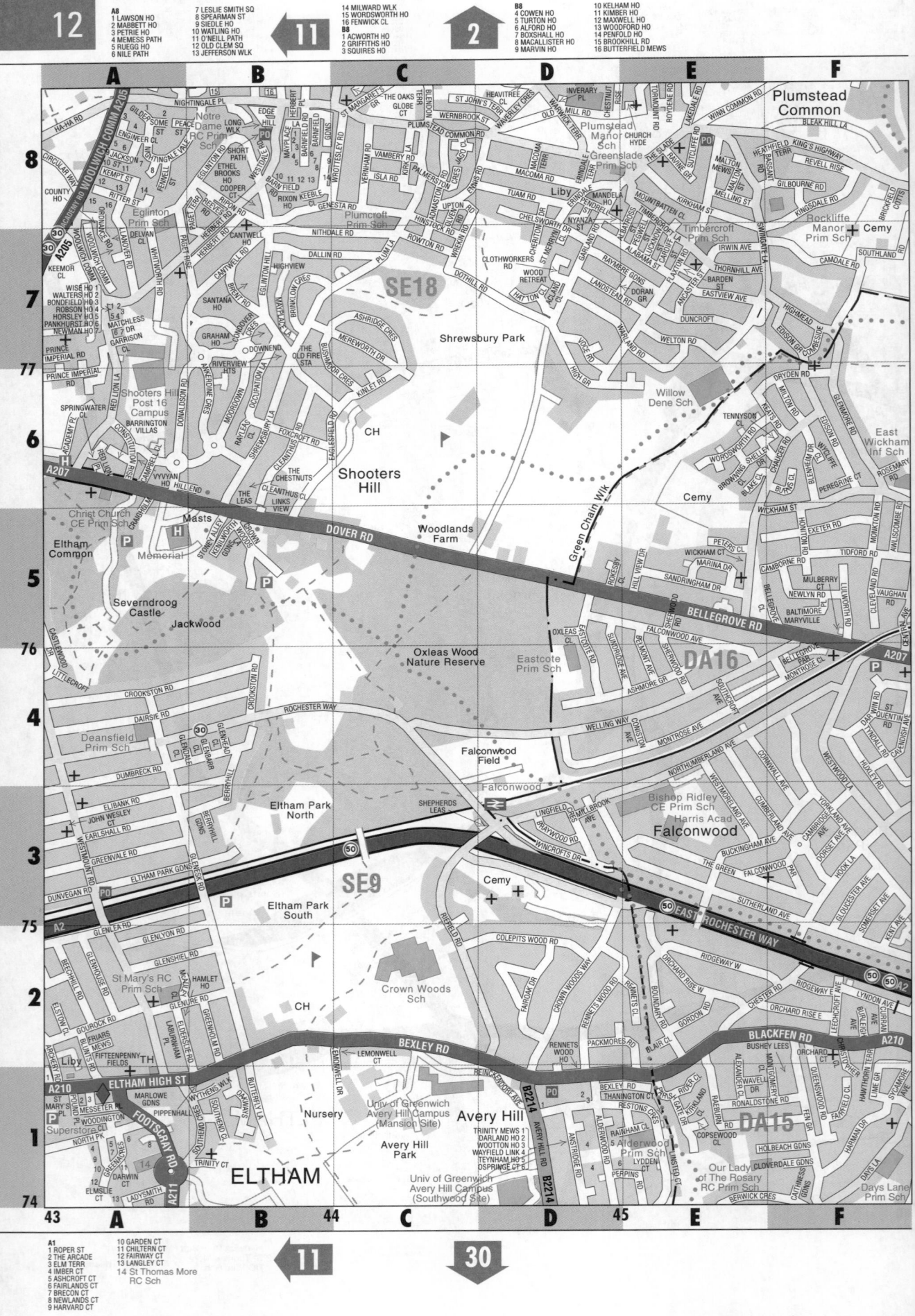

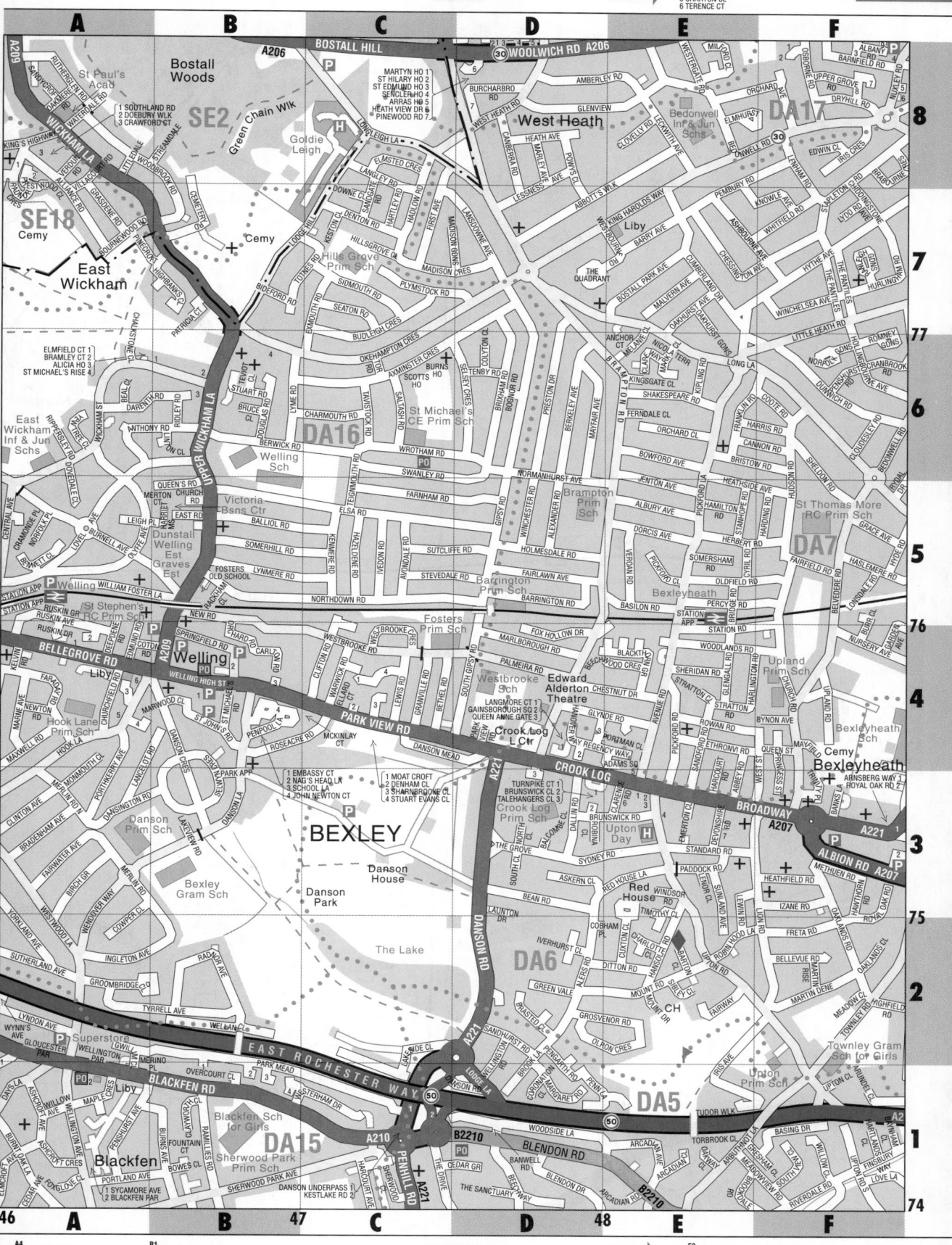

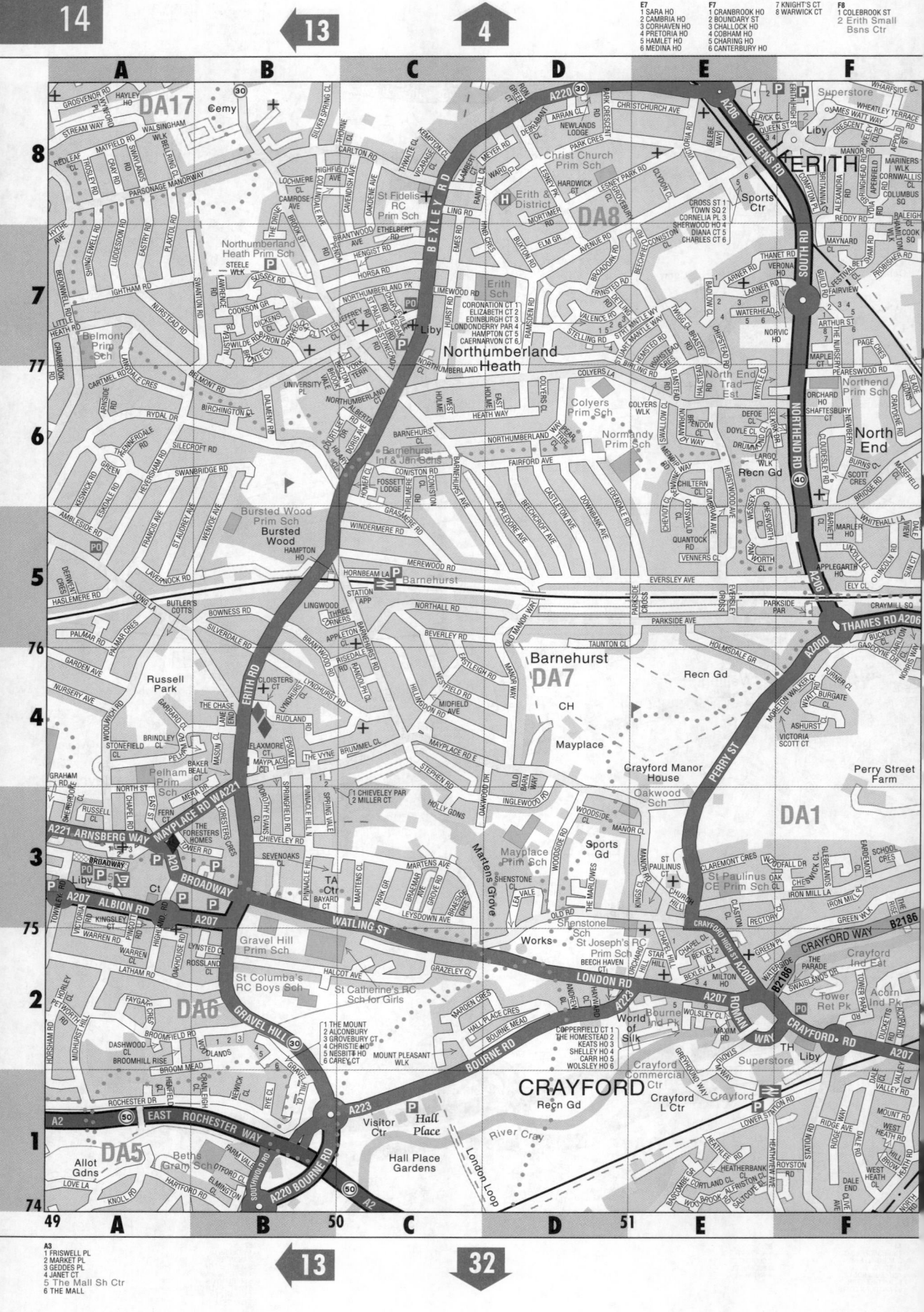

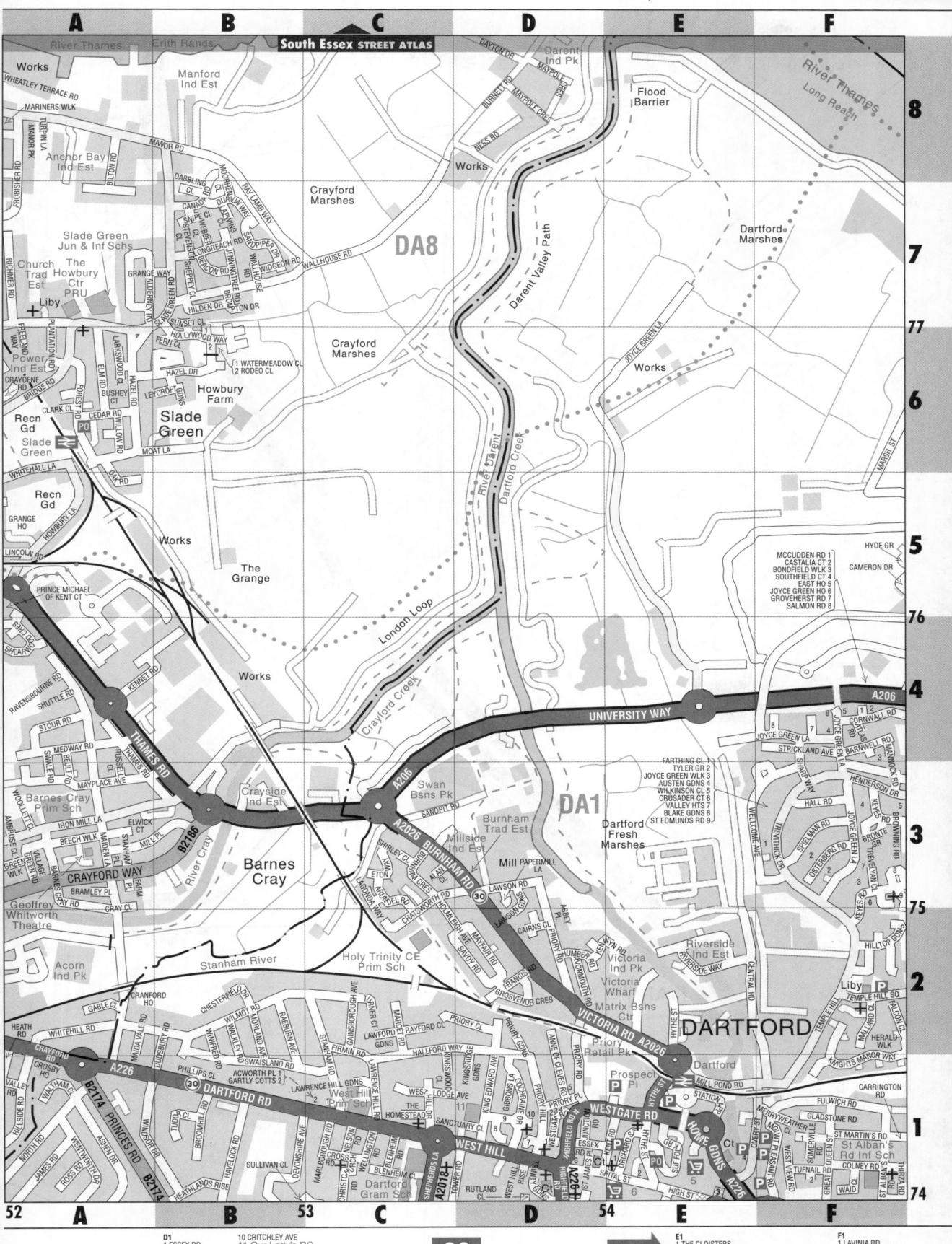

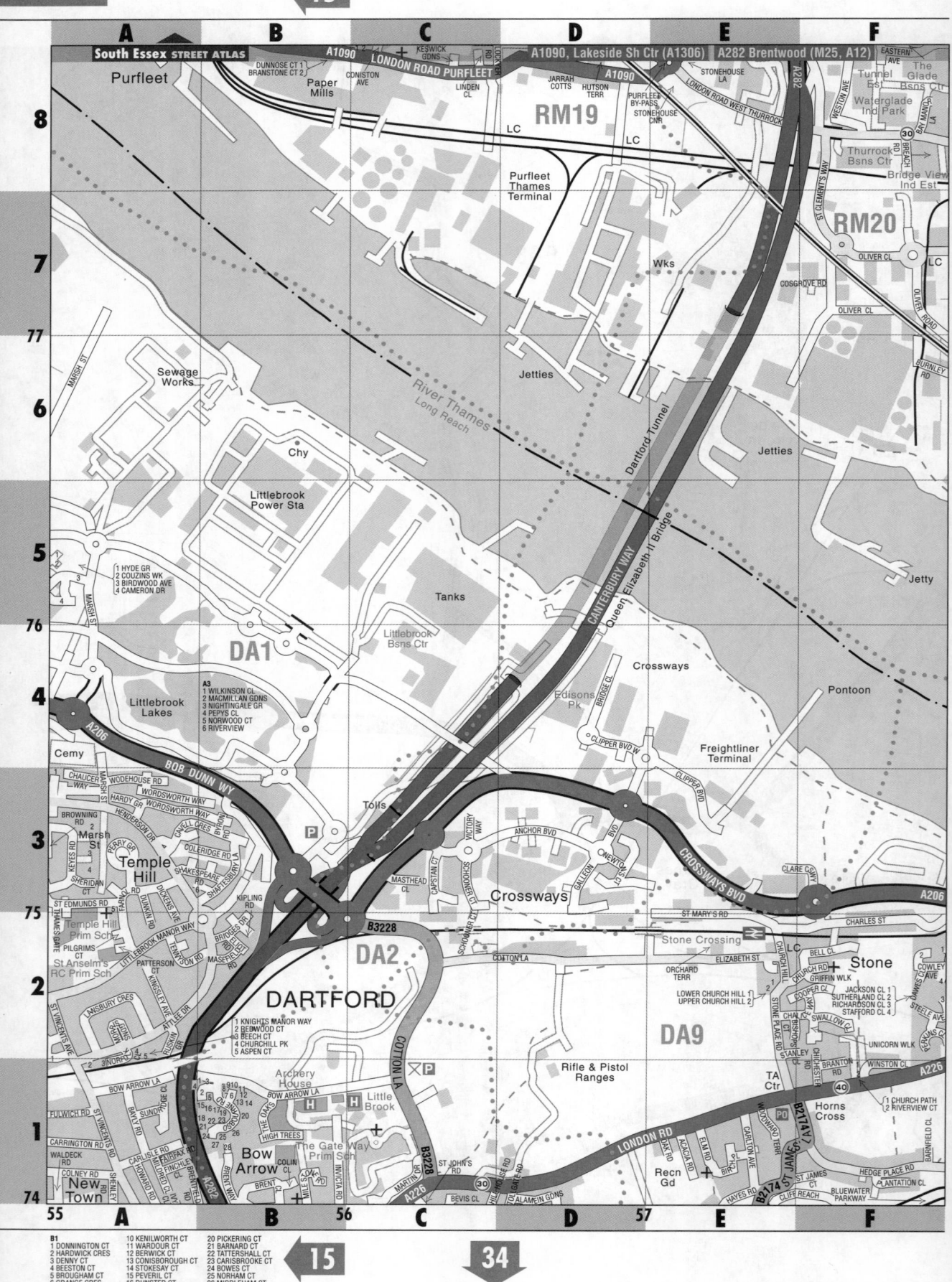

South Essex STREET ATLAS

Purfleet

A1090

DUNNOSE CT 1
BRANSTONE CT 2

LONDON ROAD PURFLEET

KESWICK GDNS

A1090, Lakeside Sh Ctr (A1306)

A282 Brentwood (M25, A12)

Paper Mills

CONISTON AVE

LINDEN CL

JARRAH COTTS

HUTSON TERR

A1090

STONEHOUSE LA

PURFLEET BY-PASS
STONEHOUSE CNR

LONDON ROAD WEST THURROCK

A282

EASTERN AVE

WESTON AVE

The Glade

Tunnel Est

Waterglade Ind Park

Thurrock Bsns Ctr

RM19

LC

LC

RAT MANOR WAY

ST CLEMENTS WAY

30

Bridge View Ind Est

RM20

OLIVER CL

Purfleet Thames Terminal

Wks

COSGROVE RD

BURNLEY RD

OLIVER CL

OLIVER CL

LC

MARSH ST

Sewage Works

River Thames
Long Reach

Jetties

Dartford Tunnel

Jetties

77

6

Chy

Littlebrook Power Sta

Jetty

1 HYDE GR
2 COUZINS WK
3 BIRDWOOD AVE
4 CAMERON DR

Tanks

Crossways

Pontoon

5

76

DA1

Littlebrook Bsns Ctr

Edisons Pk

A3
1 WILKINSON CL
2 MACMILLAN GDNS
3 NIGHTINGALE GR
4 PEPYS CL
5 NORWOOD CT
6 RIVERVIEW

Littlebrook Lakes

CLIPPER BVD W

BRIDGE CL

Freightliner Terminal

CLIPPER BVD

4

A206

Cemy

CHAUCER WAY

MARSH ST

WODEHOUSE RD

BOB DUNN WY

Tolls

P

VICTORY WAY

ANCHOR BVD

GALLEON BVD

CROSSWAYS BVD

CLARE C GNY

A206

HARDY GR

WORDSWORTH WAY

SCHOONER CT

NEWTON CT

3

BROWNING RD

Marsh St

PERRY GR

COLERIDGE RD

CAPSTAN CT

CROSSWAYS

MASTHEAD CL

SCHOONER CT

KEYES CT

SHERIDAN CT

Temple Hill

SHAKESPEARE RD

SHAFTESBURY RD

KIPLING RD

B3228

Crossways

ST MARY'S RD

75

ST EDMUNDS RD

DICKENS AVE

BRIDGES DR

MASEFIELD RD

Stone Crossing

ELIZABETH ST

CHURCH HILL

LC

BELL CL

Stone

THAMES GATE

PILGRIMS CT

St Anselm's RC Prim Sch

Temple Hill Prim Sch

LITTLEBROOK MANOR WAY

PATTERSON CT

ORCHARD TERR

LOWER CHURCH HILL
UPPER CHURCH HILL

GRIFFIN WLK

COOPER CL

CHURCH HILL

STONE PLACE RD

COWLEY AVE

JACKSON CL 1
SUTHERLAND CL 2
RICHARDSON CL 3
STAFFORD CL 4

STEELE AVE

DA2

LANSBURY CRES

ST VINCENTS AVE

DARTFORD

1 KNIGHTS MANOR WAY
2 BEDWOOD CT
3 BEECH CT
4 CHURCHILL PK
5 ASPEN CT

COTTON LA

Rifle & Pistol Ranges

DA9

STANLEY

SWALLOW

UNICORN WLK

CHICHESTER

BRANTON CT

WINSTON RD

A226

2

NORFOLK

BOW ARROW LA

Archery House

P

TA Ctr

40

Horns Cross

1 CHURCH PATH
2 RIVERVIEW CT

B2174

FULWICH RD

ST VINCENTS RD

SUNDRIDGE

BAVY RD

H

H

Little Brook

LONDON RD

HILL HOUSE RD

ACACIA RD

ELM RD

CARLTON RD

Recn Gd

ST JAMES

HEDGE PLACE RD

PLANTATION RD

1

CARRINGTON RD

WALDECK RD

COLNEY RD

CARLISLE RD

FAIRFAX RD

HOWARD RD

FINCHLEY

Bow Arrow

The Gate Way Prim Sch

COLIN CL

BRENT WAY

MILE RD

INVICTA RD

B3228

ST JOHN'S RD

A226

MARTIN

30

B2174

ST JAMES

BLUEWATER PARKWAY

New Town

SHERLEY

A282

BRENT

ALAMEIN GDNS

BEVIS CL

HAYES RD

CLIFF REACH

74

B1
1 DONNINGTON CT
2 HARDWICK CRES
3 DENNY CT
4 BEESTON CT
5 BROUGHAM CT
6 GRANGE CRES
7 ORFORD CT
8 ALNWICK CT
9 BRAMBER CT
10 KENILWORTH CT
11 WARDOUR CT
12 BERWICK CT
13 CONISBOROUGH CT
14 STOKESAY CT
15 PEVERIL CT
16 DUNSTER CT
17 CALSHOT CT
18 LYDFORD CT
19 LONGTOWN CT
20 PICKERING CT
21 BARNARD CT
22 TATTERSHALL CT
23 CARISBROOKE CT
24 BOWES CT
25 NORHAM CT
26 MIDDLEHAM CT
27 PRUDHOE CT
28 BRIDGE CT

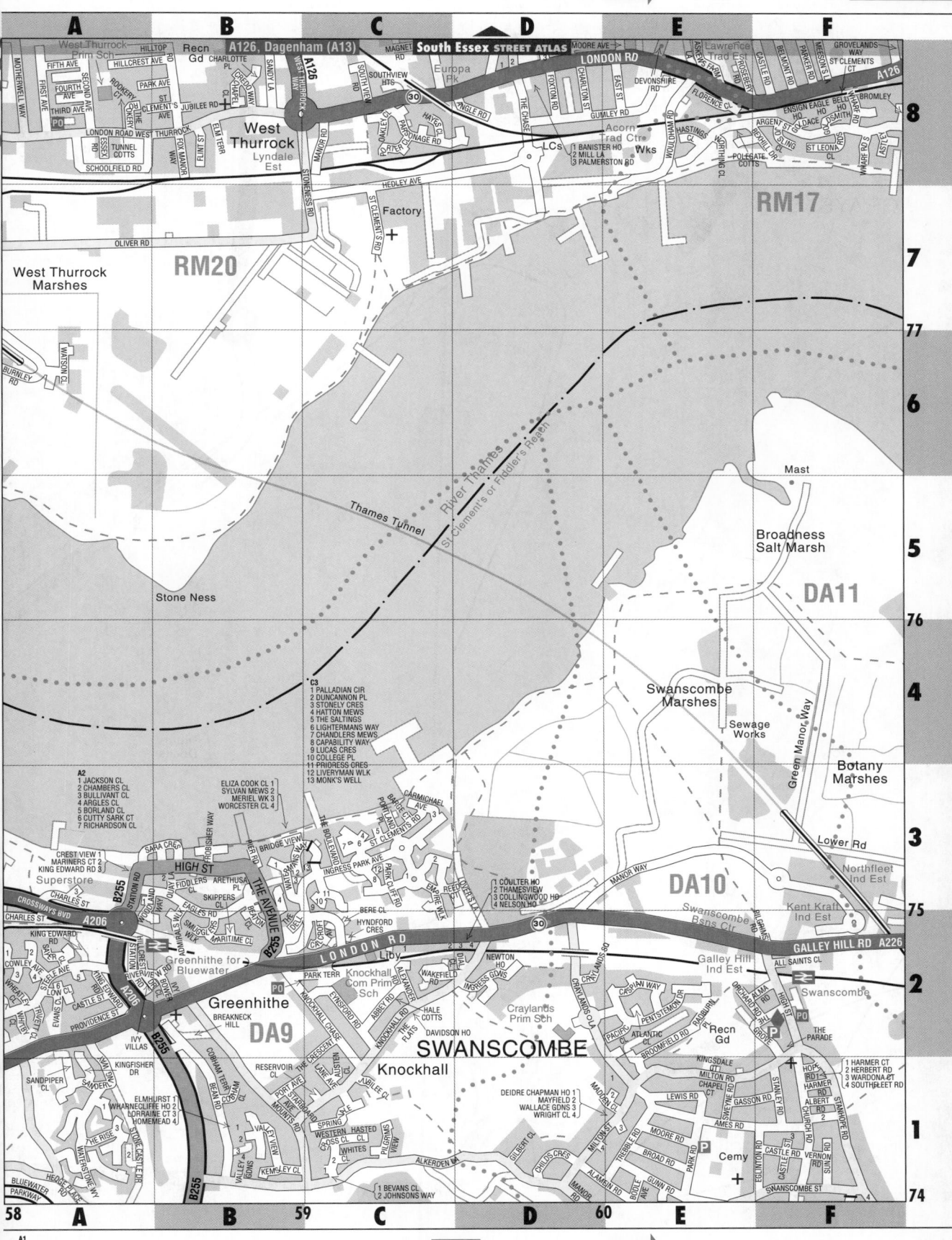

South Essex STREET ATLAS

A126, Dagenham (A13)

LONDON RD

West Thurrock

RM17

RM20

West Thurrock Marshes

77

River Thames

St Clements or Fiddler's Reach

Thames Tunnel

Mast

Broadness Salt/Marsh

DA11

Stone Ness

76

Swanscombe Marshes

Sewage Works

Botany Marshes

C3
1 PALLADIAN CIR
2 DUNCANNON PL
3 STONELY CRES
4 HATTON MEWS
5 THE SALTINGS
6 LIGHTERMANS WAY
7 CHANDLERS MEWS
8 CAPABILITY WAY
9 LUCAS CRES
10 COLLEGE PL
11 PRIORESS CRES
12 LIVERYMAN WLK
13 MONK'S WELL

Lower Rd

Northfleet Ind Est

A2
1 JACKSON CL
2 CHAMBERS CL
3 BULLIVANT CL
4 ARGLES CL
5 BORLAND CL
6 CUTTY SARK CT
7 RICHARDSON CL

ELIZA COOK CL 1
SYLVAN MEWS 2
MERIEL WK 3
WORCESTER CT 4

CARMICHAEL AVE

DA10

Swanscombe Bsns Ctr

Kent Kraft Ind Est

HIGH ST

Superstore

Manor Way

Galley Hill Ind Est

GALLEY HILL RD A226

1 COULTER HO
2 THAMESVIEW
3 COLLINGWOOD HO
4 NELSON HO

Swanscombe

Greenhithe for Bluewater

LONDON RD

Knockhall Com Prim Sch

Newton Ho

Craylands Prim Sch

Recn Gd

THE PARADE

Greenhithe

DA9

Knockhall

SWANSCOMBE

Davidson Ho

Cemy

1 HARMER CT
2 HERBERT RD
3 WARDONA CT
4 SOUTHFLEET RD

DEIDRE CHAPMAN HO 1
MAYFIELD 2
WALLACE GDNS 3
WRIGHT CL 4

1 WHARNECLIFFE HO 2
LORRAINE CT 3
HOMEMEAD 4

1 BEVANS CL
2 JOHNSONS WAY

Bluewater Parkway

A1
1 BRAMBLING CL
2 NORTHWOOD DR
3 WOLSEY CRES

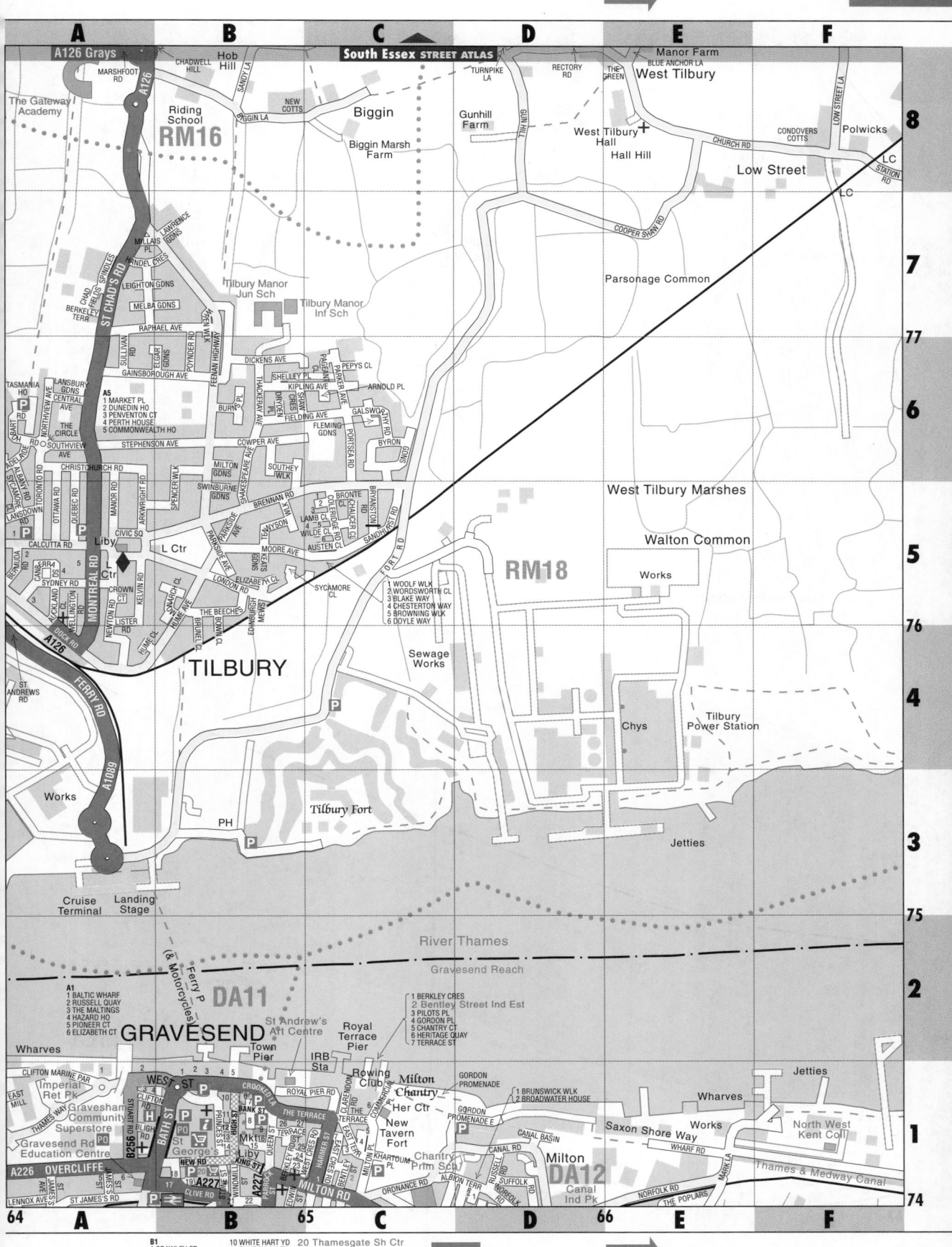

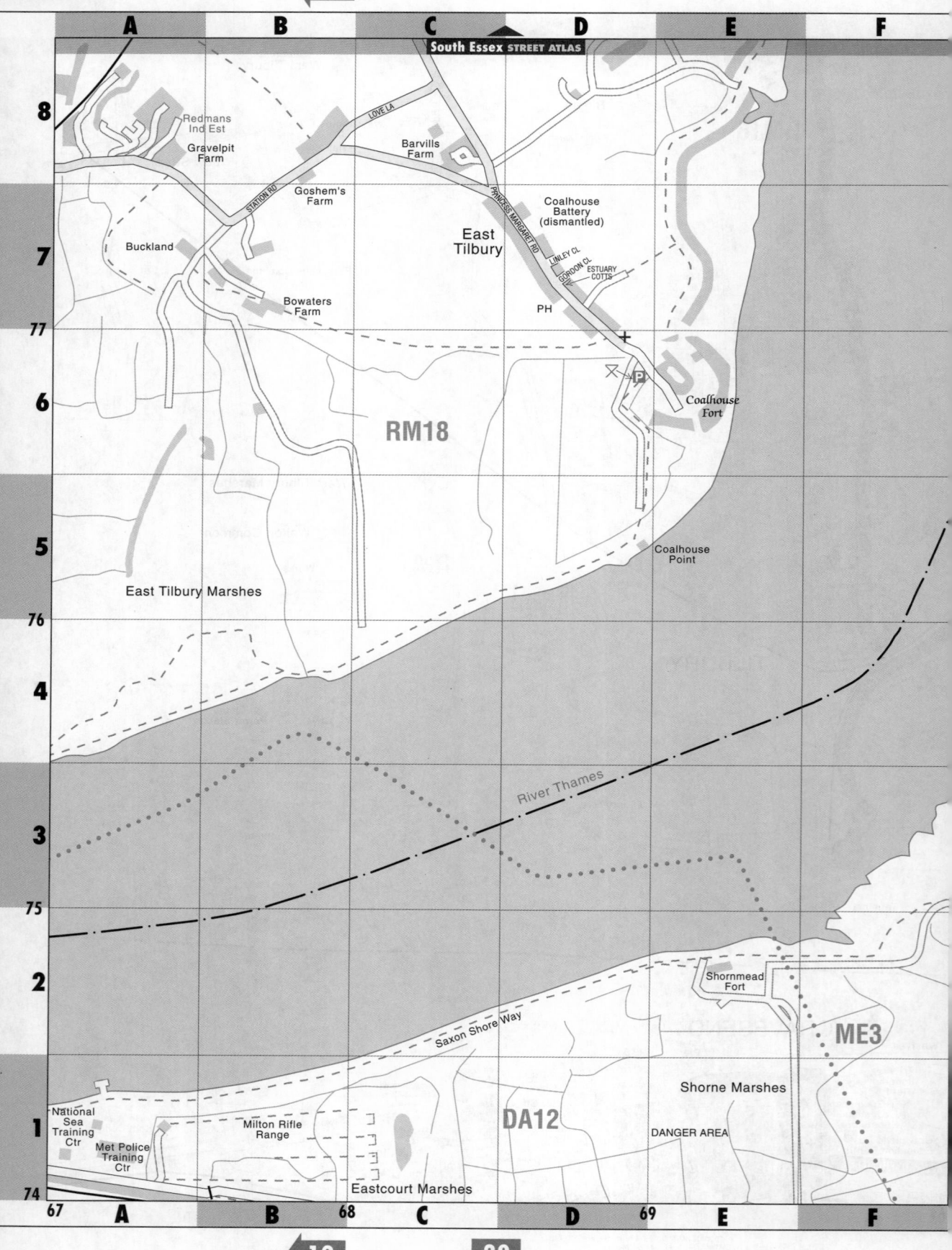

South Essex STREET ATLAS

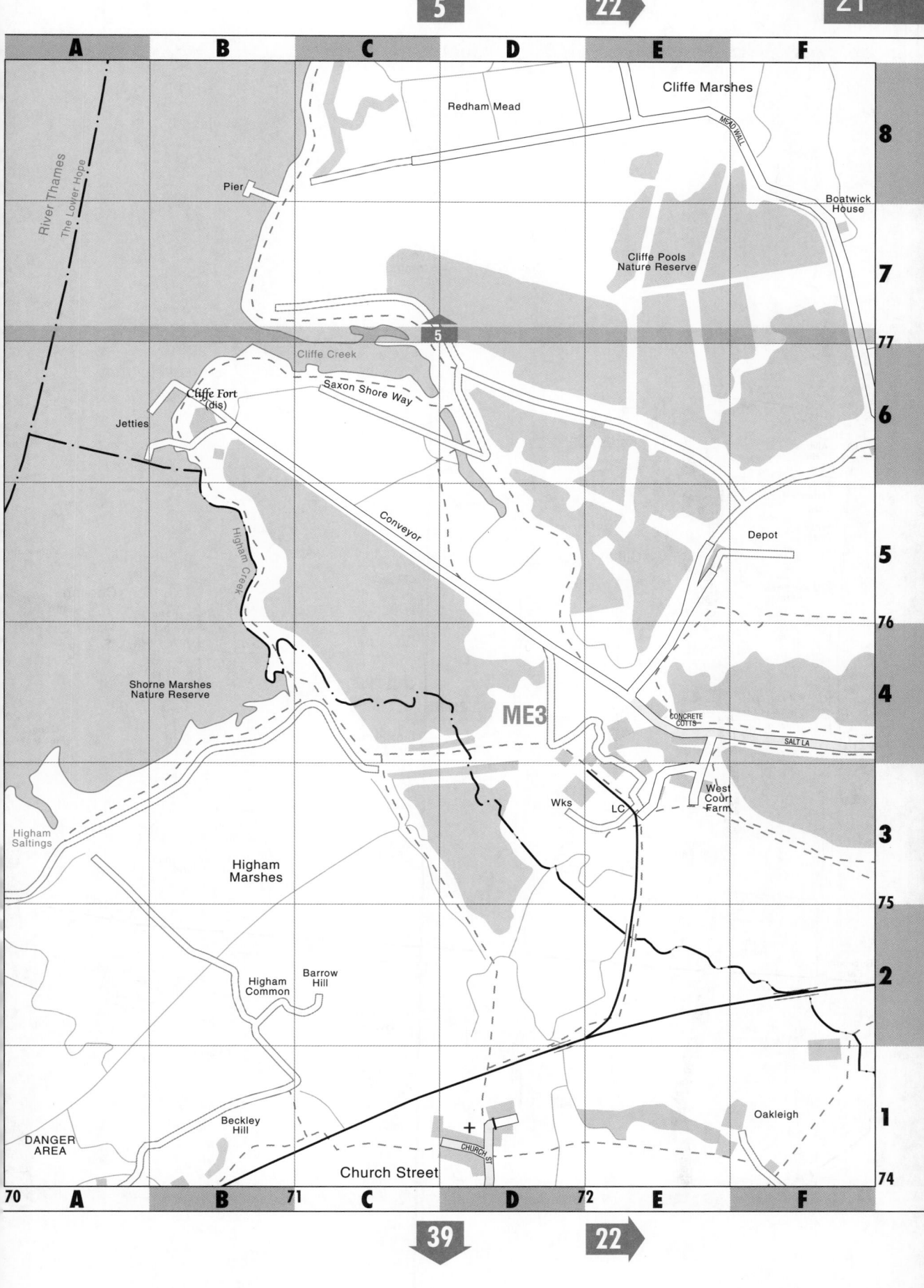

5

22

Cliffe Marshes

Redham Mead

8

MEAD WALL

Boatwick
House

Cliffe Pools
Nature Reserve

7

River Thames

The Lower Hope

Pier

77

Cliffe Creek

5

Saxon Shore Way

Cliffe Fort
(dis)

6

Jetties

Conveyor

Higham Creek

Depot

5

76

Shorne Marshes
Nature Reserve

4

ME3

CONCRETE
COTTS

SALT LA

Wks

LC

West
Court
Farm

Higham
Saltings

3

Higham
Marshes

75

Higham
Common

Barrow
Hill

2

Oakleigh

Beckley
Hill

1

DANGER
AREA

CHURCH ST

Church Street

74

70 A   B   71   C   D   72   E   F

39

22

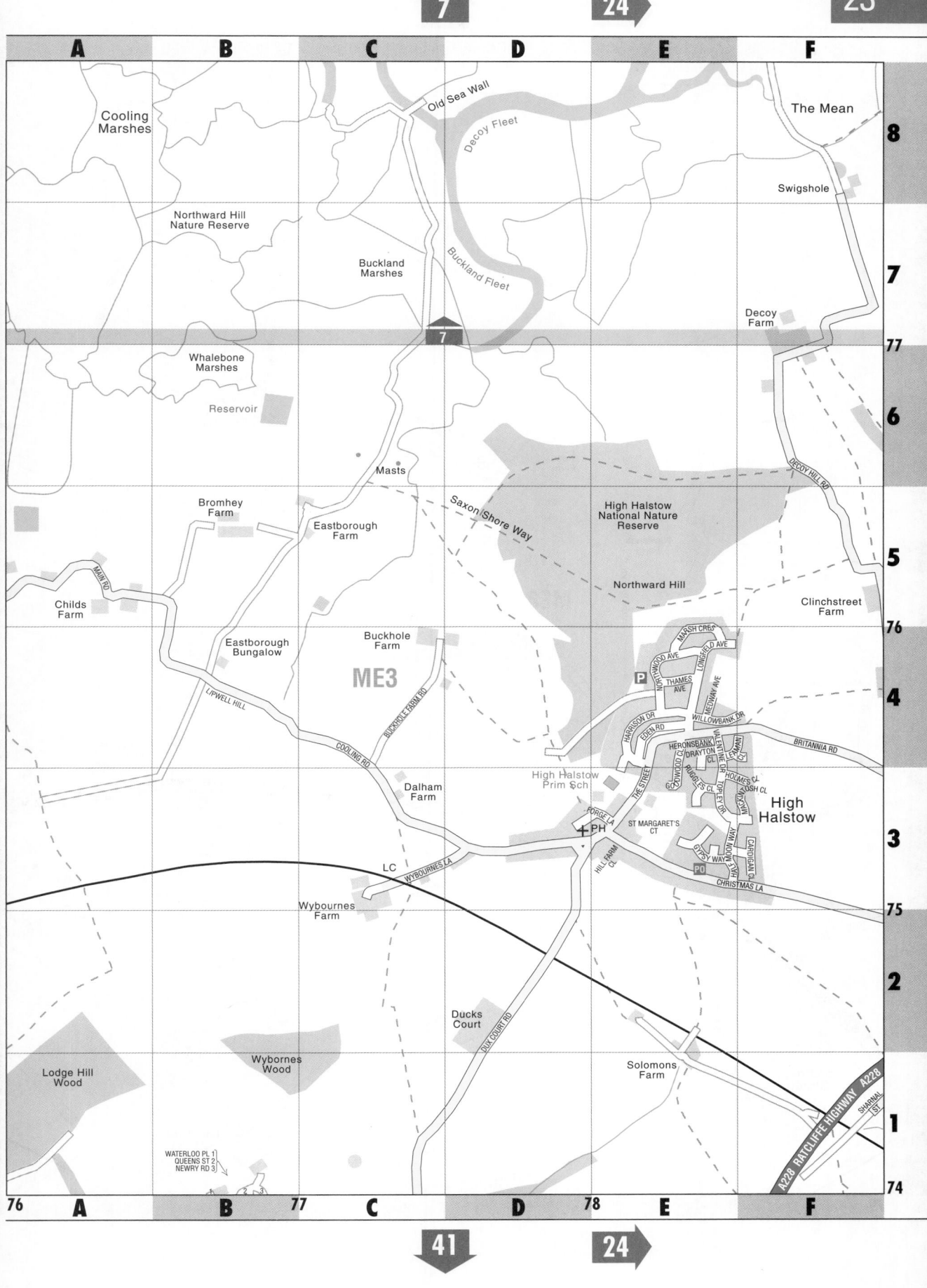

7

24

8

The Mean

Cooling
Marshes

Swigshole

Northward Hill
Nature Reserve

7

Buckland
Marshes

Old Sea Wall

Decoy Fleet

Decoy
Farm

Buckland Fleet

7

77

Whalebone
Marshes

6

Reservoir

Decoy Hill Rd

Masts

Saxon Shore Way

High Halstow
National Nature
Reserve

5

Bromhey
Farm

Eastborough
Farm

Northward Hill

Clinchstreet
Farm

76

Childs
Farm

Main Rd

Eastborough
Bungalow

Buckhole
Farm

MARSH CRES

Lipwell Hill

Buckhole Farm Rd

ME3

LONGFIELD AVE

NORTHWOOD AVE

4

P

Thames
Ave

MEDWAY AVE

Cooling Rd

WILLOWBANK DR

HARRISON DR

EDEN RD

BRITANNIA RD

Dalham
Farm

High Halstow
Prim Sch

HERONSBANK

DRAYTON
CL

VALENTINE LA

LAMAN

GOSH CL

HOLMES CL

High
Halstow

GODWOOD CT

RUGGLES CL

TOPLEY DR

THE STREET

FORGE LA

PH

ST MARGARET'S
CT

3

LC

WYBOURNES LA

HILL FARM
CL

GYPSY WAY

GYPSY WAY

CARDIGAN CL

75

PO

CHRISTMAS LA

Wybournes
Farm

2

Ducks
Court

DUX COURT RD

Lodge Hill
Wood

Wybornes
Wood

Solomons
Farm

1

A228 RATCLIFFE HIGHWAY A228

SHARNAL
ST

WATERLOO PL 1
QUEENS ST 2
NEWRY RD 3

74

41

24

23
8

A B C D E F

8

7

77
8

6

5

76

4

3

75

2

1

74

Refuse Tip

Coombe House

Mayland

Little Owls

SHAKESPEARE FARM RD

Ramsgreen

Moat Farm

MOAT FARM RD

St Mary Hoo

Ross Farm

HALL RD

ROSE COTTS

Noreland Cottage

COOMBE FARM LA

HOOPERS LA

Newlands Farm

RATCLIFFE HIGHWAY

ST MARY'S

ME3

Bell Wood

Walnut Tree Farm

NEWLANDS FARM RD

Saxon Shore Way

CLINCH ST

PH

Malmaynes Hall Farm

Fenn Street

BELLWOOD CT

Turkey Hall Farm

MALMAYNES HALL RD

A228

JACKSON'S CNR

BRITANNIA RD

Fenn Farm

SHARNAL ST

Fisher's Wood

New Barn Farm

Parbrook House

CHRISTMAS LA

PARBROOK RD

Tudor Farm

RATCLIFFE HIGHWAY

A228

SHARNAL ST

ROPER'S GREEN LA

Sharnal Street

Cold Arbour

North Street

STOKE RD

North Street Farm

Tunbridge Hill

79 A B 80 C D 81 E F

23
42

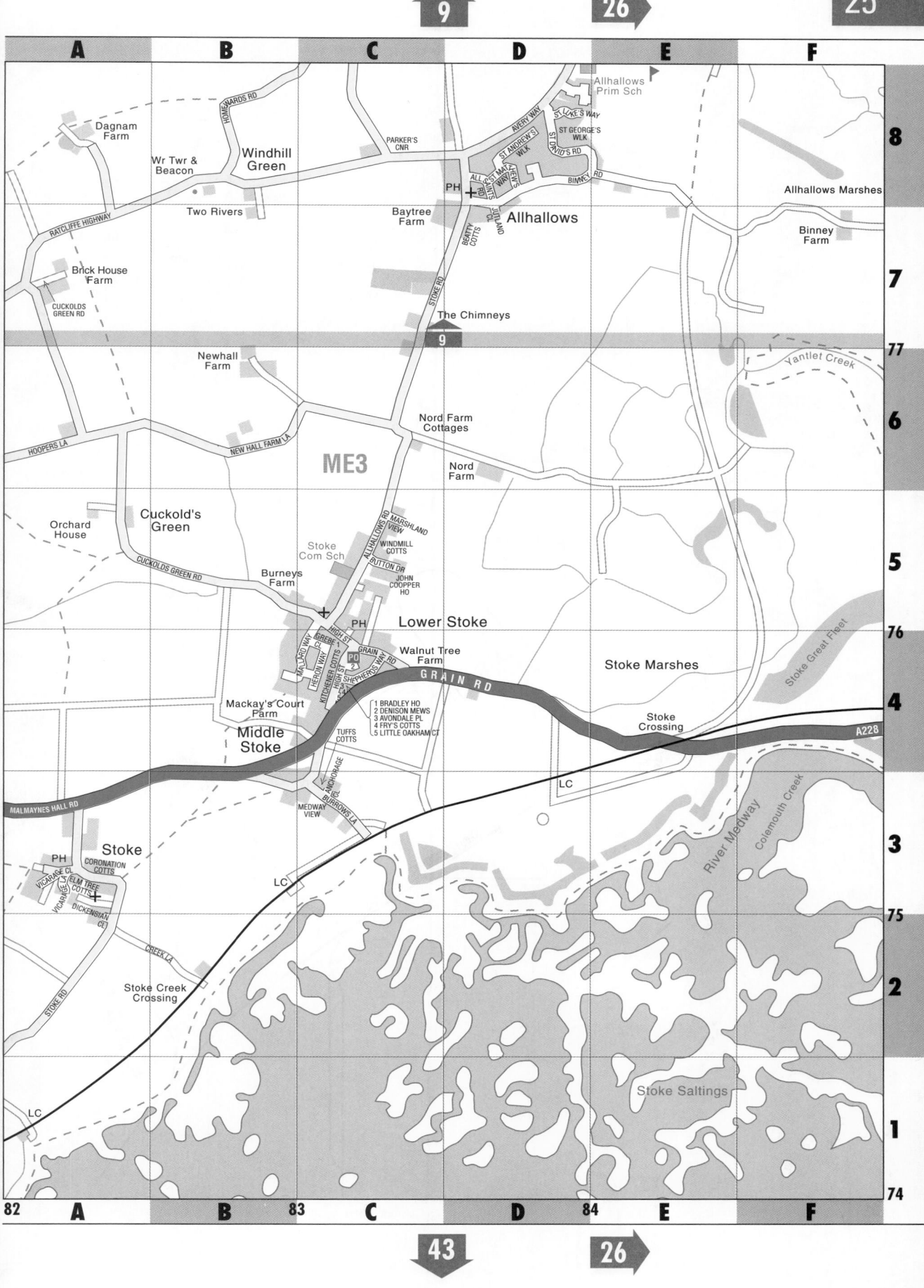

9
26

A **B** **C** **D** **E** **F**

8

Dagnam Farm

Wr Twr & Beacon

Windhill Green

HOMENARDS RD

PARKER'S CNR

Allhallows Prim Sch

ST LUKE'S WAY

ST GEORGE'S WLK

AVERY WAY

ST ANDREW'S WLK

ST MATHEWS WAY

ALL SAINTS RD

ST DAVID'S RD

BINNEY RD

Allhallows Marshes

Two Rivers

RATCLIFFE HIGHWAY

Baytree Farm

PH

BEATTY COTTS

JUTLAND

Allhallows

Binney Farm

7

Brick House Farm

STOKE RD

The Chimneys

9

CUCKOLDS GREEN RD

77

Newhall Farm

Yantlet Creek

6

HOOPERS LA

NEW HALL FARM LA

ME3

Nord Farm Cottages

Nord Farm

Orchard House

Cuckold's Green

CUCKOLDS GREEN RD

Burneys Farm

Stoke Com Sch

ALLHALLOWS RD

MARSHLAND VIEW

WINDMILL COTTS

BUTTON DR

JOHN COOPPER HO

5

Stoke Cotts

76

PH

HIGH ST

GRAIN RD

Lower Stoke

Stoke Marshes

Stoke Great Fleet

GREBE CL

MALLARD WAY

HERON WAY

KITCHENER WAY

HIGH ST

SHEYHERDS WAY

PO 2

Walnut Tree Farm

Stoke Crossing

4

Mackay's Court Farm

Middle Stoke

TUFFS COTTS

ANCHORAGE CL

BURROWS LA

1 BRADLEY HO
2 DENISON MEWS
3 AVONDALE PL
4 FRY'S COTTS
5 LITTLE OAKHAM CT

GRAIN RD

LC

A228

Coiemouth Creek

MALMAYNES HALL RD

MEDWAY VIEW

River Medway

75

PH

Stoke

CORONATION COTTS

VICARAGE CL

ELM TREE COTTS

VICARAGE LA

DICKENSIAN CL

LC

3

CREEK LA

STOKE RD

Stoke Creek Crossing

2

Stoke Saltings

LC

1

74

82 **A** **B** **83** **C** **D** **84** **E** **F**

43
26

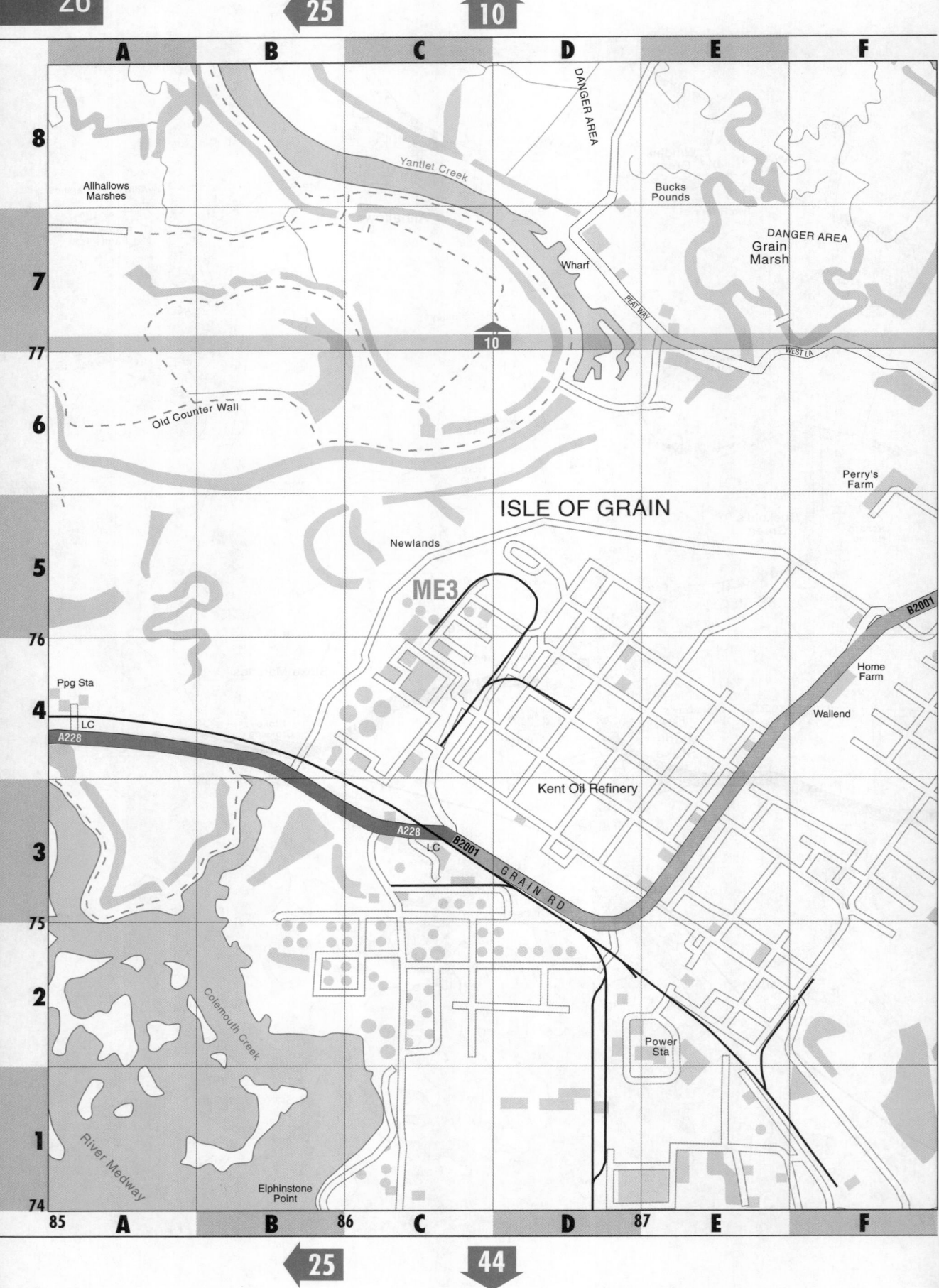

A B C D E F

8

Allhallows
Marshes

Yantlet Creek

DANGER AREA

Bucks
Pounds

DANGER AREA
Grain
Marsh

7

Wharf

PEAT WAY

WEST LA

77

6

Old Counter Wall

Perry's
Farm

ISLE OF GRAIN

5

Newlands

ME3

B2001

76

Ppg Sta

Home
Farm

4

LC

A228

Wallend

Kent Oil Refinery

A228

B2001

3

LC

GRAIN RD

75

2

Colemouth Creek

Power
Sta

1

River Medway

Elphinstone
Point

74

85 A B 86 C D 87 E F

28

A B C D E F

8

River Thames

Grain Spit

7

The Flats

Works

77

Rose Court
Farm

P

B2001

Grain

6

St James'
CE Prim Sch

WEST LA

PAWNELL RD

FRY CL

LEVETT CL

PH

PO

HIGH ST

ST JAMES CL

PINTAIL CL

BES RD

TEAL CL

Liby

CORONATION RD

CHAPEL RD

SCARSDALE

SHELLDRAKE CL

COASTGUARD
COTTS

EDINBURGH RD

GRASSMERE

GRIFFIN RD

CORINTHIAN
CT

LAPWING RD

RIVENDELL CL

CHAPEL RD

SEAVIEW

SMITHFIELD RD

5

GRAIN RD

Whitehouse
Farm

POWER STATION RD

ME3

Grain
Tower

76

PORT VICTORIA RD

Smithfield
Marshes

4

Garrison
Point

LB
Sta

GARRISON RD

SLIPWAY RD

BOATHOUSE
RD

Docks

ANCHOR LA

STOREHOUSE
WHARF

SHEERNESS

3

Chy

Grain
Power
Station

Jetty

Sheerness
Harbour Est

GREAT BASIN RD

75

House Fleet

River Medway

2

Piers

ME12

Jetty

Cockleshell
Hard

1

The
Lappel

Horseshoe
Point

74

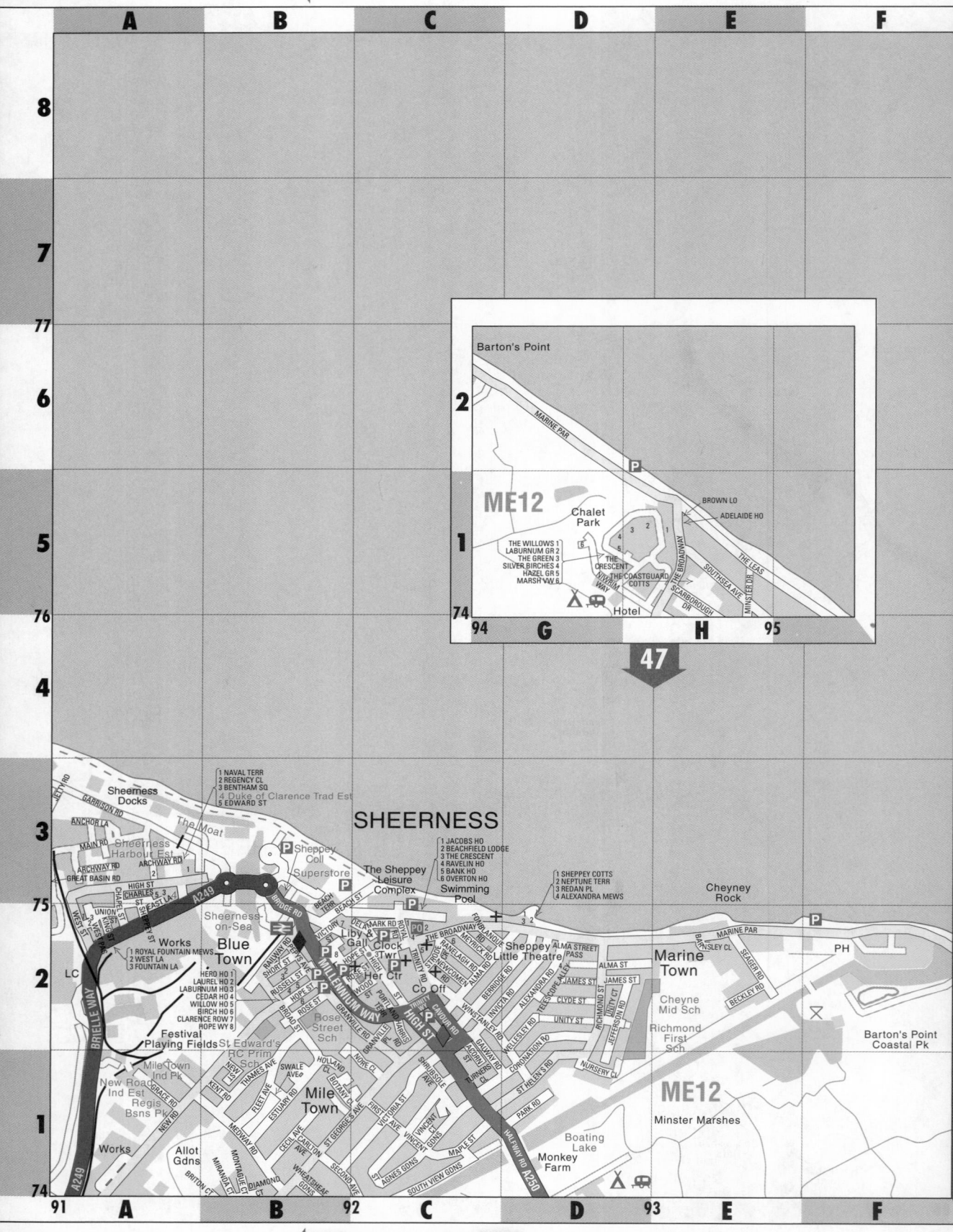

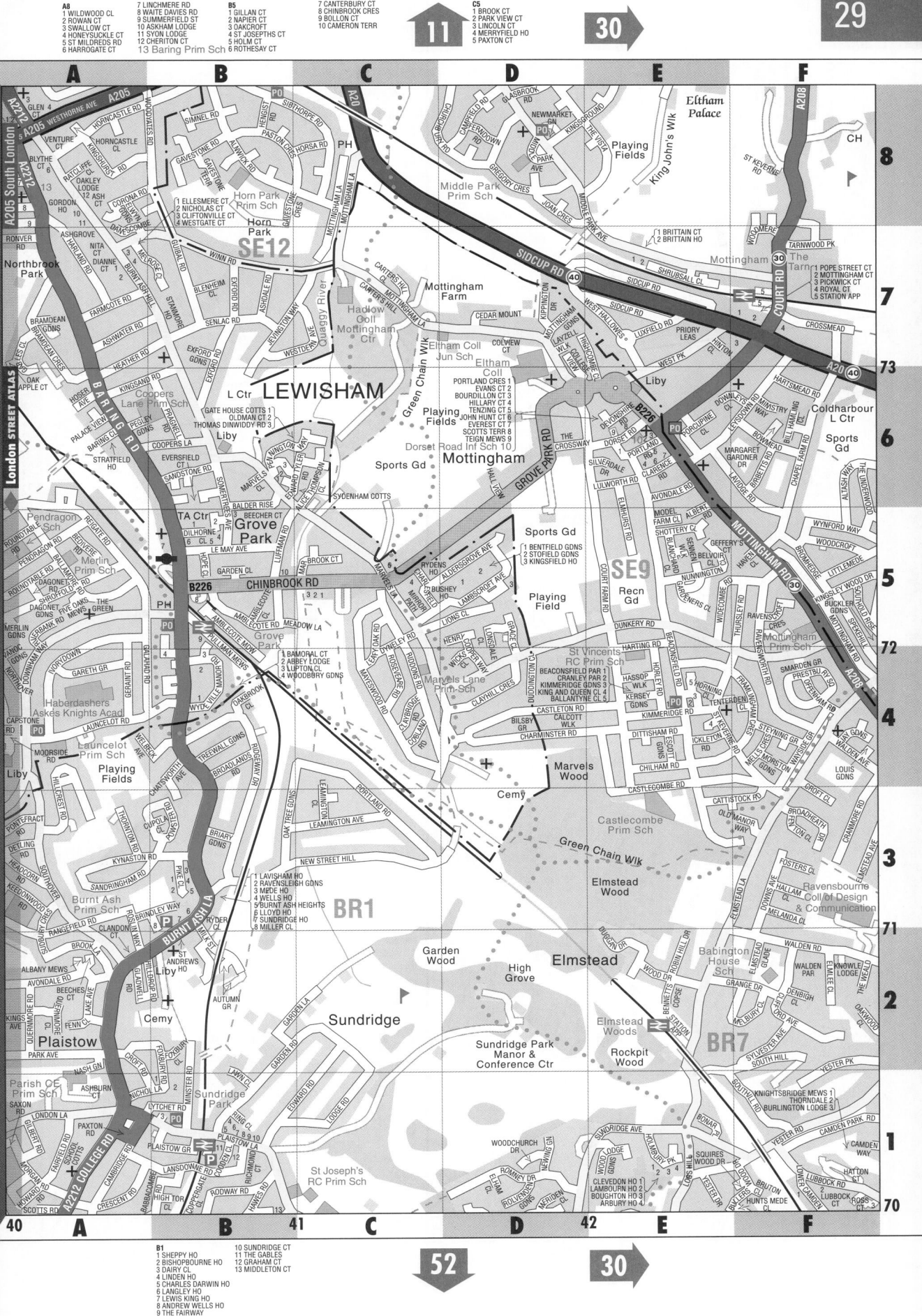

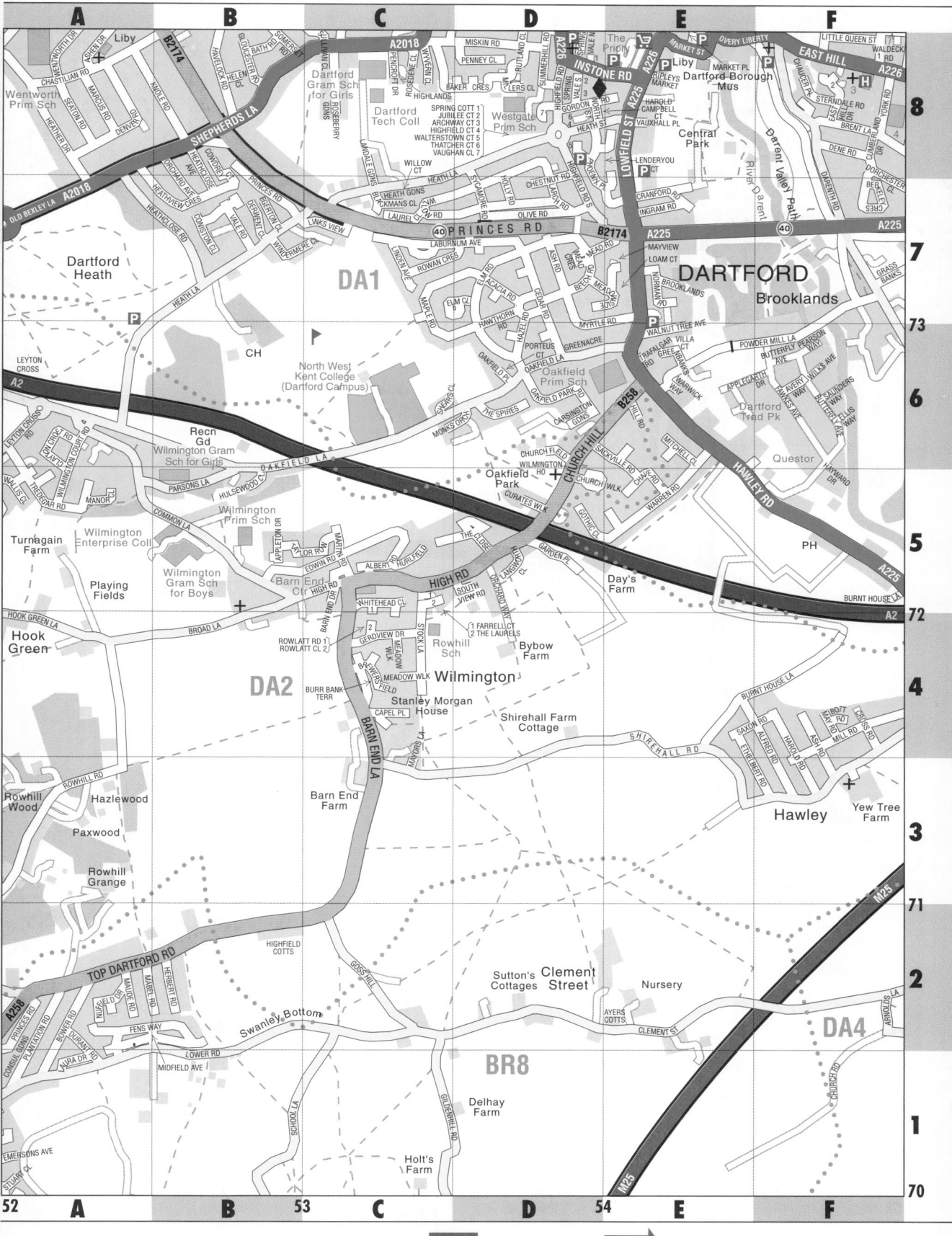

A   B   C   D   E   F

Liby
Wentworth Prim Sch
B2174
Dartford Gram Sch for Girls
Dartford Tech Coll
Dartford Heath

DA1

North West Kent College (Dartford Campus)

MISKIN RD
PENNEY CL
RUTLAND CL
Summerhill Rd
The Priory
Overy Liberty
LITTLE QUEEN ST
EAST HILL
A226
WALDECK RD
Market St
Liby
Dartford Borough Mus
Market Pl
RIPLEY'S Market
Central Park
DARTFORD
Brooklands
GRASS BANKS
Darent Valley Path
River Darent

PRINCES RD
A2018
A225
B2174
A225

SPRING COTT 1
JUBILEE CT 2
ARCHWAY CT 3
HIGHFIELD CT 4
WALTERSTOWN CT 5
THATCHER CT 6
VAUGHAN CL 7
WILLOW CT
Westgate Prim Sch

Oakfield Prim Sch
Dartford Trad Pk
Questor
Oakfield Park
WILMINGTON
CHURCH HILL
HAWLEY RD
PH
BURNT HOUSE LA
A2

A2
LEYTON CROSS
Recn Gd Wilmington Gram Sch for Girls
OAKFIELD LA
Wilmington Prim Sch
Wilmington Enterprise Coll
Turnagain Farm
Playing Fields
Wilmington Gram Sch for Boys
Barn End Ctr
HIGH RD
Whitehead Cl
Rowhill Sch
Rowhill Farm
Day's Farm
Bybow Farm

HOOK GREEN LA
BROAD LA
Hook Green
DA2
BURR BANK TERR
Stanley Morgan House
CAPEL PL
Wilmington
1 FARRELL CT
2 THE LAURELS
Shirehall Farm Cottage
SHIREHALL RD
Hawley
Yew Tree Farm
M25

Rowhill Wood
Hazlewood
Paxwood
Rowhill Grange
Barn End Farm
Barn End La
HIGHFIELD COTTS
BR8
TOP DARTFORD RD
A258
Swanley Bottom
FENS WAY
MIDFIELD AVE
LOWER RD
SCHOOL LA
GOSS HILL
GILDENHILL RD
Sutton's Cottages
Clement Street
Nursery
AYERS COTTS
CLEMENT ST
DA4
Delhay Farm
Holt's Farm
EMERSONS AVE

8
7
73
6
5
72
4
3
71
2
1
70

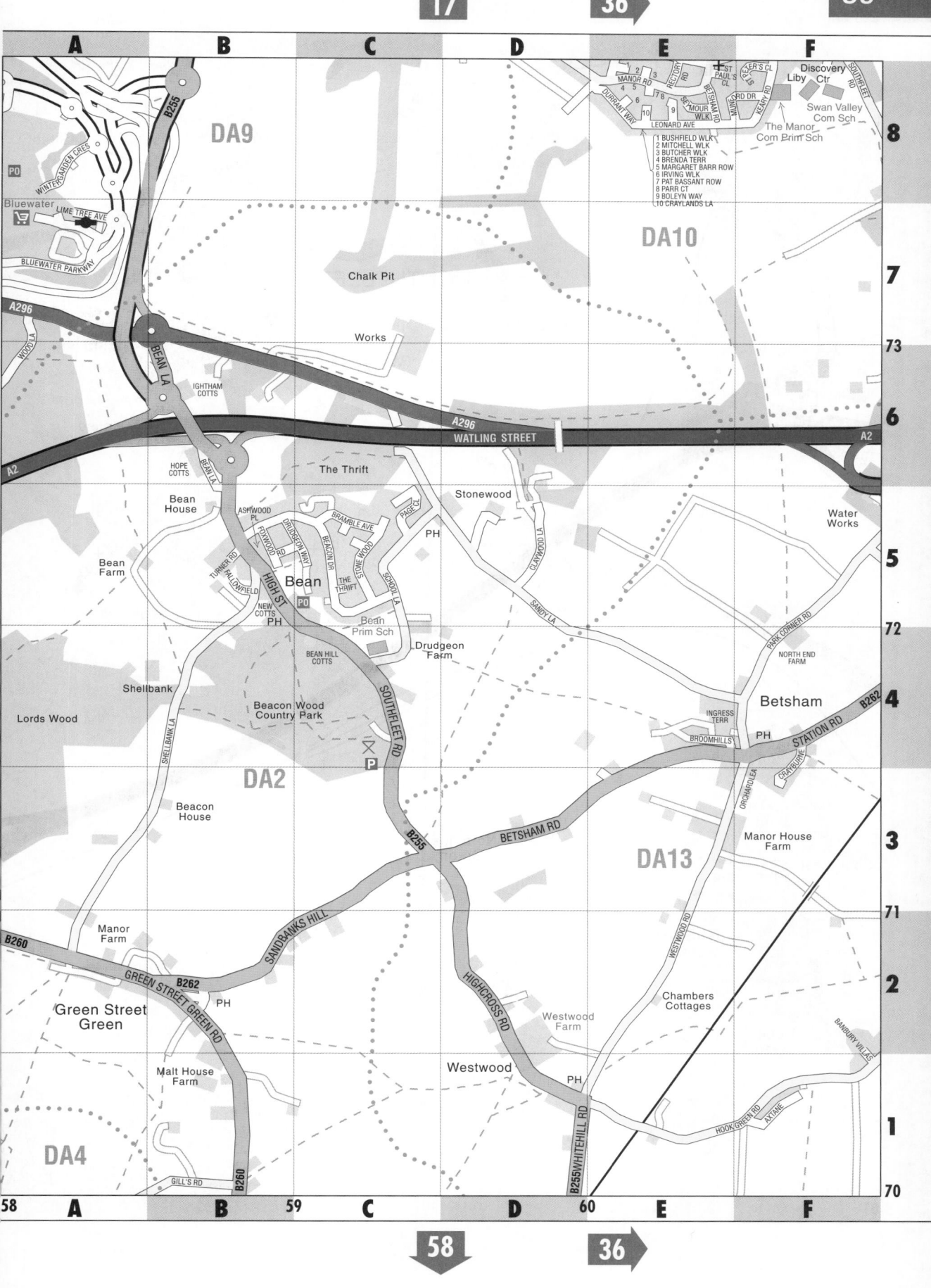

A   B   C   D   E   F

DA9

8

PO

WINTERGARDEN CRES

B255

Bluewater

LIME TREE AVE

BLUEWATER PARKWAY

7

Chalk Pit

73

A296

WOOD LA

BEAN LA

Works

DA10

1 BUSHFIELD WLK
2 MITCHELL WLK
3 BUTCHER WLK
4 BRENDA TERR
5 MARGARET BARR ROW
6 IRVING WLK
7 PAT BASSANT ROW
8 PARR CT
9 BOLEYN WAY
10 CRAYLANDS LA

Discovery Liby Ctr

Swan Valley Com Sch

The Manor Com Prim Sch

St PAUL'S CL

MANOR RD

RECTORY RD

LEONARD AVE

DURRANT WAY

MOUR WLK

BETSHAM RD

KEARY RD

SOUTHFLEET RD

ST PETER'S CL

6

A2

IGHTHAM COTTS

HOPE COTTS

BEAN LA

The Thrift

Stonewood

WATLING STREET

A296

A2

Water Works

Bean House

ASHWOOD PL

FOXWOOD RD

DRUDGEON WAY

BRAMBLE AVE

BEAN DR

PAGE CL

PH

CLAYWOOD LA

5

Bean Farm

TURNER RD

FALLOWFIELD

HIGH ST

Bean

PO

THE THRIFT

STONE WAY

SCHOOL LA

SANDY LA

72

PARK CORNER RD

NORTH END FARM

Shellbank

NEW COTTS PH

Bean Prim Sch

Drudgeon Farm

Betsham

B262

STATION RD

4

Lords Wood

SHELLBANK LA

BEAN HILL COTTS

Beacon Wood Country Park

SOUTHFLEET RD

P

INGRESS TERR

BROOMHILLS

PH

ORCHARDLEA

CRAYBURNE

DA2

Beacon House

B255

Betsham Rd

Manor House Farm

DA13

3

71

Manor Farm

B260

GREEN STREET GREEN RD

B262

PH

SANDBANKS HILL

WESTWOOD RD

Chambers Cottages

2

Green Street Green

Malt House Farm

B260

HIGHCROSS RD

Westwood Farm

BANBURY VILLAS

Westwood

PH

HOOK GREEN RD

AXTANE

1

DA4

GILL'S RD

B255 WHITEHILL RD

70

58   A   B   59   C   D   60   E   F

35

18

E5
1 EVEREST CL
2 SWALLOWFIELDS
3 DOWDING WLK
4 GREENDALE WLK
5 LANGDALE WLK
6 ROBYNS CROFT

E8
1 COMPASS CT
2 LIGHTERMAN'S MEWS
3 GALLEON MEWS
4 CAPSTAN MEWS
5 MARINERS WAY

F7
1 MAY AVE IND EST
2 HUNTSMAN HO
3 BRADBERY CT
4 BOUNDARY HO
5 ALFRED HO
6 WYCLIFFE HO

7 THANET HO
8 SOUTHFLEET RD
F8
1 CREMORNE RD
2 BYCLIFFE MEWS
3 BYCLIFFE TERR
4 PELHAM TERR

DA10

Perry Street

Sewage Works

A226

A2260

A2

NORTHFLEET

Springhead Ent Pk

St Joseph's RC Prim Sch

HARTFIELD PL

LABURNUM GR
LIME AVE

B261

Dover Rd Prim Sch

OLD RD W B261

B262

Brookvale Workshops

Cemy

MEADOW RD 1
FLEMING CT 2

Spring Head Nursery

Northfleet Tech Coll

Wombwell Park

St Margaret's Rd 1
Stanley Rd 2

Cygnet L Ctr

Liby

New House

Cécil Rd Prim Sch

DA11

Sports Gd

Superstore

Northfleet Sch for Girls

HALL RD

PEPPERHILL LA

FLEET RD

VIKING RD

Painters Ash Prim Sch

PICKWICK HO

JOHNSON HO

KENNEDY HO

PO

B262

Pepper Hill

STATION RD

A2

WATLING ST

ASHMORE GDNS 1
ROWMARSH CL 2
FOXBERRY WLK 3

NIGHTINGALE CL 1
BRIGHTLANDS 2
MALLOW CL 3

Hazells

DOWNS RD

Mast

A2

Superstore

Scadbury Manor

Northfleet Green

Southfleet

Sedley's CE Prim Sch

CHURCH ST

PH

LINCOLNSHOTT

DA13

Friary Court

Redstreet

DEAN & CHAPTER COTTS

RED ST

PH

Madam Wood

Weaver's Orch

HOOK PLACE COTTS

BANBURY VILLAS

Hook Green

THOMAS COTTS

GLOXINIA RD

BRAKEFIELD RD

BROAD DITCH RD

DA3

Brakefield House

FAIRVIEW

THE DROVE WAY

THE KNOLE

BRAMLEY RD

BURGHFIELD RD

35

59

F5
1 LAWRANCE SQ
2 BENNETT HO
3 GARDEN ROW
4 JENKINS CL
5 Shears Green
Jun & Inf Schs

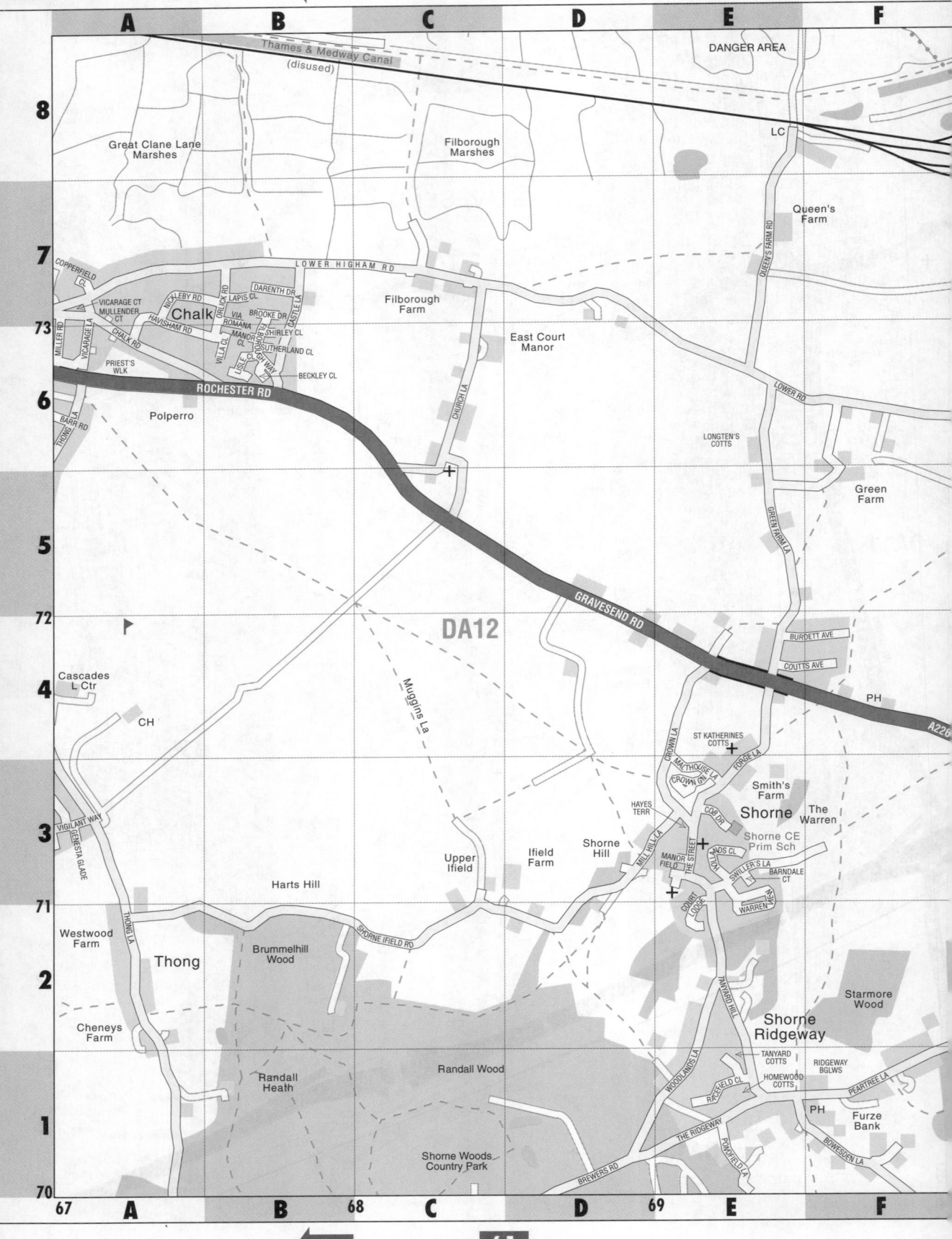

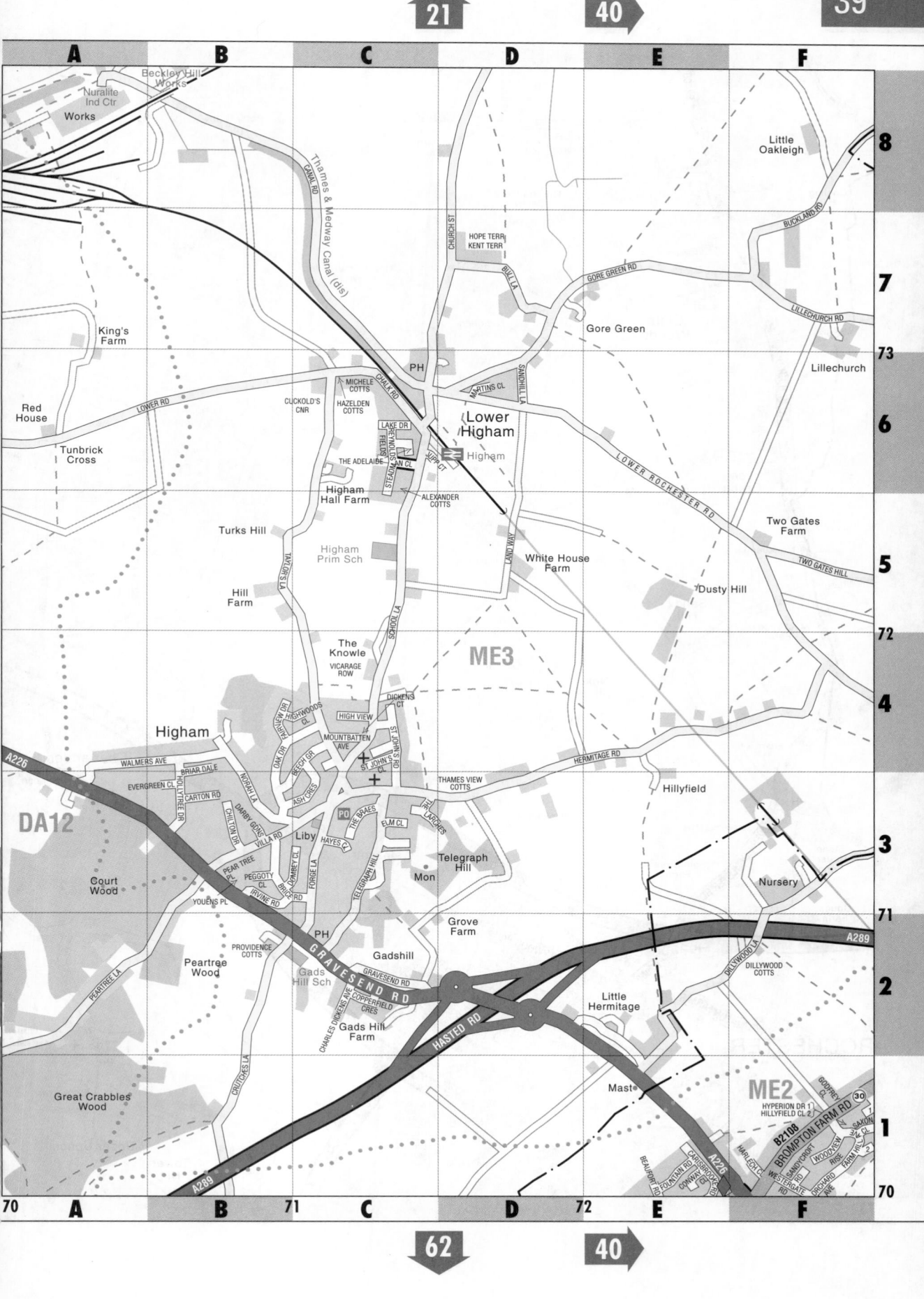

A B C D E F

8
7
73
6
5
72
4
3
71
2
1
70

Depot
Deangate Ridge Sports Gd
Deangate Wood
Deangate
CH
Tile Barn Farm
Chattenden Farm
Mast
Sundown
Mill Farm
PH
STREET FARM COTTS
Stonebridge
ME3
Hoo St Werburgh
Ratcliffe Highway
Hoo St Werburgh Prim Sch
The Hundred of Hoo Sch
Marlborough Ctr
JENNIFER CT
Broad Street
MAIN RD
1 NURSERY GDNS
2 BUTT HAW CL
HAIG VILLAS
ST WERBURGH
PO
Liby
MAIN RD
ARMYTAGE CL 1
EVEREST MEWS 2
HOO COMM
BROADWOOD
COE'S GN
SEARCHLIGHT HTS
BRANTA FIELDS
CHURCH FARM
Cockham Farm
Saxon Shore Way
Hoo Lodge
ME2
Saxon Shore Way
Cockham Wood
Gull Down Plantation
Hoo Marina Park
Works
Arethusa Venture Ctr
Lower Upnor
Hoo Marina
Pier
Upnor Reach
River Medway
7 TAPPAN DR
8 HENRIETTA CH
9 LITTLE VICTORY MOUNT
Pier
ME4
St Mary's Island CE Prim Sch
Finsborough Ness
EGRET CL 1
PARTRIDGE DR 2
MEADOWSWEET VW 3
ASTER DR 4
TEAL DR 5
EASTVIEW 6
Short Reach
ME3
Hoo Salt Marsh
The Avenue
St Mary's Island
ME7
Marina
Hoo Ness
HAVEN WAY 1
THE WHIMBRELS 2
WILLOWHERB CL 3
DEWBERRY CL 4
DOCK HEAD RD

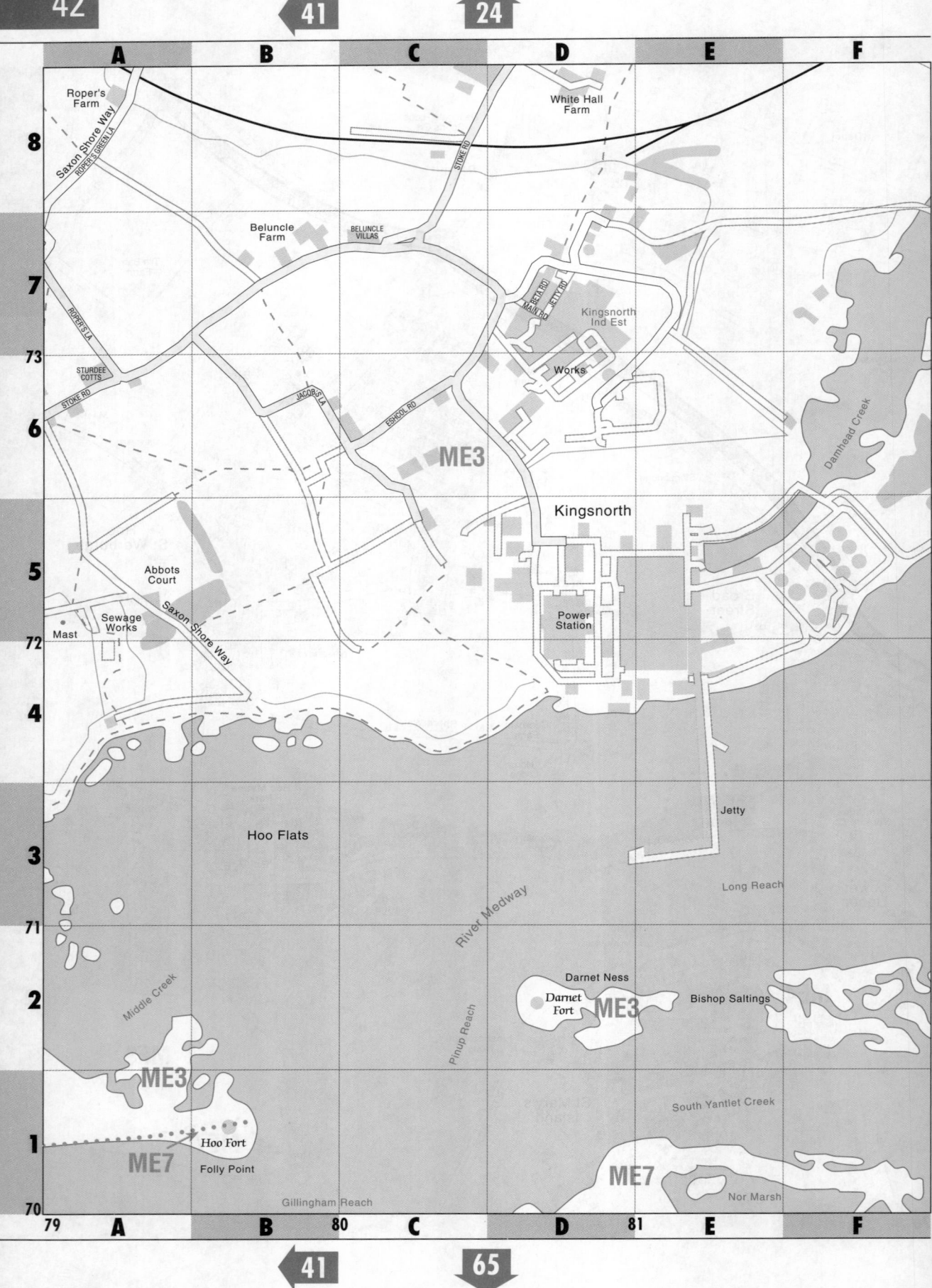

A B C D E F

Roper's Farm

White Hall Farm

8

Saxon Shore Way

ROPER'S GREEN LA

Beluncle Farm

BELUNCLE VILLAS

STOKE RD

7

ROPERS LA

BETA RD
MAIN RD
JETTY RD

Kingsnorth Ind Est

73

STURDEE COTTS

JACOB LA

Works

STOKE RD

ESHCOL RD

6

ME3

Kingsnorth

5

Abbots Court

Power Station

Mast

Sewage Works

Saxon Shore Way

72

Damhead Creek

4

Jetty

Hoo Flats

3

Long Reach

River Medway

71

Middle Creek

Pinup Reach

2

Darnet Ness

Darnet Fort

ME3

Bishop Saltings

ME3

South Yantlet Creek

1

Hoo Fort

ME7

Folly Point

ME7

Nor Marsh

70

Gillingham Reach

79 A B 80 C D 81 E F

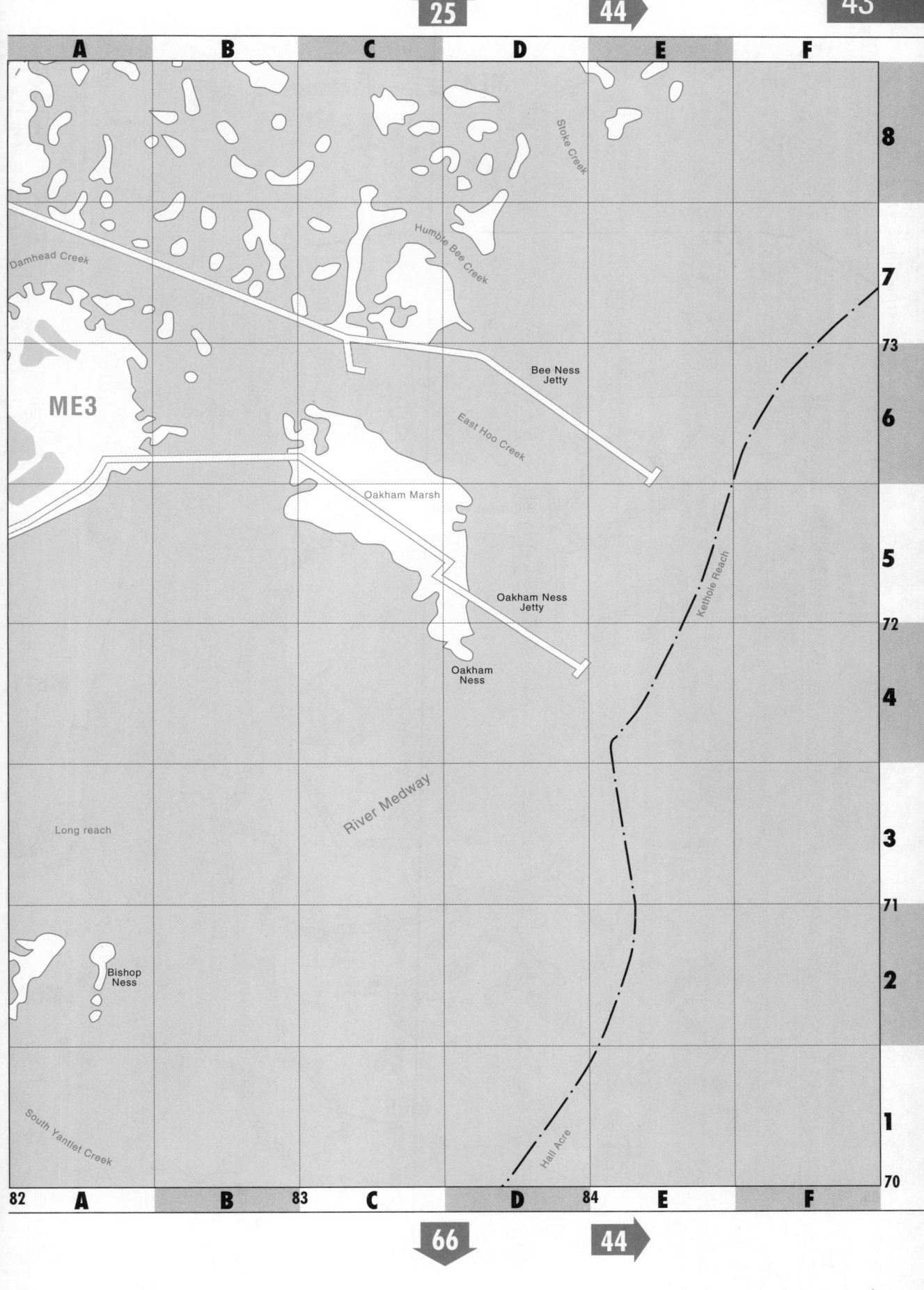

A   B   C   D   E   F

8

Stoke Creek

Humble Bee Creek

7

Damhead Creek

73

ME3

Bee Ness
Jetty

6

East Hoo Creek

Oakham Marsh

5

Oakham Ness
Jetty

72

Ketthole Reach

Oakham
Ness

4

River Medway

3

Long reach

71

Bishop
Ness

2

1

South Yantlet Creek

Hall Acre

70

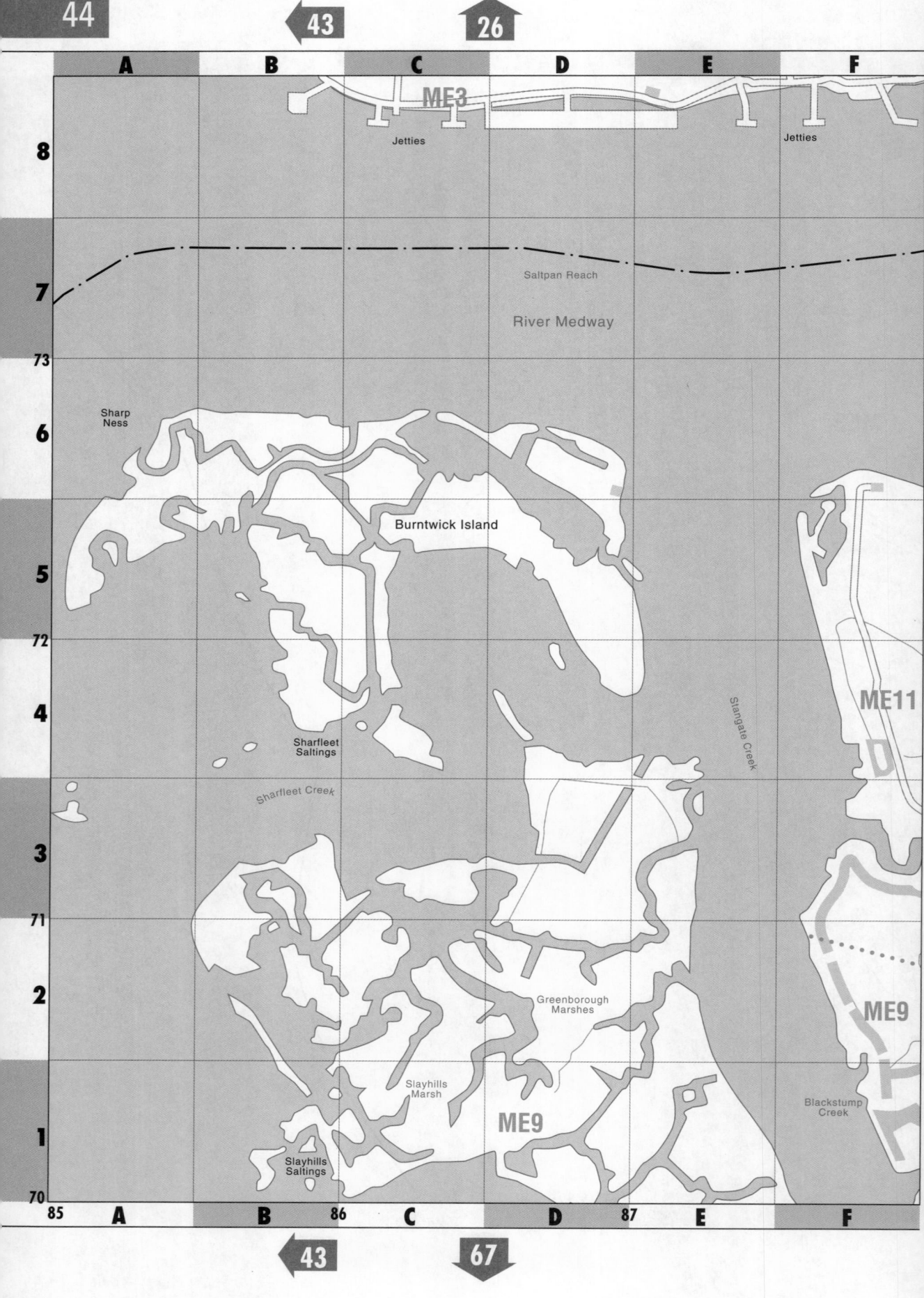

ME3

Jetties

Jetties

Saltpan Reach

River Medway

73

Sharp
Ness

Burntwick Island

ME11

72

Sharfleet
Saltings

Sharfleet Creek

Stangate Creek

71

Greenborough
Marshes

ME9

Slayhills
Marsh

ME9

Blackstump
Creek

Slayhills
Saltings

70

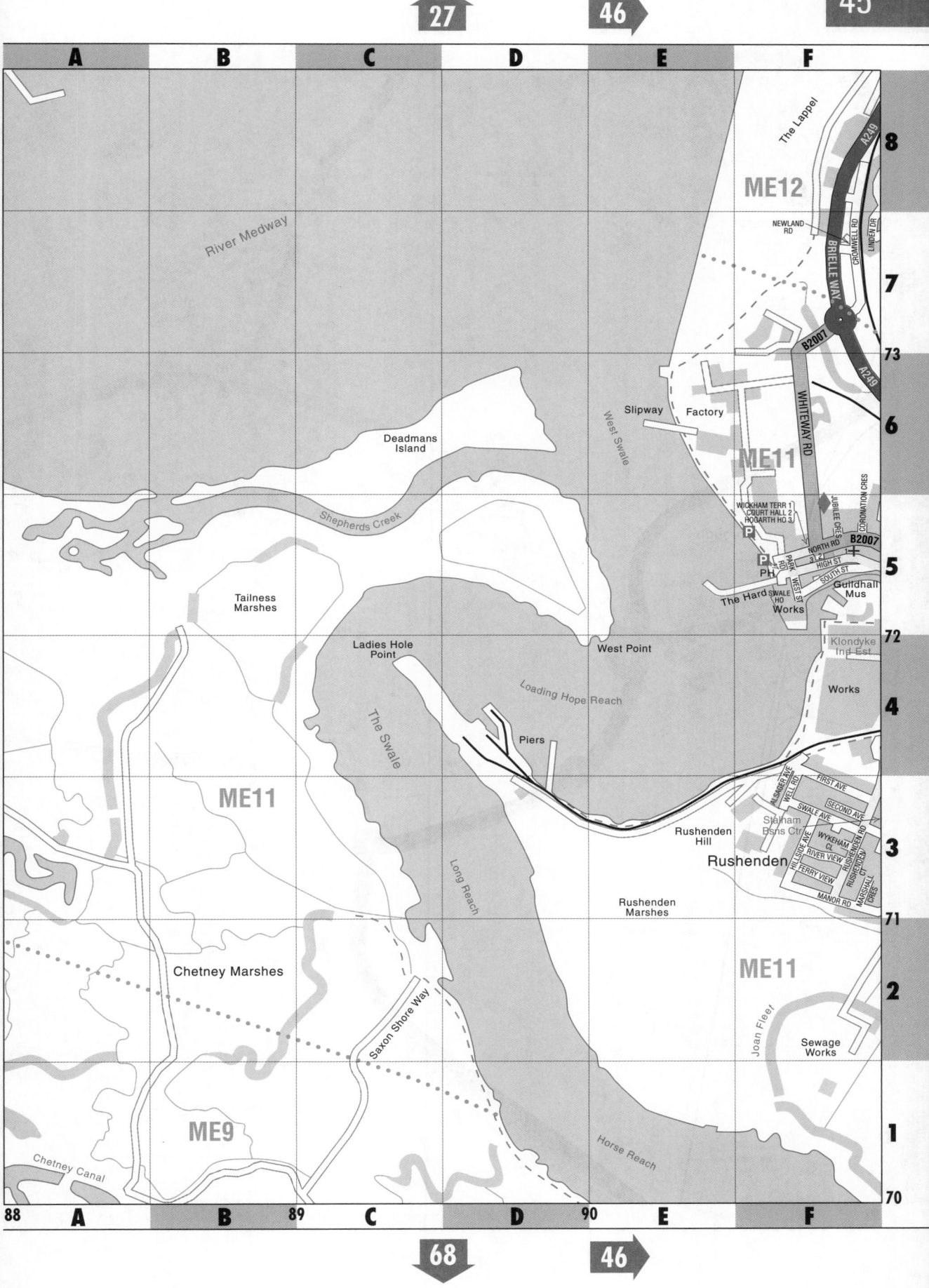

A B C D E F

8
7
73
6
5
72
4
3
71
2
1
70

The Lappel

ME12

A249
NEWLAND RD
CROMWELL RD
LINDEN DR
BRIELLE WAY
B2007
WHITEWAY RD
A249

Slipway   Factory

West Swale

ME11

WICKHAM TERR 1
COURT HALL 2
HOGARTH HO 3
P
P
PH
The Hard
SWALE HO
Works
NORTH RD
PARK
WEST ST
HIGH ST
SOUTH ST
B2007
JUBILEE CRES
CORONATION CRES
Guildhall
Mus

Klondyke
Ind Est

Works

River Medway

Deadmans
Island

Shepherds Creek

Tailness
Marshes

Ladies Hole
Point

West Point

Loading Hope Reach

Piers

The Swale

Rushenden
Hill

Stainham
Bsns Ctre

ALLSWORTH AVE
WET RD
FIRST AVE
SWALE AVE
SECOND AVE
WYKEHAM
CL
RIVER VIEW
HILLSIDE AVE
FERRY VIEW
MANOR RD
RUSHENDEN RD
RUSHENDEN CT
MARSHALL CRES

Rushenden

ME11

Long Reach

Chetney Marshes

Saxon Shore Way

Rushenden
Marshes

ME11

Joan Fleet

Sewage
Works

ME9

Horse Reach

Chetney Canal

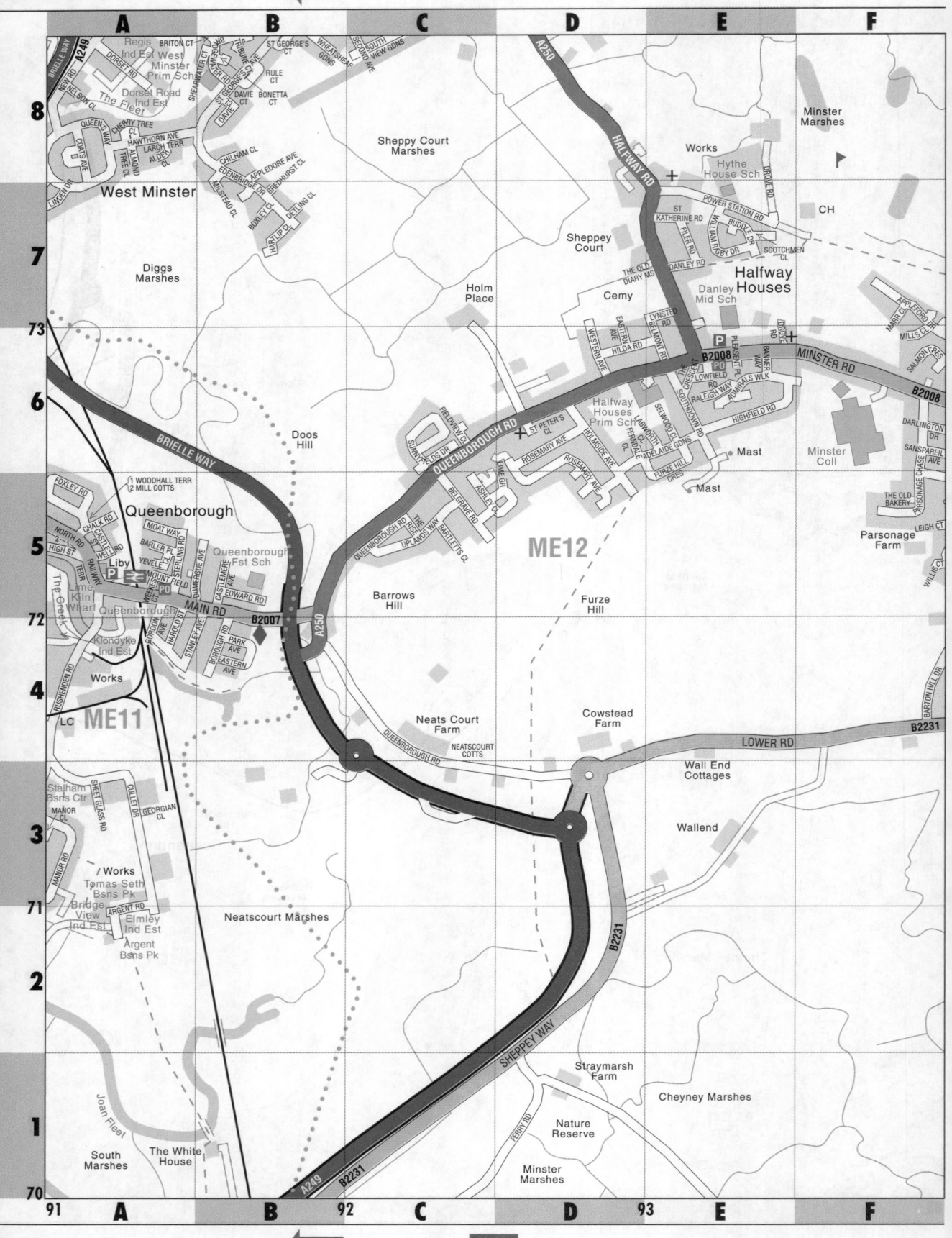

A   B   C   D   E   F

8

Leysdown-on-Sea

71

2

GROVE AVE.

EASTERN RD   P
PO
SAND CT   THE PROMENADE   MANOR WAY
B2231   LEYSDOWN RD   B2231   7
THAMES   NUTTS AVE.
CT   PH   PRIORY
PARK AVE.   WING RD   SHELLNESS RD
1   Holiday   WING RD   P
Village   73
ME12   WING RD
SHURLAND AVE.   SEAVIEW AVE.

70
03   G   H   04   6

73

Swanley Farm   Barrows Brook

NORMAN RD   Warden
Point   5
MANOR WAY
Cartts   COASTGUARD HOS
PH   Farm
WARDEN RD
WARDEN   72
WAY   Thorn
Barnland   Hill   4
Farm   THORN HILL RD
CLIFF DR.
PRESTON HALL GDNS
SEA APP.   P
ME12   ST JAMES CL.
Warden   IMPERIAL DR.   SEASALTER CL.
KNOLL WAY   WATERSIDE   JETTY RD
BUCKLERS   VIEW
EMPRESS GDNS   CL.   MELOD...   CLIFF VIEW GDNS
Rayham   WINDSOR   EMERALD VIEW
GDNS   BEACH APP.
CLARENCE GDNS   ST CLEMENTS RD   3
LEICESTER GDNS   SEA VIEW GDNS
Mustards   SEA VIEW GDNS   CONDOR CL.
PH   71
Holiday
Villages   2
B2231
SOUTHSEA GDNS   WARDEN BAY RD
Mast
MUSTARDS RD   GROVE WAY
CORONATION DR
Bay View   ST CLEMENTS   VANITY RD
B2231   CL.
DANES DR   BAY VIEW
GDNS
WARDEN VIEW GDNS   CLIFF VIEW GDNS   Cemy
LEYSDOWN RD
Rides   PH
Old Rides   Farm   Paradise   1
Farm   HARTY FERRY RD   Farm

00   A   B   01   C   D   02   E   F   70

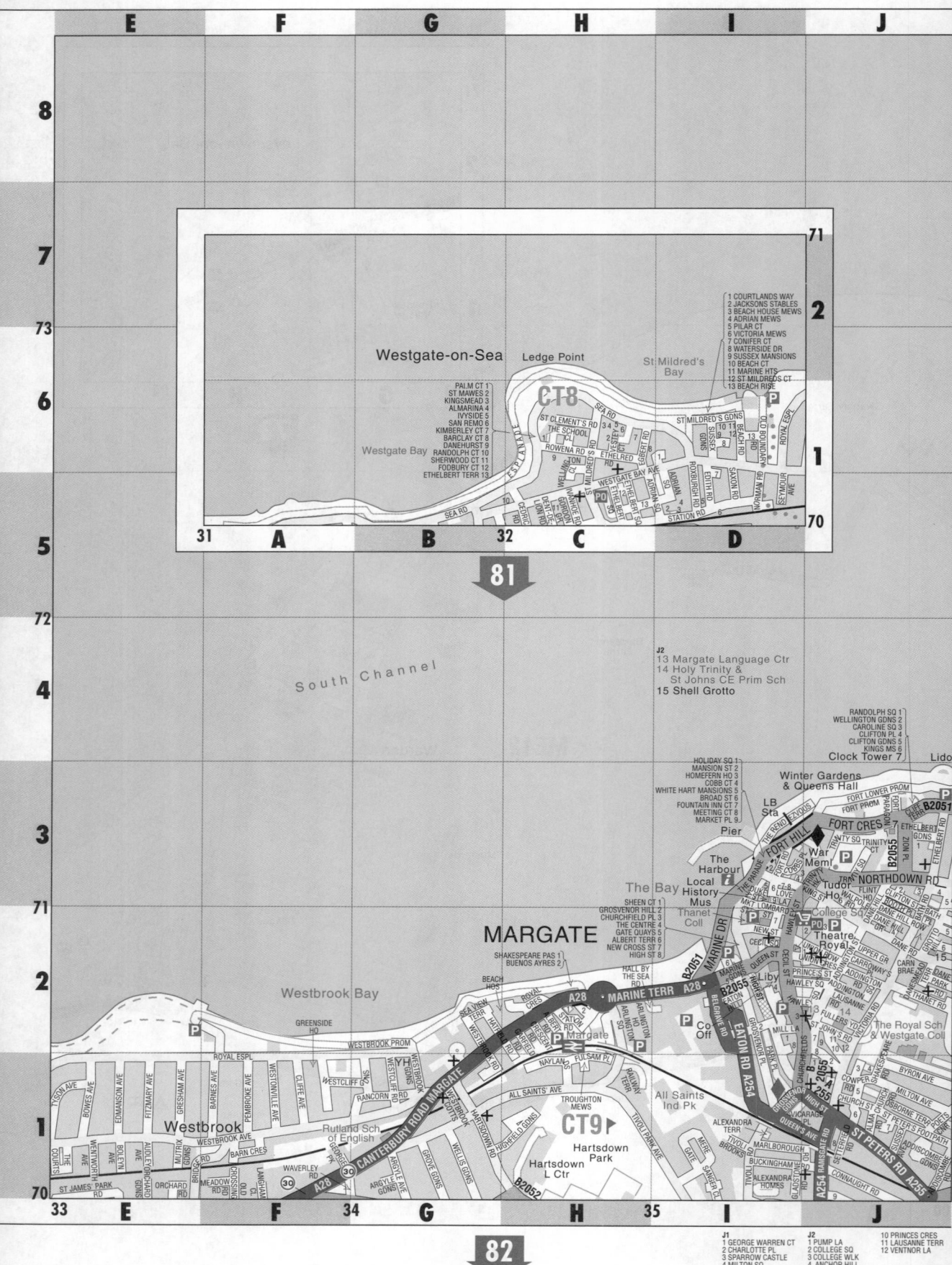

Westgate-on-Sea

Ledge Point

St Mildred's Bay

CT8

1 COURTLANDS WAY
2 JACKSONS STABLES
3 BEACH HOUSE MEWS
4 ADRIAN MEWS
5 PILAR CT
6 VICTORIA MEWS
7 CONIFER CT
8 WATERSIDE DR
9 SUSSEX MANSIONS
10 BEACH CT
11 MARINE HTS
12 ST MILDREDS CT
13 BEACH RISE

PALM CT 1
ST MAWES 2
KINGSMEAD 3
ALMARINA 4
IVYSIDE 5
SAN REMO 6
KIMBERLEY CT 7
BARCLAY CT 8
DANEHURST 9
RANDOLPH CT 10
SHERWOOD CT 11
FODBURY CT 12
ETHELBERT TERR 13

Westgate Bay

ST CLEMENT'S RD
THE SCHOOL
ST MILDRED'S GDNS
ROWENA RD
WELLINGTON
SEA RD

81

South Channel

Westbrook Bay

J2
13 Margate Language Ctr
14 Holy Trinity &
St Johns CE Prim Sch
15 Shell Grotto

RANDOLPH SQ 1
WELLINGTON GDNS 2
CAROLINE SQ 3
CLIFTON PL 4
CLIFTON GDNS 5
KINGS MS 6
Clock Tower 7
Lido

HOLIDAY SQ 1
MANSION ST 2
HOMEFERN HO 3
COBB CT 4
WHITE HART MANSIONS 5
BROAD ST 6
FOUNTAIN INN CT 7
MEETING CT 8
MARKET PL 9

Winter Gardens
& Queens Hall

LB Sta

FORT CRES

B2051

B2055

Pier

The Harbour

Local History Mus

FORT HILL

War Meml

NORTHDOWN RD

The Bay

SHEEN CT 1
GROSVENOR HILL 2
CHURCHFIELD PL 3
THE CENTRE 4
GATE QUAYS 5
ALBERT TERR 6
NEW CROSS ST 7
HIGH ST 8

Thanet Coll

Tudor Ho

College Sq

Theatre Royal

MARGATE

SHAKESPEARE PAS 1
BUENOS AYRES 2

BEACH HO

MARINE DR

MARINE TERR

A28

Liby

B2055

The Royal Sch & Westgate Coll

Westbrook

WESTBROOK PROM

P Margate

A28
Margate

Co Off

CT9 ▶

All Saints Ind Pk

ALL SAINTS AVE

TROUGHTON MEWS

Hartsdown Park
Hartsdown L Ctr

CANTERBURY ROAD MARGATE

Rutland Sch of English

ST PETERS RD A255

EATON RD A254

A254 MARGATE RD

B2052

82

J1
1 GEORGE WARREN CT
2 CHARLOTTE PL
3 SPARROW CASTLE
4 MILTON SQ
5 ARNOLD RD
6 OXFORD ST
7 HOMESTEAD CL
8 VICARAGE CRES
9 CONNAUGHT GDNS

J2
1 PUMP LA
2 COLLEGE SQ
3 COLLEGE WLK
4 ANCHOR HILL
5 GROTTO RD
6 GROTTO GDNS
7 ST JOHN'S ST
8 CHARLOTTE SQ
9 WINDSOR MEWS

10 PRINCES CRES
11 LAUSANNE TERR
12 VENTNOR LA

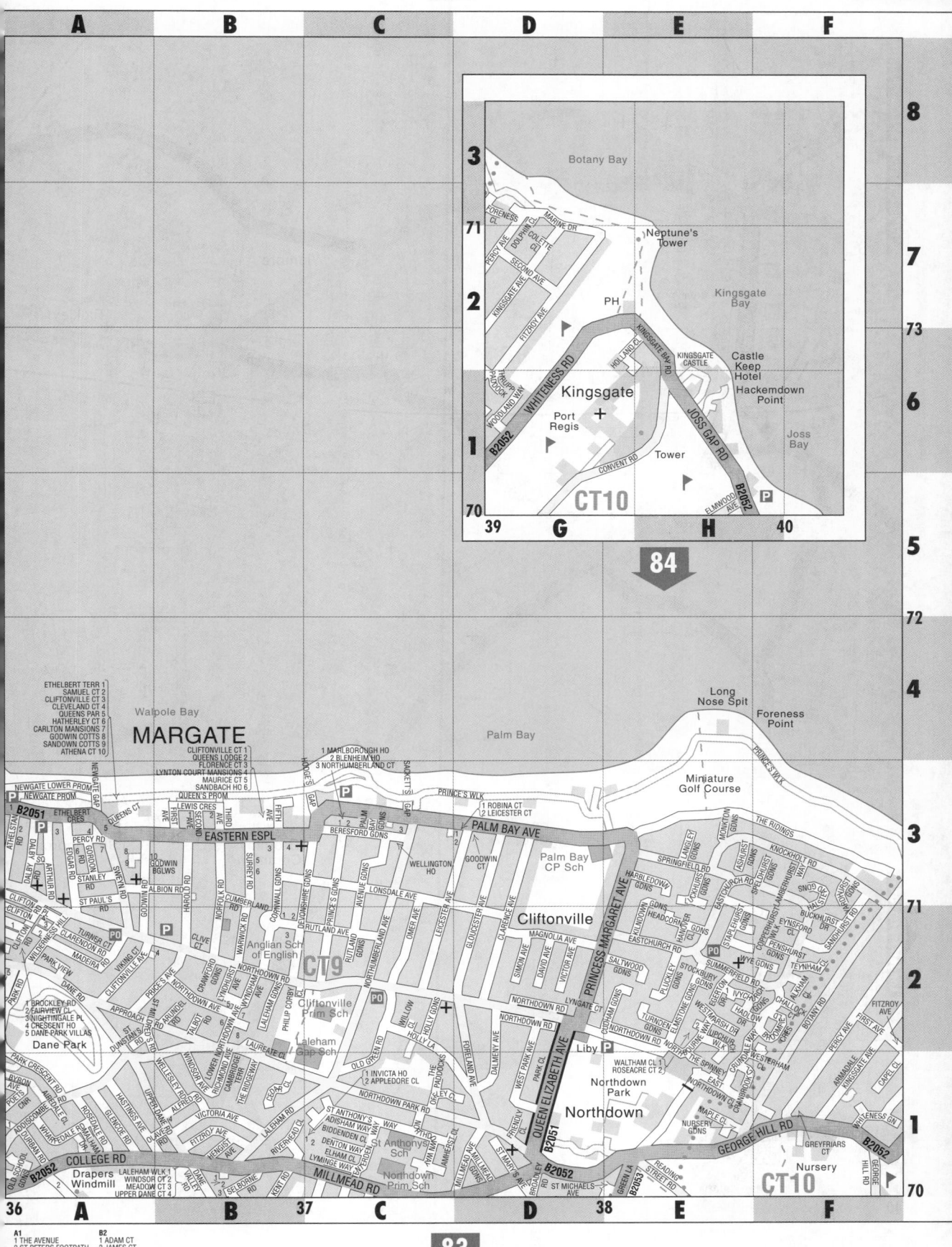

29

BR7

WIDMORE

BICKLEY

BROMLEY

BR1

BR2

Bromley Common

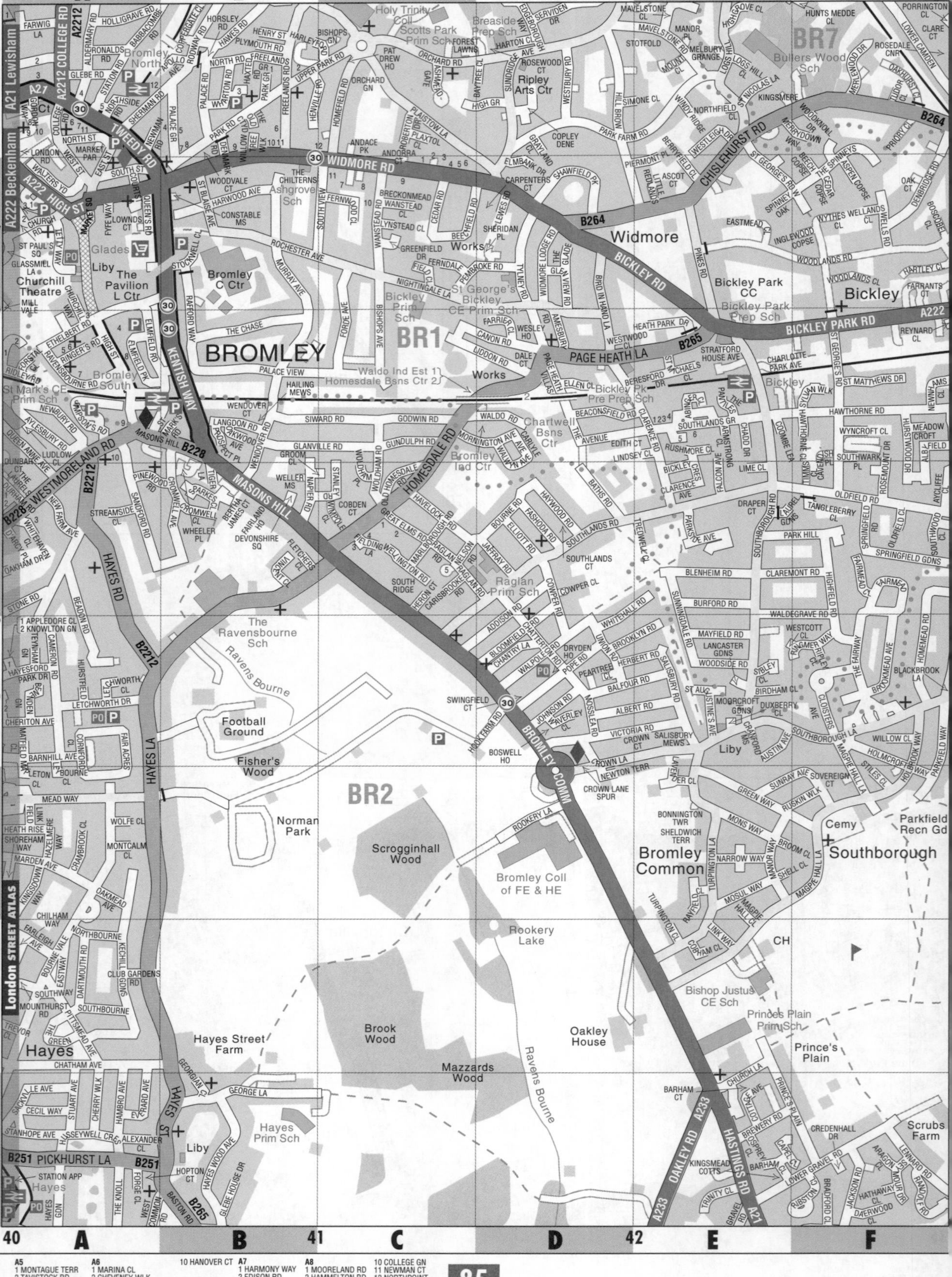

Southborough

HAYES

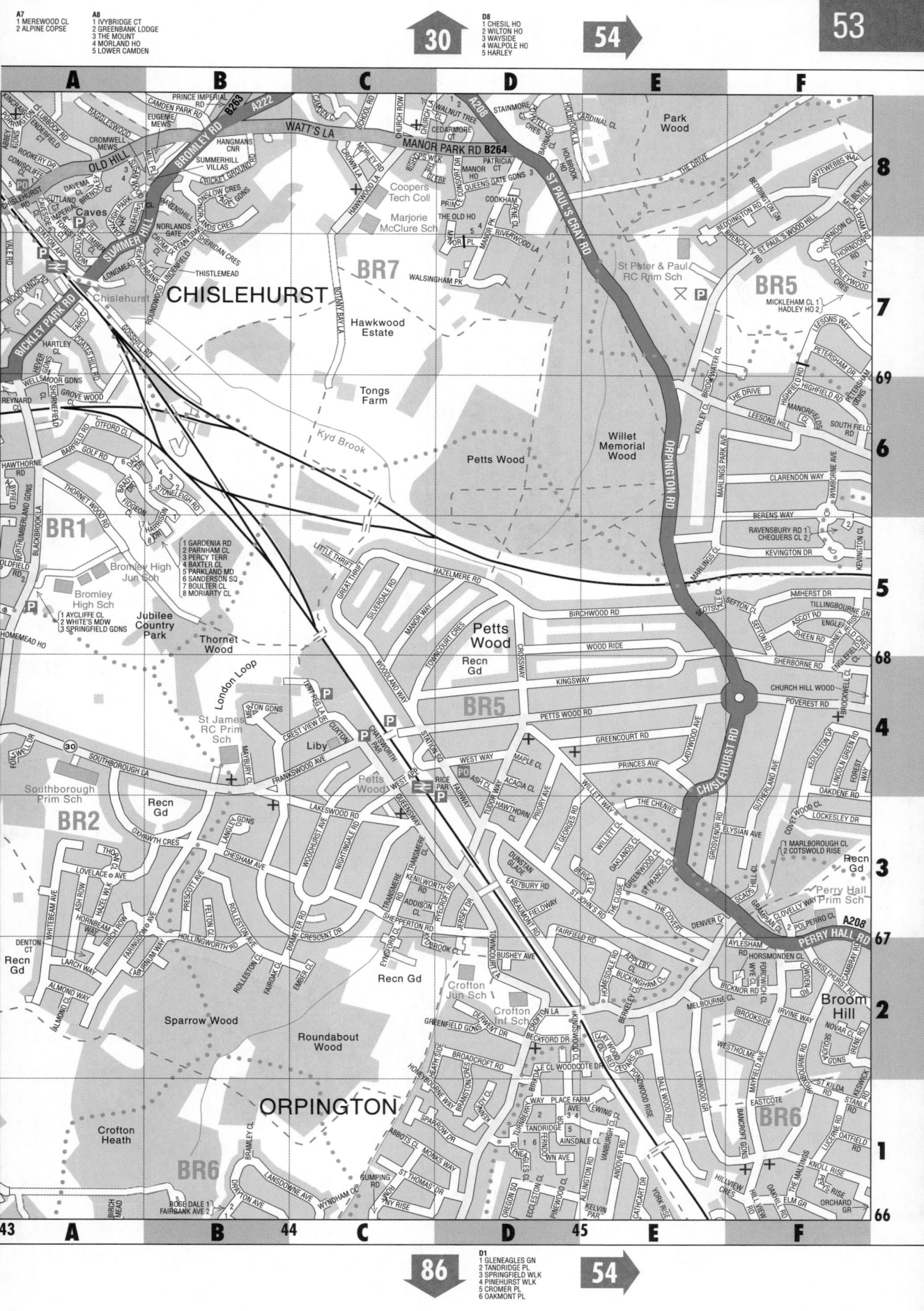

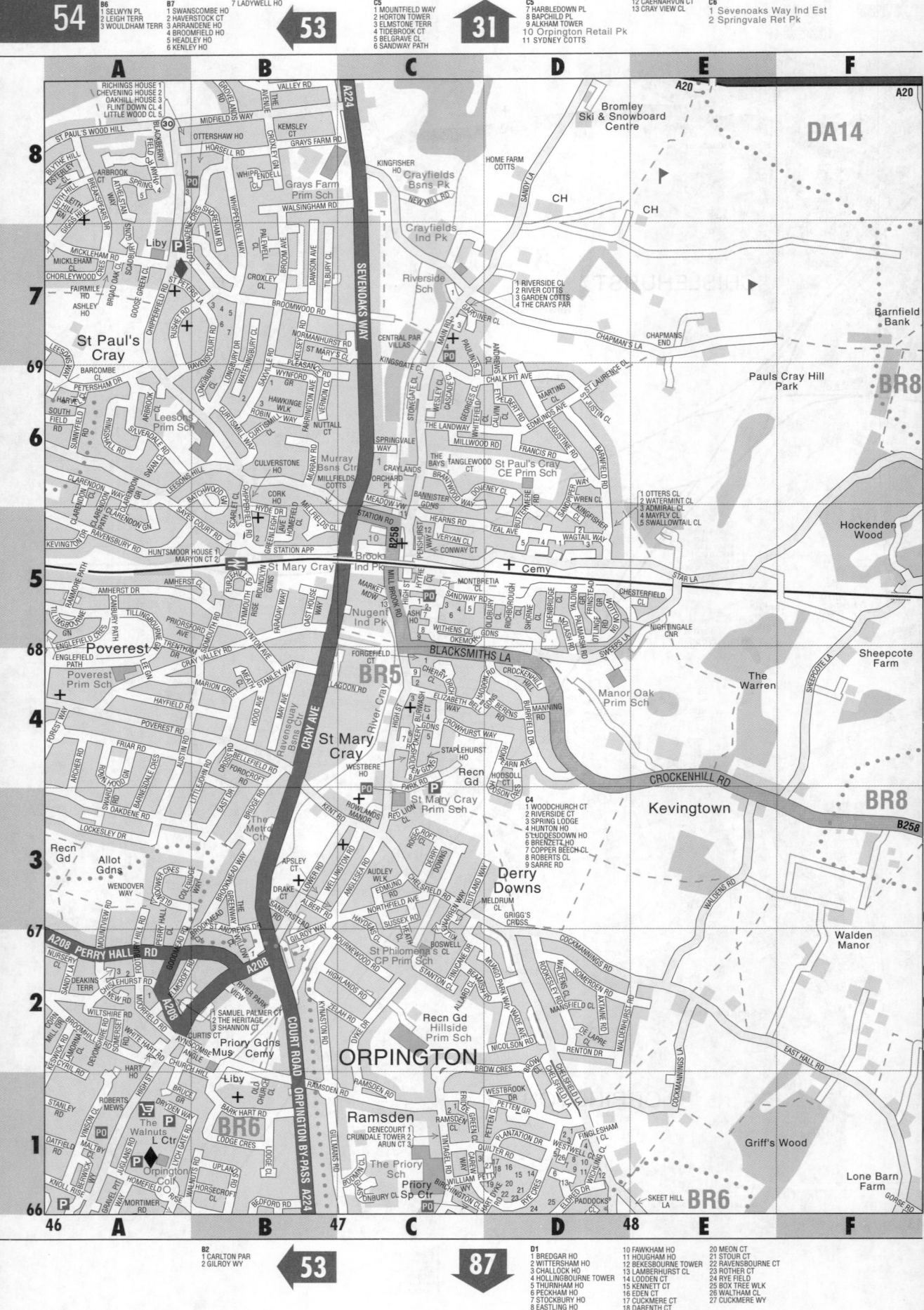

32

56
E6
1 WHITEOAK CT
2 KENNET CT
3 WHITE OAK SQ
4 ST ANDREW'S CT
5 RUXTON CT
6 BERKELEY CT

7 St Bartholomews
RC Prim Sch

55

DA14

Birchwood
Corner

Nursery

Nursery

College Rd

Egerton Ave
Spring Vale Cl
Nutley Cl

MAIN RD
B258

Hextable
Sch

SQUIRES
FIELD

8

MAIDSTONE RD

A20   B2173

Burnt House
Farm

KIDDENS

Birchwood Terr 1
Jessamine Terr 2

Oakwood
Ct

New Barn Park

New Barn Rd

Swanley New
Barn Railway

VEITCHIL
BARN

White Oak

ARCHER
WAY

B258

7

Hockenden

Hockenden La

Hockenden
House

LONDON RD

White
Oak
L Ctr

Horizon
Prim Sch

ARCHER
WAY

69

Liby

SWANLEY TECH COLL

Swanley
Tech Coll

B2173

SWANLEY LA

LULLINGSTONE RD

6

STAR LA

Civic
Ctr

LONDON RD

Park Road
Ind Est

B258

B2173

Bourne Wood

St Mary's CE
Prim Sch

Swanley

B258

High St

LONDON RD

High Firs
Prim Sch

5

SHEEPCOTE LA

WINTON
CT

WAYLANDS

68

BR5

BR8

A20

PETHAM COURT
COTTS

4

Recn
Gd

GREEN COURT RD

Crockenhill
Prim Sch

Petham
Court

Crouch
Farm

The Green

SEVEN ACRES

KIDDS
COTTS

Cemy

Gosenhill
Farm

3

CROCKENHILL RD

CRAY RD

PH

Crockenhill

CHURCH FARM CL

EYNSFORD RD

WESTED FARM
COTTS

67

Church Rd

1 HARNETTS CL
2 SCHOOL COTTS
3 CHURCH COTTS
4 ALMSHOUSES

Wested
Farm

2

Bleak House
Farm

HARVEST WAY

BR5

Allot
Gdns

DA4

1

HIGHCROFT
HALL

M25

66

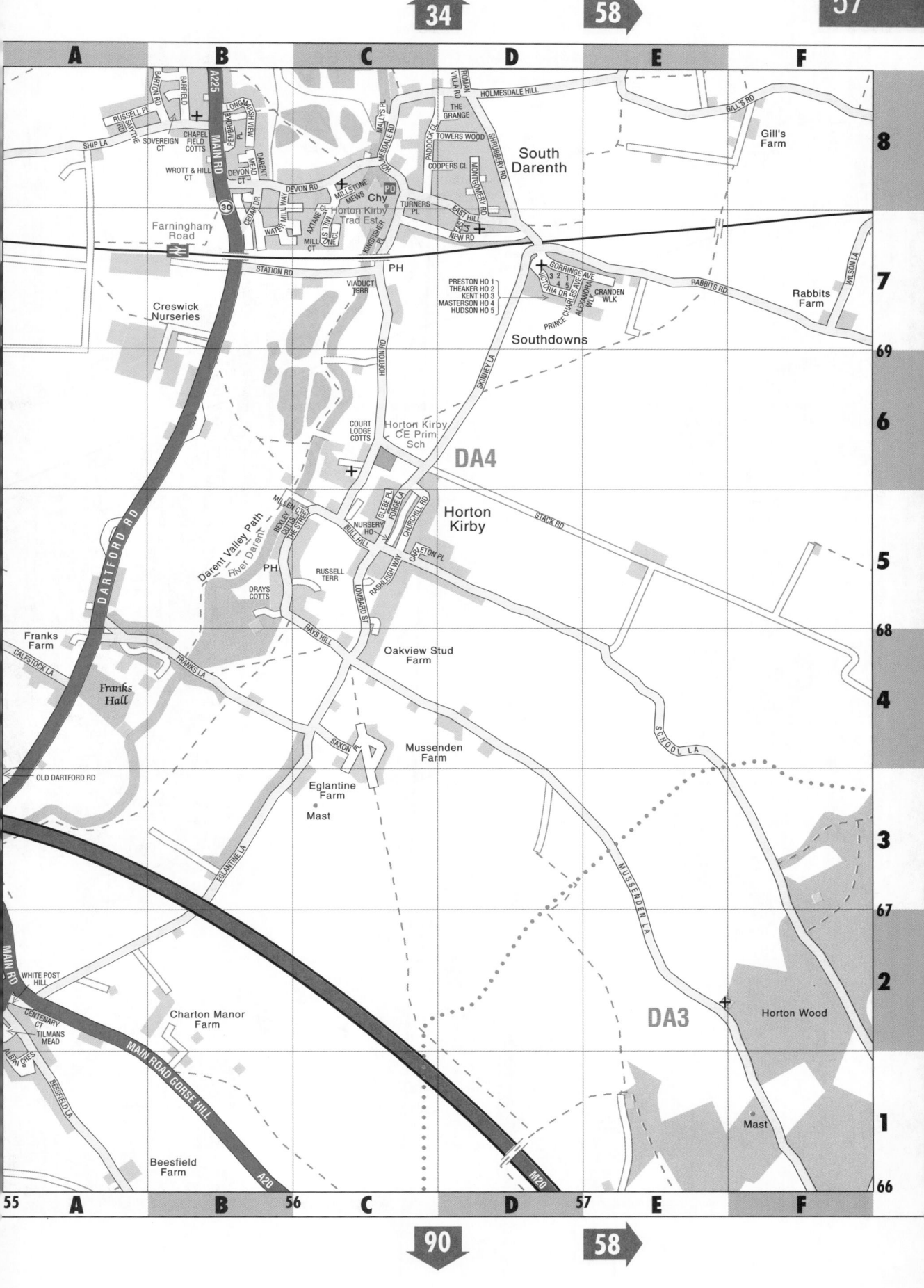

A B C D E F

8

Grubb Street

Ryecroft Farm

B260 GREEN STREET GREEN RD

Ryecrofts Wood

GILL'S RD

WILSON LA

Mile End Green

DA2

Mile End Green Cotts

B255

WHITEHILL RD

DA13

Whitehill

Longfield

7

Pinden

Pinden End Farm

B255

NORTHDOWN RD

MAIN RD

Liby

WEST SHAW

ROWANS CL

PH

PO

ESSEX RD

FOSTERS MEWS

KENT RD

LANDSEER CL

HARTLEY RD

ST MARY'S WAY

69

RABBITS RD

DA4

Dene Bottom Farm

CHEYNE WLK

CAVENDISH SQ

RUSSELL SQ

EATON SQ

STATION RD

P

P

P

Longfield

OAKWOOD RISE

COPSE SIDE

Longfield Acad

B260

6

Dean Bottom

CANADA FARM RD

FAWKHAM RD

THE CRESCENT 6

THE MEWS 1
ST JAMES SQ 2
GROSVENOR SQ 3
BEDFORD SQ 4
ST GEORGES SQ 5
SLOANE SQ 6

BRAMBLEFIELD CL

PARK DR

HOTTSFIELD

FAIRACRE PL

QUAKERS CL

NORTHFIELD

GULCROFT

CAXTON

Churchdown Wood

MERTON AVE 4 2

HAWTHORNS

PERRAN CL

VIEWPOINT CT

PITFIELD

BRAMBLEDOWN 3 1

WELL FIELD

1 SILVERDALE
2 MERRYFIELDS CL
3 EVERGLADE CL
4 FORTUNA CL

PORCHESTER CL

5

Steephill Sch

BANKSIDE

HOSELANDS VIEW

PARKFIELD

LARKS FIELD

DOWNS VALLEY

GRESHAM AVE

GRESHAM CL

WOODLAND AVE

68

Beeches Farm

Canada Farm

Hill Barn Farm

CASTLE HILL

THE OLD DOWNS

SANDSHAW CT

OLD DOWNS

WICKHAMS WAY

4

DA3

Hartley Green

DICKENS CL

GREEN WAY

STACK LA

CHURCH RD

Our Lady of Hartley RC Prim Sch

JOHNS CL

GORSE WAY

Lane Oak Farm

SCUDDERS HILL

Football Ground

Sports Club

Pennis Farm

Hartley Prim Sch

BROOMFIELDS

CULVEY CL

PO

ROUND ASH WAY

CAPT WAY

ASH RD

CARMELITE WAY

CONIFER AVE

CHERRY TREES

Liby

THE WRENS

MANOR DR

3

Nursery

VALLEY RD

FAIRBY LA

CHANTRY AVE

ST JOHN'S LA

REDHILL WOOD SCH

BILLINGS HILL

BRANCA

TATES ORCH

Hartley

67

THREE GATES RD

SCHOOL LA

THE GROVE

MANOR LA

Pennis Wood

PH

2

Fawkham CE Prim Sch

Parkfield Wood

Fawkham Manor

H

TN15

CH

Chapel Wood

Mast

Milestone Sch

1

OLIVER MILL 1
CHAPEL WOOD 2

FARM CL

CALING CROFT

2 1

CHAPEL WOOD RD

66

59
37

A B C D E F

8

WROTHAM RD
A227

Huntondown Wood

Ifield Court

New Cottages

P

Jeskyns Country Park

Henhurst Dale

Henhurst

HENHURST HILL

HENHURST RD

Winstead Hill

A2

7

CHURCH RD

Dabbs Place Farm

Jeskyns Court

Nash Street

Cozendon Wood

Tollingtrough Green

Dabbs Place

JESKYNS RD

69

NASH ST

DA12
Owletts

Jeskyns Farm

Cobham

6

Nurstead Court

The Park

Mill Hill

COPT HALL RD

Wealdway

ROUND ST

Round Street

THE STREET

BATTLE ST
SARGENTS
SCOTLAND LA

Cobham College

NURSTEAD CHURCH LA

The Beeches

Sweep's Hole

P

5

WHITE POST LA

SALLOWS

SOLE ST

Sole Street

MANOR RD

MANOR CT

STRATTON FIELDS

SOLE ST

GREENLANDS

Danes Place

Gold Street

68

Lordscroft Shaw

MAY PL

GOLD ST

4

STATION RD

THE RAILWAY SIDINGS

NURSERY RD

Meopham

P

Meopham Station

Blundells Shaw

Sole Street

Henley Street

HENLEY ST

HAY'S MEAD

JOHN'S RD

A227

EDMUND CL

EDVA RD

FAIR VIEW GDNS

NORWOOD LA

PH

DA13

Camer Farm

CAMER RD

CAMER GDNS

CAMER ST

PH

NEW RD

HOOK GREEN CT

P.O.

ARBORFIELD

PINE RISE

ADMAN CL

WALNUT TREE WAY

POPLAR WLK

Camer

Reynold's Farm

3

CHESTNUT CL

MELLIKER LA

THE MEDLARS

THE PIPPINS

THE RUSSETS

WROTHAM RD

DENESWAY

TRADESCANT DR

MULBERRY CL

LILAC PL

Hook Green

Henley Down

67

STRAND

CHINNERY CT

HUNTINGFIELD RD

HIGHFIELD RD

BEECH WAY

DORMERS DR

GREEN LA

P

Camer Country Park

2

LONGFIELD RD

B260

SCHOOL CL

THE PARADE

P

CAMER PARK RD

Henley Wood

Henley Down

Helen Allison Sch

Meopham Prim Sch

Meopham Court

Bramble Hall Farm

Oakenden

1

SHIPLEY HILLS RD

THE OLD VICARAGE

A227

THE STREET

FOXENDOWN LA

BRIMSTONE HILL

OAKENDEN RD

DEAN RD

Luddesdown

Luddesdown Court

66

59
93

A B C D E F

WATLING STREET

THONG LA

A2

Hotel

Shorne Woods
Country Park

Visitor
Ctr

P

Puckle Hill

Brewers
Wood

Boysden
Shaw

8

Park
Pale

M2

Scalers
Hill House

SCOTLAND LA

The
Mount

PALE PARK LA

WATLING ST

7

Ashenbank
Wood

P

West Park

Peggy Taylor's
Hill

CH

69

HALFPENCE LA

DA12

Cobham Hall
Sch

Cobham Hall
Sch

6

The Avenue

Cobham
Hall

Cobham Park

Deer Park

P

Cobham
Prim Sch

PH

THE STREET

LAWRENCE DR

LODGE LA

Lodge
Farm

Mausoleum

William's
Hill

Norwood Grove

5

NEW COLLEGE
OF COBHAM

Cobhambury
Farm

Winterham
Hill

Lodge Wood

Nor Wood

68

BATT'S RD

COBHAMBURY RD

4

Cobhambury
Wood

Shoulder of Mutton
Shaw

WARREN RD

ME2

Lower
Bush

BUSH RD

Bush
Farm

3

DA13

HENLEY ST

Bowman's
Hill

Red
Wood

Warren
House

67

UPPER BUSH RD

Upper
Bush

LUDDESDOWN RD

Cutter
Ridge

2

PH

Brookers
Farm

Lower
Luddesdown

BUCKLAND RD

Longbottom
Wood

NORTH DOWNS WAY

Rectory

CUTTER RIDGE RD

Little Red
Wood

Stonereed
Shaw

Dean
Farm

1

Court
Lodge

Bush
Valley

North
Wood

66

67 A B 68 C D 69 E F

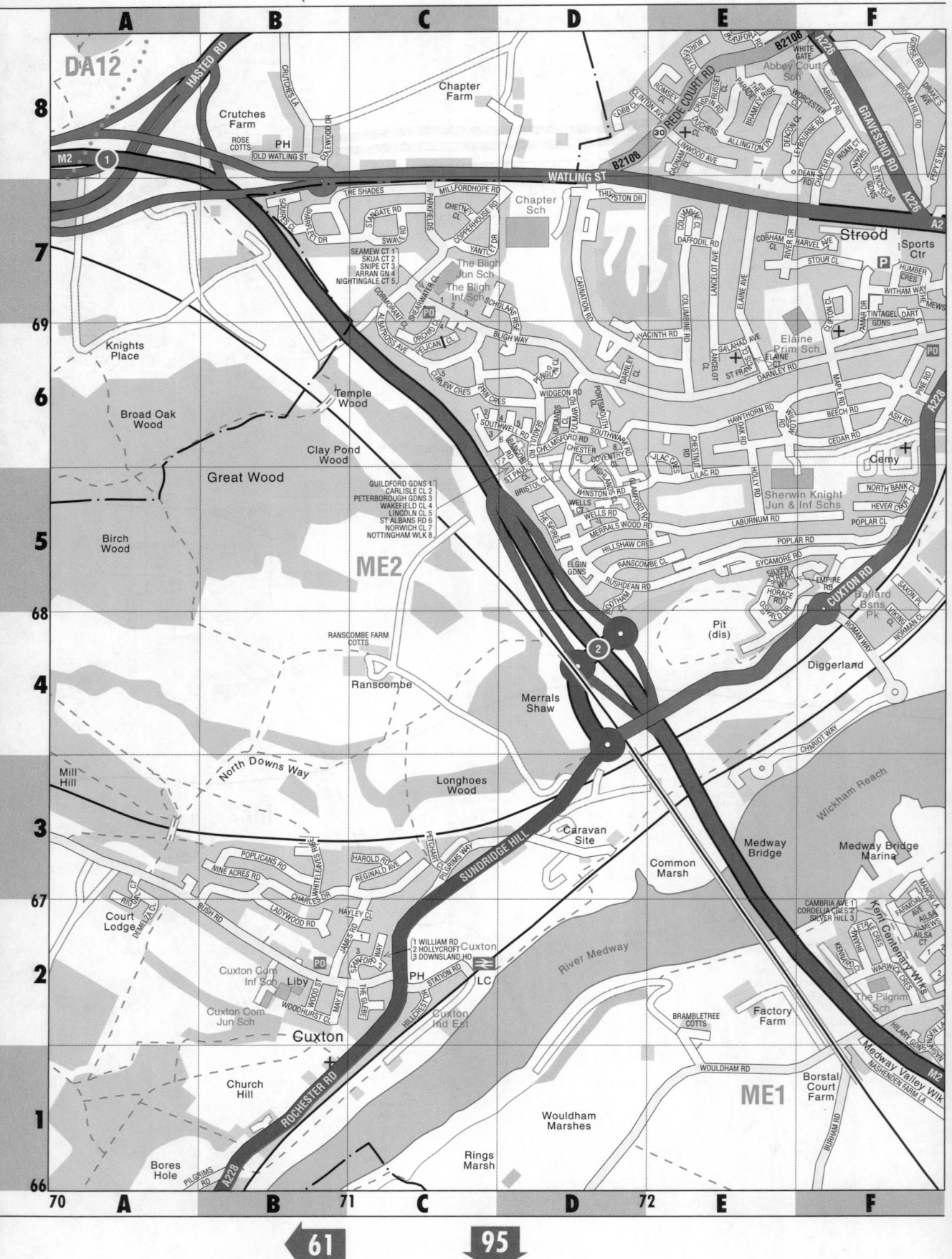

DA12

HASTED RD

Crutches
Farm

Chapter
Farm

CRUTCHES LA

CLEWDOOR DR

ROSE
COTTS

PH

OLD WATLING ST

WATLING ST

B2108

M2

Strood

Sports
Ctr

GRAVESEND RD

A226

A2

THE SHADES

MILLFORDHOPE RD

Chapter
Sch

REDE COURT RD

WHITE
GATE

Abbey Court
Sch

B2108

A226

Knights
Place

Temple
Wood

Broad Oak
Wood

Clay Pond
Wood

Great Wood

ME2

Birch
Wood

The Bligh
Jun Sch
The Bligh
Inf Sch

SEAMEW CT 1
SKUA CT 2
SNIPE CT 3
ARRAN GN 4
NIGHTINGALE CT 5

SCHOLARS RISE

BLIGH WAY

Elaine
Prim Sch

Cemy

Sherwin Knight
Jun & Inf Schs

GUILDFORD GDNS 1
CARLISLE CL 2
PETERBOROUGH GDNS 3
WAKEFIELD GDNS 4
LINCOLN CL 5
ST ALBANS RD 6
NORWICH CL 7
NOTTINGHAM WLK 8

CUXTON RD

Ballard
Bsns
Pk

Ranscombe Farm
Cotts

Ranscombe

Pit
(dis)

Diggerland

Merrals
Shaw

Mill
Hill

North Downs Way

Longhoes
Wood

Caravan
Site

Medway
Bridge

Medway Bridge
Marina

Wickham Reach

Court
Lodge

POPLICANS RD

NINE ACRES RD

BUSH RD

SUNDRIDGE HILL

Common
Marsh

PILGRIMS WAY

PETHAM GN

Cuxton Com
Inf Sch

Liby

PO

Cuxton Com
Jun Sch

Cuxton

1 WILLIAM RD
2 HOLLYCROFT
3 DOWNSLAND HO

Cuxton

PH

STATION RD

LC

Cuxton
Ind Est

River Medway

BRAMBLETREE
COTTS

Factory
Farm

The Pilgrim
Sch

Kent Cement Wks

ME1

Church
Hill

ROCHESTER RD

Wouldham
Marshes

WOULDHAM RD

Borstal
Court
Farm

Medway Valley Wlk

M2

Bores
Hole

PILGRIMS RD

A228

Rings
Marsh

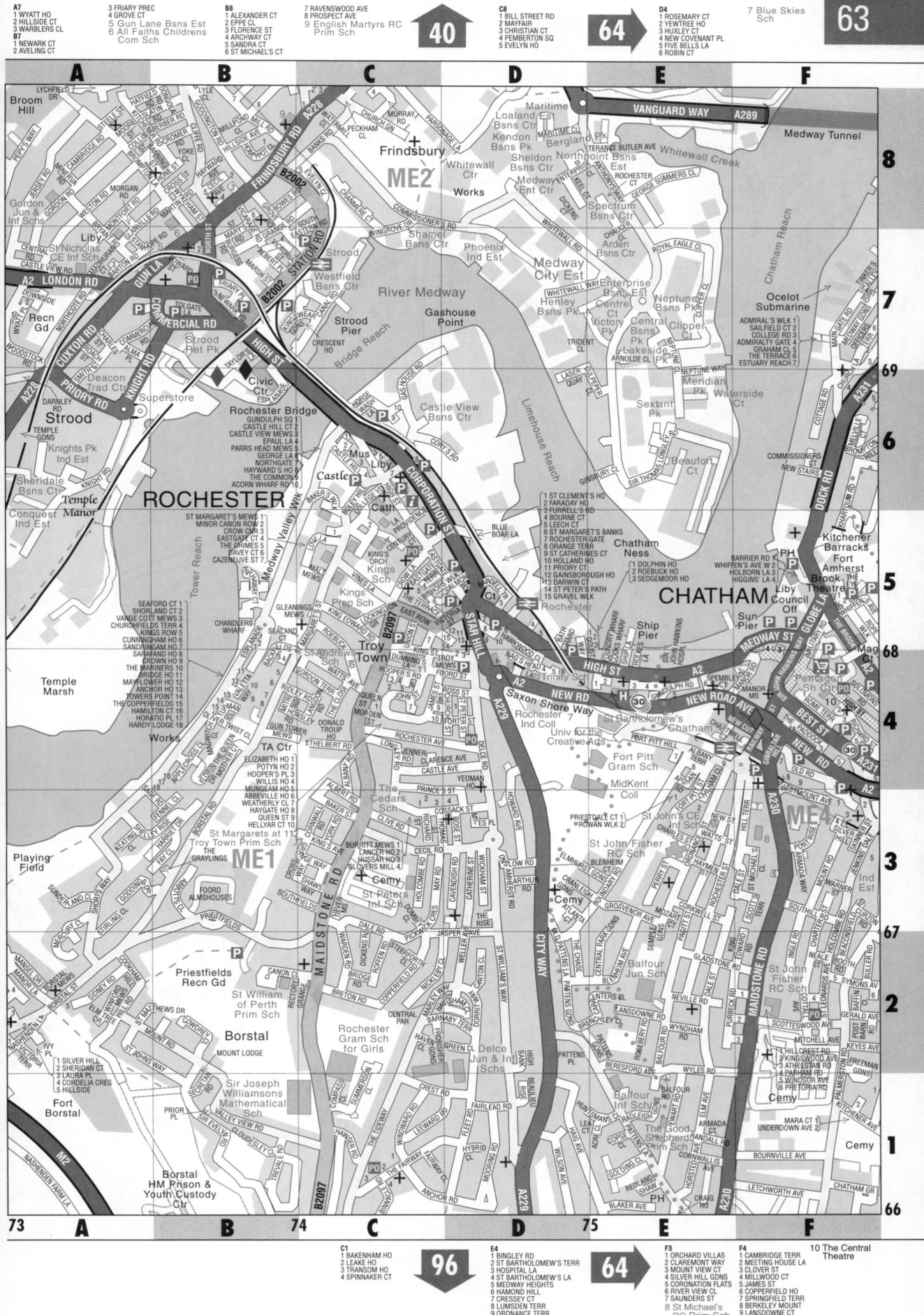

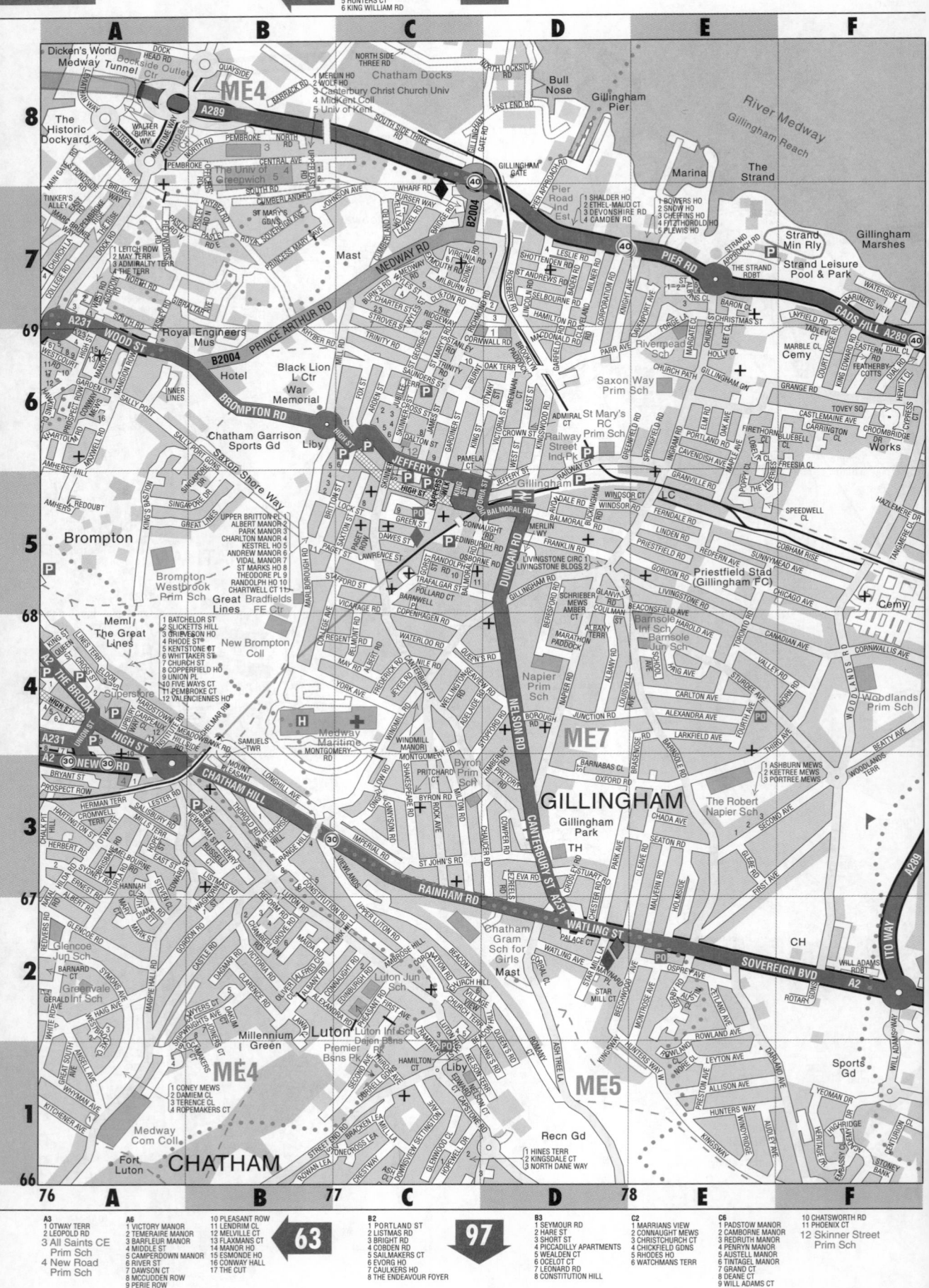

C7
1 AUGUSTA CL
2 ANNVERA HO
3 SUNDERLAND HO
4 LATIMER PL
5 HUNTERS CT
6 KING WILLIAM RD

7 FORSYTH CT

63

41

D6
1 BURNT OAK
  PRIM SCH

A3
1 OTWAY TERR
2 LEOPOLD RD
3 ALL SAINTS CE
  PRIM SCH
4 NEW ROAD
  PRIM SCH

A6
1 VICTORY MANOR
2 TEMERAIRE MANOR
3 BARFLEUR MANOR
4 MIDDLE ST
5 CAMPERDOWN MANOR
6 RIVER ST
7 DAWSON CT
8 MCCUDDEN ROW
9 PERIE ROW

10 PLEASANT ROW
11 LENDRIM CL
12 MELVILLE CT
13 FLAXMANS CT
14 MANOR HO
15 ESMONDE RD
16 CONWAY HALL
17 THE CUT

63

97

B2
1 PORTLAND ST
2 LISTMAS RD
3 BRIGHT RD
4 COBDEN RD
5 SAILMAKERS CT
6 EVORG HO
7 CAULKERS HO
8 THE ENDEAVOUR FOYER

B3
1 SEYMOUR RD
2 HARE ST
3 SHORT ST
4 PICCADILLY APARTMENTS
5 WEALDEN CT
6 OCELOT CT
7 LEONARD RD
8 CONSTITUTION HILL

C2
1 MARRIANS VIEW
2 CONNAUGHT MEWS
3 CHRISTCHURCH CT
4 CHICKFIELD GDNS
5 RHODES HO
6 WATCHMANS TERR

C6
1 PADSTOW MANOR
2 CAMBORNE MANOR
3 REDRUTH MANOR
4 PENRYN MANOR
5 AUSTELL MANOR
6 TINTAGEL MANOR
7 GRAND CT
8 DEANE CT
9 WILL ADAMS CT

10 CHATSWORTH RD
11 PHOENIX CT
12 SKINNER STREET
   PRIM SCH

A B C D E F

8

River Medway
Gillingham Reach

Nor Marsh

7

Copperhouse Marshes

Ferol
Peak

69

Cinque Port Marshes

Horrid
Hill

6

DANES HILL

Walnut Tree
Farm

Saxon Shore Way

B2004
Grange

Mill Hill

ME7

THE SPIERS

Sharp's
Green

Visitor Ctr

5

Allot Gdns
Grace
Manor

Lower
Twydall

LOWER RAINHAM RD

Riverside
Country Park

1 BUTTERMERE CL
2 PENRITH CT
3 KESWICK CT
4 BRAITHWAITE CT

LADDS
CNR

Mariners
Farm

68

Cemy
Sports
Field

Little London
Farm

Bloors
Wharf

4

CORNWALLIS
RDBT
CORNWALLIS AVE

Beechings
Way Ind Ctr

1 BISHOPBOURNE GN
2 HEADCORN RD
3 DENTON GN

Twydall
Ent Ctr

PH

BLOORS WHARF RD

ITO WAY

Featherby
Inf Sch
Featherby
Jun Sch

Liby

1 FORDWICH GN
2 BONNINGTON GN
3 SELLINGE GN

Pump
Farm

Bloors
Place

WEST MOTNEY
WAY
B2004

3

BEECHINGS WAY

Lower
Rainham

67

Twydall
Twydall
Jun Sch PIKEFIELDS 1
WOODCHURCH HO 2

King George V
Memorial Hos

Rainham
Mark
Gram Sch

Thames
View Inf Sch

THE
WILLOWS

2

St Thomas of
Canterbury
RC Prim Sch

Thames
View
Jun Sch

ME8

SOVEREIGN BVD

1 TATSFIELD CL
2 KESTON CT
3 Danecourt Com
Sch

The
Ice Bowl

Superstore

A2

NORFOLK
CL

Cozenton
Park

Liby

Rainham

1

Works

LONDON RD A2

Playing
Fields

HIGH ST A2

STATION

66

F1
1 CREVEQUER CHAMBERS
2 Rainham Sh Ctr
3 GRESHAM CL
4 HARRISON CT
5 MAPLINS CL
6 SIGNAL CT
7 SUFFOLK CT

44
68

A **B** **C** **D** **E** **F**

8

7

69

6

Millfordhope Creek

Greenborough Marshes

Slaughterhouse Point

Stangate Creek

The Shade

Millfordhope Marsh

Twinney Creek

River Medway

Halstow Creek

Barksore Marshes

Funton Creek

Callows House

Twinney Wharf

5

68

Twinney Acre

FROG FARM COTTS

Saxon Shore Way

Frog Farm

Funton Brick Works

Funton

RASPBERRY HILL LA

Saxon Shore Way

4

Sewage Works

Great Barksore

GREENWAYS

CURLEW AVE

LAPWING RD

HERON CL

THE GREEN

BELL COTTS

THE STREET

BURNTWICK DR

PH

WESTMOR

Stray Farm

CROUCH HILL

GT OWEN DR

VICARAGE LA

THE CRESCENT

VICARAGE COTTS

Little Barksore

Tiptree Hill

BASSER HILL

3

67

Holywell

Green Farm

Lower Halstow

MANORHALL RD

SCHOOL LA

SEA VIEW COTTS

CUMBERLAND DR

ME9

Tiptree

WESTFIELD COTTS

Lower Halstow Prim Sch

Elm Farm

Callum Hill

STICKFAST LA

2

BREACH LA

The Laurels

WARDWELL LA

Boxted Farm

BOXTED LA

Hawes Wood

HIGH OAK HILL

BELNOR AVE

Great Norwood

1

66

100
68

A B C D E F

8

7

69

6

5

68

4

3

67

2

1

66

Chetney Hill

The Shade

Funton Reach

River Medway

Bedlams Bottom

Raspberry Hill

Saxon Shore Way

Raspberry Hill La

Raspberry Hill Park

Saxon Shore Way

Horse Reach

Ferry Marshes

Saxon Shore Way

Marshbank

Chetney Cottages

Willow Bank Ind Est

Willow Cottages

Old Ferry Rd

Ridham Fleet

Sheppey Way

A249

Moat Farm Cottages

Orchard Farm

Reservoir

Culnell's Cottages

Culnells

ME9

Iwade

SHOOTERS CH
STANGATE DR
UPPER FANS LA

ELM TREE AVE
STANGATE DR
MAPLE CRES
SANDERLING WAY

Iwade Prim Sch

PH

THE STREET

CHURCH VIEWS

Iwade
MEADOW
EVERGREEN CL
CHETNEY
OAK WALK
YEW WALK
SHURLAND CRES
ROOKERY VW
LINK WAY
SPRINGVALE
MEADOW RISE
SHERSTONE
THE SALTINGS
SCHOOL LA
MEADOW WISE
FERRY RD
HELEN THOMPSON CL
KINGFISHER
SHELDUCK CL
TURNSTONE CL
WOODPECKER DR
School MS
PLANTATION CT
PO
Coleshall Cotts
MANSFIELD DR
COLSON DR
MAYNINS
ALFIE WAY
TERN WAY
PINTAIL DR
GREENSHANKS
WIGEON RD
CORMORANT RD
SANDPIPER LA

Coleshall Farm

Coleshall

Featherbed La

Sheppey Way

B2005
Grovehurst Rd
ME10

LC

Swale Way

Great Grovehurst

Kemsley

PO

Corbiere

Pheasants Farmhouse

Stickfast La

Cambray Farm

Cambray Cottages

Parsonage La

Layfield Cotts

Woodsvole Cotts

A249

Bramblefield La

Kemsley

Sandstone Dr

Kemsley Prim Sch

B2005

Dams Mead Cl

SQUARE RIDHAM AVE
Coldharbour La
Flanders Cl
Liege Cl
Castle Rough
Glover Cl
Coleman Dr
Grovehurst

1 OSTEND CT
2 BRUGES CT
3 MELLOR ROW
4 MONARCH DR
5 PREMIER WAY
6 EDWARD DR
7 MARTIN CT
8 ARCHER CT

88 A B 89 C D 90 E F

69
47

Stray
Marshes

Elmley Island

ME12

Old Counter Wall

Windmill Creek

Elmley Fleet

Sharfleet
Creek

Cockleshell
Creek

Wellmarsh
Creek

ME9

Peg Fleet

The Swale

Main Channel

Fowley Channel

Saxon Shore Way

69
103

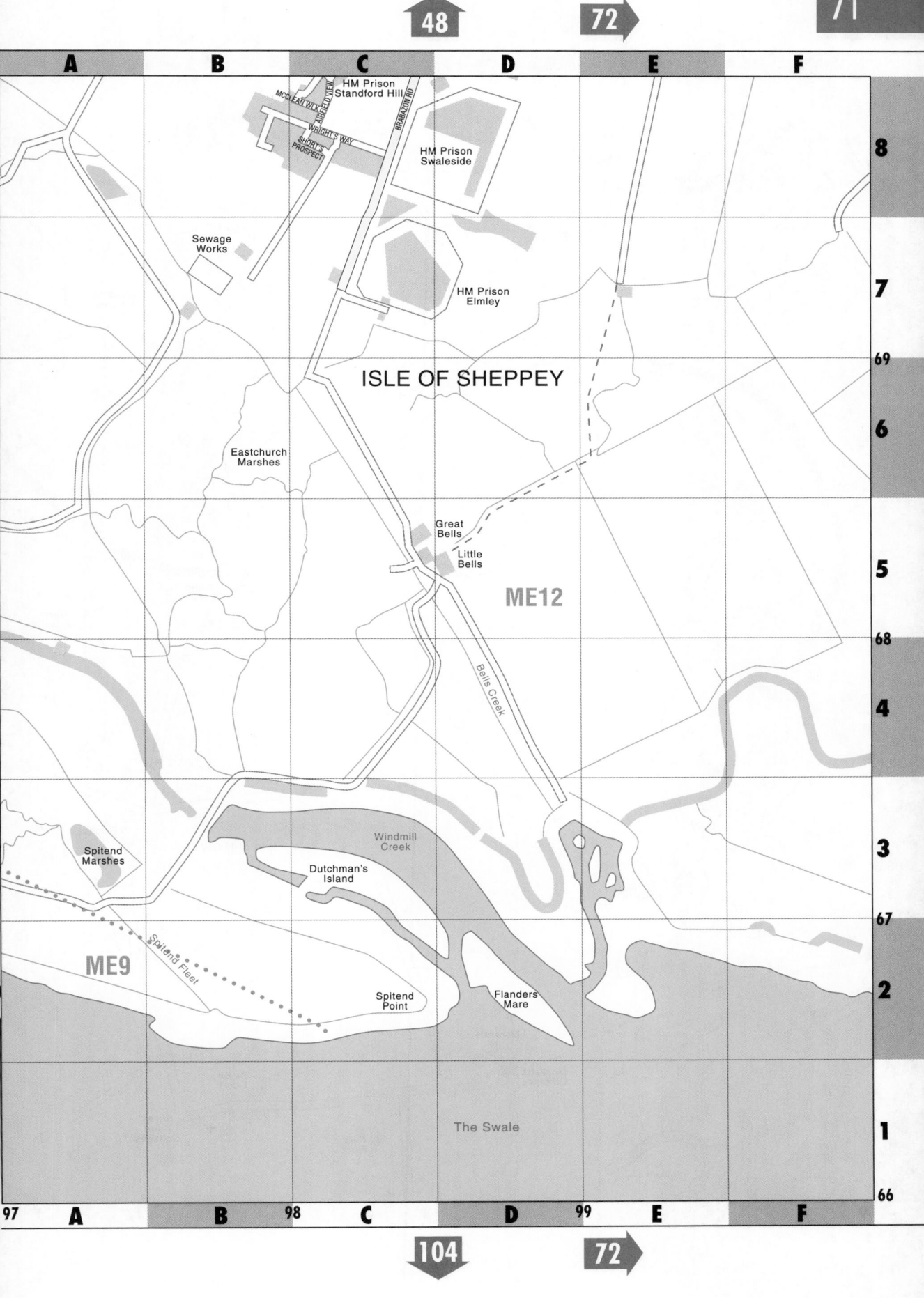

A B C D E F

8
7
69
6
5
68
4
3
67
2
1
66

HM Prison
Standford Hill

MCCLEAN WLK
ARGYLE VIEW
WRIGHT'S WAY
SHORT'S PROSPECT
BRABAZON RD

HM Prison
Swaleside

Sewage
Works

HM Prison
Elmley

ISLE OF SHEPPEY

Eastchurch
Marshes

Great
Bells

Little
Bells

ME12

Balls Creek

Windmill
Creek

Spitend
Marshes

Dutchman's
Island

ME9

Spitend Fleet

Spitend
Point

Flanders
Mare

The Swale

97 A B 98 C D 99 E F

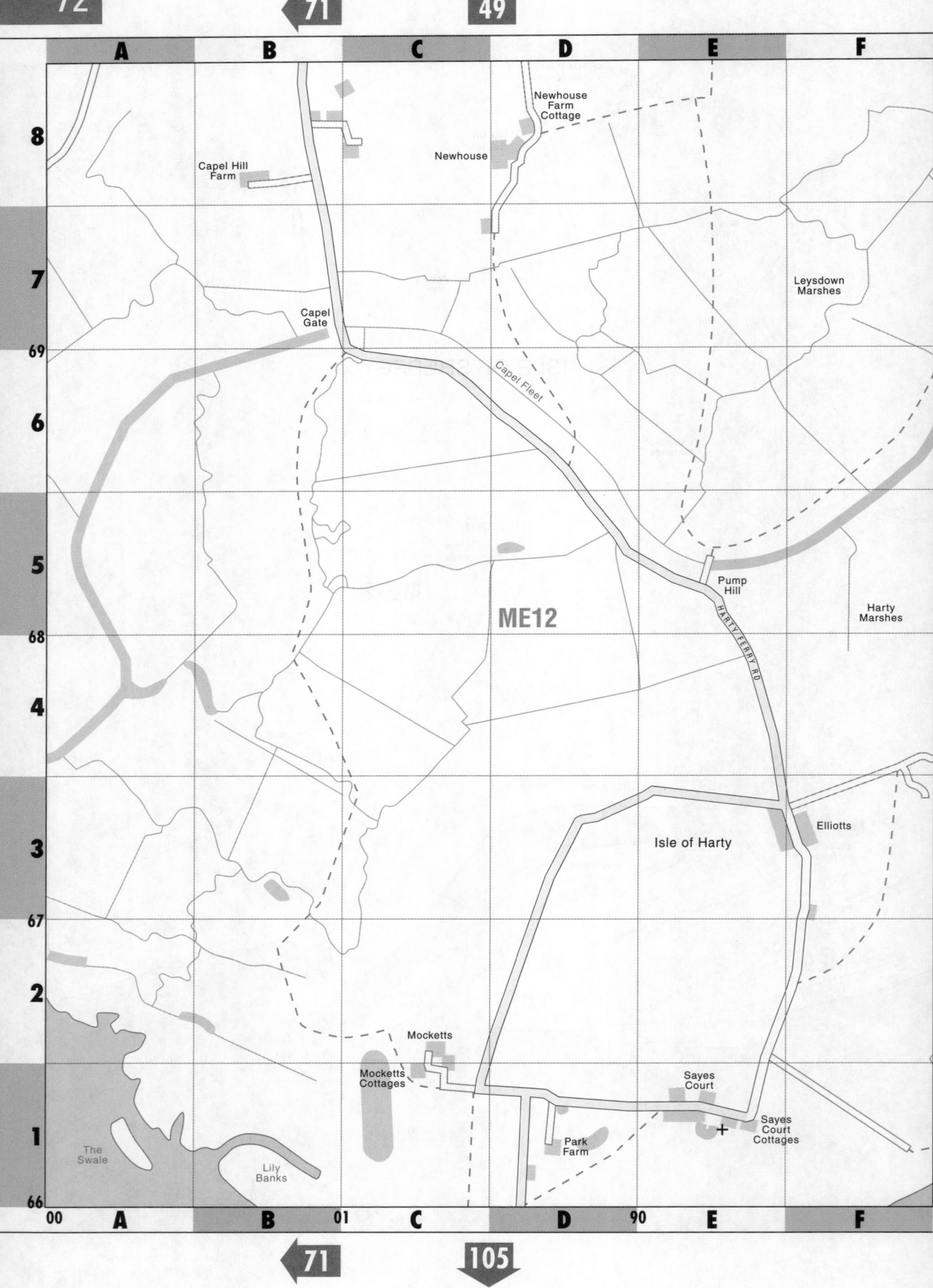

WHITSTABLE

Tankerton Bay

Kingsdown Park

1 CASTLE HO
2 MARINE HO
3 MARINE CT
4 GRAND PAVILION

WYNN ELLIS HO 1
THE BARGES 2
MARINERS LEE 3
SOUTH LODGE 4
SOUTH LODGE CL 5
THE EXCHANGE 6
TANKERTON HTS 7

Swimming Pool

Harbour

EAST QUAY

Saxon Shore Way

Castle

TANKERTON MEWS

TANKERTON CIR

B2205

TOWER PAR

TANKERTON RD

IRB Sta

Reeves Beach

St Marys RC Prim Sch

NORTHWOOD RD

D2
1 STARVATION CNR
2 NEW ST
3 FOUNTAIN ST
4 THE OLD POLICE STA
5 ST PETERS COTTS
6 HARTS LA
7 VICTORIA HO
8 THE OLD HALLS
9 ALBERT CT
10 LEGGETT'S LA
11 RED LION LA
12 WHITEPOST
13 CUSHINGS WALK
14 SQUEEZE GUT ALLEY
15 BEACH ALLEY
16 THE SALTINGS
17 HAYES ALLEY
18 EVELINGS ALLEY
19 BONNERS ALLEY
20 KNIGHTS ALLEY
21 SALT MARSH LA

HARBOUR ST

WESTGATE TERR

STRANGFORD RD
GLOUCESTER RD

Whitstable

Pettmans Mews

HIGH ST

WHITE MARSH CT

TEYNHAM RD

CLEWER THE CLOISTERS

THE BRIDGE APP

Shipwrights Lee

OXFORD ST

KING EDWARD

Railway Ave

MARINE TERR 1
COASTGUARD ALLEY 2

WAVE CREST

Thurston Park

SUMMERFIELD RD

SEAWAY COTTS

Lower Island

CT5

Church Street

WEST BEACH

WEST CLIFF

CLIFTON RD

Liby

BELMONT RD

WINDSOR

75

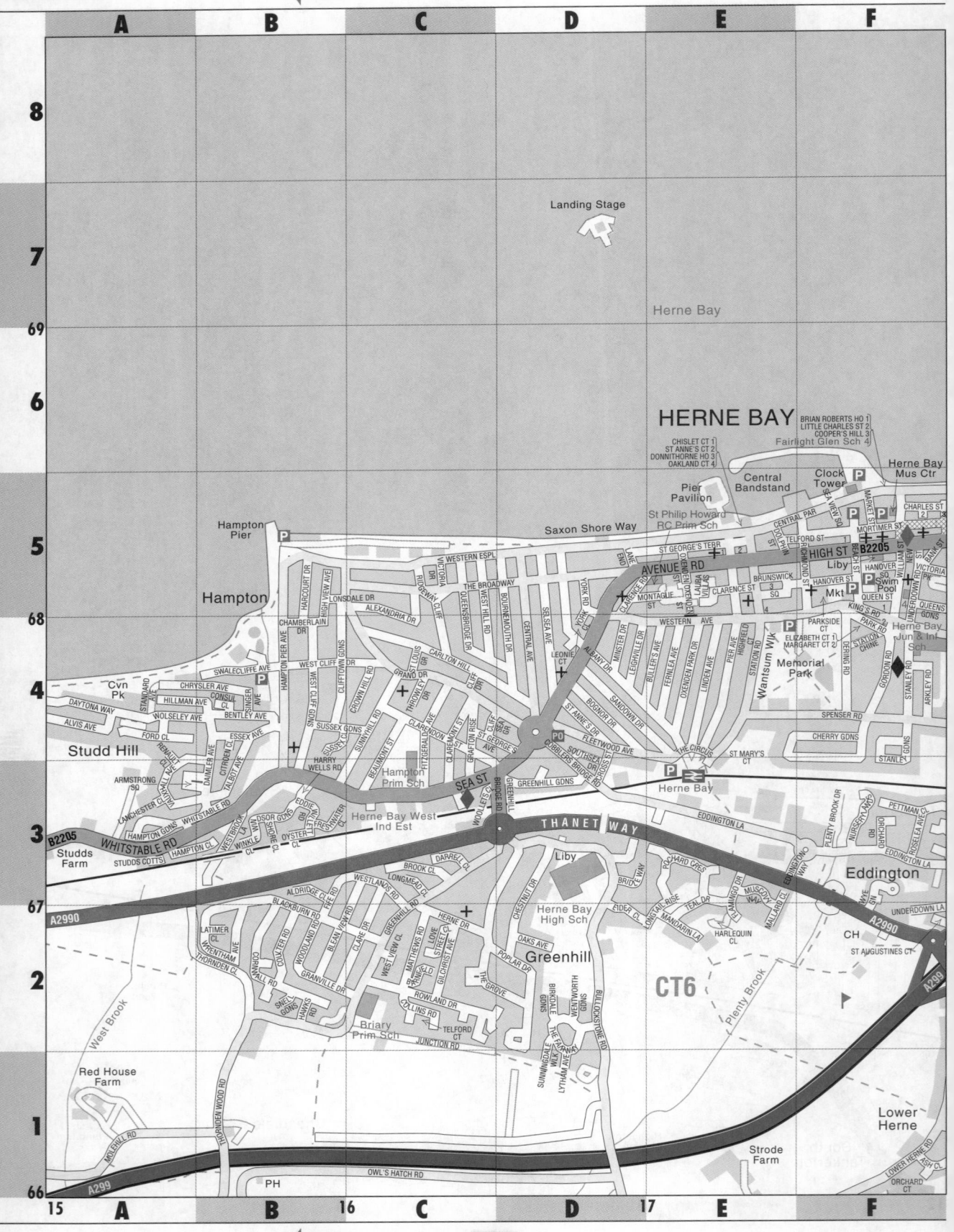

HERNE BAY

Landing Stage

Herne Bay

BRIAN ROBERTS HO 1
LITTLE CHARLES ST 2
COOPER'S HILL 3
Fairlight Glen Sch 4

CHISLET CT 1
St ANNE'S CT 2
DONNITHORNE HO 3
OAKLAND CT 4

Herne Bay
Mus Ctr

Clock
Tower

Central
Bandstand

Pier
Pavilion

St Philip Howard
RC Prim Sch

Saxon Shore Way

Hampton
Pier

CHARLES ST
1 2

HIGH ST
Liby

B2205

Hampton

Swim
Pool

Herne Bay
Jun & Inf
Sch

AVENUE RD

St GEORGE'S TERR

Western Espl

The Broadway

Mkt

Memorial
Park

Hampton Pier Ave

Cvn
Pk

Studd Hill

CHERRY GDNS

SPENSER RD

STANLEY

PO

THE CIRCUS

St MARY'S
CT

Herne Bay

Hampton
Prim Sch

SEA ST

Herne Bay West
Ind Est

THANET WAY

Eddington

B2205

WHITSTABLE RD

Studds
Farm

STUDDS COTTS

A2990

A2990

UNDERDOWN LA

Liby

Herne Bay
High Sch

CT6

Greenhill

CH

St AUGUSTINES CT

A299

Briary
Prim Sch

Red House
Farm

West Brook

Plenty Brook

Lower
Herne

Strode
Farm

ORCHARD
CT

PH

OWL'S HATCH RD

8

7

69

6

Wantsum Wlk

Beltinge Cliff

P

P

RECULVER

OCEAN

MANOR CL

HAVEN DR

MANOR RD

BISHOPSTONE
CL

HILLBOROUGH DR

BISHOPSTONE LA

Bishopstone

1 PROSPECT HILL
2 CHAPEL ST
3 CAVENDISH CT
4 HERTFORD HO

The Kings Hall

East Cliff Par

The Downs

Saxon Shore Way

The Lees

The Lees

BURLINGTON DR

HAZELMERE DR

LISMORE RD

CUNNINGHAM RD

BELTINGE RD

RECULVER

GLENBERVIE DR

FRESLANDS

PIER

WANTSUM

FINE WLK

THE PADDOCKS

SANDERLING RD

5

CHARLES ST

HIGH ST

PO

BEACON WLK

BELLE VUE

HILL TOP

BEACON HILL

ALMA RD

THURLOW AVE

ASHBEE GDNS

KNOWLER WAY

GLENBERVIE DR

GAINSBOROUGH DR

GARTH

LANCASTER GDNS

COVENTRY GDNS

KINGSTON CL

DOVER CL

PORCHMANN WAY

RECULVER RD

KENT RD

68

VICTORIA PK

SOUTH RD

CAVENDISH RD

GOSFIELD RD

CECIL PK

CECIL CT

DOUGLAS RD

OAKDALE RD

IVANHOE RD

HERNE AVE

MICKLEBURGH HILL

HILLBOROUGH RD

BELTINGE RD

DENCE PK

DENCE CL

BEACON AVE

SALISBURY RD

SEA VIEW RD

GLEN AVE

SYCAMORE CL

QUEENS AVE

REGENTS WLK

THE HORSHAMS

PO

GLENBROOK

TERMINUS RD

HOLMSCROFT

RICHMOND DR

ROWLAND CRES

ROSEBERY AVE

PUFFIN RD

PETRE

TEAL

TAMAR

WALLIS RD

BARNES

WAY

Queen Victoria Meml

H

KING EDWARD AVE

KING EDWARD CT

GRANGE RD

REEDS CL

ROSE GDNS

HILARY CL

WILLOW TREE CL

MAXTED CT

ORCHARD PK

THORNHURST

CHURCHILL AVE

OSBORNE GDNS

CLEMENTINE CL

Beltinge

NEVILLE RD

Hillborough Bsns Pk

4

QUEEN'S CT

ST ANDREWS CL

SPENSER RD

HERNEVILLE GDNS

BURTON FIELDS

MICKLEBURGH AVE

LAWRENCE GDNS

MEADOW GDNS

RECULVER

HIGHFIELDS VIEW

MACLEAN PK

HIGHFIELDS AVE

WINSTON GDNS

CHARTWELL AVE

Elm Court Farm

Sweech Bridge

Maystreet Bridge

MAY ST

SWEECHBRIDGE RD

COLLARD

MAYFIELD RD

SUNDERLAND RD

FAIROAKS

ELIZABETH WAY

ASH TREE

TALMEAD

The Willows Prim Sch

CHAMOS

NYOLA RD

ELLIOT CT

SELBY CT

CORNWALLIS CL

CAMPBELL

CORSICAN WLK

BOSHOLE LA

Sewage Works

Mast

Maystreet Cross

3

BEAUMONT

CANTERBURY RD

ST CLEMENT'S CT

PARSONAGE RD

Herne Bay Court

PRIORY LA

BOWES

B2205

BRISTOL CL

MARGATE LA

WALCOT PL

Blacksole Farm

CT6

THANET WAY

A299

67

B2205

SWALE CL

PIGEON LA

THE DOWN

HILLCROFT RD

EASTGATE CL

CAVENDOURNE

DARENTH CL

HILLBROW AVE

GREEN ACRES

ELLIS WAY

KINGSFIELD RD

GOLDFINCH

PARTRIDGE

PEARTREE RD

HELDING CL

CURLEW

PINTAIL WAY

WILLOW FARM WAY

HOOPERS LA

BOSHOLE LA

BRAMLEY GDNS

SPICERS FLD

MARGATE RD

HEART IN HAND RD

2

A291

Cemy

WINDMILL RD

SONDES CL

MILL LA

UPPER TREE DOWN

BUCKINGHAM CL

HUNTERS FORSTAL RD

BRAMBLEFIELDS

DEAN CROFT

SHERWOOD CL

GORSE LA

HARVEST CT

RYE

PLOUGH

THE MEADOWS

BARLEY CL

CHASE

MERRYWOOD GR

SILVERDALE

MAGNOLIA RISE

PO

PH

Pond Cotts

Broomfield

Heart in Hand

HEART IN HAND CNR

WINDMILL RD

MOUNT VIEW RD

Windmill

STRODE PARK RD

CHARNWOOD RD

RADNOR CL

EPPING CL

LAKE DR

STRANGFORD PL

ARDEN RD

ASHDOWN

HAWE FARM WAY

BROOMFIELD RD

HUNTERS CHASE

Oxenden House Farm

OXENDEN CNR

1

LOWER HERNE RD

A291

STRODE PARK RD

MILL VIEW RD

WOODROW CHASE

SENACRE

SCHOOL LA

Hunters Forstal

Hawe Farm

Claver House

KFORD HILL

CT3

66

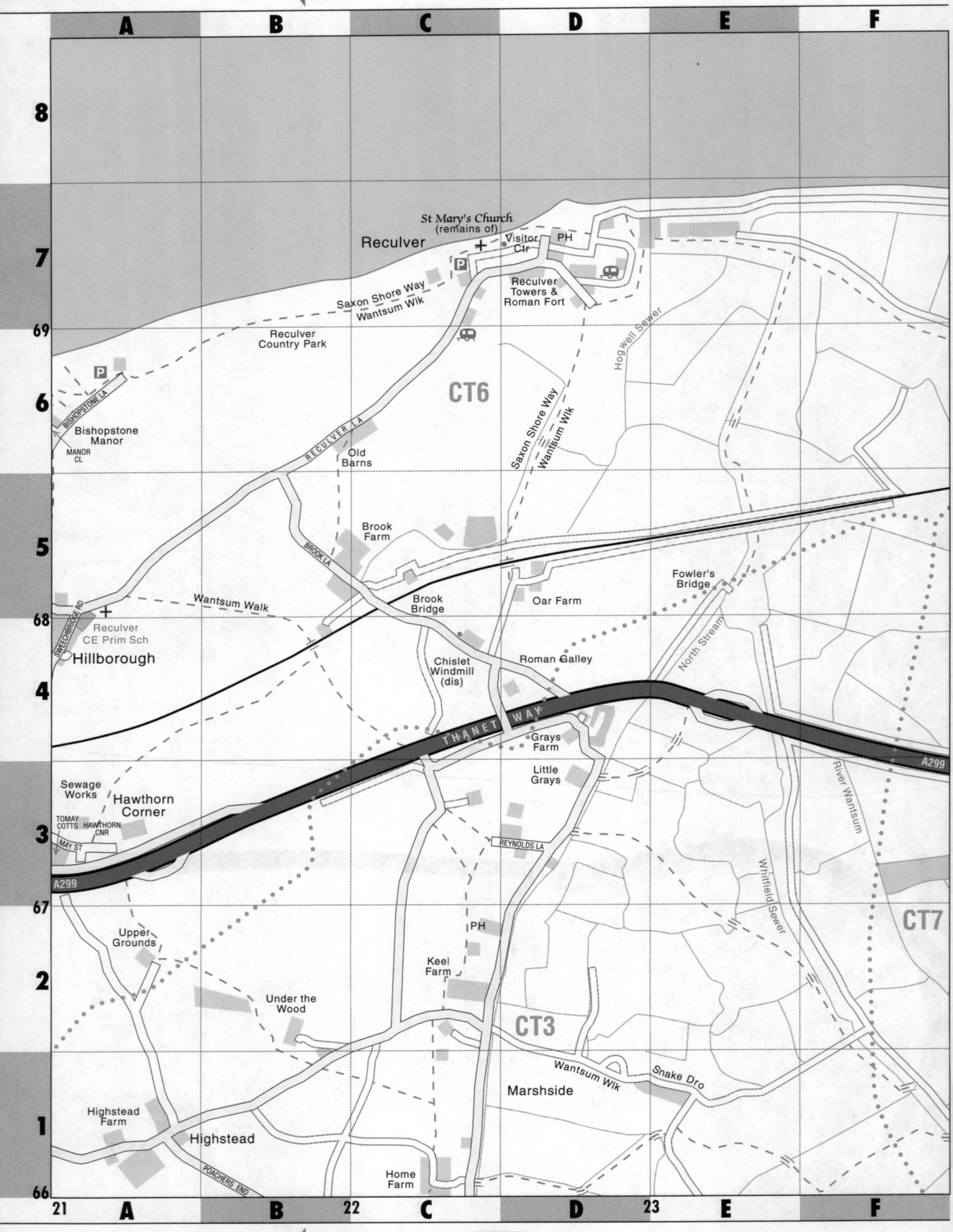

A B C D E F

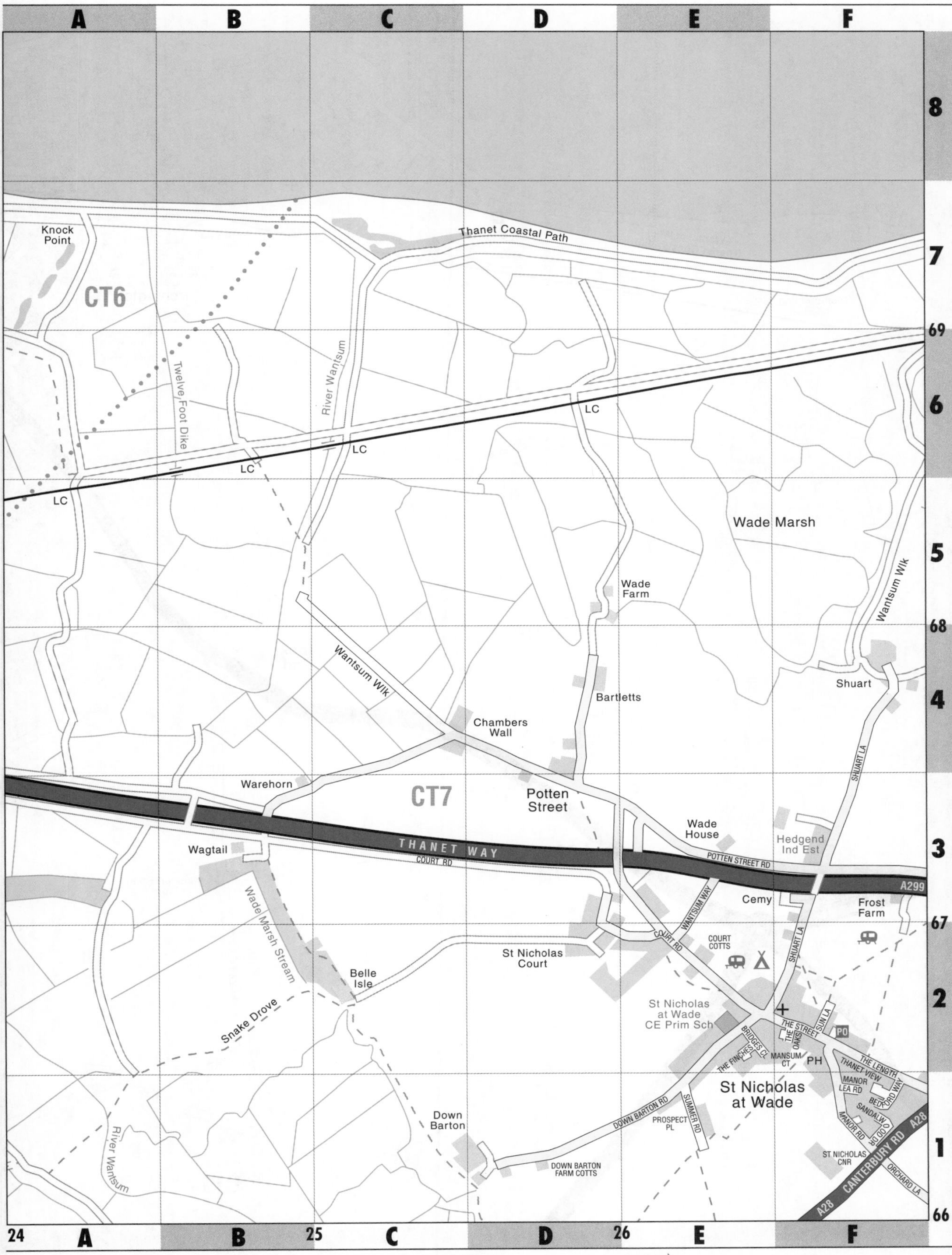

8

7

Knock Point

CT6

Thanet Coastal Path

69

LC

LC

6

LC

LC

LC

Twelve Foot Dike

River Wantsum

Wade Marsh

5

Wade Farm

Wantsum Wlk

68

4

Bartletts

Shuart

Wantsum Wlk

Chambers Wall

CT7

Potten Street

Wade House

Hedgend Ind Est

3

Warehorn

THANET WAY

COURT RD

POTTEN STREET RD

A299

SHUART LA

Wagtail

Cemy

Frost Farm

67

Wade Marsh Stream

Belle Isle

St Nicholas Court

COURT RD

WANTSUM WAY

COURT COTTS

SHUART LA

2

Snake Drove

St Nicholas at Wade CE Prim Sch

THE STREET

SUN LA

PO

THE FINCHES

BRIDGES CL

MANSUM CT

PH

THANET VIEW

THE LENGTH

BEDFORD WAY

MANOR LEA RD

St Nicholas at Wade

River Wantsum

Down Barton

DOWN BARTON RD

PROSPECT PL

SUMMER RD

MANOR RD

SANDALW...

ST. NICHOLAS CNR

CANTERBURY RD

ORCHARD LA

A28

1

DOWN BARTON FARM COTTS

66

24 A B 25 C D 26 E F

79

F8
1 DALLINGER RD
2 CARMEL CT
3 SANDPIPER CT
4 GAINSBORO RD
5 LYELL CT
6 HOMEBIRCH HO

7 BERESFORD CT

LARKESCLIFF CT 1
SEA VIEW HTS 2
APRIL RISE 3
BAY VIEW HTS 4
MCKINLAY CT 5
RINGSLOE CT 6
SHORE CL 7
FERNDOWN 8
FORELAND CT 9
HAZEL CT 10
COASTGUARD COTTS 11

Minnis Bay

Groynes

Wantsum Wlk
Thanet Coastal Path

Plumpudding
Island

Gore End
Farm

BIERCE CT 1
BIERCE CT COTTS 2
ROSSETTI CT 3
UPPER MALTINGS PL 4
THE MALTHOUSES 5
SANDLE'S RD 6

WALNUT
MEWS

Birchington-on-Sea

Birchington

FLINT COTTS 1
RANSOME WAY 2

Wade
Marsh

Brooksend Stream

Reservoirs

CT7

Great
Brooksend
Farm

Upper
Hale

Brooks
End

College
Farm

CRISPE RD

Hale

Nether Hale
Farm

Coney
Close

Monkton Road
Farm

CANTERBURY ROAD BIRCHINGTON

POTTEN STREET RD

A299
THANET WAY

St NICHOLAS
RDBT

CANTERBURY RD

A28

ORCHARD LA

A299

SEAMARK RD

PLUMSTONE RD

CT12

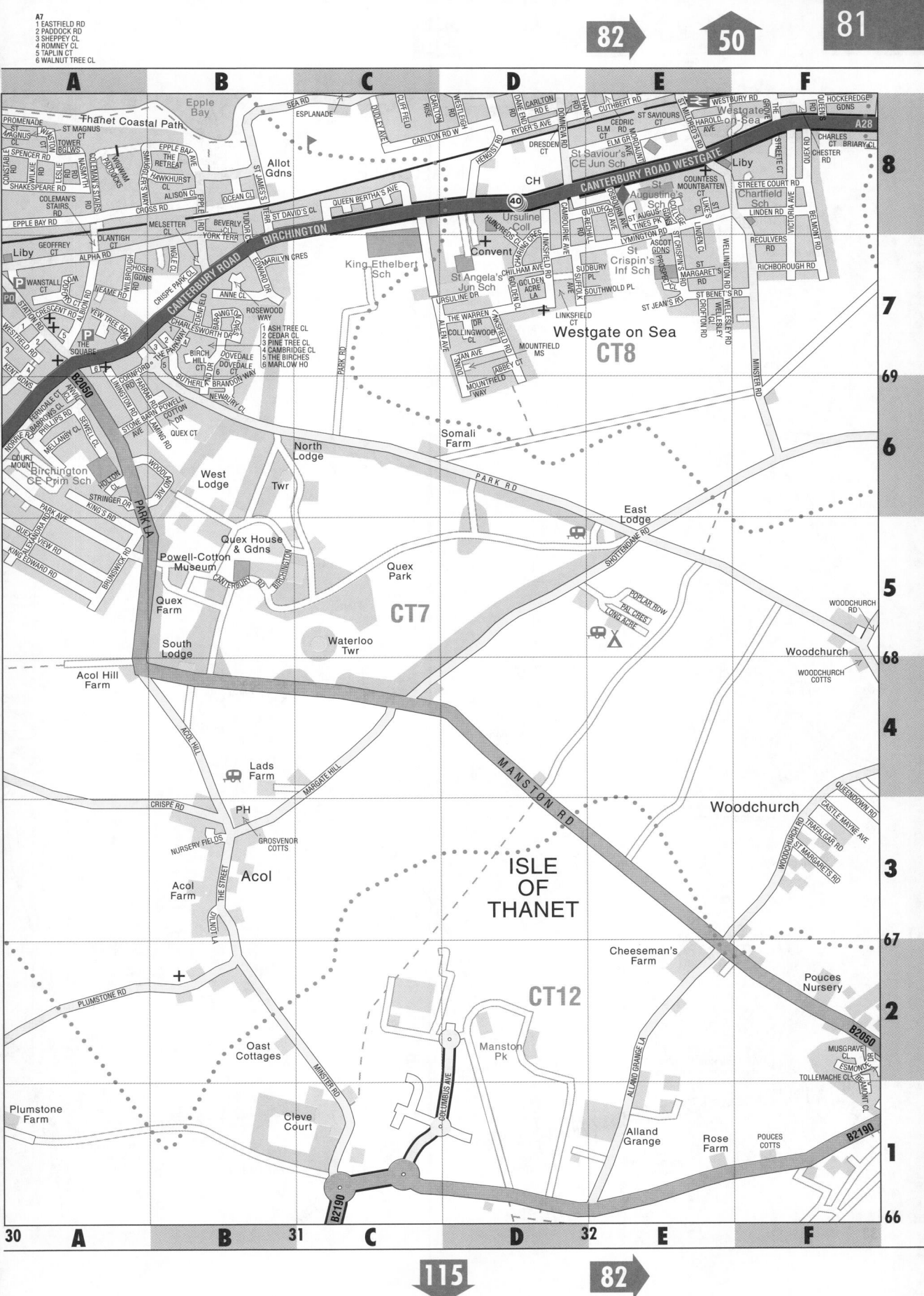

A7
1 EASTFIELD RD
2 PADDOCK RD
3 SHEPPEY CL
4 ROMNEY CL
5 TAPLIN CT
6 WALNUT TREE CL

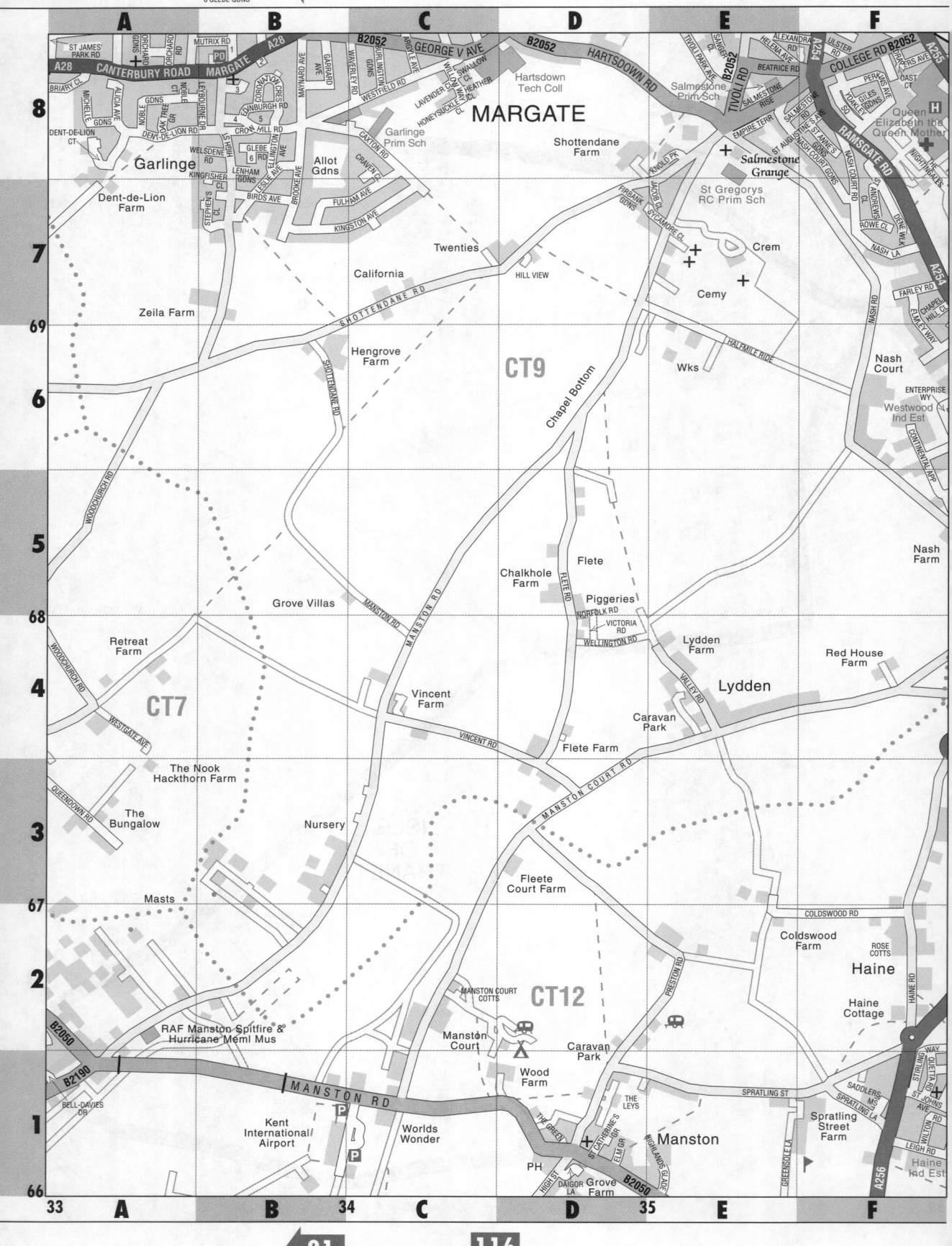

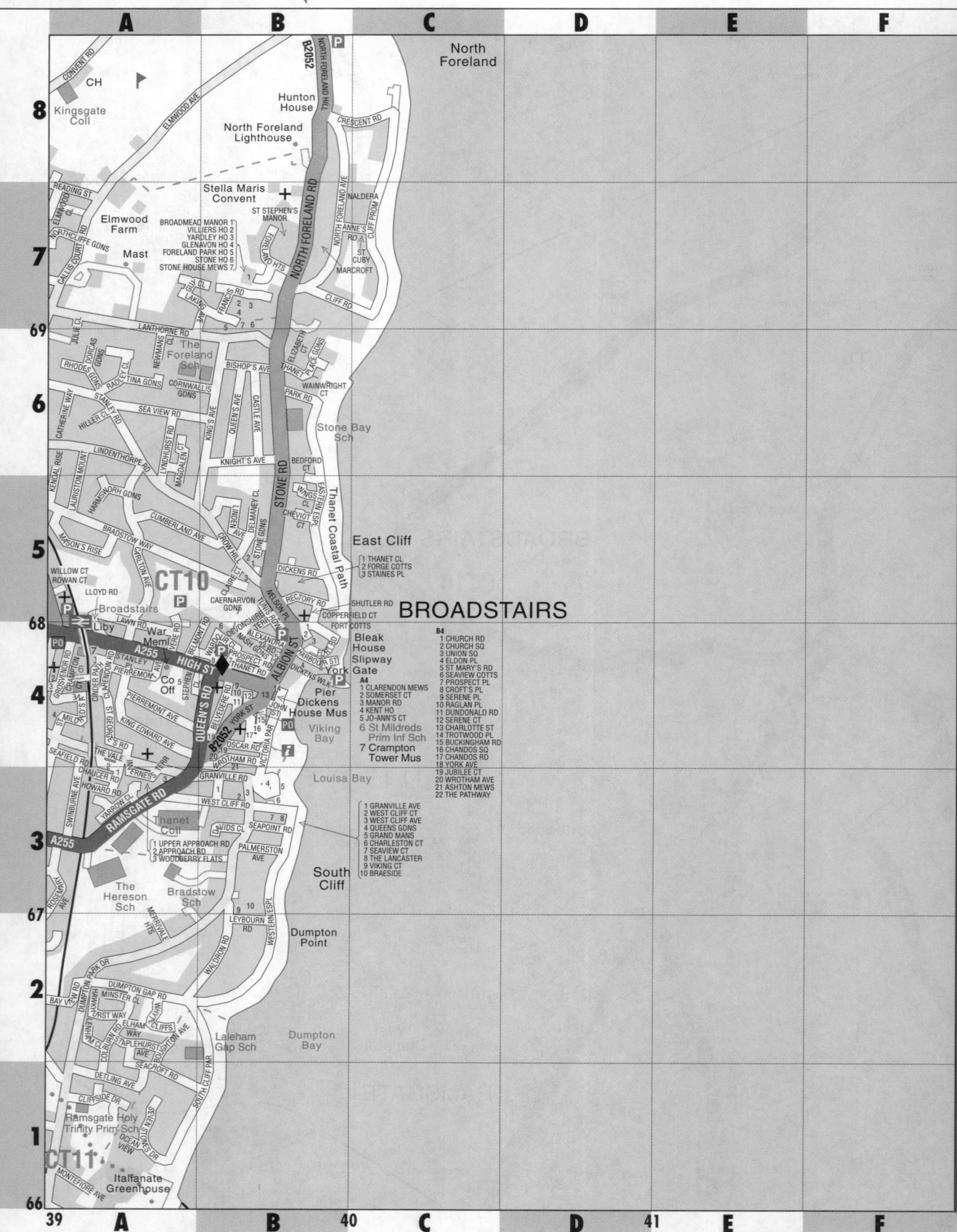

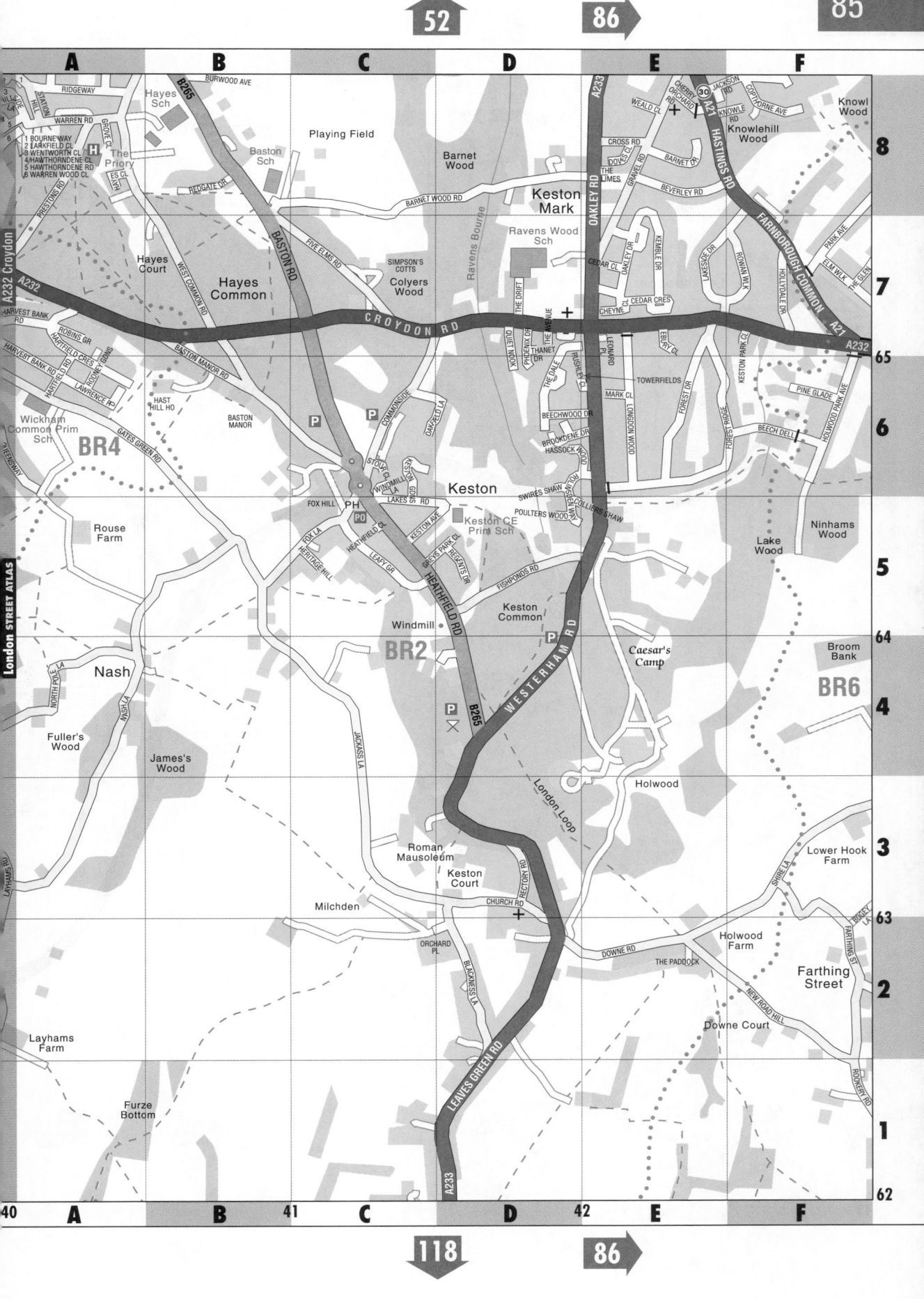

A   B   C   D   E   F

8
7
65
6
5
64
4
3
63
2
62
1

London STREET ATLAS

BURWOOD AVE
RIDGEWAY
WARREN RD
STATION HILL
ALICE LA
GROVE RD
The Priory
1 BOURNE WAY
2 LAKFIELD CL
3 WENTWORTH CL
4 HAWTHORNDENE CL
5 HAWTHORNDENE RD
6 WARREN WOOD CL
PRESTONS RD
ES LNTH
Hayes Sch
Baston Sch
B265
REDGATE DR
BASTON RD
FIVE ELMS RD
WEST COMMON RD
Hayes Court
Hayes Common
Playing Field
Barnet Wood
BARNET WOOD RD
SIMPSON'S COTTS
Colyers Wood
Ravens Bourne
Keston Mark
Ravens Wood Sch
THE DRIFT
OAKLEY RD
A233
JACKSON RD
CHERRY ORCHARD RD
WEALD CL
30
A21
COPTHORNE AVE
KNOWLE RD
CROSS RD
DOVE'S CL
GRAVEL RD
BARNET RK
THE LIMES
BEVERLEY RD
Knowl Wood
Knowlehill Wood
HASTINGS RD
FARNBOROUGH COMMON
PARK AVE
ELM WLK
THE GLEN
A232
CROYDON RD
CEDAR CL
OAKLEY DR
KEMBLE DR
LAKESIDE DR
ROWAN WLK
HOLYVALE DR
A21
A232 Croydon
A232
HARVEST BANK RD
ROBINS GR
HARTFIELD CRES
HATFIELD RD
RODNEY GDNS
LAWRENCE RD
GATES GREEN RD
HAST HILL HO
BASTON MANOR RD
BASTON MANOR
COMMONSIDE
OAKFIELD LA
THE DALE
PHOENIX DR
THE AVENUE
OAKLEY RD
THANET DR
RUSHLEY CL
LEONARD RD
LONGDON WOOD
CHEYNE CL
CEDAR CRES
TOWERFIELDS
EBURY CL
FOREST DR
KESTON PARK CL
FOREST RIDGE
PINE GLADE
HOLWOOD PARK AVE
BEECH DELL
BR4
Wickham Common Prim Sch
GREENWAYS
HARVEST BANK RD
P
P
STOVE PL
WINDMILL LA
GDNS
LAKES RD
KESTON AVE
FOX HILL
PH
PO
FOX LA
HEATHFIELD CL
HERITAGE HILL
LEAFY GR
GREYS PARK CL
REGENTS DR
FISHPONDS RD
KESTON RD
Keston CE Prim Sch
Keston
BEECHWOOD DR
BROOKDENE DR
HASSOCK WOOD
POULTERS WOOD
SWIRES SHAW
POLLARDS WOOD
COLLIERS SHAW
MARK CL
Lake Wood
Ninhams Wood
BR6
Rouse Farm
BR2
HEATHFIELD RD
Windmill
Keston Common
P
WESTERHAM RD
Caesar's Camp
Broom Bank
Nash
NORTH POLE LA
JACKASS LA
B265
P
London Loop
Holwood
Fuller's Wood
James's Wood
LAYHAMS RD
NASH LA
Roman Mausoleum
Keston Court
RECTORY RD
Milchden
Holwood Farm
SHIRE LA
Lower Hook Farm
BRIDGET RD
FARTHING ST
ORCHARD PL
BLACKNESS LA
CHURCH RD
DOWNE RD
THE PADDOCK
NEW ROAD HILL
Farthing Street
Layhams Farm
LEAVES GREEN RD
Downe Court
ROOKERY RD
Furze Bottom
A233

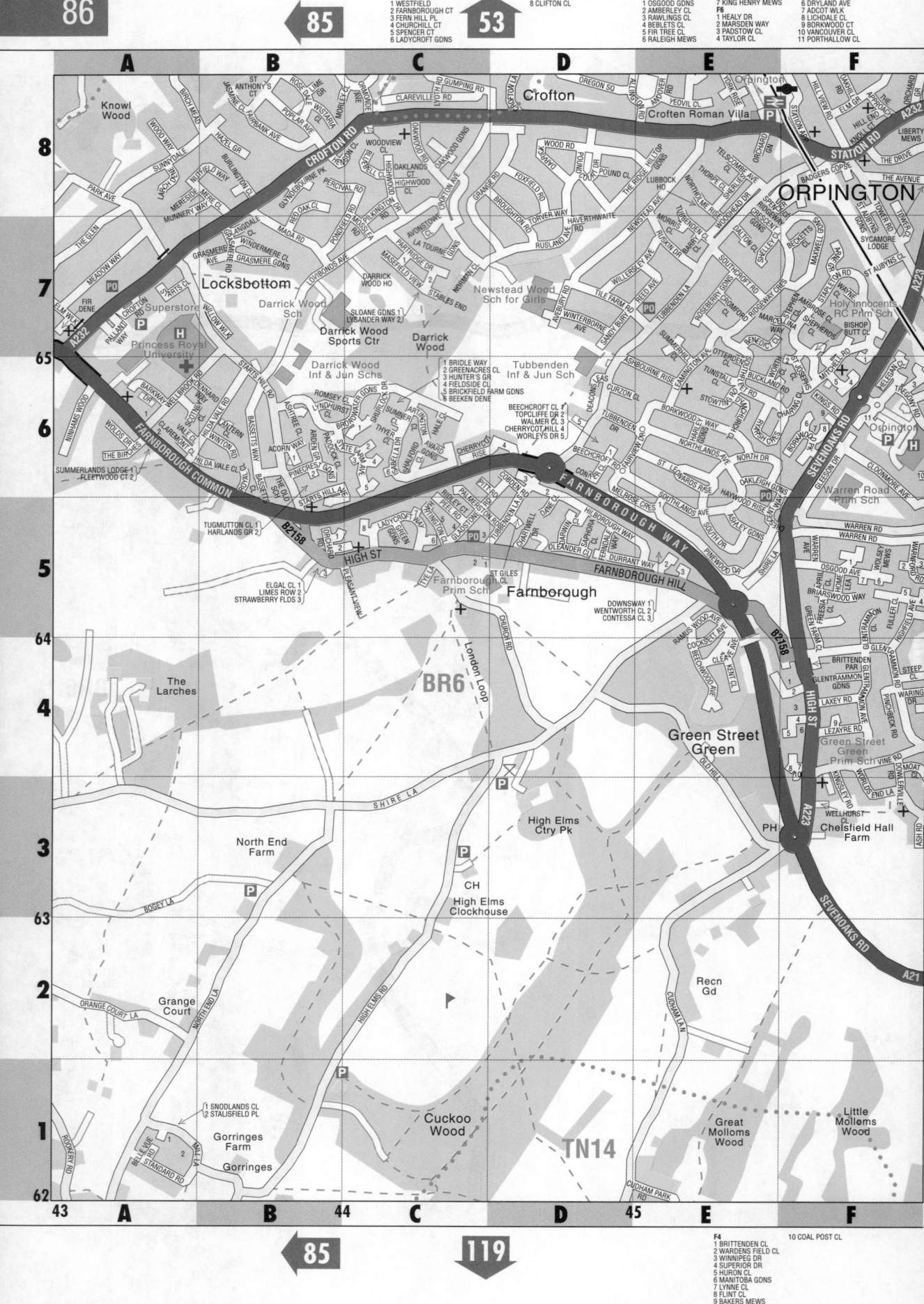

85

53

85

119

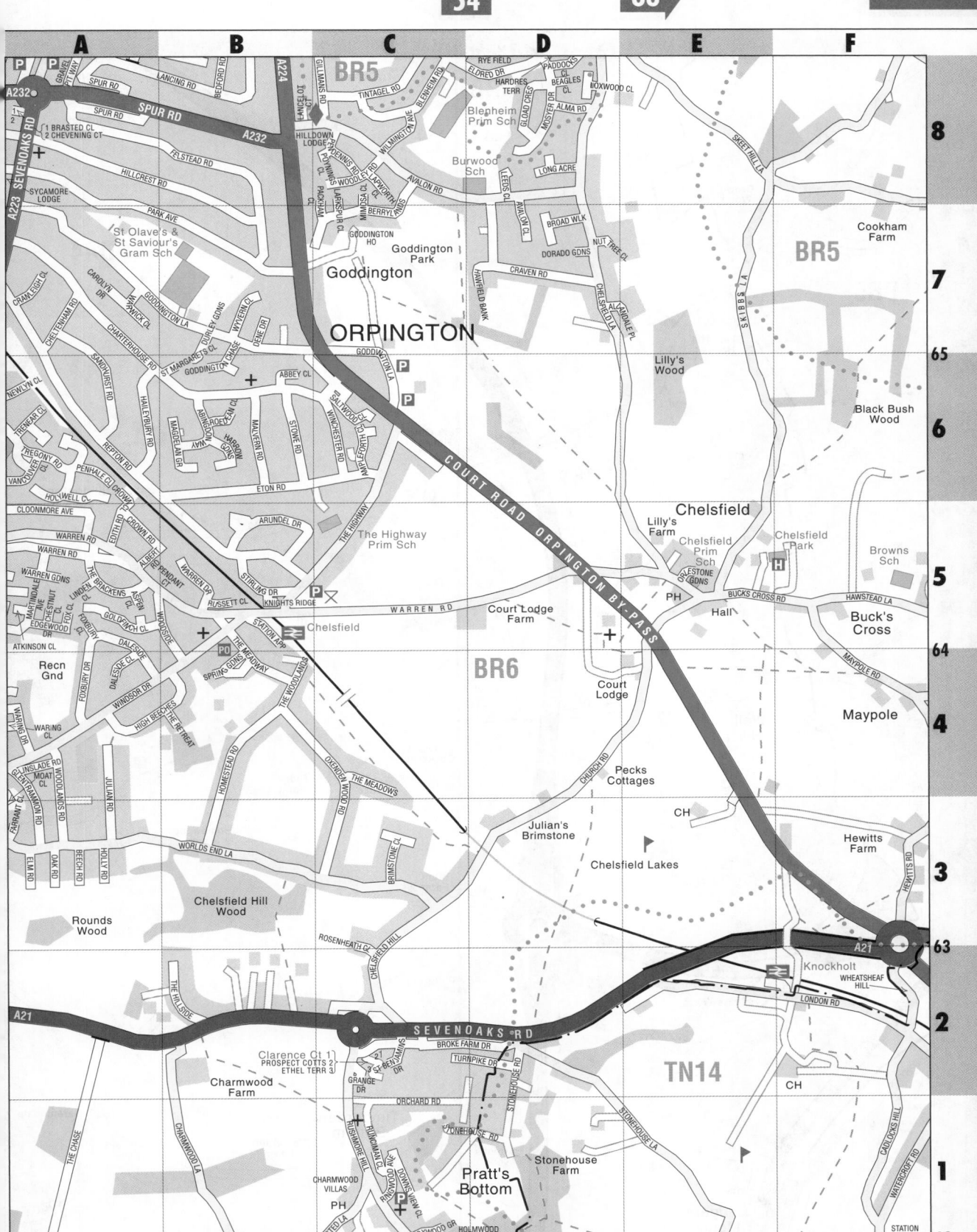

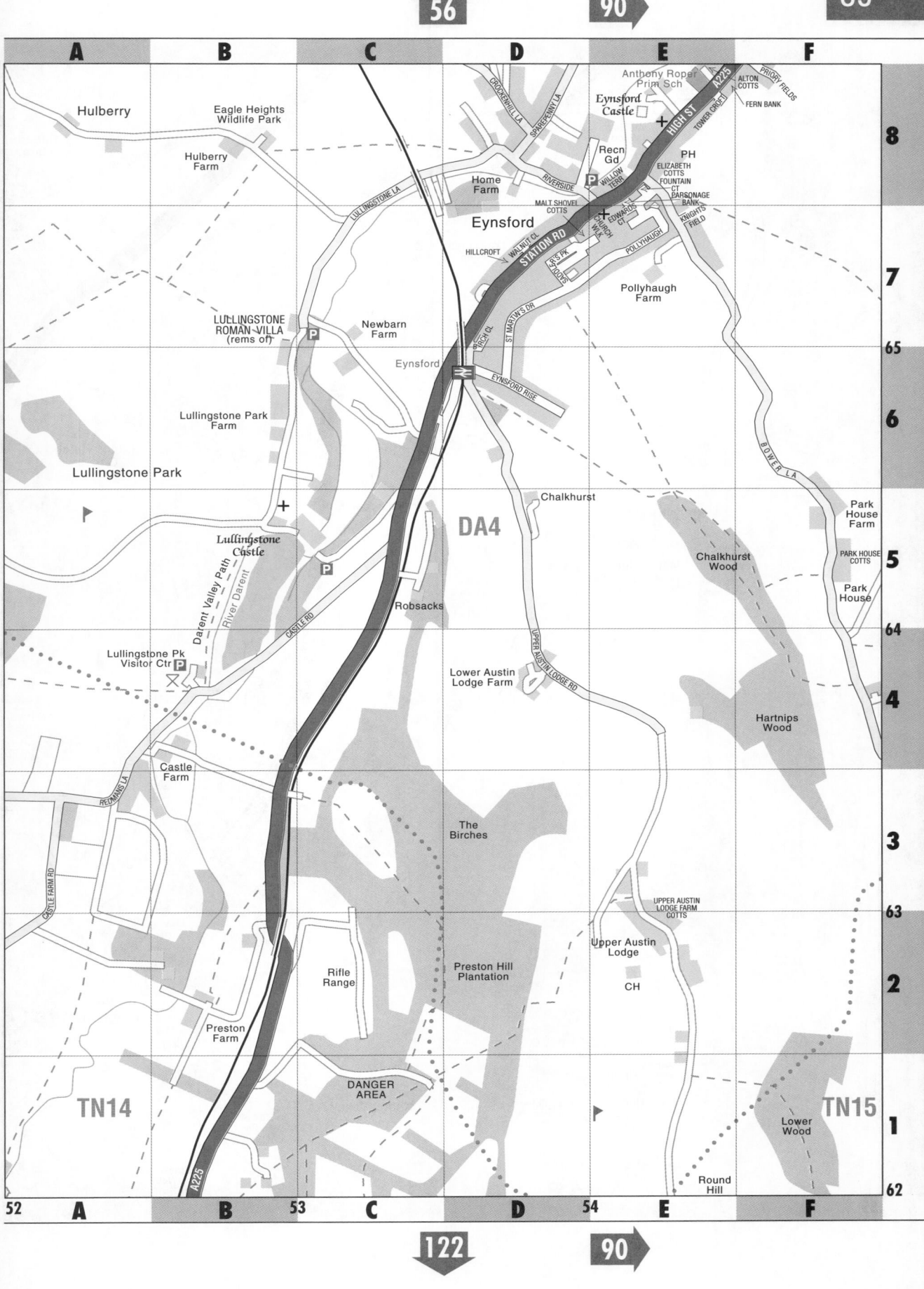

A **B** **C** **D** **E** **F**

8

Firpound Shaw

BEESFIELD LA

DONKEY LA

Alchin's Wood

Kennels

A20

M20

GABRIEL SPRING RD

Gabrielspring Wood

SPEEDGATE FARM

Speed Gate

MUSSENDEN LA

THREE GATES RD

GABRIEL SPRING ROAD (EAST)

7

Olivers Shaw

MAPLESCOMBE LA

Gorse Hill Farm

80

MAIN ROAD GORSE HILL

SCRATCHERS LA

DA3

M20

65

6

DA4

Hotel

COLIN CHAPMAN WAY

FAWKHAM RD

Brands Hatch Circuit

5

Lower Park Wood

MAPLESCOMBE FARM COTTS

West Kingsdown Farm

Grove Wood

Maplescombe

Adder Bank Shaw

Maplescombe Farm

SYMONDS CL

NEAL RD

GILLIE'S RD

VIKING WK

64

Blue Chalet Ind Pk

KELPS CL

STACKLANDS CL

OAKLANDS CL

SHERBOURNE CL

LOVELACE CL

HEVER AVE

REGE

MILLFIELD RD

PRIMMETT CL

BRAKES PL

HEVER RD

4

Bower Park Farm

BOTSOM LA

THE BRIARS

MILTON RD

MULTON RD

Florence Farm Mobile Home Pk

WELLS CT

PO P

P

WHITEGATES AVE

ASTOR RD

WOOD VIEW CL

PURSER CL

LONDON RD

WESTFIELD COTTS

WOOD RD

INKHURST

MITCHEM CL

Clearways Bsns Est

Church Wood

3

Hog Wood

Sidehilly Wood

CARTERAGE

SUSSEX CL

Clearways Mobile Home Pk

RUSHETTS RD

CHURCH RD

CHANCEL CL

63

KNATTS VALLEY RD

TN15

KAYSLAND DR

KINGSFIELD RD

KINGSINGFIELD RD

KINGFISHER DR

BAKERS AVE

Windmill Grange

SOUTHFIELDS RD

WARLAND RD

ASH TREE DR

Liby PH

West Kinsdown Ind Est

BLACKDOWN

BLACKHORN GRANGE

VERNAL CL

2

BOWER LA

High Castle Wood

MEADOW BANK CL 1

POUND BANK CL 2

BIRCHWAY 3

BEACON ROW

West Kingsdown

A20

PH

1

ASHEN GROVE RD

Ashen Grove Mobile Home Pk

East Hill

CHERRY TREE GR

East Hill Farm Caravan Pk

Knatts Valley

The Halt Caravan Pk

SCHOOL LA

THE GROVE

62

EAST HILL RD

Pasadena Caravan Pk

EAST HILL FARM PK

Stacklands Wood

55 **A** **56** **B** **C** **57** **D** **E** **F**

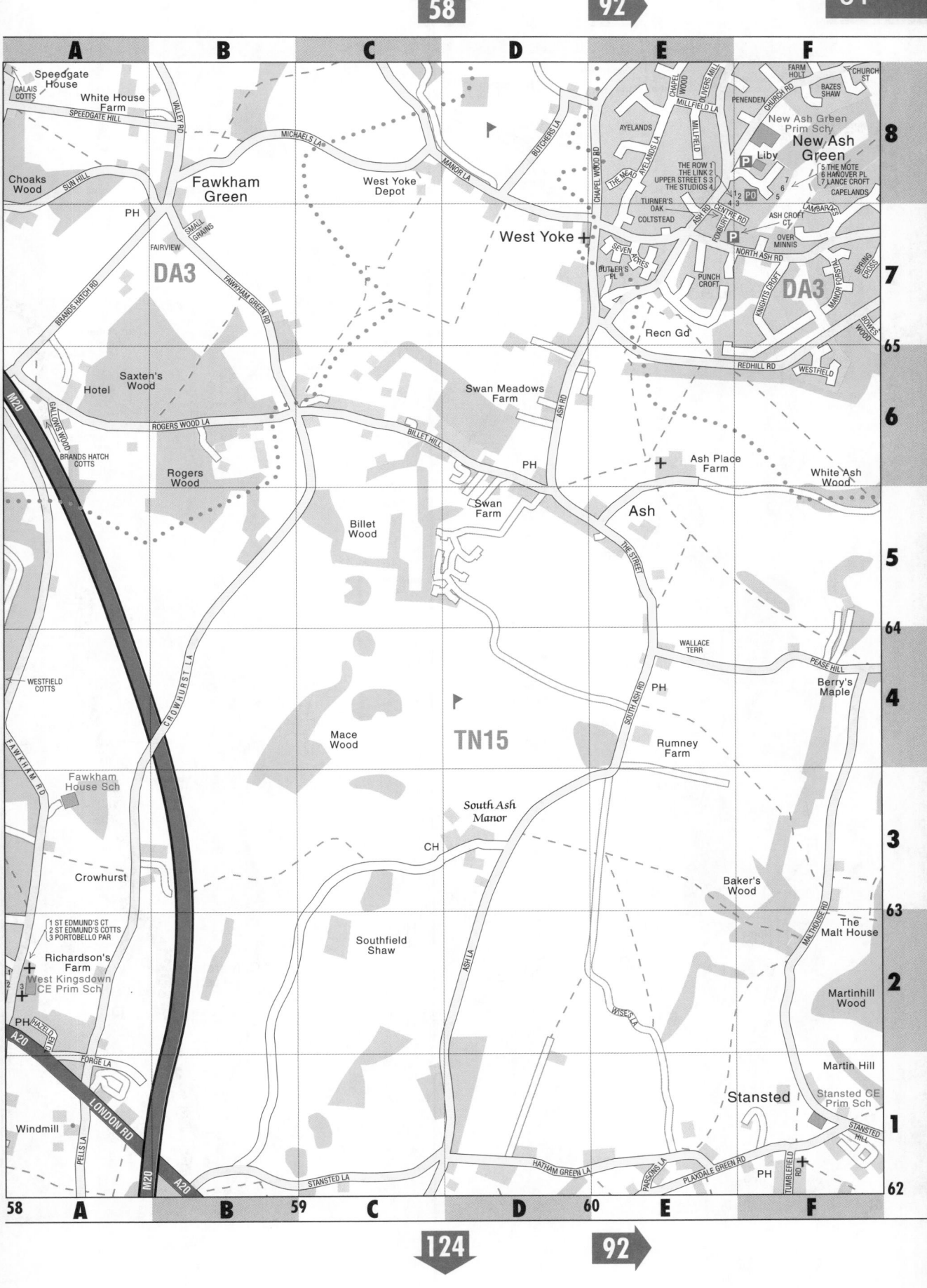

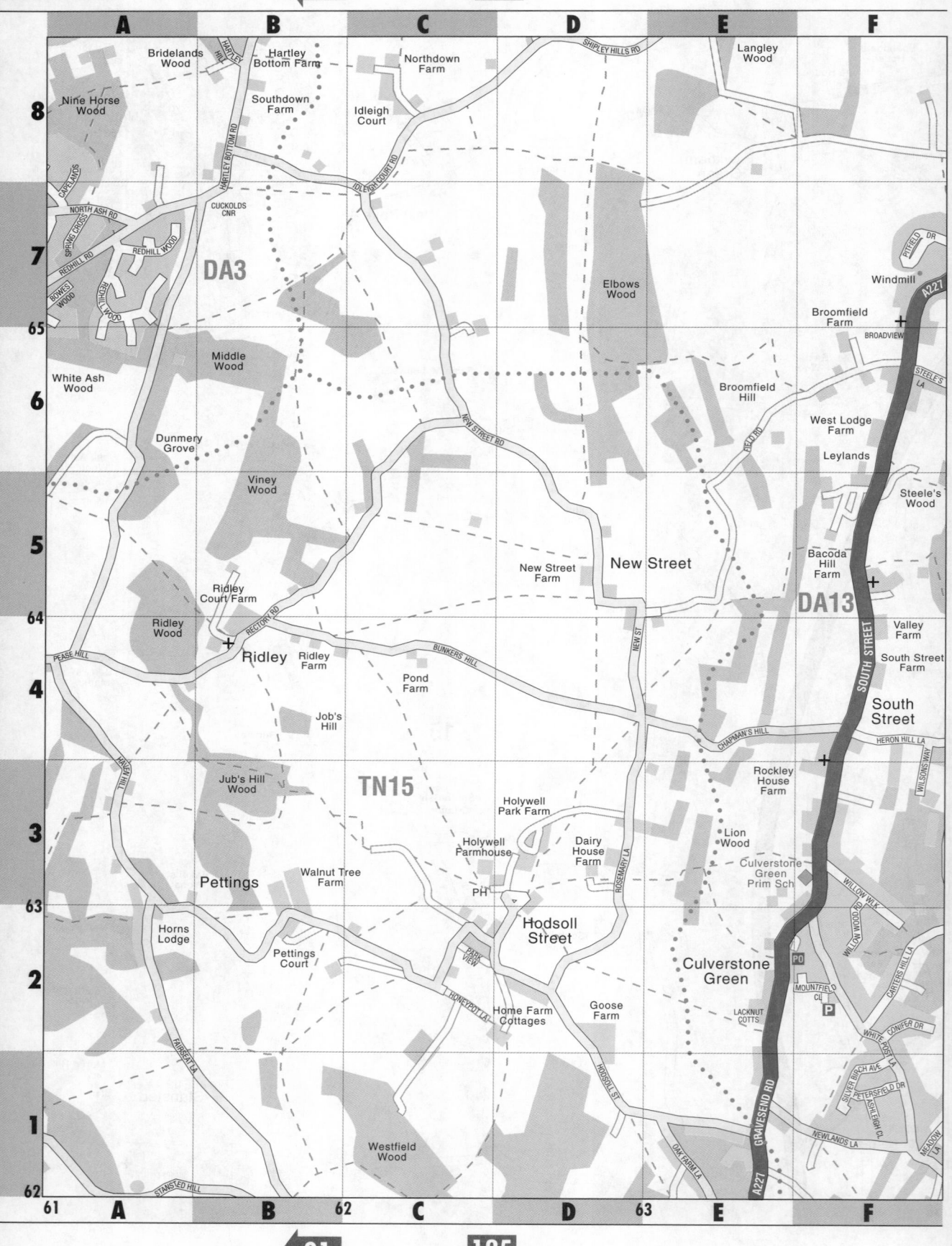

A B C D E F

8

Bridelands Wood
Hartley Bottom Farm
Northdown Farm
Shipley Hills Rd
Langley Wood

Nine Horse Wood
Southdown Farm
Idleigh Court

7

North Ash Rd
Spring Cross
Bowes Wood
Redhill Rd
Redhill Wood
CUCKOLDS CNR

DA3

Elbows Wood

Windmill
A227
PITFIELD DR
Broomfield Farm
BROADVIEW

65

White Ash Wood
Middle Wood

Broomfield Hill
STEELE'S LA

West Lodge Farm
Leylands

6

Dunmery Grove
Viney Wood

FIELD RD
Steele's Wood

5

New Street Farm
New Street
Bacoda Hill Farm
DA13

64

Ridley Court Farm
Ridley Wood
RECTORY RD
Ridley
Ridley Farm
BUNKERS HILL

NEW ST
SOUTH STREET
Valley Farm
South Street Farm

4

Pease Hill
Pond Farm
Job's Hill

CHAPMAN'S HILL
South Street
HERON HILL LA
WILSONS WAY

3

HALE HILL
Jub's Hill Wood

Holywell Park Farm
Holywell Farmhouse
PH
Dairy House Farm
ROSEMARY LA
Lion Wood
Rockley House Farm
Culverstone Green Prim Sch

TN15
Pettings
Walnut Tree Farm

63

Horns Lodge
Pettings Court
PARK VIEW
Hodsoll Street

Culverstone Green

2

FAIRSEAT LA
HONEYPOT LA
Home Farm Cottages
Goose Farm
HODSOLL ST
LACKNUT COTTS
GRAVESEND RD
MOUNTFIELD CL
P
PO
WILLOW WLK
WILLOW WOOD
CARTERS HILL LA

1

Westfield Wood
OAK FARM LA
A227
WHITE POST LA
SILVER BIRCH AVE
PETERSFIELD DR
NEWLANDS LA
CONIFER DR
ASHLEIGH CL
MEADOW
WHITE POST

62

STANSTED HILL

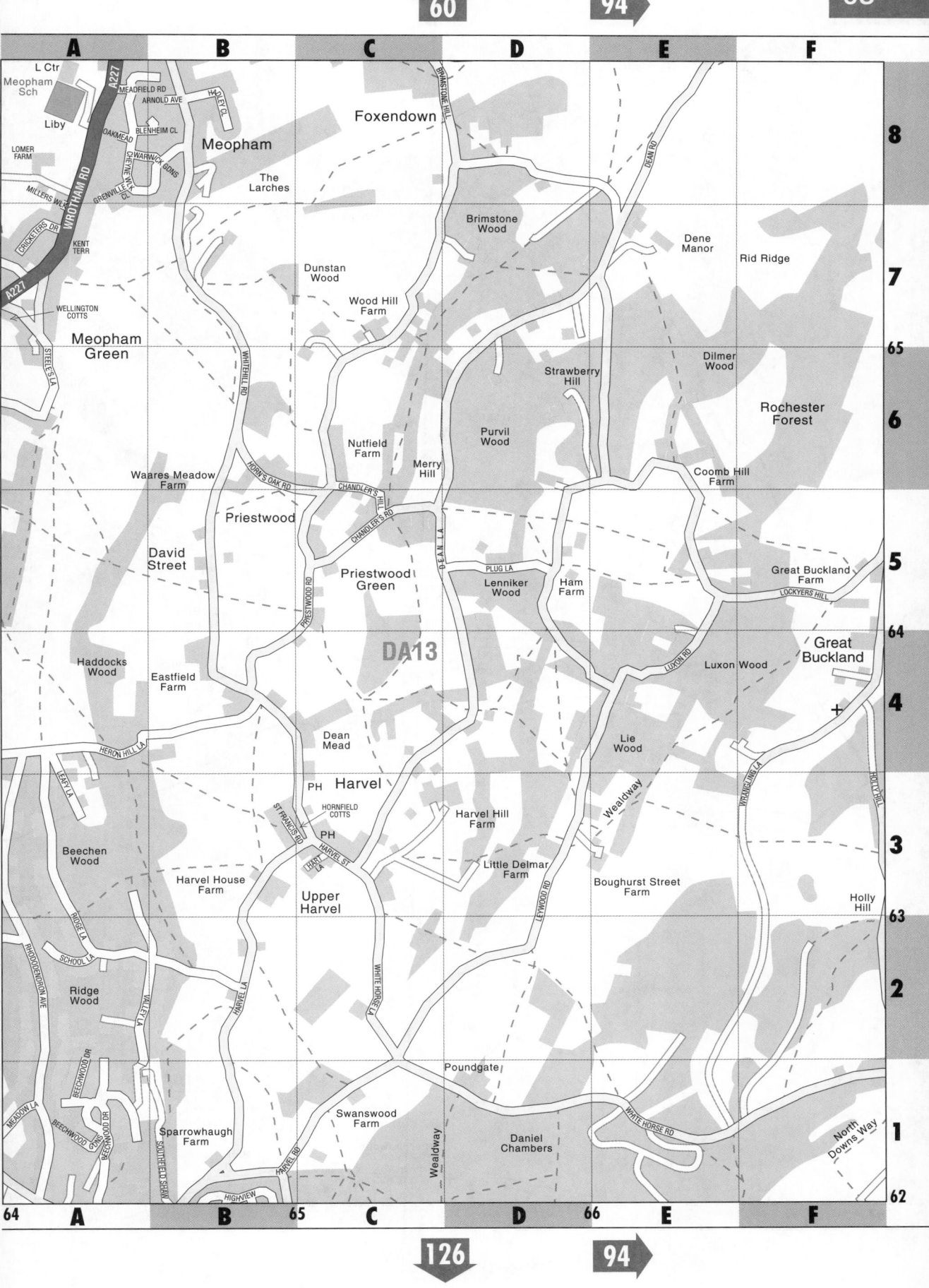

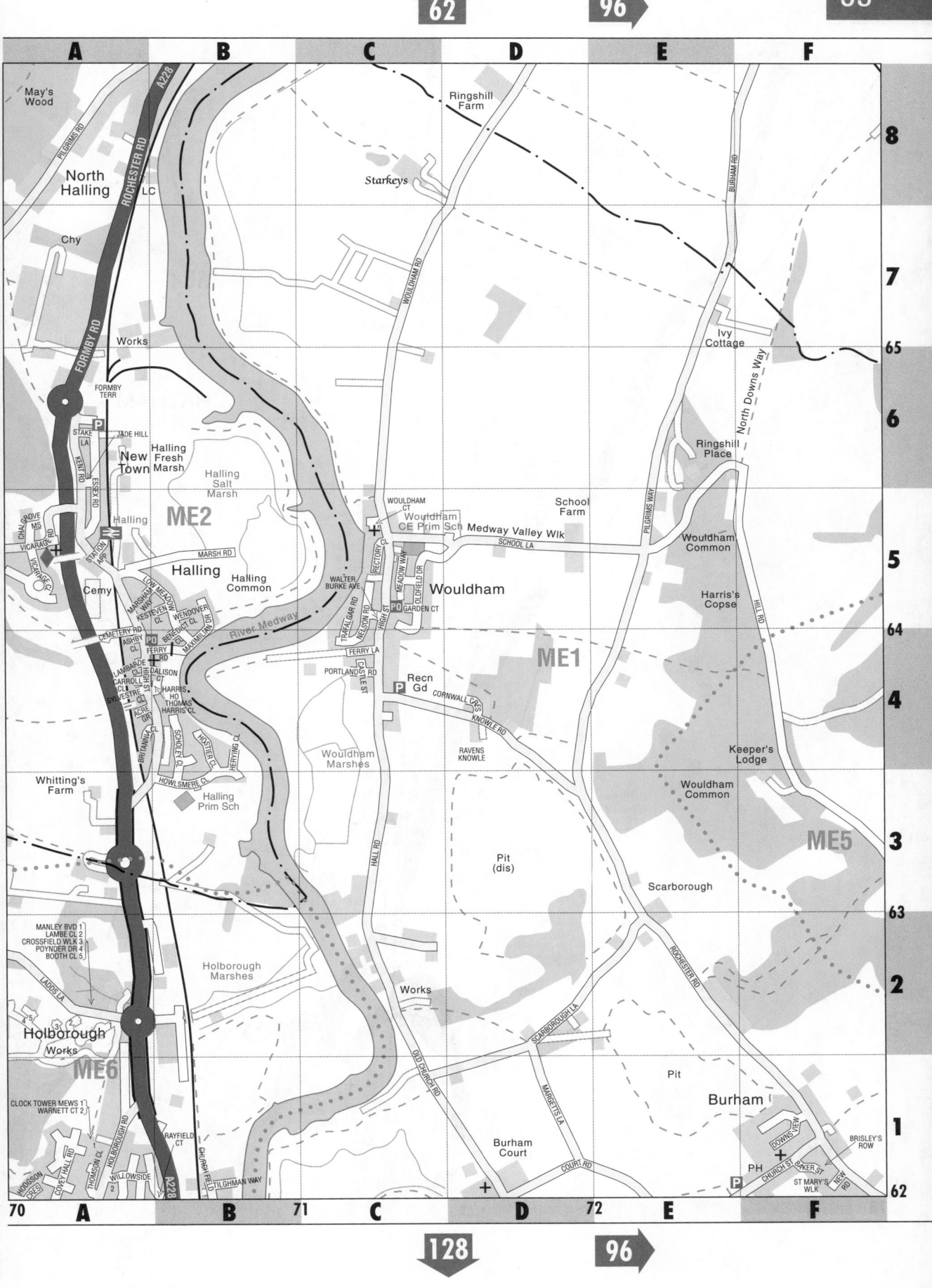

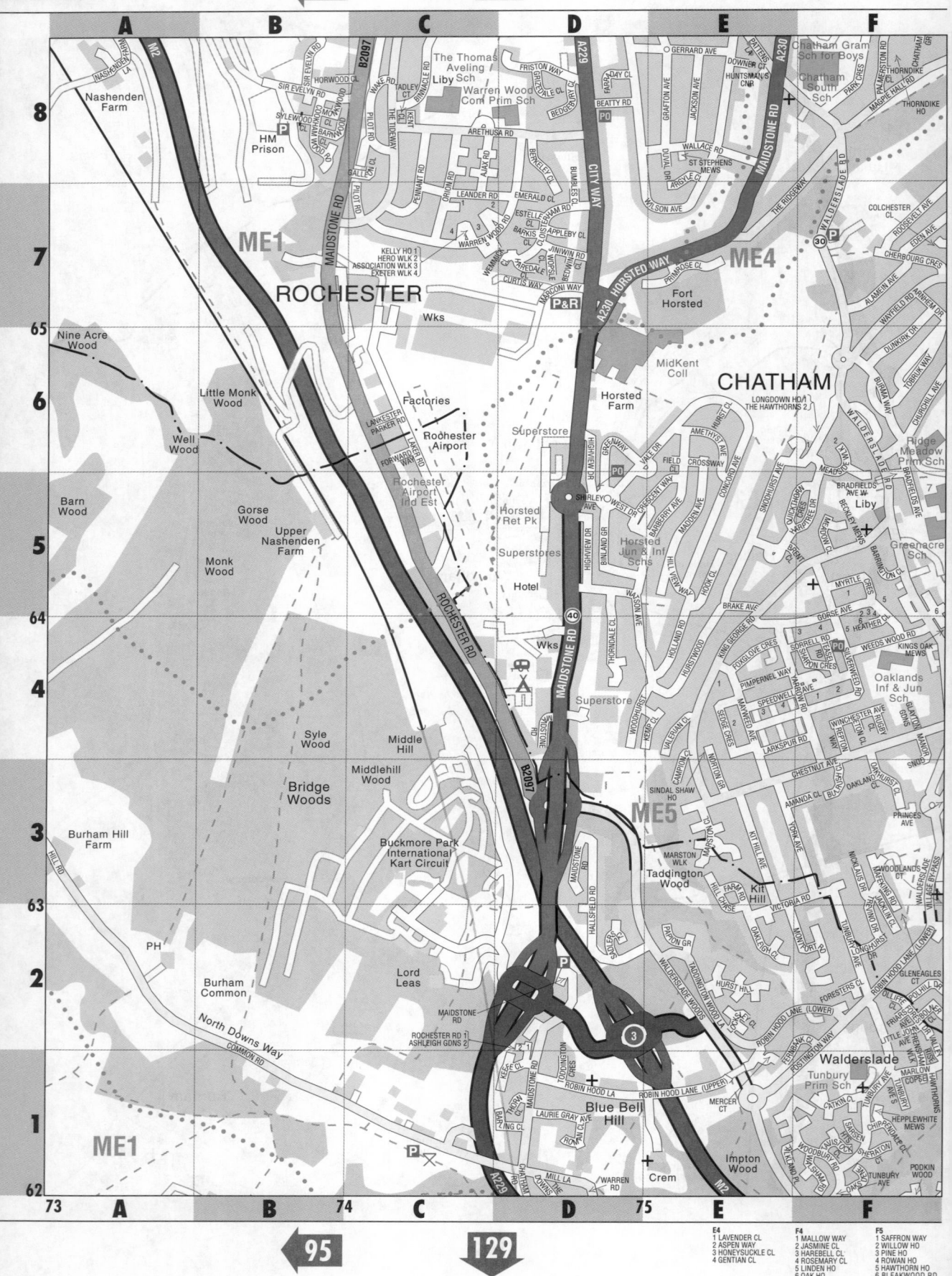

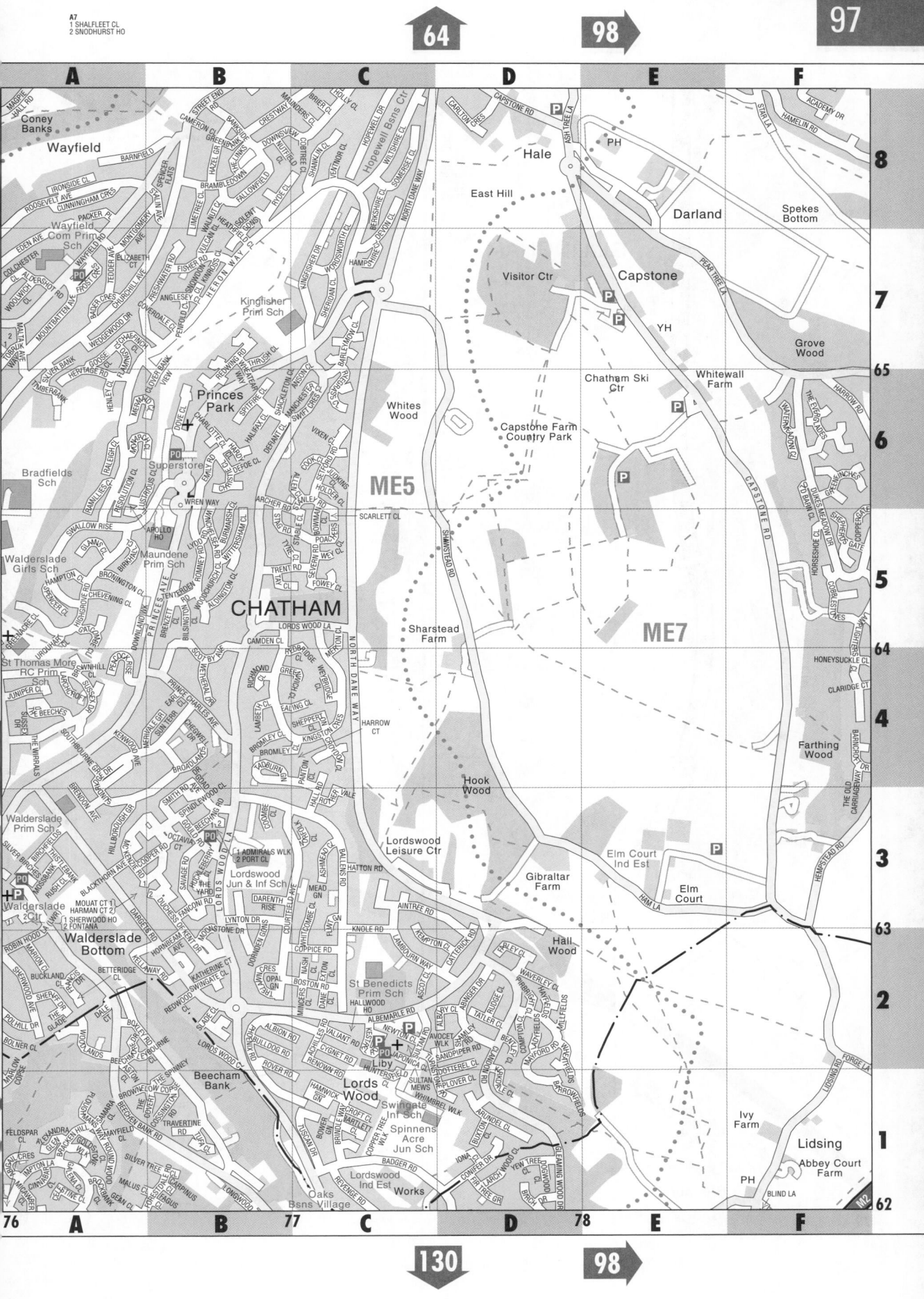

A7
1 SHALFLEET CL
2 SNODHURST HO

Coney
Banks

Wayfield

Wayfield
Com Prim
Sch

Kingfisher
Prim Sch

Princes
Park

Whites
Wood

Hale

East Hill

Visitor Ctr

Darland

Spekes
Bottom

Capstone

YH

Chatham Ski
Ctr

Whitewall
Farm

Grove
Wood

ME5

Bradfields
Sch

Superstore

Maundene
Prim Sch

Capstone Farm
Country Park

Walderslade
Girls Sch

CHATHAM

Sharstead
Farm

ME7

St Thomas More
RC Prim
Sch

HARROW
CT

Honeysuckle Cl

Claridge Ct

Hook
Wood

Farthing
Wood

Walderslade
Prim Sch

Walderslade
2 Ctr

Lordswood
Leisure Ctr

Lordswood
Jun & Inf Sch

Gibraltar
Farm

Elm Court
Ind Est

Elm
Court

Walderslade
Bottom

Hall
Wood

St Benedicts
Prim Sch

Beecham
Bank

Lords
Wood

Swingate
Inf Sch

Spinnens
Acre Jun Sch

Ivy
Farm

Lidsing

Abbey Court
Farm

Lordswood
Ind Est

Oaks
Bsns Village

Works

8
7
65
6
5
64
4
3
63
2
1
62

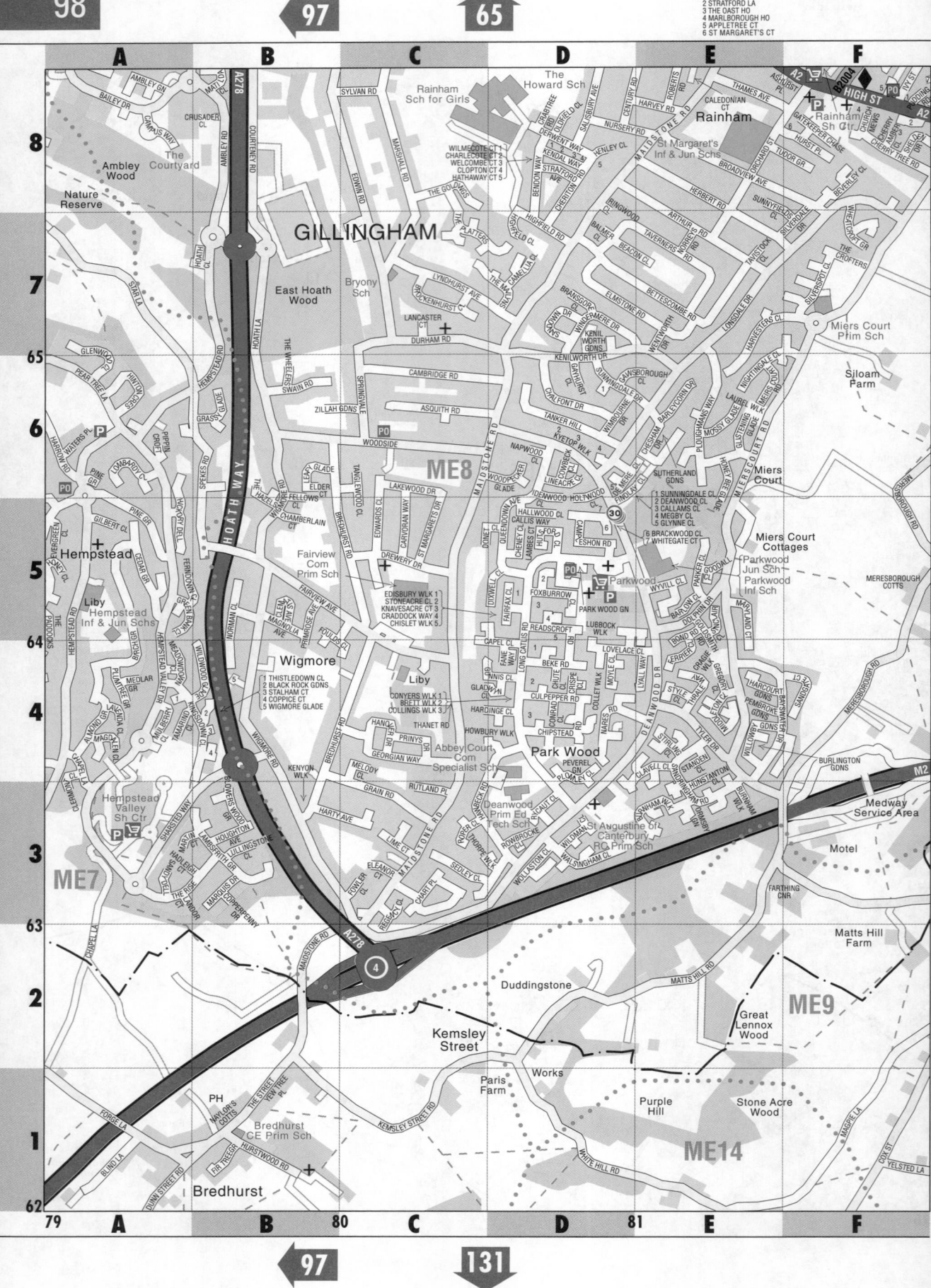

97

65

F8
1 SUNSHINE CT
2 STRATFORD LA
3 THE OAST HO
4 MARLBOROUGH HO
5 APPLETREE CT
6 ST MARGARET'S CT

7 THE OLD ORCHARD

GILLINGHAM

Rainham

Hempstead

Wigmore

Park Wood

ME8

ME7

ME9

ME14

Bredhurst

Duddingstone

Kemsley
Street

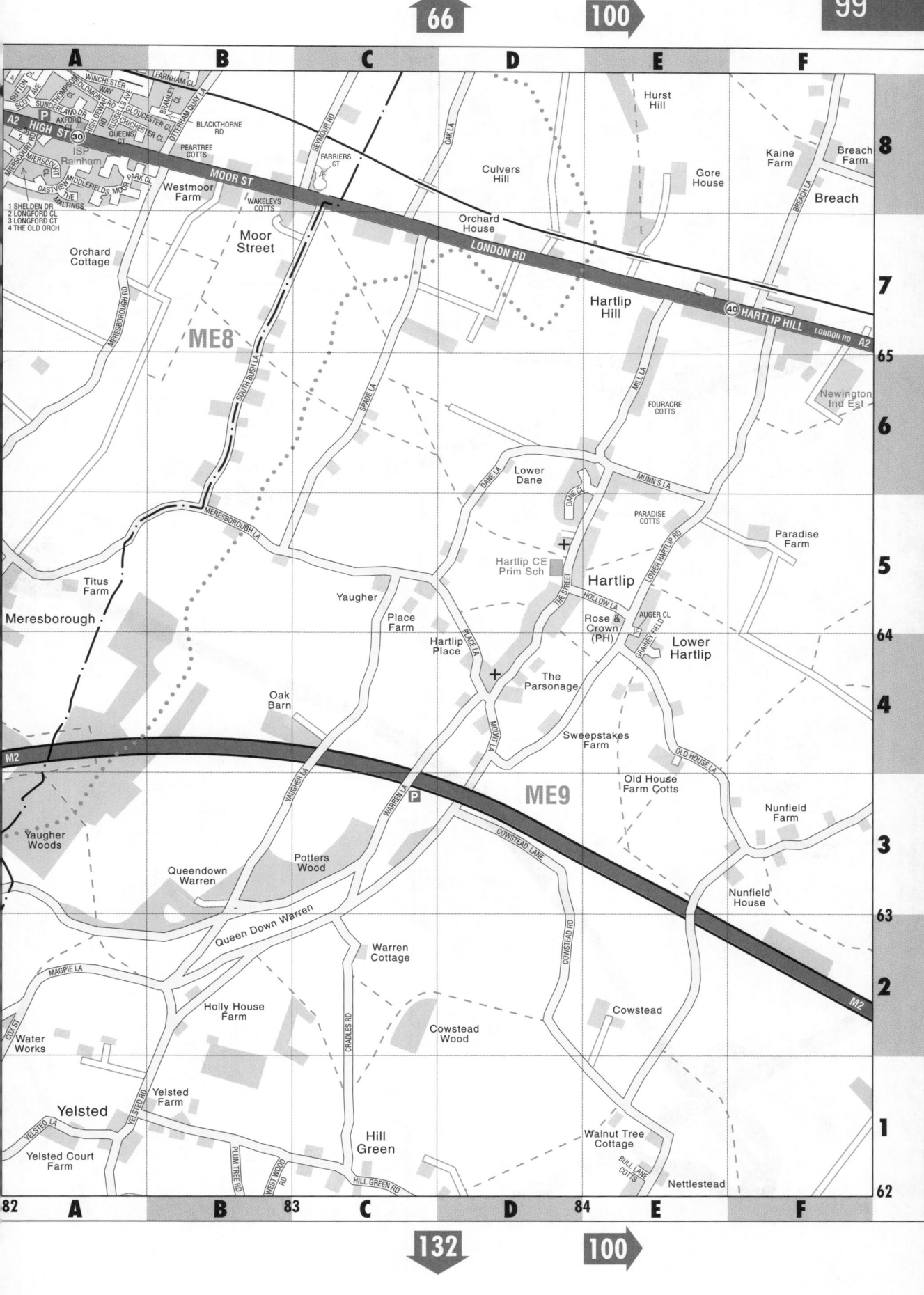

A   B   C   D   E   F

8
7
65
6
5
64
4
3
63
2
1
62

Hurst
Hill

Kaine
Farm

Breach
Farm

Breach

SUTTON
CL
SCOTT LA
WINCHESTER
CL
SOLOMON RD
SUNDERLAND CL
AXFORD
FARNHAM CL
BRAMLEY CL
GLOUCESTER
CHESTER CL
OTTERHAM QUAY LA

P

A2

HIGH ST
30

ISP
Rainham

WIERSCOTT
OASTY CT
THE
HALTINGS
MIDDLEFIELDS
PARK CL
QUEENS CL

MOOR ST

BLACKTHORNE
RD

PEARTREE
COTTS

Westmoor
Farm

WAKELEYS
COTTS

FARRIERS
CT

SEYMOUR RD

OAK LA

Culvers
Hill

Orchard
House

LONDON RD

Gore
House

1 SHELDEN DR
2 LONGFORD CL
3 LONGFORD CT
4 THE OLD ORCH

Orchard
Cottage

Moor
Street

MERESBOROUGH RD

SOUTH BUSH LA

ME8

SPADE LA

Hartlip
Hill

40   HARTLIP HILL

LONDON RD   A2

MERESBOROUGH LA

MUNN'S LA

FOURACRE
COTTS

Newington
Ind Est

Titus
Farm

Meresborough

DANE LA

Lower
Dane

DANE CL

PARADISE
COTTS

LOWER HARTLIP RD

Paradise
Farm

Yaugher

Place
Farm

PLACE LA

Hartlip CE
Prim Sch

THE STREET

Hartlip

MILL LA

HOLLOW LA

Rose &
Crown
(PH)

AUGER CL

GRANEY FIELD

Lower
Hartlip

Hartlip
Place

The
Parsonage

Oak
Barn

MOUNT LA

Sweepstakes
Farm

OLD HOUSE LA

Old House
Farm Cotts

Nunfield
Farm

M2

VAUGHER LA

WARREN LA

P

ME9

COWSTEAD LANE

Nunfield
House

Yaugher
Woods

Queendown
Warren

Potters
Wood

Queen Down Warren

Warren
Cottage

CRADLES RD

COWSTEAD RD

Cowstead

M2

MAGPIE LA

Holly House
Farm

Cowstead
Wood

COX ST

Water
Works

Yelsted

YELSTED LA

YELSTED RD

Yelsted
Farm

PLUM TREE RD

WEST WOOD LA

Hill
Green

HILL GREEN RD

Walnut Tree
Cottage

BULL LANE
COTTS

Nettlestead

Yelsted Court
Farm

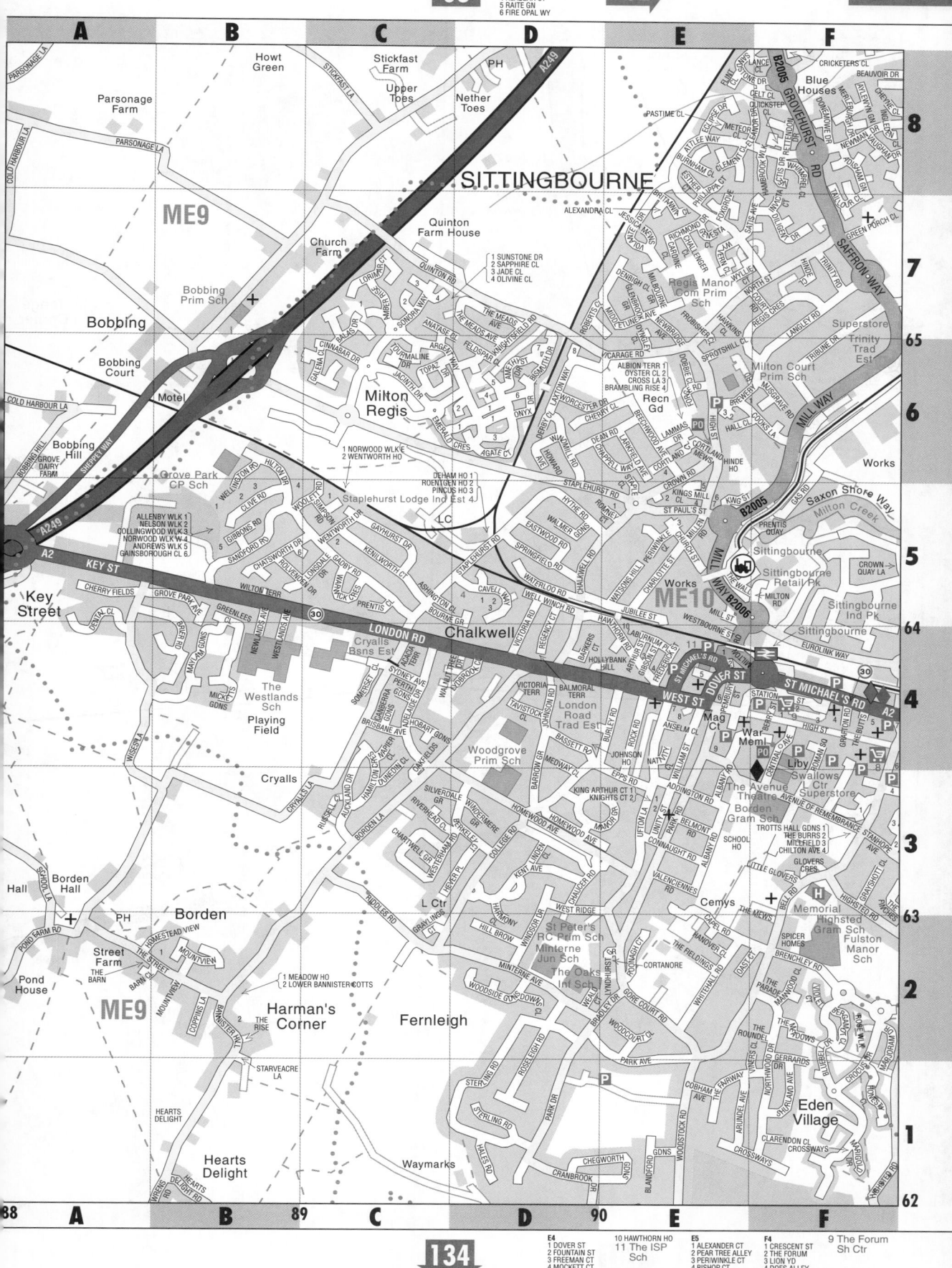

68

102

D6
1 MOONSTONE SQ
2 RUBY CL
3 AMETHYST DR
4 REALGAR CT
5 RAITE GN
6 FIRE OPAL WY
7 TRONA CT
8 PIPPIN CL

SITTINGBOURNE

ME9

Bobbing

Milton Regis

Key Street

Borden

Harman's Corner

Fernleigh

ME9

Hearts Delight

Eden Village

Chalkwell

ME10

E4
1 DOVER ST
2 FOUNTAIN ST
3 FREEMAN CT
4 MOCKETT CT
5 CHURCH ST
6 PEMBURY CT
7 WINGATE CT
8 THE CLOISTERS
9 MIDDLETON CT
10 HAWTHORN HO
11 The ISP Sch

E5
1 ALEXANDER CT
2 PEAR TREE ALLEY
3 PERIWINKLE CT
4 BISHOP CT
5 TANNERY CT
6 RIGDEN'S CT
7 GILES-YOUNG CT

F4
1 CRESCENT ST
2 THE FORUM
3 LION YD
4 DOES ALLEY
5 ST MICHAEL'S CL
6 RIVERBOURNE CT
7 CROWN QUAY LA
8 Bell Sh Ctr
9 The Forum Sh Ctr

A B C D E F

8
7
65
6
5
64
4
3
63
2
1
62

91 A B 92 C D 93 E F

Castle Rough

Saxon Shore

Kemsley Marshes

Church Marshes Country Park

Trinity Trad Est

Milton Regis

Sewage Works

Sittingbourne & Kemsley Light Rly

Saxon Shore Way

Milton Creek

Works

Eurolink North Ind Est

Nature Reserve

Little Murston

Tonge Corner Farm

Tonge Corner

Telegraph Hill

Blacketts Rd

Wilford Court

Anchor Bsns Pk

Glenmere Bsns Ctr

Stadium Way

Castle Rd

Gas Rd

Brickmakers Ind Est 1
Castleacres Ind Pk 2
Castle Road Bsns Prec 3

1 D2 Trad Est

Drywall Ind Est

Church Road Bsns Ctr

Castle Road Tech Ctr

Central Park Stad (Sittingbourne FC)

Mere Court

Bingham Rd

West Tonge Farm

Murston

Works

ME10

Eaves Ct

Eurolink Bsns Pk

Eurolink East Ind Est

East Hall

Swale Way

St Giles Houses

ME9

Dolphin Pk

West Lane Trad Est

Eurolink Ind Ctr

Murston Jun Sch

Wells Ho

Murston Inf Sch

Churchill Ho

Great Easthall Way

Swale Heritage Trail

Bunces Farm

Bayford Court

The Smeed-Dean Ctr

St Georges Bsns Pk

Eurolink Way

Tonge Rd

All Saints Rd

Lomas Rd

Tonge Mill

St Michael's Rd

Shortlands Rd

Wheatcroft Cl

Snipeshill

Scraps Hill

Lower Rd

East St

Canterbury Rd

Stones Farm

Fox Hill

Bapchild

Hempstead Farm

South Ave Jun & Inf Sch

The Finches

Canterbury Road Prim Sch

Lansdowne Prim Sch

1 Oaktree Ho
2 Birch Ho
3 Ashtree Ho
4 Willow Ho

Meadowfield Sch

Bapchild & Tonge CE Aided Sch

The Street

Hotel

London Rd A2

The Old Vicarage

Radfield

Meadowfield Sch Sports Ctr

Bapchild Court

Sittingbourne Com Coll

Morris Court

Heywood Cottages

Little Dully Cottages

Ashgores House

New Cottages

A4
1 GOSHAWK HO
2 MERLIN HO
3 FALCON HO
4 KESTREL CT
5 CROWN QUAY LA
6 RONALDS CT
7 PLAZA CT
8 Centre 2000
9 THE TURRETS

B4
1 JARRETT'S CT
2 HOMEVIEW TERR
3 HOMEVIEW
4 SMEED CL
5 PRICES CT
6 HARKNESS CT
7 DICKSON CT
8 POULSEN CT
9 THOMAS CT

C5
1 FIELDER CL
1 HUTCHINGS CL
3 HEARNE CL
4 BRACKEN CT
5 THE CEDARS

103 71

The Swale

A | B | C | D | E | F

8
Fowley Island
South Deep
Saxon Shore Way

7
Rifle Range (dis)
Luddenham Gut

65

Teynham Level

6

Little Uplees

UPLEES COTTS

Howletts

5
ME9
ME13

UPLEES RD

64

Luddenham Marshes
Poplar Hall

4
MARSH LA

UPLEES RD

3
Luddenham Court
Cherry Tree Dr

63
Swale Heritage Trail

DEERTON ST
BROOK COTTS
Elverton
PH
Hawks & Beetles Farm
Nash's Farm

2
Deerton Street
The Old Farmhouse
Wildmarsh

Lower Newlands
THE ELMS
The Old Rectory

LOWER RD
Mockbeggar
Luddenham Prim Sch

BYSING WOOD RD

1
LOWER NORTON LA
Mockbeggar Farm
BYSING WOOD COTTS
Bysing Wood

Stone Farm
BYSING WOOD RD

62
LC

97 | A | B | 98 | C | D | 99 | E | F

103 137

A   B   C   D   E   F

8

The Ferry Inn (PH)

HARTY FERRY RD

ME12

7

Uplees Marshes

The Swale

65

6

Gate House Bungalow

Oare Marshes Nature Reserve

Visitor Ctr

P

Saxon Shore Way

5

ME13

HARTY FERRY COTTS

Nagden Marshes

64

4

Broomfield Farm

Court Lodge

Norman's Hill

PH

Hollowshore

Faversham Creek

UPLEES RD

+

Pheasant Farm

Oare Creek

Ham Marshes

3

CHURCH RD

Wharf

Works

63

Oare

RUSSELL PL

PO PH

HARRISON TERR

COLEGATES CT

COLEGATES

MOUNT PLEASANT

THE STREET

Works

Ham Farm

2

COLEGATES RD

Piggery

B2045

JOHN HALL CL

Gravel Works

Windmill (dis)

Ham Farm

Ham Rd

SEAGATE RD

WESTERN LINK

MAYLAND CT

WEBB CT

WELLS WAY

PH

WINDMILL LA

OARE RD

Gate House

FAVERSHAM

The Brents

Saxon Shore Way

Faversham Creek

1

Oare Gunpowder Works Country Park

BYSING WOOD RD

B2045

WILDISH RD

IVORY CT

JOHNSON CT

BYSING WOOD RD

CHURCHILL WAY

SHERWOOD CL

Davington Prim Sch

FINCH CL

CROSTAL RD

PRIORY PL

LARKSFIELD RD

SPRINGHEAD RD

BROOK RD

UPPER BRENTS

North Quay

South Quay

Brents Ind Est

Shipyard Area

WATERSIDE CL

Wharf

Works

Sewage Works

ABBEY FIELDS

62

00   A   B   01   C   D   02   E   F

108

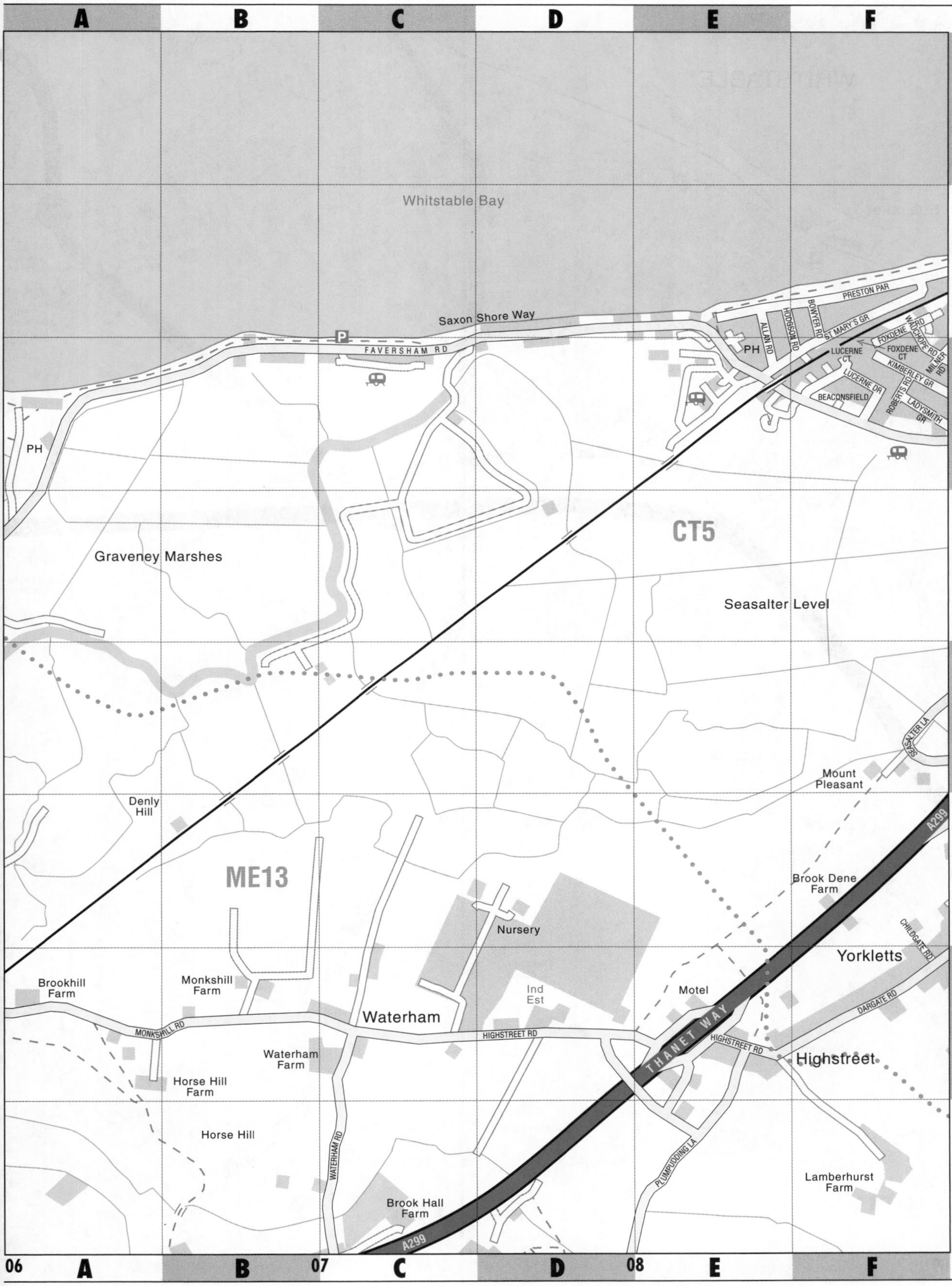

A **B** **C** **D** **E** **F**

8

7

Whitstable Bay

PRESTON PAR

Saxon Shore Way

P

FAVERSHAM RD

65

ST MARY'S GR
BOWYER RD
HUDSON RD
ALLAN RD

PH

LUCERNE
CT

FOXDENE
FOXDENE RD
CT
WILDROSE
WALMER RD
KIMBERLEY GR

6

LUCERNE DR

BEACONSFIELD

ROBERTS RD
LADYSMITH
GR

PH

CT5

Graveney Marshes

Seasalter Level

5

64

4

Denly
Hill

Mount
Pleasant

SALTER LA

A299

ME13

Brook Dene
Farm

3

CHILDGATE RD

Nursery

Yorkletts

63

Brookhill
Farm

Monkshill
Farm

Ind
Est

Motel

DARGATE RD

2

MONKSHILL RD

Waterham

HIGHSTREET RD

THANET WAY

HIGHSTREET RD

Highstreet

Waterham
Farm

Horse Hill
Farm

PLUMPUDDING LA

1

Horse Hill

Lamberhurst
Farm

Brook Hall
Farm

WATERHAM RD

A299

62

06 **A** **B** **07** **C** **D** **08** **E** **F**

140   108

107

74

D8
1 JAFFA CT
2 MARINERS CT
3 NORFOLK ST
4 WHITBOURNE CT
5 OLD PRINTWORKS CL
6 SADDLETON GR

8

WHITSTABLE

Saxon Shore Way
Saxon Shore Way

Seasalter

CLIFTON GDNS
WEST CLIFF
CLIFTON
PORTLAND
SAXON SHORE
THE CHASE
ALEXANDRA RD
ALEXANDRA RD
VULCAN CL
CANTERBURY RD
B2205
SWAN FIELD
ST JAMES
VALE RD
WICKETTS END
SWALECLIFFE
GLEBE WAY
GODFREY
CRANLEIGH
CRANLEIGH GDNS
MILLSTREAM COTTS
DOWNS AVE
FARM HO CL
INVICTA RD
Cemy
Sports Ctr
A2090
SPIRE AVE

7

Joy La
CUNDISHALL CL
NETOUR AVE
GENESTA AVE
SUNRAY AVE
VALKYRIE AVE
CYPRESS CL
DOVE CL
Joy Lane Prim Sch
SHEARWATER CT
KINGFISHER CL
GRAMMAR PL
MAUGHAM CT
ORCHARD GR
GORDON RD
GREEN LA
KENT ST
HILLVIEW RD
SUFFOLK
ST MARY'S
HAZEL CL
SADDLETON RD
NORMAN RD
CRANLEIGH CT
CRANLEIGH GDNS
KINGSLEY RD
BELTON
SYDNEY
WILLOW
MILLSTROOD RD
WILLOW
HO CL
BELLEVUE RD
Com Coll Whitstable
REGENCY CL
Mill Strood Farm
DEBO
RAH CL
GOLDEN HILL
CLIFFORD RD

PRESTON PAR
FAIRWAY CRES
ADMIRALTY WLK
SEASALTER BEACH
GEORGE'S AVE
MEDINA AVE
ST ALPHEGE
ST ALPHEGE
SOMERSET CL
SHAMROCK AVE
COLUMBIA AVE
APRIL
ROSE WAY
NORTHWAY
OSPREY CL
GRIMTHORPE AVE
BRITANNIA AVE
FIELD VIEW
MARTINDOWN RD
SPRING WLK
THE HEIGHTS
MEADOW WLK
BORSTAL HILL
PIERPOINT RD
MILLERS CT
CLOVELLY RD
Windmill Hotel
Duncan Down
ST ANDREW'S CL
HUNTERS CHASE
ST LUKE'S CL
ST VINCENT'S
ST PATRICK'S
ST MARK'S CL
ST DAVID'S CL
ST GEORGE'S CL
DOGGERELL ACRE
AURELIE WY
EVERSLEIGH RISE
Superstore
Joseph Wilson Ind Est

65

MILNER RD
GATEACRE
ASHLEY DR
FAVERSHAM RD
EDEN RD
FLORENCE RD
HAZLEMERE RD
CORDINGHAM RD
DORSET CL
CAROLINE CRES
JAYNE WLK
SANDPIPER CT
WILLOW CL
LARK CL
ANTH
SWALLOW WLK
MARTIN CL
SAND END
SHEPPEY VIEW
SHERWOOD AVE
SHERWOOD CL
THE WARREN
LONG REACH CL
LAMB'S WLK
SOUTH VIEW RD
A299
Duncan Down
HILLTOP
HUNTERS CHASE
PADDOCK CL
Mast

C6
1 LEYSDOWN VIEW
2 WARDEN POINT WAY
3 POLLARD PL
4 COLUMBINE CL
5 Chaucer Bsns Pk

South View Farm
Benacre Wood
THANET WAY

6

FREEMAN'S CL
CHANTONBURY CHASE
THE GRANGE
MARGARET'S
HERITAGE CL
PORTLIGHT PL
APPLEGARTH PK
CHURCH LA
ROWAN TREE PK
TRADEWINDS
THE OAKS
FAVOURITE RD
SPEEDWELL RD
GOLDCREST WLK
NIGHTINGALE LA
IBIS CL
MAJOR CL
BODKIN WY
WRAIK HILL
Motel
BLUEFIELD MEWS
PH
A290
MONTPELIER AVE
Seasalter Cross
Caravan Parks

A6
1 WAUCHOPE RD
2 ROYAL NAVY WY

SEASALTER LA
THANET WAY
HARRIETS CNR
PILGRIMS LA
WELLINGTON ST
SUNNYSIDE RD
MARLBOROUGH ST
WILLOW RD
ROYAL AVE
Hillside Bungalow
Clapham Hill
CT5
Seeshill Farm
Lincey
Bogshole Farm

5

CLAPHAM HILL
The Oaks
Seasalter Dairy Farm
BOGSHOLE LA
Lincey

64

Sunset Farm
Wraik Hill
Elmcroft
Court Lees Farm
Burgess Farm

4

FOX'S CROSS MILL
FOX'S CROSS
Holme Lodge Farm
PYE ALLEY LA
April Cottage
Court Lees Manor

3

DARGATE RD
GLEN WLK
BARN CL
FORD WLK
Fox's Cross Bottom
PEAN COURT RD
FOX'S CROSS RD
CARLTON RD
Oakapple Cottage
PEAN HILL
Marley Wood

63

COOMBE WLK
Ellenden Farm

2

Coombe Wood
Ellenden Wood
CT2
Works
Hempshall Wood

1

ME13
Tong Wood
Dockers Field Farm
A290
HONEY HILL

62

109
76
109
143

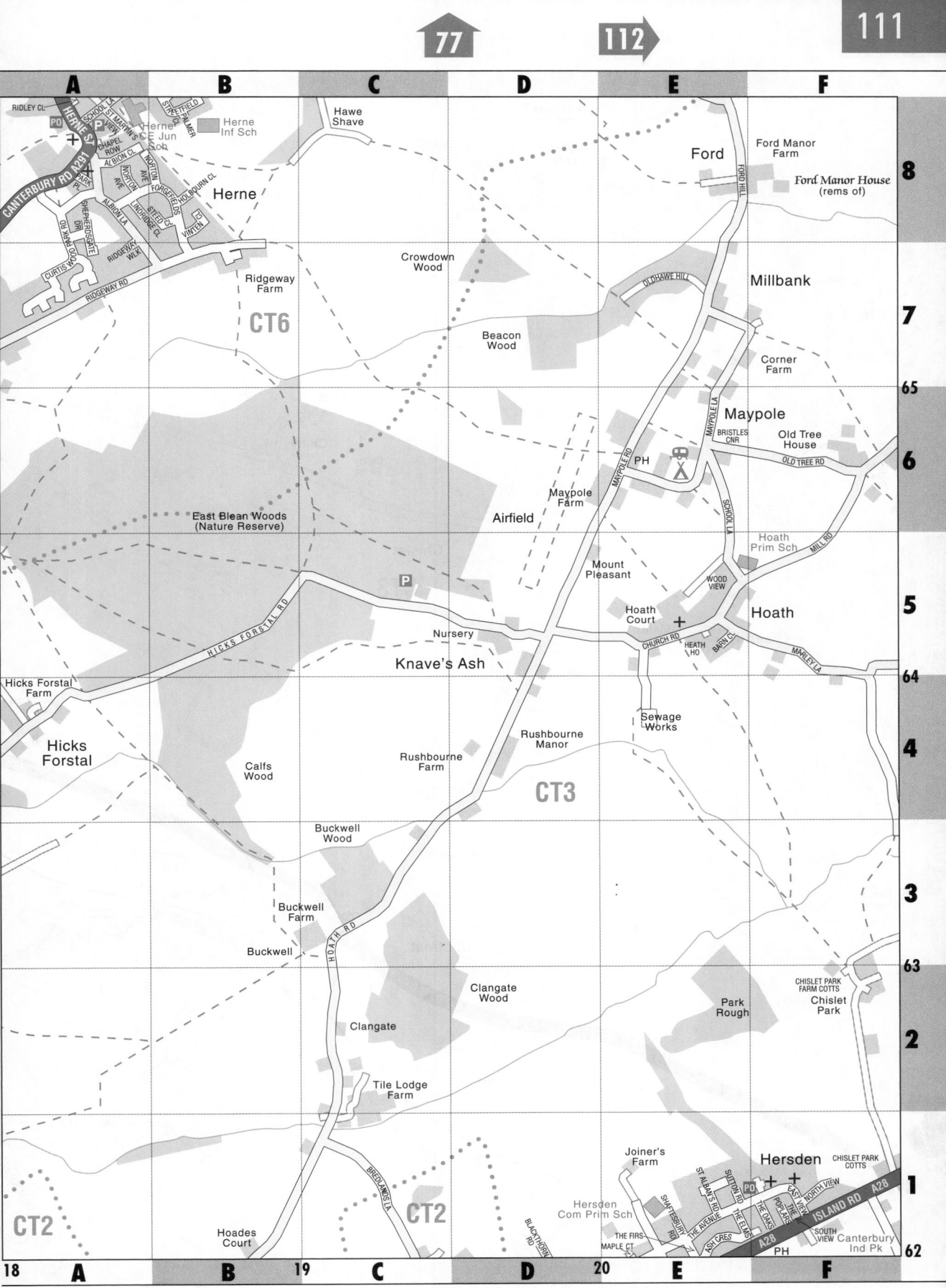

Ford
Ford Manor Farm
Ford Manor House (rems of)

8

RIDLEY CL
PO
HERNE ST
P
SCHOOL LA
ST MARTIN'S
STREETFIELD
HORNE
STREETFIELD MER
Hawe Shave

Millbank

Herne CE Jun Sch
Herne Inf Sch
CHAPEL ROW
CANTERBURY RD A291
ALBION CL
HOLBOURN CL
FORGEFIELDS
NORTON AVE
ALBION CL
CURTIS WOOD
SHEPHERDSGATE DR
OLD PARK RD
RIDGEWAY WLK
STEED CL
VINTEN
LINGHAM CL
Herne
OLDHAWE HILL

Crowdown Wood

Corner Farm

65

Ridgeway Farm
RIDGEWAY RD
CT6

Beacon Wood

Maypole
BRISTLES CNR
Old Tree House
OLD TREE RD

7

6

MAYPOLE RD
PH
Maypole Farm

SCHOOL LA
Hoath Prim Sch
MILL RD

East Bean Woods (Nature Reserve)

Airfield
Mount Pleasant
WOOD VIEW

Hoath

5

P
Hoath Court
Nursery
CHURCH RD
HEATH HO
BARN CL
MARLEY LA

64

HICKS FORSTAL RD
Knave's Ash

Hicks Forstal Farm

Sewage Works

4

Rushbourne Manor

Hicks Forstal
Calfs Wood
Rushbourne Farm
CT3

Buckwell Wood

3

Buckwell Farm
HOATH RD

CHISLET PARK FARM COTTS

63

Buckwell
Clangate Wood
Park Rough
Chislet Park

2

Clangate

Tile Lodge Farm

Joiner's Farm
Hersden
CHISLET PARK COTTS

1

CT2
BREDLANDS LA
BLACKTHORN RD
CT2
Hersden Com Prim Sch
ST ALBAN'S RD
SUTTON RD
PO
EAST VIEW
NORTH VIEW
THE POPLARS
ISLAND RD A28

Hoades Court
THE FIRS
MAPLE CT
SHAFTESBURY RD
THE AVENUE
THE ELMS
THE OAKS
ASH CRES
SOUTH VIEW
PH
A28
Canterbury Ind Pk

62

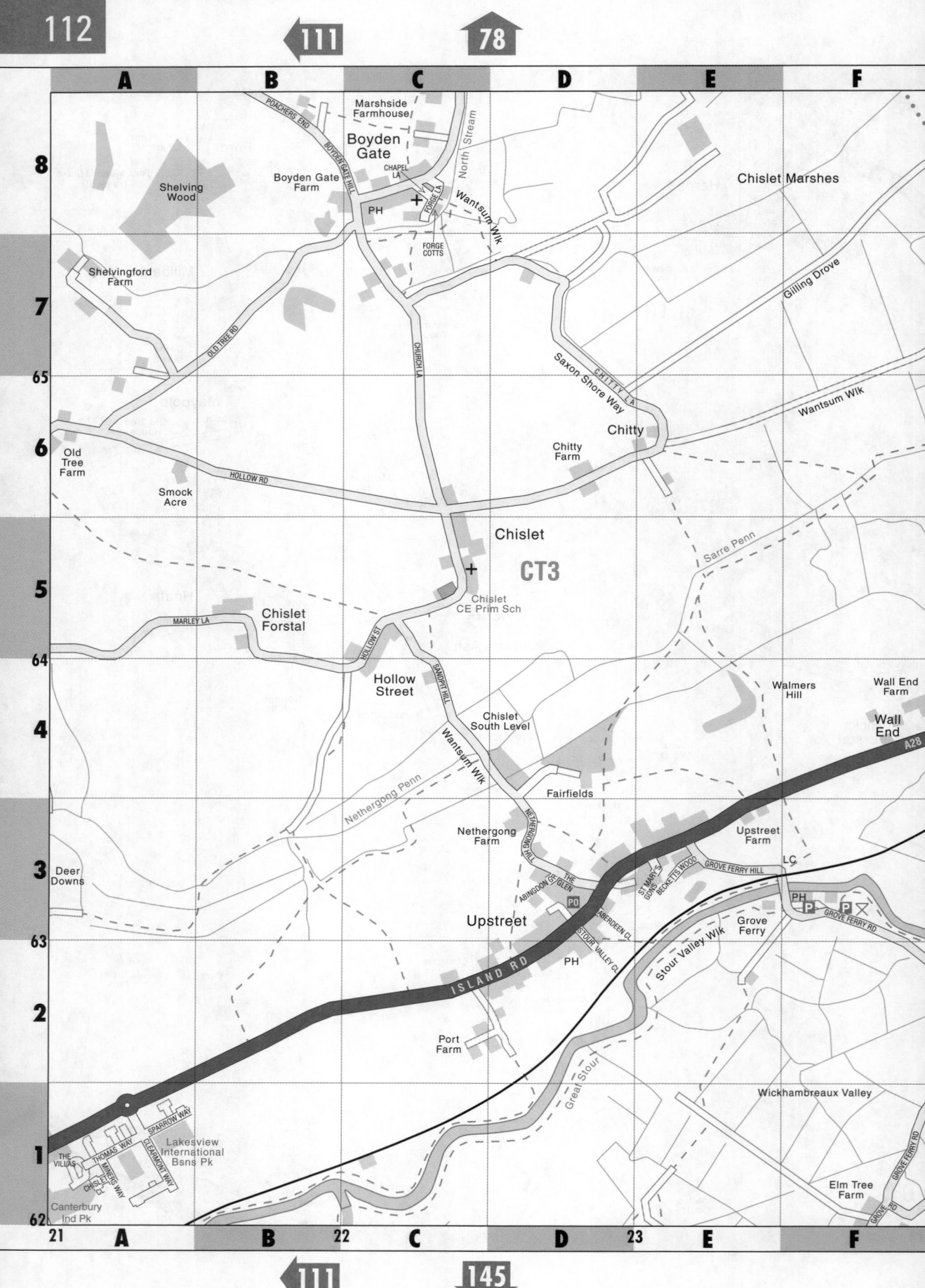

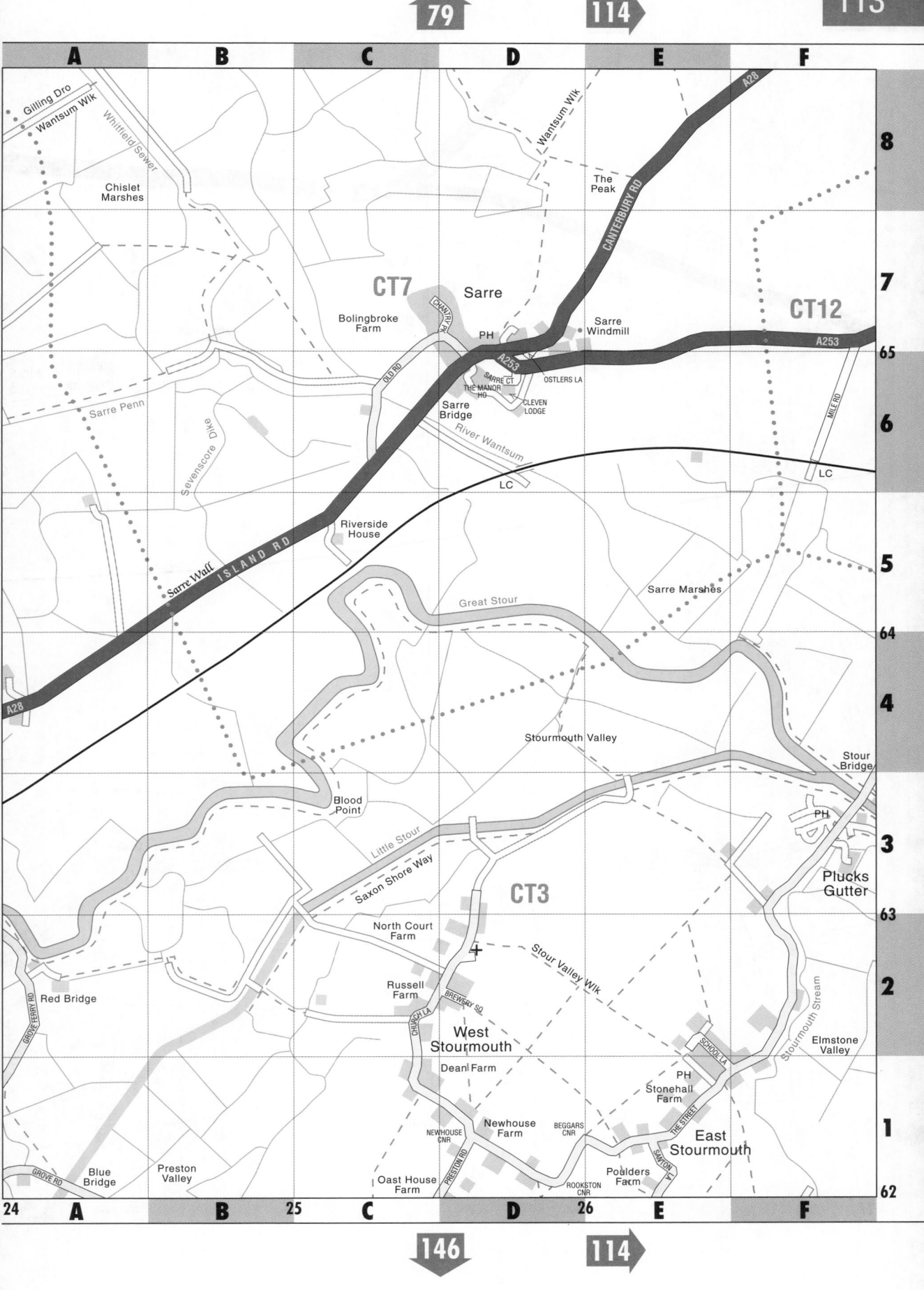

A   B   C   D   E   F

8

7

CT7   Sarre   CT12

65

6

5

64

4

3

63

2

1

62

Gilling Dro
Wantsum Wlk
Whitfield Sewer
Chislet Marshes

Wantsum Wlk
The Peak
CANTERBURY RD
A28

Bolingbroke Farm
CHANTRY PK
PH
Sarre Windmill
A253
SARRE CT
THE MANOR HO
OSTLERS LA
Sarre Bridge
CLEVEN LODGE
OLD RD
Sarre Penn
LC

A253
MILE RD
LC

Sevenscore Dike
River Wantsum
Riverside House
ISLAND RD
Sarre Wall
Great Stour
Sarre Marshes

A28
Stourmouth Valley
Stour Bridge

Blood Point
Little Stour
PH
Plucks Gutter

Saxon Shore Way
CT3
North Court Farm
Stour Valley Wlk

Grove Ferry Rd
Red Bridge
Russell Farm
BREWERY SQ
CHURCH LA
West Stourmouth
SCHOOL LA
Stourmouth Stream
Elmstone Valley

Dean Farm
PH
Stonehall Farm
THE STREET

Newhouse Farm
BEGGARS CNR
East Stourmouth
NEWHOUSE CNR
PRESTON RD
SAXON LA

Grove Rd
Blue Bridge
Preston Valley
Oast House Farm
ROOKSTON CNR
Poulders Farm

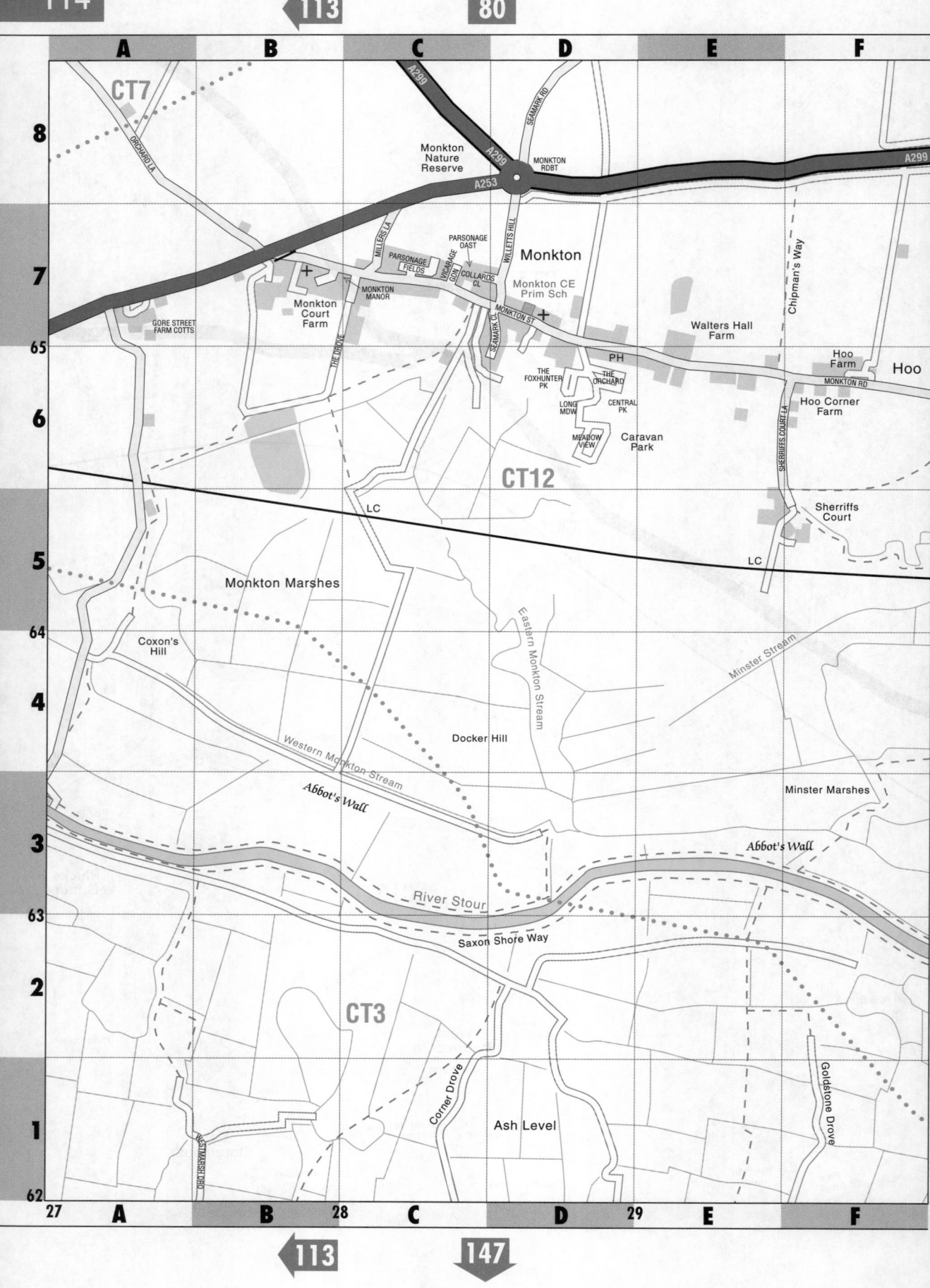

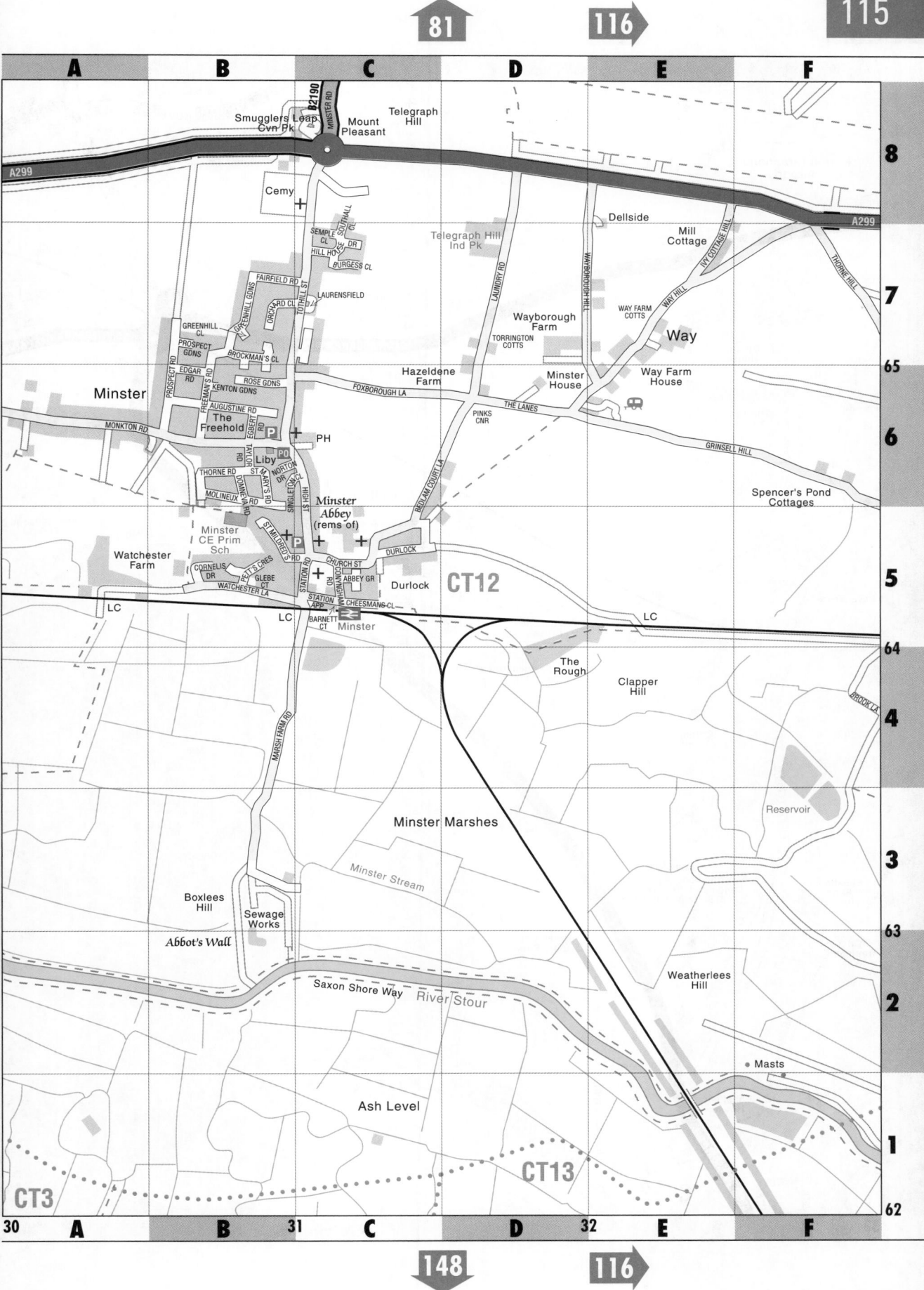

RAMSGATE

Sandwich Bay

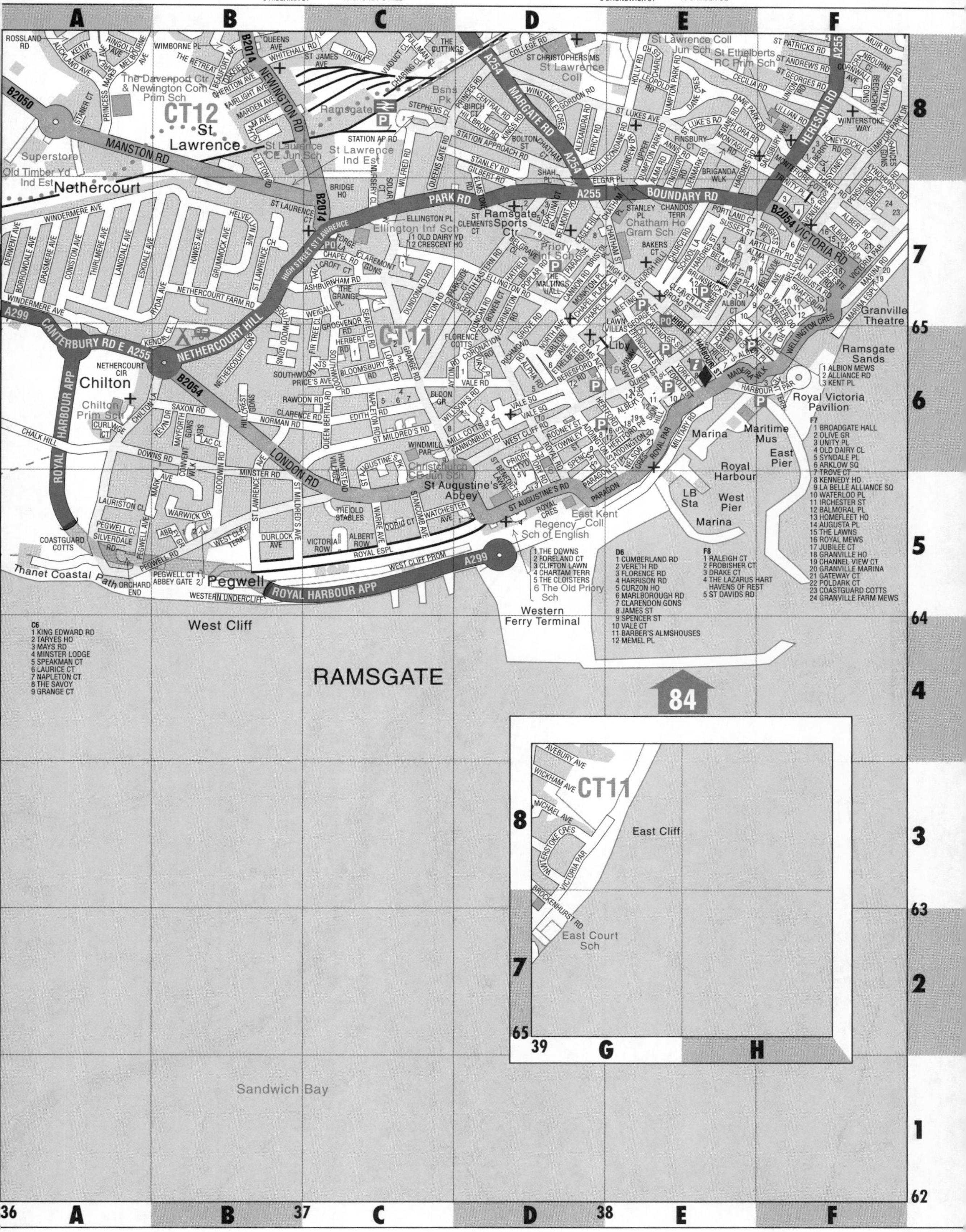

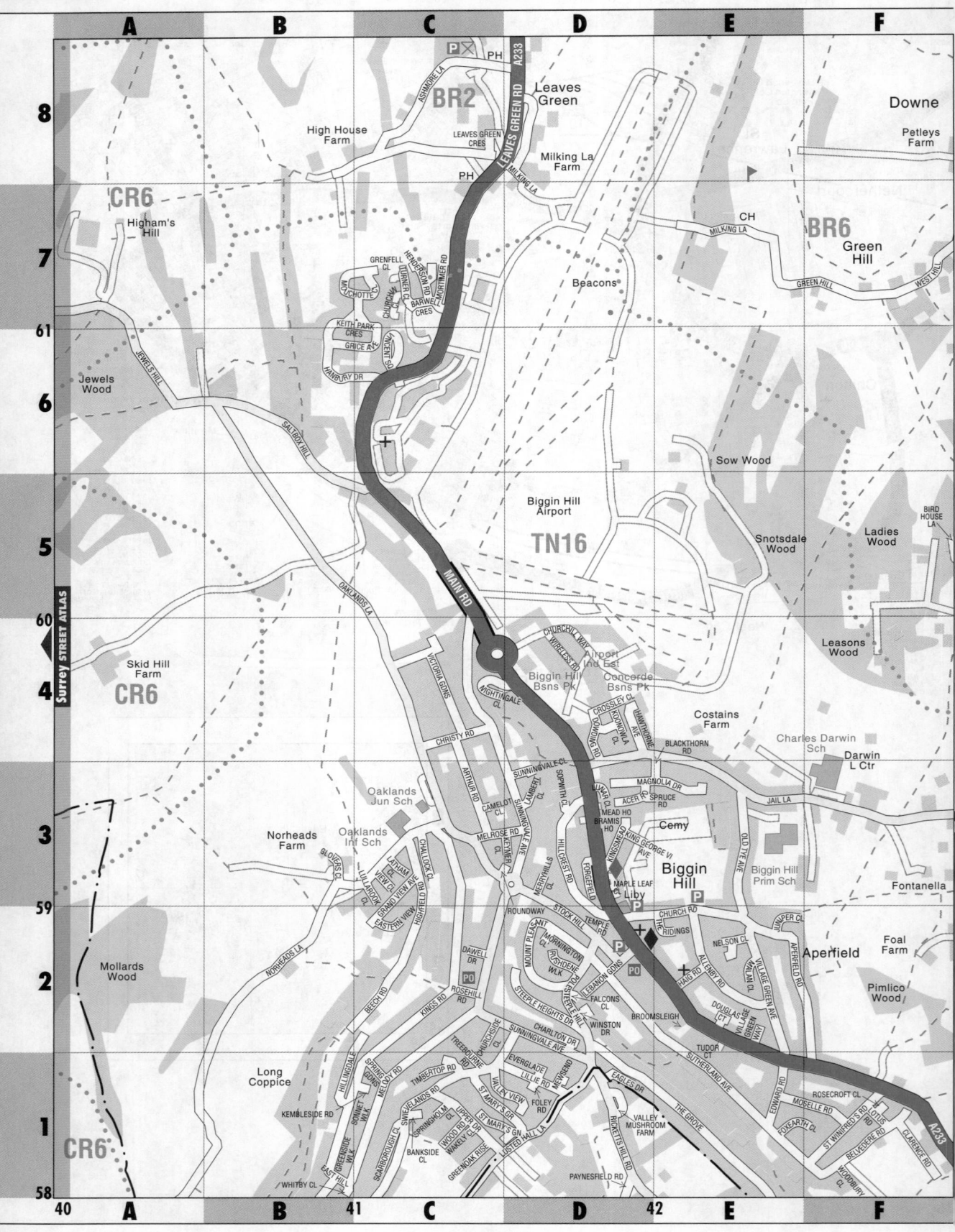

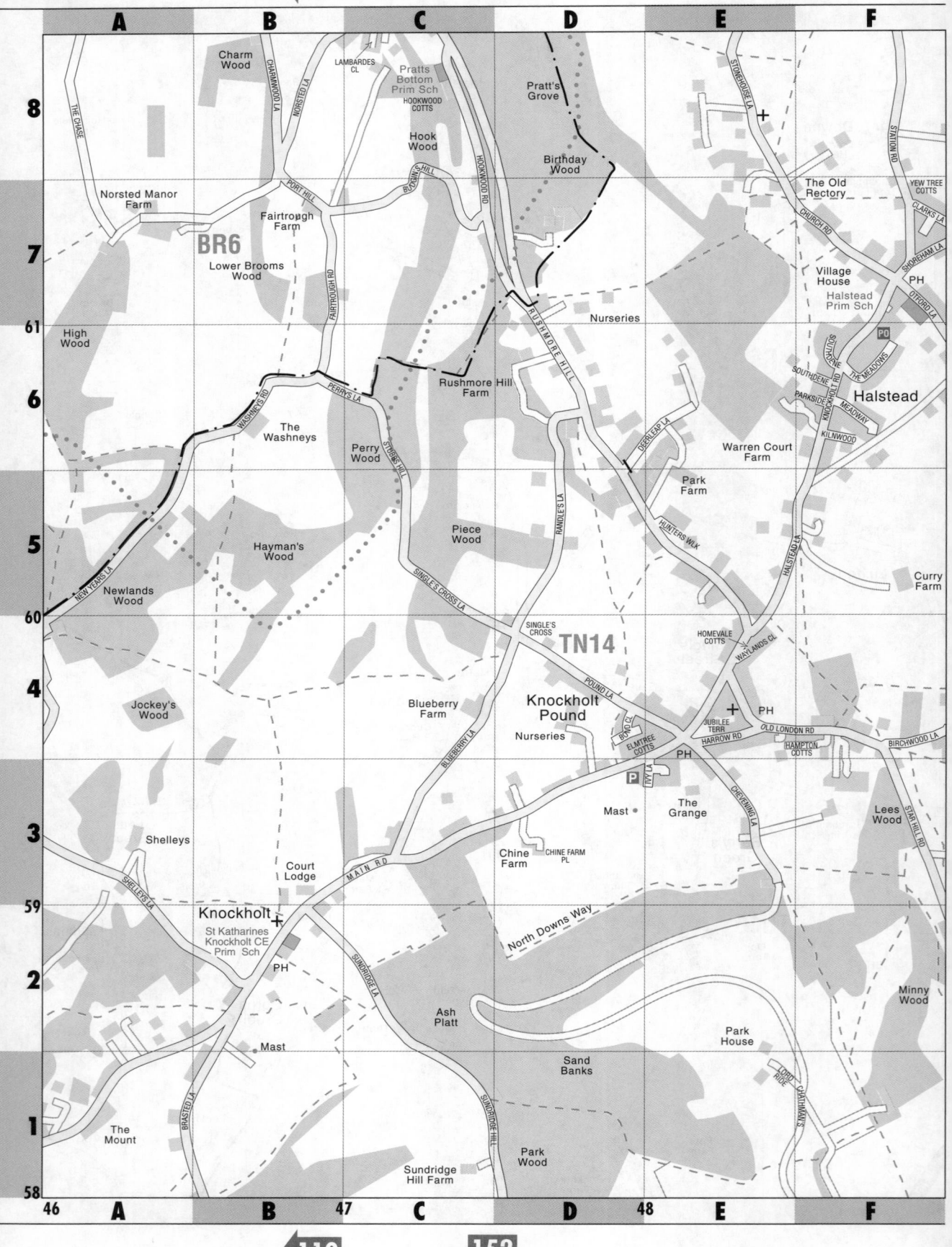

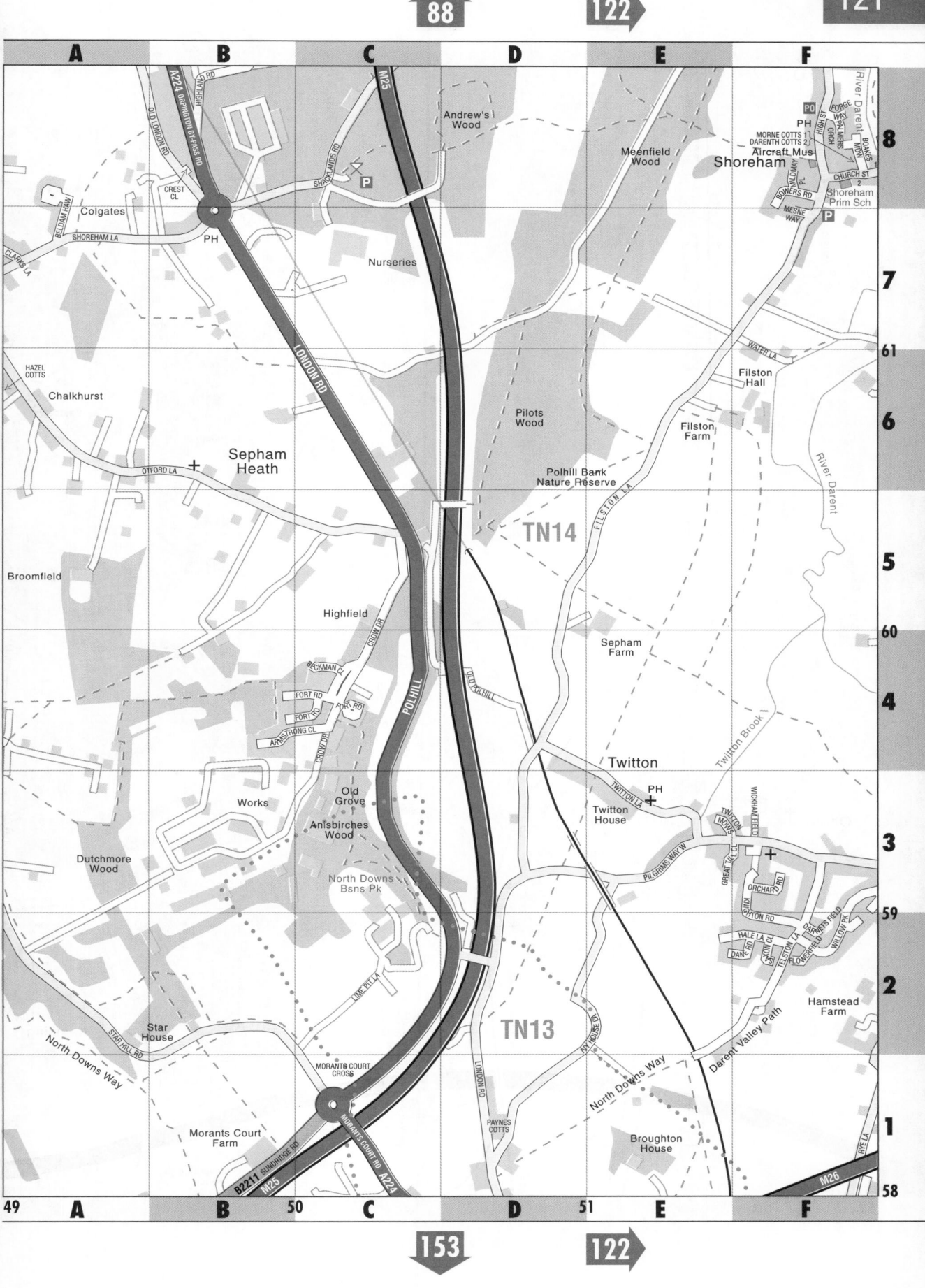

A   B   C   D   E   F

8

River Darent

PO
FORGE WAY
HIGH ST
W PALMERS ORCH
BRAKES
MKW
MORNE COTTS 1
DARENTH COTTS 2
PH
Aircraft Mus
Shoreham
CHURCH ST
2

Meenfield
Wood

Andrew's
Wood

Colgates

BELDAM HAW

CREST CL

OLD LONDON RD
HIGHLAND RD
A224 ORPINGTON BY-PASS RD

SHACKLANDS RD

M25

P

PH

SHOREHAM LA

CLARKS LA

BOWERS RD
MESNE WAY
Shoreham
Prim Sch
P

7

Nurseries

61

WATER LA

HAZEL
COTTS

Chalkhurst

Filston
Hall

6

Pilots
Wood

Filston
Farm

Sepham
Heath

OTFORD LA

LONDON RD

Polhill Bank
Nature Reserve

FILSTON LA

River Darent

5

Broomfield

TN14

60

Highfield

Sepham
Farm

4

BECKMAN CL
FORT RD
FORT RD
FORT
ARMSTRONG CL
CROWN DR

CROWN DR

POLHILL

OLD POLHILL

Twitton Brook

Twitton

TWITTON LA

PH

Twitton
House

3

Works

Old
Grove

Anisbirches
Wood

PILGRIMS WAY W

WICKHAM FIELD
TWITTON MKW
GREAT VALE CL
ORCHARD RD

59

Dutchmore
Wood

North Downs
Bsns Pk

KNIGHTON RD

DARENTS FIELD
TILSTON LA
WILLOW PK
FLOWERFIELD

HALE LA CL
DAN
DAN

Hamstead
Farm

2

STAR HILL RD

Star
House

LIME PIT LA

TN13

IVY HOUSE DR

LONDON RD

North Downs Way

Darent Valley Path

North Downs Way

MORANTS COURT
CROSS

Broughton
House

RYE LA

1

Morants Court
Farm

B2211 SUNDRIDGE RD
M25
MORANTS COURT RD A24

PAYNES
COTTS

M26

58

49   A   B   50   C   D   E   51   F

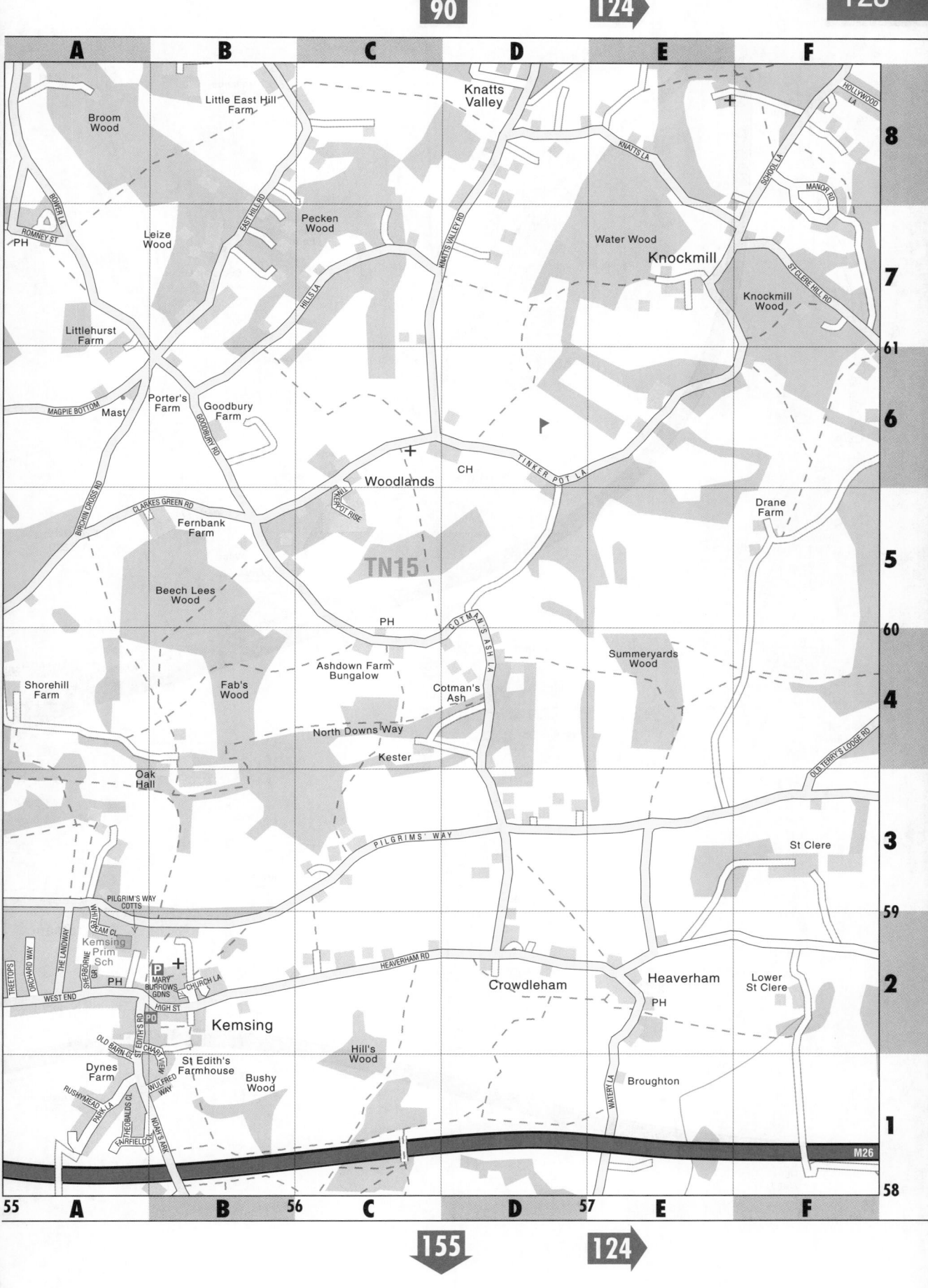

A   B   C   D   E   F

8
7
61
6
5
60
4
3
59
2
1
58

Broom Wood

Little East Hill Farm

Knatts Valley

HOLLYWOOD LA

ROMNEY ST
PH
BOWER LA

Leize Wood

EAST HILL RD

Pecken Wood

KNATTS VALLEY RD

Water Wood

Knockmill

SCHOOL LA
MANOR RD
ST CLERE HILL RD

Knockmill Wood

Littlehurst Farm

HILLS LA

MAGPIE BOTTOM
Mast

Porter's Farm

Goodbury Farm

GOODBURY RD

CH

TINKER POT LA

Drane Farm

BIRCHIN CROSS RD

CLARKES GREEN RD

Fernbank Farm

Woodlands

TINKER POT RISE

TN15

Beech Lees Wood

PH

COTMAN'S ASH LA

Summeryards Wood

Shorehill Farm

Fab's Wood

Ashdown Farm Bungalow

Cotman's Ash

OLD TERRY'S LODGE RD

Oak Hall

North Downs Way

Kester

St Clere

PILGRIMS' WAY

PILGRIM'S WAY COTTS

WHITER..
CREAM CL

Kemsing Prim Sch

THE LANDWAY
ORCHARD WAY
TREETOPS

SHERBORNE GR
PH
P
MARY BURROWS GDNS
CHURCH LA

HEAVERHAM RD

Crowdleham

Heaverham
PH
Lower St Clere

WEST END
HIGH ST
PO

Kemsing

Dynes Farm

OLD BARN CL
ST EDITH'S RD
CHART VIEW
WULFRED WAY

St Edith's Farmhouse

Bushy Wood

Hill's Wood

WATERY LA

Broughton

RUSHYMEAD LA
PARK LA
THEOBALDS CL
NOAH'S ARK
FAIRFIELD

M26

F3
1 THORNDYKE WAY
2 THOMAS WYATT WAY
3 BLACKSOLE RD
4 NEW WLK
5 RIGGS WAY
6 MOUNTAIN CL
7 St George's CE
   Prim Sch

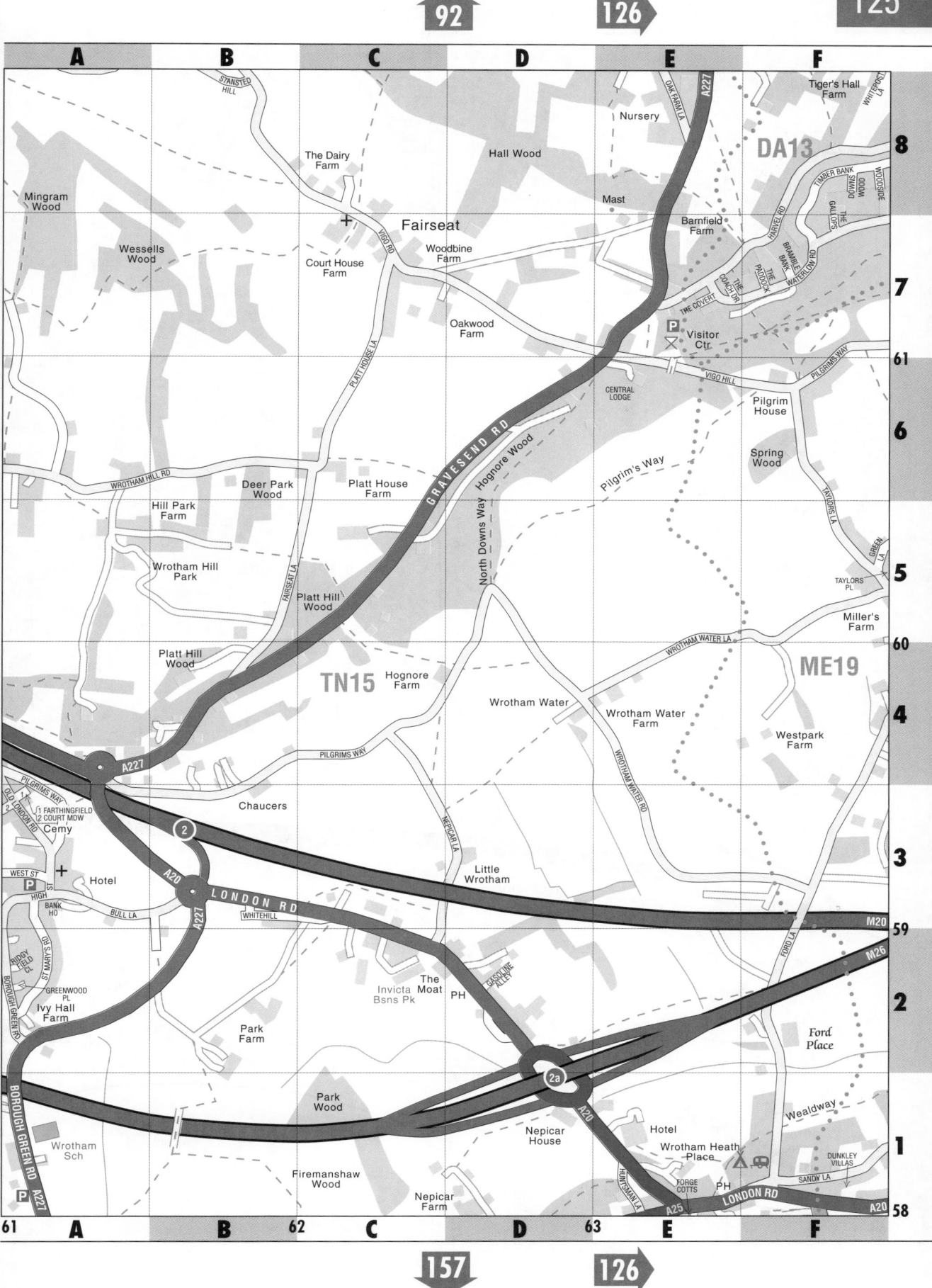

92
126

A **B** **C** **D** **E** **F**

STANSTED HILL

The Dairy Farm

Nursery

Hall Wood

Tiger's Hall Farm

WHITEPOST LA

DA13

8

Mingram Wood

Wessells Wood

Fairseat

Woodbine Farm

Mast

Barnfield Farm

TIMBER BANK

ODOM SMWD

WOODSIDE

THE GALLOPS

HARVEL RD

WATERLOW RD

THE PADDOCK

BRAMBLE BANK

THE COVERT

THE COACH DR

7

Court House Farm

Oakwood Farm

P

Visitor Ctr.

61

VIGO RD

PLATT HOUSE LA

Central Lodge

VIGO HILL

PILGRIMS WAY

Pilgrim House

Spring Wood

6

WROTHAM HILL RD

Deer Park Wood

Platt House Farm

GRAVESEND RD

Hognore Wood

Pilgrim's Way

TAYLORS LA

GREEN LA

Hill Park Farm

Platt Hill Wood

North Downs Way

TAYLORS PL

5

Wrotham Hill Park

FAIRSEAT LA

Miller's Farm

60

Platt Hill Wood

TN15

Hognore Farm

Wrotham Water

Wrotham Water Farm

WROTHAM WATER LA

ME19

Westpark Farm

4

A227

PILGRIMS WAY

Chaucers

PILGRIMS WAY

NEPICAR LA

WROTHAM WATER RD

2

OLD LONDON RD

1 FARTHINGFIELD
2 COURT MDW

Cemy

A20

2

Little Wrotham

FORD LA

M20

3

WEST ST

HIGH ST

P

Hotel

BANK HO

BULL LA

A227

LONDON RD

WHITEHILL

M26

59

RIDGY FIELD CL

GR ST MARY'S RD

GREENWOOD PL

Ivy Hall Farm

BOROUGH GREEN RD

Park Farm

The Moat

Invicta Bsns Pk

PH

GASON LA

GASON PARK

Ford Place

2

Park Wood

2a

A20

Wealdway

DUNKLEY VILLAS

BOROUGH GREEN RD

A227

Wrotham Sch

P

A227

Firemanshaw Wood

Nepicar House

Nepicar Farm

Park Wood

HUNTS MAN LA

FORGE COTTS

A25

Hotel

Wrotham Heath Place

PH

LONDON RD

SANDY LA

A20

1

58

157
126

B8
1 ADMERS WOOD
2 ADMERS WY
3 SOUTHFIELD SHAW

125

93

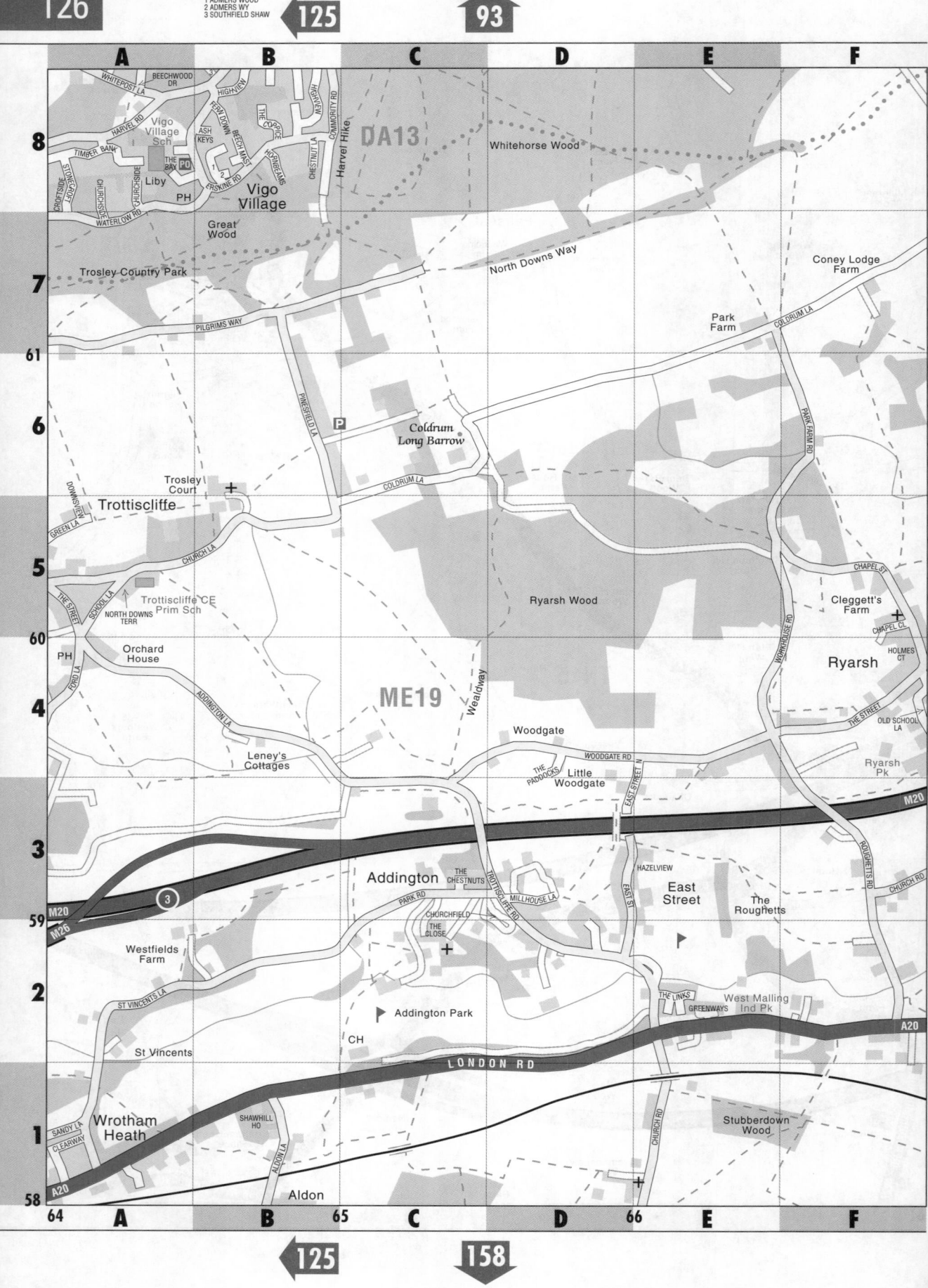

A B C D E F

8
7
61
6
5
60
4
3
59
2
1
58

67 A B 68 C D 69 E F

Birling Place Farm
Walnut Tree Farm
Dyke Place
Stalks Wood
Snodland CE Prim Sch
TOWNSEND RD
WOODLANDS AVE
CONSTITUTION HILL
Langhold House
Austen's Farm
ME6
St Katherine's Sch
Holmesdale Tech Coll
Parson's Corner
Horn Street
Ley Farm
Birling Lodge
PH
+ Birling
BULL RD
THE CLOSE
RYARSH RD
MASTERS LA
BIRLING PK
Sandhole
CH
PH
P
A228
MALLING RD
Godfreys Farm
Clacketts Farm
Old Place Farm
ME19
Birling Ashes
RSPCA Animal Ctr
P
ME20
Leybourne Way
BROOK RD
CASTLE WAY
Leybourne Lake
PH
Ryarsh Prim Sch
Stables
Birling Wood
Birling Ashes
Lunsford
Lunsford Hall
M20
Motel
Castle Lake
PARTRIDGE AVE
Grange Park Coll
CHURCH RD
+
Leybourne Pk
PARK RD
Spider's Hall
Ss Peter & Paul CE Prim Sch
PH
WILLOW RD
59
Audley House
Leybourne Castle +
LITTLE MARKET ROW 1
EVERGREEN CL 2
BROADOAK 3
Leybourne
CASTLE WAY
RECTORY LA S
Sports Gd
Nurseries
PH
GRANGE CL
Leybourne Wood
MILL BROOK
London Rd
PUMP CL
A20
ASHTON WAY
A228
SANDY LA
NORMAN RD
FARTHERWELL RD
BRICKFIELDS
RYARSH LA
P
HIGH TOWN HILL
NEVILL CT
GREBE CT 1
FALCON GN 2
BLATCHFORD CL 3
SHAFTESBURY CL 4
ADDISON CL 5
WALPOLE CL 6
COLUMBINE RD 7
COLUMBINE CL 8
TYLER CL 9
LARKSPUR RD
58

F4
1 SOUTHEY WAY
2 CRONIN CL
3 BLAKE DR
4 COLERIDGE CL
5 CHESTERTON RD
6 BROWNING CL
7 BARRIE DR
8 CHRISTIE DR

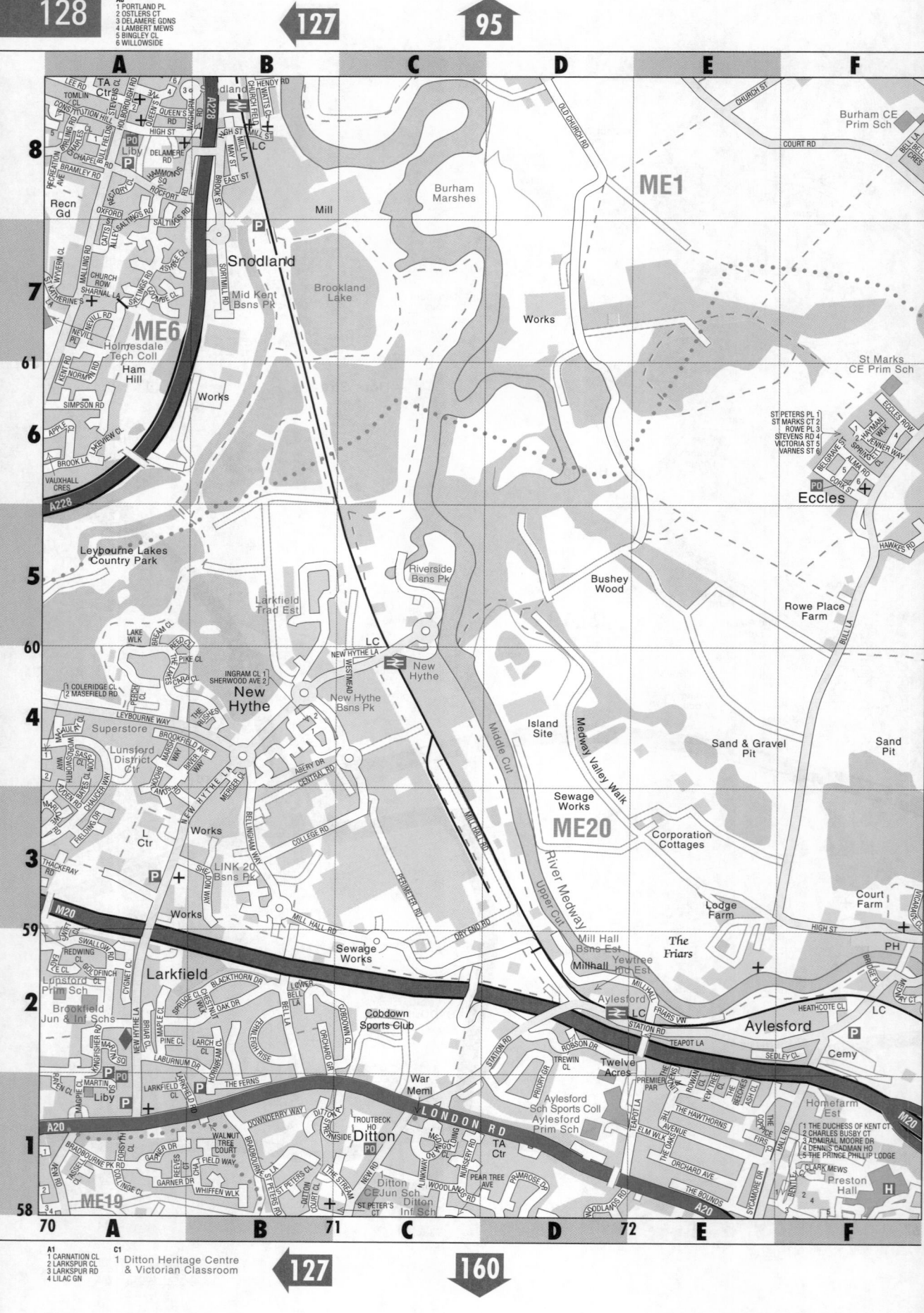

128

A8
1 PORTLAND PL
2 OSTLERS CT
3 DELAMERE GDNS
4 LAMBERT MEWS
5 BINGLEY CL
6 WILLOWSIDE

127

95

A1
1 CARNATION CL
2 LARKSPUR CL
3 LARKSPUR RD
4 LILAC GN

C1
1 Ditton Heritage Centre
& Victorian Classroom

127

160

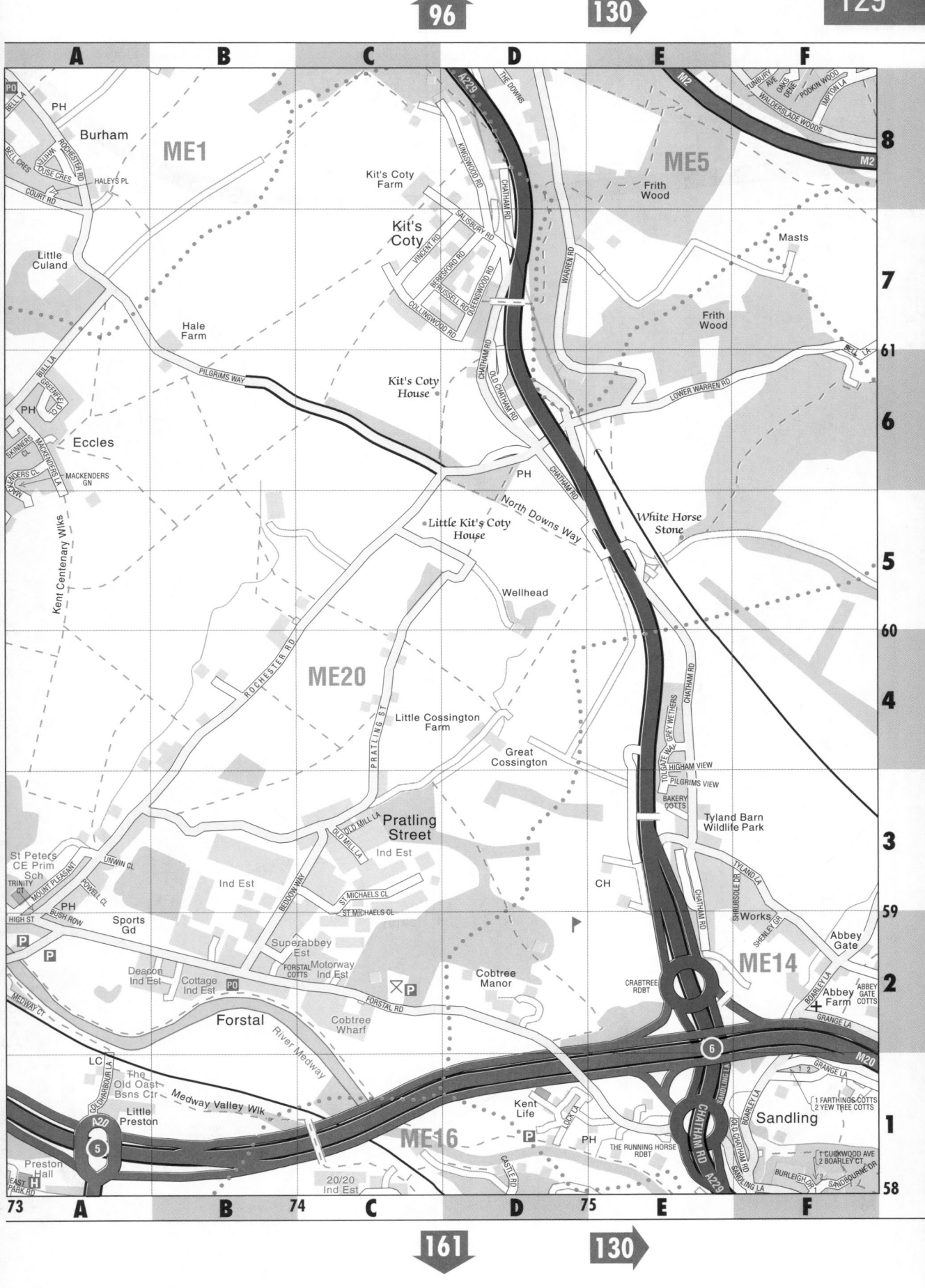

A B C D E F

8 7 61 6 5 60 4 59 3 2 1 58

Burham

ME1

Kit's Coty Farm

Kit's Coty

Kit's Coty House

Little Kit's Coty House

Wellhead

Little Culand

Hale Farm

PILGRIMS WAY

Eccles

ME20

Little Cossington Farm

Great Cossington

North Downs Way

White Horse Stone

ME5

Frith Wood

Frith Wood

Masts

Lower Warren Rd

Pratling Street

Ind Est

Ind Est

St Peters CE Prim Sch

Sports Gd

Superabbey Est

Motorway Ind Est

Deacon Ind Est

Cottage Ind Est

Forstal

FORSTAL RD

Cobtree Wharf

River Medway

Cobtree Manor

Higham View

Pilgrims View

Bakery Cotts

Tyland Barn Wildlife Park

CH

Works

ME14

Abbey Gate

Abbey Gate Cotts

CRABTREE RDBT

Crabtree Rdbt

Abbey Farm

M20

Little Preston

The Old Oast Bsns Ctr

Medway Valley Wlk

ME16

Kent Life

Sandling

The Running Horse Rdbt

CHATHAM RDBT

1 Farthings Cotts
2 Yew Tree Cotts

1 Cuckwood Ave
2 Boarley Ct

Preston Hall

20/20 Ind Est

5

6

73 74 75

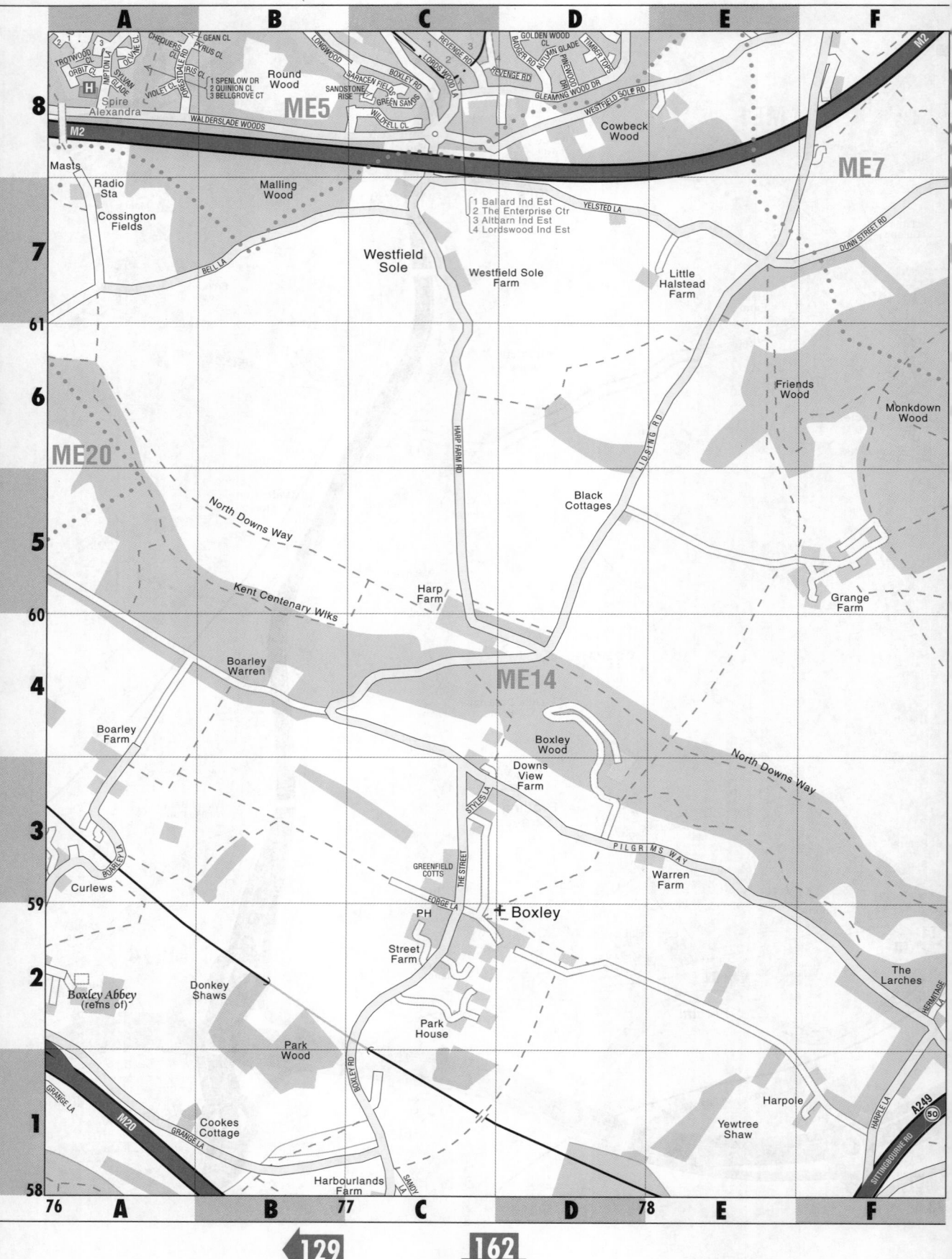

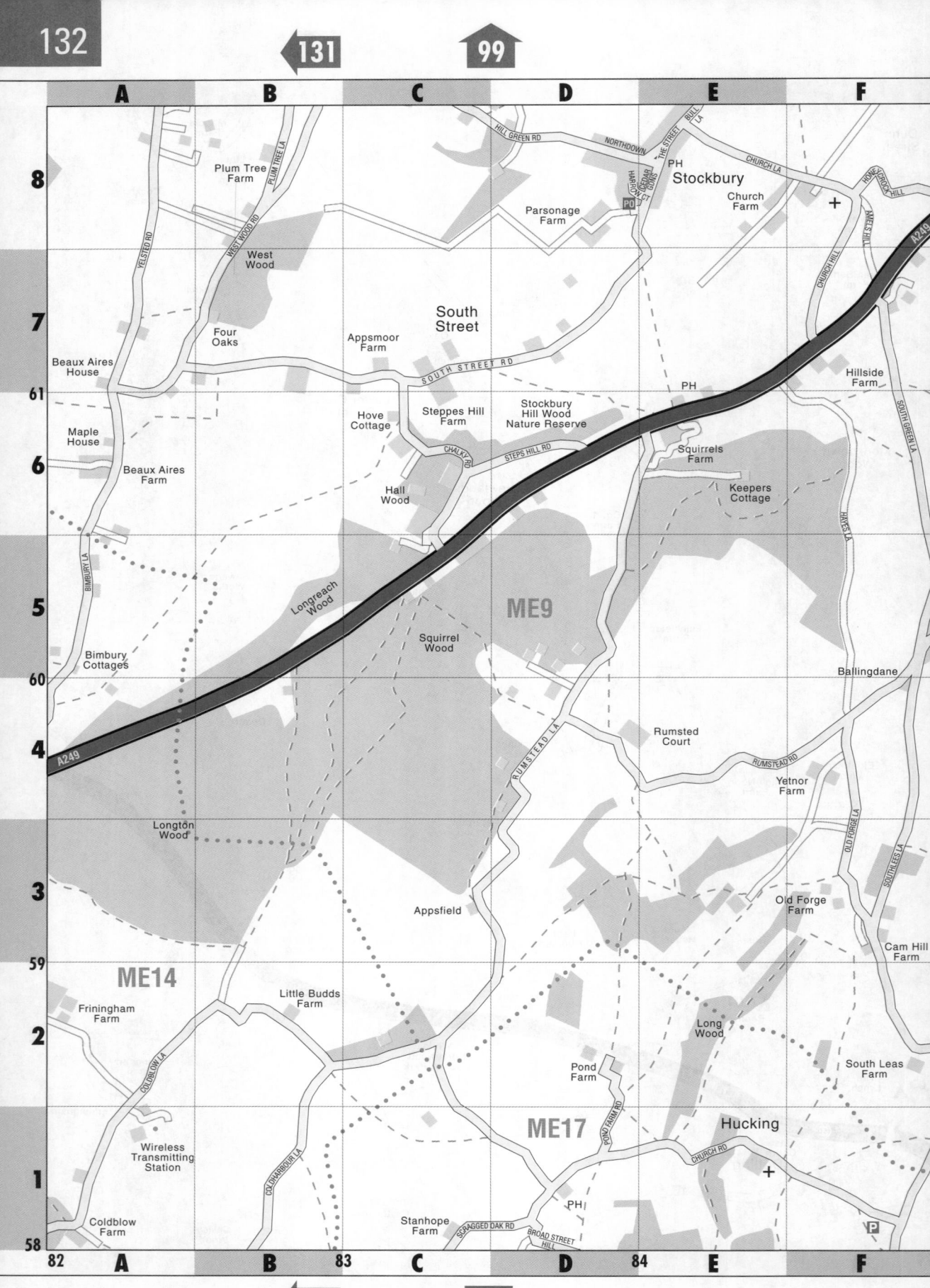

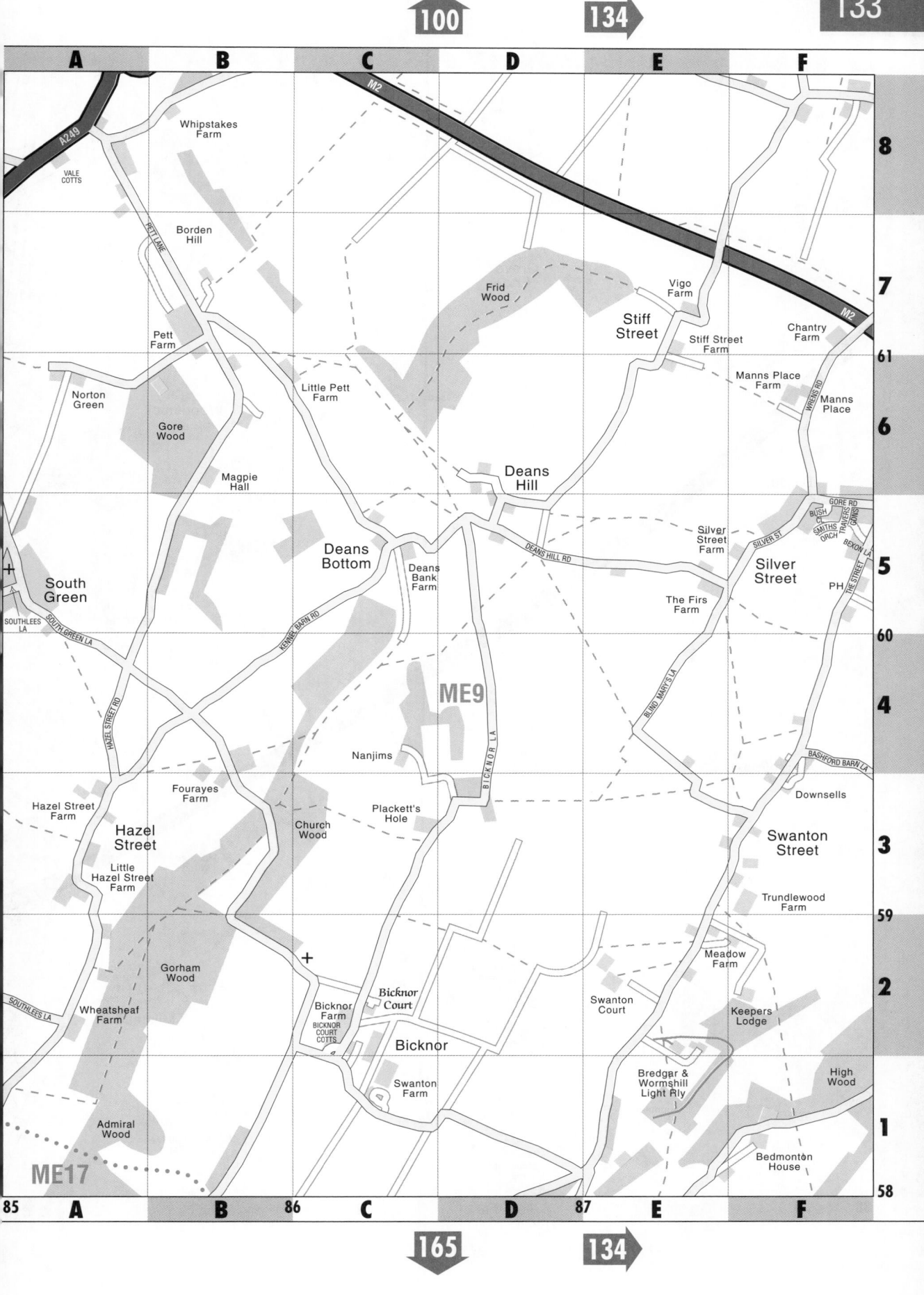

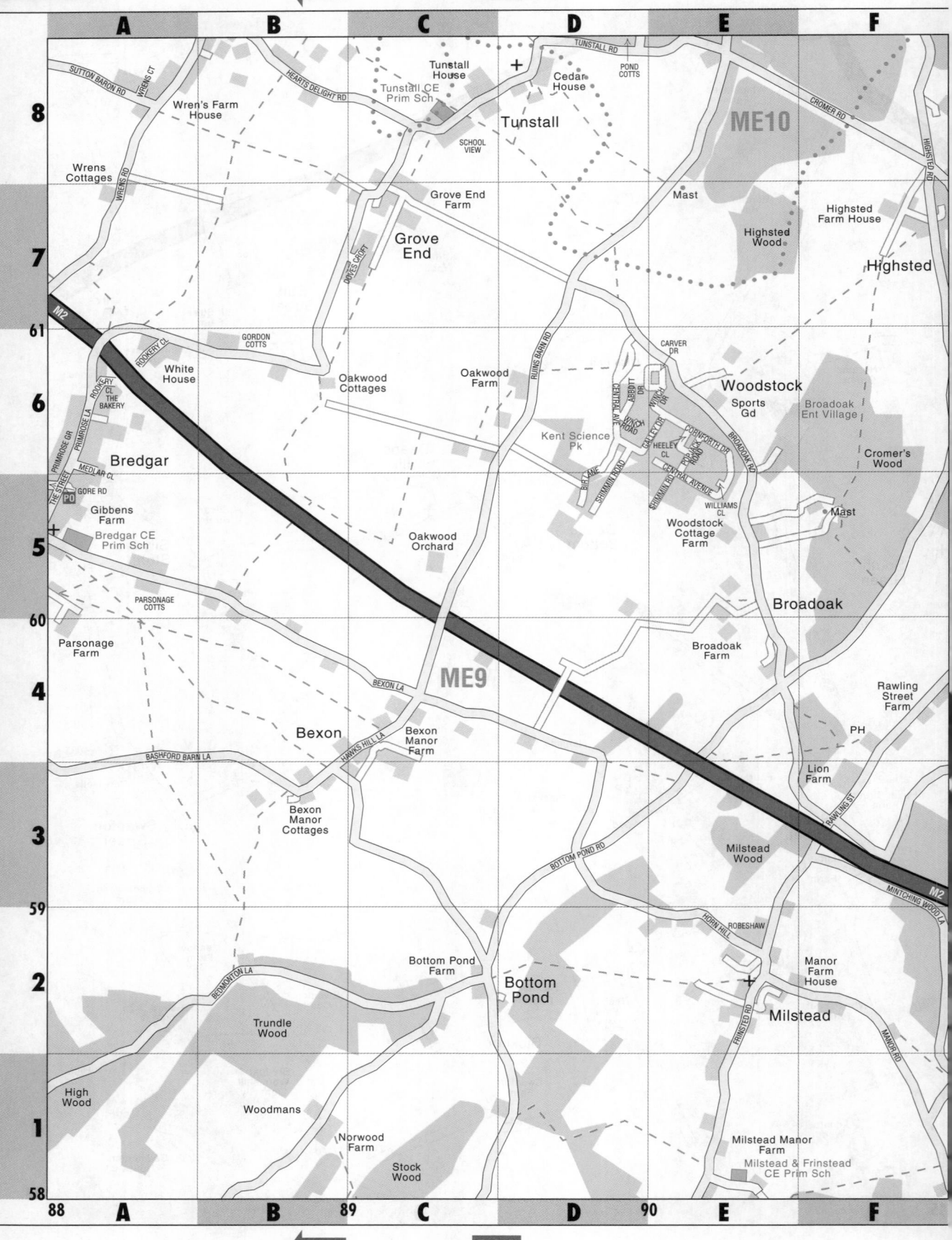

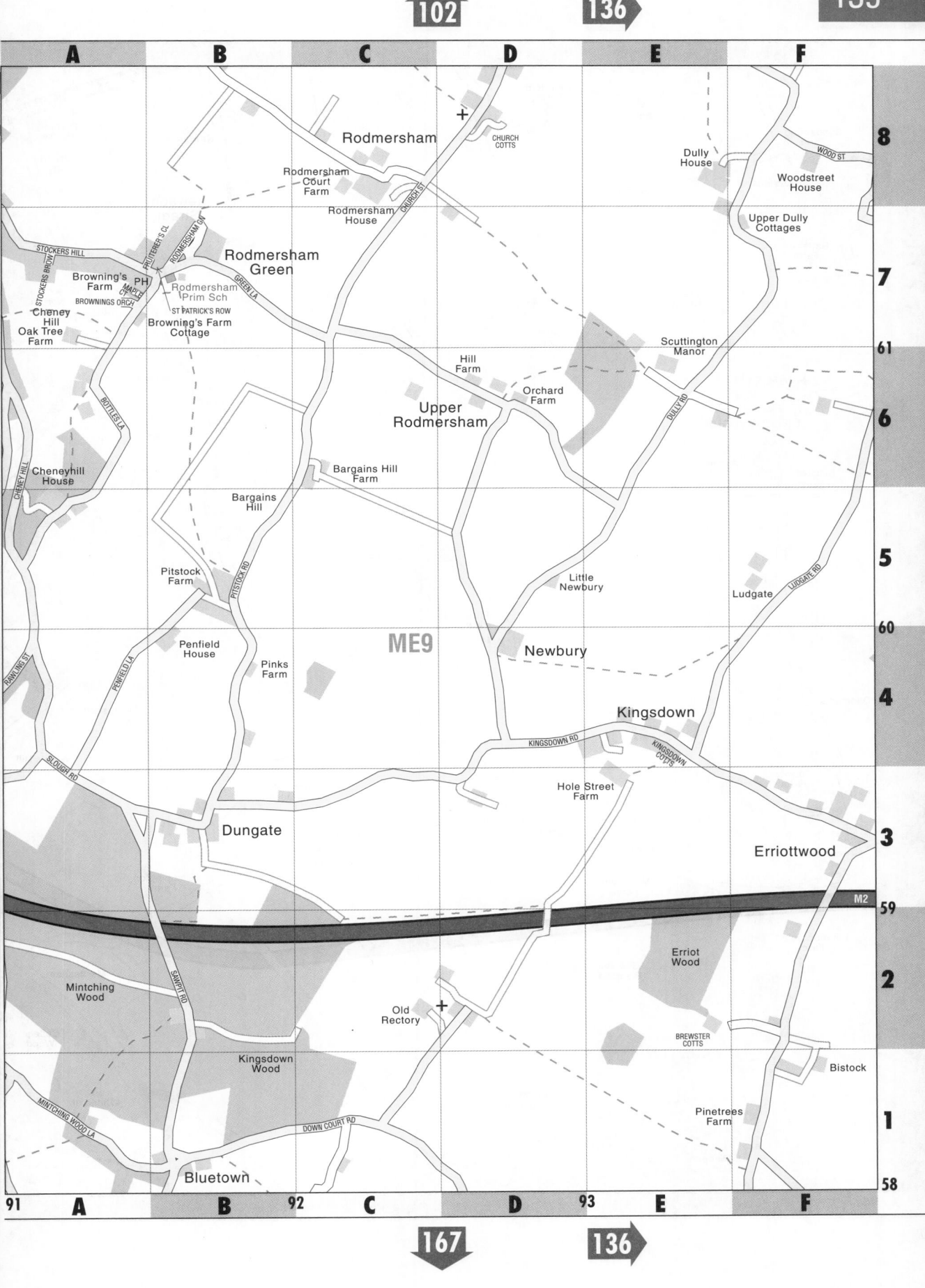

A B C D E F

8

WOOD ST
Sunderland Farm
Sunderland
CLAYFIELD RD
WOOD ST
Batteries Farm
THE STREET
PH
St Pauls Ct
Lynsted

JOHN NASH CL
GIRLS CL
BATS CL
BATTERIES TERR
Bogle
LYNSTED LA
Bogle
Swedish Houses
Lynsted & Norton Prim Sch

Cambridge Farm
CAMBRIDGE LA
Cherry Gardens
CAMBRIDGE LA

Nouds House
Upper Newlands

Orchard House
Norton Ash

LONDON RD
A2
LOWER NORTON LA

Lewson Street
LEWSON STREET RD
PH
WORLD'S END
Norton Court
THE TREFOIL
PROVENDER LA

7

61

BOGLE RD
Bumpit Farm
Nouds Farm
NOUDS RD
NOUDS LA

Tickham
Tickham Farm
Upper Tickham Cotts

6

THE VALLANCE
Aymers
Lynsted Court
Park Farm

MILL LA
TICKHAM LA

Loyterton

Green Acres
NORTON RD

ME13

5

60

Park View
ME9

Monks Farm

RUSHETT LA

4

Dadman's
Lynsted Park

Rushett
Wren's Hill

3

Colyers Farm
CHRISTOPHER'S ROW
KINGSDOWN RD
Moonfield Farm

Stuppington Cottages

HOMESTALL RD
Homestall
Stuppington Farm

M2

59

M2
Little Sharsted Farm

Sharsted Plantation

Martlesham

2

College Wood

1

Sharsted Court

Keepers Cottage

Champion Court

FAVERSHAM RD
NORTH EASTLING RD
Whitehall

ME13

58

94 A B 95 C 96 D E F

104
138

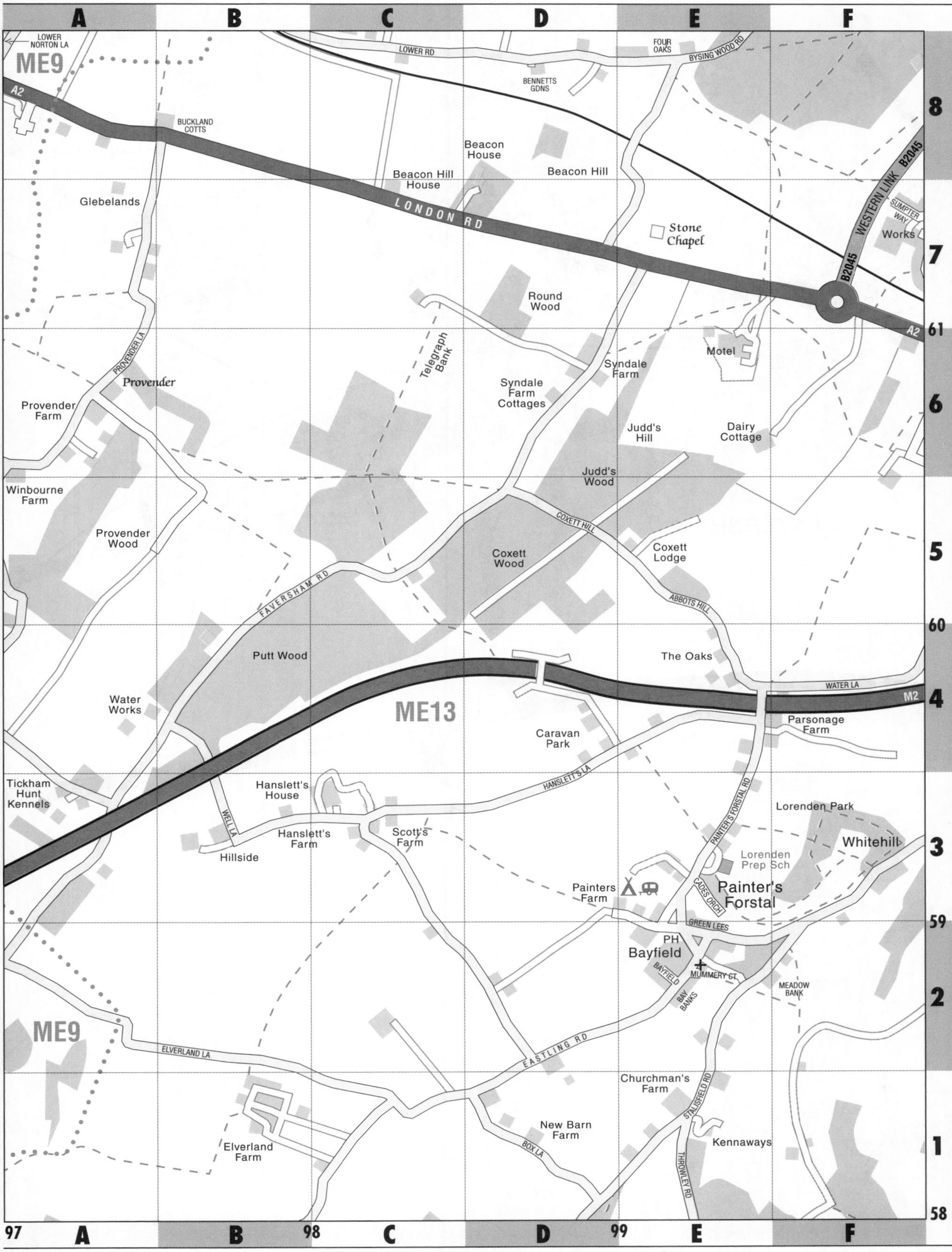
A
B
C
D
E
F
8
7
61
6
5
60
4
3
59
2
1
58
97
98
99
LOWER NORTON LA
ME9
A2
BUCKLAND COTTS
LOWER RD
BENNETTS GDNS
FOUR OAKS
BYSING WOOD RD
Beacon House
Beacon Hill House
Beacon Hill
Glebelands
LONDON RD
Stone Chapel
B2045
WESTERN LINK
SUMPTER WAY
Works
Round Wood
Telegraph Bank
PROVENDER LA
Provender
Provender Farm
Syndale Farm Cottages
Syndale Farm
Motel
Judd's Hill
Dairy Cottage
Winbourne Farm
Judd's Wood
Provender Wood
COXETT HILL
Coxett Wood
Coxett Lodge
FAVERSHAM RD
ABBOTS HILL
Putt Wood
The Oaks
WATER LA
M2
Water Works
ME13
Caravan Park
Parsonage Farm
Tickham Hunt Kennels
Hanslett's House
HANSLETT'S LA
PAINTER'S FORSTAL RD
Lorenden Park
WELL LA
Hanslett's Farm
Scott's Farm
Hillside
Whitehill
Lorenden Prep Sch
Painters Farm
CADES ORCH
Painter's Forstal
GREEN LEES
PH
Bayfield
BAYFIELD
MUMMERY CT
MEADOW BANK
BAY BANKS
ME9
ELVERLAND LA
EASTLING RD
Churchman's Farm
STALISFIELD RD
New Barn Farm
Kennaways
BOX LA
Elverland Farm
THROWLEY RD

169
138

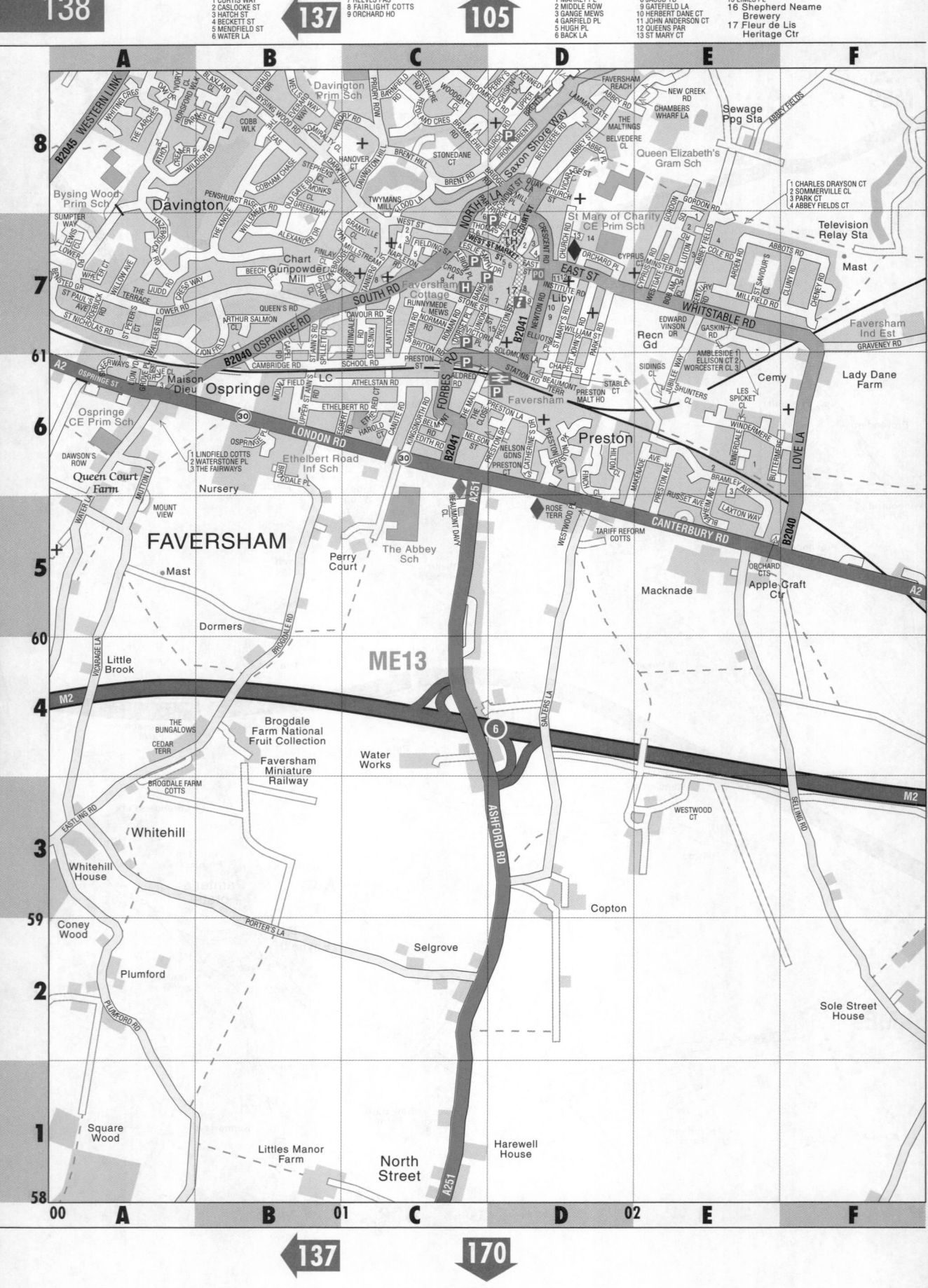

C7
1 CURTIS WAY
2 CASLOCKE ST
3 HATCH ST
4 BECKETT ST
5 MENDFIELD ST
6 WATER LA

C7
7 REEVES PAS
8 FAIRLIGHT COTTS
9 ORCHARD HO

137

105

D7
1 MARKET PL
2 MIDDLE ROW
3 GANGE MEWS
4 GARFIELD PL
5 HUGH PL
6 BACK PL

7 CROSS LA
8 JACOB YD
9 GATEFIELD LA
10 HERBERT DANE CT
11 JOHN ANDERSON CT
12 QUEENS PAR
13 ST MARY CT

14 WILLIAM GIBBS CT
15 LIMES PL
16 Shepherd Neame
   Brewery
17 Fleur de Lis
   Heritage Ctr

ME13

FAVERSHAM

Davington

Ospringe

Preston

Whitehill

North Street

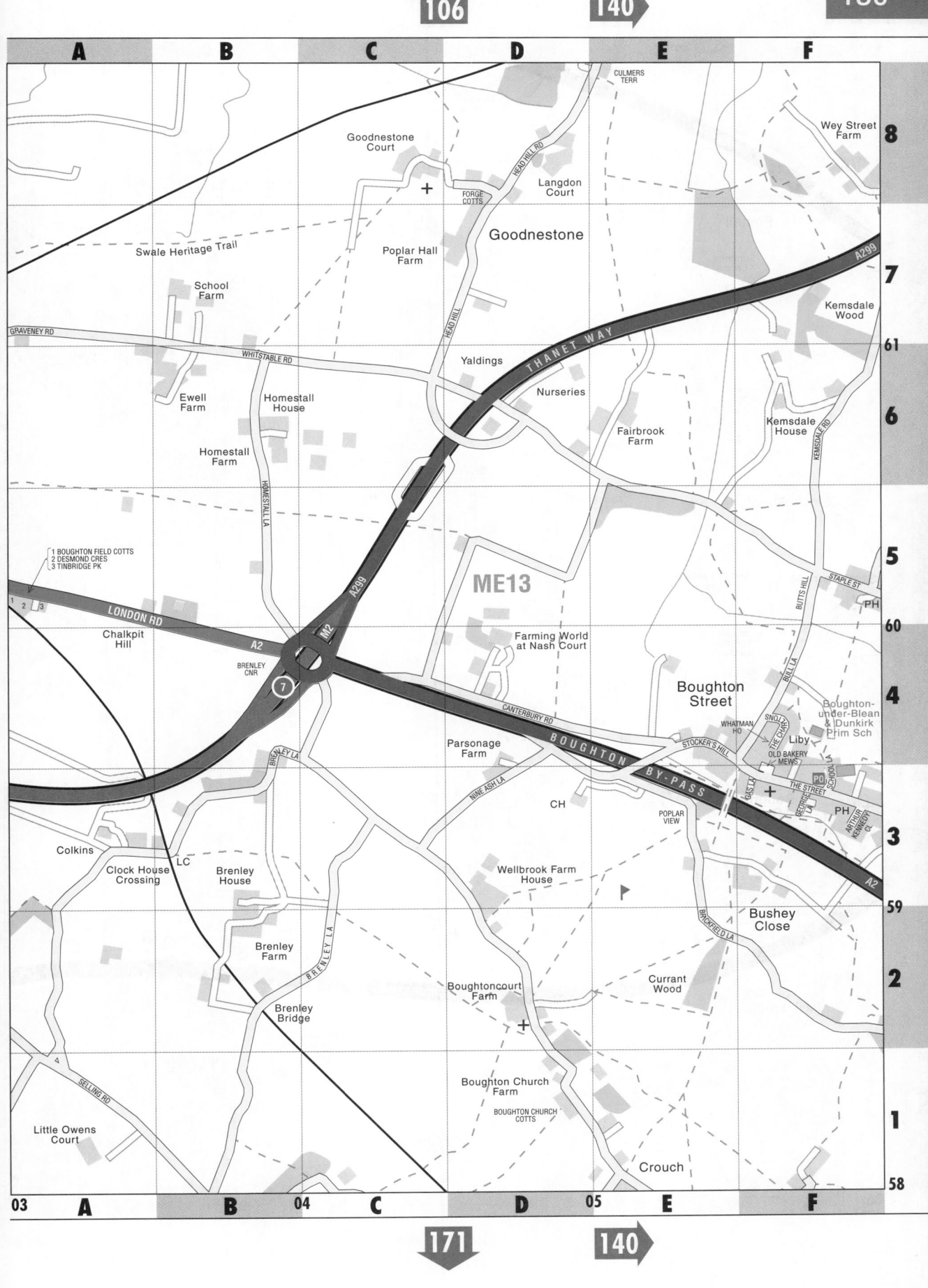

A B C D E F

8
7
61
6
5
60
4
59
2
1
58

Wey Street Farm

Goodnestone Court

Langdon Court

CULMERS TERR

FORGE COTTS

Goodnestone

HEAD HILL RD

Poplar Hall Farm

A299

Swale Heritage Trail

School Farm

Kemsdale Wood

HEAD HILL

GRAVENEY RD

WHITSTABLE RD

Yaldings

THANET WAY

Nurseries

Ewell Farm

Homestall House

Fairbrook Farm

Kemsdale House

KEMSDALE RD

Homestall Farm

HOMESTALL LA

1 BOUGHTON FIELD COTTS
2 DESMOND CRES
3 TINBRIDGE PK

ME13

BUTTS HILL

STAPLE ST

PH

1 2 3

A299

LONDON RD

A2

Chalkpit Hill

Farming World at Nash Court

M2

BRENLEY CNR

Boughton Street

Boughton-under-Blean & Dunkirk Prim Sch

BULL LA

7

WHATMAN HO

SNOUT

THE QUAR

Liby

Old Bakery Mews

CANTERBURY RD

BOUGHTON

Parsonage Farm

STOCKER'S HILL

GAS LA

THE STREET

GEORGE'S LA

PO

SCHOOL LA

BY-PASS

PH

ARTHUR

KENNEDY CL

BRENLEY LA

NINE ASH LA

CH

POPLAR VIEW

A2

Colkins

Clock House Crossing

LC

Brenley House

Wellbrook Farm House

Bushey Close

BRENLEY LA

BROOKFIELD LA

Brenley Farm

Currant Wood

Boughtoncourt Farm

Brenley Bridge

SELLING RD

Boughton Church Farm

BOUGHTON CHURCH COTTS

Little Owens Court

Crouch

139 107

A B C D E F

8

Lavender Farm
Dargate House
A299 THANET WAY
PLUMPUDDING LA
OAST COTTS
Dargate Farm
Wey Street Farm
Belvedere Farm
Fostall
Beesborough Farm
PH
Dargate
Dargate Common
A299
Summer Lees
GODFREY'S GRAVE
BUTLER'S HILL
DARGATE RD

7

KEMSDALE RD
Hernhill CE Prim Sch
SWALE VIEW
WOODLANDS
CROCKHAM RD
Bradbourne Cottages

61

MANOR COTTS
Hernhill
Blean Wood
Acorn Cottage
COURTENER RD

6

Church Farm
PH
CROCKHAM LA
Crockham Wood
Twr
Holly Hill
Church Hill
Slutsole
Crockham Farm
Holly Hill Farm
CT2
Firtree Cottages

5

Staplestreet
Mount Ephraim Wood
HOLLY HILL RD
RED RD

60

STAPLESTREET RD
Mount Ephraim Gardens
THREAD LA
Courtenay Farm
Bossenden Wood

4

ME13
Thread Wood
DAWES RD
COURTENAY RD
Bossenden Farm

Clay Pits Wood

BOUNDS LA

3

1 CHESTNUT CT
2 GROVE COURT FARM
Boughton Street
THE STREET
OAK DR
BRICKLEY CL
STONEY RD
High Wood
Dunkirk
THE RIDGEWAY
ST PAULS CRES
HIGHVIEW CL
WHEATSHEAF
ST PAULS RD
Boughton under Blean
CANTURBURY RD
COLONEL'S LA
LEACH HO
ST PETER'S
PERNLEIGH CL
COURTENAY HO
Mast
Hospital Wood

59

A2
DUNKIRK RD N
Boughton Hill
WOODSIDE
WOODSIDE COTTS
LONDON RD
PH
Horselees
WHEATSHEAF

2

HORSELEES RD
BRICKFIELD LA
Hickmans Green
BROUGHTON BY-PASS
A2
DUNKIRK RD S
Poundfall Wood
Brotherhood Woods

1

Hurst Wood
Arnolds Wood
Forester's Lodge Farm
Fishpond Wood
Iron Hill

58

06 A 07 B C 07 D 08 E F

108
142

ME13

Clay
Hill

Meadow
Grange
Nursery

CT5

Butler's Court
Wood

Denstroude

Brook
Lodge

DENSTROUDE LA

Honey
Hill

Druidstone
Park

PH

Parsonage
Farm

Honey Hill
Farm

WOODLANDS

BLEAN COMM A290

Denstroude
Farm

Nature Reserve

Mincing
Wood

Little Den
Lees

Crawford's
Rough

Great Den
Lees

North Bishopden
Wood

Grimshill
Wood

CT2

Crooked
Oak

Church
Wood

Blean Woods
Nature
Reserve

NEW RD

ME13

Manson
Wood

Landing Strip

Homestall
Wood

Willows
Wood

BOUGHTON BY-PASS

Motel

Harbledown
Lodge

Stumps
Farm

DENSTEAD LA

Staines
Farm

PH GLEMSFORD
COTTS

Upper
Harbledown

NEW COTT RD

NEW
COTTS

THE GREEN
LITTLE MEADOW

CHAUCER
MEWS

CT4

PROSPECT
COTTS

A2050

Poldhurst
Farm

A2

173
142

E1
1 ROSIERS CT
2 CROSS ST
3 LIONARD HO
4 ST DUNSTANS CT
5 WESTERLY MEWS
6 CRANMER HO
7 THE MALTINGS
8 WESTGATE CT

F1
1 ST STEPHENS HO
2 BARTON MILL CT
3 GREAT STOUR PL
4 ST STEPHENS PATHWAY
5 ST STEPHENS FIELDS
6 GAMMONS YD
7 THE MERCHANT STORE
8 KIRBY'S HEIGHTS
9 TEMPLAR CT

10 WESTSIDE APARTMENTS
11 RIVERSIDE CT
12 STERLING CT
13 STOURSIDE STUDIOS
14 WESTGATE HALL RD
15 CHANTRY CT
16 BLACKFRIARS ST
17 ST ALPHEGE LA
18 THE CLOISTERS
19 ST PETER'S ST

20 St Peters Sch of English
21 Kent Music Sch
22 Sidney Cooper Gallery
23 Kent Masonic Liby & Mus

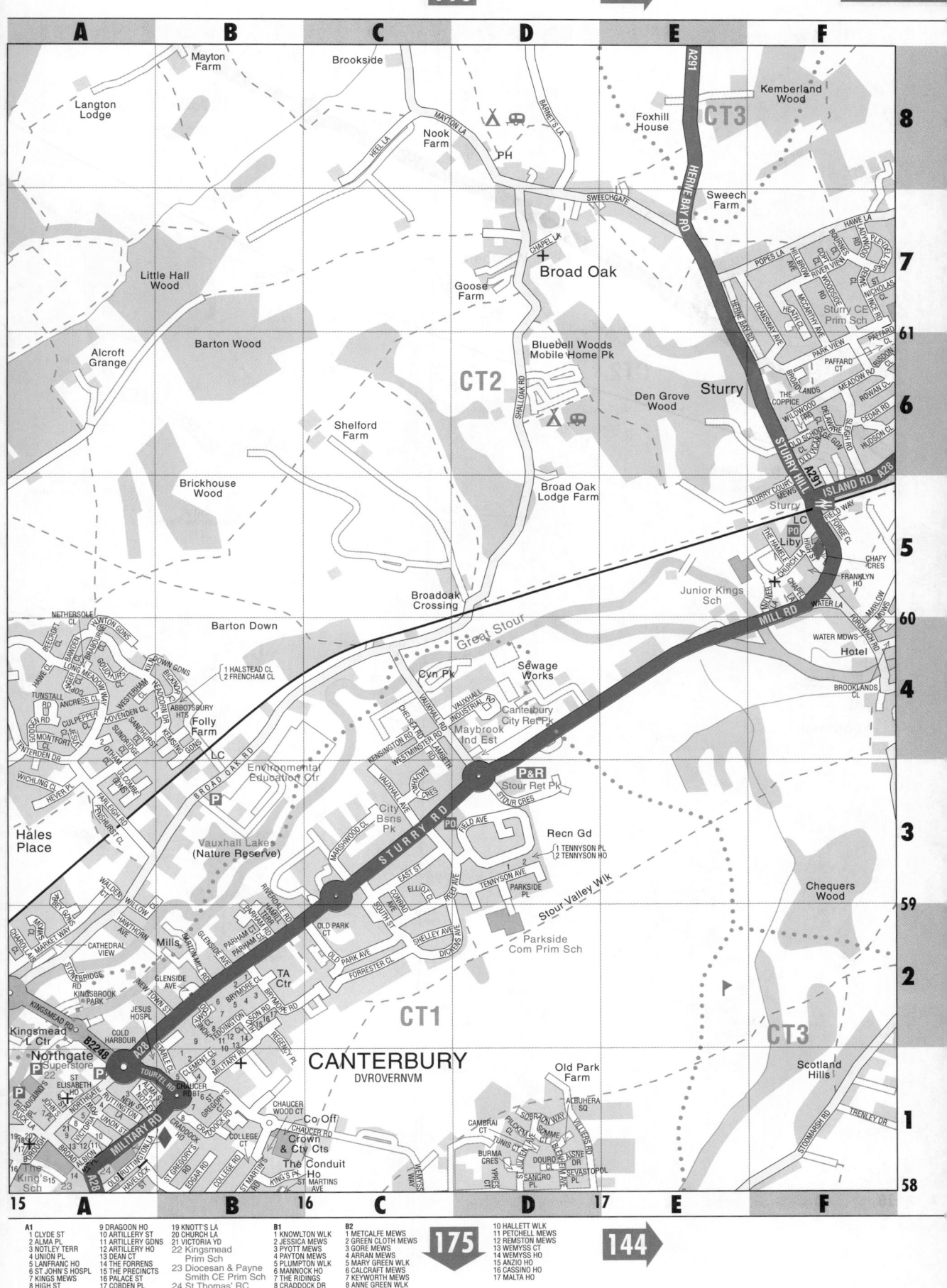

110 144

A1
1 CLYDE ST
2 ALMA PL
3 NOTLEY TERR
4 UNION PL
5 LANFRANC HO
6 ST JOHN'S HOSPL
7 KINGS MEWS
8 HIGH ST
ST GREGORY'S
9 DRAGOON HO
10 ARTILLERY ST
11 ARTILLERY GDNS
12 ARTILLERY HO
13 DEAN CT
14 THE FORRENS
15 THE PRECINCTS
16 PALACE ST
17 COBDEN PL
18 HOMESPIRE HO
19 KNOTT'S LA
20 CHURCH LA
21 VICTORIA YD
22 Kingsmead
Prim Sch
23 Diocesan & Payne
Smith CE Prim Sch
24 St Thomas' RC
Prim Sch

B1
1 KNOWLTON WLK
2 JESSICA MEWS
3 PYOTT MEWS
4 PAYTON MEWS
5 PLUMPTON WLK
6 MANNOCK HO
7 THE RIDINGS
8 CRADDOCK DR

B2
1 METCALFE MEWS
2 GREEN CLOTH MEWS
3 GORE MEWS
4 ARRAN MEWS
5 MARY GREEN WLK
6 CALCRAFT MEWS
7 KEYWORTH MEWS
8 ANNE GREEN WLK
9 GILLON MEWS
10 HALLETT WLK
11 PETCHELL MEWS
12 REMSTON MEWS
13 WEMYSS CT
14 WEMYSS HO
15 ANZIO HO
16 CASSINO HO
17 MALTA HO

175 144

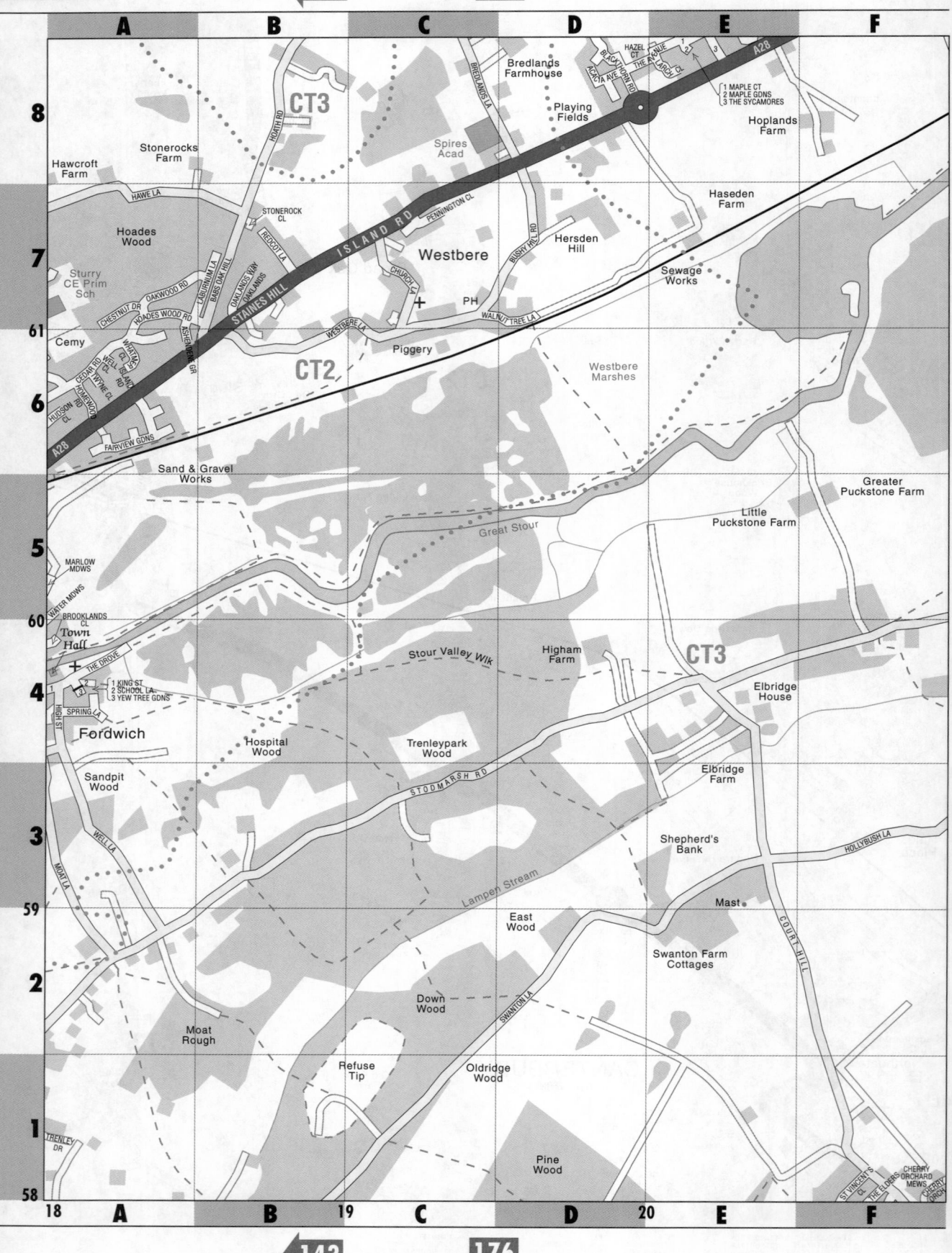

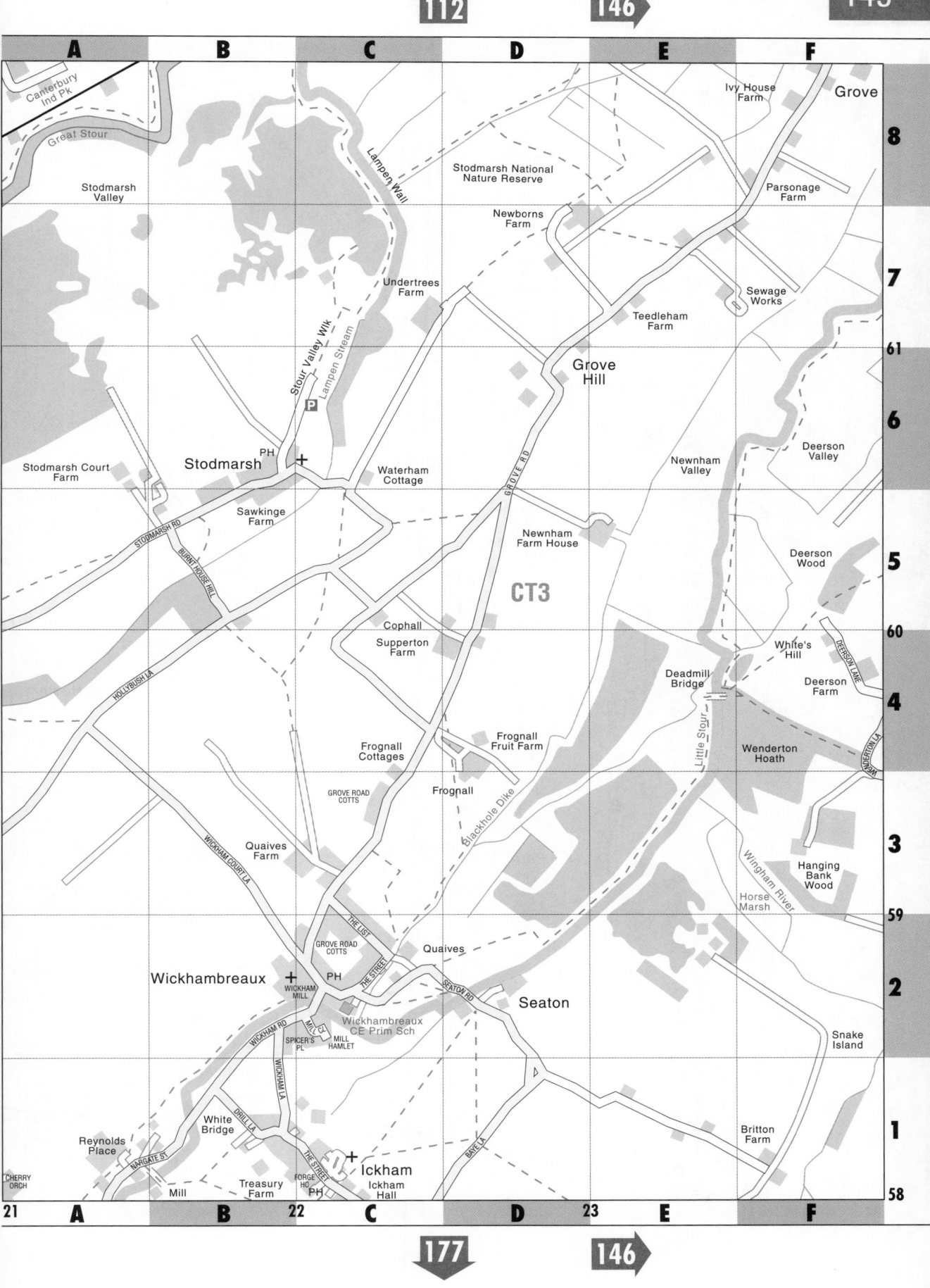

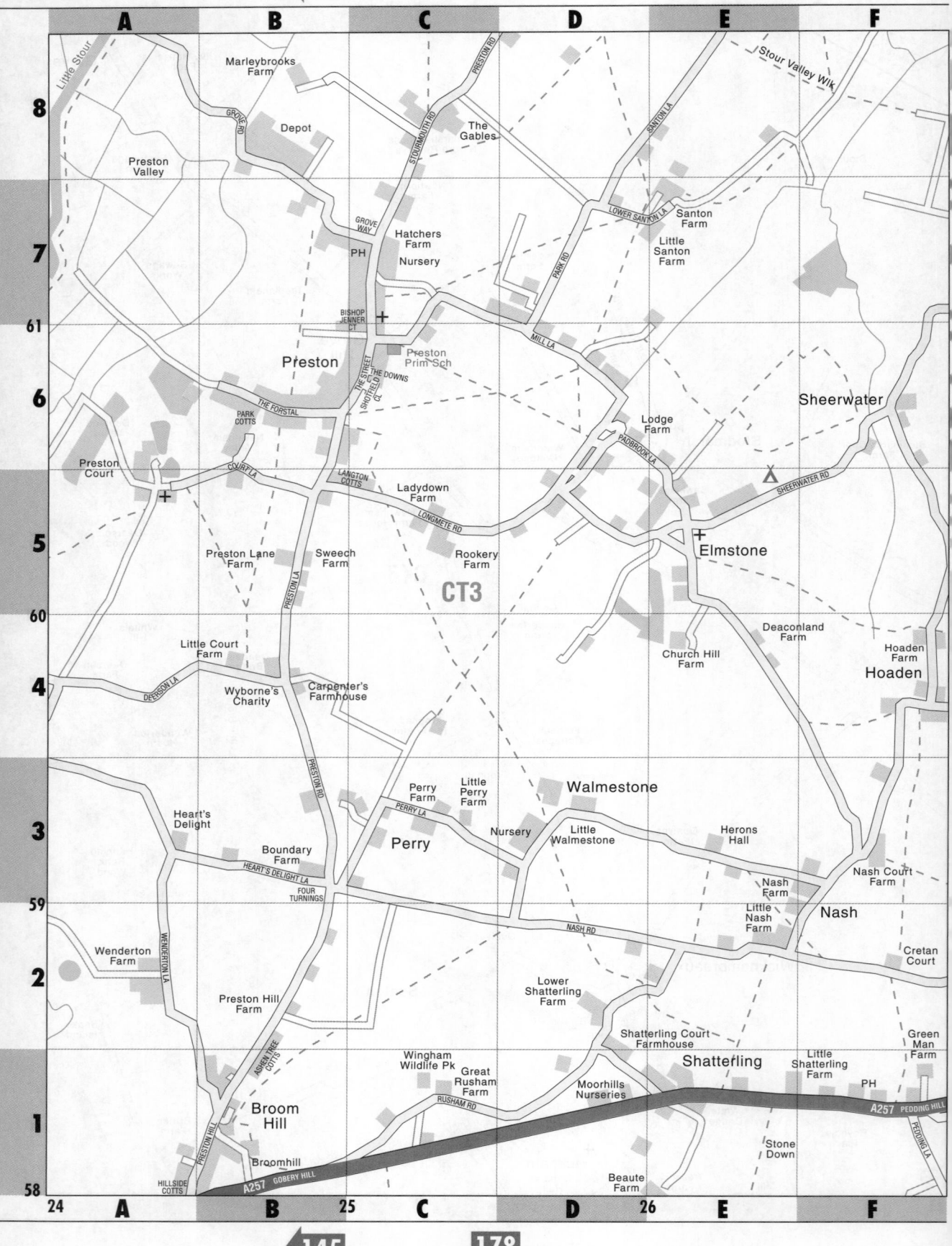

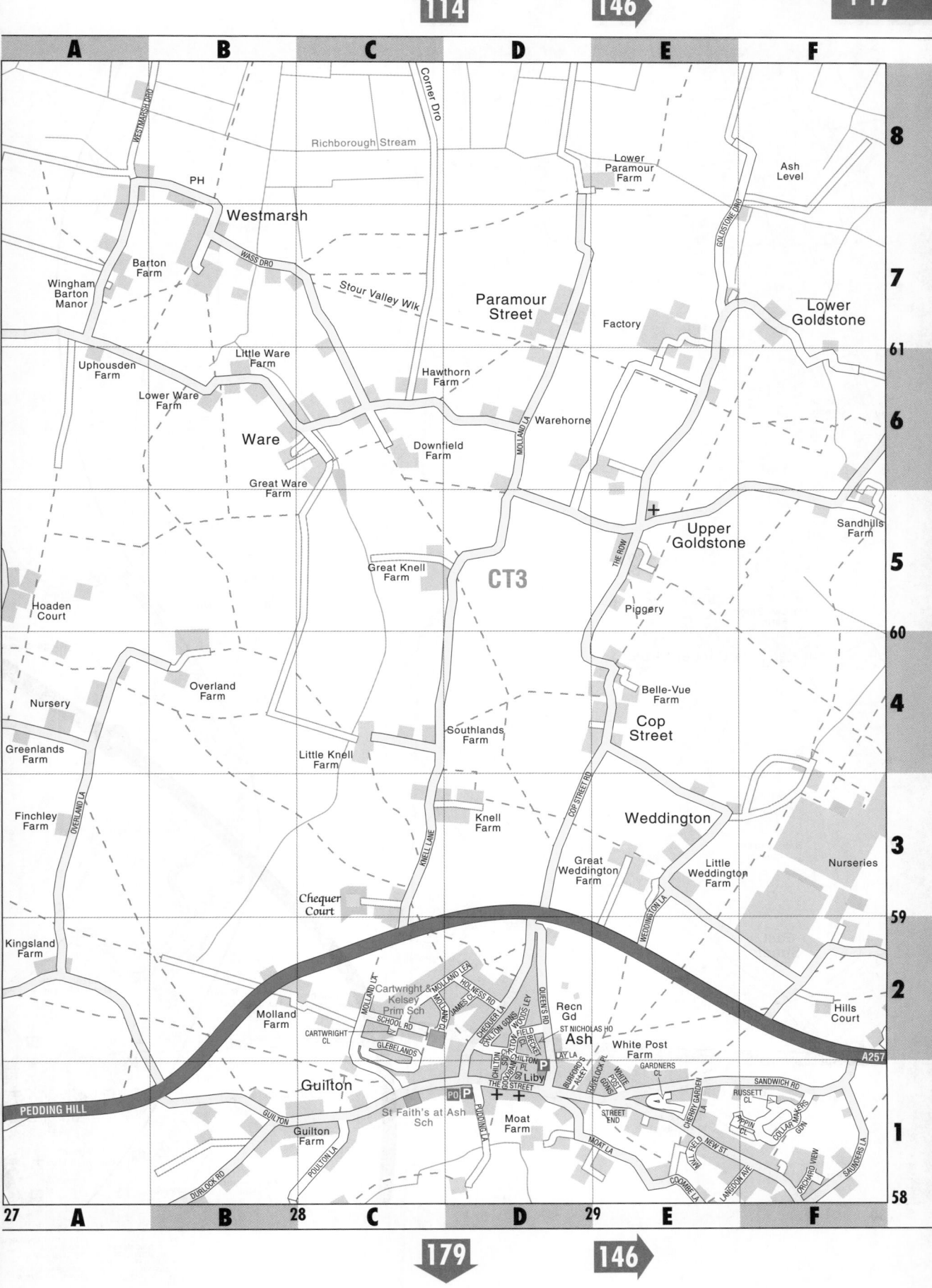

F1
1 GUESTLING MILL CT
2 CREIGHTON FLATS
3 CHURCH ST
4 VICARAGE LA
5 GUILDCOUNT LA
6 HARNET ST
7 WANTSUM MEWS
8 STOUR CT
9 LOOP COURT MEWS
10 THE OLD COACHWORKS
11 TANNERY LA
12 ST JOHN'S COTTS
13 WATTS YD
14 WHITEFRIARS WAY
15 WHITEFRIARS MDW

116

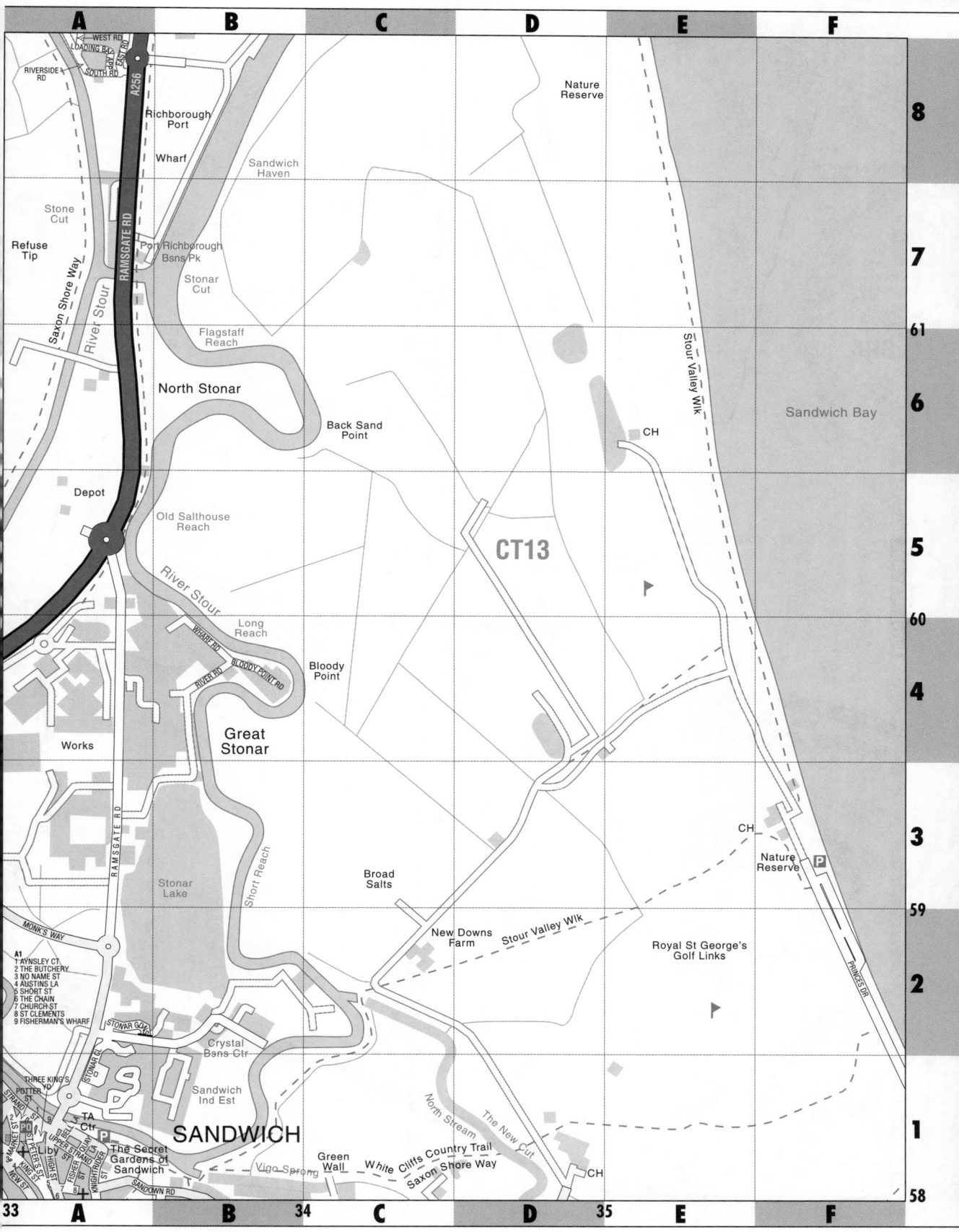

181

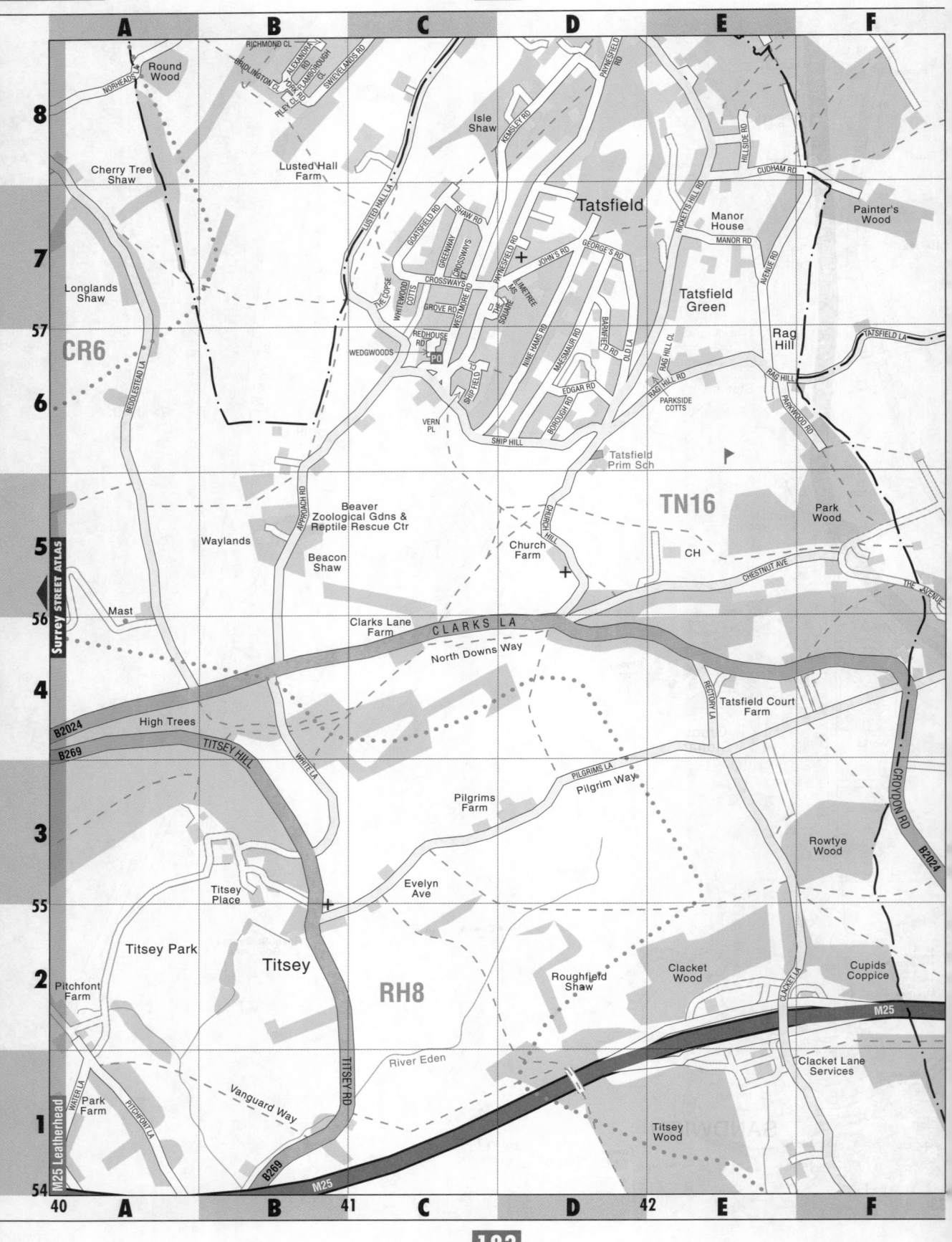

D1
1 HORTONS WAY
2 MARKET WAY
3 MORETON ALMHOUSES
4 AUSTIN CT
5 ST MARY'S CT
6 DUNCANS COTTS
7 FULLERS HILL
8 WINTERTON CT
9 QUEBEC COTTS

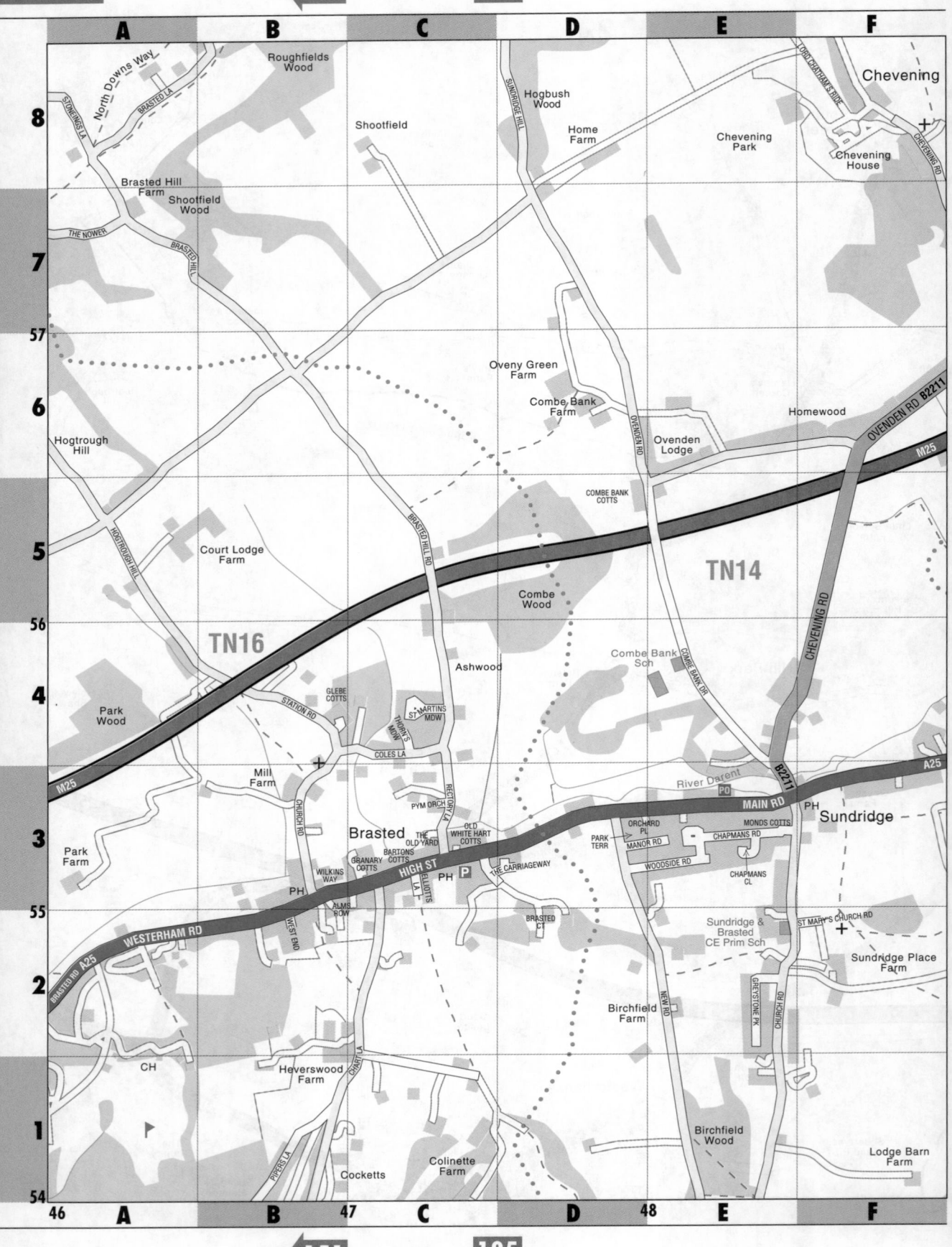

121
154

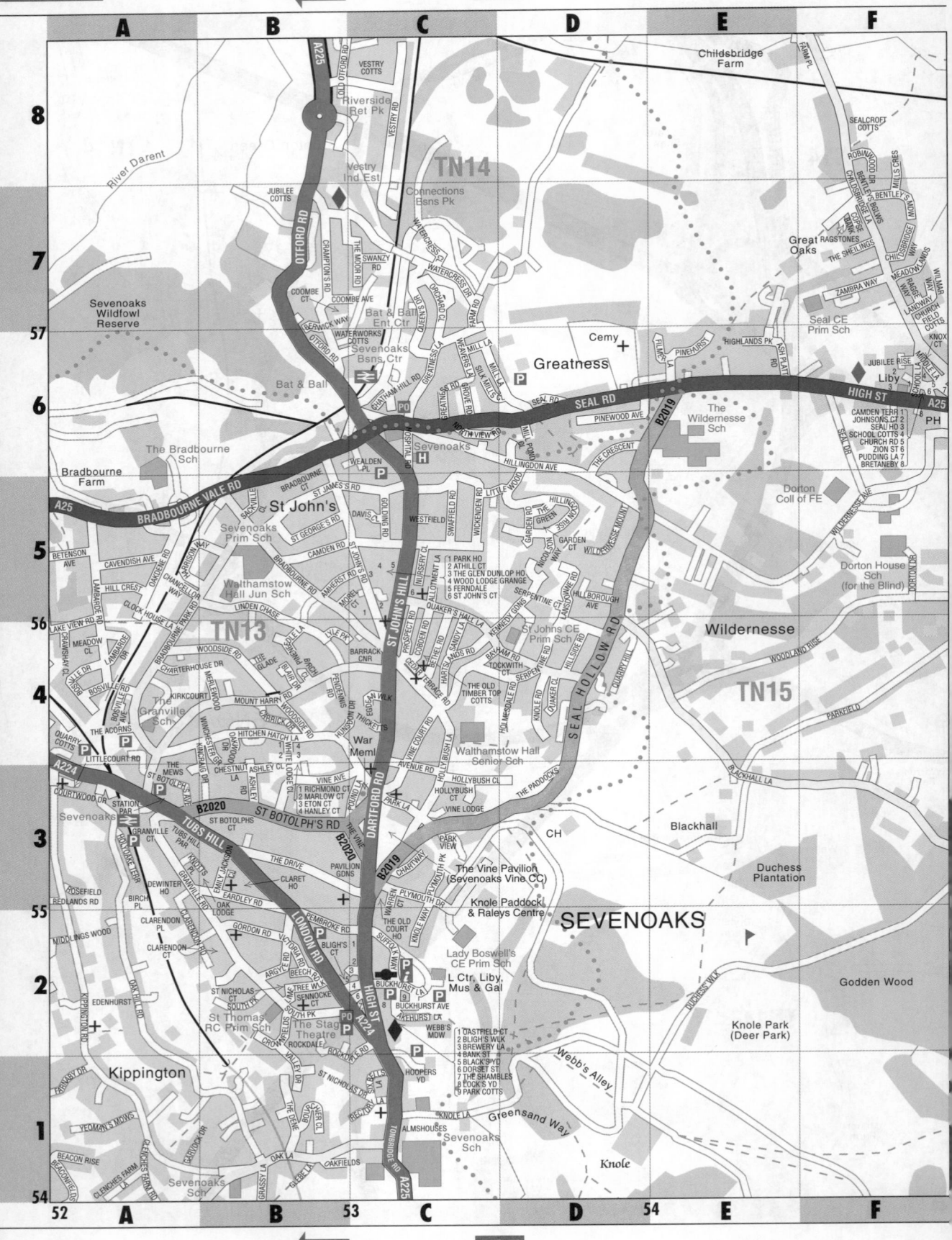

A   B   C   D   E   F

8

Noah's Ark

Cockney's Wood

Chaucer Ind Pk
Chaucer Bsns Pk

Kemsing

HONEYPOT LA

7

Penfield

Tanners Cross

WATERY LA

Stonepitts

57

Seal

CHURCH ST

Fullers Hill

Broomsleigh

GARDEN TERR

6

HIGH ST

TN15

Chart Farm

EAST POINT

Oldbury Hill

GROVE RD

MAIDSTONE RD

SANDS RD

Styants Bottom

Oldbury Wood

5

The Grove

Larchwood Farm

PILLAR BOX LA

STYANTS BOTTOM RD

CH

Styants Wood

56

PARK LA

Chance Wood

Oak Bank Hall

Seal Chart

Redhill Wood

Frankfield

SEVENOAKS RD   A25

4

HALL HILL

PH

Hanger Wood

PH

Fish Ponds Wood

3

Hall Place

BLACKHALL LA

Godden Green

CHURCH RD

St Lawrence CE Prim Sch

Raspit Hill

TAVERN COTTS

PH

STONE STREET RD

55

BACK LA

PH

Great Roger's Wood

Stone Street

PH

2

POND LA

Stake Farm

BROADHOATH

Lord's Spring Wood

Diantshatch Wood

Sevenoaks Prep Sch

Lower Bitchet

THE COPPICE

1

Rambles Wood

Bitchet Green

155
124

F7
1 STATION CT
2 STATION APP
3 SCHOOL APP
4 CLOKE MEWS
5 FOX LEA
6 FOUR WENTS CL

7 STALEYS ACRE

8

7

57

6

5

56

4

3

55

2

1

54

58   59   60

A   B   C   D   E   F

Borough Green

Works

Sand Pit

Cricketts Farm

Works

Ightham Court

Dark Hill Farm

Borough Green & Wrotham

WESTERN RD

SEVENOAKS RD

A227

MAIDSTONE RD

Bellows La

Jasmine Cotts

Wyatt Cl

Conyerd Rd

Quarry Hill Rd

Harrison Rd

Crowhurst Rd

Dryland Rd

Thong La

Basted House

Works

Basted

PH

PLOUGH HILL

MILL LA

Mill La

Bourne Green

Brookside Farm

Dux Farm

Yopps Green

Lady's Wood

Sheet Hill

Sheet Hill Farm

Bewley Farm

WINFIELD LA

River Bourne

Crowhurst Farm

Crowhurst La

Warren Farm

Ightham Warren

Prestons

TN15

Trycewell Farm

Ightham

Oldbury

Oldbury Cotts

OLDBURY LA

Oldbury Hill

Ightham Prim Sch

Oldbury

Oldbury Wood

UPPER SPRING LA

SPRING LA

REDWELL LA

OLD LA

RECTORY LA

COBS CL

JUBILEE CRES

CHAPEL ROW

CHAPEL VIEW

PH

The Street

FEN POND RD

BATES HILL

BOROUGH GREEN RD

A227

IGHTHAM BY-PASS

WALKER PL

RUSHMERE CT

DURLINGS ORCH

BUSTY LA

TRYCEWELL LA

The Glebe

FEN POND

SEVENOAKS RD

A25

COPT HALL RD

COMMON RD

NUTFIELDS

PH

SEVEN WENTS

Ightham Common

Raspit Hill

SANDY LA

SMARTS RD

TEBBS WAY

BACK LA

High Cross Rd

MOTE RD

Scathes Wood

Ivy Hatch

STONE STREET RD

PINE TREE LA

COACH RD

PH

TONBRIDGE RD

A227

Scatt's Dene

YOPPS GN

Bewley La

BEWLEY LA

SHEET HILL

BOURNE LA

Manor Farm House

Manor Farm Cotts

Patchgrove Wood

155
155
189

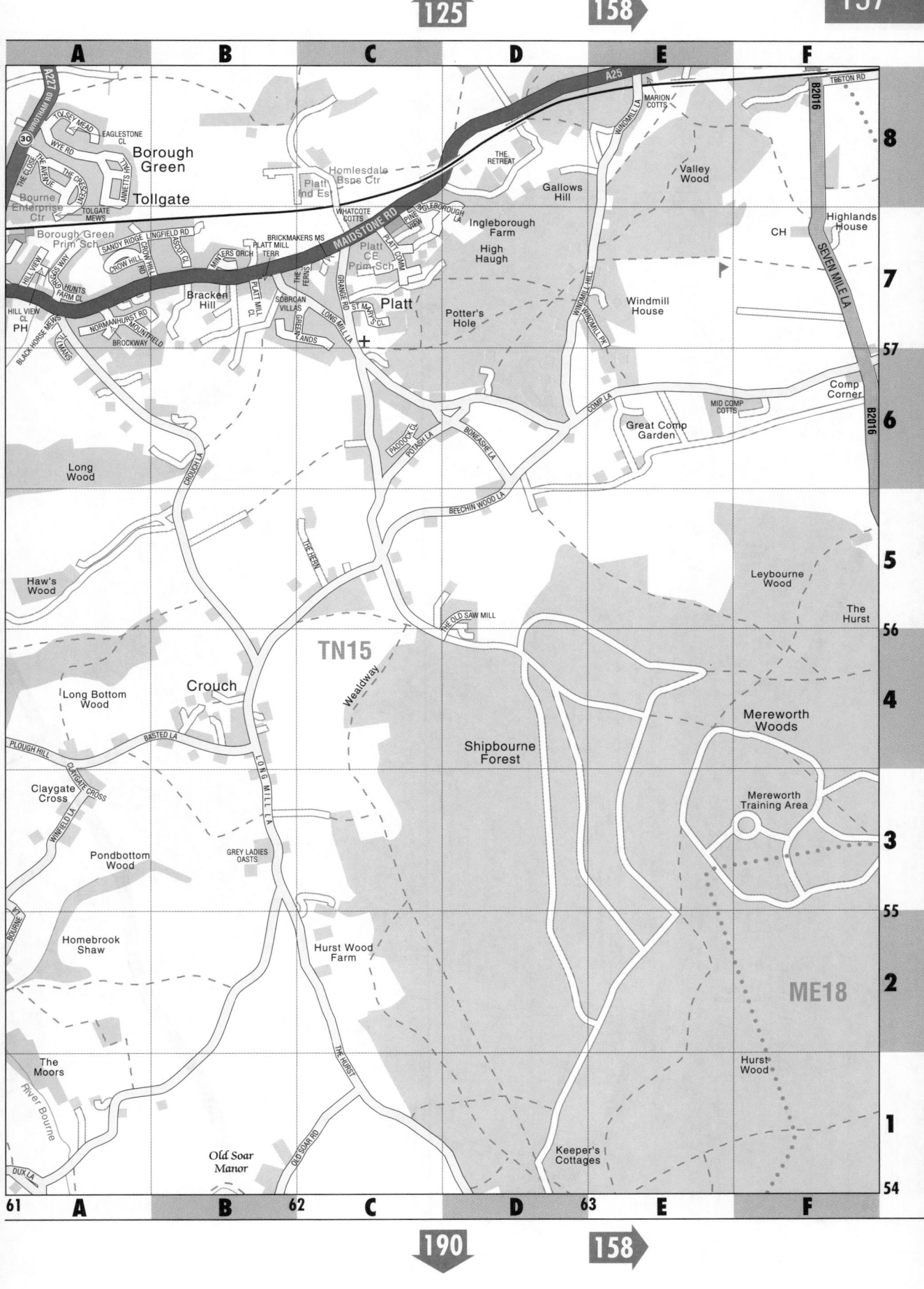

A   B   C   D   E   F

8
7
57
6
5
56
4
55
2
ME18
1
54

Borough
Green
Tollgate

A227 RD
WROTHAM RD
TOLSEY MEAD
EAGLESTONE CL
WYE RD
THE CLOSE
THE AVENUE
THE CRESCENT
ANNETTS HL
Bourne
Enterprise
Ctr
TOLGATE MEWS
Borough Green
Prim Sch
SANDY RIDGE
CROW HILL
LINGFIELD RD
ASCOT CL
CROW RD
MINERS ORCH
HILL VIEW
CROSS WAY
HUNTS FARM CL
HILL VIEW CL PH
BLACK HORSE MEWS
NORMANHURST RD
MOUNTFIELD
ST MARYS
BROCKWAY
Bracken
Hill
PLATT MILL CL
PLATT MILL TERR
SOBROAN VILLAS
GREEN LANDS
LONG MILL LA
CROUCH LA

Homesdale
Bsps Ctr
Platt
Ind Est
WHATCOTE COTTS
PINE VIEW
Platt
CE
Prim Sch
THE FREITH
GRANGE LA
ST MARY'S CL
Platt
COLEBOROUGH LA
POLEBOROUGH LA
PLATT COMM
BRICKMAKERS MS

MAIDSTONE RD
A25

THE RETREAT
Gallows
Hill
Ingleborough
Farm
High
Haugh
Potter's
Hole
MARION COTTS
WINDMILL LA
Valley
Wood
CH
WINDMILL HILL
WINDMILL PK
Windmill
House
TESTON RD
B2016
Highlands
House
SEVEN MILE LA

Long
Wood

PADDOCK CL
POTASH LA
BONEASHE LA
BEECHIN WOOD LA
COMP LA
Great Comp
Garden
MID COMP COTTS
Comp
Corner
B2016

Haw's
Wood
THE HERN
THE OLD SAW MILL
TN15
Wealdway
Leybourne
Wood
The
Hurst

Long Bottom
Wood
Crouch
BASTED LA
Mereworth
Woods
Shipbourne
Forest
Mereworth
Training Area

PLOUGH HILL
CLAYGATE CROSS
WINFIELD LA
Claygate
Cross
Pondbottom
Wood
GREY LADIES OASTS
LONG MILL LA
THE HURST
Hurst Wood
Farm

BOURNE
Homebrook
Shaw
The
Moors
River Bourne
DUX LA
OLD SOAR RD
Old Soar
Manor
Keeper's
Cottages
Hurst
Wood

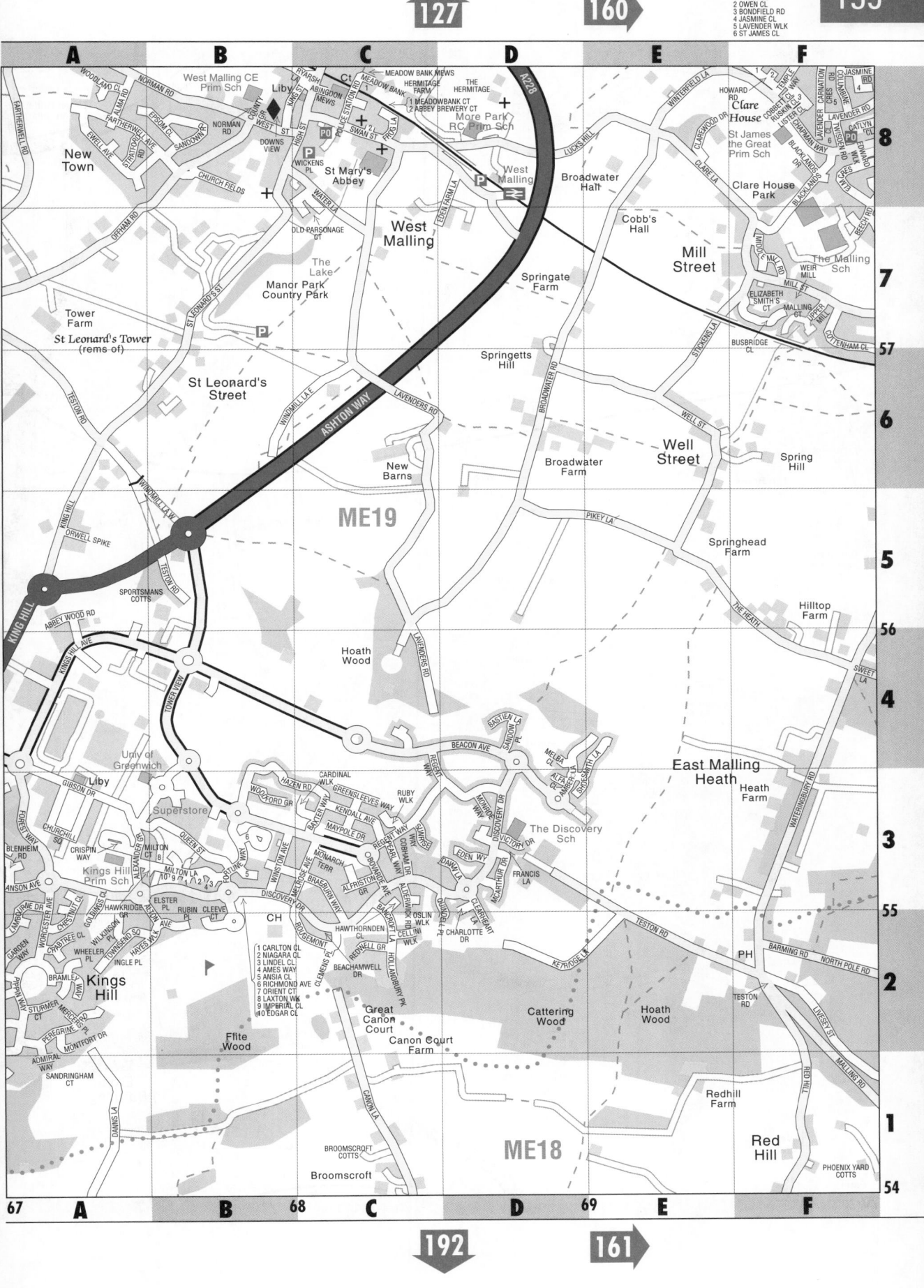

F8
1 TYLER CL
2 OWEN CL
3 BONDFIELD RD
4 JASMINE CL
5 LAVENDER WLK
6 ST JAMES CL

127   160

A   B   C   D   E   F

West Malling CE Prim Sch

Liby

New Town

MEADOW BANK MEWS
HERMITAGE FARM
THE HERMITAGE
1 MEADOWBANK CT
2 ABBEY BREWERY CT

More Park RC Prim Sch

West Malling

St Mary's Abbey

Old Parsonage

The Lake

Manor Park Country Park

Tower Farm

St Leonard's Tower (rems of)

St Leonard's Street

New Barns

ME19

Hoath Wood

Broadwater Hall

Cobb's Hall

Springate Farm

Springetts Hill

Broadwater Farm

Springhead Farm

Clare House

St James the Great Prim Sch

Clare House Park

Mill Street

The Malling Sch

Elizabeth Smith's Ct

BUSBRIDGE CL

Well Street

Spring Hill

Hilltop Farm

8

7

57

6

5

56

4

Sportsmans Cotts

Univ of Greenwich

Liby

Superstore

Kings Hill Prim Sch

Kings Hill

Flite Wood

CH

1 CARLTON CL
2 NIAGARA CL
3 LINDEL CL
4 AMES WAY
5 ANSIA CL
6 RICHMOND GR
7 ORIENT CT
8 LAXTON WLK
9 IMPERIAL CL
10 EDGAR CL

Great Canon Court

Canon Court Farm

Broomscroft Cotts

Broomscroft

Beacon Ave

East Malling Heath

Heath Farm

The Discovery Sch

Cattering Wood

Hoath Wood

Redhill Farm

Red Hill

PHOENIX YARD COTTS

ME18

55

2

1

54

67   A   68   B   C   68   D   69   E   F

192   161

159
128

A B C D E F

8 7 57 6 5 56 4 3 55 2 1 54

LILAC GN
LAVENDER RD
CATLIN CL
New Road Bsns Est
Kingsdown Ind Est
WILLOW DR
PARK FARM HOUSES
SCOTT CL
CHERRY ORCH
PEAR TREE
PRIMROSE CL
WOODLANDS RD
ACORN GR
GORSE RD
FFINCH CL
BIRCH CRES
Holt Hill
BRASSEY DR
HOLLY WOOD AVE
BRIDGET CL
MCKENZIE CL
1 WILLIAM BAKER HO
2 CLIVE HO
Royal British Legion Village
LONDON RD
A20
Bradbourne House

South Aylesford Ret Pk
Superstore
Quarry Wood Ind Est
WOOD CL
Euroway
Britannia Bsns Pk
MILLS RD
WELDERS WAY
LAKE RD
WHITEWOOD RD
WHITEWOOD POST
B2246
HERMITAGE LA

ME20

PRIORY PK
KILN BARN RD

East Malling
PH
MILL ST
CHURCH WLK
HIGH ST
THE GRANGE
Great East
COTTENH
CHAPEL ST
East Malling
ROCKS CL
Laboratories
Barming

Paris Farm
MANNINGHAM HO
GILLETTS LA
The Rocks
THE ROCKS RD
FOUR ACRES
East Malling Research
Kiln Barn

ME19

Knoxes Shaw Farm
Broke Wood
HERMITAGE CT
B2246

WATERBURY RD
Belvidere Oast Farm
EASTERFIELDS
Kiln Barn Farm
Hermitage Farm

SWEET LA
The Manor Riding Stables
L'Escargot Manor House
Fullingpits Wood

Upper Paris Farm
Luckhurst Farm
Ditton Common

Leigh Cottage
Water Tower
Cemy

Oaken Wood
REDE WOOD RD
BROOMSHAW RD
ROBERTS ORCHARD RD
BEECHWOOD RD
WESLEY
BANKY MDW
LONG RECE
MAPLESDEN

Seven Wents

ME16
HEATH RD
NORTHFIELDS
MARLBOROUGH PAR
BEVERLEY RD
HURST LA

The Lodge
Barming Prim Sch
BELMONT CL
NORTH ST
APPLE TREE CL
BELL FARM GDNS
SOUTHWOOD RD
MAYPLAND RD
ABINGDON RD
TRELLYN CL

Hall Place

NORTH POLE RD
Teston Corner
ME18
Hall Place Farm
CEDAR DR
MATTERDALE GDNS
BULL ORCH
PO
BARNED CT
A26
GLEBE LA

TONBRIDGE RD
PRIORSDEAN CL
PH
THE OLD SCHOOL
East Barming

Livesey Street
LIVESEY ST
MALLING RD
Knole Farm
LEIGH TERR
A26
CHURCH LA
SOUTH ST
Court Lodge Farm

A B C D E F

70 71 72

159
193

A3
1 SPRINGWOOD CL
2 CATHERINE CL
3 MAGNOLIA HO
4 HAWTHORNE HO
5 CHESTNUT HO
6 BIRCH HO
7 ROWAN HO
8 WILLOW HO
9 ALMOND HO
10 OAKAPPLE HO
11 LANGLEY HO
12 KINGSWOOD HO
13 HARRIETSHAM HO
14 CORIANDA DR

E2
1 MILLERS WHARF
2 MILLSTOCK TERR
3 THE MEADOWS
4 ALLNUTT MILL CL
5 BANK VIEW

E3
1 NEWTON CL
2 ORCHARD PL
3 OLDCHURCH CT
4 RYCAULT CL
5 WHITE ROCK PL
6 VICTORIA CT
7 WESTREE CT

E4
1 BIRNAM SQ
2 ROCKY HILL TERR
3 BIRKDALE CT
4 SWALLOW HO
5 ROBIN HO
6 SWIFT HO
7 PEACOCK MEWS
8 KENTISH CT

E5
1 THE MEWS
2 RUTH HO
3 CARRIE HO
4 CLAIRE HO
5 DANIEL HO

F4
3 MARKET COLONNADE
4 MARKET BLDGS
5 ROYAL STAR ARC
6 BANK ST
7 MEDWAY HO
8 WATERSIDE

F5
1 Maidstone
Mus & Gallery

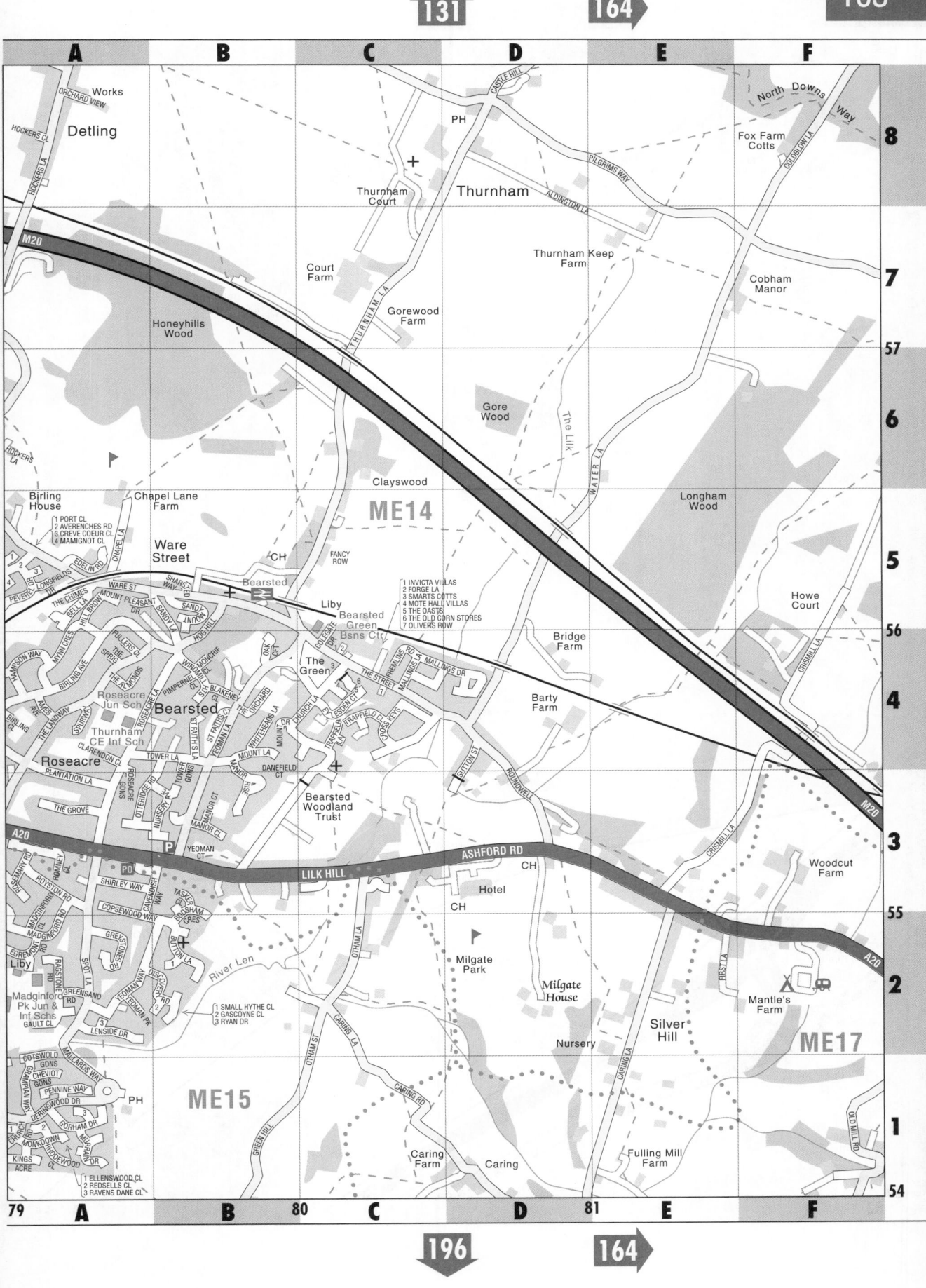

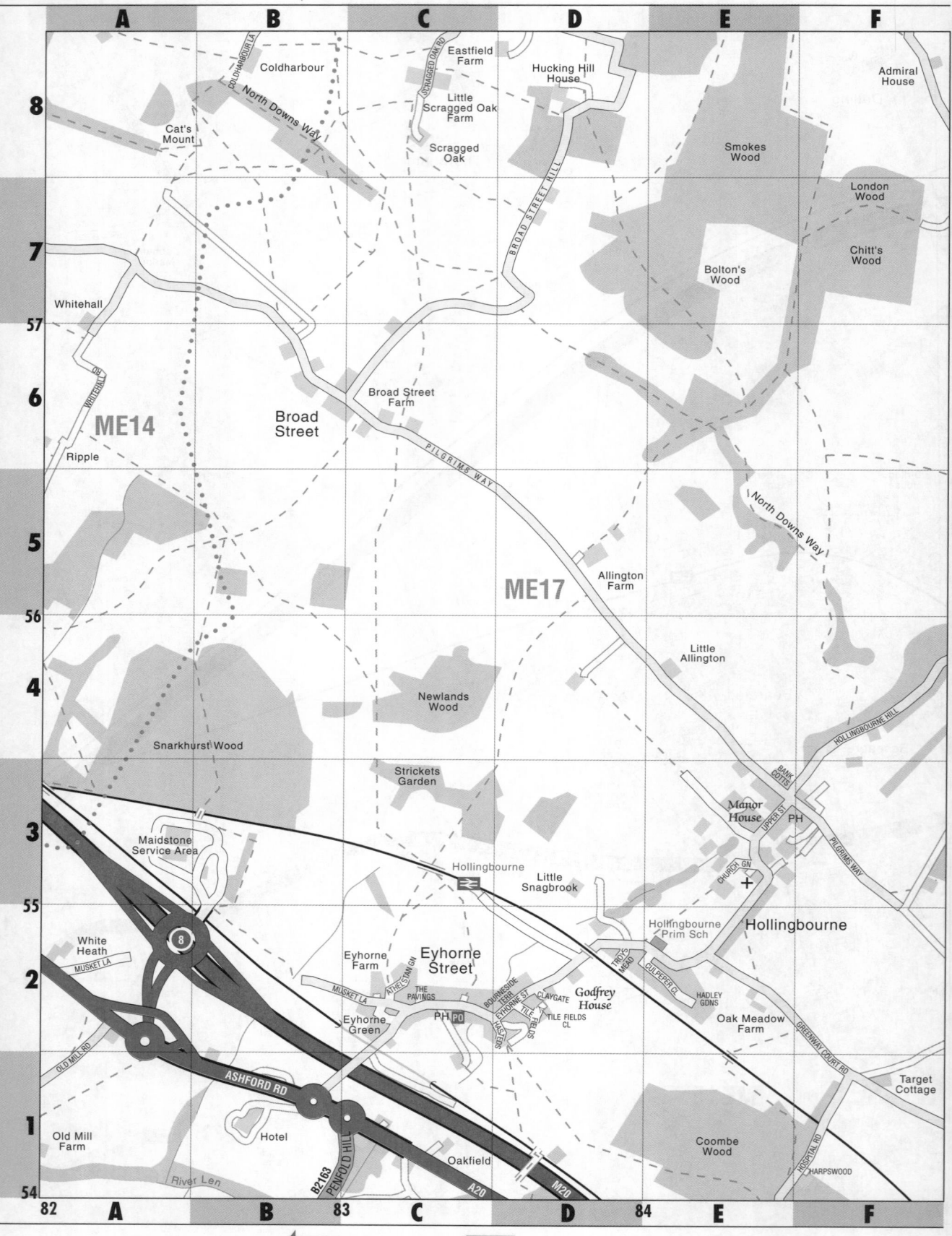

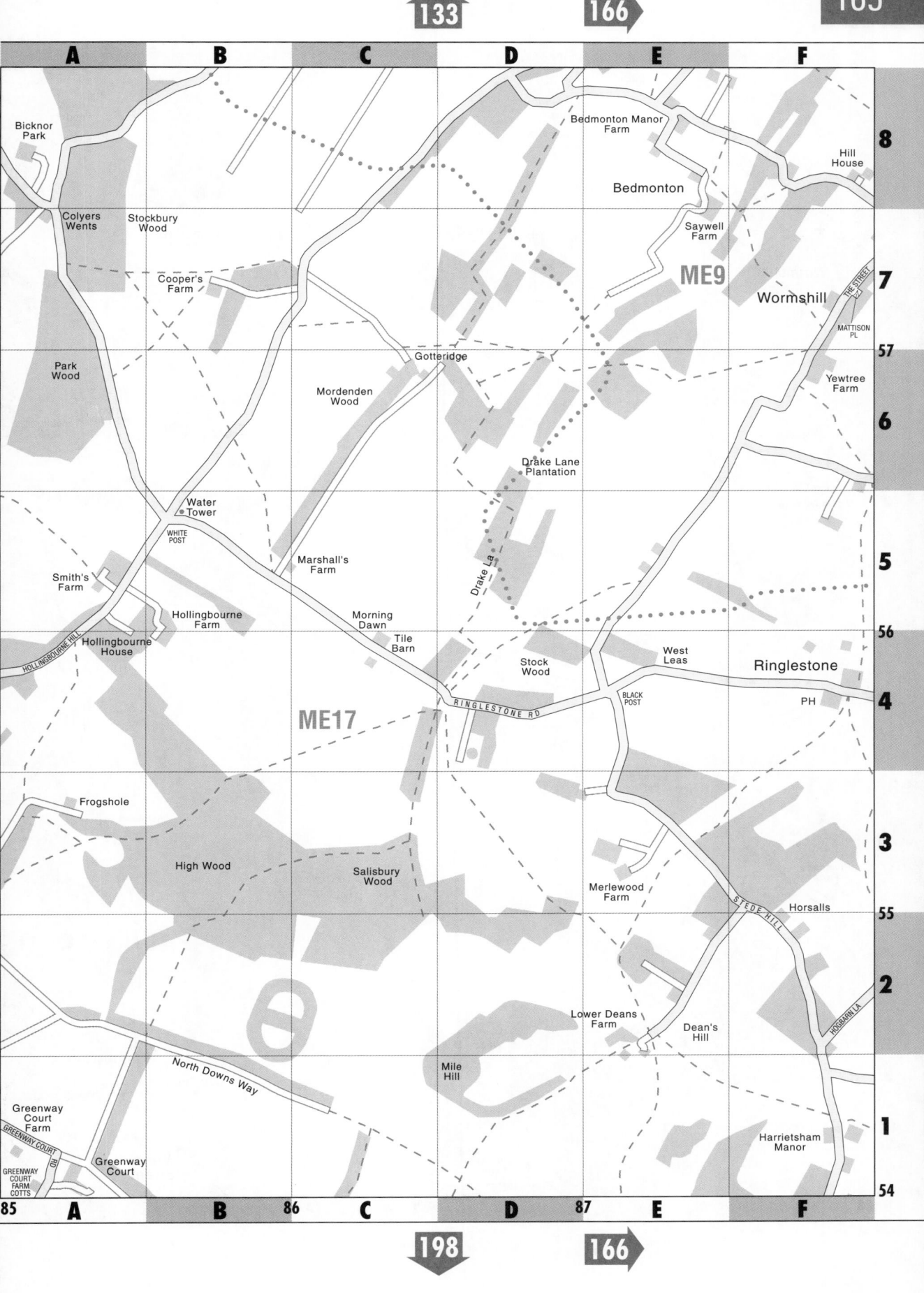

A   B   C   D   E   F

8

Bicknor Park

Bedmonton Manor Farm

Hill House

Colyers Wents

Stockbury Wood

Bedmonton

Saywell Farm

ME9

7

Cooper's Farm

Wormshill

THE STREET

MATTISON PL

57

Park Wood

Gotteridge

Mordenden Wood

Yewtree Farm

6

Drake Lane Plantation

Water Tower

WHITE POST

Marshall's Farm

Drake La

5

Smith's Farm

Morning Dawn

Tile Barn

Stock Wood

West Leas

Ringlestone

56

Hollingbourne Farm

HOLLINGBOURNE HILL

Hollingbourne House

RINGLESTONE RD

BLACK POST

PH

4

ME17

Frogshole

Merlewood Farm

Horsalls

3

High Wood

Salisbury Wood

STEDE HILL

55

2

Lower Deans Farm

Dean's Hill

HOGBARN LA

North Downs Way

Mile Hill

1

Greenway Court Farm

GREENWAY COURT RD

Harrietsham Manor

GREENWAY COURT FARM COTTS

Greenway Court

54

A   B   C   D   E   F

8

Hogshaw
Wood

Manor
Farm

FAIRVIEW
COTTS   Frinsted

Torry Hill
Park

THE STREET
DRAY'S FIELD   Wormshill

Copes
Farm

7

Kippen

Torry
Hill

57

New Purchase
Farm

6

Oorlair

ME9

Park
Farm

Timbold
Hill

COALPIT LA

Park Farm

Yoke's
Court

Sweet's
Wood

OAST
COTTS

5

Madam's
Court

Lord's
Hill

56

Ashdown
Hill

RINGLESTONE RD

4

Minnels
Farm

Lenniker
Farm

Wrinsted
Court

Ashdown

ASHDOWN RD

Lord's
Wood

3

The
Dell

HOGBARN LA

Plummers
Farm

PILGRIMS CW

Butts
Bank

55

Hogbarn

2

ME17

Stedehill
Wood

Broomy Lees
Wood

Greenways

West Street
Farm

ASHDOWN RD

1

WEST ST

West
Street

FAVERSHAM RD

54

Flint Barn
Farm

Newage
Farm

FLINT LA

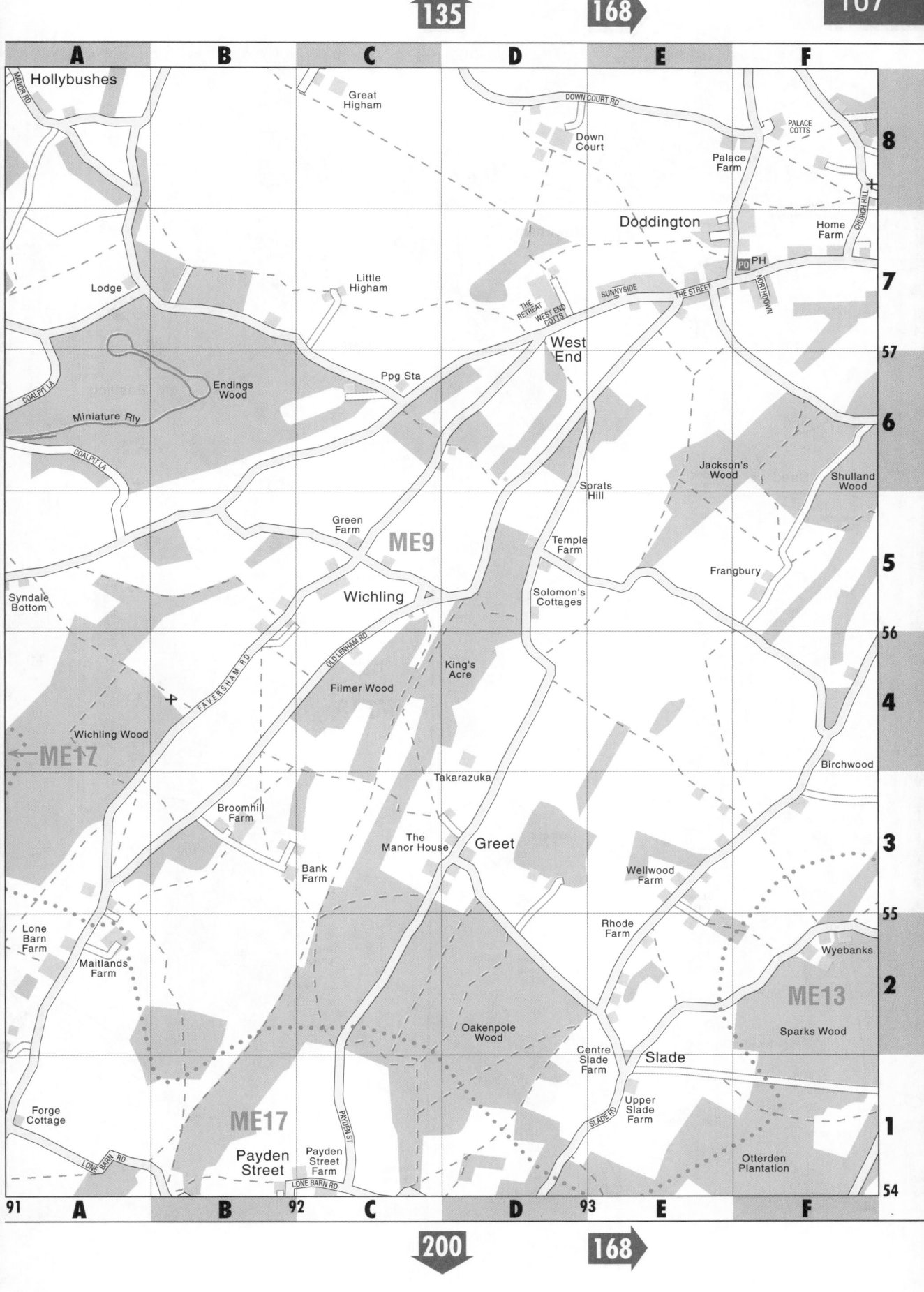

135
168

A   B   C   D   E   F

Hollybushes

MANOR RD

Great Higham

DOWN COURT RD

Down Court

PALACE COTTS

Palace Farm

8

Doddington

Home Farm

CHURCH HILL

Lodge

Little Higham

THE RETREAT

WEST END COTTS

SUNNYSIDE

THE STREET

PO PH

NORTHDOWN

7

West End

57

Ppg Sta

COALPIT LA

Endings Wood

6

Miniature Rly

Jackson's Wood

Shulland Wood

COALPIT LA

Sprats Hill

Green Farm

ME9

Temple Farm

Frangbury

5

Syndale Bottom

Wichling

Solomon's Cottages

56

FAVERSHAM RD

OLD LENHAM RD

King's Acre

Filmer Wood

4

Wichling Wood

Birchwood

ME17

Takarazuka

Broomhill Farm

The Manor House

Greet

Wellwood Farm

3

Bank Farm

55

Rhode Farm

Lone Barn Farm

Wyebanks

Maitlands Farm

ME13

2

Sparks Wood

Oakenpole Wood

Centre Slade Farm

Slade

PAYDEN ST

Forge Cottage

SLADE RD

Upper Slade Farm

ME17

1

LONE BARN RD

Payden Street

Payden Street Farm

Otterden Plantation

LONE BARN RD

54

91   A   B   92   C   D   93   E   F

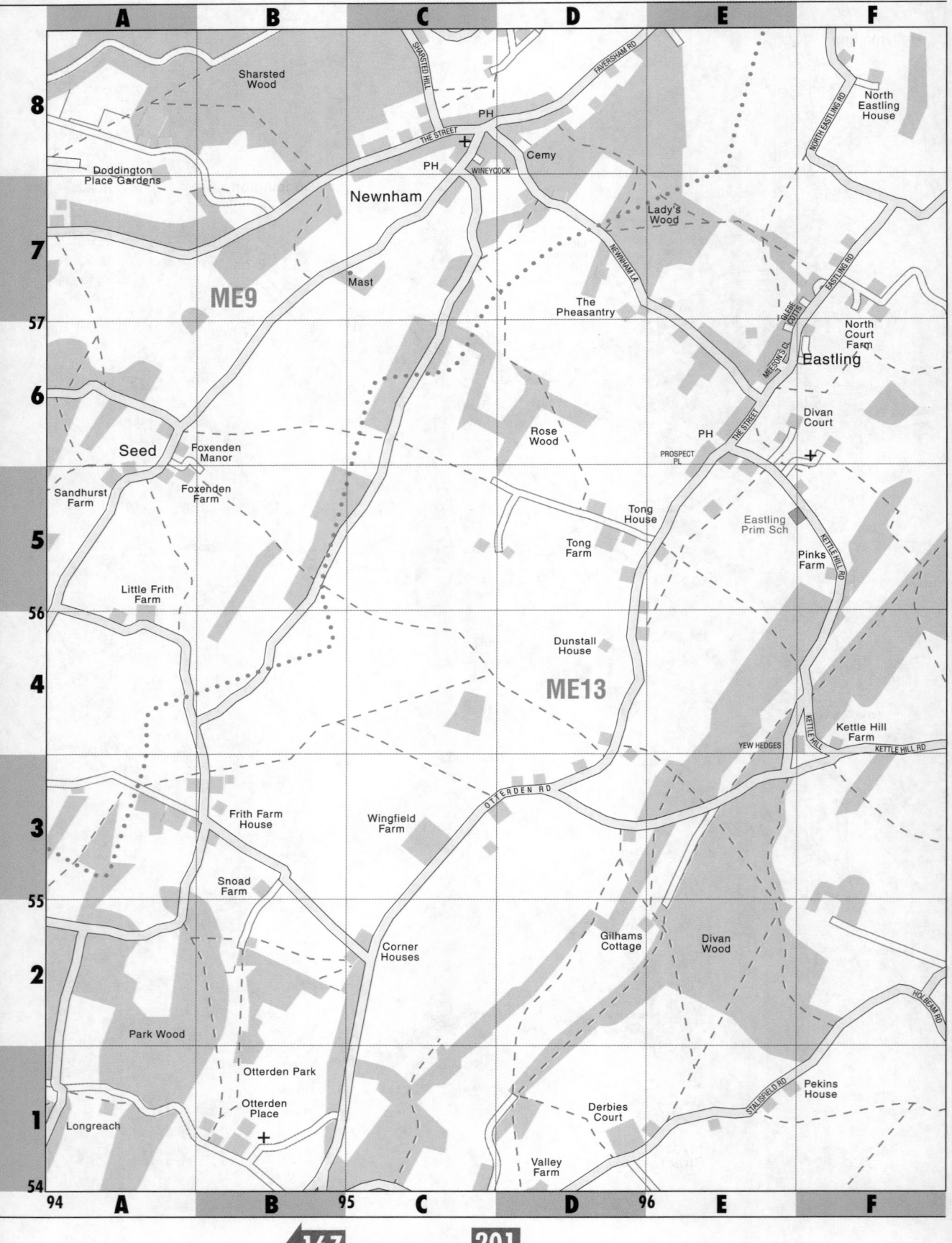

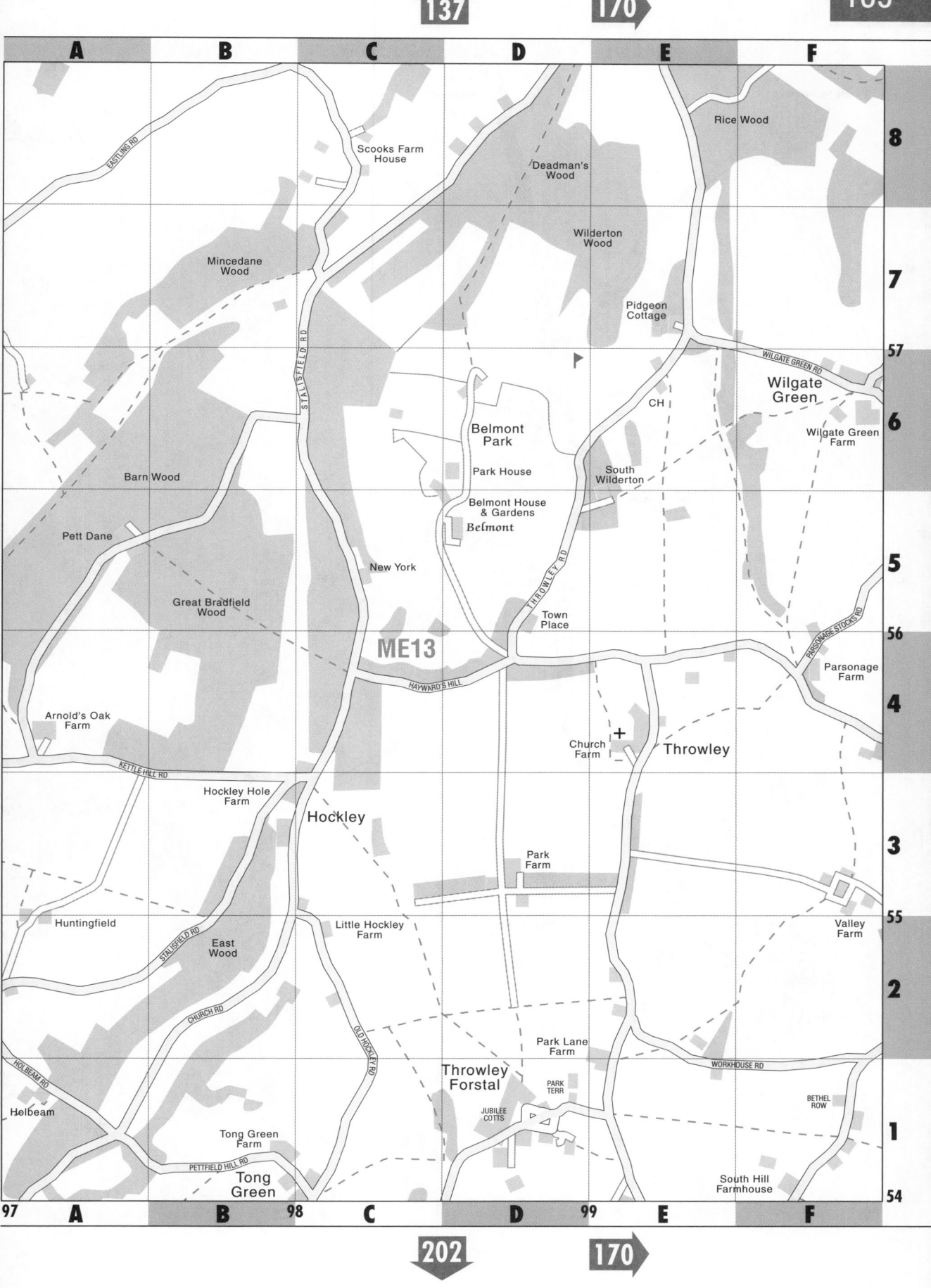

A   B   C   D   E   F

Badgin Wood

North Street

OAST COTTS

OWENS COURT COTTS

Owens Court

Saffery Farm

8

PLUMFORD RD

Gosmere

GOSMERE FARM BARNS

7

NEWHOUSE LA

NEWHOUSE FARM COTTS

Newhouse Farm

WINDING HILL

57

Throwley House

Sheldwich

6

OLD BADGINS RD

THE STOCKS

Church Plantation

Winding Hill Wood

Cobrahamsole Farm

Sheldwich Prim Sch

HUNTERS WAY

FIRST HARROW

Sheldwich Lees

LEES CHURCH RD

AMOS CL

NURSERY LA

MORGAN KIRBY'S GDN

CARRIAGE HO

Lees Court

5

ME13

Lees Court Park

56

Lords Farm

4

Little Lords

LORDS COTTS

Stocking Wood

BAGSHILL RD

Poultry Farm

ASHFORD RD

3

MILLEN'S ROW

DAYTON RD

55

Badlesmere Court

FISHER STREET RD

Black Shaw

Leaveland Court

LEAVELAND COTTS

Woods Court

2

Leaveland Wood

Badlesmere Park Wood

Holly Grove

Stringmans Farm

Workhouse Wood

1

Tenant Wood

Badlesmere

Leaveland

A251

54

00   A   B   01   C   D   02   E   F

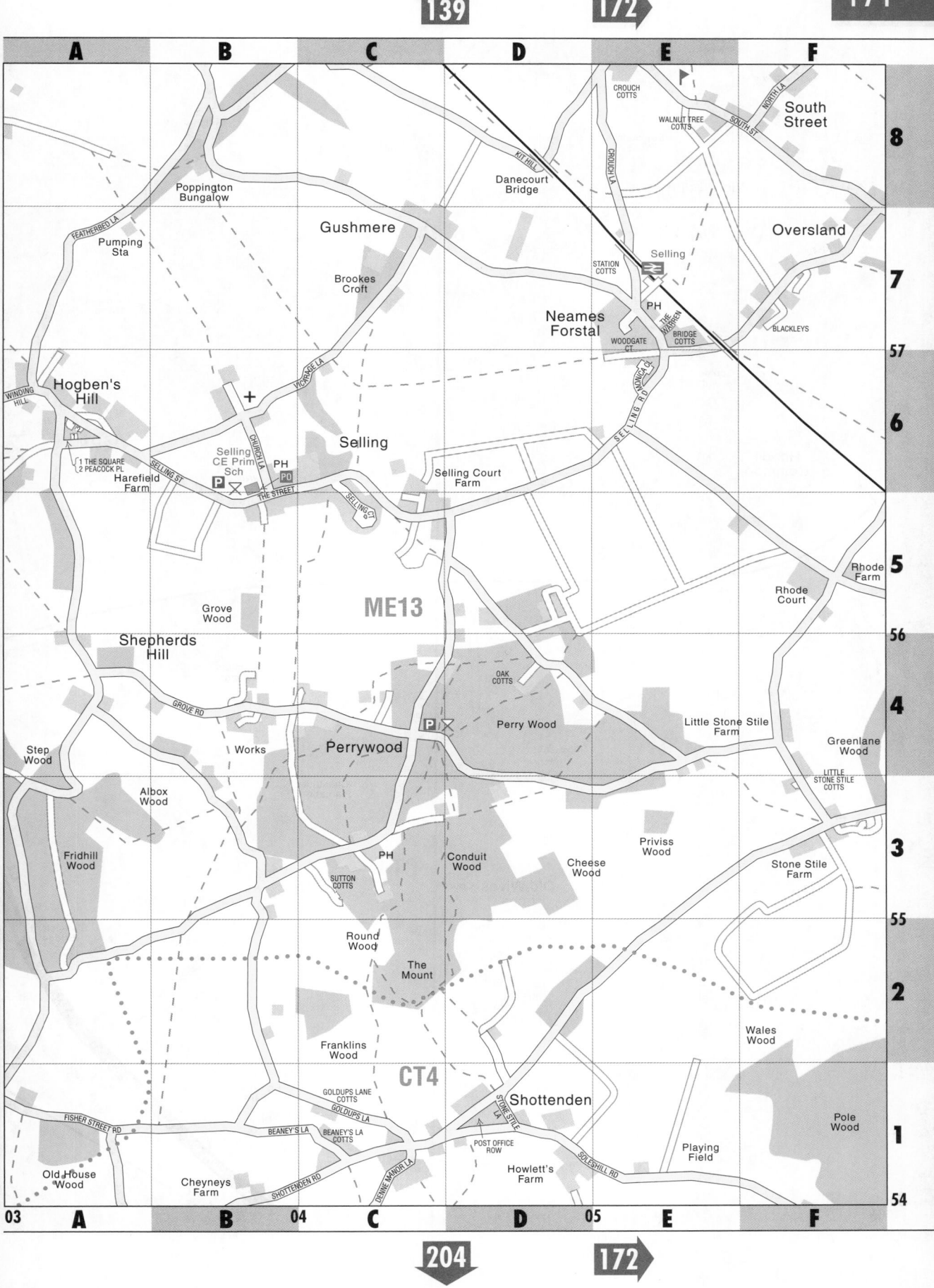

139

172

204

172

South Street

Overland

Crouch Cotts

Walnut Tree Cotts

North La

South St

Selling

Station Cotts

Blackleys

Neames Forstal

Woodgate Ct

Bridge Cotts

PH

The Warren

Poppington Bungalow

Featherbed La

Pumping Sta

Gushmere

Brookes Croft

Danecourt Bridge

Kit Hill

Crouch La

Winding Hill

Hogben's Hill

+

Worge La

Church La

Selling St

Selling CE Prim Sch

1 The Square
2 Peacock Pl

Harefield Farm

P

PH

PO

The Street

Selling

Selling Ct

Selling Court Farm

Selling Rd

Veronica La

Rhode Farm

Rhode Court

ME13

Grove Wood

Shepherds Hill

Grove Rd

Works

Step Wood

Albox Wood

Fridhill Wood

Perrywood

P

Oak Cotts

Perry Wood

Little Stone Stile Farm

Greenlane Wood

Little Stone Stile Cotts

PH

Sutton Cotts

Conduit Wood

Cheese Wood

Priviss Wood

Stone Stile Farm

Round Wood

The Mount

Franklins Wood

CT4

Wales Wood

Goldups Lane Cotts

Goldups La

Shottenden

Stone Stile La

Pole Wood

Fisher Street Rd

Beaney's La

Beaney's La Cotts

Post Office Row

Playing Field

Old House Wood

Cheyneys Farm

Shottenden Rd

Orne Manor La

Howlett's Farm

Soleshill Rd

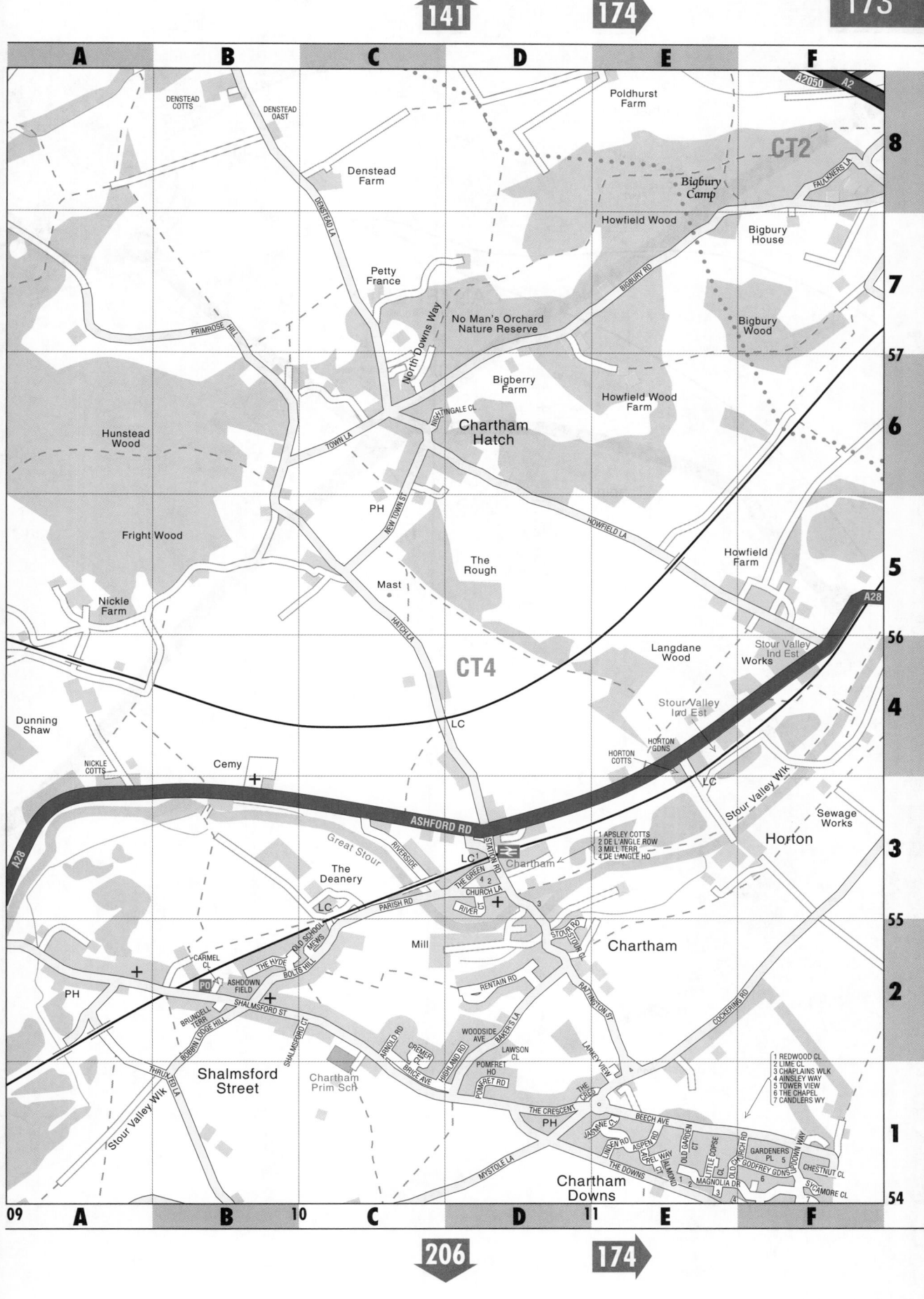

141 174

206 174

A B C D E F

8
7
57
6
5
56
4
3
55
2
1
54

A B 10 C D 11 E F

Poldhurst Farm

CT2

Bigbury Camp

Howfield Wood

Bigbury House

Bigbury Wood

Denstead Cotts

Denstead Oast

Denstead Farm

Petty France

No Man's Orchard Nature Reserve

Bigberry Farm

Howfield Wood Farm

Chartham Hatch

Hunstead Wood

Fright Wood

PH

The Rough

Howfield La

Howfield Farm

Howfield La

Mast

CT4

Langdane Wood

Stour Valley Ind Est Works

Nickle Farm

Dunning Shaw

LC

Stour Valley Ind Est

HORTON GDNS

HORTON COTTS

LC

Stour Valley Wlk

Sewage Works

Nickle Cotts

Cemy

ASHFORD RD

Horton

A28

Great Stour

RIVERSIDE

LC

The Deanery

LC

PARISH RD

THE GREEN

STATION RD

LC

CHURCH LA

RIVER

1 APSLEY COTTS
2 DE L'ANGLE ROW
3 MILL TERR
4 DE L'ANGLE HO

Chartham

Mill

STOUR RD

STOUR PL

Chartham

PH

CARMEL CL

PO

ASHDOWN FIELD

THE HYDE

BOLTS HILL

OLD SCHOOL MEWS

RENTAIN RD

BATTINGTON ST

COCKERING RD

BRUNGELL TERR

BOBBIN LODGE HILL

SHALMSFORD ST

ARNOLD RD

SHALMSFORD CT

Chartham Prim Sch

CREMER CL

BRICE AVE

HIGHLAND RD

WOODSIDE AVE

BAKER'S LA

LAWSON CL

POMFRET HO

POMFRET RD

LANKEY VIEW

1 REDWOOD CL
2 LIME CL
3 CHAPLAINS WLK
4 AINSLEY WAY
5 TOWER VIEW
6 THE CHAPEL
7 CANDLERS WY

Shalmsford Street

THRUXTED LA

Stour Valley Wlk

MYSTOLE LA

THE CRES

PH

THE CRESCENT

JASMINE CL

ASPEN RD

BEECH AVE

OLD GARDEN

LITTLE COPSE

OLD CHURCH RD

GARDENERS PL

CHESTNUT CL

SYCAMORE CL

LAUREL WAY

ALMOND

THE DOWNS

MAGNOLIA DR

GODFREY GDNS

Chartham Downs

North Downs Way

PRIMROSE HILL

DENSTEAD LA

NIGHTINGALE CL

TOWN LA

NEW TOWN ST

HATCH LA

A2050 A2

FAULKNERS LA

A28

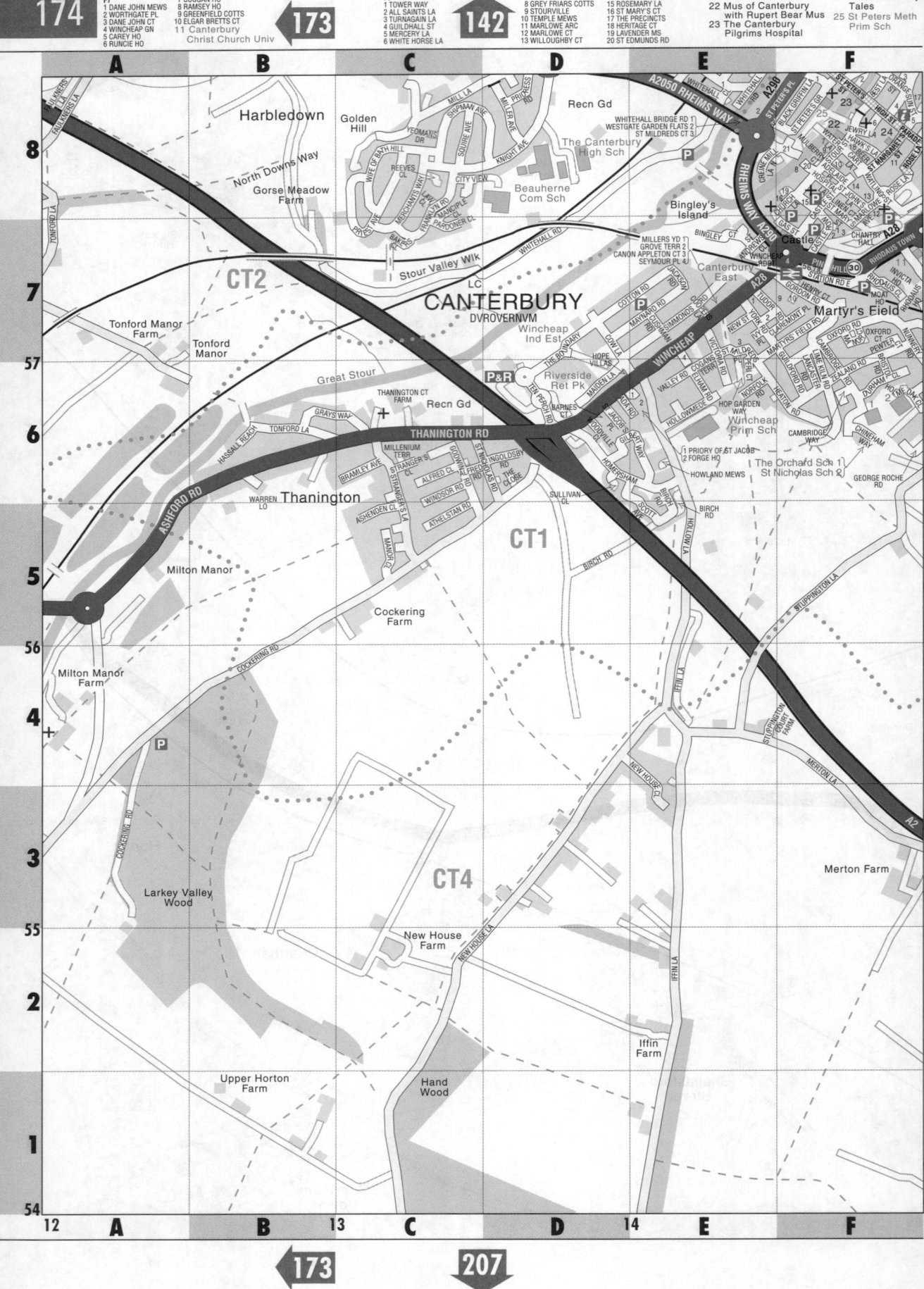

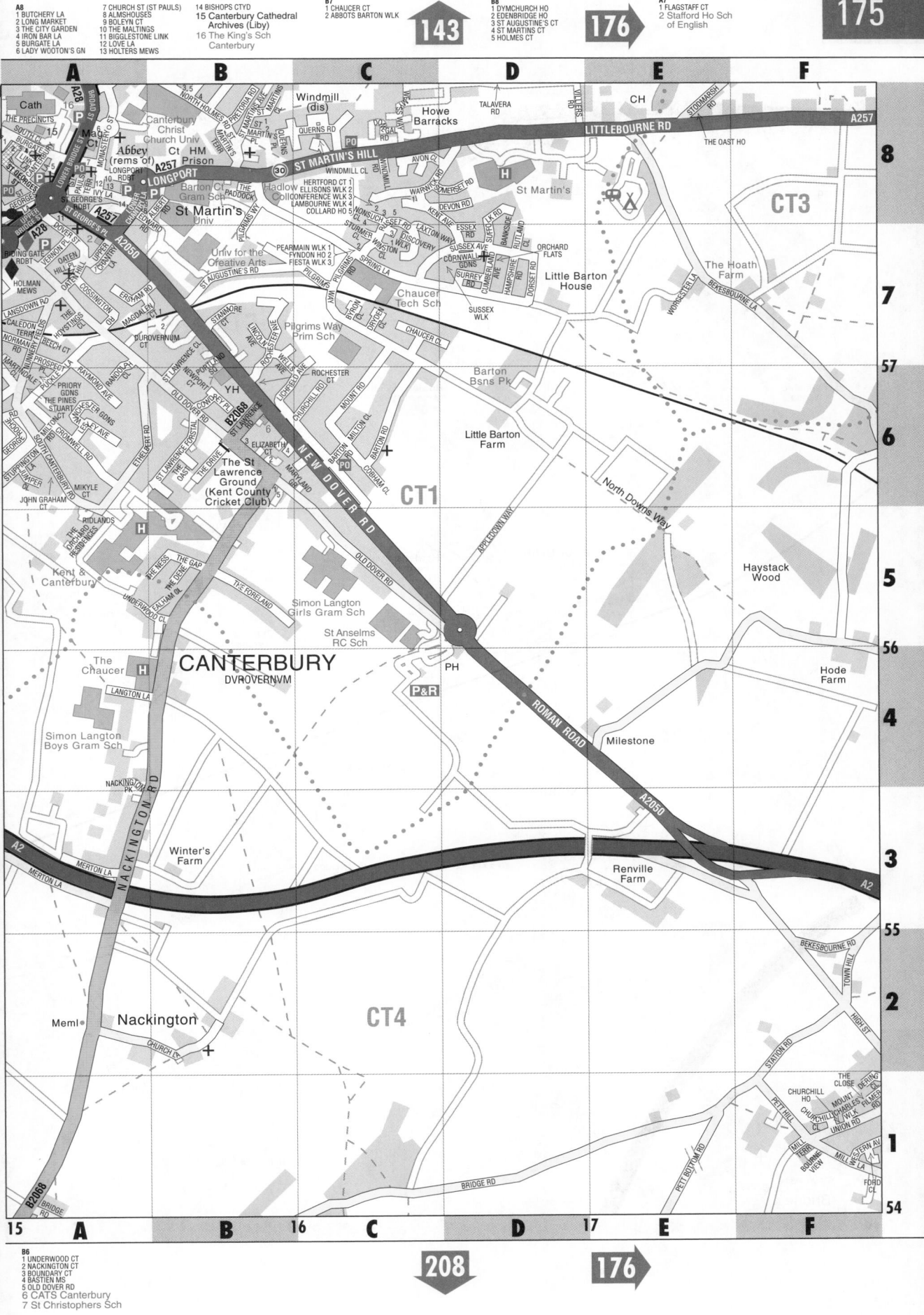

A B C D E F

LITTLEBOURNE RD
SWANTON LA
Jacob's Close
CANTERBURY RD

8

Fishpoolhill Wood
Court Wood

PINESIDE RD
HILLCREST RD
ST VINCENT'S CL
COURT MDWS
CHERRY ORCH
CHURCH RD
COURTHILL
FENHILL RD
PH
EWING CL
Littlebourne CE Prim Sch
JUBILEE RD
ELLEN CL
THE HILL
Littlebourne
Recn Gd
THE GREEN
HIGH ST
A257

Farthings Wood

7

Firdown Wood
Ponds Cottages
CT3
SCHOOL PATH
ROSE ACRE RD
ORCHARD RD
THE MALTINGS
MARGATE ST

57

Palmsted Wood
Woolton Farm
Howletts Wild Animal Park
P
SILVER DIKE

6

Conduit Wood
BEKESBOURNE LA
LACKENDEN COTTS
BEKESBOURNE LA

Lower Garrington Farm

BEKESBOURNE LA

Bekesbourne Hill
Howletts Farm

5

OAKLEIGH LANE
BEKESBOURNE HILL
PH
UNICORN COTTS
HOWLETTS OAST
Lines Wood
Upper Garrington Farm

56

Bekesbourne
SCHOOL LA
STATION RD

4

CRANMER CL 1
ASPINALL CL 2
BIFRONS RD
SCHOOL LA
Ford
Bekesbourne
LYSANDER CL
AERODROME RD

BIFRONS HILL
Patrixbourne
THE STREET
Old Palace RD
CT4
Fords
HAVILLANDS
CHALKPIT HILL

3

BIFRONS GDNS
ST MARY'S RD
Essentially Hops-Chalkpit Farm
DOWNSIDE
ADISHAM RD

55

Bifron's Park
KEEPERS HILL
BRAMLING RD

2

CONYNGHAM LA
Bridge & Patrixbourne CE Prim Sch
PATRIXBOURNE RD
North Downs Way

Recn Gd
PO
RIVERSIDE MEWS
LYNTON PL
SHEPHERDS CLOSE RD

1

KING'S RD
UNION RD
HIGH ST
WESTERN AVE
SAXON RD
GREEN CL
WINDMILL
MILLLA
BRIDGEFORD WAY
BREWERY RD
PH
BRIDGE HILL
MEADOW CL
BOURNE PK RD
Ford
Bridge
A2
Shepherd's Close

54

18 A B 19 C D 20 E F

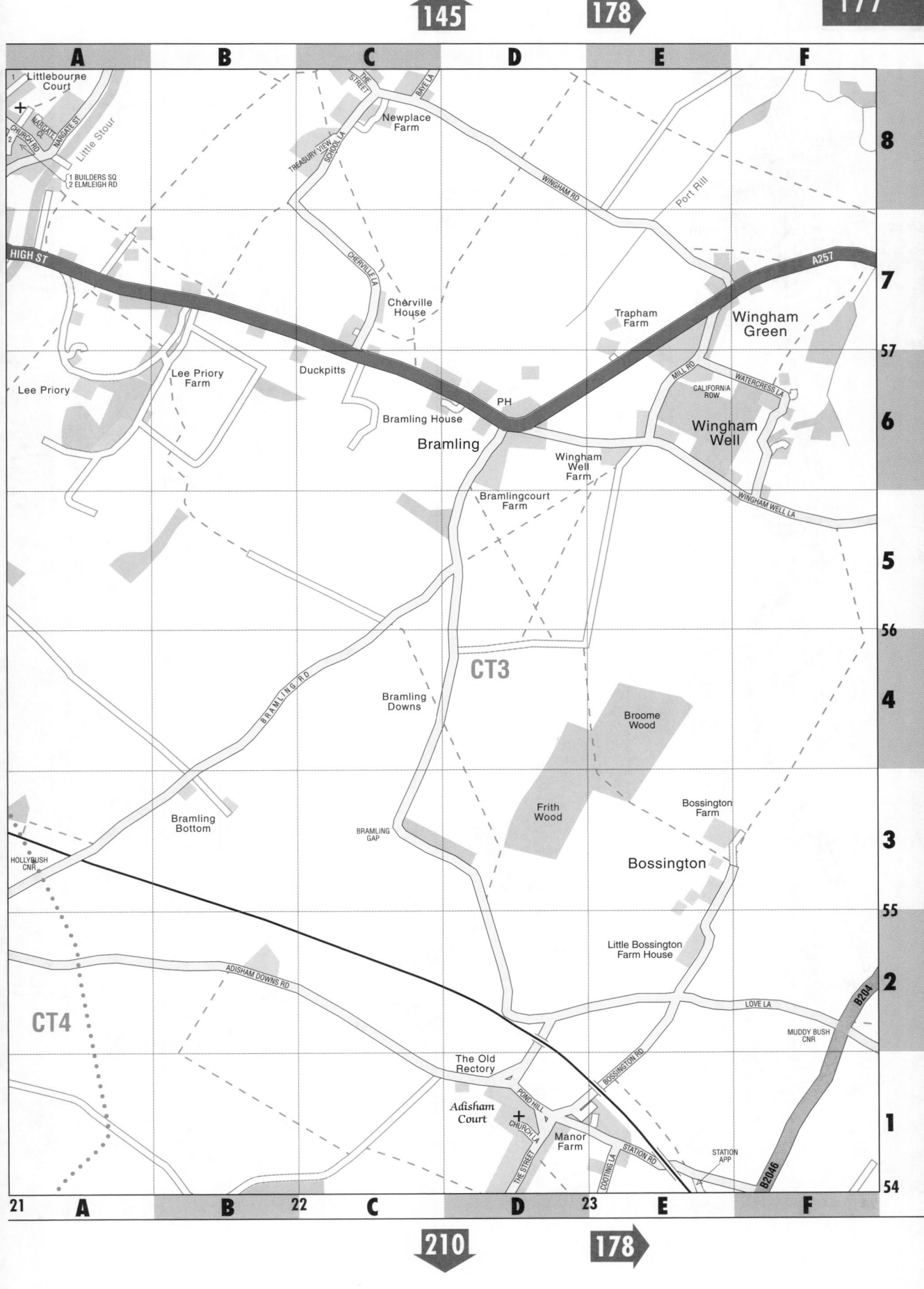

A   B   C   D   E   F

1 Littlebourne Court

MARGATE ST
MARGATE DE
CHURCH RD
2

1 BUILDERS SQ
2 ELMLEIGH RD

Little Stour

THE STREET
BAYE LA
Newplace Farm

TREASURY VIEW
SCHOOL LA

Port Rill

8

HIGH ST

CHERVILLE LA

Cherville House

A257

7

Trapham Farm

Wingham Green

57

Lee Priory

Lee Priory Farm

Duckpitts

Bramling House

PH

Wingham Well Farm

MILL RD
CALIFORNIA ROW
WATERCRESS LA

Wingham Well

6

Bramling

Bramlingcourt Farm

WINGHAM WELL LA

5

BRAMLING RD

Bramling Downs

CT3

56

Broome Wood

4

Bramling Bottom

BRAMLING GAP

Frith Wood

Bossington Farm

3

HOLLYBUSH CNR

Bossington

55

CT4

ADISHAM DOWNS RD

Little Bossington Farm House

LOVE LA

B204

MUDDY BUSH CNR

2

The Old Rectory

BOSSINGTON RD

Adisham Court

POND HILL
CHURCH LA

Manor Farm

COOTING LA

STATION RD

STATION APP

B2046

1

WINGHAM RD

54

177
146

A B C D E F

PETTS LA
GOBERY HILL
A257
8
NORTH COURT CL
COURT RD
SWELLOW PL
DREWERY CRES
MILES CT
P O
EDMUND ST
PALMER RD
ST MARY'S MDW
HIGH ST
GARDEN COTTS
Wingham River
Sewage Works
Brook Farm
Great Pedding Farm
WATERLOCK COTTS
CANTERBURY RD
VICARAGE GDNS
HARRIS'S LA
SOUTH COURT DR
COLLEGE WAY
Dambridge Farm
Wingham
CANON GN
B2046
7
Wingham Prim Sch
SEATH CNR
COURT FLATS
ORCHARD CL
MILL CT CL
Dam Bridge
Twitham
BROOK COTTS
The Groves
GROVE RD
PH
57
Recn Gd
Wingham Ind Est
POPSOL LA
STAPLE RD
BATES CL
Church Farm
6
Witherdens Hall
Twitham Court
Little Twitham Farm
SNAKES HILL
Blackney Hill
Neavy Downs
GOODNESTONE RD
57
DEAN FARM LA
Crockshard Farm
56
Bushy Rough
Twitham Hill
Crixhall Court
4
Dene Farm
DENE FARM BARNS
ADISHAM RD
Little Crockshard Farm
CROCKSHARD LA
CROCKSHARD HILL
CT3
Crixhall Rough
BUCKLAND LA
3
Works
Loverswalk Wood
Claypits
CAVE LA
55
Uffington Court
UFFINGTON CT
Church Wood
GOODNESTONE HILL
BOYES LA
PO
Yew Tree Farm
FITZWALTERS MDW
SADDLERS HILL
CATSOLE HILL
2
Fitzwalter Wood
Goodnestone CE Prim Sch
SCHOOL LA
HOSPITAL MEADOW COTTS
Goodnestone
Copman's Cottages
THE STREET
PAST TO MILL LA
PH
1
Goodnestone Park Gdns
Goodnestone House
Long Wood
Chillenden Windmill
Goodnestone Park
54
24 A 25 B C 25 D 26 E F

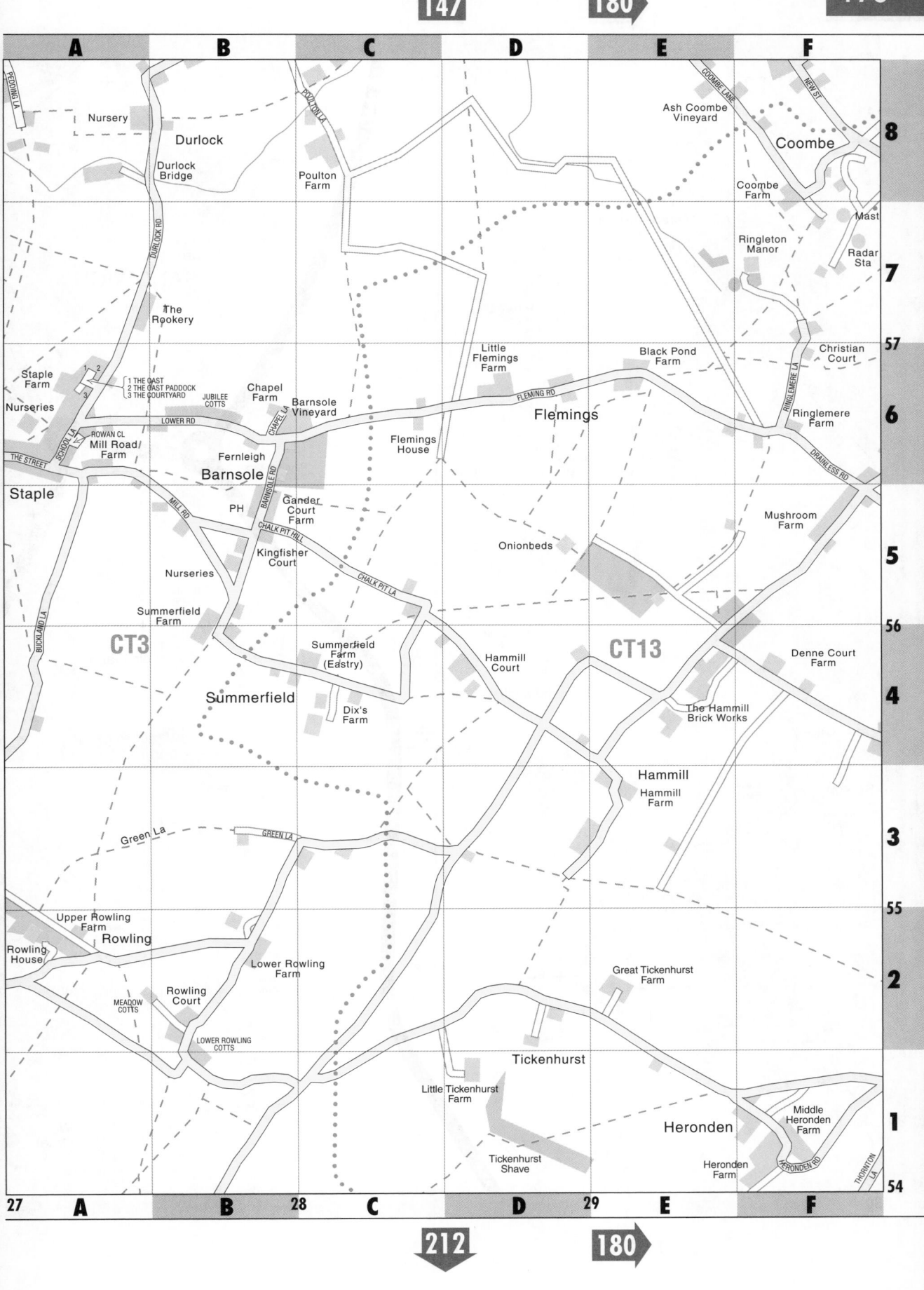

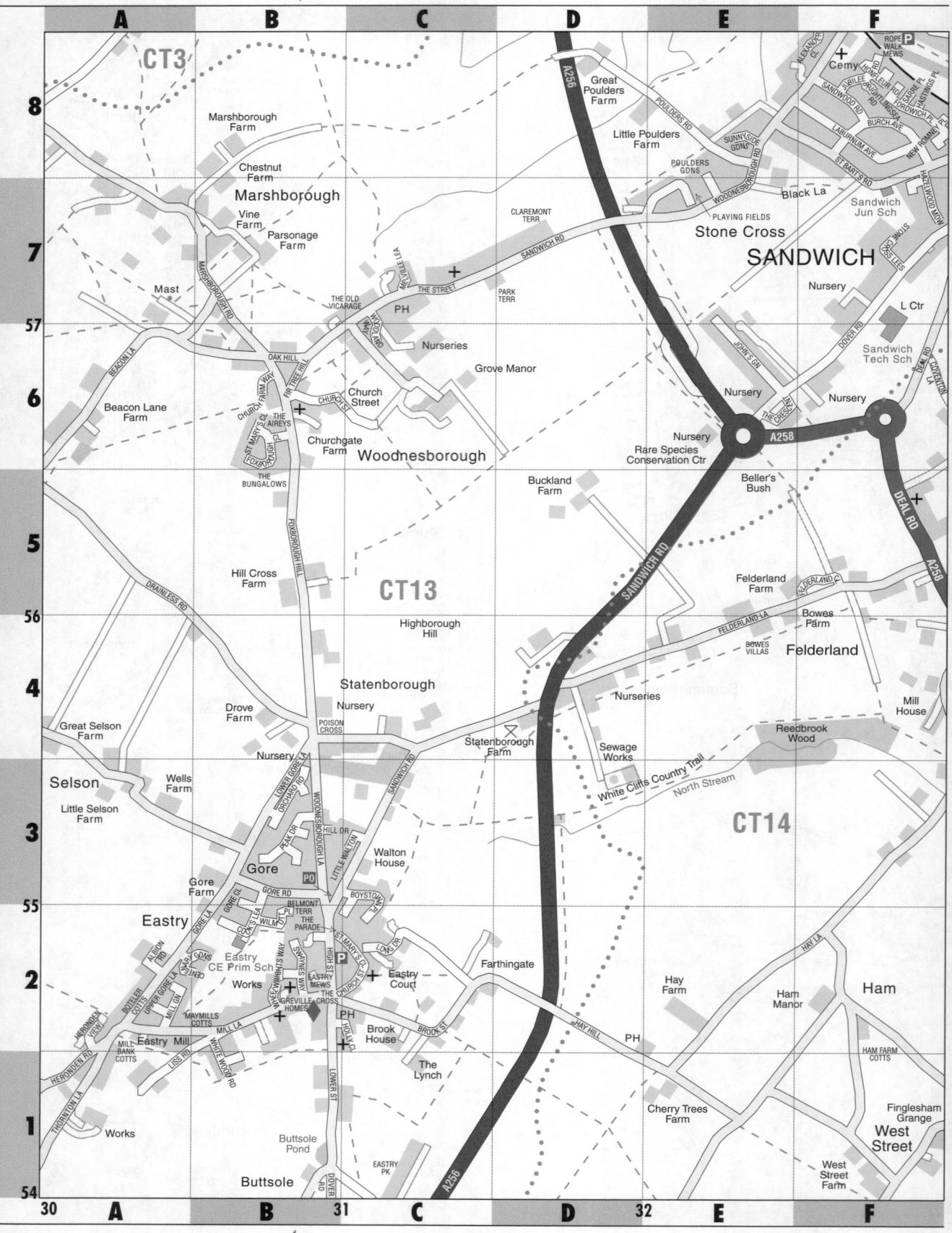

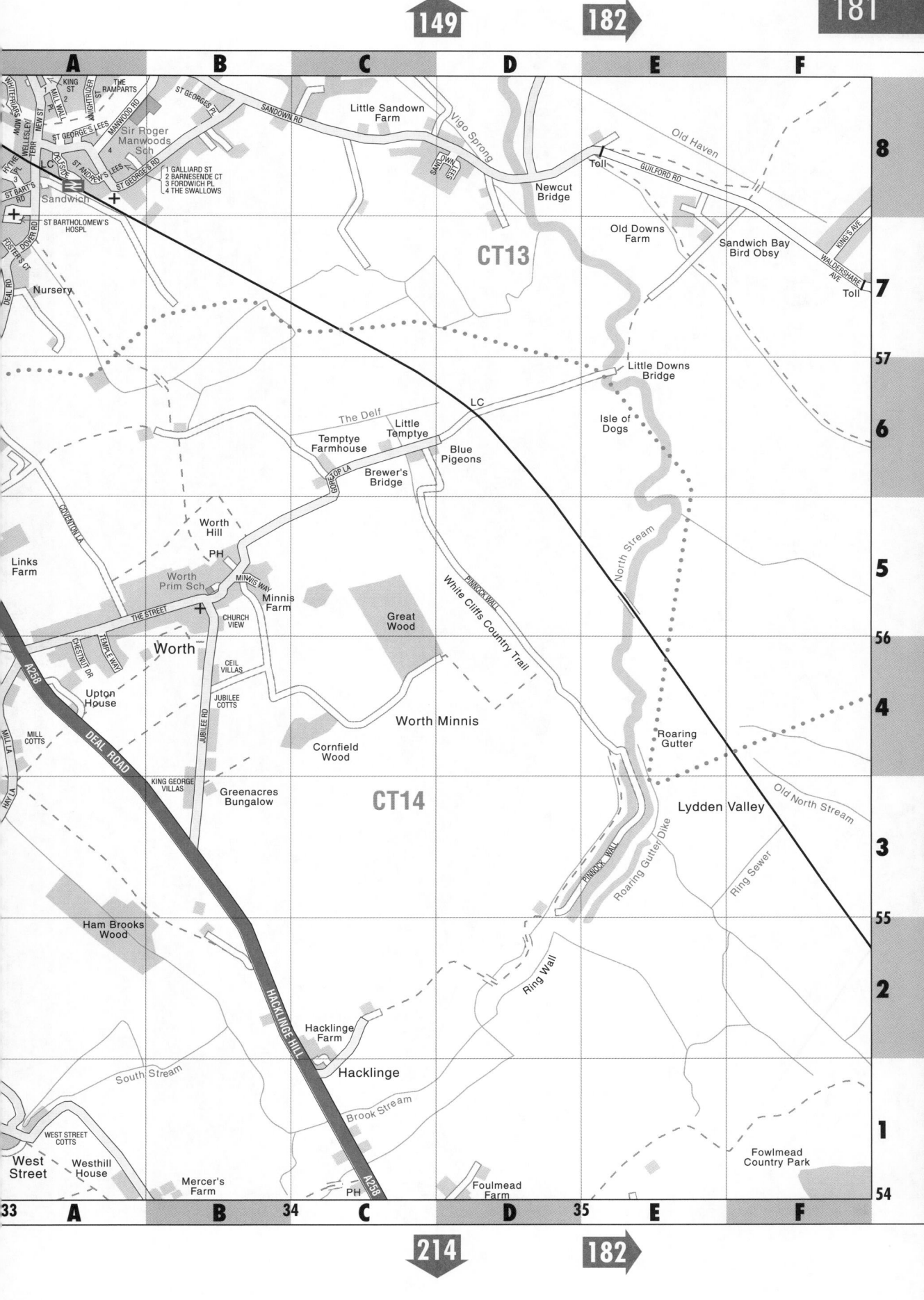

A   B   C   D   E   F

8

KING ST
MILL WALL
THE RAMPARTS
NEW ST
ST GEORGE'S PL
ST GEORGE'S LEES
SANDOWN RD
Little Sandown Farm
Vigo Sprong
Old Haven
Toll
GUILFORD RD

WHITEFRIARS MDW
WELLESLEY TERR
MANWOOD RD
Sir Roger Manwoods Sch
1 GALLIARD ST
2 BARNESENDE CT
3 FORDWICH PL
4 THE SWALLOWS
SANDOWN LEES
Newcut Bridge
Old Downs Farm
Sandwich Bay Bird Obsy
KING'S AVE
WALDERSHARE AVE

HYTHE
ST BART'S RD
ST ANDREW'S RD
DEAL RD
ST GEORGE'S RD
LC
Sandwich
St Bartholomew's Hospl
FOSTER'S CT
DOVER RD
Nursery

CT13

Toll

7

57

Little Downs Bridge

The Delf
Little Temptye
Temptye Farmhouse
Blue Pigeons
LC
Isle of Dogs

6

Brewer's Bridge
GORSOP LA
Worth Hill
PH
Worth Prim Sch
MINNIS WAY
Minnis Farm
Great Wood
White Cliffs Country Trail
PINNOCK WALL
North Stream

COVERTON LA
Links Farm
Worth
THE STREET
CHURCH VIEW
CEIL VILLAS
EMR'E WAY
CHESTNUT DR

5

56

Upton House
JUBILEE COTTS
Worth Minnis
Roaring Gutter

4

MILL COTTS
A258
DEAL ROAD
MILL LA
KING GEORGE VILLAS
JUBILEE RD
Greenacres Bungalow
Cornfield Wood

CT14

Lydden Valley
Old North Stream

PINNOCK WALL
Roaring Gutter Dike
Ring Sewer

3

55

Ham Brooks Wood
HACKLINGE HILL
Ring Wall

2

Hacklinge Farm
Hacklinge
South Stream
Brook Stream
A258

1

WEST STREET COTTS
West Street
Westhill House
Mercer's Farm
PH
Foulmead Farm
Foulmead Farm
Fowlmead Country Park

54

181

Sandwich Bay

Royal
St George's
Golf Links

KING'S AVE

COASTGUARD
COTTS

NORTH RD

PRINCES DR

Sandwich Bay
Estate

WHITEHALL

WALDERSHARE AVE

SHAWDON AVE

FAIRWAY 1
THE SANCTUARY 2
GUILFORD HO 3
THE DUNES 4

CAMBRIDGE AVE

DICKSON'S
CNR

Lyddcourt
Stile

CT13

Lydden

Mary Bax's
Stone

Saxon Shore Way

White Cliffs Country Trail

GREENACRES

Old North Stream

CT14

Tenants
Hills

Walnut Tree
Farm

REDHOUSE WALL

CH

Redhouse
Farm

GOLF RD

Penfield Sewer

CANUTE RD

SANDOWN RD

Sandown Castle
(remains of)

1 CASTLE WLK
2 CANUTE WLK

THE MARINA

GOLF CT 1
LINKS CT 2
WALCHEREN CL 3

ETHELBERT RD

GODWYN
RD

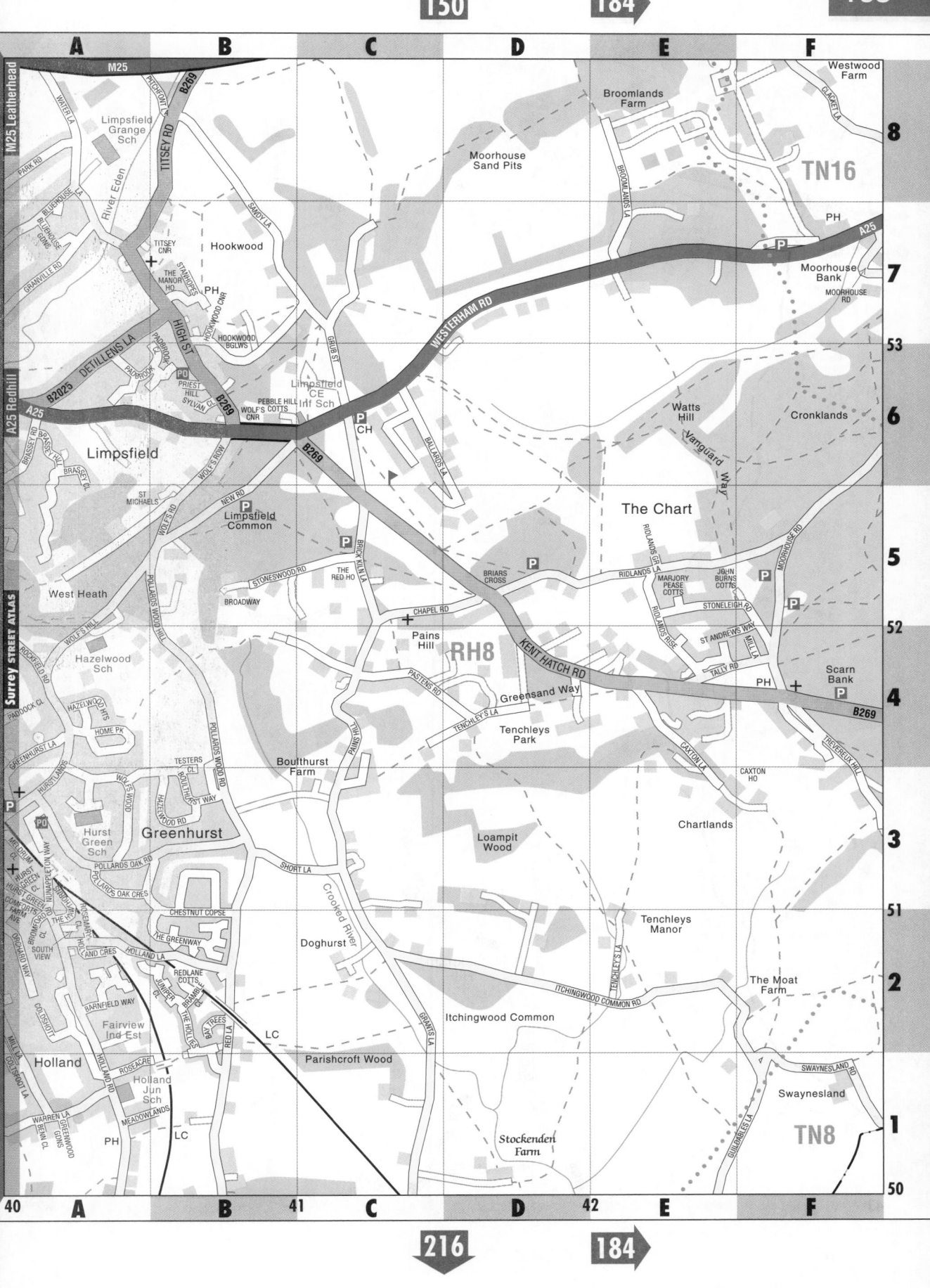

150
184
216
184

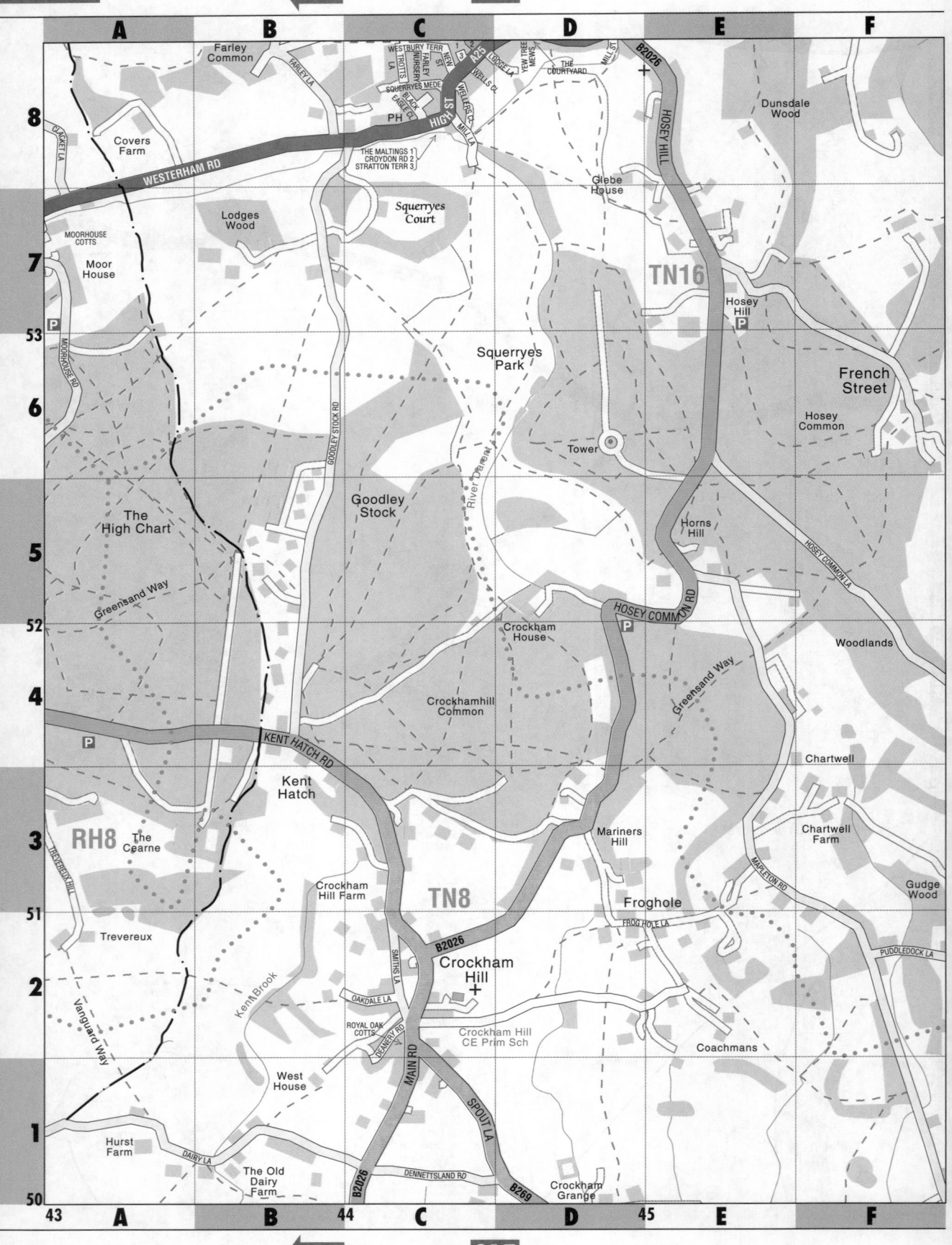

183
151

183
217

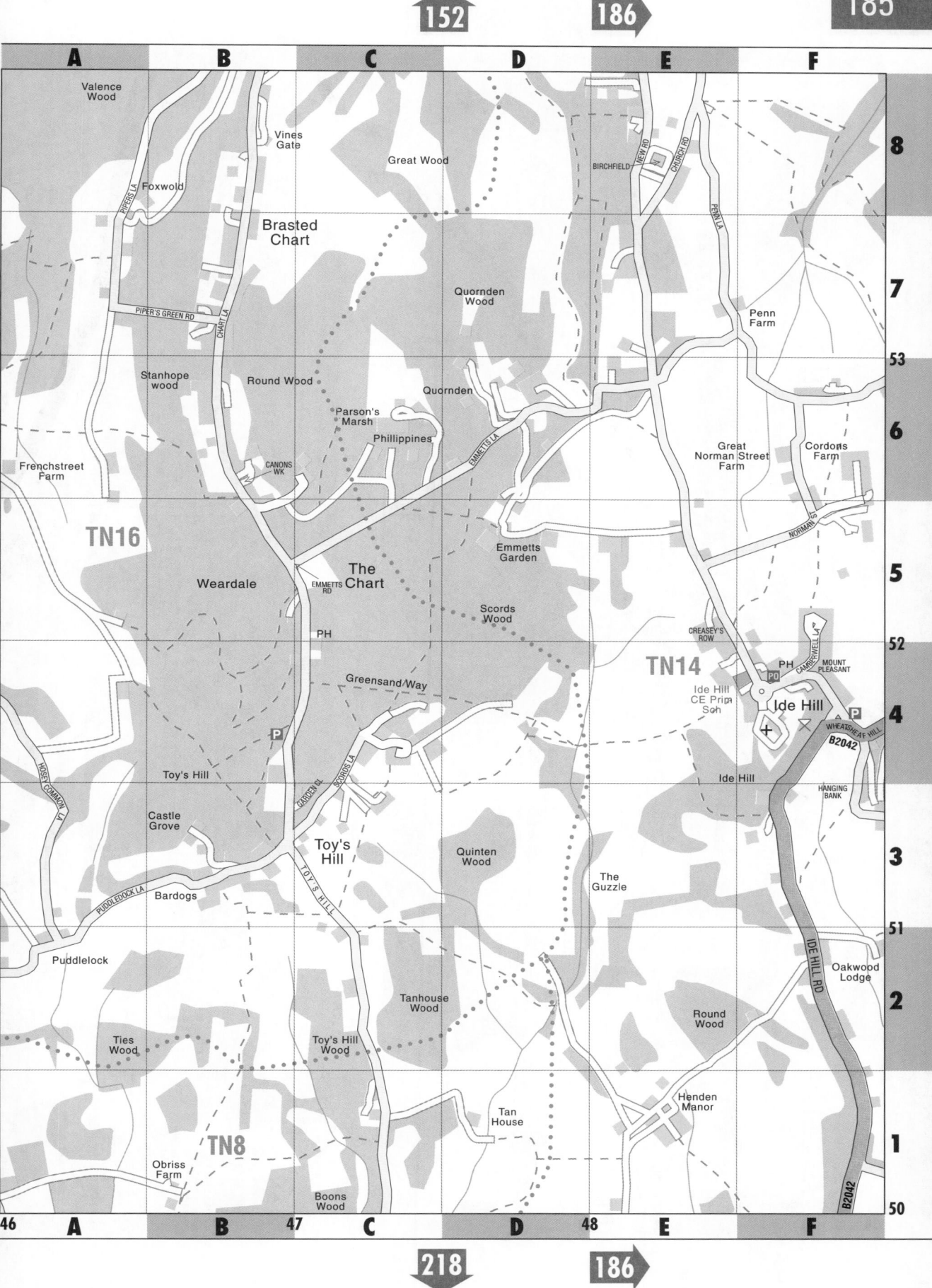

← 185
↑ 153

A   B   C   D   E   F

8

Willow Wood

Greenlane
Wood

Dibden

New
Beacon
Sch

DIBDEN LA

TN13

Hawks
Wood

Whitley

Mildridge
Wood

BACK LA

A21

SEVENOAKS BY-PASS

7

53

Whitley Forest

Mill Bank
Wood

Brook
Place

PH

TN13

OAK LA

6

Whitley
Row

Apps
Hollow

Roundabout
Wood

Dust
Wood

CHAPEL
WLK

Hyde's
Forest

Pitfield Wood

GRACIOUS LANE END

WHITE HOUSE LA

5

NIGHTINGALE LA

THE
PANTYLES

Goathurst
Common

York's
Hill

Sheephill
Wood

RYCROFT LA

WHITE HOUSE RD

52

Everlands

Bayley's
Hill

4

P

Brockhill
Wood

Stubbs Wood

TN14

Greensand Way

Hanging
Bank

Yorkshill
Farm

Harbour
Hook

Hatchlands
Farm

BAYLEY'S HILL

Wickhurst
Manor

WICKHURST RD

3

Boarhill

51

2

Bowzell
Farm

BOWZELL RD

1

Bowzell Wood

Scollops
Farm

Old House
Farm

50

49   A   B   50   C   D   51   E   F

A B C D E F

8
Fawke Farm House
Fawke Common
Bitchet Common
Broadhoath Wood

7
CHESTNUT WALK
Redlands Wood
Starvecrow House
One Tree Hill P
Shingle Hill
Wilmot Hill

53
Carter's Hill
Rooks Hill
Greensand Way
Greensand Way

6
Greensand Way
Kettleshill Farm
CARTER'S HILL
TN15
ROOKS HILL
Budd's Dell

5
Black Charles
FORGE VIEW
Absalom's Farm
Ducks Grove
Budd's Green
Cold Blows
Valley Farm
UNDERRIVER HOUSE RD
Underriver House
MOTE RD

52
Underriver
PH +
Budd's Toll

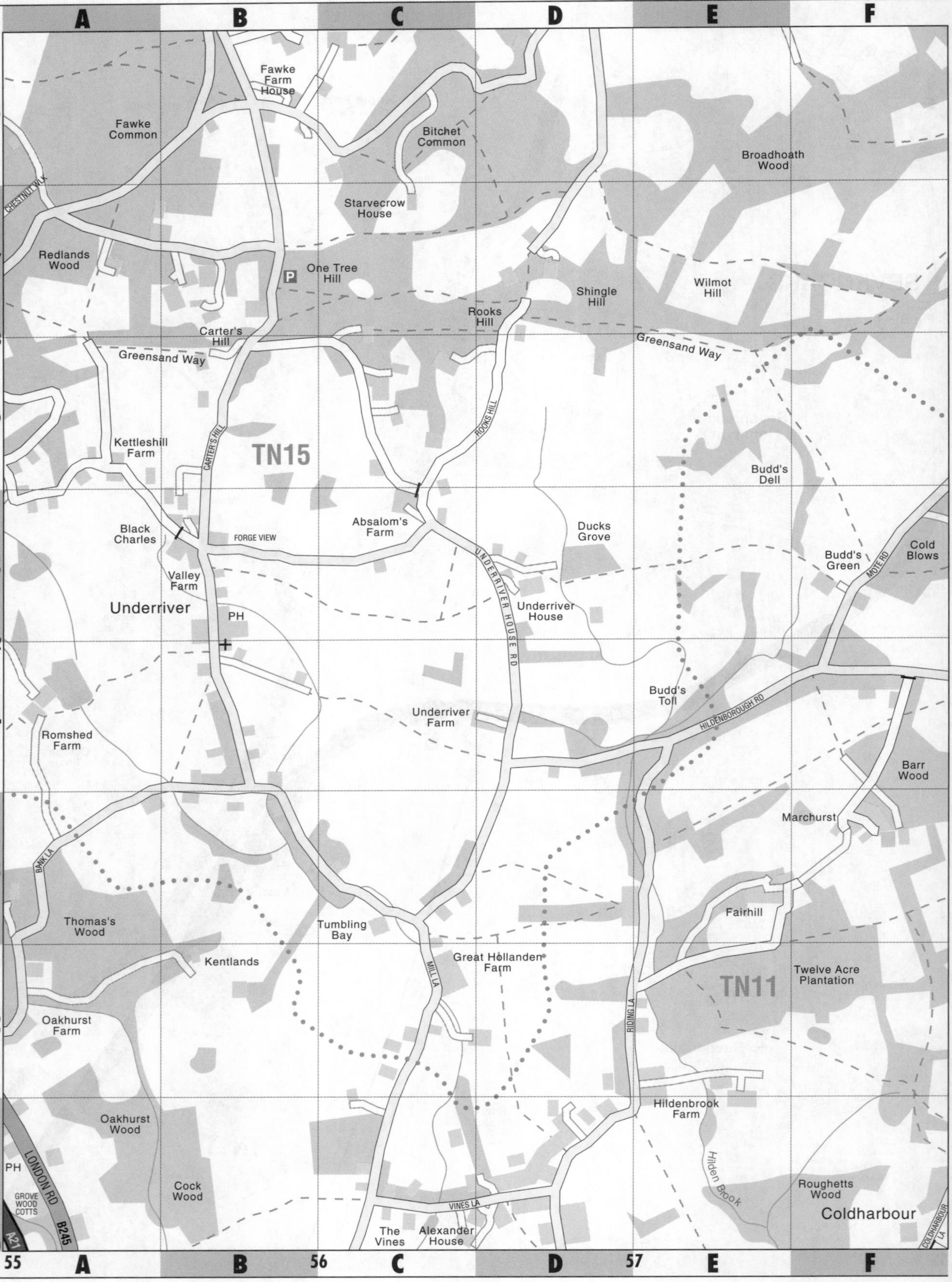

4
Romshed Farm
Underriver Farm
HILDENBOROUGH RD
Barr Wood
Marchurst

3
BANK LA
Fairhill

51
Thomas's Wood
Tumbling Bay
Kentlands
Great Hollanden Farm
TN11
Twelve Acre Plantation

2
Oakhurst Farm
MILL LA
RIDING LA

1
PH
LONDON RD
GROVE WOOD COTTS
B245
Oakhurst Wood
Cock Wood
Hildenbrook Farm
Hilden Brook
Roughetts Wood
Coldharbour

50
A21
The Vines
Alexander House
VINES LA
COLDHARBOUR LA

55 A B 56 C D 57 E F

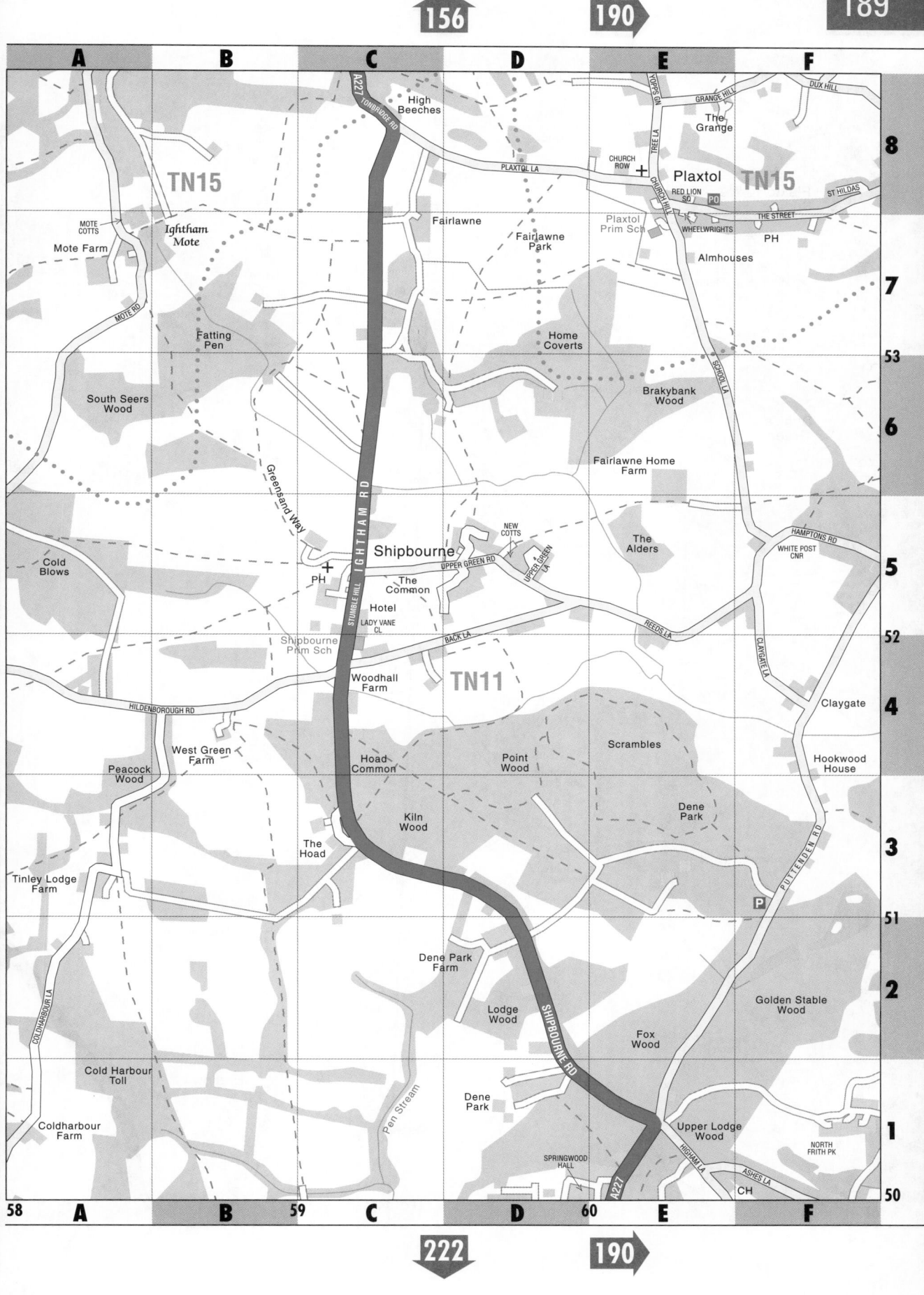

A B C D E F

8

TN15

Mote
Cotts

Mote Farm

Ightham
Mote

High
Beeches

Fairlawne

YOPPS GN

GRANGE HILL

DUX HILL

TREE LA

CHURCH
ROW

CHURCH HILL

The
Grange

Plaxtol

RED LION
SQ
PO

ST HILDAS

THE STREET

PH

TN15

Plaxtol
Prim Sch

WHEELWRIGHTS

Almhouses

PLAXTOL LA

7

53

MOTE RD

Fatting
Pen

South Seers
Wood

Fairlawne
Park

Home
Coverts

Brakybank
Wood

SCHOOL LA

6

Greensand Way

IGHTHAM RD

Fairlawne Home
Farm

5

Cold
Blows

STUMBLE HILL

PH

Shipbourne

The
Common

Hotel

LADY VANE
CL

UPPER GREEN RD

NEW
COTTS

UPPER GREEN LA

The Alders

HAMPTONS RD

WHITE POST
CNR

52

Shipbourne
Prim Sch

BACK LA

REEDS LA

CLAYGATE LA

Woodhall
Farm

TN11

Claygate

4

HILDENBOROUGH RD

West Green
Farm

Hoad
Common

Point
Wood

Scrambles

Hookwood
House

Peacock
Wood

Kiln
Wood

Dene
Park

PULTENDEN RD

3

51

Tinley Lodge
Farm

The
Hoad

COLDHARBOUR LA

Dene Park
Farm

Lodge
Wood

SHIPBOURNE RD

Fox
Wood

Golden Stable
Wood

P

2

Cold Harbour
Toll

Dene
Park

Upper Lodge
Wood

NORTH
FRITH PK

Coldharbour
Farm

Pen Stream

SPRINGWOOD
HALL

A227

HIGHAM LA

ASHES LA

CH

1

50

A B C D E F

8

DUX HILL
SHRUBSHALL MDW
BOURNE VALE
THE STREET
HYDERS FORGE
COUNCIL HOS
Plaxtol Spoute
TN15
BROOK LA
OLD SOAR RD
Broadfield Farm
Quarry Wood

SPINNERS WENTS
THE HURST
SWANTON RD

7
ALLENS LA
Allen's Farm
Wealdway
PECKHAM HURST RD
Crooked Chimneys
GOVER VIEW
Peckham Hurst

53
+ LONG MILL LA
Mills
Upper Farm
ROUGHWAY LA
Rats Castle
GOVER HILL
ME18

BARTON COTTS
Roughway
Gover Hill

6
Dunk's Green
Greensand Way
Stickland's Wood
Adams Well Farm
FORGE LA

PH
DUNK'S GREEN RD

5
Puttenden Manor Farm
Fish Farm
Hamptons
PILLAR BOX LA
PARK RD
Lavender Nursery
Oxen Hoath

52
HAMPTONS RD
OXENHOATH RD
TN11

4
River Bourne
Hamptons Park
Four Wents
Oxen Hoath Park
Park Farm
Vines Farm
MATTHEWS LA

Oxenhoath Mill Farm

3
Clearhedges Wood
Frith Wood
Mount Pleasant
Cricketers Cottage Farm
Pear Tree Farm

51
The Common
COMMON RD
CARPENTERS LA
A26

2
HIGH HOUSE LA
Stallion's Green
STEERS PL
PALMERS BROOK
LONEWOOD WAY
CEMETERY LA
PH
Cemy

1
Yewtree Wood
North Frith Farm
Hope Farm
MILL VIEW
Hadlow
HADLOW PK
MAIDSTONE RD
JAMES CL
SPAR CL
A26

THE PADDOCK
HOPE AVE
MARSHALL GDNS
TWYFORD RD
TANTER RD
SCHOOL LA
BROOKFIELDS
THE CH'RRY ORCH
GREAT ELMS
SMITHERS CL
CHESFIELD CL

50
WATER SLIPPE
FREEHOLD
THE...

61 A 62 B C 63 D E F

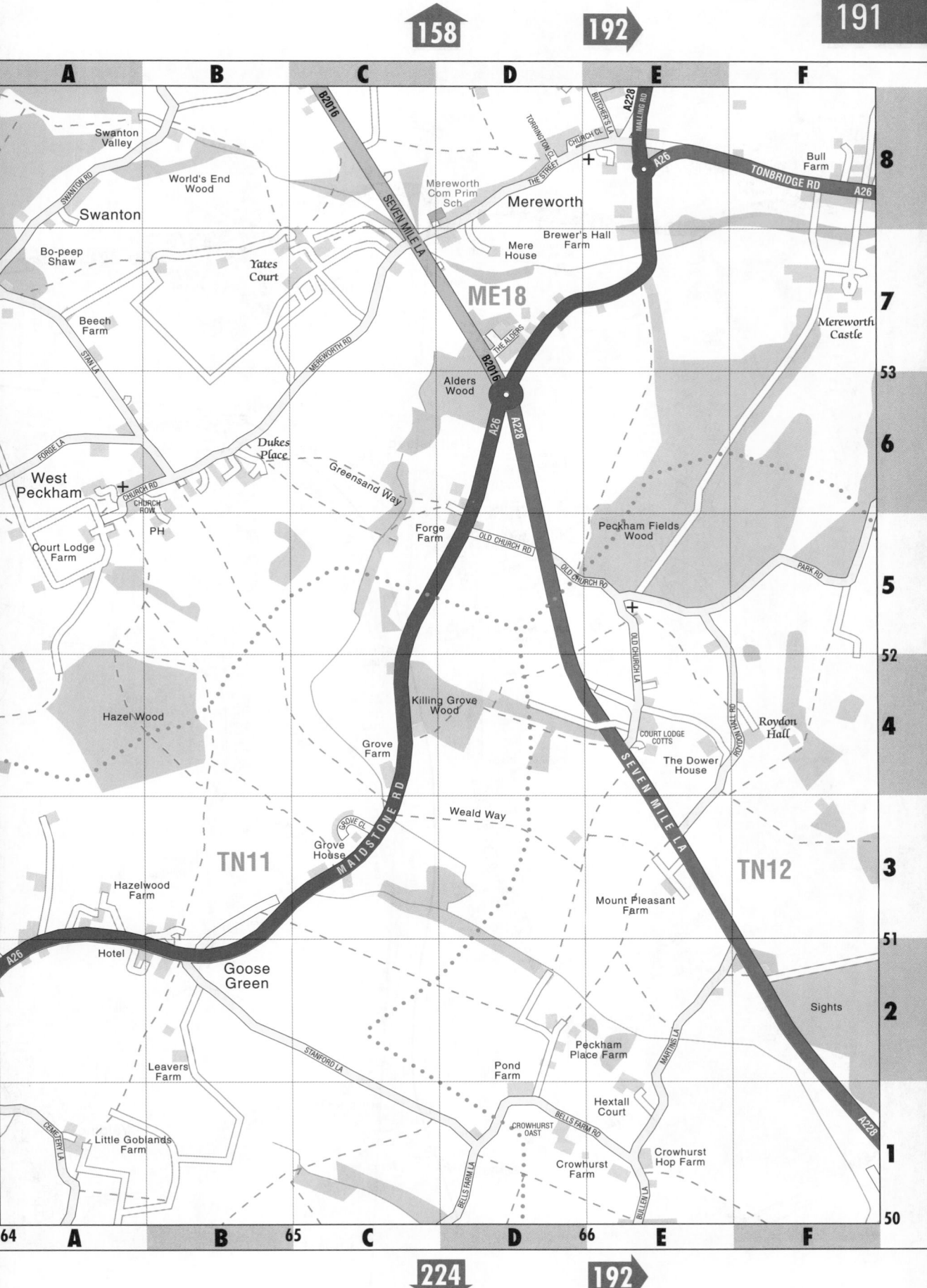

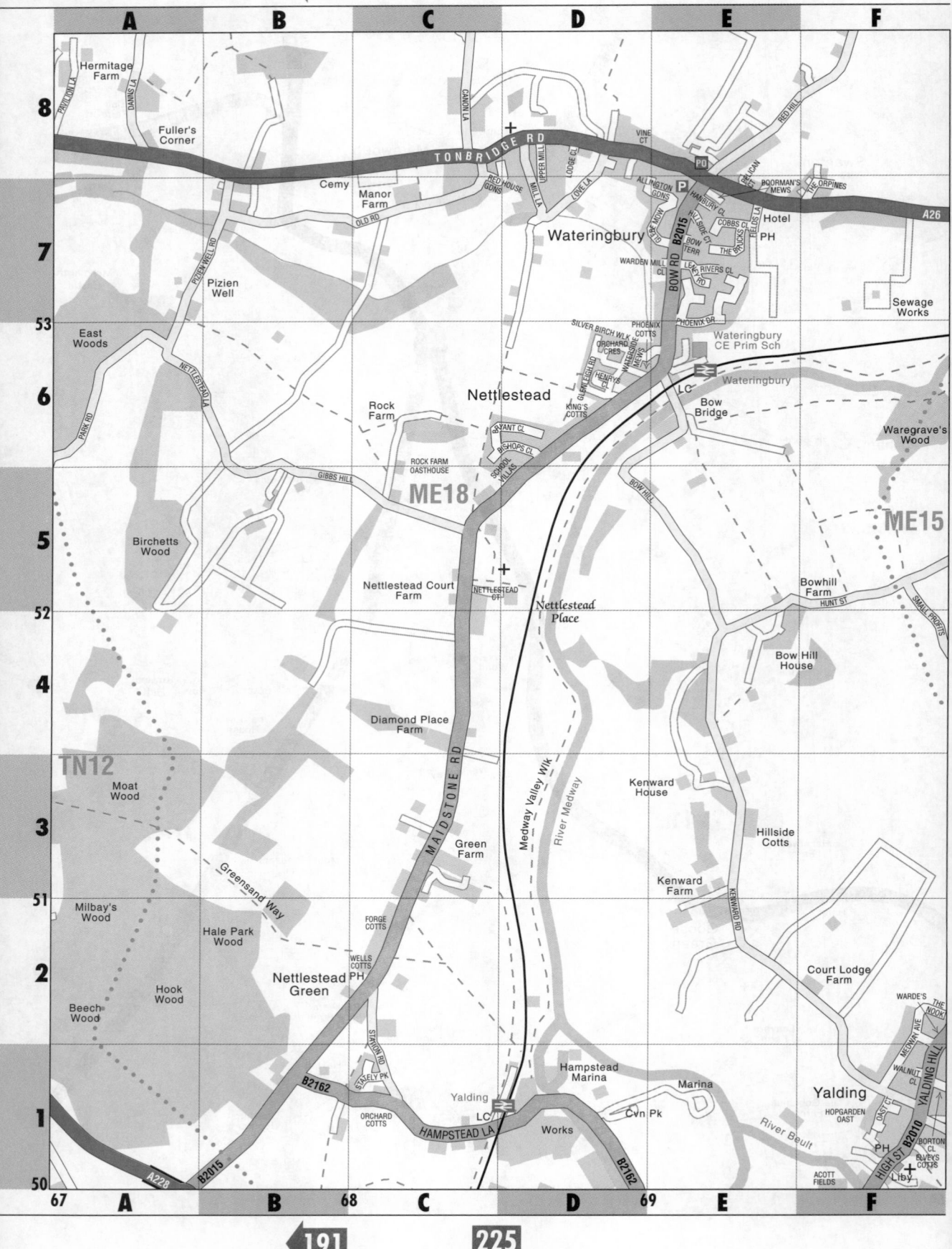

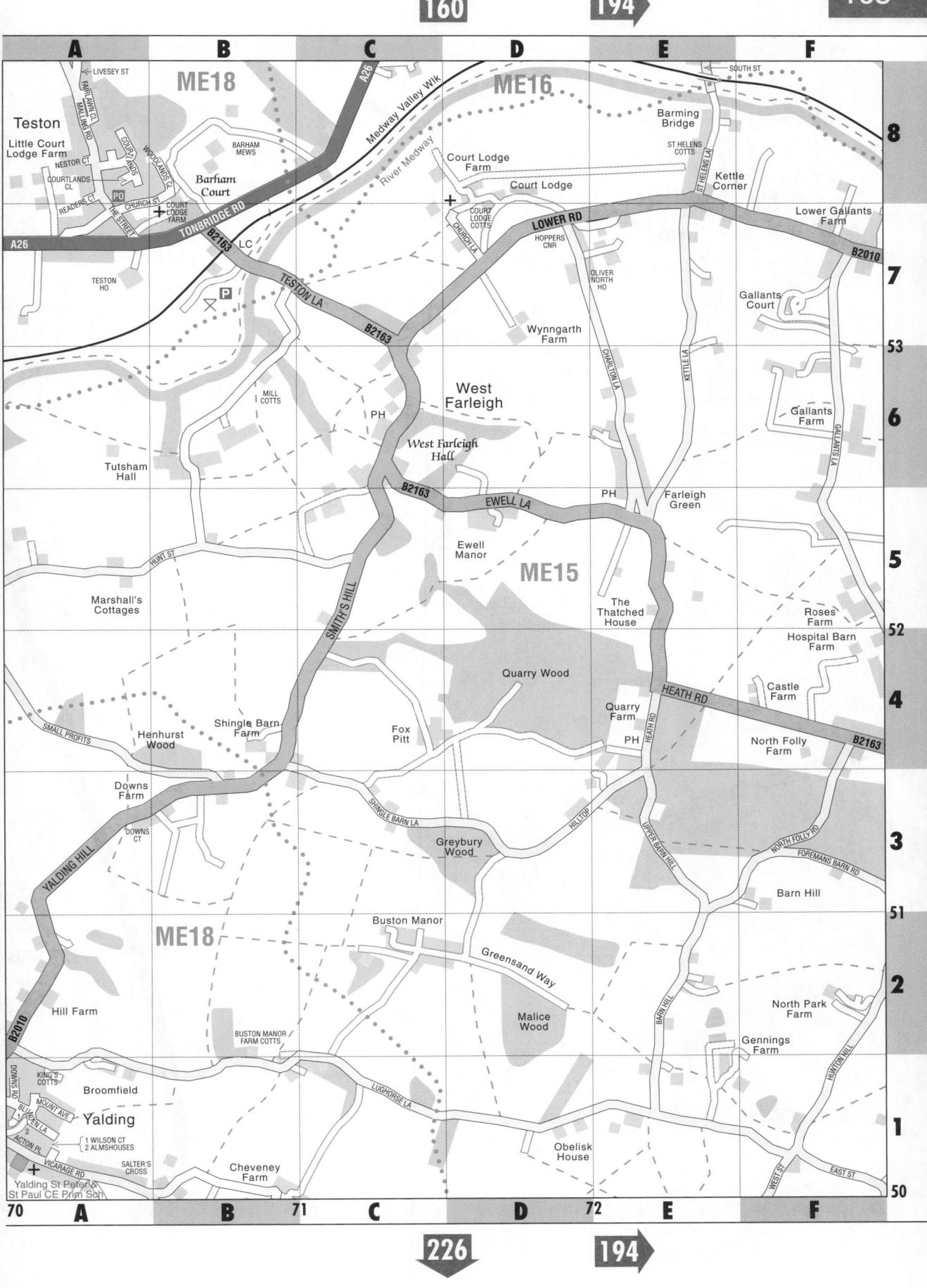

A   B   C   D   E   F

← LIVESEY ST

ME18

← FAIRLAWN CL
MALLING RD

Teston

Little Court
Lodge Farm

NESTOR CT

COPPLANDS

WOODLANDS CL

BARHAM
MEWS

ME16

Barming
Bridge

COURTLANDS
CL

READERS CT

PO

THE STREET

CHURCH ST

Barham
Court

ST HELENS
COTTS

Court Lodge
Farm

Court Lodge

Kettle
Corner

Lower Gallants
Farm

A26

TONBRIDGE RD

Court Lodge
Farm

LC

COURT
LODGE
COTTS

LOWER RD

HOPPERS
CNR

ST HELENS LA

B2010

TESTON
HO

B2163

TESTON LA

CHURCH LA

OLIVER
NORTH
HO

P

B2163

MILL
COTTS

PH

Wynngarth
Farm

West
Farleigh

CHARLTON LA

KETTLE LA

Gallants
Court

53

7

8

Gallants
Farm

6

Tutsham
Hall

West Farleigh
Hall

GALLANTS LA

HUNT ST

B2163

EWELL LA

PH

Farleigh
Green

Marshall's
Cottages

Ewell
Manor

SMITH'S HILL

ME15

PH

The Thatched
House

Roses
Farm

Hospital Barn
Farm

Quarry Wood

5

52

Shingle Barn
Farm

Fox
Pitt

Quarry
Farm

Castle
Farm

SMALL PROFITS

Henhurst
Wood

HEATH RD

Downs
Farm

SHINGLE BARN LA

PH

HEATH RD

North Folly
Farm

B2163

4

DOWNS
CT

Greybury
Wood

HILLTOP

UPPER BARN HILL

NORTH FOLLY RD

FOREMANS BARN RD

Barn Hill

3

51

YALDING HILL

ME18

Buston Manor

Greensand Way

BARN HILL

North Park
Farm

2

B2010

Hill Farm

BUSTON MANOR
FARM COTTS

Malice
Wood

Gennings
Farm

GRUMITH HILL

KING'S
COTTS

DOWNS RD

Broomfield

LUGHORSE LA

MOUNT AVE

BLUBELL LA

Yalding

1 WILSON CT
2 ALMSHOUSES

Obelisk
House

WEST ST

EAST ST

1

ACTON PL

VICARAGE RD

SALTER'S
CROSS

Cheveney
Farm

Yalding St Peter &
St Paul CE Prim Sch

50

70   A   B   71   C   D   72   E   F

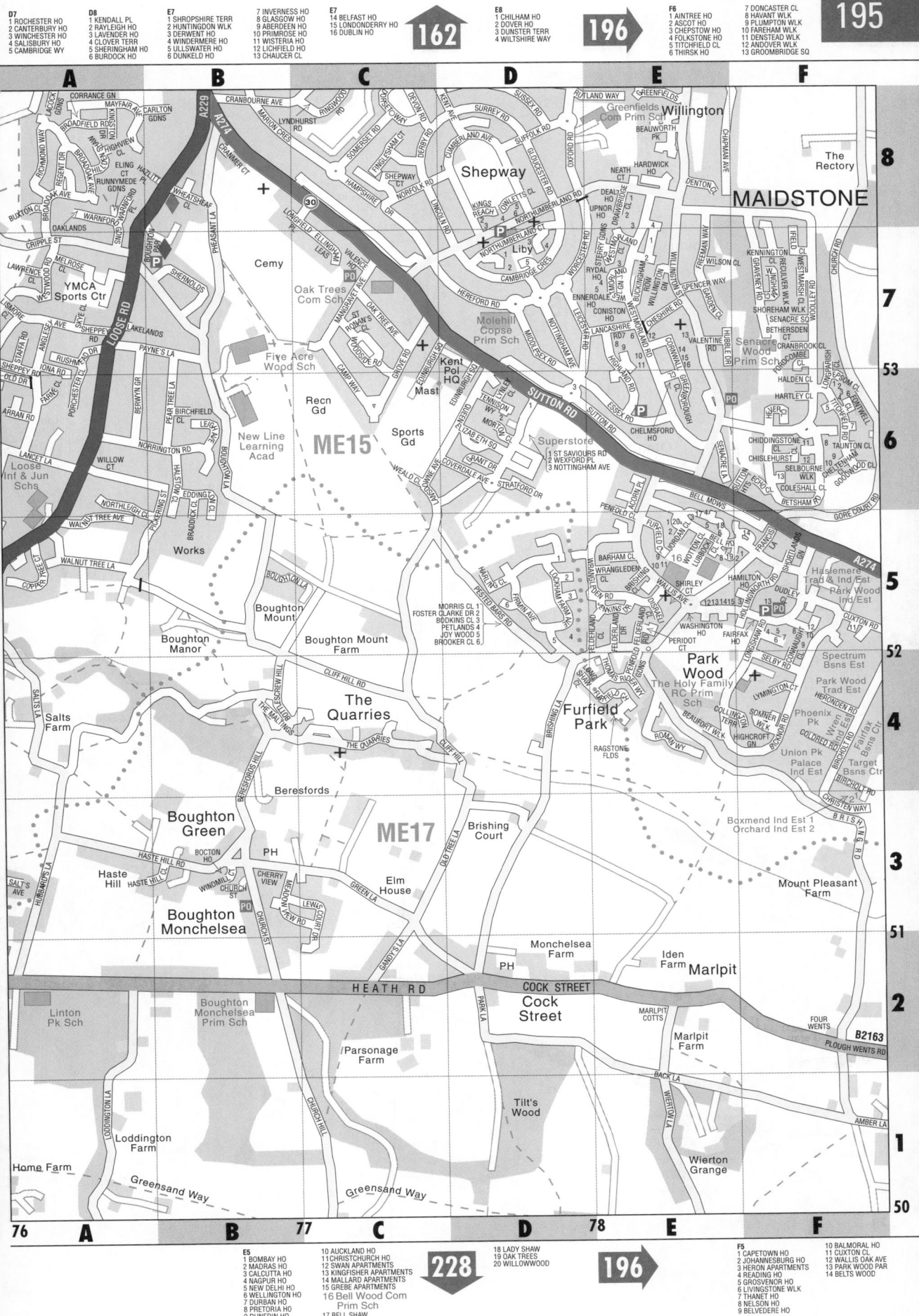

162
196

D7
1 ROCHESTER HO
2 CANTERBURY HO
3 WINCHESTER HO
4 SALISBURY HO
5 CAMBRIDGE WY

D8
1 KENDALL PL
2 RAYLEIGH HO
3 LAVENDER HO
4 CLOVER TERR
5 SHERINGHAM HO
6 BURDOCK HO

E7
1 SHROPSHIRE TERR
2 HUNTINGDON WLK
3 DERWENT HO
4 WINDERMERE HO
5 ULLSWATER HO
6 DUNKELD HO

7 INVERNESS HO
8 GLASGOW HO
9 ABERDEEN HO
10 PRIMROSE HO
11 WISTERIA HO
12 LICHFIELD HO
13 CHAUCER CL

E7
14 BELFAST HO
15 LONDONDERRY HO
16 DUBLIN HO

E8
1 CHILHAM HO
2 DOVER HO
3 DUNSTER TERR
4 WILTSHIRE WAY

F6
1 AINTREE HO
2 ASCOT HO
3 CHEPSTOW HO
4 FOLKSTONE HO
5 TITCHFIELD CL
6 THIRSK HO

7 DONCASTER CL
8 HAVANT WLK
9 PLUMPTON WLK
10 FAREHAM WLK
11 DENSTEAD WLK
12 ANDOVER WLK
13 GROOMBRIDGE SQ

228
196

E5
1 BOMBAY HO
2 MADRAS HO
3 CALCUTTA HO
4 NAGPUR HO
5 NEW DELHI HO
6 WELLINGTON HO
7 DURBAN HO
8 PRETORIA HO
9 DUNEDIN HO

10 AUCKLAND HO
11 CHRISTCHURCH HO
12 SWAN APARTMENTS
13 KINGFISHER APARTMENTS
14 MALLARD APARTMENTS
15 GREBE APARTMENTS
16 Bell Wood Com
   Prim Sch
17 BELL SHAW

18 LADY SHAW
19 OAK TREES
20 WILLOWWOOD

F5
1 CAPETOWN HO
2 JOHANNESBURG HO
3 HERON APARTMENTS
4 READING HO
5 GROSVENOR HO
6 LIVINGSTONE WLK
7 THANET HO
8 NELSON HO
9 BELVEDERE HO

10 BALMORAL HO
11 CUXTON CL
12 WALLIS OAK AVE
13 PARK WOOD PAR
14 BELTS WOOD

195
163

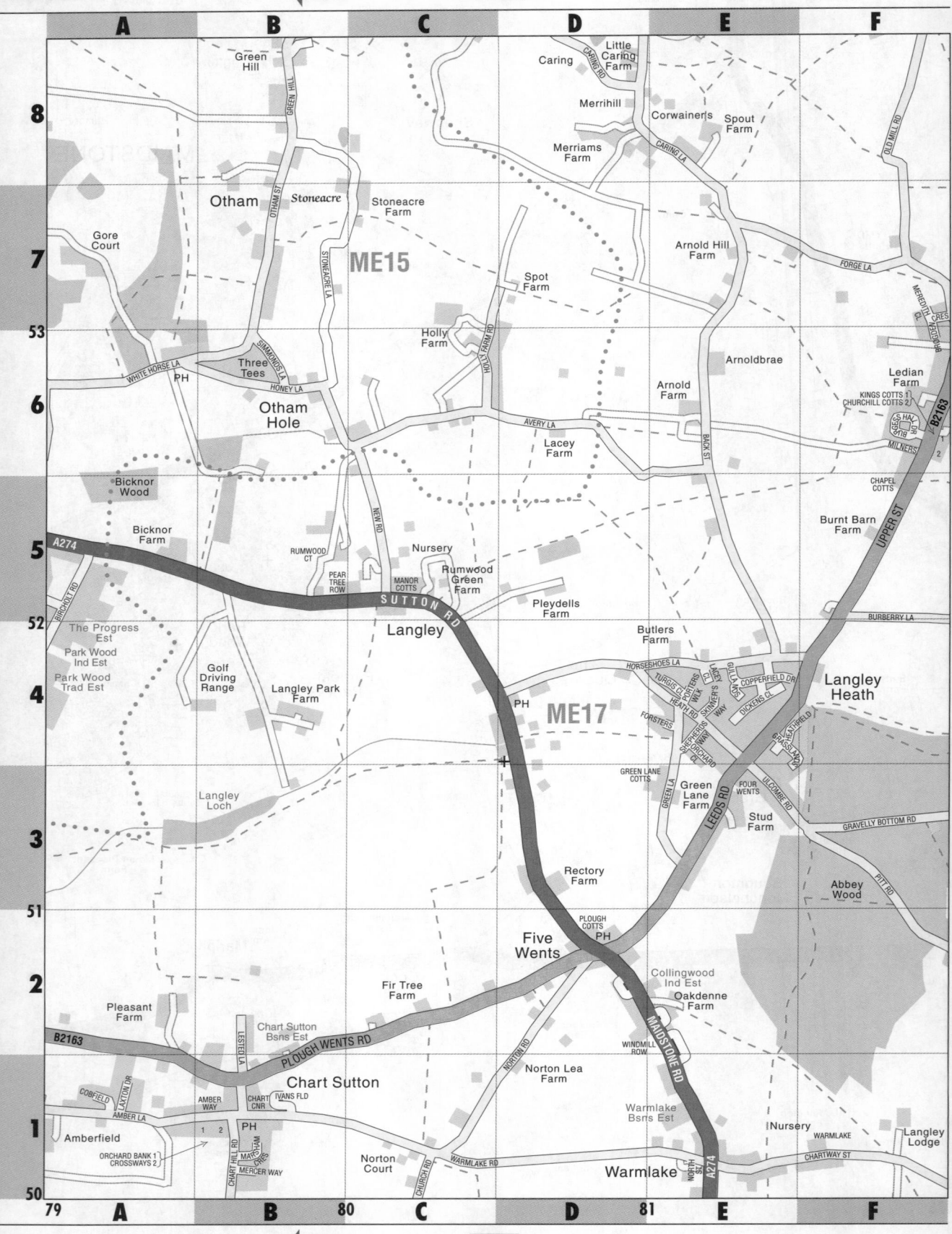

164
198

A   B   C   D   E   F

8

Warren
Wood

Sewage
Works

Leeds &
Broomfield
CE Prim
Sch

Ashbank

PH

CH

7

Leeds

ASHBANK
COTTS

Battel
Hall

Leeds
Castle

Forge
House

53

PH

LOWER ST

WYKEHAM GR

GEORGE LA

PENFOLD HILL

B2163

A20

M20

HOSPITAL RD

ASHFORD RD

GREENWAY COURT RD

GREENWAY LA

A20

M20

Abbey
Farm

The
Great
Water

CHEGWORTH
LA

6

FARMER CL

UPPER ST

Chegworth

River Len

BURBERRY LA

Church
Farm

Broomfield

Roses
Farm

5

Chegworth
Court

Park Barn
Farm

PARK BARN RD

ME17

CHEGWORTH RD

52

Scrub
Wood

BROOMFIELD RD

4

Glebe
Dene

King's
Wood

3

WATER LA

Apiary
Bsns Pk

The
Apiary

PO

WHITEHALL DR

ASHFORD DR

CHARLESFORD AVE

Kingswood

Kingswood
Prim Sch

51

Kingswood
Farm

GRAVELLY BOTTOM RD

Works

THORNEYCROFT
CL

ELDER
CL

CHESTNUT DR

LARCH CL

TALL TREES
CL

COPPERFIELD CL

THE
WYCHLINGS

BUSHY GR

IVY CL

WALDENS
MEWS

BELL WAY

THE
WALK

CAYSER DR

WILDWOOD CL

LENHAM RD

2

PITT RD

CROSS DR

Cherry
Tree
Farm

HEATHERWOOD
CL

HOLLY TREE CL

GREENSAND
RIDGE

College
Farm

1

BRIDGEFIELD

CHARTWAY ST

Chartway
Street

CHARLTON LA

Street
Farm

Manor
Farm

MORRY LA

ULCOMBE HILL

WORKHOUSE LA

CH

50

82   A   B   83   C   D   84   E   F

230
198

197
165

A   B   C   D   E   F

8

GREENWAY COURT RD

No Man's Acre

North Downs Way

Hillside Farm

Stede Hill

COLESDANE

Mount Farm

Court Lodge Farm

PILGRIMS WAY

STEDE HILL

PILGRIMS WAY

7

Greenway Forstal

GREENWAY LA

Garden of England Pk (Mobile Home Pk)

Goddington

Ockley Mead

Court Lodge

Kingboro Farm

53

A20

M20

Holm Mill

HOLM MILL LA

GODDINGTON LA

Trout Farm

Harrietsham CE Prim Sch

Harrietsham

CHIPPENDAYLE DR

CUTBUSH CL

PILGRIMS LAKES

IRELANDS

CHURCH RD

HARRISON DR

ST WELCUMES WAY

The Old Bailey

CHURCH LA

MARLEY RD

MERCER DR

6

CHEGWORTH LA

The Hampshires

WEST ST

HOOK LA

BALDWIN'S

QUESTED WAY

VENS WAY

WHEELWRIGHTS

STATION RD

FORGE MDW

CRICKETERS CL

WILLOW CL

PO

Old

NEW MDW

CHURCH CRES

DOWN HL RISE

DOWNLANDS

A20

ASHFORD RD

LENMEAD

Roebuck Bsns Park

Harrietsham

TAYLOR CT

The Bell Farm

EAST ST

CHURCH RD

RECTORY LA

Mayfield

5

WATER LANE

Waterlane Farm

Pollhill

Spion Kop Farm

River Len

Poplar Farm

Sewage Works

Cherry Tree Farm

Stubble Hill Farm

52

Cherry Gardens

WATER LANE

Works

SANDWAY RD

4

Fairbourne Mill

FAIRBOURNE LA

RUNHAM LA

3

Waterlane Cottages

Fairbourne Manor Farm

Runham Farm

The Firs

M20

51

Affers Wood

2

Heath Orchard

Gaskin Wood

Runham Wood

Wellesley House

MOUNT PLEASANT TERR

GREEN LA

SCHOOL LA

Platt's Heath Prim Sch

Mast

LENHAM RD

GREEN HILL LA

HEADCORN RD

Platt's Heath

1

Hill Farm

Fairbourne Heath

Tillman Gate Farm

Fairbourne Heath Cotts

WINDMILL HILL

PH

ELMSTONE HOLE RD

Greensand Way

Liverton Street

50

85   A   B   86   C   D   87   E   F

ME17

197
231

166
200

A B C D E F

West Street

FLINT LA

Woodside Green

8

Hilltop

Marlow Farm

Tophill Farm

Marley Court

Lea Farm

PILGRIMS WAY

7

FAVERSHAM RD

Highfield

53

Factory

North Downs Way

MARLEY RD

Marley Works

LIMETREE TERR

War Memorial

6

DICKLEY LA

M20

Dickley Wood

ASHFORD RD

HILL CRES

Cemy

Westgate House

FROGMORE WLK 1
NAPOLEON WLK 2
RIVERS WLK 3
MORELLA WLK 4

THE CLOISTERS

Swadelands Sch

MAIDSTONE RD

FORD RD

ROYTON AVE
CHILSTON RD

DOUGLAS RD

Grove House

GROOM WAY

Northdown Bsns Pk

A20

5

LOWER CL

CHERRY CL

SWADELANDS CL

MITCHELL CL

Douglas Almshouses

Atwater Liby

NORTHDOWN CL

Boldrewood Farm

Depot
GRANT'S COTTS

HAM LA

HATCH RD

BEACON RD

ROBINS AVE

HONYWOOD RD

Lenham Prim Sch

MALTHOUSE CL

HIGH ST

THE SQUARE

P

WICKHAM PL

CHURCH SQ

Lenham Ho.

LENHAM SQ GDNS

OLD ASHFORD RD

Ashmill Bsns Pk

52

Lenham

DALE TERR

ROBINS CL

MILL CL

HOUSE RD

CROFT GDNS

PO

TITHE RD

ME17

Tanyard Farm

4

OLD HAM LA

Kiln Wood

Inkstand Meadow Farm

Oxley Wood

Stour Valley Wlk

Great Stour

Nature Reserve

HEADCORN RD

Leadingcross Green

3

SANDWAY RD

Sandway

Sewage Works

51

M20

PH

LENHAM HEATH RD

2

Pleasant Farm

Home Farm

BOUGHTON RD

Ridding Farm

Mount Castle Farm

MOUNT CASTLE LA

Lewsome Farm

Chapel Farm

BOWLEY LA

M20

1

Chilston Park

Chilston Park Hotel

50

88 A B 89 C D 90 E F

232
200

199
167

A   **B**   **C**   **D**   **E**   **F**

8

LONE BARN RD

Payden Street

Bunker's Hill

PANCT ST

SLADE RD

HURSTWOOD RD

Hurst Farm

Warren Lodge Farm

ME13

7

Birch Wood

Warren Street

Stubblefield House

BUNCE COURT RD

Bunce Court

53

WARREN ST

Blue House Farm

Little Pivington Farm

6

Middleton Farm

Water Tower

PH

Oak Farm

COLD HARBOUR RD

Cold Harbour

Great Pivington Farm

HUBBARDS HILL

Glebe Farm

RAYNER HILL

5

RAYNER HILL COTTS

HIGHBOURNE PK

Waterditch Farm

WATERDITCH LA

Westbury Farm

Pilgrims' Way

ME17

North Downs Way

52

A20

Fair View

4

ASHFORD RD

New Shelve Farm

Cobham Farm

Wheatgratten Farm

Old Shelve

3

Old Shelve Farm

COUNTRY WAYS

51

2

Acton Farm

MAIDSTONE RD

TN27

YEW TREE PK

Forstal Cotts

Sand Pit

Shepherd's Farm

HART HILL

MOUNT CASTLE LA

Lenham Forstal

Bolton Farm

1

The Forstal

BULL HILL

THE FORSTAL

LENHAM FORSTAL RD

CRABTREE LA

HEATHFIELD BGLWS

ROSE LA

A20

Lenham Heath

CHARING HEATH RD

50

91   **A**   **B**   **92**   **C**   **D**   **93**   **E**   **F**

199
233

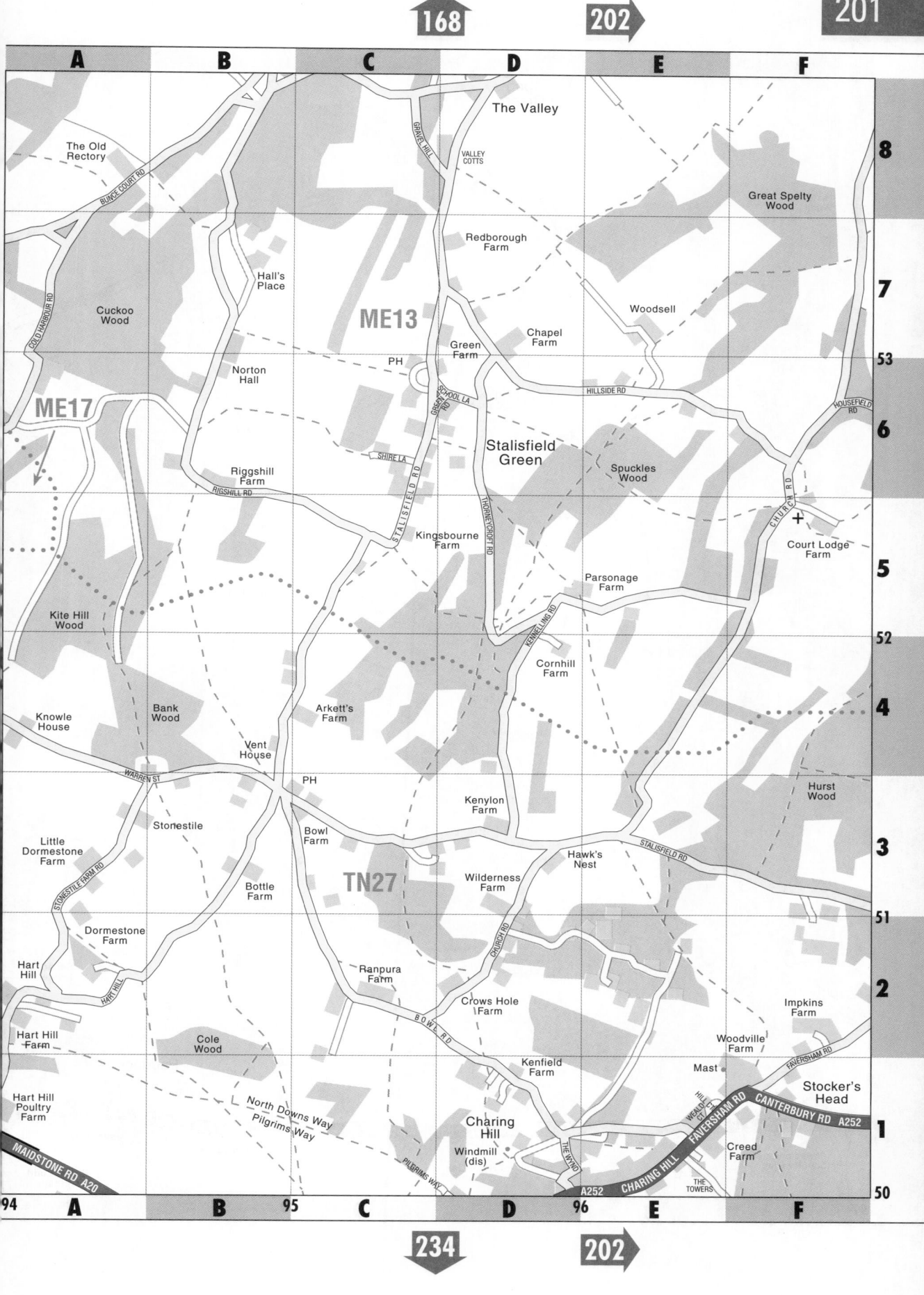

A B C D E F

8

The Valley

The Old
Rectory

GRAVEL HILL

VALLEY
COTTS

Great Spelty
Wood

BUNCE COURT RD

Hall's
Place

Redborough
Farm

7

COLD HARBOUR RD

Cuckoo
Wood

ME13

Woodsell

53

Norton
Hall

Green
Farm

Chapel
Farm

PH

ME17

SCHOOL LA

GREEN HILL

HILLSIDE RD

HOUSEFIELD
RD

6

Riggshill
Farm

SHIRE LA

Stalisfield
Green

Spuckles
Wood

CHURCH RD

RIGGSHILL RD

STALISFIELD RD

Kingsbourne
Farm

THORNEYCROFT RD

+

Court Lodge
Farm

5

Parsonage
Farm

Kite Hill
Wood

KENFIELING RD

52

Knowle
House

Bank
Wood

Arkett's
Farm

Cornhill
Farm

4

Vent
House

Hurst
Wood

WARREN ST

PH

Kenylon
Farm

STALISFIELD RD

3

Stonestile

Bowl
Farm

Hawk's
Nest

Little
Dormestone
Farm

STONESTILE FARM RD

TN27

Bottle
Farm

Wilderness
Farm

CHURCH RD

51

Dormestone
Farm

HART HILL

Ranpura
Farm

Crows Hole
Farm

Impkins
Farm

2

Hart
Hill

BOWL RD

Woodville
Farm

FAVERSHAM RD

Hart Hill
Farm

Cole
Wood

Kenfield
Farm

Mast

Stocker's
Head

CANTERBURY RD A252

CREED Farm

Hart Hill
Poultry
Farm

North Downs Way
Pilgrims Way

Charing
Hill

THE WYND

WEALD WAY

FAVERSHAM RD

1

MAIDSTONE RD A20

PILGRIMS WAY

Windmill
(dis)

A252 CHARING HILL

THE
TOWERS

50

94 A B 95 C D 96 E F

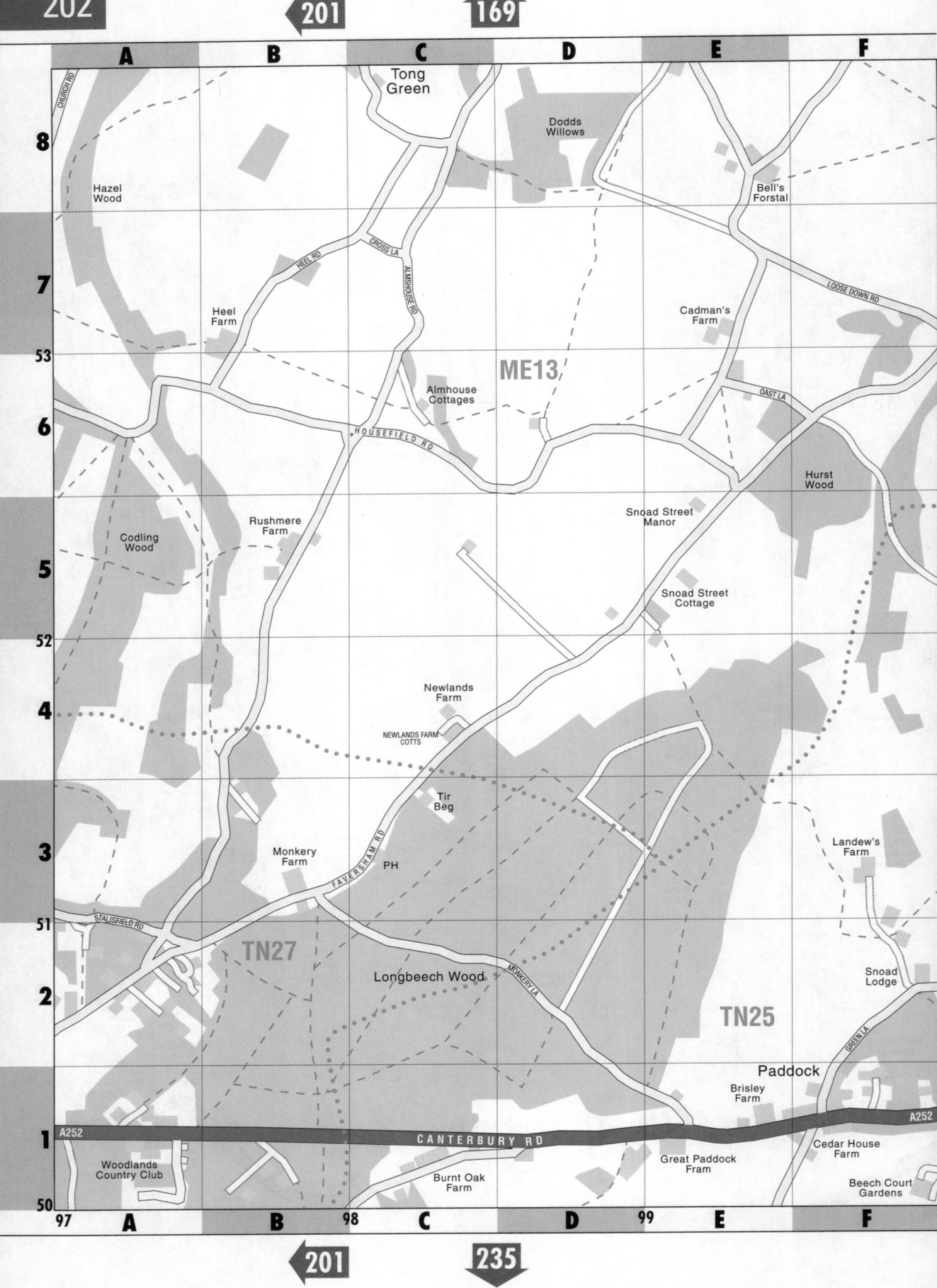

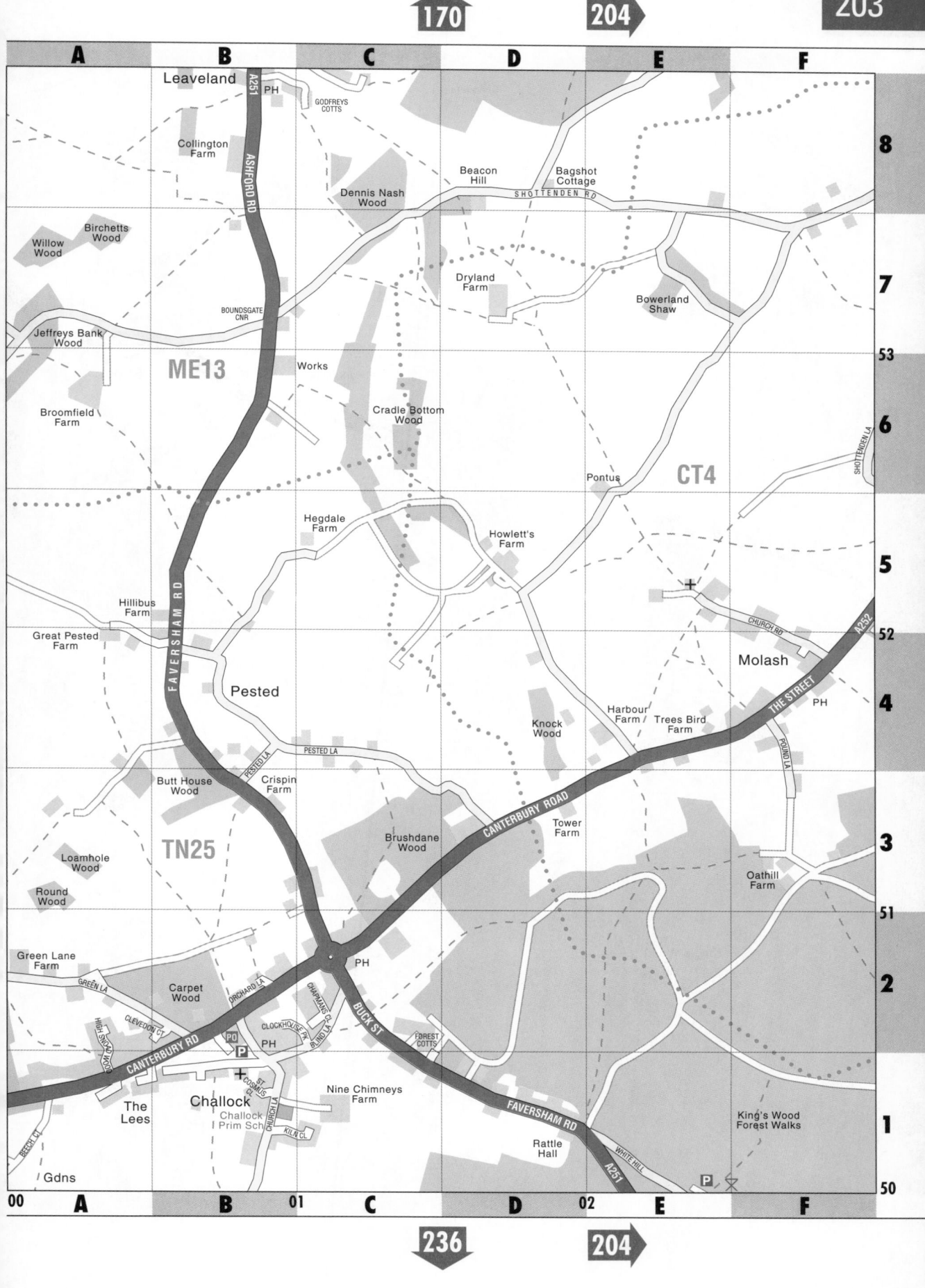

203
171

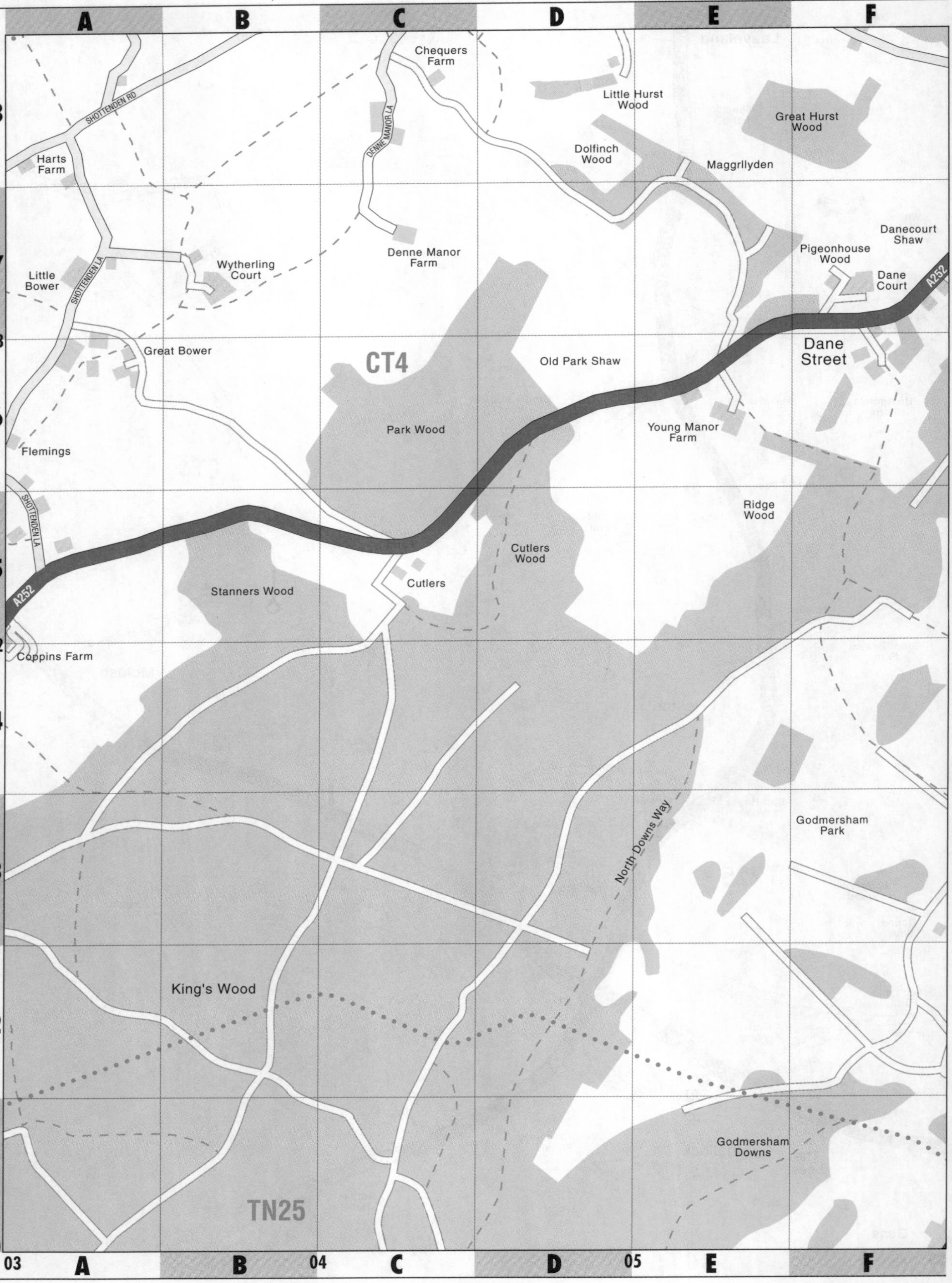

A B C D E F

8

Chequers Farm

Little Hurst Wood

Great Hurst Wood

Harts Farm

SHOTTENDEN RD

DENNE MANOR LA

Dolfinch Wood

Maggrllyden

Danecourt Shaw

7

Little Bower

SHOTTENDEN LA

Wytherling Court

Denne Manor Farm

Pigeonhouse Wood

Dane Court

A252

53

Great Bower

CT4

Old Park Shaw

Dane Street

6

Flemings

Park Wood

Young Manor Farm

Ridge Wood

SHOTTENDEN LA

A252

5

Stanners Wood

Cutlers

Cutlers Wood

52

Coppins Farm

4

North Downs Way

Godmersham Park

3

51

King's Wood

2

Godmersham Downs

1

TN25

50

03 A B 04 C D 05 E F

203
237

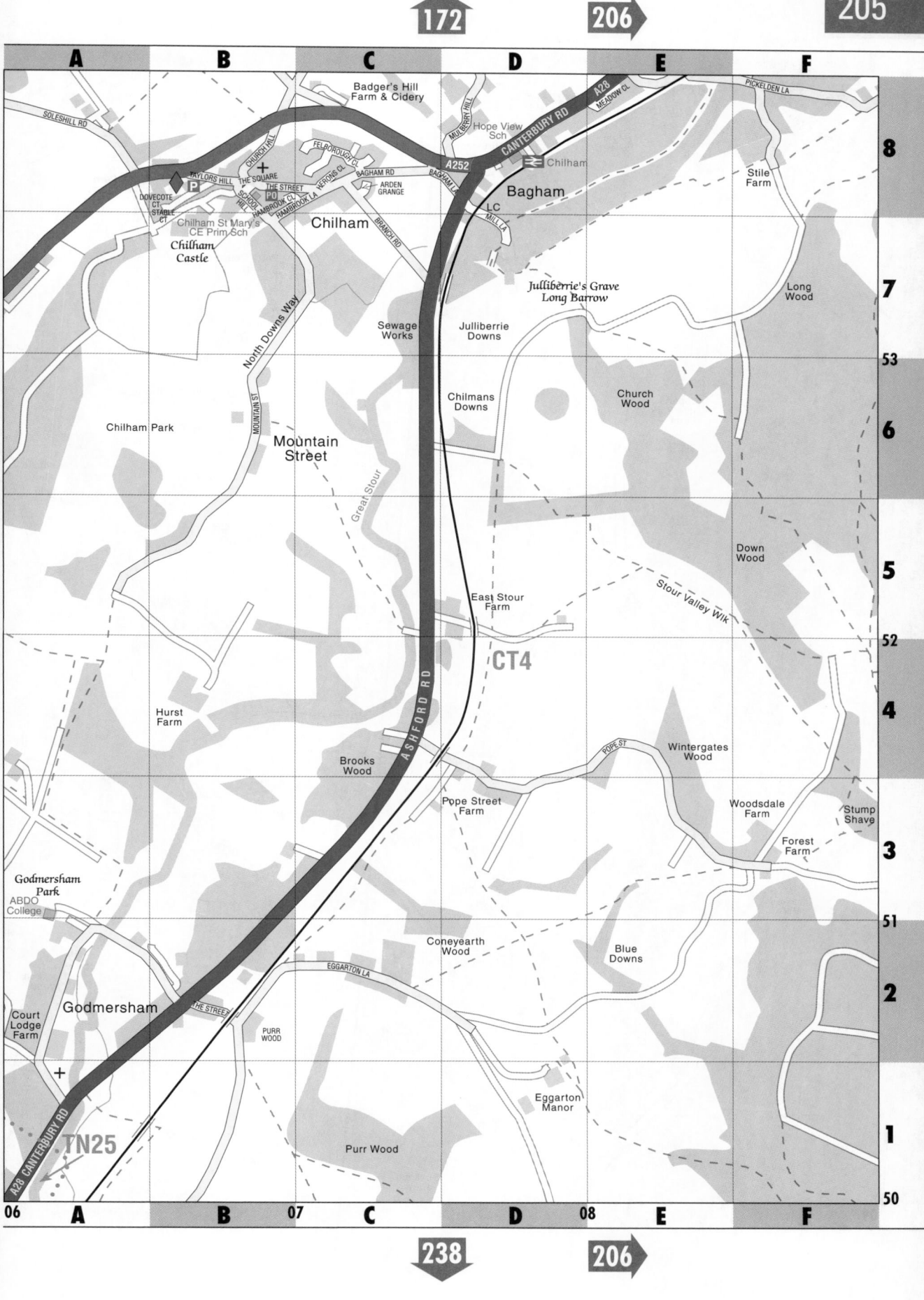

A B C D E F

8
7
53
6
5
52
4
3
51
2
1
50

06 A B 07 C D 08 E F

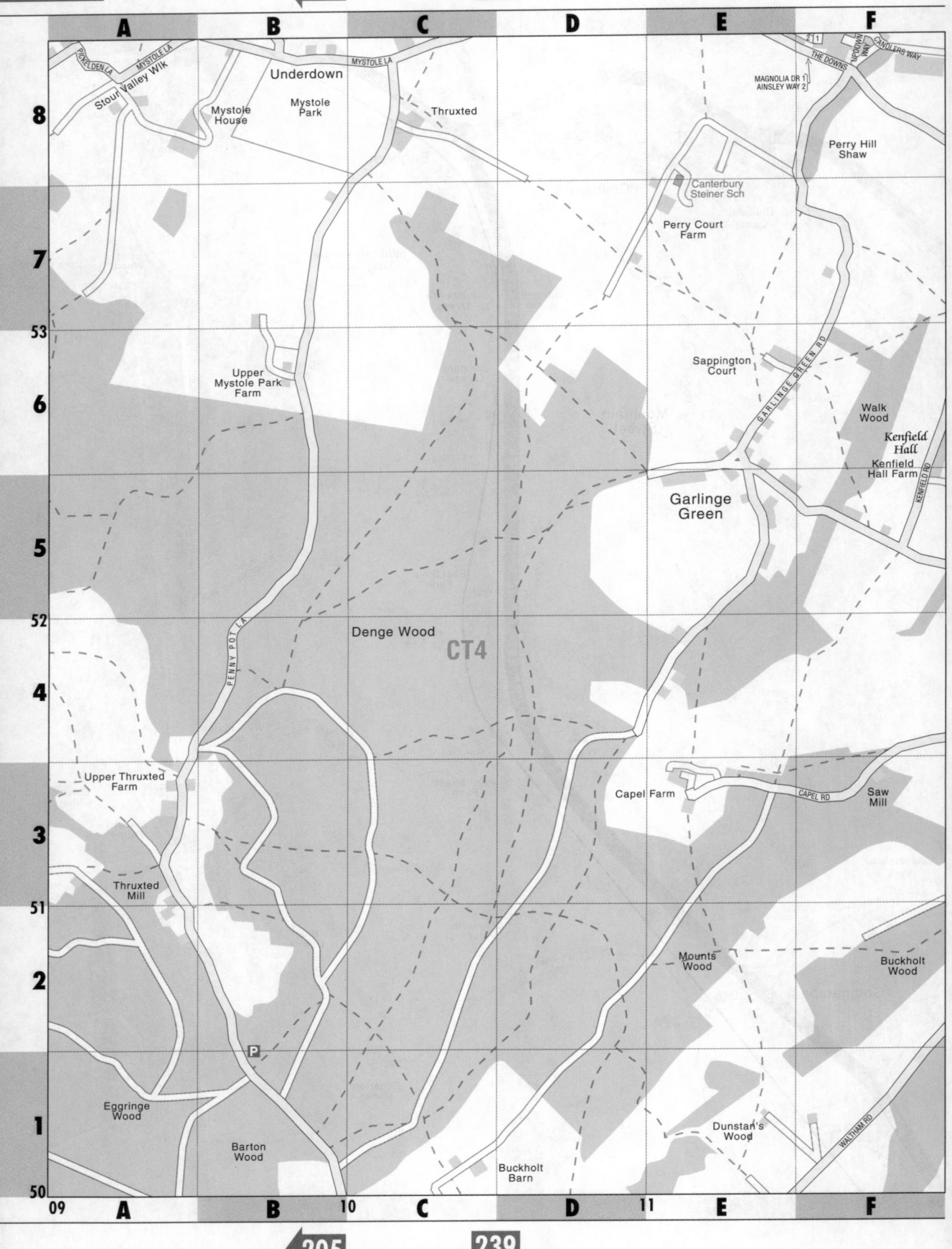

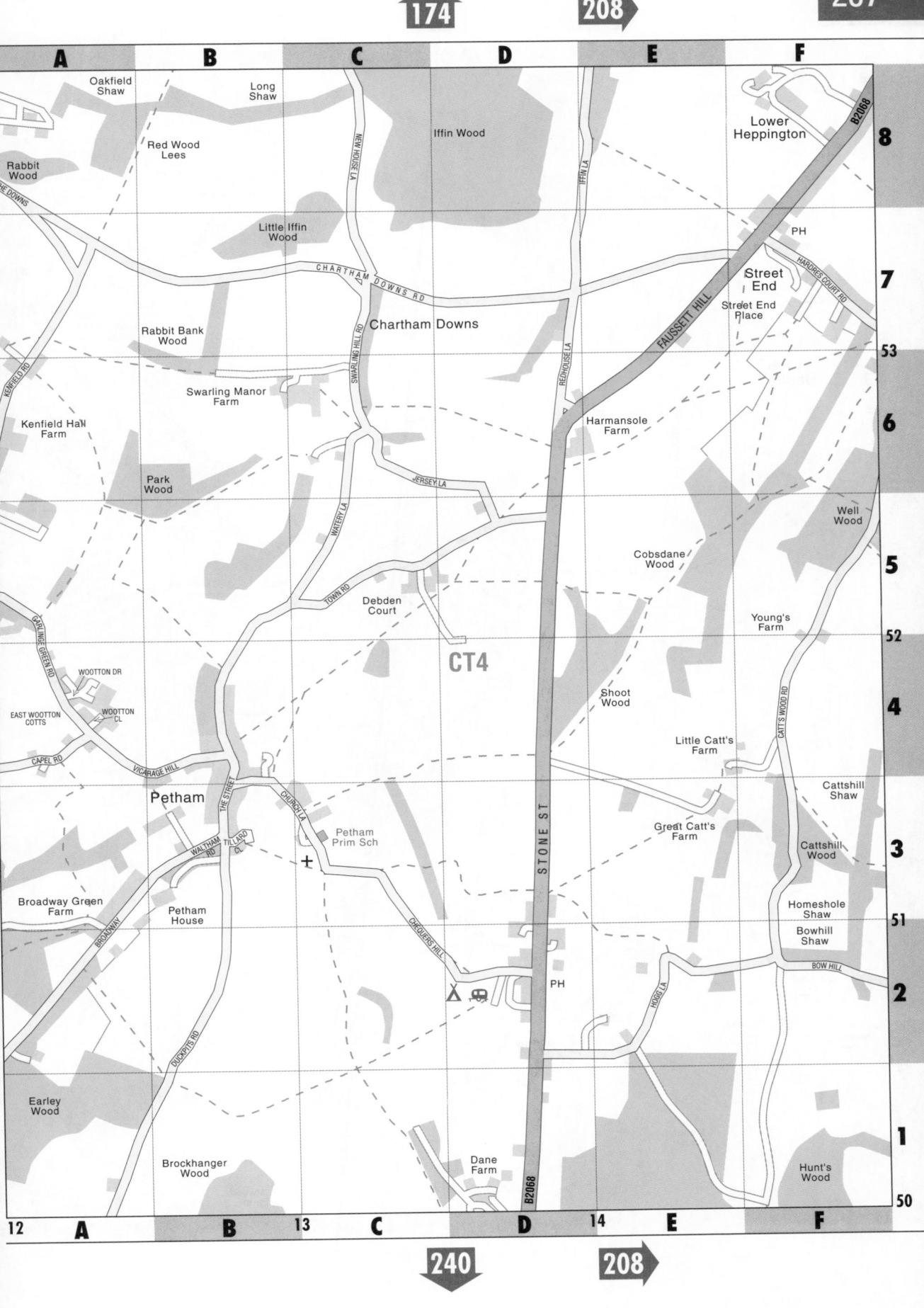

174

208

A B C D E F

8

Oakfield Shaw

Long Shaw

Iffin Wood

Lower Heppington

B2068

Red Wood Lees

Rabbit Wood

THE DOWNS

Little Iffin Wood

IFFIN LA

NEW HOUSE LA

PH

7

CHARTHAM DOWNS RD

Street End

HARDRES COURT RD

Chartham Downs

Street End Place

53

FAUSSETT HILL

Rabbit Bank Wood

SWARLING HILL RD

KENFIELD RD

6

Swarling Manor Farm

Harmansole Farm

REDHOUSE LA

Kenfield Hall Farm

JERSEY LA

Well Wood

Park Wood

WATERY LA

Cobsdane Wood

5

Young's Farm

TOWN RD

Debden Court

52

CT4

Shoot Wood

4

CARLINGE GREEN RD

WOOTTON DR

Little Catt's Farm

CATT'S WOOD RD

EAST WOOTTON COTTS

WOOTTON CL

Cattshill Shaw

CAPEL RD

VICARAGE HILL

Great Catt's Farm

Cattshill Wood

3

Petham

THE STREET

CHURCH LA

Petham Prim Sch

STONE ST

WALTHAM RD

TILLARD CL

Homeshole Shaw

Broadway Green Farm

BROADWAY

Petham House

CHEQUERS HILL

51

Bowhill Shaw

BOW HILL

PH

2

HOBB LA

DUCKPITS RD

Earley Wood

Hunt's Wood

1

Brockhanger Wood

Dane Farm

B2068

50

240

208

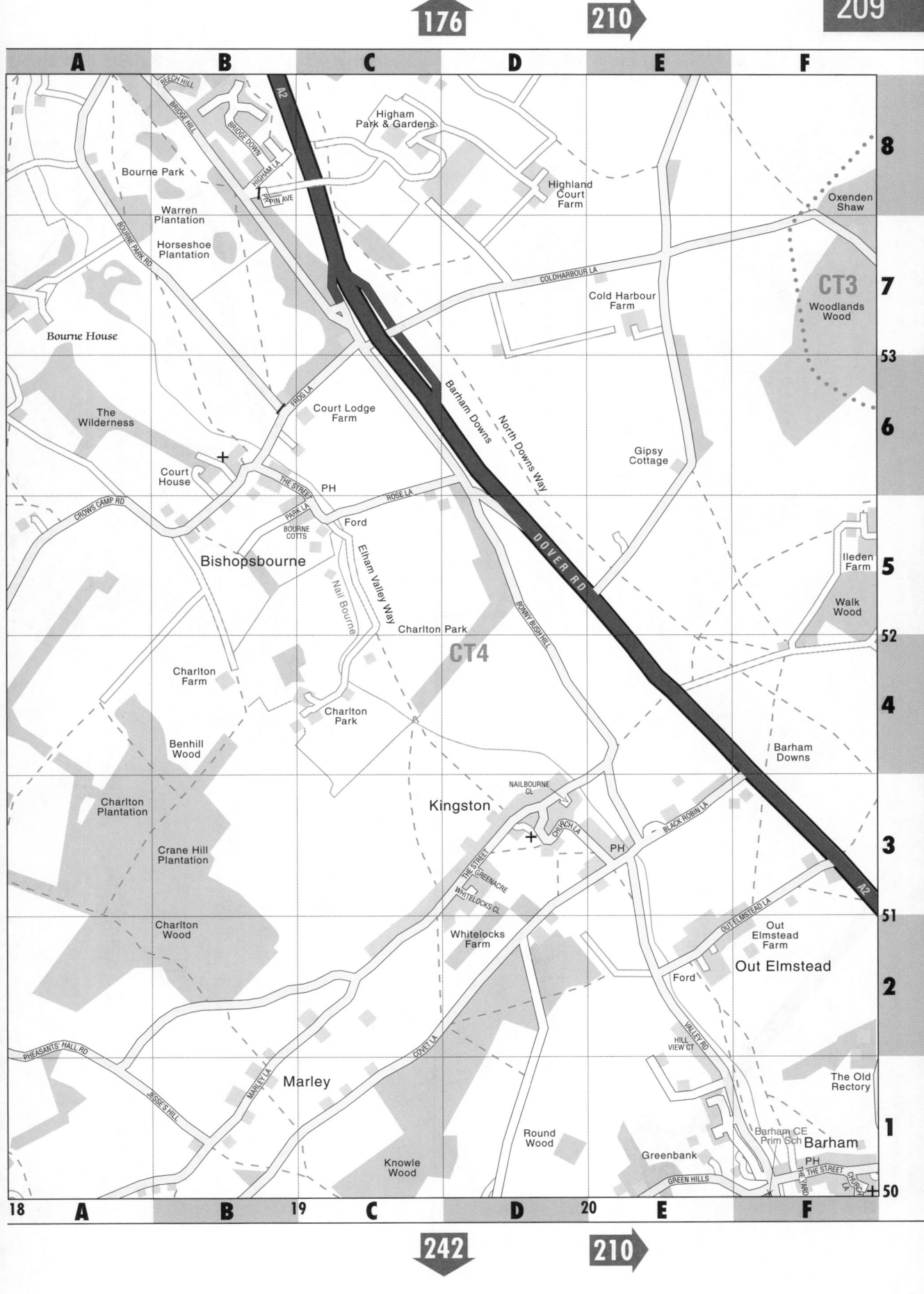

A B C D E F

8

7

53

6

5

52

4

3

51

2

1

50

BEECH HILL
BRIDGE HILL
BRIDGE DOWN
HIGHAM LA
A2
Bourne Park
Warren Plantation
Horseshoe Plantation
PIPPIN AVE
Higham Park & Gardens
Highland Court Farm
Oxenden Shaw
CT3
Woodlands Wood
COLDHARBOUR LA
Cold Harbour Farm
Bourne House
BOURNE PARK RD
The Wilderness
FROG LA
Court Lodge Farm
Barham Downs
North Downs Way
Gipsy Cottage
Court House
THE STREET
PH
ROSE LA
Ileden Farm
Walk Wood
CROWS CAMP RD
PARK LA
BOURNE COTTS
Ford
Elham Valley Way
Nail Bourne
Bishopsbourne
DOVER RD
Charlton Park
CT4
BONNY BUSH HILL
Charlton Farm
Charlton Park
Benhill Wood
Barham Downs
Charlton Plantation
Crane Hill Plantation
Kingston
NAILBOURNE CL
CHURCH LA
PH
BLACK ROBIN LA
A2
Charlton Wood
THE STREET
THE GREENACRE
WHITELOCKS CL
Whitelocks Farm
OUT ELMSTEAD LA
Out Elmstead Farm
Out Elmstead
Ford
PHEASANTS' HALL RD
MARLEY LA
Marley
COVET LA
VALLEY RD
HILL VIEW CT
The Old Rectory
JESSE'S HILL
Round Wood
Greenbank
Barham CE Prim Sch
Barham
PH
THE YARD
THE STREET
CHURCH LA
Knowle Wood
GREEN HILLS

209
177

A B C D E F

CT4

Twelve Acre Shaw

Adisham CE Prim Sch

Adisham

Bl
oodden

Adisham

B2046

Ratling Court

8

WOODLANDS RD

DONKEY LA

Woodlands Manor

7

Oxenden Wood

Cooting Farm

COOTING LA

THE STREET

53

Pitt Wood

CT3

6

Temnyson Gdns

Coleridge Gdns

Thirlmere Gdns

Buttermere Gdns

Wordsworth Gdns

Grasmere

Cornwallis Ave

1 ULLSWATER GDNS
2 ENNERDALE GDNS

DORMAN AVE N

DERWENT WAY

Kings Rd

Burgess Rd

Woodlands Wood

Windermere Gdns

Aylesham Prim Sch

5

Well Wood

Cooting Downs

Woodland Ave

NEWMAN RD

NTTLE AVE

VALE VIEW RD

CRIPPS CL

OAKSIDE RD

SNOWDOWN CT

MILNER CT

MARKET PL

BOULEVARD COURRIERES

EASTRY CT

BRIAR CL

VIRGIL CL

Aylesham

PO

Queens Rd

HYDE PL

CLARENDON RD

SPINNEY CL

ASH

HILL CRES

SYCAMORE

ELM RD

COOTING RD

COX CL

MARKET AVE S

52

HAWTHORN CL

Aylesham Ind Est

Ileden Wood

4

Aylesham Wood

COVERT RD

SPINNEY LA

Ackholt Wood

3

Barham Downs

CT4

AYLESHAM CNR

Willow Wood

POND LA

CT15

Upper Digges Farm

51

A2

Chalk Wood

2

RECTORY LA

DOVER RD

ADISHAM RD

North Downs Way

Cemy

Well Wood

Nethersole Farm

CHURCH LA

THE STREET

Aylesham Farm

Womenswold

Snow Down

1

DOVER RD

B2046

Westmore Cottages

Woolage Village

NETHERSOLE RD

THE GREEN

THE PLACE

CORAL RD

50

OLD DOVER RD

GRAVEL CASTLE RD

A2

A260

21 A B 22 C D 23 E F

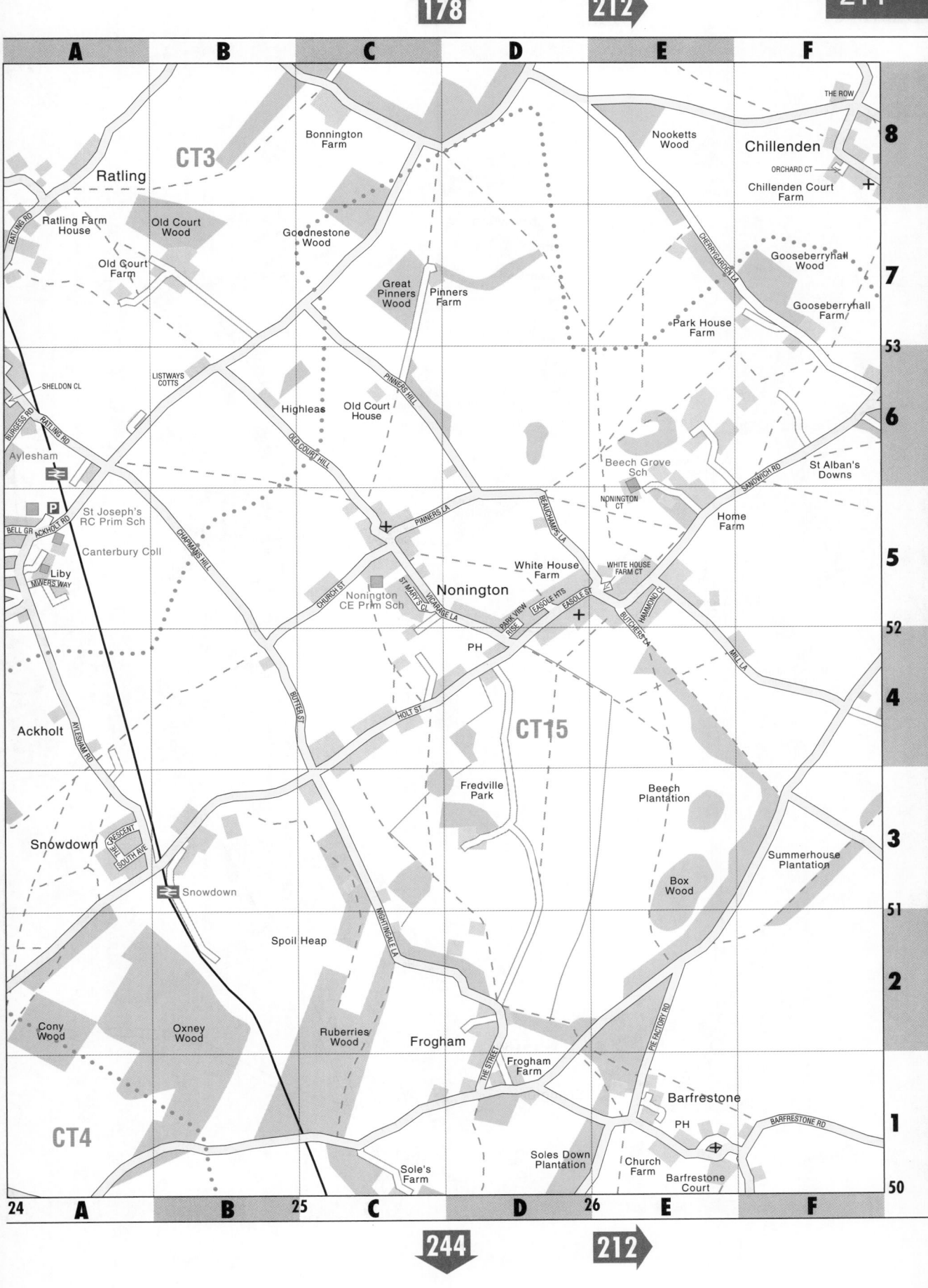

THE ROW

Nooketts Wood

Chillenden

ORCHARD CT

Chillenden Court Farm

CT3

Bonnington Farm

Ratling

Goodnestone Wood

Gooseberryhall Wood

Ratling Farm House

Old Court Wood

Gooseberryhall Farm

Old Court Farm

Great Pinners Wood

Pinners Farm

Park House Farm

SHELDON CL

LISTWAYS COTTS

Highleas

Old Court House

PINNERS HILL

Aylesham

Beech Grove Sch

NONINGTON CT

St Alban's Downs

SANDWICH RD

Home Farm

BURGESS RD

RATLING RD

St Joseph's RC Prim Sch

Canterbury Coll

Pinners La

White House Farm

WHITE HOUSE FARM CT

BEAUCHAMPS LA

BELL GR

ACKHOLT RD

CHAPMANS HILL

Liby

MWERS WAY

CHURCH ST

ST MARY'S CL

Nonington CE Prim Sch

Nonington

VICARAGE LA

PARK VIEW RISE

EASOLE HTS

EASOLE ST

HAMMOND CL

BUTCHERS LA

PH

MILL LA

Ackholt

OLD COURT HILL

BUTTER ST

HOLT ST

CT15

Fredville Park

Beech Plantation

Summerhouse Plantation

AYLESHAM RD

CRESCENT THE

SOUTH AVE

Snowdown

Box Wood

Snowdown

Spoil Heap

NIGHTINGALE LA

PRE FACTORY RD

Cony Wood

Oxney Wood

Ruberries Wood

Frogham

Frogham Farm

Barfrestone

CT4

THE STREET

Soles Down Plantation

Church Farm

PH

BARFRESTONE RD

Sole's Farm

Barfrestone Court

24

25

26

8

7

53

6

5

52

4

3

51

2

1

50

A B C D E F

211
179

A B C D E F

8

YEW TREE FARM

SHORT ST

PH

War Meml

Home Wood

Knowlton

CT13

The Warren

CT3

Home Farm

+

Black La

7

CUCKOLDS CNR

Knowlton Park

Knowlton Court

THORNTON EA

SANDWICH RD

53

The Grove

Manorial Earthworks

Shingleton Wood

6

Dover Lodge Cottages

Round Wood

Shingleton Farm

Venson Farm

St Alban's Downs

Shingleton Cottages

Thorntonhill Cottages

CT14

5

Kelk Hill

Thornton Farm

Kittington Cottages

52

Brown Pudding Plantation

Thornton Wood

Garden Wood

4

Kittington Farm

The Downs

PIKE RD

SCHOOL RD

CRANE CT

3

Beeches Farm

51

CT15

Spoil Heap

Craythorne Firs

2

POPLAR DR

CYPRESS GR

BEECH DR

ASH GR

DERBY GR

OAK GR

ROMAN WAY

SWEETBRIAR LA

Burgess Hill

Works

BARVILLE RD

CHALKER RD

ST JOHNS RD

FAIRVIEW RD

LARCH RD

MILNER RD

ADELAIDE RD

MILNER

TERRACE RD

PO

+

Elvington

Pike Road Ind Est

ELMTON LA

MILYARD WAY

WIGMORE LA

SANDWICH RD

1

BARFRESTONE RD

ADELAIDE RD

Sports Gd

50

27 A 28 B C 28 D 29 E F

211
245

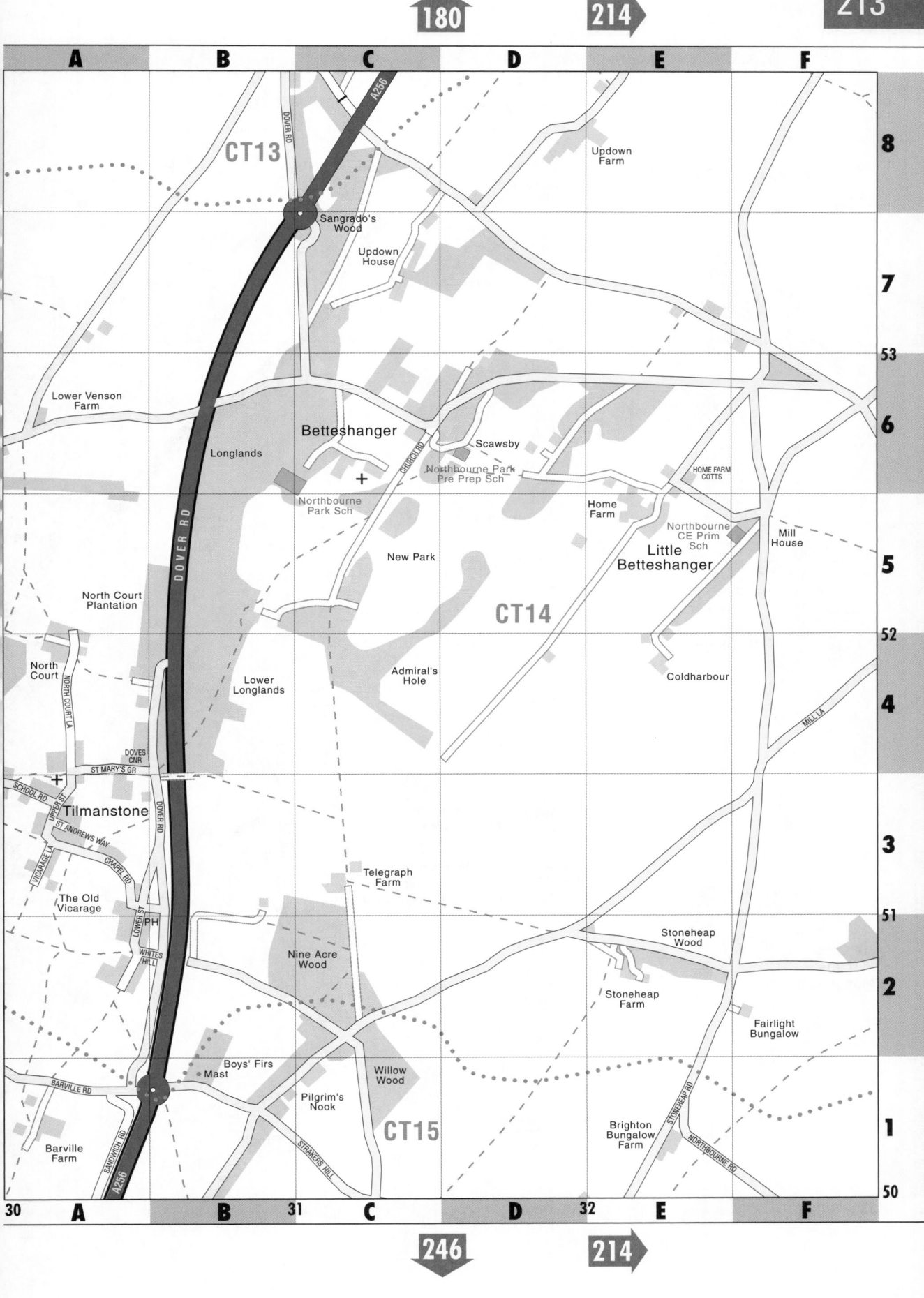

A B C D E F

8

7

53
6

CT13

Sangrado's Wood

Updown Farm

Updown House

Lower Venson Farm

Longlands

Betteshanger

Scawsby

Northbourne Park Pre Prep Sch

HOME FARM COTTS

DOVER RD

CHURCH RD

A256

Northbourne Park Sch

Home Farm

Little Betteshanger

Northbourne CE Prim Sch

Mill House

5

New Park

CT14

52
4

North Court Plantation

Admiral's Hole

Coldharbour

MILL LA

North Court

Lower Longlands

NORTH COURT LA

DOVES CNR

ST MARY'S GR

SCHOOL RD

✝ Tilmanstone

St Andrews Way

UPPER ST

VICARAGE LA

CHAPEL RD

The Old Vicarage

LOWER ST

PH

WHITES HILL

Telegraph Farm

Stoneheap Wood

51
2

Nine Acre Wood

Stoneheap Farm

Fairlight Bungalow

Boys' Firs Mast

Willow Wood

Pilgrim's Nook

CT15

Brighton Bungalow Farm

STONEHEAP RD

NORTHBOURNE RD

3

1

BARVILLE RD

SANDWICH RD

A256

STRAKERS HILL

Barville Farm

50
30 A B 31 C D 32 E F

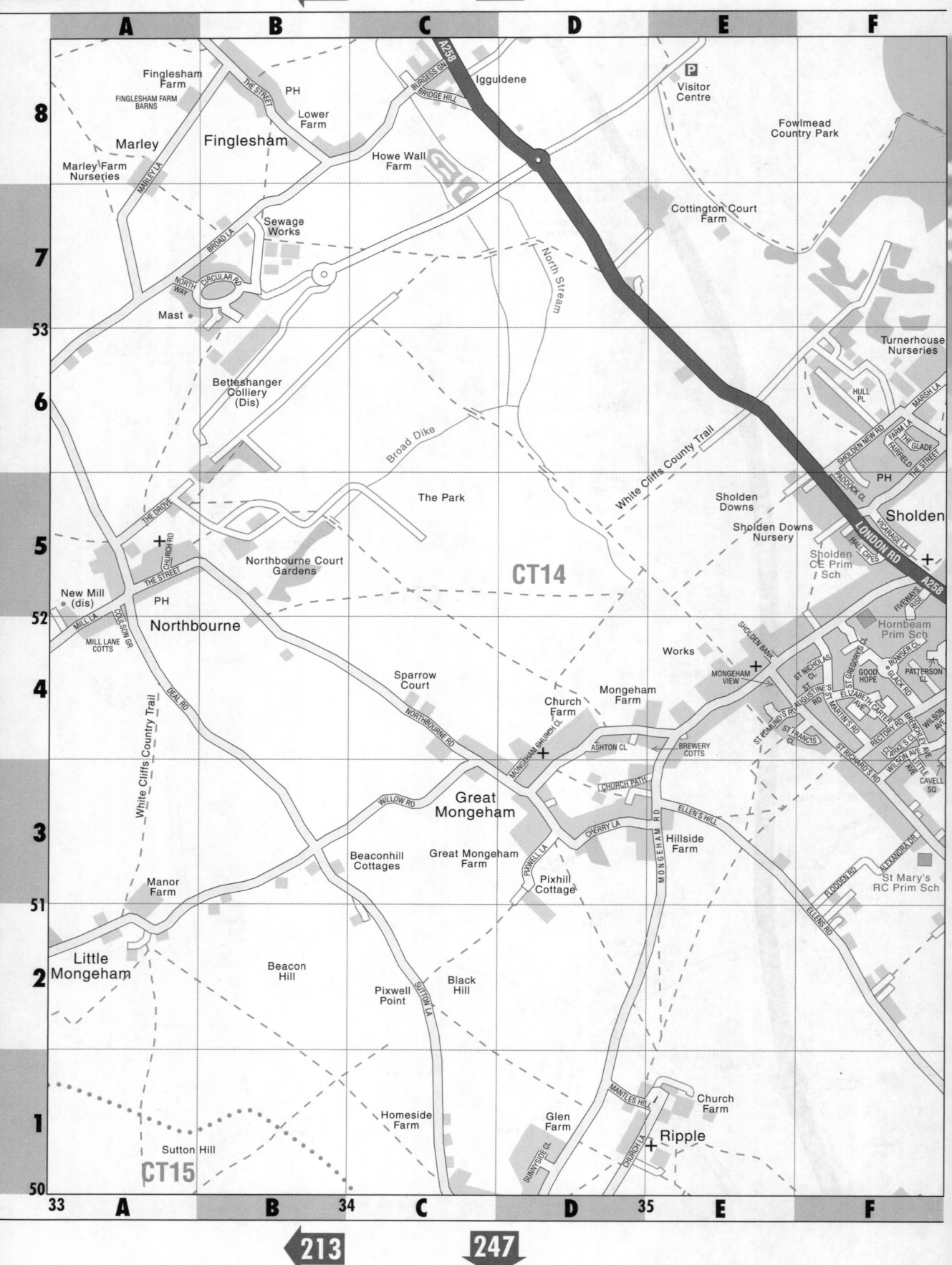

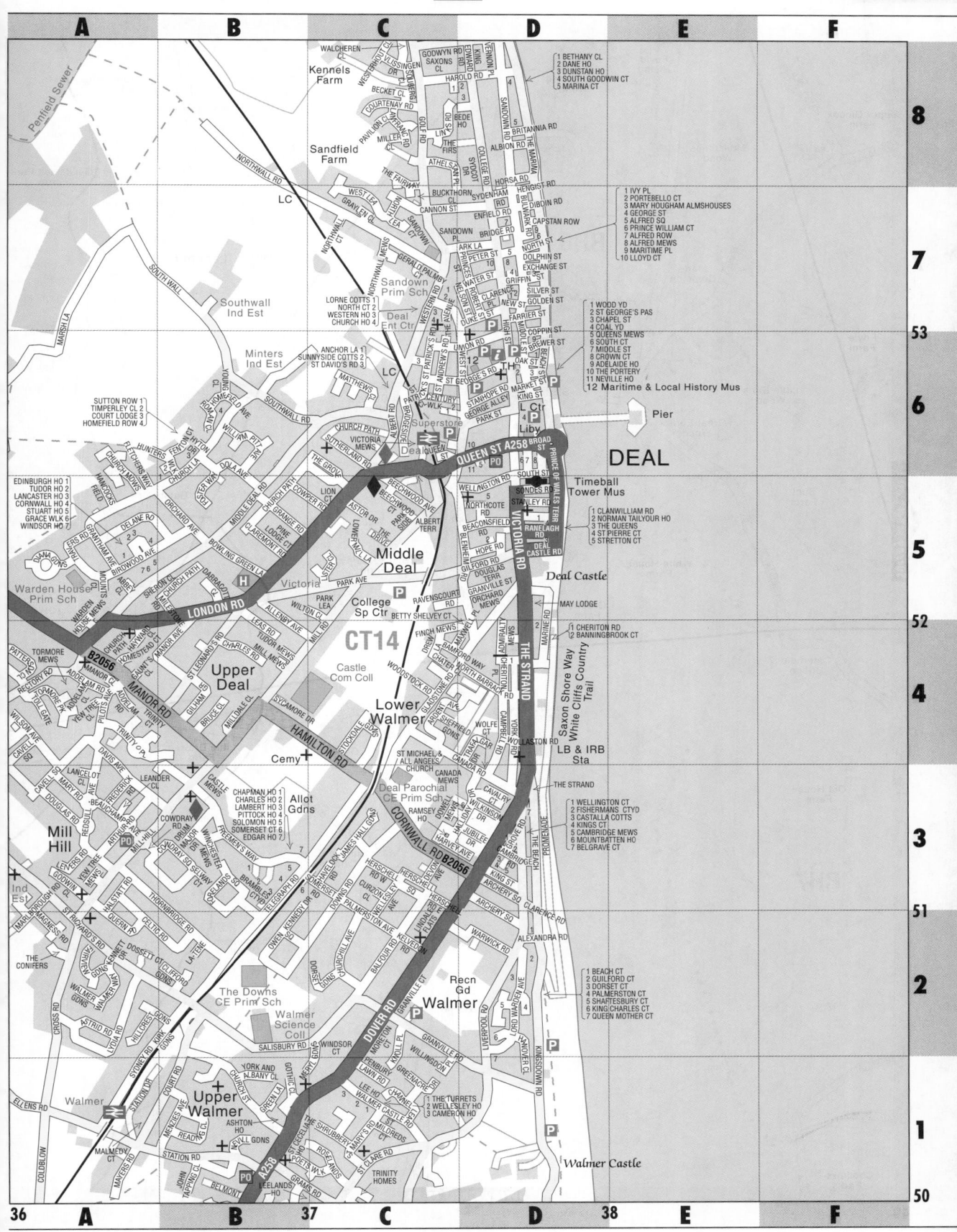

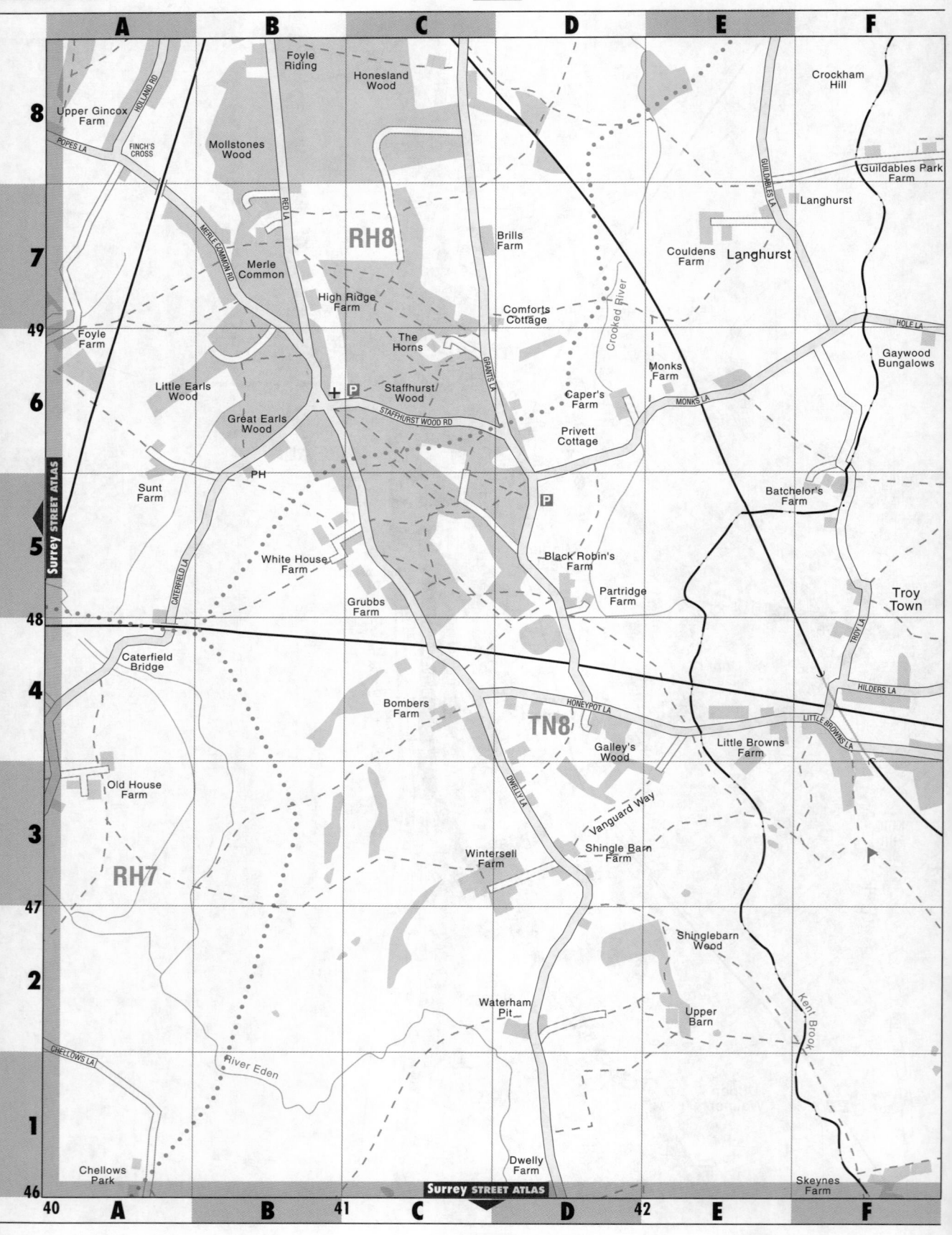

Surrey STREET ATLAS

A **B** **C** **D** **E** **F**

8 Upper Gincox Farm

POPES LA

FINCH'S CROSS

HOLLAND RD

Foyle Riding

Honesland Wood

Crockham Hill

Mollstones Wood

RED LA

GUILDABLES LA

Guildables Park Farm

7 Merle Common

MERLE COMMON RD

RH8

Brills Farm

Langhurst

Couldens Farm

Langhurst

High Ridge Farm

Comforts Cottage

49 Foyle Farm

The Horns

Crooked River

HOLE LA

Gaywood Bungalows

6 Little Earls Wood

Staffhurst Wood

Caper's Farm

Monks Farm

MONKS LA

Great Earls Wood

STAFFHURST WOOD RD

GRANTS LA

Privett Cottage

PH

P

Batchelor's Farm

Sunt Farm

CATERFIELD LA

White House Farm

P

Black Robin's Farm

Troy Town

5 Grubbs Farm

Partridge Farm

TROY LA

48 Caterfield Bridge

HILDERS LA

4 Old House Farm

Bombers Farm

HONEYPOT LA

TN8

Little Browns Farm

LITTLE BROWNS LA

Galley's Wood

Vanguard Way

DWELLY LA

Shingle Barn Farm

3 RH7

Wintersell Farm

Shinglebarn Wood

47

Kent Brook

2 Waterham Pit

Upper Barn

CHELLOWS LA

River Eden

1

Dwelly Farm

Skeynes Farm

46 Chellows Park

A **B** **C** **D** **E** **F**
40 41 42

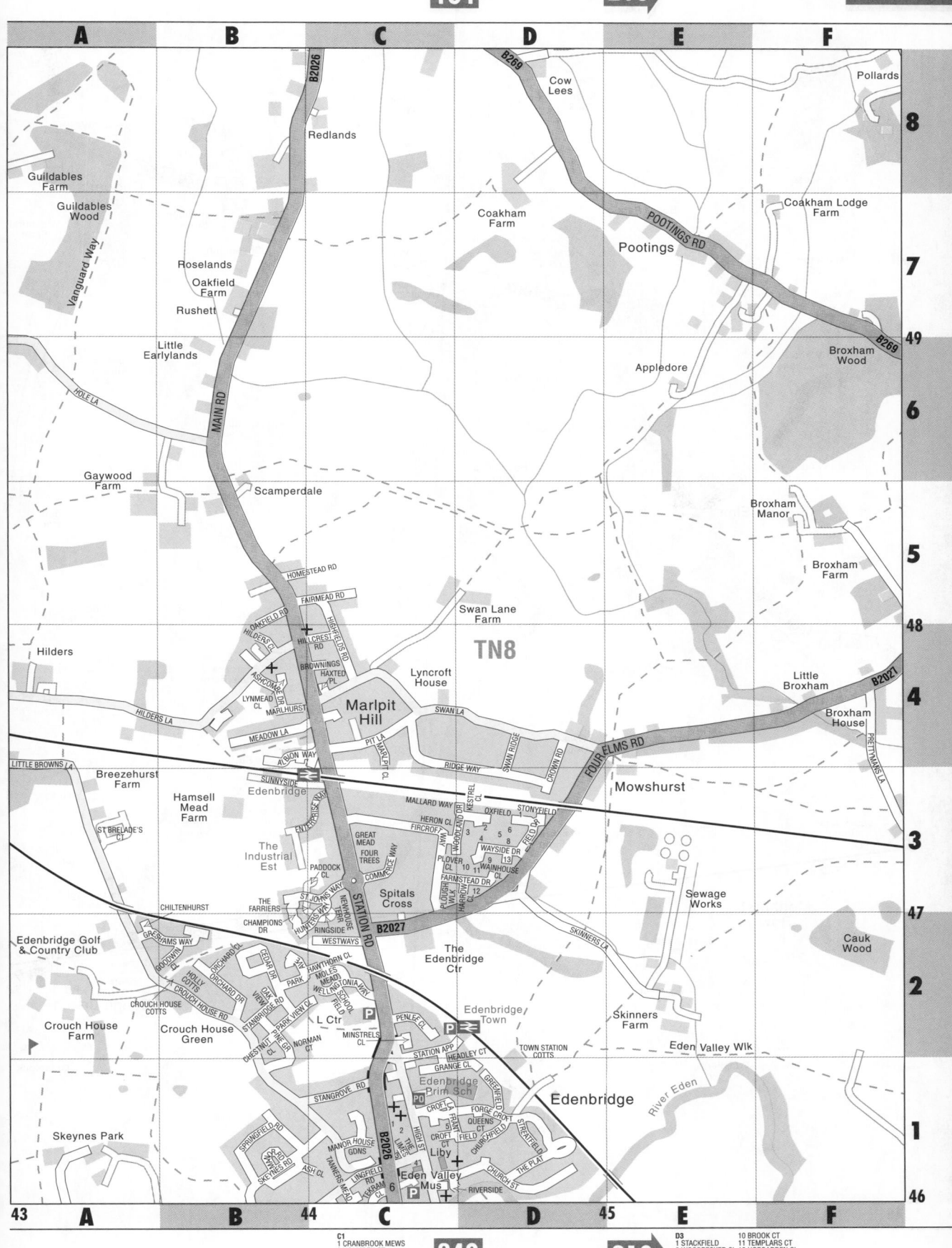

C1
1 CRANBROOK MEWS
2 HOLMDEN CT
3 THE OLD SCHOOL HO
4 LINGFIELD MEWS
5 FLORENCE COTTS
6 MONT ST AIGNAN WAY

D3
1 STACKFIELD
2 WOODPECKER CL
3 MAGPIE GN
4 SORRELL CL
5 SPEEDWELL CL
6 ROWFIELD
7 SMITHY FIELD
8 BRIAR CL
9 FOXGLOVE CL
10 BROOK CT
11 TEMPLARS CT
12 HOPGARDEN CL
13 CLOVER WLK

217
185

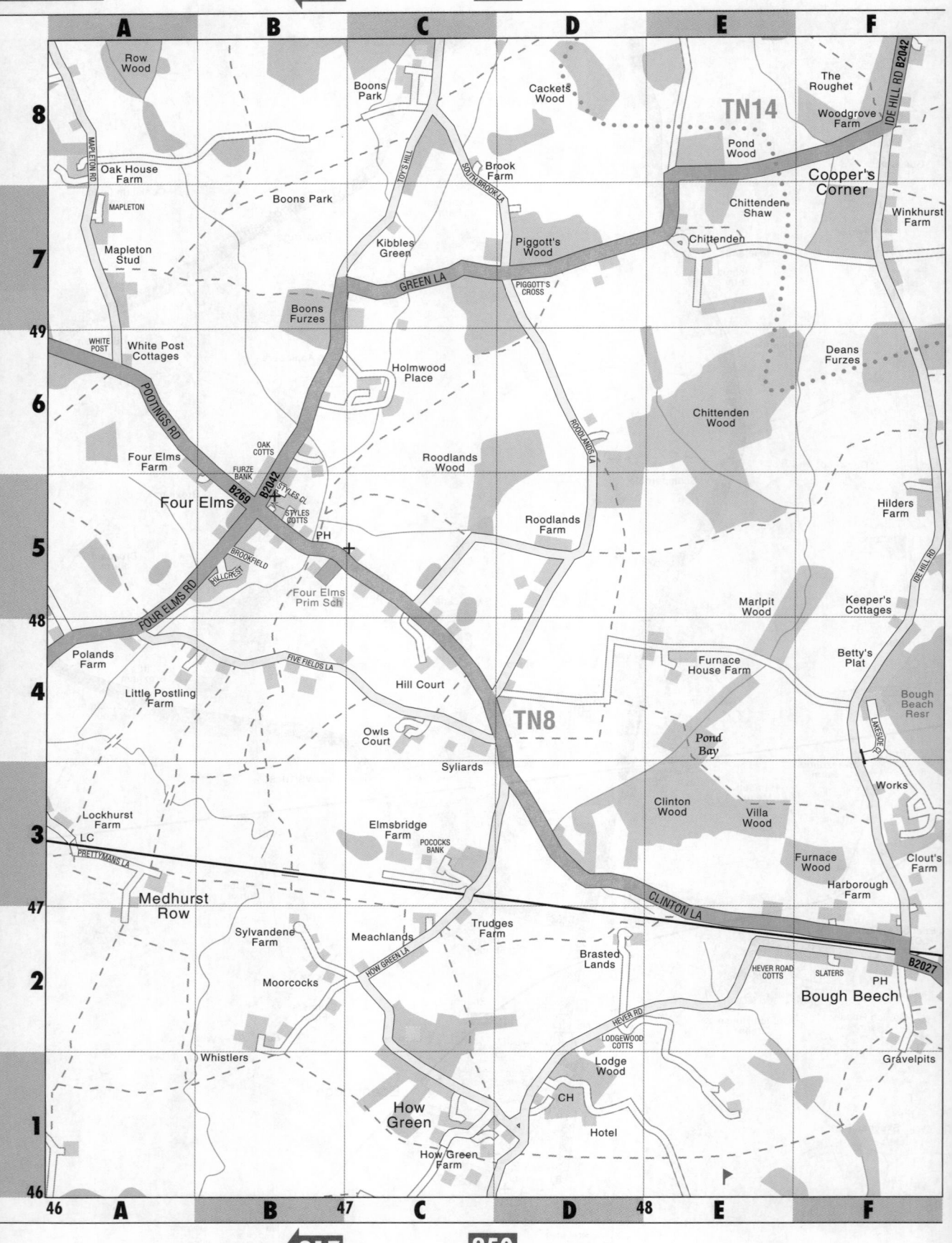

217
250

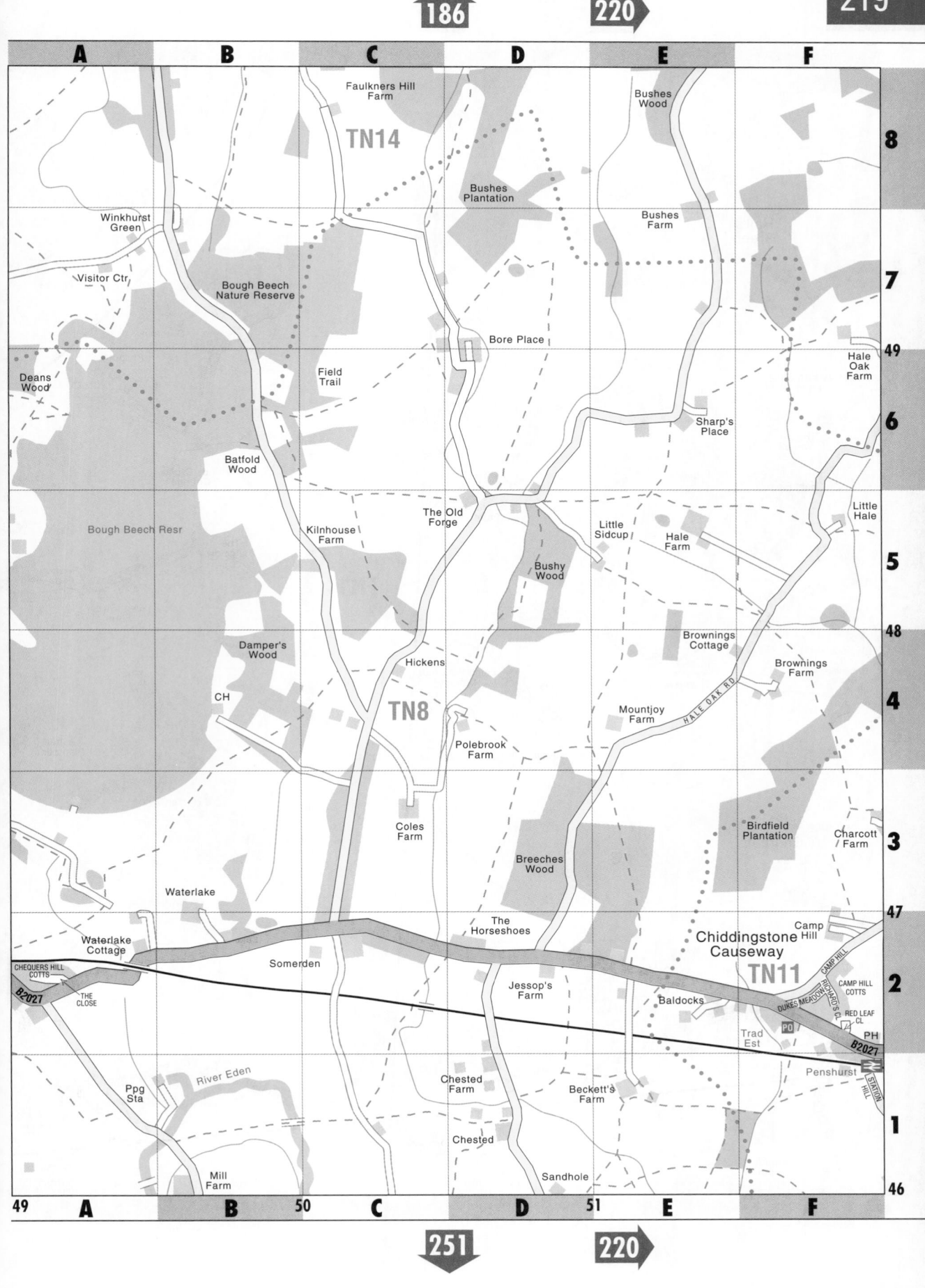

A | B | C | D | E | F

8

Faulkners Hill Farm

Bushes Wood

TN14

Bushes Plantation

Bushes Farm

7

Winkhurst Green

Bough Beech Nature Reserve

Bore Place

49

Visitor Ctr

Hale Oak Farm

Deans Wood

Field Trail

Sharp's Place

6

Batfold Wood

The Old Forge

Little Hale

Bough Beech Resr

Kilnhouse Farm

Little Sidcup

Hale Farm

5

Bushy Wood

48

Damper's Wood

Hickens

Brownings Cottage

Brownings Farm

4

CH

TN8

Mountjoy Farm

HALE OAK RD

Polebrook Farm

Birdfield Plantation

Charcott Farm

3

Coles Farm

Breeches Wood

Waterlake

47

The Horseshoes

Chiddingstone Causeway

Camp Hill

Waterlake Cottage

Somerden

Jessop's Farm

TN11

Camp Hill Cotts

2

CHEQUERS HILL COTTS

THE CLOSE

Baldocks

Red Leaf CL

B2027

PO

PH

B2027

River Eden

Chested Farm

Beckett's Farm

Penshurst

STATION HILL

1

Ppg Sta

Chested

Mill Farm

Sandhole

46

A | B | C | D | E | F

219
187

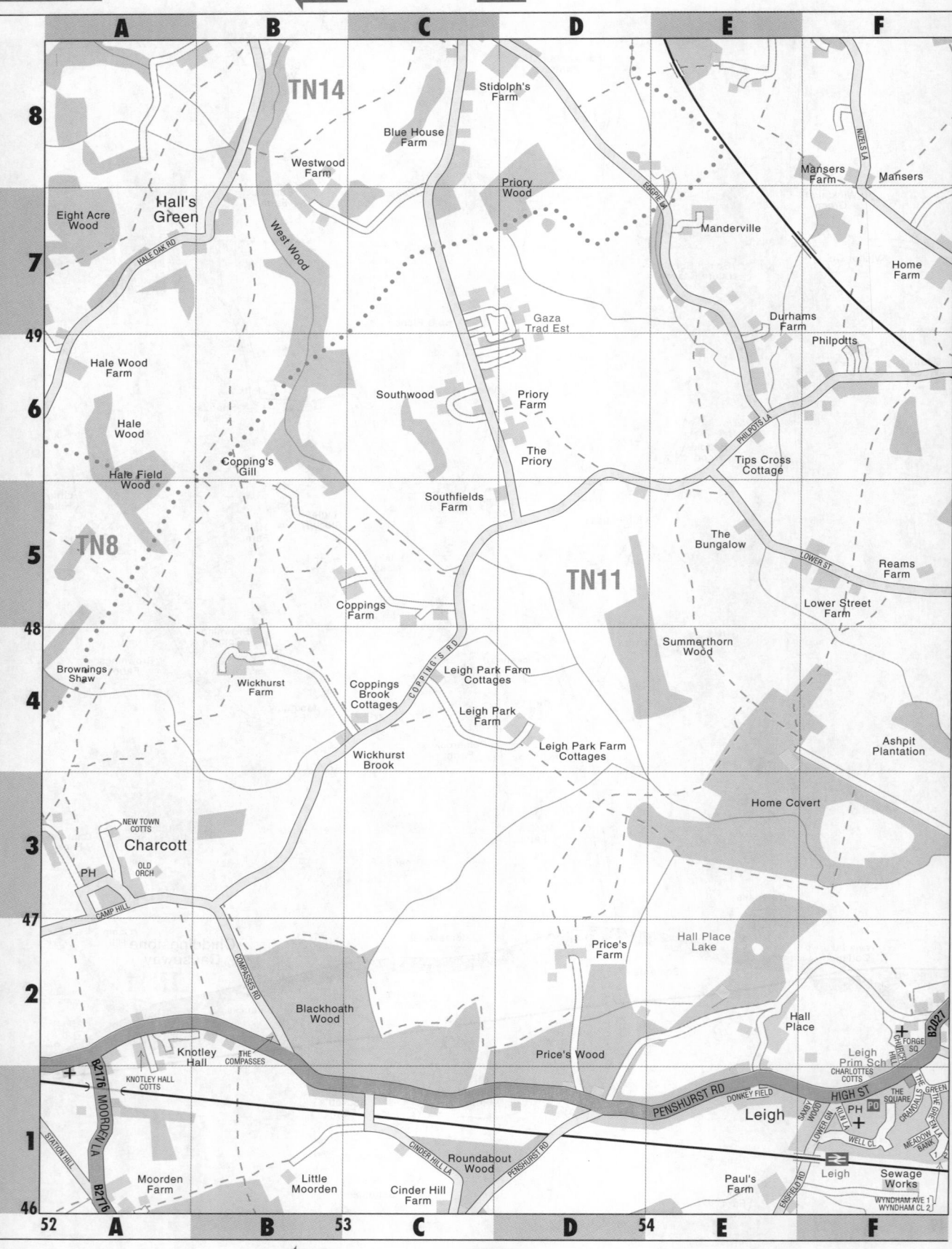

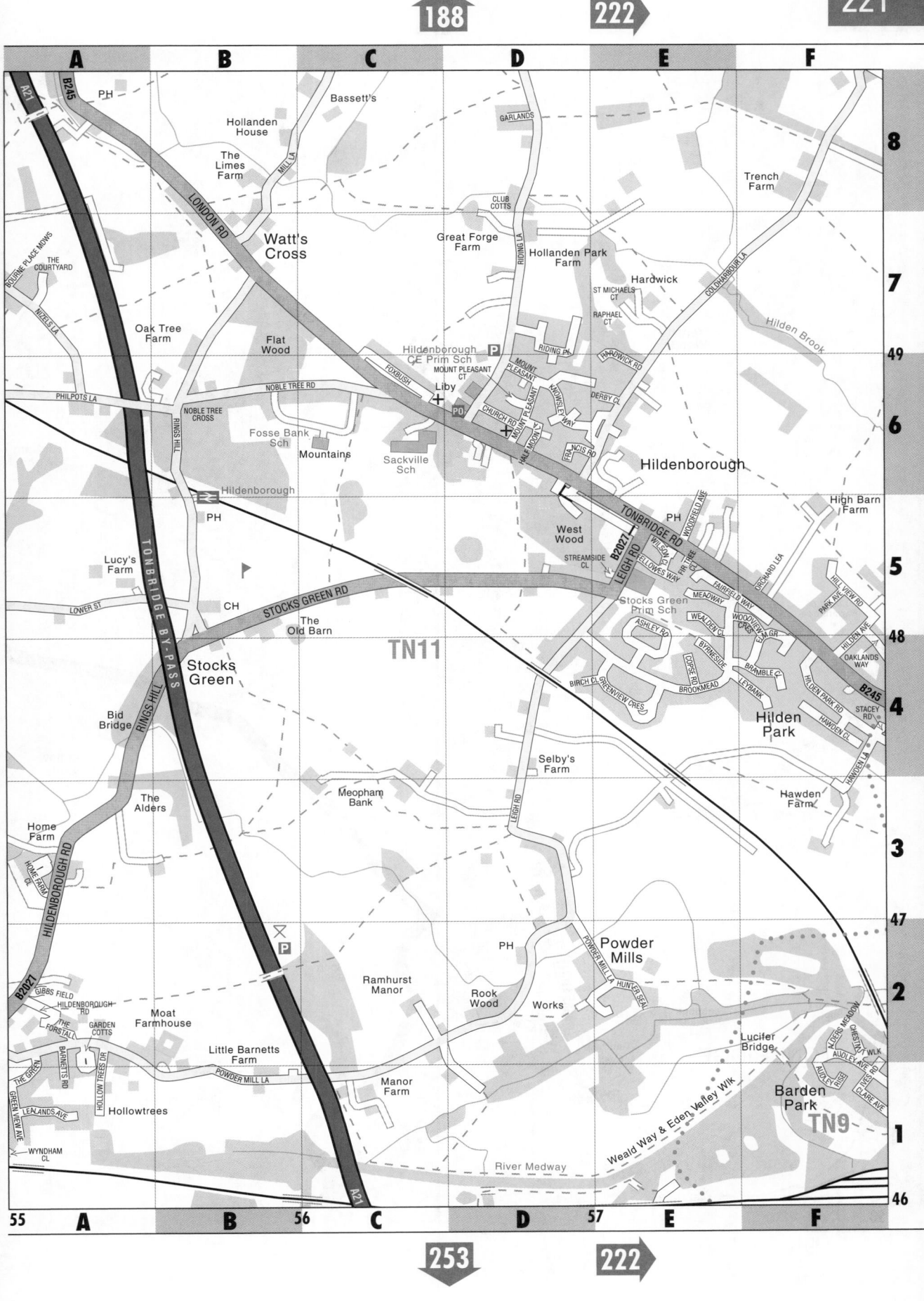

A   B   C   D   E   F

8

7

49

6

5

48

4

3

47

2

1

46

PH
Bassett's
Hollanden House
The Limes Farm
LONDON RD
Watt's Cross
GARLANDS
CLUB COTTS
Great Forge Farm
RIDING LA
Hollanden Park Farm
Hardwick
St MICHAELS CT
COLDHARBOUR LA
Trench Farm
Hilden Brook

BOURNE PLACE MEWS
THE COURTYARD
NIGELS LA
Oak Tree Farm
Flat Wood
NOBLE TREE RD
RIDING PH
RAPHAEL CT
HARDWICK RD

PHILPOTS LA
NOBLE TREE CROSS
RINGS HILL
FOXBUSH
Hildenborough CE Prim Sch
P
MOUNT PLEASANT CT
MOUNT PLEASANT
KNOWSLEY WAY
DERBY CL
Liby
PO
CHURCH RD
MOUNT PLEASANT
HALL MOON'S
FRANCIS RD
Hildenborough
High Barn Farm

Fosse Bank Sch
Mountains
Sackville Sch
TONBRIDGE RD
PH
WOODFIELD AVE
ORCHARD LEA

Hildenborough
PH
West Wood
B2027
LEIGH RD
WILSON CL
FIR TREE
FAIRFIELD WAY
MEADOW
HILL VIEW RD
PARK AVE

Lucy's Farm
STREAMSIDE CL
FELLOWES WAY
Stocks Green Prim Sch
WEALDEN CL
WOODVIEW CRES
ELM GR
HILDEN AVE

LOWER ST
CH
STOCKS GREEN RD
ASHLEY RD
CORSE RD
BRAMBLE
OAKLANDS WAY

TONBRIDGE BY-PASS
The Old Barn
TN11
BYRNESIDE
BROOKMEAD
LEYBANK
HILDEN PARK RD
B245

Stocks Green
BIRCH CL
GREENVIEW CRES
Hilden Park
STACEY RD
HAWDEN CL

Bid Bridge
The Alders
Selby's Farm
Hawden Farm

Home Farm
HILDENBOROUGH RD
RINGS HILL
Meopham Bank
LEIGH RD
LINDEN LA

B2027
GIBBS FIELD
HILDENBOROUGH RD
THE FORSTALL
GARDEN COTTS
Moat Farmhouse
Ramhurst Manor
Rook Wood
PH
Works
POWDER MILL RD
Powder Mills
HUNTER SEAL
Lucifer Bridge

THE GREEN
BARNETTS RD
HOLLOW TREES DR
LEALANDS AVE
Little Barnetts Farm
POWDER MILL LA
Manor Farm
ROGERS MEADOW
AUDLEY AVE
CHESTNUT WLK
CLARE AVE

GREEN VIEW AVE
WYNDHAM CL
Hollowtrees
Weald Way & Eden Valley Wlk
Barden Park
TN9

River Medway

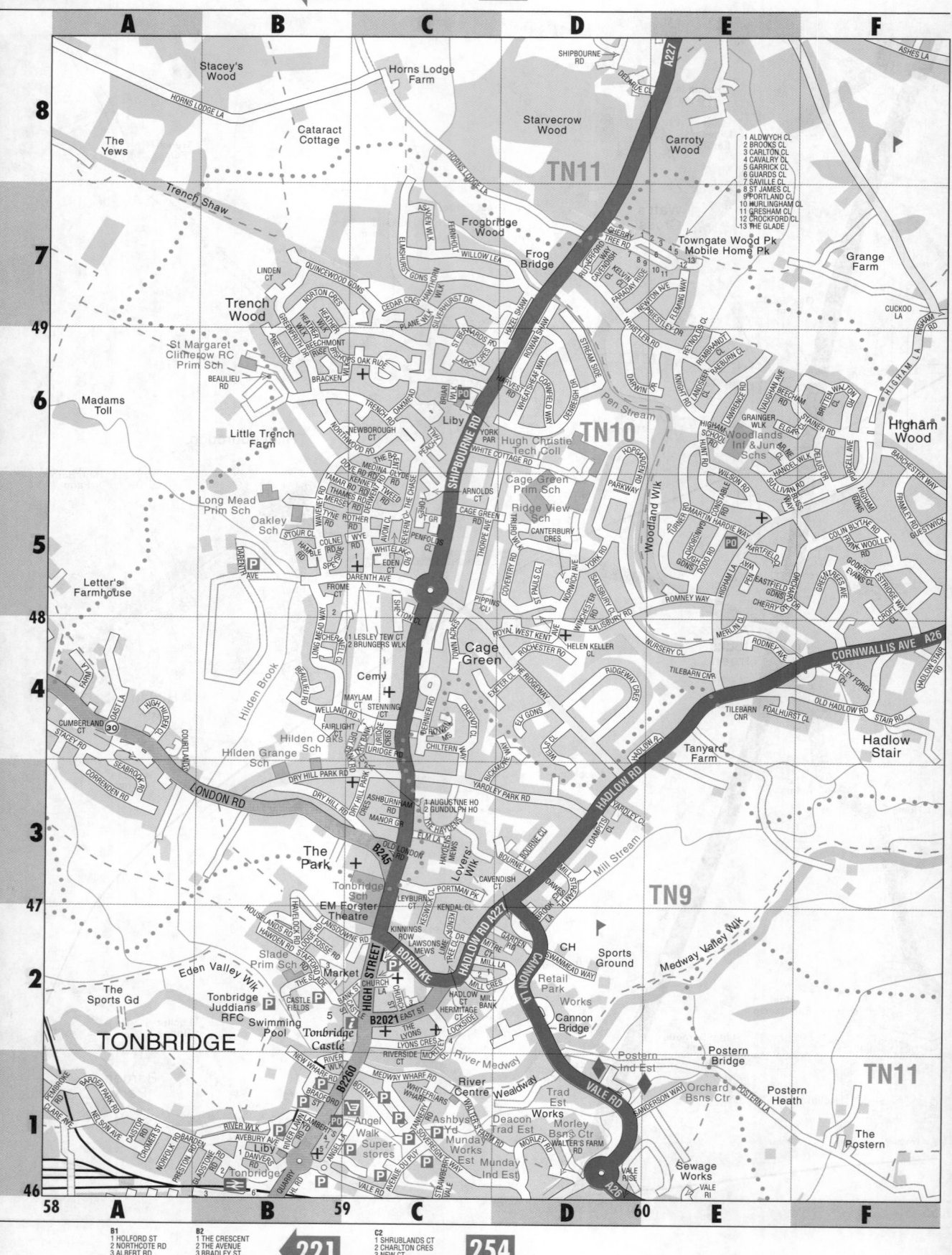

B1
1 HOLFORD ST
2 NORTHCOTE RD
3 ALBERT RD
4 ANGEL WLK
5 THE PAVILION
6 WATERLOO RD
7 Pavilion Sh Ctr

B2
1 THE CRESCENT
2 THE AVENUE
3 BRADLEY ST
4 ANNISON ST
5 Council Offs

C2
1 SHRUBLANDS CT
2 CHARLTON CRES
3 NEW CT
4 TOWN LOCK HO

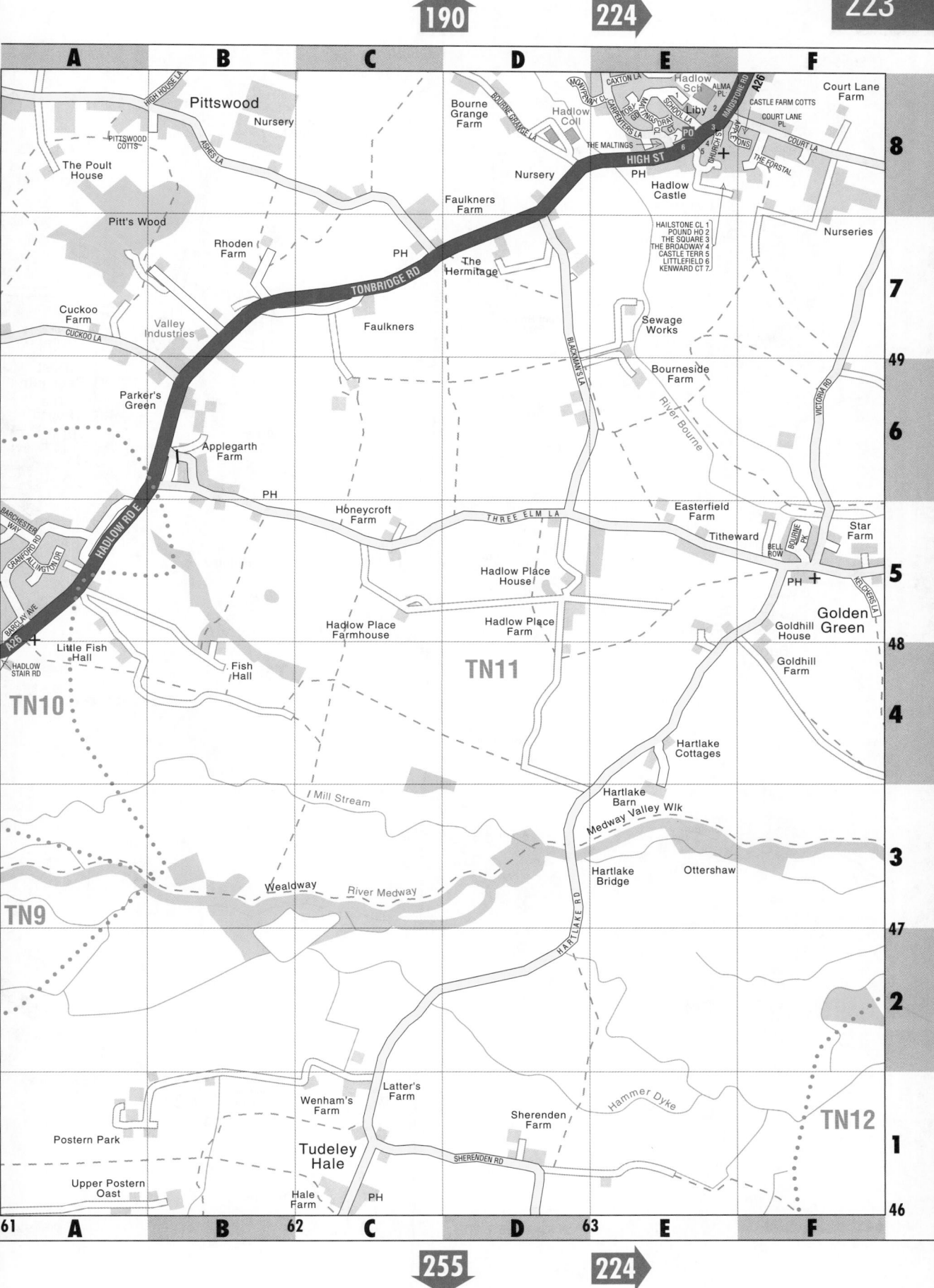

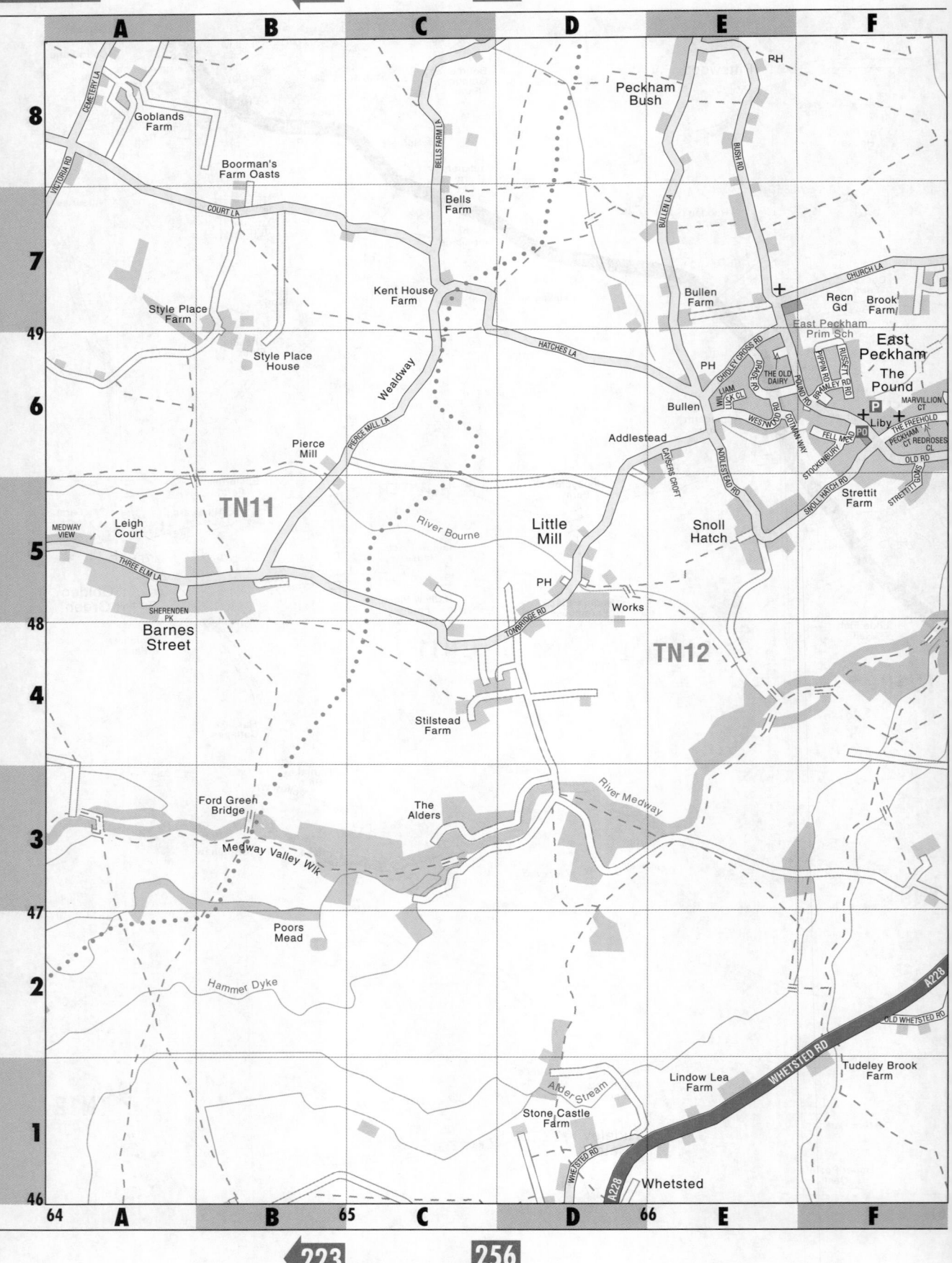

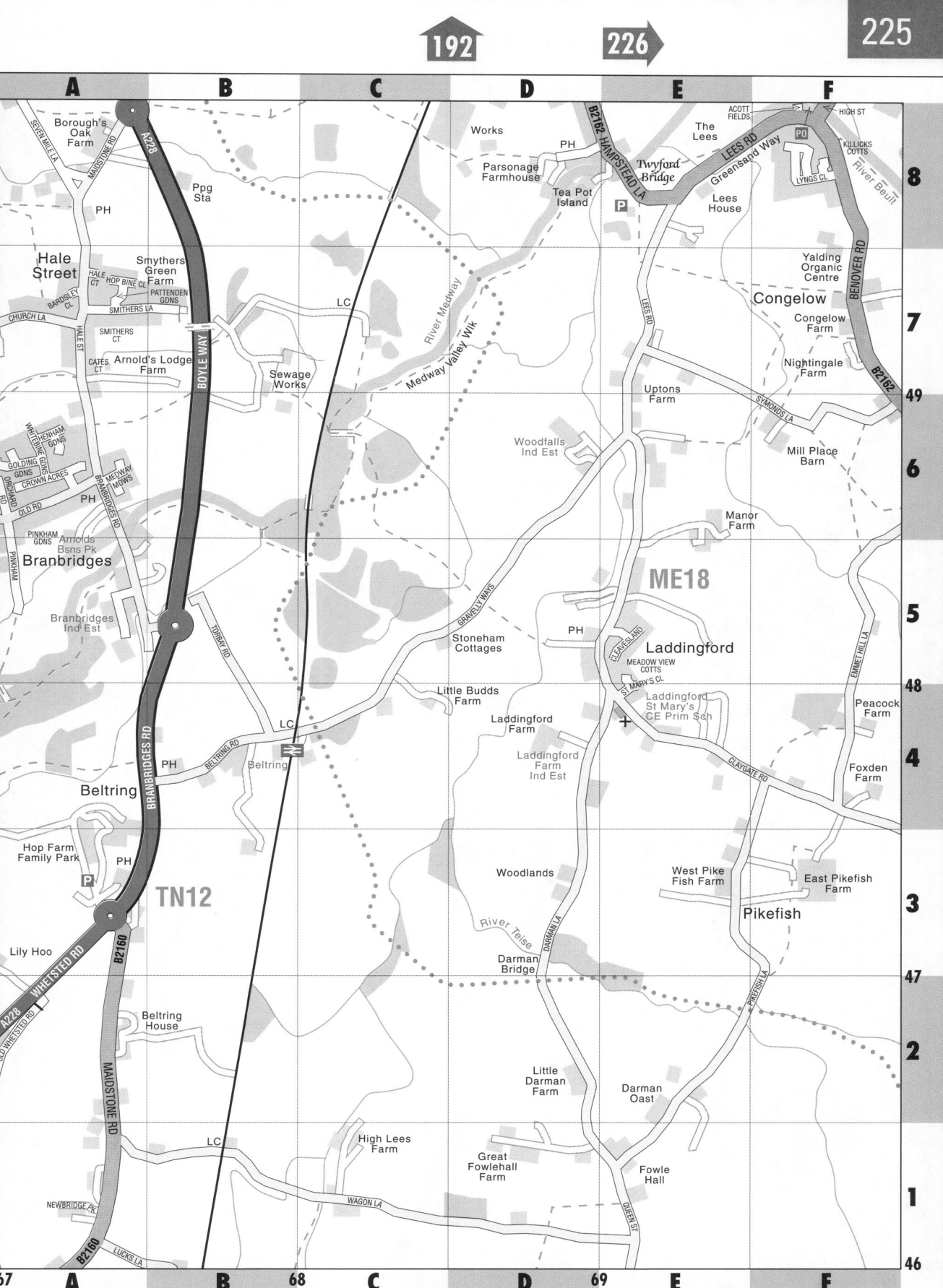

Borough's Oak Farm

SEVEN MILE LA

MAIDSTONE RD

A228

Works

B2162 HAMPSTEAD LA

PH

Parsonage Farmhouse

Tea Pot Island

Twyford Bridge

ACOTT FIELDS

LEES RD

Greensand Way

The Lees

HIGH ST

PO

LYNGS CL

KILLICKS COTTS

River Beult

BENOVER RD

B2162

8

Hale Street

Ppg Sta

PH

Smythers Green Farm

HALE CT

HOP BINE CL

PATTENDEN GDNS

SMITHERS LA

LC

P

Lees House

Yalding Organic Centre

Congelow

Congelow Farm

7

BARDSLEY CL

HALE ST

CHURCH LA

SMITHERS CT

CATES CT

Arnold's Lodge Farm

BOYLE WAY

Sewage Works

River Medway

Medway Valley Wlk

Uptons Farm

LEES RD

SYMONDS LA

Nightingale Farm

49

WHITCHENHAM GDNS

GOLDING GDNS

ORCHARD RD

CROWN ACRES

MEDWAY MDWS

BRANBRIDGES RD

OLD RD

PH

Woodfalls Ind Est

Mill Place Barn

6

PINKHAM GDNS

PINKHAM

Arnolds Bsns Pk

Branbridges

Manor Farm

Branbridges Ind Est

TORBAY RD

ME18

5

Stoneham Cottages

PH

CLEAVERSLAND

Laddingford

MEADOW VIEW COTTS

Little Budds Farm

ST MARY'S CL

48

LC

Beltring

Laddingford Farm

Laddingford St Mary's CE Prim Sch

Peacock Farm

EMMET HILL LA

4

PH

BELTRING RD

Beltring

Laddingford Farm Ind Est

CLAYGATE RD

Foxden Farm

Hop Farm Family Park

PH

P

Woodlands

West Pike Fish Farm

East Pikefish Farm

3

TN12

B2160

Lily Hoo

River Teise

DARMAN LA

Pikefish

PIKEFISH LA

47

WHETSTED RD

A228

OLD WHETSTED RD

Beltring House

Darman Bridge

2

MAIDSTONE RD

Little Darman Farm

Darman Oast

LC

High Lees Farm

Great Fowlehall Farm

Fowle Hall

1

NEWBRIDGE PK

WAGON LA

QUEEN ST

46

B2160

LUCKS LA

225
193

A B C D E F

8

Cheveney

VICARAGE RD

Hunton

+

Hunton Court Farm

BENSTED CL

Grove Farm

THE SQUARE

Scott's Farm

GROVE LA

Clock House

7

MILL LA

WEST ST

PEACE COTTS

Hunton CE Prim Sch

ME15

EAST ST

49

B2162

BENOVER RD

Durrants Farm

BISHOP'S LA

Bishops Oast

Stonewall

6

Normans

EMMET HILL LA

Benover

WATER LA

Elphicks Farm

HUNTON RD

ME18

River Beult

5

PH

Foresters Cottage Farm

Reed Court Farm

48

Rugmer Farm House

4

FORGE LA

DAIRY PL

Dairy House

DAIRY LA

Dairy Farm

Nurseries

Jarmons Farm

Den Farm

DEN LA

3

Crow Plain Farm

Den Cottages

Bentletts Farm

TN12

47

SLANGATE RD

Gain Hill Nursery

Mockbeggar

STARR COTTS

Spitzbrook

2

Nursery

Brandenbury

PROSPECT PL

Haviker Street

1

Park Cottage

Moat Farm

St Margarets Collier Street CE Sch

Green Lane Cotts

GREEN LA

B2162

+

Old Moat Farm

46

70 A B 71 C D 72 E F

225
258

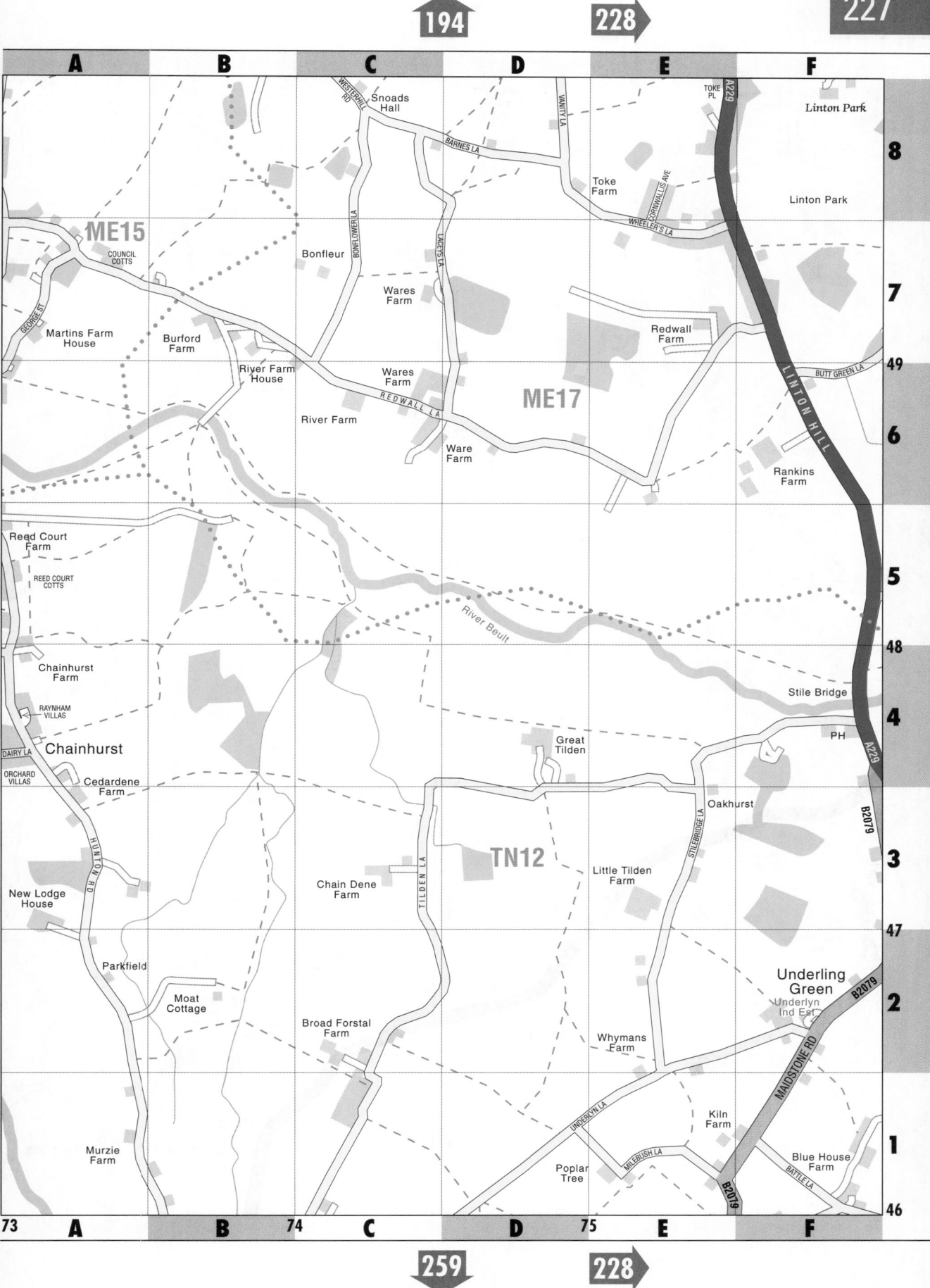

Linton Park

8

ME15

Council Cotts

Snoads Hall

Toke Farm

Linton Park

7

Bonfleur

Wares Farm

Martins Farm House

Burford Farm

River Farm House

Wares Farm

Redwall Farm

49

ME17

6

River Farm

Ware Farm

Rankins Farm

Reed Court Farm

5

River Beult

REED COURT COTTS

48

Chainhurst Farm

Stile Bridge

RAYNHAM VILLAS

4

PH

Chainhurst

Great Tilden

Oakhurst

Cedardene Farm

ORCHARD VILLAS

TN12

Little Tilden Farm

3

New Lodge House

Chain Dene Farm

47

Parkfield

Underling Green

2

Moat Cottage

Broad Forstal Farm

Whymans Farm

Underlyn Ind Est

Kiln Farm

Murzie Farm

Poplar Tree

Blue House Farm

1

46

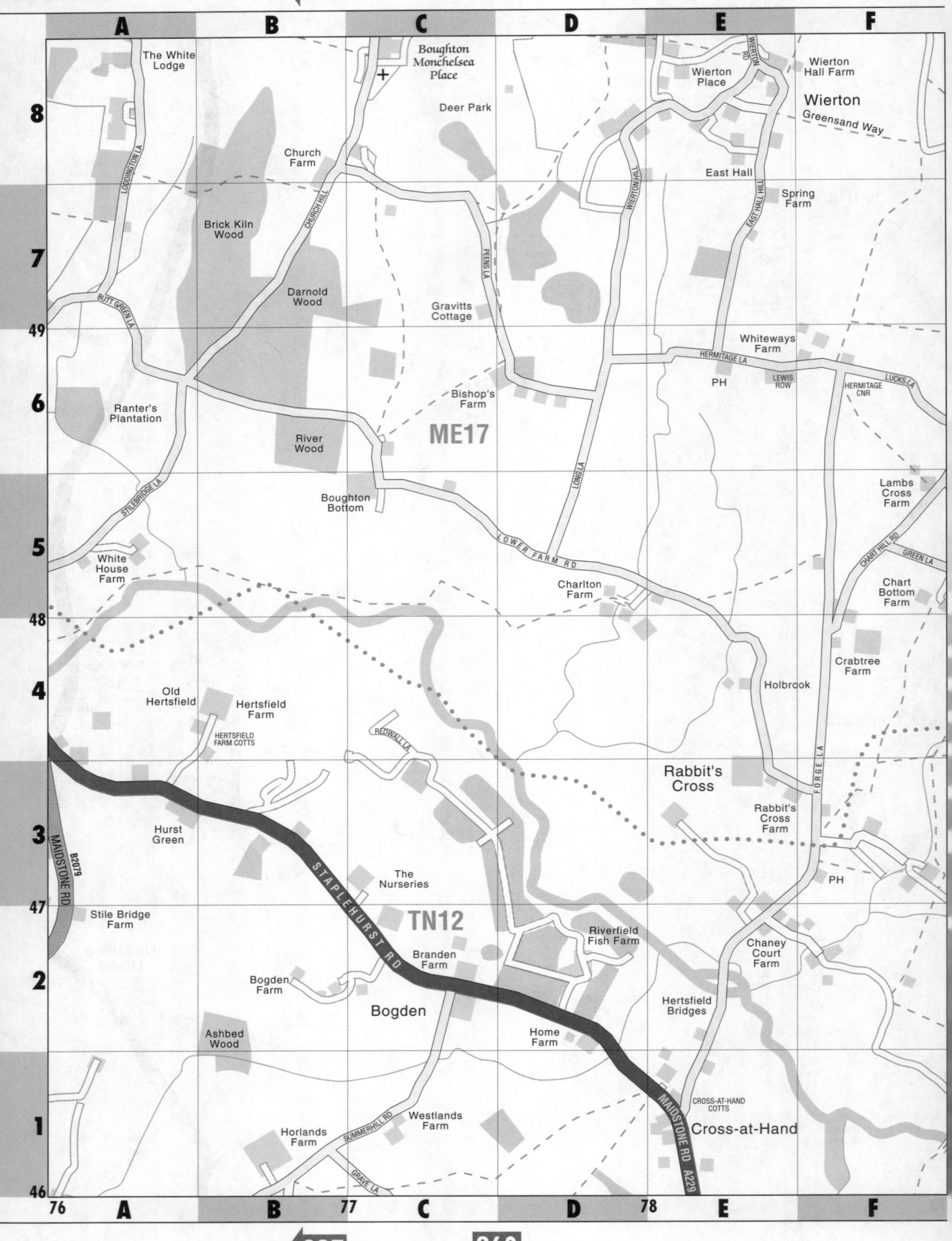

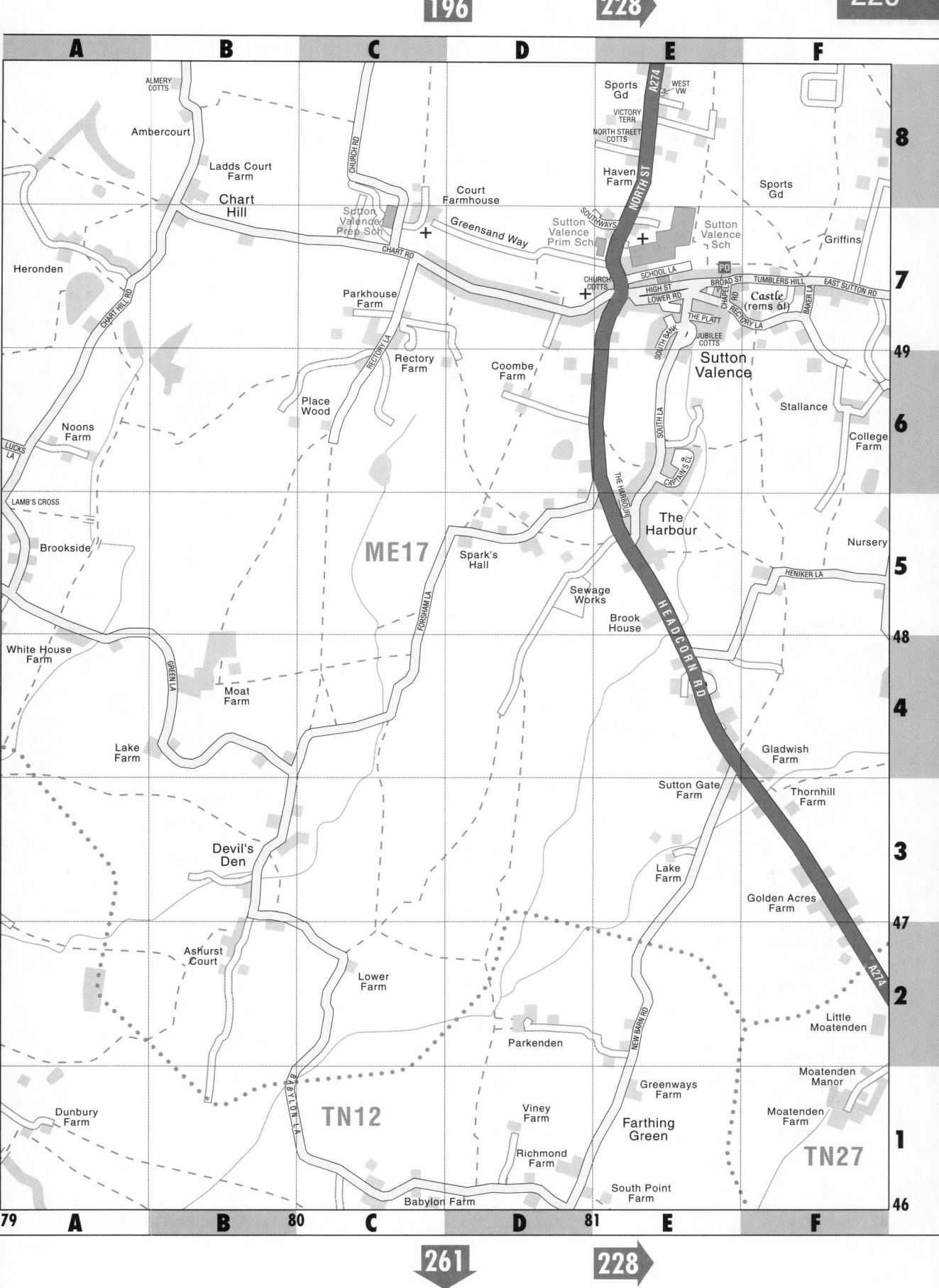

A   B   C   D   E   F

8

7

49

6

5

48

4

3

47

2

1

46

ALMERY COTTS

Ambercourt

Ladds Court Farm

Chart Hill

CHURCH RD

Court Farmhouse

Sports Gd

A274

WEST VW

VICTORY TERR

NORTH STREET COTTS

Haven Farm

NORTH ST

Sutton Valence Prep Sch

Greensand Way

CHART RD

SOUTHWAYS

Sutton Valence Prim Sch

Sutton Valence Sch

Griffins

Sports Gd

Heronden

CHART HILL RD

Parkhouse Farm

RECTORY LA

Rectory Farm

Coombe Farm

CHURCH COTTS

SCHOOL LA

BROAD ST

TUMBLERS HILL

EAST SUTTON RD

HIGH ST

CHAPEL HILL

Castle (rems of)

BAKER LA

RECTORY LA

LOWER RD

Sutton Valence

Place Wood

SOUTH BANK

THE PLATT

JUBILEE COTTS

Stallance

Noons Farm

LUCKS LA

SOUTH LA

College Farm

LAMB'S CROSS

Brookside

ME17

Spark's Hall

THE HARBOUR

CAPTAIN'S CL

The Harbour

HENIKER LA

Nursery

Sewage Works

White House Farm

FORSHAM LA

Brook House

HEADCORN RD

GREEN LA

Moat Farm

Lake Farm

Gladwish Farm

Thornhill Farm

Sutton Gate Farm

Devil's Den

Lake Farm

Golden Acres Farm

A274

Ashurst Court

Lower Farm

BABYLON LA

NEW BARN RD

Little Moatenden

Parkenden

Moatenden Manor

Dunbury Farm

TN12

Viney Farm

Greenways Farm

Moatenden Farm

Farthing Green

TN27

Richmond Farm

South Point Farm

Babylon Farm

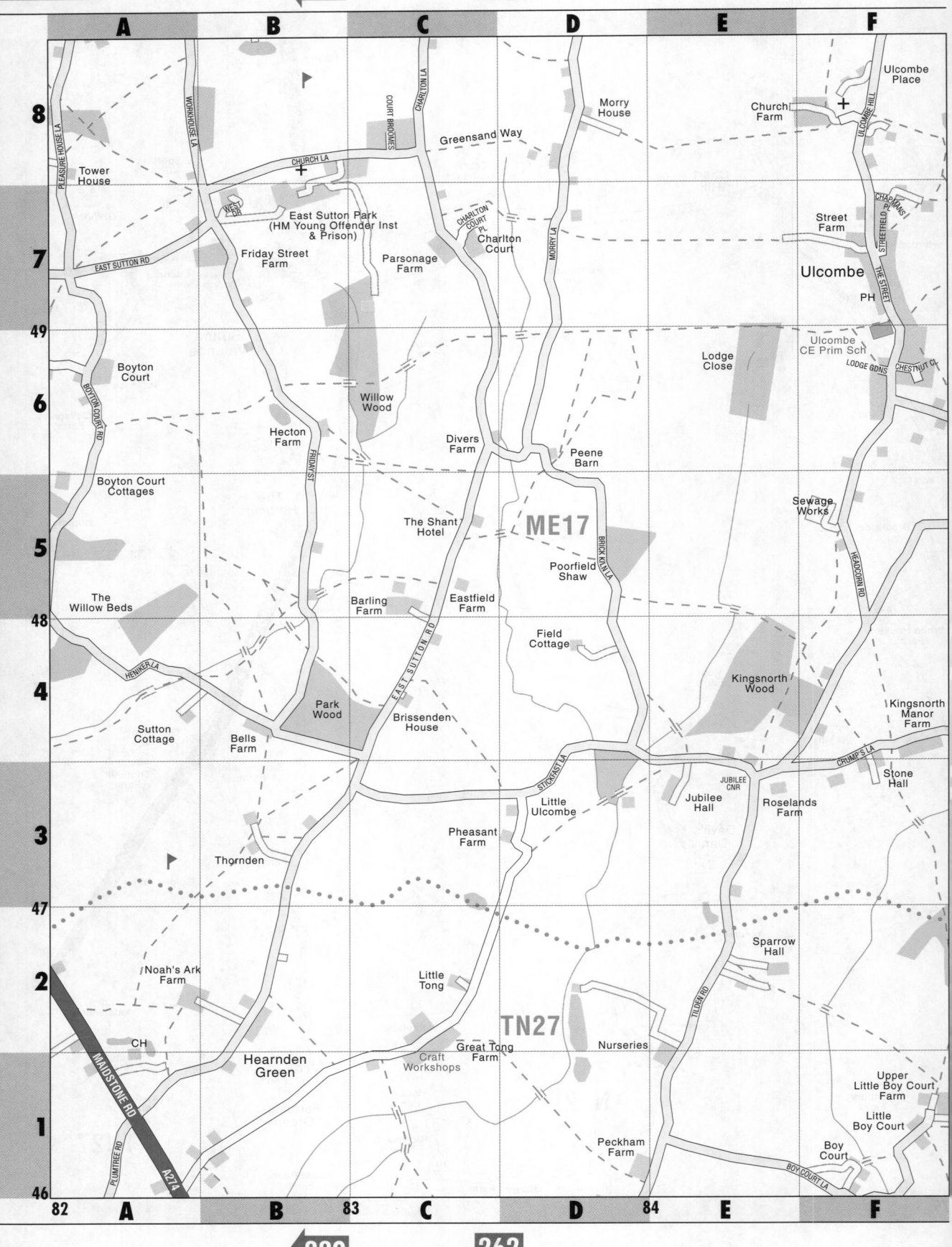

| | A | B | C | D | E | F |

Ulcombe Place
Church Farm
Morry House
Street Farm
Ulcombe
Tower House
Boyton Court
East Sutton Park (HM Young Offender Inst & Prison)
Friday Street Farm
Parsonage Farm
Charlton Court
Greensand Way
Ulcombe CE Prim Sch
Lodge Close
Hecton Farm
Willow Wood
Divers Farm
Peene Barn
Sewage Works
Boyton Court Cottages
The Shant Hotel
ME17
Poorfield Shaw
The Willow Beds
Barling Farm
Eastfield Farm
Field Cottage
Kingsnorth Wood
Kingsnorth Manor Farm
Sutton Cottage
Bells Farm
Park Wood
Brissenden House
Little Ulcombe
Jubilee Hall
Roselands Farm
Stone Hall
Thornden
Pheasant Farm
Sparrow Hall
Noah's Ark Farm
Little Tong
TN27
Nurseries
CH
Hearnden Green
Great Tong Farm
Craft Workshops
Upper Little Boy Court Farm
Little Boy Court
Peckham Farm
Boy Court

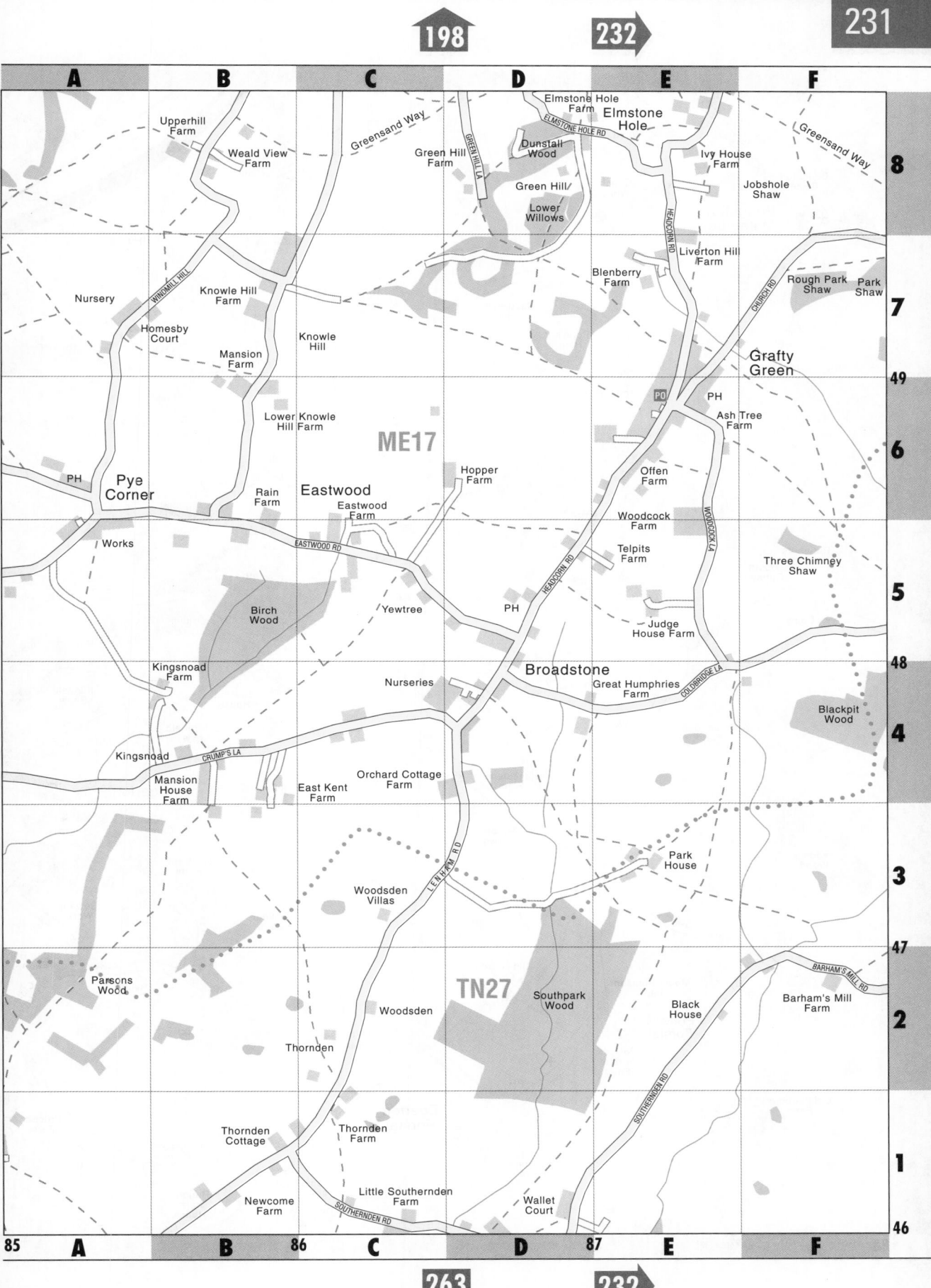

A B C D E F

8

Upperhill Farm
Weald View Farm
Greensand Way
Green Hill LA
GREEN HILL RD
Green Hill Farm
Elmstone Hole Farm
ELMSTONE HOLE RD
Dunstall Wood
Elmstone Hole
Ivy House Farm
Greensand Way
Jobshole Shaw

Nursery
WINDMILL HILL
Knowle Hill Farm
Homesby Court
Mansion Farm
Knowle Hill
Green Hill
Lower Willows
HEADCORN RD
Blenberry Farm
Liverton Hill Farm
CHURCH RD
Rough Park Shaw
Park Shaw

7

49

Lower Knowle Hill Farm
ME17
Grafty Green
PO
PH
Ash Tree Farm

6

PH
Pye Corner
Rain Farm
Eastwood
Hopper Farm
Eastwood Farm
Offen Farm
Woodcock Farm
WOODCOCK LA
Three Chimney Shaw

5

Works
EASTWOOD RD
Birch Wood
Yewtree
PH
HEADCORN RD
Telpits Farm
Judge House Farm

48

Kingsnoad Farm
Nurseries
Broadstone
Great Humphries Farm
COLDBRIDGE LA
Blackpit Wood

4

Kingsnoad
CRUMP'S LA
Mansion House Farm
East Kent Farm
Orchard Cottage Farm
LENHAM RD
Park House

3

47

Parsons Wood
Woodsden Villas
TN27
Southpark Wood
Black House
BARHAM'S MILL RD
Barham's Mill Farm

2

Woodsden
Thornden
SOUTHERNDEN RD

Thornden Cottage
Thornden Farm

1

Newcome Farm
SOUTHERNDEN RD
Little Southernden Farm
Wallet Court

46

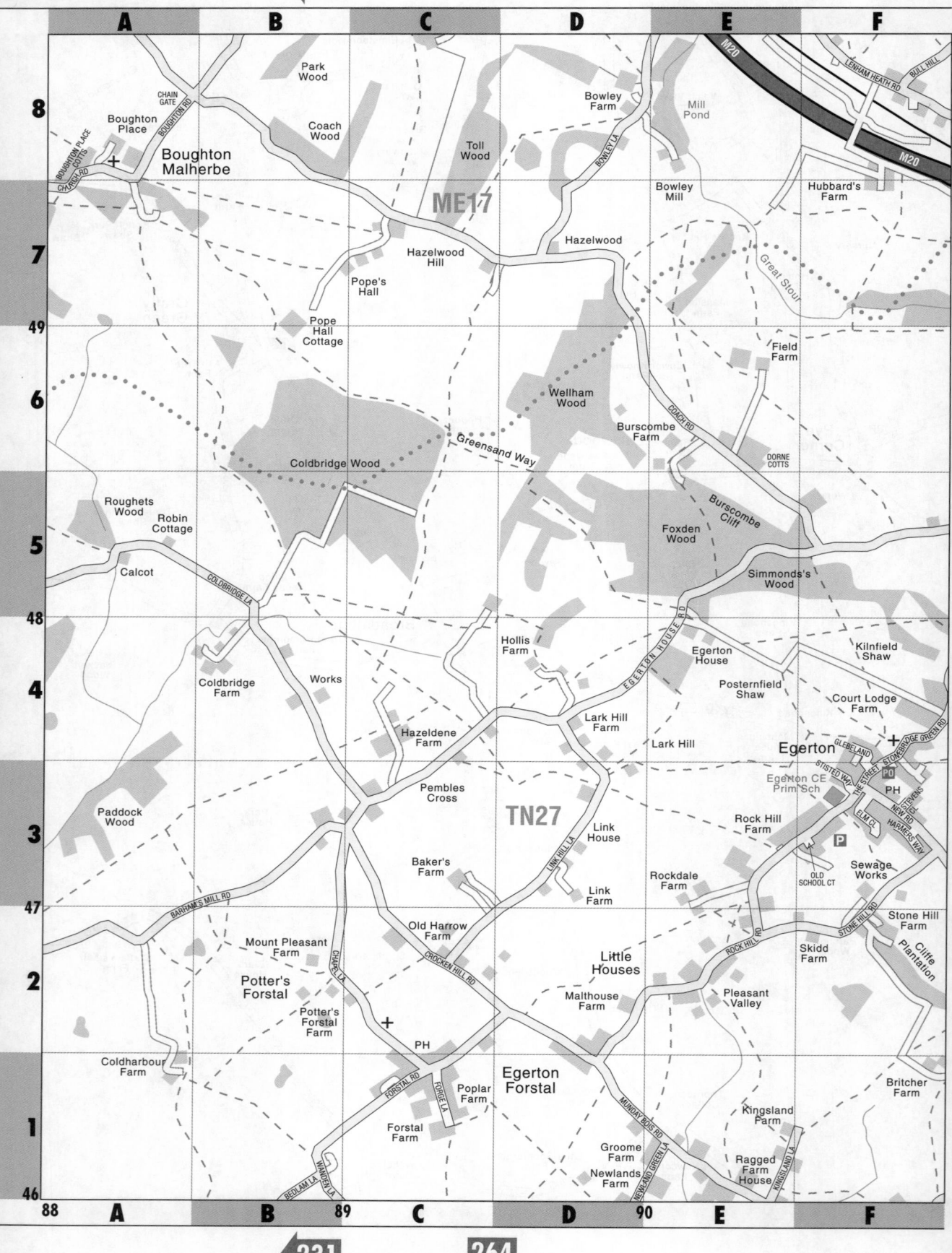

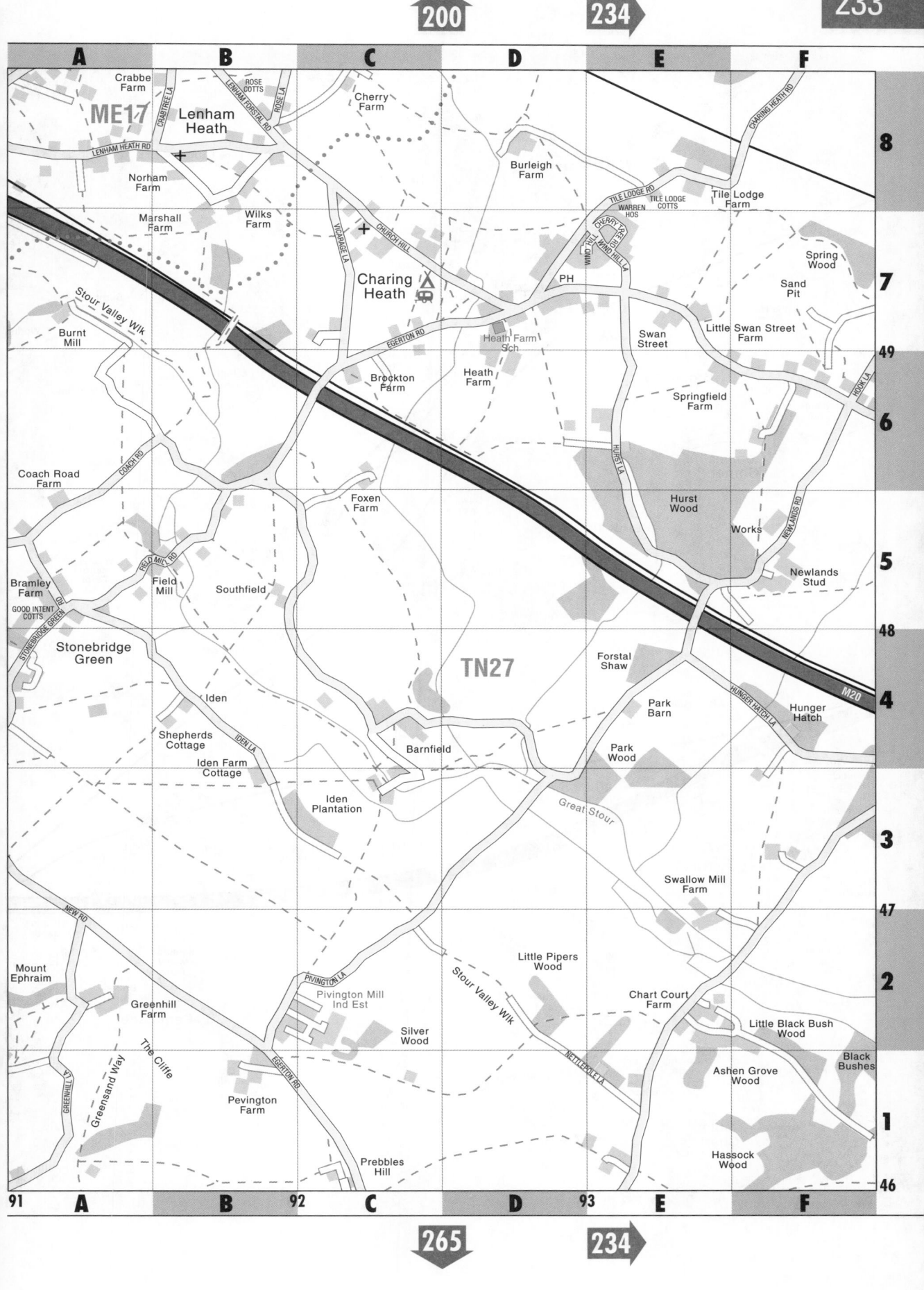

200 234

ME17

Crabbe Farm

CHARTREE LA

ROSE COTTS

Lenham Heath

ROSE LA

Cherry Farm

Burleigh Farm

CHARING HEATH RD

8

Norham Farm

LENHAM FORSTAL RD

TILE LODGE RD
Tile Lodge Cotts
Tile Lodge Farm

Marshall Farm

Wilks Farm

LENHAM HEATH RD

Spring Wood

VICARAGE LA

WARREN HOS

WIND HILL

CHERRY TREE RD

WIND HILL LA

Sand Pit

CHURCH HILL

7

Charing Heath

PH

Swan Street

Little Swan Street Farm

HOOK LA

EGERTON RD

Heath Farm Sch

49

Stour Valley Wlk

Burnt Mill

Brockton Farm

Heath Farm

Springfield Farm

6

HURST LA

Coach Road Farm

COACH RD

Foxen Farm

Hurst Wood

NEWLANDS RD

Works

FIELD MILL RD

Field Mill

Southfield

Newlands Stud

5

Bramley Farm

GOOD INTENT COTTS

STONEBRIDGE GREEN

48

Stonebridge Green

TN27

Forstal Shaw

HUNGER HATCH LA

M20

4

Iden

IDEN LA

Barnfield

Park Barn

Hunger Hatch

Shepherds Cottage

Park Wood

Iden Farm Cottage

Iden Plantation

Great Stour

3

NEW RD

Swallow Mill Farm

47

Mount Ephraim

Little Pipers Wood

Chart Court Farm

2

PIVINGTON LA

Greenhill Farm

Pivington Mill Ind Est

Stour Valley Wlk

Little Black Bush Wood

GREENHILL LA

The Cliffe

Greensand Way

EGERTON RD

Silver Wood

NETTLEPOLE LA

Black Bushes

Pevington Farm

Ashen Grove Wood

1

Prebbles Hill

Hassock Wood

46

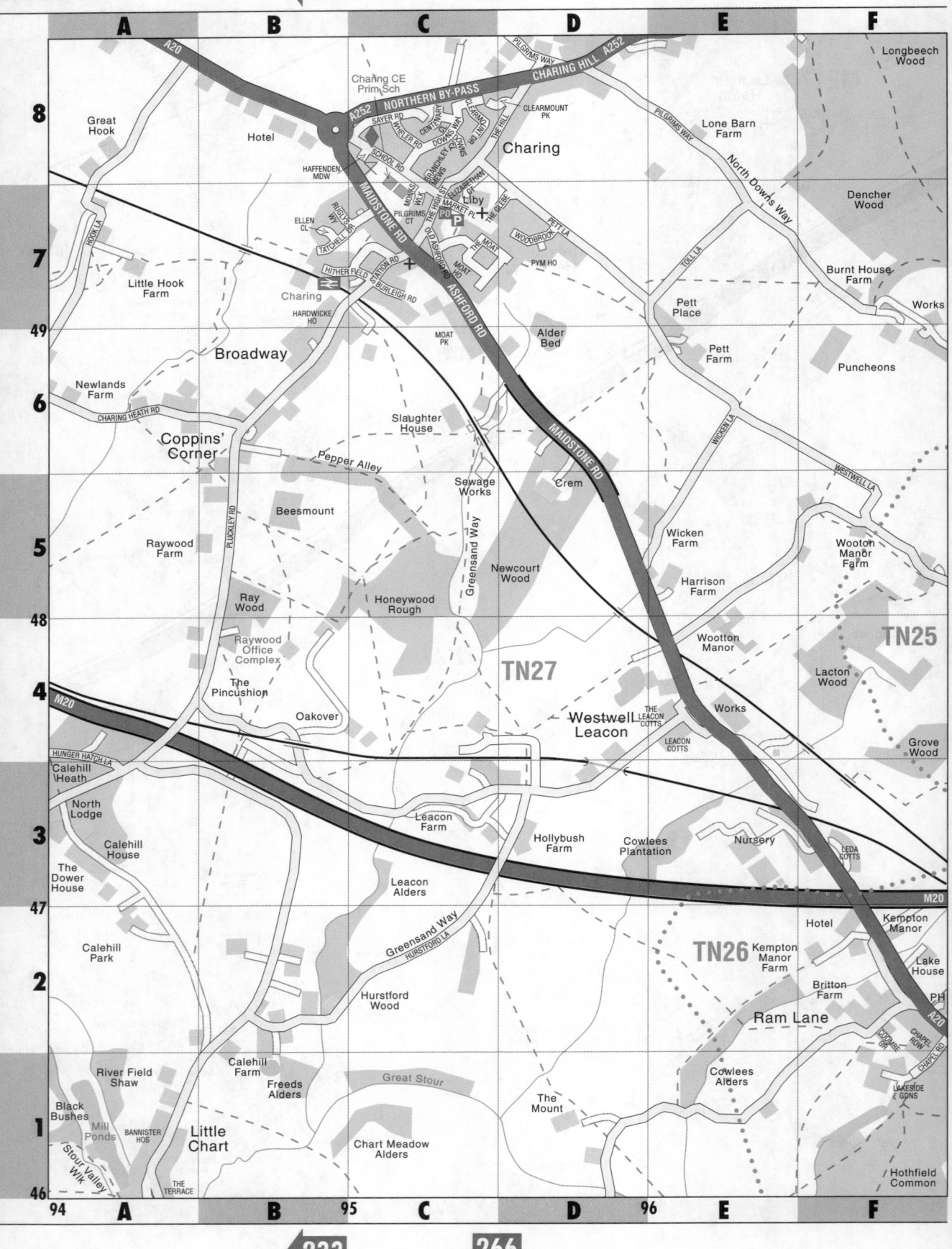

A   B   C   D   E   F

8

A20

Longbeech
Wood

Great
Hook

Hotel

Charing CE
Prim Sch

PILGRIMS WAY

CHARING HILL A252

Lone Barn
Farm

Dencher
Wood

NORTHERN BY-PASS

A252

SAYER RD
WHEELER RD

CLEARMOUNT
PK

Charing

PILGRIMS WAY

North Downs Way

7

HOOK LA

Little Hook
Farm

HAFFENDEN
MDW

MAIDSTONE RD

ELLEN
CL

RIGLESFORD

TATCHELL DR

PILGRIMS
CT

PO
P

Liby

THE HIGH
MARKET PL

THE GREBE

PETT LA

WOODBROOK

MOAT

PYM HO

TOLL LA

Pett
Place

Burnt House
Farm

Works

49

HITHER FIELD

BURLEIGH RD

HARDWICKE
HO

Charing

MOAT
PK

Alder
Bed

Pett
Farm

Puncheons

Broadway

6

Newlands
Farm

CHARING HEATH RD

Slaughter
House

Crem

MAIDSTONE RD

WICKEN LA

WESTWELL LA

Coppins'
Corner

PLUCKLEY RD

Pepper Alley

Sewage
Works

Greensand Way

Wicken
Farm

Wooton
Manor
Farm

5

Raywood
Farm

Beesmount

Honeywood
Rough

Newcourt
Wood

Harrison
Farm

Wootton
Manor

Lacton
Wood

48

Ray
Wood

Raywood
Office
Complex

TN27

Works

TN25

4

M20

The
Pincushion

Oakover

Westwell
Leacon

THE
LEACON
COTTS

LEACON
COTTS

Grove
Wood

Calehill
Heath

HUNGER HATCH LA

Leacon
Farm

Hollybush
Farm

Cowlees
Plantation

Nursery

LEDA
COTTS

North
Lodge

3

Calehill
House

Leacon
Alders

M20

47

The
Dower
House

Greensand Way

HURSTFORD LA

TN26

Kempton
Manor
Farm

Hotel

Kempton
Manor

Calehill
Park

Lake
House

2

Hurstford
Wood

Britton
Farm

A20

PH

Ram Lane

CHAPEL ROW

CHAPEL RD

River Field
Shaw

Calehill
Farm

Freeds
Alders

Great Stour

Cowlees
Alders

COOMBE DR

LAKESIDE
GDNS

1

Black
Bushes

Mill Ponds

BANNISTER
HOS

Little
Chart

Chart Meadow
Alders

The
Mount

Hothfield
Common

46

Stour Valley Wlk

THE
TERRACE

94   A   B   95   C   D   96   E   F

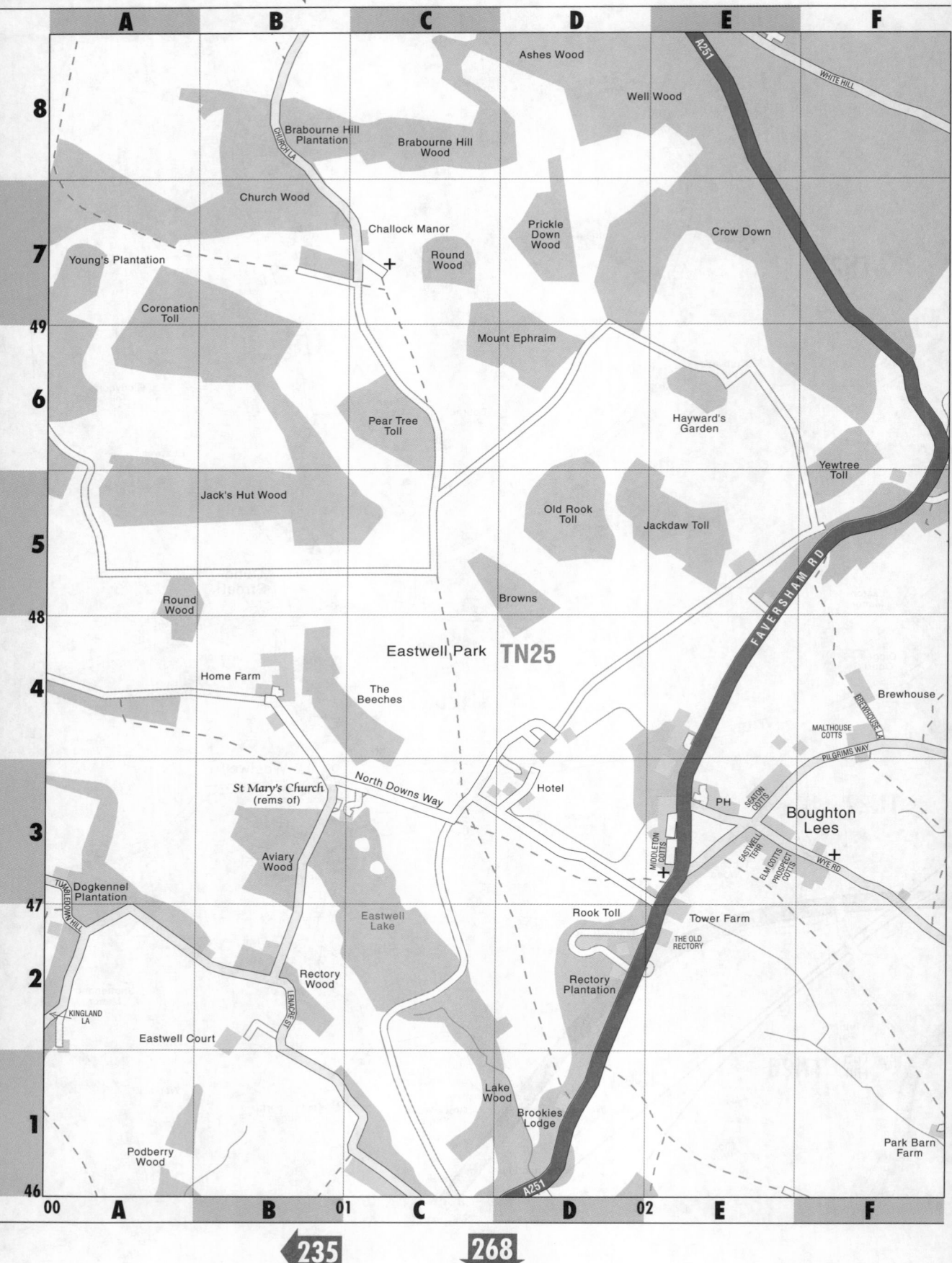

A   B   C   D   E   F

8

Ashes Wood

Well Wood

Brabourne Hill
Plantation

CHURCH LA

Brabourne Hill
Wood

Church Wood

Prickle
Down
Wood

Crow Down

A251

WHITE HILL

7

Challock Manor

Round
Wood

Young's Plantation

49

Coronation
Toll

Mount Ephraim

6

Pear Tree
Toll

Hayward's
Garden

Yewtree
Toll

Jack's Hut Wood

Old Rook
Toll

Jackdaw Toll

FAVERSHAM RD

5

Round
Wood

48

Browns

Eastwell Park   **TN25**

4

Home Farm

The
Beeches

Brewhouse

BREWHOUSE LA

MALTHOUSE
COTTS

PILGRIMS WAY

St Mary's Church
(rems of)

North Downs Way

Hotel

PH

SEATON
COTTS

Boughton
Lees

3

Aviary
Wood

MIDDLETON
COTTS

EASTWELL
TERR

ELM COTTS
PROSPECT
COTTS

WYE RD

TUTT ELDOWN HILL

Dogkennel
Plantation

47

Rook Toll

Tower Farm

Eastwell
Lake

THE OLD
RECTORY

2

Rectory
Wood

Kingland
La

LENACRE ST

Rectory
Plantation

Eastwell Court

1

Lake
Wood

Brookies
Lodge

Park Barn
Farm

Podberry
Wood

A251

46

00   A   B   01   C   D   02   E   F

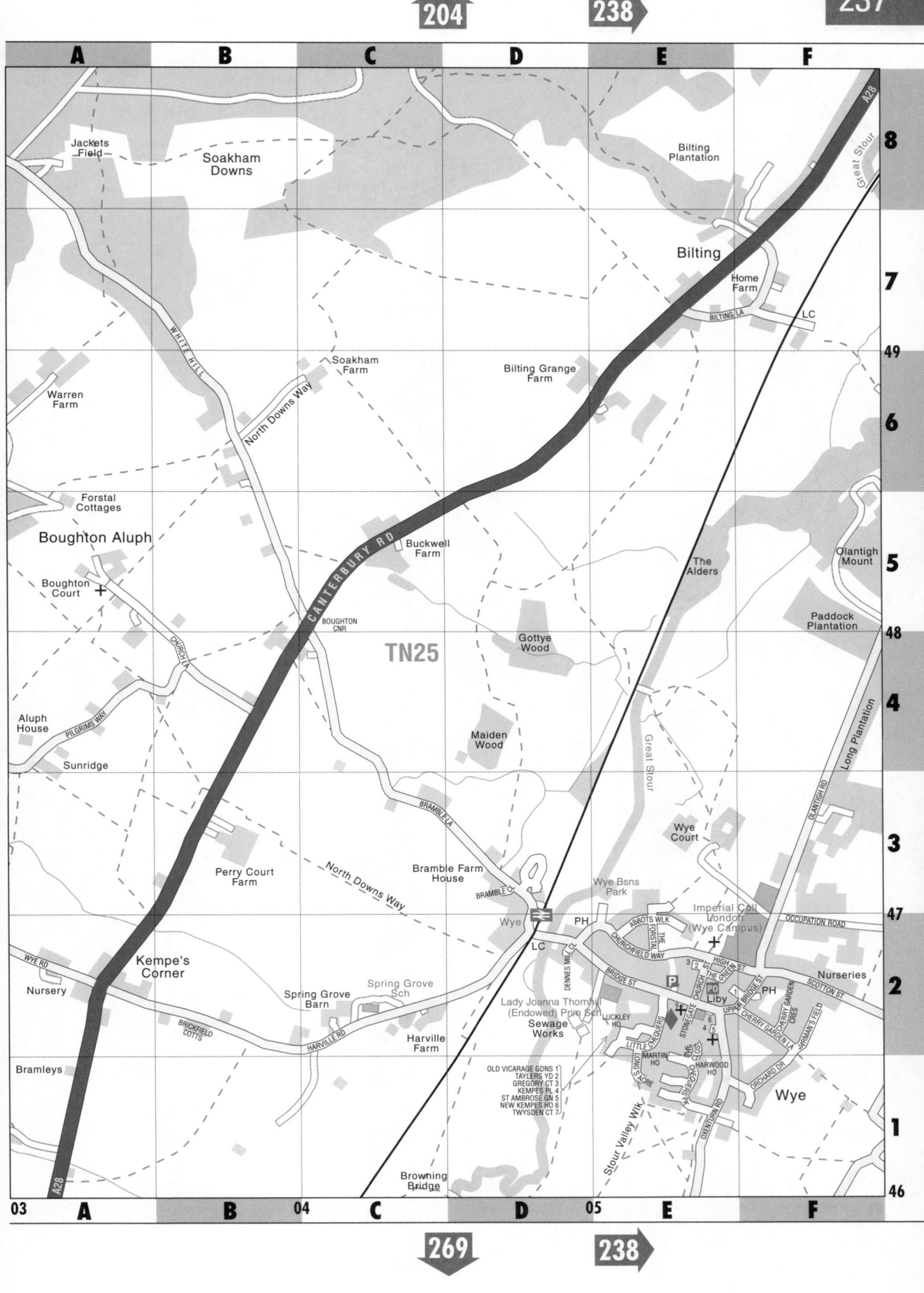

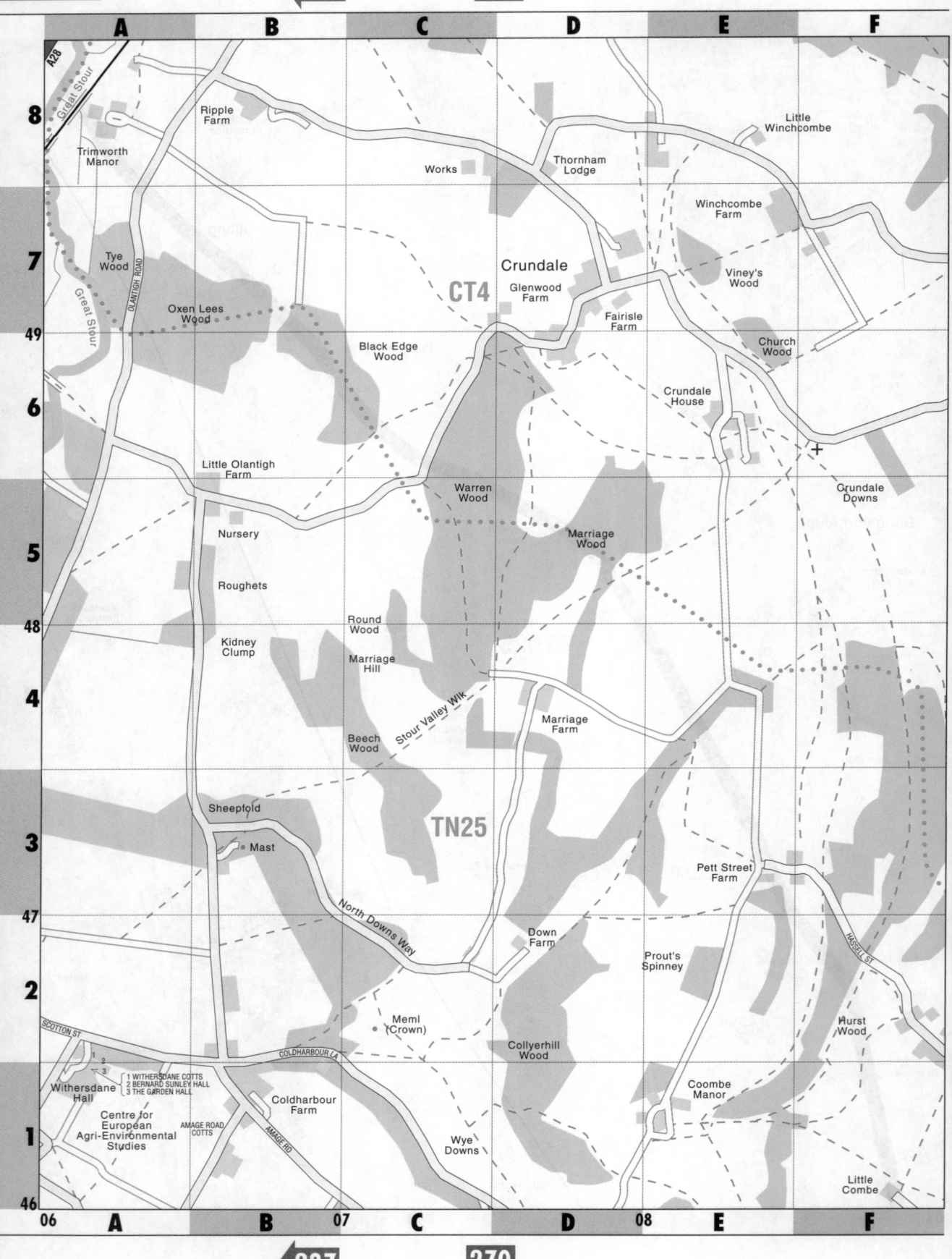

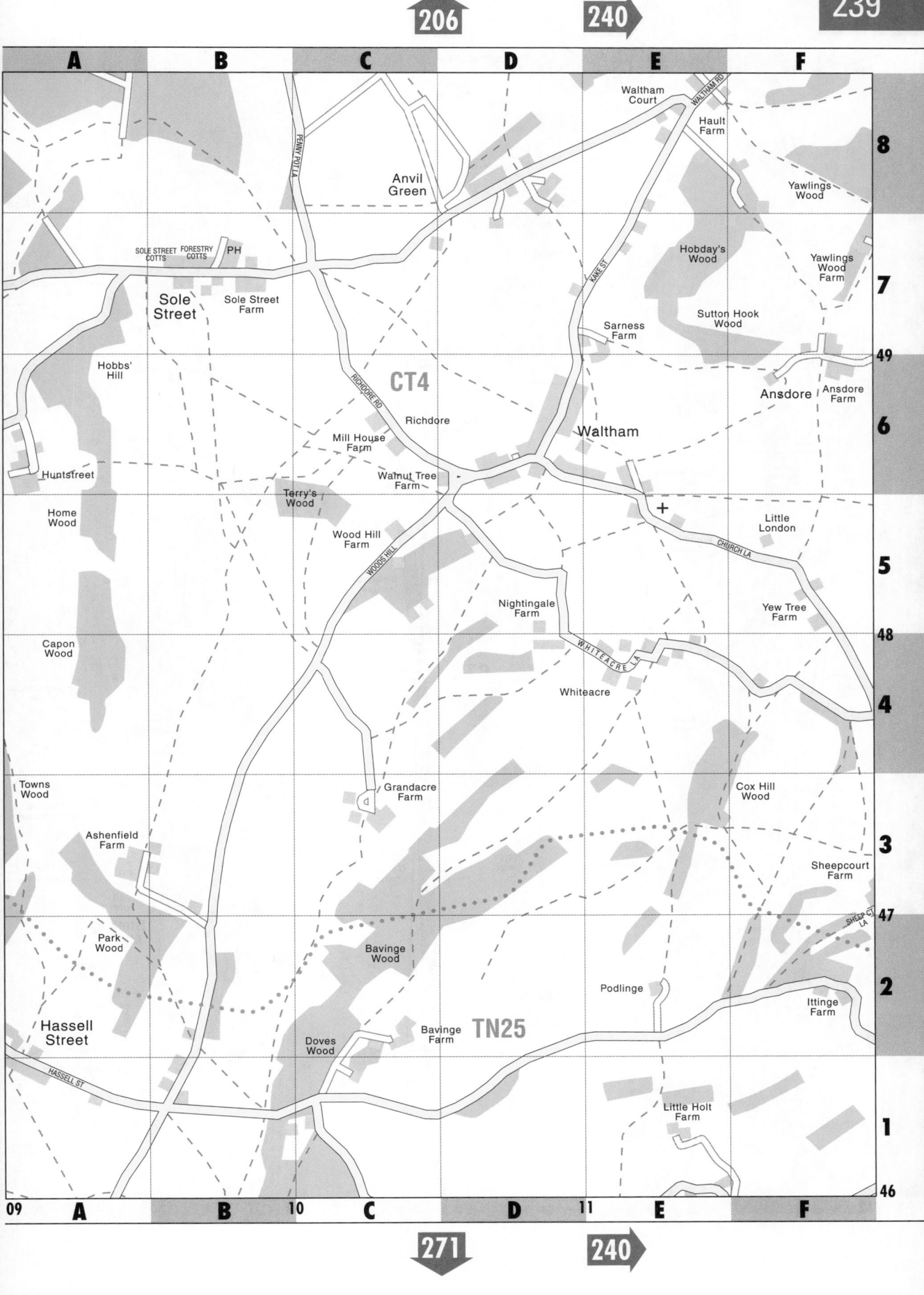

A B C D E F

8

Waltham Court

Hault Farm

Anvil Green

Yawlings Wood

SOLE STREET COTTS FORESTRY COTTS PH

Sole Street

Sole Street Farm

KAKE ST

Hobday's Wood

Yawlings Wood Farm

7

Hobbs' Hill

CT4

Richdore

RICHDORE RD

Sarness Farm

Sutton Hook Wood

49

Ansdore

Ansdore Farm

6

Huntstreet

Mill House Farm

Walnut Tree Farm

Waltham

Terry's Wood

Home Wood

Wood Hill Farm

WOODS HILL

+

Little London

CHURCH LA

5

Capon Wood

Nightingale Farm

Yew Tree Farm

48

WHITEACRE LA

Whiteacre

4

Towns Wood

Grandacre Farm

Cox Hill Wood

3

Ashenfield Farm

Sheepcourt Farm

47

SHEEP CT LA

Park Wood

Bavinge Wood

Podlinge

Ittinge Farm

2

Hassell Street

Doves Wood

Bavinge Farm

TN25

Little Holt Farm

1

HASSELL ST

46

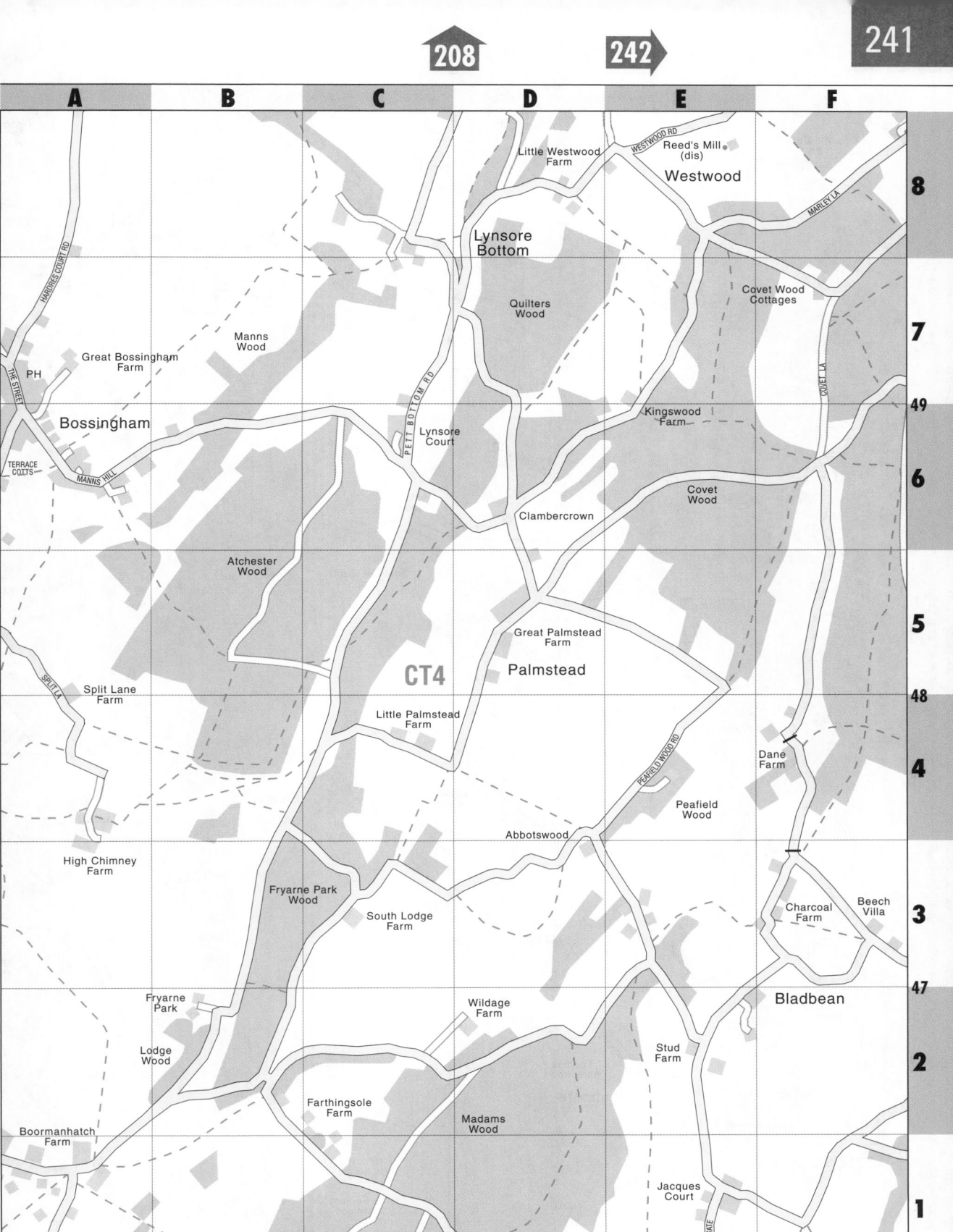

208
242

A B C D E F

8
7
49
6
5
48
4
3
47
2
1
46

Westwood Rd
Reed's Mill (dis)
Westwood
Little Westwood Farm
Marley La

Lynsore Bottom

Covet Wood Cottages

Hardres Court Rd
Manns Wood
Quilters Wood

The Street
PH
Great Bossingham Farm
Kingswood Farm
Covet La

49

Bossingham
Lynsore Court
Pett Bottom Rd

Terrace Cotts
Manns Hill
Clambercrown
Covet Wood

Atchester Wood

CT4
Great Palmstead Farm
Palmstead

Split La
Split Lane Farm
Little Palmstead Farm

Peafield Wood Rd
Dane Farm

High Chimney Farm
Abbotswood
Peafield Wood

Fryarne Park Wood
Charcoal Farm
Beech Villa

South Lodge Farm
Bladbean

Fryarne Park
Wildage Farm

Lodge Wood
Stud Farm

Farthingsole Farm
Madams Wood

Boormanhatch Farm

Jacques Court
Park Gate

15 A B 16 C D 17 E F

273
242

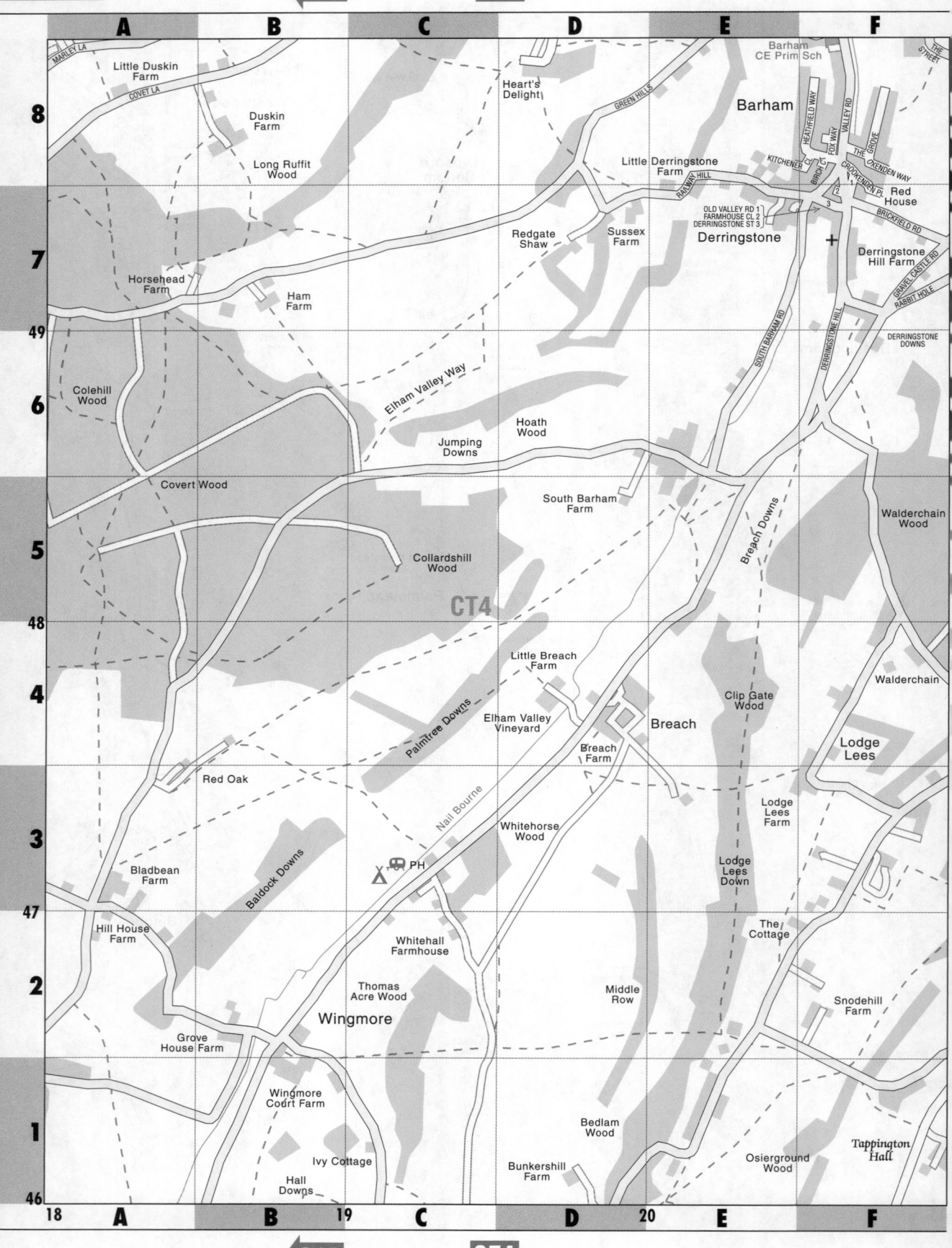

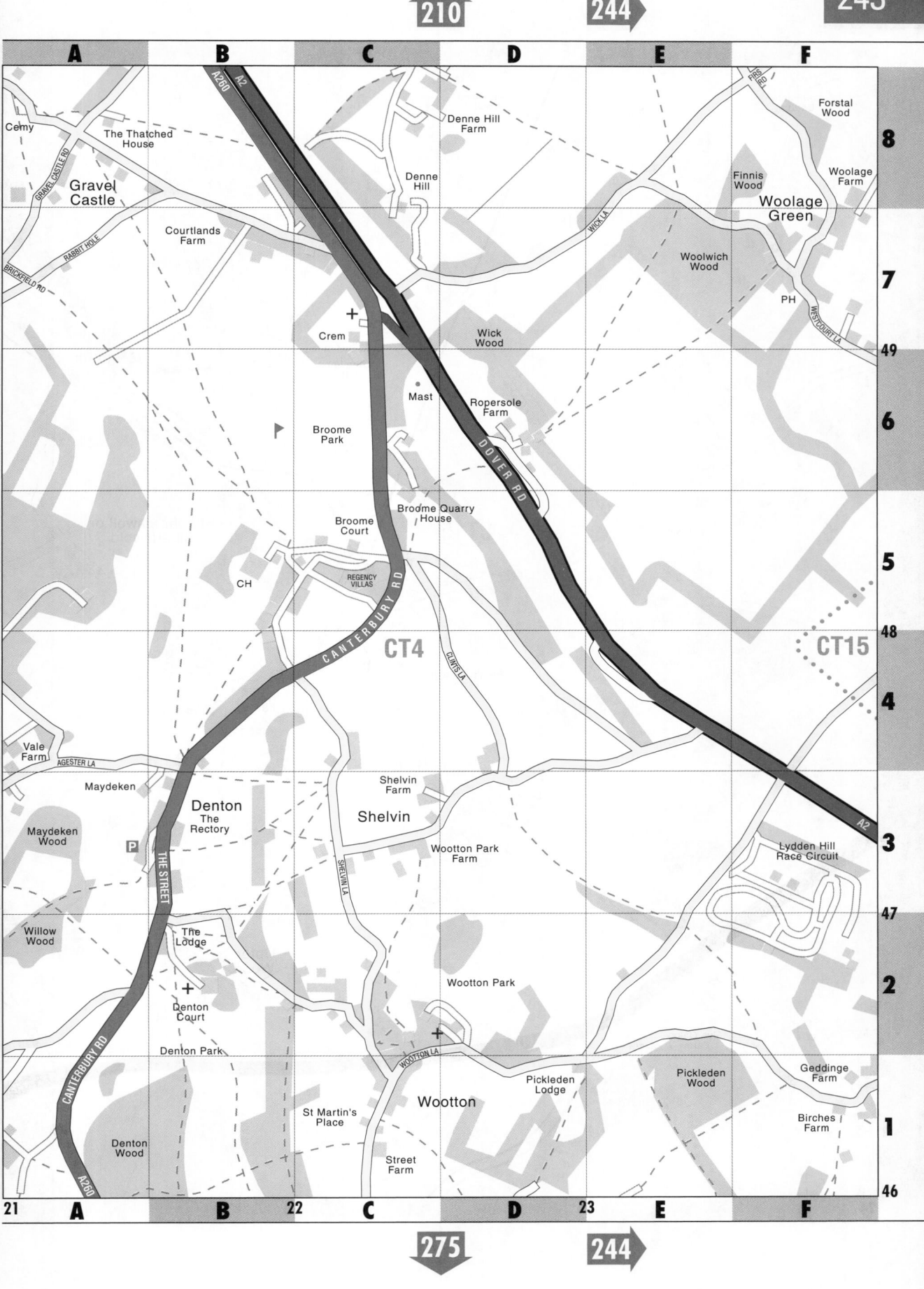

210
244

A B C D E F

8
7
49
6

5
48
4

3
47
2

1
46

CT4

CT15

Cemy
Gravel Castle
The Thatched House
GRAVEL CASTLE RD
RABBIT HOLE
BRICKFIELD RD
Courtlands Farm
A260
A2
Denne Hill Farm
Denne Hill
FIRS RD
Forstal Wood
Finnis Wood
Woolage Farm
Woolage Green
Woolwich Wood
WICK LA
PH
WESTCOURT LA
Crem
Mast
Wick Wood
Ropersole Farm
Broome Park
DOVER RD
Broome Quarry House
Broome Court
CH
REGENCY VILLAS
CANTERBURY RD
GUNS LA
Shelvin Farm
Shelvin
Wootton Park Farm
Lydden Hill Race Circuit
A2
Vale Farm
AGESTER LA
Maydeken
Denton
The Rectory
Maydeken Wood
P
THE STREET
SHELVIN LA
Willow Wood
The Lodge
Denton Court
Denton Park
CANTERBURY RD
A260
Denton Wood
St Martin's Place
Wootton
WOOTTON LA
Wootton Park
Pickleden Lodge
Pickleden Wood
Geddinge Farm
Birches Farm
Street Farm

243   211

A B C D E F

8

Leighgate Bottom

Three Barrows Down

Lower Soles Wood

CT4

Long La

Stafflands Wood

7

North Downs Way

LONG LA

49

Long Lane Farm

Golgotha

6

West Court Downs

East Kent Railway

LC

SHEPHERDSWELL RD

Crossways

CT15

Shepherdswell or Sibertswold

5

Shepherds Well

MOSWELL DR
STATION RD

GLEN   PENFOLD GDNS
EYTHORNE RD
BERNARD
MEADOW VIEW RD
ST ANDREW'S GDNS

HILL

MILL LA HACLING DANE

WESTCOURT LA

THE TERRACE
THE GRANGE

APPROACH RD

COOMBE DRIVE

SIBERT'S CL

48

PH

THE OAKLEYS

PH

PROSPECT COTTS

CHURCH HILL

MILLFIELDS

Puckland Wood

West Court Farm

WHITTINGTON TERR

P

PO

MOORLAND RD

BROOM HILL

4

Botolph Street Farm

Sibertswold CE Prim Sch

PH

Upton Court Farm

Halfway Street

Diamond Farm

COLDRED RD

Coxhill Farm

3

A2

DOVER RD

Hope Wood

COXHILL

Claysole Wood

47

Upton Wood

THE CONIFERS

CHURCH RD

2

CT4

Five Oaks Farm   Mast

A2

CHURCH RD

1

Lyddenhill Wood

LYDDEN HILL

COLDRED HILL

46

24   A   B   25   C   D   26   E   F

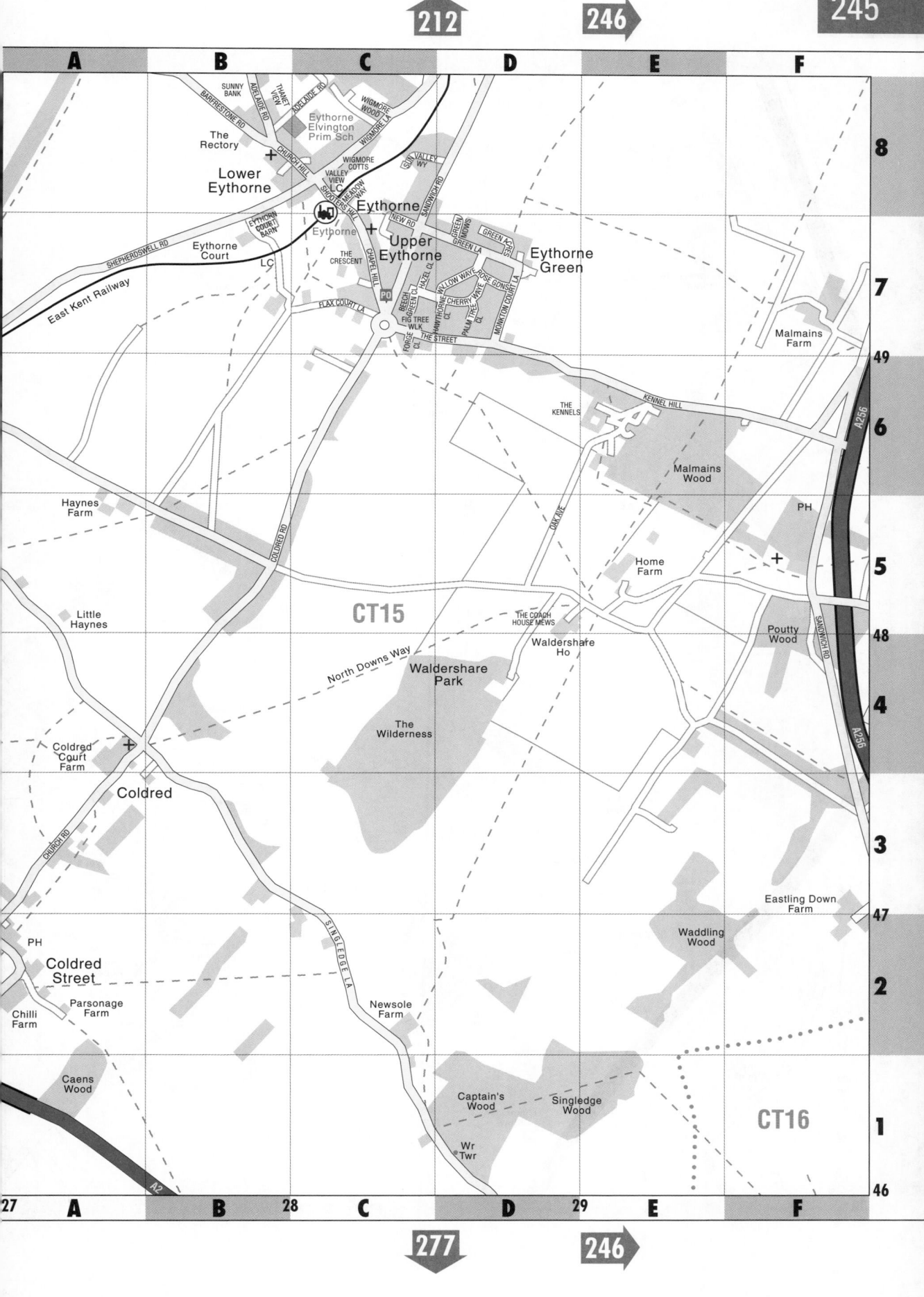

A B C D E F

8
7
49
6
5
48
4
3
47
2
1
46

SUNNY BANK
BARFRESTONE RD
ADELAIDE RD
THANET VIEW
ADELAIDE RD
WIGMORE WOOD
WIGMORE LA
Eythorne Elvington Prim Sch
WIGMORE COTTS
The Rectory
CHURCH HILL
VALLEY VIEW
Lower Eythorne
GUN VALLEY WY
SANDWICH RD
LC
MEADOW WAY
SADLERS HILL
Eythorne
Eythorne
NEW RD
GREEN MDWS
GREEN LA
GREEN LA
GREEN ACRES
Upper Eythorne
Eythorne Green
SHEPHERDSWELL RD
Eythorne Court
EYTHORN COURT BARN
LC
THE CRESCENT
CHAPEL HILL
FLAX COURT LA
PO
BEECH
GREEN CL
HAZEL CL
HAWTHORNE WY
WILLOW WAY
ROSE GDNS
MONKTON COURT LA
CHERRY
PALM TREE
PATH
CL
FIG TREE WLK
FORGE CL
THE STREET
East Kent Railway

Malmains Farm

KENNEL HILL
THE KENNELS

A256

Malmains Wood

PH

Haynes Farm
COLDRED RD
OAK AVE
Home Farm

+

CT15
SANDWICH RD

Little Haynes
Poutty Wood
48

THE COACH HOUSE MEWS
Waldershare Ho

North Downs Way
Waldershare Park

Coldred Court Farm
+

The Wilderness

A256

Coldred

CHURCH RD

Eastling Down Farm
47

PH
Coldred Street
SINGLEDGE LA
Waddling Wood

Parsonage Farm
Newsole Farm

Chilli Farm

Caens Wood

Captain's Wood
Singledge Wood
CT16

Wr Twr

A2

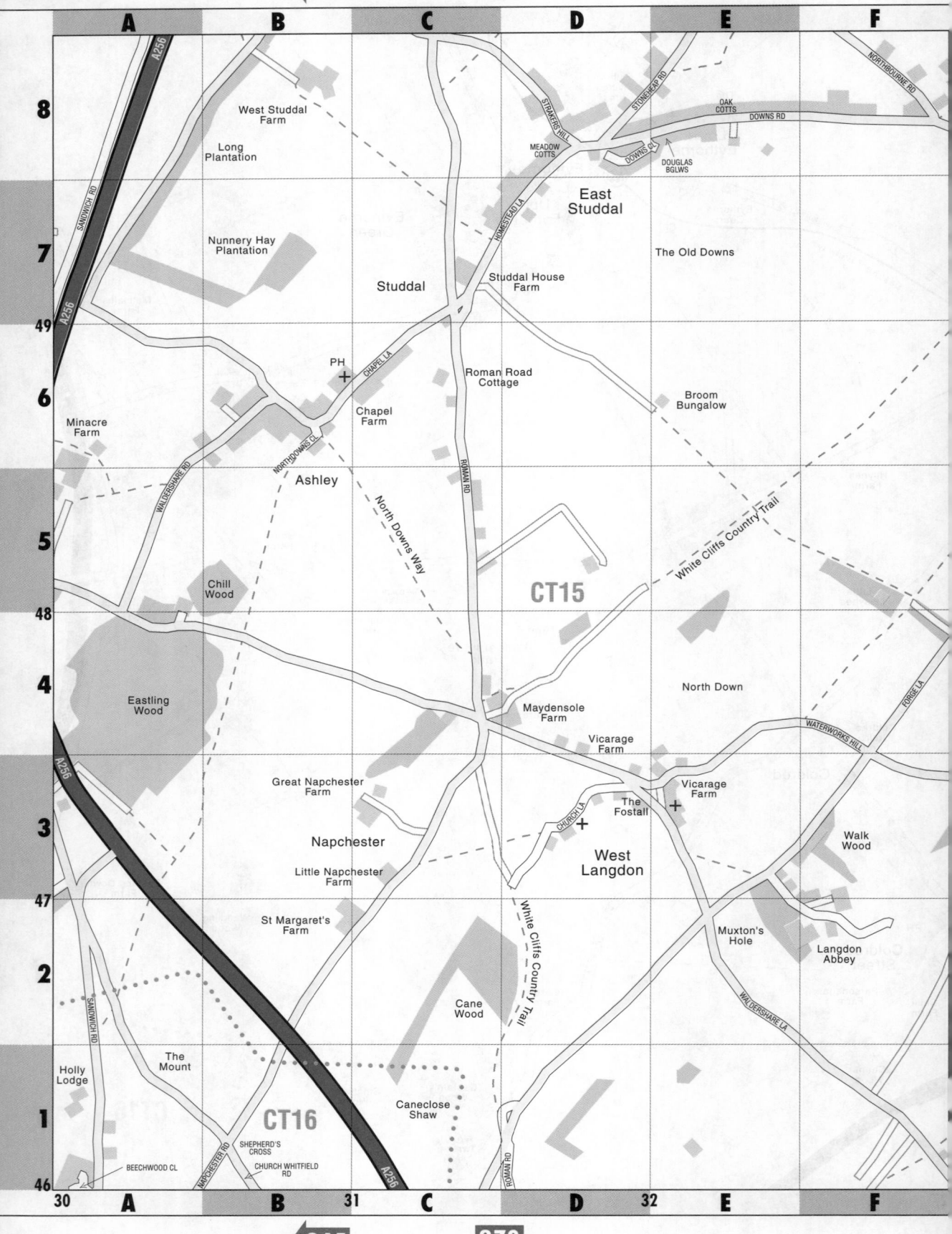

A B C D E F

White Cliffs Country Trail

CRANSWICK COTTS

SUTTON LA

MAYTREE COTTS

CHAPEL LA

CHURCH LA

PORTLAND TERR

Homestead Farm

Coldblow Farm

PH

Ripple

Ripplevale Sch

8

Sutton Vale Country Club

DOWNS RD

VALE RD

Parsonage Farm

POMMEUS LA

Ripple Farm

Upper Farm

CHURCH HILL

CROOKED S RD

RIPPLE RD

7

Sutton Court Farm

+

Sutton

Wingleton Farm

49

Holly Lodge

COLDBLOW

FORGE LA

SUTTON LANE

6

Downs

Ripple Court

RIPPLE CROSS

CT14

SUTTON LA

Sutton

The Forest

MANOR MEWS

Winkland Oaks Farm

Ringwould

CHURCH LA

+

FRONT ST

HANGMAN'S LA

BACK ST

S RISE

CHURCH HAVEN

A258

5

48

CT15

Nursery

DOVER RD

4

Appleton Manor

RINGWOULD RD

WATERWORKS HILL

Oxneybottom Wood

3

Mast

Martin

50

WATERWORKS LA

Martin Lodge

PH

THE STREET

47

The Grange

WHEATSHEAF LA

St Nicholas Church (rems of)

Martin Lodge Farm

EAST LANGDON RD

LUCERNE LA

Hollands Hill

1 MARTIN DALE CRES
2 STATION APP

2

Martin Mill

Oxney Court

Martin Mill

BARLEY CL

OLD ROMAN RD

Langdon Prim Sch

LUCERNE LA

RAILWAY COTTS

GREEN LA

GURLING RD

East Langdon

WEST SIDE

P.O.

Martin Vale

STATION RD

Mast

VICTORY RD

NELSON PARK RD

THE CHASE

1

THE STREET

Jossingblock

CHURCH FARM MS

Church Farm

A258

BERESFORD RD

46

33 A B 34 C D 35 E F

A B C D E F

8

Cold Blow
Crossing
LC

ST MARGARETS DR 1
WHITE ACRE DR 2
KINGSLAND GDNS 3
DOWNLANDS 4
THE MALTINGS 5
THISTLEDOWN 6

BLAKE CL

GRAMS RD

Hawksdown

Rays Bottom

Hawks
Hill

Hawkshill Rd

Hawkshill
House

LIVERPOOL RD

HAWKSDOWN

NEWLANDS DR

A258

SIMPSON CL

COLDBLOW

7

RIPPLE RD

Windmill
(dis)

Claytons
Hill

Knights
Bottom

Hawkshill
Down

KINGSDOWN RD

CECIL RD

WELLINGTON PARADE

DOVER RD

49

6

Knights
Hill

GLEN RD

CLAREMONT TCE

CLAREMONT RD

OSBORNE RD

BALMORAL RD

EDWARD RD

CARLTON RD

SEA RD

KING'S CL

CLIM DOWN

ST MONICAS RD

ST
MONICAS

MOUNT
PLEASANT

WATLANDS RD

BOUNDARY
RD

CHURCH CLIFF

CLIFF RD

JARVIST
PL NORTH
RD

WELLINGTON PAR

PH

Kingsdown
& Ringwould
CE Prim Sch

THE RISE

THE WEST

ST JAMES RD

SOUTH RD

Ripple
Down
House

CHURCH LA

A258

RINGWOULD RD

Woodhill
Farm

Chalk
Hill
Farm

CHALK HILL RD

ALEXANDRA RD

UPPER ST

PO

Kingsdown
Holiday Village

Kingsdown

SAXON SHORE WAY

UNDERCLIFFE RD

5

Great
Coombe

CT14

48

Wood
Hill

VICTORIA RD

HILLCREST HILL

KINGSDOWN HILL

THE AVE

Oldstairs Bay

COASTGUARD
COTTS

OLDSTAIRS RD

CH

White Cliffs Country Trail

The Swamp

4

The Lynch

Hill
Farm

Barrows
Hill

VICTORIA RD

QUEENSDOWN RD

BAYVIEW RD

NORTHMOTE RD

East Bottom
Farm

Morningside

THE LEAS

Old Parker's
Cap

3

GREEN LA

ST MARGARETS RD

Free
Down

Otty
Bottom

Kelf
Farm

OLDSTAIRS RD

East Bottom

GRANVILLE RD

47

2

East Valley
Farm

East Hill

NELSON PARK RD

CT15

1

BOYNE RD

Old Bottom
Free Down

COLLINGWOOD RD

NORWAY DRIVE

FLEET RD

Barrow
Mount

Hope
Point

46

36 A B 37 C D 38 E F

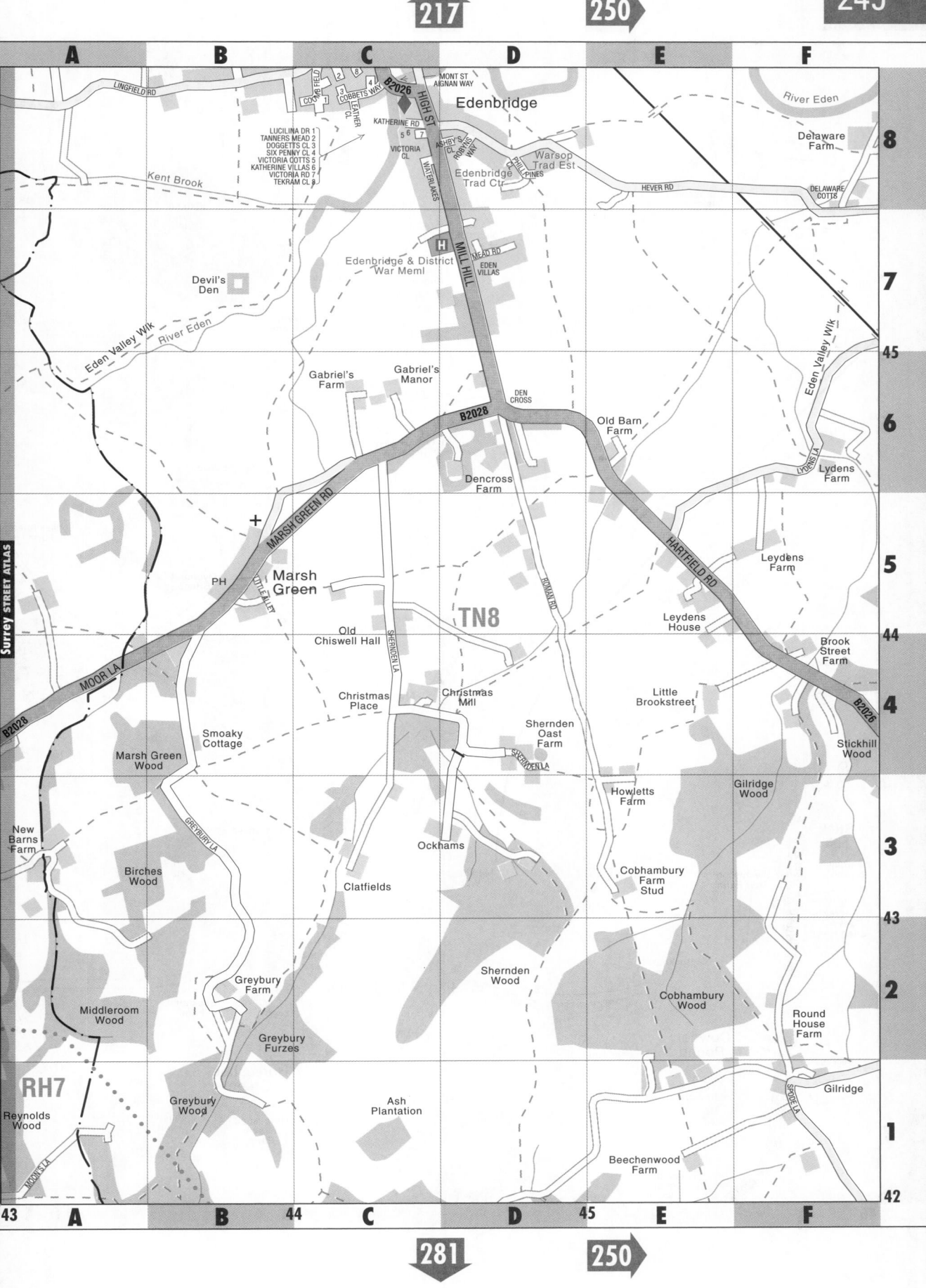

LINGFIELD RD

B2026

MONT ST AIGNAN WAY

Edenbridge

River Eden

Delaware Farm

KATHERINE RD

LUCILINA DR 1
TANNERS MEAD 2
DOGGETTS CL 3
SIX PENNY CL 4
VICTORIA COTTS 5
KATHERINE VILLAS 6
VICTORIA RD 7
TEKRAM CL 8

VICTORIA CL

Warsop Trad Est

HEVER RD

DELAWARE COTTS

Kent Brook

Edenbridge Trad Ctr

Devil's Den

H

Edenbridge & District War Meml

MILL HILL

MEAD RD

EDEN VILLAS

Eden Valley Wlk

River Eden

45

Gabriel's Farm

Gabriel's Manor

DEN CROSS

Eden Valley Wlk

7

B2028

Old Barn Farm

LYDENS LA

6

Dencross Farm

Lydens Farm

MARSH GREEN RD

+

HARTFIELD RD

Leydens Farm

PH

Marsh Green

LITTLE ALLEY

TN8

Leydens House

5

Old Chiswell Hall

SHERNDEN LA

44

Brook Street Farm

MOOR LA

Christmas Place

Christmas Mill

EDWARD RD

Little Brookstreet

B2026

4

B2028

Smoaky Cottage

Shernden Oast Farm

SHERNDEN LA

Stickhill Wood

Marsh Green Wood

Howletts Farm

Gilridge Wood

New Barns Farm

GREYBURY LA

Ockhams

Cobhambury Farm Stud

3

Birches Wood

Clatfields

43

Shernden Wood

Greybury Farm

Cobhambury Wood

Middleroom Wood

2

Greybury Furzes

ROUND HOUSE FARM

RH7

Greybury Wood

Ash Plantation

SPODE LA

Gilridge

Reynolds Wood

MOOR LA

Beechenwood Farm

1

42

43 A 44 B C 44 D 45 E F

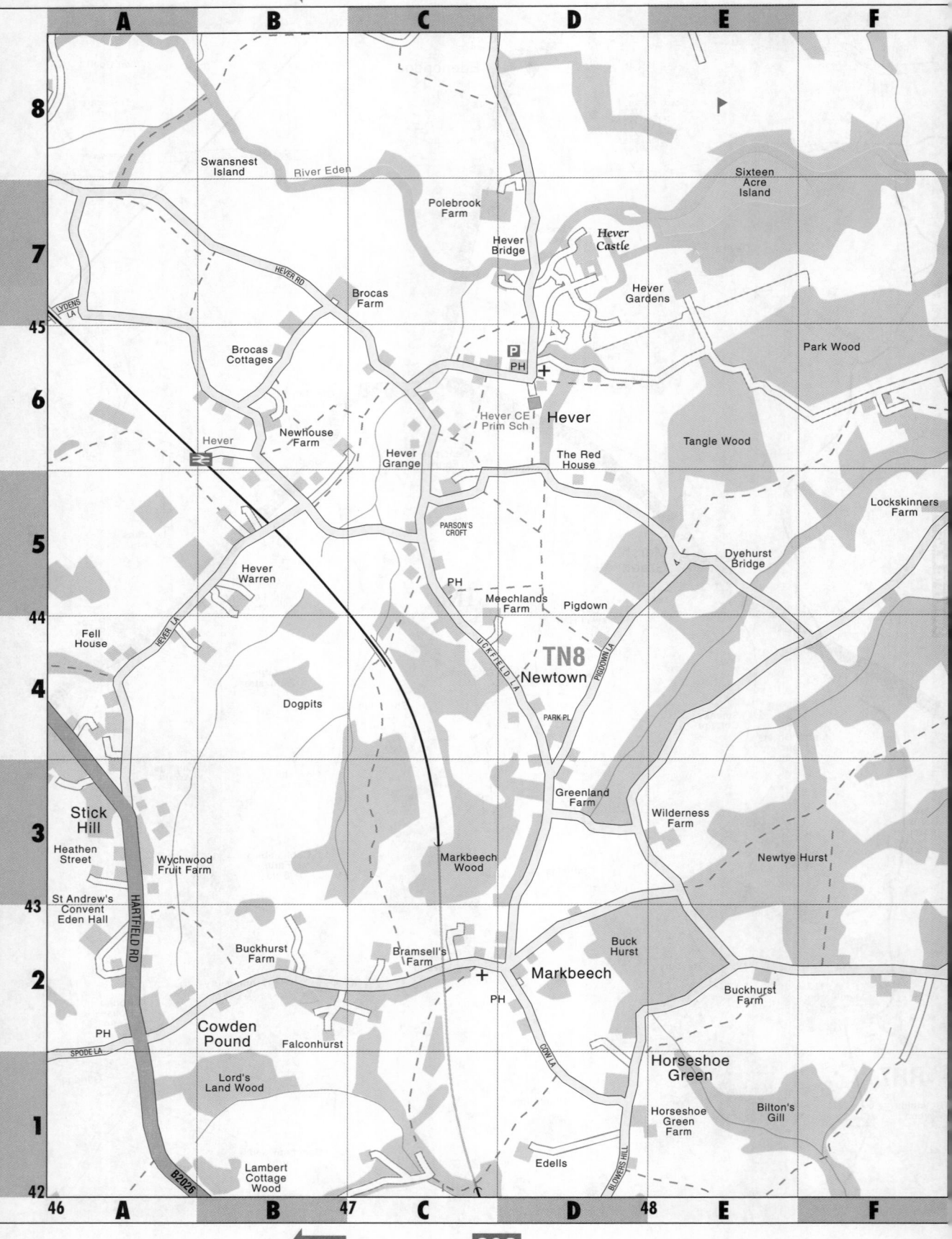

A   B   C   D   E   F

8

7

45

6

Hever

5

44

4

3

43

2

Cowden Pound

1

42

46   A   47   B   C   48   D   E   F

Swansnest Island

River Eden

Polebrook Farm

Hever Bridge

Hever Castle

Brocas Farm

Hever Gardens

Park Wood

Brocas Cottages

P

PH

P

Hever

Newhouse Farm

Hever CE Prim Sch

Hever

The Red House

Tangle Wood

Hever Grange

Locksinners Farm

PARSON'S CROFT

Dyehurst Bridge

Hever Warren

PH

Meechlands Farm

Pigdown

Fell House

TN8 Newtown

Dogpits

PARK PL

Stick Hill

Greenland Farm

Wilderness Farm

Newtye Hurst

Heathen Street

Wychwood Fruit Farm

Markbeech Wood

St Andrew's Convent Eden Hall

HARTFIELD RD

Buckhurst Farm

Bramsell's Farm

Buck Hurst

Markbeech

Buckhurst Farm

PH

PH

Falconhurst

Horseshoe Green

PH

SPODE LA

Lord's Land Wood

Horseshoe Green Farm

Bilton's Gill

B2026

Lambert Cottage Wood

Edells

HEVER RD

LYDENS LA

HEVER LA

UCKFIELD LA

PIGDOWN LA

COW LA

BLOWERS HILL

Sixteen Acre Island

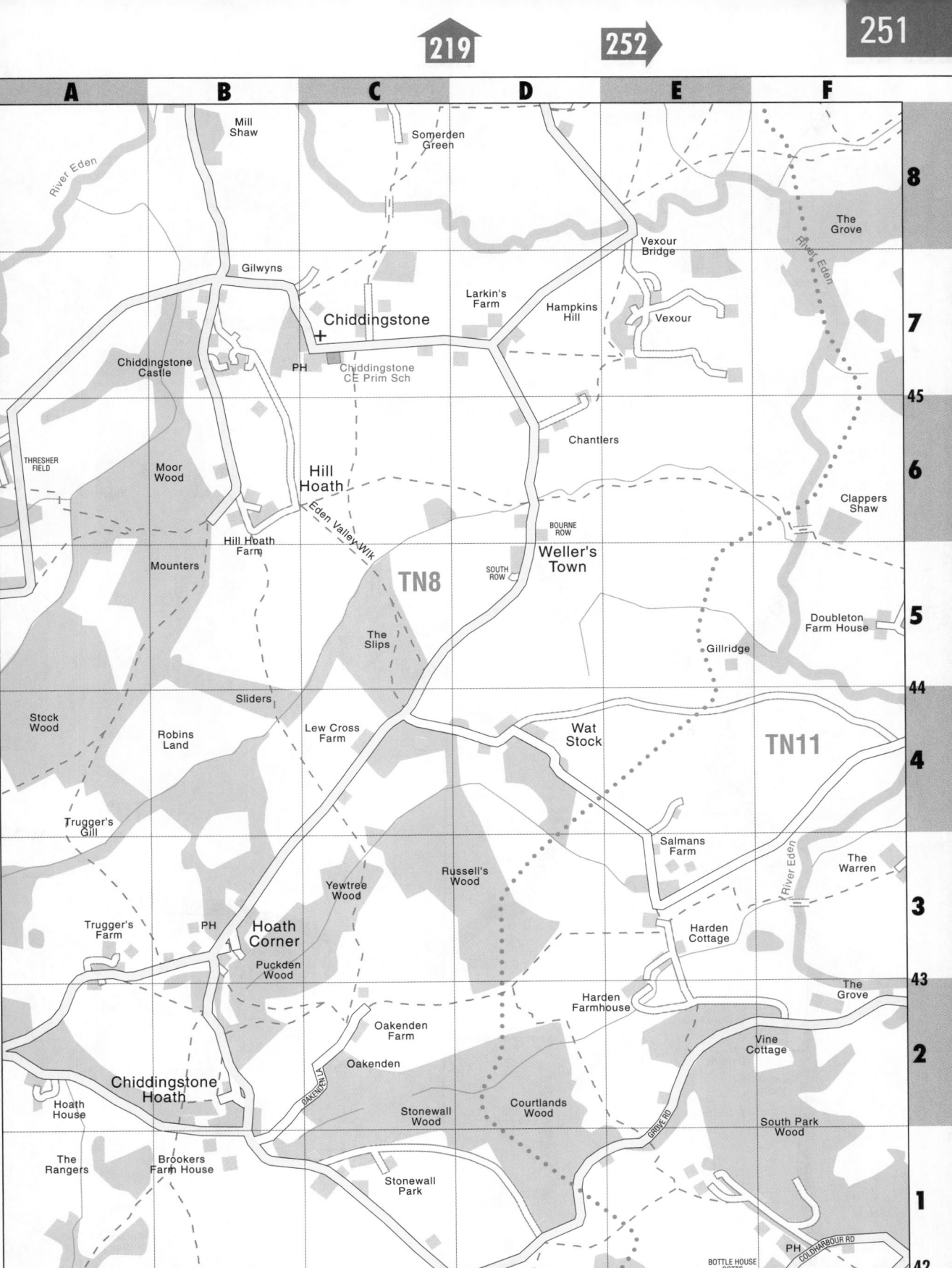

A   B   C   D   E   F

Mill
Shaw

River Eden

Somerden
Green

8

The
Grove

Vexour
Bridge

Gilwyns

7

Larkin's
Farm

Hampkins
Hill

Vexour

River Eden

Chiddingstone

PH

Chiddingstone
CE Prim Sch

45

Chiddingstone
Castle

Chantlers

6

THRESHER
FIELD

Moor
Wood

Hill
Hoath

Clappers
Shaw

Hill Hoath
Farm

Eden Valley Wlk

BOURNE
ROW

Weller's
Town

Mounters

TN8

SOUTH
ROW

5

The
Slips

Gillridge

Doubleton
Farm House

44

Sliders

Stock
Wood

Lew Cross
Farm

Wat
Stock

TN11

4

Robins
Land

Salmans
Farm

River Eden

The
Warren

Trugger's
Gill

Russell's
Wood

3

Trugger's
Farm

PH

Hoath
Corner

Yewtree
Wood

Harden
Cottage

Puckden
Wood

43

Harden
Farmhouse

The
Grove

Oakenden
Farm

Vine
Cottage

2

Chiddingstone
Hoath

BAKENDEN LA

Oakenden

Courtlands
Wood

GROVE RD

South Park
Wood

Hoath
House

Stonewall
Wood

The
Rangers

Brookers
Farm House

Stonewall
Park

1

PH   COLDHARBOUR RD

BOTTLE HOUSE
COTTS

42

49   A   B   50   C   D   51   E   F

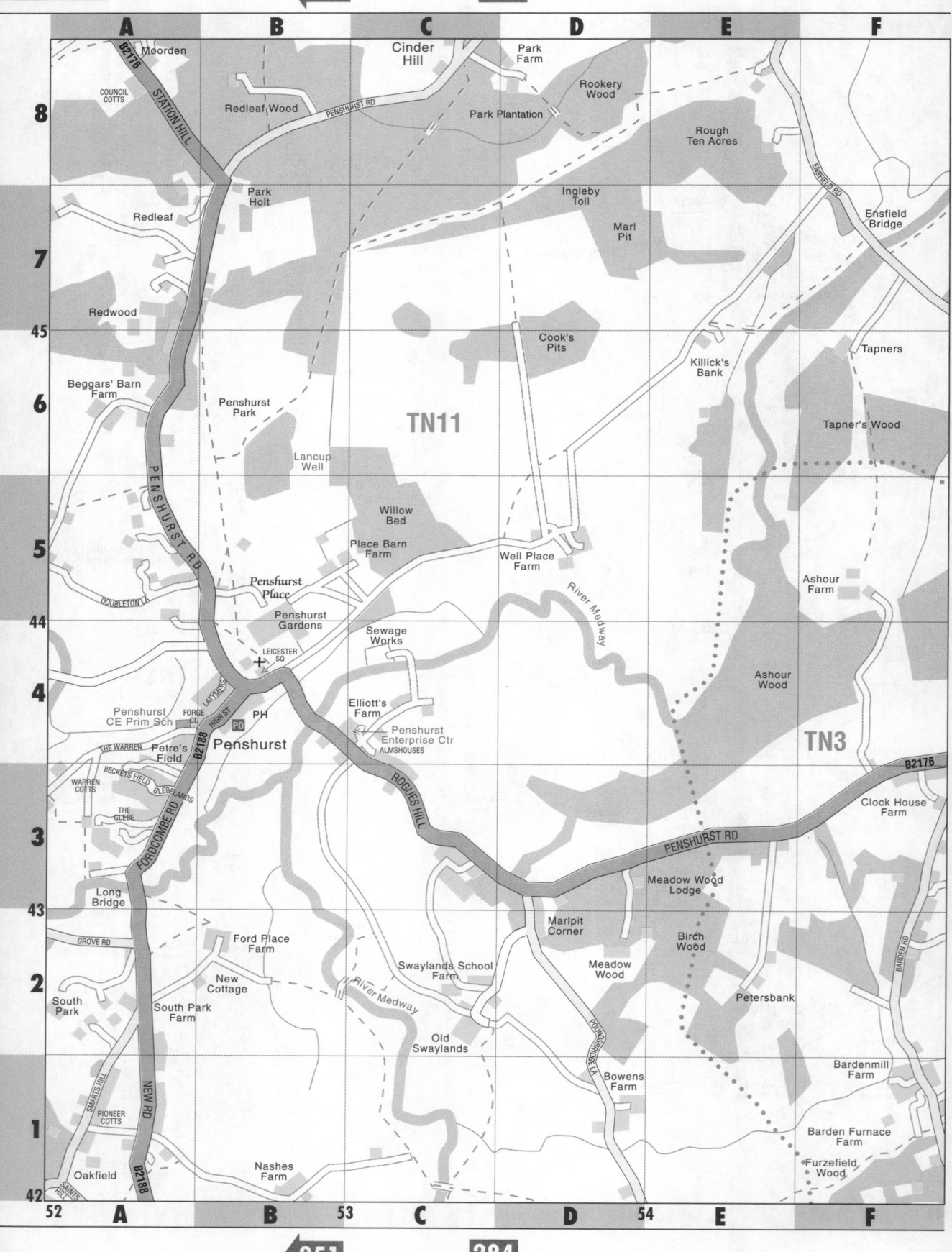

A8
1 Sussex Road Prim Sch
2 The Hayesbrook Sch

◄ 253

B8
1 ST AUGUSTINE HO
2 BECKET CT
3 QUARRY HILL PAR
4 THE LOWRY
5 BICKLEY RD
6 MONKS WLK

▲ 222

7 DEANS CT
8 MARY MAGDALENE HO
9 MERRYFIELD CT
10 TONBRIDGES CHAMBERS
11 ST GEORGES MEWS
12 GARDYNE MEWS
13 WHITE OAK CL

14 ALMSHOUSES
15 SKINNER'S TERR

TONBRIDGE

TN9

TN11

TN4

TN2

Brook Street

The Judd Sch

West Kent Coll

Tonbridge Gram Sch

Tonbridge Cottage

Mabledon Farm

Streamlands

Beeches Wood

Rook Wood

Nightingale Farm

Moat Farm

Moatenden

Forest Farm

Gorse Wood

Minepit Wood

Devil's Wood

Appletree Wood

Old Forge Farm

Honnington Farm

Coneyburrow Wood

High Wood

Brokes Mill Farm

Forge Farm

Brokes Wood

Southborough

Nursery

Great Lodge Ret Pk

Sewage Works

Royal Tunbridge Wells Bsns Pk

Colebrook Ind Est

King's Standing Ind Est

Riverdale Est

Orchard Bsns Ctr

Hillview Sch for Girls

St Stephen's Prim Sch

Woodgate

Weald of Kent Gram Sch

Somerhill Park

Somerhill

The Schools at Somerhill

Alders Wood

The Brakes

Castlehill Wood

Castle Hill

Castle Hill Farm

Pilgrim's Wood

Masts

Oast House

High Weald Landscape Trail

Tunbridge Wells Circular Walk

Tonbridge By-Pass

Pembury Rd

Woodgate Way

Five Oak Green Rd

London Rd

Quarry Hill Rd

Vauxhall La

South Frith

◄ 253

▲ 286

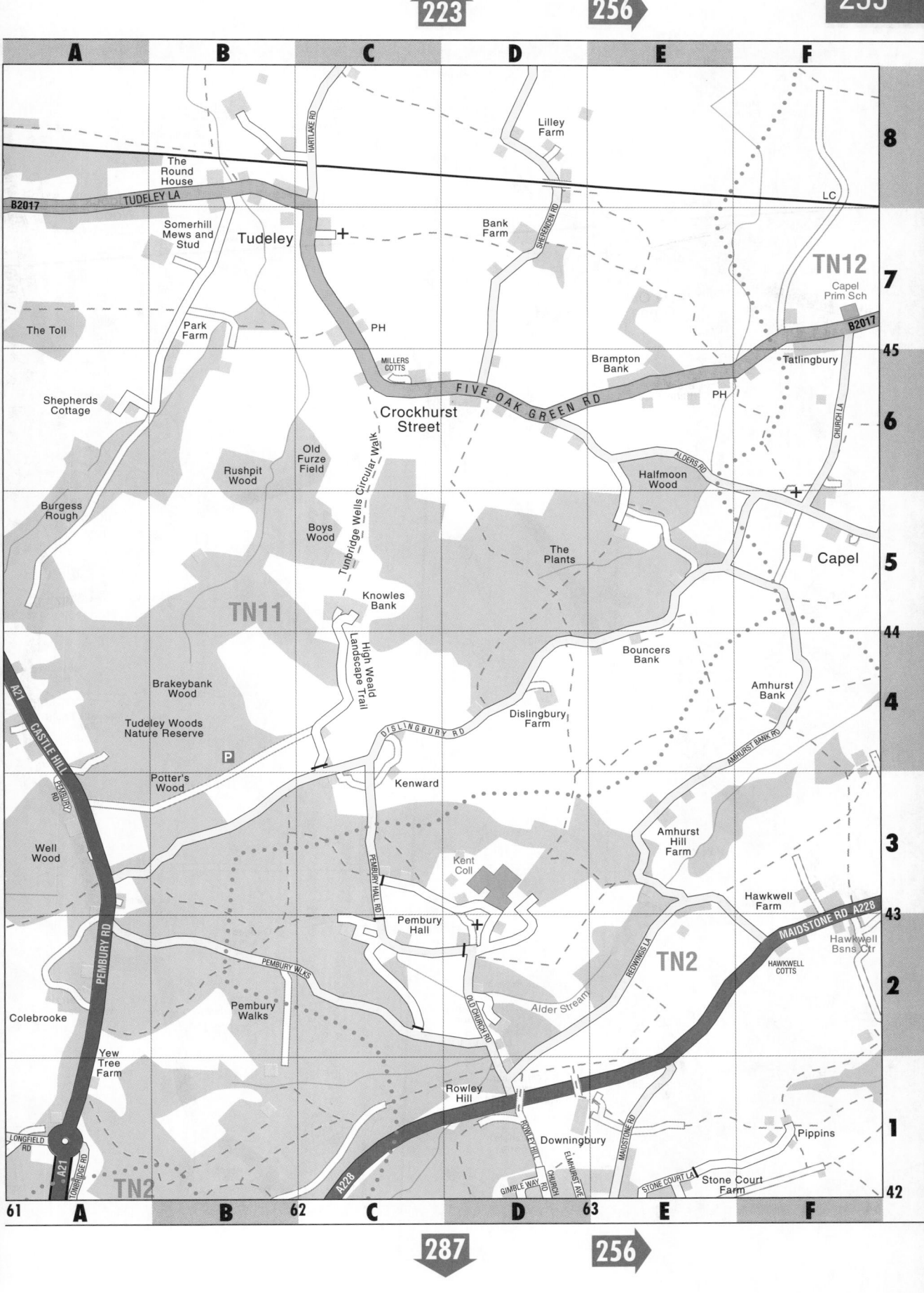

A　B　C　D　E　F

B2017
TUDELEY LA
The Round House
Somerhill Mews and Stud
Tudeley
HARTLAKE RD
Lilley Farm
SHEPHERDS RD
Bank Farm
LC
TN12
Capel Prim Sch
The Toll
Park Farm
PH
MILLERS COTTS
FIVE OAK GREEN RD
Brampton Bank
Tatlingbury
B2017
Shepherds Cottage
Crockhurst Street
PH
Rushpit Wood
Old Furze Field
ALDERS RD
Halfmoon Wood
CHURCH LA
Capel
Burgess Rough
Boys Wood
Tunbridge Wells Circular Walk
The Plants
TN11
Knowles Bank
High Weald Landscape Trail
Bouncers Bank
Amhurst Bank
Brakeybank Wood
Tudeley Woods Nature Reserve
P
Potter's Wood
DISLINGBURY RD
Dislingbury Farm
AMHURST BANK RD
A21
Well Wood
Kenward
Amhurst Hill Farm
CASTLE HILL
PEMBURY RD
Kent Coll
Hawkwell Farm
PEMBURY HALL RD
MAIDSTONE RD A228
Hawkwell Bsns Ctr
Colebrooke
Pembury Hall
TN2
HAWKWELL COTTS
PEMBURY WLKS
REDWINGS LA
Yew Tree Farm
Pembury Walks
OLD CHURCH RD
Alder Stream
Pippins
LONGFIELD RD
A21
A228
Rowley Hill
ROWLEY HILL RD
Downingbury
MAIDSTONE RD
ELMHURST AVE
STONE COURT LA
Stone Court Farm
TONBRIDGE RD
TN2
GIMBLE WAY
CHURCH

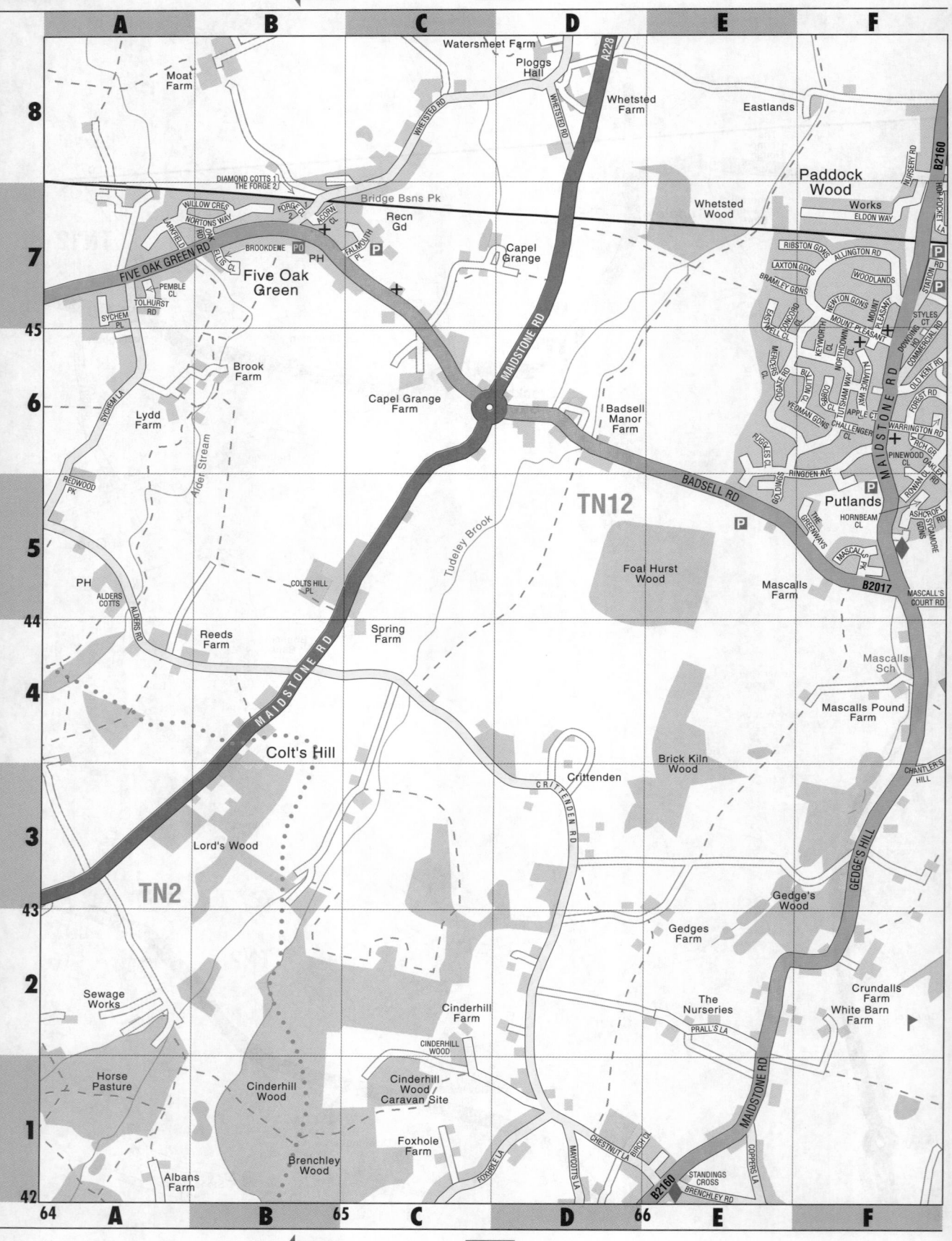

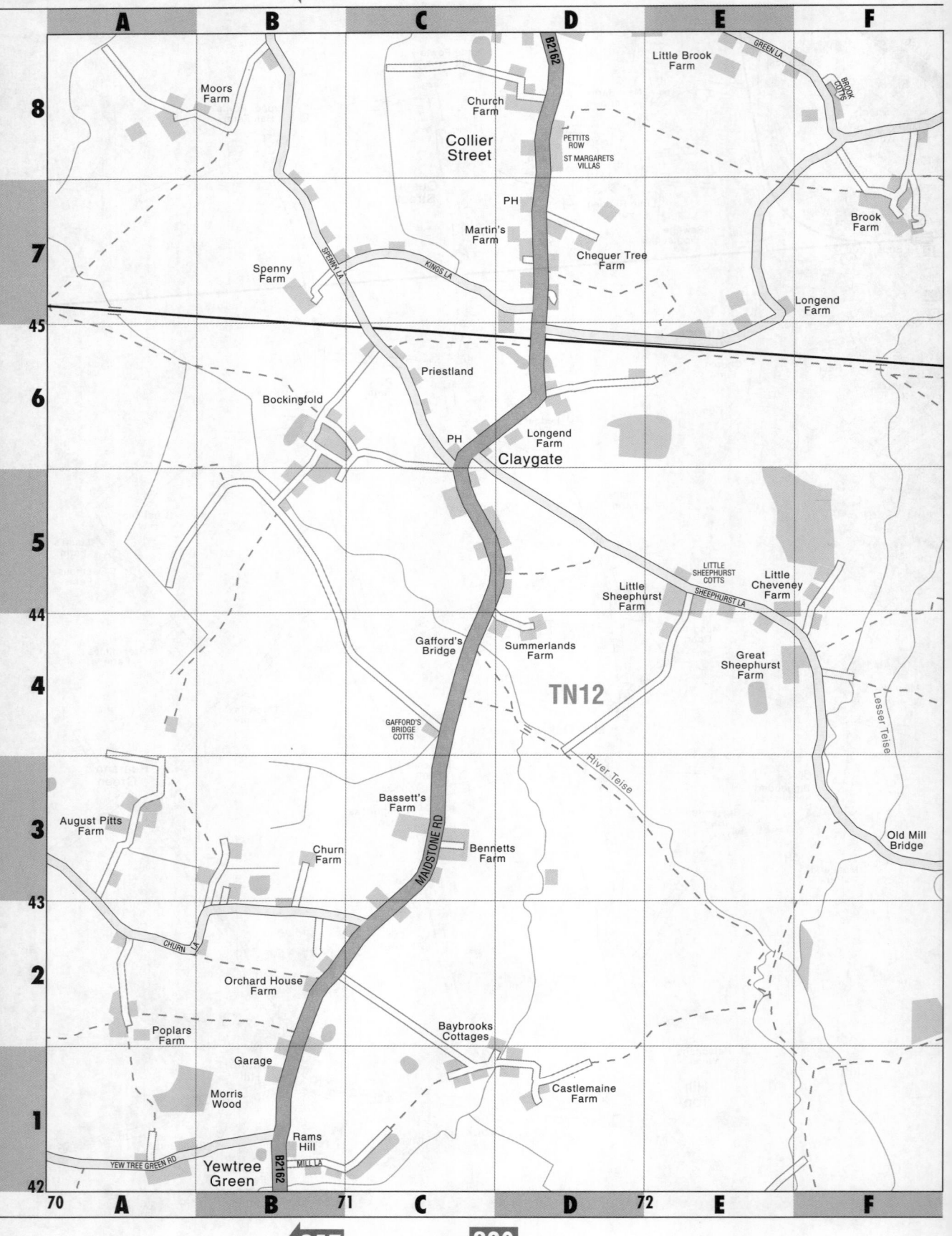

A B C D E F

8
7
45
6
44
5
4
3
43
2
1
42

Spitz Bridge
Mill Farm
Gatehouse Farm
HUNTON RD
Foundation Farm
Target Farm
ALDEN LA
LINDERLYN LA
LITTLE MILL FARM COTTS
Copt Hall Farm
Milebush
St Ann's Green
ST ANN'S GREEN LA
Milebush Farm
B2079
Little Pattenden
PATTENDEN LA
Marden Grange
Wheelbarrow Park Est
The Old Vicarage Sch
Guardian Ind Est
Church Farm
Cemy
MAIDSTONE RD
Bridgehurst Wood
Crest Ind Est
Marden
Turkey Farmhouse
MEADS CL
SOVEREIGNS WAY
MEDWAY COTTS
RAILWAY COTTS
EASON VILLAS
HOWLAND COTTS
WEST END
CHURCH GN
HIGH ST
CHAFFENDEN CL
THE OLD MKT
BARNES WLK
MEADOW VIEW
Moatlands Farm
BRAMLEY
CT LUCAS WAY
DARRELL PROS
PROVIDENCE CHAPEL
BALLARD CL
LIME CL
SUTTON FORGE
SOUTH RD
HOWLAND RD
Marden Prim Sch
CHANTRY CL
DENTRY PL
MERCHANT PL
ROUNDEL WAY
CURLHURST
STELLA CL
OAK TREE CL
Holders Farm
Hall House
Little Mountain Farm
THE COCKPIT
MAYNARDS
SUTTON CT
NAPOLEON DR
STANLEY RD
ALBION RD
JEWELL DR
GOUDHURST RD
Brooklyn Villas
CRANHAM SQ
1 ALLENS
2 MAPLESDEN
3 ALBION COTTS
4 CLAREMONT PL
Marden
Westfield Villas
SPRINGROVE COTTS
COPPER LA
Gravelpit Farm House
Westfield House
TN12
Poulters Hall
Cannon Farm
THORN RD
Longridge Farm
Roughlands Farm
PLAIN RD
The Plain
Thorn Farm
B2079
SHEEPHURST LA
Marden Beech
Marden Thorn
Widehurst
Beech Farm
Beale Farm
Susans Farm
Cornwells Farm
Springfield
Great Cheveney Farm
Widehurst Wood
Wilden Wood
WILDEN PARK RD
Cockle Wood
Great Cheveney House
B2079
Tavern Farm
Forstal Farm
SHERENDEN LA

73 A B 74 C D 75 E F

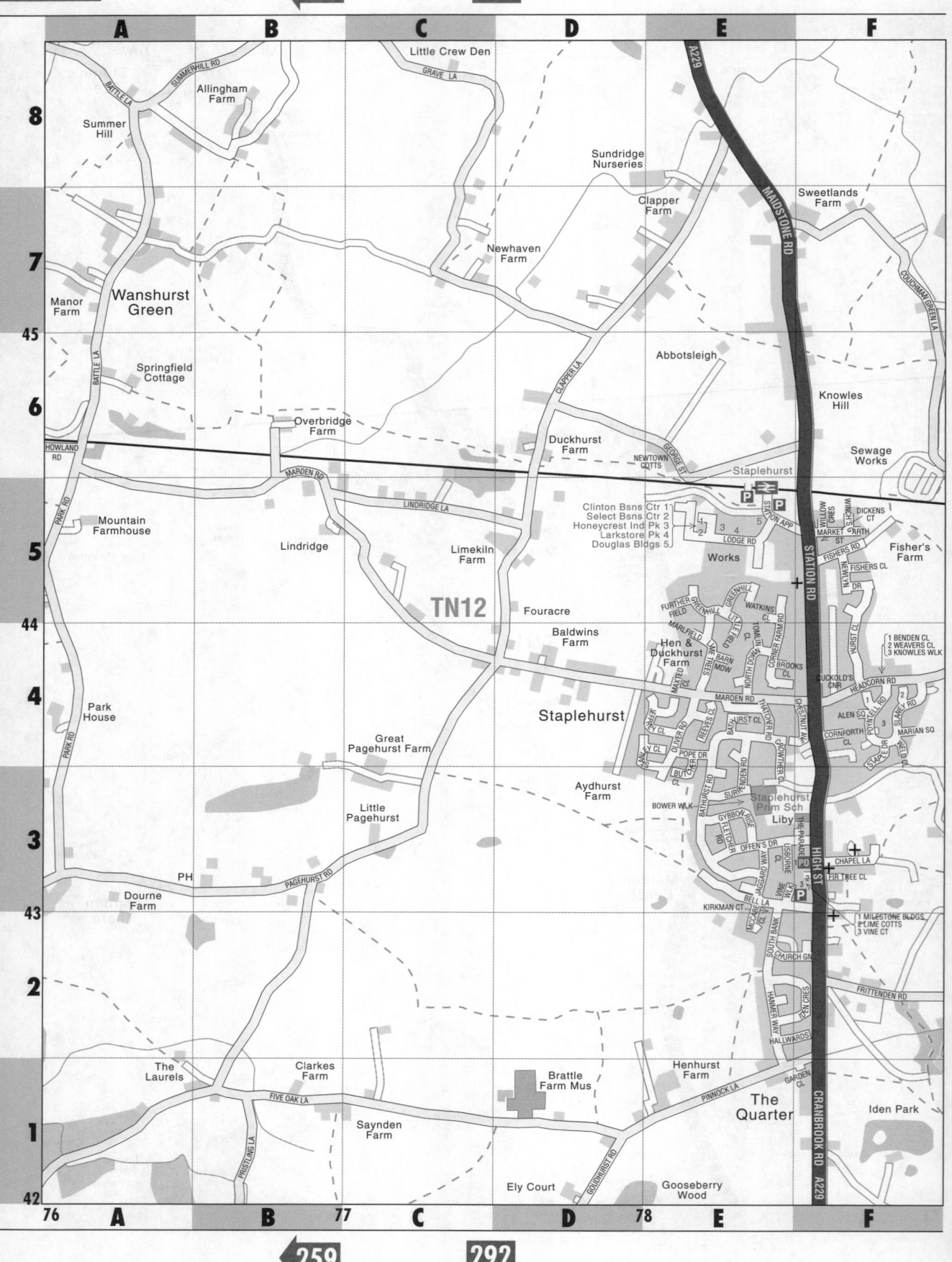

A B C D E F

Little Crew Den

GRAVE LA

Summerhill Rd

Allingham Farm

BATTLE LA

8

Summer Hill

Sundridge Nurseries

Clapper Farm

Sweetlands Farm

COUCHMAN GREEN LA

MAIDSTONE RD
A229

Newhaven Farm

7

Wanshurst Green

Manor Farm

45

Abbotsleigh

Knowles Hill

Springfield Cottage

BATTLE LA

6

Overbridge Farm

Duckhurst Farm

CLAPPER LA

GEORGE ST

Newtown Cotts

Staplehurst

Sewage Works

HOWLAND RD

MARDEN RD

Staplehurst

PARK RD

LINDRIDGE LA

Clinton Bsns Ctr 1
Select Bsns Ctr 2
Honeycrest Ind Pk 3
Larkstore Pk 4
Douglas Bldgs 5

STATION APP

STATION RD

MOTTIM

WINCH'S

MARKET ST

DICKENS CT

GARTH

SBRS

Mountain Farmhouse

Lindridge

Limekiln Farm

LODGE RD

Works

FISHERS RD

FISHERS CL

Fisher's Farm

5

44

TN12

Fouracre

Baldwins Farm

Hen & Duckhurst Farm

FURTHER FIELD

GREENHILL

WATKINS

MARLFIELD

GREENHILL

LIME TREES

LIME BARN MDW

TOMLIN

NORTH DOWN

CORNER FARM

BROOKS CL

OLD

WURST ST

NEWLYN

FISHERS CL

DR

1 BENDEN CL
2 WEAVERS CL
3 KNOWLES WLK

4

Park House

PARK RD

MAXTED

JERSEY CL

OLIVER RD

REEVES CL

BATHURST CL

THATCHER RD

MARDEN RD

CHESTNUT AVE

CROWTHER RD

CUCKOLD'S CNR

HEADCORN RD

ALEN SQ

POYNTELL CL

CORNFORTH CL

STAPLE DR

SLANEY RD

MARIAN SQ

Great Pagehurst Farm

Little Pagehurst

LY CL

POPE DR

BUTCHER RD

Aydhurst Farm

BOWER WLK

SURRENDEN RD

Staplehurst Prim Sch

Liby

THE PARADE

PO

3

PH

PAGEHURST RD

GYBBON RISE

OFFEN'S DR

USBORNE

HIGH ST

CHAPEL LA

FIR TREE CL

43

Dourne Farm

BATHURST RD

FLETCHER

BELL LA

MCCABE

MAGGART

KIRKMAN CT

SOUTH BANK

CHURCH GN

1 MILESTONE BLDGS
2 LIME COTTS
3 VINE CT

2

HANMER WAY

HALLWARDS

FRITTENDEN RD

CRANBROOK RD
A229

The Laurels

Clarkes Farm

Henhurst Farm

PINNOCK LA

The Quarter

Iden Park

1

FIVE OAK LA

PRISTLING LA

Saynden Farm

GOUDHURST RD

Brattle Farm Mus

Ely Court

Gooseberry Wood

42

76 A B 77 C D E 78 F

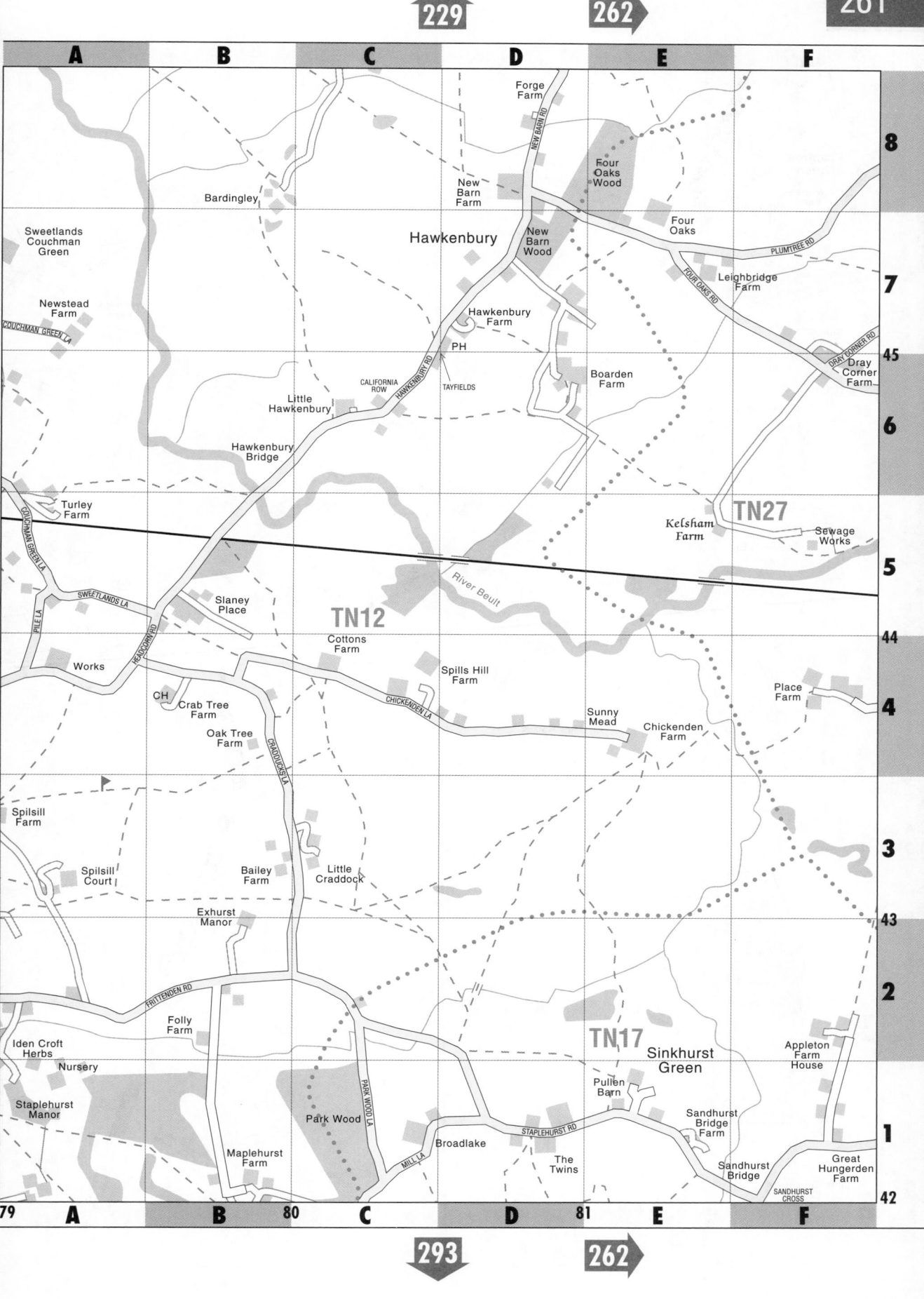

229
262

A B C D E F

8
7
45
6
5
44
4
3
43
2
1
42

Forge
Farm

New Barn Rd

Four Oaks
Wood

New
Barn
Farm

Bardingley

Hawkenbury

Four
Oaks

New
Barn
Wood

Plumtree Rd

Sweetlands
Couchman
Green

Leighbridge
Farm

Four Oaks Rd

Newstead
Farm

Hawkenbury
Farm

Dray Corner Rd

Dray
Corner
Farm

Couchman Green La

PH

Boarden
Farm

Little
Hawkenbury

California
Row

Hawkenbury Rd

TAYFIELDS

Hawkenbury
Bridge

Turley
Farm

TN27

Kelsham
Farm

Sewage
Works

Couchman Green La

Sweetlands La

Slaney
Place

TN12

River Beult

Pile La

Works

Headcorn Rd

Cottons
Farm

Spills Hill
Farm

Place
Farm

CH

Crab Tree
Farm

Chickenden La

Sunny
Mead

Chickenden
Farm

Oak Tree
Farm

Craddocks La

Spilsill
Farm

Bailey
Farm

Little
Craddock

Spilsill
Court

Exhurst
Manor

Frittenden Rd

Folly
Farm

TN17

Sinkhurst
Green

Appleton
Farm
House

Iden Croft
Herbs

Pullen
Barn

Nursery

Park Wood La

Sandhurst
Bridge
Farm

Staplehurst
Manor

Park Wood

Staplehurst Rd

Mill La

Broadlake

The
Twins

Sandhurst
Bridge

Sandhurst
Cross

Great
Hungerden
Farm

Maplehurst
Farm

79 A B 80 C D 81 E F 42

293
262

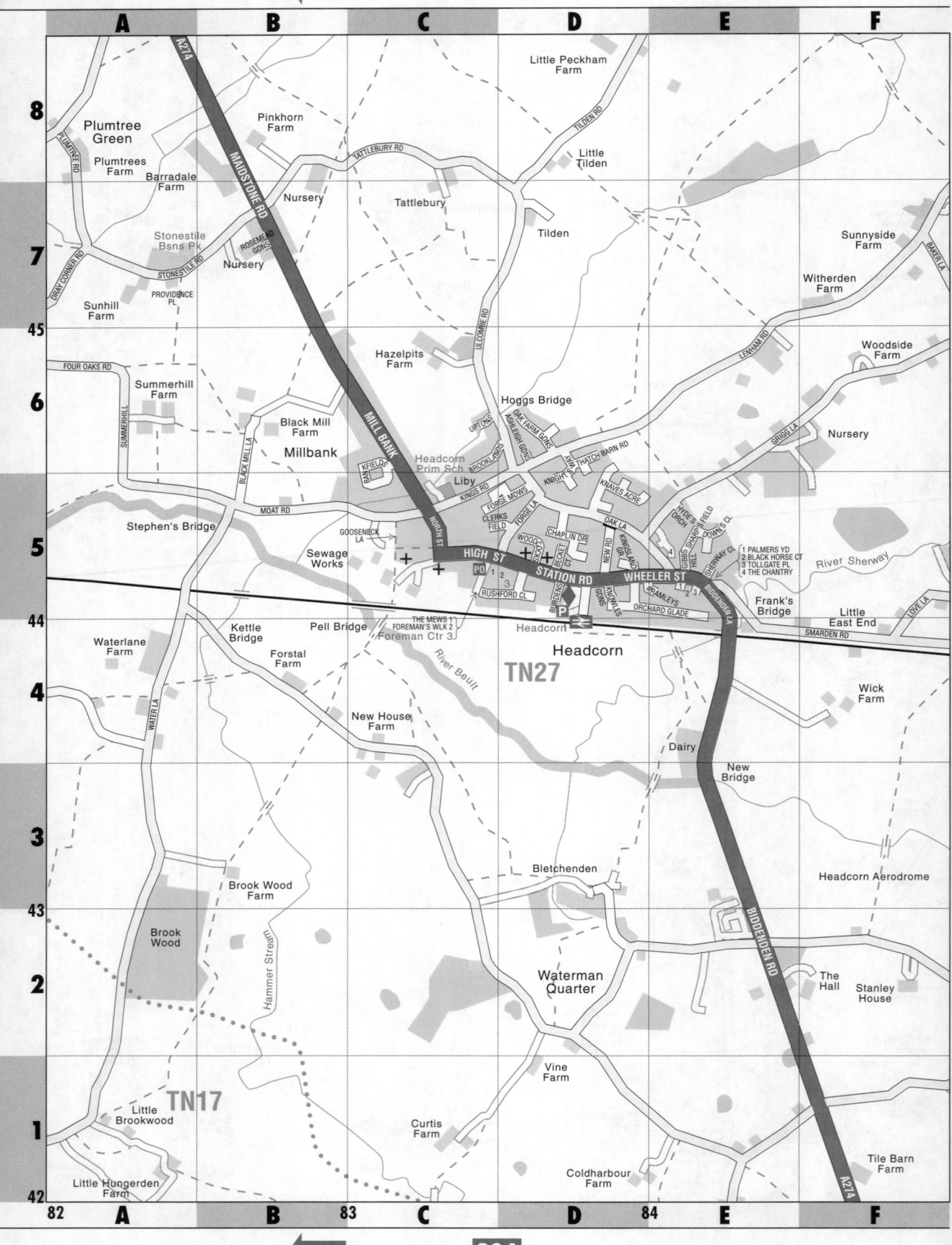

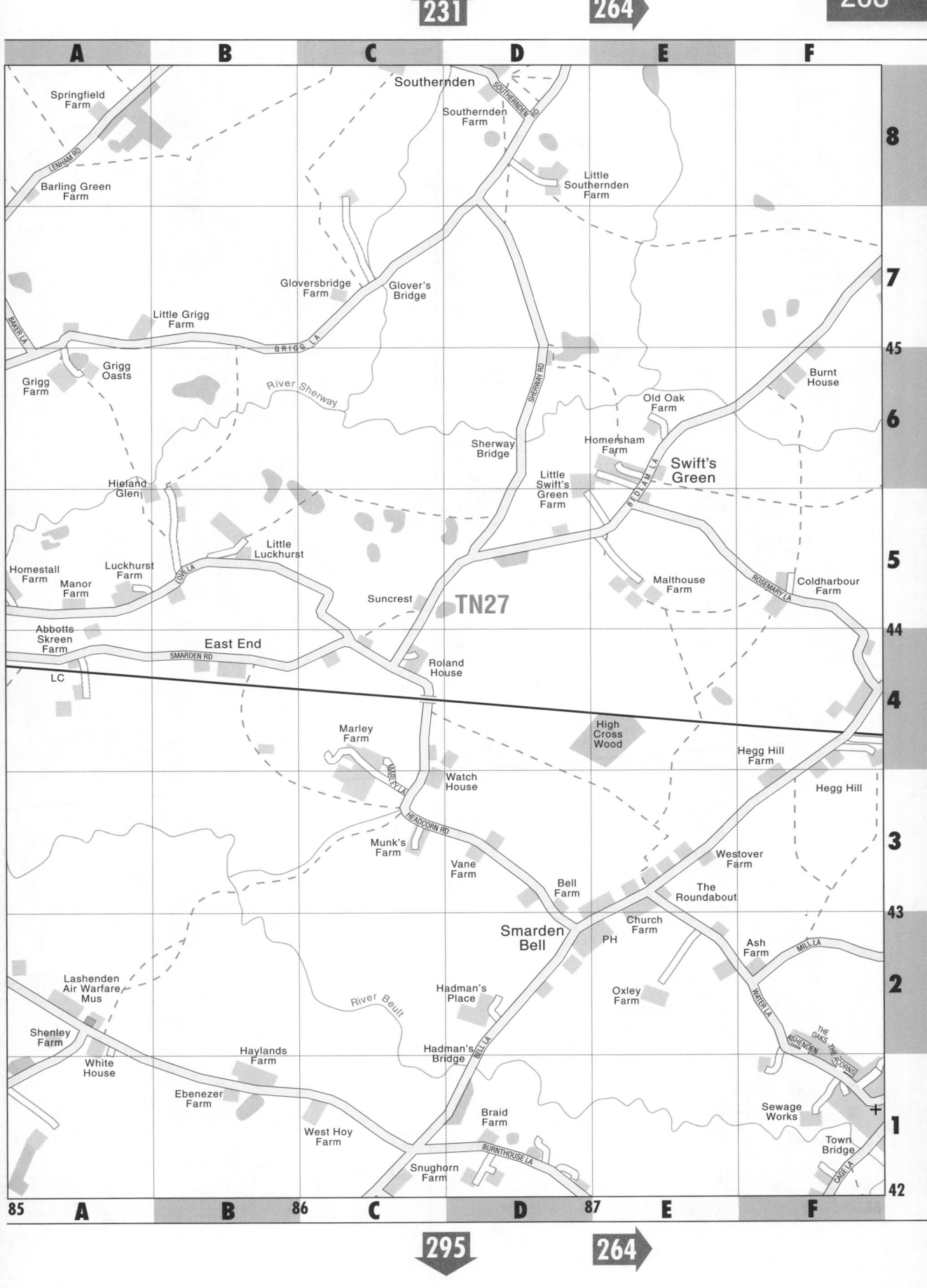

A **B** **C** **D** **E** **F**

Southernden

Springfield
Farm

8

Southernden
Farm

LENHAM RD

Barling Green
Farm

Little
Southernden
Farm

7

BAKER LA

Gloversbridge
Farm

Glover's
Bridge

Little Grigg
Farm

GRIGG LA

45

Grigg
Oasts

River Sherway

Burnt
House

6

Grigg
Farm

Old Oak
Farm

Sherway
Bridge

Homersham
Farm

Swift's
Green

SHERWAY RD

Hieland
Glen

Little
Swift's
Green
Farm

BEDLAM LA

5

Homestall
Farm

Luckhurst
Farm

Little
Luckhurst

Malthouse
Farm

ROSEMARY LA

Coldharbour
Farm

Manor
Farm

LOVE LA

Suncrest

TN27

Abbotts
Skreen
Farm

East End

SMARDEN RD

44

LC

Roland
House

High
Cross
Wood

4

Marley
Farm

Hegg Hill
Farm

MARLEY LA

Watch
House

Hegg Hill

HEADCORN RD

3

Munk's
Farm

Westover
Farm

Vane
Farm

Bell
Farm

The
Roundabout

43

Smarden
Bell

Church
Farm

Ash
Farm

MILL LA

PH

Lashenden
Air Warfare
Mus

Hadman's
Place

Oxley
Farm

WATER LA

2

River Beult

THE OAKS   THE ACORNS

Shenley
Farm

Haylands
Farm

Hadman's
Bridge

BELL LA

ASHENDEN

White
House

Sewage
Works

1

Ebenezer
Farm

Braid
Farm

Town
Bridge

West Hoy
Farm

BURNTHOUSE LA

CAGE LA

Snughorn
Farm

42

A 85 **B** 86 **C** **D** 87 **E** **F**

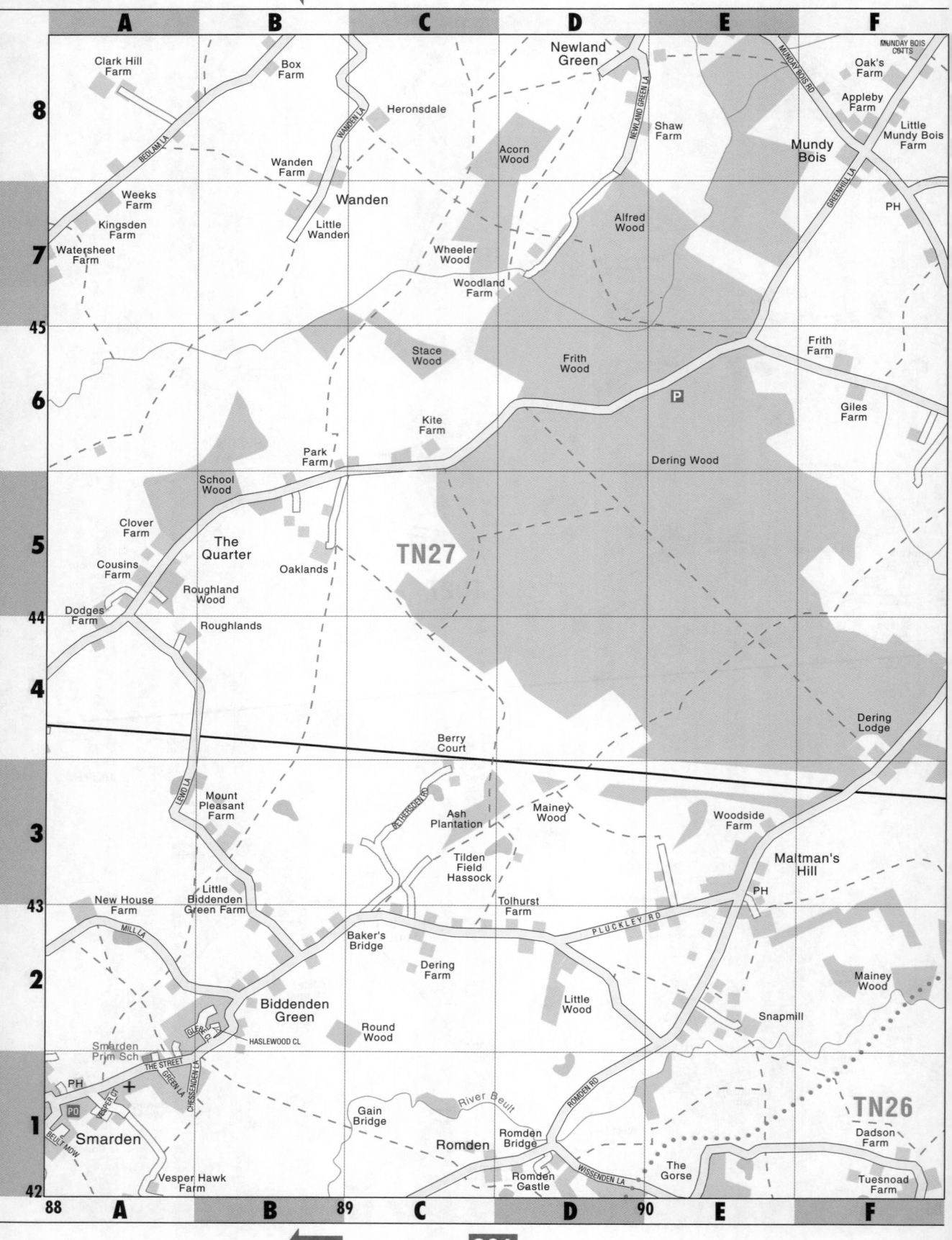

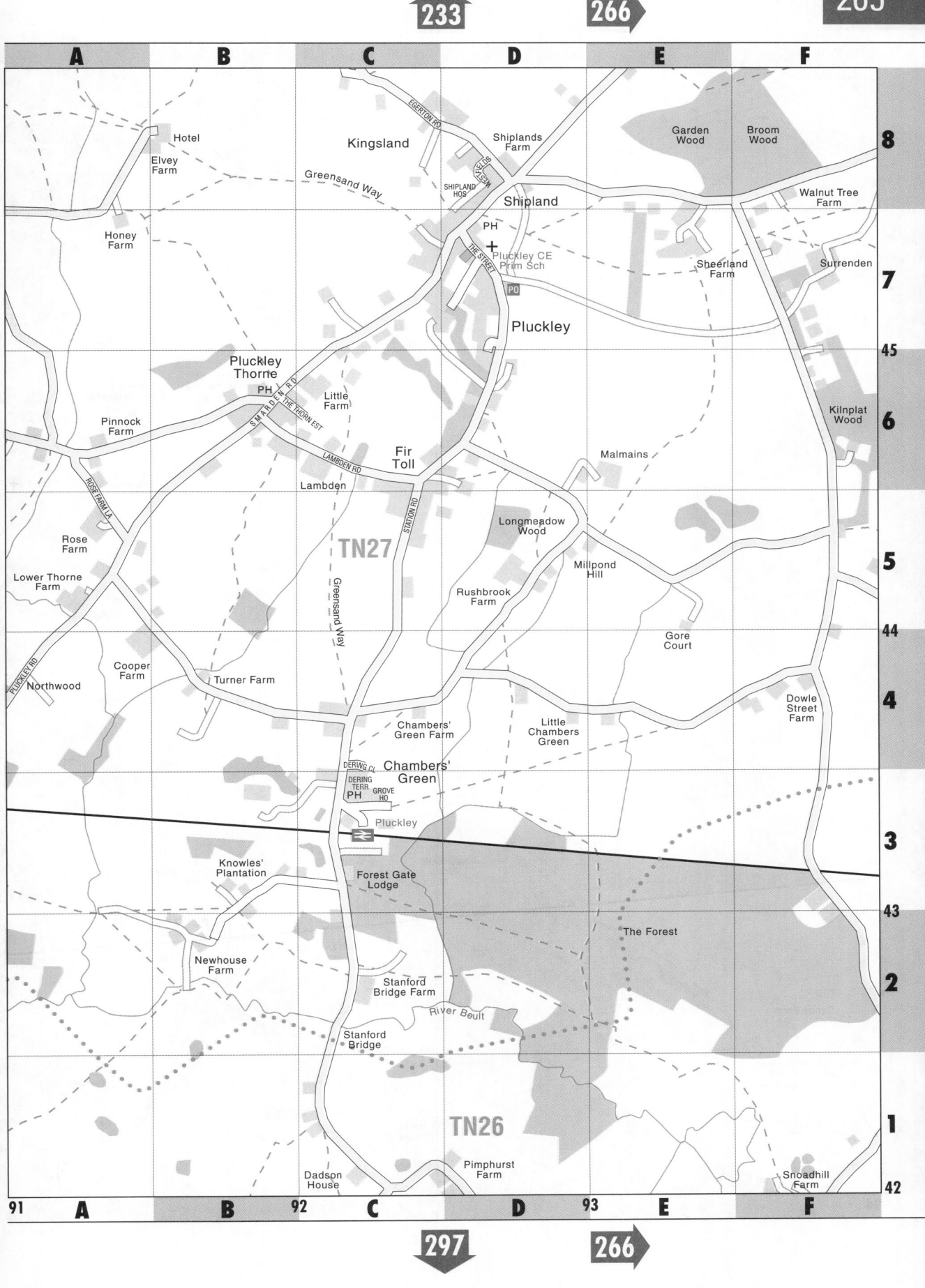

A B C D E F

8

Hotel

Kingsland

Elvey Farm

Greensand Way

Shiplands Farm

EGERTON RD

Garden Wood

Broom Wood

Honey Farm

SHIPLAND HOS

THE STREET

Shipland

Walnut Tree Farm

PH

Pluckley CE Prim Sch

Sheerland Farm

Surrenden

7

PO

Pluckley

45

Pluckley Thorne

PH

SMARDEN RD

THE THORN EST

Little Farm

6

Kilnplat Wood

Pinnock Farm

LAMBDEN RD

Fir Toll

Malmains

Lambden

Rose Farm

ROSS FARM LA

STATION RD

TN27

Greensand Way

Longmeadow Wood

Millpond Hill

5

Lower Thorne Farm

Rushbrook Farm

Gore Court

44

Cooper Farm

Turner Farm

PLUCKLEY RD

Northwood

Chambers' Green Farm

Little Chambers Green

Dowle Street Farm

4

DERING CL

Chambers' Green

DERING TERR PH

GROVE HO

Pluckley

3

Knowles' Plantation

Forest Gate Lodge

43

The Forest

Newhouse Farm

Stanford Bridge Farm

2

River Beult

Stanford Bridge

TN26

1

Dadson House

Pimphurst Farm

Snoadhill Farm

42

91 A B 92 C D 93 E F

265
234

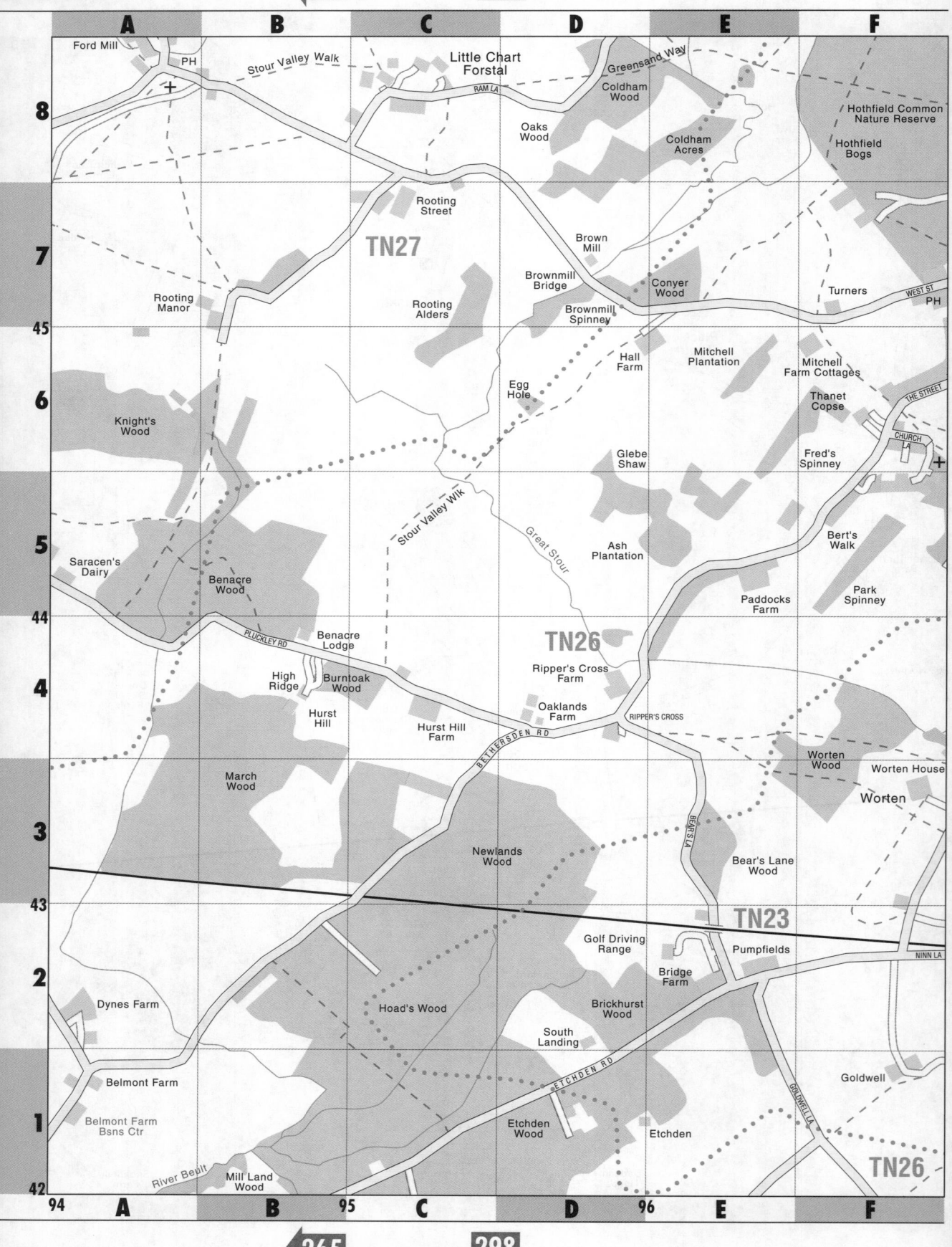

TN25

Castle Farm

Kingsland

Crouchers Manor

CH

8

A20

Ripple Court

WATERY LA

Foxenhill Toll

Beechbrook

Beechbrook Wood

7

COMMON WAY

Tollhill Wood

TN26

MAIDSTONE RD

Depot

WESTWELL LA

KINGSLAND LA

SANDYHURST LA

STATION RD

Hothfield

PLANTATION CL

SMALL CL

COACH DR

TUFTON RD

BEECH DR

PO

THANET TERR

THE STREET

MEADOW VIEW

PARK DR

SCHOOL RD

Home Farm

Mill House

Woodside

P

PH

HOWS WOOD GDNS

Potters Corner

45

6

M20

The Larches

WATERFALL RD

Broomfield Wood

Potters Corner Wood

POTTERS CNR

Hoad's Wood

Nursery

Marble Wood

Eyesend Plantation

Mansion Copse

Pigsbrook Wood

GODINTON LA

Balls Wood

Eyesend

The Warren

5

Godinton Plantation

Balls Wood

Lodge Wood

HAZEL HTS

BLOSSOM

HILL

ASHGROVE

ORCHARD HTS

West Lodge

Petts Hole

FOREST AVE

ALMOND

ROSEWOOD DR

CHERRYWOOD

WARREN VIEW

FARRIER CL

44

Worten Mill

Godinton House & Gardens

Chestnut Tell Plantation

WYNDHAM WAY

PEMBURY

PONDMOOR

WARD

WATKIN CL

A20

Goldwyn Com Spec/Sch

Jubilee Plantation

SPRINGWOOD RD

WHITEBEAM CL

SYCAMORE LA

LONG WK

SIR JOHN FOGGE AVE 1
INTELLIGENCE WK 2
LANCASTER WY 3
BRIGADIER GDNS 4

ORDINANCE WY

4

River Spinney

TN23

Great Stour

Greensand Way

MYRTLE GN

ASPEN DR

HEARTWOOD DR

EVERGREEN WY

MANOR WAY

A28

Stour Valley Wlk

SWEET BAY CRES

HOLLY MDWS

MULBERRY RD

LILAC CT

PH

LOUDON WAY

TEMPLER WAY

Willow Bed

Chart Ave

BUTTERNUT COPSE

Godinton Prim Sch

LOUDON

LOCKHOLT CL

SPRINGWOOD DR

LOUDON PATH

CEDAR

LIME CL

POPLAR

EAST LODGE RD

HORNBEAM

BRIDGE RD

3

43

MAPLE CL

THE SPINNEY

NEL CL

CHESTNUT CL

YEW

ROWAN CL

CYPRESS

JUNIPER CL

VIBURNUM CL

CHART RD

HILTON RD

St George's Bsns Ctr

Bridge Rd Ind Ctr

NINN LA

BRUNSWICK RD

Godinton Park

Cobbs Wood Ind Est

HANOVER CL

BRUNSWICK IND CTR

2

Depot

Ninn Lodge Farm

Bucksford Manor

WATERCRESS HO 1
KINGFISHER HO 2
HERON HO 3
ALDER HO 4
WILLOW HO 5
MEADOWSWEET HO 6

Fairwood Ind Pk

STAFFORD

Brookfield Ind Pk

CAPEL CL

JEFFERSON CL

WATERSIDE TERR

Bucksford Bridge

CHART RD

B2229

BEAVER LA

LEACON RD

FORD WY

Montpelier Bsns Pk

DENCORA WAY

1

Great Chart

PH

THE STREET

TOKE CL

CORONATION DR

THE PADDOCKS

SINGLETON RD

MIDDLE CL

Playing Field

HAMMANDS

HOPPERS WAY

A28

BUCKSFORD LA

Buxford Mill

P

The Wyvern Sch

Singleton Lake

COVERT 1
EGGRINGE 2
HONEYFIELD 3
SILECROFT CT 4
BROUGHTON CT 5
OAKENPOLE 6
HUNTSWOOD 7

BROOKFIELD RD

MILLBROOK

B2229

OAKLANDS

HILLBROW LA

BAILEYS FIELD

CRESSFIELD

ARLINGTON

42

97

98

99

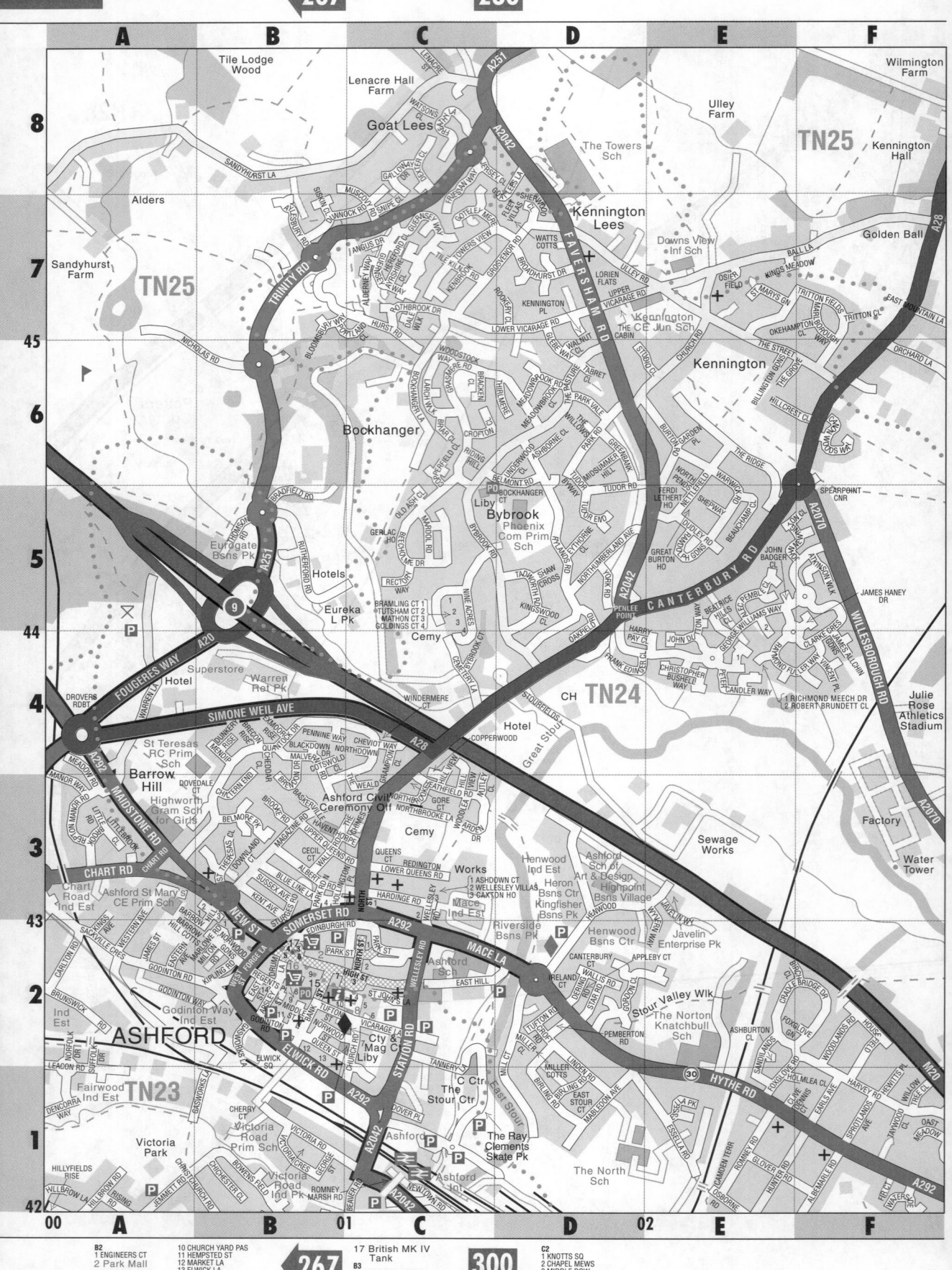

B2
1 ENGINEERS CT
2 Park Mall
3 ST GEORGE'S SQ
4 GILBERT RD
5 NEW RENTS
6 CASTLE ST
7 KINGS PAR
8 COUNTY SQ
9 TUFTON WLK

10 CHURCH YARD PAS
11 HEMPSTED ST
12 MARKET LA
13 ELWICK LA
14 REGENTS CT
15 Ashford
   Borough Mus
16 County Square
   Sh Ctr

17 British MK IV
   Tank
B3
1 BARROW HILL TERR
2 BARROW HILL PL
3 GRAVEL WLK
4 WOLSELEY PL

C2
1 KNOTTS SQ
2 CHAPEL MEWS
3 MIDDLE ROW
4 CHURCH YD
5 ASHDALE HO
6 COLLEGE CT
7 LESLEY CHALK HO
8 Ashford Sch
   of Art & Design

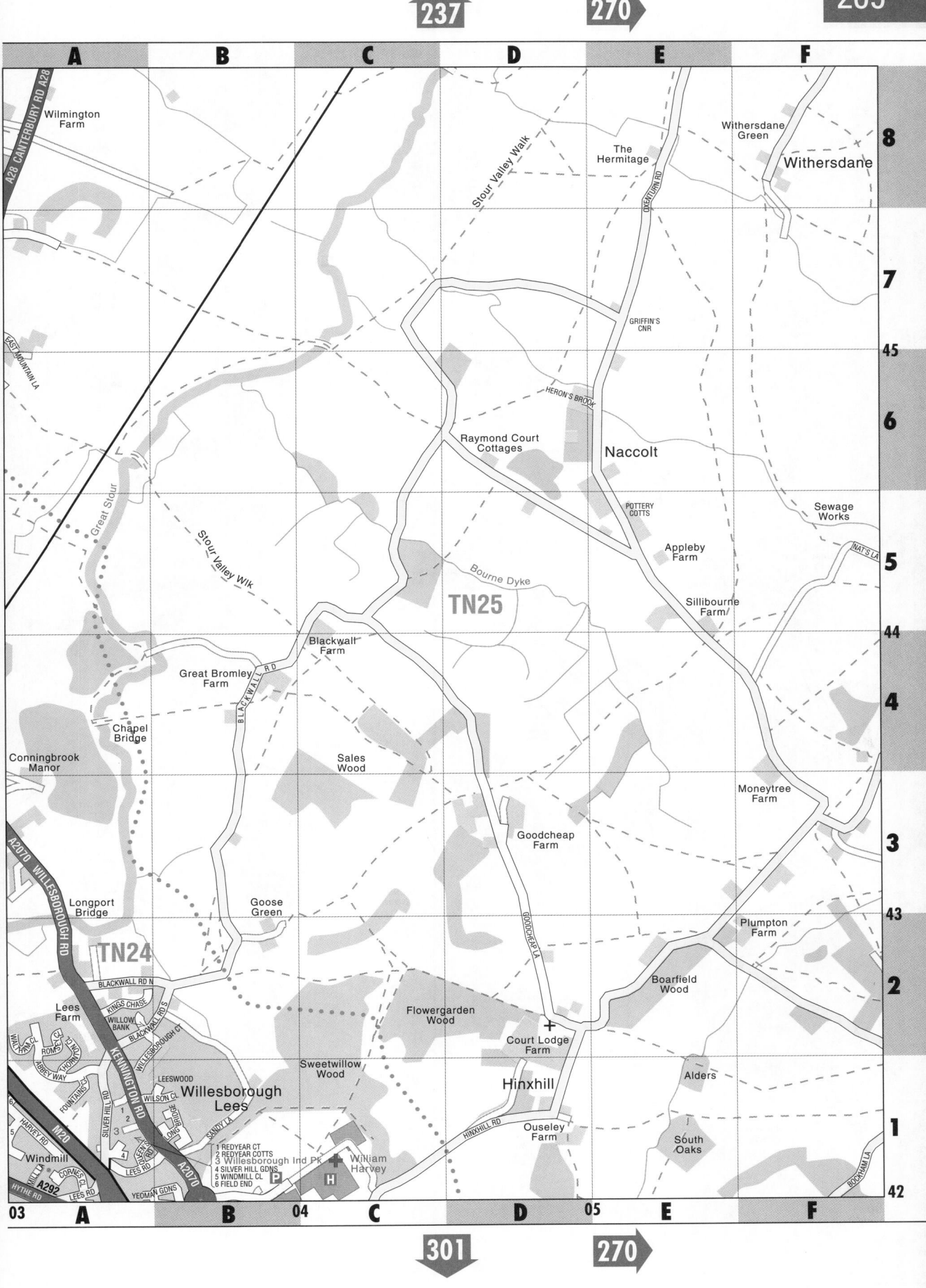

A   B   C   D   E   F

8

7

45

6

5

44

4

3

43

2

1

42

Wilmington
Farm

A28 CANTERBURY RD A28

EAST MOUNTAIN LA

Stour Valley Walk

The Hermitage

Withersdane
Green

Withersdane

OXENTURN RD

GRIFFIN'S
CNR

HERON'S BROOK

Raymond Court
Cottages

Naccolt

POTTERY
COTTS

Sewage
Works

NAT'S LA

Great Stour

Stour Valley Wlk

Bourne Dyke

TN25

Appleby
Farm

Sillibourne
Farm

Blackwall
Farm

Great Bromley
Farm

BLACKWALL RD

Chapel
Bridge

Conningbrook
Manor

Sales
Wood

Moneytree
Farm

Goodcheap
Farm

GOODCHEAP LA

A2070 WILLESBOROUGH RD

Longport
Bridge

Goose
Green

Plumpton
Farm

TN24

BLACKWALL RD N

KINGS CHASE

WILLOW
BANK

BLACKWALL RD S

BLACKWALL CT

WILLESBOROUGH CT

Lees
Farm

WALTHAM CL

HORNBEAM CL

ROMS

KENNINGTON RD

ABBEY WAY

FOUNTAINS CT

SILVER HILL RD

BOURNE

LONG

WILSON CL

LEESWOOD

SANDY LA

Boarfield
Wood

Flowergarden
Wood

Court Lodge
Farm

Sweetwillow
Wood

Willesborough
Lees

Alders

Hinxhill

1 REDYEAR CT
2 REDYEAR COTTS
3 WILLESBOROUGH IND PK
4 SILVER HILL GDNS
5 WINDMILL CL
6 FIELD END

William
Harvey

HINXHILL RD

Ouseley
Farm

South
Oaks

BOCKHAM LA

Windmill

A2070

HARVEY RD

M20

CORNES CL

LEES RD

HYTHE RD

A292

YEOMAN GDNS

LEES RD

03   A   B   04   C   D   05   E   F

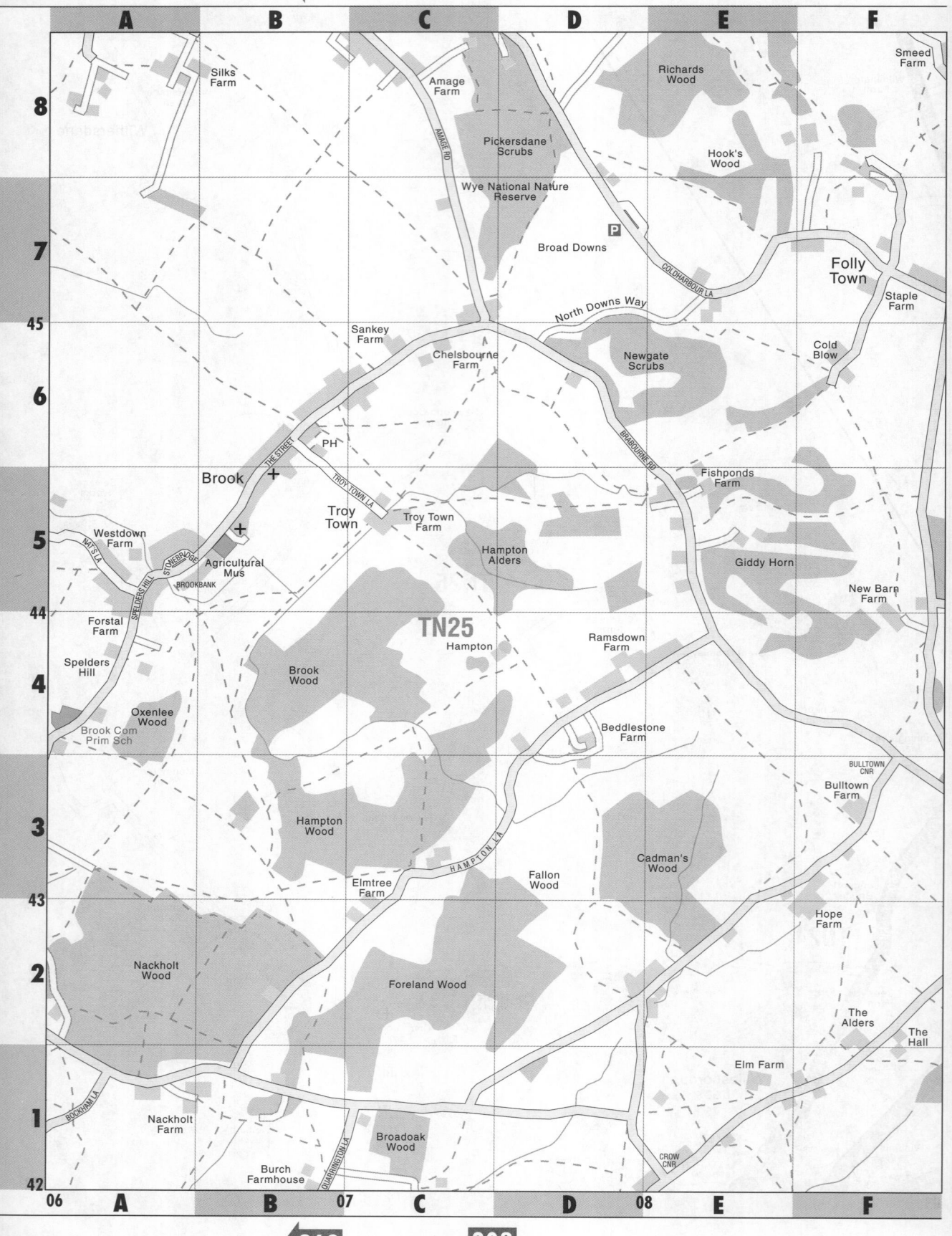

269
238

A B C D E F

8

Silks
Farm

Amage
Farm

Richards
Wood

Smeed
Farm

Pickersdane
Scrubs

Hook's
Wood

Wye National Nature
Reserve

P

7

Broad Downs

Folly
Town

COLDHARBOUR LA

Staple
Farm

45

North Downs Way

Sankey
Farm

Chelsbourne
Farm

Newgate
Scrubs

Cold
Blow

6

BRABOURNE RD

PH

THE STREET

Fishponds
Farm

Brook

Troy
Town

TROY TOWN LA

Troy Town
Farm

Hampton
Alders

Giddy Horn

New Barn
Farm

5

Westdown
Farm

MT ST LA

SPELDERS HILL

STONEBRIDGE

Agricultural
Mus

BROOKBANK

44

Forstal
Farm

TN25

Hampton

Ramsdown
Farm

4

Spelders
Hill

Oxenlee
Wood

Brook
Wood

Beddlestone
Farm

BULLTOWN
CNR

Brook Com
Prim Sch

Bulltown
Farm

3

Hampton
Wood

Cadman's
Wood

Hope
Farm

43

Elmtree
Farm

HAMPTON LA

Fallon
Wood

2

Nackholt
Wood

Foreland Wood

The
Alders

The
Hall

Elm Farm

1

BOCKHAM LA

Nackholt
Farm

Broadoak
Wood

CROW
CNR

Burch
Farmhouse

QUARRINGTON LA

42

06 A B 07 C D 08 E F

269
302

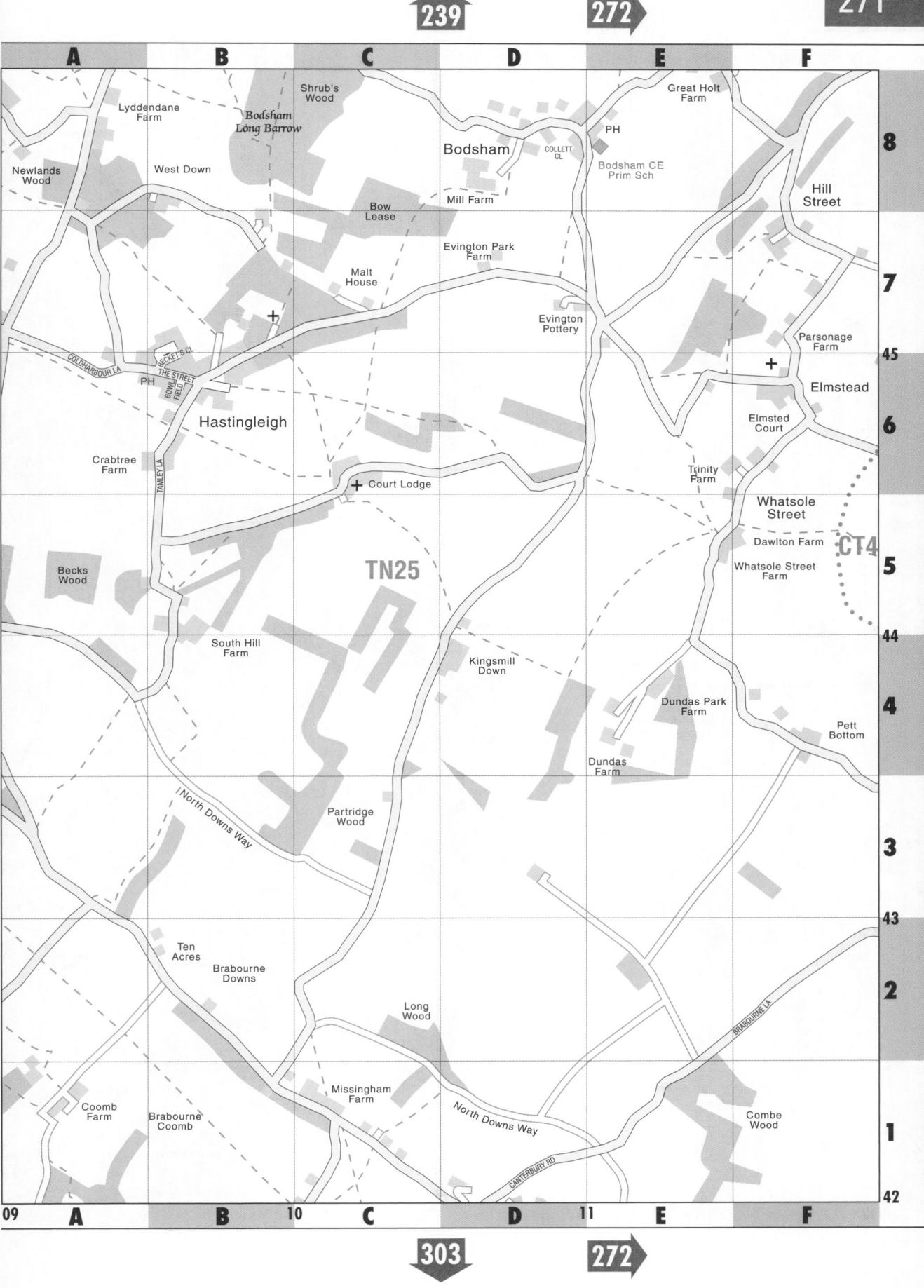

271
240

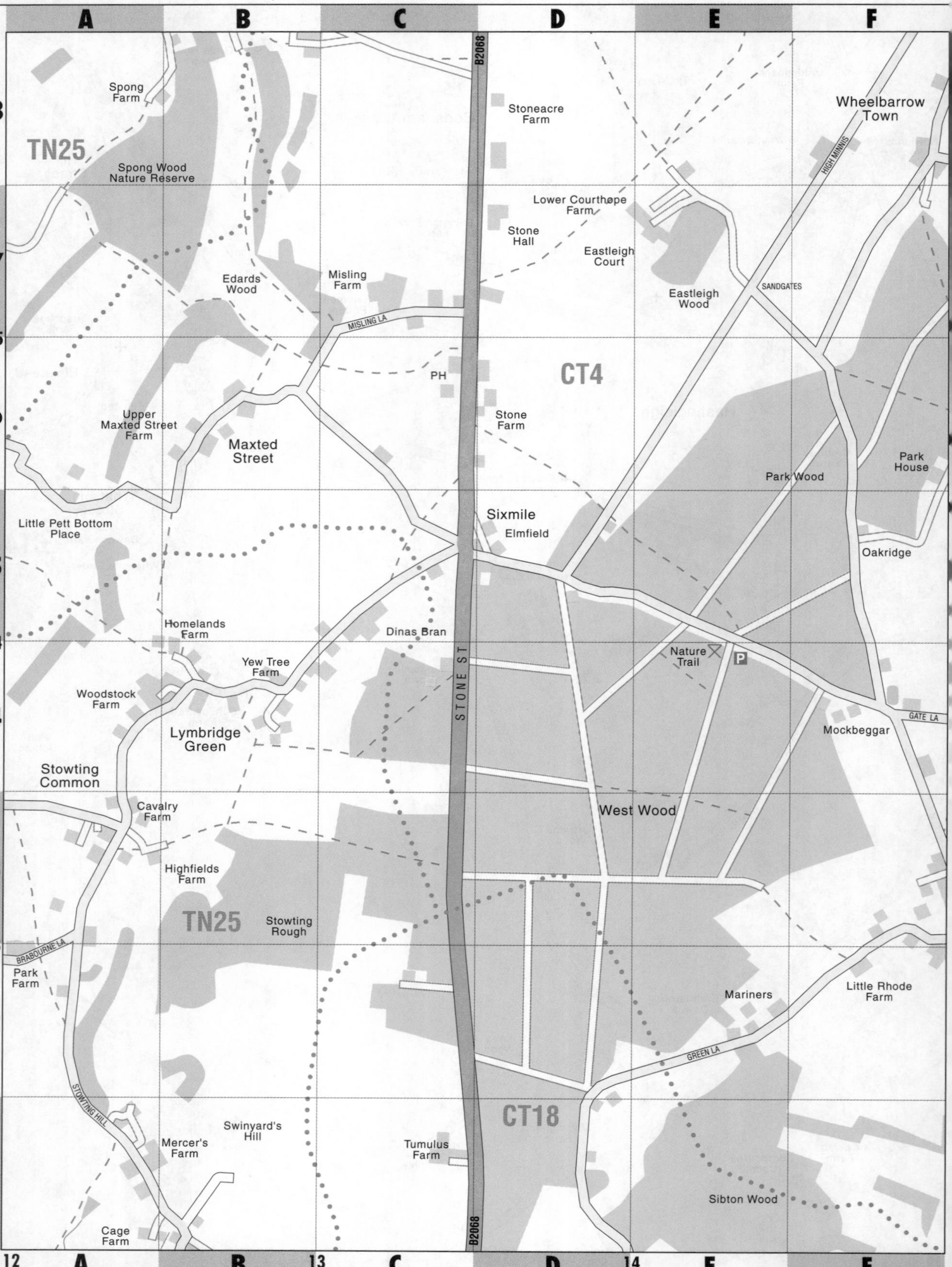

A B C D E F

8

Spong Farm

Stoneacre Farm

Wheelbarrow Town

TN25

Spong Wood Nature Reserve

Lower Courthøpe Farm

Stone Hall

Eastleigh Court

7

Edards Wood

Misling Farm

Eastleigh Wood

SANDGATES

45

MISLING LA

CT4

PH

6

Upper Maxted Street Farm

Maxted Street

Stone Farm

Park Wood

Park House

Sixmile

Elmfield

Little Pett Bottom Place

Oakridge

5

Homelands Farm

Dinas Bran

Nature Trail

P

44

Yew Tree Farm

Woodstock Farm

GATE LA

4

Lymbridge Green

Mockbeggar

Stowting Common

Cavalry Farm

West Wood

3

Highfields Farm

STONE ST

B2068

TN25

Stowting Rough

43

BRABOURNE LA

Park Farm

Mariners

Little Rhode Farm

2

GREEN LA

STOWTING HILL

CT18

Swinyard's Hill

Mercer's Farm

Tumulus Farm

1

Sibton Wood

42

12 A B 13 C D 14 E F

Cage Farm

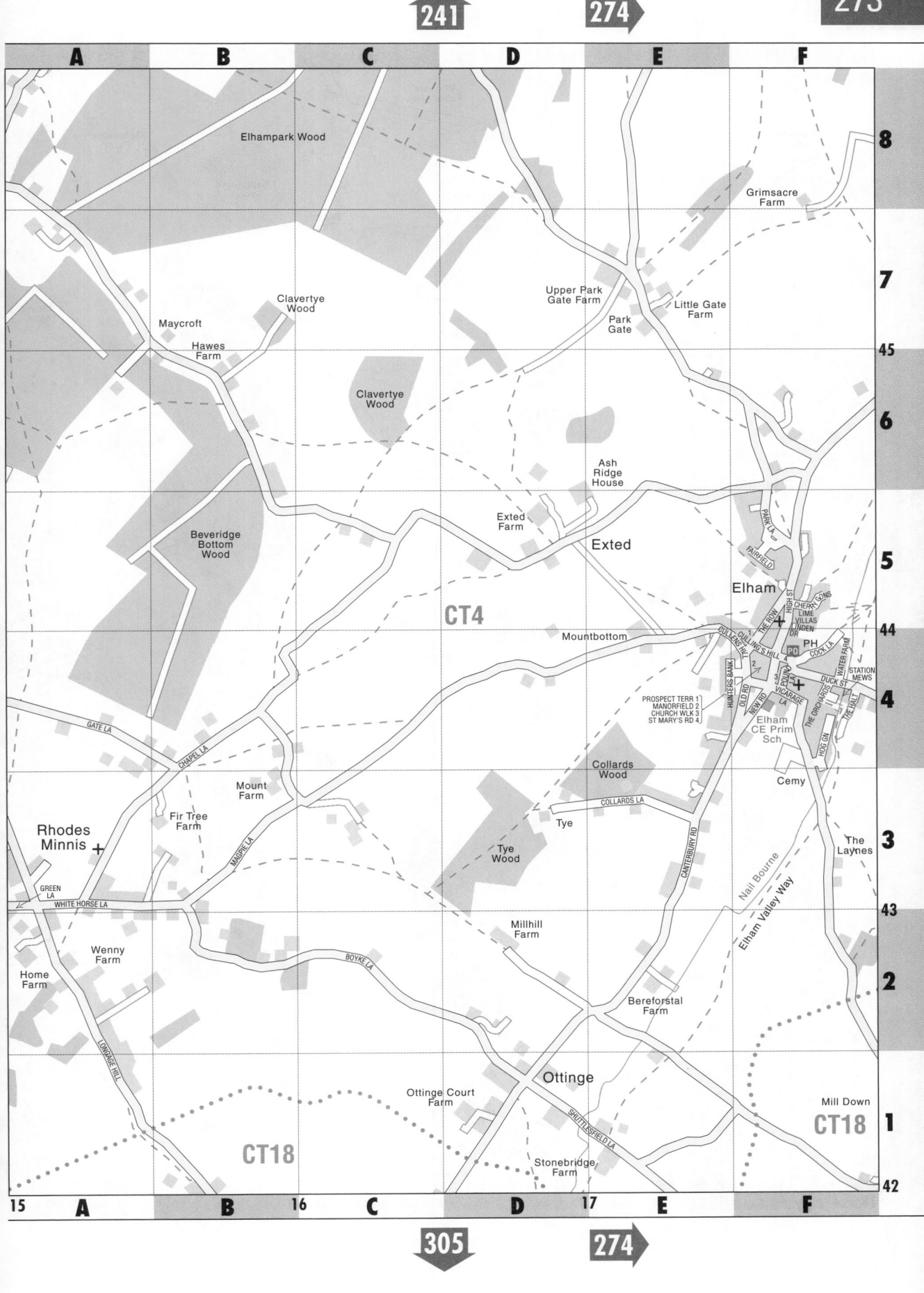

Elhampark Wood

Clavertye Wood

Maycroft

Hawes Farm

Upper Park Gate Farm

Park Gate

Little Gate Farm

Grimsacre Farm

Clavertye Wood

Ash Ridge House

Exted Farm

Exted

Beveridge Bottom Wood

PARK LA

FAIRFIELD

Elham

CT4

Mountbottom

HIGH ST

THE ROW

CHERRY'S ONS

LIME VILLAS

LINDEN DR

CULLING'S HILL

PH

PO

COCK LA

WATER FARM

HUNTERS BANK

OLD RD

NEW RD

POUND LA

VICARAGE LA

DUCK ST

STATION MEWS

THE ORCHARDS

THE HALT

PROSPECT TERR 1
MANORFIELD 2
CHURCH WLK 3
ST MARY'S RD 4

Elham CE Prim Sch

HOG GN

GATE LA

CHAPEL LA

Mount Farm

Fir Tree Farm

Collards Wood

Cemy

MAGPIE LA

Collards LA

Tye

The Laynes

Rhodes Minnis

Tye Wood

CANTERBURY RD

Nail Bourne

Elham Valley Way

GREEN LA

WHITE HORSE LA

Millhill Farm

Wenny Farm

Home Farm

BOYKE LA

Bereforstal Farm

LONGAGE HILL

Ottinge

Mill Down

CT18

Ottinge Court Farm

SHUTTLESFIELD LA

Stonebridge Farm

CT18

8

7

45

6

5

44

4

3

43

2

1

42

15 A B 16 C D 17 E F

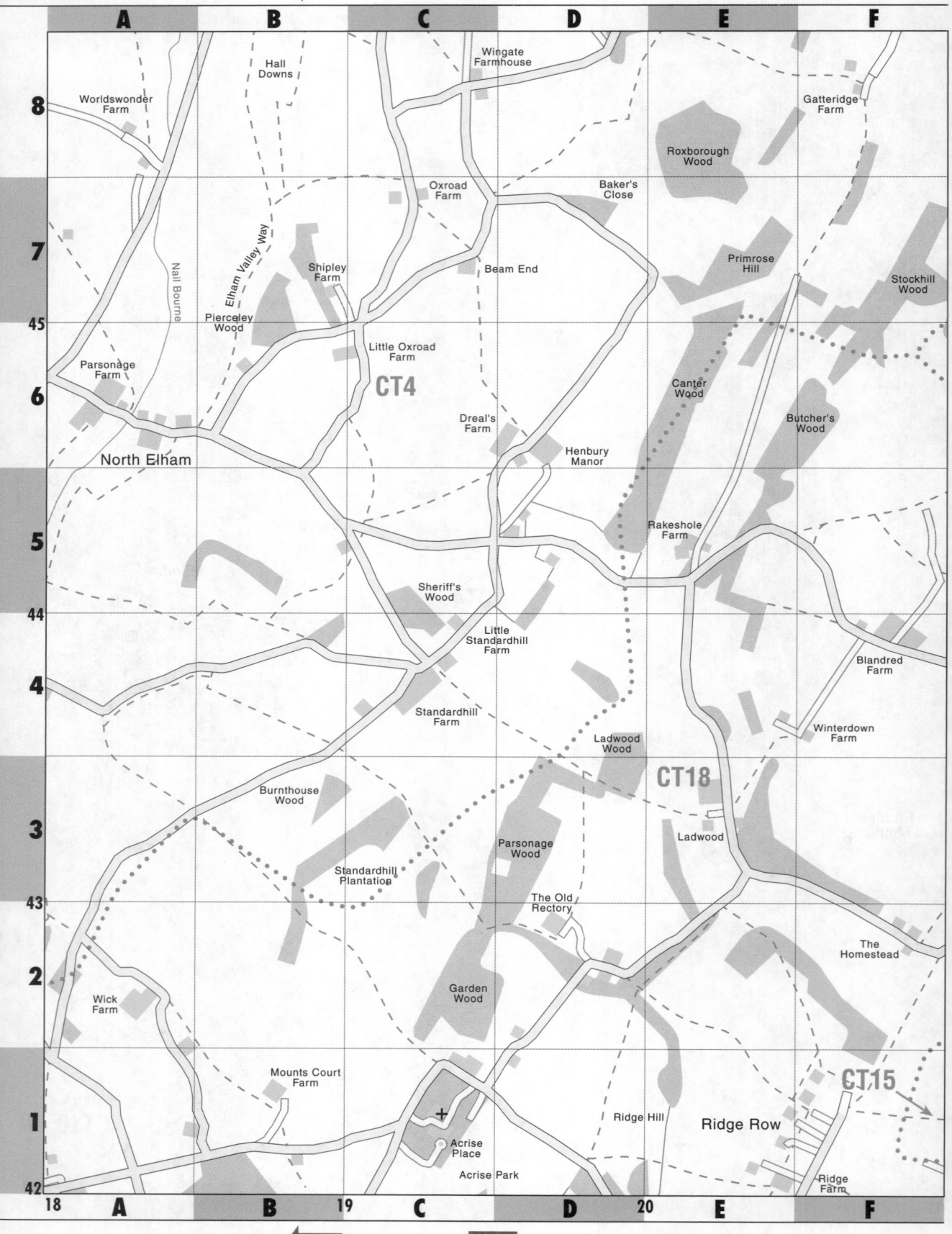

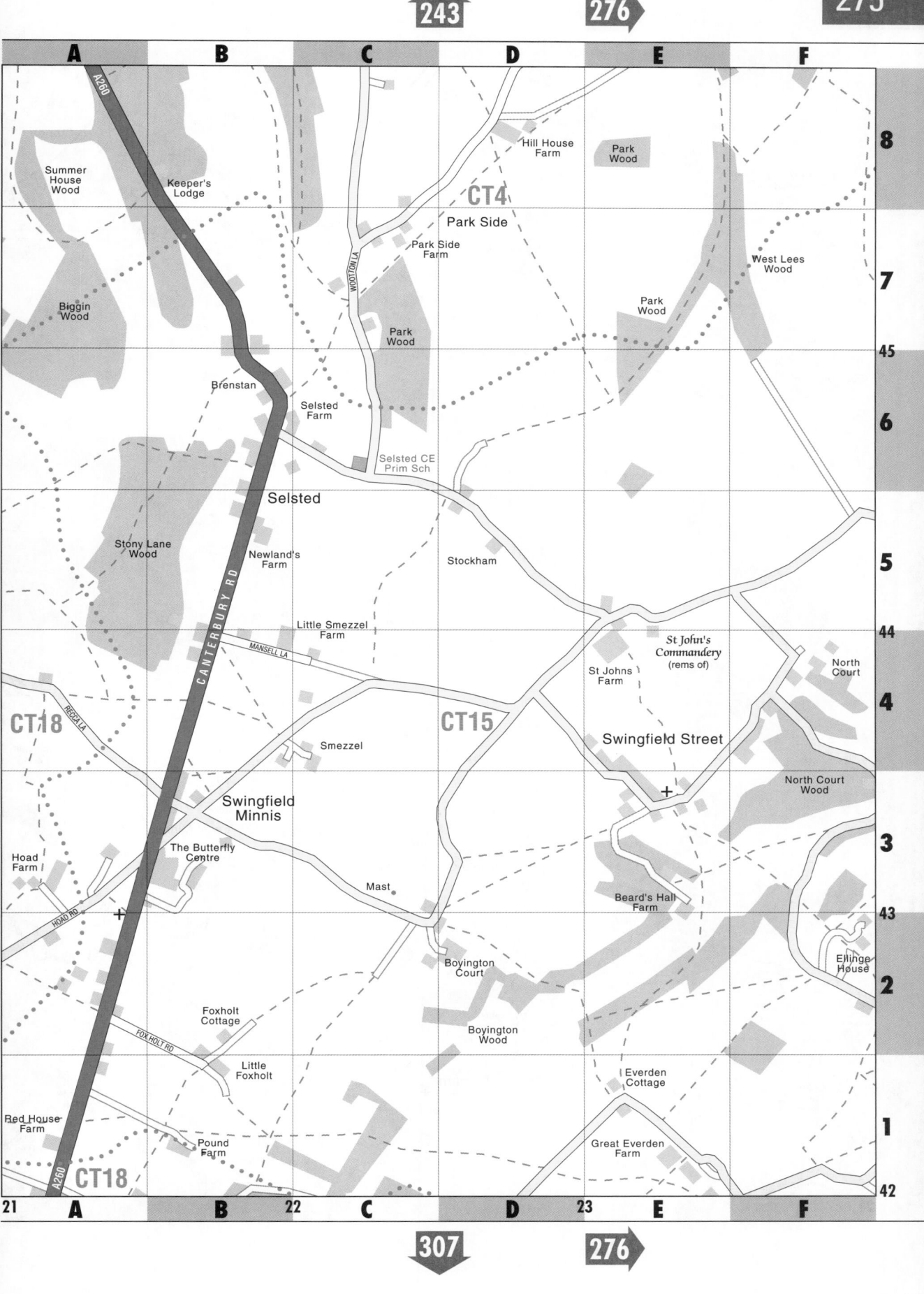

A B C D E F

8

Summer House Wood

Keeper's Lodge

Hill House Farm

Park Wood

CT4

Park Side

Park Side Farm

West Lees Wood

7

WOOTON LA

Biggin Wood

Park Wood

45

Brenstan

Park Wood

Selsted Farm

6

Selsted CE Prim Sch

Selsted

Stony Lane Wood

Newland's Farm

Stockham

5

CANTERBURY RD

Little Smezzel Farm

St John's Commandery (rems of)

North Court

44

MANSELL LA

St Johns Farm

CT18

CT15

4

REGGA LA

Smezzel

Swingfield Street

North Court Wood

Hoad Farm

Swingfield Minnis

3

HOAD RD

The Butterfly Centre

Mast

Beard's Hall Farm

43

Boyington Court

Ellinge House

2

Foxholt Cottage

FOX HOLT RD

Boyington Wood

Little Foxholt

Everden Cottage

Red House Farm

1

Pound Farm

Great Everden Farm

A260

CT18

42

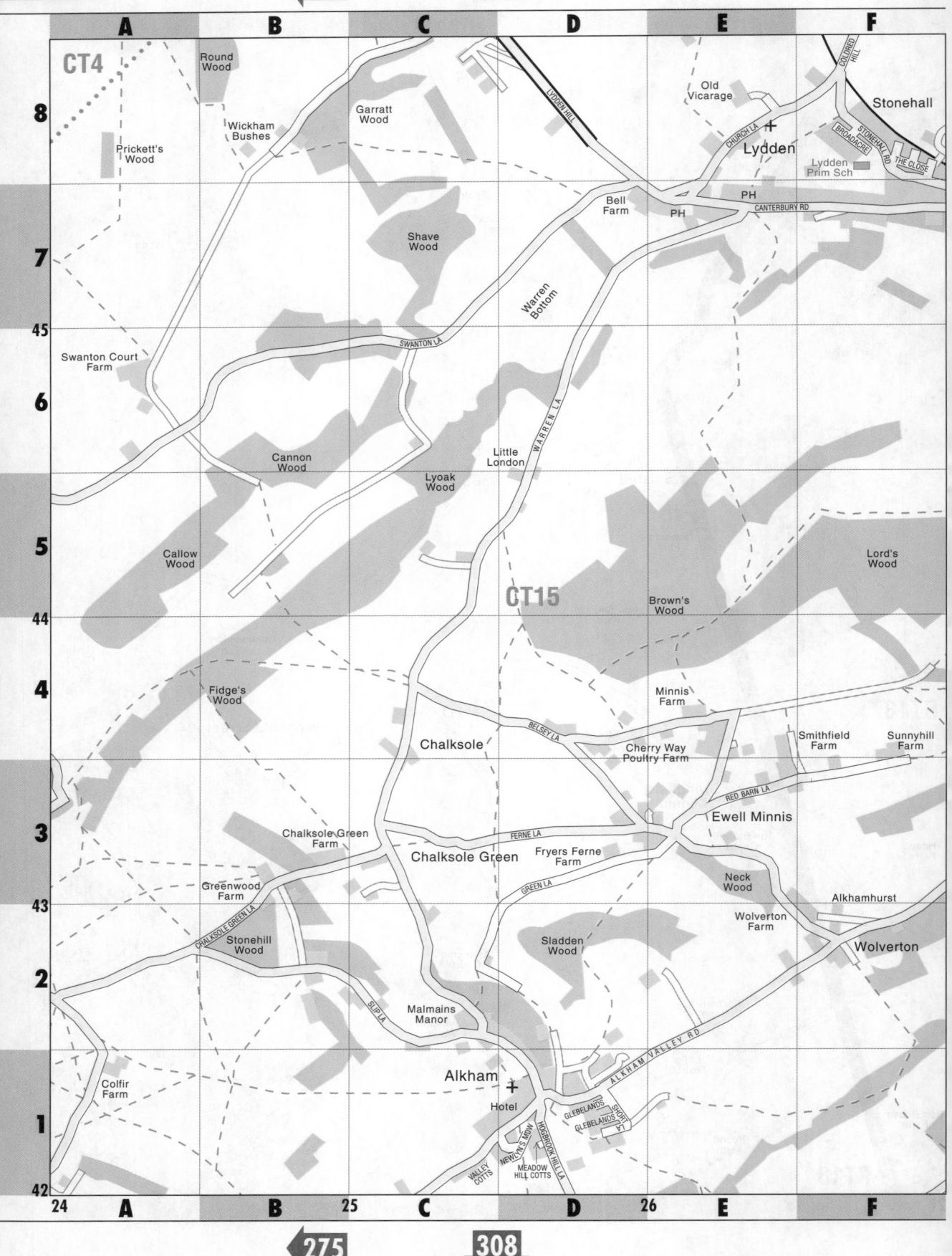

CT4

8
7
45
6
5
44
4
3
43
2
1
42

A   B   C   D   E   F

Prickett's Wood
Round Wood
Wickham Bushes
Garratt Wood
Shave Wood
Old Vicarage
Stonehall
CHURCH LA
Lydden
PH
Lydden Prim Sch
BROADACRE
STONEHALL RD
THE CLOSE
COLDRED HILL
CANTERBURY RD
Bell Farm
PH
Warren Bottom
LYDDEN HILL
SWANTON LA
Swanton Court Farm
Cannon Wood
Lyoak Wood
Little London
WARREN LA
Callow Wood
CT15
Brown's Wood
Lord's Wood
Fidge's Wood
Chalksole
BELSEY LA
Minnis Farm
Cherry Way Poultry Farm
Smithfield Farm
Sunnyhill Farm
Ewell Minnis
RED BARN LA
Chalksole Green Farm
Chalksole Green
FERNE LA
Fryers Ferne Farm
Neck Wood
Alkhamhurst
Greenwood Farm
GREEN LA
Wolverton Farm
Wolverton
CHALKSOLE GREEN LA
Stonehill Wood
SLIP LA
Malmains Manor
Sladden Wood
ALKHAM VALLEY RD
Colfir Farm
Alkham
Hotel
GLEBELANDS
GLEBELANDS
SHORT LA
NEWTON'S ROW
VALLEY COTTS
HOGBROOK HILL LA
MEADOW HILL COTTS

24   25   26
A   B   C   D   E   F

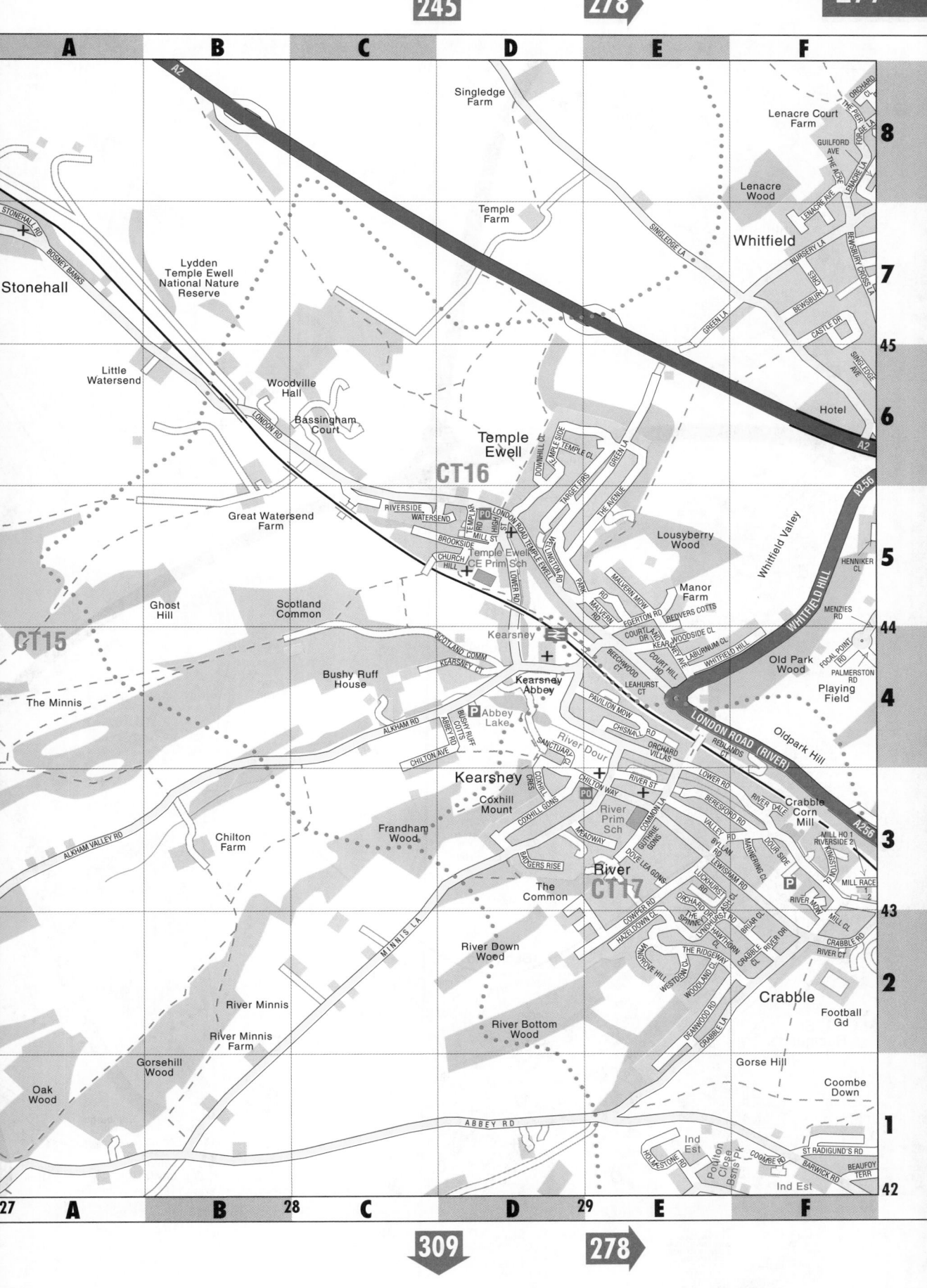

CT15

CT16

CT17

Church Whitfield

Whitfield

Pineham

Little Pineham Farm

Great Pineham Farm

Guston

Copthorne

Buckland Valley

Green Lane Hill

Long Hill

Buckland

DOVER

St Radigund's

Dover Castle

Edinburgh Hill

Bleriot Meml

B2
1 ST ANNE'S CT
2 OSPREY CT
3 MAYFIELD CT
4 MAGPIE LODGE
5 CHAFFINCH LODGE
6 HERON LODGE
7 Shatterlocks
Inf Sch

B3
1 FITZWALTER CT
2 WELLINGTON GDNS
3 BRUNSWICK GDNS
4 WASHINGTON CL
5 BOSTON CL
6 TORONTO CL
7 HUDSON CL
8 MONTREAL CL

C1
1 ALEXANDRA PL
2 BARTON VIEW TERR
3 LEIGHTON CT
4 ST ALPHEGE RD
5 SHOOTER'S HILL
6 BARTHOLOMEW ST
7 CHURCHILL ST
8 PAUL'S PL
9 MATTHEW'S PL
10 WARDEN CT
11 TEMPLAR CT
12 DOOR MEWS

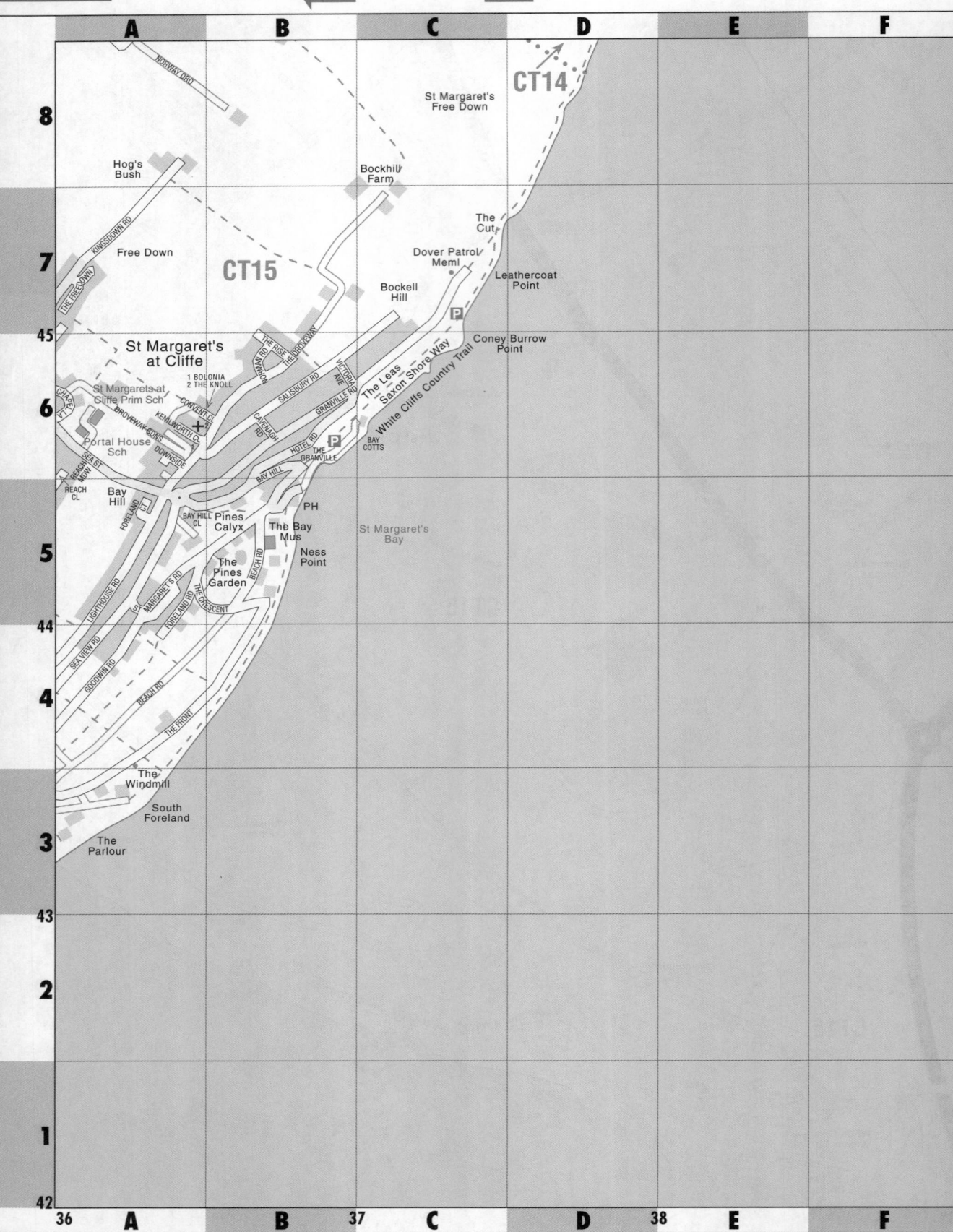

CT14

St Margaret's Free Down

Hog's Bush

Bockhill Farm

The Cut

Free Down

Dover Patrol Meml

CT15

Leathercoat Point

Bockell Hill

Coney Burrow Point

St Margaret's at Cliffe

St Margarets at Cliffe Prim Sch

1 BOLONIA
2 THE KNOLL

The Leas

Saxon Shore Way

White Cliffs Country Trail

Portal House Sch

BAY COTTS

THE GRANVILLE

Bay Hill

Pines Calyx

PH

St Margaret's Bay

The Bay Mus

The Pines Garden

Ness Point

The Windmill

South Foreland

The Parlour

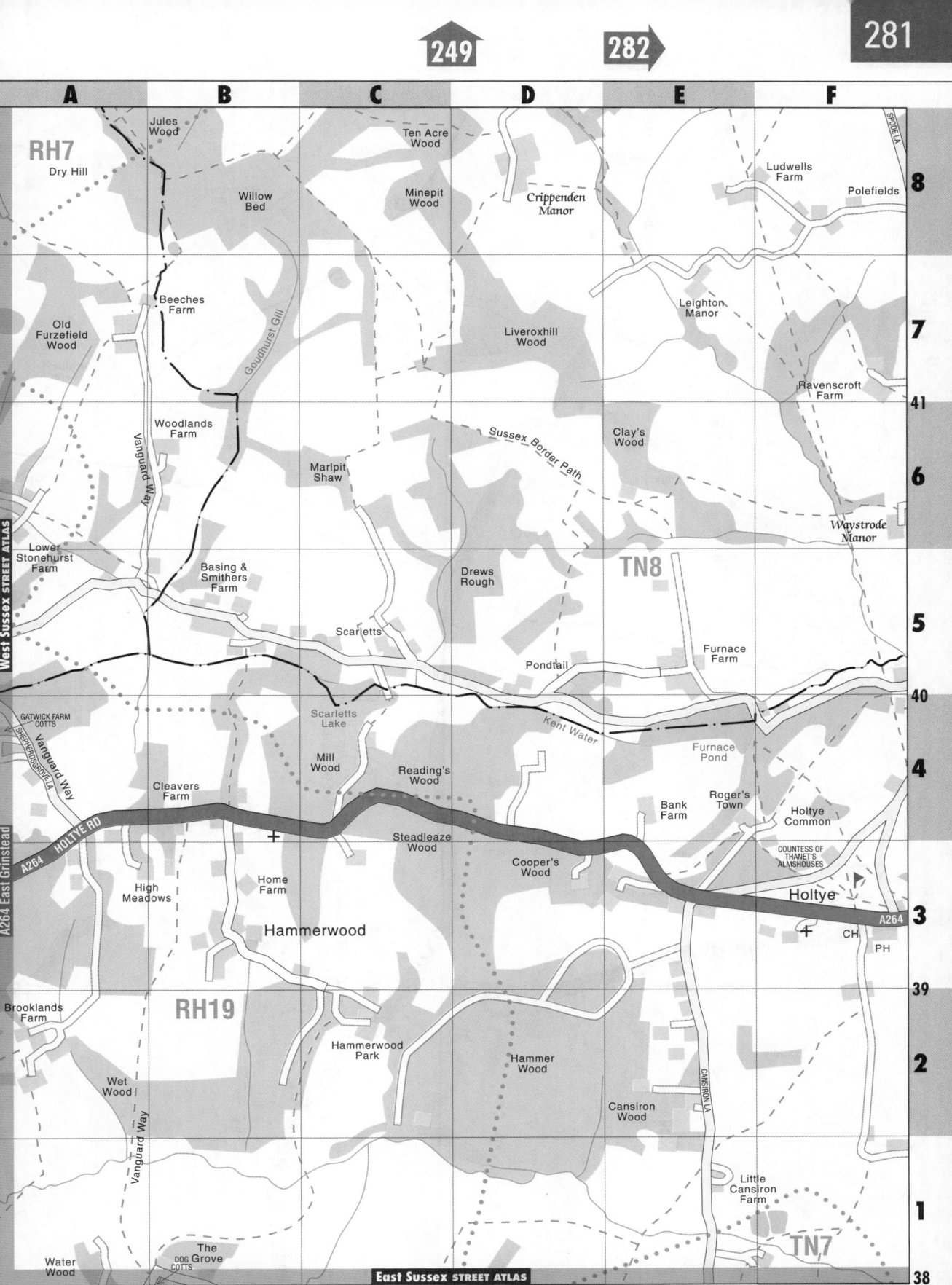

A B C D E F

RH7

Dry Hill

Jules Wood

Willow Bed

Ten Acre Wood

Minepit Wood

Crippenden Manor

Ludwells Farm

Polefields

8

Beeches Farm

Old Furzefield Wood

Goudhurst Gill

Leighton Manor

Liveroxhill Wood

Ravenscroft Farm

7

41

Woodlands Farm

Marlpit Shaw

Sussex Border Path

Clay's Wood

6

Vanguard Way

Lower Stonehurst Farm

Basing & Smithers Farm

Drews Rough

TN8

Waystrode Manor

West Sussex STREET ATLAS

Scarletts

Furnace Farm

5

Pondtail

Kent Water

40

Gatwick Farm Cotts

Scarletts Lake

Mill Wood

Reading's Wood

Furnace Pond

4

Vanguard Way

Stephens Grove La

Cleavers Farm

Steadleaze Wood

Bank Farm

Roger's Town

Holtye Common

A264 East Grinstead

A264 HOLTYE RD

High Meadows

Home Farm

Cooper's Wood

Countess of Thanet's Almshouses

Holtye

A264

3

Hammerwood

CH

PH

Brooklands Farm

RH19

39

Hammerwood Park

Wet Wood

Hammer Wood

Cansiron La

Cansiron Wood

2

Vanguard Way

Little Cansiron Farm

1

Water Wood

The Grove

Dog Cotts

TN7

38

43 A B 44 C D 45 E F

Spode La

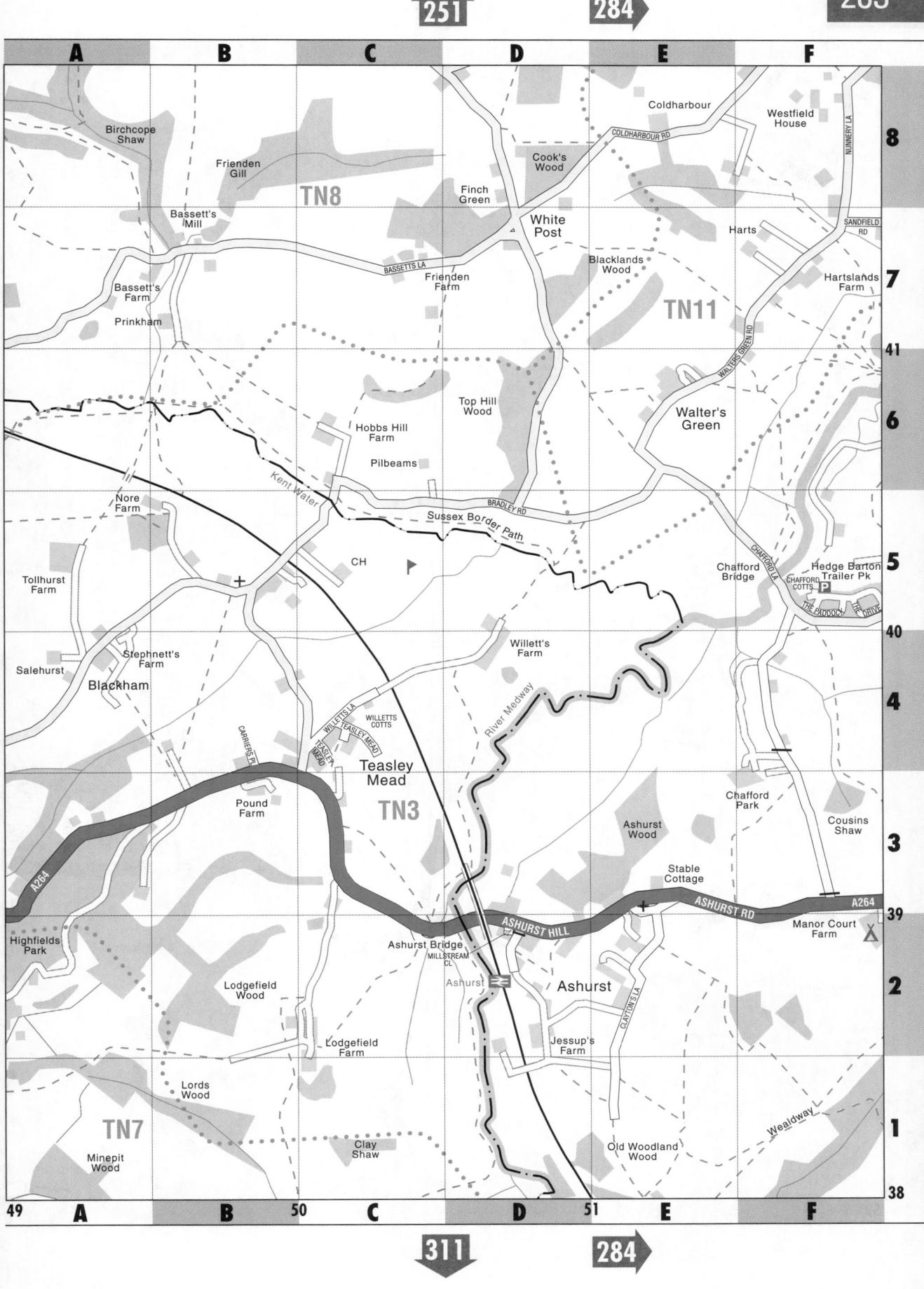

A   B   C   D   E   F

8 Birchcope Shaw

Frienden Gill

Coldharbour

Westfield House

COLDHARBOUR RD

NUNNERY LA

TN8

Cook's Wood

Bassett's Mill

Finch Green

White Post

Harts

SANDFIELD RD

BASSETTS LA

Frienden Farm

Blacklands Wood

Hartslands Farm
7

Bassett's Farm

TN11

Prinkham

WALTERS GREEN RD

41

Top Hill Wood

Walter's Green
6

Hobbs Hill Farm

Pilbeams

Kent Water

BRADLEY RD

Nore Farm

Sussex Border Path

CHAFFORD LA

Chafford Bridge

Hedge Barton Trailer Pk

Tollhurst Farm

CH

CHAFFORD COTTS

THE PADDOCK

THE DRIVE
5

Willett's Farm

40

Salehurst

Stephnett's Farm

River Medway

Blackham

CARRIERS PL

WILLETTS LA

WILLETTS COTTS

Chafford Park

Cousins Shaw
4

TEASLEY MEAD

Teasley Mead

Ashurst Wood

Pound Farm

TN3

Stable Cottage

A264

ASHURST RD

A264

Manor Court Farm
39

Highfields Park

ASHURST HILL

Ashurst Bridge

MILLSTREAM CL

Ashurst

CLAYTON'S LA

Lodgefield Wood

Ashurst

Jessup's Farm
2

Lodgefield Farm

Lords Wood

Wealdway

TN7

Old Woodland Wood

Minepit Wood

Clay Shaw
1

38

49   A   B   50   C   D   51   E   F

283
252

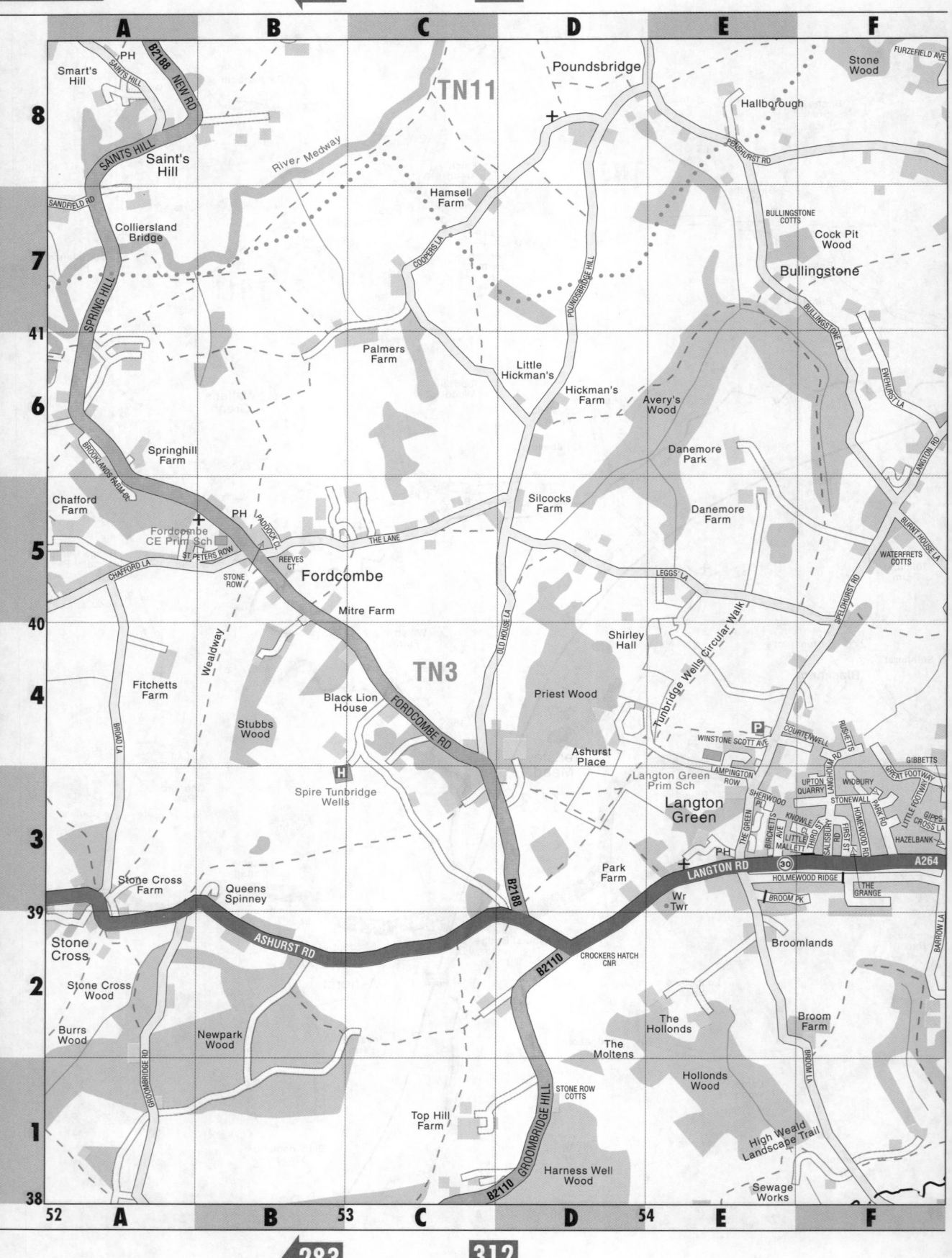

A B C D E F

8
41
7
6
5
40
4
3
39
2
1
38

283
312

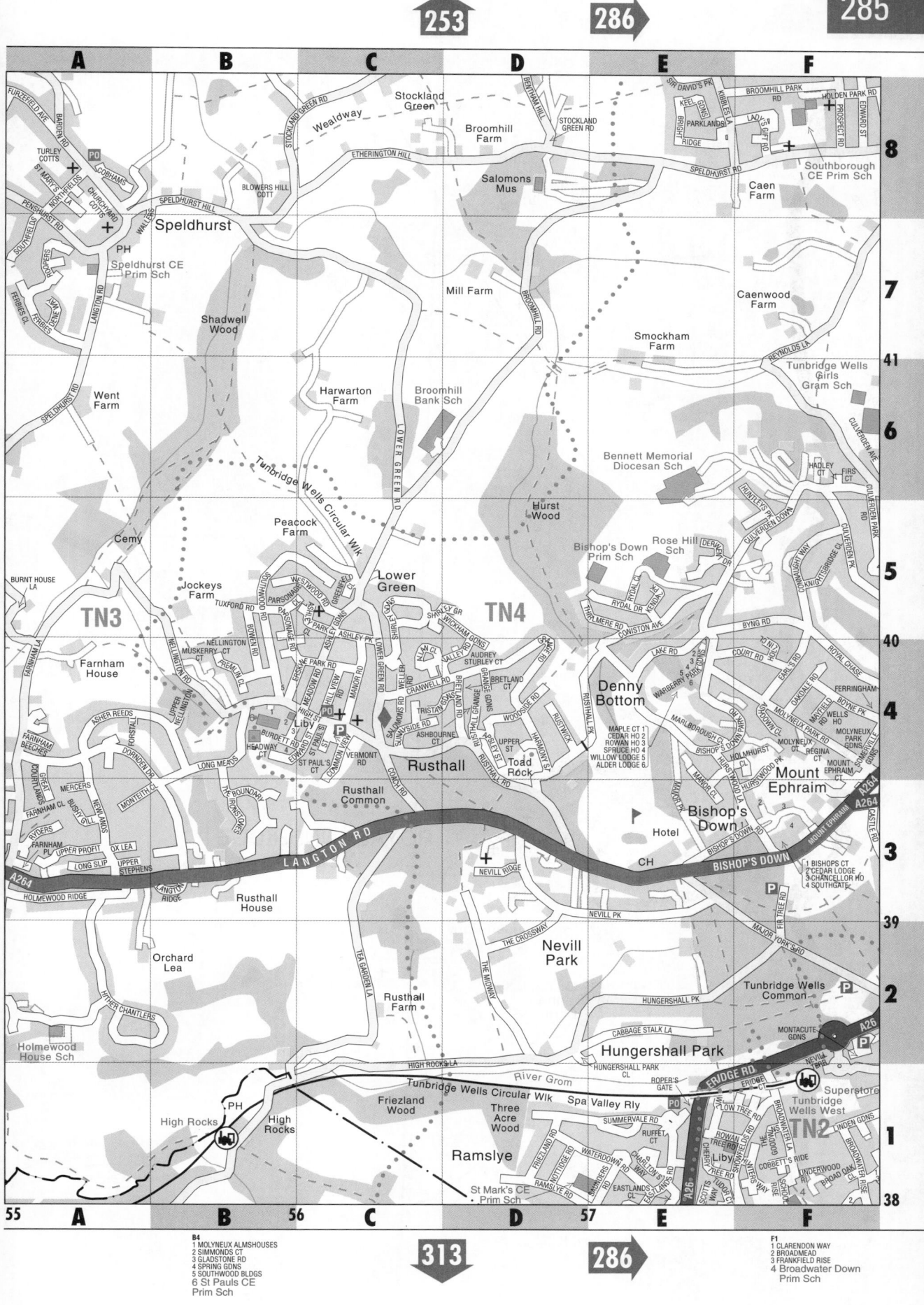

A5
1 HAMILTON HO
2 WOODBURY CL
3 ST GEORGES CT
4 EXCHANGE MEWS

285

C7
1 TAYLOR CT
2 HAROLD HO
3 OAK HO
4 CLAREMONT CT

254

A B C D E F
8 7 41 6 5 40 4 3 39 2 1 38
58 59 60
High Brooms
TN4
St Matthew's High Brooms CE Prim Sch
St Gregory's RC Comp Sch
St Augustine's RC Prim Sch
Tunbridge Wells Gram Sch for Boys
Sports Ctr
St Johns CE Prim Sch
Tunbridge Wells Girls' Gram Sch
The Skinners' Sch
St John's
Cemy
Kent & Sussex
Royal Victoria Pl
Tunbridge Wells
TN1
Calverley Park
Register Office
Mount Sion
The Pantiles
Madeira Park
The Nevill Ground (Cricket Club)
Banner Farm
Camden Park
Claremont Prim Sch
St Peter's CE Prim Sch
Tunbridge Wells Circular Wlk
Ferndale
St James' CE Jun & Inf Sch
Chilston House
The Tunbridge Wells Nuffield Hospital
ROYAL TUNBRIDGE WELLS
TN2
Hawkenbury
High Weald Landscape Trail
High Wood
Palmers Farm
TN3
Tuttys Farm
Reynards Brook Farm
Blackhurst
Muxelwell Farm
Water Tower
Beechwood Sacred Heart Sch
Tunbridge Wells High Sch
Sherwood Park
Sherwood
Sherwood Park Prim Sch
Gregg's Wood
Robin Gate
Robingate Wood
Works
Chalklin Bsns Pk
Spa Ind Pk
Tunbridge Wells Trad Pk
High Brooms Ind Pk
Orchard Bsns Ctr
LONDON RD
ST JOHN'S RD
PEMBURY RD
CALVERLEY PARK GDNS
CRESCENT RD
CHURCH RD
MOUNT EPHRAIM
MOUNT PLEASANT RD
GROVE HILL RD
PROSPECT RD
FRANT RD
A26
A264
A267
B2023
B2249
HIGH WOODS LA
HAWKENBURY RD

A2
1 CHRIST CHURCH AVE
2 CASTLE ST
3 WHITE BEAR PAS
4 WARWICK RD
5 BELGROVE
6 SPENCER MEWS
7 BERKELEY RD
8 SION WLK
9 EDEN WLK
10 CUMBERLAND GDNS
11 CUMBERLAND YD
12 CUMBERLAND MEWS
13 BEDFORD TERR
14 CHAPEL PL
15 KENTISH MANS
16 MARKET PL
17 MARKET ST
18 COACH & HORSES PAS
19 SUSSEX MEWS
20 THE PANTILES
21 REGENCY HALL
22 UNION SQ
23 CUMBERLAND COTTS

A3
1 CLANRICARDE GDNS
2 CLANRICARDE RD
3 MEREVALE HO

285

A4
1 SUFFOLK MEWS
2 ALEXANDER CT
3 LONDON RD
4 Royal Wells Coll
5 Trinity Theatre & Arts Centre

314

B3
1 CALVERLEY PARK CRES
2 MOUNT PLEASANT AVE
3 GREAT HALL ARC
4 MOUNTFIELD CT
5 THE MEWS
6 MEADOW HILL RD
7 GUILDFORD RD
8 MOUNT PLEASANT AVE
9 Great Hall Arcade

B4
1 ELIZABETH GARLICK CT
2 CAMDEN CT
3 GROVER ST
4 RICHARD BEAU NASH APARTMENTS
5 MONSON WAY
6 CADOGAN GDNS
7 CATHERINE PL
8 LANSDOWNE SQ
9 GARDEN HO
10 SPENCER MEWS

B5
1 St Barnabas CE Prim Sch

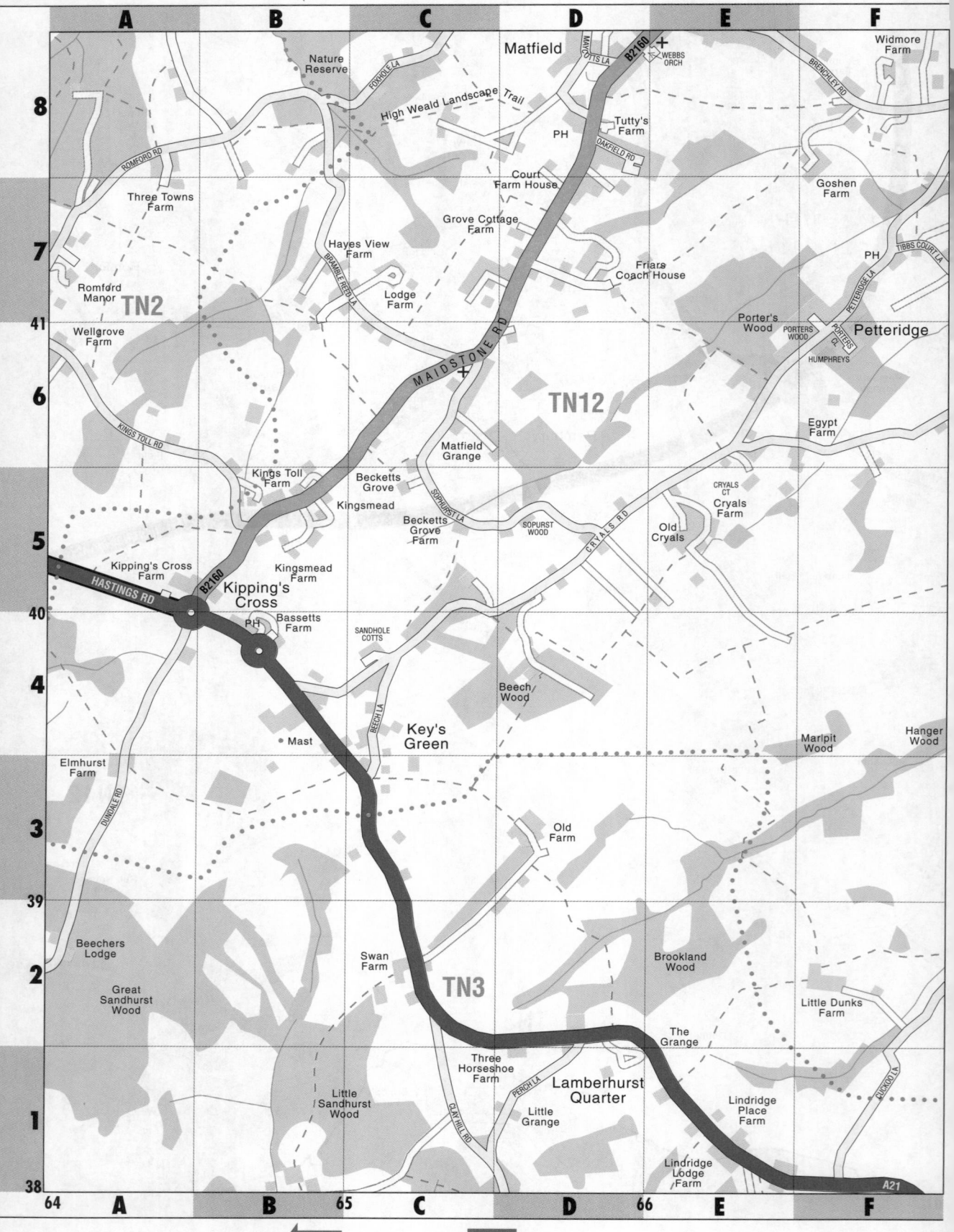

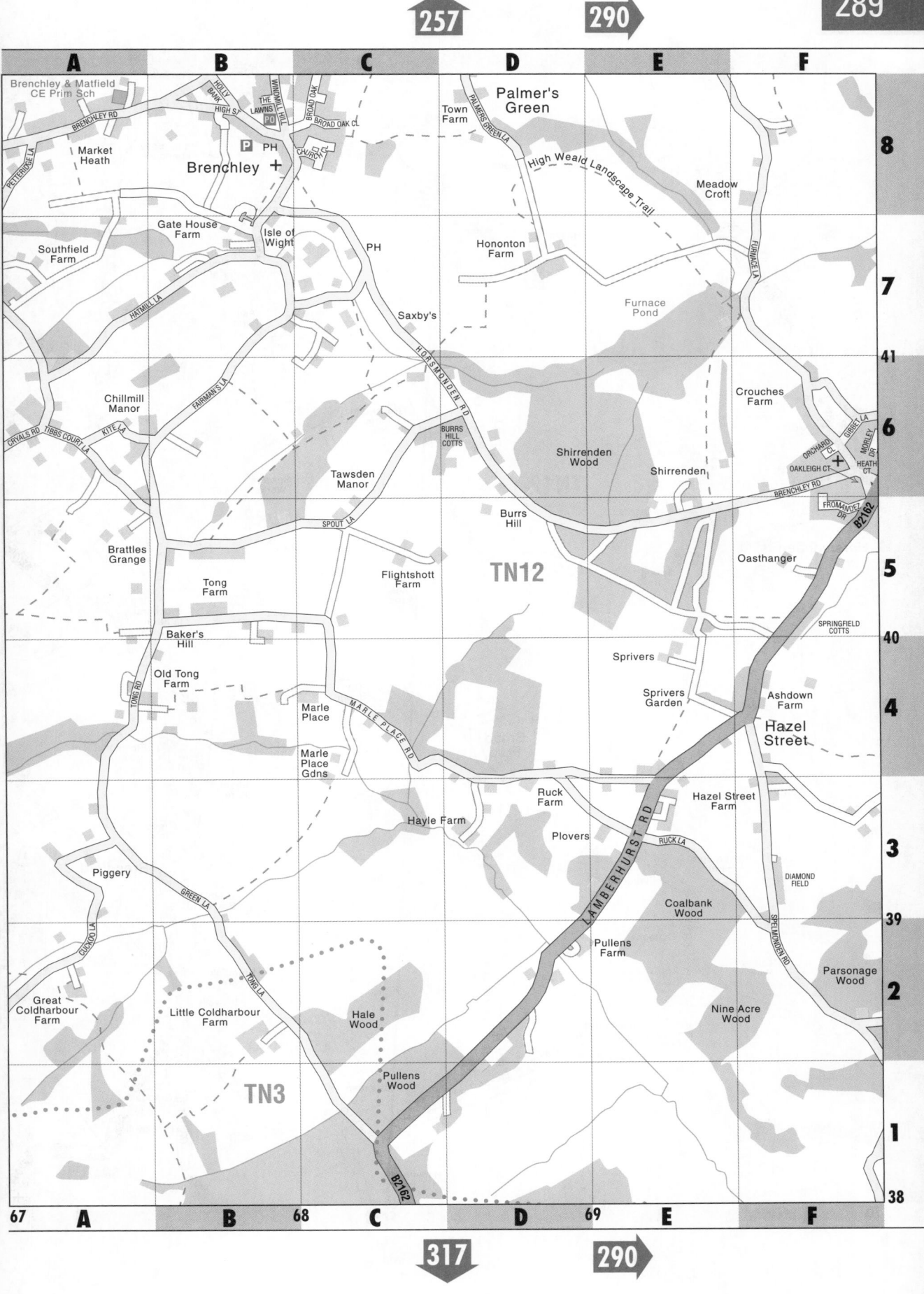

Map labels:

- Brenchley & Matfield CE Prim Sch
- Market Heath
- Brenchley
- Southfield Farm
- Gate House Farm
- Isle of Wight
- PH
- Saxby's
- Chillmill Manor
- HATMILL LA
- FARMAN'S LA
- KITE LA
- CRYALS RD
- TIBBS COURT LA
- PETTERIDGE LA
- BRENCHLEY RD
- HOLLY BANK
- HIGH ST
- WINDMILL HILL
- BROAD OAK
- BROAD OAK CL
- THE LAWNS
- PO
- CHURCH
- Town Farm
- Palmer's Green
- PALMERS GREEN LA
- High Weald Landscape Trail
- Hononton Farm
- Meadow Croft
- FURNACE LA
- Furnace Pond
- Crouches Farm
- Shirrenden Wood
- Shirrenden
- GIBBS LA
- MORLEY DR
- ORCHARD CL
- OAKLEIGH CT
- HEATH CT
- BRENCHLEY RD
- FROMANDEZ DR
- B2162
- HORSMONDEN RD
- BURRS HILL COTTS
- Tawsden Manor
- Burrs Hill
- TN12
- Oasthanger
- Brattles Grange
- SPOUT LA
- Flightshott Farm
- Tong Farm
- Baker's Hill
- Old Tong Farm
- TONG RD
- Marle Place
- Marle Place Gdns
- MARLE PLACE RD
- Sprivers
- Sprivers Garden
- SPRINGFIELD COTTS
- Ashdown Farm
- Hazel Street
- Hazel Street Farm
- Ruck Farm
- Hayle Farm
- Plovers
- RUCK LA
- LAMBERHURST RD
- DIAMOND FIELD
- Piggery
- GREEN LA
- CUCKOO LA
- TONG LA
- Great Coldharbour Farm
- Little Coldharbour Farm
- Hale Wood
- Coalbank Wood
- Pullens Farm
- SPELMONDEN RD
- Parsonage Wood
- Nine Acre Wood
- TN3
- Pullens Wood
- B2162

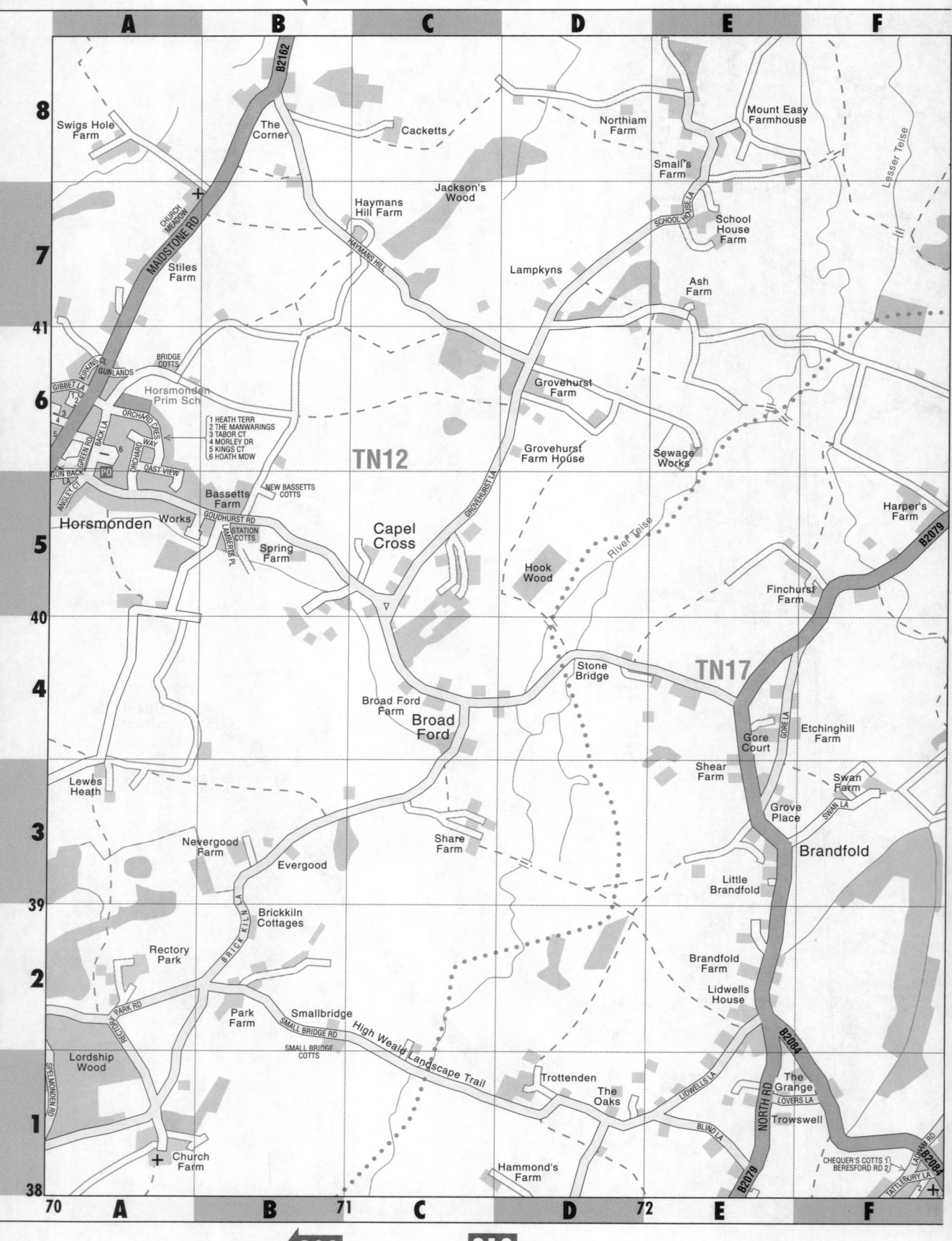

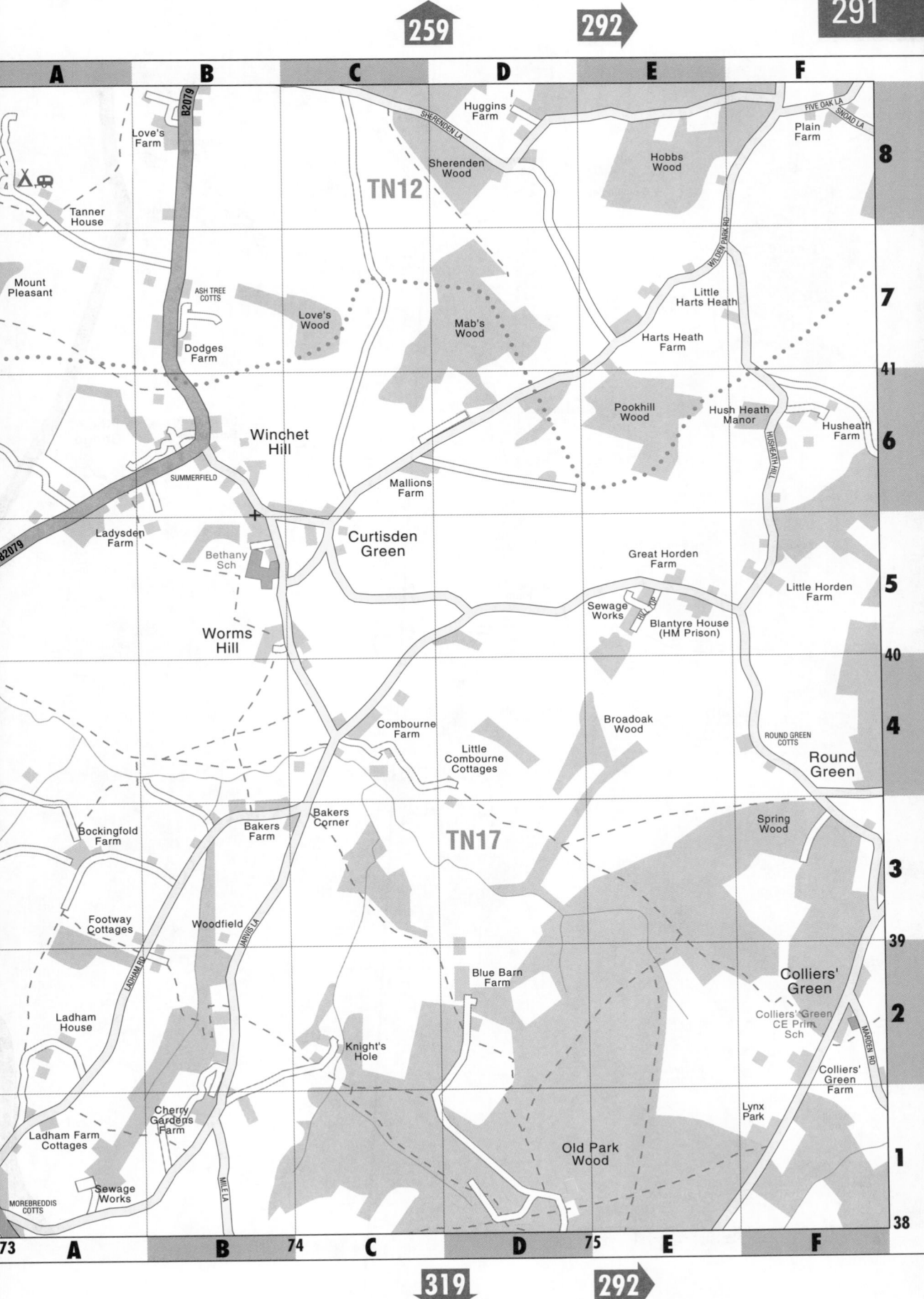

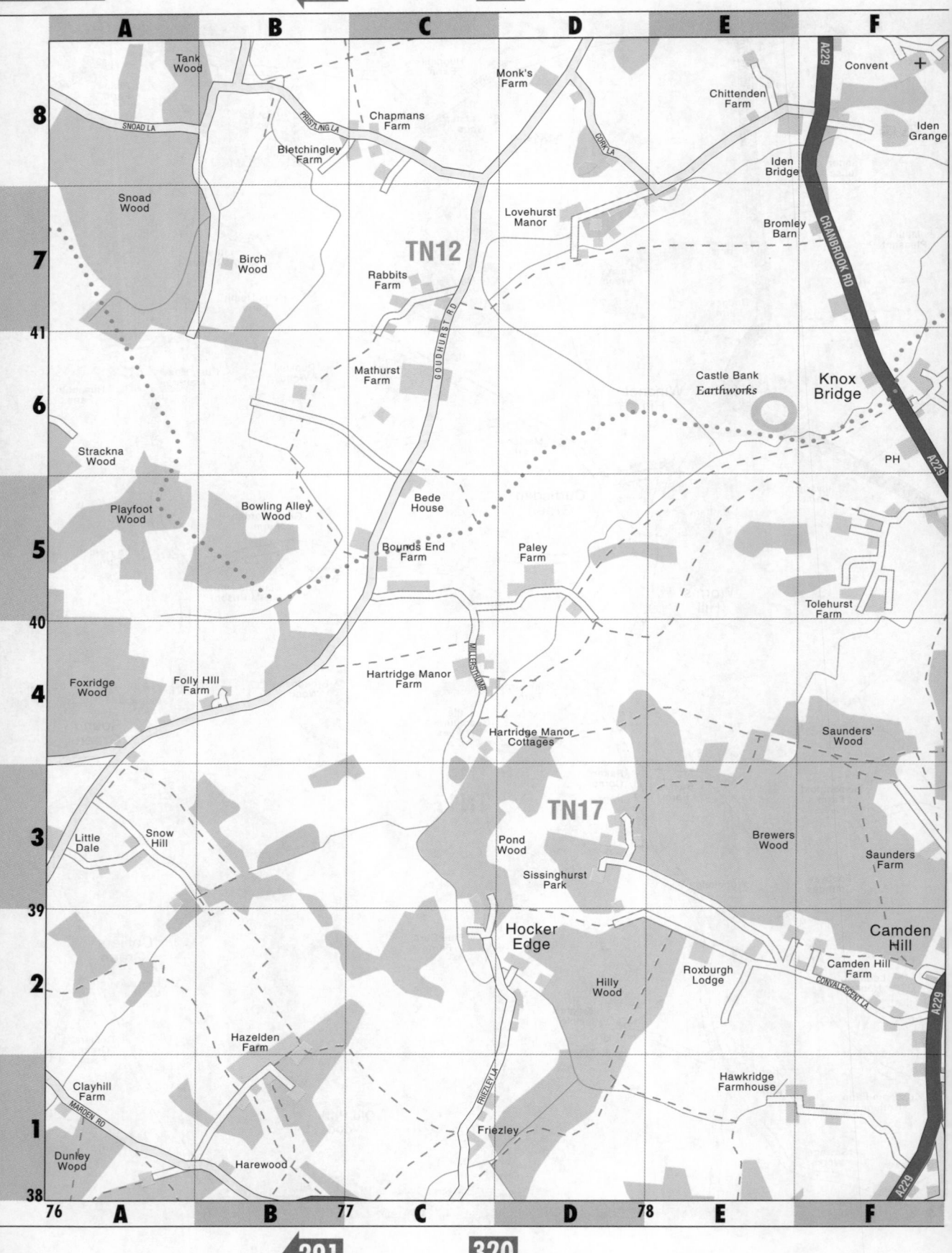

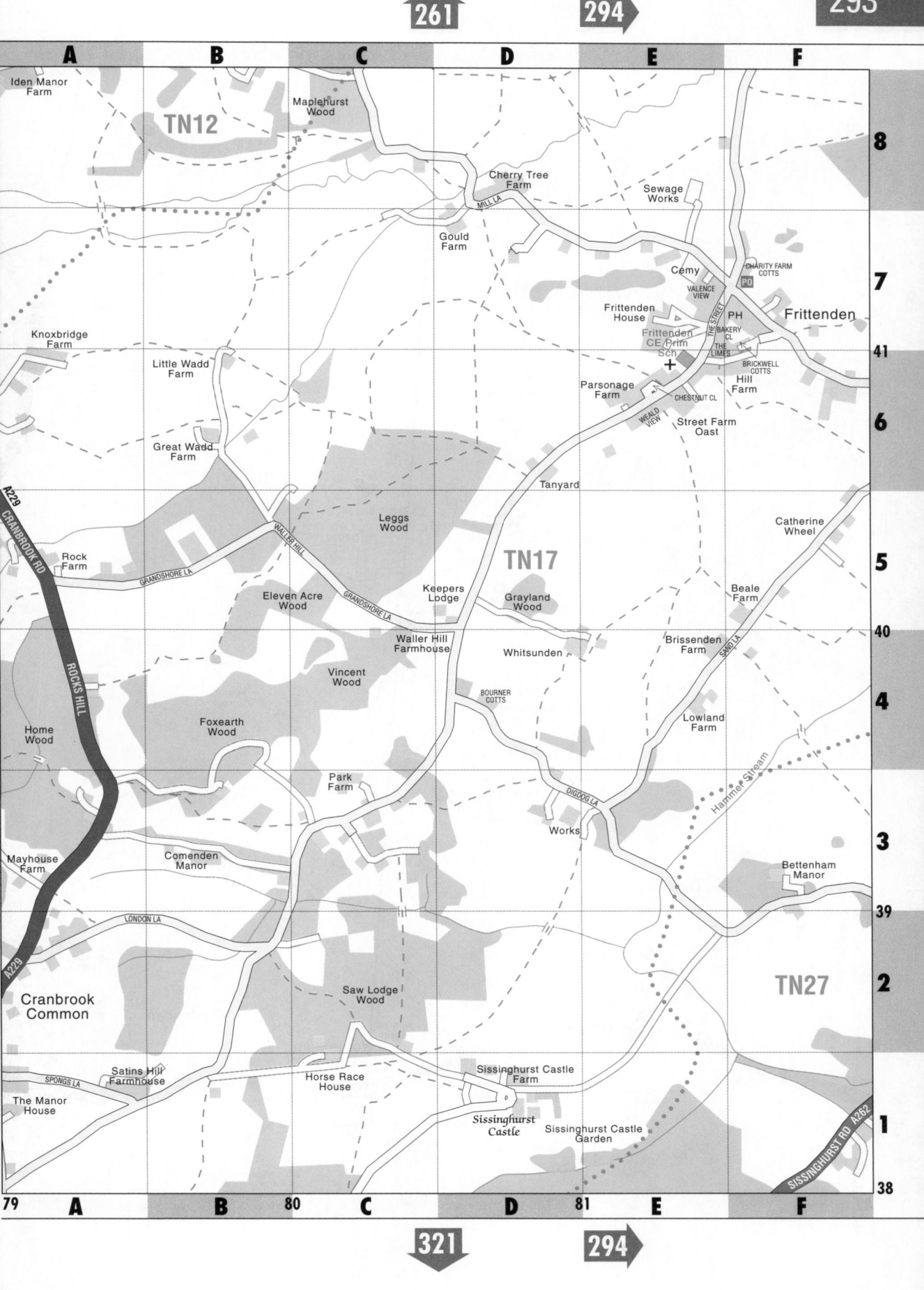

A B C D E F

8

Iden Manor
Farm

TN12

Maplehurst
Wood

Cherry Tree
Farm

Sewage
Works

7

Gould
Farm

MILL LA

Cemy

CHARITY FARM
COTTS

PO

VALENCE
VIEW

Frittenden
House

THE STREET

PH

BAKERY
CL

Frittenden

41

Knoxbridge
Farm

Little Wadd
Farm

Frittenden
CE Prim
Sch

THE
LIMES

BRICKWELL
COTTS

Parsonage
Farm

CHESTNUT CL

Hill
Farm

6

Great Wadd
Farm

WEALD
VIEW

Street Farm
Oast

Tanyard

A229

CRANBROOK RD

Rock
Farm

GRANDSHORE LA

WALLER HILL

Leggs
Wood

TN17

Catherine
Wheel

5

GRANDSHORE LA

Eleven Acre
Wood

Keepers
Lodge

Grayland
Wood

Beale
Farm

40

Waller Hill
Farmhouse

Whitsunden

Brissenden
Farm

SAND LA

ROCKS HILL

Vincent
Wood

BOURNER
COTTS

Lowland
Farm

4

Home
Wood

Foxearth
Wood

Park
Farm

DIGDOG LA

Works

Hammer Stream

3

Mayhouse
Farm

Comenden
Manor

Bettenham
Manor

39

A229

LONDON LA

2

Cranbrook
Common

Saw Lodge
Wood

TN27

SPONGS LA

Satins Hill
Farmhouse

Horse Race
House

Sissinghurst Castle
Farm

SISSINGHURST RD A262

1

The Manor
House

Sissinghurst
Castle

Sissinghurst Castle
Garden

38

A   B   C   D   E   F

8

Pound Wood

Little Bubhurst Farm

Great Bubhurst Farm

The Rustics

Hillside

Links Farm

Wick Hill

Lingfield House

BIDDENDEN RD

A274

7

Peasridge Farm

Payne Land Farm

BUBHURST LA

Ayleswade Farm

Little Ayleswade

AYLESWADE RD

41

Balcombe Barn

Old Lashenden Farm

Bounds Cross

HEADCORN RD

A274

6

Corner Farm

Pond Farm

TN17

Stone Court Farm

Little Buckhurst

SAND LA

Chanceford Farm

Lashenden

Ibornden Farm

Park Farm

5

Buckhurst

Buckhurst Farm

Hammer Stream

Buckhurst Bridge

Farm House

40

Clay Bridge

4

Hareplain

Brookwood Farm

Hareplain Farm

Claybridge Stream

Heron Cottage

Ibornden Park

3

Common Farm

Bettmans Wood Farm

West Ongley Farm

TN27

39

Little Bettenham

White House Farm

Three Chimneys

PH

East Ongley Farm

Sewage Works

MANSION HOUSE CL

THE MEADOWS

SANDEMAN WAY

CHEESELANDS

CHURCH VIEW

GLEBELANDS

Biddenden

2

Holden Farm

Nimrod Farm

Worsenden Green

WORSENDEN

CHULKHURST CL

CHULKHURST

FOSTEN LA

SISSINGHURST RD

A262 HIGH ST

1

Hammer Stream

Frogs Hole Farm

Great Batchelor's Farm

Randolph's Farm

The John Mayne CE Prim Sch

Recn Gd

Hammer Mill Farm

Worsenden Farm

38

82   A   B   83   C   D   84   E   F

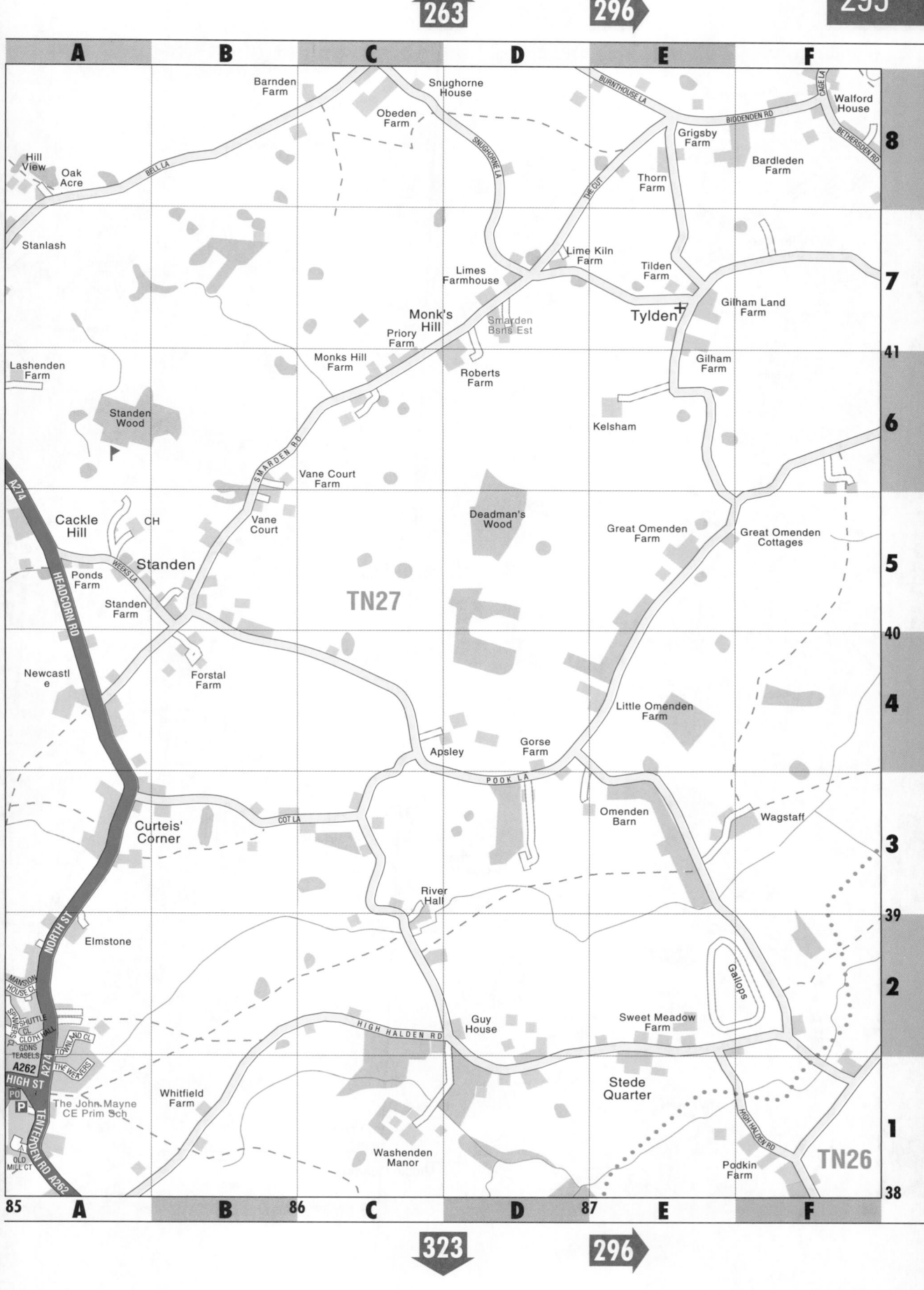

A   B   C   D   E   F

Barnden
Farm

Snughorne
House

Obeden
Farm

Hill
View

Oak
Acre

BELL LA

SNUGHORNE LA

THE CUT

BURNTHOUSE LA

BIDDENDEN RD

CAGE LA

BETHERSDEN RD

Walford
House

Grigsby
Farm

8

Thorn
Farm

Bardleden
Farm

Stanlash

Lime Kiln
Farm

Tilden
Farm

7

Limes
Farmhouse

Monk's
Hill

Smarden
Bsns Est

Tylden

Gilham Land
Farm

Lashenden
Farm

Priory
Farm

Monks Hill
Farm

Roberts
Farm

Gilham
Farm

41

Standen
Wood

SMARDEN RD

Kelsham

6

A274

Vane Court
Farm

Deadman's
Wood

Great Omenden
Farm

Great Omenden
Cottages

Cackle
Hill

CH

Vane
Court

WEEKS LA

Standen

TN27

5

Ponds
Farm

Standen
Farm

Little Omenden
Farm

40

HEADCORN RD

Newcastl
e

Forstal
Farm

4

Apsley

Gorse
Farm

POOK LA

Wagstaff

COT LA

Curteis'
Corner

Omenden
Barn

3

River
Hall

39

NORTH ST

Elmstone

Gallops

2

MANSION
HOUSE CL

SHUTTLE

CLOTH HALL

GDNS
TEASELS

WOLLAND CL

THE WEAVERS

A274

HIGH HALDEN RD

Guy
House

Sweet Meadow
Farm

A262

HIGH ST

PO

P

The John Mayne
CE Prim Sch

Whitfield
Farm

Stede
Quarter

HIGH HALDEN RD

1

TENTERDEN RD A262

OLD
MILL CT

Washenden
Manor

Podkin
Farm

TN26

38

85   A   B   86   C   D   87   E   F

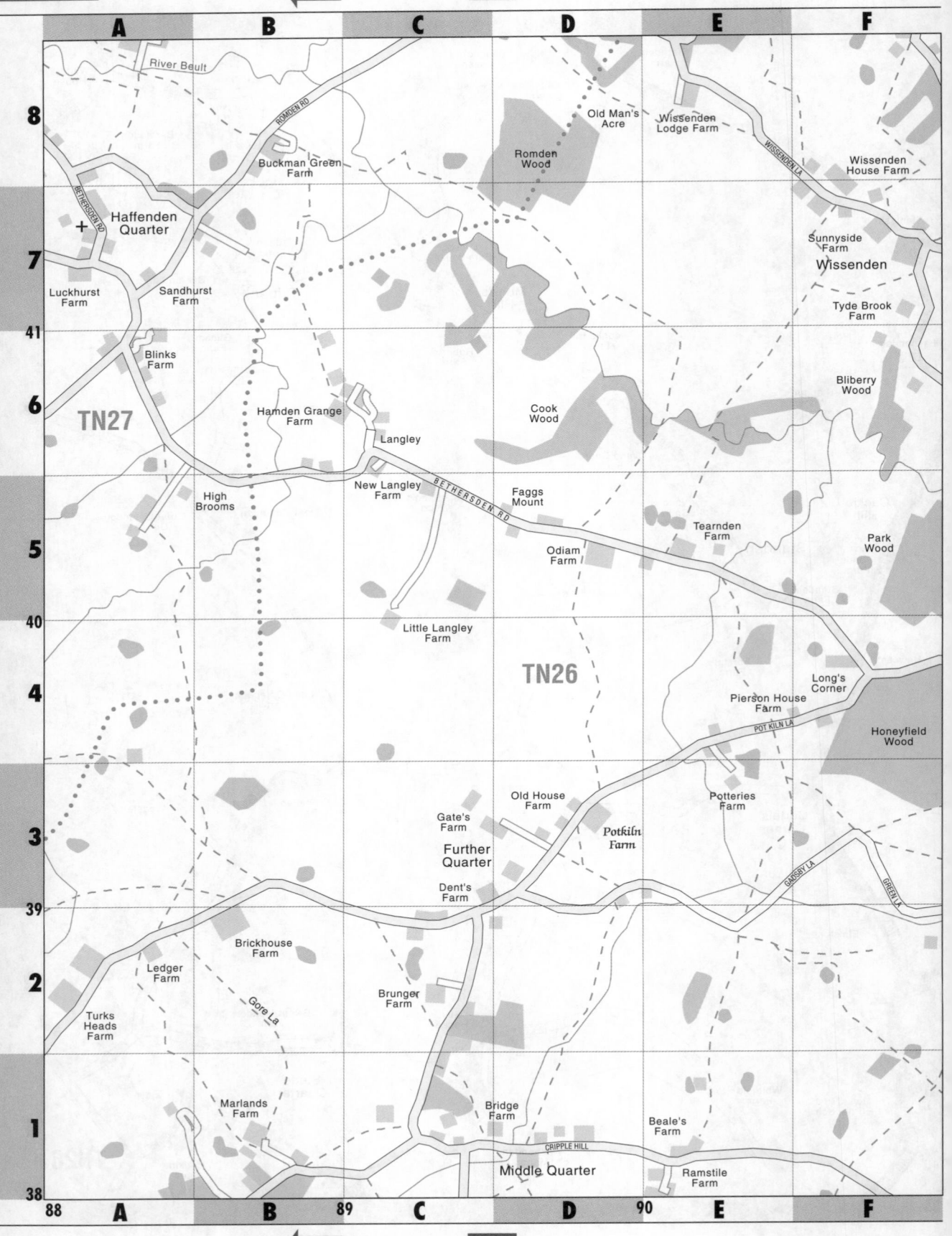

A B C D E F

8

Old Man's Acre

Romden Wood

Wissenden Lodge Farm

Wissenden House Farm

River Beult

ROMDEN RD

Buckman Green Farm

WISSENDEN LA

7

Haffenden Quarter

+

Sunnyside Farm

Wissenden

Luckhurst Farm

BETHERSDEN RD

Sandhurst Farm

Tyde Brook Farm

41

Blinks Farm

Bliberry Wood

6

TN27

Hamden Grange Farm

Cook Wood

Langley

Faggs Mount

New Langley Farm

BETHERSDEN RD

Tearnden Farm

Park Wood

5

High Brooms

Odiam Farm

40

Little Langley Farm

TN26

Long's Corner

4

Pierson House Farm

POT KILN LA

Honeyfield Wood

Old House Farm

Potteries Farm

Gate's Farm

Potkiln Farm

3

Further Quarter

Dent's Farm

GARSSY LA

GREEN LA

39

Brickhouse Farm

2

Ledger Farm

Brunger Farm

Gore La

Turks Heads Farm

Marlands Farm

Bridge Farm

Beale's Farm

1

CRIPPLE HILL

Middle Quarter

Ramstile Farm

38

88 A B 89 C D 90 E F

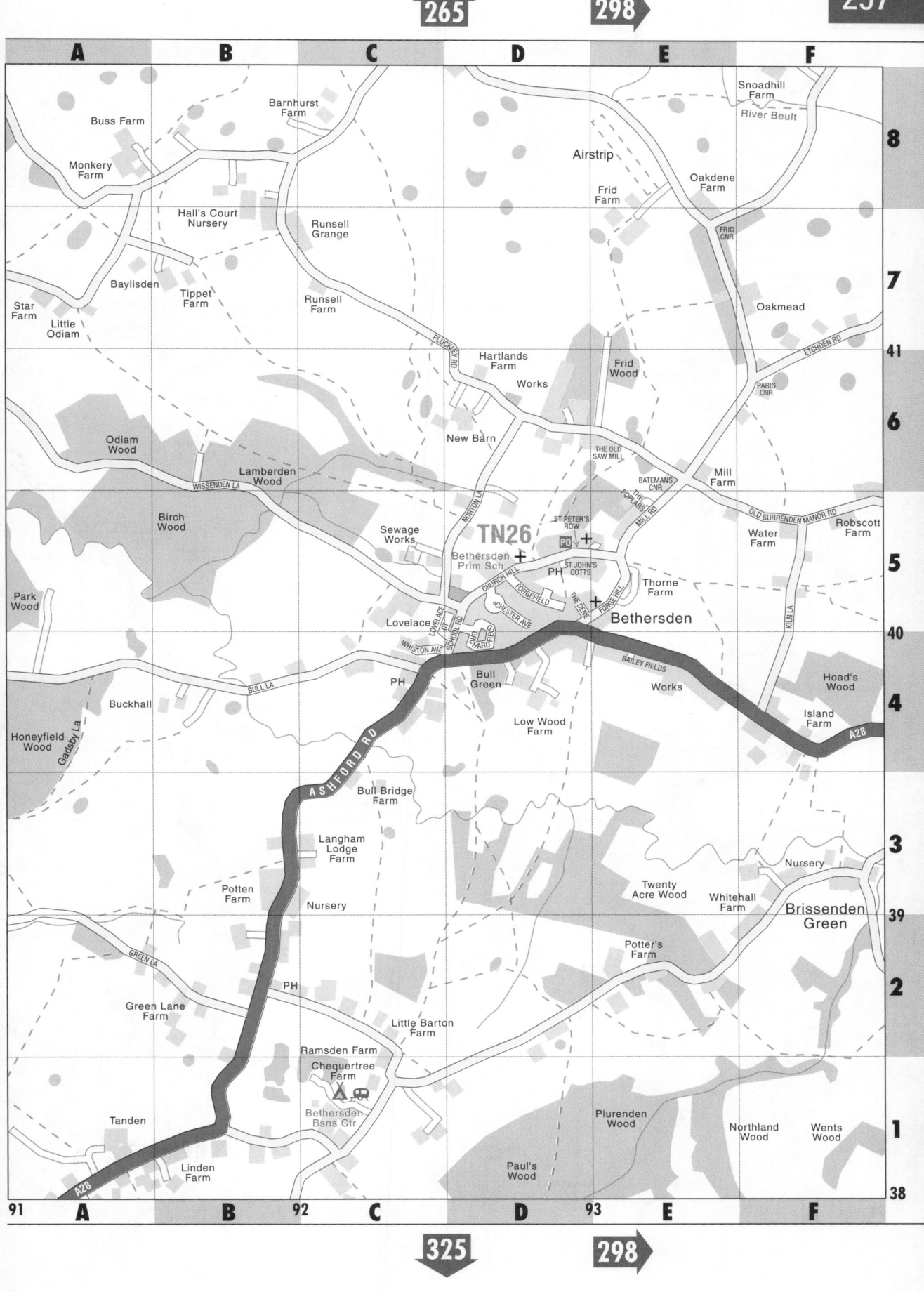

265
298

A   B   C   D   E   F

8
7
41
6
5
40
4
3
39
2
1
38

Snoadhill Farm
River Beult

Buss Farm

Monkery Farm

Barnhurst Farm

Airstrip

Frid Farm

Oakdene Farm

FRID CNR

Hall's Court Nursery

Runsell Grange

Oakmead

ETCHDEN RD

Baylisden

Tippet Farm

Runsell Farm

PLUCKLEY RD

Hartlands Farm

Works

Frid Wood

PARIS CNR

Star Farm

Little Odiam

Odiam Wood

New Barn

THE OLD SAW MILL

Mill Farm

BATEMANS CNR

THE POPLARS

MILL RD

OLD SURRENDEN MANOR RD

Lamberden Wood

WISSENDEN LA

Sewage Works

NORTON LA

TN26

St Peter's Row

PO

St John's Cotts

PH

Water Farm

Robscott Farm

Birch Wood

Bethersden Prim Sch

CHURCH HILL

FORGEFIELD

THE DENE

FORGE HILL

Thorne Farm

Park Wood

Lovelace

LOVELACE CT

SCHOOL RD

CHESTER AVE

OLD YARD

Bethersden

KILN LA

WHISTON AVE

BULL LA

PH

Bull Green

BATLEY FIELDS

Works

Hoad's Wood

Buckhall

GADSBY LA

Low Wood Farm

Island Farm

A28

Honeyfield Wood

ASHFORD RD

Bull Bridge Farm

Langham Lodge Farm

Nursery

Potten Farm

Nursery

Twenty Acre Wood

Whitehall Farm

Brissenden Green

GREEN LA

PH

Green Lane Farm

Little Barton Farm

Potter's Farm

Ramsden Farm

Chequertree Farm

Bethersden Bsns Ctr

Plurenden Wood

Northland Wood

Wents Wood

Tanden

Linden Farm

Paul's Wood

A28

325
298

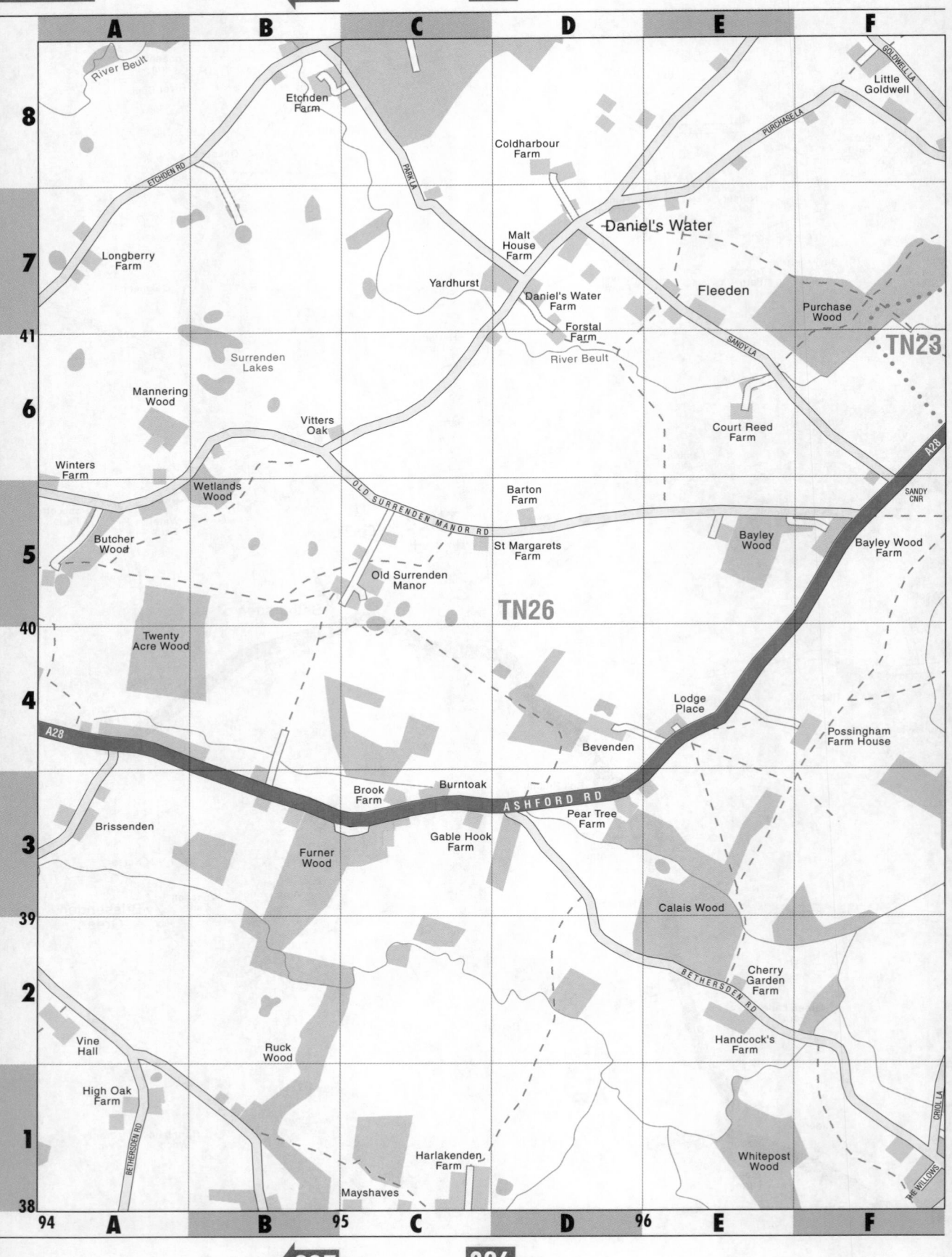

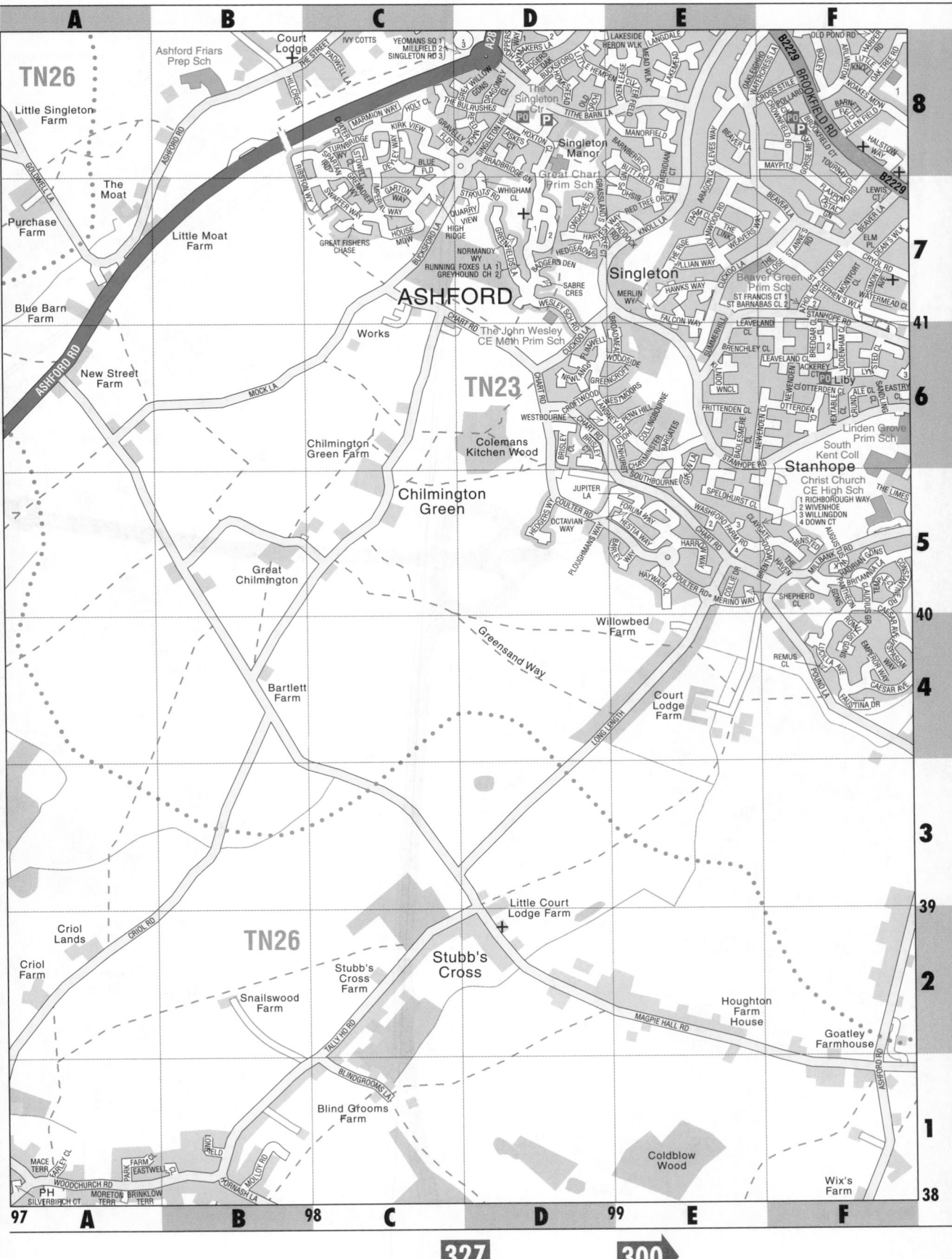

267

300
F6
1 ADISHAM GDNS
2 MONKTON CL
3 SHELDWICH CL
4 STEDDY CL

F8
1 Ashford Oaks
Com Prim Sch

299

TN26

Little Singleton Farm

The Moat

Purchase Farm

Blue Barn Farm

New Street Farm

Ashford Friars Prep Sch

Court Lodge

Little Moat Farm

Great Fishers Chase

Works

Chilmington Green Farm

Great Chilmington

Bartlett Farm

Chilmington Green

ASHFORD

The John Wesley CE Meth Prim Sch

TN23

Colemans Kitchen Wood

Greensand Way

Willowbed Farm

Court Lodge Farm

Singleton Manor

Great Chart Prim Sch

Singleton

Beaver Green Prim Sch

Stanhope

Linden Grove South Prim Sch Kent Coll

Christ Church CE High Sch
1 RICHBOROUGH WAY
2 WIVENHOE
3 WILLINGDON
4 DOWN CT

B2229

BROOKFIELD RD

Ashford Oaks

Little Court Lodge Farm

Stubb's Cross

TN26

Criol Lands

Criol Farm

Snailswood Farm

Stubb's Cross Farm

Blind Grooms Farm

Magpie Hall Rd

Houghton Farm House

Goatley Farmhouse

Coldblow Wood

Wix's Farm

Eastwell

PH

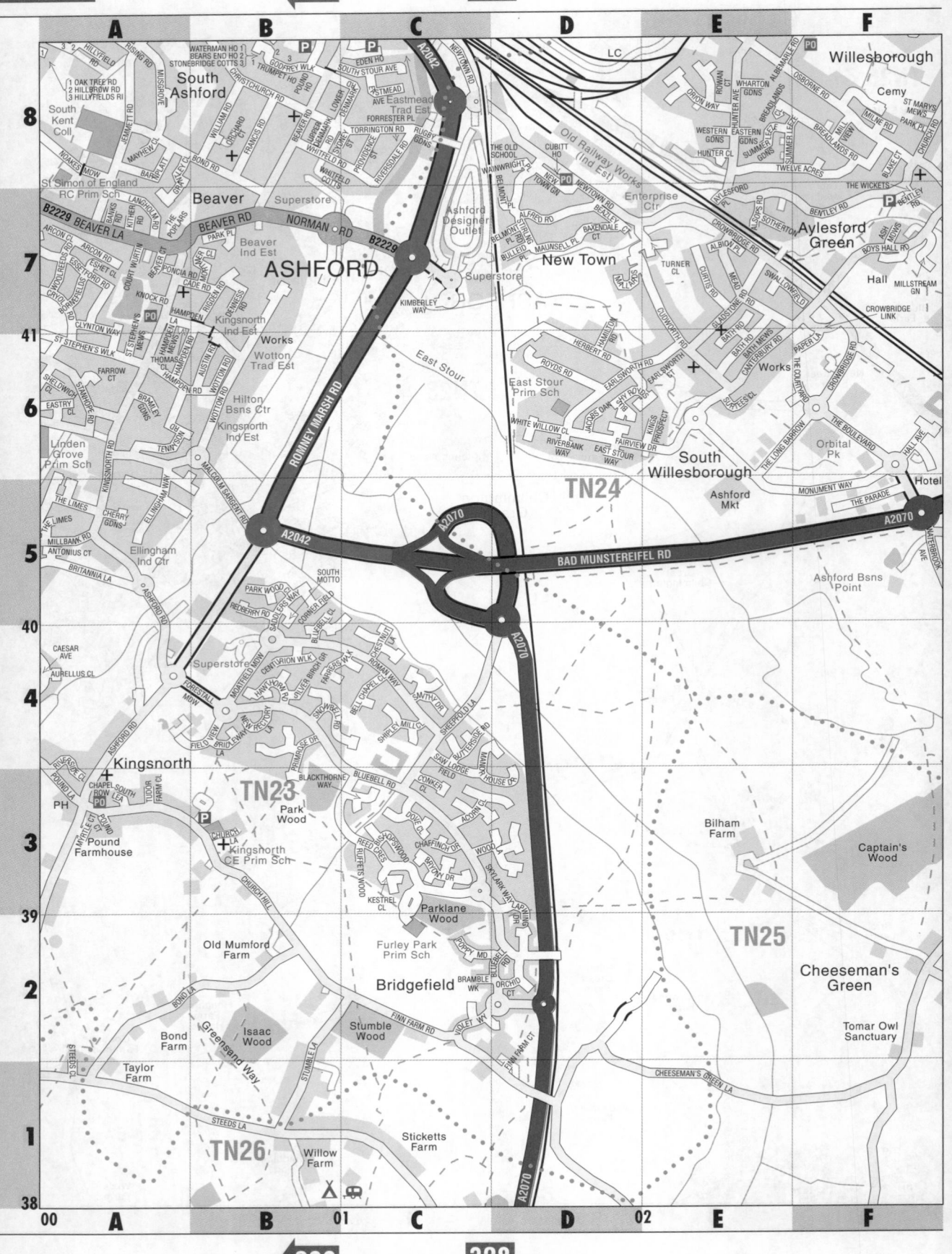

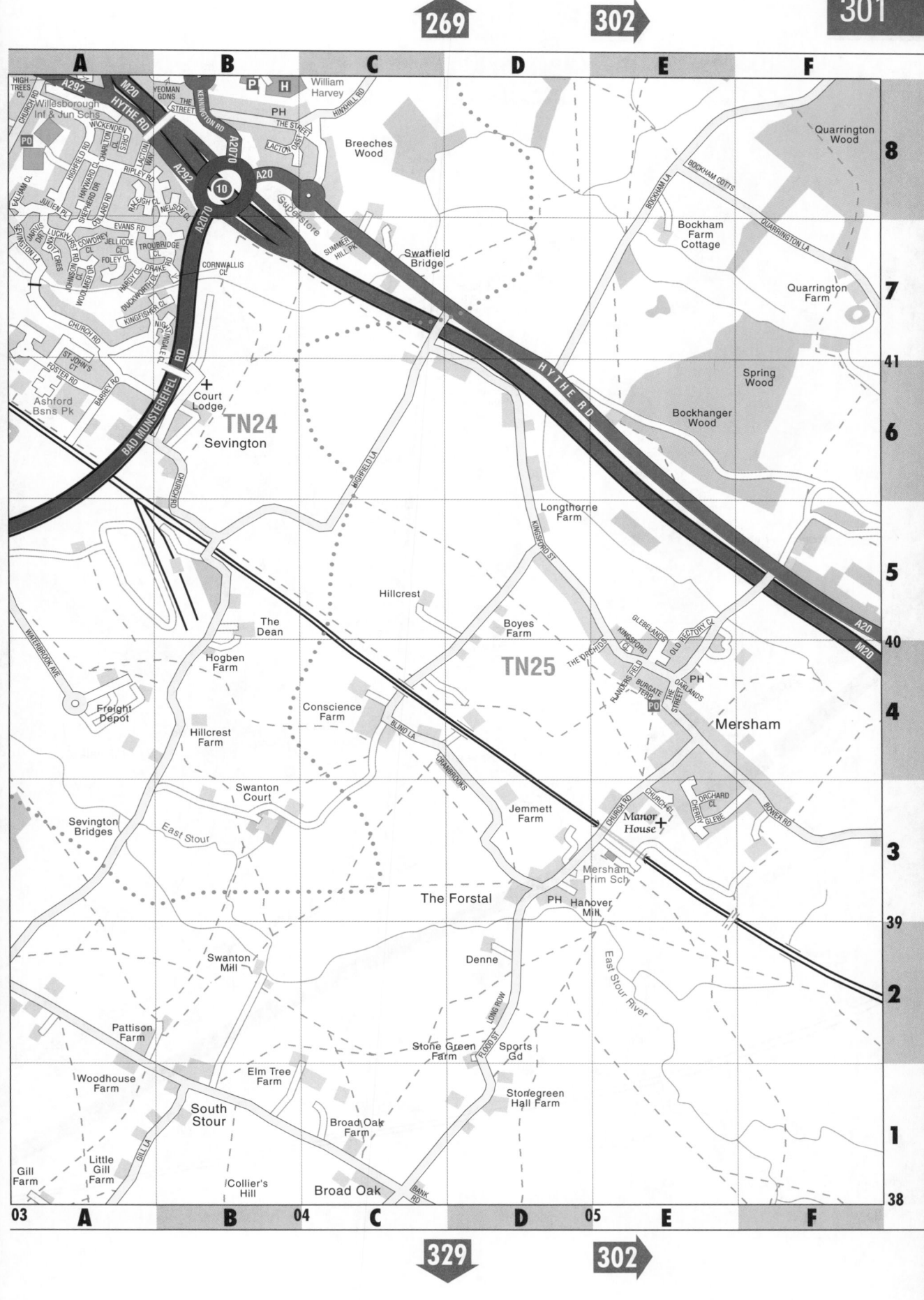

A B C D E F

8

Fallon Farmhouse

Fords Water

Waterside Farm

Bircholt Wood

Bircholt Forstal

Seeley Farm

California Farm

7

Gains Cottage

Bircholt Court

MANOR POUND LA

41

Deer Park

Brockham Farm

Chapel Farm

CANTERBURY RD

POUND LA

6

Jacob's Platation

Pemsey Farm

PH

Brabourne Lees

MOUNTBATTEN WAY

BRAMLEY CL

PROSACRE WAY

MOUNTBATTEN WAY

ORPINS CL

PO

THE LEES CL

LEES RD

Hatch Park

Mersham-le-Hatch

Court Farm

BRIDGE RD

THE WARREN

ORANGE FIELD

KNATCHBULL WAY

Warren Hill

WARREN HI

5

Barrack Wood

Joe Farm

WOOLPACK HILL

TN25

CHESTNUTS

SANDY PL

PH

Smeeth Prim Sch

OLD CALL

RAMSTONE CL

MANOR LEAZE

PLAIN RD

POUND LA

RIDGEWAY TERR

CARDLAND CL

40

A20

THE RIDGEWAY

Ridgeway

Bog Farm

Lodge House

LILYVALE COTTS

LILYVALE RD

4

M20

Home Farm

Caldecott Foundation Sch

Church Farm

CHURCH RD

Smeeth

Fishpond Wood

Scott's Hall Plantation

Lilyvale

LILYVALE RD

Lily Vale Farm

STOCK LA

The Paddocks

HYTHE RD

Scott's Hall

Washington

3

BOWER RD

STATION RD

Evegate

39

Little Stock Farm

Evegate Manor

Park Wood

Water Farm

Apple Barn

COOPER'S LA

A20

2

Park Wood Cottage

Sellindge Converter Station

CHURCH LA

1

East Stour River

Works

M20

38

Evegate Mill

06 A B 07 C D 08 E F

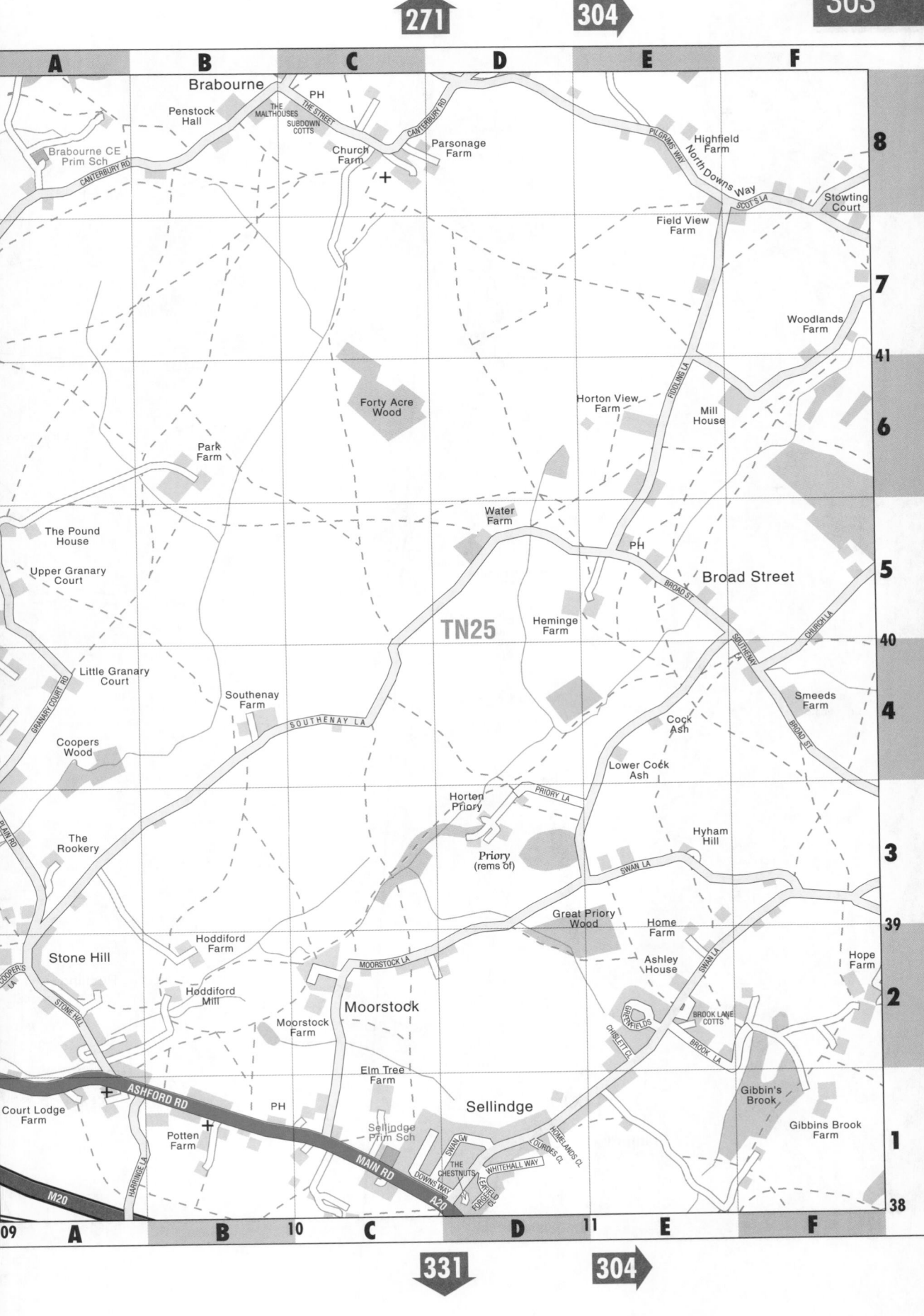

271
304
331
304

A B C D E F

8
7
41
6
5
40
4
3
39
2
1
38

Brabourne
PH
THE MALTHOUSES
Penstock Hall
THE STREET
SUBDOWN COTTS
CANTERBURY RD
Brabourne CE Prim Sch
CANTERBURY RD
Church Farm
Parsonage Farm
PILGRIMS WAY
Highfield Farm
North Downs Way
SCOT'S LA
Stowting Court
Field View Farm
Woodlands Farm
Forty Acre Wood
PIDDLING LA
Horton View Farm
Mill House
Park Farm
The Pound House
Upper Granary Court
Water Farm
PH
Broad Street
BROAD ST
TN25
Heminge Farm
SOUTHENAY LA
Little Granary Court
GRANARY COURT RD
Southenay Farm
SOUTHENAY LA
Smeeds Farm
Coopers Wood
Cock Ash
BROAD ST
CHURCH LA
Lower Cock Ash
PLAIN RD
The Rookery
Horton Priory
PRIORY LA
Hyham Hill
Priory (rems of)
SWAN LA
Great Priory Wood
Home Farm
Hope Farm
Stone Hill
Hoddiford Farm
MOORSTOCK LA
Ashley House
SWAN LA
COOPER'S LA
STONE HILL
Hoddiford Mill
Moorstock
GRENFIELDS
BROOK LANE COTTS
BROOK LA
Moorstock Farm
CHISLETT C.
Court Lodge Farm
ASHFORD RD
PH
Elm Tree Farm
Gibbin's Brook
Potten Farm
Sellindge
HOMELANDS CL
Gibbins Brook Farm
HARRINGE LA
MAIN RD
Sellindge Prim Sch
THE CHESTNUTS
SWAN GN
LOURDES CL
WHITEHALL WAY
LEACEFIELD CL
A20
M20
DOWNS WAY

09 A B 10 C D 11 E F

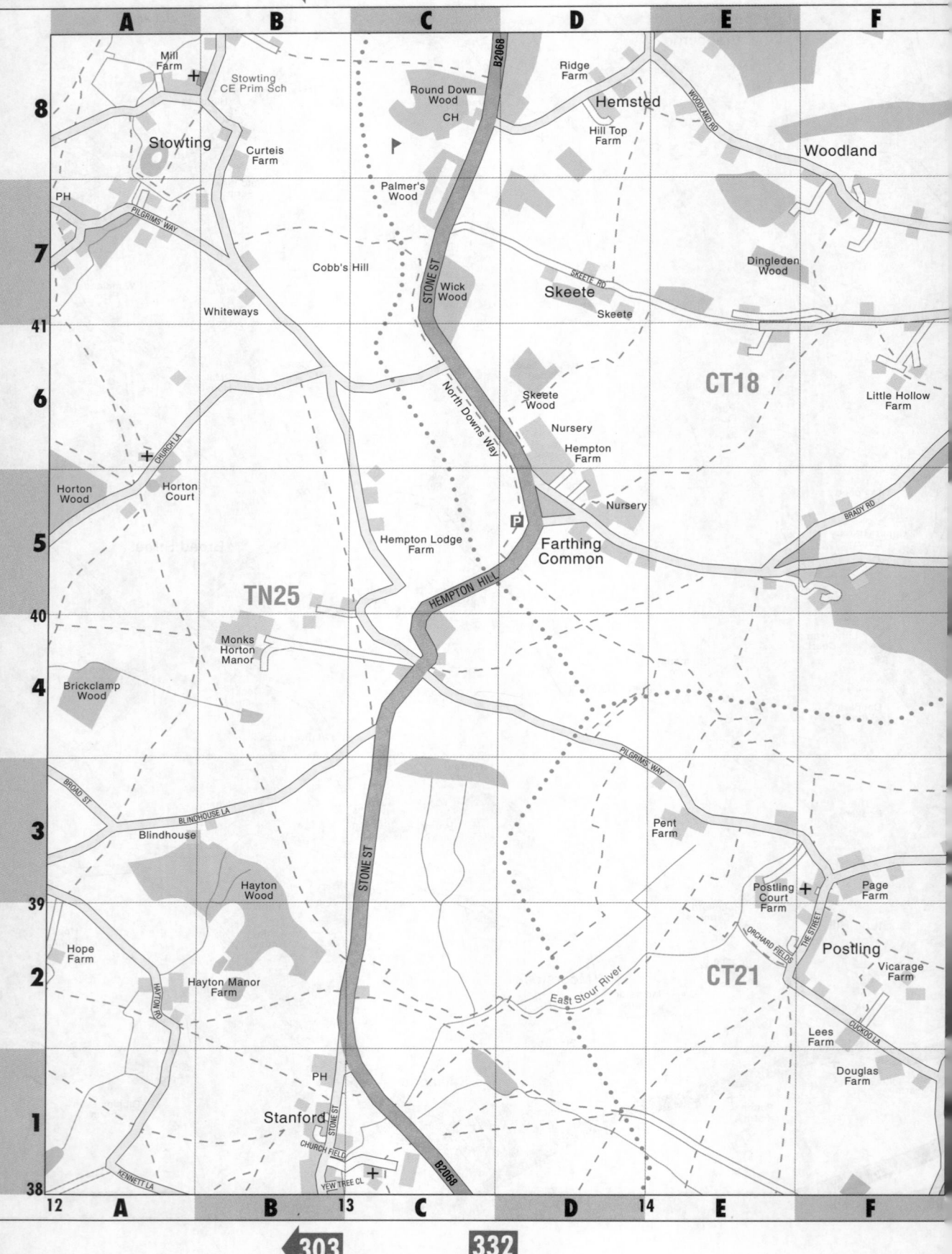

273
306

A B C D E F

8

CT4

Longage Farm

Sibton Park

Hunt's Rough Wood

YEWTREE CROSS

LONGAGE HILL

7

North Lyminge

Little Stonebridge

Great Shuttlesfield Farm

CANTERBURY RD

PLEASANT CL
ROBUS TERR
KIMBERLY TERR

WOODLAND RD

BARTON FIELD
FOX CL
BEDINGFIELD WAY
HOBBEN CL
ETHELBURGA DR
LINDEN WAY
ROBUS CL
SILVERLANDS RD
PALM TREE WAY

NORTH LYMINGE LA

WESLEY TERR

41

WOODLAND COTTS

SKEETE RD

BRADY RD

DOG KENNEL

Valley Farm

Lyminge

JAMES CT
CHURCH RD
NAILBOURNE CT

HIGH ST
CHURCH CT

WELL RD

Lyminge CE Prim Sch
PH

STATION RD

THE SIDINGS
P
PO
Liby
NASH HILL

GREENBANKS

Red House Farm

MAYFIELD RD
WENTWORTH CL
RECTORY LA

1
2

6

SPRINGSIDE TERR 1
EVERIST CT 2

Broad Street

CT18

5

Elham Valley Way

Sunningdale Farm

40

Postling Wood

Newbarn

CH

Greenloaming

4

Shearins Farm

Staple Farm

CANTERBURY RD

BADGERS BRIDGE

THE OLD

ARK COTTS

PH

TEDDARS LEAS RD

The Lince

3

Etchinghill

MERIDEN WLK
IVY CL
TOLSFO RD CL

UPSTREET

ST MARYS CL
ST MARYS DR
CHAPEL CL

HILL VIEW TERR

ST MARYS

Coombe Farm

Coombe Wood

39

WESTFIELD LA

Saxon Shore Way

Mast

Swingfield (Tolsford Hill) Radio Sta

Mast

North Downs Way

The Beeches

Little Beachborough

2

CT21

Tolsford Plantation

Tolsford Hill

Brackman's Bushes

Temple Pond

Beachborough Park

Seabrook Stream

Ashley Wood

1

38

15 A B 16 C D 17 E F

333
306

← 305
274 ▲

A B C D E F

8

Mill Down Farm

Acrise Wood

Knowl Hill

Little Knowlhill Shaw

White Gate House

Black Horse Farm

COACH RD

7

Little Shuttlesfield Farm

Lower Winterage Farm

WINTERAGE LA

Upper Winterage Farm

Bush Farm

Limes Farm

SCHOOL RD

PAY ST

41

Acrise Court

Shuttlesfield

Souge Wood

Pillars Wood

Roods Meadow

PAY ST

6

Tan Barn

Paddlesworth Court Wood

Cobham's Rough

Pay Street Farm

5

Paddlesworth Court Farm

Redsole Farm

Cemy

40

CT18

Paddlesworth

PH

Crem

WOODCOCK GDNS 1
KIRTON CL 2
ECKFORD CL 3

BENSON CL 1
HUMPHREY TERR 2
CHURCHILL WLK 3
ST LUKE'S WLK 4

4

Cole Farm

Mast

Sole Farm

BENSON LA

GILLMAN CL

MICHAEL'S CL

SISKIN CL

THE MEWE

AERODROME RD

ORR CL

3

Shearins Bungalow

Home Farm

Arpinge

White Hall

Kent Battle of Britain Mus

GARDNER CL 1
GEDDES CL 2
PROBYN MEWS 3
OSPREY CT 4

Gibraltar

39

Parsonage Farm

Lower Arpinge Farm

Elvington

Elvington Farm

Gibraltar Farm

GIBRALTAR LA

ELVINGTON LA

2

Arpine Range

Pilgrim's Way

Upper Arpinge Farm

Pigeonhouse Wood

Grove Farm

Little Dane Farm

Upper Dane Farm

1

Elham Valley Way

P

North Downs Way
Saxon Shore Way

Northcliffe

Cheriton Hill

CRETE RD W

CT19

38

PEENE COTTS

HILL LA

Peene Quarry

DANTON LA

A B C D E F

18   19   20

← 305
334 ▼

A   B   C   D   E   F

8

South Alkham

Upton Farm House

Uplands Farm

Mount Ararat

Moorlands

Lonebarn Farm

7

Drellingore Cottage Farm

Ppg Sta

Drellingore

Meggett Farm

MEGGETT LA

HOGBROOK HILL LA

Poulton Farm

Copt Hill Farm

ALKHAM VALLEY RD

41

Bramble Hill Cottage

Ferns Farm

CT15

6

5

Tumble Tye Farm

Capel Church Farm

BROADSOLE LA

PATRIFIELD COTS

FORGE FIELD

QUEEN'S LEA

LADY GATE RD

THE STREET

YOUNG'S PL

LOWSLIP HIL

Mill La

40

Hockley Sole

The Old Sch

Capel Farm

SATMORE LA

West Hougham

CROOK'S COURT LA

White Hill

GRAVEL LA

Chalk Pi Wood

4

A20

Hurst Farm

HURST LA

Hollingbury Farm

Capel House Farm

SATMAR LA

Swinge Hill

CT18

CAPEL ST

CAULDHAM LA

Channel Tunnel

SATMORE LA

Great Satmar Farm

Satmar

Dawkinge Wood

A20

3

GREEN LA

Capel-le-Ferne Prim Sch

WINEHOUSE LA

Abbot's Land Farm

39

SETH DR

ELIZA RD

Masts

PH

B2011

2

Great Cauldham Farm

LANCASTER AVE

BEATRICE RD

TELMA RD

AVONDALE RD

ALEXANDRA RD

NEW DOVER RD

Capel Court Pk

PH

Capel-le-Ferne

VICTORIA RD

CLARENCE RD

ALBERT RD

Old Dover Rd

Eagle's Nest

CAULDHAM CL

ALBANY RD

SEA VIEW CT

North Downs Way

Saxon Shore Way

East Cliff and Warren Country Park

1

REECE ADAMS HO

CAPEL ST

B2011

Battle of Britain Memorial

Steady Hole

The Warren

38

A B C D E F

8

St Radigund's
Abbey Farm

St Radigund's
Abbey
(remains of)

Sleed
Wood

POULTON CL

HOLLOW
WOOD
RD

Ind Est

Gorse
Hill

Long
Wood

COOMBE RD

P

QUEENS AVE

7

Park
Hill

Square
Wood

Long
Wood

Whinless Down

Harbour
Sch

MARKLAND

READING RD

ELM
GDNS

SUFFOLK
GDNS

ELM
PARK

MARLBOROUGH RD

NEWBURY

41

ELMS HILL

Elms
Farm

Chilverton
Elms

Elms
Wood

ELMS VALE RD

Coney
Hill

CT17

B2011

6

LOWSLIP HILL

The
Park

SKINYWAY LA

West
Down

Little Farthingloe
Farm

The Women's
Land Army
Mus

FARTHINGLOE
COTTS

Great
Farthingloe

Farthingloe

CT15

Cherry Tree
Farm

PARSONAGE
VILLAS

5

Church
Hougham

CHURCH LA

DOCTOR'S LA

FOLKESTONE RD

40

Channel Tunnel

GRAVEL LA

Mast

TV Transmitting
Station

PLOUGH HILL

A20

Round
Down

4

Motel

PH

Great
Hougham
Court
Farm

HOUGHAM COURT LA

Little
Hougham
Court

Church
Wood

P

Visitors
Centre

P

3

Court
Wood

Samphire Hoe
Country Park

39

CT18

North Downs Way
Saxon Shore Way

2

Abbot's
Cliff

Lydden
Spout

1

27 A 28 B C 28 D 29 E F

38

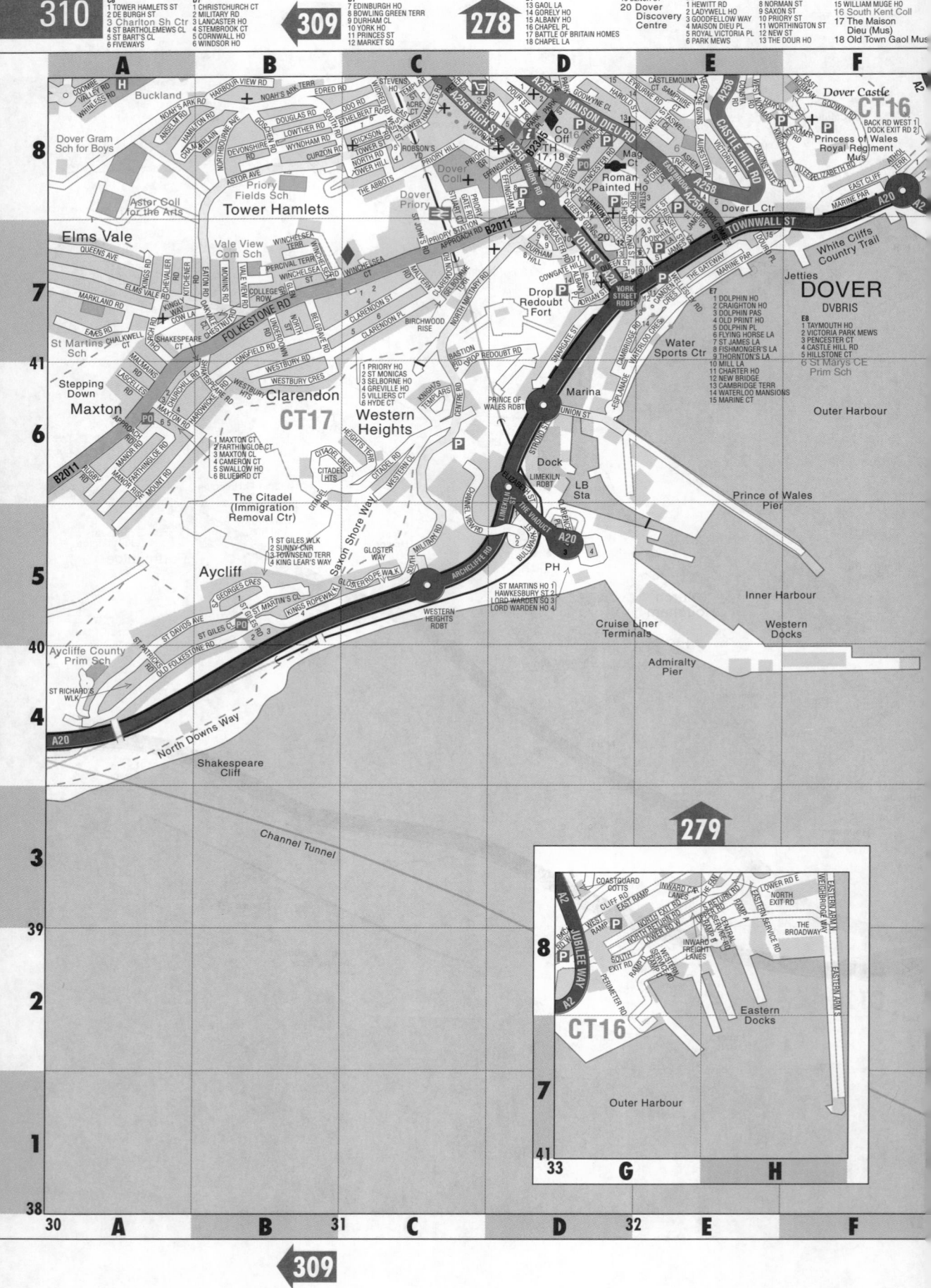

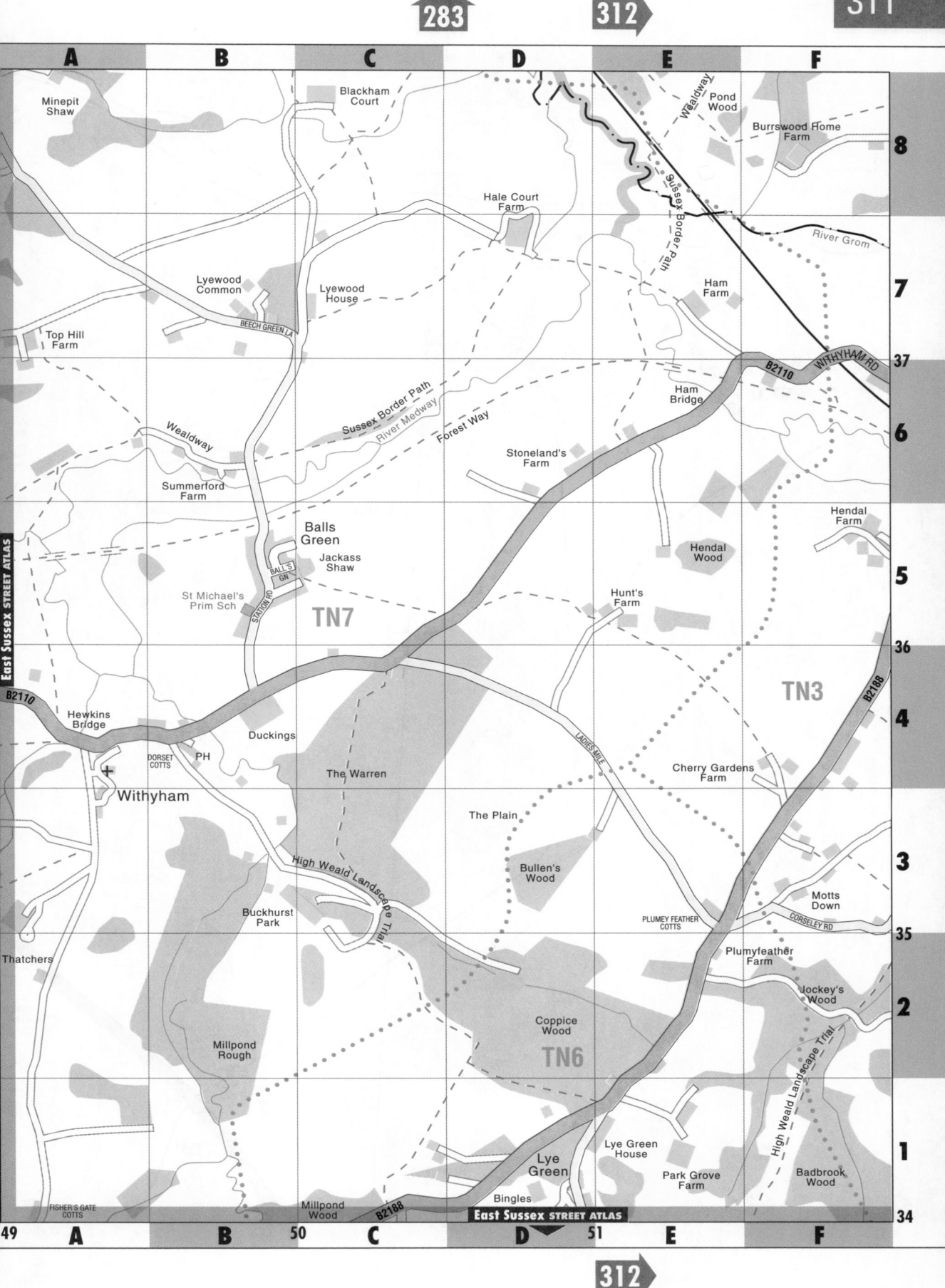

A   B   C   D   E   F

8

Minepit
Shaw

Blackham
Court

Pond
Wood

Burrswood Home
Farm

Wealdway

River Grom

Hale Court
Farm

7

Lyewood
Common

Lyewood
House

Ham
Farm

BEECH GREEN LA

Sussex Border Path

37

Top Hill
Farm

WITHYHAM RD

B2110

Wealdway

Sussex Border Path

River Medway

Forest Way

Ham
Bridge

6

Summerford
Farm

Stoneland's
Farm

Hendal
Farm

Balls
Green

Jackass
Shaw

Hendal
Wood

5

St Michael's
Prim Sch

BALL'S
GN

Hunt's
Farm

TN7

STATION RD

TN3

B2188

36

B2110

Hewkins
Bridge

Duckings

Cherry Gardens
Farm

4

DORSET
COTTS

PH

The Warren

LADIES MILE

Withyham

The Plain

Motts
Down

3

High Weald Landscape Trail

Buckhurst
Park

Bullen's
Wood

PLUMEY FEATHER
COTTS

CORSELEY RD

35

Thatchers

Plumyfeather
Farm

Jockey's
Wood

2

Millpond
Rough

Coppice
Wood

High Weald Landscape Trail

TN6

1

Lye Green
House

FISHER'S GATE
COTTS

Lye
Green

Park Grove
Farm

Badbrook
Wood

Millpond
Wood

Bingles

B2188

34

East Sussex STREET ATLAS

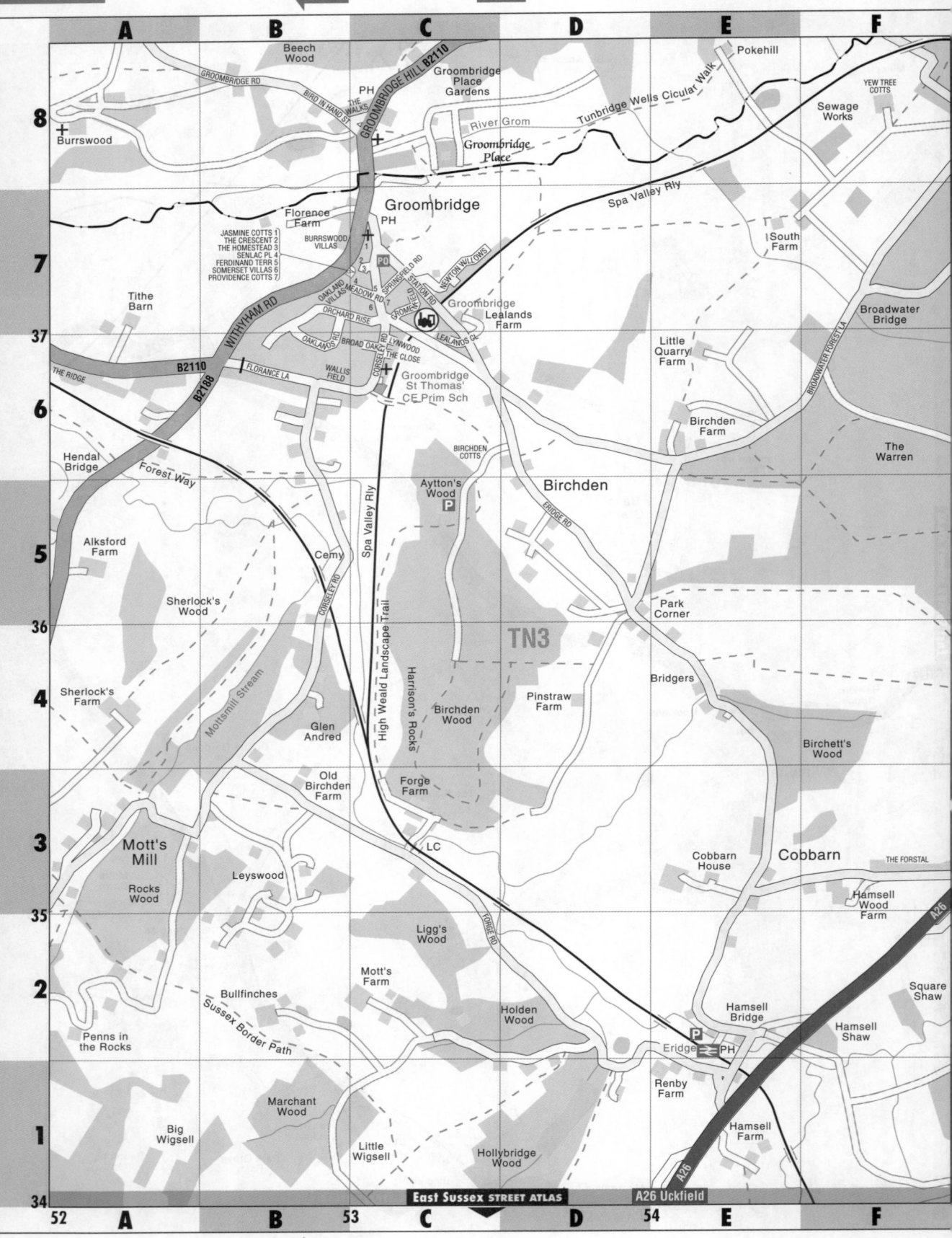

East Sussex STREET ATLAS
A26 Uckfield

Spa Valley Rly

Ramslye
Wood

TN4

RAMSLYE RD

EASTLANDS
CL

SCOTTS
WY

STUART CL

FURNIVAL
CT

BROADCROFT

BROADLN'A

Ramslye
Farm

SNOWFIELDS
RD

LNEGLA DR

BROADMEAD

ESSEX

ST GEORGE'S

8

LODGE LA

Strawberry
Hill

ERIDGE RD

A26

COURT
ROYAL

KENTISH GDNS

1 LEICESTER DR
2 DEVONSHIRE CL
3 BROADMEAD AVE

BROADWATER
CT

Broadwater
Down

Ruffet
Wood

BROADWATER DOWN

BARNFIELD

The Firs

BROADWATER FOREST LA

STRAWBERRY CL

HARGATE DR

ST MARK'S RD

HADDCROFT

Broadwater
Forest

Broadwater Down

TN2

7

Spratsbrook
Farm

Strawberry Hill
Farm

37

Broadwater
Lodge

Sprat's Brook

Hargate
Forest

Firtree
Plantation

6

The Warren

The
Roundabouts

BUNNY LA

Bohemia

5

Eridge
Rocks

TN3

Whitehill
Wood

36

Warren
Farm

PH

4

WARREN FARM LA

Eridge
Park

Eridge
Park

Eridge
Green

Crown
House

Mill
Wood

3

A26

35

Steel
Bridge

High Weald Landscape Trail

Keepers
Cottages

2

Steel Bridge
Farm

Forge
Wood

Eridge
Old Park

Bushy
Wood

Great Robbins
Shaw

Bushy
Shaw

1

34

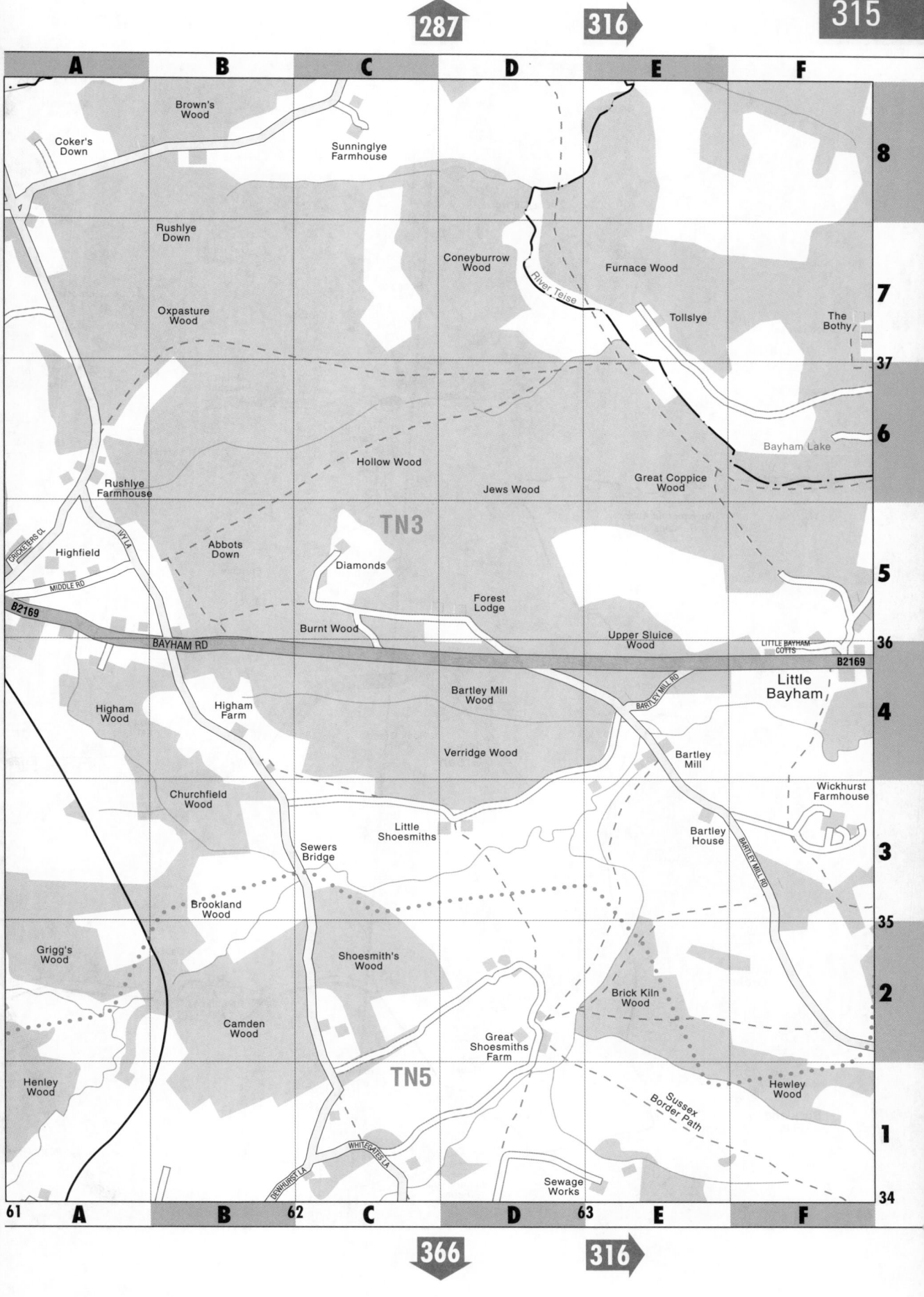

Maynards
Farm

Sandhurst

Clay Hill
Cottages

8

Tongs Wood

Uzzards

Clayhill Wood

Rear Wood

Owl House
Gardens

Stubb's Wood

Snagg's
Well

Owl
House

Cooksbroom
Wood

7

Ellis
Wood

Garden House

Owlet
Farm

37

Mount
Pleasant

MOUNT PLEASANT

Bayham
Abbey

6

Hoathly
Farm

MOUNT PLEASANT LA

CLAY HILL RD

Timberlog
Wood

River Teise

Bayham Old Abbey
(remains of)

TN3

5

Floshet
Wood

Furnace
Mill

Stumlets
Wood

BULL LANE
COTTS

36

Win
Bridge

Furnace
Farm

Sluice
Wood

4

PH

STONE
COTTS

Apps's
Wood

Hook Green
Farm

B2169

Hook
Green

FURNACE LA

Copthall
Farm

3

Skent's
Wood

Rowland
Wood

35

TREE HEATH RD

Owls Castle
Farm

Toll
Wood

Buss's
Green

2

NEILLS RD

HOGHOLE LA

Maitlands

Yew Tree Green
Farm

Stiver's
Wood

B2100

Crowhurst
House

Broadwell
Wood

BARTLEY MILL RD

TN5

SWEETINGS LA

Free
Heath

1

Buckland
Hill

Markwicks

Buckland Hill
Farm

SLEEPERS STILE RD

Hunter's Hall
Farm

B2100

Monk's
Park

34

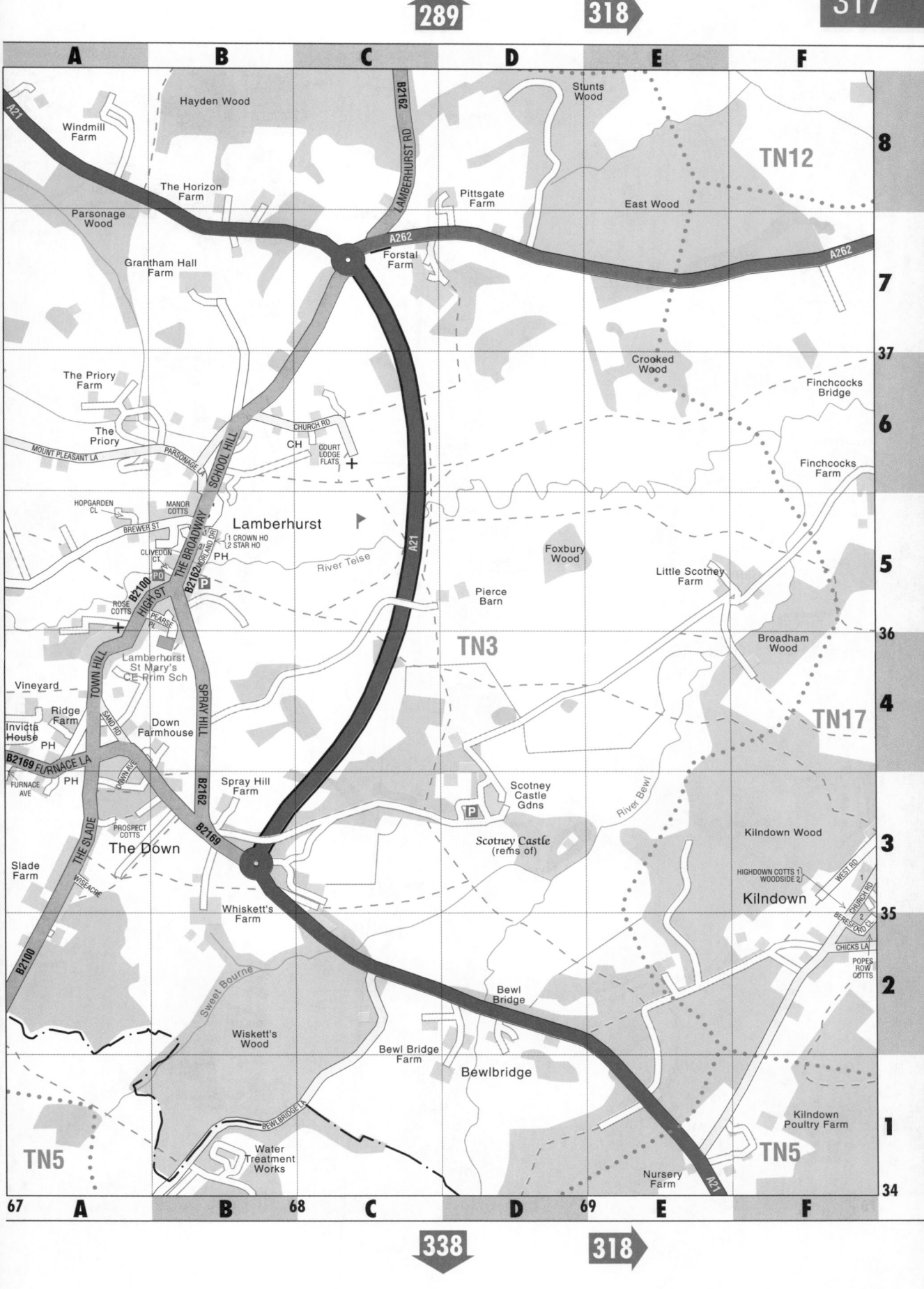

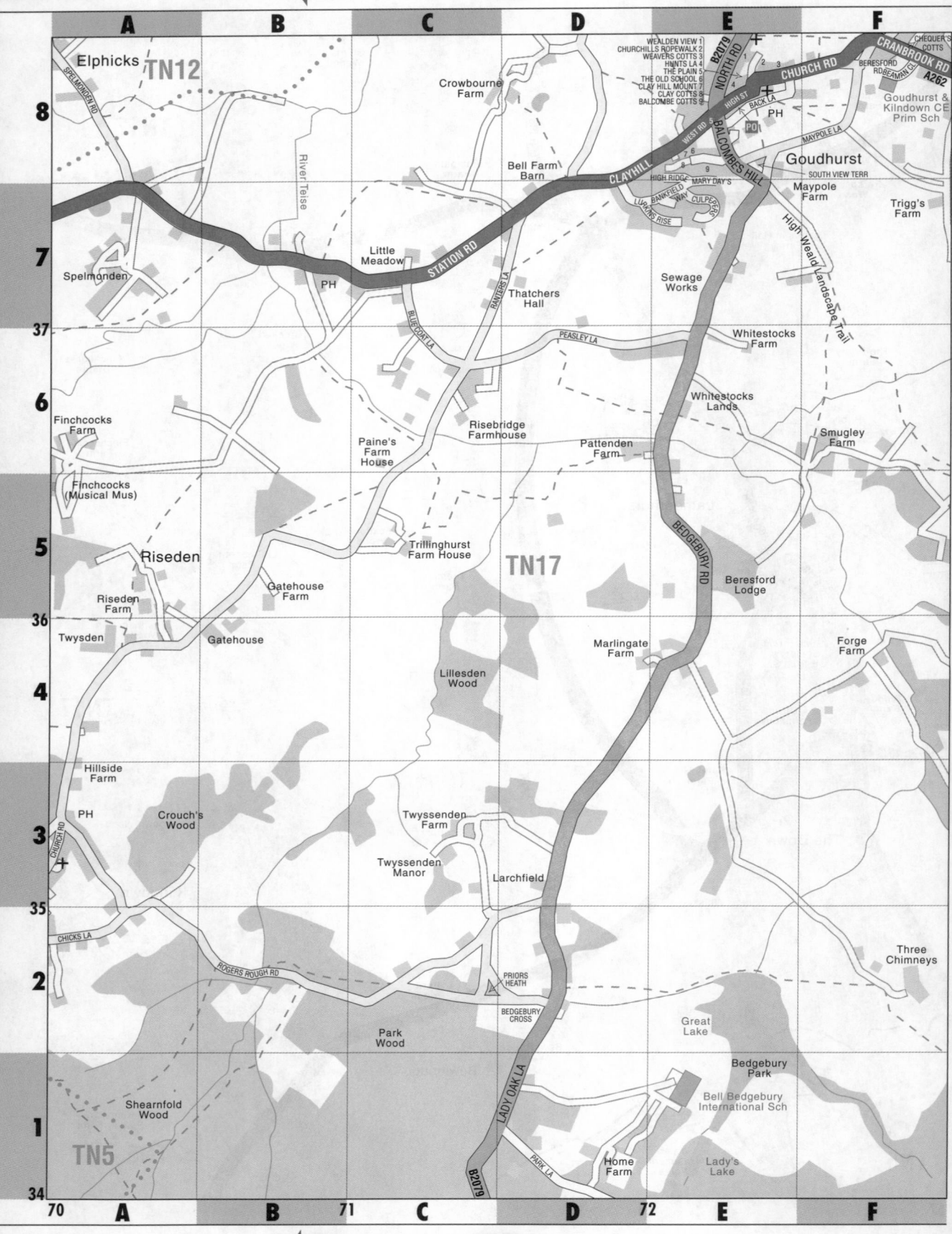

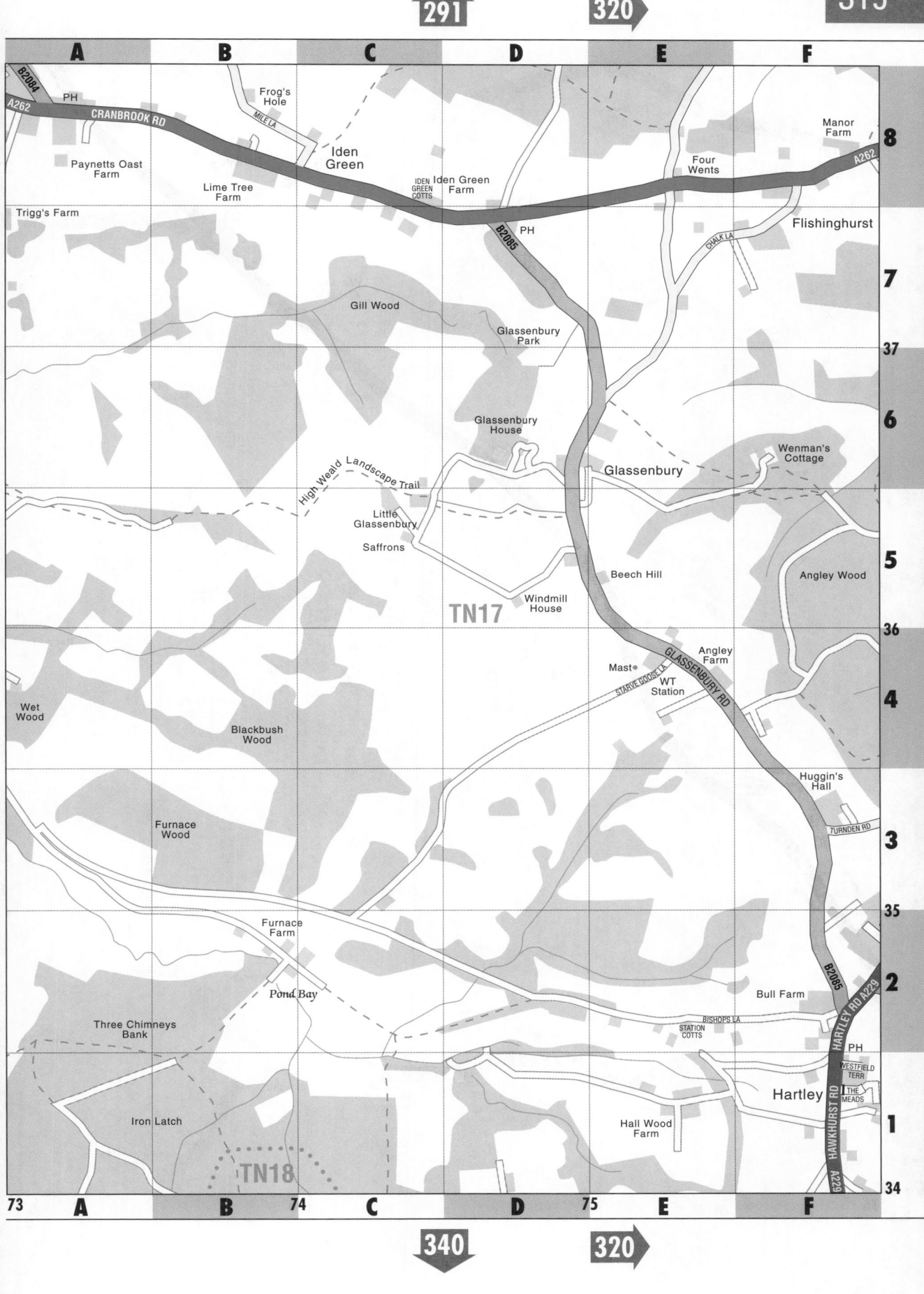

A   B   C   D   E   F

B2084

A262

PH

CRANBROOK RD

Frog's Hole

MILE LA

Paynetts Oast Farm

Lime Tree Farm

Iden Green

IDEN GREEN COTTS

Iden Green Farm

Four Wents

Manor Farm

A262

8

Trigg's Farm

B2085

PH

CHALK LA

Flishinghurst

7

Gill Wood

Glassenbury Park

37

Glassenbury House

Wenman's Cottage

6

High Weald Landscape Trail

Little Glassenbury

Saffrons

Glassenbury

Angley Wood

5

TN17

Windmill House

Beech Hill

36

Mast

WT Station

Angley Farm

GLASSENBURY RD

STARVE GOOSE LA

Angley Wood

4

Wet Wood

Blackbush Wood

Huggin's Hall

TURNDEN RD

3

Furnace Wood

35

Furnace Farm

Pond Bay

Bull Farm

B2085

HARTLEY RD A229

2

Three Chimneys Bank

BISHOPS LA

STATION COTTS

PH

WESTFIELD TERR

THE MEADS

Hartley

HAWKHURST RD

Iron Latch

Hall Wood Farm

1

TN18

A229

34

319
292

319
341

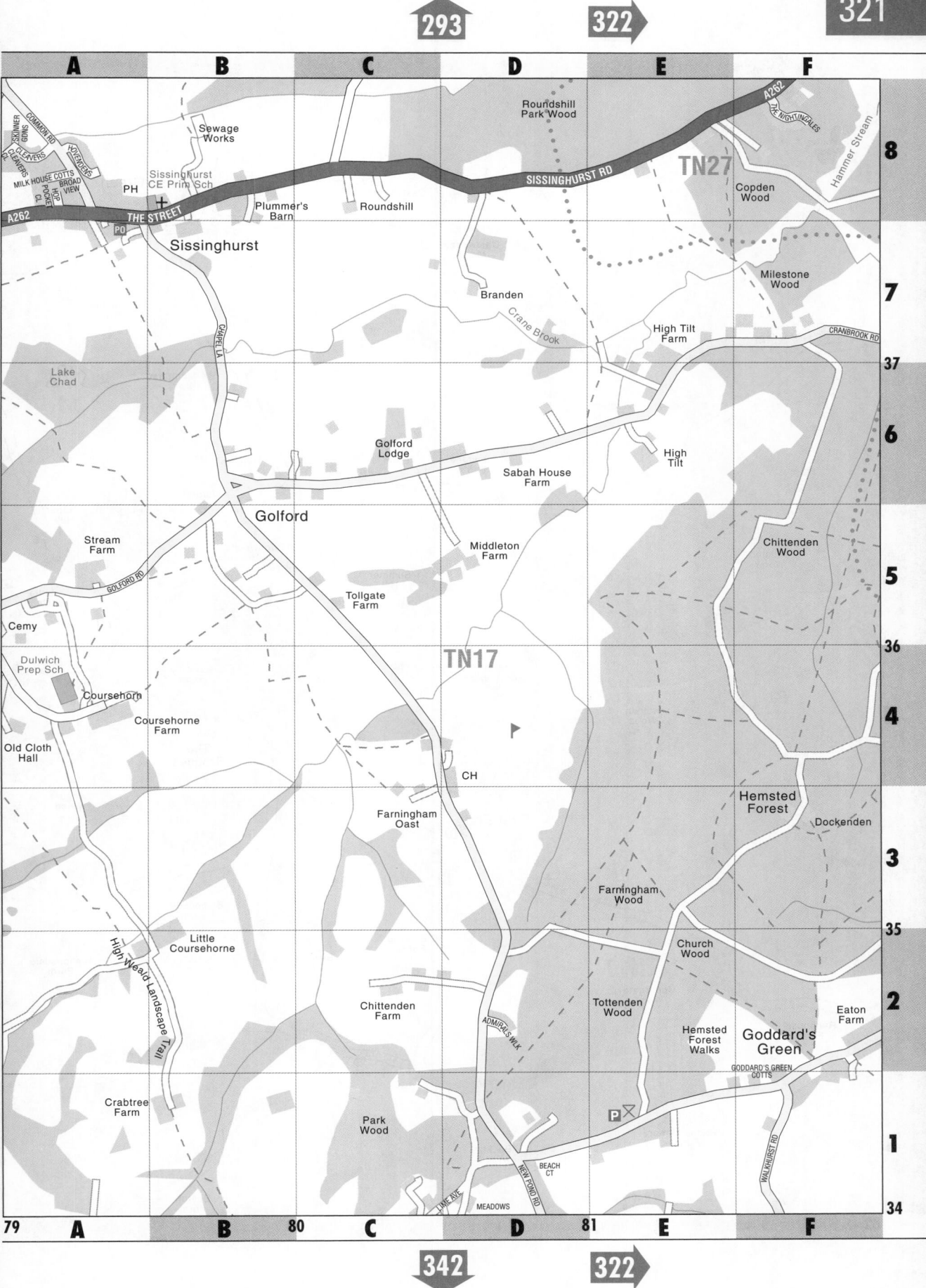

293
322
342
322

A   B   C   D   E   F

8   7   37   6   5   36   4   3   35   2   1   34

COMMON RD
SKINNER CL
SWIG CL
CLEAVERS CL
HOVENDENS
MILK HOUSE COTTS
BROAD VIEW
HOP POCKET CL
A262
PH
PO
Sissinghurst CE Prim Sch
THE STREET
Sissinghurst

Sewage Works
Plummer's Barn
Roundshill

Roundshill Park Wood
SISSINGHURST RD
TN27
Copden Wood
A262
THE NIGHTINGALES
Hammer Stream

Milestone Wood

Branden
Crane Brook
High Tilt Farm
High Tilt
CRANBROOK RD

CHAPEL LA
Lake Chad

Golford Lodge
Sabah House Farm
Chittenden Wood

Golford

Stream Farm
GOLFORD RD
Middleton Farm
Tollgate Farm
TN17

Cemy
Dulwich Prep Sch
Coursehorn
Coursehorne Farm
Old Cloth Hall

CH
Farningham Oast

Hemsted Forest
Dockenden

Farningham Wood
Church Wood

High Weald Landscape Trail
Little Coursehorne

Chittenden Farm
ADMIRAL'S WLK
Tottenden Wood
Hemsted Forest Walks
Goddard's Green
Eaton Farm
GODDARD'S GREEN COTTS
WALKHURST RD

Crabtree Farm

Park Wood
P

LIME AVE
NEW POND RD
BEACH CT
MEADOWS

79   80   81
A   B   C   D   E   F

321
294

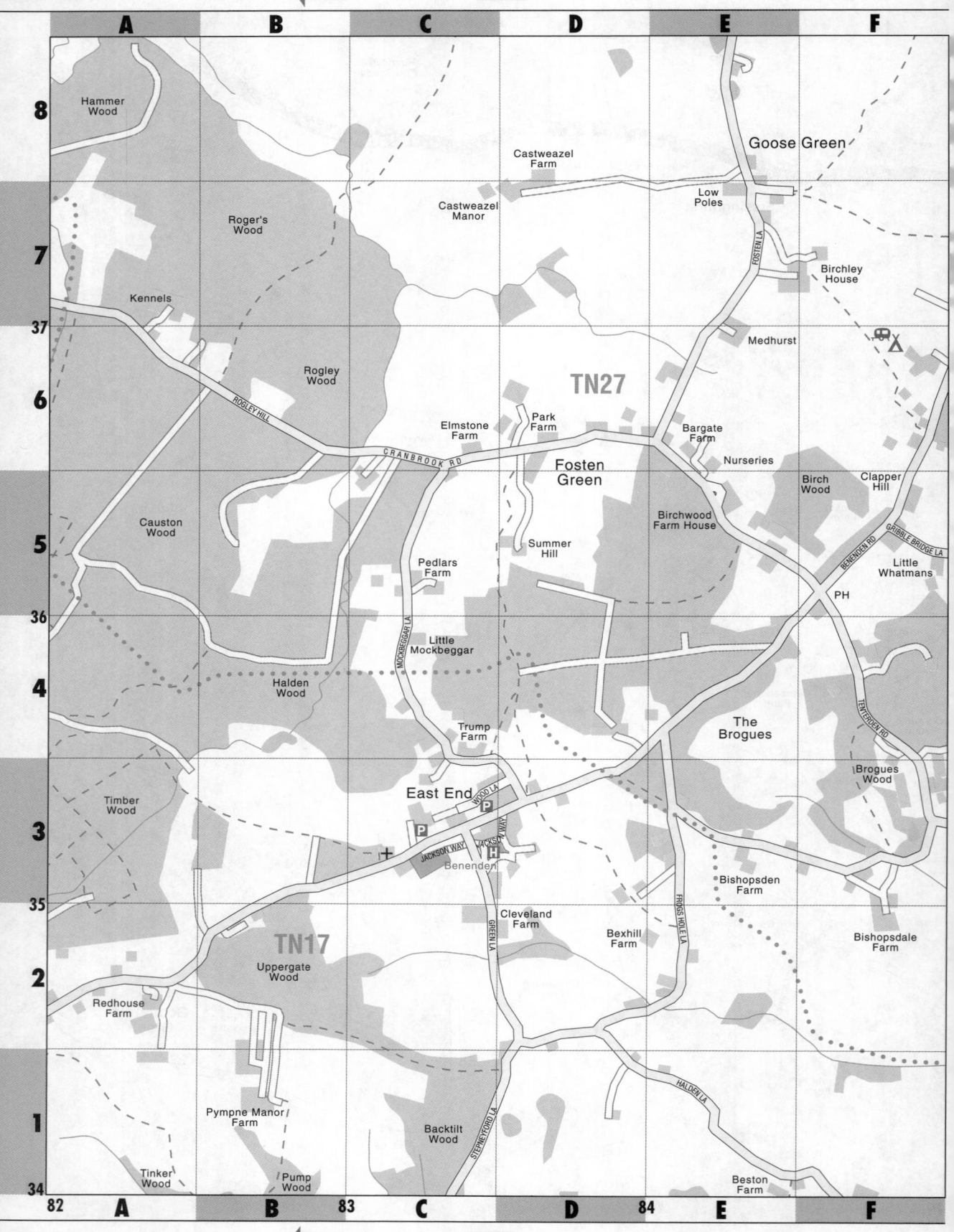

321
343

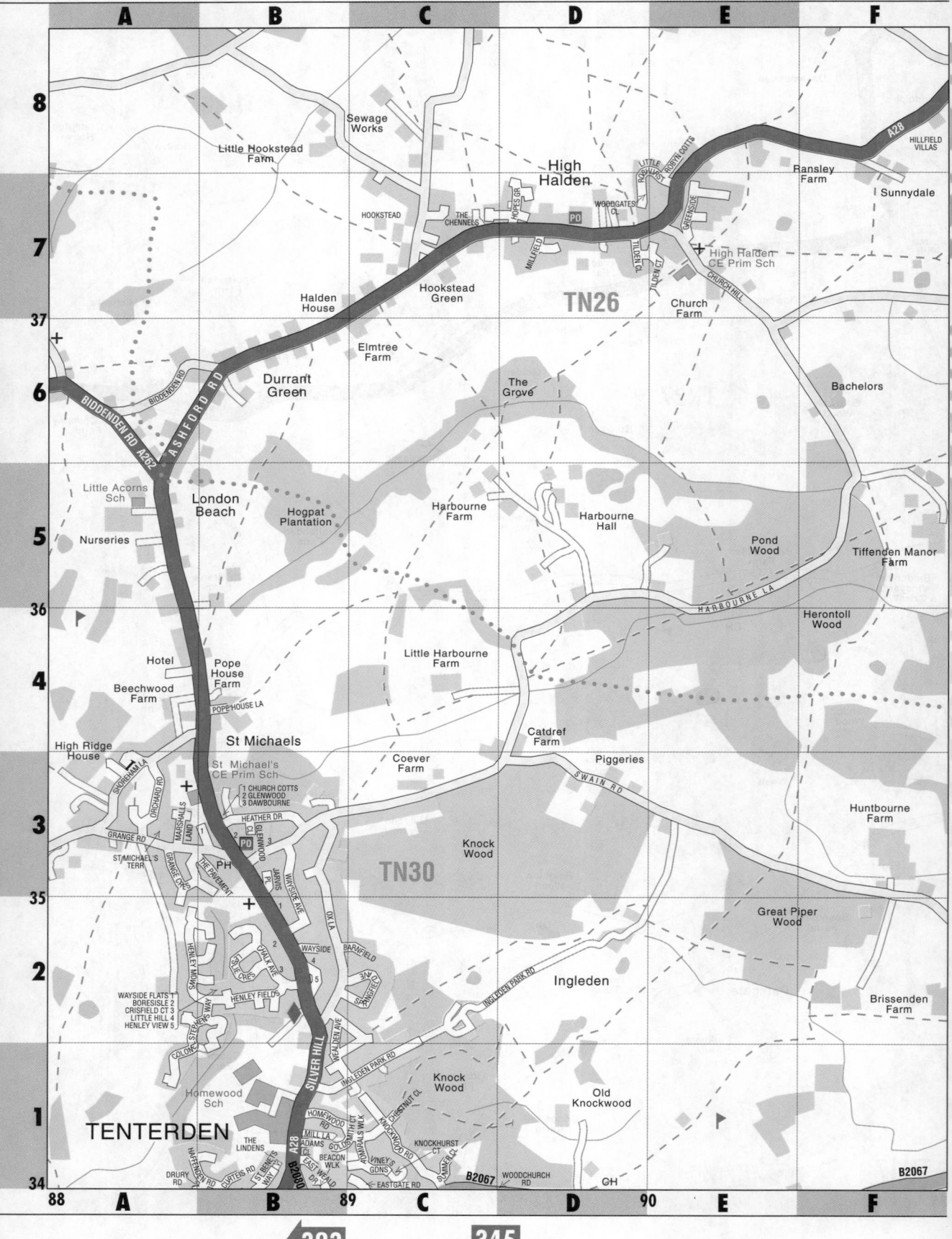

A B C D E F

8

7

37

6

5

36

4

3

35

2

1

34

88 A B 89 C 90 E F

Little Hookstead Farm

Sewage Works

HOOKSTEAD

THE CHENNELS

High Halden

PO

WOODGATES CT

LITTLE ROBIN COTTS

Ransley Farm

HILLFIELD VILLAS

Sunnydale

A28

GREENSIDE

High Halden CE Prim Sch

CHURCH HILL

Halden House

Hookstead Green

Elmtree Farm

TN26

Church Farm

Bachelors

BIDDENDEN RD

BIDDENDEN RD

ASHFORD RD

Durrant Green

A262

The Grove

Little Acorns Sch

London Beach

Hogpat Plantation

Harbourne Farm

Harbourne Hall

Pond Wood

Tiffenden Manor Farm

Nurseries

HARBOURNE LA

Herontoll Wood

Hotel

Pope House Farm

POPE HOUSE LA

Little Harbourne Farm

Beechwood Farm

Catdref Farm

Piggeries

High Ridge House

St Michaels

St Michael's CE Prim Sch

1 CHURCH COTTS
2 GLENWOOD
3 DAWBOURNE

HEATHER DR

Coever Farm

SWAIN RD

Huntbourne Farm

SHOREHAM LA

ORCHARD RD

MARSHALLS LAND

GLENWOOD
PL

PO

PH

GRANGE RD

GRANGE CT

THE PAVEMENT

JARVIS

WAYSIDE AVE

Knock Wood

TN30

St Michael's Terr

OX LA

CHALK AVE

BARNFIELD

Great Piper Wood

HENLEY MEWS

ST BEES CRES

WAYSIDE

SPRINGFIELD

2
4
5

WAYSIDE FLATS 1
BORESISLE 2
CRISFIELD CT 3
LITTLE HILL 4
HENLEY VIEW 5

HENLEY FIELDS

COLONELS STEPHENS WAY

Ingleden

INGLEDEN PARK RD

Brissenden Farm

Homewood Sch

SILVER HILL

WEALDEN LANE

INGLEDEN PARK RD

Knock Wood

Old Knockwood

TENTERDEN

THE LINDENS

HAFENDEN RD

DRURY RD

CURTEIS RD

ST BENET'S WAY

A28

B2080

MILL LA

HOMEWOOD RD

ADAMS CL

EAST WEALD

GOLDSMITH CT

GOLDS CL

BEACON WLK

KNOCKWOOD RD

CHESTNUT CL

TRAMPALS WLK

VINEY'S GDNS

KNOCKHURST CT

B2067

Knock Wood

WOODCHURCH RD

GH

B2067

EASTGATE RD

EASTGATE DRY

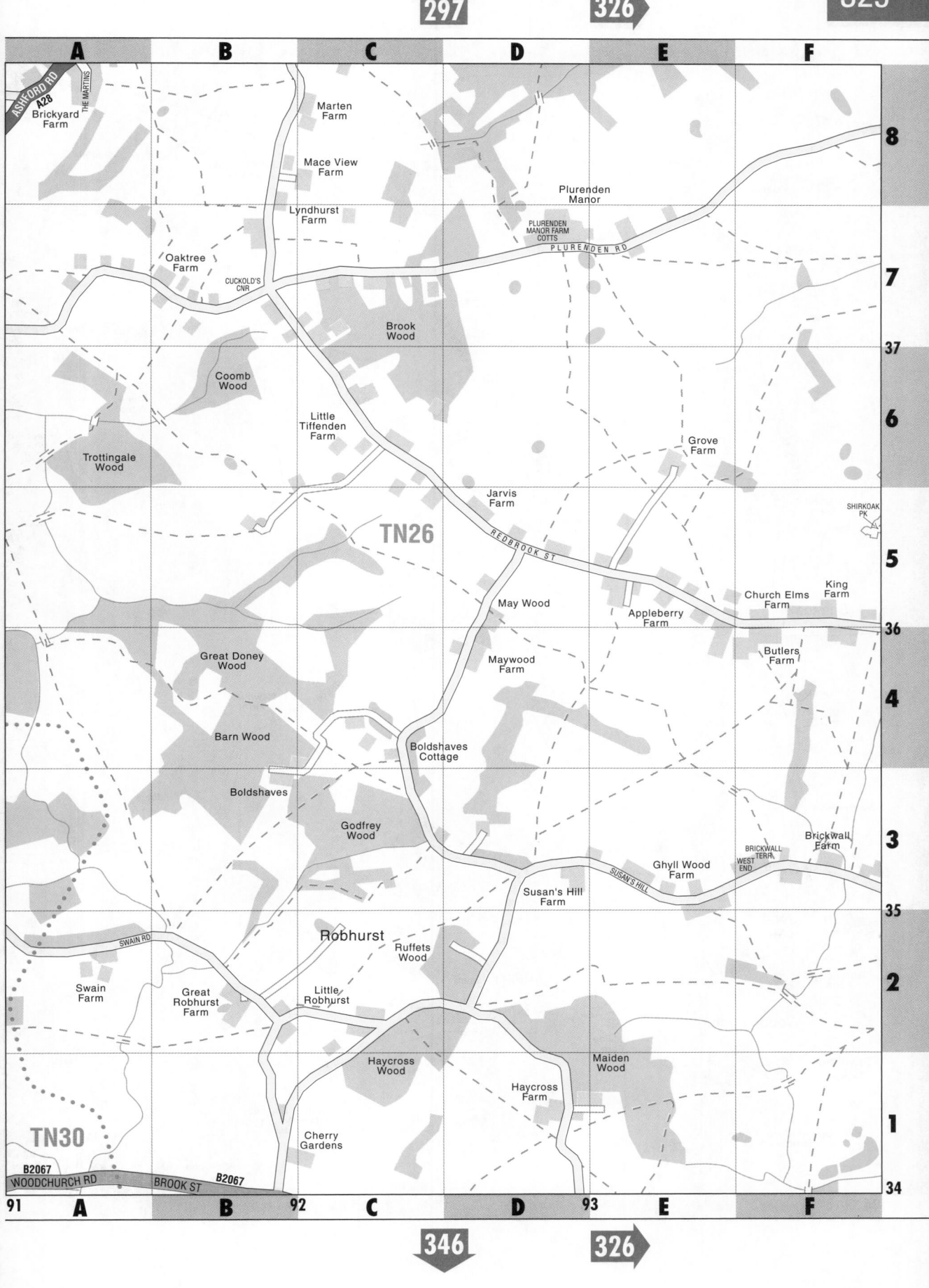

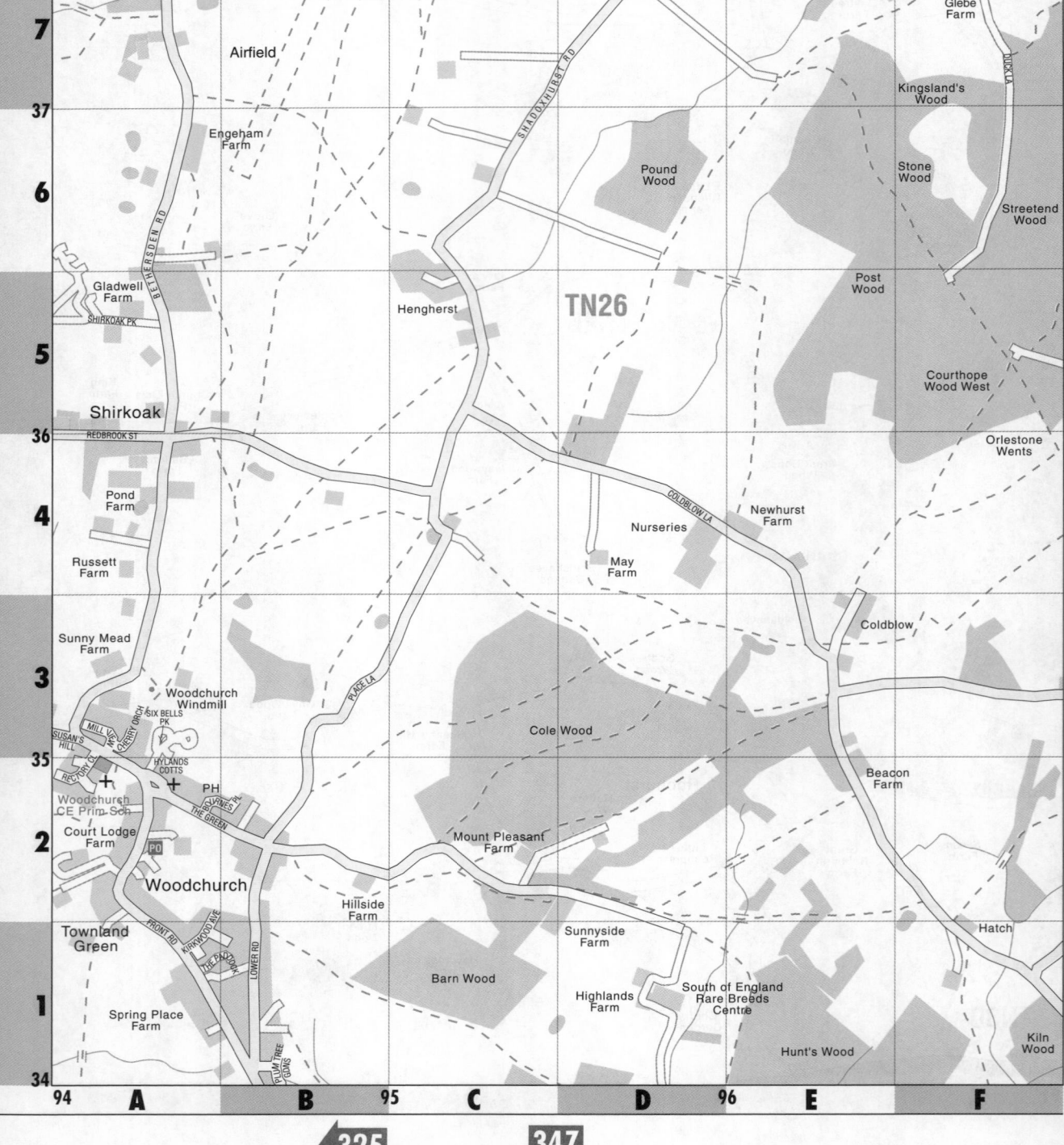

A   B   C   D   E   F

8

7

37

6

5

36

4

3

35

2

1

34

PLURENDEN RD

Great Engeham Manor

Airfield

Engeham Farm

BETHERSDEN RD

Gladwell Farm

SHIRKOAK PK

Shirkoak

REDBROOK ST

Pond Farm

Russett Farm

Sunny Mead Farm

Woodchurch Windmill

SIX BELLS PK

MILL VIEW

CURTY ORCH

SUSAN'S HILL

RECTORY CT

HYLANDS COTTS

PLACE LA

LYNES PK

THE GREEN

PH

Woodchurch CE Prim Sch

Court Lodge Farm

PO

Woodchurch

Townland Green

FRONT RD

KIRKWOOD AVE

LOWER RD

THE PADDOCK

Spring Place Farm

PLUM TREE GDNS

Harlakenden Wood

Coleham Green

SHADOXHURST RD

Pound Wood

Hengherst

TN26

Cole Wood

Mount Pleasant Farm

Hillside Farm

Barn Wood

Frightsbridge Farm

WOODCHURCH RD

CHURCH LA

RECTORY BGLWS

Colebran Wood

Glebe Farm

DUCK LA

Kingsland's Wood

Stone Wood

Streetend Wood

Post Wood

Courthope Wood West

Orlestone Wents

COLDBLOW LA

Newhurst Farm

Nurseries

May Farm

Coldblow

Beacon Farm

Sunnyside Farm

Highlands Farm

South of England Rare Breeds Centre

Hunt's Wood

Hatch

Kiln Wood

94   A   B   95   C   D   96   E   F

327 300

A B C D E F

8

CH

Braeside Farm

Meadow Farm

Sticket Wood

Hookstead Lake

Steeds La

Steeds La

BLIBY CNR

Bliby

Bliby Bsns Ctr

Greensand Way

7

Bishop's Wood

Lone Barn Farm

Brisley Farm

Bliby Wood

LITTLE ACRES

37

Brisley Wood

ROWLING ST

TN25

Stone Cross

FRITH RD

6

Highview Farm

Athans Farm

Golden Wood

Brisley La

Golden Wood Farm

Rowling Street

Newhouse Farm

BROMLEY GREEN RD

TN26

Harding's Bridge

Lamb's Wood

Honeypot

STONE CROSS RD

5

Chequertree Wood

Hall

Gorse Green Farm

Roughground Wood

Swanton Farm

36

Woodreeve Farm

CAPEL RD

Greensand Way

Dynes Farm

4

Silver Birches Mobile Homes Pk

Haberdashers' Wood

Ladswood Farm

POUNDHURST RD

New House Farm

Dicker's Wood

Dyne's Wood

3

Soaper's Wood

Packing Wood

Hollybush Farm

Stonegate Farm

Norland Wood

Saxon Shore Way

Hodge's Wood

35

2

Mast

Court Lodge Farm

Ham Street Woods National Nature Reserve

GILL LA

Horton Green

Gill Farm

Weston's Wood

Pierland Wood

Carving Wood

A2070

Huntbourne Wood

Bourne Wood

Greensand Way

Saxon Shore Way

Hibbet's Wood

Hanger Wood

Freeland Wood

1

34

00 A B 01 C D 02 E F

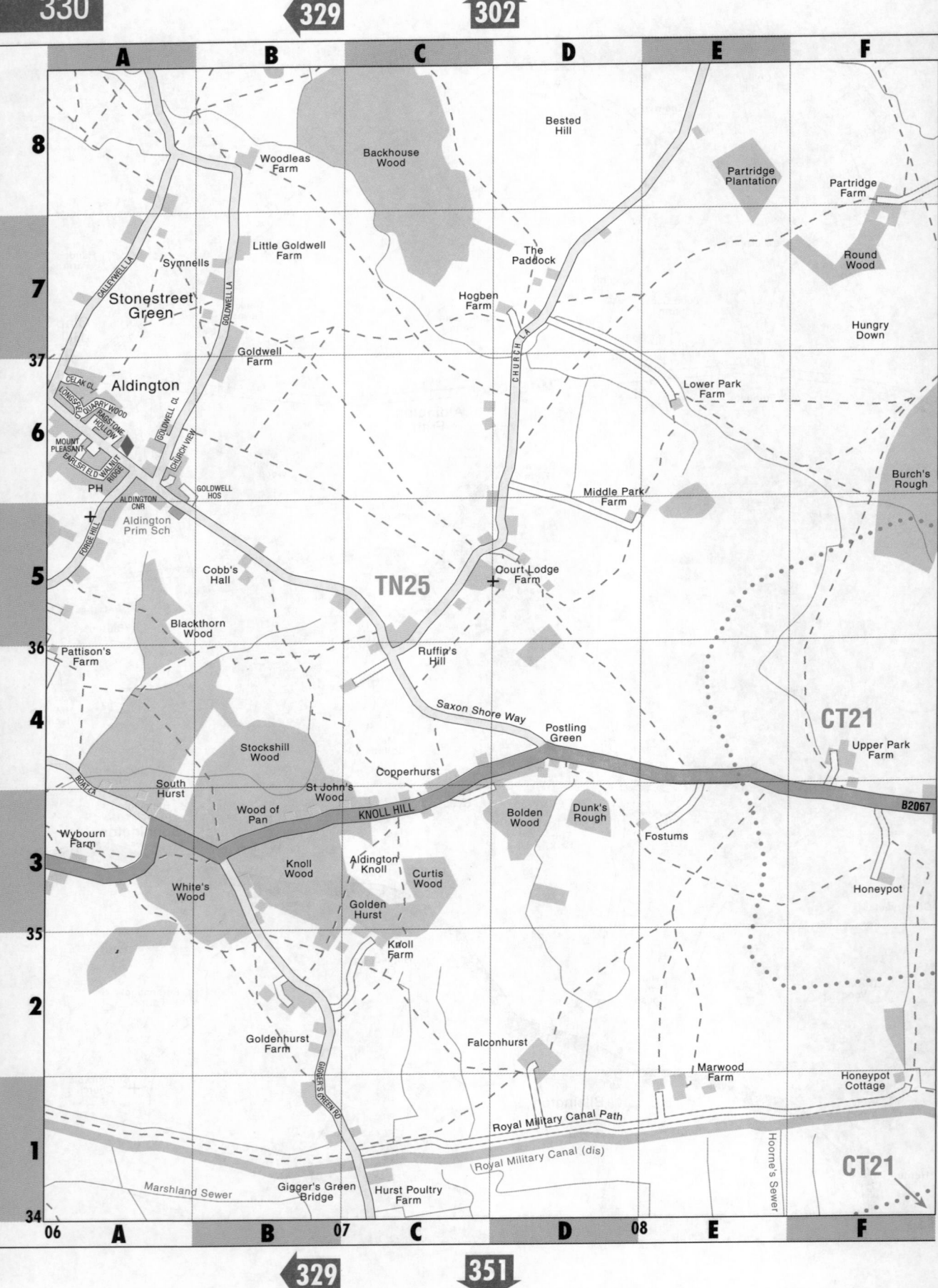

A   **B**   **C**   **D**   **E**   **F**

8

Bested
Hill

Woodleas
Farm

Backhouse
Wood

Partridge
Plantation

Partridge
Farm

Little Goldwell
Farm

7

Symnells

Round
Wood

CALLYWELL LA

Stonestreet
Green

GOLDWELL LA

The
Paddock

Hogben
Farm

Hungry
Down

37

Goldwell
Farm

CHURCH LA

Aldington

Lower Park
Farm

CELAK CL

GOLDWELL CL

6

QUARRY WOOD

FLAGSTONE
HOLLOW

CHURCH VIEW

Middle Park
Farm

Burch's
Rough

MOUNT
PLEASANT

LONGS CL

EARLSFIELD WALNUT
RIDGE

GOLDWELL
HOS

PH

ALDINGTON
CNR

FORGE HILL

Aldington
Prim Sch

Cobb's
Hall

Qourt Lodge
Farm

TN25

5

Blackthorn
Wood

36

Pattison's
Farm

Ruffin's
Hill

4

Saxon Shore Way

Postling
Green

CT21

Upper Park
Farm

Stockshill
Wood

Copperhurst

BOAT LA

South
Hurst

St John's
Wood

KNOLL HILL

Bolden
Wood

Dunk's
Rough

B2067

Wood of
Pan

Fostums

Wybourn
Farm

3

Knoll
Wood

Aldington
Knoll

Curtis
Wood

Honeypot

White's
Wood

Golden
Hurst

35

Knoll
Farm

2

Goldenhurst
Farm

Falconhurst

Marwood
Farm

Honeypot
Cottage

GIGGER'S GREEN RD

1

Royal Military Canal Path

Hoorne's Sewer

CT21

Royal Military Canal (dis)

34

Marshland Sewer

Gigger's Green
Bridge

Hurst Poultry
Farm

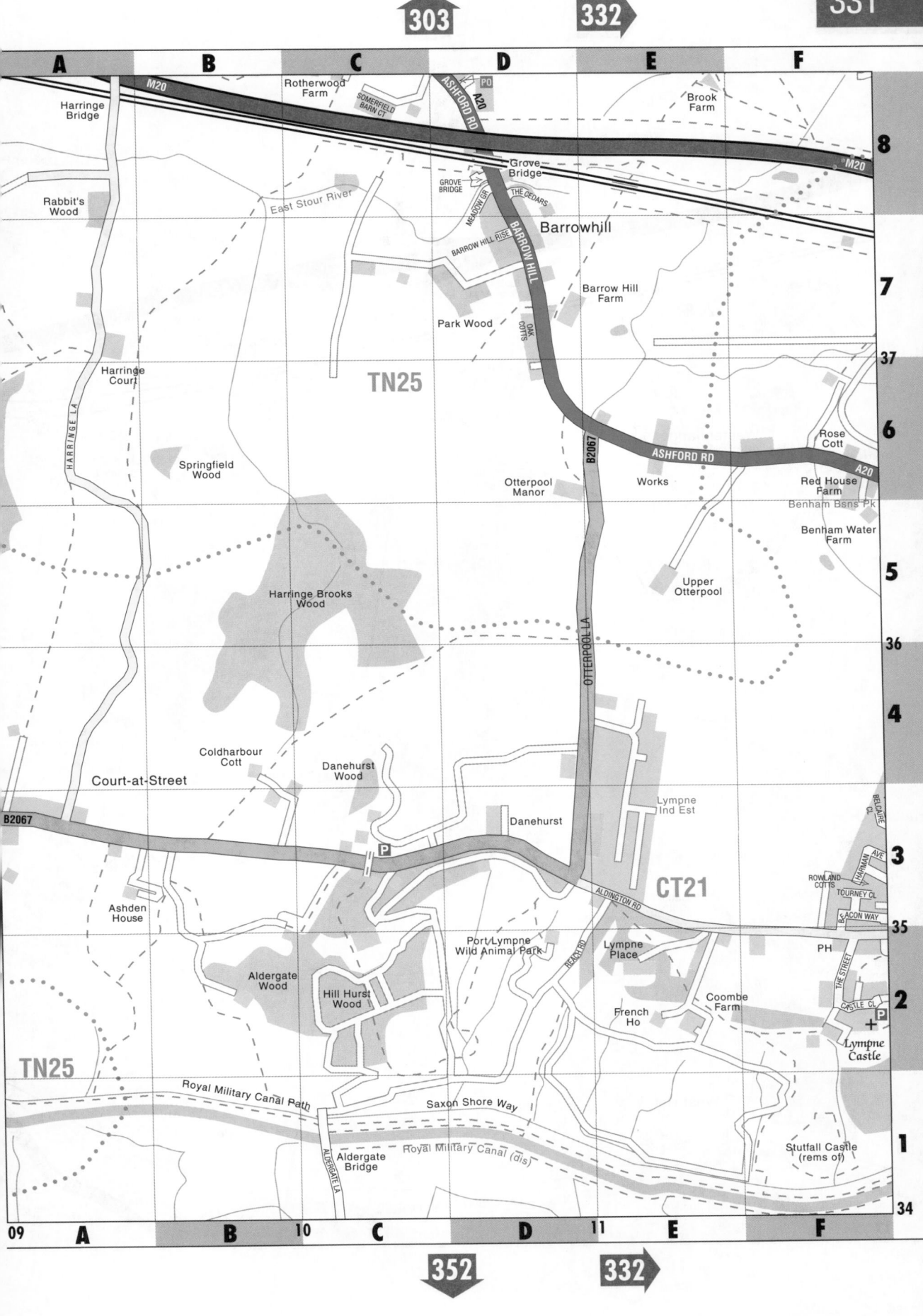

303
332

A B C D E F

8
7
37
6
5
36
4
3
35
2
1
34

09 A B 10 C D 11 E F

352
332

Harringe Bridge
M20
Rotherwood Farm
SOMERFIELD BARN CT
ASHFORD RD
A20
PO
Brook Farm
M20
Grove Bridge
GROVE BRIDGE
MEADOW GR
THE CEDARS
Barrowhill
Rabbit's Wood
East Stour River
BARROW HILL RISE
BARROW HILL
Barrow Hill Farm
Park Wood
OAK COTTS
Harringe Court
TN25
Rose Cott
Springfield Wood
B2067
ASHFORD RD
A20
Otterpool Manor
Works
Red House Farm
Benham Bsns Pk
Benham Water Farm
HARRINGE LA
Harringe Brooks Wood
Upper Otterpool
OTTERPOOL LA
Coldharbour Cott
Danehurst Wood
Court-at-Street
B2067
Danehurst
Lympne Ind Est
CT21
BELCAIRE CL
ROWLAND COTTS
HARMAN AVE
TOURNEY CL
Ashden House
P
ALDINGTON RD
BACON WAY
PH
Port Lympne Wild Animal Park
Lympne Place
REACH RD
THE STREET
Aldergate Wood
Hill Hurst Wood
French Ho
Coombe Farm
CASTLE CL
P
Lympne Castle
TN25
Royal Military Canal Path
Saxon Shore Way
ALDERGATE LA
Aldergate Bridge
Royal Military Canal (dis)
Stutfall Castle (rems of)

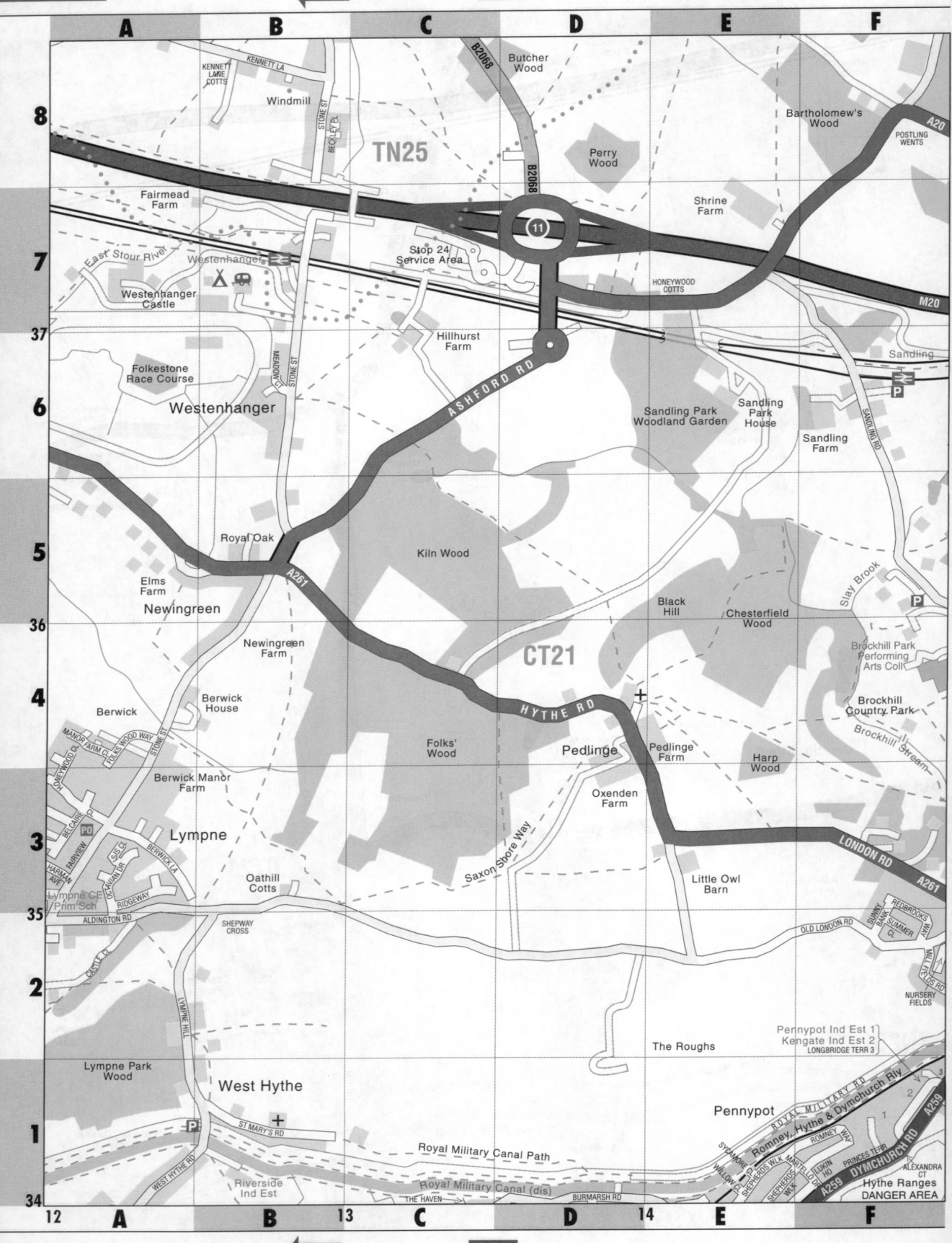

A   **B**   **C**   **D**   **E**   **F**

B2068

Butcher Wood

8

KENNETT LANE COTTS

KENNETT LA

STONE ST

BECKLEY PL

Windmill

Bartholomew's Wood

A20

POSTLING WENTS

TN25

Perry Wood

B2068

Fairmead Farm

Shrine Farm

7

East Stour River

Westenhanger

Stop 24 Service Area

11

HONEYWOOD COTTS

M20

Westenhanger Castle

37

Folkestone Race Course

Hillhurst Farm

ASHFORD RD

Sandling

P

STONE ST

MEADOW

Sandling Park Woodland Garden

Sandling Park House

6

Westenhanger

Sandling Farm

SANDLING RD

Slay Brook

Royal Oak

5

A261

Kiln Wood

Black Hill

Chesterfield Wood

P

Elms Farm

Brockhill Park Performing Arts Coll

36

Newingreen

Newingreen Farm

CT21

Brockhill Country Park

Brockhill Stream

4

Berwick

Berwick House

STONE ST

FOLKS WOOD WAY

HYTHE RD

Folks' Wood

Pedlinge

Pedlinge Farm

Harp Wood

MANOR FARM CL

ONEYWOOD CL

Berwick Manor Farm

Oxenden Farm

Little Owl Barn

LONDON RD

A261

BELCAIRE

FAIRVIEW

HARMAN

PO

S SCH CL

OCTAVIAN DR

BERWICK LA

Lympne

REDBROOKS WAY

SUNNY BANK

SUMMER CL

3

AVE

RIDGEWAY

Oathill Cotts

Saxon Shore Way

MILL RISE

35

Lympne CE Prim Sch

ALDINGTON RD

SHEPWAY CROSS

Old London RD

NURSERY FIELDS

2

CASTLE LA

LYMPNE HILL

The Roughs

Pennypot Ind Est 1
Kengate Ind Est 2
LONGBRIDGE TERR 3

Lympne Park Wood

West Hythe

Pennypot

ROYAL MILITARY RD

Romney, Hythe & Dymchurch Rly

A259

DYMCHURCH RD

1

WEST HYTHE RD

P

ST MARY'S RD

SYCAMORE CL

WILLOW

SHEPHERDS WLK

MARTELLO RD

LUKIN

PRINCES TERR

ALEXANDRA CT

Royal Military Canal Path

Hythe Ranges DANGER AREA

Riverside Ind Est

Royal Military Canal (dis)

34

THE HAVEN

BURMARSH RD

A259

12   **A**   **B**   **13**   **C**   **D**   **14**   **E**   **F**

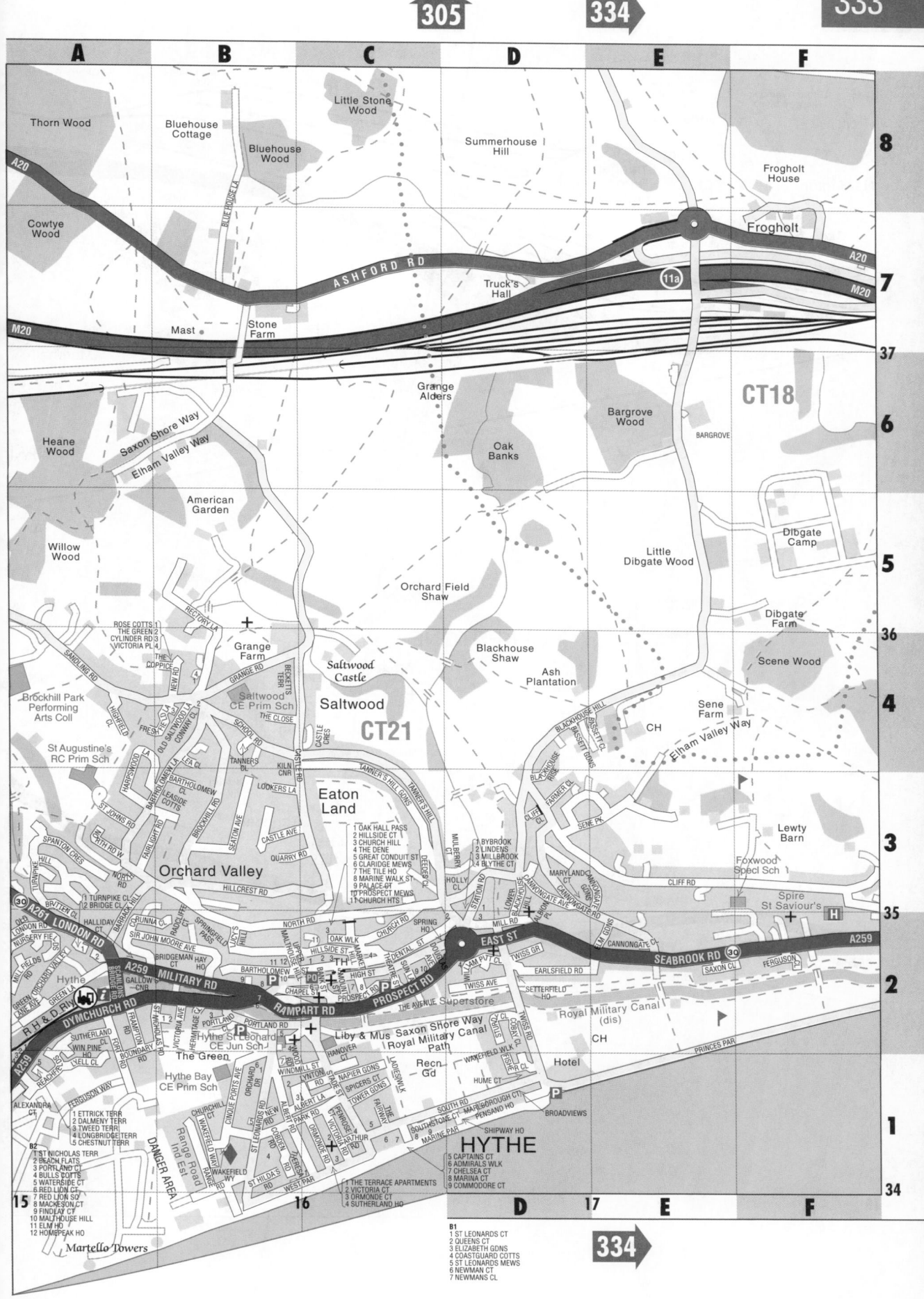

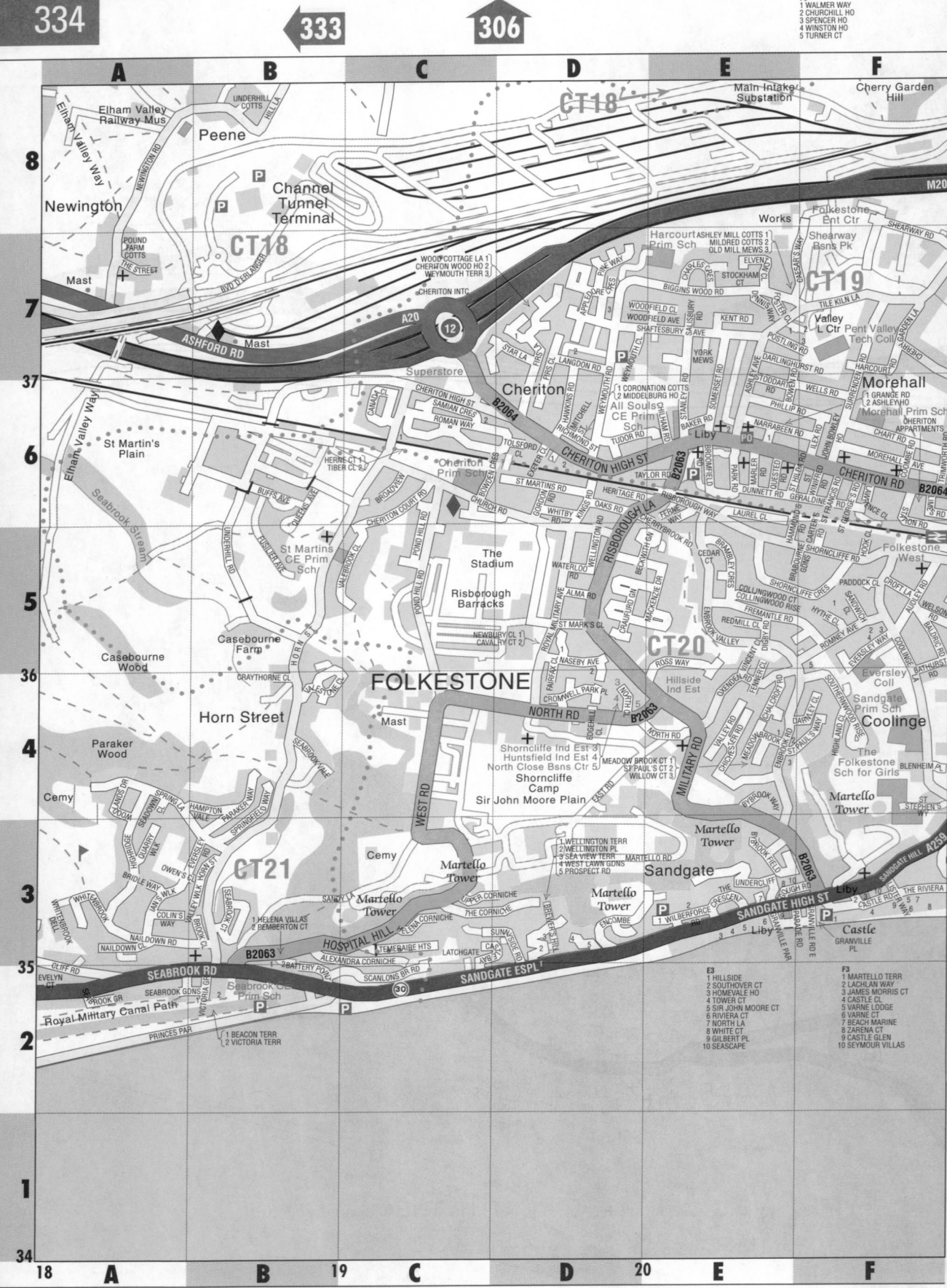

333
306

F5
1 WALMER WAY
2 CHURCHILL HO
3 SPENCER HO
4 WINSTON HO
5 TURNER CT

A **B** **C** **D** **E** **F**

Elham Valley
Railway Mus

UNDERHILL
COTTS
Peene

Channel
Tunnel
Terminal

CT18

Newington

POUND
FARM
COTTS
THE STREET
Mast

Main Intake
Substation

Cherry Garden
Hill

Works

Folkestone
Ent Ctr

Shearway
Bsns Pk

CT19

Harcourt
Prim Sch

ASHLEY MILL COTTS 1
MILDRED COTTS 2
OLD MILL MEWS 3

Valley
L Ctr Pent Valley
Tech Coll

Mast

WOOD COTTAGE LA 1
CHERITON WOOD HO 2
WEYMOUTH TERR 3

CHERITON INTC

A20

12

Cheriton

Superstore

8

7

37

Morehall

1 GRANGE RD
2 ASHLEY HO
Morehall Prim Sch

CHERITON
APPARTMENTS

All Souls
CE Prim
Sch

1 CORONATION COTTS
2 MIDDELBURG SQ

Liby
PO

St Martin's
Plain

Seabrook Stream

HERNE CT 1
TIBER CL 2

Cheriton
Prim Sch

BUFFS AVE

St Martins
CE Prim
Sch

The
Stadium

Risborough
Barracks

NEWBURY CL 1
CAVALRY CT 2

Folkestone
West

CT20

CHERITON RD
B2064

Casebourne
Wood

Casebourne
Farm

CRAYTHORNE CL

FOLKESTONE

Mast

NORTH RD

Shorncliffe Ind Est 3
Huntsfield Ind Est 4
North Close Bsns Ctr 5
Shorncliffe
Camp
Sir John Moore Plain

Hillside
Ind Est

MEADOW BROOK CT 1
ST PAUL'S CT 2
WILLOW CT 3

Eversley
Coll

Sandgate
Prim Sch

Coolinge

The
Folkestone
Sch for Girls

Martello
Tower

Paraker
Wood

Horn Street

Cemy

CT21

Cemy

Martello
Tower

1 WELLINGTON TERR
2 WELLINGTON PL
3 SEA VIEW TERR
4 WEST LAWN GDNS
5 PROSPECT RD

Martello
Tower

Martello
Tower

Sandgate

Martello
Tower

Liby

THE RIVIERA

Castle

1 HELENA VILLAS
2 PEMBERTON CT

UPPER CORNICHE

THE CORNICHE

1 WILBERFORCE RD

SANDGATE HIGH ST

Liby

GRANVILLE
PL

B2063

HOSPITAL HILL

NAILDOWN RD
NAILDOWN CL

1 BEACON TERR
2 VICTORIA TERR

Seabrook CE
Prim Sch

SEABROOK RD

Royal Military Canal Path

PRINCES PAR

SANDGATE ESPL

30

E3
1 HILLSIDE
2 SOUTHOVER CT
3 HOMEVALE HO
4 TOWER CT
5 SIR JOHN MOORE CT
6 RIVIERA CT
7 NORTH LA
8 WHITE CT
9 GILBERT PL
10 SEASCAPE

F3
1 MARTELLO TERR
2 LACHLAN WAY
3 JAMES MORRIS CT
4 CASTLE CL
5 VARNE LODGE
6 VARNE CT
7 BEACH MARINE
8 ZARENA CT
9 CASTLE GLEN
10 SEYMOUR VILLAS

6

5

36

4

3

35

2

1

34

18 **A** **B** **19** **C** **D** **20** **E** **F**

333

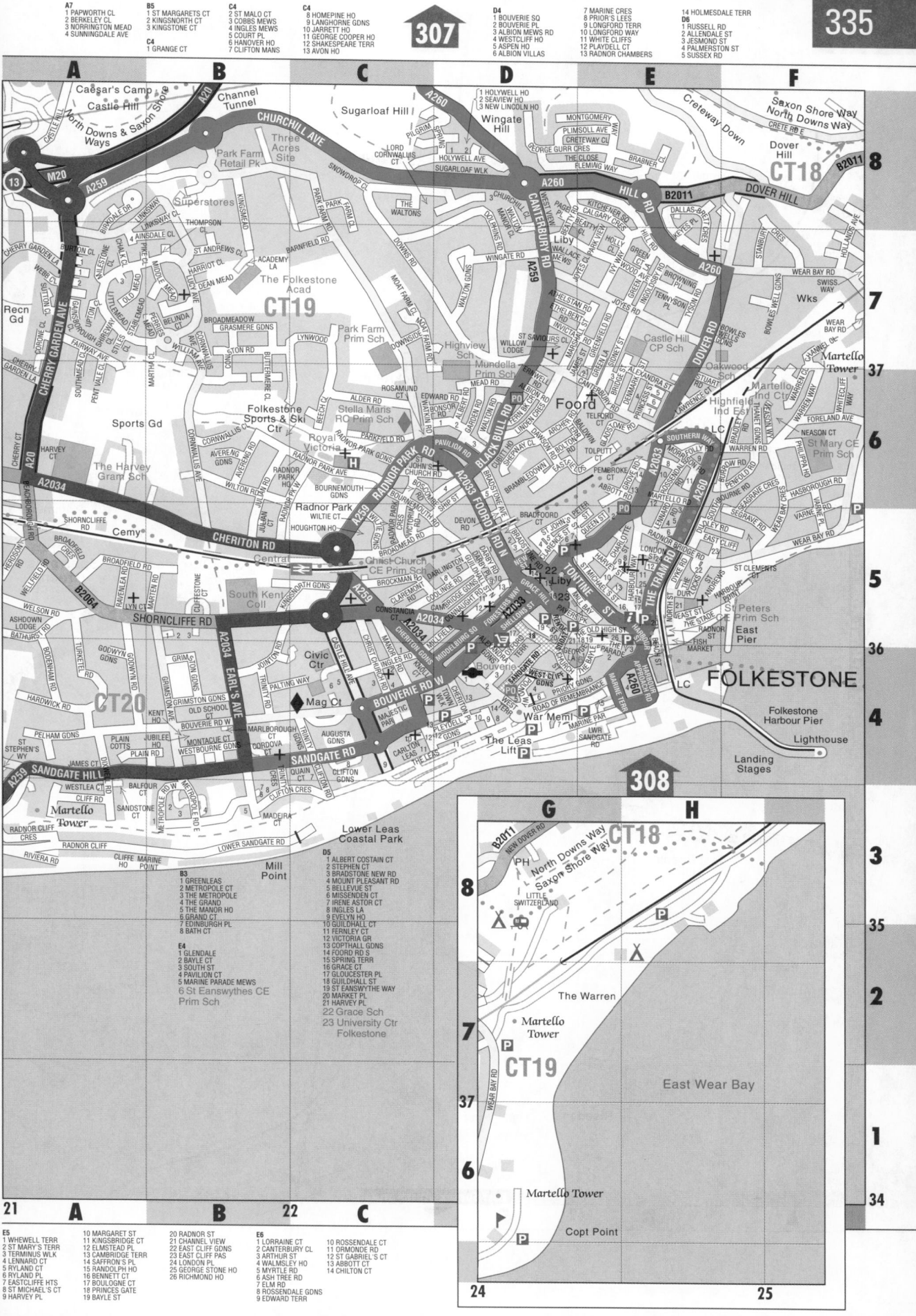

A7
1 PAPWORTH CL
2 BERKELEY CL
3 NORRINGLHAM MEAD
4 SUNNINGDALE AVE

B5
1 ST MARGARETS CT
2 KINGSNORTH CT
3 KINGSTONE ST

C4
1 GRANGE CT

C4
2 ST MALO CT
3 COBBS MEWS
4 INGLES MEWS
5 COURT PL
6 HANOVER HO
7 CLIFTON MANS

C4
8 HOMEPINE HO
9 LANGHORNE GDNS
10 JARRETT HO
11 GEORGE COOPER HO
12 SHAKESPEARE TERR
13 AVON HO

D4
1 BOUVERIE SQ
2 BOUVERIE PL
3 ALBION MEWS RD
4 WESTCLIFF HO
5 ASPEN HO
6 ALBION VILLAS

7 MARINE CRES
8 PRIOR'S LEES
9 LONGFORD TERR
10 LONGFORD WAY
11 WHITE CLIFFS
12 PLAYDELL
13 RADNOR CHAMBERS

14 HOLMESDALE TERR

D6
1 RUSSELL RD
2 ALLENDALE ST
3 JESMOND ST
4 PALMERSTON ST
5 SUSSEX RD

307

D5
1 ALBERT COSTAIN CT
2 STEPHEN CT
3 BRADSTONE NEW RD
4 MOUNT PLEASANT RD
5 BELLEVUE ST
6 MISSENDEN CT
7 IRENE ASTOR CT
8 INGLES LA
9 EVELYN HO
10 GUILDHALL CT
11 FERNLEY CT
12 VICTORIA GR
13 COPTHALL GDNS
14 FOORD RD S
15 SPRING TERR
16 GRACE CT
17 GLOUCESTER PL
18 GUILDHALL ST
19 ST EANSWYTHE WAY
20 MARKET PL
21 HARVEY PL
22 Grace Sch
23 University Ctr
Folkestone

B3
1 GREENLEAS
2 METROPOLE CT
3 THE METROPOLE
4 THE GRAND
5 THE MANOR HO
6 GRAND CT
7 EDINBURGH PL
8 BATH CT

E4
1 GLENDALE
2 BAYLE CT
3 SOUTH ST
4 PAVILION CT
5 MARINE PARADE MEWS
6 St Eanswythes CE
Prim Sch

308

E5
1 WHEWELL TERR
2 ST MARY'S TERR
3 TERMINUS WLK
4 LENNARD CT
5 RYLAND CT
6 RYLAND PL
7 EASTCLIFFE HTS
8 ST MICHAEL'S CT
9 HARVEY PL

10 MARGARET ST
11 KINGSBRIDGE CT
12 ELMSTEAD PL
13 CAMBRIDGE TERR
14 SAFFRON'S PL
15 RANDOLPH HO
16 BENNETT CT
17 BOULOGNE CT
18 PRINCES GATE
19 BAYLE ST

20 RADNOR ST
21 CHANNEL VIEW
22 EAST CLIFF GDNS
23 EAST CLIFF PAS
24 LONDON PL
25 GEORGE STONE HO
26 RICHMOND HO

E6
1 LORRAINE CT
2 CANTERBURY CL
3 ARTHUR ST
4 WALMSLEY HO
5 MYRTLE RD
6 ASH TREE RD
7 ELM RD
8 ROSSENDALE GDNS
9 EDWARD TERR

10 ROSSENDALE CT
11 ORMONDE RD
12 ST GABRIEL'S CT
13 ABBOTT CT
14 CHILTON CT

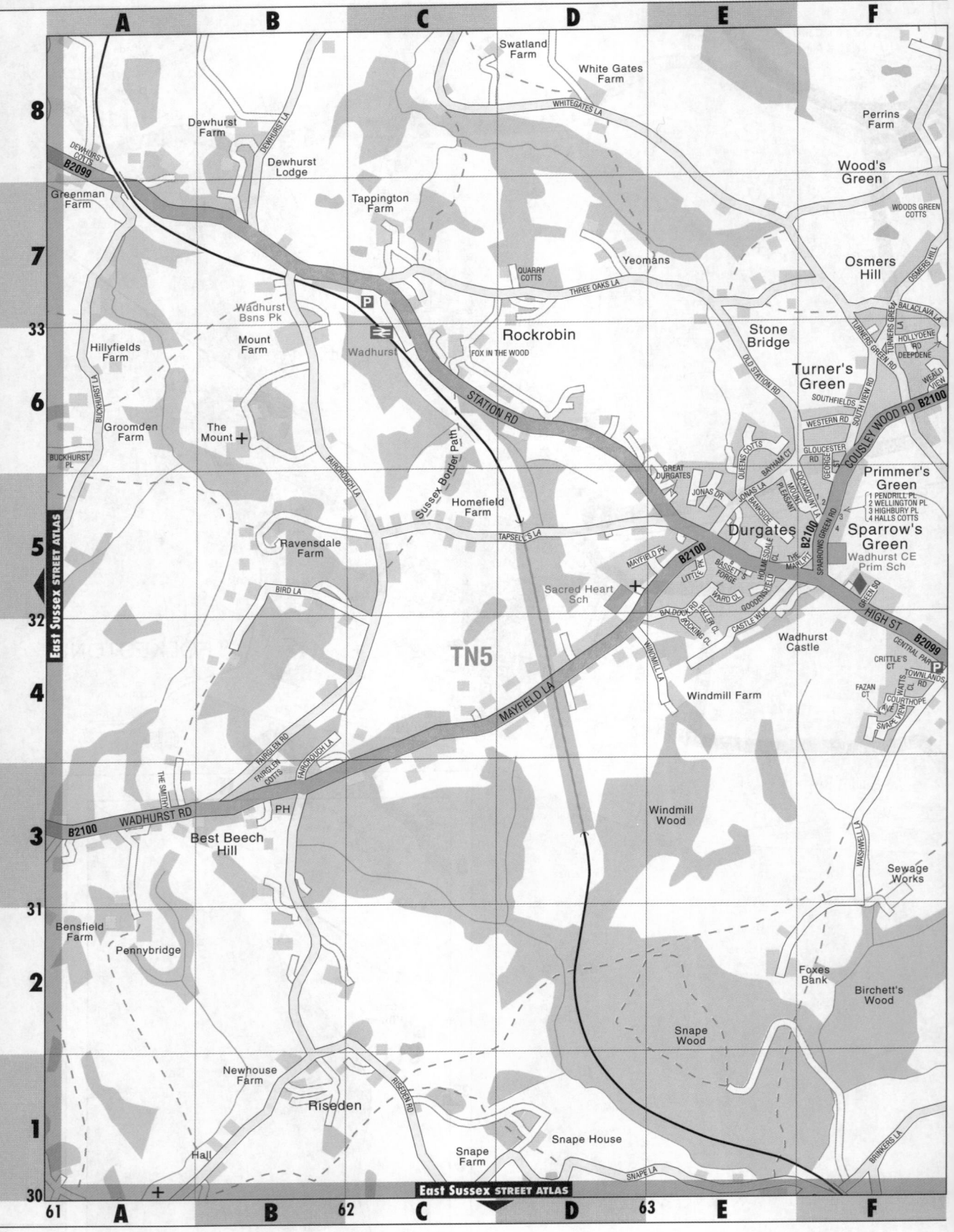

East Sussex STREET ATLAS

| | A | | B | | C | | D | | E | | F |

A   B   C   D   E   F

8

7

33

6

5

32

4

3

31

2

1

30

B2100

Newbury's

NEWBURY CTS

NEWBURY LA

The Colleens

Ladymeads Farm

BEWLBRIDGE LA

MONKS LA

Hillside Cotts

WINDMILL LA

Lower Cousley Wood

Gate House Farm

COUSLEY WOOD RD

PH

Cousley Wood

Pell Green

Great Butts

BUTTS LA

Little Butts Farm

Bewl Water

Bryant's Farm

BALACLAVA LA

PH

1
3 4
2 5

Great Pell Oast

Sussex Border Path

Newbarn

Wishdown

1 FAIR VIEW COTTS
2 DEEPDENE
3 THE LEAS
4 PELL CL
5 BIRCH KILN COTTS

Pell Bridge

Vicarage Green

BLACKSMITH'S LA

Little Pell Farm

TN5

Little Whiligh

Southfields

Chesson's Farm

CHURCH
ST   HIGH
ST

POPES GL

Liby
P

Uplands Com Coll

1 THE SQUARE
2 KINGSLEY CT

Wadhurst

WATERS COTTS

STONE CROSS RD

LAUREL BANK

LOWER HIGH ST

Foxhole

FOXHOLE LA

Long Wood

WARD'S LA

Stone Cross

Moseham

Whiligh

Birchett's Green

BIRCHETTS GREEN LA

Birchett's Green Farm

BRINKERS LA

Darby's Farm

DARBY'S LA

Holbeam Wood

Upper Wallands Farm

STONEGATE RD

Shover's Green House

HIGH ST

Cattle Breeding Ctr

Shover's Green

Normanswood

CHURCHSETTLE LA

Bugsey's Farm

Wallcrouch Farm

Wallcrouch

B2099

Walland Manor

A   B   C   D   E   F

8

Bedgebury
National Pinetum

Combwell
Wood

PARK LA

Park
House

Springwood
Lodge

Combwell Priory
Farm

TN17

Bedgebury
Park Woods

7

tonecrouch
arm House

33

LADY OAK LA

B2079

Starvegoose
Bank

Motel

6

Windmill Down

Windy
Ridge

B2079

Flimwell
Grange

Mast

5

Radio
Station

32

P

TN5

Ketley
Farm

FLIMWELL CL.

TN18

4

Sussex Border Path

Frith
Wood

Union
Street

LONDON RD

PH

3

FRUITFIELDS

RED OAST
COTTS

BLENHEIM
WAY

Downash Ho 1
Downash Ct 2

NURSERY CL.

OLD WAY

HIGH ST

BERNER'S
HILL

FORGE
COTTS

B2087

SUNNYBANK

A268

31

BROOM HILL
COTTS

UNION
ST

Flimwell

HAWKHURST RD

Mount Pleasant
Farm

GINGERBREAD LA

MEADOW VIEW

CLARKS YD

A268

2

Berner's
Hill

Quedley

Seacox
Heath

CH

West
Lodge

Ringden
Wood

Keeper's
Cottage

1

Saw Mill

TN19

Ringden
Farm

A21

Sewage Works

A21 Hastings

30

70   A   B   71   C   D   72   E   F

A B C D E F

8

Brick Kiln
Cottages

Sugarloaf
Hill

WHITELIMES

TN17

Louisa
Lodge

Hedgingford
Wood

Foresters
Cottage

TN17

Frith
Wood

PARK LA

Badger's
Oak Farm

Tubslake

7

Osborne's
Farm

HAWKHURST RD

33

Louisa
Lake

Rose's
Farm

6

Frith
Farm

Trenley
Farm

Yewtree
Farm

POTTER'S LA

Limes
Grove
Farm

5

Tanyard
Farm

STATION
COTTS

LIMES GR

Gill's
Green

SANTERS CT

32

TN18

Siseley
Farm

Gill's
Green
Farm

4

SOPER'S LA

Trewint
Farm

WELLINGTON COTTS

PH

HEARTENOAK RD

CRANBROOK RD

Soper's Lane
Farm

SLIP HILL RD

Slip
Mill

3

Little
Pix Hall
Farm

LIGHTFOOT
GN

SYDNEY TERR 1
CASTLE TERR 2
SANDROOK VILLAS 3

Springfield
Ind Est

A229

31

Elm Hill
Farm

Lightfoot
Green

CH

OAKFIELD

WESTERN RD

2

A268

Hawkhurst
Community

H

High
Street

PHILPOTT'S
CROSS

HIGH ST

THEOBALDS

P

A268

Elm Hill
House

IDDENDEN
COTTS

Marlborough
House
Sch

NORTH HILL RD

PARK VIEW

LORENDEN
PK

Seacox
Poultry Farm

COPTHALL
AVE

1

Delmonden
Manor

DELMONDEN RD

Hurstwood
Cottage

HIGHGATE HILL A229

Cockshot

Sussex Border Path

Hensill
House

TALBOT RD

30

73 A 74 B C 75 D E F

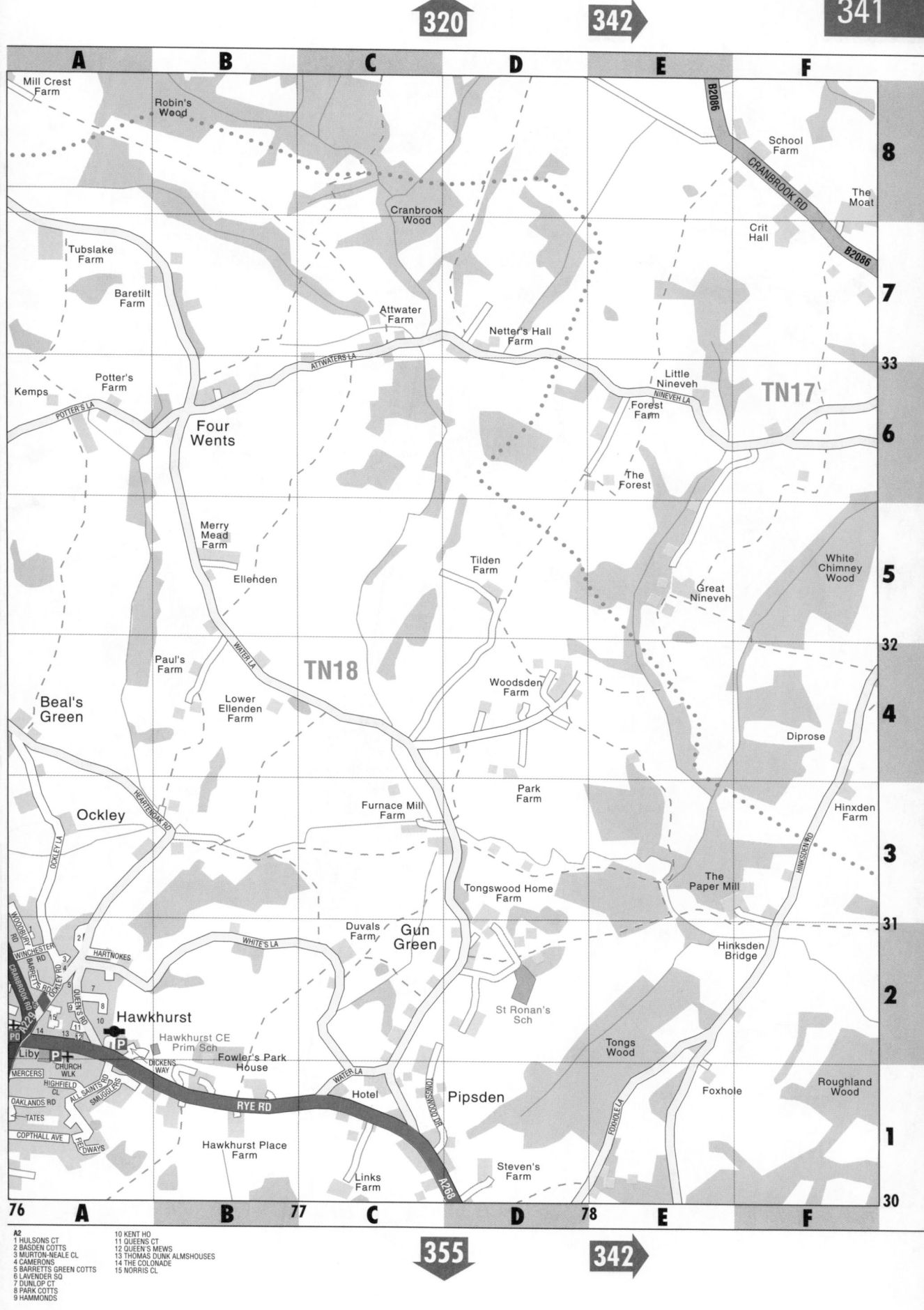

A B C D E F

8

7

33
6

5

32
4

3

31
2

1

30

76 A B 77 C D 78 E F

Mill Crest Farm
Robin's Wood
Cranbrook Wood
B2086
School Farm
CRANBROOK RD
The Moat
Crit Hall
B2086
Tubslake Farm
Baretilt Farm
Attwater Farm
Netter's Hall Farm
Little Nineveh
NINEVEH LA
TN17
Kemps
Potter's Farm
ATTWATERS LA
Forest Farm
POTTER'S LA
Four Wents
The Forest
Merry Mead Farm
Ellenden
WATER LA
Tilden Farm
Great Nineveh
White Chimney Wood
TN18
Paul's Farm
Lower Ellenden Farm
Woodsden Farm
Diprose
Beal's Green
Park Farm
Hinxden Farm
Ockley
HEARTENOAK RD
Furnace Mill Farm
Tongswood Home Farm
The Paper Mill
HINXDEN RD
OCKLEY LA
WOODBURY RD
WINCHESTER RD
BARRETT'S ROCKET ST
CRANBROOK RD
Duvals Farm
Gun Green
Hinksden Bridge
WHITE'S LA
HARTNOKES
QUEEN'S RD
Hawkhurst
Hawkhurst CE Prim Sch
St Ronan's Sch
Tongs Wood
PO
Liby
CHURCH WLK
MERCERS
HIGHFIELD CL
OAKLANDS RD
TATES
COPTHALL AVE
ALL SAINTS RD
SMUGGLERS
HEDWAYS
DICKENS WAY
Fowler's Park House
WATER LA
Hotel
Pipsden
FOXHOLE LA
Foxhole
Roughland Wood
RYE RD
Hawkhurst Place Farm
Links Farm
A268
Steven's Farm

A2
1 HULSONS CT
2 BASDEN COTTS
3 MURTON-NEALE CL
4 CAMERONS
5 BARRETTS GREEN COTTS
6 LAVENDER SQ
7 DUNLOP CT
8 PARK COTTS
9 HAMMONDS
10 KENT HO
11 QUEENS CT
12 QUEEN'S MEWS
13 THOMAS DUNK ALMSHOUSES
14 THE COLONADE
15 NORRIS CL

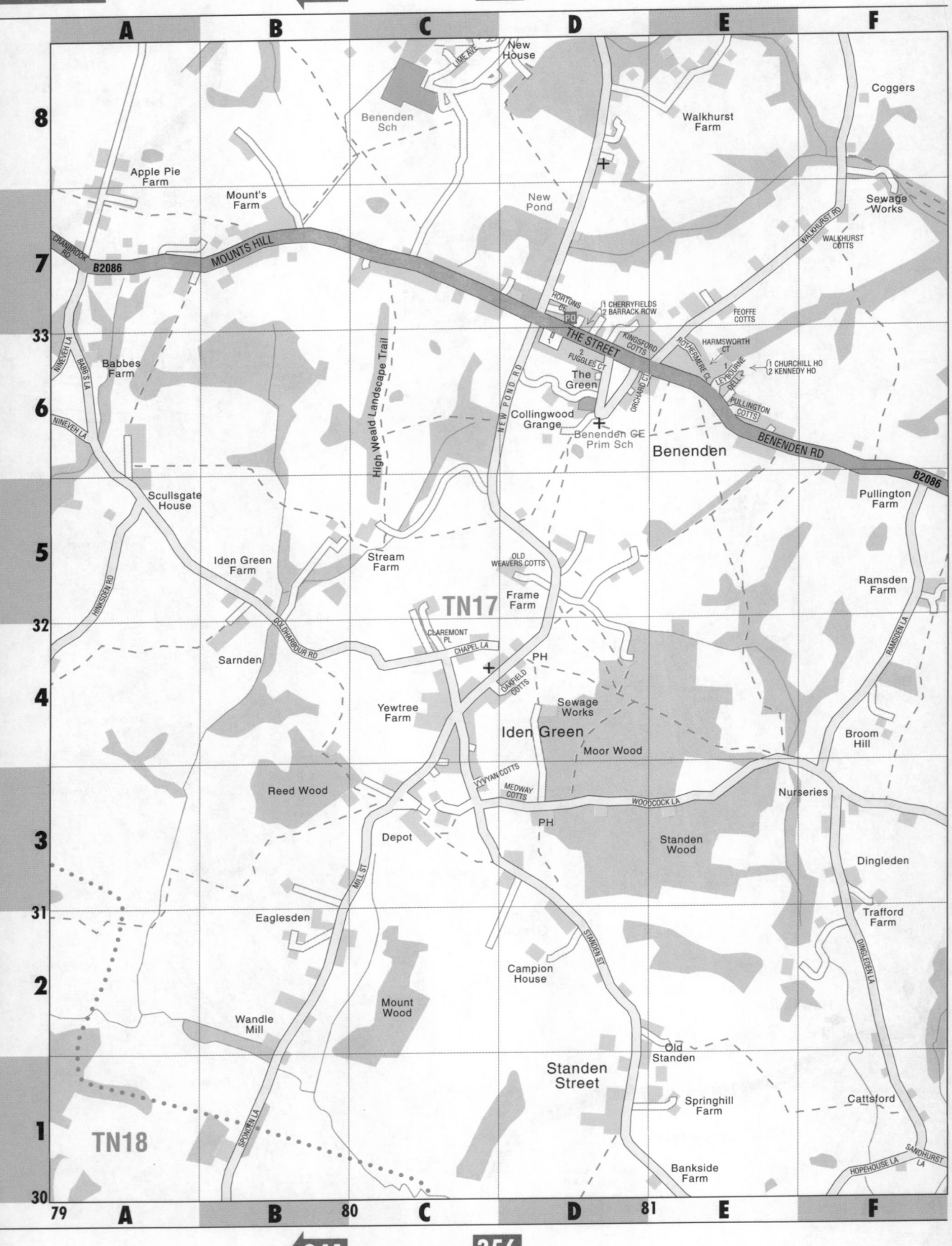

A B C D E F

8

Coggers

Apple Pie
Farm

Mount's
Farm

New
House

Benenden
Sch

Walkhurst
Farm

New Pond

Sewage
Works

7 B2086 MOUNTS HILL Walkhurst Walkhurst
Rd COTTS

CRANBROOK
RD

NINEVEH LA
BABB S LA

33

HORTONS
RD

THE STREET

1 CHERRYFIELDS
2 BARRACK ROW

FEOFFE
COTTS

Babbes
Farm

KINGSFORD
COTTS

HARMSWORTH
CT

PO

6

NINEVEH LA

High Weald Landscape Trail

NEW POND RD

1 FUGGLES CT
2

The
Green

ROTHERMERE CT

LEYBOURNE
PL 1
2

1 CHURCHILL HO
2 KENNEDY HO

ORCHARD CT

PULLINGTON
COTTS

Collingwood
Grange

Benenden CE
Prim Sch

Benenden BENENDEN RD B2086

HINKSDEN RD

Scullsgate
House

Pullington
Farm

5

Iden Green
Farm

Stream
Farm

OLD
WEAVERS COTTS

Ramsden
Farm

RAMSDEN LA

TN17

BOLD HARBOUR RD

Frame
Farm

32

CLAREMONT
PL

CHAPEL LA

PH

Sarnden

OAKFIELD
COTTS

4

Yewtree
Farm

Sewage
Works

Iden Green

Broom
Hill

Moor Wood

Nurseries

3

Reed Wood

VYVYAN COTTS

MEDWAY
COTTS

WOODCOCK LA

Depot

PH

Standen
Wood

Dingleden

MILL ST

DINGLEDEN LA

31

Eaglesden

Trafford
Farm

SPRIVERS LA

2

Wandle
Mill

Mount
Wood

Campion
House

STANDEN ST

Old
Standen

Cattsford

1

TN18

Standen
Street

Springhill
Farm

SANDHURST LA

30

Bankside
Farm

HOPEHOUSE LA

79 A 80 B C 80 D 81 E F

322
344

A B C D E F

8
7
33
6
5
32
4
3
31
2
1
30

Mount Pleasant
Farm

Colebarn
Farm

Mount Hall
Farm

Cott
Farm

Mount
Le Hoe

Stepneyford
Bridge

Halden
Place

STEPNEYFORD LA

Stumble
Wood

Nine Acre
Wood

Maplesden
Farm

Greenlane
Farm

Brick Kiln
Wood

Beacon
Wood

HALDEN LA

Rawlinson
Farm

Hole
Park

Rawlinson
Gill

Windmill
(dis)

Beacon
Hill

TN17

Halden Lane
Farm

Beacon Hall
Farm

Sewage
Works

BENENDEN RD

Ranters
Oak

Chessenden

GATEFIELD COTTS

TENTERDEN RD A28

The
Orchards

West
Cross

Windmill
Farm

C M Booth Collection
of Historic
Vehicles (Mus)

PH

HIGH ST

TANYARD

B2086

REGENT ST

Rolvenden

SPARKESWOOD AVE

SPARKESWOOD CL

WM FREDS

OLD REGENT DR

PO

Sparkeswood

Dingleden
Farm

Windmill
(dis)

Mill
House

Kemsdale
House

High Weald Landscape Trial

Rolvenden
Prim Sch

HIGH ST

PIX'S LA

LION/PENNY

+

SUMNER
CL

Old
Parsonage

The
Wilderness

MAYTHAM RD

Pookwell
Wood

Elphees

Great
Maytham
Hall

SANDHURST LA

Rowenden
Vineyard

Toad
Hall

Merrington
Place

HASTINGS RD

Devenden

Cherrygarden
Farm

Cornhill

Farnell
Wood

ALDER LA

FROG'S LA

Mallards

A28

WASSALL LA

LITTLE JOB'S
CROSS

357
344

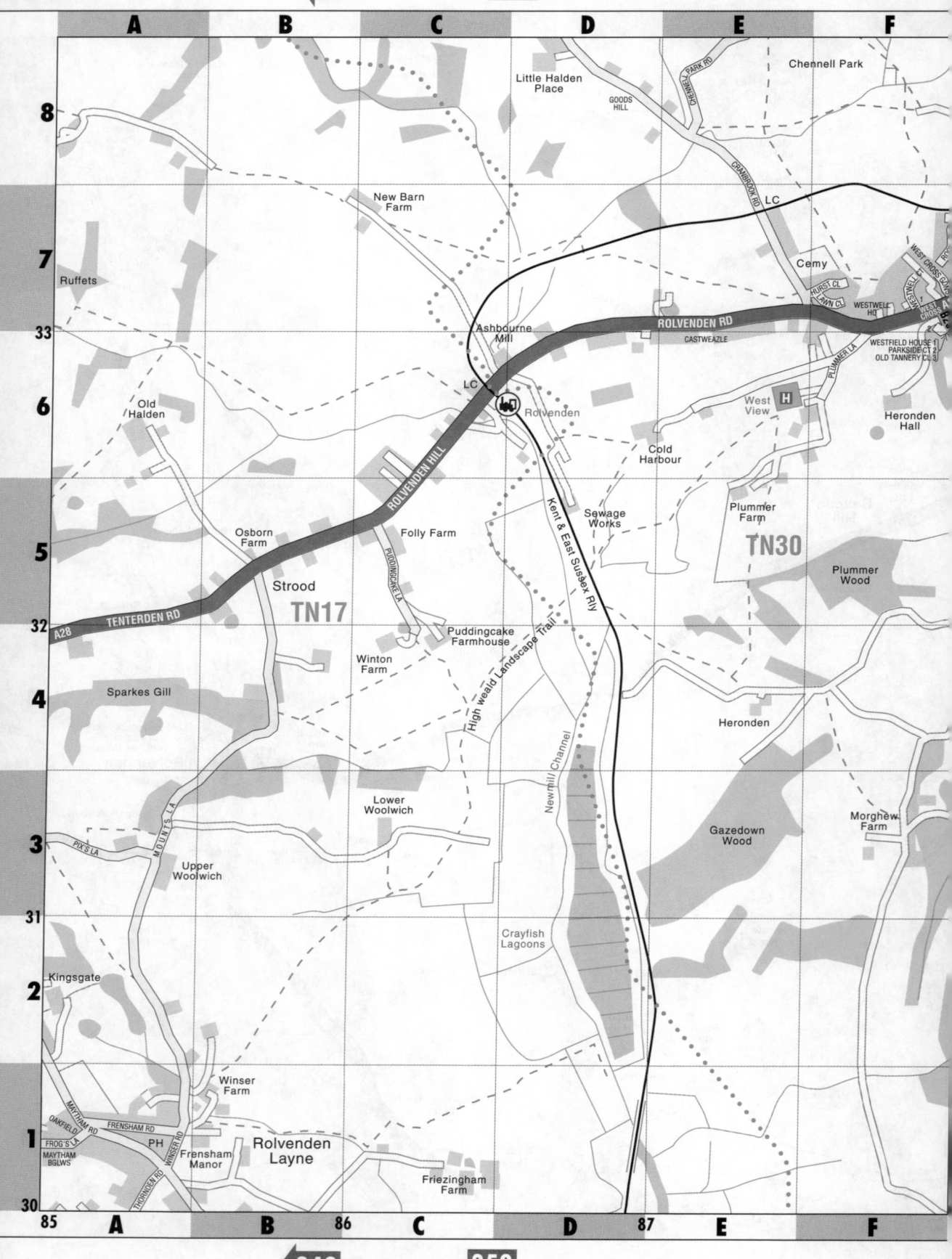

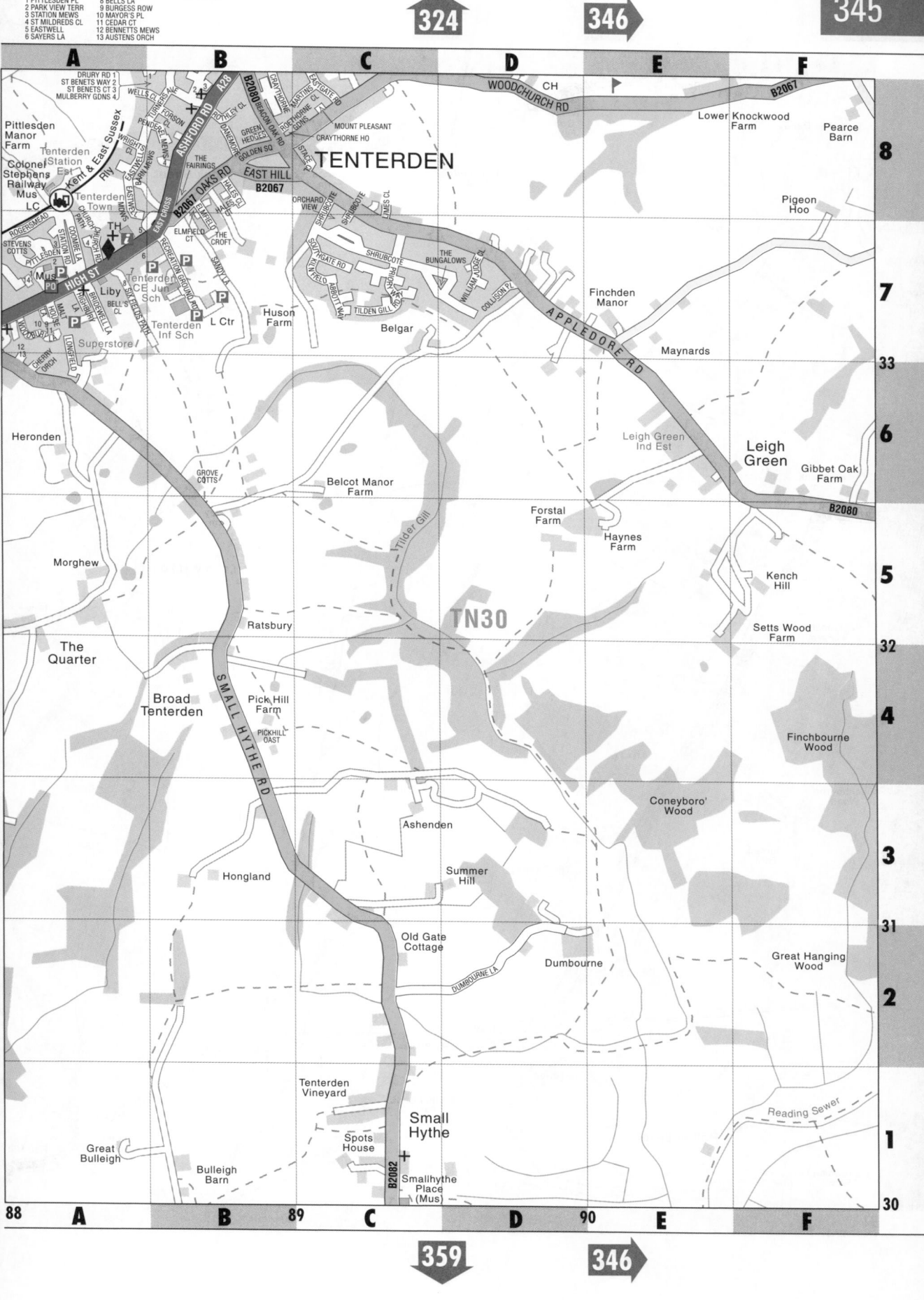

A7
1 PITTLESDEN PL
2 PARK VIEW TERR
3 STATION MEWS
4 ST MILDREDS CL
5 EASTWELL
6 SAYERS LA
7 THEATRE SQ
8 BELLS LA
9 BURGESS ROW
10 MAYOR'S PL
11 CEDAR CT
12 BENNETTS MEWS
13 AUSTENS ORCH
14 ROGERSMEAD

A   B   C   D   E   F

DRURY RD 1
ST BENETS WAY 2
ST BENETS CT 3
MULBERRY GDNS 4

WELLS CL

WOODCHURCH RD
CH

Lower Knockwood
Farm

Pearce
Barn

Pittlesden
Manor
Farm

Tenterden
Station
Est

Colonel
Stephens
Railway
Mus
LC

MOUNT PLEASANT
CRAYTHORNE HO

GREEN
HEDGES
GOLDEN SQ

TENTERDEN

8

EAST HILL

B2067

Pigeon
Hoo

ROGERSMEAD
STEVENS
COTTS
STATION RD
COOMBE LA
PITTLESDEN DR

Tenterden
Town

B2067 OAKS RD

ORCHARD
VIEW

SHRUBCOTE

Finchden
Manor

7

Mus
PO

TH

Liby
Bell's
CL

Tenterden
CE Jun
Sch

Huson
Farm

SUTTON FIELD RD

SHRUBCOTE

THE BUNGALOWS

A P P L E D O R E   R D

Maynards

33

Superstore

CHERRY
ORCH

Tenterden
Inf Sch

L Ctr

Belgar

TILDEN GILL

COLLISON PL
WILLIAM JUDGE CL

Leigh Green
Ind Est

Leigh
Green

6

Heronden

GROVE
COTTS

Belcot Manor
Farm

Forstal
Farm

Gibbet Oak
Farm

B2080

Tilder Gill

Haynes
Farm

Kench
Hill

5

Morghew

Ratsbury

TN30

Setts Wood
Farm

32

The
Quarter

Pick Hill
Farm

PICKHILL
OAST

Finchbourne
Wood

4

Broad
Tenterden

SMALL HYTHE RD

Ashenden

Coneyboro'
Wood

3

Hongland

Summer
Hill

Old Gate
Cottage

DUMBOURNE LA

Dumbourne

Great Hanging
Wood

31

Reading Sewer

2

Tenterden
Vineyard

Small
Hythe

1

Great
Bulleigh

Spots
House

B2082

Bulleigh
Barn

Smallhythe
Place
(Mus)

30

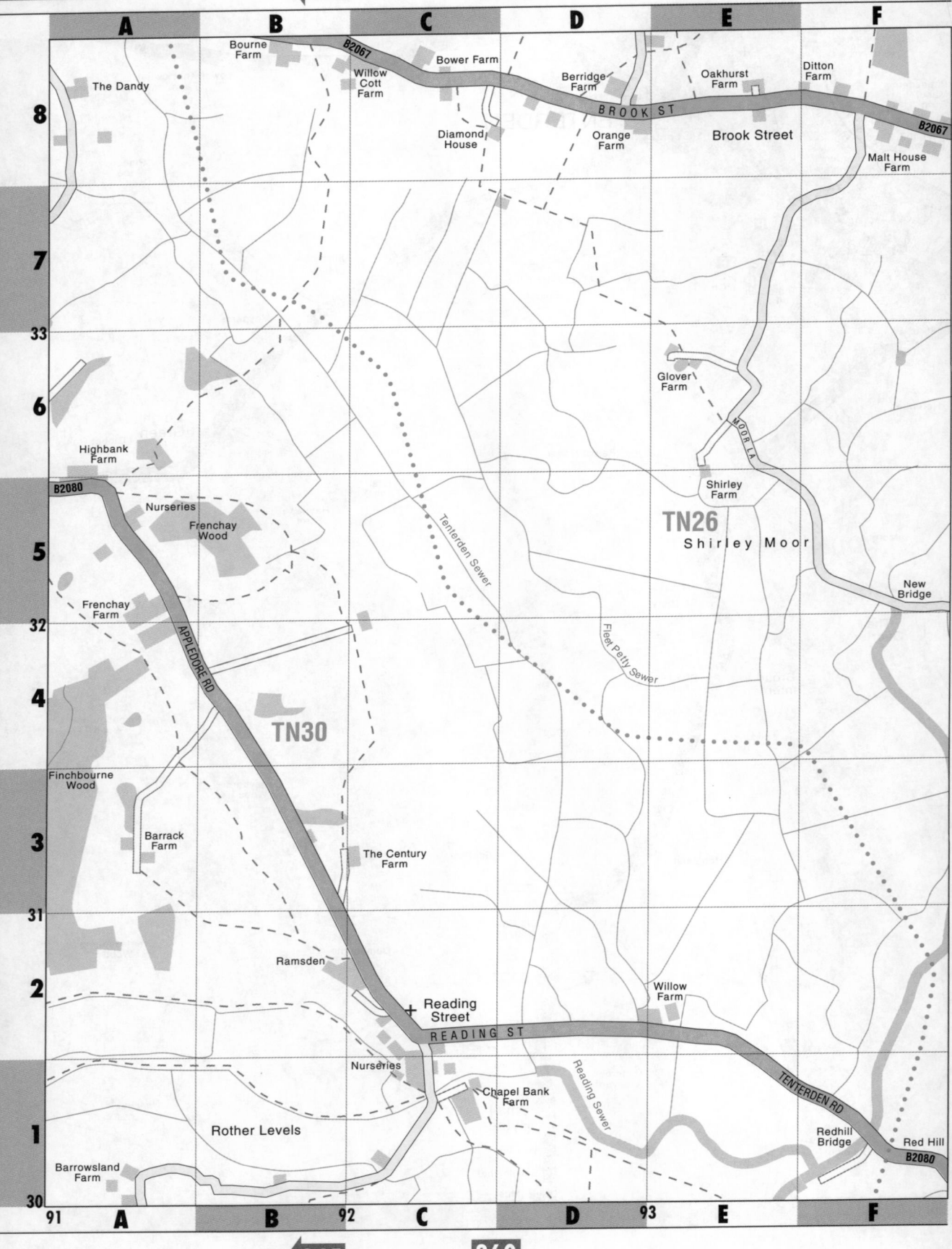

A   B   C   D   E   F

8

7

33

6

32

5

4

3

31

2

1

30

91   A   B   92   C   D   93   E   F

The Dandy

Bourne Farm

Willow Cott Farm

B2067

Bower Farm

Berridge Farm

Oakhurst Farm

Ditton Farm

BROOK ST

Brook Street

B2067

Diamond House

Orange Farm

Malt House Farm

Glover Farm

MOOR LA

Shirley Farm

TN26

Shirley Moor

Highbank Farm

B2080

Nurseries

Frenchay Wood

New Bridge

Frenchay Farm

APPLEDORE RD

Tenterden Sewer

Fleet Petty Sewer

TN30

Finchbourne Wood

Barrack Farm

The Century Farm

Ramsden

Reading Street

READING ST

Willow Farm

Reading Sewer

TENTERDEN RD

Nurseries

Chapel Bank Farm

Rother Levels

Redhill Bridge

Red Hill

B2080

Barrowsland Farm

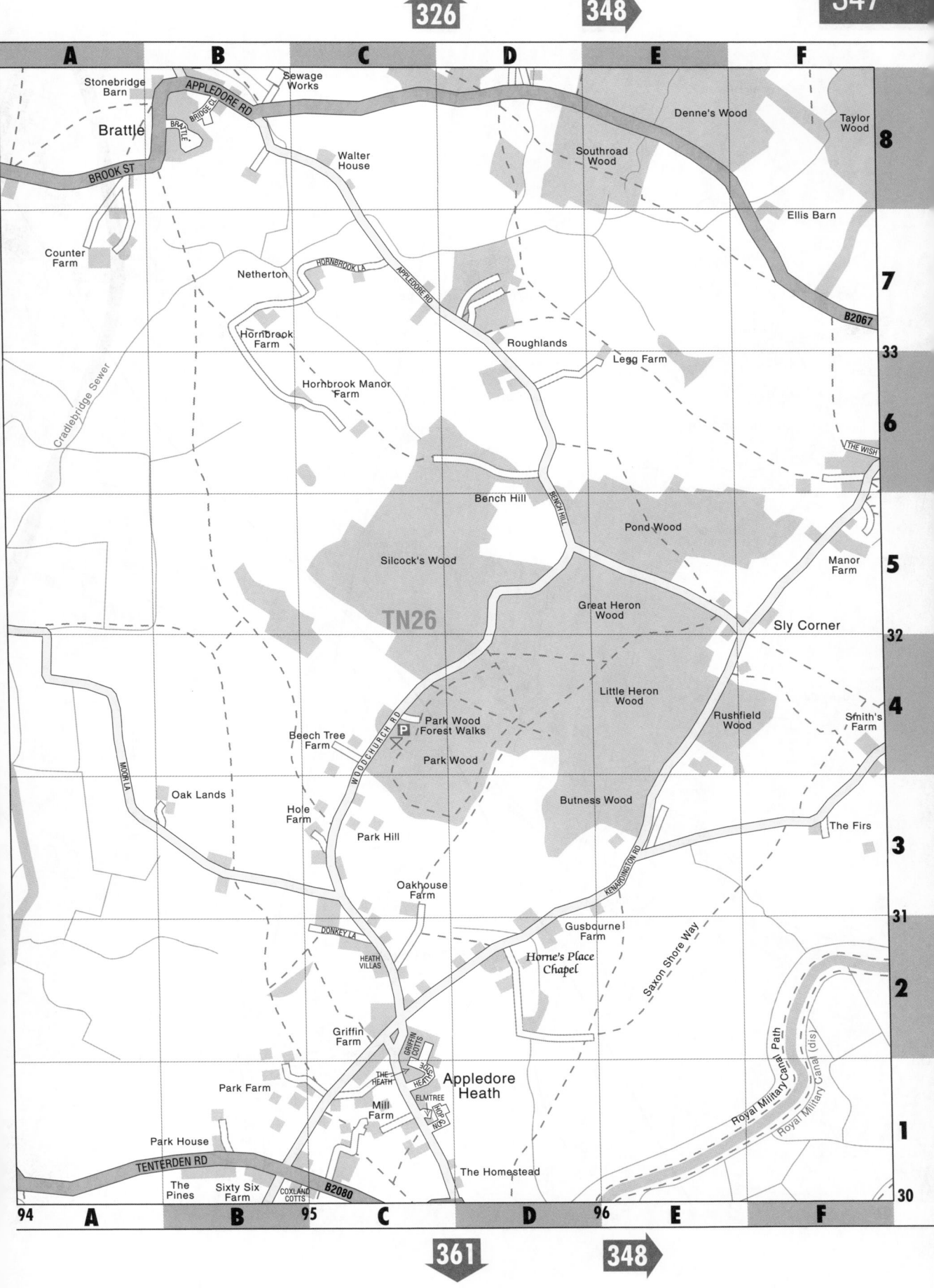

326
348

Stonebridge Barn
Sewage Works
APPLEDORE RD
Brattle
BRIDGE CL
BRATTLE
BROOK ST
Walter House
Denne's Wood
Southroad Wood
Taylor Wood

8

Counter Farm
Netherton
HORNBROOK LA
APPLEDORE RD
Ellis Barn

7

Hornbrook Farm
Roughlands
Legg Farm
B2067

33

Hornbrook Manor Farm
Cradlebridge Sewer
THE WISH

6

Bench Hill
BENCH HILL
Pond Wood
Manor Farm

Silcock's Wood
Great Heron Wood
Sly Corner
5

TN26
32

Little Heron Wood
Rushfield Wood
Smith's Farm
4

Beech Tree Farm
WOODCHURCH RD
Park Wood Forest Walks
P
Park Wood
Butness Wood
The Firs

Oak Lands
MOOR LA
Hole Farm
Park Hill
3

Oakhouse Farm
KENARDINGTON RD
Gusbourne Farm
31

DONKEY LA
HEATH VILLAS
Horne's Place Chapel
Saxon Shore Way
2

Griffin Farm
GRIFFIN COTTS
THE HEATH
HEATH
Appledore Heath
Royal Military Canal Path
Royal Military Canal (dis)

Park Farm
ELMTREE
Mill Farm
BUS STN

1

Park House
TENTERDEN RD
The Pines
Sixty Six Farm
COXLAND COTTS
B2080
The Homestead

30

94   A   B   95   C   D   96   E   F

361
348

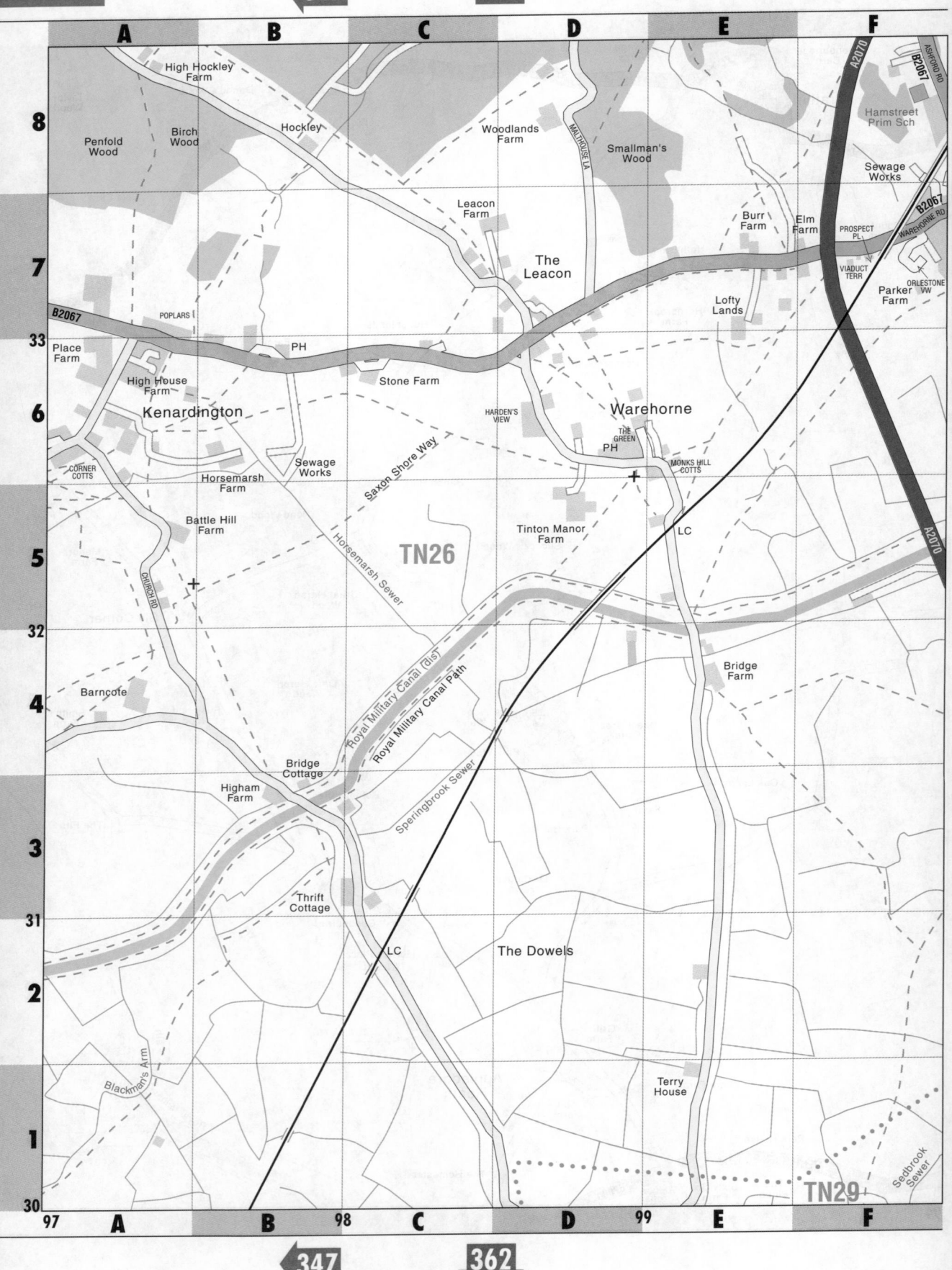

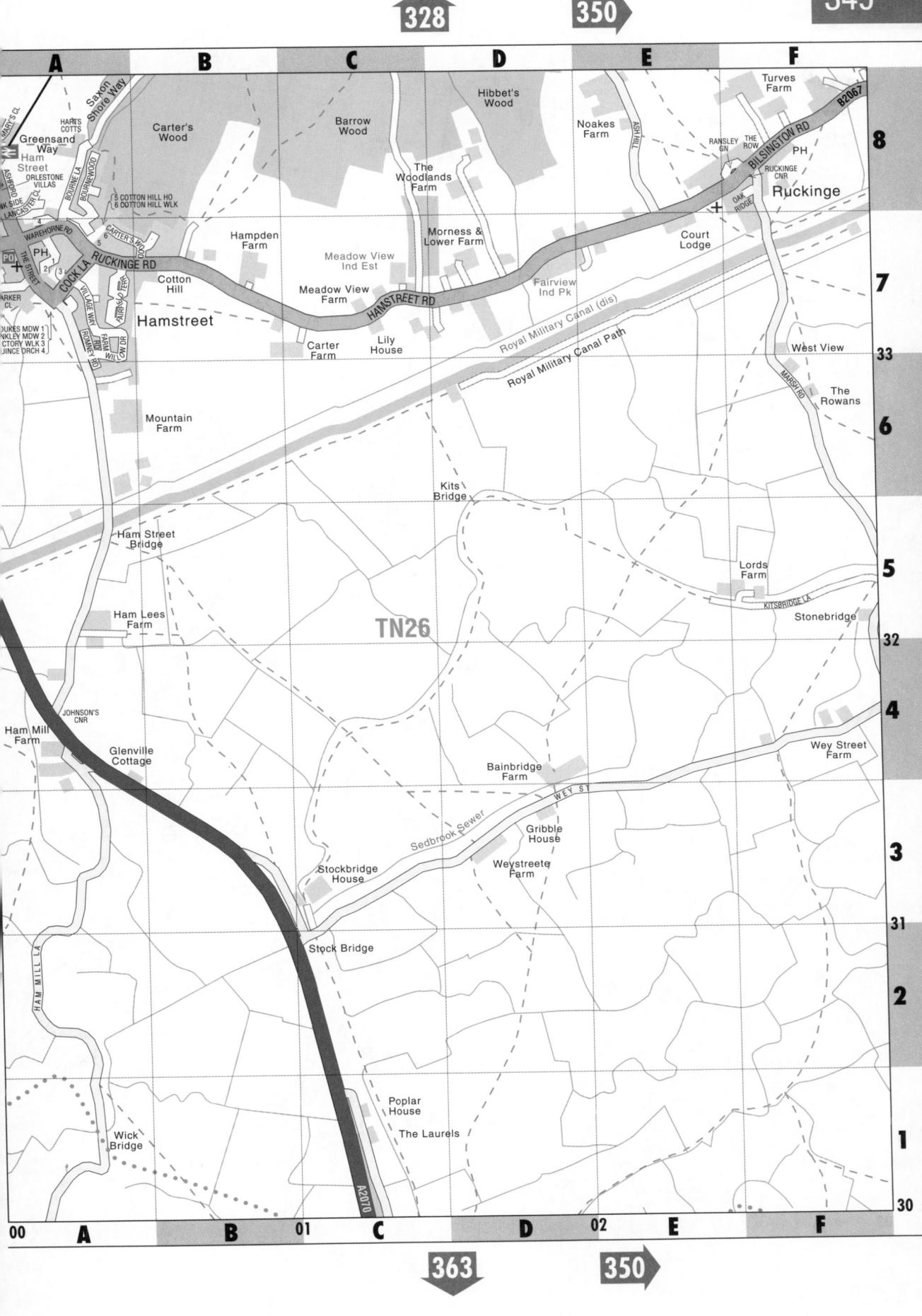

349
329

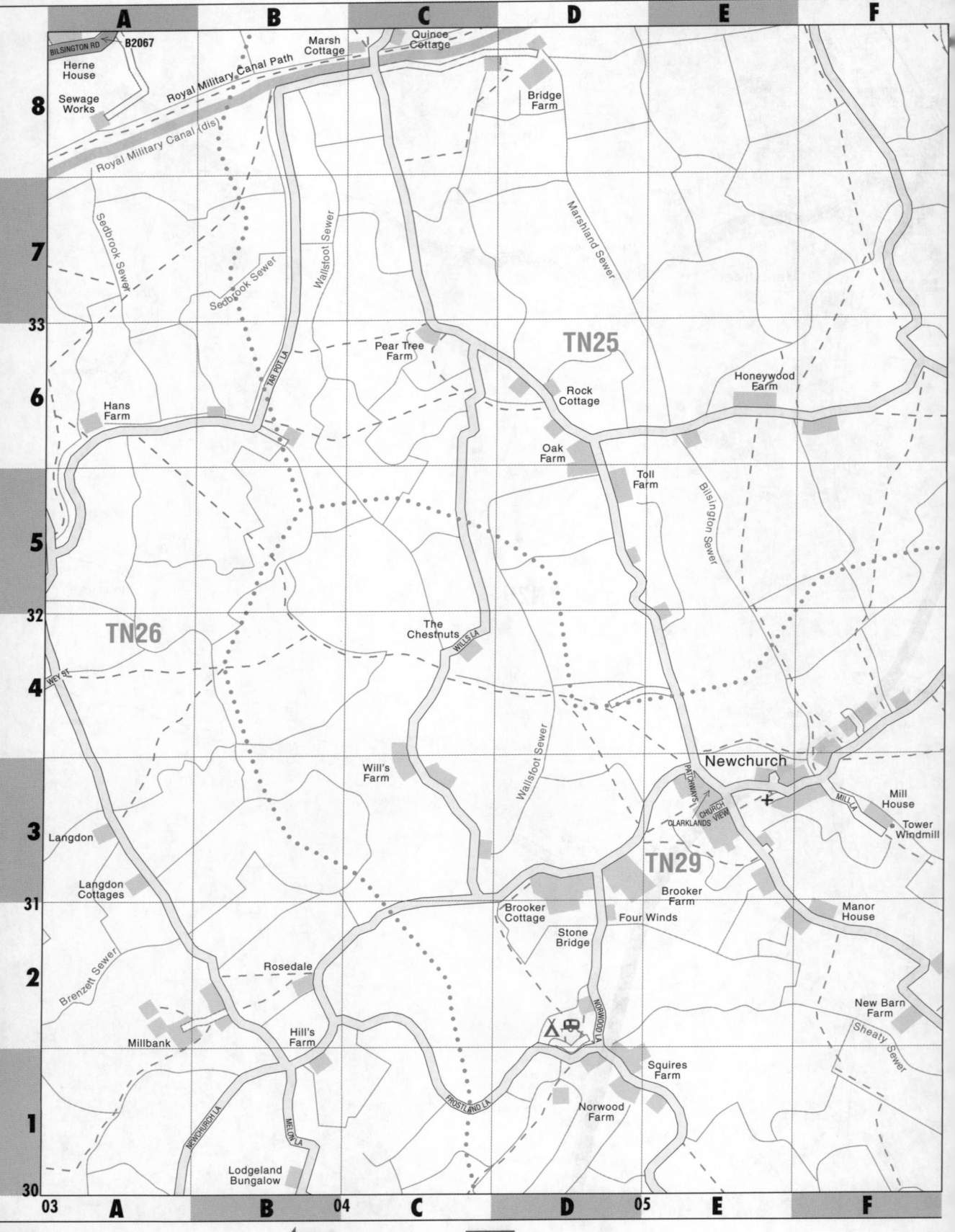

349
364

BILSINGTON RD
B2067
Herne House
Sewage Works
Royal Military Canal Path
Royal Military Canal (dis)
Marsh Cottage
Quince Cottage
Bridge Farm
Sedbrook Sewer
Sedbrook Sewer
Wallstoot Sewer
Marshland Sewer
TN25
Pear Tree Farm
Rock Cottage
Honeywood Farm
Hans Farm
Oak Farm
Toll Farm
Bilsington Sewer
TN26
The Chestnuts
WILLS LA
Will's Farm
Wallsfoot Sewer
Newchurch
Mill House
MILL LA
Tower Windmill
WEY ST
Langdon
Langdon Cottages
Brenzett Sewer
Brooker Farm
PATCHWAYS
CHURCH VIEW
CLARKLANDS
TN29
Manor House
Rosedale
Brooker Cottage
Stone Bridge
Four Winds
Millbank
Hill's Farm
New Barn Farm
Sheaty Sewer
NEWCHURCH LA
MELON LA
FROSTLAND LA
NORWOOD LA
Squires Farm
Norwood Farm
Lodgeland Bungalow

03 04 05

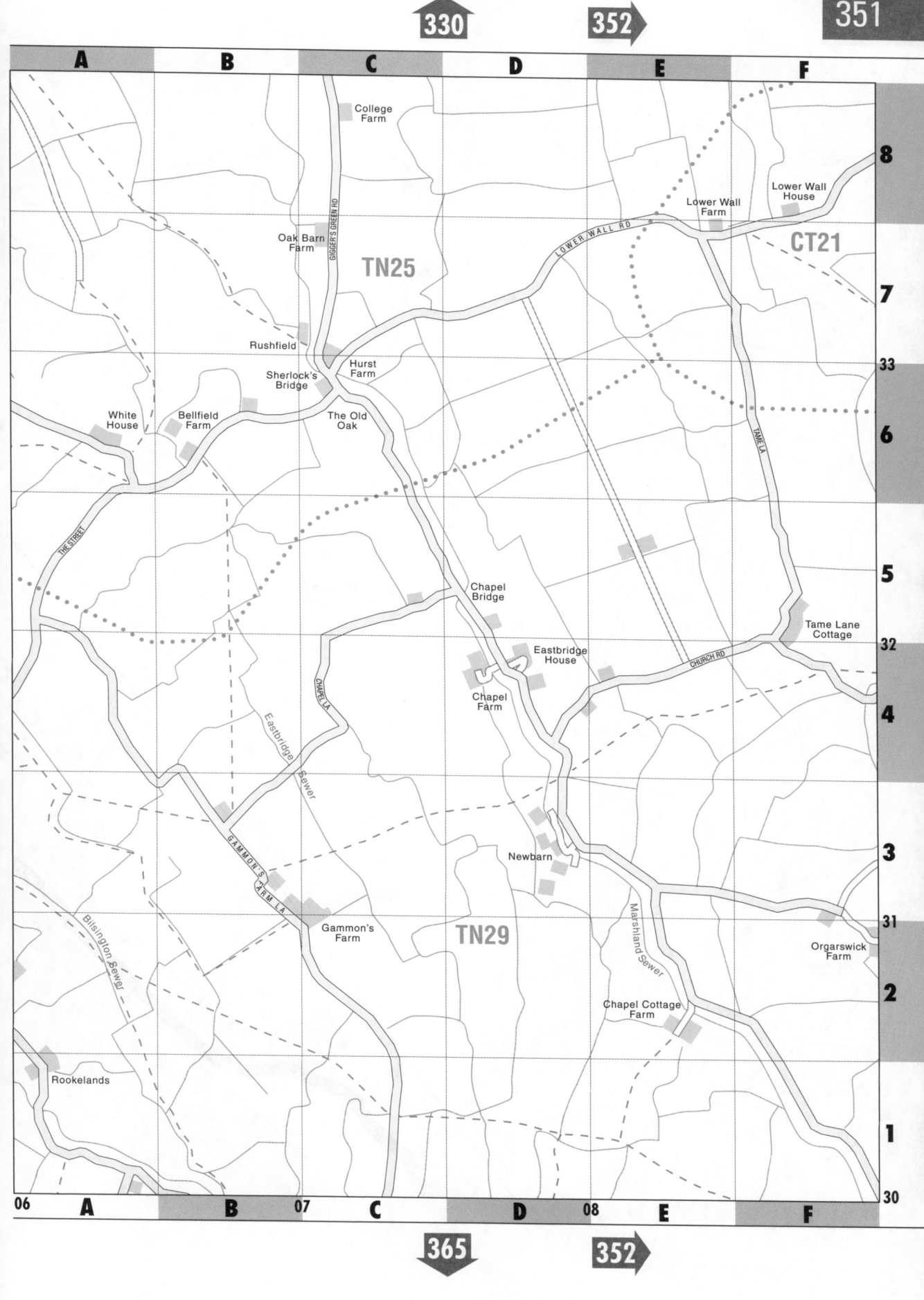

351
331

A B C D E F

8

7

33

6

32

5

4

3

31

2

1

30

09 A B 10 C D 11 E F

Tontine Farm

ALDERGATE LA

Willop Sewer (Selby Arm)

LOWER WALL RD

Selby Farm

Hoorne's Sewer

CT21

Lone Barn

Abbott's Court

Abbott's Court Cottages

SHEAR WAY

DONKEY ST

The Little Piece

Willop Sewer

Eaton Farm

Lathe Barn

Donkey Street

Hoorne's Sewer

Hoorne's Sewer

PH

Burmarsh

Forty Acre Farm

CHURCH RD

THE GREEN

PAINESFIELD CL

THORNDIKE RD

Sewage Works

Baronet Bridge

TN29

Orgarswick Farm

Hazelhurst

BURMARSH RD

Haguelands Farm

Romney, Hythe & Dymchurch Rly

Willop Basin

MARINE AVE

WILLOP WAY

WILLOP CL

A259

Hoorne's Sewer

31

LC

CROSSWAYS CL

GREEN MDWS

QUEENSWAY

QUEENSWAY

KINGSWAY

LOWER SANDS

LOWER SANDS

TOWER EST

ASPEN RD

HYTHE RD

Martello Tower

Dymchurch

TRY'N CTN GDNS

TUDOR AVE

VENTURE CL

PEAR TREE

SEA WALL

LC

WRAIGHTSFIELD AVE

THE OVAL

A259

351
366

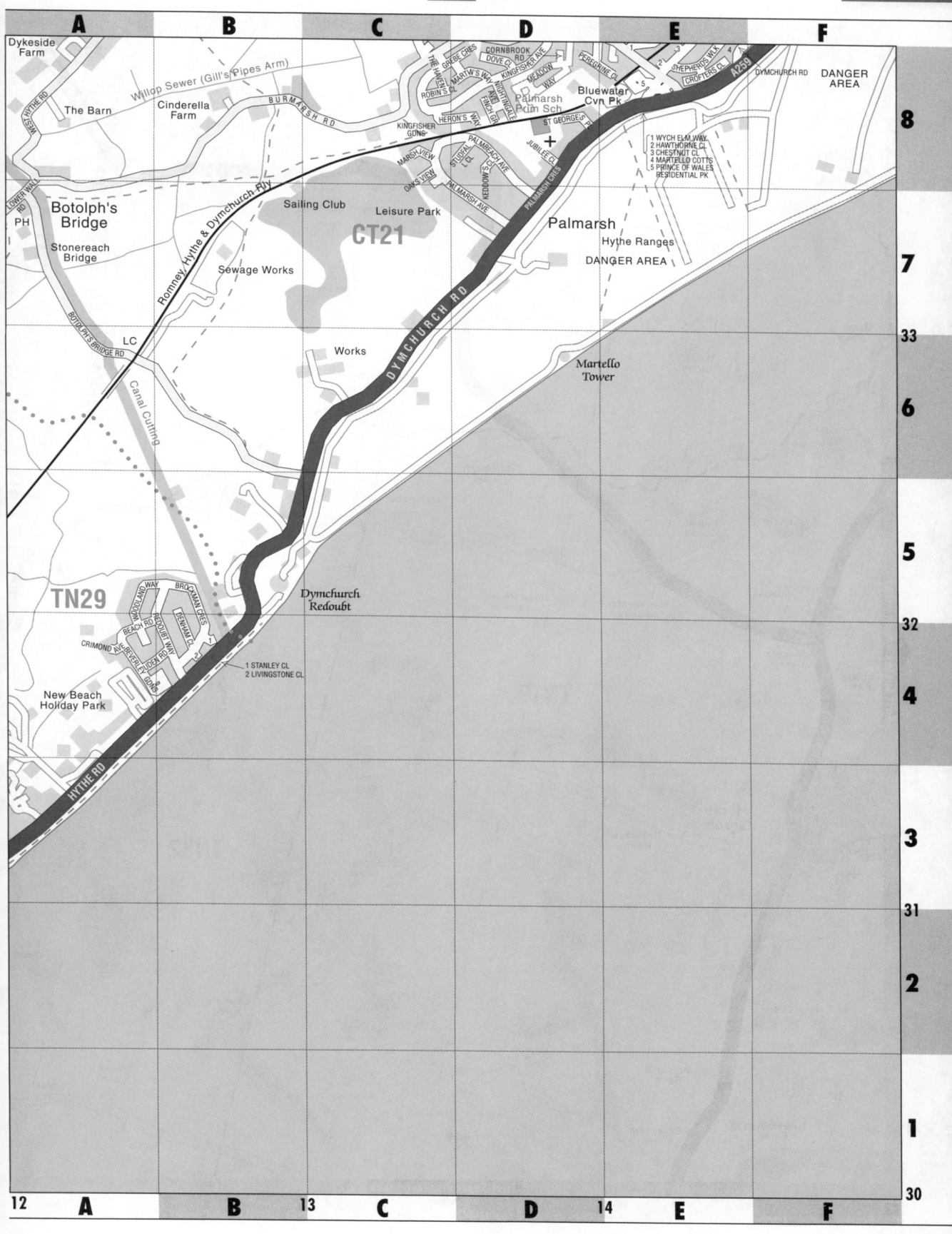

A   B   C   D   E   F

Dykeside
Farm

Willop Sewer (Gill's Pipes Arm)

CORNBROOK
RD
DOVE CL
GREBE CRES
KINGFISHER AVE
MEADOW
WAY
PEREGRINE CL

The Barn

Cinderella
Farm

BURMARSH RD

ROBIN'S CL
MARTW'S WAY
NIGHTINGALE
FINCH GR

Palmarsh
Prim Sch

Bluewater
Cvn Pk

SHEPHERDS WLK
CROFTERS CL

DYMCHURCH RD

DANGER
AREA

8

WEST HYTHE RD
HYTHE RD

KINGFISHER
GDNS

MARSH VIEW

OAKS VIEW

STUDD L CL
PALMBEACH AVE
KEDDOW'S CL

JUBILEE CL

St GEORGE'S

A259

1 WYCH ELM WAY
2 HAWTHORNE CL
3 CHESTNUT CL
4 MARTELLO COTTS
5 PRINCE OF WALES
  RESIDENTIAL PK

LOWER WALL RD
PH

Botolph's
Bridge

Sailing Club

Leisure Park

CT21

Romney, Hythe & Dymchurch Rly

PALMARSH AVE

Palmarsh

Hythe Ranges

DANGER AREA

7

Stonereach
Bridge

Sewage Works

PALMARSH CRES

BOTOLPH'S BRIDGE RD

LC

Canal Cutting

Works

DYMCHURCH RD

Martello
Tower

33

6

TN29

WOODLAND WAY
BROCKMAN CRES
BEACH RD
REDOUBT WAY
FENHAM CL

Dymchurch
Redoubt

32

5

CRIMOND AVE
BEVERLEY GDNS
PLUDEN RD

1 STANLEY CL
2 LIVINGSTONE CL

4

New Beach
Holiday Park

HYTHE RD

31

3

2

1

30

12   A   B   13   C   D   14   E   F

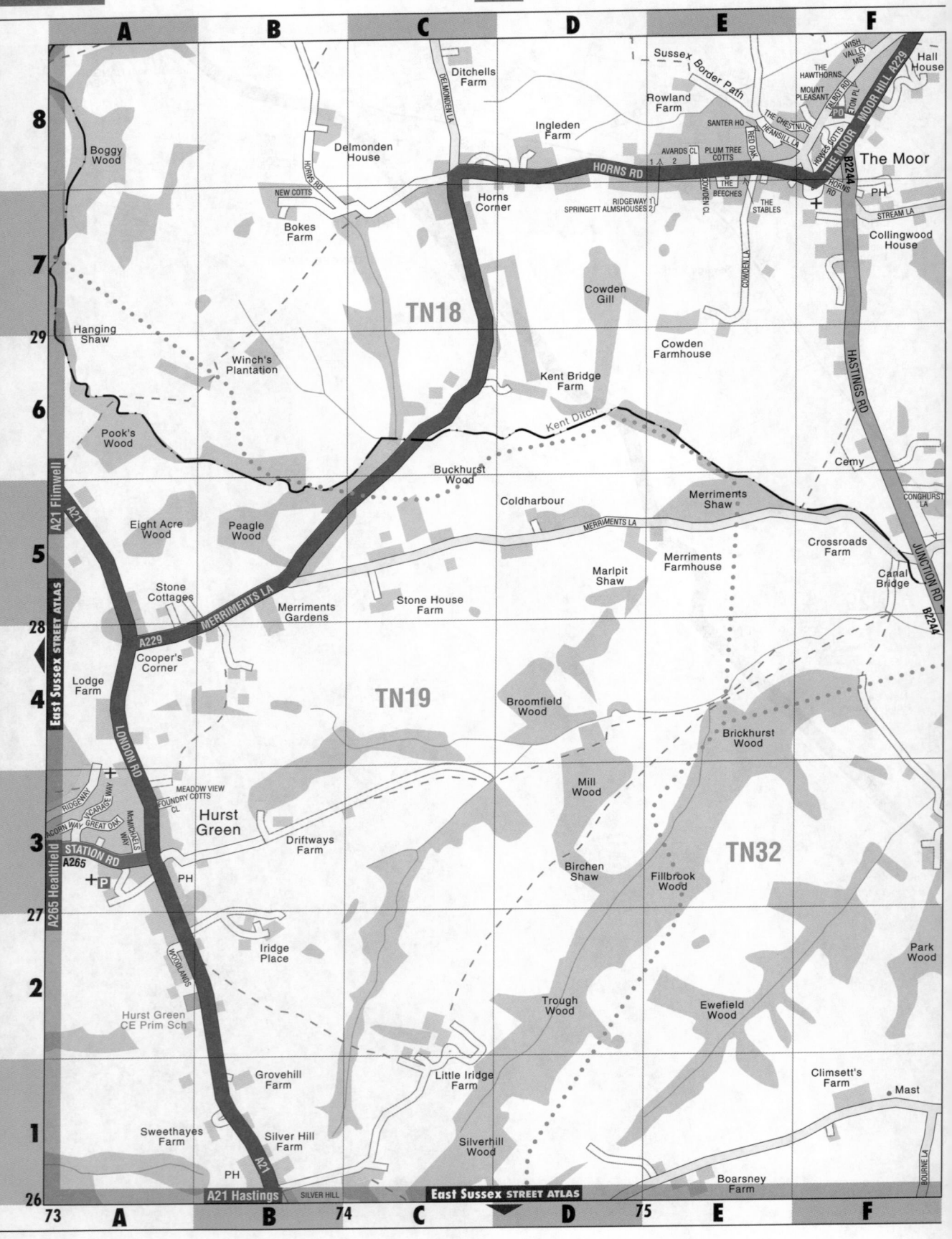

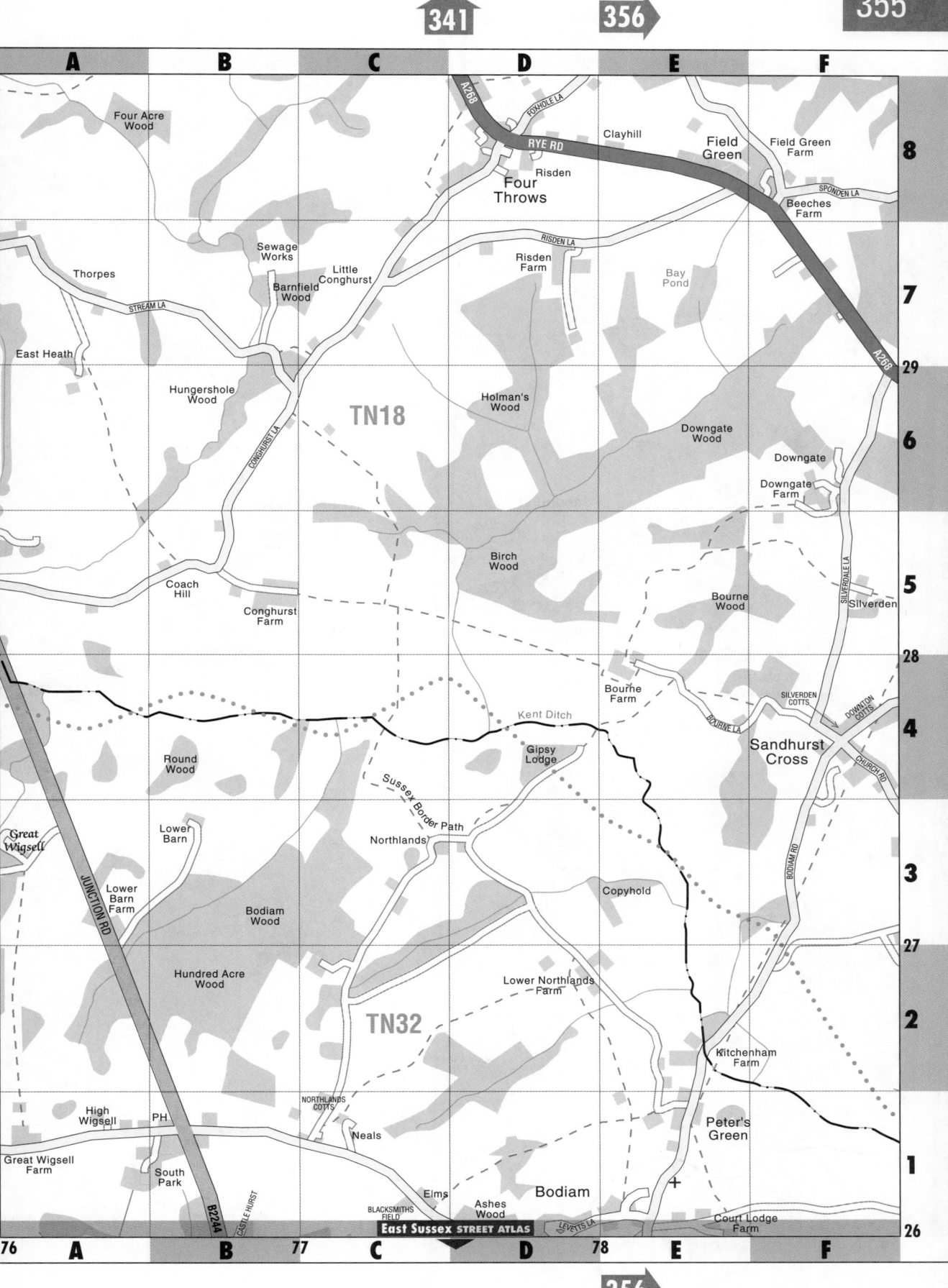

355
342

A **B** **C** **D** **E** **F**

8

Standen
Street

SPONDEN LA

Sponden
House

STANDEN ST

TN17

Hope House
Farmhouse

7

Sponden
Farmhouse

SPONDEN LA

Alderden
Manor

Reynolds
Farm

HOPEHOUSE LA

Orchard
Farm

Lords
Wood

Hopemill
Bridge

29

A268

MEGRIMS HILL

Sewage
Works

6

Malthouse
Farm

ANGEL
TERR BROOKFIELD
ANGEL
ROW

STREAM
PIT LA
PRINGFIELD RD

QUEEN ST
PH

Sandhurst

THE ROPE WLK

Sandhurst
Prim Sch

Puxtye

CROUCH LA

Hoad's
Farm

Sandhurst
Vineyards

STONE PIT LA

LOMAS LA

Lomas

OLD ORCHARD

BACK RD
PO

OAKS LONSTAL

Burnt Farm
House

BURNT HOUSE
RINGLE
GN

Sandhurst
Farm

Scurms
Farm

LINKDEN
COTTS

5

BIDJAM RD

Brickhouse
Farmhouse

Burnt Farm
House

28

TN18

Boxhurst
Farm

Linkhill

Hollowdene

TWYSDEN
COTTS
1
2

SANDHURST CL

Castlegate
Farm

4

1 BETHERINDEN COTTS
2 FORGEFIELD COTTS

Burnt House
Farm

Boxhurst

ETHNAM LA

Glassocks

CHURCH RD

Barnfield
Shaw

MARSH QUARTER LA

Little
Boxhurst

Ethnam Farm
Bungalow

3

Old Sandhurst
Place

Twisden
Plantation

Cledge
Wood

Great
Ethnam Farm

Ethnam

27

Old Place
Farm

2

Marsh Quarter
Farm

River Rother

1

Kent Ditch

Kent & East Sussex Rly

TN32

Dyneshill
Wood

26

79 **A** **B** **80** **C** **D** **81** **E** **F**

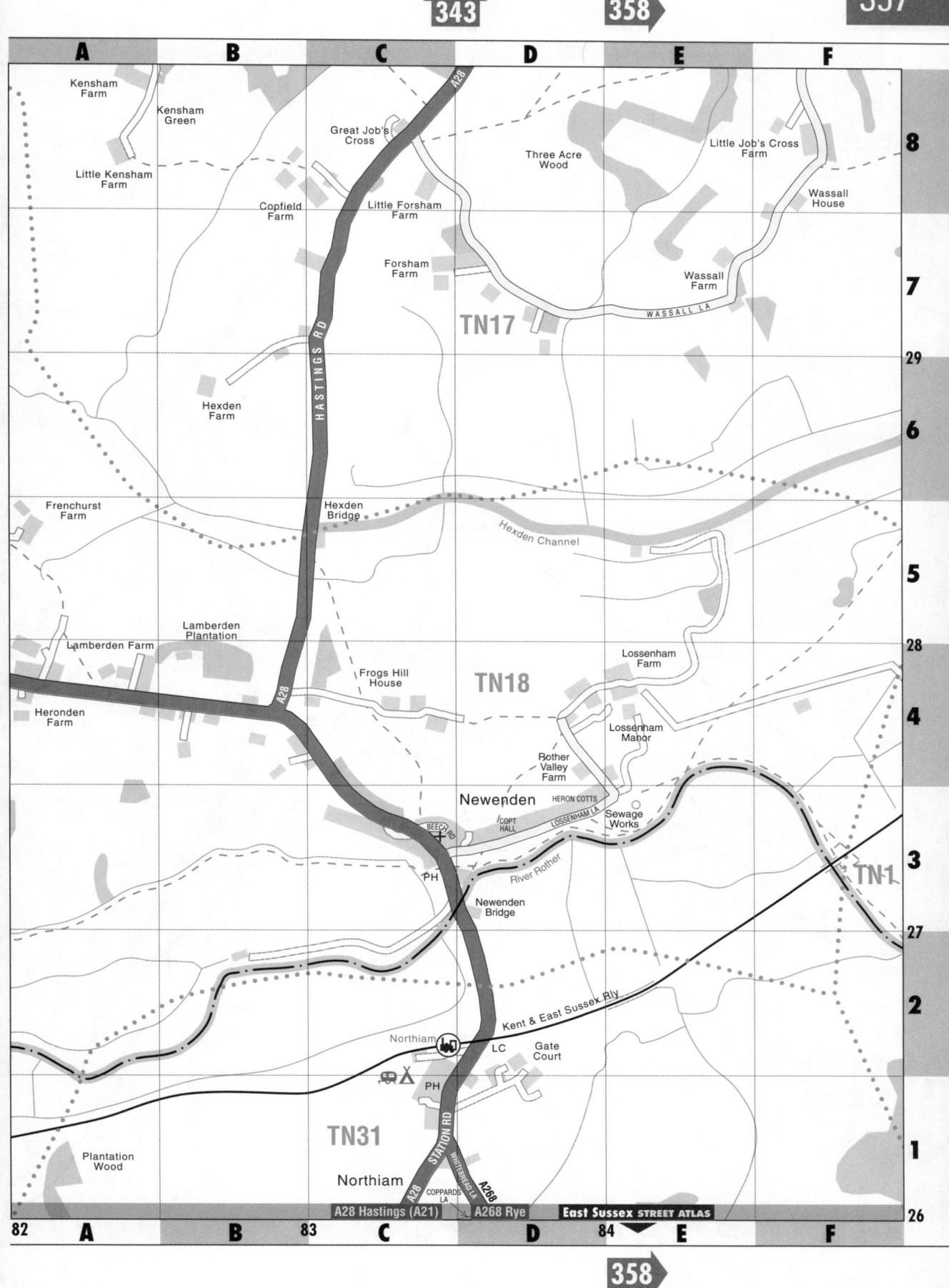

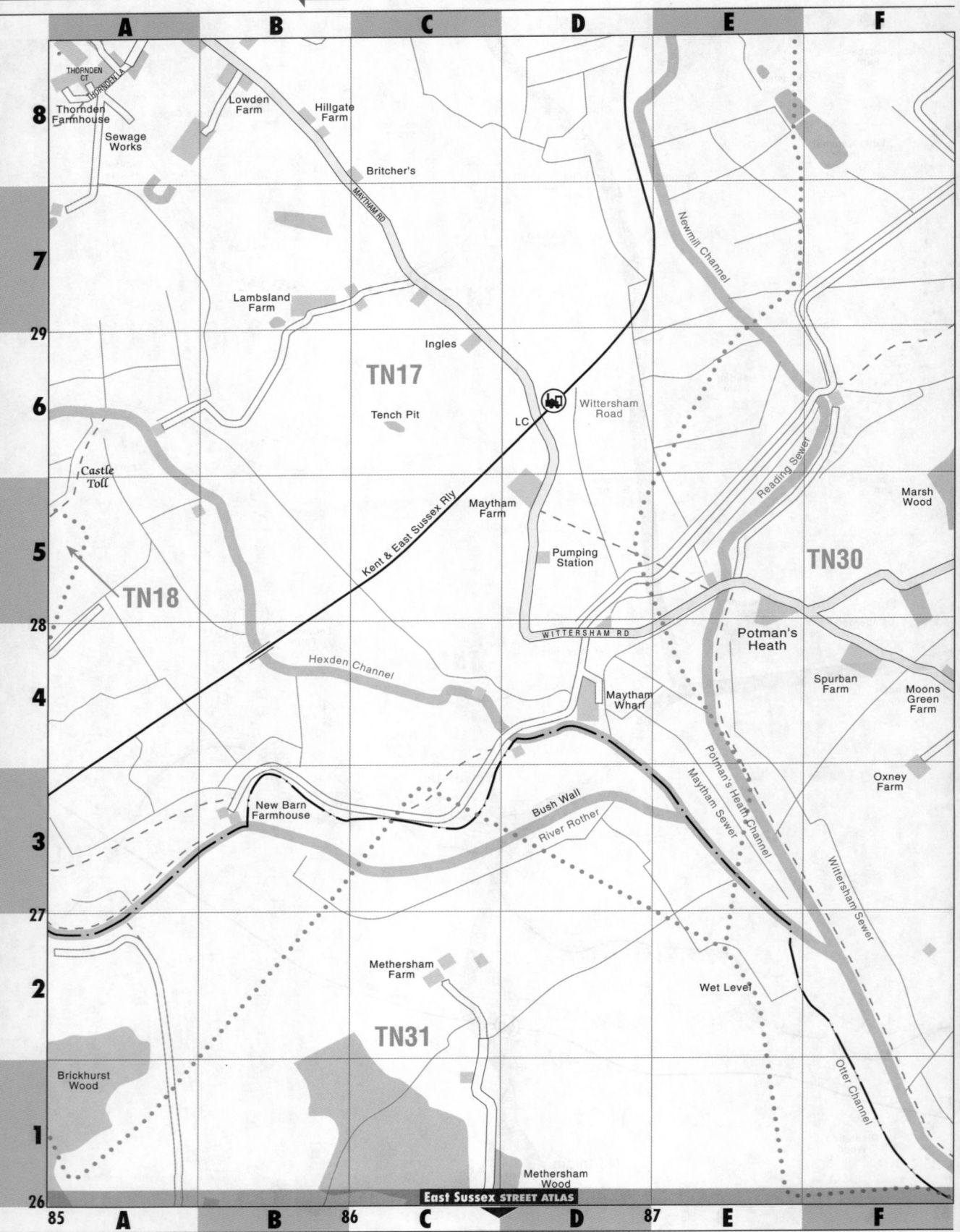

A   B   C   D   E   F

THORNDEN
CT
THORNDEN LA
Thornden
Farmhouse
Sewage
Works

Lowden
Farm
Hillgate
Farm

Britcher's

MAYTHAM RD

8

Lambsland
Farm

7

29

Ingles

TN17

6

Tench Pit

LC

Wittersham
Road

Newmill Channel

Reading Sewer

Marsh
Wood

Castle
Toll

Kent & East Sussex Rly

Maytham
Farm

TN30

5

TN18

Pumping
Station

28

Potman's
Heath

Hexden Channel

WITTERSHAM RD

Spurban
Farm

Moons
Green
Farm

4

Maytham
Wharf

Potman's Heath Channel

Maytham Sewer

Oxney
Farm

New Barn
Farmhouse

Bush Wall

River Rother

Wittersham Sewer

3

27

Methersham
Farm

Wet Level

2

TN31

Brickhurst
Wood

Otter Channel

1

Methersham
Wood

26

85   A   B   86   C   D   87   E   F

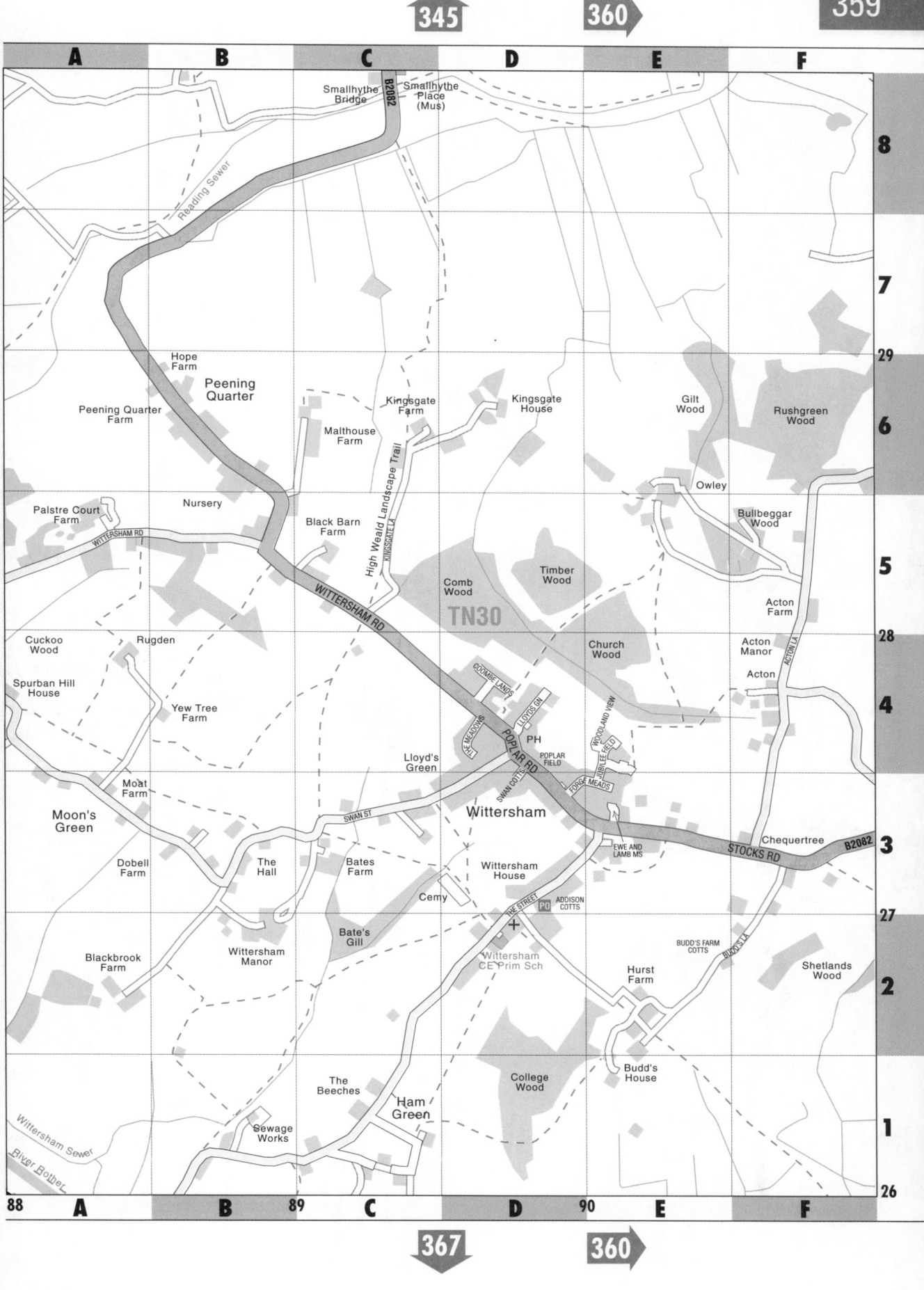

8

7

29

6

5

28

4

3

27

2

1

26

Smallhythe
Bridge
B2082
Smallhythe
Place
(Mus)

Reading Sewer

Hope
Farm

Peening
Quarter

Peening Quarter
Farm

Malthouse
Farm

Kingsgate
Farm

Kingsgate
House

Gilt
Wood

Rushgreen
Wood

High Weald Landscape Trail

KINGSGATE LA

Nursery

Owley

Bullbeggar
Wood

Palstre Court
Farm

WITTERSHAM RD

Black Barn
Farm

Comb
Wood

Timber
Wood

Acton
Farm

WITTERSHAM RD

TN30

Church
Wood

Acton
Manor

Acton

ACTON LA

Cuckoo
Wood

Rugden

Yew Tree
Farm

COOMBE LANDS

THE MEADOWS

LLOYDS GN

POPLAR RD

PH

POPLAR
FIELD

WOODLAND VIEW

JUBILEE FIELD

Spurban Hill
House

Lloyd's
Green

SWAN COTTS

FORGE MEADS

Moat
Farm

SWAN ST

Wittersham

EWE AND
LAMB MS

Chequertree

STOCKS RD

B2082

Moon's
Green

Dobell
Farm

The
Hall

Bates
Farm

Wittersham
House

Cemy

THE STREET

ADDISON
COTTS

P.O.

BUDD'S FARM
COTTS

BUDD'S LA

Shetlands
Wood

Blackbrook
Farm

Wittersham
Manor

Bate's
Gill

Wittersham
CE Prim Sch

Hurst
Farm

The
Beeches

College
Wood

Budd's
House

Ham
Green

Sewage
Works

Wittersham Sewer

River Rother

	A	B	C	D	E	F

TN26

8 High House Farm

Hayes Farm

Ramsden Farm

7

29 Stone Corner Farm

EBONY COTTS STONE CNR

HOGPOUND CNR

6 Whole Farm

Little Odiam Farm

LOWER RD

Chapel Bank

Saxon Shore Way

Reading Sewer

5 Stemp's Wood

Rosehill Farmhouse

RISE HILL

Odiam Farm

Stone Farm

Luckhurst

28 **TN30**

4 Green Acres

Maynes Farm

Isle of Oxney

Twelve Acre Wood

Curteis Wood

Luckhurst Wood

Catt Farm

Stone-in-Oxney

PH

STONE GN

FORGE MDW

THE STREET

The Stocks

Wr Twr

Lord's Wood

Scrub's Wood

CATT'S HILL

CATT'S HILL

3 STOCKS RD

Stocks Farm

WITTERSHAM RD

Four Acre Wood

QUARRY COTTS

WADDLE CNR

WATTLE CNR

TOP RD

Huggit's Farm

CHURCH HILL

Stocks Mill Windmill

Holman's Farm

27 Prospect House

Oxenden

Little Prawls Farm

KNOCK HILL

2 Tophill Farm

RYE RD

Rook Wood

Great Prawls Farm

Tighe Farm

Saxon Shore Way

Cliff Farm

1 Underhill Farmhouse

Rother Levels

Stone Cliff

26

| 91 | A | B | 92 | C | D | 93 | E | F |

B2082

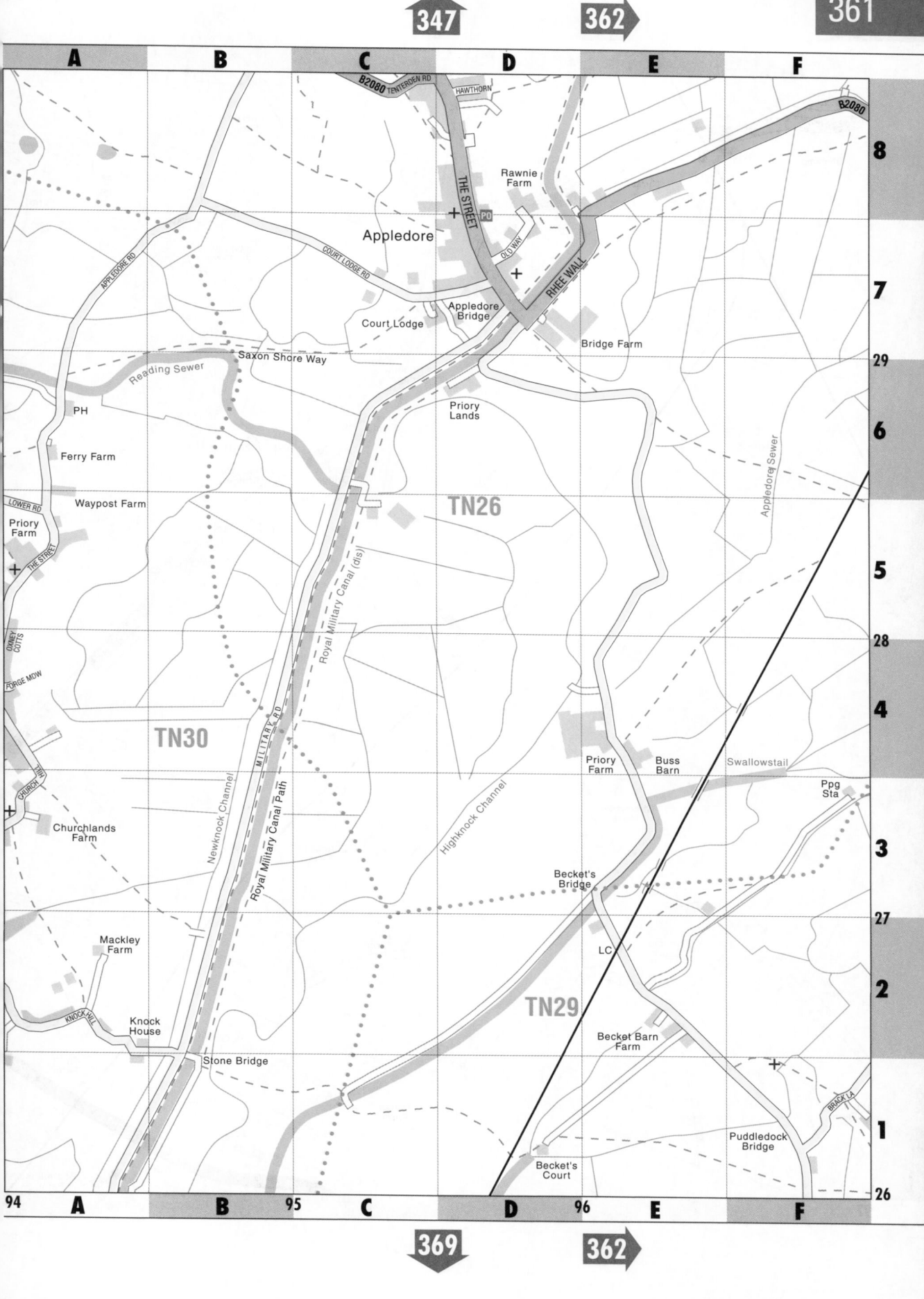

A | B | C | D | E | F

B2080 TENTERDEN RD

HAWTHORN

Rawnie
Farm

THE STREET

PO

Appledore

OLD WAY

RHEE WALK

B2080

8

APPLEDORE RD

COURT LODGE RD

Court Lodge

Appledore
Bridge

Bridge Farm

7

29

Saxon Shore Way

Reading Sewer

PH

Priory
Lands

Appledore Sewer

6

Ferry Farm

LOWER RD

Waypost Farm

TN26

Priory
Farm

THE STREET

5

ODNEY
COTTS

28

FORGE MDW

4

TN30

MILITARY RD

Royal Military Canal (dis)

Priory
Farm

Buss
Barn

Swallowstail

Ppg
Sta

CHURCH HILL

Churchlands
Farm

Newknock Channel

Royal Military Canal Path

Highknock Channel

Becket's
Bridge

3

Mackley
Farm

LC

27

KNOCK HILL

Knock
House

TN29

2

Becket Barn
Farm

BRACK LA

Stone Bridge

Puddledock
Bridge

1

Becket's
Court

26

94 | A | B | 95 | C | D | 96 | E | F

361
348

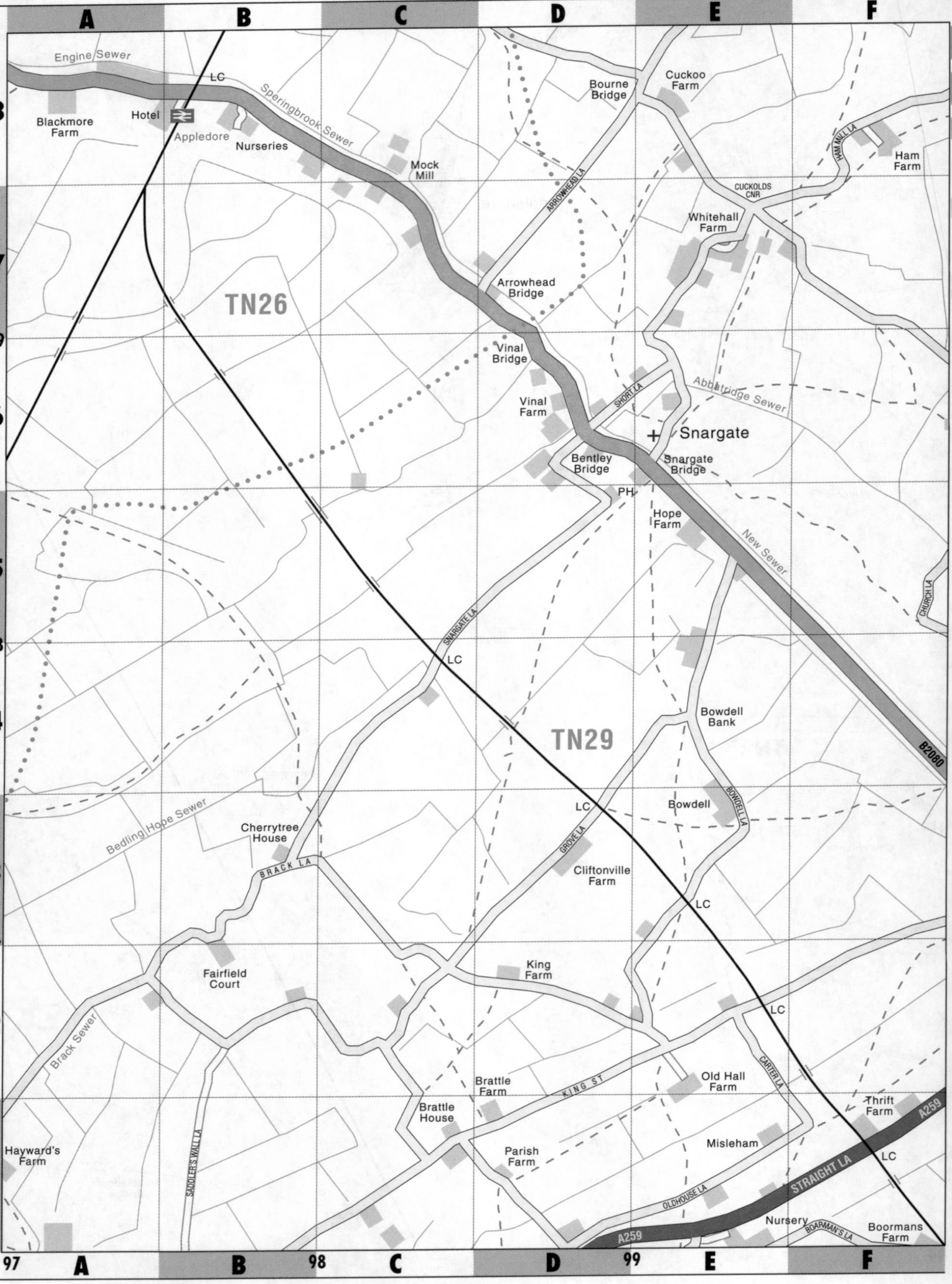

A B C D E F

8
7
29
6
5
28
4
27
3
2
1
26

Engine Sewer
LC
Speringbrook Sewer
Hotel
Appledore
Blackmore Farm
Nurseries
Mock Mill
Bourne Bridge
Cuckoo Farm
HAM MILL LA
Ham Farm
CUCKOLDS CNR
ARROWHEAD LA
Whitehall Farm
TN26
Arrowhead Bridge
Vinal Bridge
Vinal Farm
SHORT LA
Abbotridge Sewer
Bentley Bridge
Snargate
Snargate Bridge
PH
Hope Farm
New Sewer
Bedling Hope Sewer
Cherrytree House
BRACK LA
LC
SNARGATE LA
TN29
Bowdell Bank
Bowdell
BOWDELL LA
LC
Fairfield Court
Brack Sewer
SADDLER'S WALL LA
Cliftonville Farm
LC
GROVE LA
LC
King Farm
Brattle Farm
Brattle House
KING ST
Old Hall Farm
CARTER LA
Thrift Farm
A259
B2080
CHURCH LA
Hayward's Farm
Parish Farm
Misleham
LC
OLDHOUSE LA
STRAIGHT LA
A259
Nursery
BOARMAN'S LA
Boormans Farm

97 98 99

A B C D E F

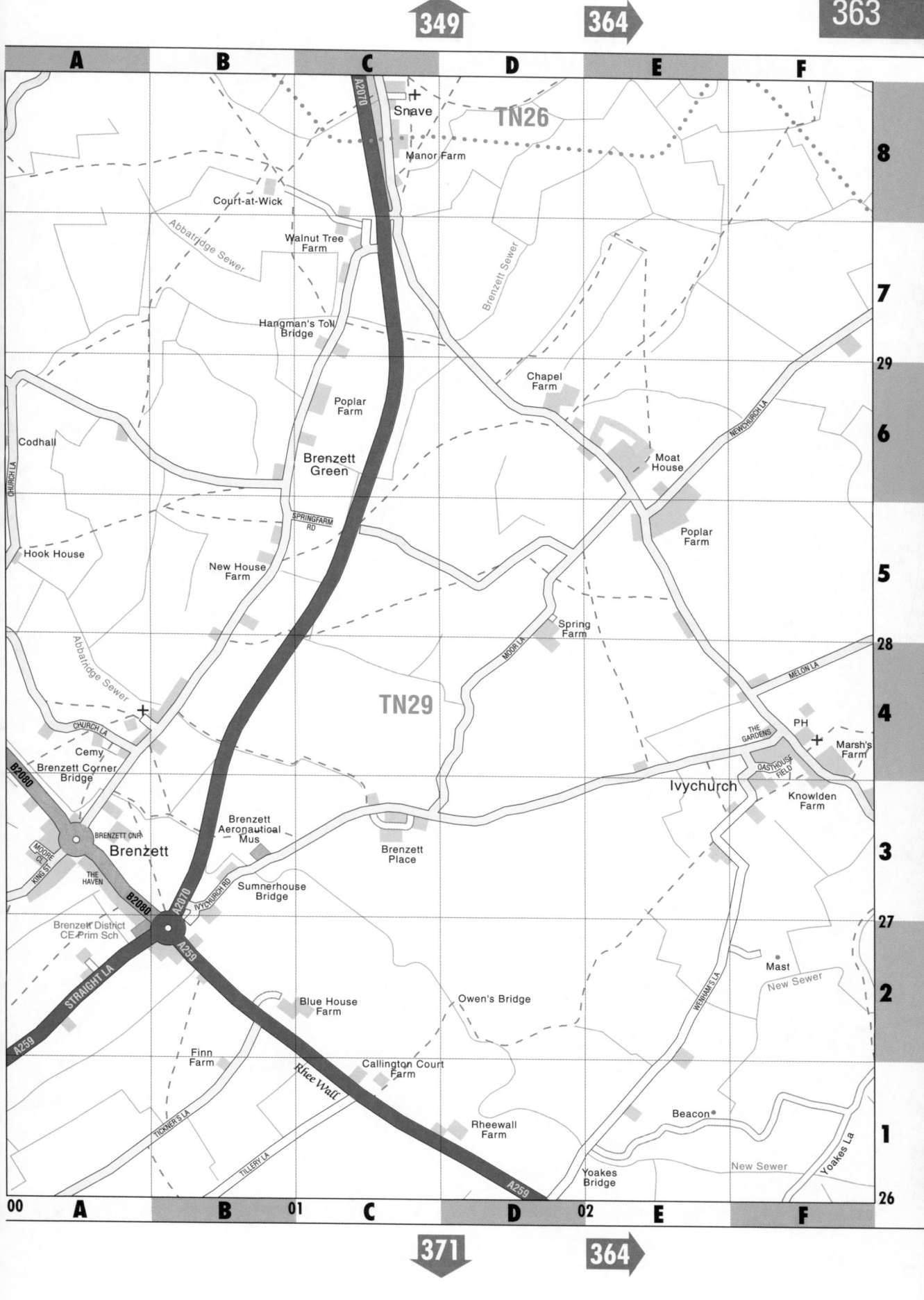
TN26

Snave

Manor Farm

Court-at-Wick

Abbatridge Sewer

Walnut Tree
Farm

Hangman's Toll
Bridge

Brenzett Sewer

Chapel
Farm

Poplar
Farm

Codhall

Brenzett
Green

Moat
House

NEWCHURCH LA

Hook House

SPRINGFARM
RD

New House
Farm

Poplar
Farm

Abbatridge Sewer

Spring
Farm

MOOR LA

MELON LA

TN29

PH

THE
GARDENS

Marsh's
Farm

CHURCH LA

Cemy

OASTHOUSE
FIELD

Brenzett Corner
Bridge

Ivychurch

Knowlden
Farm

B2080

Brenzett
Aeronautical
Mus

Brenzett
Place

MOORE
CL

BRENZETT CNR

Brenzett

KING ST

Sumnerhouse
Bridge

THE HAVEN

B2080

A2070

IVYCHURCH RD

Brenzett District
CE Prim Sch

Mast

New Sewer

WENHAM S LA

A259

STRAIGHT LA

Blue House
Farm

Owen's Bridge

A259

Finn
Farm

Rhee Wall

Callington Court
Farm

Beacon

Yoakes La

A259

Rheewall
Farm

New Sewer

TICKNER'S LA

TILLERY LA

Yoakes
Bridge

363
350

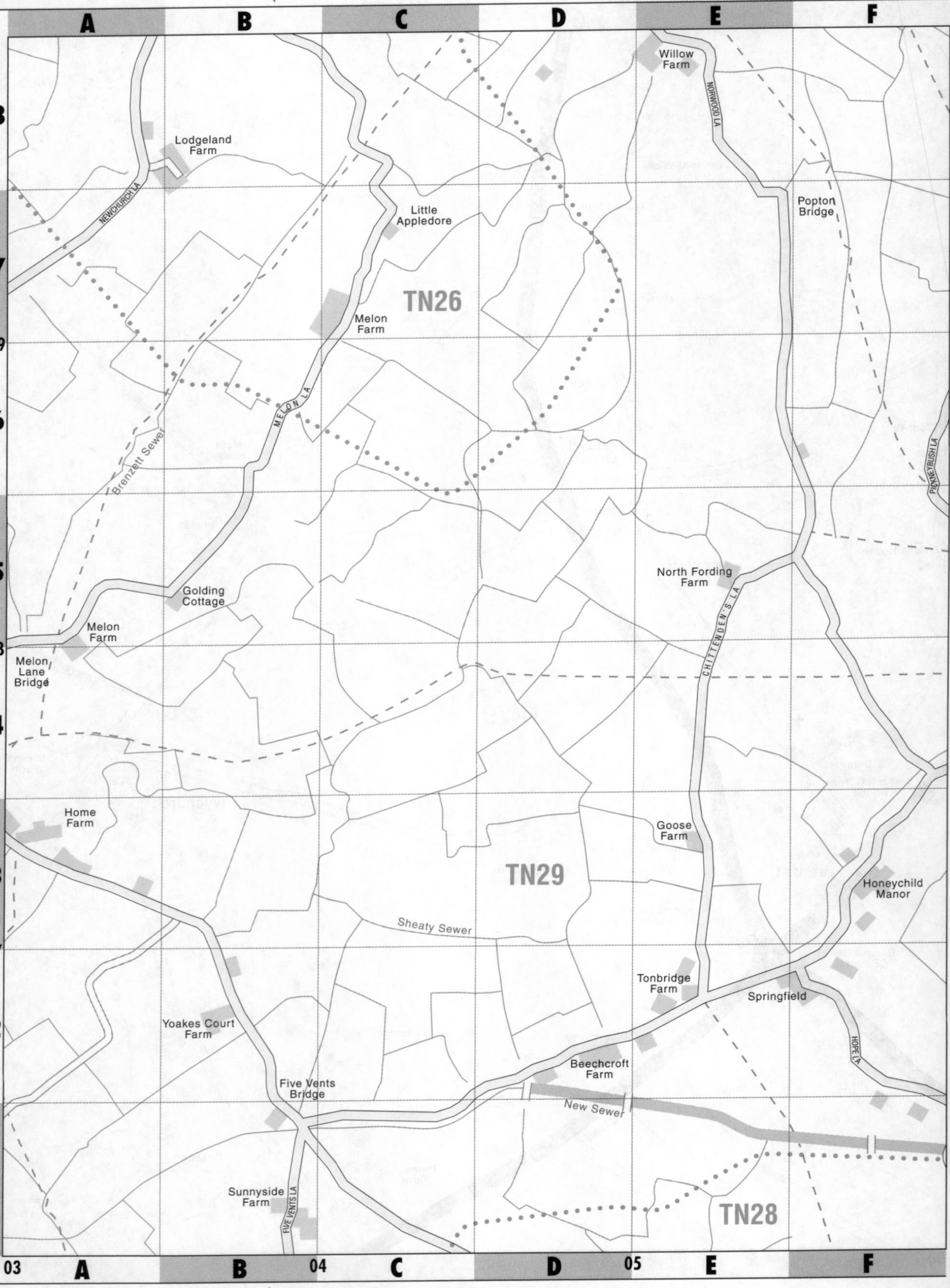

A B C D E F

8

Willow
Farm

Lodgeland
Farm

NEWCHURCH LA

NORWOOD LA

Popton
Bridge

Little
Appledore

7

TN26

29

Melon
Farm

MELON LA

6

Brenzett Sewer

PICKNEYBUSH LA

5

North Fording
Farm

Golding
Cottage

CHITTENDEN'S LA

28

Melon
Farm

Melon
Lane
Bridge

4

Home
Farm

Goose
Farm

3

TN29

Honeychild
Manor

Sheaty Sewer

27

Tonbridge
Farm

Springfield

2

Yoakes Court
Farm

HOPE LA

Beechcroft
Farm

Five Vents
Bridge

New Sewer

FIVE VENTS LA

1

Sunnyside
Farm

TN28

26

03 A B 04 C D 05 E F

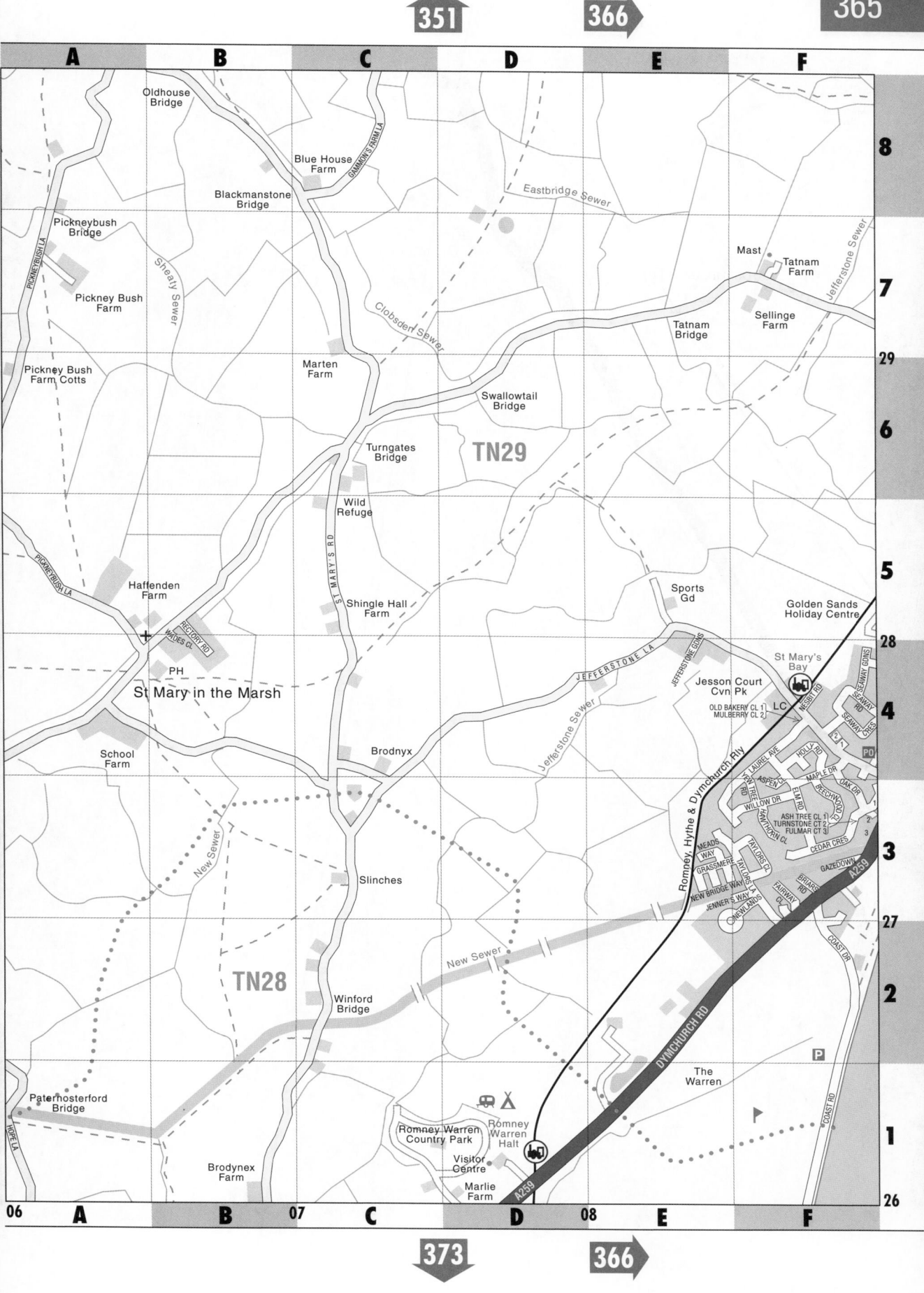

A B C D E F

8

Oldhouse
Bridge

Blue House
Farm

Blackmanstone
Bridge

GAMMON'S FARM LA

Eastbridge Sewer

Pickneybush
Bridge

Mast

Tatnam
Farm

7

Pickney Bush
Farm

Sheaty Sewer

Clobsden Sewer

Tatnam
Bridge

Sellinge
Farm

Jefferstone Sewer

29

Pickney Bush
Farm Cotts

Marten
Farm

Swallowtail
Bridge

TN29

6

Turngates
Bridge

Wild
Refuge

ST MARY'S RD

PICKNEY BUSH LA

Haffenden
Farm

RECTORY RD
WADES CL

Shingle Hall
Farm

Sports
Gd

Golden Sands
Holiday Centre

5

28

PH

St Mary in the Marsh

JEFFERSTONE LA

JEFFERSTONE GDNS

Jesson Court
Cvn Pk

OLD BAKERY CL 1
MULBERRY CL 2

St Mary's
Bay

LC

NESBIT RD

SEAWAY GDNS
SEAWAY RD
SEAWAY CRES

4

School
Farm

Brodnyx

Jefferstone Sewer

Romney, Hythe & Dymchurch Rly

LAUREL AVE
YEW TREE RD
ASPEN
ELM RD
WILLOW DR

HOLLY RD
MAPLE DR
BEECHWOOD
OAK DR

PO

New Sewer

Slinches

ASH TREE CL 1
TURNSTONE CT 2
FULMAR CT 3

HAWTHORN CL

CEDAR CRES

GAZEDOWN

A259

3

TN28

MEADS
WAY
GRASSMERE

TAYLORS CL

TAYLORS

BRIARS
RD
FAIRWAY

27

New Sewer

NEW BRIDGE WAY

JENNER'S WAY

NEWLANDS

Winford
Bridge

DYMCHURCH RD

The
Warren

P

2

Paternosterford
Bridge

HOPE LA

Romney Warren
Country Park

Romney
Warren Halt

COAST RD

COAST DR

1

Brodynex
Farm

Visitor
Centre

Marlie
Farm

A259

26

06 A B 07 C D 08 E F

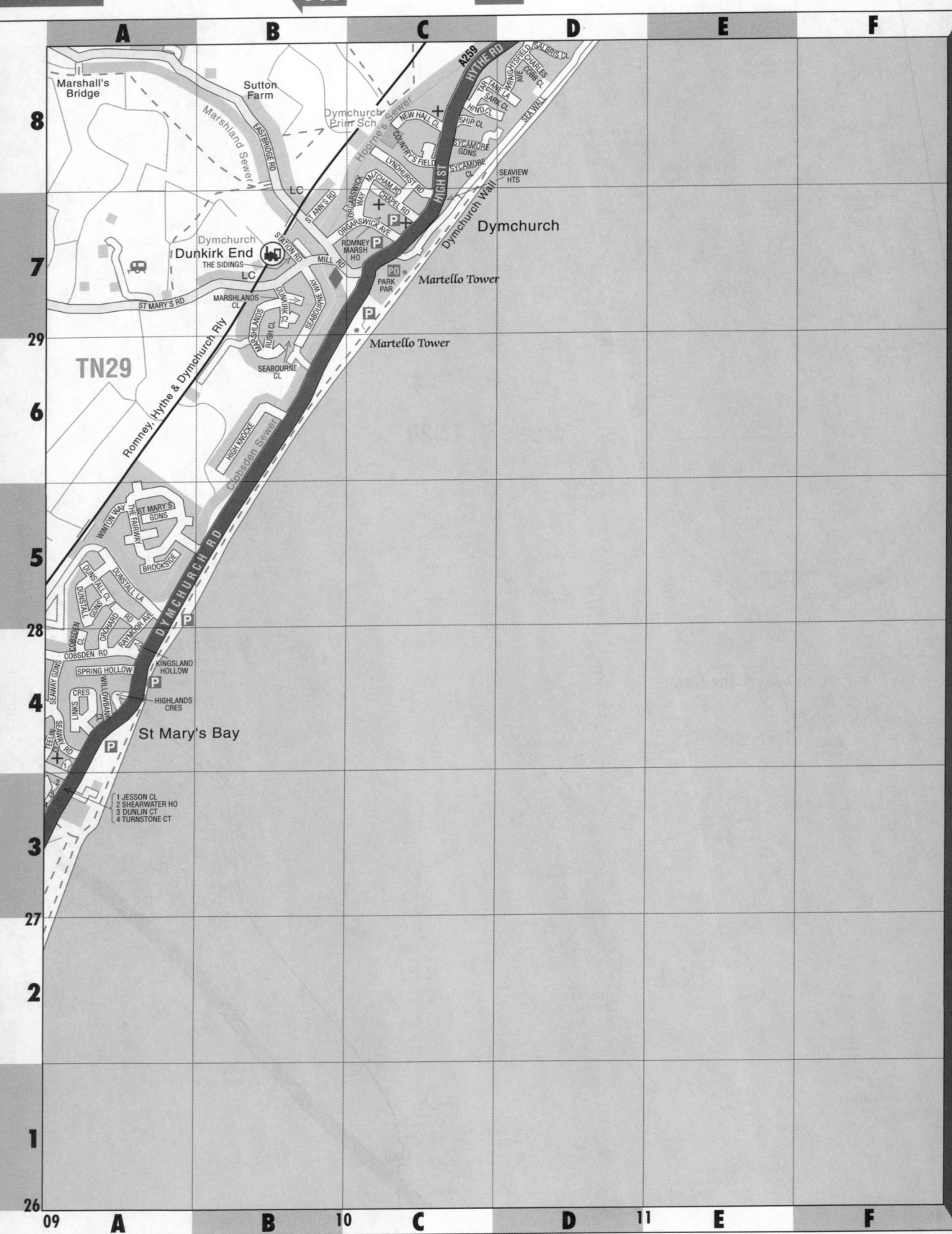

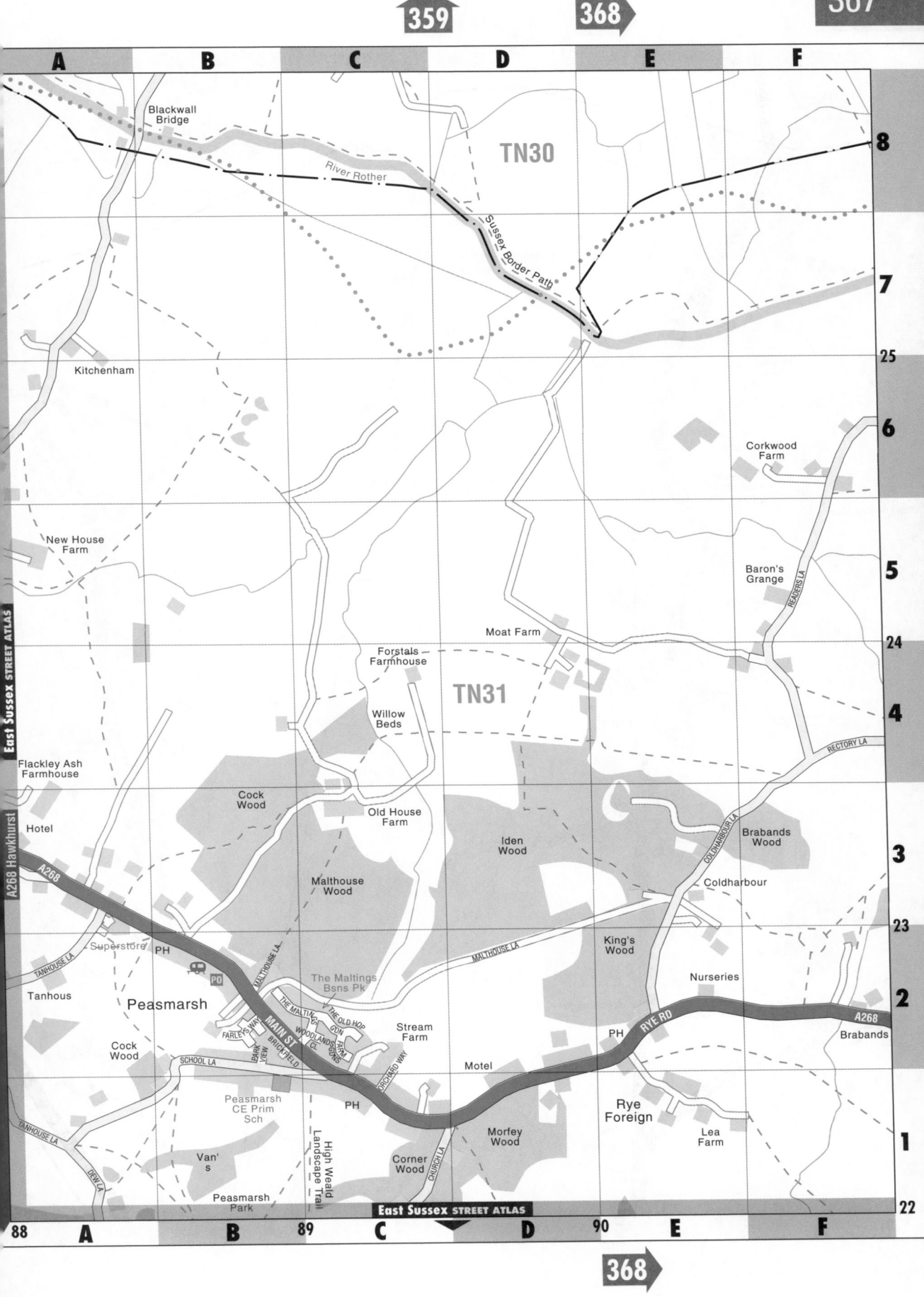

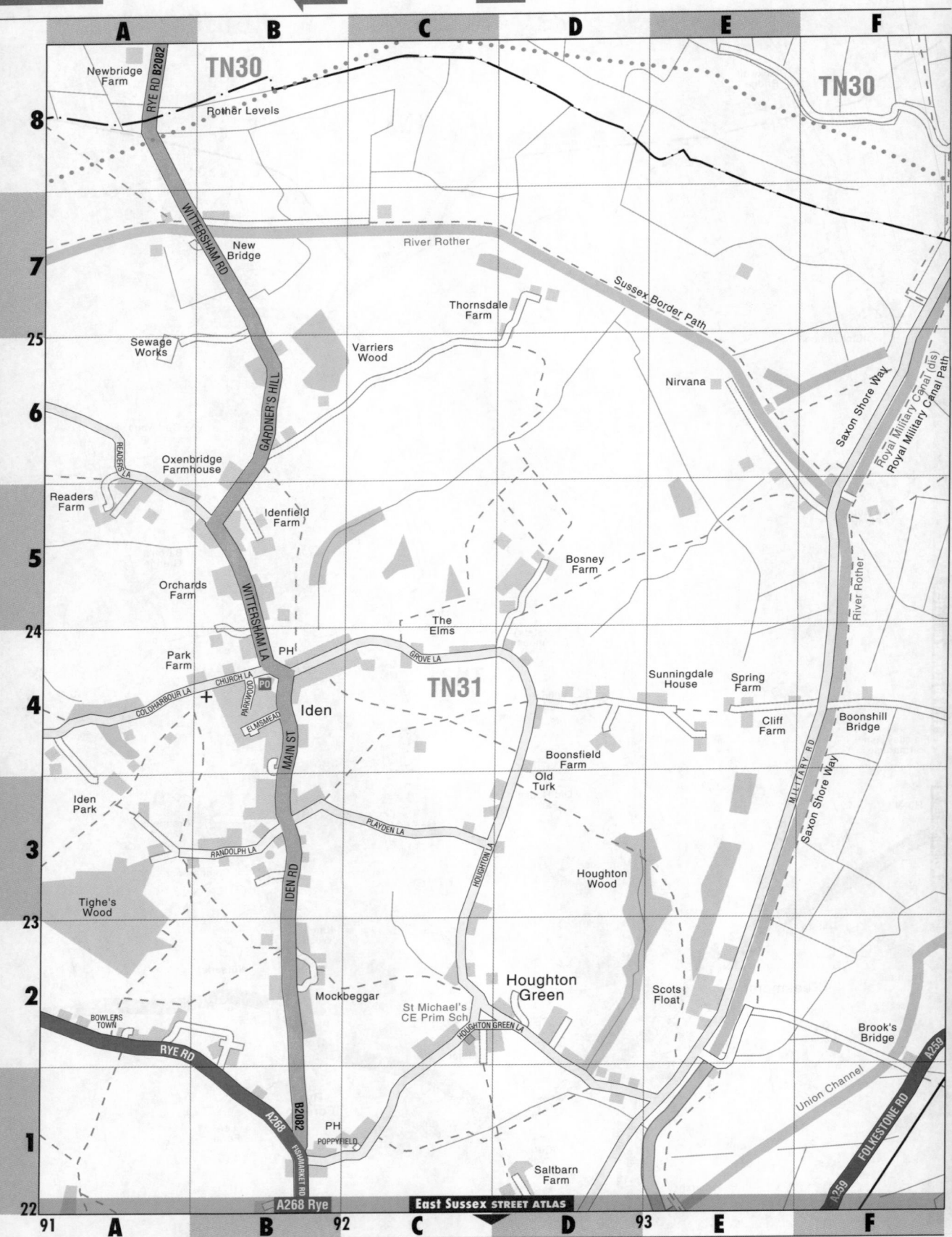

A   B   C   D   E   F

TN30

Newbridge
Farm

RYE RD B2082

Rother Levels

8

TN30

WITTERSHAM RD

New
Bridge

River Rother

7

Sussex Border Path

25

Sewage
Works

Thornsdale
Farm

GARDNER'S HILL

Varriers
Wood

Nirvana

Saxon Shore Way

Royal Military Canal (dis)
Royal Military Canal Path

6

Oxenbridge
Farmhouse

READERS LA

Readers
Farm

Idenfield
Farm

Bosney
Farm

River Rother

5

WITTERSHAM LA

Orchards
Farm

24

The
Elms

GROVE LA

Sunningdale
House

Spring
Farm

Park
Farm

PH

TN31

Cliff
Farm

Boonshill
Bridge

4

COLDHARBOUR LA

CHURCH LA

PARK LA

PO

ELMSMEAD

Iden

MAIN ST

Boonsfield
Farm

Old
Turk

Saxon Shore Way

MILITARY RD

Iden
Park

IDEN RD

PLAYDEN LA

HOUGHTON LA

Houghton
Wood

Scots
Float

Brook's
Bridge

RANDOLPH LA

3

Tighe's
Wood

23

Mockbeggar

Houghton
Green

2

BOWLERS
TOWN

RYE RD

St Michael's
CE Prim Sch

HOUGHTON GREEN LA

A259

Union Channel

FOLKESTONE RD

A268

B2082

PH
Poppyfield

Saltbarn
Farm

A259

1

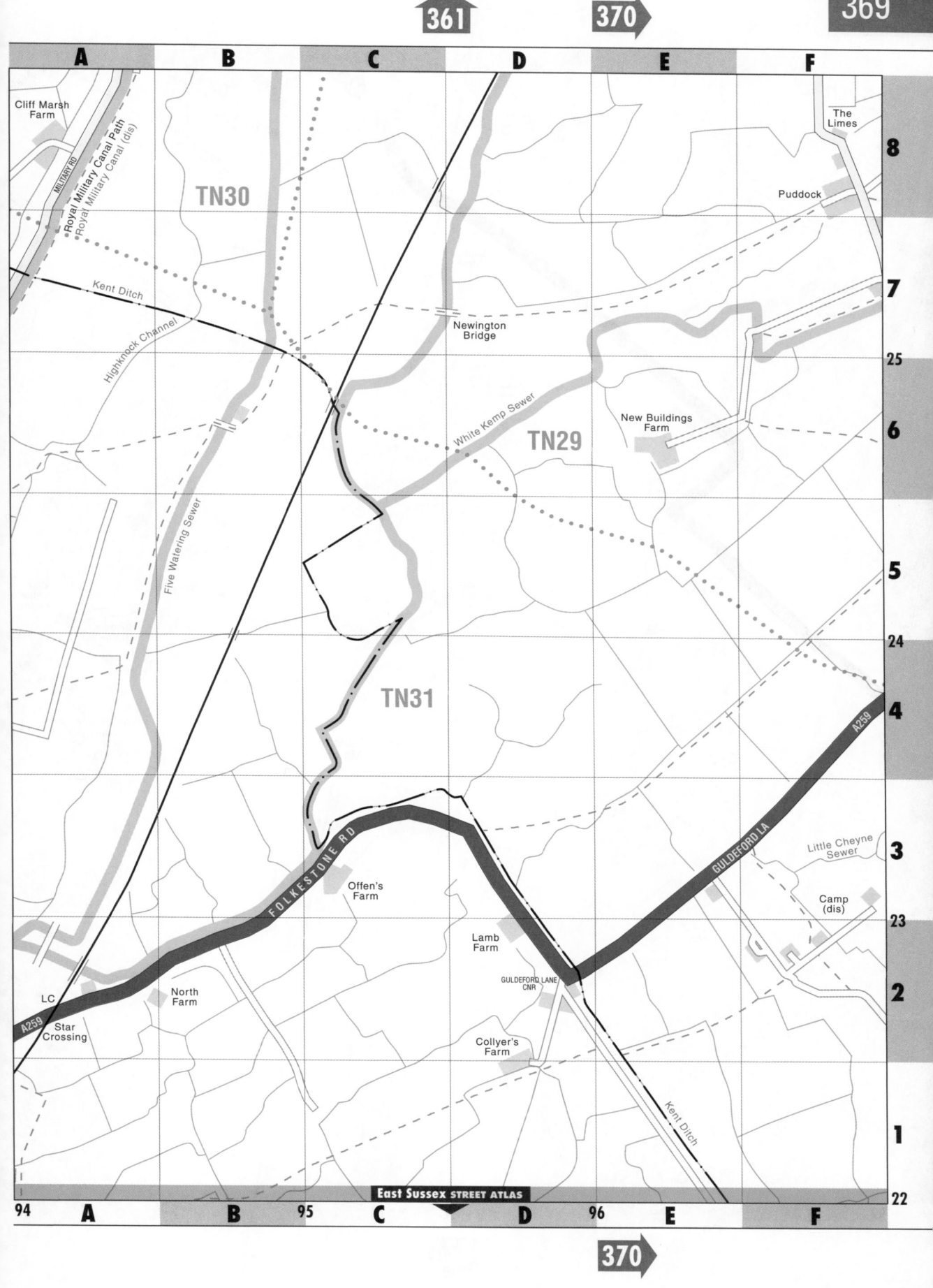

A B C D E F

8

7

25

6

5

24

4

3

23

2

1

22

Cliff Marsh Farm

MILITARY RD

Royal Military Canal Path
Royal Military Canal (dis)

TN30

Kent Ditch

Highknock Channel

Five Watering Sewer

Newington Bridge

White Kemp Sewer

TN29

New Buildings Farm

The Limes

Puddock

TN31

FOLKESTONE RD

Offen's Farm

Lamb Farm

GULDEFORD LANE CNR

GULDEFORD LA

A259

Little Cheyne Sewer

Camp (dis)

LC

A259

Star Crossing

North Farm

Collyer's Farm

Kent Ditch

369
362

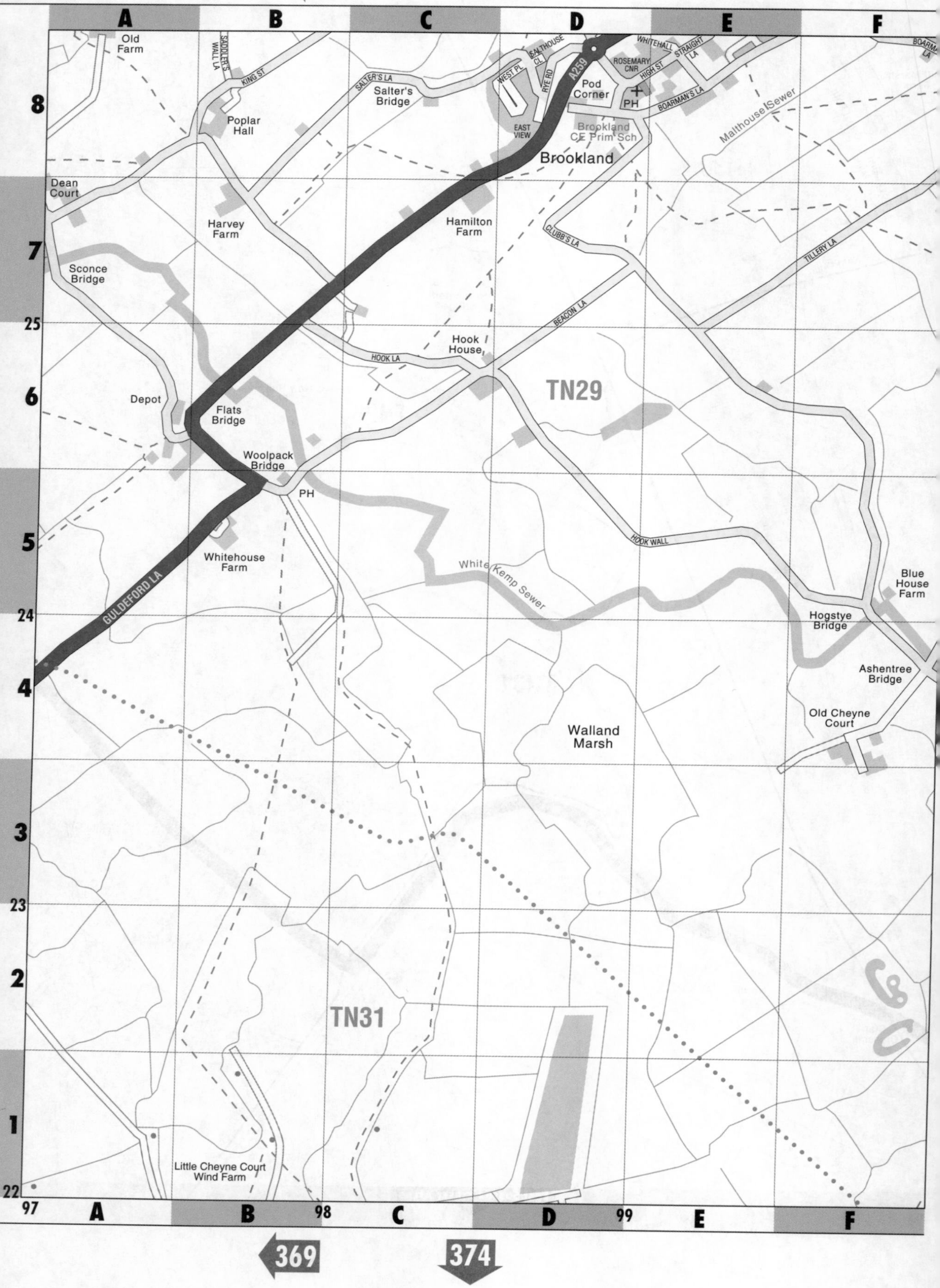

A B C D E F

8

7

25

6

5

24

4

3

23

2

1

22

Old Farm

SADDLER'S WALL LA

KING ST

Poplar Hall

Dean Court

Harvey Farm

Sconce Bridge

Depot

Flats Bridge

Woolpack Bridge

PH

Whitehouse Farm

GULDEFORD LA

Salter's Bridge

Salter's La

West Pl

East View

RYE RD

SALTHOUSE CL

A259

Pod Corner

PH

Brookland CE Prim Sch

Brookland

Whitehall

ROSEMARY CNR

HIGH ST

STRAIGHT LA

BOARMAN'S LA

Malthouse Sewer

Hamilton Farm

CLUBB'S LA

TILLERY LA

Hook La

Hook House

BEACON LA

TN29

Hook Wall

White Kemp Sewer

Blue House Farm

Hogstye Bridge

Ashentree Bridge

Old Cheyne Court

Walland Marsh

TN31

Little Cheyne Court Wind Farm

BOARM LA

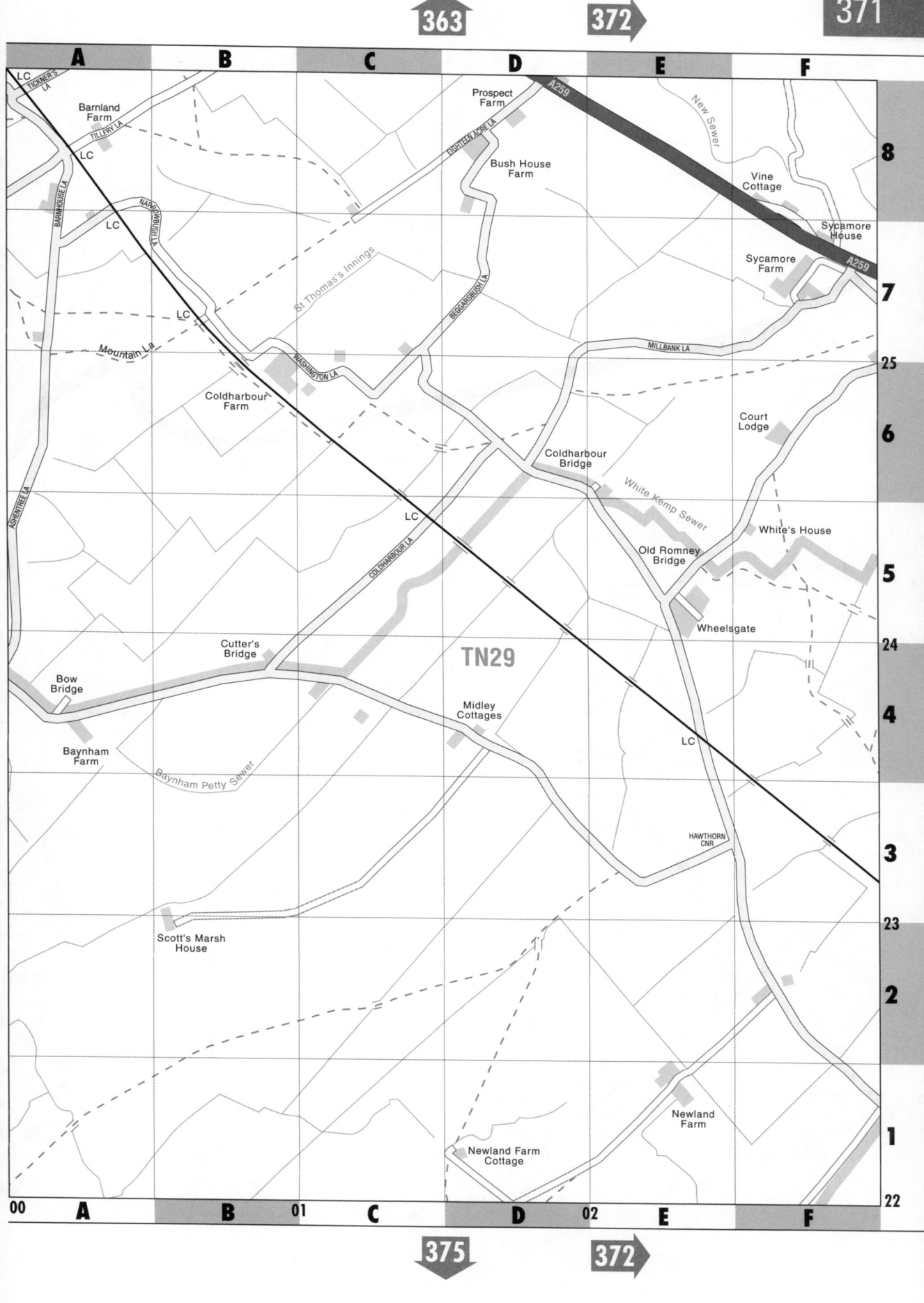

363
372

A   B   C   D   E   F

LC
TICKNER'S LA

Barnland
Farm

TILLERY LA

LC

BARNHOUSE LA

NARROWBUSH LA

LC

LC

Mountain La

St Thomas's Innings

Prospect
Farm

A259

New Sewer

Vine
Cottage

Bush House
Farm

Sycamore
House

EIGHTEEN ACRE LA

BEGGARSBUSH LA

Sycamore
Farm

A259

7

MILLBANK LA

25

WASHINGTON LA

Coldharbour
Farm

Court
Lodge

6

Coldharbour
Bridge

White Kemp Sewer

LC

White's House

ASHENTREE LA

COLDHARBOUR LA

Old Romney
Bridge

5

Cutter's
Bridge

TN29

Wheelsgate

24

Bow
Bridge

4

Midley
Cottages

Baynham
Farm

LC

Baynham Petty Sewer

HAWTHORN
CNR

3

Scott's Marsh
House

23

2

Newland
Farm

1

Newland Farm
Cottage

22

00   A   B   01   C   D   02   E   F

375
372

371 364

A B C D E F

8

TN28

Chapel Land Farm

Hope Farm

The Homestead

The Manor House

7

FIVE VENTS LA

DOWLE CL

Stone Bridge

Old Romney

THE LIMES
ST CATHERINES

Wallingham Sewer

25

ELM FIELDS

LYDD RD

SPITALFIELD LA

PRIORY CL

Spitalfield TERR

6

HAMMOND'S CNR

B2075

A259

Plumtree Farm

Isles Bridge

Kemps Hill Farm

5

Romney Farm

24

BELL CNR

Caldecot Petty Sewer

Kemps Hill Petty Sewer

4

SWAMP RD

TN29

Kemp's Hill

Mast

Swan Farm

Kingsmarsh Lane Bridge

ROMNEY RD

Dengemarsh Sewer

3

White Kemp Sewer

Castilore Farm

23

Swamp Road Bridge

Caldicott Farm

CALDECOT LA

Belgar Farm

2

Swamp Crossing Farm

LC

Swamp Crossing

Birds Kitchen

Footway Farm

CH

1

Horsebones Bridge

Westbrook Farm

LC

Caldecot Crossing

Forty Acre Farm

DENNES LA

Horses Bones Farm

B2075

22

03 A B 04 C D 05 E F

371 376

A B C D E F

8

Warren House

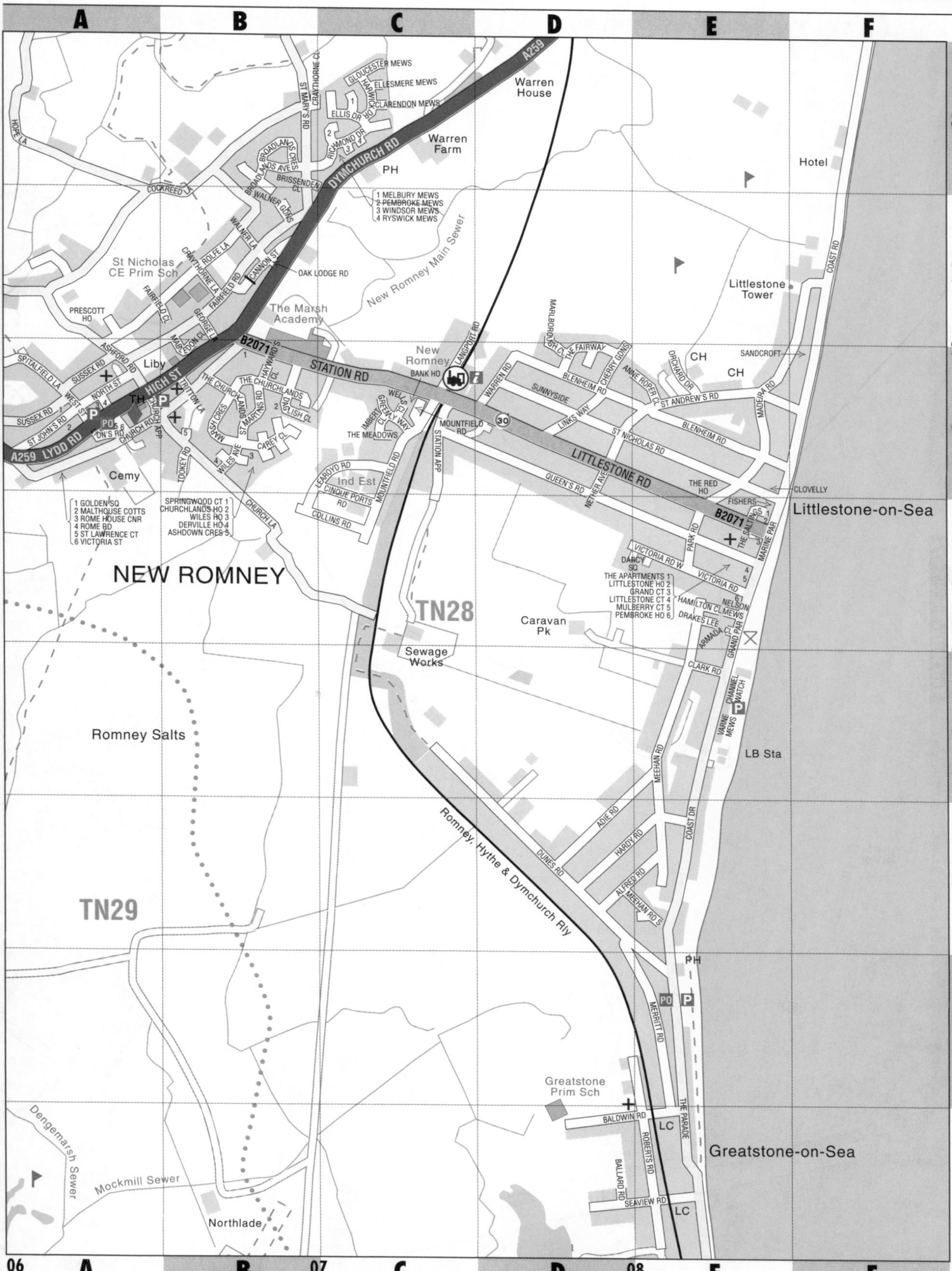

Gloucester Mews
Ellesmere Mews
Clarendon Mews

Warren Farm

Hotel

7

ST MARY'S RD
CRANTHORNE CL
HAWICK
RICHMOND DR
ELLIS DR
DYMCHURCH RD
PH

1 MELBURY MEWS
2 PEMBROKE MEWS
3 WINDSOR MEWS
4 RYSWICK MEWS

Littlestone
Tower

BRISSENDEN CL
BROADLANDS AVE
BROADLANDS CRES
WALNER GDNS
WALNER LA

OAK LODGE RD

New Romney Main Sewer

CH

SANDCROFT

CH

25

St Nicholas
CE Prim Sch

CAVENHOLME LA
ROLFE LA
FAIRFIELD RD
CANNON ST
GEORGE LA

The Marsh
Academy

New
Romney

MARLBORGH CL
THE FAIRWAY
BLENHEIM RD
CHERRY GDNS
ANNE ROPER CL
ORCHARD DR
ST ANDREW'S RD
MADEIRA DR

PRESCOTT
HO

FAIRFIELD CL
ASHFORD RD

B2071
STATION RD

BANK HO
WARREN RD

SUNNYSIDE

BLENHEIM RD

7

Liby
TH
HIGH ST
SUSSEX RD
ST JOHN'S RD
NORTH LA
SPITALFIELD LA

MARSH CRES
HAYWARD'S
THE CHURCHLANDS
ENGLISH CL
WELLS WAY
GREY'S WAY
IMBERT RD

LINKS WAY
ST NICHOLAS RD

THE RED
HO

6

A259 LYDD RD
COLN'S RD
CHURCH RD APP
WILES AVE
TOLKEY RD
CAREY CL

MOUNTFIELD
RD
30

LITTLESTONE RD

FISHERS
GS
B2071

Cemy

LEAROYD RD
CINQUE PORTS
RD
STATION APP
MOUNTFIELD RD

Ind Est

QUEEN'S RD

NETHER AVE

PARK RD
MARINE PAR
THE SALTINGS

Clovelly

Littlestone-on-Sea

1 GOLDEN SQ
2 MALTHOUSE COTTS
3 ROME HOUSE CNR
4 ROME RD
5 ST LAWRENCE CT
6 VICTORIA ST

SPRINGWOOD CT 1
CHURCHLANDS HO 2
WILES HO 3
DERVILLE HO 4
ASHDOWN CRES 5

The Meadows
CHURCH LA
COLLINS RD

VICTORIA RD W
DARCY
SQ
THE APARTMENTS 1
LITTLESTONE HO 2
GRAND CT 3
LITTLESTONE CT 4
MULBERRY CT 5
PEMBROKE HO 6

VICTORIA RD

NELSON
HAMILTON PL
DRAKES LEE

5

NEW ROMNEY

TN28

Caravan
Pk

ARMADA CL
GRAND PAR

24

Sewage
Works

CLARK RD

CHANNEL
WATCH
P

4

Romney Salts

MEEHAN RD

VARNE
MEWS

LB Sta

Romney, Hythe & Dymchurch Rly

ADIE RD

COAST DR

3

TN29

DUNES RD
HARDY RD

ALFRED RD
MEEHAN RD S

PH
PO
P

23

MERRITT RD

2

Greatstone
Prim Sch

BALDWIN RD

ALFRED RD
ROBERTS RD

THE PARADE

LC

Dengemarsh Sewer

BALLARD RD

Greatstone-on-Sea

1

Mockmill Sewer

SEAVIEW RD

LC

Northlade

06 A B 07 C D 08 E F 22

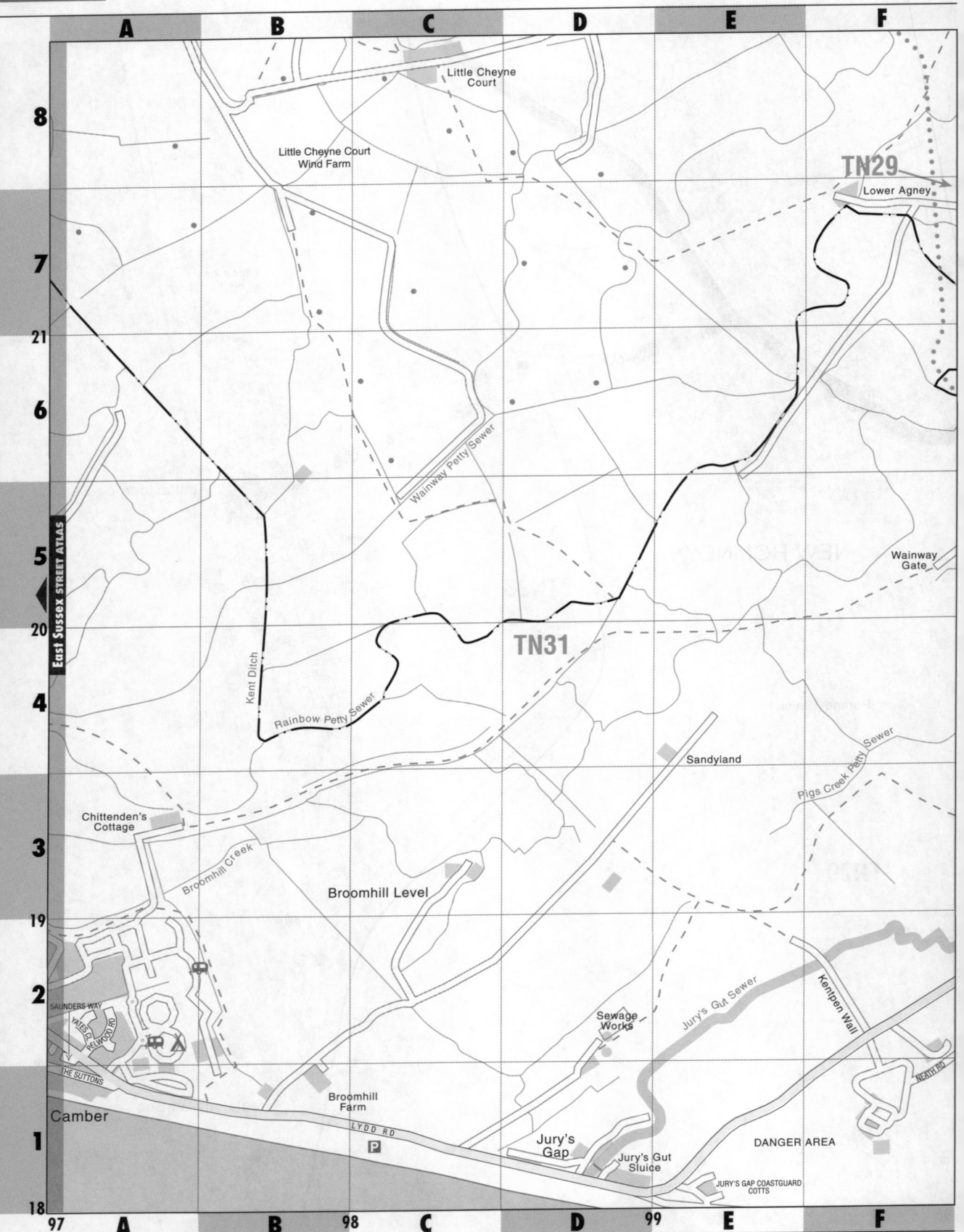

East Sussex STREET ATLAS

Little Cheyne Court

Little Cheyne Court Wind Farm

TN29

Lower Agney

Wainway Petty Sewer

Wainway Gate

TN31

Kent Ditch

Rainbow Petty Sewer

Pigs Creek Petty Sewer

Sandyland

Chittenden's Cottage

Broomhill Creek

Broomhill Level

Kentgen Wall

SAUNDERS WAY

WATES CL

PELKYD RD

THE SUTTONS

Sewage Works

Jury's Gut Sewer

NEATH RD

Camber

Broomhill Farm

LYDD RD

P

Jury's Gap

Jury's Gut Sluice

JURY'S GAP COASTGUARD COTTS

DANGER AREA

A B C D E F

8

7

21

6

Wainway Petty Sewer

Little
Scotney

Tore Petty Sewer

Nod Wall

Tore Wall

Dering Petty Sewer

TN29

Red
House

Scotney
Court
Farm

Burnthouse Wall

Oakhill Fleet

Sewage
Works

Scotney Bridge
North

Scotney

5

20

378

Scotney
Court

Scotney
Bridge South

DANGER AREA

Tore Wall

Jury's Gut Sewer

4

TN31

The
Forelands

LC

3

Works

378

19

Jury's Gap
Farm

Rosedale

DANGER AREA

NEATH RD

FERGUSON RD

LC

2

Holmstone

SOUTH BROOKS RD

Midrips

LC

LC

South
Brooks

DANGER AREA

Lydd
Ranges

1

The
Wicks

18

00 A B 01 C D 02 E F

A B C D E F

8

Westbroke Cottages
Westbroke House
Whitehall Farm
Walland Marsh
Jack's Court
CALDECOT LA
DENNES LA
ROMNEY RD
B2075
BRIDGE HOME PK
KITEWELL LA
LYDD TOWN CROSSING
LC
ASH GR
THE BEECHES

7

The Glebe
P
SAMUEL MEWS
WELTON RD
SYCAMORE
POPLAR LA
STATION RD
GILLETT RD
MEADOW VW
TACKHAM DR
Cemy
Ind Est
Hotel

21

Gravel Pits
COPPERFIELDS
CHURCH RD
CANNON ST 2
NEW ST 1
GEORGE'S
NESS RD
EASTERN RD
MILL LA
MILL RD
COLEMAN'S CL
HARDEN RD
WOOD CL
DOLPHIN RD 5
6

6

MITTELL CT
PADDOCK WALK
THE DENNIS
THE LANDS
PO
HIGH ST
TH
PARK ST
OAK LA
QUEENSWAY
QUEEN'S RD
SKINNER
PAINE AVE
Town Mus
Lydd Prim Sch
Liby
LYDD
Green Hop Farm
Denge Marsh
1 CHAPEL ROW
2 CORONATION SQ
3 OAK BGLWS
4 THE PRIORY
5 GRISBROOK RD
6 GRISBROOK FARM CL
ROBIN RD
MANOR RD
HAMILTON RD
GOULSB
P

Tourney Hall
X B2075
Pigwell
THE GREEN
GREEN WAY
TOURNEY RD
MILL BANK
QUEENSWAY INSIDE
RYDE
COLSB WAY
WHITING HO
WOLSELEY TERR
GORDON TERR
CULVER'S LA
TN29
Cockles Bridge
DUNGENESS RD

5

Lydd Camp
GALLOWAYS RD
JURY'S GAP RD

20

378
379
Dengemarsh Sewer

4

LC
LC
LC
West Ripe
LC
DANGER AREA
Works
SOUTH BROOKS RD
DENGEMARSH RD

Twr

3

LC
Action Watersports
Heron's Park - Lydd International Raceway

19

The Quob
INVICTA RD

2

Hart's Farm
Manor Farm

1

LC
Brickwall Farmhouse
DANGER AREA
Piper's Pen

18

TN28

Lydd
(London Ashford)
Airport

Mockmill Sewer

Romney Sands
Holiday Park

Romney Sands

Caravan
Park

LA ROCCO 1
LA TRAUSCO 2
LA GALAMINA 3

BEACHMONT CL

PRIOR RD

CHANNON RD

DERVILLE RD

WALLER RD

COLEVILLE CRES

BEATRICE
MEWS

HULL RD

TOBY RD

LCs

P

PH

TAYLOR RD

FORT CL

LADE FORT
COTTS

FORT CRES

LC

Lade

WILLIAMSON RD

SAXTON RD

LYDOS CL

PLEASANCE RD N

Romney, Hythe & Dymchurch Railway

THE PARADE

EDWARD RD

COAST DR

379

380

Works
(dis)

Gravel
Pits

Boulderwall
Farm

TN29

Gravel
Pits

Works

PLEASANCE ROAD CENTRAL

KERON RD

Lydd-on-Sea

DUNGENESS RD

Halfway
Bush

BATTERY RD

Mast

COASTGUARD
COTTS

Denge
Marsh

Walkers Outland
(Dungeness
Nature Reserve)

E   F   G   H   I   J

Scotney
Court

Scotney
Bridge South

DANGER AREA

Jury's Gut Sewer

West
Ripe

DANGER AREA

GALLOWAYS RD

8

LC   LC   LC
LC

The Forelands

Works

Twr

SOUTH BROOKS RD.

LC

7

19

DANGER AREA

The
Quob

6

NEATH RD

FERGUSON RD

LC

INVICTA RD

Holmstone

LC

SOUTH BROOKS RD.

LC

LC   LC

South
Brooks

LC

DANGER AREA

Lydd
Ranges

5

The
Wicks

TN29

18

375   376

4

TN31

3

17

DANGER AREA

18

TN31

2

4

99   A   B   00   C   D

1

16

01   E   F   02   G   H   03   I   J

376 377 380

A B C D E F

8
7
19
6
5
18
4
3
17
2
1
16

Works

Dengemarsh Sewer

Works (dis)

Gravel Pits

Boulderwall Farm

DUNGENESS RD

DENGEMARSH RD

GALLOWAY'S RD

Action Watersports

Heron's Park-Lydd International Raceway

Hart's Farm

Manor Farm

Brickwall Farmhouse

Piper's Pen

DANGER AREA

376 377

TN29

Walkers Outland (Dungeness Nature Reserve)

DANGER AREA

Pen Bars

04 A B 05 C D 06 E F

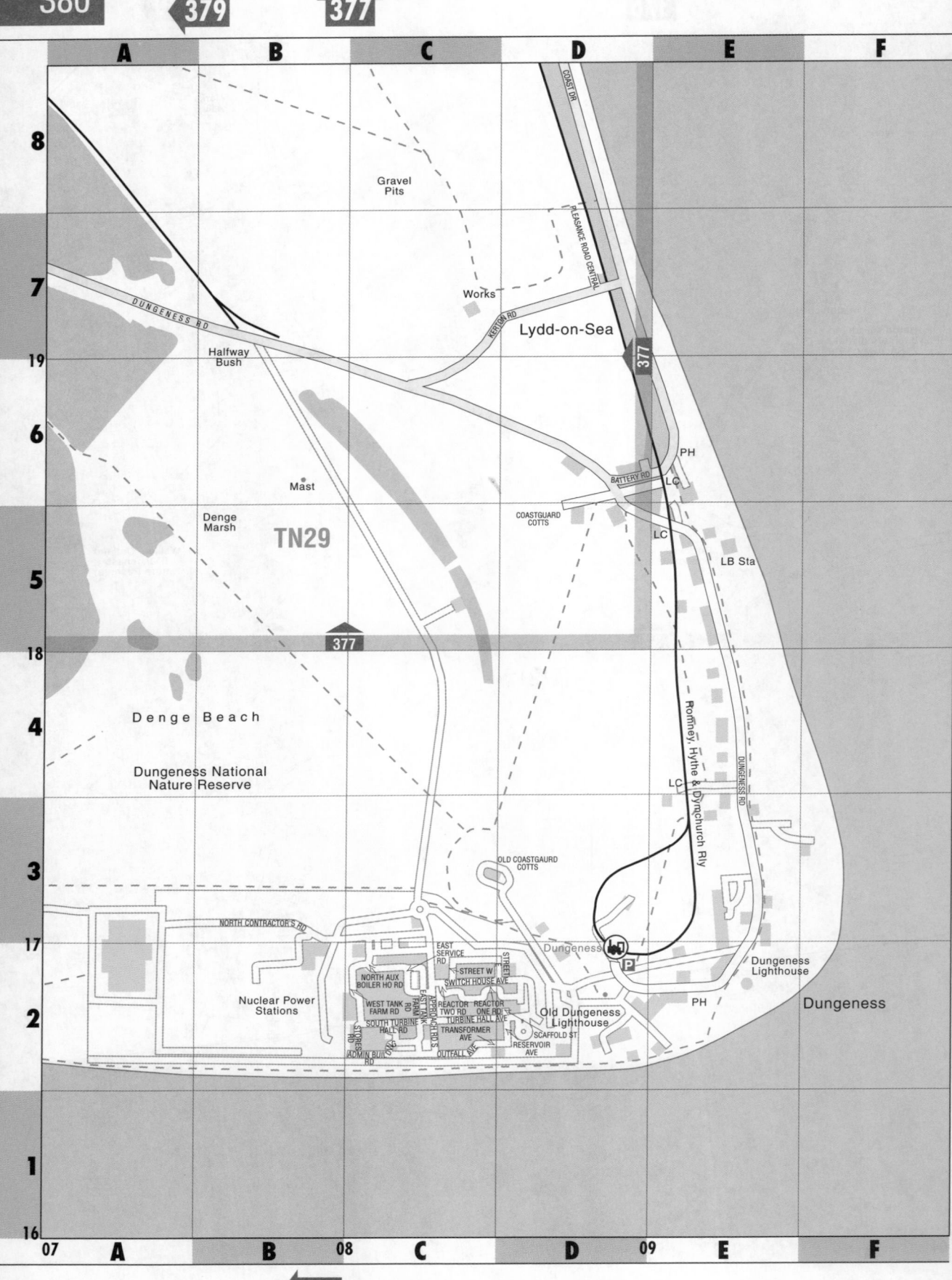

A B C D E F

8

379

7

19

6

DUNGENESS RD

Gravel
Pits

Works

KERTON RD

PLEASANCE ROAD CENTRAL

COAST DR

Lydd-on-Sea

377

PH

LC

BATTERY RD

Halfway
Bush

Mast

Denge
Marsh

TN29

COASTGUARD
COTTS

LC

LB Sta

5

18

377

Denge Beach

Dungeness National
Nature Reserve

Romney, Hythe & Dymchurch Rly

DUNGENESS RD

LC

4

3

17

OLD COASTGAURD
COTTS

Dungeness

P

Dungeness
Lighthouse

Dungeness

NORTH CONTRACTOR'S RD

EAST
SERVICE
RD

STREET W
SWITCH HOUSE AVE

STREET

Nuclear Power
Stations

NORTH AUX
BOILER HO RD

WEST TANK
FARM RD

PISGACE RD S

EAST TANK
FARM RD

REACTOR
TWO RD

REACTOR
ONE RD

TURBINE HALL AVE

Old Dungeness
Lighthouse

PH

SOUTH TURBINE
HALL RD

STORES RD

ADMIN BUILD
RD

TRANSFORMER
AVE

OUTFALL RD

SCAFFOLD ST

RESERVOIR
AVE

2

1

16

07   A   B   08   C   D   09   E   F

379

381

Index

Church Rd [6] Beckenham BR2..........**53** C6

- **Place name** May be abbreviated on the map
- **Location number** Present when a number indicates the place's position in a crowded area of mapping
- **Locality, town or village** Shown when more than one place has the same name
- **Postcode district** District for the indexed place
- **Page and grid square** Page number and grid reference for the standard mapping

Cities, towns and villages are listed in CAPITAL LETTERS

Public and commercial buildings are highlighted in **magenta** **Places of interest** are highlighted in **blue** with a star★

Abbreviations used in the index

Acad	Academy	Comm	Common	Gd	Ground	L	Leisure	Prom	Promenade
App	Approach	Cott	Cottage	Gdn	Garden	La	Lane	Rd	Road
Arc	Arcade	Cres	Crescent	Gn	Green	Liby	Library	Recn	Recreation
Ave	Avenue	Cswy	Causeway	Gr	Grove	Mdw	Meadow	Ret	Retail
Bglw	Bungalow	Ct	Court	H	Hall	Meml	Memorial	Sh	Shopping
Bldg	Building	Ctr	Centre	Ho	House	Mkt	Market	Sq	Square
Bsns, Bus	Business	Ctry	Country	Hospl	Hospital	Mus	Museum	St	Street
Bvd	Boulevard	Cty	County	HQ	Headquarters	Orch	Orchard	Sta	Station
Cath	Cathedral	Dr	Drive	Hts	Heights	Pal	Palace	Terr	Terrace
Cir	Circus	Dro	Drove	Ind	Industrial	Par	Parade	TH	Town Hall
Cl	Close	Ed	Education	Inst	Institute	Pas	Passage	Univ	University
Cnr	Corner	Emb	Embankment	Int	International	Pk	Park	Wk, Wlk	Walk
Coll	College	Est	Estate	Intc	Interchange	Pl	Place	Wr	Water
Com	Community	Ex	Exhibition	Junc	Junction	Prec	Precinct	Yd	Yard

Index of towns, villages, streets, hospitals, industrial estates, railway stations, schools, shopping centres, universities and places of interest

20/–Alb

20/20 Ind Est ME16 .. 161 C8

A

Aaron Hill Rd E6 .... 2 A8
Abberley Pk ME14.... 162 C6
Abbess Cl [12] E6......... 1 E8
Abbeville Ho ME1 ......63 C4
Abbey Brewery Ct
  ME19............... 159 C8
Abbey Cl Deal CT14 ... 215 A5
  Minster (Sheppey) ME12 .47 D6
  Orpington BR6 ....87 B6
Abbey Court Sch ME2...62 E8
Abbey Cres DA17.........4 A2
Abbey Ct
  Westgate on Sea CT8....81 D7
  Whitstable CT5..........75 A3
Abbey Dr DA2...........32 E6
Abbey Drive DA2........32 E6
Abbey Fields ME13 ....138 E7
Abbey Fields Ct ME13 .138 E7
Abbey Gate CT11 ......117 B5
Abbey Gate Cotts
  ME14................129 F2
Abbey Gdns
  Canterbury CT2....... 143 A2
  Chislehurst BR7 ....53 A8
Abbey Gr
  Minster (Thanet)
    CT12 .... 115 C5
  Ramsgate CT11 ...... 117 B5
  Woolwich SE2............3 B2
Abbeyhill Rd DA15......31 C6
Abbey Ho SE2............3 D1
Abbey Life Ct E13 ....1 B8
Abbey Lodge SE12......29 B4
Abbey Mount DA17...... 3 F1
Abbey Pl Dartford DA1...15 D2
  Faversham ME13 ..... 138 D8
Abbey Rd
  Bexley DA6, DA7........13 E3
  Erith DA17...............3 E3
  Faversham ME13 ..... 138 D8
  Gillingham ME8.........65 A2
  Gravesend DA12.........37 E7
  Kearsney CT16 .... 277 D4
  River CT15, CT17 ..... 277 D1
  Rochester ME2..........62 F8
  Swanscombe DA9........17 C2
Abbey Sch The ME13.. 138 C5
Abbey St ME13 .... 138 D8
Abbey Terr SE2 ....3 C2
Abbeyview Dr ME12 ....47 B6
Abbey Way TN24 ..... 269 A1
ABBEY WOOD 3 B3
Abbey Wood Rd
  Kings Hill ME19....... 159 A5
  Woolwich SE2............3 C2
Abbey Wood Sch SE2....3 A3
Abbey Wood Sta SE2 ....3 C3
Abbots Barton Wlk [2]
  CT1 ....175 B7
Abbotsbury Hts CT2 ...143 B4
Abbots Cl BR5...........53 C1
Abbots Court Rd ME3...41 F4
Abbots Field
  Gravesend DA12.........37 C2
  Maidstone ME16...... 161 B2
Abbots Hill ME13 ......137 E5
Abbot's Hill CT11.......117 E6
Abbots Pl CT1..........142 F1
Abbots Rd ME13........138 F7
Abbots The CT17 ..... 310 C8
Abbots Wlk TN25.......237 E2
Abbotswood Cl [7] DA17 . 3 E3
Abbott Ct [13] CT20 .....335 E6
Abbott Dr ME9 .... 134 D6
Abbott Rd
  Borough Green TN15 ...156 F7
  Folkestone CT20...... 335 E6
Abbotts Cl
  Rochester ME1..........63 B3
  Swanley BR8............56 A5
  Woolwich SE28...........3 C6
Abbott's Wlk DA7 ......13 D7
Abbott Way TN30..... 345 C7
ABDO Coll CT4 .... 205 A3
Aberdeen Cl CT3 ..... 112 D3
Aberdeen Ho [9] ME15 .195 E7
Aberford Gdns SE18....11 E6
Abergeldie Rd SE12 ....11 B1
Abery Drive ME20 .....128 B4
Abery St SE18 ....2 E2
Abigail Cres ME5........97 A1
Abingdon Gr CT3..... 112 D3
Abingdon Mews ME19 159 C8
Abingdon Rd ME16 ....160 F2
Abingdon Way BR6.....87 B6
Abinger Cl BR1..........52 E6
Abinger Dr ME5 ....97 D2
Absalom Ct ME8.........65 C2
Acacia Ave CT3....... 144 D8
Acacia Cl BR5...........53 D4
Acacia Ct DA11..........37 A8
Acacia Rd Dartford DA1..33 D7
  Stone DA9..............16 E1
Acacia Terr ME10 .... 101 C4
Acacia Way DA15.......30 F7
Acacia Wlk BR8 ....55 D7
Academy Dr ME7........64 F1
Academy La CT19 .....335 B7
Academy Pl SE18........12 A6
Academy Rd SE18 ......11 F7
Acer Ave TN2 .... 314 C8
Acer Rd TN16 .... 118 D3
Achilles Rd ME5.........97 C2
Ackerey Ct TN23 ......299 F6
ACKHOLT 211 A4
Ackholt Rd CT3....... 211 A5
Acland Cl SE18..........12 D7
ACOL....................81 B3
Acol Hill CT7 ....81 B4
Acorn Cl Chislehurst BR7 30 C3
  Five Oak Green TN12 .. 256 B7
  Hawkinge CT18....... 307 C4
  Kingsnorth TN23...... 300 C3
Acorn Gr ME20 .... 160 D8
Acorn Ind Pk DA1 ......15 A2
Acorn Pl ME15 ....195 E6
Acorn Rd Crayford DA1 ..14 F2
  Gillingham ME7.........64 F4
Acorn St ME12 ....28 C1
Acorns The
  Sevenoaks TN13...... 154 A4
  Smarden TN27 ....263 F1
Acorn Terr ME9 ....66 E2
Acorn Trad Ctr RM20....17 E8
Acorn Way
  Hurst Green TN19..... 354 A3
  Orpington BR6 ....86 B6
Acorn Wharf Rd ME1 ...63 C6
Acott Fields ME18 .....225 F8
Acre Cl ME1.............63 E1
Acre Ct CT17 .... 310 C8
Acre Gr ME2 ....95 A4
Acres Rise TN5.........338 E1
Acre The CT16 ....277 F8
Action Watersports
  TN29............... 376 D3
Acton La TN30.........359 F4
Acton Pl ME18........ 193 A1
Acton Rd CT5 ....74 D2
Acworth Ho [1] SE18....12 B8
Acworth Pl DA1 ....15 C1
Adam Cl ME17........ 194 D3
Adam Ct [1] CT9 ....51 B2
Adams Cl TN30........324 B1
Adamson Rd E16.........1 A7
Adams Sq DA6 ....13 E4
Ada Rd CT1 .... 174 D6
Adbert Dr ME15 ....194 B4
Adcot Wlk [7] BR6 ......86 F6
Addelam Cl CT14..... 215 A4
Addelam Rd CT14 .... 215 A4
Adderley Gdns SE9.....30 A4
ADDINGTON......... 126 C3
Addington La ME19....126 B4
Addington Pl CT11 ....117 E6
Addington Rd
  Margate CT9............50 J2
  Sittingbourne ME10 ... 101 E3
Addington Sq CT9......50 J2
Addington St
  Margate CT9............50 J2
  Ramsgate CT11 ...... 117 D6
Addiscombe Gdns CT9 .50 J1
Addiscombe Rd CT9....51 A1
Addison Cl
  Orpington BR5 ....53 C3
  West Malling ME19.....127 F1
Addison Cotts TN30 .. 359 D3
Addison Dr SE12 ....11 B2
Addison Rd BR2........52 D4
Addlestead Rd TN12...224 E6
Adelaide Dr ME10 .... 101 C4
Adelaide Gdns
  Halfway Houses ME12...46 E6
  [19] Ramsgate CT11.... 117 E6
Adelaide Ho Deal CT14 215 D6
  Sheerness ME12....... 28 H1
Adelaide Pl CT1 ....174 F8
Adelaide Rd
  Chislehurst BR7 ....30 B3
  Elvington CT15 .... 212 B1
  Gillingham ME7.........64 C4
  Tilbury RM18............18 F5
Adelaide The ME3......39 C6
Aden Terr [1] ME14 ... 162 A7
Adie Rd TN28......... 373 D3
ADISHAM 210 D8
Adisham CE Prim Sch
  CT3................ 210 D8
Adisham Downs Rd CT3,
  CT4 ....177 B2
Adisham Dr ME16 .....161 B7
Adisham Gdns [1]
  TN23 ....299 F6
Adisham Gn ME10.....101 F8
Adisham Rd
  Bekesbourne CT4..... 176 E3
  Wingham CT3 .... 178 A4
  Womenswold CT4, CT3. 210 C2
Adisham Sta CT3 ......210 E8
Adisham Way CT9......51 C1
Admaston Rd SE18 .....12 C8
Admers Way [2] DA13..126 B8
Admers Wood [1]
  DA13.................126 B8
Admin Building Rd
  TN29 .... 380 C2
Admiral Cl BR5.........54 D5
Admiral Ct ME7 ....64 D6
Admiral Moore Dr
  ME20................128 F1
Admirals Ct E6..........2 B7
Admiral Seymour Rd
  SE9 ....11 F3
Admirals Wlk
  Chatham ME5 ....97 B3
  Goddard's Green TN17. 321 D2
  Halfway Houses ME12...46 E6
  Hythe CT21.......... 333 C1
  Swanscombe DA9.......17 B2
  Tenterden TN30 ...... 324 C1
Admiral's Wlk ME4 .....63 F7
Admiralty Cl ME13.....138 B8
Admiralty Mews CT14 215 D4
Admiralty Rd ME2......40 F1
Admiralty Terr
  Chatham ME7 ....64 A7
  Rochester ME2..........40 F1
Admiralty Wlk CT5 ... 108 A7
Admiral Way ME19 ... 159 A1
Adrian Mews CT8 ......50 D1
Adrian Sq CT8...........50 D1
Adrian St CT17 .... 310 D7
Aerodrome Est ME14 ..131 E4
Aerodrome Rd
  Bekesbourne CT4..... 176 E3
  Hawkinge CT18....... 307 A4
Afghan Rd
  Broadstairs CT10 ....83 F8
  Chatham ME4 ....63 E4
Agate Cl E16 ....1 D7
Agate Ct ME10 .... 101 D6
Agaton Rd SE9 ....30 C6
Agester La CT4....... 243 A4
Agnes Cl E6..............2 A6
Agricultural Mus Brook★
  TN25................ 270 B5
Ailsa Court ME1........62 F2
Ailsa Mews ME1........62 F2
Ainsdale Cl
  Folkestone CT19...... 335 B7
  Orpington BR6 ....53 D1
Ainsley Way CT4 ......206 F8
Aintree Cl DA12 ....37 B5
Aintree Ho [1] ME15 ...195 F6
Aintree Rd ME5 ....97 C3
Airedale Cl Dartford DA2 34 C7
  Margate CT9...........51 A1
Aireys The CT13.......180 B6
Airfield View ME12.....71 C8
Airport Ind Est TN16 .. 118 D4
Airport Rdbt E16 ....1 D5
Aisher Rd SE28..........3 C6
Aisher Way TN13 ......153 E6
Aisne Dr CT1......... 143 D1
Ajax Rd ME1............96 C8
Akehurst La TN13 .... 154 C2
Alabama St SE18 ....12 E7
Alamein Ave ME5.......96 F7
Alamein Cl CT15.......278 F3
Alamein Gdns DA2 .....34 D8
Alamein Rd DA10.......17 D1
Alanbrooke DA12.......37 C8
Alan Cl DA1 ....15 C3
Alan Marre Ho SE7 .....11 D8
Alanthus Cl SE12 ....11 A1
Alaseun Terr ME12 .....47 A5
Alban Cres DA4 ....57 A1
Albany Cl Sidcup DA5....31 D8
  Tonbridge TN9........ 254 D7
Albany Dr CT6...........76 D4
Albany Hill TN2 ...... 286 C5
Albany Ho [15] CT17 ... 310 D7
Albany Mews BR1 ......29 A2
Albany Park Sta DA5 ...31 D6
Albany Pl CT17 .... 310 D7
Albany Rd Bexley DA17 ..13 F8
  Capel-le-Ferne CT18... 308 C1
  Chatham ME4 ....64 B2
  Chislehurst BR7 ....30 B3
  Gillingham ME7.........64 D4
  Rochester ME1.........63 C4
  Sidcup DA5 ....31 C8
  Sittingbourne ME10 ... 101 E3
  Tilbury RM18...........19 A6
Albany St ME14........162 B5
Albany Terr
  Chatham ME4 ....63 E4
  Gillingham ME7.........64 D4
Albatross Ave ME2 .....62 C6
Albatross Cl [9] E6....... 1 F8
Albatross St SE18 ......12 E7
Albemarle Rd
  Ashford TN24 ....268 F1
  Chatham ME5 ....97 C2
Alberta Cl CT16 ....278 B3
Alberta Rd DA8.........14 C6
Albert Basin Way E16 ... 2 C6
Albert Costain Ct [1]
  CT20 .... 335 D5
Albert Cotts TN1 ......286 B4
Albert Ct
  [8] Ramsgate CT12.... 117 E6
  [9] Whitstable CT5 ......74 D2
Albert Ho SE28...........2 C3
Albert La CT21 .... 333 C1

Albert Manor ME7 64 B5
Albert Murray Cl DA12 37 C8
Albert Pl ME2 63 B7
Albert Rd Ashford TN24 268 B3
Broadstairs CT10 83 E8
Bromley, Bromley Common BR2 52 D4
Bromley, Mottingham SE9 29 E5
Canterbury CT1 175 B8
Capel-le-Ferne CT18 308 C2
Chatham ME4 64 A3
Dartford DA2 33 C5
Deal CT14 215 C6
Dover CT16 278 D1
Erith DA17 3 F1
Folkestone CT19 335 D6
Gillingham ME7 64 C4
Hythe CT21 333 B1
Margate CT9 50 H2
Newham E16 1 F5
Orpington BR5 54 B3
Orpington, Green Street Green BR6 87 A5
Ramsgate CT11 117 F7
Rochester ME1 63 C3
Sidcup DA5 32 B8
Swanscombe DA10 17 F1
3 Tonbridge TN9 222 B1
Albert Reed Gdns ME15 161 E2
Albert Row CT11 117 C5
Albert St
Maidstone ME14 161 F6
Ramsgate CT11 117 E6
Royal Tunbridge Wells TN1 286 B4
Whitstable CT5 74 D2
Albert Terr Deal CT14 215 C5
Margate CT9 50 I2
Minster (Sheppey) ME12 48 A5
Albert Wlk E16 2 B4
Albion Cl CT6 111 A8
Albion Cotts TN12 259 D5
Albion Ct
Ramsgate CT11 117 E6
2 Woolwich SE18 1 E2
Albion Hill 7 CT11 117 E6
Albion Ho E16 2 B5
Albion La CT6 111 A8
Albion Mews
Ramsgate CT11 117 F6
Royal Tunbridge Wells TN1 286 C5
Albion Mews Rd 3 CT20 335 D4
Albion Pl Ashford TN24 300 E7
Canterbury CT1 143 A1
Chattenden ME2 41 A3
Faversham ME13 138 C7
Hythe CT21 333 D2
Maidstone ME14 162 B4
Newington ME9 100 B6
Ramsgate CT11 117 E6
Albion Rd Bexley DA6 14 A3
Birchington CT7 81 A7
Broadstairs CT10 83 F6
Chatham ME5 97 B2
Deal CT14 215 D8
Eastry CT13 180 A2
Folkestone CT19 335 D6
Gravesend DA12 37 C8
Marden TN12 259 D5
Margate CT9 51 B3
Ramsgate CT11 117 F7
Royal Tunbridge Wells TN1 286 C5
Albion St CT10 84 B4
Albion Terr
Gravesend DA12 19 D1
Sittingbourne ME10 101 E6
Albion Villas 6 CT20 335 D4
Albion Way TN8 217 C4
Albright Ind Est RM13 4 F8
Albuhera Sq CT1 143 D1
Albury Ave DA7 13 E5
Albury Cl ME5 97 D2
Albyfield BR1 52 F6
Alchins Cotts ME17 194 E2
Alconbury DA6 14 B2
Aldeburgh Pl SE10 1 A2
Aldeburgh St SE10 1 A1
Alder Cl
Royal Tunbridge Wells TN4 254 D1
West Minst ME12 46 A8
Aldergate La CT21 331 C1
Alder Ho TN23 267 F1
Alder La TN17 343 C1
Alder Lodge TN4 285 E4
Alderman Cl DA1 32 E8
Aldermary Rd BR1 52 A8
Alderney Gdns CT10 83 E5
Alderney Rd DA8 15 A7
Alderney Way TN24 268 C7
Alder Rd
Folkestone CT19 335 C6
Sidcup DA14 30 F5
Alders Cotts TN12 256 A5
Aldersgrove Ave SE9 29 D5
Aldershot Rd ME5 97 A7
Alders Meadow TN9 221 F2
Alders Rd TN11, TN12 255 E6
Alders The ME18 191 D7
Alder Way BR8 55 D7
Alderwick Rd ME18 159 C3
Alderwood Prim Sch SE9 12 E1
Alderwood Rd SE9 12 D1
ALDINGTON 330 A6
Aldington Cl ME5 97 B5
Aldington Cnr TN25 330 A6
ALDINGTON FRITH 329 D6
Aldington La ME14 163 D8
Aldington Prim Sch TN25 330 A5
Aldington Rd
Greenwich SE18 1 D3
Lympne CT21 331 E3
Maidstone ME14 162 F4
ALDON 126 B1
Aldon Cl ME14 162 C6
Aldon Ct ME14 162 C6
Aldon La ME19 158 C8
Aldred Rd ME13 138 C6
Aldridge Cl CT6 76 B3
Aldwick Cl SE9 30 D5
Aldwych Cl TN10 222 D7
Alec Pemble Cl TN24 268 E5
Alefe Way ME9 68 D3
Alen Sq TN12 260 F4
Alers Rd DA6 13 D2
Alestan Beck Rd E16 1 D7
Alexander Cl Hayes BR2 52 A1
Sandwich CT13 180 F8
Sidcup DA15 12 E1
Alexander Cotts ME2 39 C6
Alexander Ct
Greenwich SE3 11 B5
1 Rochester ME2 63 B8
2 Royal Tunbridge Wells TN1 286 A4
1 Sittingbourne ME10 101 E5
Alexander Dr ME13 138 B7
Alexander Gr ME18 159 A3
Alexander McLeod Prim Sch SE2 3 B1
Alexander Rd
Bexley DA7 13 D5
Chislehurst BR7 30 B3
Swanscombe DA9 17 C2
Alexandra Ave ME7 64 E4
Alexandra Cl
Sittingbourne ME10 101 E7
Swanley BR8 55 E7
Alexandra Corniche CT21 334 C3
Alexandra Ct CT21 333 A1
Alexandra Dr CT14 214 F3
Alexandra Gdns CT20 335 D4
Alexandra Glen ME5 97 A1
Alexandra Homes CT9 50 I1
Alexandra Mews ME12 28 D2
Alexandra Pl 1 CT17 278 C1
Alexandra Rd
Biggin Hill TN16 150 B8
Birchington CT7 81 A5
Broadstairs CT10 84 B4
Capel-le-Ferne CT18 308 C2
Chatham ME4 64 B2
Deal CT14 215 D2
Erith DA8 14 F8
Gravesend DA12 37 E8
Kingsdown CT14 248 C5
Margate CT9 82 E8
Ramsgate CT11 117 D8
Sheerness ME12 28 D2
Tilbury RM18 18 F5
Tonbridge TN9 254 B8
Whitstable CT5 108 C8
Alexandra St
Folkestone CT19 335 E6
Maidstone ME14 161 F6
Newham E16 1 A8
Alexandra Terr CT9 50 I1
Alexandra Wlk DA4 57 E7
Alexandria Dr CT6 76 C5
Alex Hughes Cl ME6 127 F6
Alfa Close ME19 159 D3
Alfan La DA2 32 D3
Alford Ho 6 SE18 12 B8
Alford Rd DA8 4 C1
Alford Snell Lodge TN2 286 D2
Alfred Cl
Canterbury CT1 174 C6
Chatham ME4 64 B2
Alfred Ho
Gravesend DA11 37 B6
5 Northfleet DA11 36 F7
Alfred Mews CT14 215 D7
Alfred Pl DA11 36 F7
Alfred Rd Ashford TN24 300 D7
Birchington CT7 80 D8
Canterbury CT1 174 C6
Dover CT16 278 B2
Erith DA17 3 F1
Gravesend DA11 37 B6
Greatstone-on-Sea TN28 373 D3
Hawley DA2 33 F4
Margate CT9 51 B1
Alfred Row CT14 215 D7
Alfred Sq CT14 215 D7
Alfred St RM17 18 C8
Alfriston Cl DA1 14 E1
Alfriston Gr ME19 159 C3
Alice Thompson Cl SE12 29 C6
Alicia Ave CT9 82 A8
Alicia Ho DA16 13 B6
Alison Cl Birchington CT7 81 B8
Newham E6 2 A7
Whitfield CT16 278 A6
Alison Cres CT16 278 A7
Alkerden La DA9, DA10 17 C1
ALKHAM 276 C1
Alkham Cl CT9 51 F2
Alkham Rd
Maidstone ME14 162 C5
Temple Ewell CT15, CT16 277 C4
Alkham Tower 9 BR5 54 C5
Alkham Valley Rd
Alkham CT15 276 E1
Hawkinge CT18, CT15 307 E4
Allan Cl TN4 285 C4
Allandale Pl BR6 87 D7
Allandale Rd TN2 286 D7
Alland Grange La CT12 81 E2
Allan Rd CT5 107 E6
Allard Cl BR5 54 C2
Allen Ave CT8 81 D7
Allenby Ave CT14 215 B5
Allenby Rd
Biggin Hill TN16 118 E2
Ramsgate CT12 83 C2
Woolwich SE28 2 C3
Allenby Wlk ME10 101 B5
Allen Cl ME5 97 C6
Allen Ct ME12 47 A5
Allendale Cl DA2 34 D7
Allendale St 2 CT19 335 D6
Allen Field TN23 299 F8
Allen Gardiner Ho TN2 286 C3
Allens TN12 259 D5
Allens La TN15, TN11 190 A7
Allens Mead DA12 37 F7
Allen St ME14 162 B5
Allenswood Rd SE9 11 F5
All Faiths Childrens Com Sch 6 ME2 63 B7
ALLHALLOWS 9 D1
ALLHALLOWS-ON-SEA 9 D3
Allhallows-on-Sea Est ME3 9 E4
Allhallows Prim Sch ME3 9 D2
Allhallows Rd
Lower Stoke ME3 25 C5
Newham E6 1 E7
Alliance Rd Newham E13 1 C8
Ramsgate CT11 117 F6
Woolwich SE18 13 A7
Alliance Way TN12 256 F6
ALLINGTON 161 D8
Allington Cl 6 DA12 37 F7
Allington Dr
Rochester ME2 62 E8
Tonbridge TN10 223 A5
Allington Gdns ME18 192 E7
Allington Prim Sch ME16 161 C7
Allington Rd
Gillingham ME8 65 A3
Orpington BR6 53 E1
Paddock Wood TN12 256 F7
Allington Way ME16 161 B6
Allison Ave ME7 64 E1
Allnutt Mill Cl 4 ME15 161 E2
Allotment La TN13 154 C5
All Saints' Ave CT9 50 H1
All Saints CE Prim Sch 3 ME4 64 A3
All Saints Cl DA10 17 F2
All Saints' Cl CT5 74 F1
All Saints Ind Pk CT9 50 I1
All Saints La 2 CT1 174 F8
All Saints Rd
Allhallows ME3 9 D2
Hawkhurst TN18 341 A1
Royal Tunbridge Wells TN4 286 B6
Sittingbourne ME10 102 C4
All Saints' Rd DA11 36 F7
All Saints Rise TN4 286 A6
All Saints View ME13 106 E2
All Souls CE Prim Sch CT19 334 E6
Allsworth Cl ME9 100 B6
Alma Pl
2 Canterbury CT1 143 A1
Hadlow TN11 223 E8
Ramsgate CT11 117 E7
Rochester ME2 63 A7
Alma Rd Eccles ME20 128 F6
Folkestone CT20 334 D5
Herne Bay CT6 77 C5
Margate CT9 50 J1
Orpington BR5 87 D8
Ramsgate CT11 117 E8
Sheerness ME12 28 C2
Sidcup DA14 31 A5
Swanscombe DA10 17 F2
West Malling ME19 159 A8
Almarina CT8 50 C1
Alma St Canterbury CT1 143 A1
Sheerness ME12 28 D2
Alma Street Pas ME12 28 D2
Alma The DA12 37 F4
Almery Cotts ME17 229 B8
Almond Cl
Ashford TN23 267 F5
Broadstairs CT10 83 C4
Bromley BR2 53 A2
Whitstable CT5 75 D1
Almond Ct CT4 173 E1
Almond Dr BR8 55 D7
Almond Gr ME7 98 A4
Almond Ho 9 ME16 161 A3
Almond Rd DA2 34 C8
Almonds The ME14 163 A4
Almond Tree Cl ME12 46 A8
Almond Way BR2 53 A2
Almon Pl ME1 63 D5
Almshouse Rd ME13 202 C7
Almshouses
8 Canterbury CT1 175 A8
Crockenhill BR8 55 D2
Penshurst TN11 252 C4
Sevenoaks TN13 154 C1
14 Tonbridge TN9 254 B8
Yalding ME18 193 A1
Alms Row TN16 152 B3
Alnwick Ct 8 DA2 16 B1
Alnwick Rd Eltham SE12 29 B8
Newham E16 1 C7
Alonso Ho 4 DA17 4 A1
Alpha Rd Birchington CT7 81 A7
Alpha Rd *continued*
Ramsgate CT11 117 D6
Alpine Bsns Ctr E6 2 A8
Alpine Copse 2 BR1 53 A7
Alpine Way E6 2 A8
Alsager Ave ME11 45 F3
Alsike Rd DA18 3 E3
Alsops Rd TN24 300 E7
Alston Cl ME12 47 C7
Altash Way SE9 30 A6
Altbarn Ind Est ME5 130 C8
Alton Ave ME19 159 A3
Alton Cl DA5 31 E7
Alton Cotts DA4 89 E8
Alverstone Gdns SE9 30 C7
Alvis Ave CT6 76 A4
Alwold Cres SE12 11 C1
Amage Rd TN25 270 C8
Amage Road Cotts TN25 238 B1
Amanda Cl ME5 96 F3
Amar Ct SE18 2 F2
Amardeep Ct SE18 2 F1
Ambassador Gdns E6 1 F8
Amber Cl ME9 103 D2
Amber Ct ME7 64 D5
Amber La ME17 196 A1
Amber Lane ME19 159 D3
Amberleaze Dr TN2 287 D6
Amberley Cl
2 Orpington BR6 86 F5
Tonbridge TN9 254 A8
Amberley Ct
Royal Tunbridge Wells TN4 286 C8
Sidcup DA14 31 C3
Amberley Rd SE2 13 D8
Amber Rise ME10 101 C7
Amber Way ME17 196 B1
Amblecote Cl SE12 29 B5
Amblecote Mdw SE12 29 B5
Amblecote Rd SE12 29 B5
Ambleside
Faversham ME13 138 E6
Sittingbourne ME10 102 C3
Ambleside Rd DA7 14 A5
Ambley Gn ME8 98 A8
Ambley Rd ME8 98 B8
Ambley Wood Nature Reserve* ME7, ME8 98 A8
Ambrook Rd DA17 4 A3
Ambrose Cl
Crayford DA1 15 A3
6 Newham E6 1 F8
Orpington BR6 86 F7
Ambrose Hill ME5 64 C2
Amels Hill ME9 132 F8
Ames Ave ME14 163 A4
Amesbury Rd BR1 52 D6
Ames Rd DA10 17 E1
Ames Way ME19 159 B3
Amethyst Ave ME5 96 E6
Amethyst Dr ME10 101 D6
Amherst Cl
Maidstone ME16 161 D4
Margate CT9 51 C1
Orpington BR5 54 A5
Amherst Dr BR5 54 A5
Amherst Hill
Chatham ME7 64 A6
Sevenoaks TN13 153 F4
Amherst Prim Sch TN13 153 E4
Amherst Rd
Rochester ME1 63 D3
Royal Tunbridge Wells TN4 286 A5
Sevenoaks TN13 154 B5
Amherst Redoubt ME4 64 A5
Amhurst Bank Rd TN2, TN11, TN12 255 F4
Amhurst Wlk SE28 3 A5
Amies Ho ME15 194 F3
Amos Cl Herne Bay CT6 77 C3
Sheldwich ME13 170 C5
Ampleforth Cl BR6 87 C6
Ampleforth Rd SE2 3 C4
Amsbury Rd ME15, ME17 194 B2
Amshurst Villas ME15 194 A4
Anatase Cl ME10 101 C7
Ancaster St SE18 12 E7
Anchorage Cl ME3 25 C3
Anchorage Flats TN12 257 A6
Anchorage Point Ind Est SE7 1 C3
Anchor Bay Ind Est DA8 15 A8
Anchor Bsns Pk ME10 102 B6
Anchor Bvd DA2 16 D3
Anchor Ct DA7 13 E6
Anchor Hill 4 CT9 50 J2
Anchor Ho Newham E16 1 C7
Rochester ME1 63 B4
Anchor & Hope La SE7 1 C2
Anchor La Deal CT14 215 C6
Sheerness ME12 27 F3
Anchor Rd ME1 63 C1
Ancona Rd SE18 2 D1
Ancress Cl CT2 143 A4
Andace Pk BR1 52 C8
Anderson Way DA17 4 B4
Andorra Ct BR1 52 C8
Andover Ave E16 1 D7
Andover Rd BR6 53 E1
Andover Wlk 12 ME15 195 F6
Andrew Broughton Way ME14 162 B4
Andrew Cl DA1 14 D2
Andrewes Gdns E6 1 E7
Andrew Manor ME7 64 C6
Andrew Rd TN4 286 C8
Andrews Cl
Orpington BR5 54 D6
Andrews Cl *continued*
Royal Tunbridge Wells TN2 286 D5
Andrews Pl DA2 32 E6
Andrews Wlk ME10 101 B5
Andrew Wells Ho 8 BR1 29 B1
Andringham Lodge 7 BR1 52 B8
Andwell Cl SE2 3 B4
Anemone Way CT6 110 E7
Anerley Cl ME16 161 D7
Angel Cotts ME8 66 A2
Angel Hts CT18 306 E3
Angelica Dr E6 2 A8
Angel La TN9 222 B1
Angel Row TN18 356 B5
Angel Terr TN18 356 B6
Angel Walk Shop Ctr TN9 222 C1
Angel Wlk 4 TN9 222 B1
Angerstein Bsns Pk SE10 1 A2
Angle Rd RM20 17 D8
Anglesea Ave SE18 2 B2
Anglesea Pl 19 DA11 19 B1
Anglesea Rd
Orpington BR5 54 C3
Woolwich SE18 2 B2
Anglesey Ave ME15 195 A7
Anglesey Cl ME5 97 B7
Angley Ct TN12 290 A5
Angley Rd TN17 320 C6
Angley Sch TN17 320 C5
Angley Wlk TN17 320 D6
Anglia Ctr The RM13 4 E8
Anglian Ind Est IG11 3 A8
Anglian Sch of English CT9 51 B2
Anglo Saxon Ho DA12 37 E8
Angus Dr TN24 268 C7
Ankerdine Cres SE18 12 B6
Annandale Rd DA15 30 F8
Anna Pk CT7 80 F8
Anne Boleyn Cl ME12 48 E3
Anne Cl CT7 81 B7
Anne Green Wlk 8 CT1 143 B2
Anne of Cleves Rd DA1 15 D1
Anne Roper Cl TN28 373 E6
Annesley Rd SE3 11 B6
Annesmere Gardens 1 SE3 11 D4
Anne's Rd CT10 84 C7
Annetts Hall TN15 157 A8
Annex The BR8 56 B6
Annie Rd ME6 127 F6
Annison Street 4 TN9 222 B2
Anns Rd CT11 117 E8
Ann St SE18 2 D2
Ann Stroud Ct SE12 11 A2
Annvera Ho 2 ME7 64 C7
ANSDORE 239 F6
Ansell Ave ME4 64 A1
Anselm Cl ME10 101 E4
Anselm Rd CT17 310 A8
Ansia Cl ME19 159 B3
Anson Ave ME19 158 F3
Anson Cl
Broadstairs CT10 83 D3
Chatham ME5 97 C6
Orpington BR5 54 A4
Anson Pl SE28 2 D4
Anstee Rd CT17 278 C1
Anstridge Rd SE9 12 D1
Antelope Cl CT16 278 A5
Antelope Rd SE18 1 F3
Anthony Cl TN13 153 E7
Anthony Cres CT5 108 B6
Anthony Rd DA16 13 A6
Anthony Roper Prim Sch DA4 89 E8
Anthonys La BR8 56 A8
Anthonys Way ME2 63 E8
Antolin Way CT10, CT12 83 A3
Antonius Ct TN23 300 A5
Anvil Cl CT7 81 A6
ANVIL GREEN 239 C8
Anvil Terr DA2 32 E6
Anzio Cres CT15 278 E2
Anzio Ho 15 CT1 143 B2
Apartments The TN28 373 E5
APERFIELD 118 F2
Aperfield Rd
Biggin Hill TN16 118 E2
Erith DA8 14 F8
Apiary Bsns Pk The ME17 197 B3
Apollo Ave BR1 52 B8
Apollo Ho ME5 97 A6
Apollo Way Erith DA8 4 D2
St Mary's Island ME4 41 C2
3 Woolwich SE28 2 D3
Appleby Cl ME1 96 D7
Appleby Close B5 53 E2
Appleby Ct TN24 268 D2
Appleby Rd E16 1 A7
Apple Cl Hawkinge CT18 307 B4
Snodland ME6 128 A6
Apple Craft Ctr* ME13 138 E5
Applecross Cl ME1 63 B4
Apple Ct TN12 256 F6
APPLEDORE 361 C7
Appledore Ave
Bexley DA7 14 D5
West Minst ME12 46 B8
Appledore Cl Hayes BR2 52 A4
Margate CT9 51 C1
Appledore Cres
Folkestone CT19 334 D7
Sidcup DA14 30 F5
Appledore Ct ME16 161 C7
APPLEDORE HEATH 347 C1
Appledore Rd
Appledore TN26, TN30 361 A7
Brattle TN26 347 C7
Gillingham ME8 65 A3
Tenterden TN30 345 E7
Appledore Sta TN26 362 B8
Appledown Way CT1 175 D5
Appleford Dr ME12 46 F7
Applegarth Dr DA1 33 F6
Applegarth Ho DA8 14 F5
Applegarth Pk CT5 108 A6
Applegarth Rd SE28 3 C6
Apple Orch BR8 55 D5
Appleshaw Cl DA11 37 A3
Appleton Cl DA7 14 C5
Appleton Dr DA2 33 B5
Appleton Rd SE9 11 E4
Appletons TN11 223 E8
Apple Tree Cl ME16 160 F2
Appletree Ct 5 ME8 98 F8
Apple Tree La TN2 286 D8
Appold St DA8 14 F8
Approach Rd
Broadstairs CT10 84 A4
Dover CT17 310 A6
Margate CT9 51 A2
Shepherdswell CT15 244 D5
Tatsfield CR6, TN16 150 B5
Approach Road S TN29 380 C2
Approach The BR6 86 F8
April Cl BR6 86 F5
April Rise
Birchington CT7 80 D8
Whitstable CT5 108 B7
Apsledene DA12 37 D2
Apsley Cotts CT4 173 D3
Apsley Ct Orpington BR5 54 B3
14 Ramsgate CT11 117 E7
Apsley St Ashford TN23 268 B2
Rusthall TN4 285 D4
Aragon Cl Ashford TN23 299 E7
Orpington BR2 52 F1
Arborfield DA13 60 A4
Arbroath Rd SE9 11 E4
Arbrook Cl BR5 54 A6
Arbrook Ct BR5 54 A8
Arbury Ho BR1 29 E1
Arbuthnot La DA5 13 E1
Arcade The 2 SE9 12 A1
Arcadian Ave DA5 13 E1
Arcadian Cl DA5 13 E1
Arcadian Rd DA5 13 E1
Arcadia Rd DA13 59 F8
Archbishop Courtenay CE Prim Sch (Tovil Site) ME15 161 E2
Archbishop Courtenay CE Prim Sch (Town Site) 8 ME15 162 A3
Archbishops Cres ME7 65 A5
Archbishop's Sch The CT2 142 E3
Archcliffe Rd CT17 310 C5
Archer Ct ME10 68 F2
Archer Ho ME3 40 F6
Archer Rd Chatham ME5 97 B6
Folkestone CT19 335 D6
Orpington BR5 54 A4
Archers Court Maths & Computing Coll CT16 278 B5
Archer's Court Rd CT15, CT16 278 B7
Archer Way BR8 56 A7
Archery Cl ME3 40 B7
Archery House Hospl DA2 16 B1
Archery Rd SE9 11 F2
Archery Sq CT14 215 D3
Archibald Ho ME14 162 A7
Archway Ct
Dartford DA1 33 D8
4 Rochester ME2 63 B8
Archway Rd
Ramsgate CT11 117 E6
Sheerness ME12 28 A3
Arcon Cl TN23 300 A7
Arcon Rd TN23 300 A7
Arden Bsns Ctr ME2 63 E7
Arden Cl SE28 3 D7
Arden Dr TN24 268 C3
Arden Gr BR6 86 B6
Arden Grange CT4 205 C8
Ardenlee Dr ME14 162 B5
Arden Rd
Faversham ME13 138 E7
Herne Bay CT6 77 C2
Arden St ME7 64 C6
Ardent Ave CT14 215 C4
Ardent Rd CT16 278 A5
Arethusa Pl DA9 17 B3
Arethusa Rd ME1 96 C8
Arethusa Venture Ctr* ME2 41 A3
Argali Ho 3 DA18 3 E3
Argent Bsns Pk ME11 46 A2
Argent Rd ME11 46 A2
Argent St RM17 18 B7
Argent Way ME10 101 C6
Argles Cl 4 DA9 17 A2
Argyle Ave CT9 50 G1
Argyle Cl ME1 96 E8
Argyle Gdns CT9 50 G1
Argyle Rd Newham E16 1 B7
Royal Tunbridge Wells TN4 254 A2
Sevenoaks TN13 154 B2
Whitstable CT5 74 D1
Argyll Dr CT11 83 F1
Argyll Rd SE18 2 C3
Ariel Cl DA12 37 F4
Ariel Ct 5 DA17 4 A1

Ark Cotts CT18 305 D4
Ark La CT14 215 D7
Arkley Rd CT6 76 F4
Arklow Sq 6 CT11 117 F7
Arkwright Rd RM18 19 A5
Arlington TN23 299 F8
Arlington Cl DA15 30 E8
Arlington Gdns CT9 83 C8
Arlington Ho CT9 50 H2
Arlington Sq CT9 50 H2
Arlott Cl ME14 161 F6
Armada Cl TN28 373 E5
Armada Ct ME4 63 E1
Armadale CT10 51 F1
Armada Way
Chatham ME4 63 F3
Newham E6 2 C7
Armitage Pl 5 TN18 340 F2
Armourers Wlk CT16 278 A3
Armoury Dr DA12 37 C8
Armstrong Cl
Badgers Mount TN14 121 B4
Bromley BR1 52 E6
Newham E6 1 F7
Armstrong Rd
Maidstone ME15 162 A1
Woolwich SE18 2 C3
Armstrong Sq CT6 76 A3
Armytage Cl ME3 41 E4
Arne Cl TN10 222 E6
Arne Gr BR6 86 F7
Arnhem Dr ME5 96 F7
Arnold Ave DA13 93 B8
Arnolde Cl ME2 63 E7
Arnold Pl RM18 19 C6
Arnold Rd
Chartham CT4 173 C2
Gravesend DA12 37 D6
5 Margate CT9 50 J1
Arnolds Business Park
TN12 225 A5
Arnolds Court TN10 222 C5
Arnolds La DA4 34 A2
Arnott Cl SE28 3 C5
Arnsberg Way DA6, DA7 14 A3
Arnside Rd DA7 14 A6
Arolla Rd CT6 77 C4
ARPINGE 306 C3
Arran Cl DA8 14 D8
Arrandene Ho 3 BR5 54 B7
Arran Gn ME2 62 C6
Arran Mews 4 CT1 143 B2
Arran Rd ME15 195 A6
Arras Ho Bexley SE2 13 D8
Erith SE2 3 D1
Arrowhead La TN26,
TN29 362 D7
Arsenal Rd SE9 11 F4
Arsenal Way SE18 2 C3
Artemis Cl DA12 37 E8
Arthur Ct 11 RM17 18 C8
Arthur Gr SE18 2 C2
Arthur Kennedy Cl
ME13 139 F3
Arthur Rd
Biggin Hill TN16 118 C3
Birchington CT7 80 D8
Deal CT14 215 A3
Gillingham ME8 98 E7
Hythe CT21 333 C1
Margate CT9 51 A3
Rochester ME1 63 D3
Arthur Ruxley Est DA14 31 D2
Arthur Salmon Cl
ME13 138 B7
Arthur St Erith DA8 14 F7
3 Folkestone CT19 335 E6
Gravesend DA11 37 A8
Grays RM17 18 C8
Sittingbourne ME10 101 E4
Arthur Street W DA11 37 A8
Arthur Toft Ho 6 RM17 18 B8
Artillery Gdns 11 CT1 143 A1
Artillery Ho
12 Canterbury CT1 143 A1
Woolwich SE18 2 A1
Artillery Pl SE18 2 A2
Artillery Rd CT11 117 F7
Artillery Row DA12 37 C8
Artillery St 10 CT1 143 A1
Artington Cl BR6 86 C6
Artisan Cl E6 2 B6
Arun Ct BR5 54 C1
Arundel DA14 31 A3
Arundel Ave ME10 101 E1
Arundel Cl Bexley DA5 13 F1
Chatham ME5 97 D1
Tonbridge TN9 254 A8
Arundel Ct 2 DA6 13 E3
Arundel Dr BR6 87 B5
Arundel Ho TN1 286 A3
Arundel Rd
Cliffs End CT12 116 D7
Dartford DA1 15 C3
Margate CT9 51 B2
Royal Tunbridge Wells
TN1 286 B2
Arundel Sq ME15 161 F2
Arundel St ME14 161 F6
Ascot Cl
Borough Green TN15 157 B7
Chatham ME5 97 C2
Ascot Ct Bromley BR1 52 E7
Sidcup DA5 31 F8
Ascot Gdns CT8 81 E7
Ascot Ho 2 ME15 195 F6
Ascot Rd
Gravesend DA12 37 B5
Orpington BR5 53 F5
ASH Canterbury 147 D2
Hartley 91 E5
ASHBANK 197 B7
Ashbank Cotts ME17 197 B7
Ashbee Cl ME6 128 A7
Ashbee Gdns CT6 77 C5
Ashborne Cl TN24 268 D6
Ashbourne Ave DA7 13 E7
Ashbourne Ct TN4 285 D4
Ashbourne Rise BR6 86 E6
Ashbrooke Ctr The 2
CT10 83 C4
Ashburn Ct BR1 29 A1
Ashburn Gdns CT6 77 C5
Ashburnham Cl TN13 187 C8
Ashburnham Rd
Erith DA17 4 C2
Maidstone ME14 162 B8
Ramsgate CT11 117 C7
Tonbridge TN10 222 C3
Ashburn Mews ME7 64 E3
Ashburton Cl TN24 268 E2
Ashburton Rd E16 1 A7
Ashby Cl ME2 95 A4
Ashby's Cl TN8 249 D8
Ashbys Yd TN9 222 C1
Ash Cl Ashford TN23 267 E3
Aylesford ME20 128 E1
Broadstairs CT10 83 E4
Chatham ME5 64 C1
Crabble CT17 277 E3
Edenbridge TN8 217 B1
Gillingham ME8 65 B3
Herne Bay CT6 76 F1
Orpington BR5 53 D4
Royal Tunbridge Wells
TN2 314 D7
Sidcup DA14 31 B5
Swanley BR8 55 D7
Ashcombe Dr TN8 217 B4
Ash Cres
Biddenden TN27 323 D7
Hersden CT3 111 E1
Higham ME3 39 C3
Ashcroft Ave DA15 13 A1
Ashcroft Cres DA15 13 A1
Ashcroft Ct Dartford DA1 34 A8
5 Eltham SE9 12 A1
Ash Croft Ct DA3 91 F7
Ashcroft Rd
Paddock Wood TN12 257 A5
Rochester ME2 40 B2
Ash Ct Cliffs End CT12 116 D4
Lewisham SE12 29 A8
Ashdale Ho 5 TN23 268 C2
Ashdale Rd SE12 29 B7
Ashden Wlk TN10 222 C7
Ashdown Cl
Coldblow DA5 32 C8
Herne Bay CT6 77 B2
Maidstone ME16 161 D3
Royal Tunbridge Wells
TN4 285 F4
Ashdown Cres TN28 373 B6
Ashdown Ct TN24 268 C3
Ashdown Field CT4 173 B2
Ashdown Lodge CT20 335 A5
Ashdown Rd ME17,
ME9 166 F3
Ashen E6 2 A7
Ashenden TN27 263 F2
Ashenden Cl
Canterbury CT1 174 C5
Rochester ME2 40 C2
Ashendene Gr CT2 144 A6
Ashenden Wlk TN2 286 E8
Ashen Dr DA1 15 A1
Ashen Grove Mobile Home
Pk TN15 90 B1
Ashen Grove Rd TN15 90 B1
Ashen Tree Cotts CT3 146 B1
Ashentree La TN29 371 A5
Ashen Tree La CT16 310 E8
Asher Reeds TN3 285 A4
Ashes La Plaxtol TN11 189 F1
Tonbridge TN11 223 B8
Ashfield La BR7 30 C1
Ashfield Pl BR7 30 D1
ASHFORD 268 A2
Ashford Borough Mus★ 15
TN23 268 B2
Ashford Bsns Pk TN24 301 A6
Ashford Bsns Point
TN24 300 F5
Ashford Designer Outlet
TN24 300 C7
Ashford Dr ME17 197 D3
Ashford Friars Prep Sch
TN23 299 B8
Ashford Int Sta TN24 268 C1
Ashford Mkt TN24 300 E5
Ashford Oaks Com Prim
Sch 1 TN23 299 F8
Ashford Rd
Ashford TN23 299 B8
Bethersden TN26, TN23 297 C4
Charing TN27 234 C7
Chartham CT4, CT1 173 C3
Folkestone CT18, CT19 334 B7
Godmersham CT4 205 C4
Hamstreet TN26 327 F1
Harrietsham ME17 198 C6
Kingsnorth TN23, TN26 300 A4
Maidstone, Grove Green
ME14 162 D4
Maidstone ME14 163 D3
New Romney TN28 373 A6
Sellindge TN25 303 B1
Sheldwich ME13 170 C4
Tenterden, Durrant Green
TN26, TN30 324 A6
Tenterden TN30 345 B8
Westenhanger CT21, TN25,
CT18 332 C6
Ashford St Mary's CE Prim
Sch TN23 268 A3
Ashford Sch of Art &
Design (Henwood
Campus) TN25 268 D3
Ashford Sch of Art &
Design (Tufton Campus)
8 TN25 268 C2
Ashford Sta TN24 268 C1
Ash Gr Elvington CT15 212 B2
Lydd TN29 376 D7
Maidstone ME16 161 C6
St Margaret's at Cliffe
CT15 279 F6
Ashgrove Ashford TN23 267 F5
Lewisham SE12 29 A7
Ashgrove Rd TN13 187 B7
Ashgrove Sch BR1 52 B7
Ash Ho BR5 54 C5
Ashington Cl ME10 101 C5
Ash Keys DA13 126 B8
Ash La TN15 91 D2
Ashlar Pl 4 SE18 2 B2
Ashleigh Cl DA13 92 F1
Ashleigh Commercial Est
SE18 1 D3
Ashleigh Gdns
Chatham ME5 96 D1
Headcorn TN27 262 D6
ASHLEY 246 B5
Ashley Ave CT19 334 E6
Ashley Cl
Halfway Houses ME12 46 C5
Ramsgate CT12 83 B2
Sevenoaks TN13 154 B3
Ashley Dr CT5 108 A7
Ashley Gdns
Orpington BR6 86 E5
Rusthall TN4 285 C5
Ashley Ho
Folkestone CT19 334 E6
Orpington BR5 54 A7
Ashley Mill Cotts CT19 334 E7
Ashley Park Cl TN4 285 C5
Ashley Pk TN4 285 C5
Ashley Rd
Gillingham ME8 65 C2
Sevenoaks TN13 154 B3
Tonbridge TN11 221 E5
Ashly Ct 22 DA14 31 A5
Ash Mdws TN24 300 F7
Ashmead Cl ME5 97 C3
Ashmead Gate BR1 52 C8
Ashmill Bsns Pk ME17 199 F6
Ashmore Gdns DA11 36 D5
Ashmore Gr DA16 12 E4
Ashmore La BR2 118 C8
Ash Platt Rd TN15 154 E6
Ash Rd Aylesham CT3 210 E5
Dartford DA1 33 D7
Gravesend DA12 37 C4
Hartley DA3 58 F3
Hawley DA2 33 F4
New Ash Green DA3,
TN15 91 E7
Orpington BR6 86 F3
Rochester ME2 62 F6
Sandwich CT13 148 E2
Westerham TN16 151 E2
Ashridge Cres SE18 12 C7
Ashridge House 7
DA14 30 F4
Ash Row BR2 53 A3
Ashtead Dr ME9 102 D2
Ashton Cl CT14 214 D4
Ashton Ct 4 CT10 83 E5
Ashton Ho CT14 215 B1
Ashton Mews 21 CT10 84 B4
Ashton Way ME19 159 C6
Ashtree Cl BR6 86 B6
Ash Tree Cl
Birchington CT7 81 B7
St Mary's Bay TN29 365 F3
West Kingsdown TN15 90 F2
Ash Tree Cotts TN12 291 B7
Ash Tree Dr TN15 90 F2
Ashtree Ho ME10 102 B3
Ash Tree La ME5 64 D1
Ash Tree Rd 6 CT19 335 E6
Ashtrees CT6 77 B3
ASHURST 283 D2
Ashurst Ave CT5 108 C6
Ashurst Cl DA1 14 F4
Ashurst Gdns CT9 51 E3
Ashurst Hill TN3 283 D2
Ashurst Pl ME8 98 E8
Ashurst Rd
Maidstone ME14 162 C5
Stone Cross TN3 284 B2
Ashurst Sta TN3 283 D2
Ashwater Rd SE12 29 A7
Ashwell Cl 9 E6 1 E7
Ashwood Cl ME3 40 C7
Ashwood Pl DA2 35 B5
Ashworth Avenue TN15 90 D3
Askern Cl DA6 13 D3
Askes Ct TN23 299 D8
Askews Farm La RM17,
RM20 17 E8
Askham Lodge 10 SE12 29 A8
Aspdin Rd DA11 36 E5
Aspen Cl Orpington BR6 87 A5
St Mary's Bay TN29 365 F3
Swanley BR8 55 D8
Aspen Copse BR1 52 F7
Aspen Ct DA1 16 A2
Aspen Dr Ashford TN23 267 D3
Dover CT16 278 A5
Aspen Gn DA18 3 F3
Aspen Ho
5 Folkestone CT20 335 D4
2 Sidcup DA15 31 A5
Aspen Rd Chartham CT4 173 E1
Herne CT6 110 E7
Aspen Way
2 Chatham ME5 96 E4
Royal Tunbridge Wells
TN4 254 C1
Aspian Dr ME17 194 D3
Aspinall Cl CT4 176 B4
Asquith Rd ME8 98 C6
Association Wlk ME1 96 C7
Aster Drive ME4 41 B2
Aster Rd
Hoo St Werburgh ME3 41 E3
Minster (Sheppey) ME12 47 B4
Astley RM17 17 F8
Astley Ave CT16 278 C2
Astley Ct CT16 278 C2
Astley St ME14 162 A4
Aston Cl Chatham ME5 97 A2
Sidcup DA14 31 A5
Aston Pl CT10 83 E6
Astor Ave CT17 310 B8
Astor Coll for the Arts
CT17 310 A8
Astor Ct E16 1 C7
Astor Dr CT14 215 C5
Astor of Hever Com Sch
The ME16 161 C3
Astor Rd
Broadstairs CT10 83 F8
West Kingsdown TN15 90 E4
Astra Dr DA12 37 F3
Astrid Rd CT14 215 A2
Atcost Rd IG11 3 A8
Athelstan Gn ME17 164 C2
Athelstan Pl CT14 215 C8
Athelstan Rd
Canterbury CT1 174 C5
Chatham ME4 63 F2
Faversham ME13 138 C6
Folkestone CT19 335 D7
Margate CT9 51 A3
Athelstan Way BR5 54 A8
Athena Ct CT9 51 A3
Athill Ct TN13 154 C5
Athol Pl ME13 138 A8
Athol Rd Ashford TN23 299 F7
Erith DA8 4 C1
Whitstable CT5 74 F2
Athol Terr CT16 310 F8
Atkinson Cl BR6 87 A5
Atkinson Rd
Hawkinge CT18 306 F3
Newham E16 1 C8
Atkinson Wlk TN24 268 F5
Atlanta Ct ME4 63 D3
Atlantic Cl DA10 17 E2
Atlantis Avenue E16 2 C6
Atlas Gdns SE7 1 C2
Atlas Rd DA1 15 F4
Atterbury Cl TN16 151 D1
Attlee Ave CT3 210 E5
Attlee Dr DA1 16 A2
Attlee Rd SE28 3 B6
Attlee Way ME10 101 E8
Attwaters La TN18 341 C6
Atwater Ct ME17 199 D5
Aubretia Wlk ME10 102 A3
Auckland Ave CT12 117 A8
Auckland Cl RM18 19 A5
Auckland Cres CT16 278 C3
Auckland Dr ME10 101 C3
Auckland Ho 10 ME15 195 E5
Auckland Rd TN1 286 C5
Auden Rd ME20 128 A3
Audley Ave
Gillingham ME7 64 E1
Margate CT9 50 E1
Tonbridge TN9 221 F2
Audley Cl ME16 161 B5
Audley Dr E16 1 B5
Audley Rd CT20 334 F5
Audley Rise TN9 221 F1
Audley Wlk BR5 54 C3
Audre Lorde Ho E16 1 B8
Audrey Sturley Ct TN4 285 D4
Auger Cl ME9 99 E5
Augusta Cl 1 ME7 64 C7
Augusta Gdns CT20 335 C4
Augusta Pl 14 CT11 117 F7
Augusta Rd CT11 117 F7
Augustine Ho TN10 222 C3
Augustine Rd
Gravesend DA12 37 C8
Minster (Sheppey) ME12 47 B8
Minster (Thanet) CT12 115 B6
Orpington BR5 54 D6
Augustus Wlk TN23 299 F5
Aultmore Ct TN2 286 D3
Aurelie Way CT5 108 F7
Aurellus Cl TN23 300 A4
Austell Manor 5 ME7 64 C6
Austen Cl
Swanscombe DA9 17 C1
Tilbury RM18 19 C5
Woolwich SE28 3 B5
Austen Gdns DA1 15 F3
Austen Rd DA8 14 B7
Austens Orch 13 TN30 345 A7
Austen Way ME20 127 F4
Austin Ave Bromley BR2 52 E4
Herne Bay CT6 75 F4
Austin Cl Gillingham ME5 64 E2
Sittingbourne ME10 102 A8
Austin Ct 4 TN16 151 D1
Austin Rd Ashford TN23 300 B6
Northfleet DA11 36 F7
Orpington BR5 54 A4
Austins La 4 CT13 149 A1
Austral Cl DA15 30 F5
Autumn Glade ME5 130 D8
Autumn Grove BR1 29 B2
Avalon Cl BR6 87 D7
Avalon Rd BR5, BR6 87 C8
Avard Gdns BR6 86 C6
Avards Cl TN18 354 E8
Avebury Ave
Ramsgate CT11 117 G8
Tonbridge TN9 222 B1
Avebury Rd BR6 86 D7
Aveley Cl DA8 14 F8
Aveling Cl ME3 41 D6
Aveling Ct 2 ME2 63 B7
Avenons Rd 3 E16 1 A8
Avent Wlk ME9 102 E2
Avenue du Puy TN9 222 C1
Avenue Gdns CT9 51 C3
Avenue of Remembrance
ME10 101 F3
Avenue Rd
Bexley DA7, DA6 13 E4
Dover CT16 278 C1
Erith DA8 14 D7
Herne Bay CT6 76 E5
Ramsgate CT11 117 F7
Sevenoaks TN13 154 C3
Tatsfield TN16 150 E7
Avenue The
Aylesford ME20 128 E1
Biggin Hill TN16 150 F5
Borough Green TN15 157 A8
Bromley BR1 52 D6
Deal CT14 215 C7
Gravesend DA11 37 A8
Hersden CT3 111 E1
Hill Park TN16 151 A4
Hythe CT21 333 C2
Kingsdown CT14 248 D4
1 Margate CT9 51 A1
Orpington BR6 86 F8
Orpington, Keston Mark
BR2 85 D7
Orpington, St Paul's Cray
BR5 31 B1
Sidcup DA5 31 D8
St Margaret's at Cliffe
CT15 279 F6
St Mary's Island ME4 41 C2
Swanscombe DA9 17 B2
Temple Ewell CT16 277 E5
2 Tonbridge TN9 222 B2
Avenue Theatre The★
ME10 101 F3
Averenches Rd ME14 162 F5
Avereng Gdns CT19 335 B6
Avereng Rd CT19 335 B6
Avery Cl
Allhallows-on-Sea ME3 9 E3
Maidstone ME15 161 F1
Avery Ct ME3 9 E3
AVERY HILL 12 C1
Avery Hill Rd SE9 30 D7
Avery La ME15, ME17 196 D6
Avery Way Allhallows ME3 9 D2
Dartford DA1 33 F6
Aviation Ct ME12 48 E3
Aviemore Gdns ME14 162 F4
Avington Cl ME15 161 F1
Avocet Mews SE28 2 D3
Avocet Wlk ME5 97 D2
Avon Cl Canterbury CT1 175 C8
Gravesend DA12 37 D6
Tonbridge TN10 222 C5
Avon Ct DA14 31 B5
Avondale Cl CT5 109 A8
Avondale Ct ME14 162 E5
Avondale Pl ME3 25 C4
Avondale Rd
Bexley DA16 13 C5
Bromley, Mottingham SE9 29 E6
Bromley, Plaistow BR1 29 A2
Capel-le-Ferne CT18 308 C2
Gillingham ME7 64 D5
Avon Ho 13 CT20 335 C4
Avonmouth Rd DA1 15 D2
Avon St TN1 286 C5
Avonstowe Cl BR6 86 C7
Awliscombe Rd DA16 12 F5
Axford Ct ME8 99 A8
Axminster Cres DA16 13 C6
Axtaine Rd BR5 54 D2
Axtane DA13 35 F1
Axtane Cl DA4 57 C8
AYCLIFF 310 B5
Aycliffe Cl BR1 52 F5
Aycliffe Cty Prim Sch
CT17 310 A4
Ayelands DA3 91 E8
Ayelands La DA3 91 E8
Ayers Cotts BR8 33 E2
Aylesbury Rd
Ashford TN25 268 B7
Bromley BR2 52 A6
AYLESFORD 128 E2
Aylesford Cres ME8 65 B4
AYLESFORD GREEN 300 F7
Aylesford Pl TN24 300 E7
Aylesford Prim Sch
ME20 128 D1
Aylesford Sch & Sports
Coll ME20 128 D1
Aylesford Sta ME20 128 D2
AYLESHAM 210 F5
Aylesham Cnr CT3 210 D3
Aylesham Ind Est CT3 210 E4
Aylesham Prim Sch
CT3 210 E5
Aylesham Rd
Aylesham CT15, CT3 211 A4
Orpington BR6 53 F2
Aylesham Sta CT3 211 A6
Ayleswade Rd TN27 294 E7
Aylewyn Gn ME10 101 F8
Aynscombe Angle BR6 54 A2
Aynsley Ct 1 CT13 149 A1
Ayrshire Cl TN24 268 C7
Ayton Rd CT11 117 C6
Azalea Dr BR8 55 E5

B

Babbacombe Rd BR1 29 B1
Babb's La TN17 342 A6
Babington House Sch
BR7 29 F2
Babs Oak Hill CT2 144 B7
Babylon La ME17, TN12 229 B1
Backfields ME1 63 B4
Back La
6 Faversham ME13 138 D7
Godden Green TN15 155 A2
Goudhurst TN17 318 E8
Horsmonden TN12 290 A6
Ightham TN15 156 C2
Maidstone ME17 195 E1
Minster (Sheppey) ME12 47 D6
Sevenoaks TN13, TN14 153 C1
Shipbourne TN11 189 D4
Sidcup DA5 32 A8
Back Rd
Sandhurst TN18 356 B5
Sidcup DA14 31 A4
Back Road W CT16 310 G8
Back St Leeds ME17 196 E6
Ringwould CT14 247 F5
Baddlesmere Rd CT5 75 A2
Baden Powell Ho 11
DA17 4 A3
Baden Powell Rd TN13 153 E5
Baden Rd ME7 64 D7
Bader Cres ME5 97 A7
Bader Wlk DA11 36 F5
Badger Rd ME5 97 C1
Badgers Bridge CT18 305 D4
Badgers Cl CT2 142 A7
Badgers Copse BR6 86 F6
Badgers Croft SE9 30 A5
Badgers Den TN23 299 D7
Badger's Hill Farm &
Cidery★ CT4 205 C8
Badgers Holt TN2 286 E5
BADGERS MOUNT 88 B1
Badgers Oak TN23 299 D8
Badgers Rd TN14 88 B1
Badgers Rise
Badgers Mount TN14 88 A1
Deal CT14 248 C8
Kearsney CT17 277 D3
BADLESMERE 170 C1
Badlesmere Cl TN23 299 E6
Badlow Cl DA8 14 E7
Badminton Mews E16 1 A5
Bad Munstereifel Rd TN23,
TN24 300 D5
Badsell Rd TN12 256 E5
Baffin Cl ME4 63 F2
BAGHAM 205 D8
Bagham La CT4 205 D8
Bagham Rd CT4 205 C8
Bagshaw Ho 6 BR1 52 A8
Bagshill Rd ME13 170 A3
Bailey Close SE28 2 E5
Bailey Dr ME7 65 A1
Bailey Fields TN26 297 E4
Baileys Field TN23 267 F1
Baird Ho 13 DA17 4 A3
Baird's Hill CT10 83 F6
Bairdsley Cl CT10 83 F6
Bakenham Ho 1 ME1 63 C1
Baker Beall Ct DA7 14 B4
Baker Cl ME9 103 C2
Baker Crescent DA1 33 D8
Baker Hill Cl DA11 36 F4
Baker La
Headcorn TN27 262 F7
Sutton Valence ME17 229 F7
Baker Rd
Folkestone CT19 334 E6
Woolwich SE18 11 E7
Bakers Ave TN15 90 E3
Bakers Cl CT2 174 C7
BAKER'S CROSS 320 E4
Bakers Cross TN17 320 E4
Bakers Ct CT11 117 E7
Baker's La CT4 173 D2
Bakers Mews 9 BR6 86 F4
Baker St Burham ME1 95 F1
Rochester ME1 63 C3
Baker's Wlk ME1 63 C6
Bakery Cl TN17 293 E7
Bakery Cotts ME14 129 E3
Bakery The ME9 134 A6
Balaclava La TN5 337 A6
Balas Dr ME10 101 C7
Balcaskie Rd SE9 11 F2
Balchen Rd SE3 11 D5
Balcomb Cres 4 CT9 83 C8
Balcombe Cl DA6 13 D3
Balcombe Cotts TN17 318 E8
Balcombes Hill TN17 318 E8
Balcomb Mews 3 CT9 83 C8
Balder Rise SE12 29 B6
Baldock Rd TN5 336 E4
Baldric Rd CT20 334 F5
Baldwin Rd
Greatstone-on-Sea
TN28 373 D1
Minster (Sheppey) ME12 47 D7
Baldwin's Pl ME17 198 D6
Baldwin Terr CT19 335 D6
Baldwyns Mans DA2 32 D6
Baldwyn's Pk DA5 32 D6
Baldwyn's Rd DA5 32 D6
Balfour Ct CT20 335 B3
Balfour Inf Sch ME1 63 E1
Balfour Jun Sch ME4 63 E2

Balfour Rd Bromley BR2 52 D4
Chatham ME4 63 E1
Deal CT14 215 C2
Dover CT16 278 C1
Balgowan St SE18 2 F2
Baliol Rd CT5 74 E2
Ballamore Rd BR1 29 A5
Ballantyne Close SE9 29 E4
Ballard Bsns Pk ME2 62 F5
Ballard Cl TN12 259 C6
Ballard Ct 20 DA14 31 A5
Ballard Ind Est ME5 130 C8
Ballard Rd TN28 373 D1
Ballards La RH8 183 C6
Ballard Way TN12 257 B7
Ballens Rd ME5 97 C3
Balliemoor Ct CT11 83 F1
Balliol Rd Bexley DA16 13 B5
Broadstairs CT10 83 F8
Ball La TN24 268 F7
Balls Cotts ME3 40 F4
Ball's Gn TN7 311 B5
BALLS GREEN 311 C5
Balmer Cl ME8 98 D7
Balmoral Ct SE12 29 B4
Balmoral Gdns DA5 31 F8
Balmoral Ho 10 ME15 195 F5
Balmoral Pl 12 CT11 117 F7
Balmoral Rd
Gillingham ME7 64 D5
Kingsdown CT14 248 C6
4 Margate CT9 82 B8
Sutton at Hone DA4 34 B1
Balmoral Terr ME10 101 D4
Balmoral Trad Est E6 2 F8
Baltic Ho TN1 286 B5
Baltic Rd TN9 254 B7
Baltic Wharf 1 DA11 19 A1
Baltimore Pl DA16 12 F5
Bambridge Ct ME14 161 F6
Bamford Way CT14 215 C4
Banbury Villas DA13 35 F1
Banchory Rd SE3 11 B7
Banckside DA3 58 E5
Bancroft Gdns BR6 53 F1
Bancroft La ME19 159 C2
Bancroft Rd TN15 124 F3
Bangor Rd ME2 62 D6
Banister Ho RM20 17 D8
Bank Cotts ME17 164 E3
Bankfields TN27 262 C5
Bankfield Way TN17 318 E7
Bank Ho
New Romney TN28 373 C6
Sheerness ME12 28 C2
Wrotham TN15 125 A3
Bank Hos DA2 34 A3
Bank La TN11, TN15 188 A3
Bank Rd TN25 329 E8
Bankside
Canterbury CT1 175 D7
Chatham ME5 97 B8
Durgates TN5 336 E5
Northfleet DA11 18 C1
Sevenoaks TN13 153 E6
Bank Side TN26 349 A8
Bankside Cl
Biggin Hill TN16 118 C1
Joyden's Wood DA5 32 D4
Banks La DA6 13 F3
Banks Rd Ashford TN23 300 A7
Rochester ME2 63 C8
Bank St Ashford TN23 268 B2
Chatham ME4 64 B3
Cranbrook TN17 320 C5
Faversham ME13 138 C7
Gravesend DA12 19 B1
Herne Bay CT6 76 F5
Hythe CT21 333 C2
Maidstone ME14 162 A4
Sevenoaks TN13 154 C2
Tonbridge TN9 222 C2
Banks The CT10 83 F6
Bank View 5 ME15 161 E2
Banky Fields Cl ME8 66 B1
Banky Mdw ME16 160 F3
BANNER FARM 286 C2
Banner Farm Rd TN2 286 B2
Banner Way ME12 46 E6
Banningbrook Ct CT14 215 D4
Banning St ME2 63 B8
Bannister Gdns BR5 54 C6
Bannister Hill ME9 101 B2
Bannister Hos TN26 234 A1
Bannister Rd ME14 162 A7
Bannockburn Prim Sch SE18 2 F2
Bannockburn Rd SE18 2 F2
Banstead Ct 3 BR1 52 E6
Banwell Rd DA5 13 D1
BAPCHILD 102 E3
Bapchild Pl 8 BR5 54 C5
Bapchild & Tonge CE Aided Sch ME9 102 D3
Barbados Terr 2 ME14 162 A7
Barberry Ave ME5 96 E5
Barber's Almshouses 11 CT11 117 D6
Barcham Ct ME15 194 F5
Barchester Way TN10 222 F6
Barclay Ave TN10 223 A5
Barclay Ct CT8 50 C1
Barclay Field TN15 122 E2
Barcombe Cl BR5 54 A6
Bardell Terr ME1 63 D5
Barden Ct ME14 162 B5
BARDEN PARK 221 F1
Barden Park Rd TN9 222 A1
Barden Rd
Penshurst TN3 252 F2
Barden Rd *continued*
Speldhurst TN3 285 A8
Tonbridge TN9 222 B1
Barden St SE18 12 E7
Bardsley Cl TN12 225 A7
Barfield DA4 57 B8
Barfield Rd BR1, BR7 53 A6
Barfleur Manor 3 ME7 64 A6
Barfreston Cl ME15 161 F2
BARFRESTONE 211 E1
Barfrestone Rd CT15 212 A1
Bargate Cl SE18 2 F1
Bargates TN23 299 E6
Barge Court DA9 17 C3
Bargehouse Rd E16 2 B4
Barges The CT5 74 E3
Barge Way ME10 69 B2
Bargrove CT18 333 E6
Bargrove Rd ME14 162 C5
BARHAM 242 E8
Barham CE Prim Sch CT4 242 F8
Barham Cl
Chislehurst BR7 30 B3
Gravesend DA12 37 F7
Maidstone ME15 195 E5
Orpington BR2 52 E1
Barham Court★ ME18 193 B8
Barham Ct BR2 52 E1
Barham Mews ME18 193 B8
Barham Rd
Chislehurst BR7 30 B3
Dartford DA1 34 A8
Barham's Mill Rd TN27 232 B3
Baring Cl SE12 29 A6
Baring Prim Sch 13 SE12 29 A8
Baring Rd SE12 29 A6
Barker Rd ME16 161 F3
Barkers Ct ME10 101 D4
Bark Hart Rd BR6 54 B1
BARKING 3 B8
Barkis Cl ME1 96 D7
Barkway Drive BR6 86 A6
Barler Pl ME11 46 A5
Barley Cl Herne Bay CT6 77 D2
Martin Mill CT15 247 C2
Barleycorn ME19 127 E1
Barleycorn Dr ME8 98 E6
Barley Fields ME14 162 D4
Barleymow Cl ME5 97 C7
Barley Way TN23 299 E5
Barling Cl ME5 96 D1
Barlow Cl ME8 98 E5
Barlow Dr SE18 11 E6
Barlow Way RM13 4 E8
Barlow Way S RM13 4 E7
BARMING HEATH 161 A3
Barming Prim Sch ME16 160 F2
Barming Rd ME18 159 F2
Barming Sta ME16 160 F6
Barnaby Terr ME1 63 D2
Barnard Cl
Chislehurst BR7 53 D8
Woolwich SE18 2 A3
Barnard Ct Chatham ME4 64 A2
21 Dartford DA2 16 B1
Barnberry Cl TN23 299 E8
Barn Cl Borden ME9 101 A2
Hoath CT3 111 E5
Yorkletts CT5 108 A3
Barn Cres CT9 50 F1
Barncroft Cl ME14 162 F4
Barncroft Dr ME7 97 F4
Barndale Ct DA12 38 E3
Barned Ct ME16 160 F2
BARNEHURST 14 D4
Barnehurst Ave DA7, DA8 14 C6
Barnehurst Cl DA8 14 C6
Barnehurst Inf Sch DA8 14 C6
Barnehurst Jun Sch DA8 14 C6
Barnehurst Rd DA7 14 C5
Barnehurst Sta DA7 14 C5
Barn End Ctr DA2 33 C5
Barn End Dr DA2 33 C5
Barn End La DA2 33 C4
Barnes Ave CT9 50 F1
Barnes Cl ME13 138 B8
BARNES CRAY 15 B3
Barnes Cray Prim Sch DA1 15 A3
Barnes Cray Rd DA1 15 A3
Barnes Ct
Canterbury CT1 174 D6
Newham E16 1 C8
Barnesdale Cres BR5 54 A4
Barnesende Ct CT13 181 A8
Barnes La ME17 227 D8
BARNES STREET 224 A4
Barnes Way CT6 77 F4
Barnes Wlk TN12 259 D6
Barnet Dr BR2 85 E8
Barnet's La CT2 143 D8
Barnett Cl DA8 14 F5
Barnett Ct
Minster (Thanet) CT12 115 C5
3 Ramsgate CT12 83 B1
Barnett Field TN23 299 F8
Barnetts Cl TN4 254 C1
Barnetts Rd TN11 221 A2
Barnetts Way TN4 286 C8
Barnet Wood Rd BR2 85 C8
Barney Cl SE7 1 C1
Barnfield Chatham ME5 97 A8
Gravesend DA11 37 A6
Herne Bay CT6 76 C2
Royal Tunbridge Wells TN2 313 F7
Tenterden TN30 324 C2
Barnfield Cl
Crockenhill BR8 55 C2
New Barn DA3 59 D6
Stone DA9 16 F1
Barnfield Cres TN15 122 E2
Barnfield Gdns SE18 12 B8
Barnfield Rd
Bexley DA17 13 F8
Faversham ME13 138 C8
Folkestone CT19 335 C7
Orpington BR5 54 D6
Sevenoaks TN13 153 E4
Tatsfield TN16 150 D6
Woolwich SE18 12 B8
Barnfields Ct ME10 102 D5
Barnfield Way RH8 183 A2
Barnham Dr SE28 2 F5
Barn Hill ME15 193 E2
Barnhill Ave BR2 52 A4
Barnhouse La TN29 371 A8
Barnhurst La CT18 307 A5
Barnhurst Rd ME14 162 A8
Barn Mdw
Staplehurst TN12 260 E4
Upper Halling ME2 94 E4
Barnock Cl DA1 32 E8
Barn Platt TN23 300 A8
Barnsley Cl ME12 28 E2
BARNSOLE 179 B6
Barnsole Inf Sch ME7 64 E4
Barnsole Jun Sch ME7 64 E4
Barnsole Rd
Gillingham ME7 64 E3
Staple CT3 179 B5
Barnsole Vineyard★ CT3 179 C6
Barn The ME9 101 A2
Barntye Cl CT15 278 E6
Barn Tye Cl CT15 278 E6
Barnwell Pl ME7 64 C5
Barnwell Rd DA1 15 F4
Barnwood Cl ME1 96 B8
Barn Yard The★ ME9 66 D1
Baron Cl Gillingham ME7 64 E7
Maidstone ME14 162 F5
Barons Ct TN4 286 A5
Barrack Cnr TN13 154 C4
Barrack Hill CT21 333 A2
Barrack Rd ME4 64 B8
Barrack Row
Benenden TN17 342 D6
17 Gravesend DA11 19 B1
Barrel Arch Cl TN12 259 C6
Barretts Green Cotts 5 TN18 341 A2
Barretts Rd
Hawkhurst TN18 341 A2
Sevenoaks TN13 153 E7
Barrey Rd TN24 301 A6
Barrie Dr 7 ME20 127 F4
Barrier Point Rd E16 1 C5
Barrier Rd ME4 63 F5
Barrington Cl ME5 96 F5
Barrington Cres CT7 81 B7
Barrington Prim Sch DA7 13 D5
Barrington Rd DA7 13 D5
Barrington Villas SE18 12 A6
Barrowfields ME5 97 D1
Barrow Gr ME10 101 D3
BARROW GREEN 103 D3
BARROWHILL 331 D7
BARROW HILL 268 A3
Barrow Hill
Ashford TN23 268 B2
Barrowhill TN25 331 D7
Barrow Hill Cotts TN23 268 A2
Barrow Hill Pl 2 TN23 268 B3
Barrow Hill Rise TN25 331 D7
Barrow Hill Terr 1 TN23 268 B3
Barrow La TN3 284 F2
Barrows Cl CT7 81 A6
Barr Rd DA12 37 F6
Barry Ave DA7 13 E7
Barry Cl BR6 86 E7
Barry Rd E6 1 E7
Barth Mews SE18 2 E2
Bartholomew Cl CT21 333 B3
Bartholomew La CT21 333 B3
Bartholomew St
6 Dover CT16 278 C1
Hythe CT21 333 B2
Bartholomew Way BR8 55 E6
Barth Rd SE18 2 E2
Bartlett Cl ME5 97 C1
Bartlett Dr CT5 75 A1
Bartlett Rd
Gravesend DA11 37 A7
Westerham TN16 151 C1
Bartletts Cl ME12 46 C5
Bartley Mill Rd TN3 315 F3
Barton Bsns Pk CT1 175 D6
Barton Cl Bexley DA6 13 E2
2 Newham E6 1 F7
Barton Cotts TN11 190 A6
Barton Court Gram Sch CT1 175 B8
Barton Ct 4 CT11 117 E7
Barton Field CT18 305 B7
Barton Hill Dr ME12 47 A5
Barton Jun Sch CT16 278 C2
Barton Mill Ct 2 CT2 142 F1
Barton Mill Rd CT1 143 B2
Barton Rd
Canterbury CT1 175 C6
Dover CT16 278 C2
Maidstone ME15 162 A2
Rochester ME2 63 A7
Sidcup DA14 31 E2
Sutton at Hone DA4 57 B8
Bartons Cotts TN16 152 C3
Barton's Point Coastal Pk★ ME12 28 F2
Barton View Terr 2 CT17 278 C1
Barville Rd CT15 212 E2
Barwell Crescent TN16 118 C7
Barwick Rd CT17 277 F1
Bascombe Gr DA1 14 E1
Basden Cotts 2 TN18 341 A2
Baseing Cl E6 2 A6
Bashford Barn La ME9 134 A4
Basi Cl ME2 40 C1
Basildon Rd SE2 3 A1
Basilon Rd DA7 13 E5
Basil Terr 6 ME15 162 A1
Basin Approach E16 2 B6
Basing Cl ME15 162 B3
Basing Dr DA5 13 F1
Baskerville TN24 268 B3
Basket Gdns SE9 11 E2
Basmere Cl ME14 162 C6
Bassant Rd SE18 12 F8
Basser Hill ME9 67 E3
Bassett Cl CT21 333 E4
Bassett Gdns CT21 333 D4
Bassett Rd ME10 101 D4
Bassetts Cl BR6 86 B6
Bassett's Forge TN5 336 E5
Bassetts La TN8, TN11 283 C7
Bassetts Way BR6 86 B6
BASTED 156 F4
Basted La Basted TN15 156 F5
Crouch TN15 157 B4
Bastien Lane ME19 159 D4
Bastien Mews 4 CT1 175 B6
Bastion Rd Dover CT17 310 C6
Woolwich SE2 3 A1
Baston Manor BR2 85 B6
Baston Manor Rd BR2, BR4 85 B6
Baston Rd BR2 85 B7
Baston Sch BR2 85 B8
Bat & Ball Ent Ctr TN14 154 C7
Bat & Ball Sta TN14 154 C6
Batchelors TN2 287 E8
Batchelor St ME4 64 A4
Batchwood Gn BR5 54 B6
Bateman Cnr TN26 297 E6
Bates Cl
New Hythe ME20 128 A3
Staple CT3 178 F6
Bates Hill TN15 156 C5
Bateson St 2 SE18 2 E2
Bath Ct 8 CT20 335 B3
Bath Hard ME1 63 D5
Bath Mews TN24 300 E6
Bath Pl CT9 50 J2
Bath Rd Ashford TN24 300 E6
Dartford DA1 33 B8
Margate CT9 50 J2
Baths Rd BR2 52 D5
Bath St DA11 19 B1
Bathurst Cl
Ramsgate CT12 83 B1
Staplehurst TN12 260 E4
Bathurst Rd
Folkestone CT20 335 A5
Staplehurst TN12 260 E3
Bathway 18 SE18 2 A2
Batten Cl E6 1 F7
Batteries Cl ME9 136 B8
Batteries Terr ME9 136 B8
Battery Point CT21 334 B2
Battery Rd
Lydd-on-Sea TN29 380 D6
Woolwich SE28 2 E4
Battlefields TN15 124 F3
Battle La TN12 260 A8
Battle of Britain Homes 17 CT17 310 D7
Battle of Britain Meml★ CT18 308 A1
Battle Rd DA8, DA17 4 C2
Battlesmere Rd ME3 40 B8
Battle St DA12 60 F6
Batt's Rd DA12 61 A4
Baugh Rd DA14 31 C3
Bawden Cl CT2 143 A4
Baxendale Ct TN24 300 D7
Baxter Close BR1 53 B6
Baxter Rd E16 1 C7
Baxter Way ME19 159 C3
Bayard Ct DA6 14 B3
Bay Banks ME13 137 E2
Bay Cl ME3 41 E3
Bay Cotts CT15 280 C6
Baye La CT3 145 D1
Bayeux Gdns ME7 65 A5
Bayeux Ho 11 SE7 11 C8
BAYFIELD 137 E2
Bayfield ME13 137 E2
Bayfield Rd SE9 11 D3
Bayford Rd ME10 102 A4
Bayhall Rd TN2 286 C3
Bayham Ct TN5 336 E6
Bayham Old Abbey (rems of)★ TN3 316 B5
Bayham Rd
Bells Yew Green TN3 315 B4
Royal Tunbridge Wells TN2, TN3 314 C7
Sevenoaks TN13 154 D4
Bay Hill CT15 280 B6
Bay Hill Cl CT15 280 A5
Bayle Ct 2 CT20 335 E4
Bayle St 19 CT20 335 E5
Bayle The CT20 335 E4
Bayley's Hill TN14 186 E3
Bayley Wlk SE2 3 E1
Bayliss Ave SE28 3 D6
Bayly Rd DA1 16 A1
Bay Manor La RM20 16 F8
Bay Mus The★ CT15 280 B5
Bayne Cl E6 1 F7
Baynham Cl DA5 13 F1
Bays The BR5 54 C6
Bayswater Dr ME8 98 E4
Bay The DA13 126 A8
Baytree Cl Bromley BR1 52 D8
Sidcup DA15 30 F7
Bay Trees RH8 183 B2
BAY VIEW 49 D2
Bay View Gdns ME12 49 D2
Bay View Hts CT7 80 D8
Bayview Rd
Kingsdown CT14 248 C4
Whitstable CT5 108 D7
Bay View Rd CT10 84 A2
Baywell ME19 127 E2
Bazes Shaw DA3 91 F8
Beach Alley 15 CT5 74 D2
Beacham Cl SE7 11 D8
Beachamwell Dr ME19 159 C2
Beach App ME12 49 E3
Beach Ave CT7 80 F8
Beachborough Rd CT19, CT20 335 A5
Beach Ct Deal CT14 215 D2
Eltham SE9 11 E1
Goddard's Green TN17 321 D1
Westgate on Sea CT8 50 D1
Beachfield Lodge ME12 28 C2
Beach Flats 2 CT21 333 B2
Beach Hos CT9 50 G2
Beach House Mews CT8 50 D1
Beach Marine 7 CT20 334 F3
Beachmont Cl TN28 377 E8
Beach Rd
Dymchurch TN29 353 A4
St Margaret's at Cliffe CT15 280 B5
Westgate on Sea CT8 50 D1
Beach Rise CT8 50 D1
Beach St
Folkestone CT20 335 E4
Herne Bay CT6 76 F5
Sheerness ME12 28 B2
Beach Terr ME12 28 B2
Beach The CT14 215 D3
Beach Wlk CT5 74 E3
Beacon Ave CT6 77 B5
Beacon Avenue ME19 159 D4
Beacon Cl ME8 98 D7
Beacon Dr DA2 35 C5
Beaconfields TN13 154 A1
BEACON HILL 343 A5
Beacon Hill
Gillingham ME5 64 D2
Herne Bay CT6 77 B5
Beacon Hill La ME3 40 F4
Beacon La
Brookland TN29 370 D7
Woodnesborough CT13 180 A4
Beacon Oak Rd TN30 345 B8
Beacon Rd
Broadstairs CT10 83 F7
Chatham ME5 64 C2
Erith DA8 15 B7
Herne Bay CT6 77 A5
Lenham ME17 199 C5
Beacon Rise TN13 154 A1
Beacon Row TN15 90 F2
Beacons Cl 11 E6 1 E8
Beaconsfield CT5 107 F6
Beaconsfield Ave
Dover CT16 278 C1
Gillingham ME7 64 E5
Beaconsfield Cl SE3 11 A8
Beaconsfield Gdns CT10 83 F5
Beaconsfield Par SE9 29 E4
Beaconsfield Rd
Bromley, Mottingham SE9 29 E4
Bromley, Widmore BR1 52 D6
Canterbury CT2 142 F2
Chatham ME4 63 F3
Deal CT14 215 D5
Dover CT16 278 C1
Greenwich SE3 11 A8
Maidstone ME15 161 E2
Maypole DA5 32 E6
Sittingbourne ME10 102 C4
Beacons The ME17 194 C2
Beacon Terr CT21 334 B2
Beacon Way CT21 331 F3
Beacon Wlk
Herne Bay CT6 77 A5
Tenterden TN30 324 B1
Beacon Wood Ctry Pk★ DA2 35 B4
Beadon Rd BR2 52 A4
Beagles Cl BR5 87 D8
Beagles Wood Rd TN2 287 E7
Beal Cl DA16 13 A6
BEAL'S GREEN 341 A4
Beaman Cl TN17 318 F8
Beamish Rd BR5 54 C2
Beamont Cl CT12 81 F2
Beams The ME15 162 F1
BEAN 35 C5
Bean Cl TN23 267 C1
Beane Croft 1 DA12 37 F7
Beaney's La CT4 171 C1
Beaney's La Cotts CT4 171 C1
Bean Hill Cotts DA2 35 C4
Bean La DA2 35 B6
Bean Prim Sch DA2 35 C4
Bean Rd Bexley DA6 13 D3
Swanscombe DA9 17 B1
Beanshaw SE9 30 A4
Bears End Ho TN23 300 B8
Bear's La TN23, TN26 266 E3
BEARSTED 163 B4
Bearsted Cl ME8 65 B3
Bearsted Green Bsns Ctr ME14 163 C4
Bearsted Rd ME14 162 E6
Bearsted Sta ME14 163 B5
Beaton Cl DA9 17 B2
Beatrice Gdns DA11 36 E6
Beatrice Hills Cl TN24 268 E5
Beatrice Mews TN28 377 E7
Beatrice Rd
Capel-le-Ferne CT18 308 C2
Margate CT9 82 E8
Beatty Ave ME7 64 F4
Beatty Cl CT19 335 E8
Beatty Cotts ME3 9 D1
Beatty Rd
Folkestone CT19 335 D8
Rochester ME1 96 D8
Beauchamp Ave CT14 215 A3
Beauchamp Cl TN24 268 E5
Beauchamps La CT15 211 D5
Beaufighter Rd ME19 158 E3
Beaufort E6 2 A8
Beaufort Ave CT12 117 B8
Beaufort Ct ME2 63 E6
Beaufort Rd ME2 62 E8
Beaufort Wlk ME15 195 E4
Beaufoy Rd CT17 278 A1
Beaufoy Terr CT17 277 F1
Beauherne Com Sch CT2 174 D8
Beaulieu Ave E16 1 B5
Beaulieu Rd TN10 222 B4
Beaulieu Rise ME1 63 D1
Beaulieu Road TN10, TN11 222 B6
Beaulieu Wlk ME16 161 C7
Beaumanor CT6 77 A3
Beaumanor Gdns SE9 30 A4
Beaumont Davy Cl ME13 138 C5
Beaumont Dr DA11 36 F8
Beaumont Rd
Maidstone ME16 161 B2
Orpington BR5 53 D3
Beaumont St CT6 76 C4
Beaumont Terr ME13 138 D6
Beauvoir Dr ME10 102 A8
Beauworth Pk ME15 195 E8
Beauxfield CT16 278 A7
BEAVER 300 B7
Beaverbank Rd SE9 30 D7
Beaverbrook Mews ME16 161 D3
Beaver Ct TN23 300 A7
Beaver Green Prim Sch TN23 299 E7
Beaver Ind Est TN23 300 B7
Beaver La
Ashford, Beaver TN23 300 A7
Ashford, Singleton TN23 299 F7
Ashford TN23 267 E1
Beaver Rd
Ashford TN23 300 B8
Maidstone ME16 161 B7
Beavers Lodge DA14 30 F3
Beaverwood Rd BR7 30 E2
Beaverwood Sch for Girls BR7 30 E2
Beaver Zoological Gdns & Reptile Rescue Ctr★ TN16 150 B5
Beazley Ct TN24 300 D7
Bebbington Rd 3 SE18 2 E2
Beblets Cl 4 BR6 86 F5
Beckenham Dr ME16 161 D7
Becket Ave CT2 142 D1
Becket Cl Ash CT3 147 D2
Deal CT14 215 C8
Whitstable CT5 75 B1
Becket Ct
Headcorn TN27 262 D5
2 Tonbridge TN9 254 B8
Becket Mews CT2 142 F1
Becket's Cl TN25 271 B6
Beckets Field TN11 252 A3
Beckets Pl TN14 122 C3
Beckett Cl DA17 3 F3
Becketts Cl
Coldblow DA5 32 C7
Orpington BR6 86 F7
Beckett St 4 ME13 138 C7
Becketts Terr CT21 333 B4
Becketts Wood CT3 112 E3
Beckford Dr BR5 53 D2
Beckley Cl DA12 38 B6
Beckley Hill Works ME2 39 B8
Beckley Mews ME5 96 F5
Beckley Pl TN25 332 B8
Beckley Rd ME12 28 E2
Beckman Cl TN14 121 C4
Becksbourne Cl ME14 162 A8
Becks Rd DA14 31 A5
BECKTON 2 A8
Beckton Park Sta E6 1 F6
Beckton Rd E16 1 A8
Beckton Ret Pk E6 2 A8
Beckton Sta E6 2 A8
Beckwith Gn CT20 334 E5
Beckworth Pl ME16 161 B2
Becton Pl DA8 14 C6
Bedale Wlk DA2 34 B7
Beddalls Farm Ct 7 E6 1 E8
Beddington Gn BR5 53 F8
Beddington Rd BR5 53 F8
Beddlestead La CR6 150 A6
Bedlow Way ME20 129 B3
Bede Ho CT14 215 D8
Bedens Rd DA14 31 E3
Bedford Ave ME8 65 D1
Bedford Ct CT10 84 B6
Bedford Pl ME16 161 E4
Bedford Rd Dartford DA1 34 A8
Northfleet DA11 36 F6
Orpington BR6 54 B1

Bedford Rd *continued*
Royal Tunbridge Wells TN4 . . . 254 A1
Sidcup DA15 . . . 30 E5
Bedford Sq
Longfield DA3 . . . 58 E6
Ramsgate CT12 . . . 83 B2
Bedford Terr 13 TN1 . . 286 A2
Bedford Way CT7 . . . 79 F1
Bedgebury Cl
Maidstone ME14 . . . 162 C6
Rochester ME1 . . . 96 D8
Bedgebury Cross TN17 . . . 318 D2
Bedgebury National Pinetum★ TN17 . . . 339 E8
Bedgebury Rd
Eltham SE9 . . . 11 D3
Goudhurst TN17 . . . 318 E5
Bedingfield Way CT18 305 B7
Bedivere Rd BR1 . . . 29 A5
Bedlam Court La CT12 115 C6
Bedlam La TN27 . . . 263 E6
BEDMONTON . . . 165 E8
Bedmonton La ME9 . . . 134 B2
Bedonwell Inf Sch DA17 13 E8
Bedonwell Jun Sch DA17 . . . 13 E8
Bedonwell Rd
Bexley, Bexleyheath DA7 . . . 13 F6
Bexley, West Heath DA7, DA17 . . . 13 E8
Bedson Wlk ME8 . . . 66 B1
Bedwell Rd DA17 . . . 4 A1
Bedwin Cl ME1 . . . 96 D7
Beeby Rd E16 . . . 1 B8
Beecham Rd TN10 . . . 222 E6
Beech Ave
Chartham CT4 . . . 173 E1
Sidcup DA15 . . . 31 A8
Swanley BR8 . . . 55 F5
Tatsfield TN16 . . . 150 D8
Beech Cl
Faversham ME13 . . . 138 B7
Folkestone CT19 . . . 335 C6
Royal Tunbridge Wells TN27 . . . 286 C1
Beech Copse BR1 . . . 52 F7
Beech Court Gdns★ TN25 . . . 202 F1
Beechcroft
Chislehurst BR7 . . . 30 A1
Whitstable CT5 . . . 75 D1
Beechcroft Ave DA7 . . . 14 D5
Beechcroft Cl BR6 . . . 86 D6
Beechcroft Gdns CT11 117 F8
Beechcroft Rd BR6 . . . 86 D6
Beech Ct
Canterbury CT1 . . . 175 A7
Dartford DA1 . . . 16 A1
Paddock Wood TN12 . . . 257 A7
Royal Tunbridge Wells TN2 . . . 286 D4
Beech Dell BR2, BR4 . . . 85 F6
Beech Dr
Broadstairs CT10 . . . 83 D4
Elvington CT15 . . . 212 B2
Hothfield TN26 . . . 267 A7
Maidstone ME16 . . . 161 C5
Beechen Bank Rd ME5 . 97 A1
Beechenlea La BR8 . . . 56 B6
Beecher Ct SE12 . . . 29 B5
Beeches Ct BR1 . . . 29 A2
Beeches The
Aylesford ME20 . . . 128 E1
Chatham ME5 . . . 97 A4
Hextable BR8 . . . 32 F1
Lydd TN29 . . . 376 D7
New Barn DA3 . . . 59 C7
Royal Tunbridge Wells TN2 . . . 286 D5
Sole Street DA13 . . . 60 D5
The Moor TN18 . . . 354 E7
Tilbury RM18 . . . 19 B5
Beechfield Cotts 6 BR1 . . . 52 C7
Beechfield Rd
Bromley BR1 . . . 52 C7
Erith DA8 . . . 14 E7
Beech Gr
Cliffs End CT12 . . . 116 C5
Higham ME3 . . . 39 C4
Beech Green Cl CT15 . 245 C7
Beech Green La
Cowden TN7 . . . 282 F1
Withyham TN7 . . . 311 B7
Beech Grove Sch CT15 211 E6
Beech Haven Ct DA1 . . . 14 D2
Beech Hill CT4 . . . 209 B8
Beechhill Rd SE9 . . . 12 A2
Beech Ho 7 DA15 . . . 31 A5
Beech Hurst TN2 . . . 287 D7
Beech Hurst Cl ME15 . . 162 B2
Beeching Rd ME5 . . . 97 B3
Beechings Gn ME8 . . . 65 C3
Beechings Way ME8 . . . 65 C3
Beechings Way Ind Ctr ME8 . . . 65 B4
Beechin Wood La TN15 . . . 157 D5
Beech La TN12 . . . 288 C4
Beechlands Cl DA3 . . . 59 A4
Beech Manor TN2 . . . 286 D3
Beech Mast DA13 . . . 126 B8
Beechmont Rd TN13 . . . 187 B6
Beechmont Rise TN10 222 B6
Beechmore Dr ME5 . . . 97 A2
Beecholme Dr TN24 . . 268 C5
Beech Rd
Biggin Hill TN16 . . . 118 C2
Dartford DA1 . . . 33 D7
East Malling ME19 . . . 159 F7
Herne Pound ME18 . . . 158 D2
Beech Rd *continued*
Hoo St Werburgh ME3 . . . 41 E3
Newenden TN18 . . . 357 C3
Orpington BR6 . . . 87 A3
Rochester ME2 . . . 62 F6
Sevenoaks TN13 . . . 154 B2
Beech St TN1 . . . 286 B4
Beechway
Meopham Station DA13 . . 60 B2
Sidcup DA5 . . . 13 D1
Beech Wlk
Biddenden TN27 . . . 323 D7
Crayford DA1 . . . 15 A3
Beechwood Ave
Deal CT14 . . . 215 C5
Gillingham ME5 . . . 64 D2
Orpington BR6 . . . 86 E4
Sittingbourne ME10 . . . 101 E6
Beechwood Cl
St Mary's Bay TN29 . . . 365 F3
Whitfield CT16 . . . 246 A1
Beechwood Cres DA7 . . 13 E4
Beechwood Ct
Deal CT14 . . . 215 C5
Temple Ewell CT16 . . . 277 E4
Beechwood Dr
Culverstone Green DA13 . . . 93 A1
Orpington BR2 . . . 85 D6
Beechwood Gdns DA13 93 A1
Beechwood Mews TN2 . . . 286 E4
Beechwood Rd ME16 . . 160 F3
Beechwood Rise BR7 . . . 30 B4
Beechwood Sacred Heart Sch TN2 . . . 286 E4
Beechy Lees Rd TN14 . 122 E3
Beecroft Cl CT2 . . . 143 A4
Beeken Dene BR6 . . . 86 C6
Beer Cart La CT1 . . . 174 F8
Beesfield La DA4 . . . 57 A1
Beeston Ct 4 DA1 . . . 16 B1
Begbie Rd SE3 . . . 11 C6
Beggarsbush La TN29 371 D7
Beggars Cnr CT3 . . . 113 D1
Beggars La TN16 . . . 151 E3
Begonia Ave ME8 . . . 65 C2
Beke Rd ME8 . . . 98 D4
BEKESBOURNE . . . 176 D4
BEKESBOURNE HILL . . 176 B5
Bekesbourne Hill CT4 . 176 B5
Bekesbourne La
Bekesbourne CT3, CT4 . . . 176 E6
Canterbury CT3 . . . 175 F7
Littlebourne CT3 . . . 176 F6
Bekesbourne Rd CT4 . . 175 F2
Bekesbourne Sta CT4 . . 176 B5
Bekesbourne Tower 12 BR5 . . . 54 D1
Belcaire Cl CT21 . . . 332 A3
Belcanto Theatre Acad 3 SE9 . . . 11 F1
Beldam Haw TN14 . . . 121 A8
Belfast Ho 14 ME15 . . . 195 E7
Belfield Rd TN2 . . . 287 D6
Belford Gr SE18 . . . 2 A2
Belfry Drive ME3 . . . 41 E6
Belgrave Cl
5 Orpington BR5 . . . 54 C5
Ramsgate CT11 . . . 117 D7
Belgrave Ct Deal CT14 . 215 D3
Greenwich SE7 . . . 11 C7
Belgrave Rd
Dover CT17 . . . 310 B7
Halfway Houses ME12 . . . 46 C5
Margate CT9 . . . 50 I2
Royal Tunbridge Wells TN1 . . . 286 B4
Belgrave St ME20 . . . 128 F6
Belgrove 5 TN1 . . . 286 A2
Belinda Ct CT19 . . . 335 B7
Bellarmine Cl SE28 . . . 2 F4
Bell Bedgebury International Sch TN17 . . . 318 E1
Bell Chapel Cl TN23 . . 300 C4
Bell Cl DA9 . . . 16 F2
Bell Cnr TN29 . . . 372 A4
Bell Cotts ME9 . . . 67 B3
Bell Cres ME1 . . . 128 F8
Bell-Davies Dr CT12 . . . 82 A1
Bellefield Rd BR5 . . . 54 B4
Belle Friday Cl ME9 . . 103 C2
Bellegrove Cl DA16 . . . 12 F5
Bellegrove Par DA16 . . . 12 F4
Bellegrove Rd DA16 . . . 12 E5
Bellevue Ave CT11 . . . 117 F7
Bellevue Rd Bexley DA6 . 13 F2
Minster (Sheppey) ME12 . 47 C6
Ramsgate CT11 . . . 117 F7
Whitstable CT5 . . . 108 F8
Belle Vue Rd
Farthing Street BR6 . . . 86 A1
Herne Bay CT6 . . . 77 B5
Bellevue St 5 CT20 . . 335 D5
Bell Farm Gdns ME16 . . 160 F2
Bell Farm La ME12 . . . 48 A6
Bellfield Cl SE3 . . . 11 B7
Bellflower Ave ME12 . . . 47 A4
Bellflower Cl 2 E6 . . . 1 E8
Bell Gdns BR5 . . . 54 C4
Bell Gr CT3 . . . 211 A5
Bellgrove Ct ME5 . . . 130 A8
Bell Ho Erith SE2 . . . 3 D1
Grays RM17 . . . 17 F8
Bellingham Way ME20 128 B3
Bell La Burham ME1 . . . 128 F8
Chatham ME14 . . . 130 B7
Larkfield ME20 . . . 128 B2
Maidstone ME14 . . . 163 A5
Newham E16 . . . 1 A5
Sandwich CT13 . . . 149 A1
Standen TN27 . . . 295 B8
Bell La *continued*
Staplehurst TN12 . . . 260 E3
Bellman Ave DA12 . . . 37 E7
Bell Mdw ME15 . . . 195 E6
Bellows La TN15 . . . 156 F7
Bell Rd Maidstone ME15 195 E5
Sittingbourne ME10 . . . 101 F3
Bellring Cl DA17 . . . 14 A8
Bell Row TN11 . . . 223 F5
Bell's Cl TN30 . . . 345 A7
Bells Farm La TN11 . . . 224 C8
Bells Farm Rd TN11, TN12 . . . 191 D1
Bell Shaw 17 ME15 . . . 195 E5
Bell Sh Ctr 8 ME10 . . . 101 F4
Bells La 8 TN30 . . . 345 A7
Bell's La ME3 . . . 41 E6
Bell St SE18 . . . 11 E6
BELLS YEW GREEN . . . 314 F5
Bell Water Gate SE18 . . . 2 A3
Bell Way ME17 . . . 197 E2
Bellwood Ct ME3 . . . 24 C3
Bell Wood Prim Sch 16 ME15 . . . 195 E5
Belmont CT14 . . . 215 B1
Belmont Ave DA16 . . . 12 E4
Belmont Cl ME16 . . . 160 F2
Belmont Ct
9 Maidstone ME15 . . . 162 B4
2 Ramsgate CT11 . . . 117 D7
Belmont Farm Bsns Ctr TN26 . . . 266 A1
Belmont House & Gdns★ ME13 . . . 169 D5
Belmont Par BR7 . . . 30 C3
Belmont Pl TN24 . . . 300 D7
Belmont Prim Sch DA8 . 14 A7
Belmont Rd
Ashford TN24 . . . 268 D6
Broadstairs CT10 . . . 84 A4
Chislehurst BR7 . . . 30 B3
Erith DA8 . . . 14 B6
Faversham ME13 . . . 138 C6
Gillingham ME7 . . . 64 C4
Grays RM17 . . . 17 F8
Halfway Houses ME12 . . . 46 E6
Ramsgate CT11 . . . 117 D7
Sittingbourne ME10 . . . 101 E3
Westgate on Sea CT8 . . . 81 F8
Whitstable CT5 . . . 74 D1
Belmont St CT11 . . . 117 E7
Belmont Terr CT13 . . . 180 B3
Belmont Yd 8 CT5 . . . 74 D1
Belmore Pk TN24 . . . 268 B3
Belnor Ave ME9 . . . 67 F1
Belsey La CT15 . . . 276 D4
Belson Rd SE18 . . . 1 F2
Beltana Dr DA12 . . . 37 E4
Belting Dr CT6 . . . 77 E5
BELTINGE . . . 77 E6
Beltinge Rd CT6 . . . 77 B5
Belton Cl CT5 . . . 108 E8
Belton Rd DA14 . . . 31 A4
BELTRING . . . 225 A4
Beltring Rd
Beltring TN12, ME18 . . . 225 B4
Royal Tunbridge Wells TN4 . . . 286 A6
Beltring Sta TN12 . . . 225 B4
Belts Wood 14 ME15 . . . 195 F5
Beltwood Rd DA17 . . . 4 C2
Beluncle Villas ME3 . . . 42 C7
BELVEDERE . . . 4 B2
Belvedere Cl
Faversham ME13 . . . 138 D8
Gravesend DA12 . . . 37 C7
Belvedere Ct DA17 . . . 3 F3
Belvedere Ho 9 ME15 195 F5
Belvedere Ind Est DA17 . . 4 D5
Belvedere Inf Sch DA17 . . 4 B3
Belvedere Jun Sch DA17 . 4 B3
Belvedere Link Bsns Pk DA17 . . . 4 C3
Belvedere Mews SE3 . . . 11 B7
Belvedere Rd
Bexley DA7 . . . 13 F5
Biggin Hill TN16 . . . 118 F1
Broadstairs CT10 . . . 84 B4
Erith SE28 . . . 3 D5
Faversham ME13 . . . 138 D8
Belvedere Sta DA17 . . . 4 B3
Belvoir Cl SE9 . . . 29 E5
Benacre Rd CT5 . . . 108 D6
Benares Rd SE18 . . . 2 F2
Bench Hill TN26 . . . 347 D5
Bench St 19 CT16 . . . 310 D7
Benden Cl TN12 . . . 260 F4
Bendmore Ave SE2 . . . 3 A2
Bendon Way ME8 . . . 98 D8
Benedict Cl 9 Erith DA17 3 E3
Halling ME2 . . . 95 B4
Orpington BR6 . . . 86 E7
Benedict House Prep School 26 DA14 . . . 31 A5
BENENDEN . . . 342 E6
Benenden CE Prim Sch TN17 . . . 342 D6
Benenden Gn BR2 . . . 52 A4
Benenden Hospl TN17 322 C3
Benenden Manor ME8 . . 65 B3
Benenden Rd
Benenden TN17 . . . 343 B4
Cranbrook TN17 . . . 320 E1
Fosten Green TN27 . . . 322 F5
Rochester ME2 . . . 40 C1
Benenden Sch TN17 . . . 342 C8
Bengal Rd CT12 . . . 83 A1
Benhall Mill Rd TN2, TN3 . . . 314 D8
Benham Bsns Pk CT21 331 F5
Benjamin Ct 4 DA17 . . . 13 F8
Benn Cl RH8 . . . 183 A1
Bennells Ave CT5 . . . 75 B3
Bennett Cl DA16 . . . 13 A5
Bennett Ct 16 CT20 . . . 335 E5
Bennett Ho 2 DA11 . . . 36 F5
Bennett Memorial Diocesan Sch TN4 . . . 285 E6
Bennetts Ave TN15 . . . 124 C7
Bennetts Copse BR7 . . . 29 E2
Bennetts Cotts ME7 . . 131 A8
Bennetts Gdns ME13 . 137 D8
Bennetts Mews 12 TN30 . . . 345 A7
Bennett Way DA2 . . . 34 D3
Benn Ho SE7 . . . 1 C1
BENOVER . . . 226 A6
Benover Rd ME18 . . . 225 F7
Benson Cl CT18 . . . 306 F4
Benson La CT18 . . . 306 F4
Benson Rd RM17 . . . 18 C8
Bensted TN23 . . . 299 F5
Bensted Cl ME15 . . . 226 D7
Benstede Cl CT6 . . . 77 A1
Bensted Gr ME13 . . . 138 A7
Bentfield Gdns SE9 . . . 29 D5
Bentham Hill TN3, TN4 253 D1
Bentham Rd SE28 . . . 3 B5
Bentham Sq ME12 . . . 28 A3
Ben Tillet Cl E16 . . . 1 F5
Bentley Ave CT6 . . . 76 B4
Bentley Cl
Aylesford ME20 . . . 128 F1
Chatham ME5 . . . 97 D2
New Barn DA3 . . . 59 C7
Bentley Rd TN24 . . . 300 F7
Bentleys Bglws TN15 . . 154 F7
Bentley's Mdw TN15 . . 154 F7
Bentley St DA12 . . . 19 C1
Bentley Street Ind Est DA12 . . . 19 C1
Bentlif Cl ME16 . . . 161 D5
Berber Parade SE18 . . . 11 E6
Berber Rd ME2 . . . 63 B8
Bercta Rd SE9 . . . 30 C6
Bere Cl DA9 . . . 17 C2
Berengrave La ME8 . . . 65 F2
Berengrave Nature Reserve★ ME8 . . . 66 A3
Berens Ct DA14 . . . 30 F4
Berens Rd BR5 . . . 54 D4
Berens Way BR5 . . . 53 F6
Beresford Ave ME1 . . . 63 E2
Beresford Cl TN17 . . . 317 F2
Beresford Ct 7 CT7 . . . 80 F8
Beresford Dr BR1 . . . 52 E6
Beresford Gap CT7 . . . 80 F8
Beresford Gdns CT9 . . . 51 C3
Beresford Rd
Gillingham ME7 . . . 64 D4
Goudhurst TN17 . . . 290 F1
Kit's Coty ME20 . . . 129 D7
Northfleet DA11 . . . 36 E8
Ramsgate CT11 . . . 117 D6
River CT17 . . . 277 E3
St Margaret's at Cliffe CT15 . . . 247 F1
Whitstable CT5 . . . 74 D1
Beresfords Hill ME17 . 195 B4
Beresford Square Market Pl SE18 . . . 2 B2
Beresford St SE18 . . . 2 B3
Bergamot Cl ME10 . . . 101 F2
Berger Cl BR5 . . . 53 E3
Bergland Pk ME2 . . . 63 D8
Bering Wlk E16 . . . 1 D7
Berkeley Ave DA7 . . . 13 D6
Berkeley Cl
Boughton Street ME13 . . . 140 B3
2 Folkestone CT19 . . . 335 A7
Orpington BR5 . . . 53 E2
Pembury TN2 . . . 287 E7
Rochester ME1 . . . 96 D8
Berkeley Cres DA1 . . . 33 F7
Berkeley Ct
Sittingbourne ME10 . . . 101 D3
6 Swanley BR8 . . . 55 E6
Berkeley Mount 8 ME4 63 F4
Berkeley Rd
Birchington CT7 . . . 80 F8
7 Royal Tunbridge Wells TN1 . . . 286 A2
Berkeley Terr RM18 . . . 19 A7
Berkhampstead Rd 9 DA17 . . . 4 A1
Berkley Cres DA12 . . . 19 C1
Berkley Rd DA12 . . . 19 B1
Berkshire Cl ME5 . . . 97 C8
Bermuda Rd RM18 . . . 19 A5
Bernal Cl SE28 . . . 3 D6
Bernard Ashley Dr SE7 . . 1 B1
Bernards Ct DA15 . . . 30 E7
Bernards Gdns CT15 . . 244 E5
Bernard St 24 DA12 . . . 19 B1
Bernard Sunley Hall TN25 . . . 238 A2
BERNER'S HILL . . . 339 A2
Berner's Hill TN5 . . . 339 A3
Bernersmede SE3 . . . 11 A4
Berridge Rd ME12 . . . 28 C2
Berries The CT18 . . . 307 B5
Berryfield Cl BR1 . . . 52 E7
Berryhill SE9 . . . 12 B3
Berryhill Gdns SE9 . . . 12 B3
Berrylands Hartley DA3 . . 59 A3
Orpington BR6 . . . 87 C7
Berry Rd ME3 . . . 41 E3
BERRY'S GREEN . . . 119 B2
Berry's Green Rd TN16 119 B2
Berry's Hill TN16 . . . 119 B4
Berry St ME10 . . . 101 F4
Bertha Hollamby Ct DA14 . . . 31 C3
Bertha James Ct BR2 . . . 52 B5
Bertrand Way SE28 . . . 3 C6
Bert Reilly Ho 1 SE18 . . 2 D1
Bertrey Cotts TN16 . . . 119 B3
Berwick Cres DA15 . . . 12 E1
Berwick Ct 12 DA2 . . . 16 B1
Berwick La CT21 . . . 332 A3
Berwick Rd Bexley DA16 13 B6
Newham E16 . . . 1 C7
Berwick Way
Orpington BR6 . . . 54 A1
Rochester ME2 . . . 40 D1
Sevenoaks TN14 . . . 154 B7
Berwyn Gr ME15 . . . 195 A6
Beryl Ave E6 . . . 1 E8
Beryl Ho 3 SE18 . . . 2 F1
Besant Ct 15 SE28 . . . 3 B6
BESSELS GREEN . . . 153 D3
Bessels Green Rd TN13 . . . 153 D3
Bessels Meadow TN13 153 D3
Bessels Way TN13 . . . 153 D4
Bessie Lansbury Cl E6 . . 2 A7
BEST BEECH HILL . . . 336 B3
Best La CT1 . . . 174 F8
Best St ME4 . . . 63 F4
Beta Rd ME3 . . . 42 D7
Betenson Ave TN13 . . . 153 F5
Bethany Cl CT14 . . . 215 C8
Bethany Sch TN17 . . . 291 B5
Bethel Rd Bexley DA16 . . 13 C4
Sevenoaks TN13 . . . 154 C4
Bethel Row ME13 . . . 169 F1
Betherinden Cotts TN18 . . . 356 A4
BETHERSDEN . . . 297 E5
Bethersden Bsns Ctr TN26 . . . 297 C1
Bethersden Ct ME15 . . 195 F7
Bethersden Prim Sch TN26 . . . 297 D5
Bethersden Rd
Hothfield TN26 . . . 266 D4
Shadoxhurst TN26 . . . 298 E2
Smarden TN27 . . . 264 C3
Smarden TN27, TN26 . . 296 C5
Woodchurch TN26 . . . 326 A6
Beths Gram Sch DA5 . . . 14 B1
Betjeman Cl ME20 . . . 127 F3
Betony Gdns ME14 . . . 162 F5
BETSHAM . . . 35 F4
Betsham Rd
Betsham DA13 . . . 35 D3
Erith DA8 . . . 14 F7
Maidstone ME15 . . . 195 F6
Swanscombe DA10 . . . 35 E8
Betteridge Cl ME5 . . . 97 A2
Betterton Dr DA14 . . . 31 E6
Bettescombe Rd ME8 . . 98 E7
BETTESHANGER . . . 213 C6
Betts Rd E16 . . . 1 B6
Betty Shelvey Ct CT14 215 D4
Beulah Rd TN1 . . . 286 C4
Beult Mdw TN27 . . . 264 A1
Beult Rd DA1 . . . 15 A3
Bevan Pl BR8 . . . 55 F5
Bevan Rd SE2 . . . 3 B1
Bevans Cl DA9 . . . 17 C1
Bevan Way CT3 . . . 210 E5
Bevercote Wlk 1 DA17 13 F8
Beveridge Ct 1 SE28 . . . 3 B6
Beverley Ave DA15 . . . 30 F8
Beverley Cl ME8 . . . 98 F8
Beverley Cres TN9 . . . 253 F7
Beverley Ct 8 DA14 . . . 31 B4
Beverley Gdns TN29 . . 353 A4
Beverley Ho CT2 . . . 142 F2
Beverley Rd Bexley DA7 . 14 C5
Canterbury CT2 . . . 142 E2
Maidstone ME16 . . . 160 F2
Orpington BR2 . . . 85 E8
Beverley Way CT12 . . . 83 C1
Beverly Cl CT7 . . . 81 B8
Bevile Ho RM17 . . . 18 B7
Bevis Cl DA2 . . . 34 C8
BEWLBRIDGE . . . 317 D1
Bewl Bridge Cl TN5 . . . 339 B3
Bewlbridge La
Lamberhurst TN3, TN5 . . . 317 B1
Lower Cousley Wood TN5 . . . 337 F8
Bewley La TN15 . . . 156 D2
Bewl Water Nature Reserve★ TN5 . . . 338 B7
Bewl Water Visitor Ctr★ TN3 . . . 338 B8
Bewsbury Cres CT16 . . 277 F7
Bewsbury Cross La CT16 . . . 277 F7
Bexhill Dr RM17 . . . 17 F8
BEXLEY . . . 13 C3
Bexley Cl DA1 . . . 14 E2
Bexley Coll Erith DA17 . . . 4 B1
Erith DA17 . . . 4 C2
Bexley Cotts DA4 . . . 57 C5
Bexley Gram Sch DA16 . . 13 B3
BEXLEYHEATH . . . 13 F4
Bexleyheath Sch DA6 . . . 13 F4
Bexleyheath Sta DA7 . . . 13 E5
Bexley High St DA5 . . . 32 B7
Bexley La Crayford DA1 . . 14 E2
Sidcup DA14 . . . 31 C5
Bexley Rd Eltham SE9 . . . 12 C2
4 Erith DA8 . . . 4 E1
Erith DA8 . . . 4 F1
Erith, Northumberland Heath DA8 . . . 14 C8
Bexley St CT5 . . . 74 D2
Bexley Sta DA5 . . . 32 A7
BEXON . . . 134 B4
Bexon La ME9 . . . 134 C4
Bhutan Rd CT6 . . . 77 C4
BICKLEY . . . 52 F7
Bickley Cres BR1 . . . 52 E5
Bickley Ct 2 BR1 . . . 52 E6
Bickley Park Pre Prep School BR1 . . . 52 D6
Bickley Park Prep Sch BR1 . . . 52 E6
Bickley Park Rd BR1 . . . 52 F6
Bickley Prim Sch BR1 . . 52 C7
Bickley Rd Bromley BR1 . 52 E7
5 Tonbridge TN9 . . . 254 B8
Bickley Sta BR1 . . . 52 E6
Bickmore Way TN9 . . . 222 D3
BICKNOR . . . 133 C2
Bicknor Cl CT2 . . . 143 B4
Bicknor Court Cotts ME9 . . . 133 C2
Bicknor La ME9 . . . 133 D3
Bicknor Rd
Maidstone ME15 . . . 195 F4
Orpington BR6 . . . 53 F2
BIDBOROUGH . . . 253 D3
Bidborough CE Prim Sch TN3 . . . 253 D3
Bidborough Ct TN3 . . . 253 B3
Bidborough Ridge TN4 . . . 253 E4
BIDDENDEN . . . 294 E2
Biddenden Cl
Maidstone ME15 . . . 162 F3
Margate CT9 . . . 51 C1
BIDDENDEN GREEN . . 264 B2
Biddenden La TN27 . . . 262 E5
Biddenden Rd
Headcorn TN27 . . . 262 E2
Tenterden TN30 . . . 323 E6
Tylden TN27 . . . 295 F8
Biddenden Vineyards & Cider Works★ TN27 . 323 A5
Biddenden Way
Eltham SE9 . . . 30 A4
Istead Rise DA13 . . . 36 E1
Biddulph Ho 17 SE18 . . . 1 F2
Bideford Rd DA16 . . . 13 B7
Bierce Court Cotts CT7 80 F7
Bierce Ct CT7 . . . 80 F7
Bifrons Gdns CT4 . . . 176 B3
Bifrons Hill CT4 . . . 176 B4
Bifrons Rd CT4 . . . 176 B4
Bigbury Rd CT2, CT4 . . 173 E7
BIGGIN . . . 19 C8
BIGGIN HILL . . . 118 E3
Biggin Hill Airport TN16 . . . 118 D5
Biggin Hill Bsns Pk TN16 . . . 118 D4
Biggin Hill Prim Sch TN16 . . . 118 E3
Biggin La RM16 . . . 19 B8
Biggin St CT16 . . . 310 D8
Biggins Wood Rd CT19 . . . 334 E7
Bigglestone Link 11 CT1 . . . 175 A8
Bignell Rd SE18 . . . 2 B1
Bilberry Cl ME14 . . . 162 E5
Billet Deedes Way TN25 . 329 F4
Billet Hill TN15 . . . 91 C6
Bill Hamling Cl SE9 . . . 29 F6
Billings DA3 . . . 58 F3
Billington Gdns TN24 . 268 E6
Bill Street Rd 1 ME2 . . . 63 C8
Bilsby Gr SE9 . . . 29 D4
BILSINGTON . . . 329 C1
Bilsington Cl ME5 . . . 97 B5
Bilsington Cross TN25 329 C2
BILTING . . . 237 E7
Bilting La TN25 . . . 237 E7
Bilton Rd DA8 . . . 15 A8
Bimbury La ME14, ME9 132 A5
Bindon Blood Rd CT16 278 A5
Bines The TN12 . . . 257 A5
Bingham Point 5 SE18 . . 2 B2
Bingham Rd
Rochester ME2 . . . 40 C1
Sittingbourne ME10 . . . 102 D6
Bingley Cl ME6 . . . 127 F8
Bingley Ct CT1 . . . 174 E7
Bingley Rd Newham E16 . . 1 C7
1 Rochester ME1 . . . 63 E4
Binland Gr ME5 . . . 96 D5
Binnacle Rd ME1 . . . 96 C8
Binney Rd ME3 . . . 9 D2
Binnie Cl CT10 . . . 83 F2
Binsey Wlk 1 SE2 . . . 3 C4
Birbetts Rd SE9 . . . 29 F6
Birch Cl Ashford TN24 . . 268 F2
Broadstairs CT10 . . . 83 C3
Eynsford DA4 . . . 89 D7
Matfield TN12 . . . 256 D1
New Barn DA3 . . . 59 C7
Royal Tunbridge Wells TN2 . . . 286 D7
Sevenoaks TN13 . . . 154 B4
Tonbridge TN11 . . . 221 D4
Birch Cres ME20 . . . 160 D8
Birch Ct Barham CT4 . . . 242 F8
Ramsgate CT11 . . . 117 D8
BIRCHDEN . . . 312 D5
Birchden Cotts TN3 . . 312 C6
Birchdene Dr SE28 . . . 3 A5
Birch Dr ME5 . . . 97 D1
Birches The
Birchington CT7 . . . 81 B7
Greenwich SE7 . . . 11 B8
Orpington BR6 . . . 86 A6
Swanley BR8 . . . 55 E7
Tonbridge TN9 . . . 254 B7
Birchett TN23 . . . 267 E1
Birchett La TN26 . . . 327 D3
Birchetts Ave TN3 . . . 284 E3
BIRCHETT'S GREEN . . 337 F3
Birchetts Green La TN5 . . . 338 A2
Birchfield TN14 . . . 185 E8
Birchfield Cl ME15 . . . 195 B6

Birchfields ME5 97 A3
Birch Gr Bexley DA16 13 A3
Gillingham ME7 98 A4
Birch Hill Ct CT7 81 B7
Birch Ho
6 Maidstone ME16 161 A3
Sheerness ME12 28 B2
Sittingbourne ME10 102 B3
Birchin Cross Rd TN15 123 A5
BIRCHINGTON 80 E7
Birchington CE Prim Sch CT7 81 A6
Birchington Cl
Bexley DA7 14 B6
Maidstone ME14 162 C5
Orpington BR5 54 C1
Birchington-on-Sea Sta CT7 80 F7
Birch Kiln Cotts TN5 337 A6
Birch Mead BR6 86 A8
Birchmere Bsns Pk SE28 3 D4
Bircholme TN2 286 D7
BIRCHOLT FORSTAL 302 E8
Bircholt Forstal TN25 302 E7
Bircholt Rd ME15 195 F4
Birch Pl
Sevenoaks TN13 154 A3
Stone DA9 16 E1
Birch Rd
Canterbury CT1 174 E6
Hoo St Werburgh ME3 41 E3
Paddock Wood TN12 257 A6
Whitstable CT5 109 A8
Birch Row BR2 53 A3
Birch Tree Ho 18 SE7 11 C8
Birch Tree Way ME15 162 B3
Birchway TN15 90 F2
Birch Way TN2 286 D7
Birchwood Ave
Bidborough TN4 253 E3
Sidcup DA14 31 D5
BIRCHWOOD CORNER 55 C8
Birchwood Dr DA2 32 E4
Birchwood La TN14 120 F4
Birchwood Par DA2 32 E4
Birchwood Park Ave BR8 55 F6
Birchwood Rd
Joyden's Wood DA2, BR8 32 D3
Maidstone ME16 161 C5
Orpington BR5 53 E5
Birchwood Rise CT17 310 C7
Birchwood Terr BR8 55 C8
Birchwood Wlk CT2 142 E2
Birdbrook Rd SE3 11 C4
Bird Coll (Birbeck Ctr) DA15 31 A5
Birdham Cl BR1 52 E4
Bird House La BR6 119 A5
Bird in Hand La BR1 52 D7
Bird in Hand St TN3 312 B8
Bird La TN5 336 B5
Birds Ave CT9 82 B7
Birdwood Ave
Dartford DA1 16 A5
Deal CT14 215 A5
Birkbeck Prim Sch DA14 31 B5
Birkbeck Rd DA14 31 A5
Birkdale TN1 286 B6
Birkdale Cl Erith SE28 3 D7
Orpington BR6 53 D2
Whitstable CT5 109 D8
Birkdale Ct 3 ME16 161 E4
Birkdale Dr CT19 335 A8
Birkdale Gdns CT6 76 D2
Birkdale Rd SE2 3 A2
Birken Rd TN2 286 D6
Birkhall Cl ME5 97 A5
Bir La ME9 134 D5
BIRLING 127 C6
Birling Ave
Gillingham ME8 65 E1
Maidstone ME14 163 A4
Birling Cl ME14 163 A4
Birling Dr TN2 286 A1
Birling Hill DA13, ME19, ME6 94 B1
Birling Park Ave TN2 314 B8
Birling Pk ME19 127 C5
Birling Rd
Ashford TN24 268 D1
Bexley DA8 14 E6
Leybourne ME19 127 C3
Royal Tunbridge Wells TN2 314 B8
Ryarsh ME19 127 A5
Snodland ME6 127 F7
Birnam Sq 1 ME16 161 E4
Birtrick Dr DA13 59 F4
Bishopbourne Gn ME8 65 B4
Bishop Butt Cl BR6 86 F7
Bishop Ct
4 Sittingbourne ME10 101 E5
Whitstable CT5 74 F2
Bishopden Ct CT2 142 C4
Bishop Jenner Ct CT3 146 C7
Bishop John Robinson CE Prim Sch SE28 3 C6
Bishop Justus CE Sch BR2 52 E2
Bishop La ME9 66 E3
Bishop Ridley CE Prim Sch DA16 12 E3
Bishops Ave BR1 52 C6
Bishop's Ave CT10 84 B6
BISHOPSBOURNE 209 B5
Bishopsbourne Ho 2 BR1 29 B1
Bishops Cl Eltham SE9 30 C6
Nettlestead ME18 192 D6
Bishops Ct
Royal Tunbridge Wells TN4 285 F3
Stone DA9 16 E2
Bishops Ctyd 14 CT1 175 A8
BISHOP'S DOWN 285 E3
Bishop's Down TN4 285 F3
Bishop's Down Park Rd TN4 285 F4
Bishop's Down Prim Sch TN4 285 E5
Bishop's Down Rd TN4 285 F3
Bishops Gn
Ashford TN23 299 E7
Bromley BR1 52 C8
Bishops La TN17 319 E2
Bishop's La ME15 226 D6
Bishops Mews TN9 254 C8
Bishops Oak Ride TN10 222 C6
BISHOPSTONE 77 F5
Bishopstone Dr CT6 77 F6
Bishopstone La CT6 77 F5
Bishops Way
Canterbury CT2 142 D1
Maidstone ME15 161 F4
Bishops Wlk
Chislehurst BR7 53 C8
Rochester ME1 63 C5
Bishopswood TN23 300 C3
Bismuth Dr ME10 101 D6
BITCHET GREEN 155 D1
Bittern Cl CT18 307 A3
Blackberry Field BR5 54 A8
Blackberry Way
Paddock Wood TN12 257 B6
Whitstable CT5 109 B8
Blackbrook La BR1, BR2 53 A5
Black Bull Rd CT19 335 D6
Blackburn Rd CT6 76 B2
BLACK CHARLES 188 A5
Blackdale Farm Cotts DA1 34 B6
Blackdown Dr TN24 268 B4
Black Eagle Cl TN16 184 C8
Blacketts Cotts ME9 103 B7
Blacketts Rd ME9 103 A6
BLACKFEN 13 A1
Blackfen Par DA16 13 A1
Blackfen Rd DA15 13 B1
Blackfen Sch DA15 13 B1
Blackfriars St 16 CT1 142 F1
Black Griffin La CT1 174 F8
Blackhall La TN15 154 E3
BLACKHAM 283 A4
Blackheath Bluecoat Sch SE3 11 B7
Blackheath High Sch SE3 11 A7
BLACKHEATH PARK 11 A3
Blackheath Pk SE3 11 A5
Blackheath Prep Sch SE3 11 A6
Black Horse Ct TN27 262 E5
Blackhorse Mews TN2 287 C6
Black Horse Mews TN15 157 A7
Black Horse Rd 14 DA14 31 A4
Blackhouse Hill CT18, CT21 333 D4
Blackhouse Rise CT21 333 D3
BLACKHURST 286 F5
Blackhurst La TN2 286 F6
Blacklands
East Malling ME19 159 F7
East Malling ME19 159 F8
Blacklands Dr ME19 159 F8
Blackleys ME13 171 F7
Black Lion L Ctr ME4 64 B6
Blackman Cl ME3 41 D7
Blackmans Cl DA1 33 C7
Blackman's La TN11 223 D6
Blackmanstone Way ME16 161 B7
Blackmead TN13 153 E6
Black Mill La TN27 262 B6
Blackness La BR2 85 D2
Black Post ME17 165 E4
Black Robin La CT4 209 E3
Black Rock Gdns ME7 98 B4
Blacksmith Dr ME14 162 D5
Blacksmiths Field TN32 355 C1
Blacksmiths La BR5 54 C4
Blacksmith's La TN5 337 A5
Blacksole La TN15 124 F3
Blacksole Rd 3 TN15 124 F3
Blackstable Ct CT5 108 D8
Black's Yd TN13 154 C2
Blackthorn Ave
Chatham ME5 97 A3
Royal Tunbridge Wells TN4 254 C1
Blackthorn Cl TN15 90 F2
Blackthorn Dr ME20 128 B2
Blackthorne Rd ME8 99 B8
Blackthorne Way TN23 300 C3
Blackthorn Gr DA7 13 E4
Blackthorn Rd
Biggin Hill TN16 118 E3
Hersden CT3 144 D8
Blackwall Rd TN24, TN25 269 B4
Blackwall Road N TN24 269 A2
Blackwall Road S TN24 269 A2
Blackwater Cl RM13 4 E8
BLADBEAN 241 F2
Bladindon Dr DA5 31 D8
Blainey Ho ME3 40 F6
Blair Cl DA15 12 E2
Blair Dr TN13 154 B4
Blake Cl Bexley DA16 12 E6
Deal CT14 248 C8
Blake Ct Ashford TN24 300 F8
6 Ramsgate CT11 117 D7
Blake Dr 3 ME20 127 F4
Blake Gdns DA1 15 F3
Blakemore Way DA17 3 E3
Blakeney Cl ME14 163 B4
Blaker Ave ME1 63 E1
Blaker Ct SE7 11 C7
Blake Way
Royal Tunbridge Wells TN2 286 D7
Tilbury RM18 19 C5
Blanchard Cl SE9 29 E5
Blanchard Ho BR7 30 C2
Bland Dr CT18 307 C5
Blandford Gdns ME10 101 E1
Bland St SE9 11 D3
Blanmerle Rd SE9 30 B7
Blann Cl SE9 11 D1
Blatcher Cl ME12 47 B6
Blatchford Cl ME19 127 F1
Blatchington Rd TN1 286 B1
Blaxland Cl ME13 138 B8
Bleak Hill La SE18 12 F8
Bleak Ho★ CT10 84 B4
Bleak House CT10 84 B4
Bleak Rd TN29 376 C6
Bleakwood Rd 6 ME5 96 F5
BLEAN 142 A6
Blean Comm CT2 142 A6
Blean Hill CT2 142 A5
Blean Prim Sch CT2 142 B4
Blean Rd ME8 65 C2
Blean Sq ME14 162 C6
Blean View Rd CT6 76 B2
Blean Woods Nature Reserve★ CT2 141 F4
Bledlow Cl SE28 3 C6
Blendon Dr DA5 13 D1
Blendon Rd
Maidstone ME14 162 C5
Sidcup DA5 13 D1
Blendon Terr SE18 12 C8
Blenheim Ave
Canterbury CT1 143 D1
Chatham ME4 63 E2
Faversham ME13 138 E5
Blenheim Cl
Broadstairs CT10 83 D3
Dartford DA1 15 C1
Herne Bay CT6 77 A1
Maidstone ME15 162 F3
Meopham DA13 93 B8
Blenheim Close SE12 29 B7
Blenheim Ct
Chatham ME4 63 E3
Sidcup DA15 30 D5
Blenheim Dr
Bexley DA16 12 F6
Dover CT16 278 C3
Hawkinge CT18 307 A4
Blenheim Gr DA12 37 C8
Blenheim Ho
Margate CT9 51 C3
Woolwich SE18 2 C3
Blenheim Pl CT20 334 F4
Blenheim Prim Sch BR6 87 C8
Blenheim Rd
Bromley BR1 52 E5
Dartford DA1 15 C1
Deal CT14 215 D5
Kings Hill ME19 159 A3
Littlestone-on-Sea TN28 373 D6
Orpington BR5, BR6 87 C8
Sidcup DA15 31 C7
Sittingbourne ME10 102 B2
Blenheim Way TN5 339 C3
Bleriot Meml★ CT16 278 F1
Bletchington Ct 3 DA17 4 A2
Blewbury Ho 3 SE2 3 C4
BLIBY 328 F8
Bliby Bsns Ctr TN25 328 F7
Bliby Cnr TN25 328 F8
Bligh Inf Sch ME2 62 C7
Bligh Jun Sch ME2 62 C7
Bligh Rd DA11 19 A1
Bligh's Ct TN13 154 B2
Bligh's Rd TN13 154 B2
Bligh's Wlk TN13 154 C2
Bligh Way ME2 62 D6
Blindgrooms La TN26 299 C1
Blindhouse La TN25 304 B3
Blind La Bredhurst ME7 98 A1
Challock TN25 203 C2
Gillingham ME7 97 F1
Goudhurst TN17 290 E1
Mersham TN25 301 C4
Blind Mary's La ME9 133 E4
Bliss Way TN10 222 E5
Blithdale Rd SE2 3 A2
Blockhouse Rd 7 RM17 18 C8
Blockmakers Ct ME4 64 B1
BLOODEN 210 E8
Bloody Point Rd CT13 149 B4
Bloomfield Rd
Bromley BR2 52 D4
Woolwich SE18 2 B1
Bloomfield Terr TN16 151 E2
Bloomsbury Rd CT11 117 C6
Bloomsbury Way TN24 268 B7
Bloomsbury Wlk 2 ME15 162 A4
Bloors La ME8 65 D1
Bloors Wharf Rd ME7 65 F4
Blossom La TN25 267 E5
Blowers Hil Cott TN3 285 B8
Blowers Hill TN8 282 D8
Blowers Wood Gr ME7 98 B3
Bloxam Gdns SE9 11 E2
Blue Anchor La RM18 19 E8
Bluebell Cl
Gillingham ME7 64 F6
Kingsnorth TN23 300 B4
Orpington BR6 86 C8
Bluebell Dr ME10 101 F1
BLUE BELL HILL 96 D1
Bluebell Rd TN23 300 D2
Bluebell Wlks TN12 257 A5
Bluebell Woods Mobile Home Pk CT2 143 D6
Blueberry La TN14 120 C4
Bluebird Ct CT17 310 A6
Bluebird Way SE28 2 D4
Blue Boar La ME1 63 D5
Blue Chalet Ind Pk TN15 90 D4
Blue Coat La TN17 318 C6
Blue Field TN23 299 C8
Bluefield Mews CT5 108 C6
Bluehouse Gdns RH8 183 A7
Bluehouse La RH8 183 A8
Blue House La CT21 333 B8
Blue Line La TN24 268 B4
Blue Skies Sch 7 ME1 63 D4
BLUETOWN 135 B1
BLUE TOWN 28 B2
Bluett St ME14 162 A5
Bluewater Cvn Pk CT21 353 E8
Bluewater Parkway DA9 34 E8
Bluewater Sh Ctr DA9 34 F8
Blunden La ME18 193 A1
Blunts Rd SE9 12 A2
Blythe Cl ME10 102 C5
Blythe Ct Hythe CT21 333 D2
Lewisham SE12 29 A8
Blythe Hill BR5 54 A8
Blythe Rd ME15 162 B4
Blyth Ho 5 DA8 4 E1
Blyth Rd SE28 3 C6
Boakes Mdw TN14 121 F8
Boarders La TN5 338 C3
Boarley Ct ME14 129 F1
Boarley La ME14 129 F2
Boarman's La TN29 370 E8
Boathouse Rd ME12 27 F3
Boat La TN25 330 A4
Bob Amor Cl ME13 138 E7
BOBBING 101 A7
Bobbing Hill ME9 101 A6
Bobbing Prim Sch ME9 101 B7
Bobbin Lodge Hill CT4 173 B2
Bob Dunn Way DA1 16 A3
Bockham Cotts TN25 301 E8
Bockham La
Ashford TN25 270 A1
Mersham TN25 301 E8
BOCKHANGER 268 C6
Bockhanger Ct TN24 268 D5
Bockhanger La TN24 268 C6
Bocking Cl TN5 336 E4
Bockingford La ME15 194 F8
Bocton Ho ME17 195 B3
Bodenham Rd CT20 335 A4
BODIAM 355 D1
Bodiam Cl ME8 65 C3
Bodiam Ct ME16 161 F3
Bodiam Rd TN18, TN32 355 F3
Bodkins Cl ME17 195 D5
Bodle Ave DA10 17 E1
Bodmin Cl BR5 54 C1
BODSHAM 271 D8
Bodsham CE Prim Sch TN25 271 E8
Bodsham Cres ME15 163 B3
Boevey Path
2 Bexley DA17 13 F8
Erith DA17 3 F1
Bogarde Dr ME2 40 B2
BOGDEN 228 C2
Bogey La BR6 86 A3
BOGLE 136 B8
Bogle Rd ME9 136 C7
Bognor Dr CT6 76 D4
Bognor Rd DA16 13 D6
Bogshole La
Herne Bay CT6 77 D3
Whitstable CT5 108 E4
Boley Hill ME1 63 C6
Boleyn Ave CT9 50 E1
Boleyn Ct 9 CT1 175 A8
Boleyn Rd TN15 122 E2
Boleyn Way DA10 35 E8
Bolingbroke Ho ME16 161 E3
Bolton Ct 9 SE12 29 B5
Bolner Cl ME5 96 F2
Bolonia CT15 280 A6
Bolton Rd CT19 335 D6
Bolton St CT11 117 D8
Bolts Hill CT4 173 C2
Bombay Ho 1 ME15 195 E5
Bombers La TN16 151 D7
Bonar Pl BR7 29 E1
Bonaventure Ct DA12 37 F4
Bonchester Cl BR7 30 A1
Bond Cl TN14 120 D4
Bondfield Cl TN4 254 A1
Bondfield Ho SE18 12 A7
Bondfield Rd
3 East Malling ME19 159 F8
4 Newham E6 1 F8
Bondfield Wlk DA1 15 F4
Bond La TN23 300 A2
Bond Rd Ashford TN23 300 B8
Gillingham ME8 98 E5
Bond St RM17 18 C8
Boneashe La TN15 157 D6
Boneta Rd SE18 1 F3
Bonetta Ct ME12 46 B8
Bonflower La ME17 227 C7
Bonham Dr ME10 102 B5
Bonham Way DA11 36 C6
Bonners Alley 19 CT5 74 D2
Bonney Way BR8 55 E6
BONNINGTON 329 F3
Bonnington Cross TN25 329 E3
Bonnington Gn ME8 65 C3
Bonnington Rd ME14 162 C6
Bonnington Twr BR2 52 E3
Bonny Bush Hill CT4 209 D5
Bonsor Rd CT19 335 D6
Boorman's Mews ME18 192 E7
Boorman Way CT5 108 B6
Bootham Cl ME2 62 D5
Booth Cl SE28 3 B6
Booth Close ME6 95 A2
Booth Pl CT9 50 J3
Booth Rd ME4 63 F2
BORDEN 101 B2
Borden CE Prim Sch ME9 100 F3
Borden Gram Sch ME10 101 F3
Borden La ME10, ME9 101 C3
Bordyke TN9 222 C2
Boreham Ave E16 1 A7
Boresisle TN30 324 B2
Borgard Ho SE18 11 E6
Borgard Rd SE18 1 F2
Borkwood Ct 9 BR6 86 F6
Borkwood Pk BR6 86 F6
Borkwood Way BR6 86 E6
Borland Cl 5 DA9 17 A2
Bornefields TN23 300 A7
Borough CT1 143 A1
BOROUGH GREEN 156 F8
Borough Green Prim Sch TN15 157 A7
Borough Green Rd
Borough Green TN15 156 E7
Ightham TN15 156 D6
Wrotham TN15 125 A1
Borough Green & Wrotham Sta TN15 156 F7
Borough Rd
Gillingham ME7 64 D4
Queenborough ME11 46 B4
Tatsfield TN16 150 D6
Borrowdale Ave CT11 117 A7
BORSTAL 63 B2
Borstal Ave CT5 108 D6
Borstal Hill CT5 108 D7
Borstal Mews ME1 63 A2
Borstal Rd ME1 63 B3
Borstal St ME1 63 A2
Borton Cl ME18 192 F1
Boscobel Cl BR1 52 F7
Boscombe Rd CT19 335 C6
Bosman Cl ME16 161 A1
Bosney Banks CT15 277 A7
BOSSINGHAM 241 A6
Bossingham Rd CT4 240 F3
Bossingham St CT4 240 F6
BOSSINGTON 177 E3
Bossington Rd CT3 177 E1
Bostall Hill SE2 3 B1
Bostall La SE2 3 B1
Bostall Manorway SE2 3 B2
Bostall Park Ave DA7 13 E7
Bostall Rd BR5 31 B1
Boston Cl 5 CT16 278 B3
Boston Gdns ME8 65 C1
Boston Rd ME5 97 C2
Bosville Ave TN13 154 A4
Bosville Dr TN13 154 A4
Bosville Rd TN13 154 A4
Boswell Cl BR5 54 C3
Boswell Ho BR2 52 D4
Bosworth Ho 3 DA8 4 E1
Botany TN9 222 C1
Botany Bay La BR7 53 C7
Botany Cl ME12 28 B1
Botany Rd CT10 51 F2
Boteler Cotts CT13 180 A2
Botha Rd E13 1 C8
Bothwell Cl 7 E16 1 A8
BOTOLPH'S BRIDGE 353 A7
Botolph's Bridge Rd CT21 353 A6
Botsom La TN15 90 D4
Bottle House Cotts TN11 251 F1
Bottlescrew Hill ME17 195 B4
Bottles La ME9 135 A6
BOTTOM POND 134 D2
Bottom Pond Rd ME9 134 D3
Bott Rd DA2 33 F4
Boucher Dr DA11 36 F4
BOUGH BEECH 218 F2
Bough Beech Nature Reserve★ TN14 219 B7
BOUGHTON ALUPH 237 A5
Boughton Ave CT10 84 A2
Boughton Church Cotts ME13 139 D1
Boughton Cl ME8 65 B3
Boughton Cnr TN25 237 C5
Boughton Field Cotts ME13 139 A5
BOUGHTON GREEN 195 B3
Boughton Hill ME13 140 C3
Boughton Ho BR1 29 E1
Boughton La ME15 195 B6
BOUGHTON LEES 236 E3
BOUGHTON MALHERBE 232 A8
BOUGHTON MONCHELSEA 195 B3
Boughton Monchelsea Place★ ME17 228 C8
Boughton Monchelsea Prim Sch ME17 195 B2
Boughton Par ME15 195 A7
Boughton Place Cotts ME17 232 A8
Boughton Rd
Sandway ME17 199 B2
Woolwich SE28 2 E3
BOUGHTON STREET 140 A3
BOUGHTON UNDER BLEAN 140 C3
Boughton-under-Blean & Dunkirk Prim Sch ME13 139 F3
Boulevard Courrieres CT3 210 E5
Boulevard d'Erlanger CT18 334 B7
Boulevard The
Ashford TN24 300 F6
Swanscombe DA9 17 C3
Boulogne Ct 17 CT20 335 E5
Boulter Close BR1 53 D5
Boulthurst Way RH8 183 B3
Boultwood Rd E6 1 F7
Boundary Chase CT5 109 B8
Boundary Cl ME12 47 E6
Boundary Ct 3 CT1 175 B6
Boundary Ho 4 DA11 36 F7
Boundary Rd
Chatham ME4 63 E3
Deal CT14 248 D6
Hythe CT21 333 A2
Ramsgate CT11 117 E7
Royal Tunbridge Wells TN2 286 D1
Sidcup DA15 12 E2
Boundary St 2 DA8 14 F7
Boundary The
Canterbury CT1 174 D7
Langton Green TN3 285 B3
Bounds Cross TN27 294 F7
Boundsgate Cnr ME13 203 B7
Bounds La ME13 140 A3
Bounds Oak Way TN4 253 E3
Bounds The ME20 128 E1
Bourchier Cl TN13 154 B1
Bourdillon Ct SE9 29 E6
Bournbrook Rd SE3, SE9 11 D4
Bourne Cl TN9 222 D3
Bourne Cotts CT4 209 C5
Bourne Ct ME1 63 D5
Bourne Ent Ctr TN15 157 A7
Bourne Gr ME10 101 C5
Bourne Grange La TN11 223 D8
Bourne Ind Pk DA1 14 E2
Bourne La
Cranbrook TN32 354 F1
Hamstreet TN26 349 A8
Plaxtol TN15 156 F1
Sandhurst Cross TN18 355 E4
Tonbridge TN9 222 D3
Bourne Lodge Cl CT2 142 A7
Bourne Mead DA5 14 D2
Bournemouth Dr CT6 76 D4
Bournemouth Gdns CT19 335 C6
Bournemouth Rd CT19 335 C5
Bourne Par DA5 32 B8
Bourne Park Rd CT4 209 A7
Bourne Pk TN11 223 F5
Bourne Pk Rd CT4 176 A1
Bourne Place Mdws TN11 221 A7
Bourner Cotts TN17 293 D4
Bourne Rd
Aldington Frith TN25 329 D5
Bexley DA1, DA5 14 D2
Bromley BR2 52 D5
Gravesend DA12 37 F6
Sidcup DA5 32 B8
Bourne Row TN8 251 D6
Bournes Cl CT2 143 F7
Bourneside Terr ME17 164 D2
Bournes Pl TN26 326 A2
Bourne Vale Hayes BR2 52 A2
Plaxtol Spoute TN15 190 A8
Bourne View CT4 175 F1
Bourne Way Hayes BR2 85 A8
Swanley BR8 55 C6
Bournewood TN26 349 A8
Bournewood Cl ME15 162 F1
Bournewood Rd
Orpington BR5 54 C2
Woolwich SE18, SE2 13 A7
Bournville Ave ME4 63 F1
Bouverie Pl 2 CT20 335 D4
Bouverie Road W CT20 335 C4
Bouverie Sh Ctr CT19 335 D4
Bouverie Sq 1 CT20 335 D4
Bovarde Ave ME19 159 C3
BOW ARROW 16 B1
Bow Arrow La DA2 16 A1
Bowater Pl SE3 11 B7
Bowater Rd SE18 1 D3
Bowdell La TN29 362 E3
Bowden Cres CT20 334 C6
Bowen Ct CT11 117 D7
Bowen Rd
Folkestone CT19 334 E6
Rusthall TN4 285 B4
Bowens Field TN23 268 B1
Bower Cl ME16 161 E4
Bower Gn ME5 97 C1
Bower Grove Sch ME16 161 B2
Bower La Eynsford DA4 89 F6
Maidstone ME16 161 E3
Bowerland La
Chilham CT4 172 E1
Old Wives Lees CT4 172 C2

Bower Mount Rd
ME16 161 D4
Bower Pl ME16 161 E3
Bower Rd Hextable BR8 33 A2
Smeeth TN25 302 A3
Bowers Ave DA11 36 F4
Bowers Ho ME7 64 E7
Bowers Rd TN14 121 F8
Bower St ME16 161 E4
Bowers Wlk [1] E6 1 F7
Bower Terr ME16 161 E3
Bower Wlk TN12 260 E3
Bowes Ave CT9 50 E1
Bowes Cl DA15 13 B1
Bowes Ct [24] DA2 16 B1
Bowesden La DA12 38 F1
Bowes La CT6 77 A3
Bowes Rd ME2 63 B8
Bowes Villas CT14 180 E4
Bowes Wood DA3 91 F7
Bowford Ave DA7 13 E6
Bow Hill
Lower Hardres CT4 207 F2
Wateringbury ME18 192 D5
Bowland Cl CT6 77 C2
Bowlers Town TN31 368 A2
Bowles Well Gdns
CT19 335 F7
Bowley La ME17 232 D8
Bowl Field TN25 271 B6
Bowling Green La
CT14 215 B5
Bowling Green Row [1]
SE18 1 F2
Bowling Green Terr [8]
CT17 310 D7
Bowling St CT13 148 F1
Bowl Rd TN27 201 D2
Bowls Pl TN12 257 A7
Bowman Ave E16 1 A6
Bowman Cl ME5 97 C5
Bowman Ct CT17 278 A1
BOWMANS 32 F8
Bowmans Rd DA1 32 F8
Bowmead SE9 29 F6
Bown Cl RM18 19 B5
Bowness Rd DA7 14 B5
Bow Rd ME18 192 E7
Bowser Cl CT14 214 F4
Bow Terr ME18 192 E7
Bowyer Cl E6 1 F8
Bowyer Rd CT5 107 F7
Bowzell Rd TN14 187 A2
Boxgrove Prim Sch SE2 3 C3
Boxgrove Rd SE2 3 C3
Box La ME13 137 D1
BOXLEY 130 D2
Boxley TN23 299 F8
Boxley Cl
Maidstone ME14 162 B8
West Minst ME12 46 B7
Boxley Rd Chatham ME5 97 B2
Maidstone ME14 162 B7
Boxley St E16 1 B5
Boxmend Ind Est ME15 195 F3
Boxshall Ho [7] SE18 12 B8
Boxted La ME9 67 A1
Box Tree Wlk [25] BR5 54 D1
Boyard Rd SE18 2 B1
Boyces Hill ME9 100 D6
Boy Court La TN27 230 F1
BOYDEN GATE 112 C8
Boyden Gate Hill CT3 112 B8
Boyes La CT3 178 D3
Boyke La CT4 273 C2
Boyle Ho [12] DA17 4 A3
Boyle Way TN12 225 B7
Boyne Pk TN4 285 F4
Boyne Rd CT15 248 A1
Boys Hall Rd TN24 300 F7
Boystown Pl CT13 180 C3
Boyton Court Rd ME17 230 A6
Brabazon Rd ME12 48 C1
Brabner Cl CT19 335 E8
BRABOURNE 303 B8
Brabourne Ave ME8 65 C3
Brabourne CE Prim Sch
TN25 303 A8
Brabourne Cl CT2 143 A4
Brabourne Cres DA7 13 F8
Brabourne Gdns CT20 334 E5
Brabourne La TN25 271 F2
BRABOURNE LEES 302 D5
Brabourne Rd TN25 270 D6
Bracken Cl
Ashford TN24 268 C6
Newham E6 1 F8
Royal Tunbridge Wells
TN2 286 E5
Bracken Ct
[3] Broadstairs CT10 83 E5
[4] Sittingbourne ME10 102 C5
Brackendene DA2, DA5 32 E4
Bracken Hill ME5 97 A1
Bracken Lea ME5 64 C1
Bracken Rd TN2 286 E5
Brackens The BR6 87 A5
Bracken Wlk TN10 222 B6
Brack La TN29 362 B3
Brackley Cl ME14 162 C5
Brackwood Cl ME8 98 D5
Bracondale Ave DA13 59 F8
Bracondale Rd SE2 3 A2
Bracton La DA2 32 F6
Bradbery Ct [3] DA11 36 F7
Bradbourne Ct TN13 154 B6
Bradbourne La ME20 128 B1
Bradbourne Park Rd
TN13 154 A4
Bradbourne Parkway
ME19 128 A1
Bradbourne Rd
Grays RM17 18 B8
Sevenoaks TN13 154 B5
Bradbourne Rd *continued*
Sidcup DA5 32 A8
Bradbourne Sch The
TN13 154 A6
Bradbourne Vale Rd TN13,
TN14 154 A5
Bradbridge Gn TN23 299 D8
Bradbury Ct [4] SE3 11 A7
Braddick Cl ME15 195 B6
Bradenham Ave DA16 13 A3
Bradfield Ave ME9 103 D2
Bradfield Rd
Ashford TN24 268 B5
Newham E16 1 B4
Bradfields Ave ME5 96 F5
Bradfields Avenue W
ME5 96 F5
Bradfields FE Ctr ME7 64 B5
Bradfields Sch ME5 97 A6
Bradfoord Ct CT20 335 D5
Bradford Cl BR2 52 F1
Bradfords Cl ME4 41 B2
Bradford St TN9 222 B1
Bradley Dr ME10 101 E2
Bradley House ME3 25 C4
Bradley Rd
Ashurst TN3 283 D5
Folkestone CT19 335 F6
Ramsgate CT12 83 C1
Upper Halling ME2 94 E5
Bradley St [3] TN9 222 B2
Bradley Stone Rd E6 1 F8
Bradshaw Cl ME9 66 E3
Bradstone Ave CT19 335 D6
Bradstone New Rd [3]
CT20 335 D5
Bradstone Rd CT20 335 D5
Bradstow Sch CT10 84 A4
Bradstow Way CT10 84 A5
Brady Dr BR1 53 A6
Bradymead E6 2 B7
Brady Rd CT18 305 A7
Braeburn Way ME19 159 C3
Braemar Ave DA7 14 C3
Braemar Gdns DA15 30 D5
Braeside CT10 84 B3
Braeside Ave TN13 153 F3
Braeside Cl TN13 153 F4
Braeside Cres DA7 14 C3
Braes The ME3 39 C3
Braesyde Cl DA17 3 F2
Braggs La CT6 110 E6
Braithwaite Ct ME7 65 A5
Brake Ave ME5 96 E5
Brakefield Rd DA13 36 B1
Brakes Pl TN15 90 E4
Bramber Ct [9] DA2 16 B1
Bramble Ave DA2 35 C5
Bramble Bank DA13 125 F7
Bramblebury Rd SE18 2 C1
Bramble Cl
Hurst Green RH8 183 B2
Maidstone ME16 161 B3
Tonbridge TN11 221 F4
Wye TN25 237 D3
Bramble Croft DA8 4 C2
Brambledown
Chatham ME5 97 B8
Folkestone CT19 335 D6
Hartley DA3 58 F5
Bramblefield Cl DA3 58 E6
Bramblefield La ME10,
ME9 68 E1
Bramblefields Cl CT6 77 B2
Bramblehill Rd ME13 138 C8
Bramble La
Sevenoaks TN13 187 B7
Wye TN25 237 C3
Bramble Mews [1] DA12 37 D4
Bramble Reed La
TN12 288 B7
Brambles Cl ME12 47 A5
Brambles Ctyd CT14 215 B3
Brambletree Cotts ME1 62 E2
Brambletree Cres ME1 62 F2
Bramble Wlk
Kingsnorth TN23 300 C2
Royal Tunbridge Wells
TN2 286 D7
Brambley Cres CT20 334 E5
Brambling Cl [1] DA9 17 A1
Brambling Rise ME10 101 E6
Bramdean Cres SE12 29 A7
Bramdean Gdns SE12 29 A7
Bramhope Ho [16] SE7 11 C8
Bramhope La SE7 11 B8
Bramis Ho TN16 118 D3
Bramley Ave
Canterbury CT1 174 C6
Faversham ME13 138 E6
Bramley Cl
Brabourne Lees TN25 302 E6
Eastchurch ME12 48 D3
Gillingham ME8 99 B8
Istead Rise DA13 36 F1
Newington ME9 100 A5
Orpington BR6 53 D2
Swanley BR8 55 E5
Bramley Cres ME15 162 F3
Bramley Ct Bexley DA16 13 B6
[15] Erith DA17 4 A1
Marden TN12 259 B6
Bramley Dr TN17 320 D4
Bramley Gdns
Ashford TN23 300 A6
Coxheath ME17 194 C3
Herne Bay CT6 77 D2
Paddock Wood TN12 256 E7
Bramley Pl DA1 15 A3
Bramley Rd
East Peckham TN12 224 F6
Snodland ME6 128 A8
Bramley Rise ME2 62 E8
Bramleys TN27 262 D5
Bramley Way
Eastchurch ME12 48 D3
Kings Hill ME19 159 A2
BRAMLING 177 C6
Bramling Ct TN24 268 C5
Bramling Gap CT3 177 C3
Bramling Rd CT3, CT4 177 B4
Brampton Prim Sch
DA7 13 D5
Brampton Rd DA7 13 E6
Bramshaw Rd CT2 142 E2
Bramshot Ave SE3, SE7 11 B8
Bramshott Cl ME16 161 C6
Bramston Rd ME12 47 C6
BRANBRIDGES 225 A5
Branbridges Ind Est
TN12 225 A5
Branbridges Rd TN12 225 B4
Branchley Mews TN27 234 C8
Branch Rd CT4 205 C7
Branch St CT16 278 C1
BRANDFOLD 290 F3
Brandon Rd
Dartford DA1 34 A8
Ramsgate CT12 83 A1
Brandon St DA11 37 B8
Brandon Way CT7 81 B6
Brandreth Rd E6 1 F7
Brands Hatch Circuit★
DA3 90 F6
Brands Hatch Cotts
DA3 91 A6
Brands Hatch Rd DA3 91 A7
Branham Ho [1] SE18 2 B1
Bransell Cl BR8 55 C3
Bransgore Cl ME8 98 D7
Branston Cres BR5 53 D1
Branstone Ct RM19 16 D8
Branta Fields ME3 41 E4
Brantingham Cl TN9 253 F7
Branton Rd DA9 16 F1
Brantwood Ave DA8 14 C7
Brantwood Rd DA7 14 B4
Brantwood Way BR5 54 C6
Brasenose Rd ME7 64 E4
Brasier Ct ME12 47 A5
Brassey Ave CT10 83 F3
Brassey Cl RH8 183 A6
Brassey Dr ME20 160 D8
Brassey Hill RH8 183 A6
Brassey Rd RH8 183 A6
BRASTED 152 C3
BRASTED CHART 185 B7
Brasted Cl Bexley DA6 13 D2
Orpington BR6 87 A8
Brasted Ct
Brasted TN16 152 D2
Rochester ME2 40 A1
Brasted Hill TN14 152 A7
Brasted Hill Rd TN16 152 C5
Brasted La TN14 120 A1
Brasted Rd Erith DA8 14 E7
Westerham TN16 151 E1
BRATTLE 347 A8
Brattle TN26 347 B8
Brattle Farm Mus★
TN12 260 D1
Brattle Wood TN13 187 C6
Braundton Ave DA15 30 F7
Braunstone Dr ME16 161 D7
Bray Gdns ME15 194 F5
Bray Pas E16 1 A6
Braywood Rd SE9 12 D3
BREACH Derringstone 242 E4
Newington 99 F8
Breach La ME9 67 A2
Breach Rd RM20 16 F8
Breadlands Cl TN24 300 E8
Breadlands Rd TN24 300 F8
Breakneck Hill DA9 17 B2
Breakspears Dr BR5 54 A8
Bream Cl ME20 128 A5
Breaside Prep Sch BR1 52 D8
Breckonmead BR1 52 C7
Brecon Chase ME12 47 C7
Brecon Ct [7] SE9 12 A1
Brecon Rise TN24 268 B4
Brecon Sq CT12 83 A1
BREDGAR 134 A6
Bredgar CE Prim Sch
ME9 134 A5
Bredgar Cl
Ashford TN23 299 F6
Maidstone ME14 162 C5
Bredgar Ho [1] BR5 54 D1
Bredgar Rd ME8 65 B4
Bredgar & Wormshill Light
Rly★ ME9 133 E1
BREDHURST 98 B1
Bredhurst CE Prim Sch
ME7 98 B1
Bredhurst Cl ME12 46 B7
Bredhurst Rd ME8 98 B4
Bredlands La CT3, CT2 111 C1
Breedon Ave TN4 253 F1
Bremner Cl BR8 56 A5
BRENCHLEY 289 B8
Brenchley Ave
Deal CT14 214 F4
Gravesend DA11 37 B3
Brenchley Cl
Ashford TN23 299 E6
Chislehurst BR7 53 A8
Rochester ME1 63 D2
Brenchley & Matfield CE
Prim Sch TN12 289 A8
Brenchley Rd
Gillingham ME8 65 B2
Horsmonden TN12 289 F6
Maidstone ME15 161 F2
Matfield TN12 288 F8
Sittingbourne ME10 101 F2
St Paul's Cray BR5 53 F7
Brenda Ct [4] DA14 31 A4
Brenda Terr DA10 35 E8
Brendon [16] DA14 31 A4
Brendon Ave ME5 97 A3
Brendon Cl Bexley DA8 14 E6
Royal Tunbridge Wells
TN2 286 D5
Brendon Dr TN24 268 B3
Brendon Rd SE9 30 D6
Brenley Cnr ME13 139 B4
Brenley Gdns SE9 11 D3
Brenley La ME13 139 C2
Brennan Ct ME7 64 D6
Brennan Mews ME16 161 E5
Brennan Rd RM18 19 B5
Brent Cl Chatham ME5 96 E5
Dartford DA2 16 B1
Sidcup DA5 31 E7
Brentfield Rd DA1 34 B8
Brent Hill ME13 138 C8
Brent La DA1 34 A7
Brentlands Dr DA1 34 A7
Brentor Ct TN2 286 D6
Brent Prim Sch The
DA2 34 C8
Brent Rd
Faversham ME13 138 C8
Newham E16 1 A8
Woolwich SE18 12 B7
Brents Ind Est ME13 105 D1
BRENTS THE 105 D1
Brent The Dartford DA1 34 B8
Tonbridge TN10 222 C6
Brent Way DA2 16 B1
Brentwood TN23 299 F5
Brentwood Cl SE9 30 C7
Brentwood Ho SE18 11 D7
BRENZETT 363 A3
Brenzett Aeronautical
Mus★ TN29 363 B3
Brenzett Cl ME5 97 B5
Brenzett Cnr TN29 363 A3
Brenzett District CE Prim
Sch TN29 363 A2
BRENZETT GREEN 363 C6
Brenzett Ho [6] BR5 54 C4
Bretaneby TN15 154 F6
Bretland Ct TN4 285 D4
Bretland Rd TN4 285 D4
Breton Rd ME1 63 C2
Brett Wlk ME8 98 D4
Brewer Rd ME3 40 B7
Brewers Field DA2 33 C4
Brewer's Hill CT20 334 D3
Brewers Rd DA12 61 C8
Brewer St Deal CT14 215 D6
Lamberhurst TN3 317 A5
Maidstone ME14 162 A5
Brewery Cotts CT14 214 E4
Brewery La Bridge CT4 176 A1
Sevenoaks TN13 154 C2
Brewery Rd
Orpington BR2 52 E1
Sittingbourne ME10 101 E6
Woolwich SE18 2 D1
Brewery Sq CT3 113 D2
Brewhouse La TN25 236 F4
Brewhouse Rd SE18 1 F2
Brewhouse Yd [15] DA12 19 B1
Brewster Cotts ME9 135 E2
Brian Cres TN4 286 B8
Brian Roberts Ho CT6 76 F5
Briar Cl Ashford TN24 268 C6
Aylesham CT3 210 F5
Crabble CT17 277 F2
Larkfield ME20 128 A2
[8] Marlpit Hill TN8 217 D3
Briar Dale ME3 39 B4
Briar Fields ME14 162 E5
Briar Rd DA5 32 D5
Briars Cross RH8 183 D5
Briars Rd TN29 365 F3
Briars The
West Kingsdown TN15 90 D4
Whitstable CT5 108 C6
Briars Way DA3 59 A4
Briars Wlk CT10 83 F3
Briarswood Way BR6 86 F5
Briar Wlk TN10 222 C6
Briary Cl CT9 82 A8
Briary Ct DA14 31 B3
Briary Gdns BR1 29 B3
Briary Prim Sch CT6 76 C2
Brice Ave CT4 173 C1
Brice Rd ME3 39 B3
Brick Ct RM17 18 A8
Brickenden Rd TN17 320 D4
Brickfield TN31 367 B2
Brickfield Cotts
Bexley SE18 12 F8
Wye TN25 237 B2
Brickfield Farm DA3 59 A6
Brickfield Farm Gdns
BR6 86 C6
Brickfield La ME13 139 E2
Brickfield Rd CT4 242 F7
Brickfields
Pembury TN2 287 E8
West Malling ME19 127 B1
Brick Field View ME2 40 C1
Brick Kiln La
Horsmonden TN12 290 B2
Limpsfield RH8 183 C5
Ulcombe ME17 230 D5
Brickmakers Ind Est
ME10 102 B6
Brickmakers Meadows
TN15 157 C7
Brickwall Terr TN26 325 F3
Brickwell Cotts TN17 293 F6
Brickworks Cl TN9 254 B7
Bridewell La TN30 345 A7
Bridewell Pk CT5 75 A1
BRIDGE 176 A1
Bridge App The CT5 74 F1
Bridge Bsns Pk TN12 256 C7
Bridge Cl Dartford DA2 16 D4
Hythe CT21 333 A2
Tonbridge TN9 254 C8
Woodchurch TN26 347 B8
Bridge Cotts
Horsmonden TN12 290 A6
Selling ME13 171 E7
Bridge Ct
[28] Dartford DA2 16 B1
Grays RM17 18 B8
Bridge Down CT4 209 B8
BRIDGEFIELD 300 C2
Bridgefield ME17 197 B1
Bridgefield Ct CT5 75 B3
Bridgefield Rd CT5 75 B3
Bridgeford Way CT4 176 A1
Bridge Hill Bridge CT4 209 B8
Finglesham CT14 214 C8
Bridge Ho
Ramsgate CT11 117 C7
Rochester ME1 63 B4
Royal Tunbridge Wells
TN4 286 B5
Bridge Home Pk TN29 376 D8
Bridge Ind Ctr ME15 161 E2
Bridgeland Rd E16 1 A6
Bridgeman Ct CT21 333 B2
Bridge Mill Way ME15 161 D2
Bridgen Rd DA5 31 E8
Bridge & Patrixbourne CE
Prim Sch CT4 176 A2
Bridge Pl ME20 128 F2
Bridge Rd Ashford TN23 267 F2
Bexley DA7 13 E5
Brabourne Lees TN25 302 D5
Bridge CT4 175 D1
Deal CT14 215 D7
Erith DA8 14 F6
Faversham ME13 138 D8
Gillingham ME7 64 C7
Grays RM17 18 B8
Margate CT9 50 E1
Orpington BR5 54 B3
Rochester ME1 63 C2
Sheerness ME12 28 B2
Bridge Rd Ind Ctr
TN23 267 F2
Bridges Cl CT7 79 E2
Bridges Dr DA1 16 B2
Bridgeside CT14 215 C6
Bridgeside Mews
ME15 161 E2
Bridge St Dover CT16 278 C1
Folkestone CT19 335 E6
Maidstone ME15 194 F5
Wye TN25 237 E2
Bridge View DA9 17 B3
Bridge View Ind Est
Rushenden ME11 46 A2
West Thurrock RM20 16 F8
Bridgewater Cl BR7 53 E6
Bridgewater Pl ME19 127 E2
Bridgewater Rd ME12 46 B8
Bridgeway CT5 74 F2
Bridle Way
Herne Bay CT6 76 D3
Hythe CT21 334 A3
Orpington BR6 86 C6
Bridleway Gdns CT10 83 E3
Bridleway La TN23 300 B4
Bridlington Cl TN16 150 B8
Brielle Way
Queenborough ME11,
ME12 46 A6
Sheerness ME12 28 A2
Brier Cl ME5 97 C8
Brier Rd ME10 101 B4
Brigadier Gdns TN23 267 F4
Briganda Wlk CT11 117 E8
Bright Cl DA17 3 D2
Bright Ct [8] SE28 3 C5
Brightlands DA11 36 E4
Brightlingsea Rd CT13 180 F8
Bright Rd [3] ME4 64 B2
Bright Ridge TN4 285 E8
Brights Pl CT11 117 F7
Brigstock Rd DA17 4 B2
Brimpsfield Cl SE2 3 B3
Brimp The ME3 9 D3
Brimstone Cl BR6 87 C3
Brimstone Hill DA13 93 D8
Brindle Gate DA15 30 E7
Brindle Gr CT11 83 F1
Brindle's Field TN9 254 A7
Brindle Way ME5 97 C1
Brindley Cl DA7 14 B4
Brindley Way BR1 29 A3
Brinkburn Cl SE2 3 A2
Brinkers La TN5 337 A2
Brinklow Cres SE18 12 B7
Brinklow Terr TN26 299 A1
Brionne Gdns TN9 254 D8
Brisbane Ave ME10 101 C4
Brisbane Dr CT12 83 A1
Brisbane Ho RM18 18 F6
Brisbane Rd ME4 64 A3
Briset Rd SE9 11 D3
Brishing Cl ME15 195 E5
Brishing La ME17 195 D4
Brishing Rd ME15,
ME17 195 F3
Brisley Cl TN23 299 D6
Brisley Ct TN23 299 D6
Brisley La TN26 328 D6
Brisley's Row ME1 95 F1
Brissenden Cl
Chattenden ME2 41 A3
New Romney TN28 373 B8
BRISSENDEN GREEN 297 F3
Bristles Cnr CT3 111 A6
Bristol Cl Herne Bay CT6 77 B3
Rochester ME2 62 D5
Bristol Pl CT11 117 D7
Bristol Rd
Canterbury CT1 174 F6
Gravesend DA12 37 D5
Bristow Rd DA7 13 E6
Britannia Ave CT5 108 B7
Britannia Bsns Pk
ME20 160 E7
Britannia Cl Erith DA8 14 F8
Halling ME2 95 A4
Sittingbourne ME10 101 E7
Britannia Dr DA12 37 F3
Britannia Gate E16 1 A5
Britannia La TN23 299 F5
Britannia Rd Deal CT14 215 D8
Fenn Street ME3 24 A3
Britannia Village Prim Sch
E16 1 B5
British MK IV Tank★ [15]
TN23 268 B2
Briton Ct ME12 46 B8
Briton Rd ME13 138 C7
Brittain Ct SE9 29 E7
Brittain Ho SE9 29 E7
Brittains La TN13 153 F2
Britten Cl Hythe CT21 333 A3
Tonbridge TN10 222 F6
Brittenden Cl [1] BR6 86 F4
Brittenden Par BR6 86 F4
Britton St ME7 64 B5
Brixham Rd DA16 13 D6
Brixham St E16 2 A5
Broadacre Lydden CT15 276 F8
Teynham ME9 103 D2
Broadbridge Cl SE3 11 A7
Broadcloth TN17 320 D3
Broadcroft TN2 313 F8
Broadcroft Rd BR5 53 D2
Broad Ditch Rd DA13 36 D1
Broader La ME14 131 B2
Broadfield Cres CT20 335 A5
Broadfield Rd
Folkestone CT20 335 A5
Loose ME15 195 A8
BROAD FORD 290 C4
Broadgate Hall [1]
CT11 117 F7
Broadgate Rd E16 1 D7
Broad Gr TN2 286 A1
Broadheath Dr BR7 29 F3
Broadhoath TN15 155 E1
Broadhurst Dr TN24 268 D7
Broad La Dartford DA2 33 B4
Finglesham CT14 214 B7
Fordcombe TN3 284 A4
Broadlands CT2 143 F6
Broadlands Ave TN28 373 B8
Broadlands Cres TN28 373 B8
Broadlands Dr ME5 97 B4
Broadlands Ind Est
CT2 142 A7
Broadlands Rd BR1 29 B4
Broad Lawn SE9 30 A7
Broadley Ave CT7 80 F5
Broadley Rd CT10, CT9 83 C7
Broadmead
Ashford TN23 299 E6
Royal Tunbridge Wells
TN2 313 F8
Broadmead Ave TN2 313 F8
Broadmead Manor
CT10 84 B7
Broadmeadow CT19 335 B7
Broadmead Rd CT19 335 C5
Broadmere Terr ME16 161 D3
BROADOAK 134 E5
BROAD OAK Ashford 301 C1
Sturry 143 D7
Broadoak ME19 127 E2
Broad Oak
Brenchley TN12 289 C8
Groombridge TN3 312 C6
Broadoak Ave ME15 195 A8
Broadoak Cl DA4 34 A2
Broad Oak Cl
Brenchley TN12 289 C8
Orpington BR5 54 A7
Royal Tunbridge Wells
TN2 285 F1
Broadoak Ent Village
ME9 134 F6
Broadoak Rd Erith DA8 14 D7
Sittingbourne ME9 134 E6
Broad Oak Rd CT2 143 B3
Broad Rd DA10 17 E1
Broadreach Coll SE28 2 F4
Broadsole La CT15 308 E5
Broad St
Canterbury CT1 143 A1
Deal CT14 215 D6
Margate CT9 50 I3
Ramsgate CT11 117 E7
Sellindge TN25 303 E5
Sheerness ME12 28 B2
Sutton Valence ME17 229 E7
BROADSTAIRS 84 C5
Broadstairs Rd CT10 83 E5
Broadstairs Sta CT10 84 A4
BROADSTONE 231 D4
BROAD STREET
Hoo St Werburgh 41 B5
Lyminge 305 C5
Maidstone 164 B6
Sellindge 303 F5
Broad Street Hill
ME17 164 D7
BROAD TENTERDEN 345 B4
Broadview
Folkestone CT20 334 C6
Meopham DA13 92 F6
Broad View TN17 321 A8
Broadview Ave ME8 98 E8

Broadviews CT21 333 D1
Broadwater Ct TN2 313 E8
BROADWATER DOWN 313 E7
Broadwater Down TN2 313 F8
Broadwater Down Prim Sch 4 TN2 285 F1
Broadwater Forest La TN3 313 B7
Broadwater Gdns BR6 86 C6
Broadwater Ho DA12 19 D1
Broadwater La TN2, TN4 285 F1
Broadwater Rd
East Malling ME19 159 D6
Woolwich SE28 2 D3
Broadwater Rise TN2 285 F1
BROADWAY 234 B6
Broadway Bexley DA6 13 F3
Crockenhill BR8 55 C3
Gillingham ME8 65 A3
Grays RM17 18 C8
Limpsfield RH8 183 B5
Maidstone ME14 161 F4
Petham CT4 207 A2
Tilbury RM18 18 F5
Broadway Sh Ctr ME16 161 F4
Broadway The
Broadstairs CT10 84 A4
Dover CT16 310 H8
Hadlow TN11 223 E8
Herne Bay CT6 76 C5
Lamberhurst TN3 317 B5
Minster (Sheppey) ME12 47 B6
Sheerness ME12 28 C2
Broad Wlk
Eltham SE3, SE9 11 E5
Orpington BR6 87 D7
Sevenoaks TN15 187 E7
Broadwood DA11 37 B3
Broadwood Rd ME3 41 A4
Brockbank Cl ME5 97 A1
Brockdene Dr BR2 85 D6
Brockenhurst Ave ME15 162 C1
Brockenhurst Cl
Canterbury CT2 142 E2
Gillingham ME8 98 C7
Brockenhurst Rd CT11 117 G8
Brockhill Ctry Pk★ CT21 332 F4
Brockhill Park Performing Arts Coll CT21 332 F4
Brockhill Rd CT21 333 B3
Brocklebank Ho 7 E16 2 A5
Brocklebank Rd SE7 1 B2
Brocklebank Rd Ind Est SE7 1 B2
Brockley Rd CT9 51 A2
Brockman Cres TN29 353 B4
Brockman Rd CT20 335 C5
Brockman's Cl CT12 115 B7
Brock Rd E13 1 B8
Brockway TN15 157 A7
Brockwell Cl BR5 53 F4
Brodrick Gr SE2 3 B2
Brogdale Farm Cotts ME13 138 A3
Brogdale Farm National Fruit Collection★ ME13 138 B4
Brogdale Pl ME13 138 B6
Brogdale Rd ME13 138 B5
Brogden Cres ME17 196 F7
Broke Farm Dr BR6 87 C2
Brokes Way TN4 286 B8
Brome Ho SE18 11 E6
Brome Rd SE9 11 F4
Bromford Cl RH8 183 A2
Bromhedge SE9 29 F5
Bromholm Rd SE2 3 B3
BROMLEY 52 B6
Bromley RM17 17 F8
Bromley Cl ME5 97 B4
Bromley Coll 9 BR2 52 A8
Bromley Coll of FE & HE (Rookery Lane Campus) BR2 52 D3
Bromley Comm BR2 52 D3
BROMLEY COMMON 52 E3
BROMLEY GREEN 327 E6
Bromley Green Rd TN26 328 A5
Bromley High Jun Sch BR1 53 D5
Bromley High Sch BR1 53 A5
Bromley Ind Ctr BR1 52 D6
Bromley La BR7 30 D1
Bromley Manor Mans 3 BR2 52 A6
Bromley Mus★ BR6 54 B2
Bromley North Sta BR1 52 A8
Bromley Rd BR7 53 B8
Bromley South Sta BR1 52 A6
BROMPTON 64 A5
Brompton Dr DA8 15 B7
Brompton Farm Rd ME2 40 A2
Brompton Hill ME4 63 F6
Brompton La ME2 63 A8
Brompton Rd ME7 64 B6
Brompton Villas CT15 278 E6
Brompton Westbrook Prim Sch ME7 64 A5
BROMSTONE 83 E3
Bromstone Mews CT10 83 E3
Bromstone Prim Sch CT10 83 D3
Bromstone Rd CT10 83 E3
Bronington Cl ME5 97 A5
Bronte Cl
Cliffe Woods ME3 40 B7
Bronte Cl *continued*
Erith DA8 14 B7
Lunsford ME20 127 F3
Tilbury RM18 19 C5
Bronte Gr DA1 15 F3
Bronte Sch DA11 37 A8
Bronte View DA12 37 C7
Bronze Age Way DA8, DA17 4 C3
BROOK 270 B5
Brookbank Brook TN25 270 A5
Maidstone ME14 162 A8
Brook Cl Herne Bay CT6 76 C3
Hythe CT21 334 B3
Brook Com Prim Sch TN25 270 A4
Brook Cotts
Collier Street TN12 258 F8
East Farleigh ME15 194 C7
Staple CT3 178 E6
Teynham ME9 104 A2
Brook Ct
1 Lewisham SE12 29 C5
10 Marlpit Hill TN8 217 D3
Brookdale Rd DA5 13 E1
Brookdene TN12 256 B7
Brookdene Rd SE18 2 F2
Brooke Ave CT9 82 B7
Brooke Dr DA12 38 B7
Brookend Rd DA15 30 E7
Brooker Cl ME17 195 D5
Brooke Rd TN24 268 B3
Brookes Pl ME9 100 B6
Brookfield
Four Elms TN8 218 B5
Kemsing TN15 122 E2
Sandhurst TN18 356 B5
Brookfield Ave
Dover CT16 278 B2
New Hythe ME20 128 A4
Brookfield Ct
Ashford TN23 299 F8
Royal Tunbridge Wells TN4 254 A1
Brookfield Ind Pk TN23 267 F1
Brookfield Inf Sch ME20 128 A2
Brookfield Jun Sch ME20 128 A2
Brookfield Pl CT16 278 B2
Brookfield Rd
Ashford TN23 299 F8
Dover CT16 278 A3
Brookfields TN11 190 E1
Brook Hill Cl SE18 2 B1
Brookhill Rd SE18 2 B1
Brookhurst Gdns TN4 253 E3
Brook La Bexley DA5 13 D2
Bromley BR1 29 A2
Cliffs End CT12 115 F4
Greenwich SE3 11 B5
Plaxtol Spoute TN15 190 A8
Reculver CT6 78 B5
Sellindge TN25 303 E2
Snodland ME6 128 A6
Tonbridge TN9 222 D2
BROOKLAND 370 D8
Brookland CE Prim Sch TN29 370 D8
BROOKLANDS 33 F7
Brooklands Dartford DA1 33 E7
Headcorn TN27 262 C6
Royal Tunbridge Wells TN2 286 D7
Brooklands Ave DA15 30 D6
Brooklands Cl CT2 143 F4
Brooklands Farm Cl TN3 284 A6
Brooklands Pk SE3 11 A4
Brooklands Prim Sch SE3 11 A4
Brooklands Rd ME20 128 A4
Brook Lane Cotts TN25 303 E2
Brooklyn Paddock ME7 64 D6
Brooklyn Rd BR2 52 D4
Brooklyn Villas TN12 259 C5
Brookmead TN11 221 E4
Brookmead Ave BR1 52 F4
Brookmead Cl BR5 54 B3
Brookmead Rd ME3 40 B7
Brookmead Way BR5 54 B3
Brook Pk DA1 34 A6
Brook Rd
Faversham ME13 105 D1
Lunsford ME20 127 F4
Northfleet DA11 36 E7
Royal Tunbridge Wells TN2 286 D7
Swanley BR8 55 D7
Whitstable CT5 75 C3
Brooks Cl Eltham SE9 30 A6
Staplehurst TN12 260 E4
Tonbridge TN10 222 E7
BROOKS END 80 E4
Brookside
Cranbrook TN17 320 D4
Hoo St Werburgh ME3 41 E5
Orpington BR6 53 F2
St Mary's Bay TN29 366 A5
Temple Ewell CT16 277 D5
Brookside Rd DA13 36 F1
Brooks Pl ME14 162 A4
Brook Sq SE18 11 E6
Brook St Eastry CT13 180 C2
Erith DA8 14 B7
Snodland ME6 128 B8
Tonbridge TN9 254 A8
Woodchurch TN26 346 D8
BROOK STREET
Tenterden 346 E8
Tonbridge 254 A8
Brooks Way TN29 376 C5
Brook The ME4 64 A4
Brook Theatre★ ME4 63 F5
Brook Vale DA8 14 B6
Brookvale Workshops DA11 36 C7
Brookway SE3 11 A4
Broom Ave BR5 54 B7
Broom Cl BR2 52 E3
Broomcroft Rd ME8 65 F2
BROOMFIELD Herne Bay 77 D1
Kingswood 197 D5
Broomfield TN3 314 F5
Broomfield Cres CT9 51 F2
Broomfield Gate CT5 109 D5
Broomfield Ho 4 BR5 54 B7
Broomfield Rd
Bexley DA6 14 A2
Faversham ME13 138 C8
Folkestone CT19 334 E6
Herne Bay CT6 77 C2
Kingswood ME17 197 D4
Sevenoaks TN13 153 F5
Swanscombe DA10 17 E2
Broomfields DA3 58 E4
BROOM HILL
Canterbury 146 B1
Chiselhurst 53 F2
Broomhill Bank Sch TN3 285 C6
Broom Hill Cotts TN5 339 B3
Broomhill Park Rd TN4 285 F8
Broomhill Rd
Dartford DA1 15 B1
Orpington BR6 54 A2
Royal Tunbridge Wells TN3 285 D7
Broom Hill Rd ME2 62 F8
Broomhill Rise DA6 14 A2
Broomhills DA13 35 E4
Broom La TN3 284 F1
Broomlands La RH8 183 E8
Broomleigh 3 BR1 52 A8
Broom Mead DA6 14 A2
Broom Pk TN3 284 E3
Broom Rd ME10 102 C5
Broomscroft Cotts ME18 159 C1
Broomshaw Rd ME16 160 F3
Broomsleigh TN16 118 E2
BROOM STREET 106 D2
Broomwood Cl DA5 32 D6
Broomwood Rd BR5 54 B7
Brotherhood Cl CT2 142 D4
Brougham Ct 5 DA2 16 B1
Broughton By-Pass ME13 140 C2
Broughton Ct TN23 267 E1
Broughton Rd
Orpington BR6 86 D8
Otford TN14 122 A3
Brow Cl BR5 54 D2
Brow Cres BR5 54 D2
Browndens Rd ME2 94 E4
Brownelow Copse ME5 97 B1
Brownhill Cl ME5 97 A4
Browning Cl
Bexley DA16 12 E6
6 Lunsford ME20 127 F4
Browning Pl CT19 335 E7
Browning Rd DA1 15 F3
Brownings TN8 217 C4
Brownings Orch ME9 135 A7
Browning Wlk RM18 19 C5
Brown Lo ME12 28 H1
Brown Rd DA12 37 E7
Brownspring Dr SE9 30 B5
Browns Sch BR6 87 F5
Brown St ME8 65 F1
Broxbourne Rd BR6 53 F2
Broxhall Rd CT4 208 B3
Bruce Cl Bexley DA16 13 B6
Deal CT14 215 B4
Bruce Ct 2 DA15 30 F4
Bruce Gr BR6 54 A1
Bruces Wharf Rd RM17 18 A8
Brucks The ME18 192 E7
Bruges Ct ME10 68 F1
Brummel Cl DA7 14 C4
Brundell Terr CT4 173 B2
Brunel Cl RM18 19 B4
Brunell Cl ME16 161 D5
Brunel Way ME4 64 A7
Brungers Wlk TN10 222 B5
Brunswick Cl DA6 13 D3
Brunswick Cotts ME9 103 E6
Brunswick Ct 3 CT11 117 E7
Brunswick Field ME9 103 E6
Brunswick Gdns 3 CT16 278 B3
Brunswick House Prim Sch ME16 161 E5
Brunswick Ind Ctr TN23 267 F2
Brunswick Rd
Ashford TN23 267 F2
Bexley DA6 13 E3
Birchington CT7 81 A5
Brunswick Sq CT6 76 E5
Brunswick St
Maidstone ME15 162 A3
Ramsgate CT11 117 E7
Brunswick Street E ME15 162 A3
Brunswick Terr TN1 286 A2
Brunswick Wlk 1 DA12 37 D8
Brushwood Lodge 1 DA17 4 A2
Bruton Cl BR7 29 F1
Bryanston Rd RM18 19 C5
Bryant Cl ME18 192 D6
Bryant Rd ME2 63 A7
Bryant St ME4 64 A3
Bryces Alley CT5 74 D2
Brymore Cl CT1 143 B2
Brymore Rd CT1 143 B2
Bryony Dr TN23 300 C3
Bryony Sch ME8 98 C7
Bubblestone Rd TN14 122 B3
Bubhurst La TN17 294 B7
Buckden Cl SE12 11 A1
Buckham Thorns Rd TN16 151 C1
Buckhole Farm Rd ME23 23 C4
BUCKHURST 294 C5
Buckhurst Ave TN13 154 C2
Buckhurst Dr CT9 51 F2
Buckhurst La
Rockrobin TN5 336 A6
Sevenoaks TN13 154 C2
Buckhurst Pl TN5 336 A6
Buckhurst Rd TN16 151 B7
Buckingham Ave DA16 12 E3
Buckingham Cl BR5 53 E2
Buckingham Dr BR7 30 C3
Buckingham Rd
15 Broadstairs CT10 84 B4
Gillingham ME7 64 D5
Margate CT9 50 I1
Northfleet DA11 36 D8
Royal Tunbridge Wells TN1 286 B2
Whitstable CT5 75 B2
Buckingham Row ME15 195 E7
BUCKLAND 278 C2
Buckland Ave CT16 278 B2
Buckland Cl ME5 97 A2
Buckland Cotts ME13 137 B8
BUCKLAND HILL 316 A1
Buckland Hill ME16 161 E5
Buckland Hospl CT17 278 A1
Buckland La
Maidstone ME16 161 D6
Staple CT3 179 A4
Buckland Pl ME16 161 E4
Buckland Rd
Cliffe Woods ME3 40 A8
Luddesdown DA13 94 A7
Maidstone ME16 161 E4
Orpington BR6 86 E6
BUCKLAND VALLEY 278 C4
Buckler Gdns SE9 29 F5
Bucklers Cl
Royal Tunbridge Wells TN2 286 C3
Warden ME12 49 E4
Buckles Ct DA17 3 D2
Buckley Cl DA1 14 F5
Buckmore Pk-International Kart Circuit ME5 96 C3
BUCK'S CROSS 87 F5
Bucks Cross Rd
Chelsfield BR6 87 E5
Northfleet DA11 36 F5
Bucksford La TN23 299 C7
Buck St TN25 203 C2
Buckthorn Cl CT14 215 C7
Buckthorne Ho ME12 47 A4
Buckthorne Rd ME12 47 A4
Buckthorn House DA15 30 F5
Buckwheat Ct DA18 3 D3
Budd Ho 4 SE7 1 C1
Buddle Dr ME12 46 E7
Budd's Farm Cotts TN30 359 E2
Budd's La TN30 359 F2
Budgin's Hill BR6 120 C8
Budleigh Cres DA16 13 C6
Buenos Ayres CT9 50 H2
Buffs Ave CT20 334 B6
Bugglesden Rd TN27, TN30 323 D5
Bugsby's Way SE10, SE7 1 B2
Builders Sq CT3 177 A8
Bullace La 3 DA1 15 E1
Bullbanks Rd DA17 4 C2
Bulldog Rd ME5 97 B2
Bulleid Pl TN24 300 D7
Bullen La TN12 224 E7
Buller Rd ME4 63 F2
Buller's Ave CT6 76 E4
Bullers Cl DA14 31 E3
Bullers Wood Dr BR7 29 F1
Bullers Wood Sch BR7 52 E8
Bull Fields ME6 128 A8
Bullfinch Cl
Paddock Wood TN12 257 A5
Sevenoaks TN13 153 D5
Bullfinch Cnr TN13 153 E5
Bullfinch Dene TN13 153 D5
Bullfinch La TN13 153 E5
Bull Hill Horton Kirby DA4 57 C5
Lenham Heath ME17 200 A1
Lenham ME17 232 F8
BULLINGSTONE 284 F7
Bullingstone Cotts TN3 284 E7
Bullingstone La TN3 284 F7
Bullion Cl TN12 256 F6
Bullivant Cl 3 DA9 17 A2
Bull La Bethersden TN26 297 B4
Boughton Street ME13 139 F4
Chislehurst BR7 30 D1
Eccles ME20 128 F5
Lower Higham ME3 39 D7
Wrotham TN15 125 A3
Yelsted ME9 99 E2
Bull Lane Cotts
Hook Green TN3 316 C4
Yelsted ME9 99 E1
BULLOCKSTONE 110 D8
Bullockstone Rd CT6 110 E7
Bull Orch ME16 160 F2
Bull Rd ME19 127 C5
Bulls Cotts 4 CT21 333 B2
Bulls Pl TN2 287 D6
Bulltown Cnr TN25 270 F3
Bullwark St CT17 310 D5
Bull Yd 6 DA11 19 B1
Bulrush Cl ME5 96 F3
Bulrushes The TN23 299 D8
Bulwark Rd CT14 215 D7
Bumbles Cl ME1 96 D7
Bunce Court Rd ME13, ME17 200 E7
Bungalows The
Faversham ME13 138 A4
Tenterden TN30 345 D7
Woodnesborough CT13 180 B5
Bunkers Hill
New Ash Green TN15 92 C4
Sidcup DA14 31 F5
Bunker's Hill
Dover CT17 278 B2
Erith DA17 4 A2
Bunkers Hill Ave CT17 278 B1
Bunkers Hill Rd CT17 278 A1
Bunkley Mdw TN26 349 A7
Bunny La TN3 313 E5
Bunters Hill Rd ME3 40 B4
Bunton St SE18 2 A3
Burberry La ME17 197 B5
Burcharbro Rd SE2 13 D8
Burch Ave CT13 180 F8
Burch Rd DA11 18 F1
Burdens TN27 262 D5
Burdett Ave DA12 38 F4
Burdett Cl DA14 31 E3
Burdett Rd TN4 285 B4
Burdock Ct ME16 161 A3
Burdock Ho 6 ME15 195 D8
Burford Rd BR1 52 E5
Burford's Alley CT3 147 D1
Burgate CT1 175 A8
Burgate Cl DA1 14 F4
Burgate La 5 CT1 175 A8
Burgate Terr TN25 301 E4
Burgess Cl
Minster (Thanet) CT12 115 C7
Whitfield CT16 278 B7
Burgess Gn CT14 214 C8
Burgess Hall Dr ME17 196 F6
Burgess Rd
Aylesham CT3 210 F6
Rochester ME2 63 B7
Burgess Row 9 TN30 345 A7
Burghclere Dr ME16 161 B2
Burghfield Rd DA13 36 F1
Burgoyne Ct ME14 161 F7
Burgoyne Gr CT16 278 A5
Burgoyne Hts CT15 278 E3
BURHAM 95 E1
Burham CE Prim Sch ME1 128 F8
Burham Rd ME1 95 E8
Burial Ground La ME15 161 E1
Burkeston Cl ME10 102 A8
Burleigh Ave DA15 12 F2
Burleigh Cl ME2 62 E8
Burleigh Dr ME14 129 F1
Burleigh Rd TN27 234 C7
Burley Rd Newham E16 1 C8
Sittingbourne ME10 101 E4
Burlings La TN14 119 F2
Burlington Cl
6 Newham E6 1 E7
Orpington BR6 86 B8
Burlington Dr CT6 77 D5
Burlington Gdns
Gillingham ME8 98 E4
Margate CT9 82 C8
Burlington Lodge BR7 29 F1
Burma Cres CT1 143 D1
Burman Cl DA2 34 C8
BURMARSH 352 C5
Burmarsh Cl ME5 97 B5
Burmarsh Rd
Burmarsh TN29 352 C3
Hythe CT21 353 C8
Burma Way ME5 96 F6
Burnaby Rd DA11 18 E1
Burnan Ct CT5 75 C2
Burnan Rd CT5 75 C2
Burnell Ave DA16 13 A5
Burnett Rd DA8 15 D8
Burnham Cl ME10 101 E8
Burnham Cres DA1 15 C3
Burnham Rd
Dartford DA1 15 C3
Sidcup DA14 31 E6
Burnham Trad Est DA1 15 D3
Burnham Wlk ME8 98 E3
Burnley Rd RM20 17 A6
Burns Ave DA15 13 B1
Burns Cl Bexley DA16 12 F6
Erith DA8 14 F6
Burns Cres TN9 254 A7
Burns Ho DA16 13 C6
Burns Pl RM18 19 B6
Burns Rd ME16 161 C2
Burn's Rd ME7 64 C7
Burnt Ash Heights BR1 29 B3
Burnt Ash Hill SE12 29 A7
Burnt Ash La BR1, SE12 29 B3
Burnt Ash Prim Sch BR1 29 A3
Burntash Rd ME20 160 F8
Burnt House Cl
Rochester ME2 40 C2
Sandhurst TN18 356 C5
Burnt House Hill CT3 145 B5
Burnthouse La TN27 263 D1
Burnt House La
Dartford DA1 33 F5
Hawley DA2 33 F4
Langton Green TN3 285 A5
Burnt Lodge La TN5 338 B2
Burnt Oak Jun Sch DA15 31 A7
Burnt Oak La DA15 13 A1
Burnt Oak Prim Sch 1 ME7 64 D6
Burnt Oak Terr ME7 64 D6
Burnt Oast Rd ME13 140 A3
Burntwick Dr ME9 67 B3
Burntwood Gr TN13 187 B8
Burntwood Rd TN13 187 B7
Burnup Bank ME10 102 C5
Burrage Gr SE18 2 C2
Burrage Pl SE18 2 B1
Burrage Rd SE18 2 C1
Burrard Rd E16 1 B7
Burr Bank Terr DA2 33 C4
Burr Cl DA7 13 F4
Burrfield Dr BR5 54 D4
Burritt Mews ME1 63 C3
Burrow Rd CT19 335 F6
Burrows La ME3 25 C3
Burrs Hill Cotts TN12 289 D6
Burrs The ME10 101 F3
Burrstock Way ME8 66 B2
Burrswood Villas TN3 312 B7
Bursdon Cl DA15 30 F6
Bursill Cres CT12 83 B1
Burslem Rd TN2 286 E7
Bursted Hill CT4 208 B2
Bursted Wood Prim Sch DA7 14 B5
Burston Rd ME17 194 B2
Burton Cl
Folkestone CT19 335 A7
Rochester ME3 40 C3
Burton Fields CT6 77 B4
Burton Rd TN24 268 E6
Burt Rd E16 1 C5
Burts Wharf DA17 4 C5
Burwash Ct BR5 54 C4
Burwash Rd SE18 2 D1
Burwood Ave BR2 85 B8
Burwood Ho TN2 286 E5
Burwood Sch BR6 87 D8
Busbridge Close ME19 159 F7
Busbridge Rd ME6 127 E7
Bus Bridge Rd ME15 194 E6
Bush Ave CT12 83 B1
Bush Cl ME9 133 F5
Bushell Way BR7 30 A3
Bushey Ave BR5 53 D2
Bushey Cl ME13 139 F3
Bushey Ct DA8 15 A6
Busheyfields Rd CT6 110 F6
Bushey Ho SE9 29 C5
Bushey Lees DA15 12 F1
Bushfield Wlk DA10 35 E8
Bushmeadow Rd ME8 65 F2
Bushmoor Cres SE18 12 B6
Bush Rd Cuxton ME2 62 B2
East Peckham TN12 224 E8
Bush Row ME20 129 A3
Bushy Gill TN3 285 A3
Bushy Gr ME17 197 D2
Bushy Hill Rd CT2 144 D7
Bushy Royds TN24 300 D6
Bushy Ruff Cotts CT16 277 D4
Business Acad Bexley The DA18 3 E4
BUSS'S GREEN 316 A2
Buston Manor Farm Cotts ME18 193 B2
Busty La TN15 156 D6
Butcher Cl TN12 260 E3
Butchers La
New Ash Green TN15 91 D8
Nonington CT15 211 E5
Butcher's La ME19 158 D1
Butchers Rd E16 1 A7
Butchers Yd BR6 119 A8
Butcher Wlk DA10 35 E8
Butchery La 1 CT1 175 A8
Butchery The 2 CT13 149 A1
Butler Ho 9 RM17 18 B8
Butler's Cotts DA7 14 A5
Butler's Hill ME13 140 D7
Butler's Pl DA3 91 E7
Buttercup Cl TN12 257 A5
Butterfield Mews 16 SE18 12 B8
Butterfield Sq 10 E6 1 F7
Butterfly Ave DA1 33 F6
Butterfly Centre The★ CT15 275 B3
Butterfly La SE9 12 B1
Buttermere ME13 138 E6
Buttermere Cl CT19 335 B6
Buttermere Gdns CT3 210 F6
Buttermere Rd BR5 54 D5
Butternut Copse TN23 267 D3
Butterside Rd TN23 300 C4
Butter St CT15 211 C4
Butt Field Rd TN23 299 E7
Butt Green La ME17 228 A7
Butt Haw Cl ME3 41 E5
Buttmarsh Cl SE18 2 B1
Button Dr ME3 25 C5
Button Ho ME3 40 F6
Button La ME15 163 B2
Button St BR8, DA4 56 C5
Butts Ct CT4 208 A6
Butts Hill ME13 139 F5
Butts La TN5 337 C7
Butts Mdw CT4 208 A6
BUTTSOLE 180 B1
Butts The Otford TN14 122 B2
Sandwich CT13 148 F1
Sittingbourne ME10 101 F4
Buttway La ME3 22 A6
Buxton Cl Chatham ME5 97 D1
Loose ME15 195 A8
Buxton Rd Erith DA8 14 D7
Ramsgate CT12 83 B2

Buzzard Creek Ind Est
IG11...........3 A8
BYBROOK...........268 D5
Bybrook Ct TN21.......333 D3
Bybrook Ct TN24.......268 C4
Bybrook Field CT20...334 E3
Bybrook Rd TN24.......268 E3
Bybrook Way CT20.....334 E4
Bychurch Pl 7 ME15...162 A3
Bycliffe Mews 2 DA11..36 F8
Bycliffe Terr 3 DA11...36 F8
Byland Cl SE2...........3 B3
Byllan Rd CT17........277 E3
Byng Rd TN4...........285 F5
Bynon Ave DA7.........13 F4
Byrneside TN11........221 E4
Byron Ave CT9..........50 J1
Byron Cl
　Canterbury CT1....175 C2
　Woolwich SE28.......3 C5
Byron Cres CT16......278 B4
Byron Dr DA8..........14 B7
Byron Gdns RM18......19 C6
Byron Prim Sch ME7...64 C3
Byron Rd Dartford DA1..16 B3
　Gillingham ME7......64 C3
　Maidstone ME14.....162 B7
Bysing Wood Cotts
　ME13.................104 F1
Bysing Wood Prim Sch
　ME13.................138 A8
Bysing Wood Rd ME13 138 B8
Bythorne Ct ME8........66 B1
Bywater Ho SE18........1 E3

C

Cabbage Stalk La TN4 285 E2
Cabin The TN24.........268 D7
Cables Cl DA8............4 C3
Cacket's La TN14......119 E4
CACKLE HILL...........295 A5
Cade La TN13..........187 C7
Cade Rd TN23..........300 D3
Cades Orch ME13......137 E3
Cadlocks Hill TN14.....87 F1
Cadnam Cl
　Canterbury CT2......142 E3
　Rochester ME2.......62 E8
Cadogan Ave DA2.......34 D8
Cadogan Gdns 6 TN1 286 B4
Cadogan Rd SE18........2 C3
Cadwallon Rd SE9......30 C6
Caerleon Cl DA14.......31 C3
Caerleon Terr SE2......3 B2
Caernarvon Cl Erith DA8 14 D7
　12 Orpington BR5.....54 C5
Caernarvon Dr ME15..161 F1
Caernarvon Gdns CT10 .84 B5
Caesar Ave TN23......299 F4
Caesar's Way CT19....334 E7
CAGE GREEN...........222 C4
Cage Green Prim Sch
　TN10.................222 D5
Cage Green Rd TN10 .222 C5
Cage La TN27..........263 F1
Cagney Cl ME3..........40 C3
Cairns Cl DA1...........15 C2
Cairns Mews SE18....11 E6
Caister Rd TN9........222 A1
Caithness Gdns DA15..12 F1
Calais Cotts DA3.......91 A5
Calais Hill CT2.........142 E6
CALCOTT...............110 E2
Calcott Wlk SE9.......29 D4
Calcraft Mews 6 CT1 .143 B2
Calcroft Ave DA9......11 B2
Calcutta Ho 3 ME15 .195 E5
Calcutta Rd RM18......19 A5
Caldecote Cl ME8......66 B1
Caldecott Foundation Sch
　TN25.................302 B4
Calder Rd ME14.......161 E7
Calderdale DA12.......37 E2
Calderwood St SE18....2 A2
Caldew Ave ME8.........65 C1
Caldew Gr ME10.......102 A3
Caldy Rd DA17...........4 B3
Caledonian Ct ME8.....98 B8
Calehill Cl ME14......162 C6
Caledon Terr 1........175 A7
Caley Rd TN2..........286 D7
Calfstock La DA4........56 D4
Calgary Cres CT19....335 E8
California Row
　Hawkenbury TN12....261 C6
　Wingham CT3........177 E6
Caling Croft DA3........58 F1
Caliph Cl DA12..........37 F5
Callams Cl ME8.........98 D6
Calland TN25..........302 E6
Callaways La ME9.....100 B6
Calleywell La TN25....330 A7
Callis Court Rd CT10..83 F6
Callis Grange Inf Sch
　CT10..................83 F7
Callis Way ME8.........98 D5
Calshot Ct 17 DA2......16 B1
Calverden Rd CT12.....83 A1
Calverley Cl TN1......286 C3
Calverley Park Cres 1
　TN1...................286 B3
Calverley Park Gdns
　TN1...................286 C4
Calverley Pk TN1......286 B3
Calverley Rd TN1......286 B3
Calverley St TN1......286 B4
Calvert Cl Erith DA17..4 B2
　Sidcup DA14..........31 E2

Calvert Dr DA2.........32 D6
Calverton Prim Sch E16 .1 D7
Calvin Cl BR5...........54 D6
Calydon Rd SE7..........1 B1
CAMBER................374 A1
Camber Bourne Rd
　TN25.................329 C6
Cambert Way SE3......11 B3
Camberwell La TN14 .185 F4
Camborne Manor 2
　ME7..................64 C6
Cambourne Ave CT8...81 D8
Cambrai Ct CT1........143 D1
Cambray Rd BR6........53 F2
Cambria Ave ME1.......62 F2
Cambria Cl DA15.......30 E7
Cambria Cres DA12....37 F4
Cambria Ho 2 DA6.....14 E7
Cambrian Gr DA11.....37 A8
Cambrian Rd TN4......286 C2
Cambridge Ave
　Bexley DA16...........12 F3
　Sandwich CT13......182 B5
Cambridge Barracks Rd 5
　SE18...................1 F2
Cambridge Cl CT1......81 B7
Cambridge Cres ME15 195 D7
Cambridge Dr SE12....11 A2
Cambridge Gdns
　Folkestone CT20.....335 D5
　Royal Tunbridge Wells
　TN2..................286 B2
Cambridge Gn SE28....30 B7
Cambridge Ho 7 SE18 .1 F2
Cambridge La ME9....136 C8
Cambridge Mews
　CT14.................215 D3
Cambridge Rd
　Bromley BR1..........29 A1
　Canterbury CT1.....174 F6
　Deal CT14.............215 D3
　Dover CT17...........310 D7
　Faversham ME13.....138 B6
　Gillingham ME8.......98 C6
　Rochester ME2........63 A8
　Sidcup DA14..........30 E4
　Sittingbourne ME10 .102 B3
Cambridge Row SE18...8 B1
Cambridge St TN2.....286 C3
Cambridge Terr
　1 Chatham ME4......63 F4
　13 Dover CT17........310 E7
　8 Folkestone CT20..335 E5
　Margate CT9..........51 B1
Cambridge Way
　Canterbury CT1.....174 F6
　5 Maidstone ME15 .195 D7
Cambus Rd E16..........1 A8
Camdale Rd SE18......12 F7
Camden Ave TN4......287 C6
Camden Cl Chatham ME5 97 B5
　Chislehurst BR7......53 C8
　Northfleet DA11.......36 C7
Camden Cotts TN17..320 F8
Camden Cres CT16...310 E7
Camden Ct 10 Erith DA17 .4 A1
　Pembury TN2........287 D6
　2 Royal Tunbridge Wells
　TN1..................286 B4
Camden Gr BR7.........30 B2
CAMDEN HILL.........292 F2
Camden Hill TN2......286 B3
CAMDEN PARK........286 C2
Camden Park Rd BR7..30 A1
Camden Pk TN2........286 C2
Camden Rd
　Broadstairs CT10.....83 E7
　Gillingham ME7......64 D7
　Ramsgate CT11......117 E6
　Royal Tunbridge Wells
　TN1..................286 B4
　Sevenoaks TN13.....154 B5
　Sidcup DA14..........31 F8
Camden Sq 10 CT11..117 E7
Camden St ME14.......162 A5
Camden Terr
　Ashford TN24........268 E1
　Seal TN15............154 F6
　Sissinghurst TN17...320 F8
　Royal Tunbridge Wells
Camden Way BR7....30 A1
Camellia Cl
　Gillingham ME8.......98 D7
　2 Margate CT9........82 B8
Camelot Ct
　Biggin Hill TN16.....118 C3
　Woolwich SE28........2 D4
Camel Rd E16...........1 E5
Camer Ctry Pk★ DA13 .60 C2
Camer Gdns DA13.....60 C3
Cameron Cl
　Chatham ME5........97 B8
　Joyden's Wood DA5..32 E5
Cameron Ct CT1.......310 A6
Cameron Drive DA1...16 A5
Cameron Ho CT14....215 C1
Cameron Rd BR2.......52 A4
Camerons 4 TN18....341 A2
Cameron Terr 10 SE12..29 B5
Camer Park Rd DA13..60 C2
Camer St DA13.........60 C3
Camomile Dr ME14...162 F5
Campbell Cl
　Herne Bay CT6........77 C3
　Woolwich SE18.......12 A6
Campbell Ho ME3.......40 F6
Campbell Rd
　Deal CT14............215 D4
　Hawkinge CT18......307 A5
　Maidstone ME15.....162 A3
　Northfleet DA11.......36 F8

Campbell Rd continued
　Royal Tunbridge Wells
　TN4..................286 A6
Camperdown Manor 5
　ME7..................64 A6
Campfield Rd SE9.....29 D8
Camp Hill TN11........220 A3
Camp Hill Cotts TN11..219 F2
Campion Cl
　Chatham ME5.........96 E3
　Newham E6............1 F6
　Northfleet DA11.......36 E4
Campion Cres TN17..320 A2
Campion Ct 6 RM17..18 D8
Campion Pl SE28.......3 B5
Campleshon Rd ME8..98 D5
Camp Site TN26........14 B2
Campus Way ME8......98 A8
Camp Way ME15.......195 C6
Camrose Ave DA14....14 B8
Camrose St SE2.........3 A2
Canada Cl CT19.......334 C6
Canada Farm Rd DA4..58 A6
Canada Mews CT14..215 C3
Canada Rd Deal CT14 .215 D3
　Erith DA8...............15 B7
Canada Terr 3 ME14..162 A3
Canadian Ave SE6......64 A4
Canal Basin DA12........19 D1
Canal Ind Pk 2 DA12...37 D8
Canal Rd
　Gravesend DA12......19 D1
　Higham ME3..........39 C8
　Rochester ME2........63 C7
Canberra Gdns ME10 .101 C4
Canberra Rd Bexley DA7 .13 D8
　Greenwich SE7.......11 D8
Canberra Sq RM18....19 A5
Canbury Path BR5.....54 A5
Candlers Way CT14...206 F8
Candlers Wlk 1 CT14 .206 F8
Candover Rd DA7.......13 D6
CANNING TOWN.......1 B8
Cannon Bridge Works
　TN9..................222 D2
Cannonbury Rd CT11 117 D6
Cannongate Ave CT21 333 D3
Cannongate Cl CT21..333 E2
Cannongate Gdns
　CT21.................333 E3
Cannongate Rd CT21..333 D3
Cannon Rd Bexley DA7..17 A1
　Ramsgate CT11......117 D7
Cannon St Deal CT14 .215 C2
　Dover CT16...........310 D8
　Lydd TN29............376 C6
　New Romney TN28..373 B7
Canon Appleton Ct
　.....................174 E7
Canon Cl ME1...........63 B2
Canon Gn CT3..........178 A7
Canon Jeffreys Court 13
　TN18.................340 F2
Canon La ME18........159 C1
Canon Rd BR1...........52 D6
Canons Gate Rd CT16..310 E8
Canons Walk TN16...185 B6
Canon Woods Way
　TN24.................268 F6
Cansiron La TN7, TN8..281 E2
CANTERBURY..........174 C7
Canterbury Ave DA15..31 C9
Canterbury Cathedral★
　CT1...................175 A8
Canterbury Cathedral
　Archives★ 15 CT1...175 A8
Canterbury Centre The
　(Mus)★ CT1..........142 F1
Canterbury Christ Church
　Univ (Augustine House
　Campus) 11 CT1.....174 F7
Canterbury Christ Church
　Univ (Broadstairs
　Campus) 1 CT10.....83 C4
Canterbury Christ Church
　Univ (Hall Place
　Enterprise Ctre) CT2 142 F1
Canterbury Christ Church
　Univ (Medway Campus)
　ME4..................64 B8
Canterbury Christ Church
　Univ (North Holmes
　Campus) CT1.........175 B8
Canterbury City Ret Pk
　CT1...................143 D4
Canterbury Cl
　Broadstairs CT10.....83 D5
　Dartford DA1.........34 A8
　2 Folkestone CT19 .335 E6
　7 Newham E6........1 F7
Canterbury Coll CT3..211 A5
Canterbury Cres TN10 222 D5
Canterbury Ct
　Ashford TN24........268 D2
　7 Lewisham SE12...29 B5
Canterbury East Sta
　.....................174 F7
Canterbury Environmental
　Education Ctr CT3...243 B3
Canterbury High Sch The
　CT2...................142 E5
Canterbury Hill CT2..142 E5
Canterbury Ho
　6 Erith DA8..........14 F7
　2 Maidstone ME15..195 D7
Canterbury Ind Pk
　CT3...................145 A8
Canterbury La
　CT1...................175 A8
　Gillingham ME8, ME9 ..66 C1
Canterbury Pilgrims Hospl
　The★ 23 CT1.........174 F8

Canterbury Rd
　Ashford, Kennington
　TN24.................268 E5
　Ashford TN24........300 E6
　Barham CT4..........243 C5
　Boughton Aluph TN25..237 C5
　Boughton Street ME13..139 D4
　Brabourne Lees TN25..302 F6
　Brabourne TN25.....303 C8
　Challock TN25, TN27..202 C1
　Chilham CT4..........172 F1
　Denton CT4...........243 A1
　Dunkirk ME13........140 C3
　Elham CT4............273 E3
　Etchinghill CT18.....305 D4
　Faversham ME13.....138 E5
　Folkestone CT19.....335 D7
　Folkestone, Foord CT19 335 E6
　Gravesend DA12.......37 C6
　Hawkinge CT18, CT19, CT15,
　CT4..................307 B4
　Herne Bay CT6.........77 A3
　Herne CT3, CT6......110 E5
　Littlebourne CT3.....176 C8
　Lydden CT15.........276 E7
　Lyminge CT18........305 C7
　Pembury TN2.........287 E6
　Sarre CT7.............113 E7
　Sittingbourne ME10 .102 B2
　Whitstable CT5......108 D8
　Wingham CT3........178 A7
Canterbury Rd Birchington
　CT7....................81 B5
Canterbury Road
　Birchington CT7......81 B7
Canterbury Road E CT11,
　CT12.................117 A6
Canterbury Road Margate
　CT9....................50 G1
Canterbury Road Prim Sch
　ME10.................102 B7
Canterbury Road W
　CT12.................116 D7
Canterbury Road Westgate
　CT8, CT9..............81 E8
Canterbury St ME7.....64 D7
Canterbury Steiner Sch
　CT2...................206 F2
Canterbury Tales The★ 24
　CT1...................174 F8
Canterbury Way DA1, DA2,
　RM20...................16 D5
Canterbury West Sta
　.....................142 F1
Cantelupe Rd SE18....12 B7
Cantwell Ho SE18.....12 B7
Cantwell Rd SE18.....12 B7
Canute Rd
　Birchington CT7......80 D7
　Deal CT14............182 C1
　Faversham ME13.....138 C6
Canute Wlk CT14.....182 C1
Capability Way 8 DA9 .17 C3
CAPEL................255 F5
Capel Cl Broadstairs CT10..51 F1
　Gillingham ME8.......98 D4
　Orpington BR2.........52 E1
Capel Court Pk CT18 .308 D2
CAPEL CROSS.........290 C5
Capel-le-Ferne Prim Sch
　CT18.................308 D2
Capel Pl DA2............33 C4
Capel Prim Sch TN12 .255 F7
Capel Rd
　Bromley Green TN26..328 B4
　Faversham ME13.....138 B7
　Petham CT4..........206 F3
　Sittingbourne ME10 .101 E2
Capel St CT18.........308 B3
Capetown Ho 1 ME15 195 F5
Capital Ind Est DA17...4 B3
Capstan Ct DA2.........16 C3
Capstan Ctr RM18......18 D7
Capstan Mews 4 DA11 36 E8
Capstan Row CT14...215 D7
CAPSTONE.............97 E7
Capstone Farm Ctry Pk★
　ME7...................97 D5
Capstone Rd
　Chatham ME5.........64 D1
　Gillingham ME7......97 F6
　Lewisham BR1.........29 A4
Captain's Cl ME17....229 E6
Captains Ct CT21.....333 C1
Capulet Mews E16......1 A5
Caraway Cl E13..........1 B8
Cardens Rd ME3.......40 B8
Cardiff St SE18.........12 E7
Cardigan Cl ME23.....23 F3
Cardinal Cl
　Chislehurst BR7......53 D8
　Minster (Sheppey) ME12 47 D7
　Tonbridge TN9........254 D8
Cardinal Wlk ME19...159 C3
Cardine Cl ME10......101 E2
Cardwell Prim Sch SE18 .1 E7
Carew Ho 18 SE18......1 F2
Carew Way BR5.........54 E6
Carey Cl TN28.........373 B6
Carey Ct DA6............14 B2
Carey Ho 5 CT1.......174 F7
Carey's Field TN13....153 E2
Caring La ME14, ME17..163 E1
Caring Rd ME15, ME17..163 C1
Carisbrooke Ave DA5..31 D7
Carisbrooke Ct
　23 Dartford DA2......16 B1
　20 Sidcup DA14.......31 A4
Carisbrooke Dr ME16 .161 D4

Carisbrooke Rd
　Bromley BR2...........52 C5
　Rochester ME2........39 C1
Carl Ekman Ho ME13 .36 D8
Carleton Pl DA4........57 C5
Carleton Rd DA1.......34 A8
Carlisle Cl ME2.........62 C6
Carlisle Rd DA1........16 A1
Carlsden Cl CT17.....278 A3
Carlton Ave
　Broadstairs CT10.....84 A5
　Gillingham ME7......64 E4
　Ramsgate CT11......117 D6
　Sheerness ME12......28 B1
　Stone DA9.............16 C1
Carlton Cl
　Kings Hill ME19......159 B3
　Tonbridge TN10......222 E7
Carlton Cres
　Chatham ME5.........97 D8
　Royal Tunbridge Wells
　TN1..................286 C4
Carlton Gdns ME15...195 B8
Carlton Gn DA15.......30 F4
Carlton Hill CT6........76 C4
Carlton Leas CT20....335 C4
Carlton Mans CT9......51 A3
Carlton Par 1 BR5.....54 E2
Carlton Rd
　Ashford TN23........268 A2
　Bexley DA16...........13 B4
　Erith DA8...............14 C8
　Kingsdown CT14.....248 C6
　Royal Tunbridge Wells
　TN1..................286 C4
　Sidcup DA14..........30 F3
　Whitstable CT5......108 D2
Carlton Rise CT8........81 C8
Carlton Road E CT8....81 D8
Carlton Road W CT8...81 D8
Carlyle Ave BR1........52 C6
Carlyle Rd SE28.........3 C6
Carlyle Sq CT9..........50 J3
Carman's Cl ME15,
　ME17.................194 F3
Carmel Cl CT4.........173 B2
Carmel Ct 2 CT7.......80 F8
Carmelite Way DA3....58 F4
Carmichael Avenue
　DA9....................17 C3
Carnation Cl 1 ME19 .128 A1
Carnation Cres ME19 .127 F1
Carnation Rd ME2......62 D7
Carnation St SE2........3 B1
Carn Brae CT9...........50 J2
Carnbrook Mews 2
　SE3....................11 D4
Carnbrook Rd SE3....11 D4
Carnecke Gdns SE9...11 E2
Carnet Cl DA1...........32 E8
Carnoustie Cl Erith SE28..3 D7
　Whitstable CT5......109 E8
Caroland Cl TN25.....302 D5
Caroline Cl CT5.......108 B6
Caroline Cres
　Broadstairs CT10.....83 E6
　Maidstone ME16.....161 D7
Caroline Sq CT9.........50 J3
Carolyn Dr BR6.........87 A7
Carp Cl ME20..........128 A4
Carpeaux Cl ME4.......64 A4
Carpenters Cl ME1.....63 E2
Carpenters Dr BR1.....52 D7
Carpenters La TN11..190 D1
Carpinus Cl ME5.......97 B1
Carrack Ho 1 DA8......4 E1
Carr Gr SE18.............1 E2
Carriage Ho ME13.....170 D5
Carriage Mews CT2..142 F1
Carriageway The
　TN16.................152 D2
Carrick Dr TN13......154 B4
Carrie Ho 3 ME16....161 E5
Carriers Pl TN3.......283 B4
Carriers Rd TN17....320 D5
Carrill Way DA17........3 D3
Carrington Cl DA1......31 A3
Carrington Cl ME7......64 F6
Carrington Rd DA1.....16 A1
Carroll Cl ME2...........95 C4
Carroll Gdns ME20...127 F3
Carronade Pl SE28......2 D3
Carroway's Pl CT9.....50 J2
Carsington Gdns DA1..33 D6
Carson Rd E16...........1 A8
Carston Cl SE12........11 A2
Carter Avenue TN15...90 D3
Carter Cl CT18.........307 A5
Carter La TN29.........362 E2
Carter's Hill Bromley SE9 29 C7
　Underriver TN15.....188 B6
Carters Hill Cl SE9.....29 C7
Carters Hill La DA13..92 F1
Carter's Rd CT20.....334 F5
Carter's Wood TN26..349 B7
Cartmel Rd DA7.......14 A6
Carton Cl ME1...........63 D2
Carton Rd ME3..........39 B3
Cartwright Cl CT3.....147 C2
Cartwright & Kelsey Prim
　Sch CT3..............147 C2
Carver Dr ME9.........134 E6
Carville Ave TN4......253 F1
Carvoran Way ME8.....98 C5
Cascade Cl BR5.........54 E5
Cascades L Ctr DA12...38 A4
Caslocke St 2 ME13 .138 C2
Caspian Way DA10....17 E2
Caspian Wlk E16........1 D7
Cassida Rd SE2..........3 A2
Cassino Ho 16 CT1...143 B2
Cassino Sq CT15......278 C7
Casstine Cl BR8.........32 F1

Castalia Ct DA1.........15 F4
Castalla Cotts CT14...215 D3
Casterbridge Rd SE3...11 A4
Castfield Cl ME3.......22 E1
Castile Rd 12 SE18......2 A2
Castilion Prim Sch SE28 .3 C7
Castleacres Ind Pk
　ME10.................102 B6
Castle Ave
　Broadstairs CT10.....84 B6
　Dover CT17...........278 D1
　Hythe CT21..........333 B3
　Rochester ME1.......63 C4
Castle Bay CT20......334 D3
Castle Cl
　4 Folkestone CT20..334 E4
　Lympne CT21........331 F2
Castlecombe Prim Sch
　SE9....................29 E3
Castle Com Coll CT14 .215 D4
Castle Cotts CT13.....148 E5
Castle Cres CT21......333 C4
Castle Dene ME14.....161 F8
Castle Dr Kemsing TN15 122 C2
　Whitfield CT16.......277 F7
Castle Farm Cotts
　TN11.................223 F8
Castle Farm Rd TN14..89 A3
Castlefields DA13......59 F8
Castle Fields TN9......222 B2
Castleford Ave SE9....30 B7
Castle Glen 9 CT20...334 F3
CASTLE HILL..........257 E1
Castle Hill
　Folkestone CT19,
　CT18.................335 A8
　Hartley DA3...........58 E4
　Rochester ME1.......63 C4
　Thurnham ME14.....131 D1
　Tonbridge TN4......254 D4
Castle Hill Ave CT20 .335 C4
Castle Hill CP Sch
　CT19.................335 E7
Castle Hill Ct TN11....63 C6
Castle Hill Rd 4 CT16 .310 E8
Castle Ho CT5...........74 F3
Castle Hurst TN32....355 B1
Castle La DA12..........38 B6
Castlemaine Ave CT7..81 F3
Castlemere Ave ME11..46 B5
Castle Mews CT14....215 A4
Castlemount Ct CT16 .310 E8
Castlemount Rd CT16 .278 D1
　Eynsford DA4...........89 C3
　Folkestone CT20.....334 F3
　Grays RM17............17 A3
　Hythe CT21...........333 B4
　Maidstone ME16.....161 D7
　Royal Tunbridge Wells
　TN4..................286 A3
　Sittingbourne ME10 .102 B3
　Swanscombe DA10...17 F1
　Whitstable CT5.......74 F2
Castle Road Bsns Prec
　ME10.................102 B6
Castle Road Tech Ctr
　ME10.................102 B6
Castle Rough La ME10..68 F1
Castle Row CT1.......174 F7
Castle St
　6 Ashford TN23.....268 B2
　Canterbury CT1.....174 F8
　Dover CT16...........310 E8
　Queenborough ME11..46 A5
　Rochester ME2........40 C1
　2 Royal Tunbridge Wells,
　Mount Sion TN1.....286 A2
　2 Royal Tunbridge Wells,
　Southborough TN4...253 F2
　Stone DA9.............17 A2
　Swanscombe DA10...17 F1
　Tonbridge TN9......222 C2
　Woolwich ME1.........95 C4
Castle Terr
　Hadlow TN11.........223 E8
　Hawkhurst TN18.....340 F3
Castleton Ave DA7....14 D5
Castleton Rd SE9.....29 D4
Castle View Bsns Ctr
　ME1...................63 C6
Castleview Ct CT17..278 B1
Castle View Mews ME1 63 C6
Castle View Rd ME2....63 A4
Castle Way ME19.....127 D2
Castle Wlk Deal CT14 .182 D1
　Durgates TN5........336 E4
Castlewood Dr SE9....11 F5
Castweazle TN30.....344 E6
Caterfield La RH7, RH8 216 A5
Cates Ct TN12..........225 A7
Cathcart Dr BR6........53 E1
Cathedral View CT1..143 A2
Catherine Cl 2 ME16..161 A3
Catherine of Aragon Ct
　DA15..................30 D8
Catherine Pl 7 TN1...286 B4
Catherine Rd ME3......63 D3
Catherine Way CT10...84 A6
Catkin Cl ME5...........96 F1
Catlyn Cl ME19........160 A8
CATS Canterbury 6
　CT1...................175 B6
Cattle Hill CT3.........178 D2
Catterick Rd ME5......97 D2
Cattistock Rd SE9.....29 F3
Cattle Market CT13...148 F1
Catts Alley ME6........128 A7
Catt's Hill TN30.......360 E3

Catts Pl TN12...........257 C4
Catt's Wood Rd CT4....207 F4
Cauldham Cl CT18.......308 B1
Cauldham La CT18.......308 B3
Caulkers Ho ◆ ME4....64 B2
Causeway The
 Canterbury CT1..........142 F1
 Sandwich CT13..........148 D2
Causton Rd TN17..........320 C5
Cavalry Cl TN10..........222 E7
Cavalry Ct Deal CT14....215 D3
 Folkestone CT20..........334 D5
Cave Hill ME15............161 F1
Cave La CT3...............178 D3
Cavell Cres DA1............16 A3
Cavell Sq CT14............215 A3
Cavell Way ME10.........101 D5
Cavenagh Rd CT15.......280 B6
Cavendish Ave
 Bexley DA16..............12 F4
 Erith DA8................14 C8
 Gillingham ME7...........64 E6
 Sevenoaks TN13.........154 A5
 Sidcup DA15..............31 A8
Cavendish Cl TN10........222 D7
Cavendish Ct
 Herne Bay CT6............77 A5
 Tonbridge TN9...........222 D3
Cavendish Dr TN2.........286 B1
Cavendish Pl ◆ CT11....117 C6
Cavendish Place BR1....52 F6
Cavendish Rd
 Herne Bay CT6............77 A5
 Rochester ME1............63 D3
Cavendish Sq DA3.........58 D6
Cavendish St CT11.......117 C6
Cavendish Way...........163 B3
Caversham Cl ME8........65 F1
Caveside Cl BR7...........53 A8
Cavour Rd
 Faversham ME13.........138 C7
 Sheerness ME12..........28 C2
Caxton Cl Hartley DA3....58 F5
 Tenterden TN30.........344 F7
Caxton Ho
 Ashford TN24............268 C3
 The Chart RH8...........183 F3
Caxton La Hadlow TN11 223 E8
 The Chart RH8...........183 E4
Caxton Rd CT9............82 C8
Cayser Dr ME17..........197 E2
Caysers Croft TN12.......224 E6
Cazeneuve St ME1........63 C5
Cecil Ave Gillingham ME8 65 A2
 Rochester ME2............63 B8
 Sheerness ME12..........28 B1
Cecil Burns Lodge
 TN2...................286 D2
Cecil Ct Ashford TN24....268 B3
 Herne Bay CT6............77 A4
Cecilia Gr CT10............83 F6
Cecilia Rd CT11...........117 E8
Cecil Kidby Ho TN2.......286 F6
Cecil Pk CT6...............77 A4
Cecil Rd
 Kingsdown CT14.........248 D7
 Northfleet DA11...........36 F7
 Rochester ME1............63 C3
Cecil Road Prim Sch
 DA11...................36 F7
Cecil Sq CT9...............50 I2
Cecil Sq CT9...............50 I2
Cecil Way BR2.............52 A1
Cedar Ave
 Gravesend DA12..........37 C4
 Sidcup DA15..............31 A8
Cedar Cl Ashford TN23...267 E3
 Birchington CT8...........81 B7
 Broadstairs CT10..........83 F7
 Ditton ME20.............160 D8
 Margate CT9..............51 B1
 Meopham Station DA13...60 A3
 Orpington BR2.............85 E7
 Sittingbourne ME10......102 B2
 Swanley BR8...............55 C7
Cedar Copse BR1..........52 F7
Cedar Cres
 Orpington BR2.............85 E7
 St Mary's Bay TN29......365 F7
 Tonbridge TN10.........222 D2
Cedar Ct Eltham SE9......11 E1
 Folkestone CT20..........334 E5
 ◆ Greenwich SE7..........11 C8
 Maidstone ME14.........162 B6
 Royal Tunbridge Wells
 TN4...................286 A5
 ◆ Tenterden TN30........345 A7
Cedar Dr
 Edenbridge TN8..........217 B2
 Maidstone ME16.........160 E2
 Sutton at Hone DA4.......57 B7
Cedar Gdns ME9..........132 E8
Cedar Gr Gillingham ME7 98 A5
 Sidcup DA5...............13 D1
Cedar Ho
 Royal Tunbridge Wells
 TN4...................285 E4
 Sheerness ME12..........28 B2
Cedarhurst Cotts ◆
 DA5...................32 A8
Cedarhurst Dr SE9.........11 C2
Cedar La TN27............323 D7
Cedar Lodge TN4.........285 F3
Cedarmore Ct BR7........53 C8
Cedar Mount SE9..........29 D7
Cedar Pl ◆ ◆ SE7..........1 C1
Cedar Rd Bromley BR1....52 C7
 Dartford DA1.............33 D7
 Erith DA8................15 A6
 Hoo St Werburgh ME3....41 E3
 Rochester ME2.............63 F6

Cedar Rd continued
 Sturry CT2..............144 A6
Cedar Ridge TN2..........286 D5
Cedars PRU The ME16 161 D4
Cedars Sch The ME1.......63 C3
Cedars The
 Barrowhill TN25..........331 D8
 Paddock Wood TN12.....257 A7
 ◆ Sittingbourne ME10....102 C5
Cedar Terr ME13..........138 A4
Cedar Terrace Rd
 TN13...................154 C4
Cedarview CT2............142 C1
Cedarwood Ho ME15....194 B6
Cedric Rd Eltham SE9.....30 C5
 Westgate on Sea CT8.....50 C1
Ceil Villas CT14...........181 B4
Celak Cl TN25.............330 A6
Celandine Dr SE28.........3 B5
Celestine Cl ME5...........97 A1
Celia Ave TN15.............90 E3
CELLARHILL...............103 C1
Cellini Walk ME19..........159 C2
Celt Cl ME10...............101 F8
Celtic Rd CT14............215 A2
Cement Block Cotts ◆
 RM17...................18 C8
Cemetery La
 Ashford TN24............268 C4
 Hadlow TN11.............191 A1
 Woolwich SE7.............11 E8
Cemetery Rd
 Halling ME2...............95 A4
 Snodland ME6.............94 F1
 Woolwich SE2.............13 B7
Centenary Cl TN27........234 C8
Centenary Ct DA4.........57 A2
Centenary Gdns CT13..180 A2
Central Ave Bexley DA16 13 A5
 Chatham ME4..............64 B8
 Gravesend DA12...........37 B5
 Herne Bay CT6............76 D4
 Sittingbourne ME10......101 F4
 Tilbury RM18..............19 A6
 Woodstock ME9.........134 D6
Central Bsns Pk ME2.....63 C7
Central Cl ◆ SE18.........2 B2
Central Lodge TN15......125 E6
Central Par
 Herne Bay CT6............76 E5
 Rochester ME1............63 D2
 Sidcup DA15..............31 A4
 Wadhurst TN5...........336 F4
Central Park Gdns ME4 63 E2
Central Park Stad
 ME10...................200 C6
Central Par Villas BR5...54 C7
Central Pk CT12..........114 D6
Central Rd Dartford DA1..1 E6
 New Hythe ME20.........128 B4
 Ramsgate CT11..........117 D8
 Rochester ME2............63 A7
Central Service Rd
 CT16...................310 H8
Central Terr ME3...........40 F6
Central Theatre The ★ ◆
 ME4...................63 F4
Central Way SE28...........3 B6
Centre 2000
 Maidstone ME16.........161 C8
 ◆ Sittingbourne ME10...102 A4
Centre Common Rd
 BR7...................30 C1
Centre Ct ME2.............63 E7
Centre Performing Arts
 Coll The SE18.............11 E8
 New Ash Green DA3......57 C1
Centre The Margate CT9..50 I2
 Ramsgate CT12..........83 A1
Centurian Square SE18 11 E7
Centurian Way DA18.....4 A3
Centurion Cl ME8..........64 F1
Centurion Wlk TN23.....300 B4
Century Ct ME1............63 C5
Century Rd
 Faversham ME13.........138 E7
 Gillingham ME8...........98 D1
Century Wlk CT14........215 C6
Ceres Rd ME10............102 C5
Ceres Rd SE18..............2 F2
Cerne Rd DA12.............37 E5
Cervia Way DA12..........37 F5
Chada Ave ME7............64 E3
Chadd Dr BR1.............52 E6
Chadfields RM18...........19 A7
Chadwell Hill RM17.......19 A8
Chadwick Cl DA11.........36 E5
Chadwick Ct
 ◆ Dartford DA1...........15 D1
 ◆ Woolwich SE28..........3 B5
Chadwick Way SE28.......3 D6
Chadwin Rd E13............1 B8
Chaffe's La ME9............66 E3
Chaffes Terr ME9...........66 E2
Chaffey Ho ◆ SE7..........1 C1
Chaffinch Cl ME5...........97 A7
Chaffinch Dr TN23........300 C3
Chaffinch Lodge ◆
 CT16...................278 B2
Chaffinch Way TN12.....257 A6
Chafford Cotts TN3......283 F5
Chafford La TN3..........283 F5
Chafy Cres CT2............143 F5
Chain Gate ME17.........232 A8
CHAINHURST..............227 A4
Chain The ◆ TN13........149 A1
Chalcombe Rd SE2.........3 B3
Chalcroft Rd CT20........334 E4
Chalet Cl DA5..............32 D4
Chalfont Ct ◆ DA17.......4 A1
Chalfont Dr
 Gillingham ME8............98 D6
 Herne Bay CT6............77 D2

Chalgrove Mews ME2...95 A5
Chalice Way DA9..........16 F2
CHALK...................38 A7
Chalk Ave TN30...........324 B2
Chalk Cl CT19.............335 A7
Chalk Ct RM17.............18 A8
Chalkenden Ave ME8...65 A2
Chalkers Way ME8........65 A4
Chalket La TN2............287 C5
Chalk Hill CT11, CT12...116 F6
Chalk Hill Rd CT14.......248 C5
Chalk La TN17............319 E7
Chalklin Business Park
 TN2...................286 E8
Chalk Pit Ave BR5.........54 D6
Chalkpit Hill CT4..........176 D3
Chalk Pit Hill
 Chatham ME4.............64 A3
 Staple CT3...............179 B5
Chalk Pit La CT13, CT3 179 C5
Chalk Rd Chalk DA12.....38 A6
 Lower Higham ME3........39 C6
 Newham E13..............1 C8
 Queenborough ME11......46 A5
CHALKSOLE..............276 C4
CHALKSOLE GREEN.....276 C3
Chalksole Green La
 CT15...................276 B2
Chalkstone Cl DA16......13 A6
Chalkways TN15..........122 F3
CHALKWELL..............101 D4
Chalkwell Cl CT17........101 D7
Chalkwell Rd ME10.......101 D5
Chalky Bank DA1..........37 A3
Chalky Bank Rd ME8.....65 F2
Chalky Rd ME9............132 B5
Challenge Cl DA12.........37 F4
Challenger Cl
 Paddock Wood TN12.....256 F6
 Sittingbourne ME10......101 E7
CHALLOCK...............203 B1
Challock Cl TN16..........118 C3
Challock Ct CT9............51 F2
Challock Ho
 ◆ Erith DA8..............14 F7
 ◆ Orpington BR5..........54 D1
Challock Prim Sch
 TN25...................203 B1
Chalmers Way ME8.......65 A4
Chamberlain Ave
 ME16...................161 C2
Chamberlain Cl ◆ SE28 .2 D3
Chamberlain Cl ME8......98 B5
Chamberlain Dr CT6......76 B4
Chamberlain Rd
 Chatham ME4..............64 B2
 Dover CT17..............310 B8
Chambers Avenue DA14 31 E2
Chambers Cl ◆ DA9.......17 A2
CHAMBERS' GREEN....265 C4
Chambers Wharf La
 ME13...................138 E8
Champions Drive TN8 217 F6
Chancel Cl TN15..........90 E3
Chancel Ct CT2...........142 D1
Chancellor Ho TN4.......285 F3
Chancellor Way TN13...154 A5
Chancelot Rd SE2..........3 B2
Chance Mdw CT15.......278 E6
Chancery La ME15.......162 B3
Chancery Rd ME3.........22 B5
Chanctonbury Chase
 CT5...................108 A6
Chanctonbury Cl SE9....30 B5
Chandler Ave E16..........1 A8
Chandlers Dr DA8.........4 E2
Chandler's Hill DA13....93 C5
Chandlers Mews ◆
 DA9...................17 C3
Chandler's Rd DA13......93 C5
Chandlers Wharf ME1...63 B5
Chandos Rd
 ◆ Broadstairs CT10.......84 B4
 Royal Tunbridge Wells
 TN1...................286 C5
Chandos Sq ◆ CT10......84 B4
Chandos Terr CT12.......117 E2
Channel Cl CT19..........335 F7
Channel Lea CT14.......215 C1
Channel Rd CT9...........83 A6
Channel View ◆ CT19 335 E5
Channel View Ct ◆
 CT11...................117 F7
Channel View Rd CT17 310 C5
Channel Watch TN28....373 E4
Channon Rd TN28........377 E7
Chantler's Hill TN12.....257 A4
Chantlers Mead TN8....282 A5
Chantry Ave DA3..........58 E3
Chantry Cl Sidcup DA14..31 E3
 Woolwich SE2............3 C3
Chantry Ct
 ◆ Canterbury CT1.......142 F1
 Gravesend DA12..........19 C1
Chantry Hall CT1.........174 F7
Chantry Her Ctr★ DA12 19 C1
Chantry La BR2............52 F4
Chantry Pk CT7...........113 D7
Chantry Pl
 Marden TN12............259 C6
 Sevenoaks TN13.........153 F5
Chantry Prim Sch DA12 19 C1
Chantry Rd TN25.........259 C5
Chantry The TN27.......262 E5
Chapel Alley Cotts
 TN14...................122 A8
Chapel Cl Crayford DA1 14 E2
 Etchinghill CT18.........305 D3
 Ryarsh ME19.............126 F5
 West Thurrock RM20......17 B8
Chapel Cotts ME17.......196 F5
Chapel Ct DA10............17 E1

Chapel Farm Rd SE9....29 F6
Chapel Field Cotts DA4 57 B8
Chapel Hill Crayford DA1 14 E2
 Eythorne CT15...........245 C7
 Margate CT9..............83 A6
Chapel Hill Cl CT9.........82 F7
Chapel Hos ME2...........94 E4
 Westgate on Sea CT8.....81 F8
Chapel La Blean CT2.....142 A7
 Boyden Gate CT3.........112 C8
 Bredhurst ME7............98 A2
 Broad Oak CT2..........143 D7
 Dover CT16..............310 D7
 East Studdal CT15.......246 C6
 Egerton Forstal TN27...232 B2
 Gillingham ME7...........98 A4
 Iden Green TN17.........342 C4
 Maidstone ME14.........163 A5
 Newchurch TN29.........351 C4
 Rhodes Minnis CT4......273 B4
 Ripple CT15.............247 D8
 Sissinghurst TN17.......321 B7
 Staple CT3..............179 B6
 Staplehurst TN12........260 F3
 St Margaret's at Cliffe
 CT15...................279 F6
 Sturry CT2..............143 F5
 Upper Halling ME2......94 E6
Chapel Mews ◆ TN23 268 C2
Chapel Pl
 ◆ Dover CT17...........310 B8
 Ramsgate CT11..........117 D7
 ◆ Royal Tunbridge Wells
 TN1...................286 A2
 Ticehurst TN5...........338 E1
Chapel Place La CT11 117 D7
Chapel Rd Bexley DA7....14 A3
 Dymchurch TN29.........366 C7
 Grain ME3................27 B5
 Limpsfield RH8...........183 C5
 Ram Lane TN26..........234 F1
 Ramsgate CT11..........117 D7
 Snodland ME6............128 A8
 Sutton Valence ME17...229 E7
 Tilmanstone CT14.......213 A3
 Whitfield CT16...........278 A8
Chapel Row Herne CT6 111 A8
 Ightham TN15............156 C6
 Kingsnorth TN23.........300 A3
 Lydd TN29...............376 C6
 Ram Lane TN26..........234 F2
Chapelsite Ct ◆ DA17....4 A2
Chapel St Deal CT14.....215 D6
 East Malling ME19.......160 A6
 Faversham ME13.........138 D6
 Herne Bay CT6............77 A5
 Hythe CT21.............333 B2
 Minster (Sheppey) ME12 47 D6
 Ryarsh ME19.............126 F5
 Sheerness ME12..........28 A2
Chapel The
 Chartham CT4...........173 F1
 Maidstone ME16.........161 B3
Chapel View TN15........156 C6
Chapel Wlk
 Goathurst Common
 TN14...................186 B5
 Maypole DA2..............32 E6
Chapel Wood DA3.........91 E8
Chapel Wood Rd DA3,
 TN15...................91 E8
Chaplains Wlk CT4.......173 E1
Chaplin Cl ME3............40 C3
Chaplin Court DA4.........34 A2
Chaplin Dr TN27.........262 D5
Chapman Ave ME15.....195 E8
Chapman Fields CT12 116 D5
Chapman Ho CT14.......215 B3
Chapman Rd DA17........4 B1
Chapmans Cl
 Challock TN25...........203 C2
 Sundridge TN14.........152 E3
Chapmans End BR5......54 E7
Chapmans Hill CT3,
 CT15...................211 B5
Chapman's Hill DA13,
 TN15...................92 E4
Chapman's La
 Orpington BR5, BR8.....54 D7
 Swanley BR8..............55 A7
Chapmans Pl ME17......230 F7
Chapmans Rd TN14.....152 E3
Chapman Way
 East Malling ME19.......159 F8
 Royal Tunbridge Wells
 TN2...................286 C8
Chappell Way ME10.....101 E6
Chapter Rd ME2...........62 F8
Chapter Sch ME2..........62 D7
CHARCOTT..............220 A3
Chardwell Cl E6...........1 F7
Charford Rd E16............1 A8
CHARING................234 D8
Charing CE Prim Sch
 TN27...................234 C8
Charing Cl Orpington BR6 86 F6
 Ramsgate CT12..........117 C8
Charing Cres CT8.........81 D7
CHARING HEATH........233 C6
Charing Heath Rd
 Charing Heath TN27....233 F8
 Charing TN27...........234 A6
CHARING HILL...........201 D1
Charing Hill TN27........201 E1
Charing Ho ◆ DA8........14 F7
Charing Rd ME8...........65 B3
Charing Sta TN27.........234 B7
Chariot Way ME4..........62 F4
Charity Farm Cotts
 TN17...................293 F7
Charlbury Cl ME16.......161 C3
Charldane Rd SE9.........30 B5
Charlecote Ct ME8........98 D8
Charles Busby Ct
 ME20...................128 F1

Charles Cl Sidcup DA14...31 B4
 Snodland ME6............128 A8
Charles Cobb Cl TN29 366 D8
Charles Cres CT15........245 C7
Charles Ct Erith DA8.....14 E8
 Royal Tunbridge Wells
 TN2...................286 C3
Charles Darwin Ho ◆
 BR1...................29 B1
Charles Darwin Sch
 TN16...................118 F3
Charles Dickens Ave
 ME3...................39 C2
Charles Dickens Sch The
 CT10...................83 E4
Charles Dr ME2............62 B2
Charles Drayson Ct
 ME13...................138 E7
Charlesfield SE9...........29 C5
Charles Flemwell Mews
 E16...................1 A5
Charlesford Ave ME17 197 D3
Charles Garvice Ct SE3 11 D4
Charles Grinling Wlk
 SE18...................2 A2
Charles Ho CT14..........215 B3
Charles Lister Ct CT17 278 B1
Charles Rd
 Badgers Mount TN14....88 B1
 Deal CT14...............215 B4
 Ramsgate CT11..........117 E8
Charles St Chatham ME4 63 E3
 Grays RM17..............18 C8
 Herne Bay CT6............77 A5
 Maidstone ME16.........161 E3
 Newham E16..............1 C5
 Rochester ME2............63 A7
 Royal Tunbridge Wells
 TN4...................286 A8
 Sheerness ME12..........28 A3
 Stone DA9...............16 F7
Charles Street Ctr The
 TN4...................286 A8
Charleston Ct CT10.......84 B3
Charles Whincup Rd E16 1 B5
Charlesworth Dr CT7....81 B7
Charlock Cl ME16.........161 D8
Charlock Dr ME12.........47 A4
Charlotte Cl Bexley DA6 13 F4
 Chatham ME5..............97 B6
Charlotte Ct
 Chislehurst BR7..........30 E2
 ◆ Ramsgate CT11.......117 E6
Charlotte Dr
 Gillingham ME8...........65 C1
 Kings Hill ME19..........159 D3
Charlotte Park Ave BR1 52 E6
Charlotte Pl
 ◆ Margate CT9.........50 J1
 West Thurrock RM20.....17 B8
Charlottes Cotts TN11 220 F1
Charlotte Sq ◆ CT9......50 J2
Charlotte St
 ◆ Broadstairs CT10......84 B4
 Folkestone CT20.........335 E5
 Sittingbourne ME10......101 E5
CHARLTON................11 D8
Charlton Ave CT16.......278 C1
Charlton CE Prim Sch
 CT16...................278 C1
Charlton Church La SE7 .1 C1
Charlton Ct
 Ashford TN24............301 A8
 Ramsgate CT12..........83 B2
Charlton Court Pl
 ME17...................230 C7
Charlton Cres ◆ TN9..222 C2
Charlton Ctr ◆ CT17...310 C8
Charlton Dene SE7.......11 D7
Charlton Dr TN16........118 D2
Charlton Gate Bsns Pk
 SE7...................1 C2
Charlton Gn CT16........278 C1
Charlton La
 Chartway Street
 ME17...................197 C1
 Greenwich SE7...........1 D1
 Sutton Valence ME17...230 C8
 West Farleigh ME15......193 E6
Charlton Manor ME7....64 B5
Charlton Manor Prim Sch
 SE7...................11 D7
Charlton Park La SE7....11 E8
Charlton Park Rd SE7...11 D8
Charlton Rd SE3, SE7...11 B8
Charlton Sh Ctr ◆
 CT16...................310 C8
Charlton St Grays RM20 17 D8
Charlton Sta SE7...........1 C1
Charltons The ME13.....139 F4
Charlton's Way TN4.....285 C1
Charminster TN23.......299 E6
Charminster Rd SE9......29 C4
Charmouth Rd DA16.....13 C6
Charmwood La BR6.......87 B1
Charmwood Villas BR6 .87 C1
Charne The TN14.........122 A2
Charnock BR8..............55 E5
Charnwood CT5...........75 D1
Charnwood Rd CT6.......77 B1
Charollais Cl CT2.........143 A2
Chartam Terr CT11.......117 D5
Chart Cl ME13............138 B7
Chart Cnr ME17...........196 B1
Charter Dr DA5............31 E8
Charterhouse Dr TN13 154 A4
Charterhouse Rd BR6 ...87 A6
Charter St Chatham ME4 63 F2
 Gillingham ME7...........64 C7

Chartfield Sch CT8.......81 F8
Chart Gunpowder Mill★
 ME13...................138 B7
CHARTHAM..............173 E2
CHARTHAM DOWNS 173 D1
Chartham Hatch Rd
 CT4...................207 C7
Chartham Prim Sch
 CT4...................173 C2
Chartham Sta CT4.......173 D3
CHART HILL.............229 B8
Chart Hill Rd
 Chart Sutton ME17......196 B1
 Sutton Valence ME17...229 A7
Chart La TN16...........185 B7
Charton Cl ◆ DA17.......13 B4
Chart Pl ME8..............98 C3
Chart Rd
 Ashford, Godinton Park
 TN23...................267 F2
 Ashford, Great Chart
 TN23...................267 D1
 Ashford, Stanhope
 TN23...................299 D6
 Folkestone CT19.........334 F6
 Sutton Valence ME17...229 C7
Chart Road Ind Est
 TN23...................268 A3
CHART SUTTON........196 B1
Chart Sutton Bsns Est
 ME17...................196 B2
CHART THE Limpsfield .183 E5
 Toys Hill...............185 C5
Chart View TN15.........123 B2
Chartway TN13...........154 C3
Chartway St ME17.......197 C1
CHARTWAY STREET...197 C1
Chartwell★ TN16.......184 F4
Chartwell Bsns Ctr BR1 52 E6
Chartwell Cl
 Rochester ME2............40 B1
 Sidcup SE9...............30 C6
Chartwell Ct
 Chatham ME4..............63 E4
 Maidstone ME15.........162 B3
Chartwell Dr
 Maidstone ME16.........161 B4
 Orpington BR6.............86 D5
Chartwell Gr ME10.......101 C3
Chase Sq ◆ TN1...........19 B1
Chase The Bexley DA7...14 B4
 Bromley BR1..............52 B6
 Chatham ME4..............63 D2
 Gillingham ME8...........65 A2
 Kemsing TN15...........122 E3
 Pratt's Bottom BR6.......87 A1
 Ramsgate CT11...........83 F1
 St Margaret's at Cliffe
 CT15...................247 F1
 Tonbridge TN10.........222 C5
 West Thurrock RM20.....17 D8
 Whitstable CT5..........108 C8
Chastilian Rd DA1........33 A8
Chater Cl Ashford TN23 299 C8
 Deal CT14...............215 C6
CHATHAM.................63 C6
Chatham Ave BR2........52 A2
Chatham Cl SE18..........2 B3
Chatham Ct CT11.........117 D8
Chatham Gram Sch for
 Boys ME4...............96 F8
Chatham Gram Sch for
 Girls ME5...............64 C2
Chatham Hill ME4........64 B3
Chatham Hill Rd TN14 154 C6
Chatham Ho ◆ SE18.....1 F2
Chatham House Gram Sch
 CT11...................117 E7
Chatham Pl CT11.........117 E7
Chatham Rd
 Kit's Coty ME20.........129 D6
 Maidstone ME14........129 E1
 Sandling ME14..........129 E4
Chatham Ski Ctr ME1...97 E6
Chatham South Sch
 ME4...................96 F8
Chatham St CT11.........117 E7
Chatham St ME4...........63 E4
Chatham Way
 Kit's Coty ME20.........129 D6
 Maidstone ME14........129 E1
 Sandling ME14..........129 E4
Chatsworth Ave
 Bromley BR1..............29 B4
 Sidcup DA15..............31 A7
Chatsworth Dr
 Rochester ME2............40 B1
 Sittingbourne ME10......101 B5
Chatsworth Ho ◆ BR2..52 A5
Chatsworth Inf Sch
 DA15...................31 A7
Chatsworth Par BR5......53 C4
Chatsworth Rd
 ◆ Gillingham ME7........64 C6
CHATTENDEN.............40 F4
Chattenden Ct ME4......162 B6
Chattenden La ME3.......40 F5
Chattenden Prim Sch
 ME3...................40 F4
Chattenden Terr ME3....40 F4
Chatterton Rd BR2.......52 D4
Chatwell Ct ME7..........64 C5
Chaucer Ave CT5..........75 B1
Chaucer Bsns Pk
 Kemsing TN15...........155 D8
 Whitstable CT5...........75 B1
Chaucer Cl
 Canterbury CT1..........175 C7
 ◆ Maidstone ME15......195 C4
 Rochester ME2............63 C5
 Tilbury RM18..............19 C5

Chaucer Coll CT2 . . . . . 142 D3
Chaucer Cres CT16 . . . . **278** B3
Chaucer Ct 1 CT1 . . . . **175** B7
Chaucer Hospl The
CT4 . . . . 175 A4
Chaucer Ind Pk TN15 . . 155 D8
Chaucer Mews CT2 . . . . 141 E1
Chaucer Pk DA1 . . . . 33 F8
Chaucer Rd Bexley DA16 12 F6
Broadstairs CT10 . . . . . . 84 A3
Canterbury CT1 . . . . . . 143 C1
Elvington CT15 . . . . . . 212 B2
Gillingham ME7 . . . . 64 D3
Northfleet DA11 . . . . 36 D5
Sidcup DA15 . . . . 31 C7
Sittingbourne ME10 . . . 101 D3
Chaucer Tech Sch
CT1 . . . . 175 C7
Chaucer Way
Dartford DA1 . . . . 16 A3
New Hythe ME20 . . . . . 128 A3
Chaucer Wood Ct CT1 143 B1
Chaundrye Cl SE9 . . . . . . 11 F1
Chauntler Cl E16 . . . . . . 1 B6
Chave Rd DA2 . . . . 33 E5
Cheddar CT24 . . . . . . 268 B4
Cheeselands TN27 . . . . 294 F2
CHEESEMAN'S
GREEN 300 F2
Cheeseman's Green La
TN23/TN25 . . . . 300 E1
Cheesmans Cl CT12 . . 115 C5
Cheffins Ho ME7 . . . . . . 64 E7
Chegwell Dr ME5 . . . . . . 97 B4
Chegworth Gdns ME10 101 E1
Chegworth La ME17 . . . 198 A6
Chegworth Rd ME17 . . 197 F5
Cheldoc Rise ME4 . . . . . . 41 C2
Chellows La RH7 . . . . . 216 A1
Chelmar Rd ME7 . . . . . . 64 B4
Chelmsford Cl E6 . . . . . . 1 F7
Chelmsford Ho ME15 . . 195 E6
Chelmsford Rd ME2 . . . . 62 D6
Chelsea Ct
6 Bromley BR1 . . . . . . 52 E6
Hythe CT21 . . . . 333 C1
Chelsea Rd CT1 . . . . . . 143 C4
CHELSFIELD 87 E5
Chelsfield Hill BR6 . . . . 87 C7
Chelsfield Ho ME16 . . . 161 D5
Chelsfield La
Badgers Mount BR6,
TN14 . . . . 88 B2
Chelsfield BR5, BR6 . . . . 87 D7
Orpington BR5 . . . . 54 C1
Chelsfield Park Hospl
BR6 . . . . 87 F5
Chelsfield Prim Sch
BR6 . . . . 87 E5
Chelsfield Rd BR5 . . . . . 54 C1
Chelsfield Sta BR6 . . . . . 87 B5
Chelsiter Ct DA14 . . . . . 30 F4
Chelsworth Dr SE18 . . . 12 D8
Cheltenham Cl
Gravesend DA12 . . . . . . 37 C3
Maidstone ME15 . . . . . 195 F6
Cheltenham Rd BR6 . . . . 87 A7
Cheney Cl ME8 . . . . 98 D5
Cheney Hill ME9 . . . . . . 135 A5
Cheney Rd ME13 . . . . . 138 F7
Chenies Cl TN2 . . . . . . 314 A8
Chenies The
Joyden's Wood DA2 . . . . 32 E4
Orpington BR6 . . . . 53 E3
Chennell Park Rd
TN30 . . . . 323 E1
Chennels The TN26 . . . 324 C1
Chepstow Ho **3** ME15 195 F6
Chequer La CT3 . . . . . . 147 D2
Chequers Cl
Chatham ME5 . . . . 130 A8
Istead Rise DA13 . . . . . . 59 F7
Orpington BR5 . . . . 53 F5
Chequers Ct ME2 . . . . . . 40 A1
Chequers Hill CT4 . . . . 207 C2
Chequers Hill Cotts
TN8 . . . . 219 A2
Chequers La RM9 . . . . . . 3 F8
Chequers Pk TN25 . . . . 232 F1
Chequers Rd ME12 . . . . . 47 E6
Chequers Sh Ctr ME15 162 B4
Chequer's Terr ME12 . . . 48 A5
Chequertree TN25 . . . . 329 B7
Cherbourg Cres ME5 . . . 96 F7
Cherbury Cl SE28 . . . . . . 3 D7
CHERITON 334 D6
Cheriton Appartments
CT19 . . . . 334 F6
Cheriton Ave Hayes BR2 52 A4
Ramsgate CT12 . . . . . . 117 B8
Cheriton Court Rd
CT20 . . . . 334 C6
Cheriton Ct 12 SE12 . . . 29 A8
Cheriton Dr SE18 . . . . . 12 D8
Cheriton Gdns CT20 . . 335 C4
Cheriton High St CT20 334 D6
Cheriton Intc CT19 . . . . 334 C7
Cheriton Pl Deal CT14 . 215 D4
Folkestone CT20 . . . . . 335 D4
Cheriton Prim Sch
CT20 . . . . 334 C6
Cheriton Rd Deal CT14 215 D4
Folkestone CT19, CT20 . 335 B5
Folkestone, Morehall
CT19 . . . . 334 F6
Gillingham ME8 . . . . . . 98 D8
Cheriton Way ME16 . . . 161 C7
Cheriton Wood Ho
CT19 . . . . 334 D7
Cherries The ME16 . . . 161 A2
Cherry Amber Cl ME8 . . 98 F8

Cherry Ave
Canterbury CT2 . . . . . . 142 D2
Swanley BR8 . . . . 55 D5
Cherrybrook Rd CT20 334 D6
Cherry Cl Lenham ME17 199 C5
Sittingbourne ME10 . . . 101 D6
Cherrycot Hill BR6 . . . . 86 D6
Cherrycot Rise BR6 . . . . 86 C6
Cherry Ct Ashford TN23 268 B3
Broadstairs CT10 . . . . . . 83 E7
Folkestone CT19 . . . . . 335 A6
Sidcup DA14 . . . . 31 B5
Cherrydown Rd DA14 . . . 31 D6
Cherry Dr CT2 . . . . 142 D2
Cherryfields TN17 . . . . 342 D6
Cherry Fields ME16 . . . 101 A5
Cherry Garden Ave
CT19 . . . . 335 A7
Cherry Garden Cres
TN25 . . . . 237 F2
Cherrygarden La CT15,
CT3 . . . . 211 E2
Cherry Garden La
Ash CT3 . . . . 147 E1
Folkestone CT19 . . . . . 334 F7
Wye TN25 . . . . 237 F2
Cherry Garden Rd CT2 142 D2
Cherry Gdns
Ashford TN23 . . . . 300 A5
Broadstairs CT10 . . . . . . 83 C5
Elham CT4 . . . . 273 F5
Herne Bay CT6 . . . . 76 F4
Littlebourne-on-Sea
TN28 . . . . 373 D6
Teynham ME9 . . . . 103 C2
Cherry Glebe TN25 . . . 301 E3
Cherry Gr
Elvington CT15 . . . . . . 212 B2
Tonbridge TN10 . . . . . 222 B5
Cherry Hill Ct ME9 . . . 100 B6
Cherry La CT14 . . . . . . 214 D3
Cherry Orch
Ditton ME20 . . . . 160 C8
Greenwich SE7 . . . . 11 C8
Littlebourne CT3 . . . . . 144 F1
Old Wives Lees CT4 . . . 172 C2
Tenterden TN30 . . . . . 345 A6
Whitstable CT5 . . . . . . 109 C8
Woodchurch TN26 . . . . 326 A3
CHERRY ORCHARD . . . 161 B4
Cherry Orchard Cl BR5 54 C4
Cherry Orchard La
TN25 . . . . 329 E4
Cherry Orchard Mews
CT3 . . . . 144 F1
Cherry Orchard Prim Sch
SE7 . . . . 11 C7
Cherry Orchard Rd BR2 85 E8
Cherry Orchard Way
ME16 . . . . 161 B3
Cherry Orch The TN11 190 E1
Cherry Rd ME3 . . . . 41 E3
Cherry Tree Ave CT16 278 C1
Cherry Tree Cl
Grays RM17 . . . . 18 C8
Teynham ME9 . . . . 103 D2
West Minst ME12 . . . . . 46 A8
Cherry Tree Ct 19 SE7 . . 11 C8
Cherry Tree Dr ME13 . 104 F3
Cherry Tree Gdns CT12 83 F3
Cherry Tree Gr TN15 . . . 90 B1
Cherry Tree La DA2 . . . . 32 F5
Cherry Tree Rd
Charing Heath TN27 . . . 233 E7
Gillingham ME8 . . . . 98 F8
Royal Tunbridge Wells
TN2 . . . . 285 E1
Tonbridge TN10 . . . . . 222 D7
Cherry Trees DA3 . . . . . . 58 F4
Cherry View ME17 . . . . 195 B3
Cherry Waye CT15 . . . . 245 D5
Cherry Wlk BR2 . . . . 52 A1
Cherrywood Dr DA11 . . . 36 F5
Cherrywood Rise TN25 267 F4
Cherville La CT3 . . . . . . 177 C7
Chervilles ME16 . . . . . . 161 A2
Chervil Mews SE28 . . . . 3 B5
Cherwell Cl TN10 . . . . . 222 B4
Chesfield Cl TN11 . . . . . 190 F1
Chesham Ave BR5 . . . . . 53 B3
Chesham Dr ME8 . . . . . . 98 E6
Cheshire Rd
Maidstone ME15 . . . . . 195 E7
Maidstone, Willington
ME15 . . . . 162 E2
Cheshunt Cl DA13 . . . . . 60 A3
Cheshunt Rd DA17 . . . . . 4 A1
Chesil Ho 1 BR7 . . . . . . 53 B8
CHESLEY 100 A3
Chessenden La TN27 . . 264 A1
Chessington Ave DA7 . . 13 E7
Chester Ave
Bethersden TN26 . . . . . 297 D5
Royal Tunbridge Wells
TN2 . . . . 286 D2
Chester Cl ME2 . . . . 62 D6
Chesterfield Cl BR5 . . . 54 D5
Chesterfield Dr
Dartford DA1 . . . . 15 B2
Sevenoaks TN13 . . . . . 153 D5
Chesterford Ho SE18 . . . 11 D7
Chester Rd
Gillingham ME7 . . . . . . 64 D2
Sidcup DA15 . . . . 12 E2
Westgate on Sea CT8 . . . 81 F8
Chesterton Rd
Cliffe ME3 . . . . 22 B6
5 Lunsford ME20 . . . . 127 F4
Chesterton Way RM18 . . 19 C5
CHESTFIELD 75 E1
Chestfield Cl ME8 . . . . . 65 E2
Chestfield Rd CT5 . . . . 109 C5
Chestfield & Swalecliffe
Sta CT5 . . . . 75 D2

Chestnut Ave
Blean CT2 . . . . 142 A7
Chatham ME5 . . . . 96 F3
Hill Park TN16 . . . . . . 151 A6
Royal Tunbridge Wells
TN4 . . . . 286 B8
Staplehurst TN12 . . . . . 260 F4
Stone DA9 . . . . 34 F8
Tatsfield CT16 . . . . 150 E5
Chestnut Cl
Ashford TN23 . . . . 267 E3
Chartham CT4 . . . . 173 F1
Edenbridge TN8 . . . . . 217 B2
Frittenden TN17 . . . . . 293 E6
Hythe CT21 . . . . 353 E8
Kings Hill ME19 . . . . . 159 A2
Northfleet DA11 . . . . . . 18 F1
Orpington BR6 . . . . 87 A5
Royal Tunbridge Wells
TN4 . . . . 286 B8
Sidcup DA15 . . . . 31 A6
Tenterden TN30 . . . . . 324 C1
Ulcombe ME17 . . . . . . 230 F6
Whitfield CT16 . . . . . . 278 A8
Chestnut Copse RH8 . 183 B2
Chestnut Ct
Boughton Street
ME13 . . . . 140 A3
Royal Tunbridge Wells
TN2 . . . . 314 A8
Chestnut Dr Bexley DA7 13 E4
Broadstairs CT10 . . . . . . 83 D4
Coxheath ME17 . . . . . . 194 B3
Herne Bay CT6 . . . . 76 D3
Kingswood ME17 . . . . . 197 D2
Sturry CT2 . . . . 144 A7
Worth CT14 . . . . 181 A4
Chestnut Gr DA2 . . . . . . 32 E4
Chestnut Ho 6 ME16 . 161 A3
Chestnut La
Kingsnorth ME23 . . . . . 300 C4
Matfield TN12 . . . . . . 256 D1
Sevenoaks TN13 . . . . . 154 B3
Vigo Village DA13 . . . . 126 B8
Chestnut Pl TN8 . . . . . 282 A6
Chestnut Rd
Dartford DA1 . . . . 33 D7
Dover CT17 . . . . 310 B7
Rochester ME2 . . . . 62 E6
Chestnuts Royal BR7 . . 30 D1
Chestnut St ME9 . . . . . 100 E4
Chestnuts The
Addington ME19 . . . . . 126 C3
Brabourne Lees TN25 . . 302 D5
Chislehurst BR7 . . . . . . 30 D1
7 Erith DA17 . . . . 3 F1
Sellindge TN25 . . . . . . 303 D1
The Moor TN18 . . . . . . 354 F8
Woolwich SE18 . . . . 12 B6
CHESTNUT STREET . . . 100 D5
Chestnut Terr 333 A1
Chestnut Wlk
Larkfield ME20 . . . . . . 128 B2
Sevenoaks TN15 . . . . . 187 F6
Tonbridge TN9 . . . . . . 221 F2
Chestnut Wood La
ME9 . . . . 100 D4
Cheswick Cl DA1 . . . . . 14 F3
Chesworth Cl DA8 . . . . . 14 E1
Chetney Cl ME2 . . . . 62 C7
Chetney View ME9 . . . . 68 D4
Chetwood Wlk 15 E6 . . . 1 E8
Chevalier Rd CT17 . . . 310 A7
Chevender Rd BR7 . . . . . 30 B1
Cheveney Wlk 2 BR2 . 52 A6
CHEVENING 152 F7
Chevening Cl ME5 . . . . . 97 A5
Chevening Ct BR6 . . . . . 87 A8
Chevening House BR5 . . 53 E1
Chevening La TN14 . . . 120 E3
Chevening Prim Sch
TN13 . . . . 153 B5
Chevening Rd
3 Greenwich SE10 . . . . 1 A1
Sevenoaks TN13, TN14 . 153 B6
Sundridge TN14 . . . . . 152 F4
Chevenings The DA14 . . 31 C5
Cheviot Cl Bexley DA7 . 14 F5
Tonbridge TN9 . . . . . . 222 C4
Cheviot Ct CT10 . . . . . . 84 B6
Cheviot Gdns ME15 . . . 163 A4
Cheviot Ho 6 DA11 . . . . 18 F1
Cheviot Way TN24 . . . . 268 C4
Chevron Cl ME5 . . . . . . 97 B4
Chevron Ho RM17 . . . . . 18 B7
Cheyne Cl Orpington BR2 85 E7
Sittingbourne ME10 . . . 101 F8
Cheyne Mid Sch ME12 . 28 D2
Cheyne Rd ME12 . . . . . . 48 D3
Cheyne Wlk
Longfield DA3 . . . . 58 D6
Meopham DA13 . . . . . . 93 A8
Chicago Ave ME7 . . . . . 64 F5
Chichester Cl
Ashford TN23 . . . . 268 B1
Gillingham ME8 . . . . . . 99 A8
Greenwich SE3 . . . . 11 C6
Newham E6 . . . . 1 E7
Chichester Ct 3 DA16 . 12 A3
Chichester Dr TN13 . . . 153 F2
Chichester Rd
Folkestone CT20 . . . . . 334 E4
Ramsgate CT12 . . . . . . 83 B1
Stone DA9 . . . . 16 F1
Tonbridge TN9 . . . . . . 254 B4
Chichester Rise DA12 . . 37 D4
Chichester Wharf 14 DA8 4 F1
Chichester Wlk 2 CT12 83 B1
Chickenden La NT17 . . 261 C4
Chickfield Gdns 4 ME5 64 C2
Chicks La TN17 . . . . . . 317 F2
Chiddingfold Cl ME12 . 47 D6
CHIDDINGSTONE 251 C7

Chiddingstone Ave DA7 13 F7
Chiddingstone Castle★
TN8 . . . . 251 B7
CHIDDINGSTONE
CAUSEWAY 219 F2
Chiddingstone CE Prim
Sch TN8 . . . . 251 C7
Chiddingstone Cl
ME15 . . . . 195 F6
CHIDDINGSTONE
HOATH 251 A2
Chidley Cross Rd TN12 224 E6
Chieveley Dr TN2 . . . . . 286 D1
Chieveley Par DA7 . . . . 14 B4
Chieveley Rd DA7 . . . . . 14 B3
Chiffinch Gdns DA11 . . 36 E5
Childgate Rd CT5 . . . . . 107 F2
Childs Cres DA10 . . . . . 17 D1
Childscroft Rd ME8 . . . . 65 F2
Childs Way TN15 . . . . . 124 F3
CHILHAM 205 C7
Chilham Ave CT8 . . . . . . 81 D7
Chilham Cl Chatham ME4 63 E3
Sidcup DA15 . . . . 31 F8
West Minst ME12 . . . . . 46 B8
Chilham Ho
1 Maidstone ME15 . . 195 E8
Rochester ME2 . . . . 40 C1
Chilham Rd Bromley SE9 29 E4
Folkestone CT19 . . . . . 334 E6
Gillingham ME8 . . . . . . 65 A3
Maidstone ME16 . . . . . 161 C7
Chilham St Mary's CE Prim
Sch CT4 . . . . 205 B8
Chilham Sta CT4 . . . . . 205 D8
Chilham Way BR2 . . . . . 52 A2
CHILLENDEN 211 F8
Chillenden Windmill★
CT3 . . . . 178 F1
Chillington Cl ME2 . . . . 94 E4
Chillington St ME14 . . 161 F6
Chilliwack Rd ME3 . . . . 40 F5
CHILMINGTON
GREEN 299 C5
Chilston Ct TN4 . . . . . . 286 A5
Chilston Rd
Lenham ME17 . . . . 199 D5
Royal Tunbridge Wells
TN4 . . . . 286 A5
Chiltern Cl Bexley DA7 . 14 E6
Maidstone ME15 . . . . . 162 F1
Chiltern Ct 11 SE9 . . . . 12 A1
Chiltern End TN24 . . . . 268 B3
Chiltern Rd DA11 . . . . . 36 E5
Chilterns DA14 . . . . 31 A3
Chilterns, The BR1 . . . . 52 B7
Chiltern Way TN9 . . . . 222 C4
Chiltern Wlk TN2 . . . . . 286 D4
CHILTON 117 A6
Chilton Ave
Sittingbourne ME10 . . . 102 A3
Temple Ewell CT16 . . . 277 C4
Chilton Cl
14 Folkestone CT20 . . 335 E6
Gillingham ME8 . . . . . . 65 C1
Chilton Dr ME3 . . . . 39 B3
Chilton Field CT3 . . . . . 147 D2
Chilton Gdns CT3 . . . . 147 D2
Chilton La CT11 . . . . . . 117 A6
Chilton Pl CT3 . . . . 147 D2
Chilton Prim Sch CT11 117 A6
Chilton Sq CT3 . . . . 147 D2
Chilton Way CT17 . . . . 277 D3
Chimes The
Ashford TN24 . . . . 268 C3
Hoo St Werburgh ME3 . . 41 E6
Maidstone ME14 . . . . . 163 A5
Rochester ME1 . . . . 61 E4
Chine Farm Pl TN14 . . 120 D3
Chineham Way CT1 . . . 174 F6
Chinnery Ct DA14 . . . . . 60 A2
Chippendale Cl ME5 . . . 96 F1
Chippendayle Dr
ME17 . . . . 198 D6
Chipperfield Rd BR5 . . . 54 A7
Chippie's Way CT13 . . . 148 F1
CHIPSTEAD 153 C5
Chipstead Cl ME16 . . . 161 D6
Chipstead La TN13 . . . 153 D5
Chipstead Park Cl
TN13 . . . . 153 C5
Chipstead Pk TN13 . . . 153 C5
Chipstead Place Gdns
TN13 . . . . 153 D5
Chipstead Rd Erith DA8 . 14 E7
Gillingham ME8 . . . . . . 98 D4
Chipstead Sq TN13 . . . 153 C5
CHISLEHURST 53 B7
Chislehurst Caves★
BR7 . . . . 53 A8
Chislehurst Cl ME15 . . 195 F6
Chislehurst High St
BR7 . . . . 30 B2
Chislehurst Rd
Bromley BR1, BR2 . . . . . 52 E8
Orpington BR6 . . . . 54 A2
Orpington, Broom Hill
BR6 . . . . 53 F7
Orpington, Petts Wood BR5,
BR6 . . . . 53 E4
Sidcup DA14 . . . . 31 A3
Chislehurst & Sidcup Gram
Sch DA15 . . . . 31 B4
Chislehurst Sta BR7 . . . 53 A7
Chislehurst (St Nicholas)
CE Prim Sch 1 BR7 . . . 30 C1
CHISLEHURST WEST . . 30 A3
CHISLET 112 D5

Chislet CE Prim Sch
CT3 . . . . 112 C5
Chislet Cl CT3 . . . . 112 A1
Chislet Ct CT6 . . . . 76 C5
CHISLET FORSTAL . . . 112 B5
Chislet Park Cotts CT3 111 F1
Chislet Cl CT25 . . . . . . 303 E2
Chislet Wlk ME8 . . . . . . 98 D5
Chisnall Rd CT17 . . . . . 277 E4
Chiswell Sq SE3 . . . . . . 11 B5
Chittenden's La TN29 . . 364 E5
CHITTY 112 D6
Chitty La CT3 . . . . 112 D6
Chorleywood Cres BR5 54 A7
Christchurch Ave CT3 . 14 E8
Christ Church Ave **1**
TN1 . . . . 286 A2
Christ Church CE High Sch
TN23 . . . . 299 B5
Christ Church CE Jun Sch
CT11 . . . . 117 C6
Christ Church CE Prim Sch
CT20 . . . . 335 C5
Christ Church CE Sch
SE18 . . . . 12 A4
Christ Church Cres **2**
DA12 . . . . 37 C8
Christchurch Ct
3 Chatham ME5 . . . . 64 C2
1 Dover CT17 . . . . . . 310 D7
Christchurch Ho **11**
ME15 . . . . 195 E5
Christ Church Prim Sch
DA8 . . . . 14 D8
Christchurch Rd
Ashford TN23 . . . . 300 B8
Dartford DA1 . . . . 15 C1
Sidcup DA15 . . . . 30 F5
Tilbury RM18 . . . . 19 A6
Christchurch Way
CT16 . . . . 278 B3
Christen Way ME15,
ME17 . . . . 195 F3
Christian Ct 3 ME2 . . . 63 C8
CHRISTIAN FIELDS 37 C4
Christian Fields Ave
DA12 . . . . 37 C4
Christie Cl ME5 . . . . 97 B6
Christie Dr 8 ME20 . . . 127 F4
Christie Ho DA14 . . . . . 14 B2
Christies Ave TN14 . . . . 88 B1
Christmas La ME3 . . . . . 23 F3
Christmas St ME7 . . . . . 64 E7
Christmas Tree Farm★
BR6 . . . . 119 A7
Christopher Bushell Way
TN24 . . . . 268 E4
Christopher Ct DA15 . . . 12 F2
Christopher's Row
ME9 . . . . 136 A3
Christy Rd TN16 . . . . . 118 C4
Chrysler Ave CT6 . . . . . 76 B4
Chudleigh 7 ME8 . . . . . 64 A8
Chulkhurst TN27 . . . . 294 F1
Chulkhurst TN27 . . . . 294 F1
Church Alley **1** DA11 . . 19 B1
Church App TN28 . . . . 373 A6
Church Ave DA14 . . . . . . 31 B3
Churchbury Rd SE9 . . . . 29 D8
Church Cl
Brenchley TN12 . . . . . . 289 C8
Cliffe ME3 . . . . 22 B6
Mereworth ME18 . . . . . 191 D8
Mersham TN25 . . . . . . 301 E3
Church Cliff CT14 . . . . 248 D6
Church Cotts
Cranbrook TN17 . . . . . 320 D5
Crockenhill BR8 . . . . . . 55 D2
Rodmersham ME9 . . . . 135 D8
Shoreham TN14 . . . . . 122 A8
Sutton Valence ME17 . . 229 E7
Tenterden TN30 . . . . . 324 B3
Church Court Gr CT10 . 83 E6
Church Cres ME17 . . . . 198 F6
Church Ct Dartford DA2 . 33 D5
Lyminge CT18 . . . . . . 305 C6
Church Farm Cl
Crockenhill BR8 . . . . . . 55 D3
Hoo St Werburgh ME3 . . 41 E4
Churchfarm Mews
CT15 . . . . 247 A1
Church Farm Rd ME9 . . 66 E3
Church Farm Way
CT13 . . . . 180 B6
Churchfield
Dartford DA2 . . . . 33 D6
Sevenoaks TN13 . . . . . 153 F5
Snodland ME6 . . . . 95 B1
Stanford TN25 . . . . . . 304 B1
Church Field Cotts
TN15 . . . . 154 F7
Churchfield Pl CT9 . . . . 50 I2
Churchfield Rd DA16 . . 13 A4
Churchfields
Broadstairs CT10 . . . . . . 83 F7
Margate CT9 . . . . 50 J1
Church Fields ME19 . . . 159 B8
Churchfields Terr ME1 . 63 B4
Churchfields Way TN25 237 E2
Church Gn
Hollingbourne ME17 . . . 164 E3
Marden TN12 . . . . 259 C6
Rochester ME2 . . . . 63 C8
Staplehurst TN12 . . . . . 260 E2
Church Haven CT14 . . . 247 F5

Church Hill
Bethersden TN26 . . . . . 297 D5
Boughton Street ME13 . 140 A5
Canterbury CT2 . . . . . . 142 C1
Charing Heath ME17,
TN27 . . . . 233 C7
Chatham ME5 . . . . 64 C2
Chilham CT4 . . . . 205 B8
Crayford DA1 . . . . 14 E2
Cudham TN14, TN16 . . . 119 C4
Dartford DA2 . . . . 33 D6
Doddington ME9 . . . . . 167 F4
Eythorne CT15 . . . . . . 245 C8
Hawkinge CT18 . . . . . . 307 D4
High Halden TN26 . . . . 324 E7
Hythe CT21 . . . . 333 C2
Kingsnorth TN23 . . . . . 300 B3
Leigh TN11 . . . . 220 F2
Linton ME17 . . . . 228 B7
Loose ME17 . . . . 195 C1
Orpington BR6 . . . . 54 A2
Plaxtol TN15 . . . . 189 E8
Ramsgate CT11 . . . . . . 117 E7
Shepherdswell CT15 . . 244 D4
Stockbury ME9 . . . . . . 132 F7
Stone DA9 . . . . 16 E2
Stone in Oxney TN30 . . 360 F3
Sutton CT15 . . . . 247 A7
Tatsfield TN16 . . . . . . 150 D5
Temple Ewell CT16 . . . 277 D5
Woolwich SE18 . . . . 1 F3
Church Hill Wood BR5 . 53 F4
Church Ho CT14 . . . . . 215 C3
CHURCH HOUGHAM . . . 309 B5
Church Hts CT21 . . . . . 333 C2
Church Hyde SE18 . . . . 12 E8
Churchill Ave
Chatham ME5 . . . . 97 A7
Deal CT14 . . . . 215 C2
Folkestone CT19 . . . . . 335 C8
Herne Bay CT6 . . . . 77 D4
Churchill Bsns Ctr
TN16 . . . . 151 D1
Churchill CE Prim Sch
TN16 . . . . 151 C2
Churchill Cl Bridge CT4 175 F1
Dartford DA1 . . . . 34 B7
Folkestone CT19 . . . . . 335 D8
St Margaret's at Cliffe
CT15 . . . . 279 F5
Churchill Cotts ME17 . 196 F6
Churchill Ct
Hythe CT21 . . . . 333 B1
4 Orpington BR6 . . . . 86 C5
1 Ramsgate CT11 . . . 117 D7
Westerham TN16 . . . . . 151 D1
Churchill Ho
Benenden TN17 . . . . . 342 E6
Bridge CT4 . . . . 175 F1
2 Folkestone CT20 . . 334 F5
Maidstone ME16 . . . . . 161 B2
Sittingbourne ME10 . . . 102 A2
Teynham ME9 . . . . 103 C3
1 Woolwich SE18 . . . . 2 B2
Churchill Pk DA1 . . . . . 16 A2
Churchill Rd
Canterbury CT1 . . . . . . 175 C6
Dover CT17 . . . . 310 A6
Grays RM17 . . . . 18 D8
Horton Kirby DA4 . . . . . 57 C5
Minster (Sheppey) ME12 .47 D6
Newham E16 . . . . 1 C7
Northfleet DA11 . . . . . . 36 F7
Churchill Sch The
CT18 . . . . 307 A4
Churchill Sq ME19 . . . . 159 A3
Churchills Ropewalk
TN17 . . . . 318 E8
Churchill St **3** CT16 . . 278 C1
Churchill Theatre
BR1 . . . . 52 A7
Churchill Way
Biggin Hill TN16 . . . . . 118 D4
Bromley BR1 . . . . 52 A7
Faversham ME13 . . . . . 105 B1
Churchill Wlk CT18 . . . 306 F4
Churchin Cl TN16 . . . . 118 C7
Church La Adisham CT3 177 D1
Aldington ME25 . . . . . . 330 D7
Barham CT4 . . . . 209 F1
Boughton Aluph TN25 . 237 B4
Boyden Gate CT3 . . . . 112 C2
Brenzett TN29 . . . . . . 362 F5
Canterbury CT1 . . . . . . 174 F8
20 Canterbury, Northgate
CT1 . . . . 143 A1
Capel TN12 . . . . 255 C6
Chalk DA12 . . . . 38 C6
Challock TN25 . . . . . . 236 B8
Chartham CT4 . . . . 173 D3
Chatham ME4 . . . . 63 F6
Chislehurst BR7 . . . . . . 53 C8
Church Hougham CT15 . 309 B5
Deal CT14 . . . . 215 B6
East Peckham TN12 . . . 224 F7
Frant TN3 . . . . 314 B4
Harrietsham ME17 . . . 198 E6
Hothfield TN26 . . . . . . 266 F6
Iden TN31 . . . . 368 B4
Kemsing TN15 . . . . . . 123 B2
Kingsnorth TN23 . . . . . 300 B3
Kingston CT4 . . . . 209 D3
Lower Hardres CT4 . . . 175 B2
Lydden CT15 . . . . 276 B8
Maidstone, Bearsted
ME14 . . . . 163 C4
Maidstone ME16 . . . . . 160 E1
Newington ME9 . . . . . . 100 B6
Orpington BR2 . . . . 52 E1
Peasmarsh TN31 . . . . . 367 C1

Church La continued
Petham CT4 . . . . 207 C3
Ringwould CT14 . . . . . . 247 F5
Ripple CT14 . . . . 214 D1
Selling ME13 . . . . 171 B6
Shadoxhurst TN26 . . . . 327 A7
Stockbury ME9 . . . . . . 132 E8
Stourmouth CT3 . . . . . . 113 C2
Stowting TN25 . . . . 304 A6
Sturry CT2 . . . . 143 F5
Sutton Valence ME17 . . 230 B8
Tonbridge TN9 . . . . 222 C2
Trottiscliffe ME19 . . . . 126 B5
Waltham CT4 . . . . 239 F5
Westbere CT2 . . . . 144 C7
West Farleigh ME15 . . . 193 D7
West Langdon CT15 . . . 246 D3
Whitstable CT5 . . . . . . 108 A6
Womenswold CT4 . . . . . 210 D2
Churchlands ME14 . . . . 162 B5
Churchlands Ho TN28 . 373 B6
Churchlands The TN28 373 B6
Church Manorway DA8 . . 4 D3
Church Manor Way SE18,
  SE2 . . . . 3 A2
Church Marshes Ctry Pk★
  ME10 . . . . 102 A7
Church Mdws CT14 . . . 215 A6
Church Meadow TN12 290 A7
Church Mews
  Gillingham ME8 . . . . . . 98 F8
  Iwade ME9 . . . . 68 E4
Church Path Deal CT14 215 B5
  Gillingham ME7 . . . . . . 64 E6
  Great Mongeham CT14 . 214 D3
  Northfleet DA11 . . . . . . 18 C1
  Stone DA9 . . . . 16 F1
Church Rd
  Ashford, Aylesford Green
    TN24 . . . . 301 A7
  Ashford, Kennington
    TN24 . . . . 268 E6
  Ashford TN23 . . . . 268 C2
  Ashford, Willesborough
    TN24 . . . . 301 A8
  Bexley DA7, DA6 . . . . . 13 F4
  Bexley, Welling DA16 . . 13 B5
  Biggin Hill TN16 . . . . . 118 E2
  Bitchet Green TN15 . . . 155 E3
  Brasted TN16 . . . . 152 B3
  ■ Broadstairs CT10 . . . 84 B4
  Bromley BR1, BR2 . . . . 52 A7
  Burmarsh TN29 . . . . . . 351 C4
  Charing TN27 . . . . 201 D2
  Chart Sutton ME17 . . . 196 C1
  Chelsfield BR6 . . . . 87 D4
  Coldred CT15 . . . . 245 A3
  Crockenhill BR8 . . . . . . 55 D2
  Dover CT17 . . . . 310 A7
  Eastchurch ME12 . . . . . 48 D2
  Eastling ME13 . . . . 169 B2
  Erith DA8 . . . . 4 D1
  Faversham ME13 . . . . . 138 D7
  Faversham, Oare ME13 105 B3
  Faversham, The Brents
    ME13 . . . . 138 D8
  Folkestone CT20 . . . . . 334 C6
  Goudhurst TN17 . . . . . 318 F8
  Grafty Green ME17 . . . 231 F7
  Gravesend DA12, DA13 . . 37 D1
  Halstead TN14 . . . . . . 120 F7
  Harrietsham ME17 . . . . 198 E6
  Hartley DA3 . . . . 59 A2
  Hawley DA4 . . . . 33 F1
  Henhurst DA13 . . . . 60 C8
  Hoath CT3 . . . . 111 E5
  Hucking ME17 . . . . 132 E1
  Hythe CT21 . . . . 333 C2
  Kenardington TN26 . . . 348 A5
  Kilndown TN17 . . . . . . 317 F3
  Lamberhurst TN3 . . . . . 317 C6
  Littlebourne CT3 . . . . . 177 A8
  Lydd TN29 . . . . 376 C6
  Lyminge CT18 . . . . 305 C7
  Maidstone ME15 . . . . . 195 F7
  Maidstone, Tovil ME15 . 161 E2
  Margate CT9 . . . . 50 J1
  Mersham TN25 . . . . . . 301 E3
  Molash CT4 . . . . 203 F5
  New Romney TN28 . . . . 373 A6
  Northbourne, Betteshanger
    CT14 . . . . 213 C6
  Northbourne CT14 . . . . 214 A5
  Offham ME18 . . . . 158 D8
  Orpington BR6 . . . . 86 D5
  Orpington, Keston BR2 . 85 D3
  Paddock Wood TN12 . . 257 B6
  Pembury TN2 . . . . 255 D1
  Pembury TN2 . . . . 287 D8
  Ramsgate CT11 . . . . . . 117 E7
  Royal Tunbridge Wells,
    Southborough TN4 . . 253 F2
  Royal Tunbridge Wells
    TN1 . . . . 286 A3
  Ryarsh ME19 . . . . 127 A3
  Sandhurst Cross TN18 . 355 F4
  Seal TN15 . . . . 155 A3
  Sevenoaks Weald TN14 187 B3
  Sevington TN24 . . . . . . 301 B6
  Sidcup DA14 . . . . 31 A4
  Sittingbourne ME9 . . . 102 E5
  Sittingbourne, Murston
    ME10 . . . . 102 B5
  Smeeth TN25 . . . . 302 C4
  Stalisfield Green ME13 . 201 F5
  Stone DA9 . . . . 16 F1
  Sundridge TN14 . . . . . 152 E2
  Sutton at Hone DA4 . . . 34 A2
  Sutton Valence ME17 . . 229 C8
  Swanley Village BR8 . . . 56 D8
  Swanscombe DA10 . . . . 17 F1

Church Rd continued
  Tenterden TN30 . . . . . 345 A7
  Tilbury RM18 . . . . 18 F6
  Tonbridge TN11 . . . . . . 221 D6
  West Kingsdown TN15 . . 90 E3
  West Peckham ME8 . . . 191 A6
  West Tilbury RM18 . . . . 19 E8
Church Road Bsns Ctr
  ME10 . . . . 102 B6
Church Row
  Chislehurst BR7 . . . . . . 53 C8
  Plaxtol TN15 . . . . 189 E8
  Snodland ME6 . . . . 128 A7
  West Peckham ME18 . . 191 B6
Church Row Mews BR7 30 C1
Church St (St Pauls) ■
  CT1 . . . . 175 A8
Churchsettle La TN5 . . 337 C1
Churchside DA13 . . . . . 126 A8
Churchside Cl TN16 . . . 118 C2
Church Sq
  ■ Broadstairs CT10 . . . 84 B4
  Lenham ME17 . . . . 199 D5
Church St
  Broadstairs CT10 . . . . . 83 C6
  Burham ME1 . . . . 95 F1
  Canterbury CT2 . . . . . . 142 E1
  Chatham ME4 . . . . 64 A4
  Cliffe ME3 . . . . 22 B5
  Cowden TN8 . . . . 282 B5
  Deal CT14 . . . . 215 B1
  Dover CT16 . . . . 310 D7
  Eastry CT13 . . . . 180 C2
  Edenbridge TN8 . . . . . 217 D1
  Faversham ME13 . . . . . 138 D8
  Folkestone CT20 . . . . . 335 D4
  Gillingham ME7 . . . . . . 64 E6
  ■ Grays RM17 . . . . 18 C8
  Hadlow TN11 . . . . 223 E8
  Hoo St Werburgh ME3 . 41 E5
  Lower Higham ME3 . . . . 39 D7
  Maidstone, Boughton
    Monchelsea ME17 . . 195 B2
  Maidstone, Loose ME15 194 F5
  Maidstone ME14 . . . . . 162 A4
  Maidstone, Tovil ME15 . 161 E2
  Margate CT9 . . . . 50 J1
  Minster (Thanet) CT12 . 115 C5
  Newham E16 . . . . 2 B5
  Nonington CT15 . . . . . 211 C5
  Northfleet DA13 . . . . . . 36 A3
  Rochester ME1 . . . . 63 D4
  Rodmersham ME9 . . . . 135 C8
  ■ Sandwich CT13 . . . . 149 A1
  ■ Sandwich, The Butts
    CT13 . . . . 148 F1
  Seal TN15 . . . . 155 A7
  Shoreham TN14 . . . . . . 122 A8
  ■ Sittingbourne ME10 101 E4
  Sittingbourne ME10 . . 101 E5
  Teston ME18 . . . . 193 A8
  Ticehurst TN5 . . . . 338 D1
  Tonbridge TN9 . . . . . . 222 C2
  Wadhurst TN5 . . . . 337 A4
  Whitstable CT5 . . . . . . 74 F1
  Woodnesborough CT13 180 B6
  Wye TN25 . . . . 237 E2
CHURCH STREET
  Gravesend 21 C1
  Whitstable 74 F1
Church Street
  Hartley DA3 . . . . 59 A1
  New Ash Green DA3 . . . 91 B8
Church Terr
  Chatham ME5 . . . . 64 C2
  Minster (Sheppey) ME12 .47 C7
Church Trad Est DA8 . . . 15 A7
Church View
  Aldington TN25 . . . . . . 330 A6
  Biddenden TN27 . . . . . 294 F2
  ■ Dartford DA1 . . . . . . 15 E1
  Herne Bay CT6 . . . . 77 C4
  Newchurch TN29 . . . . . 350 E3
  Swanley BR8 . . . . 55 D6
  Worth CT14 . . . . 181 B5
Church Way CT5 . . . . . . 75 D3
CHURCH WHITFIELD 278 B8
Church Whitfield Rd
  CT16 . . . . 278 B8
Church Wlk
  Dartford DA2 . . . . 33 D5
  East Malling ME19 . . . . 160 A7
  Elham CT4 . . . . 273 F4
  Eynsford DA4 . . . . 89 E7
  Gravesend DA12 . . . . . 37 D7
  Hawkhurst TN18 . . . . . 341 A1
Church Wood Cl CT2 . . 142 B2
Churchwood Dr CT5 . . . 75 D1
Churchyard Cotts TN3 285 A8
Churchyard Pas 10
  TN23 . . . . 268 B2
Church Yd 4 TN23 . . . 268 C2
Churn La TN12 . . . . . . 258 A2
Chute Cl ME8 . . . . 98 D4
Chyngton DA15 . . . . . . 30 F5
**Cicero Languages
  International** 2 TN4. 286 B5
Cimba Wood DA12 . . . . 37 E4
CINDER HILL 252 C8
Cinder Hill La TN11 . . . 252 C7
Cinderhill Wood TN12 256 C2
Cinderhill Wood Cvn Site
  TN12 . . . . 256 C1
Cinder Path CT10 . . . . . 84 A4
Cinnabar Cl ME5 . . . . . . 97 A1
Cinnabar Dr ME10 . . . . 101 C6
Cinnamon Gr ME16 . . . 161 A3
Cinque Ports Ave
  CT21 . . . . 333 B1
Cinque Ports Rd TN28 373 C5
Circle The RM18 . . . . . . 19 A6
Circular Rd Dover CT16 279 B1
  Finglesham CT14 . . . . . 214 B7
Circular Way SE18 . . . . 12 A8

Circus The CT6 . . . . 76 E4
Cirrus Cres DA12 . . . . . 37 E3
Citadel Cres CT17 . . . . 310 B6
Citadel Hts CT17 . . . . . 310 B6
Citadel Rd CT17 . . . . . . 310 B6
**Citadel The (Immigration
  Removal Ctr)** CT17 . . 310 B5
Citroen CT1 . . . . 76 B4
City Bsns Pk CT1 . . . . . 143 C3
City Garden The 3
  CT1 . . . . 175 A8
City View CT2 . . . . 174 C8
City Way ME1 . . . . 63 D2
Civic Sq RM18 . . . . 19 A5
Civic Way TN1 . . . . 286 A5
CJ Gallards Almshouses
  TN4 . . . . 286 A8
Clacket La
  Tatsfield TN16 . . . . 150 E2
  Westerham TN16 . . . . . 184 A8
Clacketts Farm ME19 . . 127 B5
Claire Ct Birchington CT7 80 F7
  Broadstairs CT10 . . . . . 84 B5
Claire Ho 4 ME16 . . . . 161 C8
Clancy Gdns TN17 . . . . 320 B5
Clandon Cl BR1 . . . . 29 A2
Clandon Rd ME5 . . . . . . 97 D2
Clanricarde Gdns 1
  TN1 . . . . 286 A3
Clanricarde Rd 2 TN1 286 A3
Clanwilliam Rd CT14 . . 215 D5
CLAPHAM HILL 108 D5
Clapham Hill CT5 . . . . . 108 D5
Claphatch La TN5 . . . . 338 A5
CLAP HILL 329 F7
Clapper Hill CT14 . . . . 240 B3
Clapper La TN12 . . . . . 260 D6
Clara Pl SE18 . . . . 2 A2
Clare Ave TN9 . . . . 221 F1
Clare Cnr SE9 . . . . 30 B8
Clare Ct BR7 . . . . 52 F8
Clare Dr CT6 . . . . 76 C2
Clare La ME19 . . . . 159 E8
Claremont Cl
  Kingsdown CT14 . . . . . 248 C6
  Newham E16 . . . . 2 A5
  Orpington BR6 . . . . 86 A6
Claremont Cres DA1 . . . 14 E3
Claremont Ct 4 TN2 . 286 C7
Claremont Gdns
  Ramsgate CT11 . . . . . . 117 C7
  Royal Tunbridge Wells
    TN2 . . . . 286 B2
Claremont Pl
  Canterbury CT1 . . . . . . 174 F7
  ■ Gravesend DA11 . . . . 37 B8
  Iden Green TN17 . . . . . 342 C4
  Marden TN12 . . . . 259 D4
Claremont Prim Sch
  TN2 . . . . 286 B2
Claremont Rd
  Bromley BR1 . . . . 52 F5
  Deal CT14 . . . . 215 B5
  Folkestone CT20 . . . . . 335 C5
  Hextable BR8 . . . . 32 E1
  Kingsdown CT14 . . . . . 248 C6
  Maidstone ME14 . . . . . 162 B5
  Royal Tunbridge Wells
    TN1 . . . . 286 B2
Claremont St
  Herne Bay CT6 . . . . 76 C4
  Newham E16 . . . . 2 A4
Claremont Terr CT13 . 180 D7
Claremont Way 2 ME4 63 F3
Clarence Ave
  Bromley BR1 . . . . 52 E5
  Margate CT9 . . . . 51 D2
  Rochester ME1 . . . . 63 C4
Clarence Cres DA14 . . . 31 B5
Clarence Ct
  2 Grays RM17 . . . . 18 B8
  Maidstone ME14 . . . . . 162 E4
  Sidcup CT BR6 . . . . 87 C2
Clarence Gdns ME12 . . 49 E3
Clarence Lodge TN1 . . 286 A3
Clarence Pl Deal CT14 . 215 D7
  Dover CT17 . . . . 310 D5
  Gravesend DA12 . . . . . 37 B7
Clarence Rd Bexley DA6 13 B5
  Biggin Hill TN16 . . . . . 118 F1
  Bromley, Mottingham SE9 29 E6
  Bromley, Widmore BR1 . 52 E6
  Capel-le-Ferne CT18 . . 308 B2
  Chatham ME4 . . . . 64 B2
  Deal CT14 . . . . 215 D3
  Grays RM17 . . . . 18 B8
  Herne Bay CT6 . . . . 76 D5
  Ramsgate CT11 . . . . . . 117 C6
  Royal Tunbridge Wells
    TN1 . . . . 286 A3
  Sidcup DA14 . . . . 31 B5
Clarence Row
  Gravesend DA12 . . . . . 37 B8
  Royal Tunbridge Wells
    TN1 . . . . 286 A3
  Sheerness ME12 . . . . . 28 B2
Clarence St
  Folkestone CT20 . . . . . 335 D5
  Herne Bay CT6 . . . . 76 E5
CLARENDON 310 B6
Clarendon Cl
  Maidstone ME14 . . . . . 163 A4
  Orpington BR5 . . . . 54 A6
  Sittingbourne ME10 . . 101 F1
Clarendon Ct TN13 . . . 154 A2
Clarendon Dr ME2 . . . . 40 A1
Clarendon Gdns
  Dartford DA2 . . . . 34 D8
  ■ Ramsgate CT11 . . . . 117 D6
  Royal Tunbridge Wells
    TN2 . . . . 286 A1
Clarendon Gn BR5 . . . . 54 A5
Clarendon Gr BR5 . . . . 54 A5

**Clarendon House Gram
  Sch** 15 CT11 . . . . 117 E6
Clarendon Mews
  ■ Broadstairs CT10 . . . 84 A4
  New Romney TN28 . . . . 373 C8
  Sidcup DA5 . . . . 32 B7
Clarendon Path BR5 . . . 54 A6
Clarendon Pl
  Dover CT17 . . . . 310 C7
  Joyden's Wood DA2 . . . 32 E3
  Maidstone ME14 . . . . . 162 A4
  Sevenoaks TN13 . . . . . 154 A2
Clarendon Rd
  Aylesham CT3 . . . . 210 F5
  Broadstairs CT10 . . . . . 84 A4
  Dover CT17 . . . . 310 C7
  Gravesend DA12 . . . . . 19 C1
  Margate CT9 . . . . 51 A2
  Sevenoaks TN13 . . . . . 154 A2
Clarendon St
  Dover CT17 . . . . 310 C7
  Herne Bay CT6 . . . . 76 C4
Clarendon Way
  Royal Tunbridge Wells
    TN2 . . . . 286 A1
  St Paul's Cray BR5, BR7 . 53 C1
Clare Rd CT5 . . . . 74 E2
Claret Ho TN13 . . . . . . 154 B3
Clareville Rd BR5 . . . . . 86 C8
Clare Way Bexley DA7 . . 13 E6
  Sevenoaks TN13 . . . . . 187 C8
Clarewood Dr ME19 . . . 159 E8
Claridge TN1 . . . . 286 B6
Claridge Ct ME7 . . . . . . 97 F4
Claridge Ct ME7 . . . . . . 97 F4
Claridge Mews CT21 . . 333 C2
Clarkbourne Dr RM17 . . 18 D8
Clark Cl DA8 . . . . 15 A6
Clarke Cres TN24 . . . . . 268 F4
Clarke's Cl CT14 . . . . . . 214 F4
Clarkes Green Rd
  TN15 . . . . 123 B5
Clarklands TN29 . . . . . 350 E3
Clark Mews ME20 . . . . 128 F1
Clark Rd TN28 . . . . 373 E4
Clarks La
  Halstead TN14 . . . . . . 120 F7
  Titsey CR6, RH8, TN16 . 150 C4
Clarks Yard TN5 . . . . . . 339 A3
Clark's Yd TN5 . . . . 339 A3
Claston Cl DA1 . . . . 14 E3
Claudius Gr TN23 . . . . . 299 F5
Clavadal Rd TN12 . . . . 257 A7
Clavell Cl ME18 . . . . 98 E4
Claxfield Cotts ME9 . . . 103 A2
Claxfield Rd ME9 . . . . . 136 A8
Claybridge Rd SE12 . . . 29 C4
Clay Cotts TN17 . . . . . . 318 E8
Claydon Mews SE18 . . . . 2 A1
Clayfarm Rd SE9 . . . . . . 30 C6
CLAYGATE 258 D6
Claygate Ashford TN23 . 299 F5
  Eyhorne Street ME17 . . 164 D2
Claygate Cross TN15 . . 157 A3
Claygate La TN11 . . . . 189 F4
Claygate Rd TN12 . . . . 226 B2
Clayhill TN17 . . . . 318 D8
Clayhill Cres SE9 . . . . . . 29 D4
Clay Hill Mount TN17 . 318 E8
Clay Hill Rd TN3 . . . . . . 316 D6
Claymill Ho 2 SE18 . . . . 2 C1
Clayton Cl 3 E6 . . . . 1 F7
Clayton Croft Rd DA2 . . 33 A6
Clayton's La TN3 . . . . . 283 E2
Claytonville Terr DA17 . . 4 C4
Clay Wood Cl BR6 . . . . . 53 E2
Clayworth Cl DA15 . . . . 13 B1
Cleanthus Cl SE18 . . . . 12 B6
Cleanthus Rd SE18 . . . . 12 B6
Clearheart Lane ME19 159 D3
Clearmont Way CT3 . . . 112 A1
Clearmount Dr TN27 . . 234 C8
Clearmount Pk TN27 . . 234 D8
Clearway ME1 . . . . 126 A1
Clearways Bsns Est
  TN15 . . . . 90 E3
**Clearways Mobile Home
  Pk** SE12 . . . . 90 D3
Cleave Ave BR6 . . . . 86 E4
Cleave Rd ME7 . . . . 64 E3
Cleaver La CT11 . . . . . . 117 E7
Cleavers TN17 . . . . 321 A8
Cleavers Cl TN17 . . . . . 321 A8
Cleavesland ME18 . . . . 225 E5
Cleeve Ave TN2 . . . . . . 286 D2
Cleeve Ct ME10 . . . . . . 101 E8
Cleeve Park Gdns DA14 31 B6
Cleeve Park Sch DA14 . 31 C5
Clegg Ho SE3 . . . . 11 B3
Clematis Ave ME8 . . . . . 98 B5
Clemens Pl ME7 . . . . . . 159 C2
Clement Cl
  Canterbury CT1 . . . . . . 143 B1
  Sittingbourne ME10 . . 101 E8
Clement Ct ME5 . . . . . . 161 D5
Clementine Cl CT6 . . . . 77 D4
Clements Ave E16 . . . . . 1 A6
Clement's Rd CT12 . . . . 83 C2
Clement St BR8, DA4 . . . 33 E2
CLEMENT STREET 33 D2
Cleminson Ct DA14 . . . 31 D2
Clenches Farm La
  TN13 . . . . 154 A1
Clenches Farm Rd
  TN13 . . . . 154 A1
Clendon Way SE18 . . . . . 2 D2
Clerke Dr ME10 . . . . . . 102 A8
Clerks Field TN27 . . . . . 262 D5
Clermont Cl ME7 . . . . . 98 A4
Clevedon Cl TN25 . . . . . 203 B2
Clevedon Ho BR1 . . . . . 29 E1
Cleveland TN2 . . . . 286 D4
Cleveland Cl CT16 . . . . 278 B3

Cleveland Ct CT9 . . . . . 51 A3
Cleveland Ho
  Maidstone ME16 . . . . . 161 B2
  ■ Northfleet DA11 . . . . 18 D1
Cleveland Rd
  Bexley DA16 . . . . 12 F5
  Gillingham ME7 . . . . . . 64 D6
Cleveley Lo CT11 . . . . . 83 E2
Clevely Cl ME7 . . . . 1 C2
Cleven Lodge CT7 . . . . 113 D6
Cleve Rd DA14 . . . . 31 D5
Cleves Rd TN15 . . . . . . 122 E2
Cleves View 4 DA1 . . . . 15 D1
Cleves Way TN23 . . . . . 299 E8
Clewer Ho 8 SE2 . . . . . . 3 D4
Clewer Lo CT5 . . . . 74 F2
Clewson Rise ME14 . . . 162 B8
Cliff Ave CT6 . . . . 77 C5
Cliff Cl CT21 . . . . 333 D3
Cliff Dr Herne Bay CT6 . . 76 C4
  Warden ME12 . . . . 49 E4
CLIFFE 22 B5
Cliffe Ave CT9 . . . . 50 F1
Cliffe Ct ME3 . . . . 22 B5
Cliffe Ho
  Folkestone CT20 . . . . . 335 A3
  St Margaret's at Cliffe
    CT15 . . . . 279 F6
**Cliffe Pools Nature
  Reserve**★ ME3 . . . . 5 E1
Cliffe Rd Deal CT14 . . . 248 D6
  Rochester ME2 . . . . 40 A1
  Rochester ME2 . . . . 63 B8
Cliffestone Ct CT20 . . . 335 B5
CLIFFE WOODS 40 B7
Cliffe Woods Cty Prim Sch
  ME3 . . . . 40 C8
Cliff Field CT8 . . . . 81 C8
Cliff Gdns ME12 . . . . . . 47 E7
Cliff Hill ME17 . . . . 195 D4
Cliff Hill Rd ME17 . . . . 195 C4
Clifford Ave BR7 . . . . . . 29 F2
Clifford Gdns CT14 . . . 215 B2
Clifford Ho 6 ME14 . . . 162 A4
Clifford Rd CT5 . . . . . . 108 F8
Clifford Way ME15 . . . . 161 E2
Cliff Prom CT10 . . . . . . 84 C7
Cliff Rd Birchington CT7 . 80 F8
  Broadstairs CT10 . . . . . 84 B7
  Dover CT15, CT16 . . . . 279 C1
  Folkestone CT20 . . . . . 335 A3
  Hythe CT21 . . . . 333 E3
  Whitstable CT5 . . . . . . 74 F3
Cliff Reach DA9 . . . . . . 16 F1
Cliff Sea Gr CT6 . . . . . . 76 C4
CLIFFS END 116 D6
Cliffs End Gr CT12 . . . . 116 D5
Cliffs End Rd CT12 . . . . 116 E5
Cliffside Dr CT10 . . . . . 84 A1
Cliff St CT11 . . . . 117 E6
Cliff Terr CT9 . . . . 50 J3
Clifftown Gdns CT6 . . . 76 B4
Cliff View Gdns
  Leysdown-on-Sea
    ME12 . . . . 49 D1
  Warden ME12 . . . . 49 E4
Cliff View Rd CT12 . . . . 116 D6
Clifton Cl
  Maidstone ME14 . . . . . 162 B5
  8 Orpington BR6 . . . . . 86 C5
  Rochester ME2 . . . . 62 F7
Clifton Cotts TN12 . . . . 286 D8
Clifton Cres CT20 . . . . . 335 B3
Clifton Gdns
  Canterbury CT2 . . . . . . 142 D2
  Folkestone CT20 . . . . . 335 C4
  Margate CT9 . . . . 50 J3
  Whitstable CT5 . . . . . . 108 D8
Clifton Gr DA11 . . . . . . 37 B8
Clifton Lawn CT11 . . . . 117 D5
Clifton Mans 7 CT20 . . 335 C4
Clifton Marine Par
  DA11 . . . . 18 F1
Clifton Pl Margate CT9 . 51 A3
  Royal Tunbridge Wells
    TN1 . . . . 286 B2
Clifton Rd Bexley DA16 . 13 C4
  Folkestone CT20 . . . . . 335 C4
  Gillingham ME7 . . . . . . 64 C7
  Gravesend DA11 . . . . . 19 A1
  Margate CT9 . . . . 51 A2
  Ramsgate CT11 . . . . . . 117 B8
  Royal Tunbridge Wells
    TN2 . . . . 286 C2
  Sidcup DA14 . . . . 30 E4
  Whitstable CT5 . . . . . . 74 D1
Clifton St CT9 . . . . 50 J3
CLIFTONVILLE 51 D2
Cliftonville Ave
  Margate CT9 . . . . 51 A2
  Ramsgate CT12 . . . . . . 83 B1
Cliftonville Ct
  Lewisham SE12 . . . . . . 29 A7
  Margate, Cliftonville CT9 51 B3
  Margate CT9 . . . . 51 A3
Cliftonville Prim Sch
  CT9 . . . . 51 C2
Clim Down CT14 . . . . . 248 D6
Clinch Cl 15 E16 . . . . 1 A8
Clinch St ME3 . . . . 24 A4
Clinton Ave Bexley DA16 13 A3
  Rochester ME2 . . . . 62 A1
Clinton Bsns Ctr TN12 260 E5
Clinton Cl ME17 . . . . . . 194 B3
Clinton La TN8 . . . . 218 E3
Clints La CT4 . . . . 243 D4
Clipper Bvd DA9 . . . . . . 16 E3
Clipper Bvd W DA2 . . . . 16 D4
Clipper Cl ME2 . . . . 63 E7
Clipper Cres DA12 . . . . 37 C4
Clipper Ct ME2 . . . . 63 E7

Clive Dennis Ct TN24 . . 268 E1
Clivedon Court TN3 . . . 317 B5
Clive Ho ME20 . . . . 160 F8
Clive Rd Cliffs End CT12 116 D6
  Erith DA17 . . . . 4 A2
  Gravesend DA11 . . . . . 19 B1
  Margate CT9 . . . . 83 A5
  Rochester ME1 . . . . 63 C3
  Sittingbourne ME10 . . 101 B5
Clock Ho The DA15 . . . 31 A7
Clockhouse
  Ashford TN23 . . . . 267 F1
  Royal Tunbridge Wells
    TN2 . . . . 286 F6
Clock House La TN13 . . 154 A4
Clockhouse Pk TN25 . . 203 C2
Clock House Rise
  ME17 . . . . 194 C2
Clock Tower★ CT9 . . . . . 50 J3
Clock Tower Mews
  Snodland ME6 . . . . 95 A1
  Woolwich SE28 . . . . 3 B6
Clocktower Par CT2 . . 142 A6
Cloisterham Rd ME1 . . . 96 D7
Cloisters Ave BR2 . . . . . 52 F4
Cloisters Ct DA7 . . . . . . 14 B4
Cloisters The
  18 Canterbury CT1 . . . 142 F1
  ■ Dartford DA1 . . . . . . 15 E1
  Lenham ME17 . . . . 199 C5
  Ramsgate CT11 . . . . . . 117 D5
  8 Sittingbourne ME10 101 E4
  Whitstable CT5 . . . . . . 74 F2
Cloke Mews 4 TN15 . . 156 F7
Cloonmore Ave BR6 . . . 86 F6
Clopton Ct ME8 . . . . 98 D8
Close The
  Addington ME19 . . . . . 126 C2
  Ashford TN23 . . . . 299 F7
  Birling ME19 . . . . 127 B5
  Borough Green TN15 . . 157 A8
  Bough Beech TN8 . . . . 219 A2
  Bridge CT4 . . . . 175 F1
  Canterbury CT1 . . . . . . 174 D6
  Canterbury, Hales Place
    CT2 . . . . 142 F4
  Canterbury, St Dunstan's
    CT2 . . . . 142 C3
  Cudham TN16 . . . . 119 B3
  Dartford DA2 . . . . 33 D5
  Faversham ME13 . . . . . 138 C6
  Folkestone CT19 . . . . . 335 E6
  Groombridge TN3 . . . . 312 C6
  Hythe CT21 . . . . 333 B4
  Ightham TN15 . . . . 156 D6
  Lydden CT15 . . . . 276 F8
  New Barn DA3 . . . . 59 B7
  Orpington BR5 . . . . 53 E3
  Rochester ME1 . . . . 63 C4
  Royal Tunbridge Wells
    TN2 . . . . 286 C8
  Sevenoaks TN13 . . . . . 153 E3
  Sidcup DA14 . . . . 31 B3
  ■ Sidcup, Old Bexley
    DA5 . . . . 32 A8
  Wye TN25 . . . . 237 E2
Cloth Hall Gdns TN27 . 295 A2
Clothier Ho SE7 . . . . 1 E1
Clothworkers Rd SE18 . 12 D7
Cloudberry Cl ME1 . . . . 161 D6
Cloudesley Cl ME1 . . . . 63 B1
Cloudesley Close 9
  DA14 . . . . 30 F4
Cloudesley Rd
  Bexley DA7 . . . . 13 F6
  Erith DA8 . . . . 14 F6
Clouston Cl CT18 . . . . . 307 B5
Clovelly TN28 . . . . 373 E6
Clovelly Dr ME12 . . . . . 47 B8
Clovelly Rd Bexley DA7 . 13 E8
  Whitstable CT5 . . . . . . 108 D7
Clovelly Way BR6 . . . . . 53 F3
Clover Bank View ME5 . 97 B6
Clover Cl ME12 . . . . 49 E3
Clover Ct 12 Grays RM17 18 D8
  Sittingbourne ME10 . . 102 B5
Cloverdale Gdns DA15 . 12 F1
Clover Lay ME5 . . . . 66 B2
Cloverlay Ind Pk ME8 . 66 C1
Clover Rd ME3 . . . . 41 E3
Clover Rise CT5 . . . . . . 75 B1
Clover St 3 ME4 . . . . . . 63 F4
Clovers The DA11 . . . . . 18 B2
Clover Terr 4 ME15 . . 195 D8
Clover Way TN12 . . . . . 257 A5
Clover Wlk 13 TN8 . . . 217 D3
Clowes Ct CT2 . . . . 142 C4
Clubb's La TN29 . . . . . 370 D7
Club Cotts TN11 . . . . . 221 C8
Club Gardens Rd BR2 . . 52 A2
Cluny Rd ME13 . . . . . . 138 F7
Clyde Rd TN10 . . . . 222 C6
Clydesdale Ho DA18 . . . . 3 E4
Clyde St
  ■ Canterbury CT1 . . . . 143 A1
  Sheerness ME12 . . . . . 28 C2
Clydon Cl DA8 . . . . 14 E8
Clynton Way TN23 . . . . 300 A7
**C M Booth Collection of
  Historic Vehicles (Mus)**★
  TN17 . . . . 343 C4
Coach Dr TN26 . . . . . . 267 E7
Coach Dr The DA13 . . . 125 E7
Coach & Horses Pas 18
  TN2 . . . . 286 A2
Coach House Mews 8
  BR1 . . . . 52 A6
Coach House Mews The
  CT15 . . . . 245 D5
Coach Rd
  Charing Heath TN27 . . 233 A6
  Densole CT18 . . . . 306 F8
  Egerton ME17, TN27 . . 232 C6
  Ightham TN15 . . . . 156 B2

Coach Rd *continued*
Rusthall TN4 . . . . . . 285 C3
Coach Yd The ME16 . .161 B3
Coal Ct RM17 . . . . .18 A8
Coalhouse Fort★ RM18 20 E6
Coalpit La ME9 . . . . . .167 A6
Coal Post Cl 10 BR6 . . .86 F4
Coast Dr
Greatstone-on-Sea
TN28 . . . . .373 C3
Lydd-on-Sea TN29 . .380 D8
St Mary's Bay TN29 . .365 F2
Coastguard Alley CT5 . .74 C1
Coastguard Cotts
Birchington CT7 . . . . . .80 D8
Conyer ME9 . . . . . . .103 E6
Dover CT16 . . . . . . .310 G8
Grain ME3 . . . . .27 B5
Herne Bay CT6 . . . . . .75 F4
4 Hythe CT21 . . . . .333 B1
Kingsdown CT14 . . . .248 D4
Leysdown-on-Sea ME12 . .73 E4
Lydd-on-Sea TN29 . .380 D5
Minster (Sheppey) ME12 .48 C5
23 Ramsgate, East Cliff
CT11 . . . . .117 F7
Ramsgate, Pegwell
CT11 . . . . .117 A5
Sandwich CT13 . . . . .182 A8
Coastguard Cotts The
ME12 . . . . .28 H1
Coastguard Hos ME12 . .49 C1
Coast Rd TN28 . . . . . .373 F7
Coates Hill Rd BR1 . . . .53 A7
Coats Ave ME12 . . . . . .46 A8
Cobay Cl CT21 . . . . . .333 D2
COBBARN 312 F3
Cobb Cl ME2 . . . . .62 D8
Cobb Ct ME4 . . . . .50 I3
Cobbets Way TN8 . . . .249 C8
Cobbett Rd ME19 . . . . .159 F8
Cobbett Rd SE9 . . . . . .11 E4
Cobbett's Ride TN2 . . .285 C1
Cobblers Bridge Rd
CT6 . . . . .76 D3
Cobblestones ME7 . . . .97 F5
Cobbs Cl
Paddock Wood TN12 . .256 F6
Wateringbury ME18 . . .192 E7
Cobbs Hill CT4 . . . . . .172 C2
Cobbs Mews 3 CT20 . .335 C4
Cobbs Pl CT9 . . . . .50 I3
Cobbs Wood Ind Est
TN23 . . . . .267 F2
Cobb Wlk ME13 . . . . . .138 B8
Cobden Ct Bromley BR2 . .52 C5
9 Woolwich SE28 . . . .3 C5
Cobden Pl 17 CT1 . . . .143 A1
Cobden Rd
4 Chatham ME4 . . . . .64 B2
Hythe CT21 . . . . . . .333 B1
Orpington BR6 . . . . . .86 D6
Sevenoaks TN13 . . . .154 C4
Cobdown Cl ME20 . . . .128 C2
Cobdown Gr ME8 . . . . . .66 A2
Cob Dr DA12 . . . . .38 E3
Cobfield ME17 . . . . . . .196 A1
COBHAM 60 F6
Cobham Ave ME10 . . . .101 E1
Cobhambury Rd DA12 . .61 B4
Cobham Chase ME13 . .138 B8
Cobham Cl Bromley BR2 . .52 C2
Canterbury CT1 . . . . .175 C6
Maidstone ME16 . . . .161 E4
Rochester ME2 . . . . . .62 E7
2 Sidcup DA15 . . . . .13 B1
Swanscombe DA9 . . . .17 B1
Cobham Coll★ DA12 . . .60 F5
Cobham Ct ME19 . . . . .159 C3
Cobham Hall Sch DA12 .61 C6
Cobham Ho 4 DA8 . . . .14 F7
Cobham Pl DA6 . . . . . . .13 D2
Cobham Prim Sch DA12 61 A5
Cobham Rise ME7 . . . . .64 F5
Cobhams TN3 . . . . . . .285 A8
Cobham Terr DA9 . . . . .17 E1
Cobland Rd SE12 . . . . .29 C4
Cobs CT15 . . . . .156 C6
Cobsden Cl TN29 . . . . .366 A4
Cobsdene DA12 . . . . . . .37 D2
Cobsden Rd TN29 . . . . .366 A4
Cobtree Cl ME5 . . . . . . .97 C8
Cobtree Rd ME17 . . . . .194 C3
Cobtree Wharf ME20 . .129 C2
Cobweb Cnr 142 B4
Cochraine Drive DA1 . .15 D1
Cockerhurst Rd TN14 . .88 E2
Cockering Rd
Canterbury CT1, CT4 . .174 B4
Chartham CT4 . . . . . .173 E2
Cock La Elham CT4 . . . .273 F4
Hamstreet TN26 . . . . .349 A7
Cockmannings La BR5 . .54 E1
Cockmannings Rd BR5 .54 D2
Cockmount La TN5 . . . .336 F5
Cockpit The TN12 . . . .259 C8
Cockreed La TN28 . . . .373 B7
Cocksett Ave BR6 . . . . .86 E4
COCKSHOT 340 F1
Cock St ME17 . . . . . . .195 D2
COCK STREET 195 D2
Cocksure La DA14 . . . . .32 A4
Coddown Sports Club
ME20 . . . . .128 C2
Codrington Cres DA12 .37 D3
Codrington Gdns DA12 .37 D3
Codrington Rd CT11 . . .117 D7
Coe's Green ME3 . . . . . .41 A4
Cogans Terr CT1 . . . . .174 E6
Cogate Rd TN12 . . . . .256 E6
Coggan Ho 7 CT1 . . . .174 F7
Cokers Yd TN4 . . . . . . .254 A1
Colburn Rd CT10 . . . . . .84 A2

Colchester Cl ME5 . . . . . .97 A7
Cold Arbor Rd TN13 . . .153 D3
COLDBLOW 32 D7
Coldblow Cl CT14 . . . . .215 A1
Cold Blow Cres DA5 . . . .32 C7
Coldblow La
Hucking ME14 . . . . . .132 A2
Woodchurch TN26 . . . .326 D4
Coldbridge La TN27 . . .232 B5
COLDHARBOUR 188 F1
Cold Harbour
Lenham 200 F6
Sittingbourne 100 F6
Cold Harbour CT1 . . . .143 A2
Coldharbour Crest SE9 30 A5
Coldharbour La
Bridge CT4, CT3 . . . . .209 D7
Forstal ME20 . . . . . . .129 A1
Hastingleigh TN25 . . . .271 A6
Hucking ME14, ME9 . . .132 B1
Old Romney TN29 . . . .371 C5
Peasmarsh TN31 . . . . .367 E3
Rainham RM13 . . . . . . .4 F6
Shipbourne TN11 . . . .189 A2
Sittingbourne ME10 . . . .68 F1
Sittingbourne ME10 . . . .69 A1
Tonbridge TN11 . . . . .221 E7
Wye TN25 . . . . .238 B2
Cold Harbour La ME3 . .100 F6
Coldharbour L Ctr SE9 . .29 F6
Coldharbour Rd
Ashurst TN8, TN11 . . .283 E8
Gravesend DA11 . . . . . .37 A4
Iden Green TN17 . . . . .342 B4
Northfleet DA11 . . . . . .36 F5
Cold Harbour Rd
ME13 . . . . .201 A7
COLDRED 245 A3
Coldred Hill CT15 . . . .244 F1
Coldred Rd
Coldred CT15 . . . . . .245 B5
Maidstone ME15 . . . . .195 F4
Shepherdswell CT15 . .244 B3
COLDRED STREET 245 A2
Coldrum La ME19 . . . . .126 C6
Coldrum Long Barrow★
ME19 . . . . .126 C6
Coldshott RH8 . . . . . . .183 A2
Coldswood Rd CT12 . . . .82 F2
Colebrooke Ct DA14 . . . .31 B4
Colebrook Ind Est TN2 254 E1
Colebrook St ME4 . . . . .286 C8
Colebrook St 1 DA8 . . .14 F8
Cole Cl SE28 . . . . .3 B5
Colegate Dr ME14 . . . .163 C4
Colegates Cl ME13 . . . .105 B2
Colegates Ct ME13 . . . .105 B2
Colegates Rd ME13 . . . .105 A2
Coleman Cres CT1 . . . . .83 C1
Coleman Dr ME10 . . . . .68 F1
Coleman Rd DA17 . . . . . .4 A2
Colemans TN29 . . . . . .376 D7
Colemans Heath SE9 . . .30 B5
Coleman's Stairs Rd
CT7 . . . . .79 B8
Coleman's Yd 3 CT11 117 C6
Colepits Wood Rd SE9 . .12 D2
Coleraine Rd 1 SE3 . . . .11 A8
Cole Rd ME13 . . . . . . .138 E7
Coleridge Cl 4 ME20 . .127 F4
Coleridge Gdns CT3 . . .210 F6
Coleridge Rd
Dartford DA1 . . . . . . .16 B3
Tilbury RM18 . . . . . . .19 C5
Coleridge Way BR6 . . . .54 A3
Coles Ct TN2 . . . . .286 C3
Colesdane ME17 . . . . . .198 E8
Coleshall Cl ME5 . . . . . .195 F6
Coleshall Cotts ME9 . . . .68 D3
Coles La TN16 . . . . . . .152 C4
Cole Terr ME17 . . . . . .199 C4
Colets Orch TN14 . . . . .122 B3
Colette Ct CT10 . . . . . . .51 G2
Coleville Cres TN8 . . . .377 E7
Colewood Dr ME2 . . . . . .62 B8
Colewood Rd CT5 . . . . . .75 E3
Colfe's Sch SE12 . . . . . .11 B1
Colfe Way ME10 . . . . . .102 A8
Colin Blythe Rd TN11 222 F5
Colin Chapman Way
DA3 . . . . .90 C6
Colin Cl DA2 . . . . .16 B1
Colin's Way CT21 . . . . .334 A3
Collard Cl CT6 . . . . .77 A4
Collard Ho CT1 . . . . . .175 C8
Collard Pl CT18 . . . . . .307 A5
Collard Rd TN24 . . . . . .301 A8
Collards Cl CT12 . . . . .114 C7
Collards La CT4 . . . . . .273 E3
Collar Makers Gn CT3 .147 F1
College Ave
Gillingham ME7 . . . . . .64 B4
Maidstone ME15 . . . .161 F3
Tonbridge TN9 . . . . . .254 A7
College Cotts ME16 . . .161 F3
College Ct
6 Ashford TN23 . . . .268 C2
Canterbury CT1 . . . . .143 B1
6 Maidstone ME15 . .162 A3
College Dr TN2 . . . . . .286 D4
College Gdns CT8 . . . . .81 B8
College Gn 10 BR1 . . . .52 A8
College Pl 10 DA9 . . . . .17 C3
College Rd Bromley BR1 .29 A1
Canterbury CT1 . . . . .143 B1
Chatham ME4 . . . . . . .64 A2
Deal CT14 . . . . .215 D8
Hextable BR8 . . . . . . .32 F1
Maidstone ME15 . . . .161 F2
Margate CT9 . . . . .51 A1
New Hythe ME20 . . . .128 B3
Northfleet DA11 . . . . . .18 B2
Ramsgate CT11 . . . . . .83 E1
Sittingbourne ME10 . . .101 D3

College Row CT17 . . . .310 B7
College Sq 2 CT5 . . . . . .50 J2
College Square Sh Ctr
CT9 . . . . .50 J2
College View SE9 . . . . . .29 D7
College Way CT3 . . . . . .178 A7
College Wlk
4 Maidstone ME15 . .162 A3
3 Margate CT9 . . . . .50 J1
College Yd ME1 . . . . . . .63 C6
Coller Cres DA2 . . . . . . .34 E3
Collett Cl TN15 . . . . . .122 E2
Collett Cl ME25 . . . . . .271 D4
Collett Wlk ME8 . . . . . . .98 D4
Collie Dr TN23 . . . . . . .299 E5
Collier Cl E6 . . . . .2 B6
COLLIERS' GREEN 291 F2
Colliers' Green CE Prim
Sch TN17 . . . . .291 F2
Colliers Shaw BR2 . . . . .85 D5
COLLIER STREET 258 C8
Collindale Ave Erith DA8 14 B8
Sidcup DA15 . . . . . . .31 A2
Collingbourne TN23 . . .299 E6
Collinge Cl ME9 . . . . . .128 A1
Collinge Wlk ME8 . . . . . .98 D4
Collington Cl DA12 . . . .37 B6
Collington Ho 3 SE7 . .11 B8
Collington Terr ME15 . .195 E4
Comp La TN15 . . . . . . .157 E6
Compton Cl ME5 . . . . . .97 D2
Compton Pl DA8 . . . . . .14 F8
Concord Ave ME5 . . . . . .96 E5
Concord Cl
Paddock Wood TN12 . .256 E7
Royal Tunbridge Wells
TN2 . . . . .286 C4
Concorde Bsns Pk
CT16 . . . . .118 D4
Concorde Dr E6 . . . . .1 F8
Concrete Cotts ME3 . . . .21 E4
Condor Cl ME12 . . . . . . .49 E3
Condover Cres SE18 . . .12 B7
Condovers Cotts RM18 . .19 F8
Conduit Ho The★ CT1 143 B1
Conduit Rd SE18 . . . . . . .2 B1
Conduit St ME13 . . . . .138 D8
Coneyburrow Rd TN2 . .286 E5
Coney Mews ME4 . . . . . .64 A1
Conference Rd SE2 . . . . .3 C2
Conference Wlk CT1 . . .175 C8
CONGELOW 225 F7
Conghurst La TN18 . . . .355 B6
Congleton Gr SE18 . . . . .2 C1
Congo Rd SE18 . . . . .2 D1
Congress Rd SE2 . . . . . . .3 C2
Congreve Rd SE9 . . . . .11 F4
Congreve Wlk 6 E16 . . . .1 F8
Conifer Ave DA3 . . . . . . .58 E3
Conifer Cl BR6 . . . . .86 D6
Conifer Ct CT8 . . . . .50 D1
Conifer Dr Chatham ME7 .97 C8
Culverstone Green DA13 .92 F2
Conifers The
Deal CT14 . . . . .215 A2
Shepherdswell CT15 . .244 F2
Conifer Way BR8 . . . . . .55 C8
Conisborough Ct 13
DA2 . . . . .16 B1
Coniscliffe Cl BR7 . . . . .53 A8
Coniston Ave
Bexley DA16 . . . . . . .12 C4
Purfleet RM19 . . . . . .16 C8
Ramsgate CT11 . . . . .117 A7
Royal Tunbridge Wells
TN4 . . . . .285 E5
Coniston Cl Bexley DA7 .14 C6
Dartford DA1 . . . . . . .33 B7
Erith DA8 . . . . .14 E7
Gillingham ME7 . . . . . .65 A6
Coniston Dr CT3 . . . . . .210 F6
Coniston Ho ME15 . . . .195 E4
Coniston Rd Bexley DA7 .14 C6
Folkestone CT19 . . . . .335 B7
Conker Cl TN23 . . . . . .300 C3
Connaught Bridge E16 . .1 D6
Connaught Cl ME15 . . . .195 E4
Connaught Gdns 9 CT9 50 J1
Connaught Mews
2 Chatham ME4 . . . . .64 C2
Woolwich SE18 . . . . . . .2 A1
Connaught Pk★ CT16 278 D1
Connaught Rd
Chatham ME4 . . . . . . .64 C2
Dover CT16 . . . . .278 D1
Folkestone CT20 . . . . .335 D5
Gillingham ME7 . . . . . .64 D5
Margate CT9 . . . . .50 J1
Newham, Silvertown E16 . .1 D5
Sittingbourne ME10 . . .101 E3
Woolwich SE18 . . . . . . .2 B1
Connaught Way TN4 . . .285 F5
Connections Business Park
TN14 . . . . .154 C7
Conqueror Dr ME7 . . . . .65 A6
Conquest Ind Est ME2 . .63 A5
Conrad Ave CT1 . . . . . .143 C3
Conrad Cl ME8 . . . . .98 D4
Consort Cl ME14 . . . . . .162 B5
Constable Ave E16 . . . . . .1 B5
Constable Mews BR1 . . .52 B7
Constable Rd
Birchington CT7 . . . . . .81 A8
Northfleet DA11 . . . . . .36 E5
Tonbridge TN10 . . . . .222 E5
Constable's Rd CT16 . .310 E8
Constance Grove 8
DA1 . . . . .15 D1
Constance St E16 . . . . . .1 E5
Constancia CT20 . . . . .335 C5
Constantine Rd TN23 . .299 F5
Constitutional Hill Rd
TN4 . . . . .253 F1
Constitution Cres DA12 37 B7
Constitution Hill
8 Chatham ME5 . . . . .64 C5
Gravesend DA12 . . . . . .37 C7

Constitution Hill *continued*
Snodland ME6 . . . . . .128 A8
Constitution Rd ME5 . . . .64 B2
Constitution Rise SE18 12 A6
Consul Cl CT6 . . . . .76 B4
Consul Gdns BR8 . . . . . .33 A1
Contessa CT9 . . . . .82 F6
Continental App CT9 . . .82 F6
Convalescent La TN17 292 F2
Convent Cl CT15 . . . . . .280 B6
Conventina Ho 3
CT11 . . . . .117 D7
Convent Rd CT10 . . . . . .51 G1
Convent Wlk CT11 . . . .117 D7
Conway Cl BR5 . . . . .54 C5
Conway Gdns RM17 . . . .18 B7
Conway Hall 16 ME7 . .64 A6
Conway Mews ME7 . . . . .64 A6
Conway Prim Sch 5
SE18 . . . . .2 E2
Conway Rd
Maidstone ME16 . . . .161 C6
Woolwich SE18 . . . . . . .2 E2
CONYER 103 F5
Conyerd Rd TN15 . . . . .156 F6
Conyer Rd ME9 . . . . . . .103 F4
Conyers Wlk ME8 . . . . . .98 D4
Conyngham Cl ME8 . . . . .83 B2
Conyngham La CT4 . . . .176 A2
Conyngham Rd
Herne Bay CT6 . . . . . .77 D5
Minster (Thanet) CT12 . .115 C5
Cooden Cl Bromley BR1 . .29 B1
Gillingham ME8 . . . . . .66 A2
Cook Cl ME5 . . . . .97 C6
Cookham Dene CT7 BR7 .53 D8
Cookham Rd ME1 . . . . . .63 A2
Cookham Rd DA14, BR8 .55 A8
Cookham Wood Rd
ME1 . . . . .96 B8
Cookhill Rd SE2 . . . . .3 B3
Cooks La ME10 . . . . . . .101 F6
Cook's Lea CT13 . . . . . .180 B2
Cookson Gr DA8 . . . . . . .14 B7
Cook Sq DA8 . . . . .14 F7
Cooks Wharf ME1 . . . . . .63 E4
Coolfin Rd E16 . . . . .1 F7
COOLING 22 F5
Cooling Castle★ ME3 . .22 E4
Cooling Cl ME14 . . . . . .162 C6
Cooling Comm ME3 . . . .40 D8
COOLINGE 334 F4
Coolinge La CT20 . . . . .334 F4
Coolinge Rd CT20 . . . . .335 D5
COOLING STREET 22 D2
Cooling St ME3 . . . . .22 D2
COOMBE 179 F8
Coombe Ave TN14 . . . . .154 B7
Coombe Cl Chatham ME5 97 B3
Dover CT17 . . . . .278 A1
Snodland ME6 . . . . . .128 A7
Coombe Ct Dover CT17 278 A1
Sevenoaks TN14 . . . . .154 B7
Coombe Dr
Shepherdswell CT15 . .244 E5
Sittingbourne ME10 . . .102 C4
Coombe Farm La ME3 . .24 E6
Coombe Gr TN26 . . . . .234 F2
Coombe La
Ash CT13, CT3 . . . . . .179 E8
Tenterden TN30 . . . . .348 A7
Coombe Lands TN30 . . .359 D4
Coombe Lea BR1 . . . . . .52 B8
Coombe Lodge SE7 . . . .11 C8
Coombe Rd
Crabble CT17 . . . . . . .277 F2
Dover CT15, CT17 . . . .309 E8
Folkestone CT19 . . . . .334 F6
Gravesend DA12 . . . . . .37 C6
Hoo St Werburgh ME3 . .41 E5
Maidstone ME15 . . . .161 F2
Otford TN14 . . . . . . .122 C4
Coombe Valley Rd
CT17 . . . . .278 A1
Coombe Way TN18 . . . .307 A1
Coombe Wlk CT15 . . . .108 A2
Coombe Wood La
CT18 . . . . .300 D2
Coomb Field TN8 . . . . .249 C8
Coombfield Dr DA2 . . . . .34 B4
Cooper Cl DA9 . . . . .16 F2
Cooper Ct SE18 . . . . . . .12 B8
Cooper Rd Chatham ME5 97 B3
Snodland ME6 . . . . . .127 F6
Coopers Cl DA4 . . . . .57 D8
COOPER'S CORNER . . .218 F8
Coopers Cotts DA4 . . . . .34 A4
Coopers Dr DA2 . . . . . . .32 E6
Cooper Shaw Rd RM18 .19 F7
Cooper's Hill CT6 . . . . . .76 F5
Coopers La
Canterbury CT1 . . . . .174 C7
Lewisham SE12 . . . . . .29 C5
Poundsbridge TN11,
TN3 . . . . .284 C2
Cooper's La TN25 . . . . .302 F2
Coopers Lane Prim Sch
SE12 . . . . .29 C5
Cooper's Rd DA12 . . . . . .37 C7
Coopers Tech Coll BR7 . .53 C8
COOPER STREET 148 C6
Cooper Street Drove
CT3 . . . . .148 B4
Coote Rd DA7 . . . . .13 F6
Cooting La CT3 . . . . . . .210 D8
Cooting Rd CT3 . . . . . . .210 E4
Copenhagen Rd ME7 . . .64 C4

Copinger Cl CT2 . . . . . .143 A4
Copland Ave ME12 . . . . .47 C6
Copley Dene BR1 . . . . . .52 D8
Coppards La TN31 . . . . .357 D1
Copper Beech Cl
Gravesend DA12 . . . . . .37 D8
7 Orpington BR5 . . . . .54 C4
Copper Beech View
TN9 . . . . .254 A8
Copperfield ME12 . . . . . .48 F5
Copperfield Cl
Ashford TN24 . . . . . .268 C6
Chalk DA12 . . . . .38 A7
Kingswood ME17 . . . . .197 D2
Copperfield Cres ME3 . .39 C2
Copperfield Ct
Broadstairs CT10 . . . . .84 B5
Crayford DA1 . . . . . . .14 E2
Copperfield Dr ME17 . .196 C6
Copperfield Ho 6 ME4 .63 F4
Copperfield Rd Erith SE28 3 C4
Rochester ME1 . . . . . .63 C2
Copperfields
2 Dartford DA1 . . . . .15 E1
Kemsing TN15 . . . . . .122 F2
Lydd TN29 . . . . .376 B6
Royal Tunbridge Wells
TN2 . . . . .314 B8
Copperfields Cl TN15 . .122 F2
Copperfields Orch
TN15 . . . . .122 F2
Copperfields Sh Ctr 8
DA1 . . . . .15 E1
Copperfields The ME1 . .63 B4
Copperfields Wlk
TN15 . . . . .122 F2
Copperfield Way BR7 . . .30 C2
Coppergate
Canterbury CT2 . . . . .142 F2
Gillingham ME7 . . . . . .97 F5
Coppergate Cl BR1 . . . . .52 B8
Copperhouse La ME7 . . .65 B6
Copperhouse Rd ME2 . . .62 C7
Copperhurst Wlk CT9 . .51 F2
Copper La TN12 . . . . . .259 E5
Copperpenny Dr ME7 . . .98 B3
Copper Tree Ct ME15 . .195 A5
Copper Tree Wlk ME5 . .97 C1
Copperwood TN24 . . . . .268 C4
Coppice Cl ME7 . . . . . . .98 B4
Coppice Rd ME5 . . . . . . .97 C2
Coppice The
Aylesford ME20 . . . . .128 E1
Bitchet Green TN15 . . .155 D1
Hythe CT21 . . . . .333 B4
Joyden's Wood DA5 . . .32 D5
Pembury TN2 . . . . . . .287 D2
Sturry CT2 . . . . .143 F6
Vigo Village DA13 . . . .126 B8
Coppice View ME14 . . . .162 E6
Copping's Rd TN11 . . . .220 F1
COPPINS' CORNER 234 A6
Coppins La ME9 . . . . . .101 B2
Coppin St CT14 . . . . . .215 D6
Coppock Cl 1 CT12 . . . .83 B1
Copse Bank TN15 . . . . .154 F7
Copse Cl Greenwich SE7 .11 B8
Rochester ME1 . . . . . .63 C1
Copsehill ME19 . . . . . .127 E2
Copse Rd TN11 . . . . . . .221 E4
Copse Side DA3 . . . . . . .58 E6
Copse The
Ashford TN23 . . . . . .267 D3
Hoo St Werburgh ME3 . .41 E3
Tatsfield TN16 . . . . . .150 C7
Copsewood Cl DA15 . . . .12 E1
Copsewood Way ME15 163 A3
COP STREET 147 E4
Cop Street Rd CT3 . . . .147 D3
Copt Cl CT2 . . . . .143 E7
Coptefield Dr DA17 . . . . .3 E3
Copt Hall TN18 . . . . . . .357 D3
Copthall Ave TN18 . . . .341 A1
Copthall Gdns 13 CT20 335 D5
Copt Hall Rd
Ightham TN15 . . . . . .156 A4
Sole Street DA13 . . . . . .60 B5
Copthorne Ave BR2 . . . . .85 F8
Coralline Wlk 4 SE2 . . . .3 C4
Coral Pk ME14 . . . . . . .162 B5
Coral Reef ME12 . . . . . .47 B5
Corben Cl ME16 . . . . . .161 B6
Corbridge Ho SE2 . . . . . .3 C3
Corbylands Rd DA15 . . . .30 E7
Cordelia Cres ME1 . . . . .62 F2
Cordingham Rd CT5 . . .108 A6
Cordova Ct CT20 . . . . . .335 B4
Corelli Rd SE18, SE3 . . . .11 E6
Corhaven Ho DA8 . . . . . .14 E7
Corianda Dr 14 ME16 . .161 A3
Corinthian Ct ME5 . . . . .27 B5
Corinthian Manorway
DA8 . . . . .4 D2
Corinthian Rd DA8 . . . . . .4 D2
Cork Ho BR5 . . . . .54 B6
Cork La TN12 . . . . .292 C6
Cork St ME20 . . . . .128 F6
Corkwell St ME4 . . . . . . .63 E3
Cormorant Cl ME2 . . . . . .62 C7
Cormorant Way CT16 . . .77 F4
Cornbrook Rd CT21 . . . .353 D8
Cornel Ho 4 DA15 . . . . . .31 A5
Cornelia Pl DA8 . . . . . . .14 E8
Cornelis Dr CT12 . . . . . .115 B5
Cornell Cl DA14 . . . . . . .31 E2
Corner Cotts TN26 . . . . .348 A6
Corner Farm Rd TN12 .260 E4
Corner Rd TN23 . . . . . .300 B5

Corner Gn SE3.........11 A5
Cornes CI TN24.......269 A1
Cornfield Way TN10..222 D6
Cornflower CI ME14..162 E4
Cornford CI Hayes BR2..52 A4
　Pembury TN2........287 B6
Cornford La TN2.......287 B5
Cornford Pk TN2......287 C6
Cornford Rd CT7.......81 A7
Cornforth CI TN12....260 F4
Cornforth Dr ME9....134 C6
Corniche The CT20...358 C3
Corn Mill Dr BR6......54 A2
Cornwall Ave
　Bexley DA16........12 F4
　Ramsgate CT11.....117 F8
Cornwall CI ME15....195 E7
Cornwall Cres ME1....95 D4
Cornwall Dr BR5......31 C3
Cornwall Gdns
　Canterbury CT1....175 D7
　Margate CT9........51 B3
Cornwall Ho Deal CT14 215 A5
　[5] Dover CT17......310 D7
Cornwallis Ave
　Aylesham CT3......210 F6
　Chatham ME4.......63 E1
　Folkestone CT19...335 B6
　Gillingham ME8.....65 A4
　Herne Bay CT6.....77 C3
　Linton ME17.......227 E8
　Sidcup SE9.........30 D6
　Tonbridge TN10....222 C3
Cornwallis Circ CT5...74 D1
Cornwallis CI
　Ashford TN24......301 B7
　Erith DA8..........14 F8
　Folkestone CT19...335 B6
Cornwallis Cotts ME17 194 E2
Cornwallis Gdns CT10..84 A6
Cornwallis Rd
　Maidstone ME16...161 D4
　Woolwich SE18......2 B3
Cornwallis Rdbt ME8...65 A4
Cornwallis Sch ME15..194 F2
Cornwallis Wlk SE9...11 F4
Cornwall Rd
　Dartford DA1.......15 F4
　Deal CT14..........215 C3
　Gillingham ME7.....64 D6
　Herne Bay CT6.....76 B2
　Rochester ME1......63 C3
Cornwell Ave DA12....37 C5
Corona SE12..........29 A8
Corona Terr ME6.....127 F6
Coronation CI
　Bexley DA5.........13 D1
　Broadstairs CT10...83 E7
Coronation Cotts
　Folkestone CT19...334 D6
　Stoke ME3..........25 A3
　Ticehurst TN5......338 F2
Coronation Cres
　Margate CT9.........82 B8
　Queenborough ME11..45 F5
Coronation Ct DA8....14 D7
Coronation Dr
　Ashford TN23......267 C1
　Leysdown-on-Sea ME12..49 D2
Coronation Flats [5]
　ME4...............63 F3
Coronation Rd
　Chatham ME5.......64 C2
　Grain ME3..........27 B5
　Ramsgate CT11....117 D6
　Sheerness ME12....28 D1
Coronation Sq TN29..376 C6
Corone CT19.........335 A7
Corporation Rd ME7...64 C6
Corporation St ME1...63 C6
Corral CI ME5.........64 D2
Corral Hts [13] ME4...4 E1
Corrall Almshouses [5]
　ME15...............162 A3
Corrance Gn ME15...195 A8
Correnden Rd TN10...222 A3
Corseley Rd TN3......312 B5
Corsican Wlk CT6.....77 C3
Cortanore ME10......101 C7
Cortland CI Crayford DA1 14 E1
　Sittingbourne ME10...101 E6
Cortland Mews ME10..101 E6
Corunna CT21........333 A2
Corunna PI CT15.....278 E3
Corylus Dr CT5.......108 A7
Cory's Rd ME1........63 D6
Cosgrove Road RM20..16 F7
Cossack St ME1.......63 D3
Cossington Rd
　Canterbury CT1....175 A7
　Chatham ME5.......97 B1
Costells Mdw TN13...151 D1
Cosway Cotts TN25...329 C1
Cot La TN27..........295 B3
Cotleigh Ave DA5.....31 D6
Cotmandene Cres BR5..54 A4
Cotman's Ash La TN15 123 D4
Cotman Way TN12....224 D6
Coton Rd DA16........13 A4
Cotswold CI
　Ashford TN24......268 B4
　Bexley DA7.........14 E5
Cotswold Gdns ME15..163 A2
Cotswold Rd DA16.....36 E5
Cotswold Rise BR6....53 F3
Cottage Ave BR2......52 B2
Cottage Field CI DA14..31 C7
Cottage Ind Est ME20..139 E2
Cottage Rd Chatham ME4 63 F6
　Ramsgate CT11.....117 E6
Cottage Row CT13...148 F1

Cottall Ave ME4.......63 F2
Cottenham CI ME19..159 F7
Cottington Rd CT12...116 B5
Cotton Hill Ho TN26..349 A7
Cotton Hill Wlk TN26.349 A7
Cotton La DA2, DA9...16 C2
Cotton Rd CT1........174 E7
Couchman Green La
　TN12..............260 F7
Coulman St ME7.......64 D5
Coulson Gr CT14.....214 A5
Coulter Ho DA9.......17 C2
Coulter Rd
　Ashford TN23......299 D5
　Herne Bay CT6......76 B2
Coulters CI ME14....162 D5
Coulton Ave CT14.....36 E7
Coultrip CI ME12......48 B5
Council Ave DA11.....18 C1
Council Cotts
　Chainhurst ME15...227 A7
　Chiddingstone Causeway
　　TN11..............252 A8
　Coxheath ME15....194 A4
Council Hos TN15....190 A8
Countess Mountbatten Ct
　CT8...............81 E8
Countess of Thanet's
　Almshouses TN8...281 F3
Country's Field TN29..366 C8
Country Ways ME17..200 D3
County Gate SE9......30 C5
County Ho SE18.......12 A8
County Rd
　Maidstone ME14...162 A5
　Newham E6.........2 B8
County Sq [8] TN23..268 B2
County Square Sh Ctr [16]
　TN25..............268 B2
Coupland PI SE18......2 C1
Courier Rd RM13......4 D8
Course The SE9.......30 A4
COURT-AT-STREET..331 A4
Courtaulds CI SE28....3 A5
Court Ave DA17........3 F1
Court Broomes ME17..230 C8
Court Cotts
　St Nicholas at Wade
　　CT7...............79 E2
　Wingham CT3......178 A7
Court Cres BR8.......55 E5
Court Dr ME16........161 D4
Courtenay Ho ME13..140 C3
Courtenay Rd
　Boughton Street CT2,
　　ME13.............140 E5
　Deal CT14.........215 C8
　Maidstone ME15...161 F2
Courtenay Rd ME8.....98 B8
Courten Rd CT2......140 F6
Courtenwell TN3.....284 F7
Court Farm Rd SE9...29 E5
Courtfield Ave ME5....97 B3
Court Flats CT3......178 A7
Court Hall ME11.......45 F5
Court Hill Ho CT16...277 E4
Courthope TN12......257 A6
Courthope Ave TN5...336 F4
Court La Detling ME14 131 C5
　Hadlow TN11.......224 B7
　Preston CT3........146 B6
Courtland Ave CT16..278 A6
Courtland Dr CT16...277 E4
Courtland Gr SE28.....3 D6
Courtlands
　Chislehurst BR7.....30 B2
　Deal CT14..........248 D6
　Herne Bay CT6......77 B3
　Teston ME18.......193 A8
　Tonbridge TN10....222 A3
Courtlands Ave SE12..11 B2
Courtlands CI
　Cliffs End CT12....116 E5
　Teston ME18.......193 A8
Courtlands Farm TN7320 A3
Courtlands Way CT8...50 D1
Court Lane PI TN11...223 F8
Courtlet Dr DA8.......14 B6
Court Lodge Deal CT14 215 B6
　Erith DA17..........4 A1
　Shorne DA12........38 E2
Court Lodge Cotts
　East Farleigh ME15..194 A7
　Horton Kirby DA4...57 C6
　Mereworth ME18...191 E4
　West Farleigh ME15..193 D7
Court Lodge Farm
　ME18..............193 B7
Court Lodge Flats TN3 317 C6
Court Lodge Rd
　Appledore TN26....361 C7
　Gillingham ME7.....64 F6
Court Mdw
　Gillingham ME8......65 B2
　Wrotham TN15......124 F3
Court Mdws CT3......176 F8
Court Mews DA11......18 B1
Court Mount CT7......81 A6
Court PI [5] CT20....335 C4
Court Rd Burham ME1..128 F8
　Dartford DA2........34 E3
　Deal CT14..........215 B1
　Eltham SE9.........29 F7
　Royal Tunbridge Wells
　　TN4...............285 F4
　Sittingbourne ME10..101 F7
　St Nicholas at Wade CT7..79 E2
Court Rd (Orpington By-
　Pass)
　Chelsfield BR6, TN14..87 D3
　Orpington BR6......54 B2

Court Royal TN2......313 E8
Court St Bromley BR1..52 A7
　Faversham ME13...138 D7
Courts The CT9.......50 E1
Courtstreet BR1......52 A7
Court Tree Dr ME12...48 B5
Courtwood Dr TN13..154 A3
Cour Wurtin TN23....300 A7
Courtyard Gdns TN15..124 F3
Courtyard Mews BR5...31 A1
Courtyard The TN8...300 D5
Courtyard The ME8....98 A8
Courtyard The
　Staple CT3.........179 A6
　Watt's Cross TN11..221 A7
　Westerham TN16...184 D8
Court Yd SE9.........11 F1
COUSLEY WOOD.....337 C7
Cousley Wood Rd TN5 337 C7
Couthurst Rd SE3....11 B7
Coutts Ave DA12......38 E4
Couzins Walk DA1.....16 A5
Covelees Wall E6......2 A7
Coventon La CT14....181 A5
Coventry CI
　[9] Newham E6......1 F7
　Rochester ME2......62 B8
Coventry Gdns CT6....77 E5
Coventry Rd TN10...222 D5
Coverdale Ave ME15..195 D6
Coverdale CI ME5.....97 B7
Covert TN23..........267 E1
Covert Rd CT3........210 E4
Covert The Chatham ME5 97 B1
　Orpington BR6......53 E3
　Vigo Village DA11, DA13 125 E7
Covesfield DA11.......36 F8
Covet La CT4.........209 C2
Covet Wood CT4......53 D1
Covey Hall Rd ME6....95 A1
Cowan CI E6..........1 E8
Cowbeck CI ME8......98 D6
COWDEN.............282 A6
Cowden CI TN18.....354 E8
Cowden Cross TN18..282 C7
Cowden Mews TN18..354 E7
COWDEN POUND....250 B2
Cowden Rd
　Maidstone ME14...162 C5
　Orpington BR6......53 F2
Cowden Sta TN8.....282 D8
Cowdray Rd CT14...215 A3
Cowdray Sq CT14...215 A3
Cowdrey CI
　Ashford TN24......301 A7
　Maidstone ME16...161 B2
　Rochester ME1......63 B2
Cowdrey Ct DA1.......33 B8
Cowdrey PI CT1......175 B6
Cowdreys TN9........254 C8
Cowen Ho [4] SE18...12 B8
Cowgate Hill CT17...310 D7
Cowgate La CT18.....307 C5
Cow La Canterbury CT1 174 D7
　Horseshoe Green TN8 250 D1
Cow Leaze E6.........2 A7
Cowley Ave DA9......17 A2
Cowley Rise CT9......83 C8
Cowper Ave RM18.....19 B6
Cowper CI Bexley DA16 13 A2
　Bromley BR2........52 D5
　Whitstable CT5.....75 D3
Cowper Rd Bromley BR2 52 D5
　Crabble CT17.......277 E3
　Deal CT14..........215 C5
　Erith DA17..........4 A2
　Gillingham ME7.....64 D3
　Margate CT9........50 J1
　Sittingbourne ME10..102 B4
Cowstead La ME14....99 D3
Cowstead Rd ME9.....99 D2
Cox Dr CT18.........307 A5
Coxes Ave CT12.......83 B3
Coxes La CT12........83 B3
Coxett Hill ME13.....137 D5
Cox Gdns ME8........65 A2
Cox's CI ME6.........127 F8
Cox St ME14..........131 E6
Coxwell Rd SE18......2 D1
Cozenton CI ME8......65 E1
CRABBLE.............277 F2
Crabble Ave CT17....278 A2
Crabble CI CT17.......277 F2
Crabble Corn Mill★
　CT17..............277 F2
Crabble Hill CT16, CT17 278 A2
Crabble La CT17......277 E2
Crabble Mdws CT17..278 A3
Crabble Rd CT17......278 A3
Crabbs Croft CT [7] BR6 86 C5
Crabtree CI ME19.....159 A2
Crabtree La ME17....233 B8
Crabtree Manorway N
　DA17.............4 C5
Crabtree Manorway S
　DA17.............4 C3
Crabtree Rd ME8......98 D8
Crabtree Rdbt ME14..129 E2
Craddock Dr [8] CT1..143 B1
Craddock Ho CT1.....143 B1
Craddock Rd CT1....143 B1
Craddock Way ME8...98 D5
Cradducks La TN12...261 B4
Cradle Bridge Dr TN24 268 F2

Cradles Rd ME9........99 C2
Cradley Rd SE9........30 D7
Crafford St CT16.....278 D1
Craft Workshops TN27 230 C1
Cragie Wlk ME8.......98 E4
Craigerne Rd SE3....11 B7
Craig Ho Greenwich SE3..11 B7
　Rochester ME1......63 E1
Craigholm SE18.......12 A6
Craighton Ho [2] CT16 310 E7
Craigie Ct DA1........34 A8
Craigton Rd SE9......11 F3
Crales Ho SE18........1 E1
Cramonde PI DA16...13 A5
Crampton Ct CT10...84 A4
Cramptons TN17......322 D5
Crampton's Rd TN14..154 B7
Crampton Tower Mus★ [7]
　CT10..............84 A4
Cranborne Ave ME15 162 C1
Cranbourne Wlk CT2...142 E3
Cranbourne Ave ME15 195 B8
Cranbourne CI CT11..117 F8
CRANBROOK.........320 C6
Cranbrook CE Prim Sch
　CT17..............320 D5
Cranbrook CI
　Gillingham ME8......65 C3
　Hayes BR2..........52 A3
　Maidstone ME15...195 F7
　Margate CT9........51 E1
CRANBROOK
　COMMON..........293 A2
Cranbrook Dr ME10..101 D1
Cranbrook Ho [14] ME4..14 F7
Cranbrook Mews [1]
　TN8...............217 C1
Cranbrook Mus★
　TN17..............320 D5
Cranbrook Rd
　Benenden TN17....341 F8
　Bexley DA7.........13 F6
　Fosten Green TN27..322 C6
　Goudhurst TN17....319 A8
　Hawkhurst TN18....340 F4
　Knox Bridge TN12, TN17 292 F7
　Parkgate TN30.....323 C1
　Tenterden TN30....344 E7
Cranbrooks TN17.....301 D4
Cranbrook Sch TN17..320 D5
Crandalls TN11........220 F1
Cranden Wlk DA4.....57 E7
Crane Ho [11] TN18..340 F2
Crane House Gdns [10]
　TN18..............340 F2
Crane La TN17........320 D5
Cranford CI ME8......65 D1
Cranford Ho DA1.....15 A2
Cranford Mews BR2...52 E4
Cranford Rd
　Dartford DA1........33 E7
　Tonbridge TN10....223 A5
Cranham Sq TN12...259 C5
Cranleigh CI
　Orpington BR6......87 A7
　Sidcup DA5.........14 B1
Cranleigh Ct CT5....108 E8
Cranleigh Dr
　Swanley BR8.......55 E5
　Whitfield CT16.....278 B7
Cranleigh Gdns
　Chatham ME4.......63 D3
　Maidstone ME16...161 C2
　Whitstable CT5.....108 E8
Cranley Par SE9......29 E4
Cranley Rd E13........1 B8
Cranmer CI CT4......176 B4
Cranmer Ct ME15....195 B8
Cranmere Ct ME2.....63 C8
Cranmer Ho [6] CT2..142 E1
Cranmer Rd TN13....153 E4
Cranmore Rd BR7....29 F3
Cranstone Ct [12] DA14 31 B4
Cranswick Cotts CT14 247 C8
Cranwell Rd TN4.....285 C4
Crates Yd TN4.......286 A5
Crathie Rd SE12......11 B1
Craufurd Gn CT20...334 D5
Craven CI CT9........82 C8
Craven Rd BR6.......87 D7
Crawford Ave [9] DA1..15 D1
Crawford Gdns CT9...51 B2
Crawford Rd CT10....83 F5
Crawfords BR8........32 E1
Crawley CI [1] DA11...19 B1
Crawshay CI TN13...154 A4
Cray Ave BR5.........54 B4
Cray Bldgs DA14......31 C2
Craybrooke Rd DA14..31 B4
Crayburne DA13......35 F4
Craybury End SE9.....30 C6
Cray CI DA1..........15 A3
Craydene Rd DA8.....14 F8
Crayfields Bsns Pk BR5 54 C8
Crayfields Ind Pk BR5..54 C7
CRAYFORD...........14 D1
Crayford
　Maidstone ME14...162 C6
　Newham E6.........1 F7
Crayford Commercial Ctr
　DA1..............14 E1
Crayford High St DA1..14 E2
Crayford Ind Est DA1..14 F2
Crayford L Ctr DA2...14 E1
Crayford Rd DA1......14 E2
Crayford Sta DA1.....14 E1
Crayford Way DA1....15 A3
Craylands BR5........54 C6
Craylands La DA10...17 D2
Craylands Lane DA10..35 E8
Craylands Prim Sch
　DA10.............17 D2
Craylands Sq DA10...17 D2

Crayleigh Terr DA14...31 C2
Craymill Sq DA1......14 F5
Cray Rd Crockenhill BR8..55 C3
　Erith DA17.........14 A8
　Sidcup DA14........31 C2
Crayside Ind Est DA1..15 B3
Crays Par The BR5....54 C7
Craythorne TN30.....345 B8
Craythorne CI
　Hythe CT21........334 B4
　New Romney TN28..373 B8
Craythorne Ho TN30..345 B8
Craythorne La TN28..373 B7
Cray Valley Rd BR5....54 C5
Cray View CI [13] BR5..54 C5
Creasey's Row TN14..185 C5
Credenhall Dr BR2....52 F1
Credo Way RM20......17 B8
Creek La ME3.........25 B2
CREEKMOUTH.........2 F8
Creek The DA11.......18 B2
Creek Way RM13.......4 E8
Creighton Flats [2]
　CT13..............148 F1
Creine Mill Lane N
　CT1..............174 E8
Cremer CI CT4.......173 C2
Cremer PI ME13.....138 A8
Cremers Rd ME10....102 B5
Cremorne Rd [1] ME4..36 F8
Crendon Pk TN4......286 A8
Crescent Ave RM17...18 D8
Crescent Cotts TN13..153 E7
Crescent Ct
　[1] Grays RM17....18 D8
　Sidcup DA15........31 A5
Crescent Dr BR5......53 C3
Crescent Gdns BR8...55 C7
Crescent Ho
　Margate CT9........51 A2
　Ramsgate CT12....117 C2
　Rochester ME2......63 C7
Crescent Rd
　Birchington CT7.....81 A7
　Broadstairs CT10...84 C8
　Bromley BR1........29 A1
　Erith DA8..........14 F8
　Faversham ME13...138 D7
　Margate CT9........50 H2
　Ramsgate CT11....117 D6
　Royal Tunbridge Wells
　　TN1...............286 B3
　Sidcup DA15........30 F5
　Woolwich SE18......2 B2
Crescent St [1] ME10..101 F4
Crescent The
　Aylesham CT15....211 A3
　Bidborough TN4....253 E4
　Borough Green TN15..157 A8
　Boughton Street ME13 140 A3
　Chartham CT4......173 D1
　Chatham CT4.......173 D1
　Eythorne CT15.....245 C7
　Folkestone CT20...334 E3
　Groombridge TN3...312 C7
　Halfway Houses ME12..46 E6
　Longfield DA3......58 E6
　Lower Halstow ME9..67 C3
　Maidstone ME14...161 F8
　Northfleet DA11.....36 F6
　Sandwich CT13.....180 E6
　Sevenoaks TN13...154 D6
　Sheerness ME12....28 C2
　Sheerness ME12....28 G1
　Sidcup DA5.........31 C8
　Sidcup DA14........30 F4
　Sittingbourne ME10..69 A1
　St Margaret's at Cliffe
　　CT15..............280 A5
　St Mary's Island ME4..41 B1
　Swanscombe DA9...17 C2
　Teynham ME9.......103 D3
　[1] Tonbridge TN9..222 B2
Crescent Way
　Chatham ME5.......96 D5
　Orpington BR6......86 E5
Cressey Ct [7] ME4...63 E4
Cressfield TN23......267 F1
Cressingham Ct [1] DA17 4 A3
Cress Way ME13......138 A7
Cresta CI CT6........75 F4
Crest Ave RM17.......18 B7
Crest CI TN14.......121 B8
Crest Ind Est TN12..259 C6
Crest Rd ME1........63 C1
Crest View DA9......17 A3
Crest View Dr BR5....53 C4
Crestway ME5........97 B8
Crete Hall Rd DA11...18 E1
Crete Road E CT18,
　CT19.............307 D1
Crete Road W CT18..307 C1
Creteway CI CT19....335 E8
Creton St SE18........2 A1
Creve Coeur CT [1] ME8..65 E1
Crevequer Chambers [1]
　ME8..............65 E1
Cricketers CI
　Bells Yew Green TN3..315 A5
　Erith DA8..........4 E1
　Harrietsham ME17..198 D6
　Hawkinge CT18.....307 B6
　Sittingbourne ME10..101 F8
Cricketers Dr [3] DA1..93 A7
Cricket Ground Rd BR7 53 B8
Cricket Hall Rd ME20..53 A2
Crimond Ave TN29...353 A4
Criol Rd TN26.......299 A2
Cripple Hill TN26....296 D1
Cripple St ME15......195 A4
Cripps CI CT3........210 E5
Cripps' La CT15......279 F6
Crisfield Ct TN30....324 B2
Crismill La ME14.....163 F4

Crispe CI ME8.........98 D4
Crispe Park CI CT7....81 B7
Crispe Rd CT7........81 A3
Crispin CI DA13......138 D8
Crispin Ct ME17......194 C3
Crispin Rd ME2........62 E8
Crispin Way ME19...159 A3
Critchley Ave DA [10]..15 D1
Crittall's Cnr DA14....31 C1
Crittenden Bglws
　ME15..............194 A4
Crittenden Cotts ME15 194 A4
Crittenden Rd TN12..256 D3
Crittle's Ct TN5......336 F4
Crockenhall Way DA13..36 E1
CROCKENHILL.........55 D3
Crockenhill Hill BR8...54 E4
Crockenhill La BR8, DA4 56 C2
Crockenhill Prim Sch
　BR8...............55 C3
Crockenhill Rd BR8, BR6 54 E4
Crocken Hill Rd TN27..232 C2
Crockers Hatch Cnr
　TN3..............284 D2
Crockford CI TN10...222 E7
CROCKHAM HILL....184 C2
Crockham Hill CE Prim
　Sch TN8..........184 C2
Crockham La ME13...140 B6
Crockham Rd ME13..140 C6
Crockham Way SE9...30 A4
CROCKHURST
　STREET...........255 C6
Crockshard Hill CT3..178 B4
Crockshard La CT3...178 A4
Crocus Dr ME9/ME10..101 F2
Croft CI Bromley BR7..29 F3
　Chatham ME5.......97 C1
　Erith DA17..........3 F1
　Tonbridge TN10....222 F5
Croft Ct TN8.........217 C1
Crofters CI TN21.....353 E8
Crofters The ME8.....98 F7
Croft Gdns ME17....199 D4
Croft La
　Edenbridge TN8....217 C1
　Folkestone CT20...334 F5
CROFTON............86 D8
Crofton Ave
　Orpington BR5, BR6..86 C8
　Sidcup DA5.........31 D8
Crofton CI TN24.....268 C6
Crofton Inf Sch BR5...53 D2
Crofton Jun Sch BR5..53 D2
Crofton La BR5, BR6...53 C2
Crofton Rd
　Orpington BR6......86 B8
　Westgate on Sea CT8..81 E7
Crofton Roman Villa★
　BR6..............86 E8
Croft Rd Ashford TN24..268 D2
　Bromley BR1........29 A2
　Westerham TN16...151 C1
Croftside DA13......126 A8
Croft's PI [3] CT10...84 B4
Croft The
　Leybourne ME19...127 E2
　Swanley BR8........55 C6
　Tenterden TN30....345 B7
Croft Way
　Sevenoaks TN13...153 F2
　Sidcup DA15........30 C6
Croftwood TN23.....299 D6
Croidene Ct ME4......47 A6
Cromarty CI [8] BR1..52 C7
Crombie CI CT18.....307 B5
Crombie Rd DA15.....30 D7
Cromer PI [5] BR6....53 D1
Cromer Rd
　Rochester ME2......63 B8
　Sittingbourne ME9,
　　ME10.............134 F8
Cromer St TN9.......222 A1
Cromford CI BR6......86 E7
Cromlix CI BR7.......53 B7
Crompton Gdns ME15 162 B3
Cromwell Ave BR2....52 B5
Cromwell CI BR2......52 B5
Cromwell Mews BR7..53 A8
Cromwell Park PI
　CT20.............334 D4
Cromwell Rd
　Canterbury CT1....175 A6
　Maidstone ME14...162 B6
　Royal Tunbridge Wells
　　TN2...............286 C3
　West Minst ME12...45 F7
　Whitstable CT5.....74 E1
Cromwell Terr ME4....64 A3
Cronin CI [2] ME20..127 F4
Crooked La DA11, DA12..19 B1
Crooked South Rd
　CT14..............247 E7
Crookenden PI CT4..242 F8
Crook Log DA6.......13 D3
Crook Log L Ctr DA6..13 D4
Crook Log Prim Sch
　DA6..............13 D3
Crook Rd TN12.......257 D1
Crook's Court La CT15 308 F4
Crookston Rd SE9....12 A4
CROOK THE.........205 F2
Croombridge Dr ME7..64 F6
Croombs Rd E16......1 C8
Crosby House DA1....15 A1
Crosier CI SE3........11 E6
Crosier Ct ME9.......66 E3
Crosley Rd ME7......64 D3
CROSS-AT-HAND....228 C1
Cross-at-Hand Cotts
　TN12..............228 C2
Crossbrook Rd SE3...11 E4
Cross Ct [11] SE28....3 B6
Cross Dr ME17......197 B1

Crossfield Walk ME6 95 A2
Cross Keys
Maidstone ME14 163 C4
Sevenoaks TN13 187 A8
Cross Keys Cl TN13 187 A8
Cross La
7 Faversham ME13 138 D7
Sidcup DA5 31 F8
Sittingbourne ME10 101 E6
Throwley Forstal ME13 202 C7
Ticehurst TN5 338 D2
Cross Lane E DA12 37 B6
Cross Lane Gdns TN5 338 D1
Cross Lane W DA11 37 B6
Crossley Ave CT6 75 F4
Crossley Cl TN16 118 D4
Crossmead SE9 29 F7
Cross Rd Birchington CT7 81 B8
Dartford DA1 15 C1
Deal CT14 215 A2
Hawley DA2 33 F4
Northfleet DA11 18 F1
Orpington, Keston Mark BR2 85 E8
Orpington, St Mary Cray BR5 54 B4
Sidcup DA14 31 B4
Cross St
2 Canterbury CT2 142 E1
Chatham ME4 64 A4
Erith DA8 14 E8
Gillingham ME7 64 C6
27 Gravesend DA12 19 B1
Herne Bay CT6 76 D3
Maidstone ME14 162 A6
Rochester ME2 63 B8
Cross Stile TN23 299 F8
Cross The CT13 180 B2
Crossway Chatham ME5 96 E6
Erith SE28 3 D7
Orpington BR5 53 D4
Cross Way ME1 63 C3
CROSSWAYS 16 D3
Crossways
Canterbury CT2 142 F4
Chart Sutton ME17 196 B1
Hextable BR8 32 F1
Sittingbourne ME10 101 F1
Tatsfield TN16 150 C7
Crossways Ave CT9 83 A5
Crossways Bvd DA2, DA9 16 E3
Crossways Cl TN29 352 E2
Crossways Ct TN16 150 C7
Crossway The
Bromley SE9 29 D6
Royal Tunbridge Wells TN4 285 D2
CROUCH 157 B4
Crouch Cotts ME13 171 E8
Crouch Croft SE9 30 A5
Crouch Hill Ct ME9 67 C3
Crouch House Cotts TN8 217 B2
Crouch House Rd TN8 217 B2
Crouch La Crouch TN15 157 B6
Linkhill TN18 356 D6
Selling ME13 171 E8
Crowbridge Link TN24 300 F7
Crowbridge Rd TN24 300 F6
Crow Cnr
Brabourne TN25 270 E1
Rochester ME1 63 C5
Crowden Way SE28 3 C6
CROWDLEHAM 123 D2
Crow Dr TN14 121 C4
Crowfoot Cl SE28 2 E5
Crow Hill
Borough Green TN15 157 A7
Broadstairs CT10 84 B5
Crow Hill Rd
Borough Green TN15 157 A7
Margate CT9 82 B8
Crowhurst La
Basted TN15 156 E4
West Kingsdown TN15 91 B4
Crowhurst Oast TN12 191 D1
Crowhurst Rd TN15 156 F6
Crowhurst Way BR5 54 C4
Crow La ME1 63 C5
Crown Acres TN12 225 A6
Crown Cl BR6 87 A6
Crown Ct Bromley BR2 52 E4
Cranbrook TN17 320 C5
Deal CT14 215 D6
Eltham SE12 11 B1
Tilbury RM18 19 A5
Crownfield Rd TN23 299 F8
Crownfields
Maidstone ME14 162 F4
Sevenoaks TN13 154 B2
Crown Gdns CT2 142 E1
Crown Gn DA12 38 E3
Crown Hill Rd CT6 76 C4
Crown Ho
Lamberhurst TN3 317 B5
Rochester ME1 63 B4
Crown La Bromley BR2 52 D4
Chislehurst BR7 53 C8
Shorne DA12 38 E4
Stelling Minnis CT4 240 E3
Crown Lane Spur BR2 52 D3
Crown Quay La 5 ME10 102 A4
Crown Rd Grays RM17 18 A8
Marlpit Hill TN8 217 D4
Orpington BR6 87 A5
Shoreham TN14 88 F1
Sittingbourne ME10 101 E6
Crown St ME7 64 D6
Crown Woods La SE18 12 B5
Crown Woods Sch SE9 12 C2
Crown Woods Way SE9 12 D2
Crows Camp Rd CT4 209 A5
Crowther Cl TN12 260 E4
Croxley Cl BR5 54 B7
Croxley Gn BR5 54 B8
Croyde Cl DA15 30 D8
Croydon Cl ME5 97 C4
Croydon Rd
Hayes BR2, BR4, BR6 85 C7
Tatsfield TN16 150 F3
Westerham TN16 151 B2
Crozier Ho SE3 11 B4
Cruden Rd DA12 37 F6
Cruise Liner Terminals CT17 310 E5
Crumpsall St SE2 3 C2
Crump's La ME17 231 B4
CRUNDALE 238 D7
Crundale 2 ME14 162 A5
Crundale Cl TN23 299 F6
Crundale Rd ME8 65 C3
Crundale Tower BR5 54 C1
Crundale Way CT9 51 E1
Crundwell Rd TN4 253 F1
Crusader Cl ME8 98 B8
Crusader Ct DA1 15 F3
Crusoe Rd DA8 4 D1
Crutches La ME3, ME2 39 B1
Cryalls Bsns Est ME10 101 C4
Cryalls La ME10, ME9 101 C3
Cryals Ct TN12 288 E5
Cryals Rd TN12 288 D5
Cryol Rd TN23 300 A7
Crystal Bsns Ctr CT13 149 B2
Crystal Ho 2 SE18 2 F1
Ctr for European Agri-Environmental Studies TN25 238 A1
Cubitt Ho CT19 335 D6
Cuckmere Ct 17 BR5 54 D1
Cuckmere Way 27 BR5 54 D1
Cuckolds Cnr
Chillenden CT3 212 A7
New Ash Green DA3 92 B7
Snargate TN29 362 E7
Cuckold's Cnr
High Halden TN26 325 B7
Lower Higham ME3 39 C6
Staplehurst TN12 260 F4
CUCKOLD'S GREEN 25 A5
Cuckolds Green Rd ME3 25 B5
Cuckoo La
Ashford, Singleton TN23 299 E7
Ashford TN23 299 D6
Lamberhurst TN12 289 A2
Postling CT21 304 F2
Tonbridge TN11 223 A7
Cuckoowood Ave ME14 129 F1
CUDHAM 119 D4
Cudham CE Prim Sch TN16 119 A3
Cudham Cl ME14 162 C6
Cudham Gdns CT9 51 E2
Cudham Lane N TN14 119 D7
Cudham Lane S TN14 119 D2
Cudham Park Rd TN14 86 E1
Cudham Rd Downe BR6 119 B7
Tatsfield TN16 150 E8
Cudworth Rd TN24 300 E7
Cuff Cres SE9 11 D1
Cugley Rd DA2 34 C8
Culcroft DA3 58 F6
Cullens Hill CT4 273 F4
Cullet Dr ME11 46 A3
Culling's Hill CT4 273 F4
CULMERS 106 E1
Culmers Terr ME13 139 E8
Culpeper Cl
Hollingbourne ME17 164 E2
Rochester ME2 63 E6
Culpepers TN17 318 E7
Culpepper Cl CT2 143 A4
Culpepper Rd
Coxheath ME17 194 B3
Gillingham ME8 98 D4
Culter Field TN23 299 E8
Culverden Ave TN4 286 A6
Culverden Down TN4 285 F5
Culverden Park Rd TN4 285 F5
Culverden Pk TN4 285 F5
Culverden Sq TN4 286 A5
Culverden St TN1 286 A4
Culver's La TN29 376 D5
CULVERSTONE GREEN 92 E2
Culverstone Green Prim Sch DA13 92 F3
Culverstone Ho BR5 54 B6
Culverton Ct 19 DA14 31 A4
Culvey Cl DA3 58 E4
Cumberland Ave
Bexley DA16 12 F3
Broadstairs CT10 84 A5
Canterbury CT1 175 D7
Gravesend DA12 37 C8
Maidstone ME15 195 D8
Cumberland Cotts 23 TN1 286 A2
Cumberland Ct
Sevenoaks TN13 153 E7
Tonbridge TN10 222 A4
Cumberland Dr
Dartford DA1 33 F8
Erith DA7 13 E7
Lower Halstow ME9 67 C3
Cumberland Gdns 10 TN1 286 A2
Cumberland Ho SE28 2 D4
Cumberland Mews 12 TN1 286 A2
Cumberland Rd
Chatham ME4, ME7 64 B7
Gillingham ME7 64 C7
Margate CT9 51 B3
Cumberland Rd *continued*
Newham E13 1 B8
1 Ramsgate CT11 117 D6
Cumberland Villas 5 DA12 37 C8
Cumberland Wlk TN1 286 A2
Cumberland Yd 11 TN1 286 A2
Cumbrian Ave DA7 14 E5
Cundishall Cl CT5 108 C8
Cundy Rd E16 1 C7
Cunningham Cl TN4 286 B7
Cunningham Cres
Birchington CT7 80 E7
Chatham ME5 97 A8
Cunningham Ho ME1 63 B4
Cunningham Rd TN4 286 B7
Cupar Pl ME3 41 B8
Cupola Cl BR1 29 B3
Curates Wlk DA2 33 D5
Curlew Ave ME9 67 B3
Curlew Cl Erith SE28 3 D6
Herne Bay CT6 77 C2
Curlew Cres ME2 62 C6
Curlew Pl CT18 307 A3
Curlews The DA12 37 D6
Curlinge Ct CT11 117 A6
Curran Ave DA15 12 F2
Currie Rd TN4 286 A5
CURTEIS' CORNER 295 A3
Curteis Rd TN30 324 B1
Curtis Ct BR6 54 A2
CURTISDEN GREEN 291 C5
Curtis La CT4 240 D2
Curtismill Cl BR5 54 B6
Curtismill Way BR5 54 B6
Curtis Rd TN24 300 E7
Curtis Way
1 Faversham ME13 138 C7
Rochester ME1 96 D7
7 Woolwich SE28 3 B6
Curtis Wood Park Rd CT6 111 A7
Curtis Wood Pk Rd CT6 110 E7
Curtis Wood Rd CT6 110 F7
Curzon Cl Deal CT14 215 C3
Orpington BR6 86 D6
Curzon Ct SE9 30 C5
Curzon Dr RM17 18 C7
Curzon Ho 5 CT11 117 D6
Curzon Rd Chatham ME4 63 F3
Dover CT17 310 B8
Maidstone ME14 162 A6
Cushings Wlk 13 CT5 74 D2
Cushman Rd CT1 174 F7
CUSTOM HOUSE 1 C7
Custom House for Excel Sta E16 1 B6
Cutbush Almshouses
3 Maidstone ME14 162 A4
1 Maidstone ME15 162 A3
Cutbush Cl ME17 198 D6
Cutbush & Corrall Ct 1 ME14 162 B4
Cutbush Ho 2 ME15 162 A3
Cuthbert Rd CT8 81 E8
Cutmore St DA11 37 B8
Cutter Cl ME2 40 F3
Cutter Ho 6 DA8 4 E1
Cutter Ridge Rd DA13 61 A1
Cut The
17 Chatham ME4/ME7 64 A6
Tylden TN27 295 E8
Cuttings The CT12 117 C8
Cutty Sark Ct 6 DA9 17 A2
CUXTON 62 B2
Cuxton BR5 53 C4
Cuxton Cl Bexley DA6 13 E2
11 Maidstone ME15 195 F5
Cuxton Com Inf Sch ME2 62 B2
Cuxton Com Jun Sch ME2 62 B2
Cuxton Ind Est ME2 62 C2
Cuxton Rd
Maidstone ME15 195 F5
Rochester ME2 62 F5
Cuxton Sta ME2 62 C2
Cyclamen Rd BR8 55 D5
Cygnet Cl ME20 128 A2
Cygnet Gdns DA11 36 F6
Cygnet L Ctr DA11 36 E5
Cygnet Rd ME5 97 C2
Cygnet Way TN23 267 F1
Cylinder Rd CT21 333 B4
Cypress Ave
Ashford TN23 267 E2
Hoo St Werburgh ME3 41 E3
Cypress Cl CT5 108 C7
Cypress Ct ME7 64 F6
Cypress Gr
Elvington CT15 212 B2
Royal Tunbridge Wells TN2 314 C8
Cypress Rd ME2 40 C1
Cypress Tree Cl DA15 30 F7
CYPRUS 2 B6
Cyprus Ct ME13 138 E7
Cyprus Pl E6 2 A6
Cyprus Rd ME13 138 E7
Cyprus Sta E6 2 A6
Cyril Hall Ct DA11 18 F1
Cyril John Gange Lodge TN2 286 D2
Cyril Lodge 6 DA14 31 A4
Cyril Rd Bexley DA7 13 E5
Orpington BR6 54 A2

D

D2 Trad Est ME10 102 B6
Dabbling Cl DA8 15 B7
Daerwood Cl BR2 52 F1
Daffodil Rd ME2 62 E7
Daglish Cl TN28 373 B6
Dagmar Rd ME4 64 B2
Dagonet Gdns BR1 29 A5
Dagonet Rd BR1 29 A5
Dahlia Dr BR8 55 F7
Dahlia Rd SE2 3 B2
Daigor La CT12 82 D1
Daimler Ave CT6 76 B3
Dainton Cl 2 BR1 52 B8
Daintons Cotts 2 TN18 340 F2
Dairsie Ct 4 BR1 52 C7
Dairsie Rd SE9 12 A4
Dairy Cl 3 Bromley BR1 29 B1
Sutton at Hone DA4 34 B1
Dairy La
Chainhurst TN12 226 F4
Crockham Hill TN8 184 B1
Woolwich SE18 1 F2
Dairy Pl TN12 226 F4
Daisy Munns Ho SE9 30 C7
Dajen Bsns Pk ME4 64 C1
Dalberg Way SE2 3 D3
Dalby Rd CT9 51 A3
Dalby Sq CT9 51 A3
Daleacres Cvn Pk CT21 352 E7
Dale Cl Crayford DA1 14 F1
Greenwich SE3 11 A4
Dale Ct Bromley BR1 52 D6
Chatham ME5 97 A2
Dale End DA1 14 F1
Dalemain Mews E16 1 A5
Dale Rd Crayford DA1 14 F1
Northfleet DA13 36 A4
Rochester ME1 63 C3
Swanley BR8 55 C6
Daleside BR6 87 A5
Daleside Cl BR6 87 A4
Dale St Chatham ME4 63 E2
Royal Tunbridge Wells TN1 286 B4
Dale The BR2 85 D6
Dale View DA8 14 F5
Dale Wlk Ashford TN24 268 C7
Dartford DA2 34 C7
Dalewood ME10 102 A2
Dale Wood Rd BR6 53 E1
Dalison Ct ME2 95 B4
Dallas-Brett Cres CT19 335 E8
Dallinger Rd 1 CT7 80 F8
Dallin Rd Bexley DA6 13 D3
Woolwich SE18 12 B7
Dalmatia Ct CT17 278 A1
Dalmeny Ave CT9 51 D1
Dalmeny Rd DA8 14 B6
Dalmeny Terr CT21 333 A1
Dalton Cl BR6 86 E7
Dalton Ct 7 CT11 117 E7
Daltons Rd BR6, BR8 88 C7
Dalton St ME7 64 C6
Daly Drive BR1 53 A6
Dame Janet Com Jun Sch CT12 83 B2
Dame Janet Inf Sch CT12 83 B2
Damerham Cl CT2 142 E3
Damiem Cl ME4 64 A2
Damigos Rd DA12 37 F7
Damon Cl DA14 31 B5
Damon Ct DA14 31 B5
Damson Ct BR8 55 D5
Damson Dr ME3 41 E3
DANAWAY 100 C3
Danaway Cotts ME9 100 C3
Dando Cres SE3 11 B4
Dan Dr ME13 138 A8
Dane Cl Chatham ME5 97 C2
Hartlip ME9 99 D6
Orpington BR6 86 D5
Sidcup DA5 32 A8
Danecourt Com Sch ME8 65 A2
Dane Court Gdns CT10 83 D5
Dane Court Gram Sch CT10 83 E4
Dane Court Rd CT10 83 C6
Dane Cres CT11 117 E8
Dane Ct Coxheath ME17 194 C2
Tilmanstone CT14 212 F4
Danedale Ave ME12 47 F6
Dane End Rd CT8 81 D8
Danefield Ct ME14 163 B4
Dane Gdns CT9 83 B8
Dane Hill CT9 50 J3
Dane Hill Gr CT9 50 J2
Dane Hill Row CT9 50 J2
Danehill Wlk DA14 31 A5
Dane Ho CT14 215 D8
Danehurst CT8 50 C1
Dane John Ct 3 CT1 174 F7
Dane John Gdns★ CT16 174 F7
Dane John Mews 1 CT1 174 F7
Dane La ME9 99 D6
Danemore TN30 345 B8
Dane Mount CT9 83 C8
Dane Park Rd
Margate CT9 50 J2
Ramsgate CT11 117 E8
Dane Park Villas CT9 51 A2
Dane Pk ME15 194 C6
Dane Rd Birchington CT7 80 D7
Dane Rd *continued*
Margate CT9 51 A2
Otford TN14 121 F2
Ramsgate CT11 117 E8
Dane Rise CT9 83 C8
Danes Cl DA11 36 C5
Danescombe SE12 29 A7
Danes Ct CT16 278 D2
Danes Dr ME12 49 D2
Danes Hill ME7 65 A6
Danes Mead ME10 68 F1
Danesmead Terr CT9 50 J2
DANE STREET 204 F6
Dane Valley Rd CT10, CT9 83 C8
Daniel Ho 5 ME16 161 E5
Daniels Ct CT5 74 C1
DANIEL'S WATER 298 D7
Danley Mid Sch ME12 46 E7
Danley Rd ME12 46 E7
Danns La ME18, ME19 159 A1
Dansington Rd DA16 13 A3
Danson Cres DA16 13 B4
Danson House★ DA6 13 C3
Danson La DA16 13 B3
Danson Mead DA16 13 C4
Danson Prim Sch DA16 13 A3
Danson Rd Bexley DA5 13 D1
Bexley DA5, DA6 13 C2
Danson Underpass DA5 13 C1
Danson Way ME8 65 D2
Danton La CT18 306 C1
Danvers Rd TN9 222 B1
Darby Gdns ME3 39 B3
Darby Pl CT20 335 D5
Darby Rd CT20 335 D5
Darby's La TN5 337 B2
D'arcy Pl BR2 52 A5
Darcy Sq TN28 373 E5
Darent Cl TN13 153 C5
DARENTH 34 B4
Darenth Ave TN10 222 C5
Darenth Cl CT6 77 B3
Darenth Cotts TN14 121 F8
Darenth Ct 18 BR5 54 D1
Darenth Ctry Pk★ DA2 34 D6
Darenth Dr DA12 38 B7
Darenth Gdns TN16 151 D1
Darenth Hill DA2 34 C3
Darenth La TN13 153 E6
Darenth Park Ave DA2 34 D6
Darenth Prim Sch DA2 34 E2
Darenth Rd Bexley DA16 13 A6
Dartford DA1 33 F7
Darenth Rd S DA2 34 B4
Darenth Rise ME5 97 B3
Darenth Way TN14 122 A8
Darenth Wood Rd DA2 34 E6
Darent Ind Pk DA8 15 D8
Darent Mead DA4 57 B8
Darent Valley Hospl DA2 34 E7
DARGATE 140 E7
Dargate Cl ME16 161 D7
Dargate Rd
Dargate CT2, ME13 140 F7
Yorkletts CT5 108 A3
Dargets Rd ME5 97 A3
Dark Hill ME13 138 C8
DARLAND 97 E8
Darland Ave ME7 64 E1
Darland Ho SE9 12 D1
Darlinghurst Rd CT19 334 E7
Darlington Dr ME12 47 A6
Darlington St CT20 335 D5
Darlton Cl DA1 14 F4
Darman La TN12, ME18 225 D3
Darnets Field TN14 121 F2
Darnley Cl
Broadstairs CT10 83 F3
Folkestone CT20 334 F4
Rochester ME2 62 D6
Darnley Ct DA11 37 A8
Darnley Dr TN4 253 E4
Darnley Rd
Gravesend DA11 37 A8
1 Grays RM17 18 B8
Rochester ME2 62 E6
Darnley St DA11 37 B8
Darns Hill BR8 55 C2
Darracott Cl CT14 215 B5
Darrell Cl CT6 76 C3
Darren Gdns CT10 83 F2
Darrick Wood Ho BR6 86 C7
Darrick Wood Inf & Jun Schs BR6 86 B6
Darrick Wood Rd BR6 86 D8
Darrick Wood Sch BR6 86 B7
Darrick Wood Sports Ctr BR6 86 B7
Dart Cl ME2 62 F7
DARTFORD 15 E2
Dartford Borough Mus★ DA1 33 E8
Dartford Gram Sch DA1 15 C1
Dartford Gram Sch for Girls DA1 33 C8
Dartford Rd
Coldblow DA5 32 C7
Dartford DA1 15 B1
Farningham DA4 57 A5
Sevenoaks TN13 154 C3
Dartford Sta DA1 15 E1
Dartford Technology Coll DA1 33 C8
Dartford Trad Pk DA1 33 F6
Dartmouth Rd BR2 52 A2
Darwin Cl BR6 86 D5
Darwin Coll CT2 142 E5
Darwin Ct Eltham SE9 12 A1
Rochester ME1 63 D5
Darwin Dr TN10 222 D6
Darwin L Ctr TN16 118 F3
Darwin Rd Bexley DA16 12 F4
Darwin Rd *continued*
Birchington CT7 80 F8
Canterbury CT2 142 E5
Tilbury RM18 18 F6
Daryngton Ave CT7 80 C7
Dashmonden Cl ME2 40 C2
Dashwood Cl DA6 14 A2
Dashwood Rd DA11 37 A6
Davall Ho 10 RM17 18 B8
Davema Cl BR7 53 A8
Davenport Ave ME7 64 E7
Davenport Rd DA14 31 E6
Davey Ct ME1 63 C5
David Ave CT9 51 D2
David Coffer Ct DA17 4 B2
David Ho 23 DA14 31 A5
David Ramsey Ho SE18 2 D2
Davids Cl CT10 84 B3
Davidson Ho DA9 17 C2
Davidson Rd CT2 142 D1
DAVID STREET 93 B5
Davie Cl ME12 46 B8
Davie Ct ME12 46 B8
DAVINGTON 138 A8
Davington Hill ME13 138 C8
Davington Prim Sch ME13 138 C8
Davis Ave Deal CT14 215 A4
Northfleet DA11 36 E7
Davis Cl TN13 154 C5
Davis Way DA14 31 E2
Davy's Pl DA12 37 E2
Dawbourne TN30 324 B3
Dawell Dr TN16 118 C2
Dawes Cl DA9 16 F2
Dawes Close TN9 222 D3
Dawes Rd CT2, ME13 140 C4
Dawes St ME7 64 C5
Dawn La ME18 159 D3
Dawn Rise ME12 48 F6
Dawson Ave BR5 54 B7
Dawson Cl SE18 2 C2
Dawson Ct 7 ME7 64 A6
Dawson Dr BR8 32 E1
Dawson Rd CT19 335 D6
Dawson's Row ME13 138 A6
Day Ho 2 ME14 162 B4
Days La DA15 30 E8
Days Lane Prim Sch DA15 12 F1
Daytona Way CT6 76 A4
Dayton Dr DA8 15 D8
Dayton Rd ME13 170 C3
Deacon Cl ME2 62 E8
Deacon Ind Est ME20 129 A2
Deacons Leas BR6 86 D6
Deacon Trad Ctr ME2 63 A6
Deacon Trad Est TN9 222 D1
Deakin Leas TN9 254 B7
Deakins Terr BR6 54 A2
DEAL 215 E6
Deal Castle★ CT14 215 D5
Deal Castle Rd CT14 215 D5
Deal Ent Ctr CT14 215 C7
Deal Ho ME15 195 E8
Deal Maritime & Local History Mus★ 12 CT14 215 D6
Deal Parochial CE Prim Sch CT14 215 C3
Deal Rd
Northbourne CT14 214 A4
Sandwich CT13, CT14 180 F5
Deal Sta CT14 215 C6
Dean & Chapter Cotts DA13 36 B2
Dean Croft CT6 77 B2
Dean Ct 13 CT1 143 A1
Deane Cl CT5 108 E7
Deane Ct 8 ME7 64 C6
Deanery Rd TN8 184 C2
Dean Hill CT4, TN25 240 B2
Dean La DA13 93 C5
Dean Mead CT19 335 B7
Dean Rd
Luddesdown DA13 93 E8
Rochester ME2 62 F8
Sittingbourne ME10 101 E6
Woolwich SE28 3 A6
DEANS BOTTOM 133 C5
Deans Ct 7 TN9 254 B8
Deansfield Prim Sch SE9 12 A4
DEANS HILL 133 D6
Deans Hill Rd ME9 133 D5
Deans Mill Ct CT1 142 F1
Dean St ME15 194 C6
DEAN STREET 194 D7
Deansway Ave CT2 143 F7
Dean's Wlk TN23 299 F7
Deanwood Cl ME8 98 D6
Deanwood Dr ME8 98 E4
Deanwood Prim Education Tech Sch ME8 98 D3
Deanwood Rd CT17 277 E2
Deborah Cl CT5 108 F7
Debrabant Cl DA8 14 D8
De Burgh Hill CT17 278 C1
De Burgh St 2 CT17 310 C8
Decimus Pl TN1 286 B4
Decoy Hill Rd ME23 23 F6
Deedes Cl CT21 333 C3
Deepdene TN5 337 A6
Deepdene Rd DA16 13 A4
Deerhurst Cl DA3 59 C6
Deerhurst Gdns ME16 161 D4
Deering Cl ME4 41 B2
Deerleap La TN14 120 E6
Deerson La CT3 146 A4
Deerton St ME9 104 A2
DEERTON STREET 104 A2

Defence Cl SE28. . . . . 2 E5
Defiance Wlk SE18. . . . . 1 F3
Defiant Cl ME5. . . . . 97 B6
Defoe Cl Chatham ME5. . . 97 B6
  Erith DA8. . . . . 14 F6
Degema Rd BR7. . . . . 30 B3
Deham Ho ME10. . . . . . . 101 D5
De Haviland Drive 8
  SE18. . . . . 2 B1
De Havilland Cl ME13. . . 307 B4
De Havilland Rd ME14. . . 176 E3
Deidre Chapman Ho
  DA10. . . . . 17 E1
Delacourt Cl CT12. . . . . . 116 D5
Delacourt Rd SE3. . . . . . . 11 B7
Delafield Rd SE7. . . . . 1 C1
Delagarde Rd TN16. . . . . 151 D1
Delamark Rd ME12. . . . . . 28 C2
Delamere Gdns 3
  ME6. . . . . 128 A8
Delamere Rd ME6. . . . . . 128 A8
Delane Rd CT14. . . . . . . 215 A5
Delane Row CT4. . . . . . . 173 D3
De l'Angle Ho CT4. . . . . . 173 D3
De l'Angle Row CT4. . . . 173 D3
De Lapre Cl BR5. . . . . 54 D2
Delarue Cl TN11. . . . . . . 222 D8
Delaware Cl CT2. . . . . . . 143 F6
Delaware Cotts TN16. . . 249 F8
Delce Jun & Inf Schs
  ME1. . . . . 63 D2
Delce Rd ME1. . . . . 63 D4
Delfside CT13. . . . . 181 A8
Delf St CT13. . . . . 148 F1
Delisle Rd SE28. . . . . 2 E4
Delius Dr TN10. . . . . 222 F6
Dell Dr TN2. . . . . 286 D4
Dell The Maypole DA5. . . 32 F7
  Swanscombe DA9. . . . . . . 17 B2
  Woolwich SE2. . . . . 3 A1
Delmaney Cl CT10. . . . . . . 84 B5
Delmar Cl CT5. . . . . 75 D3
Delme Cres SE3. . . . . 11 B5
Delmonden La TN18. . . . 354 C8
Delmonden Rd TN18. . . 340 B1
De Luci Rd ME3. . . . . 4 C1
De Lucy Prim Sch SE2. . . . 3 B4
De Lucy St SE2. . . . . 3 A1
Delvan Cl SE18. . . . . 12 A7
Delves Ave TN2. . . . . 286 C1
Demelza Cl ME2. . . . . 62 A2
De Mere Cl ME8. . . . . 98 D6
Demozay Cl CT18. . . . . . 307 A4
Denbeigh Dr TN10. . . . . . 222 B6
Denberry Dr DA14. . . . . . . 31 B5
Denbigh Ave ME8. . . . . . . 65 D1
Denbigh Cl Bromley BR7 29 F2
  Sittingbourne ME10. . . . . 101 E7
Denbigh Rd
  Ramsgate CT12. . . . . 83 A1
  Royal Tunbridge Wells
  TN4. . . . . 286 C7
Denbridge Rd BR1. . . . . . 52 F7
Dence Cl CT6. . . . . 77 B5
Dence Pk CT6. . . . . 77 B4
Dencorra Way TN23. . . . 268 A1
Den Cross TN8. . . . . 249 D6
Dene Ave DA15. . . . . 31 B8
Dene Cl DA2. . . . . 32 E4
Denecourt BR5. . . . . 54 C1
Dene Dr New Barn DA3. . . 59 B7
  Orpington BR6. . . . . 52 A7
Dene Farm Barns CT3 178 A4
Dene Farm La CT3. . . . . . 178 A4
Dene Holm Rd DA11. . . . . 36 E5
Dene Lodge Cl TN15. . . 156 F7
Dene Rd DA1. . . . . 33 F8
Denesfield St TN13. . . . . 153 C4
Denesway DA13. . . . . 60 B3
Dene The
  Betheisden TN26. . . . . . . 297 D5
  Canterbury CT1. . . . . 175 B5
  Hythe TN21. . . . . 333 C2
  Sevenoaks TN13. . . . . . . 154 B1
Dene Way TN3. . . . . 285 A7
Dene Wlk Longfield DA3. . 58 E6
  Margate CT9. . . . . 82 F7
Dengemarsh Rd TN29 379 A7
Denham Cl Bexley DA16 . 13 C4
  Dymchurch TN29. . . . . . . 353 B4
Denham Rd ME9. . . . . . . 100 B7
Denham St 2 SE10. . . . . . . 1 A1
Denison Mews ME3 . . . . 25 C4
Deniston Ave DA5. . . . . . 31 E7
Den La TN12. . . . . 226 C3
Denmark Ho 10 SE18. . . . 1 E2
Denmark Rd
  Bromley BR1. . . . . 52 B8
  Ramsgate CT11. . . . . 117 E8
Denmark St
  Folkestone CT19. . . . . . . 335 E6
  Newham E13. . . . . 1 B8
Dennard Way BR6. . . . . . . 86 A6
Denne Cl CT2. . . . . 143 F7
Denne Manor La CT4. . . 204 C8
Dennes La TN29. . . . . . . 376 C8
Dennes Mill La TN25. . . 237 D2
Denness Rd TN23. . . . . . 300 B7
Dennettsland Rd TN8. 184 C1
Denning Cl ME16. . . . . . 161 B4
Dennington Ct TN4. . . . 254 A2
Dennis Cadman Ho
  ME20. . . . . 128 F1
Dennis Rd DA11. . . . . 37 B5
Dennis Way TN19. . . . . . 334 E7
Dennis Wilcocks Cl
  ME9. . . . . 100 B6
DENNY BOTTOM. 285 E4
Denny Cl 13 E6. . . . . 1 E8
Denny Ct 3 DA2. . . . . 16 B1
DENSOLE. 307 A8
Densole La CT18. . . . . . . 307 A8

Densole Way CT18 . . . . 307 A8
Denstead Cotts CT4. . . . 173 B8
Denstead Ct CT2. . . . . . 142 C4
Denstead La ME13 173 C7
Denstead Oast CT4. . . . . 173 B8
Denstead Wlk 11 ME15 195 F6
DENSTROUDE. 141 C8
Denstroude La CT2. . . . 141 D8
Dental Cl ME10. . . . . . . 101 A5
Dental St CT21. . . . . 333 C2
Dent-de-Lion Ct CT9. . . . 82 A8
Dent-de-Lion Rd
  Margate CT9. . . . . 82 A8
  Westgate on Sea CT8. . . . 50 C1
DENTON Dover. 243 B3
  Gravesend. 37 E8
Denton Cl ME15. . . . . . . 195 E8
Denton Court Rd DA12. . 37 E8
Denton Ct BR2. . . . . 53 A2
Denton Gn ME8. . . . . 65 B4
Denton Rd Bexley DA16. . 13 C7
  Dartford DA1. . . . . 32 E8
  Maypole DA5. . . . . 32 E7
Denton St DA12. . . . . 37 E8
Denton Terr DA5. . . . . . . 32 E6
Denton Way CT9. . . . . 51 C1
Denver Cl BR6. . . . . 53 E3
Denver Ind Est RM13. . . . 4 F8
Denver Rd DA1. . . . . 33 A8
De Quincey Mews E16. . . 1 A5
Derby Cl
  Sittingbourne ME10 . . . 101 D6
  Tonbridge TN11. . . . . . . 221 E6
Derby Rd Gillingham ME5 64 E2
  Grays RM17. . . . . 18 B8
  Maidstone ME15. . . . . . . 195 C8
Derby Road Bridge
  RM17. . . . . 18 B8
Derifall Cl E6. . . . . 1 F8
Dering Ct Bridge CT4. . . 175 F1
  Pluckley TN27. . . . . 265 C4
Dering Rd
  Ashford TN24. . . . . 268 D2
  Bridge CT4. . . . . 176 A1
  Herne Bay CT6. . . . . 76 F4
Derings The TN29. . . . . 376 B6
Dering Terr TN27. . . . . . 265 C3
Dering Way DA12. . . . . . . 37 F7
Deringwood Dr ME15. 162 F1
Dernier Rd TN10, TN9. . 222 C4
Derrick Gdns SE7. . . . . . . 1 C3
DERRINGSTONE. 242 E7
Derringstone Downs
  CT4. . . . . 242 F6
Derringstone Hill CT4 242 F6
Derringstone St CT4. . . 242 F7
DERRY DOWNS. 54 D3
Derry Downs BR5. . . . . . . 54 C3
Derville Ho TN28. . . . . . . 373 B6
Derville Rd TN29. . . . . . . 377 E2
Derwent Ave CT11. . . . . 117 A2
Derwent Cl DA1. . . . . 33 B7
Derwent Cres DA7. . . . . 14 A5
Derwent Dr
  Orpington BR5. . . . . 53 D2
  Royal Tunbridge Wells
  TN4. . . . . 285 E5
Derwent Ho 3 ME15. . . 195 E7
Derwent Rd TN10. . . . . . 222 C5
Derwent Way
  Aylesham CT3. . . . . 210 F6
  Gillingham ME8. . . . . 98 D8
Desmond Cres ME13 . . 139 A5
D'Este Rd CT19. . . . . . . 117 F7
Detillens La RH8. . . . . . . 183 A6
DETLING. 131 B1
Detling Ave CT10. . . . . . 84 A1
Detling Cl
  Gillingham ME8. . . . . 65 C2
  West Minst ME12. . . . . . . 46 B7
Detling Hill ME14. . . . . 131 B2
Detling Rd Bromley BR1 . 29 A3
  Erith DA8. . . . . 14 D7
  Northfleet DA11. . . . . 36 D7
Devalls Cl E6. . . . . 2 A6
Devenish Rd SE2. . . . . 3 A4
Devon Ave CT14. . . . . . . 215 C3
Devon Cl Chatham ME5. . 97 C7
  Gillingham ME8. . . . . 65 F1
Devon Ct Ramsgate CT12 83 B2
  Sutton at Hone DA4. . . . . 57 B8
Devon Gdns CT7. . . . . . . 80 F7
Devon Rd
  Canterbury CT1. . . . . . . 175 D8
  Folkestone CT19. . . . . . . 335 D5
  Maidstone ME15. . . . . . . 195 C8
  Sutton at Hone DA4. . . . . 57 C8
Devonshire Ave DA1. . . 15 B1
Devonshire Cl TN2. . . . 313 F8
Devonshire Gdns CT9. . 51 C3
Devonshire Rd
  Bexley DA6. . . . . 13 C3
  Bromley SE9. . . . . 29 E6
  Dover CT17. . . . . 310 B8
  Gillingham ME7. . . . . 64 D7
  Gravesend DA12. . . . . . . 37 B6
  Newham E16. . . . . 1 A7
  West Thurrock RM20. . . . 17 E8
Devonshire Sq BR2. . . . 52 B5
Devonshire Terr CT10. . 84 B5
De Warren Ho 3 DA11 .18 D1
Dewberry Cl ME4. . . . . . 41 B1
Dewberry Gdns E6. . . . . 1 E8
Dewhurst Cotts TN5. . . 336 A8
Dewhurst La TN5. . . . . . 336 B8
De Winter Ho TN13. . . . 154 A3
Dew La TN31. . . . . 367 A1
Dewlands Ave DA2. . . . . 34 B8
Dexter Cl TN25. . . . . . . 268 C8
Dexter Ho 2 DA18. . . . . . 3 E3
Deyley Way TN23. . . . . . 299 C8
Dhekelia Rd ME14. . . . . . 162 A7

Dial Cl Gillingham ME7 . . . 64 F6
  Swanscombe DA9. . . . . . . 17 D2
Dial Rd ME7. . . . . 64 F6
Diameter Rd BR5. . . . . . . 53 C3
Diamond Cotts TN12. . . 256 B7
Diamond Ct ME12. . . . . . 28 B1
Diamond Field TN12. . . 289 F3
Diamond Rd CT5. . . . . . . 74 E2
Diana Cl DA14. . . . . 31 E6
Diana Ct DA8. . . . . 14 E8
Diana Gdns CT14. . . . . . 215 A5
Diana Rd ME4. . . . . 64 A2
Dianne Ct SE12. . . . . 29 A7
Dianthus Cl SE2. . . . . 3 B1
Dibden La TN13, TN14. . 186 E5
Dibdin Rd CT14. . . . . . . 215 D7
Dickens Ave
  Canterbury CT1. . . . . . . 143 D2
  Dartford DA1. . . . . 16 A3
  Tilbury RM18. . . . . 19 B6
Dickens Cl Erith DA8. . . . 14 E7
  Hartley DA3. . . . . 58 F4
  Langley Heath ME17. . . . 196 E4
Dickens Ct Higham ME3. 39 C4
  Rochester ME2. . . . . 63 D8
  Staplehurst TN12. . . . . . 260 F5
Dickens Dr
  Chislehurst BR7. . . . . 30 C2
  West Malling ME19. . . . 127 F1
Dickens Ho 3 DA17. . . . . 3 F1
Dickens House Mus★
  CT10. . . . . 84 B4
Dickensian Cl ME3. . . . . 25 A2
Dickens Rd
  Broadstairs CT10. . . . . . . 84 B5
  Gravesend DA12. . . . . . . 37 E7
  Maidstone ME14. . . . . . . 161 E8
  Rochester ME1. . . . . 63 C8
Dickens Way TN18. . . . . 341 A2
Dickens Wlk CT10. . . . . . 84 B4
Dickens World★ ME4. . 64 A8
Dickley La ME17. . . . . . . 199 A6
Dickson Ct 7 ME10. . . . . 102 B4
Dickson Ho SE18. . . . . . . 11 E6
Dickson Rd Dover CT17 310 C8
  Eltham SE9. . . . . 11 A4
Dicksons Bourne TN25 329 F6
Dickson's Cnr CT13. . . 182 A6
Dieu Stone La CT16. . . . 310 E8
Digby Rd CT20. . . . . 334 E5
Digdog La TN12, TN17. 293 D3
Diggerland★ ME2. . . . . 62 F1
Dignals CT18. . . . . 65 F2
Dignash TN25. . . . . 235 E2
Dilhorne Cl SE12. . . . . . . 29 B5
Diligent Dr ME10. . . . . . 101 F7
Dillon Way TN2. . . . . 286 D7
Dillywood Cotts ME3. . . 39 F2
Dilly Wood Fields ME3. 40 A3
Dillywood La ME3. . . . . . 39 F2
Dilnot La CT7. . . . . 81 B3
Dimmock Cl TN12. . . . . 257 B7
Dingleden La TN17. . . . 342 F2
Diocesan & Payne Smith
  CE Prim Sch 23 CT1. 143 A1
Dippers CT15. . . . . 122 F2
Discovery Dr ME9. . . . . 159 B3
Discovery Prim Sch SE28 2 E5
Discovery Rd ME15. . . . 163 B2
Discovery Sch The
  ME18. . . . . 159 D3
Discovery Wlk CT1. . . . 175 C2
Dislingbury Rd TN11. . . 255 C4
Disraeli Cl
  Maidstone ME15. . . . . . . 195 E5
  Woolwich SE28. . . . . 3 C5
Dittisham Rd SE9. . . . . . 29 E4
DITTON. 128 C1
Ditton CE Jun Sch
  ME20. . . . . 128 C1
Ditton Court Cl ME20. 128 B1
Ditton Heritage Ctr &
  Victorian Classroom★ 1
  ME20. . . . . 128 C1
Ditton Inf Sch ME20. . . 128 C1
Ditton Pl ME20. . . . . . . 128 B1
Ditton Rd DA6. . . . . 13 E2
Dixon Cl
  Maidstone ME15. . . . . . . 161 F2
  4 Newham E16. . . . . 1 F7
Dixon Ho SE2. . . . . 3 C1
Dixwell Cl ME8. . . . . 98 D5
Dixwell Rd CT20. . . . . . . 335 A4
Dobbie Cl ME10. . . . . . . 101 E6
Dobell Rd SE9. . . . . 11 F2
Dobells TN17. . . . . 320 D4
Dobson Rd DA12. . . . . . . 37 E3
Dock Approach Rd
  RM17. . . . . 18 E8
Dock Exit Rd CT16. . . . . 310 F8
Dock Head Rd
  Chatham ME4. . . . . 64 A8
  St Mary's Island ME4. . . . 41 A1
Docklands Light Railway
  E16. . . . . 1 B5
Dockland St E16. . . . . 2 A1
Dock Rd Chatham ME4. . 63 F6
  Grays RM17. . . . . 18 D8
  Tilbury RM18. . . . . 18 E5
Dockside Outlet Ctr
  ME4. . . . . 64 A8
Dockside Rd E16. . . . . . . 1 D6
Doctor Hope's Rd
  TN17. . . . . 320 D4
Doctor's La CT15. . . . . . 309 B5
DODDINGTON. 167 E7
Doddington Ct ME16. . 161 E1
Doddington Place Gdns★
  ME9. . . . . 168 A2
Doddington Rd ME8. . . . 65 D3
Dodd Rd TN10. . . . . 222 C5
Dodd's La CT16. . . . . . . 278 A5
Doebury Wlk SE18. . . . . 13 A8
Does Alley 4 ME10. . . . 101 F4

Dog Cotts RH19. . . . . . . 281 B1
Doggerel Acre CT5. . . . 108 F7
Doggetts Cl TN8. . . . . . . 249 C8
Doggetts Row ME3. . . . . 27 B6
Dog Kennel La CT18. . . 305 B7
Dogwood Cl
  Chatham ME5. . . . . 97 D1
  Northfleet DA11. . . . . 36 F4
Dola Ave CT14. . . . . 215 B6
Dolphin Cl
  Broadstairs CT10. . . . . . . 51 G3
  Erith DA8. . . . . 3 D7
  Tonbridge TN9. . . . . 254 A8
  6 Newham E16. . . . . 1 A8
Dolphin Dr ME8. . . . . 98 E5
Dolphin Ho
  1 Dover CT17. . . . . 310 E7
  Rochester ME1. . . . . 63 E5
Dolphin La CT16. . . . . . . 310 E7
Dolphin Pas 3 CT16. . . 310 E7
Dolphin Pk ME10. . . . . . 102 B5
Dolphin Pl 5 CT16. . . . . 310 E7
Dolphin Rd Lydd TN29. 376 C6
  Sittingbourne ME10. . . . . 102 B5
Dolphins Rd CT19. . . . . 335 D7
Dolphin St Deal CT14. . 215 D7
  Herne Bay CT6. . . . . 76 E5
Dombey Cl Higham ME3 39 C3
  Rochester ME1. . . . . 63 C3
Domneva Rd
  Minster (Thanet)
  CT12. . . . . 115 B6
  Westgate on Sea CT8. . . . 81 D8
Domonic Dr SE9. . . . . . . 30 B5
Donald Biggs Dr DA12 .37 D8
Donald Moor Ave ME9 103 C2
Donaldson Rd SE18. . . . 12 A6
Donald Troup Ho ME1 .63 C4
Doncaster Cl 7 ME15 195 F6
Donegal Rd CT1. . . . . . . 175 C8
Donemowe Dr ME10. . . 101 F8
Donet Cl ME8. . . . . 98 C5
Dongola Rd ME2. . . . . . . 40 B1
Donkey Field TN11. . . . 220 E1
Donkey La
  Adisham CT3. . . . . 210 C8
  Appledore Heath TN26. . 347 C2
  Maplescombe DA4. . . . . . 35 D2
Donkey St TN21, TN29. 352 E5
DONKEY STREET. . . . 352 D5
Donnahay Rd CT12. . . . 83 C3
Donnington Ct 1 DA2. .16 B1
Donnington Rd TN13. 153 D7
Donnithorne Ho CT6. . . 76 E5
Doon Brae TN4. . . . . 254 A2
Dorado Gdns BR6. . . . . . 87 D7
Doran Gr SE18. . . . . 12 E7
Dorcas Gdns CT10. . . . 84 A6
Dorchester TN1. . . . . . . 286 B6
Dorchester Ave DA5. . . 31 B8
Dorchester Cl
  Cliffe Woods ME3. . . . . . . 40 B7
  Dartford DA1. . . . . 33 B7
  Orpington BR5. . . . . 31 B1
Dorchester Rd DA12. . . 37 D5
Dorcis Ave DA7. . . . . 13 E5
Doria Dr DA12. . . . . 37 F5
Doric Ave TN4. . . . . 253 F1
Doric Cl TN4. . . . . 253 F1
Doric Ct CT11. . . . . 117 C5
Dorin Ct TN2. . . . . 286 C3
Doris Ave DA8. . . . . 14 C6
Dorking Rd TN1. . . . . . . 286 C6
Dorman Avenue N CT3 210 E6
Dorman Avenue S CT3 210 F5
Dormers Dr DA13. . . . . . 60 B2
Dornberg Cl SE3. . . . . . . 11 A7
Dornberg Rd SE3. . . . . . 11 B7
Dornden Dr TN3. . . . . . . 285 A4
Dornden Gdns ME5. . . . 97 B2
Dorne Cotts TN27. . . . . 232 E6
Dorney Rise BR5. . . . . . . 53 F5
Dorothy Ave TN17. . . . . 320 E4
Dorothy Dr CT12. . . . . . 83 C2
Dorothy Evans Cl DA7 14 B3
Dorrit Way
  Chislehurst BR7. . . . . 30 C2
  Rochester ME1. . . . . 63 D2
Dorset Ave DA16. . . . . . 12 F3
Dorset Cl CT5. . . . . 108 B7
Dorset Cotts TN7. . . . . . 311 B4
Dorset Cres DA12. . . . . 37 E4
Dorset Ct Deal CT14. . . 215 C3
  Ramsgate CT12. . . . . 83 B2
Dorset Gdns
  Birchington CT7. . . . . 80 F7
  Deal CT14. . . . . 215 C2
Dorset Pl ME13. . . . . . . 138 C7
Dorset Rd Bromley SE9. . 29 E6
  Royal Tunbridge Wells
  TN2. . . . . 286 D2
  West Minst ME12. . . . . . . 46 A8
Dorset Road Ind Est
  ME12. . . . . 46 A8
Dorset Road Inf Sch
  SE9. . . . . 29 E6
Dorset Sq ME8. . . . . 65 D1
Dorset St TN13. . . . . . . 154 C7
Dorset Way ME15. . . . . 195 C8
Dorton Coll of FE
  TN15. . . . . 154 F5
Dorton Dr TN15. . . . . . . 154 F5
Dorton House Sch (for the
  Blind) TN15. . . . . 154 F5
Dorville Rd SE12. . . . . . 11 A2
Dossett Ct CT14. . . . . . . 215 A3
Dothill Rd SE18. . . . . 12 C7
Dotterel Cl ME5. . . . . 97 D2
Doubleday Dr ME9. . . . 102 E2
Doubleton La TN11. . . . 252 A5
Douglas Almshouses
  ME17. . . . . 199 D5
Douglas Ave
  Hythe TN21. . . . . 333 C2
  Whitstable CT5. . . . . 74 E1

Douglas Bglws CT15. . . 246 E8
Douglas Bldgs TN12. . . 260 E5
Douglas Cl CT10. . . . . . . 83 E5
Douglas Ct TN16. . . . . . 118 D5
Douglas Rd Bexley DA16 13 B6
  Deal CT14. . . . . 215 A3
  Dover CT17. . . . . 310 B8
  Herne Bay CT6. . . . . 77 A4
  Lenham ME17. . . . . 199 D5
  Maidstone ME16. . . . . . . 161 E3
  6 Newham E16. . . . . 1 A8
  Tonbridge TN9. . . . . 254 A8
Douglas Terr CT14. . . . . 215 D5
Doug Siddons Ct 12
  RM17. . . . . 18 C8
Dour Ho The 13 CT16. 310 D8
Dour Mews 12 CT16. . . 278 C1
Douro Cl CT1. . . . . 143 D1
Douro Pl CT16. . . . . 310 E7
Douro Stables TN4. . . . 286 A4
Dour Side CT17. . . . . . . 277 F3
Dour St CT16. . . . . 310 D8
Doust Way ME1. . . . . 63 D5
Dove App E6. . . . . 1 E8
Dove Cl Chatham ME5. . 97 B6
  Hythe TN21. . . . . 353 D8
  Kingsnorth TN23. . . . . . . 300 C3
  Whitstable CT5. . . . . 108 C7
Dovecote Cl CT14. . . . . 205 B8
Dove Ct 6 CT11. . . . . . . 117 E7
Dovedale Ct7. . . . . 81 B7
Dovedale Rd DA2. . . . . . 34 C7
Dovedale Ct
  Ashford TN24. . . . . 268 B4
  Birchington CT7. . . . . 81 B7
Dovedale Rd DA2. . . . . . 34 C7
Dove Lea Gdns CT17. . 277 E3
Doveney Cl BR5. . . . . 54 D6
DOVER. 310 F7
Dover Castle & Princess of
  Wales Regiment Mus★
  CT16. . . . . 310 F8
Dover Coll CT17. . . . . . . 310 C8
Dove Rd TN10. . . . . 222 C6
Dover Discovery Ctr★ 20
  CT16. . . . . 310 D8
Dover Gram Sch for Boys
  CT17. . . . . 310 A8
Dover Gram Sch for Girls
  CT16. . . . . 278 C1
Dover Hill CT19. . . . . . . 335 F8
Dover Ho
  2 Maidstone ME15. . . . . 195 E8
  Rochester ME2. . . . . 40 C1
Dover L Ctr CT17. . . . . 310 E8
Dover Mus★ CT16. . . . 310 D7
Dover Patrol SE3. . . . . . 11 B5
Dover Patrol Meml★
  CT15. . . . . 280 C7
Dover Pl TN23. . . . . 268 C1
Dover Priory Sta CT17 310 C8
Dover Rd Barham CT4 . 210 A1
  Bishopsbourne CT4. . . . . 209 D5
  Dover CT15. . . . . 278 E4
  Folkestone CT19, CT20. 335 E7
  Northfleet DA11. . . . . 36 D8
  Ringwould CT14. . . . . 248 A6
  Sandwich CT13. . . . . 180 F6
  St Margaret's at Cliffe
  CT15. . . . . 279 D6
  Tilmanstone CT13, CT14 213 B5
  Woolage Green CT4. . . . . 243 D6
  Woolwich DA16. . . . . 12 C5
Dover Road Com Prim Sch
  DA11. . . . . 36 E7
Dover Road E DA11. . . . 36 F7
Dover St
  Canterbury CT1. . . . . . . 175 A7
  1 Maidstone ME16. . . . . 161 C2
  Sittingbourne ME10. . . . . 101 E4
Dover Trade Ctr CT15 278 C6
Dover Transport Mus★
  CT16. . . . . 278 A5
Doves Cl BR2. . . . . 85 E8
Doves Cnr CT14. . . . . . . 213 A4
Doves Croft ME9. . . . . . 134 C7
Dowding Ho TN12. . . . . 256 F6
Dowding Rd TN16. . . . . 118 D4
Dowding Way TN2. . . . . 254 E1
Dowell Mews CT14. . . . 215 C3
Dower Ho The DA14. . . 31 F5
Dower House Cres
  TN4. . . . . 253 E3
Dowgate Cl TN9. . . . . . . 254 D7
Dowle Cl TN29. . . . . 372 A7
Dowlerville Rd BR6. . . . . 86 F4
Dowling Cl ME6. . . . . . . 127 E7
Dowling Ho DA17. . . . . . 3 F3
Downage The DA11. . . . 37 A6
Downash Ct TN5. . . . . . . 339 A3
Downash Ho TN5. . . . . . 339 A3
Down Ave TN3. . . . . 317 A4
Downbank Ave DA7. . . . 14 D5
Down Barton Farm Cotts
  CT7. . . . . 79 D1
Down Barton Rd CT7. . 79 E1
Down Court Rd ME9. . . 135 C1
Down Ct TN23. . . . . 299 E5
Downderry Lavender
  Nursery★ TN11. . . . . . 190 D5
Downderry Way ME20 128 B1
DOWNE. 119 A8
Downe Ave TN14. . . . . . 119 D8
Downe Cl DA16. . . . . . . 13 C7
Downe Ho 10 SE7. . . . . 11 C8
Downend. 12 B7
Downe Prim Sch BR6. . 119 A8
Downer Ct ME1. . . . . 96 E8
Downe Rd
  Cudham BR6, TN14. . . . 119 C5
  Farthing Street BR2. . . . . 85 E2

Down House Mus★
  BR6. . . . . 119 A7
Downings E6. . . . . 2 A7
Downings The CT6. . . . . 77 A2
Down La TN3. . . . . 314 B1
Downland Ct TN4. . . . . . 268 B3
Downlands Deal CT14. . 248 B8
  Harrietsham ME17. . . . . . 198 F6
Downland Wlk ME5. . . . 97 A5
Downleys Cl SE9. . . . . . . 29 B8
Downman Rd SE9. . . . . . 11 E4
Downs Ave Bromley BR7 29 F3
  Dartford DA1. . . . . 34 A8
  Whitstable CT5. . . . . 87 B8
Downs CE Prim Sch The
  CT14. . . . . 215 B2
Downs Cl Charing TN27 234 C8
  East Studdal CT15. . . . . . 246 D8
  Hawkinge CT18. . . . . 307 A4
  Maidstone ME14. . . . . . . 162 B8
  Sittingbourne ME10. . . . . 101 D2
Down's Cl TN27. . . . . . . 262 E5
Downs End CT14. . . . . . . 215 C2
Downs Rd ME18. . . . . . . 193 B3
Downside
  Bekesbourne CT4. . . . . . 176 E3
  Folkestone CT19. . . . . . . 335 C7
  Rochester ME2. . . . . 63 A7
  St Margaret's at Cliffe
  CT15. . . . . 280 A6
Downside Rd CT16. . . . . 278 B6
Downsland Ho ME2. . . . 62 C2
Downs Pk CT6. . . . . 77 A5
Downs Rd
  Canterbury CT2. . . . . . . 142 F4
  Deal CT14. . . . . 215 C3
  East Studdal CT15. . . . . . 246 E8
  Folkestone CT19. . . . . . . 335 C7
  Istead Rise DA13. . . . . . . 36 D3
  Maidstone ME14. . . . . . . 162 B8
  Ramsgate CT11. . . . . 117 B6
  Yalding ME18. . . . . 193 A1
Downs The
  Chartham CT4. . . . . 173 E1
  Chatham ME5. . . . . 96 D1
  Preston CT3. . . . . 146 C6
  Ramsgate CT11. . . . . 117 D5
Downs Valley DA3. . . . . 58 E5
Downsview
  Chatham ME5. . . . . 97 C8
  Trottiscliffe ME19. . . . . . 126 A5
Downs View
  Burham ME1. . . . . 95 F1
  West Malling ME19. . . . . 159 B8
Downsview Cl BR8. . . . . 55 F6
Downs View Inf Sch
  TN4. . . . . 268 E7
Downsview Prim Sch
  BR8. . . . . 56 A6
Downs View Rd TN13. . 153 F2
Downs View Rd ME14. 162 B8
Downsway BR6. . . . . 86 E5
Downs Way
  Charing TN27. . . . . 234 C8
  Sellindge TN25. . . . . 303 C1
Downs Wood DA3. . . . . 125 F8
DOWN THE. 317 A3
Downton Cotts TN18. . 355 F4
Doyle Cl DA8. . . . . 14 B5
Doyle Way RM18. . . . . . 19 C5
Drage Rd TN12. . . . . 224 E6
Dragonfly Ct TN23. . . . 299 D8
Dragonfly Way TN18. . 307 B4
Dragoon Ho 9 CT1. . . . 143 A1
Drainless Rd TN13. . . . 180 A5
Drake Ave ME12. . . . . . . 47 D5
Drake Cres SE28. . . . . . . 3 C7
Drake Ct Orpington BR5 . 54 B3
  3 Ramsgate CT11. . . . . . 117 E8
Drake Hall E16. . . . . 1 B5
Drake Mews 5 BR2. . . . 52 C5
Drake Point 12 DA8. . . . 4 E1
Drake Rd TN24. . . . . 301 B7
Drake's Ave ME2. . . . . . . 62 F8
Drakes Cl ME9. . . . . 66 E2
Drakes Lee TN28. . . . . . 373 E5
Draper Cl DA17. . . . . 3 F2
Draper Ct BR1. . . . . 52 E5
Drapers Almshouses
  CT9. . . . . 83 A8
Drapers Ave CT9. . . . . . 82 F8
Drapers Ct CT9. . . . . 83 A8
Drapers Mills Prim Sch
  CT9. . . . . 83 A8
Draper St 3 TN4. . . . . . 253 F2
Drapers Windmill★
  CT9. . . . . 51 A1
Drawbridge Cl ME15. . 195 E8
Drawell Cl SE18. . . . . 2 E1
Dray Corner Rd TN27. 261 F7
Dray Ct TN11. . . . . 223 E8
Drays Cotts DA4. . . . . . . 57 B5
Dray's Field ME9. . . . . . 166 A7
Drayton Ave BR6. . . . . . 53 B1
Drayton Cl ME23. . . . . . 23 E4
Drayton Rd TN9. . . . . . . 254 C8
Dreadnought Ave ME12 47 A6
Dresden Ct CT8. . . . . 81 D8
Drewery Dr ME8. . . . . . . 98 C5
Drew La CT14. . . . . 215 C4
Drew Prim Sch E16. . . . . 1 C5
Drew Rd E16. . . . . 1 C5
Driffield Gdns TN9. . . . 253 F7
Drift The BR2. . . . . 85 D7
Drill La CT3. . . . . 145 B1
Drive The Ashurst TN3. 283 F1
  Bexley DA5. . . . . 31 D8
  Broadstairs CT10. . . . . . . 83 F6
  Canterbury CT1. . . . . . . 175 B6
  Chislehurst BR7. . . . . 53 C8
  Deal CT14. . . . . 215 C5
  Erith DA8. . . . . 14 B8
  Gravesend DA12. . . . . . . 37 E4
  New Barn DA3. . . . . 59 B6

Drive The *continued*
Orpington BR6 . . . . .86 F8
Royal Tunbridge Wells
TN2 . . . . 286 B1
Sevenoaks TN13 . . . . 154 B3
Sidcup DA14 . . . . .31 B4
St Paul's Cray BR7 . . . . .53 F6
Tonbridge TN9 . . . . 254 B7
Whitstable CT5 . . . . 109 D8
Drop Redoubt Fort★
CT17 . . . . 310 D7
Drop Redoubt Rd
CT17 . . . . 310 D7
Drove Rd ME12 . . . . .46 E6
Drovers Rdbt TN24 . . . 268 A4
Drove The
Fordwich CT2 . . . . 144 A4
Monkton CT12 . . . . . . 114 B6
Northbourne CT14 . . . 214 A5
Whitfield CT16 . . . . . . 278 A8
Whitstable CT5 . . . . . . 109 D8
Droveway Gdns CT15 . 280 A6
Droveway The CT15 . . 280 B6
Drove Way The DA13 . . .36 E1
Drudgeon Way DA2 . . . .35 B5
Druidstone Pk★ CT2 .141 F7
Drum La TN23 . . . . 268 B2
Drum Major Dr CT14 . 215 B3
Drummond Cl DA8 . . . .14 E6
Drury Rd TN30 . . . . 324 B1
Dry Bank Ct TN10 . . . . 222 C4
Dry Bank Rd TN10 . . . 222 C4
Drybeck Ave CT11 . . . 116 F7
Dryden Cl CT1 . . . . 175 C7
Dryden Ho BR2 . . . . .52 D4
Dryden Pl BR18 . . . . . . .19 B6
Dryden Rd Bexley DA16 . .12 F6
Dover CT16 . . . . 278 B3
Dryden Way BR5 . . . . . .54 A1
Dry End Rd ME20 . . . . 128 C3
DRYHILL 153 B3
Dryhill La TN14 . . . . . . 153 B3
Dryhill Nature Reserve★
TN14 . . . . 153 B3
Dry Hill Park Cres
TN10 . . . . 222 C3
Dry Hill Park Rd TN10 .222 B3
Dryhill Rd DA17 . . . . . . .13 F8
Dry Hill Rd TN10 . . . . . 222 B3
Dryland Ave 6 BR6 . . . .86 F6
Dryland Rd
Borough Green TN15 . . 156 F6
Snodland ME6 . . . . 127 F8
Drywall Ind Est ME10 . 102 B6
Dublin Ho 10 ME15 . . . 195 E7
Duchess of Kent Ct The
ME20 . . . . 128 F1
Duchess of Kent Dr
ME5 . . . . .97 B3
Duchess' Wlk TN15 . . . 154 E2
Ducie Ho 9 SE7 . . . . . . .11 C8
Ducketts Rd DA1 . . . . . .14 F2
Duck La Canterbury CT1 143 A1
Shadoxhurst TN26 . . . . 326 F7
Duck St CT4 . . . . 273 F4
Duckpits Rd CT4 . . . . . 240 A6
Duck St CT4 . . . . 273 F4
Duckworth Cl CT24 . . . 301 B7
Duddington Cl SE9 . . . . .29 D4
Dudely Rd DA11 . . . . . . .36 E8
Dudley Ave CT8 . . . . . . .81 C8
Dudley Cl ME15 . . . . . . 195 F5
Dudley Keen Ct TN9 . . 254 E8
Dudley Lodge TN2 . . . . 286 C4
Dudley Rd
Ashford TN24 . . . . 268 C5
Folkestone CT19 . . . . . 335 E5
Royal Tunbridge Wells
TN1 . . . . 286 A4
Dudsbury Rd
Dartford DA1 . . . . .15 B2
Sidcup DA14 . . . . .31 B2
Duggan Dr BR7 . . . . . . .29 E2
Duke of Clarence Trad Est
The ME12 . . . . .28 A3
Duke of Wellington Ave
SE18, SE28 . . . . .2 C3
Duke of York's Royal
Military Sch CT15 . . 278 F4
Dukes Mdw TN26 . . . . 349 A7
Dukes Meadow TN11 . 219 F2
Dukes Meadow Dr ME7 .97 F6
Dukes Orch DA5 . . . . . . .32 C7
Dukes Rd TN1 . . . . 286 C5
Duke St Deal CT14 . . . 215 D7
Margate CT9 . . . . .50 I3
Dukes Wlk 7 ME15 . . . 162 A4
Dukeswood CT5 . . . . . . 109 D6
Dully Rd Lynsted ME9 . 135 E6
Sittingbourne ME9 . . . . 102 E1
Dulverton Prim Sch
SE9 . . . . .30 D6
Dulverton Rd SE9 . . . . . .30 D6
Dulwich Prep Sch
TN17 . . . . 321 A4
Dumbourne La TN30 . 345 D2
Dumbreck Rd SE9 . . . . .12 A4
Dumergue Ave ME11 . . .46 B5
DUMPTON 83 E2
Dumpton Gap Rd CT10 .84 A2
Dumpton Cl CT11 . . . . . .83 E1
Dumpton Park Dr CT10,
CT11 . . . . .84 A2
Dumpton Park Rd
CT11 . . . . 117 E8
Dumpton Park Sta CT11 83 F1
Dunbar Ct BR2 . . . . .52 A5
Dunblane Rd SE9 . . . . . .11 E5
Duncan Cl CT5 . . . . 108 D7
Duncan Dr CT7 . . . . .80 E8
Duncan Ho 2 SE7 . . . . .11 B8
Duncannon Place 2
DA9 . . . . .17 C3

Duncan Rd
Gillingham ME7 . . . . . . .64 D5
Ramsgate CT11 . . . . . . 117 D7
Whitstable CT5 . . . . . . 108 D7
Duncans Cotts 6
TN16 . . . . 151 D1
Duncroft SE18 . . . . .12 E1
Dundale Rd TN12, TN3 288 A3
Dundonald Cl 7 E6 . . . . .1 E7
Dundonald Rd
11 Broadstairs CT10 . . . .84 B4
Ramsgate CT11 . . . . . . 117 C7
Dunedin Cl ME10 . . . . 101 C3
Dunedin Dr CT16 . . . . 278 B3
Dunedin Ho
9 Maidstone ME15 . . . 195 E5
Newham E16 . . . . .1 F5
2 Tilbury RM18 . . . . . . .19 A5
Dunedin Rd CT12 . . . . . .83 A1
Dunera Dr ME14 . . . . . 162 A7
Dunes Rd TN28 . . . . . . 373 D3
Dunes The CT13 . . . . . 182 A7
Dunkel Ho 6 ME15 . . . 195 E7
Dunkery Rd SE9 . . . . . . .29 C5
Dunkery Rise TN24 . . . 268 A6
Dunkin Rd DA1 . . . . .16 A3
Dunkirk CI
Dymchurch TN29 . . . . . 366 B7
Gravesend DA12 . . . . . . .37 C3
Dunkirk Dr ME5 . . . . . . .96 F6
DUNKIRK END 366 B7
Dunkirk Road N ME13 .140 B2
Dunkirk Road S ME13 .140 B1
Dunkirk Sq CT15 . . . . . 278 F3
Dunkley Villas TN15 . . 125 F1
DUNK'S GREEN 190 A4
Dunk's Green Rd TN11 190 A5
Dunlin Ct TN29 . . . . . . 366 A3
Dunlin Dr ME4 . . . . .41 C2
Dunlop Ct 7 TN18 . . . . 341 A2
Dunlop Rd RM18 . . . . . . .18 F6
Dunnett Rd CT19 . . . . 334 E6
Dunning's La ME1 . . . . . .63 C4
Dunnings The ME16 . . 161 A2
Dunn Lodge TN2 . . . . . 286 D2
Dunnock Rd
Ashford TN25 . . . . 268 B7
Newham E6 . . . . .1 E7
Dunnose Ct RM19 . . . . . .16 B8
DUNN STREET
Gillingham 131 A8
Westwell 235 E5
Dunn Street Rd ME7 . 131 A8
Dunoon Cotts BR6 . . . 119 A5
Dunoon Ct CT11 . . . . . . .83 F1
Dunorlan Farm TN2 . . 286 E4
Dunorlan Farm Cotts
TN2 . . . . 286 E4
Dunstable Ct 5 SE3 . . . .11 A7
Dunstall Cl TN29 . . . . . 366 A5
Dunstall Gdns TN29 . . 366 A5
Dunstall La TN29 . . . . . 366 A5
Dunstall Welling Est
DA16 . . . . .13 B5
Dunstan Ave CT8 . . . . . .81 D7
Dunstan Glade BR5 . . . .53 D3
Dunstan Gr TN4 . . . . . . 286 B6
Dunstan Ho CT14 . . . . 215 D8
Dunstan Rd TN4 . . . . . 286 B6
Dunster Ct 16 DA12 . . . .18 B1
Dunster Terr 3 ME15 .195 E8
DUNTON GREEN 153 E8
Dunton Green Prim Sch
TN13 . . . . 153 E7
Dunton Green Sta
TN13 . . . . 153 E7
Dunvegan Rd SE9 . . . . .11 F3
Dunwich Rd DA7 . . . . . .13 F6
Dupree Rd SE7 . . . . .1 B1
Durant Rd BR8 . . . . .33 A2
Durban Cl CT12 . . . . . . .83 A2
Durban Cres CT16 . . . 278 C4
Durban Ho 7 ME15 . . . 195 E5
Durban Rd CT9 . . . . .51 A1
DURGATES 336 E5
Durham Cl
Canterbury CT1 . . . . . . 174 F6
9 Dover CT17 . . . . 310 D7
Maidstone ME15 . . . . . 162 E1
Durham Hill CT17 . . . . 310 D7
Durham Rd Bromley BR2 52 A5
Gillingham ME8 . . . . . . .98 C7
Sidcup DA14 . . . . .31 B3
Durham Rise SE18 . . . . . .2 D1
Duriun Way DA8 . . . . . . .15 B7
Durley Gdns BR6 . . . . . .87 B7
Durling Ct ME4 . . . . .66 A1
Durlings Orch TN15 . . 156 D6
DURLOCK 179 B8
Durlock Ct CT12 . . . . . 115 C5
Durlock Ave CT11 . . . . 117 B5
Durlock Rd CT3 . . . . . . 179 B7
Durlocks The CT19 . . . 335 E5
Durndale La ME16 . . . . .36 E4
Durnford Cl CT2 . . . . . 142 E2
Durovernum Ct CT1 . . 175 A7
DURRANT GREEN 324 B6
Durrant Way
Orpington BR6 . . . . .86 D5
Swanscombe DA10 . . . . .35 E8
Durrell Gdns ME5 . . . . . .64 E1
Dursley Cl SE3 . . . . .11 C5
Dursley Gdns SE3 . . . . .11 D6
Dursley Rd SE3 . . . . .11 C5

Duval Dr ME1 . . . . .96 E8
Duvard's Pl ME9 . . . . . 100 F1
Duxberry Cl BR2 . . . . . .52 E4
Dux Court Rd ME23 . . . .23 D2
Duxford Ho 12 SE2 . . . . .3 D4
Dux Hill TN15 . . . . 189 F8
Dux La TN15 . . . . 156 F1
Dwelly La TN8 . . . . 216 D3
Dyke Dr BR5 . . . . .54 C2
Dyke Rd CT19 . . . . 335 E5
Dykewood Cl DA5 . . . . .32 E5
Dylan Rd DA17 . . . . .4 A3
DYMCHURCH 366 C7
Dymchurch Cl BR6 . . . .52 A8
Dymchurch Ho 1 CT1 175 B8
Dymchurch Martello
Tower★ TN29 . . . . . 366 C7
Dymchurch Prim Sch
TN29 . . . . 366 C8
Dymchurch Rd
Hythe CT21, TN29 . . . . 353 C6
St Mary's Bay TN29,
TN28 . . . . 366 A5
Dymchurch Sta★
TN29 . . . . 366 B7
Dyneley Rd SE12 . . . . . .29 C5
Dynes Rd TN15 . . . . . . 122 E2
Dynevor Rd TN4 . . . . . 286 C5
Dyngley Cl ME10 . . . . . 101 E6

E

EACH END 148 B1
Eadred Way ME10 . . . . .69 A1
Eagle Cl ME9 . . . . 128 A2
Eagle Cotts 8 CT11 . . . 117 D7
Eagle Heights Wildlife
Pk★ DA4 . . . . .89 B8
Eagle Hill CT11 . . . . . . 117 D7
Eagle Ho RM17 . . . . .17 F8
Eagles Cl ME10 . . . . . . 102 C4
Eagles Dr TN16 . . . . . . 118 D1
Eaglesfield Rd SE18 . . . .12 B6
Eagles Rd DA9 . . . . .11 C2
Eaglestone CT15 . . . . . 157 A8
Eagle Way DA11 . . . . . . .18 A2
Ealdham Prim Sch SE9 11 C3
Ealdham Sq SE9 . . . . . . .11 C3
Ealham Cl
Ashford TN24 . . . . 301 A8
Canterbury CT4 . . . . . . 175 B5
Ealing Cl ME5 . . . . .97 C4
Eardemont Cl DA1 . . . . .14 F3
Eardley Point 9 SE18 . . .2 B2
Eardley Rd Erith DA17 . . .4 A1
Sevenoaks TN13 . . . . . 154 B3
Earl Cl ME5 . . . . .97 B4
Earl Rd DA11 . . . . .36 E6
Earl Rise SE18 . . . . .2 D2
Earls Ave TN24 . . . . . . 268 F1
Earl's Ave CT20 . . . . . . 335 B4
Earlsfield TN25 . . . . . . 330 A6
Earlsfield Rd CT20 . . . 333 D2
Earlshall Rd SE9 . . . . . . .12 A3
Earl St ME14 . . . . 161 F4
Earlsworth Ct TN24 . . 300 D6
Earlsworth Rd TN24 . . 300 D6
Easole Hts CT15 . . . . . 211 D5
Easole St CT15 . . . . . . 211 D5
Eason Villas TN12 . . . . 259 D6
EAST BARMING 160 F1
East Beckton District Ctr
E6 . . . . .1 F8
East Blean Woods (Nature
Reserve)★ CT3, CT6 .111 B6
East Borough Prim Sch
ME14 . . . . 162 B5
Eastbridge Rd TN29 . . 366 B8
Eastbrook Pl CT16 . . . 310 E8
Eastbrook Rd SE3 . . . . . .11 B6
Eastbury Rd Newham E6,2 A7
Orpington BR5 . . . . .53 D3
EASTCHURCH 48 E3
Eastchurch CE Prim Sch
ME12 . . . . .48 E3
Eastchurch Rd
Margate CT9 . . . . .51 E3
Minster (Sheppey) ME12 .48 B5
East Cliff Dover CT16 . 310 F8
Folkestone CT19 . . . . . 335 E5
East Cliff Gdns 22
CT19 . . . . 335 E5
East Cliff Par CT6 . . . . . .77 A5
East Cliff Pas 23 CT19 335 E5
East Cliff Rd TN4 . . . . . 286 A6
East Cliff & Warren Ctry
Pk★ CT18 . . . . 308 D1
Eastcombe Ave SE7 . . . .11 B8
Eastcote BR6 . . . . .53 F1
Eastcote Prim Sch
DA16 . . . . .12 D4
Eastcote Rd DA16 . . . . .12 D5
Eastcourt Gn ME8 . . . . .65 B4
Eastcourt La
Gillingham, Lower Twydal
ME7, ME8 . . . . .65 C5
Gillingham ME8 . . . . . . .65 B3
East Court Sch CT11 . . 117 F7
East Crescent Rd DA12 .19 C1
East Cross TN30 . . . . . 345 B7
East Ct 4 ME15 . . . . . . 162 A1
East Dr BR5 . . . . .54 B3
EAST END Benenden . . 322 C3
Headcorn 263 B4
East End Rd ME4, ME7 . .64 D5
Easterfields ME19 . . . . 160 C5
Eastern Arm N CT16 . . 310 H8
Eastern Arm S CT16 . . 310 H8

Eastern Ave
Ashford TN23 . . . . 268 A2
Halfway Houses ME12 . .46 D6
Queenborough ME11 . . .46 B4
West Thurrock RM20 . . .16 F8
Eastern Espl
Broadstairs CT10 . . . . . .84 B5
Margate CT9 . . . . .51 B3
Eastern Gdns TN24 . . . 300 E8
Eastern Rd
Leysdown-on-Sea ME12 .49 G2
Lydd TN29 . . . . 376 D7
Eastern Service Rd
CT16 . . . . 310 H8
Eastern View TN16 . . . 118 C2
Eastern Way Erith SE28 . .3 D5
1 Grays RM17 . . . . .18 A8
EAST FARLEIGH 194 B7
East Farleigh Prim Sch
ME15 . . . . 194 B6
East Farleigh Sta
ME16 . . . . 194 B8
Eastfield Gdns TN10 . . 222 E5
Eastfield Ho ME16 . . . 161 B2
Eastfield Rd 1 CT7 . . . . .81 A7
Eastfields CT19 . . . . . . 335 D6
Eastgate ME1 . . . . .63 C5
Eastgate Cl 1 Erith SE28 . .3 D7
Herne Bay CT6 . . . . .77 B3
Eastgate Ct ME1 . . . . . . .63 C5
Eastgate Rd TN30 . . . . 345 C8
Eastgate Terr ME1 . . . . .63 C5
East Gn ME10 . . . . .69 A1
East Hall Hill ME17 . . . 228 E7
East Hall La ME10 . . . . 102 C5
East Hall Rd BR5 . . . . . .54 F2
East Ham Ind Est E6 . . . .1 E8
East Ham Manor Way E6 2 A7
EAST HILL 90 B1
East Hill Ashford TN24 . 268 C2
Biggin Hill TN16 . . . . . 118 B1
Dartford DA1 . . . . .33 F8
Sutton at Hone DA4 . . . .57 D7
Tenterden TN30 . . . . . . 345 B8
East Hill Dr DA1 . . . . . . .33 F8
East Hill Farm Cvn Pk
TN15 . . . . .90 B1
East Hill Farm Pk TN15 90 B1
East Hill Rd TN15 . . . . 123 B7
East Ho DA1 . . . . .15 F4
East Holme DA8 . . . . . . .14 D6
Eastwell CT7 . . . . .81 A5
Maidstone ME14 . . . . . 162 C5
Paddock Wood TN12 . . 256 E6
Shadoxhurst TN26 . . . . 299 B1
EAST LANGDON 247 A1
East Langdon Rd
Guston CT15 . . . . 278 F7
Martin Mill CT15 . . . . . 247 B2
Eastleigh Rd DA7 . . . . . .14 C4
EASTLING 168 F6
Eastling Cl ME8 . . . . . . .65 D3
Eastling Ho 8 BR5 . . . . .54 D1
Eastling Prim Sch
ME13 . . . . 168 F5
Eastling Rd
Eastling ME13 . . . . 168 F7
Painters Forstal ME13 . . 137 D3
East Lodge Rd TN23 . . 267 F3
EAST MALLING 160 A7
EAST MALLING
HEATH 159 E4
East Malling Research
ME19 . . . . 160 C6
East Malling Sta ME19 160 A6
East Mascalls 17 SE7 . . .11 C8
Eastmead Ave TN23 . . 300 C8
Eastmead Cl 1 BR1 . . . .52 E7
Eastmead Trad Est
TN23 . . . . 300 C8
East Mill DA11 . . . . .18 F1
East Milton Rd DA12 . . .37 D8
Eastmoor Pl SE7 . . . . . . .1 D3
Eastmoor St SE7 . . . . . . .1 D3
East Mountain La
TN24 . . . . 268 F7
East Norman Rd CT16 . 278 E1
Eastnor Rd SE9 . . . . .30 C7
East Northdown Cl CT9 51 E1
Easton's Cnr TN25 . . . . 329 F4
East Park Rd ME20 . . . 161 A8
EAST PECKHAM 224 F6
East Peckham Prim Sch
TN12 . . . . 224 F7
East Point TN15 . . . . . 155 A6
East Quay CT5 . . . . .74 D3
East Ramp CT16 . . . . . 310 G8
East Rd Bexley DA16 . . . .13 B5
Chatham ME4 . . . . .64 A7
Folkestone CT20 . . . . . 334 D4
Sandwich CT13 . . . . . . 149 A8
East Rochester Way
Coldblow DA1 . . . . .32 D8
Sidcup DA5, DA15 . . . . .13 C1
East Row ME1 . . . . .63 C5
EASTRY 180 B2
Eastry CE Prim Sch
CT13 . . . . 180 B2
Eastry Cl Ashford TN23 . 300 A6
Maidstone ME16 . . . . . 161 C7
Eastry Ct CT3 . . . . 210 F5
Eastry Mews CT13 . . . 180 B2
Eastry Pk CT13 . . . . . . 180 C1
Eastry Rd DA8 . . . . .14 B7
East Service Rd TN29 . 380 C2
East St Addington ME19 126 D3
Ashford TN23 . . . . 268 B2
Bexley DA7 . . . . .14 A3

East St *continued*
Bromley BR1 . . . . .52 A7
Canterbury CT1 . . . . . . 143 C3
Chatham ME4 . . . . .64 A3
Dover CT17 . . . . 310 C8
Faversham ME13 . . . . . 138 D7
Folkestone CT19 . . . . . 335 E5
Gillingham ME7 . . . . . . .64 D6
Grays RM20 . . . . .17 E8
Harrietsham ME17 . . . . 198 E5
Herne Bay CT6 . . . . .77 A5
Hunton ME15 . . . . 226 F7
Hythe ME21 . . . . 333 D2
Sittingbourne ME10 . . . 102 A4
Snodland ME6 . . . . 128 B8
Snodland ME6 . . . . 222 C2
EAST STOURMOUTH 113 C1
East Stour Ct TN24 . . . 268 D1
East Stour Prim Sch
TN24 . . . . 300 D6
East Stour Way TN24 . 300 D6
EAST STREET Ditton 126 E3
Sandwich 148 A2
East Street N ME19 . . . 126 D3
EAST STUDDAL 246 D7
East Sutton Park (HM
Young Offender Inst &
Prison) ME17 . . . . . . 230 B7
East Sutton Rd
Sutton Valence ME17 . . 230 A7
Sutton Valence ME17,
TN27 . . . . 230 C4
East Tank Farm Rd
TN29 . . . . 380 C2
East Terr
Gravesend DA12 . . . . . . .19 C1
Sidcup DA15 . . . . .30 E7
East Thamesmead Bsns Pk
DA18 . . . . .3 F4
East Thurrock Rd RM17 18 C8
Eastview ME4 . . . . .41 B2
East View
Brookland DA29 . . . . . 370 D8
Hersden CT3 . . . . 111 F1
Eastview Ave SE18 . . . . .12 E1
Eastway BR2 . . . . .52 A2
East Weald Dr TN30 . . 324 B1
Eastwell 5 TN30 . . . . . 345 A8
Eastwell Barn Mews
TN30 . . . . 345 A8
Eastwell Mdws TN30 . 345 A8
Eastwell Terr TN25 . . . 236 C3
EAST WICKHAM 13 A7
East Wickham Inf Sch
DA16 . . . . .12 F6
East Wickham Jun Sch
DA16 . . . . .13 A6
EASTWOOD 231 C6
Eastwood Cotts ME9 . 103 E6
Eastwood Rd
Eastwood ME17 . . . . . . 231 C5
Sittingbourne ME10 . . . 101 D5
Grain ME3 . . . . .27 B5
Margate CT9 . . . . .82 B8
Edinburgh Sq ME15 . . 195 C7
Edinburgh Wlk 5 CT9 . .82 A8
Edington Rd SE2 . . . . . . .3 B3
Edisbury Wlk ME8 . . . . .98 D5
Edison Gr SE18 . . . . .12 F7
Edison Rd Bexley DA16 . .12 F6
2 Bromley BR2 . . . . . . .52 A7
Edith Cavell Way SE18 . .11 E6
Edith Ct BR1 . . . . .52 D6
Edith Pond Ct SE9 . . . . .30 B6
Edith Rd
Faversham ME13 . . . . . 138 C6
Orpington BR6 . . . . .87 B5
Ramsgate CT11 . . . . . . 117 C6
Westgate on Sea CT8 . . .50 D1
Ediva Rd DA13 . . . . .60 A4
Edmanson Ave CT9 . . . .50 E1
Edmund Cl
Maidstone ME16 . . . . . 161 A3
Meopham Station DA13 . .60 A4
Edmund Hurst Dr E6 . . . .2 B8
Edmund Rd Bexley DA16 13 A4
Orpington BR5 . . . . .54 C3
Edmunds Ave BR5 . . . . .54 D6
Edmund St CT3 . . . . . . 178 A8
Edna Rd ME14 . . . . 161 F8
Edred Rd CT17 . . . . 310 B8
Edward Alderton Theatre★
DA7 . . . . .13 D4
Edward Ct Chatham ME5 64 C1
2 Newham E16 . . . . .1 A8
Edward Dr
Birchington CT7 . . . . . . .81 B7
Sittingbourne ME10 . . . .68 F1
Edward Harvey Ct DA17 . 3 F1
Edward Rd
Biggin Hill TN16 . . . . . 118 E1
Bromley BR1 . . . . .29 C1
Canterbury CT1 . . . . . . 175 A8
Chislehurst BR7 . . . . . . .30 A3
Folkestone CT19 . . . . . 335 D6
Kingsdown CT14 . . . . . 248 C6
Queenborough ME11 . . .46 B5
Edwards Cl ME8 . . . . . . .98 C5
Edwards Gdns BR8 . . . .55 D5
Edwards Rd
Dover CT16 . . . . 310 D8
Erith DA17 . . . . .4 A2
Edward St Chatham ME4 64 A3
Rochester ME2 . . . . .63 D7
Royal Tunbridge Wells
TN4 . . . . 285 F8
Rusthall TN4 . . . . 285 C4
Sheerness ME12 . . . . . . .28 A3
Edward Terr 9 CT20 . . 335 E6

Dri–Edw 397

Eden Ct
1 Hawkhurst TN18 . . . 340 F2
16 Orpington BR5 . . . . .54 D1
Tonbridge TN10 . . . . . . 222 C5
Edendale Rd DA7 . . . . . .14 D5
Eden Farm La ME19 . . 159 C3
Edenfield CT17 . . . . .81 B7
Eden Ho TN23 . . . . 300 C8
Edenhurst TN13 . . . . . 154 A2
Eden Pl DA12 . . . . .37 B8
Eden Rd
High Halstow ME23 . . . .23 E4
Joyden's Wood DA5 . . . .32 D4
Royal Tunbridge Wells
TN1 . . . . 286 A2
Whitstable CT5 . . . . . . 108 A2
Edensmuir Ct SE3 . . . . .11 A7
Eden Valley Mus★
TN8 . . . . 217 C1
EDEN VILLAGE 101 F1
Eden Villas TN8 . . . . . . 249 D7
Eden Way ME19 . . . . . . 159 D3
Eden Wlk 9 TN1 . . . . . 286 A2
Edgar Cl
Kings Hill ME19 . . . . . . 159 B3
Swanley BR8 . . . . .55 F6
Whitstable CT5 . . . . .75 D3
Edgar Ho CT14 . . . . . . 215 B3
Edgar Rd
Canterbury CT1 . . . . . . 143 B1
Dover CT17 . . . . 278 B1
Kemsing TN15 . . . . 122 E2
Margate CT9 . . . . .51 A3
Minster (Thanet) CT12 . 115 B6
Tatsfield TN16 . . . . 150 D6
Edgeborough Way BR1 52 D8
Edgebury BR7, SE9 . . . . .30 B4
Edgebury Prim Sch
BR7 . . . . .30 C4
Edge End Rd CT10 . . . . .83 F4
Edgefield Cl DA1 . . . . . . .34 B7
Edge Hill SE18 . . . . .12 B8
Edgehill Cl CT20 . . . . . 334 D4
Edge Hill Ct DA14 . . . . .30 F4
Edgehill Gdns DA13 . . . .59 F8
Edgehill Rd BR7 . . . . . . .30 C4
Edgeler Ct ME6 . . . . . . 127 F7
Edger Pl 5 ME15 . . . . . 162 A4
Edgeway Dr BR6 . . . . . . .87 A5
Edgewood Dr BR6 . . . . .87 A5
Edgeworth Rd SE9 . . . . .11 D3
Edgington Way DA14 . . .31 D1
Edinburgh Cl DA8 . . . . . .14 D7
Edinburgh Ho
Deal CT14 . . . . 215 A5
7 Dover CT17 . . . . 310 D7
Edinburgh Mews RM18 .19 B5
Edinburgh Pl 7 CT20 . 335 B3
Edinburgh Rd
Ashford TN24 . . . . 268 B2
Chatham ME4 . . . . .64 C2
Gillingham ME7 . . . . . . .64 D5

Edward Tyler Rd SE12...29 C6
Edward Vinson Dr
  ME13........................138 E7
Edward Wlk ME19......159 F8
Edwina Ave ME12......47 A7
Edwin Arnold Ct DA15..30 F4
Edwin Cl DA7..............13 E8
Edwin Petty Pl DA2....34 C8
Edwin Rd Dartford DA2..33 C5
  Gillingham ME8............98 C8
Edwins Pl ME9.........100 C7
Edwin St
  Gravesend DA12............37 B8
  Newham E16.................1 A8
Edyngham Cl ME10....102 A8
Effingham Cres CT17..310 D8
Effingham St
  Dover CT17................310 D8
  Ramsgate CT11...........117 E6
Egbert Rd
  Birchington CT7...........80 D8
  Faversham ME13...........138 C6
  Minster (Thanet) CT12. 115 B6
  Westgate on Sea CT8.....50 C1
Egdean Wlk TN13......154 C1
EGERTON....................232 F4
Egerton Ave BR8.........55 F8
Egerton CE Prim Sch
  TN27.......................232 F3
Egerton Cl DA1..........33 B7
Egerton Dr CT9...........51 E2
EGERTON FORSTAL. 232 D1
Egerton House Rd
  TN27.......................232 E4
Egerton Rd
  Charing Heath TN27......233 C7
  Maidstone ME14...........161 E7
  Pluckley TN27.............233 B1
  Temple Ewell CT16.......277 E5
Eggarton La CT4........205 C2
Eggpie La TN11, TN14..220 E7
Eggringe TN23...........267 E3
Egham Rd E13..............1 B8
Eglantine La DA4........57 B3
Eglinton Hill SE18.......2 A1
Eglinton Prim Sch SE18 12 A8
Eglinton Rd
  Swanscombe DA10.........17 F1
  Woolwich SE18.............2 A2
Egremont Rd ME15....162 F2
Egret Cl ME4.............41 B2
Eider Cl CT6.............76 D2
Eighteen Acre La
  TN29.......................371 D8
Eileen Ct SE12...........29 C6
Eisenhower Dr E6.........1 E8
Elaine Ave ME2..........62 E7
Elaine Ct ME2............62 E7
Elaine Prim Sch ME2....62 E6
Elbourne Trad Est DA17..4 B3
Elbury Dr E16.............1 A7
Elder Cl
  Kingswood ME17..........197 D2
  Sidcup DA15...............30 F7
Elder Ct ME8..............98 B6
Elderslie Rd SE9.........12 A2
Elders The CT3..........144 F1
Eldon Gr CT11...........117 D6
Eldon Pl CT10............84 B4
Eldon St ME4.............64 A4
Eldon Way TN12..........256 F7
Eldred Dr BR5.............87 D8
Eleanor Ct ME8...........98 C3
Eleanor Dr ME10........101 E8
Eleanor Smith Sch E16..1 C8
Eleanor Wlk SE18.........1 F2
Elford Cl SE3.............11 C3
Elford Rd ME3.............22 B5
Elfrida Cl CT9............83 C8
Elgal Cl BR6..............86 B5
Elgar Bretts Ct CT1...174 F7
Elgar Cl TN10...........222 E6
Elgar Gdns RM18..........19 B6
Elgar Pl CT11...........117 D7
Elgin Gdns ME2...........62 D5
ELHAM.....................273 F5
Elham CE Prim Sch
  CT4.......................273 F5
Elham Cl Bromley BR1...29 D1
  Gillingham ME8............65 B3
  Margate CT9...............51 C1
Elham Rd CT1............174 E6
Elham Valley Railway
  Mus★ CT18................334 A8
Elham Valley Vineyard★
  CT4.......................242 D4
Elham Way CT10...........84 A2
Elibank Rd SE9...........12 A3
Eling Ct ME15...........195 A8
Eliot Coll CT2...........142 E4
Eliot Rd DA1..............16 B2
Elizabethan Ct TN27...234 C7
Elizabeth Carter Ave
  CT14......................214 F4
Elizabeth Cl ME19......19 B5
Elizabeth Cotts DA4....89 E8
Elizabeth Ct
  Broadstairs CT10..........84 B6
  Canterbury CT1...........175 B6
  Chatham ME5..............97 A7
  Dartford DA2..............34 D3
  Erith DA8..................14 D7
  Gillingham ME8.............65 C1
  Gravesend DA11..........19 A1
  Herne Bay CT6.............76 F5
Elizabeth Dr CT18......308 B2
Elizabeth Fry Ct TN18..11 E6
Elizabeth Garlick Ct
  TN1.......................286 B4
Elizabeth Garrett Anderson
  Ho 4 A3

Elizabeth Gdns
  CT21......................333 B1
Elizabeth Ho
  Maidstone ME14...........162 A6
  Rochester ME1.............63 C4
Elizabeth Huggins Cotts
  DA11........................37 B6
Elizabeth Kemp Ct
  CT12.......................83 C1
Elizabeth Pl DA4.........56 E3
Elizabeth Rd CT11......117 F6
Elizabeth Smith's Ct
  ME19......................159 F7
Elizabeth St
  Dover CT17...............310 D6
  Stone DA9..................16 E2
Elizabeth Terr SE9......11 F1
Elizabeth Way
  Herne Bay CT6.............77 B3
  Orpington BR5.............54 C4
Eliza Cook Cl DA9........17 B3
Ellard Ct DA16............13 C4
Ellen Ave CT11...........83 E2
Ellenborough Rd DA14..31 E3
Ellen Cl Bromley BR1....52 D6
  Charing TN27.............234 B7
Ellen Ct CT3.............176 F8
Ellenden Ct CT2.........142 C4
Ellen's Hill CT14.......214 E3
Ellen's Pl ME9...........100 C6
Ellens Rd CT14..........214 F2
Ellenswood Cl ME15....163 A1
Ellen Wilkinson Prim Sch
  E6...........................1 E8
Ellerman Rd RM18........18 F5
Ellerslie DA12............37 B8
Ellerslie Ct DA12........37 B8
Ellesmere Ct SE18.......5 A3
Ellesmere Mews TN28 373 C4
Ellingham Ind Ctr
  TN23......................300 A5
Ellingham Leas ME15.195 C2
Ellingham Way TN23...300 A5
Ellington Ave CT9........82 B8
Ellington Inf Sch CT11 117 C7
Ellington Pl CT11.......117 C7
Ellington Rd CT11.......117 D7
Ellington Sch for Girls
  CT12.......................83 D2
Elliot Cl CT1............143 C3
Elliot Ct CT6.............77 C4
Elliots Mill ME13.......138 D7
Elliott Park Sch CT10...47 K7
Elliott Rd BR2............52 D5
Elliotts La TN16.........152 C3
Elliott St DA12...........37 D8
Ellis Cl Eltham SE9......30 C6
  Five Oak Green TN12....256 B7
  Swanley BR8...............55 D5
Elliscombe Mount SE7..11 C8
Elliscombe Rd SE7......11 C8
Ellis Ct DA1...............34 B7
Ellis Dr TN28............373 C8
Ellis Ho ME14............162 B4
Ellison Cl CT5...........75 C1
Ellison Ct ME13.........138 C6
Ellison Rd DA15..........30 D7
Ellisons Wlk CT1........175 C8
Ellison Way ME8..........66 A2
Ellis Rd CT5...............75 A3
Elliston Ho SE18..........2 A2
Ellis Way Dartford DA1..33 F6
  Herne Bay CT6.............77 C2
Elm Ave Chatham ME4...63 E1
  Chattenden ME3...........41 A4
Elmbank Dr ME1...........52 D7
Elmbourne Dr DA17.......4 B2
Elmbrook Gdns SE9......11 B3
Elm Cl Dartford DA1......33 C7
  Egerton TN27.............232 F3
  Higham ME3................39 C3
Elm Cotts
  Boughton Lees TN25....236 E3
  Swanley Village BR8......56 B8
Elm Court Ind Est ME7..97 E3
Elm Cres ME19...........159 F8
Elmcroft Ave DA15.......13 A1
Elmcroft Rd BR6..........54 A2
Elm Ct CT8................81 E8
Elmdene Rd SE18..........2 B1
Elm Dr BR8................55 D7
Elmfield Gillingham ME8 65 A3
  Tenterden TN30..........345 B8
Elmfield Cl
  Gravesend DA11...........37 B7
  Sevenoaks Weald TN14. 187 B2
Elmfield Ct Bexley DA16 .13 B6
  Coxheath ME17...........194 C3
  Tenterden TN30..........345 B8
Elmfield Pk BR1..........52 A6
Elmfield Rd BR1..........52 A6
Elm Fields TN29..........372 A6
Elm Gdns CT21...........333 E2
Elm Gr Erith DA8.........14 D7
  Maidstone ME15..........162 B3
  Manston CT12..............82 D1
  Orpington BR6.............53 F1
  Sittingbourne ME10.....102 B4
  Tonbridge TN11..........221 F5
  Westgate on Sea CT8.....81 E8
Elm Ho CT21.............333 B2
Elmhurst Bexley DA17....13 E8
  Swanscombe DA9..........17 B1
Elmhurst Ave ME2.......287 D8
Elmhurst Gdns ME4.....63 B2
Elmhurst Rd TN25.......267 F4
Elmhurst SE9.............29 E5
Elmington Cl DA5.........14 B1
Elm La
  Minster (Sheppey)
  ME12.......................47 A5
  Tonbridge TN10..........222 C3
Elmleigh Rd CT3.........177 A8

Elmley Cl E6...............1 E8
Elmley Ind Est ME11....46 A2
Elmley Marshes Nature
  Reserve★ ME12...........69 F4
Elmley Rd ME12...........47 D3
Elmley St SE18.............2 D2
Elmley Way CT9...........82 F6
Elm Par DA14..............31 A4
Elm Park Gdns CT17....309 F7
Elm Pl TN23..............299 F4
Elm Rd Aylesham CT3...210 E5
  Dartford DA1...............33 D7
  Erith DA8..................15 A6
  Folkestone CT19.........335 E6
  Gillingham ME7.............64 E6
  Gravesend DA12............37 C5
  Grays RM17.................18 C8
  Hoo St Werburgh ME3.....41 E3
  Orpington BR6.............87 A3
Royal Tunbridge Wells
  TN4.......................253 F1
  Sidcup DA14................31 A4
  St Mary's Bay TN29.....365 F3
  Stone DA9..................16 E1
  Westerham TN16..........151 E2
Elms Ave CT11...........117 D6
Elms Hill CT15...........309 D6
Elmshurst Gdns TN10. 222 C7
Elmslie Ct SE9............12 A1
Elmsmead TN31..........368 B4
ELMSTEAD Ashford.....271 F6
  Lewisham...................29 E3
Elmstead Cl TN13.......153 E5
Elmstead Glade BR7.....29 F2
Elmstead La BR7.........29 F3
Elmstead Pl CT20.......335 E5
Elmstead Rd DA8.........14 E6
Elmstead Woods Sta
  BR7........................29 E4
Elmsted Cres DA16.......13 C8
Elms The Hersden CT3. 111 E1
  Teynham ME9.............104 A2
ELMSTONE.................146 E5
Elmstone Cl ME16.......161 B2
Elmstone Gdns CT9......51 C2
ELMSTONE HOLE........231 E8
Elmstone Hole Rd
  Fairbourne Heath
  ME17......................198 D1
  Platt's Heath ME17.....231 D8
Elmstone La ME16.......161 B2
Elmstone Rd
  Gillingham ME8.............98 D7
  Ramsgate CT11...........117 D7
Elmstone Terr BR5......54 C5
ELMS VALE................310 A7
Elms Vale Rd CT15,
  CT17......................309 E7
Elm Terr Eltham SE9....12 A1
  West Thurrock RM20......17 B8
Elmton La CT15..........212 C1
Elmtree TN26............347 C1
Elm Tree Ave ME4........68 D4
Elmtree Cotts TN14....120 D4
Elm Tree Ct SE9..........35 A3
Elm Tree Ct CT9...........51 C8
Elm Tree Dr ME1..........63 A2
Elmway ME12.............47 A5
Elm Wlk Aylesford ME20 128 E1
  Orpington BR6.............85 F7
Elmwood Ave CT10........84 A8
Elmwood Cl CT10.........84 A7
Elm Wood Cl CT5.........75 C2
Elmwood Dr DA5..........31 E8
Elmwood Rd ME3..........40 F6
Elm Wood Way CT5.......75 C2
ELPHICKS.................318 A8
Elphick's Pl TN2........314 B8
Elrick Cl DA8.............14 E8
Elsa Rd DA16.............13 C5
Elsinore Ho SE18..........1 E2
Elster Pl ME19...........159 B3
Elstow Cl SE9.............11 F2
Elstree Gdns DA17.........3 E2
Elswick Sq TN25.........268 B2
Elswyn Ho DA14...........31 A5
ELTHAM....................11 E1
Eltham CE Prim Sch
  SE9........................11 F2
Eltham Coll SE9...........29 D6
Eltham College Jun Sch
  SE9........................29 D7
Eltham Green Rd SE9...11 C3
Eltham Green Sch SE9..11 D1
Eltham High St SE9.....11 F1
Eltham Hill SE9...........11 E2
Eltham Hill Tech Coll
  SE9........................11 E2
Eltham Palace★ SE9....11 E1
Eltham Palace Rd SE9...11 C1
Eltham Park Gdns SE9..12 A3
Eltham Rd SE12, SE9...11 B2
Eltham Sta SE9...........11 F2
Elventon Cl CT19.......334 E7
Elverland La ME13,
  ME9.......................137 B2
ELVINGTON Eythorne.212 C1
  Hawkinge.................306 C2
Elvington Cl ME16......161 D5
Elvington La CT18......306 E2
Elwick Cl DA1.............15 A3
Elwick La TN23..........268 B2
Elwick Rd TN23..........268 B2
Elwill Way DA13..........59 F8
Elwyn Gdns SE12.........29 A8
Ely Cl Erith DA8..........14 F5
  Gillingham ME8.............65 C2
Ely Ct TN1................286 B4
Ely Gdns TN10...........222 D4
Elysian Ave BR5..........53 F3
Embassy Ho SE9...........11 F2
Embassy Ct Bexley DA16 13 B4

Embassy Ct continued
  Sidcup DA14................31 B5
Ember Cl BR5..............53 C2
Emblin Ct DA14...........31 A4
Emelina Way CT5........108 B6
Emerald Cl Newham E16...1 E7
  Rochester ME1.............96 D7
Emerald Cres ME10......101 C6
Emerald View ME10.......49 E4
Emersons Ave BR8........32 F1
Emerton Cl DA6...........13 E3
Emerton Rd DA12..........37 F6
EM Forster Theatre★
  TN9.......................222 C2
Emily Jackson Cl TN13 154 B3
Emily Jackson Ho
  TN13......................154 B3
Emily Rd ME5.............97 B6
Emmanuel Ho ME2........2 D1
Emmerson Gdns CT5.....75 D3
Emmet Hill La ME8.....225 F5
Emmetts Garden★
  TN14......................185 D5
Emmetts La TN14,
  TN16......................185 D6
Emmetts Road TN16... 185 C5
Emperor Way TN23......299 F4
Empire Road ME2.........62 F5
Empire Terr CT9..........82 E8
Empire Walk DA9..........17 C3
Empress Dr BR7..........30 B2
Empress Gdns ME12.....49 D4
Empress Rd DA12..........37 E8
Emsworth Gr ME14......162 D6
Enbrook Rd CT20........334 E4
Enbrook Valley CT20...334 E5
Encombe CT20...........334 D3
Endeavour Foyer The
  ME4........................64 B2
Enderfield Ct BR7........53 A8
Enfield Rd CT14..........215 D7
Engineer Cl SE18........12 A8
Engineers Ct TN23......268 E2
Englefield Cl BR5........53 F5
Englefield Cres
  Cliffe Woods ME3.........40 B7
  Orpington BR5.............54 A5
Englefield Path BR5.....54 A5
English Martyrs RC Prim
  Sch ME9.....................63 B8
Ennerdale ME13.........138 C6
Ennerdale Gdns CT15...210 F6
Ennerdale Ho TN13....195 E7
Ennerdale Rd DA7........14 A6
Ennis Rd SE18............12 C8
Ensfield Rd Leigh TN11 220 E1
  Tonbridge TN11..........253 A6
Ensign Ho RM17..........17 F8
Enslin Rd SE9.............30 A8
Enterprise Bsns Est
  ME2........................63 E7
Enterprise Cl ME2.......63 D8
Enterprise Ctr TN24....300 E7
Enterprise Ctr The
  ME5.......................130 C8
Enterprise Rd
  Maidstone ME15..........162 A1
  Margate CT9...............83 A6
Enterprise Way
  Margate CT9...............83 A6
  Marlpit Hill TN8.........217 C3
Enticott Cl CT5...........75 A1
Epaul La ME1..............63 C6
Eppe Cl ME2...............63 B8
Epple Bay Ave CT7.......81 B8
Epple Bay Rd CT7.........81 A8
Epple Rd CT7..............81 A8
Epps Rd ME10............101 E3
Epsom Cl Bexley DA7....14 B4
  Maidstone ME15..........195 F6
  West Malling ME19......159 B8
Epstein Rd SE28...........3 B5
Erebus Dr SE28............2 C4
Erica Ct BR8...............55 E5
Eric Rd CT17.............278 B2
Eridge Ct TN2............285 F1
Eridge Green Ho
  ME4........................64 B2
ERIDGE GREEN.........313 B3
Eridge Green BR5........54 C1
Eridge Rd
  Groombridge TN3........312 D5
Royal Tunbridge Wells TN2,
  TN4.......................285 E1
  Eridge Sta TN3..........312 E2
Erindale SE18............12 D8
Erindale Terr SE18......12 D8
ERITH.......................4 C1
Erith Cl ME14............162 A8
Erith & District Hospl
  DA8........................14 D8
Erith High St DA8.........4 E1
Erith Mus★ DA8...........4 E1
Erith Playhouse★ DA8...4 E1
Erith Rd Bexley DA7.....14 B4
  Erith DA8, DA17..........4 B1
Erith Sch DA8.............14 F8
Erith Small Bsns Ctr
  DA8........................14 F8
Erith St CT17............278 B1
Erith Sta DA8.............4 E1
Ermington Rd SE9.......30 C6
Ernest Dr ME16.........161 B5
Ernest Rd ME4............64 A3
Ernwell Rd CT19........335 D6
ERRIOTTWOOD..........135 F3
Ersham Rd CT1..........175 A7
Erskine Cl SE9............29 E6
Erskine Park Rd TN4..285 C1
Erskine Rd DA13........126 B8
Erwood Rd SE7.............1 E1
Escott Gdns SE9..........29 E4
Escreet Gr SE18..........2 A2
Eshcol Rd ME3............42 C6
Esher Cl DA5..............31 E7

Eshet Cl TN23...........300 A7
Eskdale Ave CT11.......117 A7
Eskdale Cl DA2...........34 C7
Eskdale Rd DA7...........14 A6
Esmonde Dr CT12.........81 F2
Esmonde Ho ME7..........64 A6
Esplanade Dover CT17. 310 D6
  Rochester ME1.............63 B8
  Westgate on Sea CT8.....50 C1
Essella Pk CT1...........268 E1
Essella Rd CT24.........268 E1
Essenden Rd CT1..........4 A1
Essentially Hops★
  CT4.......................176 D3
Essetford Rd TN23......300 A7
Essex Ave CT6.............76 B4
Essex Cl TN2.............313 F8
Essex Gdns CT7...........80 F6
Essex Rd
  Canterbury CT1...........175 D7
  Dartford DA1...............15 D1
  Gravesend DA11............37 A7
  Halling ME2................95 A6
  Longfield DA3.............58 D7
  Maidstone ME15..........195 E6
  Westgate on Sea CT8.....81 F8
  West Thurrock RM20......17 A8
Essex St CT5.............108 C8
Estelle Cl ME1............96 D7
Esther Ct ME10..........101 E8
Estridge Way TN10.....222 F5
Estuary Cl CT5............75 C2
Estuary Cotts RM18......20 D7
Estuary Rd ME11.........28 B1
Estuary Reach ME4......63 F6
Etchden Rd TN26........298 A8
ETCHINGHILL...........305 C3
Etfield Gr DA14...........31 B3
Ethelbert Cres CT9......51 A3
Ethelbert Gdns CT9.....50 J3
Ethelbert Rd
  Birchington CT7...........80 D8
  Bromley BR1...............52 A6
  Canterbury CT1...........175 B6
  Deal CT14................182 C1
  Dover CT17...............310 C8
  Erith DA8..................14 C7
  Faversham ME13..........138 C6
  Folkestone CT19.........335 D7
  Hawley DA2................33 E3
  Margate CT9...............50 J3
  Orpington BR5.............54 D6
  Ramsgate CT11...........117 D6
  Rochester ME1.............63 C4
Ethelbert Road Inf Sch
  ME13......................138 C6
Ethelbert Sq CT8.........50 C1
Ethelbert Terr
  Margate CT9...............51 A3
  Westgate on Sea CT8.....50 C1
Ethel Brooks Ho SE18..12 B8
Ethelburga Dr CT18....305 D7
Ethel-Maud Ct ME7......64 D7
Ethel Rd
  Broadstairs CT10..........83 F5
  Newham E16.................1 B7
Ethelred Ct ME13.......138 C6
Ethelred Rd CT8..........50 C1
Ethel Terr BR6............87 C2
Etherington Hill TN3 285 C8
Ethnam La TN18.........356 E4
Ethronvi Rd DA7..........13 E4
Eton Cl ME5...............96 F4
Eton Ct TN13............154 B4
Eton Rd BR6...............87 B6
Eton Way DA1.............15 C3
Ettrick Terr CT21.......333 E2
Eugenie Mews BR7........53 B8
Eureka Leisure Pk
  TN24......................268 E6
Eurogate Bsns Pk
  TN24......................268 E6
Eurolink Bsns Pk
  ME10......................102 B5
Eurolink E ME10.........102 C5
Eurolink N ME10.........102 C7
Eurolink Way ME10.....101 F4
Europa Pk RM20...........17 C8
Europa Trad Est DA8.....4 D1
Europe Rd SE18............1 F3
Euroway ME20............160 E8
Eustace Pl SE18...........1 F2
Evanlode Ho SE2..........3 C4
Evans Cl DA9..............17 A2
Evans Ct SE9..............29 E6
Evans Rd TN24...........301 A7
Eva Rd ME7................64 D3
Evelings Alley CT5......75 C2
Evelyn Cl ME2.............63 C8
Evelyn Ct CT21..........334 A2
Evelyn Denington Rd E6.1 F8
Evelyn Ho
  Folkestone CT20.........335 D5
  Rochester ME2.............63 C8
Evelyn Rd
  Maidstone ME16..........161 E3
  Newham E16.................1 B5
  Otford TN14..............122 C2
Evenden Ho TN17........320 D5
Evenden Rd DA13........60 A2
Evenhill Rd CT3..........176 E8
Everard Ave BR2..........52 A1
Everard Way ME13......138 B8
Everest Cl DA11..........36 E5
Everest Ct SE9............29 E6
Everest Dr ME3...........41 E4
Everest La ME2...........40 B1
Everest Mews ME3........41 E4
Everest Pl BR8............55 D5
Everest Rd SE9............11 F2
Everett Wlk DA17.........3 F1
Everglade TN16..........118 D1
Everglade Ct DA3.........58 F5

Everglades The ME7....97 F6
Evergreen Cl
  Gillingham ME7.............98 A5
  Higham ME3................39 B3
  Iwade ME9..................68 D4
  Leybourne ME19..........127 E2
Evergreen Way TN23...267 E3
Everist Ct CT18.........305 C6
Eversfield Ct SE12.......29 B6
Eversleigh Rise CT5...108 F7
Eversley Ave DA7, DA8..14 E5
Eversley Cl ME1.........161 C6
Eversley Coll CT20......334 F4
Eversley Cross CT14...14 E5
Eversley Rd
  Greenwich SE7............11 B8
  Hythe CT21...............334 B3
Eversley Way CT20.....334 F5
Evesham Rd DA12........37 D6
Evington Pottery★
  TN25......................271 D7
Evison Cl CT16..........278 B2
Evorg Ho ME4.............64 B2
Evry Rd DA14.............31 C2
Ewart Rd ME4.............63 E1
Ewehurst La TN3........284 F6
Ewe & Lamb Mews
  TN30......................359 E3
Ewell Ave ME19.........159 A8
Ewell La ME15...........193 D5
EWELL MINNIS..........276 E3
Ewing Cl TN12...........257 A6
ExCeL London★ E16......1 B6
Excel Waterfront E16....1 B6
Exchange Mews
  TN4.......................286 A5
Exchange St CT14......215 D7
Exchange The CT5.......74 F2
Exedown Rd TN15......124 C4
Exeter Cl
  Folkestone CT19.........334 D6
  Newham E6.................1 F7
  Tonbridge TN10..........222 D4
Exeter Rd Bexley DA16..12 F5
  Gravesend DA12............37 D5
  Newham E16.................1 A8
Exeter Wlk ME1...........96 C7
Exford Gdns SE12.........29 B7
Exford Rd SE12...........29 B7
Exmoor Rise TN24......268 A4
Exmouth Rd
  Bexley DA16...............13 C7
  Gillingham ME7.............64 C7
  Grays RM17.................18 B8
EXTED.....................273 E5
Exton Cl ME5.............97 C2
Exton Gdns ME14.......162 F5
Eye The ME4..............63 F5
Eyhorne St ME17.......164 D2
EYHORNE STREET.....164 C2
Eylesden Ct ME14......163 C4
EYNSFORD..................89 D7
Eynsford Castle★ DA4..89 E8
Eynsford Rd Margate CT9 51 F2
  Orpington BR5.............54 C3
Eynsford Cres DA5.......31 D7
Eynsford Rd
  Crockenhill BR8...........55 E3
  Eynsford DA4..............56 F1
  Maidstone ME16..........161 D7
  Swanscombe DA9..........17 C2
Eynsford Rise DA4.......89 D6
Eynsford Sta DA4.........89 D6
Eynsham Dr SE2...........3 C3
Eynswood Dr DA14........31 C3
Eythorn Court Barn
  CT15......................245 B7
EYTHORNE................245 C8
Eythorne Cl TN24.......268 D5
Eythorne Elvington Prim
  Sch CT15.................245 D7
EYTHORNE GREEN.....245 D7
Eythorne Rd CT15......244 E6
Eythorne Sta★ CT15..245 C8

F

Fackenden La TN14....122 C7
Factory Rd Newham E16..1 E5
  Northfleet DA11...........18 C1
Faesten Way DA5.........32 C5
Faggs Wood Forest Wlks★
  TN26......................327 D5
Fagus Cl ME5..............97 B1
Fairacre CT10.............83 E4
Fairacre Pl DA3............58 E6
Fair Acres BR2............52 A4
Fairacres Cl CT16.......77 C4
Fairbank Ave BR6.........86 B8
FAIRBOURNE HEATH .198 C4
Fairbourne Heath Cotts
  ME17......................198 B1
Fairbourne La ME17....198 C4
Fairby La DA3.............58 F3
Fairby Rd SE12...........11 B2
Faircrouch La TN5.......336 B5
Fairfax Bsns Ctr ME15 .195 F4
Fairfax Cl
  Folkestone CT20.........334 D5
  Gillingham ME8.............98 C5
Fairfax Dr CT6............77 F5
Fairfax Gdns SE3.........11 C6
Fairfax Ho ME15.........195 F5
Fairfax Mews E16.........1 B5
Fairfax Rd RM18..........18 F6
Fairfax Road DA1.........16 A1
FAIRFIELD.................83 E4
Fairfield Deal CT14.....214 F6
  Elham CT4................273 F5
Fairfield Ave TN2.......286 C5

Fairfield Cl
 Kemsing TN15 . . . . 123 A1
 New Romney TN28 . . . 373 B7
 Sidcup DA15 . . . . 12 F1
Fairfield Cres TN9 . . . . 254 C8
Fairfield Gr SE7 . . . . 11 D8
Fairfield Pk CT10 . . . . . . 83 E4
Fairfield Rd Bexley DA7 . . 13 F5
 Borough Green TN15 . . 156 F8
 Broadstairs CT10 . . . . . 83 E4
 Bromley BR1 . . . . 29 A1
 Minster (Thanet) CT12 . 115 B7
 New Romney TN28 . . . 373 B7
 Orpington BR5 . . . . 53 D3
 Ramsgate CT11 . . . . 83 E2
Fairfields CT4 . . . . 37 E3
Fairfield Terr TN26 . . . 349 A1
Fairfield Way TN11 . . . 221 F5
Fairford Ave DA7 . . . . . 14 D6
Fairglen Cotts TN5 . . . 336 B3
Fairglen Rd TN5 . . . . . . 336 B4
Fairhurst Dr ME15 . . . 194 B4
Fairings The TN30 . . . . 345 B8
Fairland Ho BR2 . . . . 52 B5
Fairlands Ct 6 SE9 . . . . 12 A1
Fairlawn Greenwich SE7 . 11 C8
 Whitstable CT5 . . . . 75 C6
Fairlawn Ave DA7 . . . . . 13 D5
Fairlawn Cl ME18 . . . . 193 A8
Fairlawn Rd SE7 . . . . . . 11 C7
Fairlawn Rd CT12 . . . . . 83 B3
Fairlead Rd ME1 . . . . . . 63 D1
Fairleas ME10 . . . . 102 B2
Fairlight Ave CT12 . . . . 117 B8
Fairlight Cl TN4 . . . . . . 254 A2
Fairlight Cotts 8
 ME13 . . . . 138 C7
Fairlight Cross DA3 . . . . 59 C6
Fairlight Ct TN10 . . . . . 222 B4
Fairlight Glen Sch CT6 . . 76 F5
Fairlight Rd CT21 . . . . . 333 A3
Fairman's La TN12 . . . 289 B6
Fairmead BR1 . . . . 52 F5
Fairmead Cl BR1 . . . . . . 52 F5
Fairmead Rd TN8 . . . . 217 C5
Fairmile Ho BR5 . . . . . . 54 A7
Fairmile Rd CT21 . . . . . 286 E5
Fairmont Cl DA17 . . . . . . 3 F1
Fairoak Cl BR5 . . . . 53 B2
Fairoak Dr SE9 . . . . 12 D2
Fairoaks CT6 . . . . 77 B3
FAIRSEAT 125 C7
Fairseat La
 Fairseat TN15 . . . . 125 B5
 Stansted TN15 . . . . 92 A1
Fairservice Cl ME10 . . 102 C5
Fair St CT10 . . . . 83 E4
Fairthorn Rd SE7 . . . . . . 1 C7
Fairtrough Rd BR6 . . . 120 B7
Fairview Erith DA8 . . . . 14 F7
 Hawkhurst TN18 . . . . . 340 F2
 Lympne CT21 . . . . 332 A3
 New Ash Green DA3 . . . 91 B7
Fairview Ave ME8 . . . . . 63 D2
Fairview Cl Margate CT9 51 A2
 Tonbridge TN9 . . . . . . 254 B7
Fairview Com Prim Sch
 ME8 . . . . 98 C5
Fairview Cotts
 Maidstone ME15 . . . . . 194 F5
 Wormshill ME9 . . . . . . 166 C7
Fair View Cotts TN5 . . 337 A6
Fairview Dr
 Ashford TN24 . . . . 300 D6
 Higham ME3 . . . . 39 B4
 Orpington BR6 . . . . 86 D6
Fairview Gdns
 Deal CT14 . . . . 215 A2
 Meopham Station DA13 . 58 A4
 Sturry CT2 . . . . 144 A6
Fairview Ind Pk
 Rainham RM13 . . . . 4 D8
 Ruckinge TN26 . . . . . . 349 D7
Fairview Rd
 Elvington CT15 . . . . . . 212 B1
 Istead Rise DA13 . . . . . 36 E1
 Sittingbourne ME10 . . 102 A3
Fairview Trad Est RH8 183 A2
Fairwater Ave DA16 . . . 13 A3
Fairway Bexley DA6 . . . . 13 E2
 Orpington BR5 . . . . 53 D4
 Sandwich CT13 . . . . . . 182 A7
Fairway Ave CT19 . . . . 335 A7
Fairway Cl
 Rochester ME1 . . . . 63 C1
 St Mary's Bay TN29 . . 365 F3
Fairway Cres CT5 . . . . . 108 A7
Fairway Ct 12 SE9 . . . . . 12 A1
Fairway Dr Dartford DA2 34 B8
 Erith SE28 . . . . 3 F7
Fairways Ct 11 DA11 . . . 37 B8
Fairways The
 Faversham ME13 . . . . . 138 A6
 Royal Tunbridge Wells
 TN4 . . . . 286 A7
Fairway The
 Bromley, Southborough
 BR1 . . . . 52 F4
 9 Bromley, Sundridge
 BR1 . . . . 29 B1
 Deal CT14 . . . . 215 C8
 Gravesend DA11 . . . . . . 37 B6
 Herne Bay CT6 . . . . 76 D2
 Hythe CT21 . . . . 333 C1
 Littlestone-on-Sea
 TN28 . . . . 373 D6
 Rochester ME1 . . . . 63 C1
 Sittingbourne ME10 . . 101 E1
 St Mary's Bay TN29 . . 366 A5
Fairwood Ind Est TN23 268 A1
Fairwood Ind Pk TN23 267 F2
Falcon Ave Bromley BR1 52 E5
 Grays RM17 . . . . 18 C7

Falcon Cl Dartford DA1 . 15 F2
 Herne CT6 . . . . 110 F7
Falcon Ct ME10 . . . . . . 102 A2
Falcon Gdns ME10 . . . . 47 D7
Falcon Gn ME20 . . . . . 127 F1
Falcon Ho 3 ME4 . . . . 102 A4
Falcon Mews DA11 . . . . 36 E7
Falcons CT16 . . . . 118 D2
Falcon Way TN23 . . . . . 299 E7
FALCONWOOD 12 C5
Falconwood Ave DA16 . . 12 C5
Falconwood Par DA16 . 12 D3
Falconwood Sta SE9 . . . 12 D3
Falkland Rd ME5 . . . . . . 96 E1
Fallowfield Bean DA2 . . 35 B5
 Chatham ME5 . . . . 97 B8
 Sittingbourne ME10 . . 102 A2
Fallowfield Cl ME14 . . 162 E4
Falmouth Pl TN12 . . . . 256 C7
Fanconi ME6 . . . . 97 B3
Fancy Row ME14 . . . . . 163 C5
Fane Way ME8 . . . . 98 D4
Fantail Cl SE28 . . . . 3 C7
Fan The CT16 . . . . 310 H8
Fant La ME16 . . . . 161 B2
Faraday Ave DA14 . . . . . 31 B6
 Rochester ME1 . . . . 63 D5
Faraday Ho Erith DA17 . . 4 A3
 Rochester ME1 . . . . 63 D5
Faraday Lodge TN2 . . . 286 E5
 Maidstone ME14 . . . . . 162 C7
Faraday Rd Bexley DA16 13 A4
 Maidstone ME14 . . . . . 162 C7
Faraday Ride TN10 . . . 222 D7
Faraday Way
 Greenwich SE18 . . . . 1 D3
 Orpington BR5 . . . . 54 B5
Fareham Wlk 10 ME15 195 F6
Faringdon Ave BR2 . . . . 53 A3
Farington Cl ME16 . . . 161 B4
Farjeon Rd SE18, SE3 . . 11 D6
Farleigh Ave ME15 . . . . 82 A2
Farleigh Ct ME16 . . . . 161 A2
Farleigh Hill ME15 . . . 161 E1
Farleigh Hill Ret Pk
 ME15 . . . . 161 E1
Farleigh La ME16 . . . . 161 A1
Farleigh Rd CT2 . . . . . 143 A3
Farleigh Trad Est
 ME15 . . . . 161 E1
Farley Cl Chatham ME5 . 97 D2
 Shadoxhurst TN26 . . . . 299 A1
Farleycroft TN16 . . . . . 151 C1
Farley La TN16 . . . . . . 184 B8
Farley Nursery TN16 . . 184 C8
Farley Rd
 Gravesend DA12 . . . . . . 37 F7
 Margate CT9 . . . . 82 F7
Farleys Way TN31 . . . . 367 B2
Farlow Cl DA11 . . . . 36 F5
Farm Ave BR8 . . . . 55 C6
Farm Cl TN23 . . . . 299 E7
Farmcombe Cl TN2 . . . 286 B2
Farmcombe La TN2 . . . 286 B2
Farmcombe Rd TN2 . . 286 C2
Farmcote Rd SE12 . . . . . 29 A7
Farm Cres ME10 . . . . . 102 A2
Farmcroft DA11 . . . . 37 A6
Farmdale Ave ME1 . . . . 62 F2
Farmdale Rd SE10 . . . . . 1 A1
Farmer Cl Hythe CT21 . 333 D1
 Leeds ME17 . . . . 197 A6
Farm Gdns TN31 . . . . . 367 C2
Farm Ground Cl TN9 . . 254 E8
Farm Hill Ave ME2 . . . . 39 F1
Farm Holt DA3 . . . . 58 F1
Farmhouse Cl CT4 . . . . 242 F7
Farm House Cl CT5 . . . 108 F8
Farming World at Nash
 Court ★ ME13 . . . . . . 139 D4
Farm La Deal CT14 . . . 214 F6
 Tonbridge TN10 . . . . . 222 A4
Farmland Wlk BR7 . . . . 30 B3
Farm Pl DA1 . . . . 15 A3
Farm Place CT5 . . . . . . 154 F8
Farm Rd Chatham ME5 . . 96 E3
 Hamstreet TN26 . . . . . 349 A7
 Sevenoaks TN14 . . . . . 154 C7
Farmstead Dr TN8 . . . . 217 D3
Farm Vale DA5 . . . . 14 B1
Farnaby Dr TN13 . . . . . 154 A1
Farnaby Rd SE9 . . . . . . 11 C3
FARNBOROUGH 86 D5
Farnborough Cl ME16 161 C2
Farnborough Comm
 BR6 . . . . 86 B6
Farnborough Ct 2 BR6 86 C5
Farnborough Hill BR6 . . 86 E5
Farnborough Prim Sch
 BR6 . . . . 86 D5
Farnborough Way BR6 . 86 D5
Farncombe Way CT16 278 B7
Farne Cl ME15 . . . . 195 A6
Farnham Beeches
 TN3 . . . . 285 A4
Farnham Cl
 Gillingham ME8 . . . . . . 66 B1
 Langton Green TN3 . . . 285 A4
Farnham La TN3 . . . . . 285 A4
Farnham Pl TN3 . . . . . 285 A3
Farnham Rd DA16 . . . . 13 C5
FARNINGHAM 56 F2
Farningham Cl ME14 . . 162 C6
Farningham Hill Rd
 DA4 . . . . 56 E7
Farningham Road Sta
 DA4 . . . . 57 B7
Farningham Wood ★ BR8,
 DA4 . . . . 56 D5
Farnol Rd DA1 . . . . 16 A3
Faro Cl BR1 . . . . 53 A7
Farraday Cl ME1 . . . . . . 96 D8
Farrance Cl TN1 . . . . . 286 B4
Farrant Cl BR6 . . . . 87 A3
Farrants Ct BR1 . . . . . . 52 F7

Farrar Rd CT7 . . . . 81 A6
Farrell Ct DA2 . . . . 33 C5
Farrell Wlk TN23 . . . . 300 B4
Farrers Wlk TN23 . . . . 300 B4
Farrier Cl Ashford TN23 267 F5
 Bromley BR1 . . . . 52 D6
 Maidstone ME14 . . . . . 162 E5
Farriers Cl 3 DA12 . . . . 37 F7
Farriers Ct ME8 . . . . . . 99 C8
Farrier St CT14 . . . . . . 215 D7
Farriers The TN8 . . . . . 217 B3
Farrington Ave BR5 . . . . 54 B6
Farrington Pl BR7 . . . . . 30 D1
Farringtons Sch BR7 . . . 30 D1
Farrow Ct TN23 . . . . . . 300 A6
Farthely Ct 3 DA15 . . . . 30 F4
Farthing Cnr ME9 . . . . . 98 E3
Farthing Cl DA1 . . . . 15 F3
FARTHING COMMON . . 304 D5
Farthingfield TN15 . . . 125 A3
FARTHING GREEN 229 E1
Farthing Hill TN5 . . . . 338 E1
FARTHINGLOE 310 E5
Farthingloe Cotts
 CT15 . . . . 309 F5
Farthingloe Rd CT17 . . 310 A4
Farthings Cotts ME14 . 129 F1
Farthings Ct TN2 . . . . . 142 C4
Farthing St BR6 . . . . . . 85 F2
FARTHING STREET 85 F2
Farwell Rd DA14 . . . . . . 31 C4
Farwig La BR1 . . . . 52 A8
Fashoda Rd BR2 . . . . . . 52 D5
Fauchon's Cl ME14 . . . 162 F4
Fauchon's La ME14 . . . 162 F4
Faulkners La CT2 . . . . . 142 A1
Faussett Hill CT4 . . . . 207 E7
Faustina Dr TN23 . . . . 299 F4
F Ave SE18 . . . . 2 B3
FAVERSHAM 138 A5
Faversham Cottage Hospl
 ME13 . . . . 138 C7
Faversham Ind Est
 ME13 . . . . 138 F7
Faversham Miniature Rly ★
 ME13 . . . . 138 M3
Faversham Reach
 ME13 . . . . 138 D8
Faversham Sta ME13 . . 138 B8
Faversham Stone Chapel ★
 ME13 . . . . 137 E7
Favourite Rd CT5 . . . . . 108 B6
Fawkes Ave DA1 . . . . . . 33 F6
Fawkham Ave DA3 . . . . . 59 C6
Fawkham CE Prim Sch
 DA3 . . . . 58 B1
FAWKHAM GREEN 91 B8
Fawkham Green Rd
 DA3 . . . . 58 B1
Fawkham Ho 10 BR5 . . 54 D1
Fawkham House Sch
 TN15 . . . . 91 D3
Fawkham Manor Hospl
 DA3 . . . . 58 C1
Fawkham Rd
 Longfield DA3 . . . . 58 D6
 West Kingsdown TN15 . . 91 A4
Fawley Cl ME14 . . . . . . 161 E7
Fay Cl ME1 . . . . 63 B3
Faygate Cres DA6 . . . . . 14 A2
Fazan Ct TN5 . . . . 336 F4
Fearon St SE10 . . . . 1 A1
Featherbed La
 Iwade ME9 . . . . 68 C2
 Selling ME13 . . . . 171 A7
Featherby Cotts ME7 . . 64 F6
Featherby Inf Sch ME8 . 65 A3
Featherby Jun Sch ME8 65 A3
Featherby Rd ME8 . . . . 65 A3
Federation Rd SE2 . . . . . 3 C2
Feenan Highway RM18 . 19 B6
Felborough Cl CT4 . . . 205 C8
FELDERLAND 180 F4
Felderland Cl
 Maidstone ME17 . . . . . 195 E5
 Sandwich CT14 . . . . . . 180 F5
Felderland Dr ME17 . . 195 E5
Felderland La CT14 . . . 180 E4
Felderland Rd ME17 . . 195 E5
Feldspar Cl
 Chatham ME5 . . . . 97 A1
 Sittingbourne ME10 . . 101 D6
Felhampton Rd SE9 . . . 30 B5
Felix Manor BR7 . . . . . . 30 E2
Felixstowe Ct E16 . . . . . 2 B5
Felixstowe Rd SE2 . . . . . 3 B3
Fell Mead TN12 . . . . . . 224 F6
Fellowes Way TN11 . . . 221 E5
Fellows Cl ME8 . . . . 98 B6
Felltram Way SE7 . . . . . . 1 A1
Felma Ho 12 SE7 . . . . . 11 C8
Felspar Cl SE18 . . . . 2 F3
Felstead Rd BR6 . . . . . . 87 B8
Felsted Rd E16 . . . . 1 F7
Felton Cl BR5 . . . . 53 B3
Felton Ho SE3 . . . . 5 B3
Felton Lea DA14 . . . . . . 30 F3
Fendyke Rd DA17 . . . . . . 3 D3
Fen Gr DA15 . . . . 12 F1
Fen Mdw TN15 . . . . . . 124 C1
Fenn Cl BR1 . . . . 29 A2
Fennel Cl ME16 . . . . . . 161 B3

Fennell Cl ME1 . . . . 63 B3
Fennell St SE18 . . . . . . 12 A8
Fenner Cl CT20 . . . . . . 334 E4
Fenners Marsh DA12 . . 37 F7
Fenn St ME3 . . . . 24 B4
FENN STREET 24 B4
Fenoulhet Way CT6 . . . 77 A5
Fen Pond Rd TN15 . . . 156 C7
Fen Pond Road TN15 . 156 D6
Fens Way BR8 . . . . 33 A2
Fenton Cl BR7 . . . . 29 F3
Fenton Ct CT14 . . . . . . 215 B6
Fenwick Cl 16 SE18 . . . 12 A8
Feoffe Cotts TN17 . . . . 342 E7
Ferbies TN3 . . . . 285 A7
Ferbies CT3 . . . . 285 A7
Ferby Ct 3 DA15 . . . . . . 30 F4
Ferdi Lethert Ho TN24 268 E5
Ferdinand Terr TN3 . . . 312 C7
Ferguson Ave DA12 . . . 37 C4
Ferguson Cl CT21 . . . . 333 F2
Ferguson Rd TN29 . . . . 378 F6
Ferguson Way CT21 . . 333 A1
Fern Bank DA4 . . . . 89 E8
Fernbank Cl ME5 . . . . . 96 F2
Fern Bank Cres CT19 . 335 D6
Fern Cl Erith DA8 . . . . . 15 B6
 Hawkinge CT18 . . . . . . 307 C6
 Whitstable CT5 . . . . 75 C1
Fern Ct Bexley DA7 . . . . 14 A3
 Broadstairs CT10 . . . . . 84 B5
 Dover CT16 . . . . 278 D1
FERNDALE 286 D5
Ferndale Bromley BR1 . . 52 C7
 Royal Tunbridge Wells
 TN2 . . . . 286 D5
 Sevenoaks TN13 . . . . . 154 C5
Ferndale Ct Bexley DA7 . 13 E6
 Halfway Houses ME12 . . 46 D6
 Royal Tunbridge Wells
 TN2 . . . . 286 C4
Ferndale Ct CT7 . . . . . . 81 A6
Ferndale Point TN2 . . . 286 C4
Ferndale Rd
 Gillingham ME7 . . . . . . 64 E5
 Gravesend DA12 . . . . . . 37 B6
Ferndale St E6 . . . . 2 B7
Ferndale Way BR6 . . . . . 86 D5
Ferndell Ave DA5 . . . . . 32 D5
Ferndene DA3 . . . . 59 D6
Ferndown CT7 . . . . 80 D8
Ferndown Ave BR6 . . . . 53 D1
Ferndown Cl ME7 . . . . . 98 A5
Ferndown Rd SE9 . . . . . 29 D8
Ferne La CT15 . . . . 276 D3
Ferne Way CT20 . . . . . 334 E6
Fernfield CT18 . . . . 307 C6
Fernfield La CT18 . . . . 307 C7
Fernheath Way DA2 . . . 32 D3
Fern Hill Pl 3 BR5 . . . . 54 D1
Fernhill Rd ME16 . . . . 161 A2
Fernhill St E16 . . . . 1 F5
Fernholt TN10 . . . . 222 C7
Fernhurst Cres TN4 . . 254 A2
Fernlea Ave CT6 . . . . . . 76 E4
FERNLEIGH 101 C2
Fernleigh Cl ME13 . . . 140 B3
Fernleigh Rise ME20 . . 128 B2
Fernley Ct 11 CT20 . . . 335 D5
Fernside La TN13 . . . . 187 D6
Ferns The
 Larkfield ME20 . . . . . . 128 B1
 Platt TN15 . . . . 157 C7
 Royal Tunbridge Wells
 TN1 . . . . 286 C4
Fern Wlk ME10 . . . . . . 102 C5
Fernwood Cl BR1 . . . . . 52 C7
Ferranti Cl SE18 . . . . 1 D3
Ferrier Cl ME8 . . . . 98 E4
Ferrier Point 8 E16 . . . . 1 A8
Ferringham TN4 . . . . . 285 F4
Ferry La Rainham RM13 . 4 E7
 Wouldham ME1 . . . . . . 95 C4
Ferry La Ind Est RM13 . . 4 F8
Ferry Pl SE18 . . . . 2 A3
Ferry Rd Halling ME2 . . 95 B4
 Iwade ME9 . . . . 68 E4
 Queenborough ME11,
 ME12 . . . . 46 D1
 Tilbury RM18 . . . . 19 A4
Ferry View ME11 . . . . . 45 F3
Festival Ave DA3 . . . . . . 59 D6
Festival Cl Erith DA8 . . . 14 F7
 Sidcup DA5 . . . . 31 D7
Festoon Way E16 . . . . . . 1 D6
Ffinch Cl ME20 . . . . . . 160 D8
Fiddlers Cl DA9 . . . . 17 B3
Fiddling La TN25 . . . . . 303 E6
Fidgeon Cl BR1 . . . . 53 A6
Field Ave CT1 . . . . 143 D3
Field Cl Bromley BR1 . . . 52 C7
 Chatham ME5 . . . . 96 E6
Field Court DA11 . . . . . . 36 F6
Field Dr TN8 . . . . 217 D3
Field End TN24 . . . . . . 269 A1
Field End Pl ME13 . . . . 140 A3
Fielder Cl 1 ME10 . . . . 102 C5
Fieldfare Rd SE28 . . . . . . 3 C6
FIELD GREEN 355 E8
Fielding Ave RM18 . . . . 19 B6
Fielding Dr ME20 . . . . 128 A3
Fielding La BR2 . . . . 52 C5
Fielding St ME13 . . . . . 138 C7
Fieldings The ME10 . . . 101 E5
Field Mill Rd ME7 . . . . 233 B5
Field Rd DA13, TN15 . . . 92 C6
Fieldside Cl BR6 . . . . . . 86 C6
Fields La ME18 . . . . . . 192 E7
Field View
 Kingsnorth TN23 . . . . . 300 B4
 Whitstable CT5 . . . . . . 108 B7
Fieldview ME12 . . . . 46 C6
Fieldway BR5 . . . . 53 D3

Field Way CT2 . . . . 143 F5
Fieldways TN18 . . . . . . 341 A1
Fieldworks Rd ME7 . . . . 64 A7
Fiennes Way TN13 . . . 187 C8
Fiesta Dr RM9 . . . . 4 C8
Fiesta Wlk CT5 . . . . . . 108 B6
Fife Rd Herne Bay CT6 . 76 B3
 Newham E16 . . . . 1 A8
Fifteenpenny Fields
 SE9 . . . . 12 A2
Fifth Ave Margate CT9 . 51 B3
 West Thurrock RM20 . . . 17 A8
FIG STREET 187 A7
Fig Tree Rd CT10 . . . . . 83 F7
Fig Tree Wlk CT15 . . . . 245 C7
Fiji Terr ME14 . . . . 162 A7
Filborough Way DA12 . . 38 B6
Filer Rd ME12 . . . . 46 E7
Filey Cl TN16 . . . . 150 B8
Filmer La TN14 . . . . . . 154 E6
Filmer Rd CT4 . . . . 175 F1
Filston La TN14 . . . . . . 121 C5
Filston Rd DA8 . . . . 4 C1
Finchale Rd SE2 . . . . 3 A3
Finch Cl ME13 . . . . 48 A2
Finchcocks Musical Mus ★
 TN17 . . . . 318 A5
Finch Ct
 Maidstone ME14 . . . . . 161 E7
 Sidcup DA14 . . . . 31 B5
Finches The
 Sittingbourne ME10 . . 101 F3
 St Nicholas at Wade CT7 79 E2
Finch Gr CT21 . . . . 353 D8
Finchley Cl DA1 . . . . . . 16 A1
Finchley Rd RM17 . . . . . 18 B8
Finch Mews CT14 . . . . 215 C4
Finch's Cross RH8 . . . . 216 A8
Findlay Cl ME8 . . . . 98 D6
Findlay Dr 9 CT21 . . . . 333 B2
FINGLESHAM 214 B8
Finglesham Cl BR5 . . . . 54 D1
Finglesham Ct ME15 . . 195 C8
Finglesham Farm Barns
 CT14 . . . . 214 A8
Finlay Cl ME13 . . . . . . 138 B7
Finlay Ct 4 DA14 . . . . . . 24 A3
Finn Farm Ct TN23 . . . 300 D1
Finn Farm Rd TN23 . . . 300 C2
Finsbury Ct CT11 . . . . 117 E8
Finsbury Rd CT11 . . . . 117 E8
Finsbury Way DA5 . . . . 13 F1
Fintonagh Dr ME14 . . 162 B6
Finucane Dr BR5 . . . . . . 54 C2
Finwell Rd ME8 . . . . 66 A2
Firbank Cl TN16 . . . . 1 D8
Firbank Gdns CT9 . . . . 82 D7
Firbanks CT5 . . . . 108 F8
Fircroft Way TN8 . . . . . 217 C3
Fir Ct TN24 . . . . 268 F1
Fir Dene BR6 . . . . 86 A7
Firecrest Cl DA3 . . . . . . 59 B6
Fire Opal Way 6
 ME13 . . . . 101 D6
Firepower: The Royal
 Artillery Mus &
 Greenwich Heritage
 Ctr ★ SE18 . . . . 2 B3
Firethorn Cl ME7 . . . . . 64 E6
Firmin Ave ME17 . . . . 195 D5
Firmingers Rd BR6 . . . . 88 C5
Firmin Rd DA1 . . . . 15 E2
Firs Cl Aylesford ME20 . 128 E1
 Folkestone CT19 . . . . . 334 D7
Firs Ct TN4 . . . . 285 F6
Firs La CT19 . . . . 334 D7
Firs Rd CT4 . . . . 210 F1
First Ave Bexley DA7 . . . 13 C7
 Broadstairs CT10 . . . . . 51 F2
 Chatham ME4 . . . . 64 C2
 Eastchurch ME12 . . . . . 48 E5
 Gillingham ME7 . . . . . . 64 E3
 Margate CT9 . . . . 51 B3
 Northfleet DA11 . . . . . . 36 E7
 Rushenden ME11 . . . . . 45 F3
 West Thurrock RM20 . . . 17 A8
First La ME17 . . . . 163 E2
First St TN3 . . . . 284 F3
FIR TOLL 265 C6
Firtree Cl CT21 . . . . . . 333 D1
Fir Tree Gr
 Bredhurst ME7 . . . . 98 B1
 Chatham ME5 . . . . 97 B1
Fir Tree Hill CT13 . . . . 180 B6
Fir Tree Rd TN4 . . . . . . 285 F3
Fisher Cl CT21 . . . . 333 D1
Fishermans Ctyd CT14 215 D3
Fisherman's Wharf 9
 CT13 . . . . 149 A1
Fishermans Wlk SE28 . . 2 B4
Fishermen's Hill DA11 . 18 B2
Fisher Rd
 Canterbury CT2 . . . . . . 142 D1
 Chatham ME5 . . . . 97 B7
Fishers TN28 . . . . 373 C6
Fishers Cl TN12 . . . . . . 260 F5
Fisher's Gate Cotts
 TN7 . . . . 311 A1
Fishers Rd TN12 . . . . . 260 F5
Fisher St
 Maidstone ME14 . . . . . 162 A6
 Newham E16 . . . . 1 A8
 Sandwich CT13 . . . . . . 181 D5
Fisher Street Rd ME13 170 E2

Fisher's Way DA17 . . . . . 4 C5
Fishguard Way E16 . . . . 2 B5
FISHINGHURST 319 F7
Fish Market CT19 . . . . 335 E5
Fishmarket Rd TN31 . . 368 B1
Fishmonger's La 8
 CT16 . . . . 310 E7
Fishponds Rd BR2 . . . . 85 D5
Fitzgerald Ave CT6 . . . . 76 C4
Fitzgilbert Cl ME7 . . . . 65 A5
Fitzmary Ave CT9 . . . . . 50 E1
Fitzroy Ave
 Broadstairs CT10 . . . . . 51 G2
 Margate CT9 . . . . 51 B1
 Ramsgate CT12 . . . . . . 83 B2
Fitzroy Ct DA1 . . . . 34 B7
Fitzroy Rd CT5 . . . . 74 F2
Fitzthorold Ho ME7 . . . 64 E7
Fitzwalter Ct 1 CT16 . . 278 E1
Fitzwalter Rd TN3 . . . . 178 D2
Fitzwilliam Mews E16 . . 1 A5
Fitzwilliam Rd ME14 . . 162 F5
Five Acre Wood Sch
 ME15 . . . . 195 B7
Five Arches Bsns Est
 DA14 . . . . 31 D3
Fiveash Rd DA11 . . . . . . 36 F6
Five Bells La 5 ME1 . . . 63 D4
Five Elms Rd BR2 . . . . . 85 C7
Five Fields La TN8 . . . . 218 B4
FIVE OAK GREEN 256 B7
Five Oak Green Rd
 Capel TN11, TN12 . . . 255 D6
 Tonbridge TN11 . . . . . 254 F7
Five Oaks Mews BR1 . . 29 A5
Five Vents La TN29 . . . 372 B8
Fiveways 6 CT17 . . . . . 310 C8
Five Ways TN1 . . . . 286 B4
Five Ways Ct ME4 . . . . . 64 A4
Fiveways Rise CT14 . . . 214 F5
FIVE WENTS 196 D2
Five Wents BR8 . . . . 56 A7
Flack Gdns ME3 . . . . . . 41 E5
Flagstaff Ct 1 CT1 . . . 175 A7
Flamborough Cl TN16 . 150 B8
Flamingo Cl ME5 . . . . . 97 A7
Flamingo Dr CT6 . . . . . 76 E3
Flamsteed Rd SE7 . . . . . 1 E1
Flanders Cl ME10 . . . . . 68 F1
Flanders Field TN25 . . . 301 N1
Flats The
 Gravesend DA12 . . . . . . 37 E8
 Swanscombe DA9 . . . . . 17 C2
Flax Court La CT15 . . . 245 C7
Flaxman Ct
 13 Chatham ME5 . . . . . 64 A6
 Erith DA21 . . . . 4 A1
Flaxman Dr ME16 . . . . 161 C6
Flaxmore Ct DA7 . . . . . 14 B4
Flaxmore Pl TN4 . . . . . 254 A2
Flaxpond Rd TN23 . . . 299 F7
Flaxton Rd SE18 . . . . . . 12 E7
FLEEDEN 298 E2
Fleet Ave Dartford DA2 . 34 C7
 Sheerness ME12 . . . . . 28 B1
Fleet Dale Par DA2 . . . . 34 C7
Fleetdown Inf Sch DA2 34 C6
Fleetdown Jun Sch
 DA2 . . . . 34 C6
FLEET-DOWNS 34 D7
Fleet Ho DA13 . . . . 36 B2
Fleet Rd Dartford DA2 . . 34 C7
 Northfleet DA11 . . . . . . 36 C6
 Rochester ME1 . . . . 63 D1
St Margaret's at Cliffe
 CT15 . . . . 248 A1
Fleets La CT2 . . . . 142 F7
Fleet Terr DA11 . . . . 36 D7
Fleet Villas TN24 . . . . . 268 D7
Fleetwood Ave CT6 . . . . 76 D4
Fleetwood Cl
 Minster (Sheppey)
 ME12 . . . . 47 B6
 Newham E16 . . . . 1 D8
Fleetwood Ct
 1 Newham E6 . . . . 1 F8
 Orpington BR6 . . . . 86 A6
Fleming Cl DA11 . . . . . 36 C7
Fleming Gdns RM18 . . . 19 C6
Fleming Ho SE2 . . . . 3 C1
Fleming Rd CT13, CT3 . 179 D6
FLEMINGS 179 D6
Fleming Way Erith SE28 . 3 A8
 Folkestone CT19 . . . . . 335 A4
 Tonbridge TN10 . . . . . 222 E2
Fletcher Cl E6 . . . . 2 B6
Fletcher Gardens ME6 127 F8
Fletcher Rd
 Staplehurst TN12 . . . . 260 E3
 Whitstable CT5 . . . . . . 75 B1
Fletchers Cl BR2 . . . . . . 52 B5
Fletchers Way CT14 . . . 215 A5
Fletching Rd SE7 . . . . . . 11 D8
Flete Rd CT9 . . . . 29 D8
Fleur de Lis Heritage Ctr ★
 17 ME13 . . . . 138 D7
FLIMWELL 339 C3
Flimwell TN23 . . . . 299 D6
Flimwell Cl TN5 . . . . . . 339 D4
Flint Cl Orpington BR6 86 E4
 Sittingbourne ME10 . . 101 D8
Flint Cotts CT7 . . . . 80 F6
Flint Down Cl BR5 . . . . 54 A8
Flint Gn ME5 . . . . 97 C3
Flint Gr CT10 . . . . 83 E5
Flint Ho CT9 . . . . 50 J3
Flint La Lenham ME17 . 166 C1
 Woodside Green ME17 . 199 C8
Flintmill Cres SE3, SE9 . 11 E5
Flint St RM20 . . . . 17 B8

Floathaven Cl SE28 . . . . 3 A3
Floats The TN13 . . . . . 153 E6
Flodden Rd CT14 . . . . 214 F3
Flood Hatch ME15 . . . 161 D2
Flood La ME13 . . . . . . 138 C8
Flood St TN25 . . . . . . 301 D2
Florance La TN3 . . . . . 312 B6
Flora Rd CT11 . . . . . . 117 E8
Flora St DA17 . . . . 3 F1
Florence Ave CT5 . . . . 108 B7
Florence Cl RM17, RM20 17 E8
Florence Cotts
  5 Edenbridge TN8 . . 217 C1
  Ramsgate CT11 . . . . . 117 D6
Florence Ct CT9 . . . . . . 51 B3
Florence Farm Mobile
  Home Pk TN15 . . . . . . .90 D4
Florence Ho SE18 . . . . . 11 F6
Florence Rd
  4 Bromley BR1 . . . . 52 A8
  Erith DA17, SE2 . . . . . . 3 C2
  Maidstone ME16 . . . . 161 A8
  3 Ramsgate CT11 . . 117 D6
Florence St **3** ME2 . . . 63 B8
Florida Cl CT16 . . . . . 278 B3
Florin Dr ME1 . . . . 63 B4
Flowerfield TN14 . . . . 121 F2
Flowerhill Way DA13 . . 36 E1
Flower Rise ME14 . . . 161 F7
Floyd Cl TN4 . . . . 286 A7
Floyd Rd SE7 . . . . .1 C1
Flume End ME15 . . . . 161 D2
Flyers Way The TN16 . 151 D1
Flying Horse La **6**
  CT16 . . . . 310 E7
Foads Hill CT12 . . . . . 116 D6
Foads La CT12 . . . . . . 116 D5
Foalhurst Cl TN10 . . . 222 E4
Focal Point Rd CT16 . 277 F4
Fodbury Ct CT8 . . . . . . 50 C1
Foley Cl TN24 . . . . . . 301 A7
Foley Ct DA1 . . . . 34 B7
Foley Rd TN16 . . . . . . 118 D1
Foley St ME14 . . . . . . 162 A5
FOLKESTONE 335 F4
Folkestone Acad CT19 335 B7
Folkestone Central
  CT19 . . . . 335 C5
Folkestone Ent Ctr
  CT19 . . . . 334 F8
Folkestone Martello
  Tower★ CT19 . . . . . 335 G6
Folkestone Race Course
  CT21 . . . . 332 A6
Folkestone Rd
  Brookland TN31 . . . . 369 B3
  Church Hougham CT15 309 D4
  Dover CT17, CT15 . . . 310 B7
Folkestone Sch for Girls
  The CT20 . . . . 334 F4
Folkestone Sports & Ski
  Ctr CT19 . . . . 335 B6
Folkestone West Sta
  CT20 . . . . 334 F5
Folkstone Ho **4** ME15 195 F6
Folkstone, St Martins CE
  Prim Sch CT18 . . . . . 334 F1
Folks Wood Way CT21 332 A4
Folly Rd CT20 . . . . . . 335 E6
FOLLY TOWN 270 F7
Fonblanque Rd ME12 . .28 C2
Fontana ME5 . . . . .97 A3
Fontwell Cl ME15 . . . . 195 F6
Fontwell Dr BR2 . . . . . . 53 A4
FOORD 335 D5
Foord Almshouses ME1 63 B3
Foord Cl DA2 . . . . 34 E6
Foord Rd ME17 . . . . . 199 D5
Foord Road N CT19,
  CT20 . . . . 335 D5
Foord Road S **14** CT20 335 D5
Foord St ME1 . . . . .63 D4
Footbury Hill Rd BR6 . . 54 A2
FOOTS CRAY 31 B2
Foots Cray High St
  DA14 . . . . 31 D2
Foots Cray La DA14 . . .31 C7
Foots Cray Meadows★
  DA14 . . . . 31 D4
Footscray Rd SE9 . . . . .30 C7
Forbes Rd ME13 . . . . . 138 C6
FORCE GREEN 151 E4
Force Green Farm Cotts
  TN16 . . . . 151 E4
Force Green La TN16 . 151 E4
FORD 111 E8
Ford Cl Bridge CT4 . . . 175 F1
  Herne Bay CT6 . . . . . . 76 A4
Ford Ho **2** SE18 . . . . . 2 B1
Fordingbridge Cl
  ME16 . . . . 161 B5
Ford La
  Trottiscliffe ME19 . . . 126 A4
  Wrotham Heath TN15,
  ME19 . . . . 125 F2
Fordoun Rd DA11 . . . . .83 F5
Ford Rd DA11 . . . . 18 B2
Fords Park Rd E16 . . . . .1 A7
Ford Way TN23 . . . . . 267 F1
FORDWICH 144 A4

Fordwich Cl
  Maidstone ME16 . . . . 161 B7
  Orpington BR6 . . . . . . 53 F2
Fordwich Dr ME2 . . . . .40 A2
Fordwich Gn ME8 . . . . .65 C3
Fordwich Gr CT10 . . . . 83 E7
Fordwich Pl CT13 . . . . 180 F8
Fordwich Rd CT2 . . . . 143 F4
Ford Wlk CT5 . . . . 108 A3
Foreland Ave
  Folkestone CT19 . . . . 335 F6
  Margate CT9 . . . . .51 D1
Foreland Ct
  Birchington CT7 . . . . . .80 D8
  Ramsgate CT11 . . . . . 117 D5
  St Margaret's at Cliffe
  CT15 . . . . 280 A5
Foreland Hts CT10 . . . .84 B7
Foreland Park Ho CT10 84 A7
Foreland Rd CT15 . . . . 280 A4
Foreland Sch The CT10 .84 A6
Forelands Sq CT14 . . . 215 B3
Foreland St SE18 . . . . . . 2 D2
Foreland The CT11 . . . 175 B5
Foreman Ctr TN27 . . . 262 D5
Foremans Barn Rd
  ME15 . . . . 193 F3
Foreman's Wlk TN27 . 262 D5
Foreness Cl CT10 . . . . . 51 G3
Forestall Mdw TN23 . . 300 B4
Forest Ave TN25 . . . . . 267 E4
Forest Cotts TN25 . . . 203 C2
Forestdale Rd ME5 . . . 130 A8
Forest Dene TN2 . . . . 286 C1
Forest Dr Chatham ME5 . 96 F2
  Orpington BR2 . . . . . . 85 C6
Foresters Cl ME4 . . . . .96 F2
Foresters Cres DA7 . . . 14 B3
Foresters Homes The
  DA7 . . . . 14 B3
Foresters Way CT20 . . 335 D5
Forest Gr TN10 . . . . . 222 C5
Forest Hill ME15 . . . . 161 F1
Forest Lawns BR1 . . . . 52 C8
Forest Rd Erith DA8 . . . 15 A6
  Paddock Wood TN12 . . 257 A6
  Royal Tunbridge Wells
  TN2 . . . . 286 C1
Forest Ridge TN2 . . . . .85 F6
Forestry Cotts CT4 . . . 239 B7
Forest Way Eltham DA15 30 D8
  Kings Hill ME19 . . . . . 159 A3
  Orpington BR5 . . . . . . 53 F4
  Pembury TN2 . . . . . . 287 D8
  Royal Tunbridge Wells
  TN2 . . . . 286 D1
Forge Cl Eythorne CT15 245 C4
  Five Oak Green TN12 . 256 B7
  Hayes BR2 . . . . 52 A1
  Penshurst TN11 . . . . . 252 B4
  Sellindge TN25 . . . . . 303 D1
  Sturry CT2 . . . . 143 F5
Forge Cotts
  Boyden Gate CT3 . . . . 112 C8
  Broadstairs CT10 . . . . .84 B5
  Faversham ME13 . . . . 139 D8
  Flimwell TN5 . . . . . . 339 C3
  Nettlestead Green
  ME18 . . . . 192 C2
  Wrotham Heath TN15 . 125 E1
Forge Croft TN8 . . . . . 217 D1
Forgefield
  Bethersden TN26 . . . . 297 D5
  Biggin Hill TN16 . . . . 118 D3
Forge Field CT15 . . . . 308 E5
Forgefield Cotts TN26 356 A4
Forgefield Ct BR5 . . . . 54 C4
Forgefields CT6 . . . . . 111 B8
Forge Hill
  Aldington TN25 . . . . . 330 A5
  Bethersden TN26 . . . . 297 E5
Forge Ho
  Canterbury CT1 . . . . . 174 E6
  Ickham CT3 . . . . 145 C1
Forge La Ashford TN23 . 268 B2
  Benover ME14 . . . . . 226 B4
  Boxley ME14 . . . . 130 C2
  Boyden Gate CT3 . . . . 112 C8
  Bredhurst ME7 . . . . . .98 A1
  East Farleigh ME15 . . 194 C7
  Egerton Forstal TN27 . 232 C1
  Gillingham ME7 . . . . . .64 E7
  Gravesend DA12 . . . . .37 F6
  Headcorn TN27 . . . . . 262 D5
  Higham ME3 . . . . .39 C3
  High Halstow ME23 . . . 23 E3
  Horton Kirby DA4 . . . . .57 C5
  Leeds ME17 . . . . 196 F7
  Maidstone ME14 . . . . 163 C4
  Rabbit's Cross ME17,
  TN12 . . . . 228 F3
  Ramsgate CT11 . . . . . 117 C7
  Shorne DA12 . . . . 38 C3
  Sutton CT15 . . . . 247 A6
  Upchurch ME9 . . . . . . 66 F3
  West Kingsdown TN15 . 91 A1
  West Peckham ME18 . 191 A6
  Whitfield CT16 . . . . . 278 A8
  Whitstable CT5 . . . . . 108 D8
Forge Mdw
  Harrietsham ME17 . . . 198 D6
  Stone in Oxney TN30 . 361 A4
Forge Meadows TN27 262 D5
Forge Meads TN30 . . . 359 E4
Forge Path CT16 . . . . . 278 A8
Forge Pl **4** DA12 . . . . 37 F7
Forge Rd Cobham TN3 . 312 C2
  Royal Tunbridge Wells
  TN4 . . . . 254 A1
  Sittingbourne ME10 . . 101 E6
Forge Sq TN11 . . . . . 220 F2
Forge The TN12 . . . . . 256 B7
Forge View TN15 . . . . 188 B5

Forge Way
  Paddock Wood TN12 . 257 A7
  Shoreham TN14 . . . . 121 F8
Formation The E16 . . . . 2 B4
Formby Rd ME2 . . . . . . 95 A7
Formby Terr ME2 . . . . . 95 A6
Forrens The **14** CT1 . 143 A1
Forrester Cl CT1 . . . . 143 C2
Forsham La ME17 . . . . 229 C5
Forson Cl TN30 . . . . . 345 B8
FORSTAL 129 B2
Forstal Cl BR2 . . . . 52 A6
Forstal Cotts
  Forstall ME20 . . . . . 129 B2
  Lenham Heath ME17 . 200 A1
Forstall TN3 . . . . 285 A4
Forstall La ME17 . . . . 194 D4
Forstall The TN11 . . . . 221 A2
Forstal Rd
  Egerton Forstal TN27 . 232 C1
  Forstall ME20 . . . . . 129 C2
  Woolage Village CT4 . 210 E1
FORSTAL THE 301 D3
Forstal The
  Cobham TN3 . . . . . . 312 F3
  Hadlow TN11 . . . . . 223 F8
  Lenham Heath ME17 . 200 A1
  Pembury TN2 . . . . . . 287 B8
  Preston CT3 . . . . . . 146 B6
  Wye TN25 . . . . 237 C2
Forsters ME17 . . . . . . 196 E4
Forsyth CL ME19 . . . . 128 A1
Forsyth St **7** CT7 . . . . 64 C7
Fort Amherst★ ME4 . . 63 F5
Fort Burgoyne (Casemated
  Barracks) CT15 . . . . 278 E2
Fort Burgoyne Rd
  CT16 . . . . 278 E1
Fort Cl TN29 . . . . 377 E6
Fort Cotts CT10 . . . . . .84 B4
Fort Cres CT10 . . . . . . .50 J3
Fort Hill CT9 . . . . 50 J3
Fortis Cl E16 . . . . 1 C7
Fort Lower Prom CT9 . .50 J3
Fort Luton★ ME4 . . . . .64 A1
Fort Paragon CT9 . . . . 50 J3
Fort Pitt Gram Sch ME4 63 E4
Fort Pitt Hill ME1, ME4 . 63 E4
Fort Pitt St ME4 . . . . . 63 E3
Fort Prom CT9 . . . . . . 50 J3
Fort Rd
  Badgers Mount TN14 . 121 C4
  Broadstairs CT10 . . . . .84 B4
  Hythe CT21 . . . . 333 A2
  Margate CT9 . . . . .50 J3
  Tilbury RM18 . . . . 19 C5
Fortrye Cl DA11 . . . . . . 36 E6
Fort St Newham E16 . . . . 1 B5
  Rochester ME1 . . . . . . 63 D4
Fortuna Cl DA3 . . . . . . 58 F5
Fortuna Ct CT11 . . . . . 117 D7
Fortune Way ME19 . . . 159 B3
Fortune Wlk **7** SE28 . . 2 D3
Forty Acre La ME17 . . . . 1 A8
Forty Acres Hill ME12 . 47 C4
Forty Acres Rd CT2 . . 142 C4
Forum Sh Ctr The **9**
  ME10 . . . . 101 F4
Forum The **2** ME10 . 101 F4
Forum Way TN23 . . . . 299 E5
Forward Way ME1 . . . . 96 C6
Fossdene Prim Sch SE7 . 1 B1
Fossdene Rd SE7 . . . . . . 1 B1
Fosse Bank Cl TN9 . . . 254 A7
Fosse Bank Sch TN11 . 221 C6
Fossett Lodge DA7 . . . . 14 C6
Fossington Rd DA17 . . . 3 D2
FOSTALL 140 A7
Fostall Gn TN23 . . . . . 299 F7
Fostall Rd ME13 . . . . . 105 C7
FOSTEN GREEN 322 D6
Fosten La TN27 . . . . . 322 E7
Foster Cl CT19 . . . . . . 334 E4
Foster Clarke Dr ME17 195 D5
Foster Clark Est ME15 . 162 B2
Foster Rd TN24 . . . . . 301 A6
Foster's Ave CT10 . . . . 83 E7
Fosters Cl BR7 . . . . 29 F3
Fosters Mews DA3 . . . . 58 E7
Fosters Old School
  DA16 . . . . 13 B5
Fosters Prim Sch DA16 .13 C4
Foster St ME15 . . . . . 162 A3
Foster Way CT14 . . . . 215 B3
Fostington Way ME5 . . 96 F1
Fougeres Way TN24 . . 268 A4
Foulds Cl ME8 . . . . 98 B5
Founder Cl E6 . . . . 2 B7
Foundry Cl TN19 . . . . 354 A3
Foundry Wharf ME1 . . . 63 E4
Fountain Ct
  Eynsford DA4 . . . . . . .89 C8
  Sidcup DA15 . . . . 13 B1
Fountain Inn Ct CT9 . . 50 I3
Fountain La
  Maidstone ME15 . . . . 161 A2
  Sheerness ME12 . . . . .28 A2
Fountain Rd ME2 . . . . . 39 E1
Fountains Cl TN24 . . . 269 A1
Fountain St
  2 Sittingbourne
  ME10 . . . . 101 E4
  3 Whitstable CT5 . . 74 D2
Fountain Wlk DA11 . . . 18 F1
Fouracre Cotts ME9 . . . 99 E6
Four Acres ME19 . . . . 160 B5
FOUR ELMS 218 A5
Four Elms Hill ME3 . . . 40 E4
Four Elms Prim Sch
  TN8 . . . . 218 B5
Four Elms Rd TN8 . . . . 217 D4
Four Elms Rdbt ME3 . . 40 E4

Four Horseshoes Pk
  ME13 . . . . 106 D1
Four Oaks ME13 . . . . . 137 E8
Four Oaks Rd TN12,
  TN27 . . . . 261 E7
Fourth Ave
  Eastchurch ME12 . . . . 48 F5
  Gillingham ME7 . . . . . .64 E4
  West Thurrock RM20 . . 17 A8
FOUR THROWS 355 D8
Four Trees ME8 . . . . . 217 C3
Four Turnings CT3 . . . 146 B3
FOUR WENTS 341 B6
Four Wents
  Langley Heath ME17 . 196 C5
  Maidstone ME15 . . . . 161 A2
Four Wents Cl **6** TN15 156 F7
Fourwents Rd ME3 . . . . 41 D7
Fowey Cl ME5 . . . . .97 C5
Fowler Cl Gillingham ME8 98 C3
  Sidcup DA14 . . . . 31 E3
Fowlmead Ctry Pk★
  CT14 . . . . 214 E8
Foxborough Cl CT13 . . 180 B6
Foxborough Hill CT13 . 180 B5
Foxborough La CT12 . 115 C6
Foxburrow CT ME8 . . . .98 D5
Foxbury DA3 . . . . 91 E7
Foxbury Ave BR7 . . . . . 30 B6
Foxbury Cl Bromley BR1 . 29 B2
  Orpington BR6 . . . . . . 87 A5
Foxbury Dr BR6 . . . . . . 87 A4
Foxbury Rd BR1 . . . . . . 29 B2
Foxbury Wlk DA11 . . . . 36 F3
Foxbush TN11 . . . . . . 221 C6
Fox Cl Lymynge CT18 . 305 B7
  Newham E16 . . . . 1 A8
  Orpington BR6 . . . . . . 87 A5
Foxcroft Rd SE18 . . . . . 12 B5
Foxden Dr ME15 . . . . 162 F1
Foxdene Cl CT5 . . . . . 107 F6
Foxdene Rd CT5 . . . . . 107 F6
Foxdown Cl CT2 . . . . . 142 E2
Foxearth Cl TN16 . . . . 118 C1
FOXENDOWN 93 C8
Foxendown La DA13 . . 60 B1
Foxes Dale SE3 . . . . . . 11 A6
Foxfield Prim Sch SE18 . .2 C1
Foxfield Rd BR6 . . . . . .86 D8
Foxglove Cl
  9 Marlpit Hill TN8 . 217 D3
  Sidcup DA15 . . . . 13 A1
Foxglove Cres ME5 . . . .96 E4
Foxglove Gn TN24 . . . 268 F2
Foxglove Rd TN24 . . . 268 E1
Foxglove Rise ME14 . . 161 E7
Foxgloves The TN12 . . 257 B5
Foxgrove ME10 . . . . . 101 E7
Foxgrove Path SE28 . . . .2 E7
Foxgrove Rd CT5 . . . . . 75 A1
Fox Hill Keston BR2 . . . 85 C5
  Sittingbourne ME10,
  ME9 . . . . 102 D3
Foxhole La
  Four Throws TN18 . . . 355 D8
  Hawkhurst TN18 . . . . 341 E1
  Matfield TN12 . . . . . 288 C8
  Wadhurst TN5 . . . . . 337 B4
Foxhole Rd SE9 . . . . . . 11 E2
Fox Hollow Cl **2** SE18 . .2 E1
Fox Hollow Dr DA7 . . . . 13 D4
Fox Holt Rd CT15 . . . . 275 B2
Foxhome Cl BR7 . . . . . . 30 A2
Fox House Rd DA17 . . . . 4 B1
Foxhunter Pk The
  CT12 . . . . 114 D6
Fox in the Wood TN5 . 336 C6
Fox La BR2 . . . . 85 C5
Fox Lea **5** TN15 . . . . 156 F7
Foxley Rd ME11 . . . . . . 46 A5
Fox Manor Way RM20 . 17 B8
Fox's Cross CT5 . . . . . 108 B4
Fox's Cross Hill CT5 . . 108 A3
Fox's Cross Rd CT5 . . 108 C3
Fox St ME7 . . . . 64 C6
Foxtail Cl ME4 . . . . 41 B2
Foxton Ho E16 . . . . .2 A4
Foxton Rd RM20 . . . . . 17 D8
Fox Way CT4 . . . . 242 F8
Foxwood Gr
  Northfleet DA11 . . . . . 36 E7
  Pratt's Bottom BR6 . . . 87 C1
Foxwood Rd DA2 . . . . . 35 B5
Foxwood Specl Sch
  CT21 . . . . 333 F3
Foxwood Way DA3 . . . . 59 D7
Framley Rd TN10 . . . . 222 F5
Framlingham Cres SE9 29 F4
Frampton Rd CT21 . . . 333 A2
France Rd CT16 . . . . . 278 A5
Frances Gdns CT11 . . 117 F8
Frances St SE18 . . . . . . 1 F2
Francis Ave DA7 . . . . . 14 A5
Francis Cl CT12 . . . . . 116 D5
Francis Ct **7** DA8 . . . . 4 E1
Francis Dr ME5 . . . . . . 97 A2
Francis La
  Kings Hill ME19 . . . . 159 D3
  Maidstone ME15 . . . . 195 F5
Francis Rd
  Ashford TN23 . . . . . . 300 B8
  Broadstairs CT10 . . . . .84 B7
  Dartford DA1 . . . . 15 D2
  Orpington BR5 . . . . . . 54 D6
  Tonbridge TN11 . . . . 221 D6
Frankapps Cl ME9 . . . 100 B6
Frank Burton Cl **5** SE7 . 1 B1
Frank Edinger Ct TN24 268 D4
Frankfield Rise TN2 . . 286 A1
Frank Godley Ct DA14 . 31 B3
Frank Martin Ct ME14 . 162 D4
Franklin Pas SE9 . . . . . 11 E4
Franklin Rd Bexley DA7 .13 E6
  Gillingham ME7 . . . . . .64 D5

Franklin Rd continued
  Gravesend DA12 . . . . .37 D3
  Maypole DA2 . . . . 36 E6
Franklins Cotts ME15 . 194 C5
Franklyn Ho CT2 . . . . 143 F5
Franklyn Rd CT2 . . . . 174 C8
Franks Ct ME8 . . . . 65 B2
Frank's Hollow Rd
  TN3 . . . . 253 C2
Franks La DA4 . . . . 57 B4
Frankswood Ave BR5 . . 53 C4
Frank Walters Bsns Pk The
  CT10 . . . . 83 D7
Frank Woolley Rd
  TN10 . . . . 222 F5
FRANT 314 C3
Frant CE Prim Sch
  TN3 . . . . 314 B4
Frant Cotts TN5 . . . . . 338 E1
Frant Ct TN3 . . . . 314 B3
Frant Field TN3 . . . . . 217 C1
Frant Green Rd TN3 . . 314 B3
Frant Rd TN2, TN3 . . . 314 A7
Frant Sta TN3 . . . . . . 314 B4
Fraser Cl Coldblow DA5 . 32 C7
  Newham E6 . . . . 1 E7
Fraser Ho **3** SE18 . . . . 2 A2
Fraser Rd
  Erith DA8 . . . . 4 D1
  Gillingham ME7 . . . . . .64 C4
Freathy La TN25 . . . . 268 C8
Freda Cl CT10 . . . . 83 F1
Frederick Andrews Ct
  RM17 . . . . 18 D8
Frederick Ho **4** SE18 . . 1 E3
Frederick Pl **2** SE18 . . 2 B1
Frederick Rd
  Deal CT14 . . . . 215 A3
  Gillingham ME7 . . . . . .64 C4
Frederick St ME10 . . . 101 E4
Freedown The CT15 . . 280 A7
FREE HEATH 316 C1
Free Heath Rd TN3,
  TN5 . . . . 316 C3
Freehold The
  East Peckham TN12 . . 224 F6
  Hadlow TN11 . . . . . . 190 D1
Freeland Ct **24** DA14 . .31 A5
Freelands Gr BR1 . . . . .52 B8
Freelands Rd
  Bromley BR1 . . . . 52 B8
  Snodland ME6 . . . . . 127 F8
Freeland Way DA8 . . . . 15 A6
Freeman Ct **3** ME10 . 101 E4
Freeman Gdns ME4 . . . 63 F2
Freeman Rd DA12 . . . . 37 E5
Freeman's Cl CT5 . . . . 108 A6
Freeman's Rd CT12 . . 115 B6
Freeman Way ME15 . . 195 E7
Freemasons Rd E16 . . . .1 B7
Freemen's Way CT14 . 215 B3
Freesia Cl
  Gillingham ME7 . . . . . .64 F6
  Orpington BR6 . . . . . . 86 F5
Freight La TN17 . . . . . 320 C3
Fremantle Ho RM18 . . . 18 F6
Fremantle Rd Erith DA17 . 4 A2
  Folkestone CT20 . . . . 334 E5
Fremlin Cl TN4 . . . . . . 285 B4
Fremlins Rd ME14 . . . 163 C4
Fremlin Walk Sh Ctr
  ME14 . . . . 161 F4
Frencham Cl CT2 . . . . 143 A4
French's Row ME9 . . . 103 D2
FRENCH STREET . . . 184 F6
Frensham Cl ME10 . . . 102 B4
Frensham Rd
  Rolvenden TN17 . . . . 344 A1
  Sidcup SE9 . . . . 30 D6
Frensham Wlk ME5 . . . 96 F1
Freshfield La CT21 . . . 333 B4
Freshland Rd ME16 . . . 161 B4
Freshlands CT6 . . . . . . 77 E5
Freshwater Cl CT6 . . . . 76 B3
Freshwater Rd ME5 . . . 97 B7
Freta Rd DA6 . . . . 13 F2
Frewing Cl BR7 . . . . . . 30 A3
Friar Rd BR5 . . . . 54 A4
Friars Ave ME8 . . . . . . .96 F2
Friars Cl CT5 . . . . 75 A1
Friars Mews SE9 . . . . . 12 A2
Friars Pk ME20 . . . . . 128 E2
Friars The★ ME20 . . . 128 E2
Friars The CT1 . . . . . . 142 F1
Friars Way Dover CT16 278 A3
  Royal Tunbridge Wells
  TN2 . . . . 286 D6
Friars Wlk SE2 . . . . .3 D1
Friary Pl **3** ME2 . . . . . 63 B7
Friary Prec ME2 . . . . . . 63 B7
Friary Way CT2 . . . . . 142 D2
Friday Rd DA8 . . . . .4 D1
Friday St ME17 . . . . . 230 B6
Frid Cnr TN26 . . . . . . 297 E7
Friendly Cl CT9 . . . . . . 51 D1
Friends Ave CT9 . . . . . 83 D8
Friesian Way TN24 . . . 268 C8
Friezland Rd TN4 . . . . 285 D1
Friezley La TN17 . . . . 292 C1
Frimley Ct DA14 . . . . . 31 C3
FRINDSBURY 63 C8
Frindsbury Hill ME2 . . . 40 C1
Frindsbury Rd ME2 . . . 63 B8
Frinstead Dr BR5 . . . . . 54 D5
Frinstead Wlk ME16 . . 161 B7
FRINSTED 166 C7
Frinsted Cl ME8 . . . . . . 65 C3
Frinsted Rd Erith DA8 . 14 D7
  Milstead ME9 . . . . . . 134 E2
Frinton Rd DA14 . . . . . 31 E6
Friston Way ME1 . . . . . 96 C5
Friswell Pl **1** DA6 . . . 14 A3
Frith Bsns Ctr TN25 . . 329 B6
Frith Rd
  Aldington Frith TN25 . 329 C6
  Dover CT16 . . . . 278 C1

Frithwood Cl ME15 . . . 162 F1
FRITTENDEN 293 E5
Frittenden CE Prim Sch
  TN17 . . . . 293 E6
Frittenden Cl TN23 . . . 299 E6
Frittenden Rd
  Rochester ME2 . . . . . . 40 D2
  Staplehurst TN12 . . . 261 B2
Frobisher Cl ME10 . . . 101 E7
Frobisher Ct
  3 Dartford DA1 . . . 15 D1
  2 Ramsgate CT11 . 117 F8
Frobisher Gdns ME1 . . .63 C2
Frobisher Rd Erith DA8 . 15 A7
  Newham E6 . . . . 2 A7
Frobisher Way
  Gravesend DA12 . . . . .37 E3
  Swanscombe DA9 . . . . 17 B3
Frog Farm Cotts ME9 . .67 A4
FROGHAM 211 C2
FROGHOLE 184 D3
Frog Hole La TN8,
  TN16 . . . . 184 D2
FROGHOLT 333 F7
Frog La
  Bishopsbourne CT4 . . 209 C6
  Rainham RM13 . . . . 4 D8
  Royal Tunbridge Wells
  TN1 . . . . 286 A2
  West Malling ME19 . . 159 C8
Frogmore Wlk ME17 . . 199 C5
Frognal Ave DA14 . . . . 31 A2
Frognal Cl ME9 . . . . . 103 B2
Frognal Cnr BR7 . . . . . 30 F7
Frognal Gdns ME9 . . . 103 C2
Frognal La ME9 . . . . . 103 B2
Frognal Pl DA14 . . . . . 31 A3
Frogs Hole La TN17,
  TN27 . . . . 322 E3
Frog's La TN17 . . . . . 343 E1
Froissart Rd SE9 . . . . . 11 E2
Fromandez Dr TN12 . . 289 F5
Frome Ct TN10 . . . . . 222 B5
Front Brents ME13 . . . 138 D8
Front Rd TN26 . . . . . . 326 A1
Front St CT14 . . . . . . 247 F5
Front The CT15 . . . . . 280 A4
Frost Cres ME5 . . . . . . 97 A7
Frostland La TN26,
  TN29 . . . . 350 C1
Froyle Cl ME16 . . . . . 161 C6
Fruiterer's Cl ME9 . . . 135 B7
Fruitfields TN5 . . . . . 339 C3
Fry Cl ME3 . . . . 27 A6
Fry's Cotts ME3 . . . . . . 25 C4
Frythe Cl TN17 . . . . . 320 D4
Frythe Cres TN17 . . . . 320 D4
Frythe Way TN17 . . . . 320 D4
Frythe Wlk TN17 . . . . 320 D4
Fuchsia St SE2 . . . . 3 B1
Fuggles Cl TN12 . . . . 256 E6
Fuggles Ct TN17 . . . . 342 D6
Fulbert Dr ME14 . . . . 162 F5
Fulbert Rd CT16 . . . . . 278 B5
Fulham Ave CT9 . . . . . .82 C7
Fuller Cl Durgates TN5 . 336 E5
  Orpington BR6 . . . . . . 86 F5
Fullers Cl ME14 . . . . . 163 A4
Fullers Hill **7** TN16 . 151 D1
Fullers Yd CT9 . . . . 50 J2
Fulmar Cl TN29 . . . . . 365 F3
Fulmar Mews CT18 . . . 307 A3
Fulmar Rd ME2 . . . . . . 62 D6
Fulmar Way CT6 . . . . . .77 F4
Fulmer Rd E16 . . . . 1 D8
Fulsam PI CT9 . . . . 50 H1
Fulston Manor Sch
  ME10 . . . . 101 F2
Fulston Pl ME10 . . . . . 102 A3
Fulthorp Rd SE3 . . . . . 11 A5
Fulwich Rd DA1 . . . . . . 15 F1
Furfield Chase ME15 . 195 E4
Furfield Cl ME17 . . . . 195 E5
FURFIELD PARK 195 D4
Furley Park Prim Sch
  TN23 . . . . 300 C2
Furnace Ave TN3 . . . . 317 A3
Furnace La
  Hook Green TN3 . . . . 316 E4
  Horsmonden TN12 . . 289 F7
Furner Cl DA1 . . . . 14 F4
Furness Sch BR8 . . . . . 32 F2
Furnival Ct TN2 . . . . . 313 F8
Furrell's Rd ME1 . . . . . 63 D5
FURTHER QUARTER . 296 C3
Furze Bank TN8 . . . . . 218 B5
Furzefield Ave TN3 . . . 285 A8
Furzefield Cl BR7 . . . . . 30 B2
Furzefield Rd SE3 . . . . 11 B7
Furze Hill Cres ME12 . . 46 E6
Furzehill Sq BR5 . . . . . 54 B5
Fusilier Ave CT20 . . . . 334 B5
Fyfe Way BR2 . . . . .52 A7
Fyndon Ho CT1 . . . . . 175 C7

G

Gable Cl DA1 . . . . 15 A2
Gables Cl SE12 . . . . . . 29 A7
Gables The
  11 Bromley BR1 . . . 29 B1
  New Barn DA3 . . . . . . 58 B5
Gabriel Gdns DA12 . . . 37 E3
Gabriel's Hill ME15 . . 162 A4
Gabrielspring Rd DA3 . .90 D8
Gabriel Spring Rd (East)
  DA3 . . . . 90 F8
Gadby Rd ME10 . . . . . 101 C5
Gadsby La TN26 . . . . 296 F3
Gads Hill ME7 . . . . 64 F6

Gads Hill Sch ME3......39 C2
Gadwall Cl E16............1 B7
Gadwall Way SE28.........2 D4
Gafford's Bridge Cotts
　TN12..............258 C4
Gagetown Terr **1**
　ME14..............161 F7
Gainsboro Rd **4** CT7...80 F8
Gainsborough Ave
　Dartford DA1.........15 C2
　1 Margate CT9.......83 C8
　Tilbury RM18.........19 B6
Gainsborough Cl
　Folkestone CT19.....335 A7
　Gillingham ME8.......98 D6
　Sittingbourne ME10..101 B5
Gainsborough Ct **3**
　BR2...............52 C5
Gainsborough Dr
　Herne Bay CT6........77 E5
　Maidstone ME16......161 B4
　Northfleet DA11......36 D5
Gainsborough Gdns
　TN10..............222 E5
Gainsborough Ho ME1..63 D5
Gainsborough Sq DA7..13 D4
Gaitskell Rd SE9.......30 C7
Galahad Ave ME2.......62 E6
Galahad Rd BR1........29 A4
Galena Cl Chatham ME5..97 A1
　Sittingbourne ME10..101 C6
Galena Ho **4** SE18......2 F1
Gallants La
　Coxheath ME15......194 A2
　East Farleigh ME15..193 F6
Galleon Bvd DA2.......16 D3
Galleon Cl Erith DA8....4 D2
　Rochester ME1........96 C5
Galleon Mews **3** DA11..36 E8
Galleon Way ME2.......40 F3
Galley Dr ME9.........134 E6
Galley Hill Rd DA11,
　DA10..............17 F2
Galley Hill Trad Est
　DA10..............17 E2
Galliard St CT13.......181 A8
Gallions Mount Prim Sch
　SE18...............2 F1
Gallions Prim Sch E6...2 B7
Gallions Rd SE7........2 B2
Gallions Reach Sh Pk E6 2 C8
Gallions Reach Sta E6..2 B6
Gallions View Rd SE28..2 E4
Gallon Cl SE7...........1 C2
Gallops The DA13.....125 F7
Gallosson Rd SE18.....2 E2
Galloway Dr
　Ashford TN25........268 C8
　Dartford DA1.........32 E8
Galloways Rd TN29....376 C5
Gallow's Cnr CT21....333 A2
Gallows Wood DA3.....91 A6
Gallus Sq SE3.........11 B4
Gallwey Ave CT7.......80 E7
Galsworthy Cl SE28....3 B5
Galsworthy Cres SE3...11 C6
Galsworthy Rd RM18...19 C6
Galton Ho SE18........11 F6
Galway Rd ME12.......28 C1
Games Ho **7** SE7.......11 C8
Gammon's Farm La
　TN29..............351 B3
Gammons Way **6** CT2..142 F1
Gandy's La ME17......195 C2
Gange Mews **3** ME13 138 D7
Gann Rd CT5...........74 F2
Gaol La **13** CT16.......310 D7
Gap The Blean CT2.....142 A7
　Canterbury CT1......175 B5
Garden Ave DA7........14 A4
Garden Cl
　Lewisham SE12........29 B5
　Maidstone ME15......195 E7
　Rough Common ME13..142 A2
　Staplehurst TN12.....260 F1
　Toy's Hill TN16......185 C3
Garden Cotts
　Leigh TN11..........221 A2
　Orpington BR5........54 C7
　Wingham CT3.........178 A7
Garden Ct **10** Eltham SE9 12 A1
　Sevenoaks TN13.....154 D5
　Wouldham ME1........95 C5
Gardeners Cl SE9......29 C5
Gardeners Pl CT4.....173 F2
Garden Hall The TN25 238 A4
Garden Ho **9** TN1.....286 C4
Gardenia Cl ME2........40 B2
Gardenia Road BR1....53 B5
Garden La BR1.........29 B2
Garden of England Pk
　(Mobile Home Pk)
　ME17..............198 B7
Garden Pl Ashford TN24 268 E6
　Dartford DA2.........33 D5
Garden Rd Bromley BR1.29 B2
　Folkestone CT19.....335 D6
　Royal Tunbridge Wells
　TN1...............286 B4
　Sevenoaks TN13.....154 D5
　Tonbridge TN9.......222 D2
Garden Row **3** DA11....36 F5
Garden St Chatham ME7.64 A6
　Royal Tunbridge Wells
　TN1...............286 B4
Gardens The
　Coxheath ME17......194 C3
　Ivychurch TN29......363 F4
Garden Terr TN15.....155 A6
Garden Way ME19.....158 F2
Gardiner Cl BR5........54 C7
Gardiner Ho **8** SE18....11 E7
Gardiner's Hill TN31...368 B6
Gardiner St ME7.......64 C6

Gardner Cl CT18.......306 F3
Gardners Cl CT3.......147 E1
Gardyne Mews **12** TN9 254 B8
Gareth Gr BR1..........29 A4
Garfield Pl **4** ME13...138 D7
Garfield Rd
　Gillingham ME7........64 D6
　Margate CT9..........50 H2
Garganey Wlk SE28.....3 D6
Gargery Cl **2** DA12....37 F7
Garibaldi St SE18......2 E2
Garland Rd SE18......12 D7
Garlands TN11........221 D8
GARLINGE............82 A8
GARLINGE GREEN....206 E5
Garlinge Green Rd
　CT4...............206 E6
Garlinge Prim Sch CT9 .82 B8
Garlinge Rd TN4......254 A1
Garner Cl RM18........18 F5
Garner Dr ME19.......128 A1
Garnett Cl SE9.........11 F4
Garnet Wlk **9** E6........1 E8
Garrard Ave CT9.......82 B8
Garrard Cl Bexley DA7..14 A4
　Chislehurst BR7........30 B3
Garrick Cl TN10.......222 E7
Garrick Dr SE28........2 D3
Garrick St **18** SE18....19 B1
Garrington Cl ME14...162 C6
Garrison Cl SE18......12 A7
Garrison Rd ME12......27 F3
Garrolds Cl BR8........55 D7
Garrow DA3............59 B6
Garside Cl SE28........2 D3
Garth Rd TN13.........187 C2
Gartly Cotts DA1......15 C1
Garton Way TN23.....299 C2
Garvary Rd E16.........1 B7
Garvock Dr TN13......154 A1
Gascoyne Ave ME15...163 B2
Gascoyne Dr DA1......14 F4
Gas House Rd ME1......63 C6
Gaskin Rd ME13.......138 E7
Gas La ME13...........139 F3
Gasoline Alley TN15...125 D2
Gas Rd ME10...........101 F5
Gasson Rd DA10........17 E1
Gassons Rd ME6.......127 E8
Gas St CT1............174 F7
Gatcombe Cl
　Chatham ME5..........97 A5
　Maidstone ME16......161 B5
Gatcombe Rd E16.......1 A5
Gateacre Ct **14** DA14...31 B4
Gateacre Rd CT5......108 A6
Gate Farm Rd TN3,
　TN11..............253 C4
Gatefield Cotts TN17..343 F4
Gatefield La **8** ME13 .138 D7
Gate House Cotts SE12.29 B6
Gatehouse Farm Cotts
　TN3...............253 C4
Gatekeeper Chase ME8 98 F8
Gate La CT4..........273 A4
Gate Quays CT9........50 J2
Gates Green Rd BR2,
　BR4...............85 A6
Gateway Acad The
　RM16...............19 A8
Gateway Bsns Ctr **8**
　SE28...............2 D3
Gateway Ct **21** CT11..117 F7
Gateway Par DA12.....37 F4
Gateway Prim Sch The
　DA2...............16 B1
Gateway The CT16....310 E7
Gatland La ME16......161 B2
Gatling Rd SE2.........3 A1
Gattons Way DA14.....31 F4
Gatwick Farm Cotts
　RH19..............281 A4
Gatwick Rd DA12......37 B6
Gault Cl ME15........163 A2
Gaunt's Cl CT14......215 A4
Gautrey Sq **5** E6........1 F7
Gavestone Cres SE12..29 B8
Gavestone Rd SE12....29 B8
Gavestone Terr SE12..29 B8
Gavin Ho SE18..........2 E2
Gayhurst Cl ME8........98 D6
Gayhurst Dr ME10.....101 C5
Gaylor Rd RM18.......18 F6
Gayton Rd SE2..........3 C3
Gaza Trad Est TN11...220 D7
Gazedown TN29.......365 F3
Gaze Hill Ave ME10...102 A3
Gazelle Glade DA12....37 F3
Gazen Salts Nature
　Reserve* CT13......148 F2
Gean Cl ME5..........130 A8
Geddes Cl CT18.......306 F3
Geddes Pl **3** DA6.......14 A3
Gedge's Hill TN12....256 F3
Geffery's Ct SE9.......29 C5
General Gordon Pl **2**
　SE18...............2 B2
Genesta Ave CT5.....108 B7
Genesta Cl ME10......101 C7
Genesta Glade DA12...38 A3
Genesta Rd SE18......12 C8
Geneva Ave ME8.......65 A2
Gentian Cl
　4 Chatham ME5......96 E4
　Maidstone ME14......162 C5
Geoffrey Ct CT7........81 A7
Geoffrey Whitworth
　Theatre* DA1........15 A3
George Akass Ho **3**
　SE18...............2 C1
George Alley CT14....215 D6
George Cooper Ho **11**
　CT20..............335 C4

George Crooks Ho **7**
　RM17..............18 B8
George Gurr Cres
　CT19..............335 D8
George Hill Rd CT10,
　CT9...............51 E1
George La
　Boughton Street
　ME13..............139 F3
　Folkestone CT20.....335 D4
　Hayes BR2............52 B1
　Leeds ME17..........197 B7
　New Romney TN28....373 B7
　Rochester ME1........63 C6
George Marsham Ho
　ME15..............194 F3
George Parris Ct ME12 47 C6
George Pk CT9.........50 F1
George Roche Rd CT1 175 A6
George's Ave CT5.....108 A7
Georges Cl BR5........54 C6
George's Rd TN16.....150 D7
George St
　Ashford TN23........268 B1
　Chainhurst ME15.....227 A7
　Deal CT14...........215 D7
　Dover CT17..........278 C1
　Grays RM17...........18 A8
　Maidstone ME15......162 A3
　Ramsgate CT11......117 E7
　Royal Tunbridge Wells
　TN2...............286 C3
　Sittingbourne ME10..102 B4
　Sparrow's Green TN5..336 F5
　Staplehurst TN12....260 E6
　Tonbridge TN9.......254 B8
George Stone Ho **25**
　CT20..............335 C4
George Summers Cl
　ME2...............63 E8
George V Ave CT9......82 C8
George Warren Ct **1**
　CT9...............50 J1
George Williams Way
　TN24..............268 E5
George Wood Ct TN29 376 C6
Georgian Cl Hayes BR2..52 B1
　Rushenden ME11......46 A3
Georgian Dr ME17....194 D3
Georgian Way ME8.....98 C4
Georgia Pl TN2.......286 C4
Geraint Rd BR1........29 A4
Gerald Ave ME4........63 F2
Geraldine Rd CT19....334 F6
Gerald Palmby Ct
　CT14..............215 C7
Gerald Rd DA12........37 E8
Gerda Rd SE9..........30 C6
Gerdview Dr DA2.......33 C4
Gerlac Ho TN24.......268 C5
Gerrard Ave ME1.......96 E8
Gerrard Ho **4** BR2.....52 C5
Gerrards Dr ME10.....101 F2
Gertrude Rd DA17......4 A2
Gibbet La TN12.......289 F6
Gibbetts TN3..........284 F3
Gibbons La DA1........15 D1
Gibbons Rd ME10.....101 B5
Gibbs Field TN11.....221 A4
Gibbs Hill
　Headcorn TN27......262 E5
　Nettlestead ME18....192 B5
Gibraltar Ave ME7.....64 B7
Gibraltar Hill ME4.....63 F4
Gibraltar La
　Hawkinge TN18......307 A2
　Maidstone ME14......161 F8
Gibraltar Sq CT15....278 E3
GIBRALTER..........306 F3
Gibson Cl DA11........36 F5
Gibson Dr ME19......158 F4
Gibson Ho ME3.........40 F6
Gibson St ME10......101 E4
Gidd's Pond Cotts
　ME14..............162 E6
Giddyhorn La ME16...161 C5
Gideon Cl DA17........4 B2
Gifford Cl ME8........65 C3
Gigger's Green Rd
　TN25..............351 C2
Giggs Hill BR5.........54 A8
Gighill Rd ME20......127 F4
Gilbert Cl Gillingham ME7 98 A5
　Swanscombe DA10....17 D1
　Woolwich SE18........11 F6
Gilbert Pl **9** CT20....334 E3
Gilbert Rd
　4 Ashford TN24....268 B2
　Bromley BR1..........29 A1
　Erith DA17............4 A3
　Ramsgate CT11......117 E7
Gilbert Terr **2** ME14 .161 F7
Gilbert Way CT1......174 E6
Gilbourne Rd SE18....12 F8
Gilchrist Ave CT6......76 C2
Gilchrist Cotts TN14..187 C2
Gildenhill Rd BR8......33 C1
Gilderstone St SE18...12 A8
Giles Field DA12.......37 F7
Giles Gdns CT9.........82 F8
Giles La CT2..........142 D4
Giles-Young Ct **7**
　ME10..............101 E5
Gilford Rd CT14......215 D5
Gilham Gr CT14......215 B4
Gillan Ct **1** SE12......29 B5
Gill Ave Newham E16...1 A7
　Rochester ME2........40 D2
Gill Cres DA11.........36 F5
Gill Ct **2** SE18..........2 C2
Gillett Rd TN29......376 D7
Gilletts La ME15.......160 A6
Gillies Ct DA14........30 E4
Gillies Rd TN15........90 E5

GILLINGHAM..........64 D3
Gillingham Gate ME7..64 C8
Gillingham Gate Rd
　ME7...............64 C8
Gillingham Gn ME7....64 E6
Gillingham Sta ME7...64 D5
Gill La
　Aldington Frith TN25..329 A8
　Ruckinge TN26......328 C2
Gillman Cl CT18......306 F4
Gillmans Rd BR5.......54 B1
Gillon Mews **9** CT1...143 E7
GILL'S GREEN.......340 F5
Gill's Rd
　Green Street Green
　DA2...............35 B1
　Sutton at Hone DA4...57 F8
Gills Terr.............66 C3
Gill The TN2..........287 E8
Gilroy Way
　2 Orpington BR5.....54 B2
　Orpington BR5........54 B2
Gimble Way TN2......255 D1
Gingerbread La TN18 .339 F2
Ginsbury Cl ME2......163 E6
Gipps Cross La TN3...284 F3
Gipsy La RM17.........18 C8
Gipsy Rd DA16........13 D5
Giralda Cl E16..........1 D8
Giraud Dr ME13......138 B8
Glack Rd CT14........214 F4
Glade Bsns Ctr The
　RM20..............16 F8
Glades Sh Ctr BR1.....52 A7
Glades The DA12.......37 D2
Gladeswood Rd DA17...4 B2
Glade The Bromley BR1.52 D7
　Chatham ME5..........97 A2
　Deal CT14...........214 F6
　Greenwich SE7.........11 C7
　Sevenoaks TN13......154 B4
　Tonbridge TN10......222 E7
　Whitstable CT5........74 D2
Gladiator St SE1.......11 B8
Gladstone Dr ME10...102 C4
Gladstone Rd
　Ashford TN24........300 E7
　Broadstairs CT10......83 F4
　Chatham ME4..........63 D2
　Dartford DA1.........15 F1
　Deal CT14...........215 C6
　Folkestone CT19.....335 E6
　Maidstone ME14......162 A6
　Margate CT9..........50 I1
　Orpington BR6........86 C5
　3 Rusthall TN4.......285 B4
　Tonbridge TN9.......222 B1
　Whitstable CT5........74 D2
Gladwell Rd BR1.......29 A2
Gladwyn Cl ME8........98 D4
Glamford Rd ME2.......62 D5
Glamis Cl ME5.........97 A5
Glanfield Ct TN1.....286 C5
Glanville Rd
　Bromley BR2..........52 B6
　Gillingham ME7........64 D5
　Rochester ME2........63 A8
Glasbrook Rd SE9......29 D8
Glasgow Ho **8** ME15 .195 E7
GLASSENBURY.......319 E6
Glassenbury Rd TN17..319 E4
Glassmill La BR2.......52 A7
Glass Yd SE18..........2 A3
Glastonbury Cl BR5....54 C1
Glayton Gdns ME5......96 F4
Gleaming Wood Dr
　ME5...............130 D8
Gleaners Cl ME14.....162 E4
Gleanings Mews ME1...63 C5
Glebe Cl Smarden TN27 264 B2
　St Margaret's at Cliffe
　CT15..............279 F6
Glebe Cotts
　Brasted TN16........152 B4
　Eastling ME13.......168 E7
Glebe Ct CT12........115 B5
Glebefield The TN13..153 F4
Glebe Gdns
　Lenham ME17........199 E5
　6 Margate CT9.......82 B8
Glebe Ho **7** SE18.......2 A2
Glebe House Dr BR2...52 B1
Glebe La
　Maidstone ME16......161 A1
　Sevenoaks TN13.....154 B1
　Sittingbourne ME10..102 B2
Glebeland TN27......232 F4
Glebelands
　Alkham CT15........276 D1
　Ash CT3.............147 C2
　Bidborough TN3......253 C3
　Biddenden TN27.....294 F1
　Crayford DA1..........14 F3
　Mersham TN25.......301 E4
　Penshurst TN11......252 A3
Glebe Mdw ME18......192 E7
Glebe Pl DA4..........57 C5
Glebe Rd Bromley BR1..52 A8
　Gillingham ME7........64 E3
　Margate CT9..........82 B8
　Northfleet DA11.......36 F7
　Sevenoaks Weald TN14 187 B3
Glebe The
　Bidborough TN3......253 D3
　Charing TN27........234 D7
　Chislehurst BR7.......53 C8
　Cuxton ME2...........62 C2
　Pembury TN2........287 D8
　Penshurst TN11......252 A3
Glebe Way
　Ashford TN24........268 D6
　Erith DA8.............14 E8
　Whitstable CT5......108 D8
Gleeson Dr BR6........86 F6

Glemsford Cotts CT2 .141 E1
Glenalvon Way **7** SE18..1 D7
Glen Ave CT6...........77 C5
Glenavon Rd CT10......84 B7
Glenbarr Cl SE9.......12 B4
Glenbervie Dr CT6.....77 E5
Glenbrook Cl CT6......77 D5
Glenbrook Rd ME10...101 E7
Glencairne Cl E16......1 D8
Glencoe Jun Sch ME4 .64 A2
Glencoe Rd
　Chatham ME4..........64 A2
　Margate CT9..........51 A1
Glen Ct Lewisham SE12 .29 A8
　Sidcup DA14..........31 A4
Glendale
　1 Folkestone CT20...335 E4
　Swanley BR8..........55 F4
Glendale Cl SE9.......12 A4
Glendale Ct TN2......286 D6
Glendale Rd Erith DA8...4 C2
　Minster (Sheppey) ME12 47 B7
　Northfleet DA11.......36 E5
Glendale Way SE28.....3 C6
Glendower Cres BR6...54 A3
Glendown Rd SE2.......3 A1
Glen Dunlop Ho The
　TN13..............154 C5
Gleneagles Cl BR6.....53 D1
Gleneagles Dr ME5.....96 F2
Gleneagles Dr ME5.....162 A1
Gleneagles Gn **1** BR6..53 D1
Glenesk Rd SE9........12 B3
Glenfield Rd CT16....278 C8
Glengall Rd DA7.......13 E4
Glen Gr CT17.........310 E7
Glenhead Cl SE9.......12 B4
Glen Ho **6** E16..........2 C1
Glenhouse Rd SE9.....12 A4
Glenhurst Ave CT5.....31 F7
Glen Iris Ave CT2.....142 C2
Glen Iris Cl CT2......142 C2
Glenister St E16........2 A4
Glenlea Rd SE9........12 A3
Glenleigh Rd ME18....192 D6
Glenluce Rd SE3.......11 A8
Glenlyon Rd SE9.......12 A4
Glenmere Row SE12....11 A1
Glenmere Pk ME10....102 C6
Glenmere Rd DA16.....12 F6
Glenmount Path **3** SE18 2 C1
Glen Rd CT14.........248 C6
Glenrose Cl DA14......31 B3
Glenshiel Rd SE9......12 A2
Glenside CT5..........109 A8
Glenside Ave CT1.....143 B2
Glen The
　Minster (Sheppey)
　ME12..............47 B7
　Orpington BR6........86 A7
　Shepherdswell CT15..244 D5
　Upstreet CT3.........112 D3
Glentrammon Ave BR6.86 F4
Glentrammon Cl BR6...86 F4
Glentrammon Gdns BR6 86 F4
Glentrammon Rd BR6...86 F4
Glenure Rd SE9........12 A4
Glenview SE2.........13 D8
Glen View DA12........37 C7
Glen View Rd BR1......52 D7
Glen Wlk CT5.........108 A3
Glenwood Cl
　Chatham ME5..........64 C1
　Gillingham ME7........98 A7
　Maidstone ME16......161 C5
　Tenterden TN30......324 B3
Glenwood Ct **18** DA14...31 A4
Glenwood Dr ME12....47 C6
Glimpsing Gn DA18.....3 E3
Glistening Glade ME8 ..98 F4
Gload Cres BR5........87 B8
Globe Ct SE18.........12 C8
Globe La ME4..........63 F5
Globe Yd **13** DA11......19 B1
Gloster Ct CT18......307 B3
Gloster Ropewalk
　CT17..............310 C5
Gloster Way CT17....310 C5
Gloucester Ave
　Bexley DA16..........12 F3
　Broadstairs CT10......83 F3
　Margate CT9..........51 D2
　Sidcup DA15..........30 E6
Gloucester Cl ME8.....99 A8
Gloucester Ct RM18...18 F5
Gloucester Mews
　TN28..............373 C8
Gloucester Par DA15...13 A2
Gloucester Pl **17** CT20 335 D5
Gloucester Rd
　Dartford DA1.........33 B8
　Erith DA17............3 F1
　Gravesend DA12.......37 C4
　Maidstone ME15......195 D8
　Turner's Green TN5...336 F6
　Whitstable CT5........74 F2
Glover Cl
　Sittingbourne ME10...68 F1
　Woolwich SE2..........3 C2
Glover Rd TN24......268 E1
Glovers Cl TN16......118 B3
Glovers Cres ME10...101 F3
Glovers Mill ME4......63 D3
Gloxinia Rd DA13......96 B4
Glyn Davies Cl TN13 ..153 E7
Glyndebourne Pk BR6.86 B8
Glynde Rd DA7........13 E4
Glyndon Rd SE18.......2 C2
Glyn Dr DA14..........31 B4
Glynne Cl ME8.........98 D6
Goad Ave ME5..........97 B3

GOATHURST
　COMMON...........186 B5
GOAT LEES..........268 C8
Goat Lees La TN25....268 D8
Goatsfield Rd TN16...150 C7
Gobery Hill CT3......146 B1
Goddards CT1.........146 B1
Goddard St ME3.......320 B4
GODDARD'S GREEN...321 F2
Goddard's Green Cotts
　TN17..............321 F1
GODDEN GREEN.....155 B3
Godden Rd
　Canterbury CT2......143 A4
　Snodland ME6........127 F8
Godden Way ME8.......65 A3
Goddings Dr ME1......63 A3
GODDINGTON.........87 C7
Goddington Chase BR6 87 B6
Goddington Rd BR6....87 C7
Goddington La
　Harrietsham ME17...198 B6
　Orpington BR6........87 A7
Goddington Rd ME2....63 B8
Godfrey Cl ME2........39 F1
Godfrey Evans Cl TN10 222 F5
Godfrey Gdns CT4....173 F1
Godfrey Hill SE18......1 E2
Godfrey Ho CT5......108 B8
Godfrey Rd SE18.......1 F2
Godfreys Cotts ME13 .203 C8
Godfrey Wlk TN23....300 B8
Godfrey's Grave ME13 140 B7
GODINGTON PARK*...267 E2
Godinton House & Gdns*
　TN23..............267 C4
Godinton La TN23,
　TN26..............267 D5
Godinton Prim Sch
　TN23..............267 D3
Godinton Rd TN23....268 A2
Godinton Way Ind Est
　TN23..............268 B2
GODMERSHAM.......205 A2
Godstow Rd SE2........3 C4
Godwin Bglws CT9.....51 B3
Godwin Cl Deal CT14..215 A3
　Sittingbourne ME10...68 F1
Godwin Cotts CT9......51 A3
Godwin Ho SE18.......11 F6
Godwin Rd Bromley BR2 52 C6
　Canterbury CT1......174 C6
　Dover CT16..........310 F8
　Margate CT9..........51 A3
Godwyne Cl CT16.....310 D8
Godwyne Ct CT16.....278 D1
Godwyne Rd CT16.....278 D1
Godwyn Gdns CT20...335 A4
Godwyn Rd Deal CT14.215 A3
　Folkestone CT20.....335 A4
Gogway CT4..........240 B5
Goldace RM17.........17 F8
Goldcrest Cl Newham E16 1 B8
Goldcrest Dr ME4......41 C2
Goldcrest Wlk CT5....108 B6
Golden Acre La CT8....81 D7
Golden Cl CT8..........81 D7
GOLDEN GREEN.....223 F5
Golden Hill CT5......108 F6
Golden Plover Cl E16...1 A7
Golden Sq
　New Romney TN28....373 A6
　Tenterden TN30......345 B8
Golden St CT14.......210 D7
Golden Wood ME5....130 D8
Goldfinch Cl
　Faversham ME13.....105 C1
　Herne Bay CT6........77 C2
　Larkfield ME20......128 A2
　Orpington BR6........87 A5
　Paddock Wood TN12..257 A5
Goldfinch Rd SE28......2 D3
Gold Hill TN25.......235 D4
Goldie Leigh Hospl SE2 13 C8
Golding Cl Ditton ME20 128 C1
　Rochester ME1........63 E1
Golding Gdns TN12...225 A6
Golding Rd TN13......154 C5
Goldings TN12.......256 E5
Goldings Cl TN24.....268 C5
Goldings The ME8......98 C8
Goldmark Ho SE3......11 B4
Goldsel Rd BR8.........55 E5
Goldsmid Rd TN9.....254 C8
Goldsmid St **3** SE18....2 E1
Goldsmith RM17.......17 F8
Goldsmith Cl TN30...324 B1
Goldsmith Rd ME8.....98 C5
Gold St DA12, DA13....60 E4
Goldstone Dro CT3...147 E7
Goldstone Wlk ME5....97 A1
GOLD STREET........60 E4
Goldsworth Dr ME2....40 A1
Goldthorne Cl ME14...162 C5
Goldups La CT4.......171 C1
Goldups Lane Cotts
　CT4...............171 C1
Goldwell Cl TN25.....330 A6
Goldwell Hos TN25...330 A6
Goldwell La
　Aldington TN25.......330 B7
　Great Chart TN23, TN26 298 F5
Goldwing Cl E16........1 A7
Goldwyn Com Specl Sch
　TN23..............267 B4
Golf Cl CT14.........182 C5
Golf Links Ave DA11...37 B3
GOLFORD............321 B5
Golford Rd TN17.....320 F4

Golf Rd Bromley BR1 . . . . . 53 A6
Deal CT14 . . . . 215 C8
Golf Road Pl CT14 . . . . 215 C8
GOLGOTHA 244 F6
Gollogly Terr 8 SE7 . . . . 1 C1
Gooch Cl ME16 . . . . . . 161 D8
Goodall Cl ME8 . . . . 98 E5
Goodban Sq CT3 . . . . . 147 D1
Goodbury Rd TN15 . . . . 123 B6
Goodcheap La TN25 . . 269 D2
Goodensfield TN5 . . . . 336 E5
Goodfellow Way 3
CT16 . . . . 310 D8
Good Hope CT14 . . . . .214 F4
Gooding Ho SE7 . . . . 1 C1
Good Intent Cotts
TN27 . . . . 233 A5
Goodley Stock Rd TN8,
TN16 . . . . 184 B6
Goodmead Rd BR6 . . . . 54 A2
GOODNESTONE
Faversham 139 D7
Wingham 178 D2
Goodnestone CE Prim Sch
CT3 . . . . 178 C2
Goodnestone Hill CT3 178 D2
Goodnestone Park Gdns ★
CT3 . . . . 178 C1
Goodnestone Rd
Sittingbourne ME10 . . 102 A4
Wingham CT3 . . . . . . 178 B5
Good Shepherd Prim Sch
The ME4 . . . . 63 E1
Goods Hill TN30 . . . . . 344 D8
Goods Station Rd TN1 286 B4
Goodtrees La TN8 . . . . 282 B2
Goodwin Ave CT5 . . . . . 75 E2
Goodwin Cl TN8 . . . . . 217 B2
Goodwin Ct CT9 . . . . . . 51 D3
Goodwin Dr
Maidstone ME14 . . . . 162 B8
Sidcup DA14 . . . . .31 D6
Goodwin Pk CT9 . . . . . 83 A5
Goodwin Rd
Cliffe Woods ME3 . . . . 40 B7
Ramsgate CT11 . . . . . 117 B5
St Margaret's at Cliffe
CT15 . . . . 280 A4
Goodwins The TN2 . . . 285 F1
Goodwood Cl
High Halstow ME23 . . . .23 E4
Maidstone ME15 . . . . 195 F6
Goodwood Cres DA12 . . 37 C2
Goodworth Rd TN15 . .124 F3
Goosander Way SE28 . . . . 2 D3
Goose Cl ME5 . . . . 97 A7
Goose Farm CT2 . . . . . 143 D7
Goosefields ME13 . . . . 106 E1
GOOSE GREEN
Biddenden 322 E8
Hadlow 191 B2
Goose Green Cl BR5 . . . 54 A7
Gooseneck La TN27 . . 262 C5
Goose Sq 8 E6 . . . . 1 F7
Gordon Ave ME11 . . . . .46 A4
Gordon Cl
Ashford TN24 . . . . . . 268 D2
East Tilbury RM18 . . . . 20 D7
Sittingbourne ME10 . . . 36 E5
Gordon Cotts ME9 . . . 134 B6
Gordon Ct ME17 . . . . . 194 E4
Gordon Gr CT8 . . . . 50 C1
Gordon Ho SE12 . . . . . . 29 A8
Gordon Jun Sch ME2 . . 63 A8
Gordon Inf Sch ME2 . . . 63 A8
Gordon Pl DA12 . . . . . . 19 C1
Gordon Prim Sch SE9 . . 11 F3
Gordon Promenade
DA12 . . . . 19 C1
Gordon Promenade E
DA12 . . . . 19 D1
Gordon Rd
Canterbury CT1 . . . . . 174 F7
Chatham, Luton ME4 . . 64 B2
Chatham ME4 . . . . 64 A7
Dartford DA1 . . . . 33 D8
Dover CT16 . . . . 278 A5
Erith DA17 . . . . 4 C2
Faversham ME13 . . . . 138 E8
Folkestone CT20 . . . . 334 D6
Gillingham ME7 . . . . . 64 E5
Herne Bay CT6 . . . . . . 76 F4
Hoo St Werburgh ME3 . 41 D5
Margate CT9 . . . . 51 A3
Margate, Westwood CT9 .83 A5
Northfleet DA11 . . . . . 36 E8
Ramsgate CT11 . . . . . 117 D8
Rochester ME2 . . . . . . 63 A8
Royal Tunbridge Wells
TN4 . . . . 286 C7
Sevenoaks TN13 . . . . 154 B2
Sidcup DA15 . . . . .12 E2
Whitstable CT5 . . . . . 108 D8
Gordon Sq
Birchington CT7 . . . . . .80 F7
Faversham ME13 . . . . 138 E7
Gordon Terr Lydd TN29 376 C5
Rochester ME1 . . . . . . 63 C4
Gordon Way BR1 . . . . . 52 A8
GORE 180 B3
Gore Cl CT13 . . . . 180 B3
Gore Cotts Dartford DA2 34 C4
Upchurch ME9 . . . . . . 66 E1
Gore Court Rd
Maidstone ME15 . . . . 195 F5
Sittingbourne ME10 . . 101 E2
Gore Ct TN24 . . . . 268 C2
Gore End Cl CT7 . . . . . 80 F7
Gore Farm CT13 . . . . 180 B3
Gore Farm Cotts DA2 . 34 C5
Gore Green Rd ME3 . . . 39 C1

Gore La Brandfold TN17 290 E4
Eastry CT13 . . . . 180 B2
Gorely Ho 14 CT17 . . . 310 D7
Gore Mews 3 CT1 . . . 143 B2
Gore Rd Dartford DA2 . 34 C6
Eastry CT13 . . . . 180 B3
Silver Street ME9 . . . 133 F5
Gore Street Farm Cotts
CT12 . . . . 114 A7
Gore Terr CT13 . . . . . 180 B3
Goretop La CT14 . . . . 181 C6
Gorham Cl ME6 . . . . . 127 F7
Gorham Dr
Maidstone ME15 . . . . 163 A1
Tonbridge TN9 . . . . . 254 E8
Gorman Rd SE18 . . . . . . 1 F2
Gorrell Rd CT5 . . . . . . 74 E1
Gorringe Ave DA4 . . . . 57 D7
Gorse Ave ME5 . . . . . . 96 F5
Gorse Cl E16 . . . . 1 A7
Gorse Cres ME20 . . . . 160 D8
Gorse La CT6 . . . . 77 C2
Gorse Mead TN23 . . . 299 F8
Gorse Rd Orpington BR5 . 88 A8
Rochester ME2 . . . . . . 62 F8
Royal Tunbridge Wells
TN2 . . . . 286 E5
Sittingbourne ME10 . . 102 C5
Gorse Way DA3 . . . . . . 59 A4
Gorse Wood Rd
Hartley DA3 . . . . 59 A5
New Barn DA3 . . . . . . 59 A6
Gorst St ME7 . . . . 64 C5
Goschen Rd CT17 . . . . 310 B8
Gosfield Rd CT6 . . . . . .77 A4
Goshawk Ho 1 ME6 . . 102 A4
GOSMERE 170 E7
Gosmere Farm Barns
Doddington ME13 . . . 167 E2
Sheldwich ME13 . . . . 170 E7
Gossage Rd SE18 . . . . . 2 D1
Gosselin St CT5 . . . . . 108 E8
Goss Hall La CT3 . . . . 148 A2
Goss Hill BR8, DA2 . . . .33 C2
Gosshill Rd BR7 . . . . . .53 A7
Gossington Cl BR7 . . . .30 A4
Goteley Mere TN24 . . 268 C7
Gothic Cl Dartford DA1 . 33 D5
Deal CT14 . . . . 215 B1
Gothic Cotts TN26 . . . 235 A1
GOUDHURST 318 F8
Goudhurst Cl
Canterbury CT2 . . . . . 143 A4
Maidstone ME16 . . . . 161 E4
Goudhurst & Kilndown CE
Prim Sch TN17 . . . . . 318 F8
Goudhurst Rd
Cranbrook TN17 . . . . 320 D8
Gillingham ME8 . . . . . 65 B3
Horsmonden TN12 . . . 290 B5
Knox Bridge TN12,
TN17 . . . . 292 C6
Marden TN12 . . . . . . 259 B5
Gouge Ave DA11 . . . . . 36 E7
Gough Rd CT20 . . . . . 334 E3
Gould Rd ME5 . . . . 97 B3
Gourock Rd SE9 . . . . . .12 A2
Gover Hill TN11, ME18 . 190 E6
Gover View TN11 . . . . 190 E7
Gower Ho ME14 . . . . . 162 A6
Grace Ave Bexley DA7 . 13 F5
Maidstone ME16 . . . . 161 D6
Grace Cl SE9 . . . . 29 D5
Grace Ct 16 CT20 . . . 335 D5
Grace Hill CT20 . . . . . 335 D5
Grace Mdw CT16 . . . . 278 A7
Grace Rd ME12 . . . . . . 28 A1
Grace Sch 22 CT20 . . 335 D5
Grace Wlk CT14 . . . . . 215 A5
Gracious La TN13 . . . 187 B5
Gracious Lane Bridge
TN13 . . . . 187 A4
Gracious Lane End
TN14 . . . . 186 F5
Grafton Ave ME1 . . . . .96 E8
Grafton Rd
Broadstairs CT10 . . . . 83 F8
Sittingbourne ME10 . . 101 F4
Grafton Rise CT6 . . . . .76 C4
Graham Cl ME4 . . . . . . 63 F6
Graham Ct 12 BR1 . . . 29 E1
Graham Ho SE18 . . . . . 12 B7
Graham Rd DA7 . . . . . . 14 A3
GRAIN 27 B6
Grainey Field ME9 . . . . 99 E4
Grainger Wlk TN10 . . 222 E6
Grain Rd Gillingham ME8 . 98 C3
Grain ME3 . . . . 26 D3
Grampian Cl
Orpington BR6 . . . . . . 53 F3
Royal Tunbridge Wells
TN2 . . . . 286 D5
Grampian Way ME15 . 163 A1
Grampion Ct TN24 . . . 268 C4
Gram Sch for Girls
Wilmington The DA2 . . .33 B5
Grams Rd CT14 . . . . . 248 C8
Granada Ho 8 ME15 . 162 A4
Granada St 9 ME15 . . 162 A4
Granary TN12 . . . . . . 257 B6
Granary Cl
Gillingham ME8 . . . . . .65 C1
Maidstone ME16 . . . . 162 E5
Granary Cotts TN16 . . 152 C3
Granary Court Rd
TN25 . . . . 303 A4
Granary Pl CT5 . . . . . 108 D8
Granby Ho 8 SE18 . . . . 1 F2
Granby Rd Eltham SE9 . 11 F4
Northfleet DA11 . . . . . 18 D1
Woolwich SE18 . . . . . . 2 B3
Grand Ct
6 Folkestone CT20 . . 335 B3

Grand Ct continued
7 Gillingham ME7 . . . 64 C6
Littlestone-on-Sea TN28 373 E5
Grand Depot Rd SE18 . . . 2 A1
Grand Dr CT6 . . . . 76 C4
Grand Mans CT10 . . . . 84 B3
Grand Par TN28 . . . . . 373 E6
Grand Pavilion CT5 . . . 74 F3
Grandshore La TN17 . 293 B5
Grandsire Gdns ME3 . . 41 E6
Grand View Ave TN16 . 118 C3
GRANGE 65 B6
Grange Cres
6 Dartford DA2 . . . . . 16 B1
Erith SE28 . . . . 3 C7
Tenterden TN30 . . . . 324 A3
Grange Ct
1 Folkestone CT20 . . 335 C4
9 Ramsgate CT11 . . 117 C6
Grange Dr Bromley BR7 . 29 F2
Pratt's Bottom BR6 . . . .87 C2
Grange Gdns ME4 . . . 285 D4
Grange Hill
Chatham ME5 . . . . . . 64 B3
Plaxtol TN15 . . . . . . 189 E8
Grangehill Pl SE9 . . . . 11 F4
Grangehill Rd SE9 . . . 11 F3
Grange Ho Erith DA8 . . 15 A5
Gravesend DA11 . . . . . 37 A8
Maidstone ME16 . . . . 161 A2
Grange La Boxley ME14 130 A1
Hartley DA3 . . . . 59 B2
Grange Park Coll
ME19 . . . . 127 B3
Grange Rd
Broadstairs CT10 . . . . 83 F6
Deal CT14 . . . . 215 B5
Folkestone CT19 . . . . 334 E6
Gillingham ME7 . . . . . 65 A6
Gravesend DA11 . . . . . 37 A8
Grays RM17 . . . . .18 B8
Herne Bay CT6 . . . . . .77 C4
Hythe CT21 . . . . 333 B4
Orpington BR6 . . . . . . 86 C8
Platt TN15 . . . . 157 C7
Ramsgate CT11 . . . . . 117 C6
Rochester ME2 . . . . . . 63 B7
Rusthall TN4 . . . . . . 285 D4
Sevenoaks TN13 . . . . 187 A8
Tenterden TN30 . . . . 323 F3
Grange The
East Malling ME19 . . . 160 A7
Langton Green TN3 . . 284 F3
Ramsgate CT11 . . . . . 117 C6
Shepherdswell CT15 . . 244 D5
Sutton at Hone DA4 . . 57 D8
Westerham TN16 . . . . 151 C1
West Kingsdown TN15 . 90 F2
Whitstable CT5 . . . . . 108 A4
Grange Way
Broadstairs CT10 . . . . 83 F2
Erith DA8 . . . . 15 A7
Hartley DA3 . . . . 58 F3
Rochester ME1 . . . . . . 63 C3
Grangeways DA11 . . . 36 F4
Grangewood DA5 . . . . 31 F7
Granite St SE18 . . . . . . 2 F1
Grant Cl CT10 . . . . . . .83 E6
Grant Dr ME15 . . . . . 195 D6
Grantham Ave CT14 . . 215 A4
Grantley Cl TN23 . . . . 300 A8
Granton Rd DA14 . . . . .31 C2
Grant Rd ME3 . . . . 40 C3
Grant's Cotts ME17 . . 199 B5
Grants La TN8, RH8 . . 216 C6
Granville Ave
Broadstairs CT10 . . . . 84 B3
Ramsgate CT12 . . . . . 83 B1
Granville Cl ME13 . . . 138 C7
Granville Ct Deal CT14 215 C2
Erith SE2 . . . . 3 D1
Maidstone ME14 . . . . 162 A6
Sevenoaks TN13 . . . . 154 A3
Granville Dr CT6 . . . . . 76 B2
Granville Farm Mews 24
CT11 . . . . 117 F7
Granville Ho 18 CT11 . 117 F7
Granville Marina 20
CT11 . . . . 117 F7
Granville Mews DA14 . 31 A4
Granville Par CT20 . . . 334 E3
Granville Pl
Folkestone CT20 . . . . 334 F3
Sheerness ME12 . . . . 28 C2
Granville Rd
Bexley DA16 . . . . .13 C4
Broadstairs CT10 . . . . 84 B3
Deal CT14 . . . . 215 C2
Gillingham ME7 . . . . . 64 E5
Kingsdown CT14 . . . . 248 D3
Limpsfield RH8 . . . . . 183 A7
Maidstone ME14 . . . . 162 A6
Northfleet DA11 . . . . . 36 F7
Royal Tunbridge Wells
TN1 . . . . 286 C5
Sevenoaks TN13 . . . . 154 A3
Sheerness ME12 . . . . 28 C2
Sidcup DA14 . . . . 31 B4
St Margaret's at Cliffe
CT15 . . . . 280 B6
Westerham TN16 . . . . 151 C1
Granville Road E CT20 334 F3
Granville Sch The
TN13 . . . . 154 A4
Granville St Deal CT14 215 D5
Dover CT16 . . . . 278 C1
Granville The CT15 . . 280 B6

Granville Theatre ★ 25
CT11 . . . . 117 F7
Grapple Rd ME14 . . . . 162 A7
Grasdene Rd SE18 . . . .13 A7
Grasmere Ave
Orpington BR6 . . . . . . 86 B7
Ramsgate CT11 . . . . . 117 A7
Grasmere Gdns
Folkestone CT19 . . . . 335 B7
Orpington BR6 . . . . . . 86 B7
Grasmere Gr ME2 . . . . 40 C2
Grasmere Pk CT5 . . . 109 B8
Grasmere Rd
Ashford TN24 . . . . . . 268 C6
Bexley DA7 . . . . .14 C5
Orpington BR6 . . . . . . 86 B7
Whitstable CT5 . . . . . 109 B8
Grasmere Way CT5 . . 210 F6
Grass Banks DA1 . . . . .33 F7
Grasshaven Way SE28 . . 2 F5
Grassington Rd 11
DA14 . . . . .31 A4
Grasslands
Ashford TN23 . . . . . . 299 D7
Langley Heath ME17 . . 196 E4
Grassmere
Leybourne ME19 . . . . 127 F2
St Mary's Bay TN29 . . 365 E3
Grassy Glade ME7 . . . . 98 B6
Grassy La TN3 . . . . . . 187 B8
Grave La TN12 . . . . . . 260 C8
GRAVEL CASTLE 243 A8
Gravel Castle Rd CT4 . 243 A8
Gravel Hill Bexley DA6 . .14 B2
Stalisfield Green ME13 . 201 C8
Gravel Hill Cl DA6 . . . . 14 B1
Gravel Hill Prim Sch
DA6 . . . . .14 B3
Gravel La CT15 . . . . . 309 A4
Gravelly Bottom Rd
ME17 . . . . 197 B2
Gravelly Field TN23 . . 299 C8
Gravelly Fields TN23 . 299 C8
Gravelly Ways TN12 . . 225 D5
Gravel Pit Way BR6 . . . 54 A1
Gravel Rd Orpington BR2 85 E8
Sutton at Hone DA4 . . 34 B1
Gravel Wlk
3 Ashford TN23 . . . . 268 A3
Rochester ME1 . . . . . . 63 D5
Gravelwood Cl BR7 . . . 30 C5
GRAVENEY 106 E2
Graveney Cl ME13 . . . . 40 C7
Graveney Prim Sch
ME13 . . . . 106 E1
Graveney Rd
Faversham ME13 . . . . 138 F7
Maidstone ME15 . . . . 195 F7
GRAVESEND 19 B2
Gravesend Gram Sch
DA12 . . . . 37 D8
Gravesend Gram Sch for
Girls DA12 . . . . .37 A7
Gravesend Rd
Higham ME2, ME3,
DA12 . . . . 39 C2
Rochester ME2 . . . . . . 62 F8
Shorne DA12 . . . . 38 D5
Vigo Village TN15 . . . 125 D6
Gravesend Rd Education
Ctr DA11 . . . . .19 A1
Gravesend Sta DA11 . . 19 A1
Graves Est DA16 . . . . . 13 B5
Gravesham Com Hospl
DA11 . . . . 19 A1
Gravesham Ct 8 DA12 . 37 D8
Gray Cl CT18 . . . . 307 C5
Gray Ho SE2 . . . . .3 D1
Grayland Cl BR1 . . . . . 52 D8
Graylands RM17 . . . . . .17 E8
Graylen Cl CT14 . . . . . 215 C7
Graylings Ct ME10 . . . 101 C2
Graylings The ME1 . . . .63 B3
Grayne Ave ME3 . . . . . 27 B5
GRAYS 18 A7
Grays Farm Prim Sch
BR5 . . . . 54 B8
Grays Farm Rd BR5 . . . 54 B8
Grayshott Cl ME10 . . . 101 F3
Grays Rd TN16 . . . . . . 151 D7
Grays Sh Ctr RM17 . . . 18 A8
Grays Sta RM17 . . . . . .18 A8
Graystone Rd CT5 . . . . 75 A2
Grays Way CT1 . . . . . . 174 B6
Grazeley Cl DA6 . . . . . .14 C2
Great Ash BR7 . . . . 30 A1
Great Basin Rd ME12 . .27 F2
Great Bounds Dr TN4 . 253 E6
Great Brooms Rd TN4 286 C8
GREAT BUCKLAND 93 F4
Great Burton Rd TN24 268 E5
GREAT CHART 267 C1
Great Chart Prim Sch
TN23 . . . . 299 D8
Great Comp Garden ★
TN15 . . . . 157 E6
Great Conduit St CT21 333 C2
Great Courtlands TN3 285 A3
Great Durgates TN5 . . 336 F5
Great Easthall Way
ME10 . . . . 102 D4
Great Elms TN11 . . . . 190 E1
Great Elms Rd BR2 . . . 52 C5
Great Fishers TN23 . . 299 C7
Great Footway TN3 . . 284 F3
Great Hall Arc 3 TN1 286 B3
Great Hall Arcade 9
TN1 . . . . 286 B3
Great Harry Dr SE9 . . .30 A5
Great Ivy Mill Cotts
ME15 . . . . 194 F7
Great Lines ME7 . . . . . 64 B5
Great Lodge Ret Pk
TN2 . . . . 254 E1

Great Mead TN8 . . . . . 217 C3
GREAT MONGEHAM . . 214 C3
GREATNESS 154 D6
Greatness La TN14 . . . 154 C6
Greatness Rd TN14 . . . 154 C6
Great Oak
Hurst Green TN19 . . . 354 A3
Royal Tunbridge Wells
TN2 . . . . 286 D6
Great Oaks Small Sch
CT12 . . . . 116 B2
Great Queen St ME14 . 53 F1
Great South Ave ME4 . 64 A1
GREAT STONAR 149 B4
GREATSTONE-ON-
SEA 373 E1
Greatstone Prim Sch
TN28 . . . . 373 D2
Great Stour Pl 3 CT2 . 142 F7
Great Thrift BR5 . . . . . 53 C5
Great Till Cl TN14 . . . 121 E3
Greatwood BR7 . . . . . . 30 A1
Grebe Apartments 15
ME15 . . . . 195 E5
Grebe Cl
Hawkinge CT18 . . . . . 307 A4
Lower Stoke ME3 . . . . 25 C4
Grebe Cres CT21 . . . . 353 C8
Grebe Ct ME20 . . . . . 127 F1
Grecian Cl TN1 . . . . . 286 B2
Grecian St ME14 . . . . 162 A6
Greenacre Dartford DA1 33 D6
Kingston CT4 . . . . . . 209 D3
Greenacre Cl
Chatham ME5 . . . . . . 97 A5
Swanley BR8 . . . . 55 E5
Greenacre Dr
Chatham ME5 . . . . . . 97 B8
Greenacres Deal CT14 . 182 B4
Greenacres Sch ME5 . . 96 F5
Green Acres CT18 . . . 245 D7
5 Sidcup DA14 . . . . . 30 F4
Green Acres Cl CT6 . . . 77 B3
Greenacres Prim Sch
SE9 . . . . 30 A6
Greenbank
Ashford TN24 . . . . . . 268 D6
Chatham ME5 . . . . . . 97 A8
Green Bank Cl ME7 . . . 98 A5
Greenbank Lodge 2
BR7 . . . . 53 A8
Greenbanks
Dartford DA1 . . . . 33 E6
Lyminge CT18 . . . . . . 305 C6
Greenbay Rd SE7 . . . . .11 D7
Greenborough Cl
ME15 . . . . 195 E6
Green Cl
Hawkinge CT18 . . . . . 307 B4
Rochester ME1 . . . . . . 63 D2
Green Cloth Mews 2
CT1 . . . . 143 B2
Greencourt Rd SE3 . . . 53 E4
Green Court Rd BR8 . . 55 D3
Greencroft CT13 . . . . 299 E6
Greencroft Cl E16 . . . . . 1 D8
Green Ct Bridge CT4 . . 176 A1
Folkestone CT19 . . . . 335 E7
Greendale Wlk 4 DA11 36 E5
Green Dell CT2 . . . . . . 142 F4
Green Farm Cl BR6 . . . 86 F5
Green Farm La DA12 . . 38 E5
Greenfield Cl
Eccles ME20 . . . . 129 A6
Rusthall TN4 . . . . . . 285 C5
Greenfield Cotts
Boxley ME14 . . . . . . 130 C3
9 Canterbury CT1 . . 174 F7
Greenfield Ct SE9 . . . . 29 E5
Greenfield Dr BR1 . . . . 52 C7
Greenfield Gdns BR5 . . 53 D2
Greenfield Rd
Folkestone CT19 . . . . 335 E7
Gillingham ME7 . . . . . 64 D6
Joyden's Wood DA2 . . .32 D3
Ramsgate CT12 . . . . . 83 C2
Greenfields
Maidstone ME15 . . . . 195 E8
Sellindge TN25 . . . . . 303 E2
Greenfields Cl ME3 . . . 40 D3
Greenfields Com Prim Sch
ME15 . . . . 195 E8
Green Fields La TN23 . 299 C7
Greenfields Sch TN27 . 323 C6
Greenfinches
Gillingham ME7 . . . . . 97 F6
New Barn DA3 . . . . . . 59 B6
Greenfrith Dr TN10 . . 222 B6
Green Gates CT16 . . . 278 A8
Green Gdns BR6 . . . . . 86 C5
Greenhaven Dr SE28 . . 3 B7
Green Hedges TN30 . . 345 B8
GREENHILL 76 C2
GREEN HILL TN12 . . . 118 F7
Greenhill TN12 . . . . . 260 E5
Green Hill
Biggin Hill BR6 . . . . . 118 F7
Maidstone ME15 . . . . 163 B1
Woolwich SE18 . . . . . . 1 F1
Greenhill Bridge Rd
CT6 . . . . .76 D3
Greenhill Cl CT12 . . . 115 B7
Greenhill Cts SE18 . . . . 1 F1
Greenhill Gdns
Herne Bay CT6 . . . . . . 76 D3
Minster (Thanet) CT12 . 115 B7
Greenhill Rd
Herne Bay CT6 . . . . . . 76 C2
Northfleet DA11 . . . . . 36 F6

Greenhill Rd continued
Otford TN14 . . . . 122 C5
Greenhill Road TN14 . 122 C4
Green Hills CT4 . . . . . 242 D8
Greenhill Terr SE18 . . . 1 F1
GREENHITHE 17 B2
Greenhithe 3 ME15 . . 162 A3
Greenhithe Cl DA15 . . 30 E8
Greenhithe for Bluewater
Sta DA9 . . . . .17 A2
Greenholm Rd SE9 . . . 12 B2
Greenhouse La CT2 . . 142 E2
GREENHURST 183 B3
Greenhurst La
Limpsfield RH8 . . . . . 183 A4
Oxted RH8 . . . . 183 A3
Greening St SE2 . . . . . . 3 C2
Green La Alkham CT15 . 276 D3
Ashford TN23 . . . . . . 299 E5
Bethersden TN26 . . . . 297 A2
Broadstairs CT10 . . . . 83 E5
Capel-le-Ferne CT18 . . 308 B3
Challock TN25 . . . . . . 203 A2
Cliffe ME3 . . . . .22 B6
Collier Street TN12 . . . 258 E8
Deal CT14 . . . . 215 B1
Dover CT15 . . . . 278 B3
East End TN17 . . . . . . 322 C2
Eltham BR7, SE9 . . . . .30 B5
Eythorne CT15 . . . . . 245 D7
Folkestone CT19 . . . . 335 E7
Four Elms TN8 . . . . . 218 C2
Goodnestone CT3 . . . 179 B3
Grain ME3 . . . . .27 B5
High Halden TN26 . . . 296 F3
Hythe CT21 . . . . 333 A2
Lamberhurst TN12 . . . 289 B3
Langley Heath ME17 . . 196 E3
Maidstone ME17 . . . . 195 C3
Margate CT9 . . . . .83 E8
Meopham Station DA13 .60 B2
Old Wives Lees CT4 . . 172 C2
Paddock Wood TN12 . . 257 A5
Platt's Heath ME17 . . 198 F2
Rhodes Minnis CT4,
CT18 . . . . 272 E2
Rodmersham ME9 . . . 135 B7
Smarden TN27 . . . . . 264 A1
St Margaret's at Cliffe
CT15 . . . . 247 F1
Sutton Valence ME17 . 229 B4
Temple Ewell CT16 . . . 277 E6
Trottiscliffe ME19 . . . 126 A5
Whitfield CT16 . . . . . 277 E7
Whitstable CT5 . . . . . 108 D8
Greenlands Platt TN15 157 C7
Sole Street DA12 . . . . .60 D4
Greenlands Rd TN15 . . 155 B8
Green Lane Ave CT21 . 333 A2
Green Lane Bsns Pk
SE9 . . . . .30 A6
Green Lane Cotts
Collier Street TN12 . . . 226 D1
Langley Heath ME17 . . 196 E3
Green La The TN1 . . . 220 F1
Green Lawns 10 SE18 . . 2 B2
Greenlaw St SE18 . . . . . 2 A3
Greenleas
1 Folkestone CT20 . . 335 B3
Pembury TN2 . . . . . . 287 C6
Green Leas CT5 . . . . . . 75 D1
Green Lees ME13 . . . . 137 E2
Greenlees Cl ME10 . . . 101 B5
Greenleigh Ave BR5 . . 54 B5
Greenly Way TN28 . . . 373 C6
Green Mdws
Dymchurch TN29 . . . . 352 D2
Eythorne CT15 . . . . . 245 D7
Greenoak Rise TN16 . . 118 C1
Green Park Com Prim Sch
(Lower) CT16 . . . . . . 278 B4
Green Park Com Prim Sch
(Upper) CT16 . . . . . . 278 C4
Green Pl DA1 . . . . 14 E2
Green Porch Cl ME10 . 101 F7
Green Rd Birchington CT7 80 F8
Horsmonden TN12 . . . 290 A6
Stalisfield Green ME13 . 201 C6
Greensand Rd ME15 . . 163 A2
Greensand Ridge
ME17 . . . . 197 E2
Green Sands ME5 . . . . 130 C8
Green's Cotts ME15 . . 194 A4
Greens End SE18 . . . . . 2 B2
Greenshanks ME3 . . . . 68 C3
Greenshields Ind Est E16 1 A4
Greenside
High Halden TN26 . . . 324 E7
Maidstone ME15 . . . . 162 B3
Sidcup DA5 . . . . 31 E7
Swanley BR8 . . . . 55 D7
Greenside Ho CT9 . . . . 50 F1
Greenside Wlk TN16 . . 118 B1
Greenslade Prim Sch
SE18 . . . . .12 D8
Greensleeves Way
ME19 . . . . 159 C3
Greensole La CT12 . . . 82 E1
Green Sq TN5 . . . . . . 336 F5
Green St ME7 . . . . 64 C5
GREEN STREET GREEN
Hartley 35 A2
Orpington 86 E4
Green Street Green Prim
Sch BR6 . . . . 86 F4
Green Street Green Rd DA1,
DA2 . . . . 34 D4
Green The
Bexley, Bexleyheath
DA7 . . . . .14 A4
Bexley, Falconwood DA16 12 E3
Biddenden TN27 . . . . 323 D6
Blean CT2 . . . . 142 A6
Burmarsh TN29 . . . . . 352 C4

Green The *continued*
Chartham CT4 173 D3
Dartford DA2 34 D6
East Farleigh ME15 194 B7
Frant TN3 314 C3
Harbledown CT2 141 E1
Hayes BR2 52 A2
Hythe CT21 333 B4
Langton Green TN3 284 E3
Leigh TN11 220 F1
Lewisham BR1 29 A5
Littlebourne CT3 176 F7
Lower Halstow ME9 67 B3
Lydd TN29 376 B5
Manston CT12 82 D1
Orpington BR5 31 B1
Sevenoaks TN13 154 D5
Sheerness ME12 28 H1
Sidcup DA14 31 A4
Warehorne TN26 348 D6
Westerham TN16 151 D1
West Tilbury RM18 19 E8
Woodchurch TN26 326 A2
Woolage Village CT4 210 E1
Wye TN25 237 E2
Greentrees Ave TN10 222 F5
Green Vale DA6 13 D2
Greenvale Gdns ME8 65 B2
Greenvale Inf Sch ME4 64 A2
Greenvale Rd SE9 12 A3
Green View Ave TN11 221 A1
Greenview Cres TN11 221 E4
Greenview Wlk ME8 65 A4
Greenway Chatham ME5 96 D6
Chislehurst BR7 30 B3
Cranbrook TN17 320 B4
Faversham ME13 138 B8
Tatsfield TN16 150 C7
Green Way Bromley BR2 52 E3
Eltham SE9 11 D2
Hartley DA3 58 E4
Lydd TN29 376 C5
Maidstone ME16 161 B3
Royal Tunbridge Wells TN2 286 E8
Greenway Court Farm Cotts ME17 165 A1
Greenway Court Rd ME17 165 A1
Greenway La ME17 198 A7
Greenways
Addington ME19 126 E2
Lower Halstow ME9 67 B3
Maidstone ME14 162 F5
New Barn DA3 59 D6
Sittingbourne ME10 102 B3
Greenways The TN12 256 F5
Greenway The
Orpington BR5 54 B3
Oxted RH8 183 B2
GREENWICH 1 A3
Greenwich Cl
Chatham ME5 97 B4
Maidstone ME16 161 D4
Greenwich Com Coll [1] SE18 2 C2
Greenwich Cres E6 1 E8
Greenwich Hts SE18 11 E7
Greenwich Sh Pk SE7 1 B2
Green Wlk DA1 14 F3
Greenwood Cl
Orpington BR5 53 E3
Sidcup DA15 31 A6
Greenwood Gdns RH8 183 A1
Greenwood Ho [8] RM17 18 B8
Greenwood Pl TN15 125 A2
Greenwood Rd DA5 32 D4
Greenwood Way TN13 153 F2
GREET 167 D3
Greggs Wood Rd TN2 286 E7
Gregor Mews SE3 11 A7
Gregory Cl
Gillingham ME8 98 E4
Sittingbourne ME10 102 A8
Gregory Cres SE9 29 D8
Gregory Ct TN25 237 E2
Gregory Ho SE3 11 B5
Grenada Rd SE7 11 C7
Grenadier Cl
Gillingham ME8 66 B2
Maidstone ME15 162 F2
Grenadier St E16 2 A5
Grenadier Way TN23 299 C8
Grenfell Cl TN16 118 C7
Grenham Bay Ave CT7 80 E8
Grenham Rd CT7 80 F8
Grenville Cl DA13 93 A8
Grenville Gdns CT7 80 E8
Grenville Way CT10 83 E4
Gresham Ave
Hartley DA3 58 F4
Margate CT9 50 E1
Gresham Cl
[3] Gillingham ME8 65 F1
Sidcup DA5 13 F1
Tonbridge TN10 222 E7
Gresham Rd
Coxheath ME17 194 D3
Newham E16 1 B7
Greshams Way TN8 217 A2
Gresswell Cl DA14 31 A5
Greville Ho CT17 310 C7
Greville Homes CT13 180 B2
Greybury La TN8 249 B3
Greyfriars Cl ME16 161 D5
Grey Friars Cotts [8] CT1 174 F8
Greyfriars Ct CT10 51 F1
Greyhound Chase TN23 299 D7
Greyhound Way DA1 14 E1
Grey Ladies Oasts TN15 157 B3
Greys Park Cl BR2 85 D5
Greystone Pk TN14 152 E2
Greystones Cl TN15 122 E2
Greystones Rd
Cliffs End CT12 116 D5
Maidstone ME15 163 A2
Grey Wethers ME14 129 E4
Grey Willow Gdns TN23 299 D8
Gribble Bridge La TN27 323 B5
Grice Ave TN16 118 C6
Grice Cl CT18 306 F3
Grieveson Ho ME4 64 A4
Grieves Rd DA11 36 F5
Griffin Cotts TN26 347 C2
Griffin Manor Way SE28 2 D3
Griffin Rd SE18 2 D2
Griffin's Cnr TN25 269 E7
Griffin St CT14 215 D7
Griffin Way SE28 2 E3
Griffin Wlk DA9 16 F2
Griffiths Ho [2] SE18 12 B8
Grigg La TN27 263 C7
Grigg's Cross BR5 54 D3
Griggs Way TN15 157 A7
Grimsby Gr E16 2 B4
Grimshill Ct CT2 142 C4
Grimshill Rd CT5 108 E8
Grimston Ave CT20 335 B4
Grimston Gdns CT20 335 B4
Grimthorpe Ave CT5 108 C7
Grinling Ho [6] SE18 2 A2
Grinsell Hill CT12 115 E6
Grisbrook Farm Cl TN29 376 D6
Grisbrook Rd TN29 376 D6
Grizedale Cl ME1 96 D8
Gromenfield TN3 312 C7
GROOMBRIDGE 312 C7
Groombridge Cl DA16 13 A2
Groombridge Hill TN3 284 D1
Groombridge Pl★ TN3 312 C8
Groombridge Place Gdns★ TN3 312 C8
Groombridge Rd TN3 284 A1
Groombridge St Thomas' CE Aided Prim Sch TN3 312 C6
Groombridge Sq [13] ME15 195 F6
Groombridge Station★ TN3 312 C7
Groom Cl BR2 52 B5
Groom Way ME17 199 E6
Grosmont Rd SE18 2 F1
Grosvenor Ave ME4 63 E3
Grosvenor Bridge TN1 286 B5
Grosvenor Cotts CT7 81 B3
Grosvenor Cres DA1 15 D2
Grosvenor Gdns CT9 50 I1
Grosvenor Hill CT9 50 I2
Grosvenor Ho [5] ME15 195 F5
Grosvenor Manor DA5 32 D6
Grosvenor Pk TN1 286 A4
Grosvenor Pl CT9 50 I2
Grosvenor Rd
Ashford TN24 268 D7
Bexley DA6 13 E2
Broadstairs CT10 84 A4
Erith DA17 14 A8
Gillingham ME7 65 A1
Orpington BR5 53 E3
Ramsgate CT11 117 C7
Royal Tunbridge Wells TN1 286 A4
Whitstable CT5 108 D7
Grosvenor Sq DA3 58 E6
Grosvenor Wlk TN1 286 A4
Grotto Gdns [6] CT9 50 J2
Grotto Hill CT9 50 J2
Grotto Rd [5] CT9 50 J2
GROVE 145 F8
Grove Ave
Leysdown-on-Sea ME12 49 G2
Royal Tunbridge Wells TN1 286 A2
Grove Bridge TN25 331 D8
Grovebury Cl DA8 14 D8
Grovebury Ct DA6 14 B2
Grovebury Rd SE2 3 B4
Grove Cl
Faversham ME13 138 A6
Goose Green TN11 191 C3
Hayes BR2 85 A8
Grove Cotts TN30 345 B6
Grove Court Farm ME13 140 A3
Grove Ct Greenwich SE3 11 A6
[4] Rochester ME2 63 B7
Grove Dairy Farm ME9 101 A6
GROVE END 134 C7
Grove Ferry Hill CT3 112 E3
Grove Ferry Rd CT3 113 A2
Grove Gdns CT9 50 G1
GROVE GREEN 162 E5
Grove Green La ME14 162 E5
Grove Green Rd ME14 162 F5
Groveherst Rd DA1 15 F4
GROVE HILL 145 D6
Grove Hill Gdns TN1 286 B2
Grove Hill Ho TN1 286 B3
Grove Hill Rd TN1 286 B3
Grove Ho TN27 265 C3
Grovehurst Ave ME10 68 F1
Grovehurst La TN12 290 C5
Grovehurst Rd ME10, ME9 68 E2
Grove La
Brookland TN29 362 D3
Hunton ME15 226 D7
Iden TN31 368 C4
Grovelands ME17 199 E5
Grovelands Rd BR5 31 A1
Grovelands Way RM17 17 F8
Grove Market Pl SE9 11 F1
GROVE PARK 29 B5
Grove Park Ave ME10 101 B5
Grove Park CP Sch ME10 101 B6
Grove Park Rd SE9 29 D6
Grove Park Sta SE12 29 B5
Grove Pl ME13 138 A6
Grove Rd
Bexley, Bexleyheath DA7 14 C3
[8] Bexley, West Heath DA17 13 F8
Chatham ME4 64 B2
Deal CT14 215 D3
Folkestone CT20 335 E6
Gillingham ME7 65 A6
Grays RM17 18 C8
Maidstone ME15 195 C7
Northfleet DA11 18 B2
Penshurst TN11, TN8 251 E2
Preston CT3 146 B8
Ramsgate CT11 117 D6
Rochester ME2 63 B8
Seal TN15 155 B5
Selling ME13 171 B4
Sevenoaks TN14 154 C6
Staple CT3 178 F6
Tatsfield TN16 150 C7
Upper Halling ME2 94 E5
Wickhambreaux CT3 145 D6
Grove Road Cotts
Wickhambreaux CT3 145 C2
Wickhambreaux, Frognall CT3 145 C3
Grover St [3] TN1 286 B4
Groves The ME6 127 F7
Grove Terr CT1 174 E7
Grove The
Ashford TN24 268 E6
Barham CT4 242 F8
Bexley DA6 13 D3
Biggin Hill TN16 118 E1
Deal CT14 215 C6
Dover CT16 278 C1
Fawkham Green DA3 58 A2
Gravesend DA12 37 B8
Herne Bay CT6 76 C2
Maidstone ME14 163 A3
Pembury TN2 287 D8
Sidcup DA14 31 E4
Swanley BR8 55 F6
Swanscombe DA10 17 F2
Westgate on Sea CT8 81 F8
West Kingsdown TN15 90 F1
Grove Vale BR7 30 A2
Groveway ME12 49 F2
Grove Way CT3 146 C7
Grove Wood Cl BR1 53 A6
Grove Wood Cotts TN11 188 A1
Grovewood Ct ME14 162 E4
Grovewood Dr ME14 162 E4
GRUBB STREET 58 B8
Grub St RH8 183 C6
Grummock Ave CT11 117 B7
Grundy's Hill [13] CT11 117 E6
Guardian Ct ME8 65 C1
Guardian Ind Est TN12 259 C7
Guards Cl TN10 222 E7
Guernsey Way TN24 268 C7
Guestling Mill Ct [1] CT13 148 F1
Guestwick TN10 222 F5
Guibal Rd SE12 29 B7
Guildables La RH8, TN8 216 E7
Guildcount La [5] CT13 148 F1
Guildford Ave CT8 81 E8
Guildford Gdns ME2 62 C6
Guildford Lawn [1] CT11 117 E6
Guildford Rd
Canterbury CT1 174 F6
Newham E6 1 F7
[7] Royal Tunbridge Wells TN1 286 B3
Guildhall Ct [10] CT20 335 D5
Guildhall Mus★
Queenborough ME11 45 F5
Rochester ME1 63 C6
Guildhall St
[4] Canterbury CT1 174 F8
[18] Folkestone CT20 335 D5
Guildhall Street N CT19, CT20 335 D5
Guild Rd Erith DA8 14 F7
Greenwich SE7 11 D8
Guilford Ave CT16 278 A8
Guilford Ct CT14 215 D2
Guilford Ho CT13 182 A7
Guilford Rd CT13 181 E8
GUILTON 147 C1
Guilton CT3 147 B1
Guiness Dr ME2 40 B2
Guldeford La TN29, TN31 369 F3
Guldeford Lane Cnr TN31 369 D2
Gulland Ho [4] ME14 162 B4
Gullands ME17 196 E4
Gulliver Rd DA15 30 E6
Gumley Rd RM20 17 E8
Gumping Rd BR5, BR6 86 C8
Gun Back La TN12 290 A5
Gundulph Ho TN10 222 C3
Gundulph Rd
Bromley BR2 52 C6
Rochester ME1 63 E4
Gundulph Sq ME1 63 C6
Gunfleet Cl DA12 37 E8
GUN GREEN 341 C2
Gun Hill RM18 19 D8
Gun La ME2 63 B7
Gunlands TN12 290 A6
Gun Lane Bsns Est [5] ME2 63 B7
Gunner La SE18 2 A1
Gunnery Terr SE18 2 C3
Gunning St SE18 2 E2
Gunnis Cl ME8 98 D4
Gunn Rd DA10 17 E1
Gun Tower Mews ME1 63 B4
Gurdon Rd SE7 1 B1
Gurling Rd CT15 247 F1
GUSHMERE 171 C7
GUSTON 278 E6
Guston CE Prim Sch CT15 278 E3
Guston Rd
East Langdon CT15 279 A8
Maidstone ME14 162 C6
Guthrie Gdns CT17 277 E3
Guy Barnett Gr SE3 11 A4
Guy Cl CT10 84 A7
Gwillim Cl DA15 13 A2
Gwynn Rd DA11 36 C6
Gwyn Rd CT12 83 C2
Gybbon Rise TN12 260 E3
Gybbons Rd TN17 343 F3
Gypsy Cnr CT5 109 D3
Gypsy Way ME23 23 E3

H

Haberdashers Askes Knights Acad BR1 29 A4
Hackfield TN23 267 F1
Hackington Cl CT2 142 E4
Hackington Pl CT2 142 F2
Hackington Rd CT2 142 E7
Hackington Terr CT2 142 F2
HACKLINGE 181 C1
Hacklinge Hill CT14 181 B2
Hackney Rd ME16 161 C2
Hadden Rd SE28 2 E3
Haddon Dene Sch CT10 83 F4
Haddon Gr DA15 31 A8
Haddon Rd BR5 54 C4
Hadleigh Ct ME7 98 A3
Hadleigh Gdns CT6 77 B5
Hadleigh Wlk [1] E6 1 F7
Hadley Cl DA13 93 B8
Hadley Ct TN4 285 F6
Hadley Gdns ME17 164 E2
Hadley House BR5 53 F7
Hadley Rd DA17 3 F2
HADLOW 190 E1
Hadlow Coll
Canterbury CT1 175 B8
Hadlow TN11 223 D8
Hadlow Coll Mottingham Ctr SE12 29 C7
Hadlow Ct TN9 222 C2
Hadlow Dr CT9 51 E2
Hadlow Pk TN11 190 E1
Hadlow Rd Bexley DA16 13 C7
Maidstone ME14 162 C5
Sidcup DA14 31 A4
Tonbridge TN9 222 D3
Hadlow Road E TN10, TN11 223 A5
Hadlow Sch TN11 223 E8
HADLOW STAIR 222 F4
Hadlow Stair Rd TN10 222 F4
Hadlow Way DA13 36 E1
Hadrian Gdns TN23 299 F5
Haffenden Cl TN12 259 D6
Haffenden Mdw TN27 234 C8
HAFFENDEN QUARTER 296 A7
Haffenden Rd TN30 324 B1
Ha-Ha Rd SE18 11 F8
Haig Ave
Chatham, Luton ME4 64 A2
Chatham ME1 63 D1
Gillingham ME7 64 E4
Haig Ct BR7 30 B3
Haig Gdns DA12 37 C8
Haig Rd TN16 118 E2
Haig Villas ME3 41 A5
Haileybury Rd BR6 87 A6
Hailey Rd DA18 4 A4
Hailey Rd Bsns Pk DA18 4 A4
Hailing Mews BR2 52 B6
Hailstone Cl TN11 223 E8
Haimo Prim Sch SE9 11 D2
Haimo Rd SE9 11 D2
Hainault St SE9 30 B7
HAINE 82 F2
Haine Ind Est CT12 82 F1
Haine Rd CT12, CT10 82 F2
Halcot Ave DA6 14 C2
Haldane Gdns DA11 36 C7
Haldane Rd SE28 3 D6
Halden Cl ME15 195 F6
Halden La TN17 343 F6
HALE Birchington 80 B4
Chatham 97 D8
Hale Cl BR6 86 C6
Hale Cotts DA9 17 C2
Hale Ct TN12 225 A7
Hale La TN14 121 F2
Hale Oak Rd
Hall's Green TN8, TN14 219 E4
Sevenoaks Weald TN14 187 B1
Hale Rd ME3 40 C7
Hales Cl TN30 345 B8
Hales Ct TN30 345 B8
Hales Dr CT2 142 F3
HALES PLACE 143 A3
Hales Rd ME10 101 D1
Hale St TN12 225 A7
HALE STREET 225 A7
Haleys Pl ME1 129 A8
Halfmile Ride CT9 82 E6
Half Moon La TN11 221 D6
Half Moon Way ME23 23 E3
Halford Cl CT6 77 B2
Halfpence La DA12 61 B7
Halfpenny Cl ME16 161 A2
HALFWAY HOUSES 46 E7
Halfway Houses Prim Sch ME12 46 D6
Halfway Rd ME12 46 D8
Halfway St DA15 30 E7
HALFWAY STREET 244 D4
Halifax Cl ME5 97 B6
Halifield Dr DA17 3 E3
Hallam Cl BR7 29 F3
Hall Ave TN24 300 F6
Hall by the Sea Rd CT9 50 H2
Hall Cl ME10 101 E6
Hall Cres CT14 214 F5
Hallcroft Ct CT11 117 C7
Hallett Wlk [10] CT1 143 B2
Hallford Way DA1 15 C2
Hallgate SE3 11 A4
Hall Hill TN15 155 C4
Halliday Ct CT21 333 A2
Halliday Dr CT14 215 D3
HALLING 95 B5
Halling Prim Sch ME2 95 B3
Halling Sta ME2 95 A5
Hall Place Cres DA1, DA5 14 D2
Hall Place & Gdns★ DA5 14 C1
Hall Rd Aylesford ME20 128 F1
Chatham ME5 97 C3
Dartford DA1 15 F3
High Halstow ME3 24 C6
Northfleet, Pepper Hill DA11 36 C5
Northfleet, Wombwell Park DA11 36 D6
Wouldham ME1 95 C3
Halls Cotts TN5 336 F5
Hallsfield Rd ME5 96 D2
HALL'S GREEN 220 A7
Hall's Hole Rd TN2 286 E4
Hallsville Prim Sch E16 1 A7
Hall The SE3 11 A4
Hall View SE9 29 D6
Hallwards TN12 260 E2
Hallwood Cl ME8 98 D5
Hallwood Ho ME5 97 C2
Hallywell Cres E6 1 F8
Halons Rd SE9 30 A8
Halsbrook Rd SE3 11 D4
Halstatt Rd CT14 215 A3
HALSTEAD 120 F6
Halstead Cl CT2 143 B4
Halstead Gdns CT9 51 F3
Halstead La TN14 120 E5
Halstead Prim Sch TN14 120 F7
Halstead Rd DA8 14 E6
Halstead Wlk ME16 161 C7
Halstow Cl ME15 195 B6
Halstow Prim Sch [9] SE10 1 A1
Halstow Rd SE10, SE3 1 A1
Halstow Way TN23 299 F8
Halt Cvn Pk The TN15 90 E1
Halt Robin Rd DA17 4 B2
Halt The Elham CT4 273 F4
Whitstable CT5 109 A7
HAM 180 F2
Hambledon Ct ME16 161 B3
Hambledown Rd DA15 30 E8
Hamble Rd TN10 222 B5
Hambro Ave BR2 52 A1
Hambrook Cl CT4 205 B8
Hambrook La CT4 205 C8
Hambrook Wlk ME10 101 F8
Hamele The CT2 143 F5
Hamelin Rd ME7 97 F8
Hamerton Rd DA11 18 B2
Ham Farm Cotts CT14 180 F2
HAM GREEN Upchurch 66 F6
Wittersham 359 C1
Hamill Terr CT1 143 B2
Hamilton Cl
Littlestone-on-Sea TN28 373 E5
Ramsgate CT12 83 B1
Snodland ME6 127 F7
Hamilton Cres ME10 101 C3
Hamilton Ct
Chatham ME5 64 C1
Rochester ME1 63 B4
Royal Tunbridge Wells TN4 286 A5
Hamilton Ho
Coxheath ME17 194 C3
Maidstone ME15 195 F5
[1] Royal Tunbridge Wells TN4 286 A5
Hamilton Rd
Ashford TN24 300 D6
Bexley DA7 13 E5
Deal CT14 215 C4
Dover CT17 310 B8
Gillingham ME7 64 D7
Lydd TN29 376 C6
Sidcup DA15 31 A4
Whitstable CT5 74 D1
Hamilton Wlk DA8 14 F7
Ham La Gillingham ME7 97 E3
Lenham ME17 199 C5
Hamlea Cl SE12 11 A2
Hamlet Est DA8 4 D1
Hamlet Ho Eltham SE9 12 A2
[5] Erith DA8 14 E7
HAMLET OF SHELLNESS 73 E5
Hamlin Rd TN13 153 E6
Hamlyn Ct TN13 153 E6
Hammelton Rd [2] BR1 52 A8
Hammerton Close DA5 32 E5
HAMMERWOOD 281 B3
Hammerwood Pk★ RH19 281 C2
HAMMILL 179 E3
Ham Mill La TN26, TN29 349 A2
Hammond Cl CT15 211 E5
Hammonds [9] TN18 341 A2
Hammond's Cnr TN29 372 E6
Hammond's Rd CT20 334 E5
Hammonds Sq ME6 128 A8
Hammond Way [2] SE28 3 B6
Hamond Hill [6] ME4 63 E4
Hampden La TN23 300 A7
Hampden Mews TN23 300 A7
Hampden Rd TN23 300 A6
Hampden Way ME19 158 F3
Hampshire Cl ME5 97 C7
Hampshire Dr ME15 195 C8
Hampshire Rd CT1 175 D7
Hampshires The ME17 198 C6
Hampson Way ME14 163 A4
Hampstead Cl SE28 3 B5
Hampstead La ME18 192 C1
HAMPTON 76 B5
Hampton Cl
Chatham ME5 97 A5
Herne Bay CT6 76 A3
Hampton Cotts TN14 120 F4
Hampton Cres DA12 37 E6
Hampton Ct DA8 14 D7
Hampton Gdns CT6 76 A3
Hampton Ho DA7 14 B5
Hampton La TN25 270 C3
Hampton Pier Ave CT6 76 B4
Hampton Prim Sch CT6 76 C4
Hampton Rd ME14 162 C6
Hamptons Rd TN11 190 B5
Hampton Vale CT21 334 B4
Ham Rd ME13 105 C1
Ham River Hill ME3 40 A6
Ham St Woods National Nature Reserve★ TN26 328 B2
Ham Shades Cl [1] DA15 31 A5
Ham Shades La CT5 75 A1
HAMSTREET 349 B7
Hamstreet Prim Sch TN26 348 F8
Hamstreet Rd
Bromley Green TN26 327 E5
Hamstreet TN26 349 C7
Ham Street Sta TN26 349 A8
Hamwick Gn ME5 97 C1
Hanameel St E16 1 B5
Hanbury Cl ME18 192 E7
Hanbury Dr TN16 118 B6
Hanbury Wlk DA5 32 E5
Hancock Cl ME3 40 B1
Hancocks Field CT14 215 A5
Handel Cres RM18 19 A7
Handel Wlk TN10 222 E6
Hands Wlk E16 1 A7
Hanes Dene ME2 94 F5
Hang Grove Hill BR6 119 B6
Hanging Bank TN14 185 F3
Hangmans Cnr BR7 53 B8
Hangman's La CT14 247 F5
Hanley Ct TN13 154 B4
Hanmer Way TN12 260 E2
Hannah Cl ME4 64 A3
Hanover Ave E16 1 A5
Hanover Cl
Ashford TN23 267 F2
Deal CT14 215 D2
Margate CT9 51 E2
Sittingbourne ME10 101 E2
Hanover Ct
Broadstairs CT10 83 F4
[10] Bromley BR2 52 A6
Faversham ME13 138 B8
Hythe CT21 333 C1
Maidstone ME14 162 B5
Hanover Dr
Chislehurst BR7 30 C4
Gillingham ME8 98 C4
Hanover Gn ME20 127 F3
Hanover Ho [6] CT20 335 C4
Hanover Pl
Canterbury CT2 142 F2
New Ash Green DA3 91 F8
Hanover Rd
Coxheath ME17 194 C3
Royal Tunbridge Wells TN1 286 A4
Hanover Sq CT6 76 F5
Hanover St CT6 76 F5
Hanover Way DA7 13 D4
Hanscomb Ho CT2 142 E2
Hanslett's La ME13 137 D3
Hansol Rd DA6 13 E2
Hansom Terr [1] BR1 52 B8
Hanson Dr ME15 194 F3
Hanway ME8 65 A2
Harbex Cl DA5 32 B8
HARBLEDOWN 174 B8
Harbledown Gdns CT9 51 E3
Harbledown Ho ME16 161 B2
Harbledown Manor ME8 65 B3
Harbledown Pk CT2 142 C1
Harbledown Pl [7] BR5 54 C5
Harborough Ave DA15 30 F8
Harbour Approach Rd CT20 335 E4
HARBOURLAND 162 B8
Harbourland Cl ME14 162 B8

Harbourne La TN26,
TN30 . . . . .324 E5
Harbour Par CT11 . . . .117 E6
Harbour Point CT19 . . .335 F5
Harbour Sch CT15 . . . .309 E7
Harbour St
  Broadstairs CT10 . . . .84 B4
  Folkestone CT20 . . . .335 E5
  Ramsgate CT11 . . . . .117 E6
  Whitstable CT5 . . . . . . .74 D2
HARBOUR THE 229 E5
Harbour The ME17 . . . .229 E5
Harbour Twrs 16 CT11 117 E6
Harbour View Rd CT17 310 D8
Harbour Way CT20 . . .335 E5
Harcourt Ave DA15 . . . .31 C8
Harcourt Dr
  Canterbury CT2 . . . . . .142 D2
  Herne Bay CT6 . . . . . . .76 B5
Harcourt Gdns ME8 . . .98 E4
CT19 . . . . .334 E7
Harcourt Prim Sch
Harcourt Rd Bexley DA6 .13 E3
  Folkestone CT19 . . . . .334 F7
Harden Ct 11 SE18 . . . . .1 E2
Harden Rd Lydd TN29 . .376 D7
  Northfleet DA11 . . . . . . .36 F6
Harden's View TN26 . .348 D6
Hardie LE ME19 . . . . . .127 F1
Hardinge Ave TN4 . . . .253 E3
Hardinge Cl ME8 . . . . . .98 D4
Hardinge Cres SE18 . . . .2 C3
Hardinge Rd TN24 . . . .268 C3
Hardinge St SE18 . . . . . .2 B3
Harding Ho 9 SE18 . . . .1 F2
Harding Rd DA7 . . . . . . .13 F5
Hardman Rd SE7 . . . . . . .1 B1
Hardres Court Rd CT4 208 A3
Hardres Rd CT11 . . . . .117 E8
Hardres St CT11 . . . . .117 E7
Hardres Terr BR5 . . . . . .87 D8
Hardstown ME4 . . . . . . .64 A4
Hardwick Cres 3 DA2. .16 B1
Hardwicke Ho TN27 . . .234 B7
Hardwicke Rd CT17 . . .310 B6
Hardwick Ho ME15 . . . .195 E8
Hardwick Rd
  Folkestone CT20 . . . . .335 A4
  Tonbridge TN11 . . . . . .221 E6
  Northfleet DA11 . . . . . . .36 E6
Hardy Ave Newham E16. . .1 A5
  Northfleet DA11 . . . . . . .36 E6
Hardy Cl Ashford TN24 . .301 A7
  Canterbury CT2 . . . . . .142 C1
  Chatham ME5 . . . . .97 B6
Hardy Gr ME1 . . . . .16 A3
Hardy Lodge ME1 . . . . . .63 B4
Hardy Rd
  Greatstone-on-Sea
  TN28 . . . . .373 D3
  2 Greenwich SE3 . . . .11 A8
  St Margaret's at Cliffe
  CT15 . . . . .279 E8
Hardy St ME14 . . . . . .162 A6
Harebell Cl
  3 Chatham ME5 . . . . .96 F4
  Maidstone ME14 . . . . .162 E5
  Minster (Sheppey) ME12 .47 A4
Harebell Dr E6 . . . . .2 A8
Harebrook CT11 . . . . . . .83 F1
Haredale Cl ME1 . . . . . . .96 D7
Harefield Rd DA15 . . . . .31 D5
Harenc Sch DA14 . . . . . .31 C3
HAREPLAIN 294 C4
Harescroft TN2 . . . . . . .313 F7
Hare St 2 Chatham ME4 .64 B3
  Woolwich SE18 . . . . .2 A3
Harewood Lincoln Ho 4
  DA11 . . . . .18 D1
Harfst Way BR8 . . . . . . .55 C8
Hargate Cl TN12 . . . . . .313 F8
Hargood Rd SE3 . . . . . . .11 C6
Harkness Ct 6 ME10 .102 B4
Harkness Dr CT2 . . . . . .142 E2
Harland Ave DA15 . . . . .30 E6
Harland Rd SE12 . . . . . .29 A7
Harlands Gr BR6 . . . . . . .86 B6
Harland Way TN4. . . . . .253 F4
Harlech Cl ME2 . . . . .39 F1
Harlequin Cl CT6 . . . . . .76 E2
Harlequin Ho 11 DA18 . .3 E3
Harley 5 BR7 . . . . .53 D8
Harley Gdns BR6 . . . . . .86 A6
Harling Cl ME17 . . . . . .195 D5
Harlinger St SE18 . . . . . . .1 E2
Harlington Rd DA7 . . . . .13 E4
Harman Ave
  Gravesend DA11 . . . . . .37 B3
  Lympne CT21 . . . . . . .331 F3
Harman Ct ME5 . . . . . . .97 B3
Harman Dr DA15 . . . . . .12 F1
HARMAN'S CORNER . .101 B2
Harmer Ct
  Royal Tunbridge Wells
  TN4 . . . . .254 A2
  Swanscombe DA10 . . . . .17 F1
Harmer Rd DA10 . . . . . .17 F1
Harmer St ME12 . . . . . .19 C1
Harmers Way TN27 . . . .232 F3
Harmony Cl ME10 . . . . .101 D3
Harmony St TN4 . . . . . .285 D4
Harmony Way 11 BR1,
  BR2 . . . . .52 A7
Harmsworth TN17 . . . .342 E6
Harmsworth Gdns CT10 84 A5
Harness Rd SE28 . . . . . . .3 A4
Harnet St 6 CT13 . . . . .148 F1
Harnetts Cl BR8 . . . . . . .55 D2
Harold Ave Erith DA17. . . .3 F1
  Gillingham ME7 . . . . .64 E4

Harold Ave continued
  Westgate on Sea CT8 . . . .81 E8
Harold Campbell Ct
  DA1 . . . . .33 D8
Harold Ct ME13 . . . . . .138 C6
Harold Gibbons Ct SE7 .11 C8
Harold Ho 2 TN2 . . . . .286 C7
Harold Rd
  Birchington CT7 . . . . . . .80 E8
  Cuxton ME2 . . . . .62 C3
  Deal CT14 . . . . .215 D8
  Hawley DA2 . . . . .33 F4
  Margate CT9 . . . . .51 B3
  Sittingbourne ME10 . . . .102 B4
Harold's Rd CT16 . . . . .310 E8
Harper Rd
  Ashford TN23 . . . . . . .299 F8
  Newham E6 . . . . .1 F7
Harp Farm Rd ME14 . . .130 C6
Harple La ME14 . . . . . .130 F1
Harps Ave ME12 . . . . . . .47 C6
Harpswood ME17 . . . . .164 F1
Harpswood La CT21 . . .333 A4
Harptree Dr ME5 . . . . . .96 F5
Harraden Rd SE3 . . . . . .11 C6
Harrier Dr ME10 . . . . . .102 A2
Harrier Mews SE28 . . . . .2 F6
Harrier Way E6 . . . . .1 F8
Harries Rd TN24 . . . . . .286 E7
Harriestsham Sta
  ME17 . . . . .198 D6
Harriet Dr ME1 . . . . .63 B3
Harriet Mews DA16 . . . .13 B5
Harriets Cnr CT5 . . . . . .108 B5
HARRIETSHAM 198 D5
Harrietsham CE Prim Sch
  ME17 . . . . .198 D6
Harrietsham Ho 13
  ME16 . . . . .161 A3
Harringe La CT21,
  TN25 . . . . .331 A6
Harrington Ho 7 ME1 . .52 A8
Harrington Way SE18 . . . .1 D3
Harriot Cl CT19 . . . . . . .335 B7
Harris Cl DA11 . . . . .36 F5
Harris Gdns ME10 . . . . .102 C5
Harris Ho ME2 . . . . .95 B4
Harrison Ct 4 ME8 . . . .65 F1
Harrison Dr
  Harrietsham ME17 . . . .198 E6
  High Halstow ME23 . . . . .23 E4
Harrison Drive BR1. . . . .53 B5
Harrison Rd
  Borough Green TN15 . . .156 F7
  4 Ramsgate CT11 . . . .117 D6
Harrison Terr ME13 . . . .105 A2
Harrison Way TN13 . . . .154 A5
Harris Pl ME15 . . . . . . .161 E1
Harris Rd Bexley DA7 . . . .13 F6
  Sheerness ME12 . . . . . .28 C2
Harris's Alley CT3 . . . . .178 A7
Harrogate Ct 6 SE12 . .29 A8
Harrowby Gdns DA11 . .36 E6
Harrow Cl TN8 . . . . . . .217 D3
Harrow Ct Chatham ME5 .97 C4
  Stockbury ME9 . . . . . . .132 D8
Harrow Dene CT10 . . . .83 E6
Harrow Gdns BR6 . . . . . .87 B6
Harrow Manor Way SE2 .3 C3
Harrow Rd
  Gillingham ME7 . . . . .97 F6
  Halstead TN14 . . . . . .120 E4
Harrow Way
  Ashford TN23 . . . . . . .299 E5
  Maidstone ME14 . . . . .162 E5
Harry Pay Cl TN24 . . . .268 C4
Harrys Rd ME9 . . . . . . .103 D3
Harry Wells Rd CT6. . . . .76 B3
Hart Cl CT18 . . . . .307 A4
Hart Dyke Cres BR8 . . . .55 C6
Hart Dyke Rd
  Orpington BR5 . . . . .54 C1
  Swanley BR8 . . . . .55 D6
Hartfield Cl TN10 . . . . .222 E6
Hartfield Cres BR4. . . . . .85 A7
Hartfield Pl DA11. . . . . . .36 D8
Hartfield Rd
  Cowden TN8 . . . . .282 C6
  Hayes BR4. . . . . .85 A6
  Stick Hill TN8. . . . . . . .250 A2
Hartford Rd DA5 . . . . . .14 A1
Hartford Wlk 13 DA17 . . .4 A1
Hart Hill TN27 . . . . .201 A2
Hart Ho BR6. . . . . .54 A2
Harting Rd SE9 . . . . .29 C5
Hartington Cl BR6. . . . . .86 C5
Hartington Rd E16. . . . . . .1 B7
Hartington St ME4 . . . . .64 A3
Hartlake Rd TN11. . . . . .223 D3
Hartlands Cl DA5 . . . . . .13 F1
Hart Lane DA13 . . . . . . .93 C3
Hartlepool Ct E16 . . . . . .2 B4
HARTLEY Cranbrook. . . .319 F1
  New Barn 58 F3
Hartley Bottom Rd DA3 59 C2
Hartley Cl Bromley BR1. .52 F7
  Maidstone ME15. . . . . .195 H6
Hartley Court Gdns
  TN17 . . . . .320 A3
HARTLEY GREEN 58 E4
Hartley Hill DA3. . . . . . . .59 A1
Hartley Mews ME8 . . . . .65 B3
Hartley Prim Sch DA3 . .58 F3
Hartley Rd Bexley DA16. .13 C7
  Hartley TN17 . . . . .320 A3
  Longfield DA3. . . . . .58 F7
  Westerham TN16 . . . . .151 D2
HARTLIP 99 E5
Hartlip La ME12 . . . . . . .46 B7
Hartlip Endowed CE Prim
  Sch ME9 . . . . .99 D5

Hartlip Hill ME9 . . . . . . .99 F7
Hartmann Rd E16 . . . . . .1 E5
Hartnokes TN18 . . . . . .341 A2
Hartnup St ME16 . . . . .161 C2
Hartpiece Cl ME8. . . . . . .65 F2
Hartridge Farm ME15. .194 A7
Harts Cotts TN26 . . . . .349 H1
Hartsdown L Ctr CT9 . .50 H1
Hartsdown Rd CT9 . . . . .82 D8
Hartsdown Tech Coll
  CT9. . . . . .82 D8
Hart Shaw DA3. . . . . . . .59 B7
Hartshill Rd DA11. . . . . .36 F6
Harts La 6 CT5 . . . . . . .74 D2
Hartslands Rd TN13. . .154 C4
Hartslock Dr DA18, ME2. .3 D4
Hartsmead Rd SE9 . . . . .29 F6
Hart St ME1 . . . . .161 F3
Harty Ave ME8 . . . . .98 B3
Harty Ferry Cotts
  ME13. . . . . .105 C5
Harty Ferry Rd ME12 . . .72 E4
Harty Ferry View CT5. .108 C5
Harty Terr ME12 . . . . . . .48 A5
Harvard Ct 9 SE9 . . . . .12 A1
HARVEL 93 C3
Harvel Ave ME2 . . . . . . .62 F7
Harvel Cl BR5, BR7. . . . . .54 A6
Harvel Cres SE2. . . . . .3 D1
Harvel La DA13 . . . . .93 B2
Harvel Rd DA13 . . . . . .126 A8
Harvel St DA13 . . . . .93 C3
Harvest Bank Rd BR4. . .85 A7
Harvesters Cl ME8. . . . . .98 E7
Harvesters Way ME14 .162 D4
Harvest La CT4 . . . . . . .240 E5
Harvest Rd TN10 . . . . . .222 D6
Harvest Ridge ME19 . .127 D2
Harvest Way
  Ashford TN23 . . . . . . .299 D7
  Crockenhill BR8 . . . . . . .55 D2
  Hawkinge CT18. . . . . . .307 B4
Harvey Ave CT14 . . . . .215 C4
Harvey Ct CT19 . . . . . .335 A6
Harvey Dr
  Sittingbourne ME10 . . . .102 A2
  Whitstable CT5 . . . . . . .75 B1
Harvey Gdns SE7 . . . . . .1 C1
Harvey Gram Sch The
  CT19. . . . . .335 A6
Harvey Pl 9 CT20 . . . .335 E5
Harvey Point 9 E16. . . . .1 A8
Harvey Rd
  Ashford TN24 . . . . . . .268 F1
  Gillingham ME8. . . . . . . .98 E8
Harvey St ME20 . . . . . .335 E5
Harville Rd TN25 . . . . .237 C2
Harvill Rd DA14 . . . . . . .31 E3
Harwich St CT5 . . . . . .108 D8
Harwick Dr TN28 . . . . .373 D8
Harwood Ave ME1. . . . . .52 B7
Harwood Ct 3 RM17. . .18 C8
Harwood Ho ME25. . . . .237 E1
Harwood Rd ME16. . . . .161 A3
Hasborough Rd CT19. .335 F6
Haskard Cl CT18. . . . . .306 F4
Haslemere Rd DA7 . . . .14 A5
Haslemere Trad & Ind Est
  ME15 . . . . .195 F5
Hasler Cl SE18 . . . . .3 C6
Hasletts Cl TN1. . . . . . .286 B6
Haslewood Cl TN27. . . .264 B2
Hassall Reach CT1. . . . .174 B6
Hassall St TN25 . . . . . .238 F2
HASSELL STREET 239 A2
Hassendean Rd SE3 . . . .11 B7
Hassock Wood BR2. . . . .85 E6
Hassop Wlk SE9 . . . . . . .29 A4
Hasted Cl DA9. . . . . .17 C1
Hasted Rd Greenwich SE7 1 D1
  Higham ME3 . . . . .39 D2
  Newington ME9 . . . . . .100 B7
Hasteds ME17 . . . . . . .164 D2
Haste Hill Ct ME17. . . . .195 B3
Haste Hill Rd ME17 . . . .195 B3
Hast Hill Ho BR2 . . . . . .85 B6
HASTINGLEIGH 271 B6
Hastings Ave CT9. . . . . .51 A1
Hastings Cl RM17. . . . . .17 E8
Hastings Ho SE18 . . . . . .1 F2
Hastings Pl CT13 . . . . .180 F8
Hastings Rd
  Maidstone ME15. . . . . .162 B3
  Newenden TN17, TN18 . .357 C6
  Orpington BR2 . . . . .85 E8
  Pembury, Kipping's Cross
  TN2 . . . . .287 F5
  Pembury TN2 . . . . .287 D6
  The Moor TN18 . . . . . .354 F6
Hastings St SE18 . . . . . . .2 C3
Hatches La TN11, TN12 224 D6
Hatch La CT4. . . . . .173 C5
Hatch Rd ME17 . . . . . . .199 C5
Hatch St 3 ME13 . . . . .138 C7
Hatfield Ct SE3. . . . . .11 A7
Hatfield Rd Margate CT9 50 G2
  Ramsgate CT11 . . . . . .117 D7
  Rochester ME2 . . . . . . .62 E3
Hatham Green La TN15 91 D1
Hathaway Ct
  Gillingham ME8. . . . . . . .98 D8
  Rochester ME1 . . . . . . .63 B5
Hatherall Rd ME14 . . . .162 B6
Hatherley Cres DA14. . . .31 A6
Hatherley Ct CT9 . . . . . .51 A3
Hatherley Rd DA14 . . . .31 A5
Hathern Gdns SE9 . . . . .30 A4

Hatmill La TN12 . . . . . .289 A7
Hattersfield Cl DA17. . . . .3 F2
Hatton Cl
  Northfleet DA11 . . . . . . .36 E5
  Woolwich SE18 . . . . . . .12 D7
Hatton Ct DA11. . . . . . . .29 F1
Hatton Mews 4 DA9. . . .17 C3
Hatton Rd ME5 . . . . .97 C3
Havant Wlk 8 ME15. . .195 F6
Havelock Pl CT3. . . . . . .147 E1
Havelock Rd
  Bromley BR2. . . . . .52 C5
  Dartford DA1 . . . . .15 B1
  Deal CT14 . . . . .215 C3
  Erith DA17. . . . . .3 F2
  Northfleet DA11 . . . . . . .36 F7
  Tonbridge TN9. . . . . . . .222 B2
Havelock St CT1. . . . . .143 A1
Haven Cl Eltham SE9 . . . .29 F5
  Istead Rise DA13 . . . . . .59 F8
  Rochester ME1. . . . . . . .63 C2
  Sidcup DA14 . . . . .31 C2
  Swanley BR8. . . . . .55 F7
Haven Dr
  Hawkinge CT18 . . . . . .307 A4
  Herne Bay CT6 . . . . .77 F6
Havengore Ave DA12 . . .37 E8
Haven Hill TN15 . . . . . . .92 A3
Haven Lodge 9 SE18. . . .2 B2
Haven St ME3 . . . . .40 C5
Haven The
  Ashford TN23 . . . . . . .299 F5
  Brenzett TN29. . . . . . . .363 A3
  Hythe CT21 . . . . .353 C8
Haventhorpe TN24 . . . .268 C3
Haven Way ME4 . . . . . . .41 B1
Havering Cl TN2. . . . . . .286 F6
Haverstock Ct 2 BR5 . .54 B7
Haverthwaite Rd BR6. . .86 D7
HAVIKER STREET. 226 E1
Havisham Cl ME1. . . . . . .63 D2
Havisham Rd DA12 . . . . .38 A7
Havock La 11 ME14. . . .161 F4
Hawbeck Rd ME8. . . . . . .98 C3
Hawden La TN11 . . . . . .221 F4
Hawden La TN11 . . . . . .221 F4
Hawden Rd TN9 . . . . . .222 B2
Hawe Cl CT2 . . . . .143 A4
Hawe Farm Way CT6 . . .77 B2
Hawe La CT2 . . . . .144 A7
Hawes Ave ME8. . . . . . .117 B7
Hawes Rd BR1 . . . . .52 B8
Hawfield Bank BR6. . . . .87 D7
Hawk Cl CT5 . . . . .108 C7
Hawks Way TN23 . . . . .299 E7
Hawkwell Bsns Ctr
  TN2 . . . . .255 F2
Hawkwell Cotts TN2. . .255 F2
Hawkwood ME16. . . . . .161 B5
Hawkwood Cl ME1 . . . . .63 D5
Hawkwood La BR7 . . . . .53 C8
HAWLEY 33 F3
Hawley Cl ME16 . . . . . .161 A4
Hawley Rd DA1, DA2,
  DA4. . . . . .34 A4
Hawley Sq CT9 . . . . . . .50 J2
Hawley St CT9 . . . . .50 J2
Hawley Terr DA2 . . . . . . .34 A4
Hawley Vale DA2. . . . . . .34 A4
Hawser Rd ME1. . . . . . . .63 C1
Hawstead La BR6. . . . . . .87 F5
Hawthorn ME26 . . . . . .361 D8
Hawthorn Ave
  Canterbury CT2 . . . . . .143 A2
  West Minst ME12 . . . . . .46 A8
Hawthorn Cl
  Aylesham CT3 . . . . . . .210 E4

Hawthorn Cl continued
  Crabble CT17 . . . . . . .277 E2
  Edenbridge TN8 . . . . . .217 C2
  Gravesend DA12. . . . . . .37 C4
  Hythe CT21 . . . . .353 E8
  Orpington BR5 . . . . .53 D3
  Ramsgate CT11 . . . . . . .83 E1
  St Mary's Bay TN29 . . . .365 F3
Hawthorn Cnr
  Herne Bay CT6 . . . . .78 A3
  Old Romney TN29. . . . .371 A3
HAWTHORN CORNER . .78 A3
Hawthorn Cotts
  DA16 . . . . .13 A4
Hawthornden Cl ME19 159 C3
Hawthorndene Cl BR2. .85 A8
Hawthorndene Rd BR2 .85 A8
Hawthorne Ave
  Biggin Hill TN16 . . . . . .118 D4
  Gillingham ME8. . . . . . . .65 C2
Hawthorne Cl
  Bromley BR1. . . . . .52 F6
  Eythorne CT15 . . . . . . .245 D7
Hawthorne Ho 4
  ME16. . . . . .161 A3
Hawthorne Rd ME1 . . . .52 F6
Hawthorn Ho
  5 Chatham ME5 . . . . .96 F5
  10 Sittingbourne ME10 101 E4
Hawthorn La TN13. . . . .153 F5
Hawthorn Pk BR8 . . . . . .56 A7
Hawthorn Pl DA8. . . . . . . .4 C1
Hawthorn Rd Bexley DA6 13 F7
  Dartford DA1 . . . . .33 D7
  Kingsnorth TN23 . . . . . .300 B4
  Rochester ME2 . . . . . . .62 E6
  Sittingbourne ME10 . . . .101 E4
Hawthorn Wlk
  Royal Tunbridge Wells
  TN2 . . . . .286 E8
  Tonbridge TN10. . . . . . .222 C7
Haxted Pl TN8. . . . . . . .217 C4
Haxted Rd TN8 . . . . .52 B8
Hayday Rd E16 . . . . .1 A8
Haydens Cl BR5 . . . . . . .54 C3
Haydens Mews TN9 . . .222 C3
Haydens The TN9 . . . . .222 C3
Haydon Cl ME1 . . . . . . .161 B4
HAYES 52 A8
Hayes Alley 17 CT5 . . . .74 D2
Hayesbrook Sch The 2
  TN9. . . . . .254 A8
Hayes Cl Hayes BR2 . . . . .85 A8
  High ham ME3 . . . . .39 C3
  West Thurrock RM20 . . . .17 C8
Hayes Cotts ME10 . . . . .101 E4
Hayesden La TN11, TN3 253 D5
Hayesford Park Dr BR2 52 A4
Hayes Gdn BR2 . . . . .52 A1
Hayes La Hayes BR2 . . . . .52 A4
  Stockbury ME9 . . . . . . .132 F6
Hayes Prim Sch BR2. . . .52 B1
Hayes Rd Bromley BR2. . .52 C5
  Stone DA9 . . . . .34 E8
Hayes Sch BR2. . . . . .85 B8
Hayes St BR2. . . . . .52 A1
Hayes Terr DA12 . . . . . .38 E3
Hayes Wlk ME19 . . . . . .159 A2
Hayes Wood Ave BR2. . .85 B8
Hayfield ME1 . . . . .127 E2
Hayfield Rd BR5. . . . . . . .54 A4
Hayfields ME5. . . . . .97 D2
Haygate Rd ME1 . . . . . . .63 C4
Hay Hill CT13, CT14. . . .180 D2
Hay Ho CT14 . . . . .180 F2
Hay La CT14. . . . . .180 F7
Hayle Mill Cotts ME15 .194 F8
Hayle Mill Rd ME15. . . .194 F6
Hayle Rd ME15 . . . . . . .162 A3
Hayley Cl ME2. . . . . .62 C2
Hayley Ho DA17 . . . . . . .14 A8
Haymakers La TN23 . . .299 D8
Haymans Hill TN12 . . . .290 C7
Hayman Wlk ME20. . . . .128 F6
Haymen St ME4 . . . . . . .63 B3
Haynes Ho 3 ME14. . . .162 B4
Haynes Rd
  Gravesend DA11. . . . . . .37 A6
  Northfleet DA11 . . . . . . .36 F5
Hayrick Cl ME14. . . . . . .162 E5
Haysden Ctry Pk★
  TN11. . . . . .253 D8
Haysel ME10 . . . . .102 A2
Hay's Mead DA13. . . . . . .60 F3
Hays Rd ME6 . . . . .127 F6
Hayton Rd TN25 . . . . . .304 A2
Haywain Cl
  Ashford TN23 . . . . . . .299 C5
  Maidstone ME14. . . . . .162 F4
  Paddock Wood TN12. . . .257 A5
Hayward Ave ME2 . . . . . .63 B8
Hayward Cl
  Ashford TN24 . . . . . . .301 A8
  Crayford DA1 . . . . .14 D2
  Deal CT14 . . . . .215 A4
Hayward Dr DA1 . . . . . . .33 F6
Hayward's Cl TN28 . . . .373 B6
Hayward's Hill ME13. . .169 C4
Hayward's Ho ME1. . . . . .63 B5
Haywood Ho BR2. . . . . . .52 D5
Haywood Rise BR6 . . . . .86 E5
Hazard Ho 4 DA11. . . . . .19 A1
Hazebrouck Rd ME13. .138 A7

Hazel Ave
  Hoo St Werburgh ME3 . . .41 E8
  Maidstone ME16 . . . . . .161 C5
Hazelbank TN3 . . . . . . .284 F3
Hazel Cl CT15 . . . . .245 C7
Hazel Cotts TN14 . . . . .121 A6
Hazel Ct Birchington CT7 .80 D8
  Hersden CT3 . . . . .144 D8
Hazelden Cl TN15 . . . . . .91 A2
Hazelden Cotts ME2. . . .39 C6
Hazeldene Rd DA16 . . . .13 C5
Hazeldown Cl CT17. . . .277 E2
Hazel Dr DA8. . . . . .15 B6
Hazel End BR8. . . . . .55 E4
Hazel Gr Chatham ME5. . .97 B8
  Orpington BR6 . . . . .86 B8
  Sheerness ME12 . . . . . .28 G1
Hazel Hts TN25 . . . . . . .267 E5
Hazelmere 8 DA14. . . . .31 A4
Hazelmere Rd BR5 . . . . .53 D5
Hazelmere Way BR2. . . .52 A3
Hazel Rd Dartford DA1. . .33 D6
  Erith DA8. . . . . .15 A6
Hazel Shaw TN10 . . . . .222 D7
Hazels The ME8 . . . . . . .98 B5
HAZEL STREET
  Horsmonden 289 F4
  Sittingbourne 133 A3
Hazel Street Rd ME9 . .133 A4
Hazelview ME19 . . . . . .126 E3
Hazel Wlk
  Broadstairs CT10 . . . . . .83 C4
  Bromley BR2. . . . . .53 A3
HAZELWOOD 119 D8
Hazelwood Cl TN2. . . . .286 D8
Hazelwood Cotts TN5 338 D1
Hazelwood Dr ME16 . . .161 B4
Hazelwood Hts RH8 . . .183 A4
Hazelwood Mdw CT13 .180 F7
Hazelwood Rd
  Downe TN14 . . . . .119 D8
  Oxted RH8. . . . . .183 B3
Hazelwood Sch RH8. . .183 A4
Hazen Rd ME19. . . . . . .159 B3
Hazen Road ME19 . . . .159 B3
Hazlemere Dr
  Gillingham ME7. . . . . . . .65 A5
  Herne Bay CT6 . . . . .77 D5
Hazlemere Rd CT5 . . . .108 A7
Hazling Dane CT15 . . . .244 F5
Hazlitt Ct 4 SE28 . . . . . .3 C5
Hazlitt Dr ME16 . . . . . .161 D5
Hazlitt Pl ME15 . . . . . . .195 B8
HEADCORN 262 D4
Headcorn Dr CT2 . . . . .143 B4
Headcorn Gdns CT9 . . . .51 E2
Headcorn Prim Sch
  TN27. . . . . .262 C5
Headcorn Rd
  Bromley BR1. . . . . .29 A3
  Gillingham ME8. . . . . . . .65 B4
  Lashenden TN27. . . . . .295 A5
  Platt's Heath ME17. . . .198 F1
  Smarden Bell TN27. . . .263 C3
  Staplehurst TN12 . . . . .261 B4
  Sutton Valence ME17 . . .229 E4
  Ulcombe ME17 . . . . . . .230 F5
Headcorn Sta TN27 . . .262 D4
Head Hill ME13 . . . . . . .139 D7
Head Hill Rd ME13. . . . .139 D8
Headingley Rd ME16 . .161 B6
Headley Ct TN8 . . . . . . .217 C2
Headley Ho 5 BR5. . . . . .54 B7
Head Race The ME5. . .161 D2
Headstock Rise ME3. . . .41 E7
Headway Ct TN4 . . . . . .285 B4
Healy Dr 1 BR6. . . . . . . .86 F6
Heansill La TN18 . . . . . .354 E8
Heard Way ME10 . . . . .102 B5
HEARNDEN GREEN. . . .230 B1
Hearne Cl ME10. . . . . . .102 B5
Hearne Cl 3 ME10 . . . .102 C5
Hearns Rd BR5 . . . . .54 C5
Heartenoak Rd TN18 . .341 B3
Heart in Hand Cnr CT3 .77 F2
Heart in Hand Rd CT6 . .77 F2
HEARTS DELIGHT 101 B1
Heart's Delight La CT3 146 B3
Hearts Delight Rd ME9 101 B1
Heathwood Dr TN23 . .267 E3
Heath Ave DA7 . . . . .13 D8
Heath Cl Orpington BR5 .54 C3
  Sturry CT2. . . . . .143 F7
  Swanley BR8. . . . . .55 E7
Heathclose Ave DA1. . . .33 B8
Heathclose Rd DA1. . . . .33 B7
Heathcote 1 ME20 . . . .128 F2
Heath Ct
  Horsmonden TN12 . . . .289 F6
  St Margaret's at Cliffe
  CT15 . . . . .279 F6
Heathdene Dr DA17 . . . .4 B2
Heathend Rd DA5 . . . . . .32 E7
Heatherbank
  Chislehurst BR7 . . . . . . .53 A7
  Eltham SE9 . . . . .11 F5
Heather Bank TN12. . . .257 B6
Heatherbank Cl DA1 . . .14 E1
Heather Cl Chatham ME5 96 F4
  Margate CT9. . . . . .82 C8
  Newham E6. . . . . .2 F7
  Sittingbourne ME10 . . . .102 A3
Heather Dr Dartford DA1 33 A8
  Maidstone ME16 . . . . . .162 B2
  Tenterden TN30 . . . . . .324 B3
Heather End BR8. . . . . . .55 D5
Heather Rd SE12 . . . . . .29 A7
Heatherside Rd DA14. . .31 C5
Heathers The TN17 . . . .320 A3
Heather Wlk TN10 . . . . .222 B6
Heatherwood Cl ME17 197 E2
Heath Farm Sch TN27. .233 D7

Heathfield
Chislehurst BR7 . . . . .30 C2
Langley Heath ME17. . 196 E4
Heathfield Ave
Dover CT16. . . . . 278 B2
Maidstone ME14. . . . . 162 C7
Heathfield Bglws
ME17. . . . . 200 B1
Heathfield Cl
Chatham ME5 . . . . .97 B7
Maidstone ME14. . . . . 162 B7
Newham ME16. . . . . .1 D8
Orpington BR2 . . . . .85 C5
Heathfield Ct DA14. . . .31 B3
Heathfield La BR7 . . . . .30 C2
Heathfield Rd
Ashford TN24 . . . . 268 C3
Bexley DA6 . . . . .13 F3
Maidstone ME14. . . . . 162 C7
Orpington BR2 . . . . .85 D5
Sevenoaks TN13 . . . . . 153 F5
Heathfields TN2. . . . . 286 D4
Heathfield Terr
Bexley SE18. . . . . .12 F8
Swanley BR8. . . . . .55 D7
Heathfield Way CT4 . .242 E8
Heath Gdns DA1. . . . . .33 C7
Heath Gr ME16 . . . . . 161 A2
Heath Ho CT1 . . . . . . .111 E5
Heath House DA15. . .30 F4
Heath La DA1, DA2 . . . .33 B7
Heathlands Rise DA1. . .15 B1
Heathlee Rd DA1. . . . . .14 E1
Heathley End BR7 . . . . .30 C2
Heathorn St ME14. . . 162 B5
Heath Park Dr BR1 . . . .52 E6
Heath Rd Coldblow DA5. .32 C7
Coxheath ME17. . . . . . 194 C3
Crayford DA1. . . . . .14 F1
East Farleigh ME15 . . . 193 E4
Langley Heath ME17. . 196 E4
Maidstone, Cock Street
    ME17. . . . . 195 C2
Maidstone, East Barming
    ME16. . . . . .160 F3
Heath Rise BR2. . . . . . .52 A3
HEATH SIDE. 32 F5
Heathside TN26 . . . . . 347 C1
Heath Side BR5. . . . . . .53 C2
Heathside Ave
Bexley DA7. . . . . .13 E5
Coxheath ME17. . . . . . 194 C4
Heath St DA1. . . . . .33 D8
Heath Terr TN12. . . . . 290 A6
Heath The
Appledore Heath
    TN26 . . . . 347 C1
Well Street ME19 . . . . .159 F5
Whitstable CT5. . . . . . . .75 B1
Heathview TN4. . . . . . 253 F2
Heathview Ave DA1 . . .14 E1
Heathview Cres DA1. . .33 B7
Heath View Dr SE2 . . . .13 D8
Heath Villas
Appledore Heath
    TN26 . . . . 347 C2
Woolwich SE18. . . . . .2 F1
Heathway SE3. . . . . . . .11 A7
Heath Way DA7, DA8 . .14 D6
Heathwood Gdns
Swanley BR8. . . . . .55 C7
Woolwich SE7. . . . . .1 E1
Heathwood Wlk DA5 . .32 E7
Heaton Rd CT1. . . . . . 174 F6
HEAVERHAM. 123 C2
Heaverham Rd TN15. . 123 C2
Heavitree Cl SE18 . . . . .2 D1
Heavitree Rd SE18. . . . .2 D1
Hectorage Rd TN9. . . . 254 D8
Hector St SE18 . . . . .2 E2
Hedge Barton Trailer Pk
    TN3. . . . . .283 F1
Hedgend Ind Est CT7 . .79 F3
Hedge Place Rd DA9 . .17 A1
Hedgerows TN23 . . . . 299 D7
Hedgerows The DA11. .36 E6
Hedgerow The ME14 .162 E5
Hedgers Way TN23 . . 299 D5
Hedges The ME14. . . . 162 A7
Hedley Ave RM20. . . . . .17 C8
Hedley St ME14. . . . . . 162 A6
Heeley Cl ME9. . . . . . . 134 E6
Heel La CT2. . . . . 143 C4
Heel Rd ME13 . . . . 192 A2
Hegarty Court ME6 . . . .94 F1
Heights Terr CT17 . . . . 310 C6
Heights The
Greenwich SE7. . . . . .1 C1
Whitstable CT5. . . . . . . 108 C6
Helding Cl CT6 . . . . .77 B2
Helegan Cl BR6. . . . . . . .86 F6
Helena Ave CT9 . . . . . . .82 E8
Helena Corniche CT20 334 C3
Helen Allison Sch DA13 60 A2
Helena Rd CT18 . . . . . . 308 C2
Helena Villas CT21. . . .334 B3
Helen Cl DA1. . . . . .14 A1
Helen Ct DA14. . . . . . . .31 B4
Helen Keller Cl TN10 . 222 D4
Helen St SE18 . . . . .2 B2
Helen Thompson Cl
    ME9. . . . . .68 E4
Hellegan Cl BR6. . . . . . .86 F6
Hellyar Ct ME1. . . . . . . .63 C4
Helmdon Cl CT12. . . . . .83 C2
Helvellyn Ave CT11. . . .117 B7
Hemmings Cl DA14. . . .31 B6
HEMPSTEAD. 98 A5
Hempstead Inf Sch
    ME7. . . . . .98 A5
Hempstead Jun Sch
    ME7. . . . . .98 A5
Hempstead La ME9. . .102 E3

Hempstead Rd ME7,
    ME8. . . . . .98 A5
Hempstead Valley Dr
    ME7. . . . . .98 A4
Hempstead Valley Sh Ctr
    ME7. . . . . .98 A3
Hempted St TN23. . . .268 B2
Henbane Cl ME14 . . . .162 E5
Henderson Dr DA1. . . .16 A3
Henderson Rd TN16. . 118 C7
Hendley Dr TN17. . . . . 320 C5
Hendry Ho ME3. . . . . . . .40 F6
Hendy Rd ME6 . . . . . . 128 B8
Henfield Cl DA5. . . . . . .14 A1
Hengist Ave CT9. . . . . . .51 B1
Hengist Rd
Birchington CT7 . . . . . . .80 C7
Deal CT14. . . . . 215 D7
Eltham SE12 . . . . .29 B8
Erith DA8. . . . . .14 C7
Westgate on Sea CT8. . .81 D8
Hengrove Ct DA5. . . . . .31 E1
Henham Gdns TN12 . . 225 A6
HENHURST. 60 E8
Henhurst Hill DA12. . . .60 D8
Henhurst Rd
Gravesend DA13. . . . . . .37 E1
Henhurst DA12. . . . . . . .60 E8
Heniker La ME17. . . . . 230 A4
Henley Bsns Pk ME2. . .63 D7
Henley Cl Chatham ME5. .97 A6
Gillingham ME8. . . . . . . .98 D8
Royal Tunbridge Wells
    TN2. . . . . 286 C4
Henley Ct DA5. . . . . . . .31 F8
Henley Deane DA11 . . .36 E4
Henley Fields
Maidstone ME14. . . . . 162 E6
Tenterden TN30 . . . . . . 324 B2
Henley Mdws TN30 . . 324 A2
Henley Rd Newham ME1. .1 F4
Paddock Wood TN12. . 257 A7
Henley St DA13. . . . . . . .60 F3
HENLEY STREET. 60 F3
Henley View TN30. . . . 324 B2
Henniker Cl CT16. . . . . 278 A5
Henniker Cotts TN17 . 320 A3
Henrietta Chase ME4 . .41 B2
Henry Addlington Cl E6 . 2 B8
Henry Cooper Way SE9 29 D4
Henry Ct CT1. . . . . .174 F7
Henrys Cl ME14 . . . . . . 192 D6
Henry St Bromley BR1 . .52 B8
Chatham ME4 . . . . .64 B3
Gillingham ME8. . . . . . . .66 A1
Grays RM17. . . . . .18 C8
Henson Cl BR6 . . . . .86 B8
Henville Rd BR1. . . . . . .52 B8
Henwick Prim Sch
    SE9. . . . . .11 E4
Henwick Rd SE9 . . . . . .11 E4
Henwood TN24. . . . . . 268 D3
Henwood Bsns Ctr
    TN24. . . . . 268 D2
HENWOOD GREEN. . .287 E6
Henwood Green Rd
    TN2. . . . . .287 E6
Henwood Ind Est
    TN24. . . . . 268 D3
Henwoods Cres TN2. . 287 D6
Henwoods Mount TN2 287 E6
Herald Wlk DA1 . . . . . . .15 F2
Herbert Dane Ct ME13. . . . . 138 D7
Herbert Pl SE18 . . . . . . .12 B8
Herbert Rd
Ashford TN24 . . . . 300 D6
Bexley DA7 . . . . .13 E5
Bromley BR2 . . . . .52 E4
Chatham ME4 . . . . .64 A3
Gillingham ME8. . . . . . . .98 E8
Hextable BR8 . . . . .33 B2
Ramsgate CT11 . . . . . . 117 C6
Swanscombe DA10. . . . .17 F1
Woolwich SE18. . . . . . . .12 B8
Herbert St CT17. . . . . . 278 B1
Herdsdown ME3. . . . . . .41 D5
Herdson Rd CT20. . . . . 335 A5
Hereford Cl
Ashford TN24 . . . . 268 C7
Gillingham ME8. . . . . . . .65 D2
Hereford Gdns CT7. . . .80 F6
Hereford Rd ME15. . . . 195 D7
Hereson Rd CT11. . . . . 117 F8
Hereson Sch The CT10. .84 A3
Hereward Ave CT7 . . . .80 E8
Heritage Cl CT5 . . . . . . 108 A6
Heritage Ct ME13 . . . . 174 F8
Heritage Dr ME7 . . . . . .64 F1
Heritage Gdns CT16 . .310 E8
Heritage Hill BR2. . . . . .85 C5
Heritage Quay DA12. . .19 C1
Heritage Rd
Chatham ME5 . . . . .97 A6
Folkestone CT20. . . . . . 334 D6
Heritage The BR6. . . . . .54 A2
Herlun Way ME7 . . . . . .65 A6
Herman Terr ME4 . . . . . .64 A3
Hermitage Cl
Hythe CT21. . . . . 333 B2
Woolwich SE2 . . . . .3 C3
Hermitage Cnr ME17 . 228 F6
Hermitage Ct
Maidstone ME16. . . . . .160 F5
Tonbridge TN9. . . . . . . 222 C2
Hermitage Farm ME19 159 C8
Hermitage La
Boxley ME14 . . . . .130 F2
Detling ME14 . . . . 131 B4

Hermitage La continued
Maidstone ME16, ME20 .160 F6
Rabbit's Cross ME17 . . 228 E6
Hermitage Rd ME3 . . . .39 E4
Hermitage The ME19. 159 D8
HERNE. 111 B8
Herne Ave CT6 . . . . .77 A4
HERNE BAY. 76 E6
Herne Bay High Sch
    CT6. . . . . .76 D3
Herne Bay Inf Sch CT6. .76 F4
Herne Bay Jun Sch CT6 76 F4
Herne Bay Mus Ctr
    CT6. . . . . .76 F5
Herne Bay Mus & Gall
    CT6. . . . . .76 F5
Herne Bay Rd
Sturry CT3. . . . . 110 E2
Whitstable CT5. . . . . . . .75 C3
Herne Bay Sta CT6 . . . .76 E3
Herne Bay West Ind Est
    CT6. . . . . .76 C3
Herne CE Jun Sch CT6 111 A8
Herne Cl CT19. . . . . 334 C6
Herne Dr CT6 . . . . .76 C2
Herne Inf Sch CT6. . . . 111 B8
HERNE POUND. 158 D2
Herne Rd ME8. . . . . .65 C2
Herne St CT6. . . . . 111 A8
Herneville Gdns CT6. . .77 B4
Herne Windmill CT6. . .77 B2
HERNHILL. 140 B6
Hernhill CE Prim Sch
    ME13. . . . . 140 B6
Hern The TN15 . . . . 157 C5
Hero Ho ME12. . . . . .28 B2
Heron Apartments
    ME15. . . . . .195 F5
Heron Bsns Ctr TN24. . 268 D3
Heron Cl
Lower Halstow ME9 . . . .67 B3
Marlpit Hill TN8. . . . . . . 217 C3
Heron Cotts TN8 . . . . . 357 D3
Heron Cres DA14 . . . . . .30 E4
Heron Ct BR2 . . . . .52 C5
HERONDEN. 179 E1
Heronden Rd
Eastry CT13 . . . . .179 F1
Maidstone ME15. . . . . 195 H8
Heronden View CT13 . 180 A2
Heron Dr ME12 . . . . .47 B5
Heron Forestall Ave
    CT18 . . . . 307 B4
Herongate Rd BR8 . . . . .32 E2
Heron Hill DA17 . . . . .3 F2
Heron Hill La DA13 . . . .93 A4
Heron Ho Ashford TN23 267 F1
Sidcup DA14 . . . . .31 A4
Heron Lodge CT16. .278 B2
Heron Rd ME20. . . . . . 127 F1
Heronsbank ME3 . . . . . .23 E4
Heron's Brook TN25 . 269 E6
Herons Ct CT4. . . . . 205 C8
Heronsgate Prim Sch
    SE28. . . . . .2 D3
Herons Park - Lydd Int
    Raceway TN29. . . . . . 376 C3
Herons Swimming Pool
    CT6. . . . . .76 F5
Herons Way TN2. . . . . 287 E8
Heron's Way CT21. . . . 353 D8
Heron Way Chatham ME5 97 B7
Lower Stoke ME3. . . . . . .25 C4
Heron Wlk TN23 . . . . . 299 E8
Hero Wlk ME1. . . . . .96 C7
Herringham Rd SE7 . . . .1 B7
Herschell Rd CT7. . . . . . .80 F8
Herschell Road E
    CT14 . . . . 215 C3
Herschell Road W
    CT14 . . . . 215 C3
Herschell Sq CT14. . . . 215 C3
HERSDEN. 111 F1
Hersden Com Prim Sch
    CT3. . . . . 111 E1
Hertford Ct CT1 . . . . . . 175 C8
Hertford Ho
Herne Bay CT6. . . . . .77 A5
Ramsgate CT11. . . . . 117 E6
Hertford Pl CT11. . . . . . 117 E6
Hertford Rd CT9. . . . . . .83 C8
Hertford St CT11. . . . . . 117 E6
Herts Cres ME15. . . . . . 194 F3
Hertsfield Ave ME4. . . .40 A2
Hertsfield Farm Cotts
    TN12. . . . . 228 B4
Hervey Rd SE3 . . . . .11 B6
Herying Cl ME2. . . . . . . .95 B4
Hesketh Ave DA2. . . . . .34 B7
Heskett Pk TN2 . . . . . . 287 E6
Hestia Way TN23 . . . . 299 E5
HEVER. 250 D6
Hever Ave TN15 . . . . . . .90 E4
Hever Castle & Gdns
    TN8. . . . . 250 D7
Hever CE Prim Sch
    TN8. . . . . 250 D6
Hever Cl ME15. . . . . . . .195 F6
Hever Court Rd DA12. . .34 C3
Hever Croft Eltham SE9. .30 A4
Rochester ME2. . . . . .47 C3
Hever Gdns Bromley BR1 53 A7
Maidstone ME15. . . . . 195 F6
Heverham Rd SE18. . . . .2 E2
Hever Ho ME2. . . . . .40 C1
Hever La TN8. . . . . 250 A4
Hever Mews ME1. . . . . .63 C3
Hever Pl
Canterbury CT2. . . . . . . 143 A3
Sittingbourne ME10 . . . 101 D3
Hever Rd
Bough Beech TN8. . . . . 218 D2
Hever TN8. . . . . 250 B7

Hever Rd continued
West Kingsdown TN15 . . .90 E4
Hever Road Cotts TN8 218 E2
Heversham Rd DA7. . . . .14 A6
Hever Sta TN8. . . . . 250 B6
Heverswood TN14. . . . . .88 A3
Hever Wood Rd TN15. . .90 E4
Hewett Ho SE18 . . . . . . .2 B1
Hewett Pl BR8. . . . . .55 D5
Hewett Rd Gillingham ME7 64 F6
Maidstone ME16. . . . . . 161 D7
Hewitt Cl Gillingham ME7 64 F6
Maidstone ME16. . . . . . 161 D7
Hewitt Rd CT16. . . . . . . 310 D8
Hewitts Pl TN24. . . . . . 268 F1
Hewitts Rd BR6, TN14 . .87 F3
HEXTABLE. 32 E1
Hextable Cl
Ashford TN23. . . . . 299 F6
Maidstone ME16. . . . . . 161 D7
Hextable Com Prim Sch
    BR8. . . . . .32 F2
Hextable Sch BR8 . . . . .55 F8
Heyford Cl CT18. . . . . . 307 B4
Hibbs Cl BR8. . . . . .55 D7
Hibernia Dr DA12. . . . . .37 F5
Hibernia Point SE2 . . . .3 D4
Hibernia St CT11. . . . . .117 E6
Hickin Cl SE7. . . . . .1 D2
Hickman Cl E16. . . . . . . .1 D8
Hickory Dell ME7. . . . . .98 A5
HICKS FORSTAL. 111 A4
Hicks Forstal Rd CT3. . 111 B5
Hide E6. . . . . .2 A7
Higgins' La ME4. . . . . . . .63 F5
HIGHAM. 39 B4
Higham Cl ME15. . . . . . 161 E2
Higham Gdns TN10. . . 222 F5
Higham La Bridge CT4 . 209 B8
Tonbridge TN10, TN11 . 222 F6
Higham Prim Sch ME3 . .39 C5
Higham Rd Cliffe ME3 . . .22 A4
Rochester ME3. . . . . .40 C3
Tonbridge TN11. . . . . . 222 F7
Higham School Rd
    TN10. . . . . 222 E6
Higham Sta ME3. . . . . . .39 D6
Higham View ME14. . . 129 E4
HIGHAM WOOD. 222 F6
High Bank ME1. . . . . . . .63 D2
High Banks ME15. . . . . 194 F5
Highbanks Cl DA16. . . . .13 B7
High Beeches
Orpington BR6. . . . . .87 A4
Royal Tunbridge Wells
    TN2. . . . . 286 D6
Sidcup DA14 . . . . .31 E3
Highberry ME19 . . . . . . 127 E2
Highbourne Pk ME17 . 200 C5
Highbrook Rd SE3. . . . . .11 A4
HIGH BROOMS. 286 C8
High Brooms Ind Pk
    TN2. . . . . .286 C8
High Brooms Rd TN4 . 286 C7
High Brooms Sta TN2 . 286 C7
Highbury Gdns CT12. . .83 B3
Highbury La TN30 . . . . 345 A7
Highbury Pl TN5 . . . . . .336 F5
Highbury Wlk CT12. . . .83 B2
Highcombe SE7 . . . . . . .11 B8
Highcombe Cl SE9 . . . . .29 E7
High Croft Cotts BR8 . .56 A5
Highcroft Gn ME15 . . . 195 F4
Highcroft Hall BR8 . . . . .55 D1
Highcross Rd DA13. . . . .35 D2
High Cross Rd TN15. . . 156 B1
High Dewar Rd ME1. . . .90 A8
Highdown Cotts TN17 .317 F3
High Elms ME8. . . . . .65 E1
High Elms Ctry Pk
    BR6. . . . . .86 D3
High Elms Rd BR6. . . . . .86 C2
Highfield Ave Erith DA8 .14 B8
Orpington BR6. . . . . .86 F5
Highfield Cl
Gillingham ME8. . . . . . . .98 D7
Hawkhurst TN18. . . . . . 341 A1
Hythe CT21. . . . . 333 A4
Pembury TN2 . . . . 287 D6
Ramsgate CT12. . . . . . . .83 B3
Rough Common CT2. . . 142 B3
Highfield Cotts DA2 . . .33 B2
Highfield Ct
Dartford DA1. . . . . .33 D8
Herne Bay CT6 . . . . .76 E4
Margate CT9 . . . . .51 B2
Ramsgate CT12. . . . . . . .83 B2
Highfield Gdns CT9. . . .50 H1
Highfield Ind Est CT19 335 F6
Highfield La TN24,
    TN25 . . . . 301 C6
Highfield Rd
Ashford TN24 . . . . 301 A8
Bexley DA6 . . . . .13 F2
Biggin Hill TN16 . . . . . . 118 C3
Bromley BR1. . . . . .52 F5
Dartford DA1 . . . . .33 D8
Gillingham ME8. . . . . . . .98 D7
Halfway Houses ME12. . .46 E6
Kemsing TN15. . . . . . . 122 F3
Ramsgate CT12. . . . . . . .83 B3
Royal Tunbridge Wells
    TN4 . . . . 286 C7
St Paul's Cray BR7. . . . . .53 F6
Highfield Road N DA1 . .33 D7
Highfields Ave CT6. . . . .77 D4
Highfields Rd TN8. . . . . 217 C4
Highfields View CT6. . . .77 C4
High Firs BR8 . . . . .55 E5
High Firs Prim Sch BR8 55 F5
Highgate Ct ME16. .340 F2
Highgate Hill TN18. . . . 340 F1
Highgate Rd CT5. . . . . . .75 B1
High Gr Bromley BR1 . . .52 D8

High Gr continued
Woolwich SE18. . . . . . . .12 D6
Highgrove TN2. . . . . . . 314 A5
Highgrove Cl BR7 . . . . . .52 E8
Highgrove Rd ME5 . . . . .97 A5
HIGH HALDEN. 324 D7
High Halden CE Prim Sch
    TN26. . . . . 324 E7
High Halden Rd TN26,
    TN27 . . . . 295 C2
HIGH HALSTOW. 23 F3
High Halstow National
    Nature Reserve ME3 23 E5
High Halstow Prim Sch
    ME23. . . . . .23 E3
High Hilden Cl TN10. . . 222 A4
High House La TN11. . . 190 C2
High Knocke TN29. . . . 366 B6
Highland Cl CT20. . . . . 334 F4
Highland Rd
Badgers Mount TN14 . . 121 B8
Bexley DA6 . . . . .14 A3
Chartham CT4. . . . . 173 D1
Maidstone ME15. . . . . 195 E6
Royal Tunbridge Wells
    TN2. . . . . 286 D7
Highlands Dartford DA1. .33 C8
Royal Tunbridge Wells
    TN2. . . . . 286 D7
Highlands Cl ME2. . . . . .62 D5
Highlands Cres TN29 . 366 A4
Highlands Glade CT12. .82 E1
Highlands Hill BR8. . . . .56 A8
Highlands Pk TN15. . . . 154 E6
Highlands Rd BR5. . . . . .54 C2
High Mdw CT17. . . . . . 278 C1
Highmead SE18 . . . . . . .12 F7
High Meads Rd E16 . . . . .1 D7
High Minnis CT4 . . . . . .272 F8
High Oak Hill ME9. . . . . 100 D8
Highpoint TN24. . . . . . 268 D3
High Point CT9. . . . . . . .30 E5
Highpoint Bsns Village
    TN25. . . . . 268 D3
High Rd DA2. . . . . .33 C5
Highridge
Gillingham ME7. . . . . . . .64 F1
Hythe CT21. . . . . 334 A3
High Ridge
Ashford TN23. . . . . 299 C7
Goudhurst TN17. . . . . . 318 E8
Highridge Cl ME14 . . . 162 F5
High Rocks TN3 . . . . . . 285 B1
High Rocks La TN3,
    TN4. . . . . .285 C1
High Rocks Sta TN3 285 B1
High St The TN27. . . . . 234 C7
High Snoad Wood
    TN25 . . . . 203 A1
High St Ashford TN23. . 268 C2
Aylesford ME20. . . . . . . 128 F3
Bean DA2. . . . . .35 B5
Bidborough TN3 . . . . . . 253 C3
Biddenden TN27 . . . . . 294 F1
Borough Green TN15 . . 156 F7
Brasted TN14, TN16 . . 152 C3
Brenchley TN12. . . . . . 289 B8
Bridge CT4 . . . . 176 A1
Broadstairs CT10 . . . . . .84 A4
Broadstairs, St Peter's
    CT10 . . . . .83 E5
Bromley BR1. . . . . .52 A6
Brookland TN29 . . . . . . 370 E8
Canterbury CT1. . . . . . 174 F8
Chatham, Brompton ME7 64 A6
Chatham ME4. . . . . .64 A4
Cowden TN8 . . . . 282 B5
Cranbrook TN17 . . . . . . 320 C4
Dartford DA1. . . . . .15 C1
Deal CT14. . . . . 215 D6
Dover CT16. . . . . 310 C8
Downe BR6. . . . . 119 A8
Dymchurch TN29. . . . . 366 C8
Eastchurch ME12 . . . . . .48 D3
East Malling ME19 . . . . 160 A6
Eastry CT13 . . . . 180 B2
Edenbridge TN8 . . . . . . 217 C1
Elham CT4. . . . . 273 F5
Eynsford DA4. . . . . .89 E8
Farningham DA4. . . . . . .56 F2
Flimwell TN5. . . . . 339 C3
Fordwich CT2. . . . . 144 A4
Forstal ME20. . . . . 129 A3
Frant TN3 . . . . 314 C4
Gillingham ME7. . . . . . . .64 C5
Gillingham, Rainham ME8 98 F8
Goudhurst TN17 . . . . . . 318 E8
Grain ME3. . . . . .27 B6
Gravesend DA11. . . . . . .19 B1
Grays RM17. . . . . .18 A4
Hadlow TN11. . . . . 223 E8
Halling ME2. . . . . .95 A4
Hawkhurst TN18. . . . . . 340 E2
Headcorn ME17. . . . . . 262 C5
Herne Bay CT6. . . . . .76 F5
Hythe CT21. . . . . 333 C2
Kemsing TN15. . . . . . . 123 B2
Lamberhurst TN3 . . . . . 317 B5
Leigh TN11. . . . . 220 F1
Lenham ME17 . . . . 199 D5
Limpsfield RH8 . . . . 183 B7
Littlebourne CT3. . . . . . 176 F7
Lower Stoke ME3 . . . . . . .25 C4
Lydd TN29. . . . . 376 C6
Lyminge CT18 . . . . 305 C6
Maidstone ME14. . . . . . 161 F4
Manston CT12. . . . . 116 D8
Marden TN12 . . . . 259 D6
Margate CT9. . . . . .50 I2
Margate, Garlinge CT9. . .81 B4
Minster (Sheppey) ME12 .47 D6
Minster (Thanet) CT12. 115 D1
Newington ME9 . . . . . . 100 C6
New Romney TN28 . . . 373 B6
Northfleet DA11. . . . . . . .18 C1

High St continued
Orpington, Broom Hill
    BR6. . . . . .54 A1
Orpington, Farnborough
    BR6. . . . . .86 C5
Orpington, Green Street Green
    BR6. . . . . .86 F4
Orpington, St Mary Cray
    BR5. . . . . .54 C4
Otford TN14 . . . . 122 A3
Pembury TN2 . . . . 287 C6
Penshurst TN11. . . . . . 252 B4
Queenborough ME11 . . .45 F5
Ramsgate CT11 . . . . . . 117 E7
Rochester ME1. . . . . . . .63 C6
Rochester, Strood ME2. .63 B7
Rochester, Upper Upnor
    ME2. . . . . .40 F1
Rolvenden TN17 . . . . . . 343 E4
Royal Tunbridge Wells
    TN1 . . . . 286 A2
Rusthall TN4 . . . . 285 C4
Sandwich CT13 . . . . . . 149 A1
Seal TN15 . . . . 154 F6
Sevenoaks, Chipstead
    TN13 . . . . 153 C5
Sevenoaks TN13 . . . . . 154 C2
Sheerness, Blue Town
    ME12 . . . . .28 A3
Sheerness ME12. . . . . . .28 C2
Shoreham TN14 . . . . . . .88 F1
Sidcup DA14 . . . . .31 A4
Sittingbourne, Milton Regis
    ME10 . . . . 101 E6
Snodland ME6. . . . . 128 A8
Staplehurst TN12 . . . . . 260 F3
St Margaret's at Cliffe
    CT15 . . . . 279 F6
Sturry CT2. . . . . 143 F5
Sutton Valence ME17 . . 229 E7
Swanley BR8. . . . . .55 F5
Swanscombe DA10. . . . .17 F2
Swanscombe, Greenhithe
    DA9 . . . . .17 B3
Temple Ewell CT16 . . . 277 D5
Tenterden TN30 . . . . . . 345 A4
Ticehurst TN5 . . . . 338 C1
Tonbridge TN9. . . . . . . 222 C2
Wadhurst TN5. . . . . 336 F4
Westerham TN16 . . . . . 184 C8
West Malling ME19. . . . 159 C8
Whitstable CT5. . . . . . . .74 D2
Wingham CT3 . . . . 178 A8
Wouldham ME1. . . . . . . .95 C5
Wrotham TN15. . . . . . . 125 A3
Wye TN25 . . . . 237 E2
Yalding ME18. . . . . 192 F1
HIGHSTEAD. 78 A1
Highstead Cres DA8. . . .14 E7
HIGHSTED. 134 F7
Highsted Gram Sch
    ME10. . . . . 101 F2
Highsted Rd ME9, ME10 101 F1
HIGHSTREET. 107 D2
HIGH STREET. 340 D2
Highstreet Rd
Waterham ME13 . . . . . . 107 D2
Yorkletts CT5, ME13. . . 107 E2
High Street St Gregory's
    CT1 . . . . 143 A1
High Street St Lawrence
    CT11. . . . . .117 B7
High Tor Cl BR1. . . . . . . .29 B1
High Tor View SE28 . . . .2 E5
High Trees DA2 . . . . .16 B1
High Trees Cl TN24. . . . 301 A8
Highview
Vigo Village DA13. . . . . 126 B8
Woolwich SE18. . . . . . . .12 B7
High View ME3. . . . . . . .39 C4
High View Ave CT6. . . . .76 B5
Highview Cl
Boughton Street
    ME13 . . . . 140 B3
Loose ME15 . . . . 195 A8
Highview Dr ME5. . . . . . .96 D5
Highview Rd
Minster (Sheppey)
    ME12. . . . . .47 C7
Sidcup DA14 . . . . .31 B4
Highview Sch CT19 . . . 335 D6
Highway Prim Sch The
    BR6. . . . . .87 C5
Highway The BR6 . . . . . .87 C5
Highwood Cl BR6. . . . . .86 C8
Highwood Dr BR6. . . . . .86 C8
Highwoods Cl ME3. . . . .39 C4
High Woods La TN3 . . . 287 B3
Highworth Gram Sch for
    Girls TN24. . . . . 268 C2
Hilary Cl Bexley DA8. . . .14 C6
Herne Bay CT6. . . . . .77 C4
Hilary Gdns ME1 . . . . . . .62 F1
Hilbert Cl TN2. . . . . 286 C5
Hilbert Rd TN2 . . . . 286 C5
Hilborough Way BR6. . .86 D5
Hilda May Ave BR8 . . . . .55 E7
Hilda Rd Chatham ME4. .64 C3
Halfway Houses ME12. . .46 D6
Hilda Vale Cl BR6. . . . . . .86 A6
Hilda Vale Rd BR6. . . . . .86 B6
Hilden Ave TN11. . . . . . 221 F4
HILDENBOROUGH. . . 221 E6
Hildenborough CE Prim
    Sch TN11. . . . . 221 D6
Hildenborough Cres
    ME16. . . . . 161 C7
Hildenborough Rd
Leigh TN11 . . . . 221 A3

Hildenborough Rd continued
Shipbourne TN11, TN15 188 E4
Hildenborough Sta
TN11 221 B6
Hildenbrook Farm
TN11 188 E2
Hilden Dr DA8 15 B7
Hildenfields TN10 222 A4
Hilden Grange Sch
TN10 222 B3
Hilden Oaks Sch TN10 222 B3
HILDEN PARK 221 F4
Hilden Park Rd TN11 221 F4
Hilders CI TN8 217 B4
Hildersham CI CT10 83 E5
Hilders La TN8 217 A4
Hilderstone Coll [2]
CT20 83 F5
Hillary Ave DA11 36 E5
Hillary Ct SE9 29 E6
Hillary Rd ME14 162 A7
Hill Ave CT15 244 E5
HILLBOROUGH 78 A4
Hillborough Ave TN13 154 D5
Hillborough Bsns Pk
CT6 77 F4
Hillborough Dr CT6 77 F5
Hillborough Gr ME5 97 A3
Hillborough Rd CT6 77 B5
Hill Brow Bromley BR1 52 D8
Crayford DA1 14 F1
Maidstone ME14 163 A5
Sittingbourne ME10 101 D2
Hillbrow Ave
Herne Bay CT6 77 B2
Sturry CT2 143 F7
Hillbrow CI DA5 32 D4
Hillbrow La TN23 267 F1
Hillbrow Rd
Ashford TN23 268 A1
Ramsgate CT11 117 D8
Hillbury Gdns TN5 338 D1
Hill Chase ME5 96 E3
Hill CI Chislehurst BR7 30 B3
Istead Rise DA13 36 E1
Hill Cres Aylesham CT3 210 E5
Coldblow DA5 32 C7
Lenham ME17 199 D5
Hillcrest Ashford TN23 299 B8
Four Elms TN8 218 B5
Hill Crest
Royal Tunbridge Wells
TN4 286 B8
Sevenoaks TN13 154 A5
Sidcup DA15 31 B8
Hillcrest Ave RM20 17 A8
Hillcrest CI TN24 268 E6
Hillcrest Dr Cuxton ME2 62 C2
Royal Tunbridge Wells
TN2 286 D7
Stone DA9 17 A3
Hillcrest Gdns
Deal CT14 215 A2
Ramsgate CT11 117 B6
Hillcrest Rd
Biggin Hill TN16 118 D3
Bromley BR1 29 A4
Chatham ME4 63 F2
Dartford DA1 32 F8
Hythe CT21 333 B3
Kingsdown CT14 248 D4
Littlebourne CT3 176 E8
Marlpit Hill TN8 217 C4
Orpington BR6 87 A8
Hillcroft DA4 89 D7
Hillcroft Rd
Herne Bay CT6 77 B3
Newham E6 2 B8
Hill Ct Charing TN27 201 E1
Chattenden ME3 40 F4
Hilden Shaw ME15 195 A8
Hilldown Lodge BR6 87 B8
Hill Dr CT13 180 B3
Hilldrop Rd BR1 29 B2
Hill End Orpington BR6 86 F8
Woolwich SE18 12 A6
Hiller CI CT10 84 A6
Hill Farm ME23 23 E3
Hillfield Rd TN13 153 E7
Hillfield PI TN13 153 E7
Hillfield Villas TN26 324 F8
Hillgarth TN4 286 A8
HILL GREEN 99 C1
Hill Green Rd ME9 132 D8
HILL HOATH 251 C6
Hill House Dr CT12 115 C7
Hill House Rd DA2 34 C8
Hillingdale TN16 118 B1
Hillingdon Ave TN13 154 D6
Hillingdon Rd
Bexley DA7 14 C4
Gravesend DA11 37 B6
Hillingdon Rise TN13 154 D5
Hill La CT18 306 B1
Hillman Ave CT6 76 A4
HILL PARK 151 B4
Hill Rd Burham ME5 96 A4
Dartford DA2 33 E6
Folkestone CT19 338 E6
Folkestone, Foord CT19 335 E7
Rochester ME1 63 A2
Wouldham ME1 95 F5
Hillreach SE18 1 F1
Hill Rise Ashford TN25 267 E6
Dartford DA2 34 E3
Hillsgrove CI DA16 13 C7
Hills Grove Prim Sch
DA16 13 C7
Hill Shaw DA3 58 F3
Hillshaw Cres ME2 62 D5
Hillside Dartford DA2 34 E3

Hillside continued
Erith DA17 4 C2
Farningham DA4 56 F2
[1] Folkestone CT20 334 E3
Rochester ME1 63 A2
Tonbridge TN9 254 A7
Hillside Ave
Canterbury CT2 142 C2
Gravesend DA12 37 D6
Rochester ME3 63 B8
Rushenden ME11 45 F3
Hillside Cotts
Newbury TN5 337 B8
Wingham CT3 146 A1
Hillside Ct Hythe CT21 333 C2
[2] Rochester ME2 63 A7
Swanley BR8 56 A5
Wateringbury ME18 192 E7
Hillside Dr DA12 37 A4
Hillside La ME4 85 A8
Hillside Prim Sch BR5 54 C2
Hillside Rd Chatham ME4 64 A4
Dartford DA1 15 A1
Dover CT17 278 A2
Kemsing TN15 122 F2
Minster (Sheppey) ME12 47 B7
Sevenoaks TN13 154 D4
Stalisfield Green ME13 201 E6
Tatsfield TN16 150 E8
Whitstable CT5 75 A1
Hillside St CT21 333 C2
Hillside Terr DA12 37 B7
Hillside The BR6 87 B2
Hills La TN15 123 C7
Hillsley Ct [1] DA14 31 A4
Hill St TN1 286 B5
Hillstone Ct [5] CT16 310 E8
Hill Terr ME4 63 F3
Hill The Charing TN27 234 D8
Cranbrook TN17 320 D4
Littlebourne CT3 176 F8
Northfleet DA11 18 C1
HILL TOP 257 B1
Hilltop Tonbridge TN9 254 B7
West Farleigh ME15 193 D3
Whitstable CT5 108 D7
Hill Top TN17 291 E5
Hill Top Cotts ME17 194 E2
Hilltop Gdns
Dartford DA1 15 F2
Orpington BR6 86 E8
Hilltop Ho CT2 142 C3
Hilltop Prim Sch ME2 40 C1
Hilltop Rd
Minster (Sheppey)
ME12 47 A5
Rochester ME2 40 C1
West Thurrock RM20 17 B8
Hill Top Rd CT6 77 B5
Hill View Ashford TN24 268 C3
Basted ME15 156 F4
Borough Green TN15 157 A7
Margate CT9 82 D7
Hill View CI TN15 157 A7
Hillview Cres BR6 53 F1
Hill View Ct CT4 209 E2
Hill View Dr Bexley DA16 12 E5
Woolwich SE28 2 E5
Hillview Ho DA12 37 C7
Hillview Rd
Canterbury CT2 142 C3
Eltham BR7 30 A4
Whitstable CT5 108 D7
Hill View Rd
New Barn DA3 59 B6
Orpington BR6 86 F8
Rusthall TN4 285 C4
Tonbridge TN11 221 F5
Hillview Sch for Girls
TN9 254 D8
Hill View Terr CT18 305 D3
Hill View Way ME5 96 E5
Hilldyeal Rd TN14 122 C4
Hillyfield CI ME2 39 F1
Hillyfield Rd TN23 300 A8
Hillyfields Rise TN23 268 A1
Hilton Bsns Ctr TN23 300 B6
Hilton CI ME13 138 D6
Hilton Dr ME10 101 B6
Hilton Rd Ashford TN23 267 F2
Cliffe Woods ME3 40 B7
Hinchliffe Way CT9 83 D8
Hind CI TN29 366 C8
Hind Cres DA14 14 D7
Hinde CI ME10 101 F7
Hinde Ho ME10 101 E6
Hines Terr ME5 64 C5
Hinksden Rd TN17,
TN18 341 F3
Hinksey Path SE2 3 D3
Hinstock Rd SE18 12 C7
Hinton CI SE9 29 E7
Hinton Cres ME7 98 A6
HINXHILL 269 D1
Hinxhill Rd TN24, TN25 269 D1
Hirst CI CT16 278 B4
Historic Dockyard The *
ME4 64 A8
Hitchen Hatch La
TN13 154 B4
Hither Chantlers TN3 285 A2
Hither Farm Rd SE3 11 C4
Hither Field TN27 234 C7
Hive The DA11 18 B1
HOADEN 146 F4
Hoades Wood Rd CT2 144 A7
Hoad Rd CT15, CT18 275 A2
Hoads Wood Gdns
TN25 267 E6
HOATH 111 F5
Hoath CI ME8 98 B7
HOATH CORNER 251 B3

Hoath Farm The CT3 175 F7
Hoath La ME8 98 B7
Hoath Mdw TN12 290 A6
Hoath Prim Sch CT3 111 E5
Hoath Rd CT3 111 C3
Hoath Way ME7 98 B5
Hobart Cres CT16 278 A4
Hobart Gdns ME10 101 C4
Hobart Rd
Ramsgate CT12 83 A1
Tilbury RM18 19 A6
Hoblands End BR7 30 E2
HOCKENDEN 55 B6
Hockenden La BR8 55 B7
HOCKER EDGE 292 D2
Hockeredge Gdns CT8 81 F8
Hockers CI ME14 163 A8
Hockers La ME14 163 A8
HOCKLEY 169 C3
Hoddesdon Rd DA17 4 A1
Hodge's Gap CT9 51 C3
Hodgkins CI SE28 3 D6
Hodgson Cres ME6 95 A1
Hodgson Rd CT5 107 F7
Hodsoll Ct BR5 54 D4
Hodsoll St TN15 92 D1
Hodson Cres ME5 54 D3
Hogarth CI
Herne Bay CT6 77 E5
Newham E16 1 D8
Hogarth Ho ME11 45 F5
Hogarn La ME14 166 A3
Hogben CI CT18 305 B7
Hogg La CT4 207 E2
Hog Gn CT4 273 F4
Hog Hill ME14 163 B5
Hoghole La TN3 316 F2
Hog La DA11 36 D5
Hogpound Cnr TN30 360 B6
Hogs Orch BR8 36 A8
Hogtrough Hill TN16 152 A5
Holbeach Gdns DA15 12 F1
Holbeam Rd ME13 169 A1
Holborn Coll SE7 1 D2
Holborn La ME4 63 F5
Holborn Rd E13 1 B8
HOLBOROUGH 95 A2
Holborough Rd ME6 95 A1
Holbrook CI TN6 201 B8
Holbrook Dr CT12 83 B1
Holbrook Ho BR7 53 D8
Holbrook La BR7 30 D1
Holbrook Way BR2 52 F4
Holburne CI SE3 11 C6
Holburne Gdns SE3 11 D6
Holburne Rd SE3 11 D6
Holcombe CI TN16 151 D1
Holcombe Rd
Chatham ME4 63 F2
Rochester ME1 63 C3
Holcote CI DA17 3 E3
Holden Cnr TN4 253 F1
Holdenhurst TN23 299 E6
Holden Park Rd TN4 286 A8
Holden Rd TN4 253 F1
Holder CI ME5 97 C6
Holding St ME8 65 F1
Hole La TN8 217 A6
Hole Park * TN17 343 C6
Holford St [1] TN9 222 B1
Holgate St SE7 1 D3
Holiday Sq CT9 50 I3
HOLLAND 183 A1
Hollandbury Pk ME19 159 C2
Holland CI
Broadstairs CT10 51 G2
Sheerness ME12 28 B1
Holland Cres RH8 183 A2
Holland Ho ME1 63 D5
Holland Jun Sch RH8 183 A1
Holland La RH8 183 A1
Holland Rd Chatham ME5 96 E4
Maidstone ME14 162 B5
Oxted RH8 183 A1
Hollands Ave CT19 335 F7
Hollands CI DA12 38 E3
Hollicondane Rd CT11 117 E8
Hollies Ave DA15 30 F7
Hollies The
Gravesend DA12 37 D2
Hurst Green RH8 183 B2
New Barn DA3 59 C6
Sidcup DA15 31 A8
Holligrave Rd BR1 52 A8
Hollin CI ME4 285 F4
HOLLINGBOURNE 164 E2
Hollingbourne Ave CT7 13 F6
Hollingbourne Hill
ME17 164 F4
Hollingbourne Prim Sch
ME17 164 E2
Hollingbourne Sta
ME17 164 C3
Hollingbourne Tower [4]
BR5 54 D1
Hollington Ct BR7 30 D1
Hollington PI TN24 300 A8
Hollingworth Ct ME14 162 C3
Hollingworth Rd
Maidstone ME15 195 D5
Orpington BR2, BR5 53 B2
Hollingworth Way
TN16 151 D1
Hollow La
Canterbury CT1 174 E5
Hartlip ME9 99 E5
Snodland ME6 127 F6
Hollow Rd CT3 112 B6

Hollow St CT3 112 C5
HOLLOW STREET 112 C4
Hollow Trees Dr TN11 221 A1
Hollow Wood Rd CT17 309 E8
Holly Bank TN12 289 B8
Hollybank Hill ME10 101 D4
Hollybrake CI BR7 30 D1
Hollybush CI TN13 154 C3
Hollybush Cnr CT4 177 A3
Hollybush St TN13 154 C3
HOLLYBUSHES 167 A8
Hollybush La
Chelsfield BR6 88 A4
Wickhambreaux CT3 145 A4
Holly Bush La TN13 154 C3
Hollybush Rd DA1 33 C7
Holly CI Broadstairs CT10 83 C4
Chatham ME5 97 C8
Eastry CT13 180 B2
Folkestone CT19 335 A6
Hythe CT21 333 B3
Holly Cl [1] DA4 31 B4
Hollydale Dr BR2 85 F7
Hollydene ME5 336 F6
Holly Dr ME12 47 B4
Holly Farm Rd ME15 196 C6
Holly Gdns Bexley DA7 14 C3
Maidstone ME14 162 B7
Margate CT9 51 C2
Holly Hill DA13 93 F3
Holly Hill Rd
Erith DA8, DA17 4 B1
Hernhill ME13 140 D5
Holly La CT9 51 C2
Holly Mdws TN13 267 D3
Holly Rd Dartford DA1 33 D7
Orpington BR6 87 A3
Ramsgate CT11 117 E8
Rochester ME2 40 D2
Rochester, Strood ME2 62 C5
St Mary's Bay TN29 365 F4
Hollyshaw TN12 286 C2
Hollyshaw Ct TN12 286 C2
Hollytree Ave BR8 55 E7
Holly Tree CI ME7 197 E2
Hollytree Dr ME3 39 B3
Hollytree Par DA14 31 C2
Hollywood La
Knockmill TN15 123 F8
Rochester ME2 40 C2
Hollywood Way DA8 15 B6
Holman Mews CT1 175 A4
Holmbury Manor [2]
DA14 31 A4
Holmbury Pk BR7 29 E1
Holmcroft Way BR2 52 F4
Holm Ct [5] SE12 29 B5
Holmdale Rd BR7 30 C3
Holmden Ct [2] TN8 217 C1
Holmdene Ct [5] BR1 52 E6
Holme Oak CI CT1 174 F6
Holmes CI ME23 23 E3
Holmes Ct
[5] Canterbury CT1 175 B8
Ryarsh ME19 126 F4
Holmesdale Rd
Durgates TN5 336 E5
Maidstone ME15 194 F3
Holmesdale Hill DA4 57 D8
Holmesdale Rd
Bexley DA7 13 D5
Sevenoaks TN13 154 D4
Sutton at Hone DA4 57 C8
Holmesdale Tech Coll
ME6 127 F7
Holmestone Rd CT17 277 E1
Holmes Way CT21 83 A3
Holmewood House Sch
TN3 285 A2
Holmewood Rd TN4 286 C7
Holmewood Ridge
TN3 284 F3
Holmhurst CI TN4 285 F4
Holmhurst Rd DA17 4 B1
Holmlea CI TN24 268 E1
Holmleigh Ave DA1 15 C2
Holm Mill La ME17 198 B6
Holm Oak Gdns CT10 83 F4
Holmoaks
Gillingham ME8 65 E2
Maidstone ME14 162 C5
Holmscroft Rd CT6 77 D5
Holmsdale Gr DA1, DA7 14 E4
Holmside ME7 64 E3
Holmside Ave ME12 46 D6
Holm Wlk SE3 11 A5
Holmwood Cotts BR6 87 C1
Holmwood Ct DA14 30 D3
Holmwood Rd TN23 299 E7
Holmwood Villas [8] SE7 1 A1
Holness Rd E13 147 D2
Holstein Way [6] DA18 3 E3
Holt CI Ashford TN23 299 C8
Sidcup DA14 31 E4
Holt St CT15 211 C4
Holt Wood Ave ME20 160 E8
Holtwood CI ME8 98 D6
HOLTYE 281 F3
Holtye Cres ME15 162 B2
Holtye Rd RH19 281 A4
Holwood Park Ave BR2,
BR4 85 F6

Holy Family RC Prim Sch
SE3 11 C1

Holy Family RC Prim Sch
The ME15 195 F4
Holyhead CI [3] E6 1 F8
Holy Innocents RC Prim
Sch BR6 86 F7
Holyoake Terr TN13 154 A3
Holyrood Dr ME12 47 A5
Holyrood Mews E16 1 A5
Holy Trinity CE Prim Sch
Dartford DA1 15 C2
Gravesend DA12 37 C8
Holy Trinity Coll Prep Sch
BR1 52 C8
Holy Trinity Lamorbey CE
Prim Sch DA15 31 A3
Holy Trinity & St Johns CE
Prim Sch [4] CT9 50 J2
Holywell Ave CT19 335 D8
Holywell CI
Greenwich SE3 11 A8
Orpington BR6 87 A6
Holywell Ho CT19 335 D8
Holywell La ME9 66 A6
Holywell Prim Sch ME9 66 F3
Homebirch Ho [6] CT7 80 F8
Homedean Rd TN13 153 C4
Home Farm BR6 88 A5
Home Farm CI TN11 221 A3
Home Farm Cotts
East Studdal CT14 213 E6
Orpington BR5 54 D8
Home Farm Ct TN3 314 C4
Homefarm Est ME20 128 F1
Home Farm La TN2 286 B8
Homefern Ho CT9 50 I3
Homefield Ave CT14 215 B6
Homefield CI
Orpington BR5 54 B5
Swanley BR8 55 F6
Homefield Dr ME8 66 B2
Homefield Rd
Bromley BR1 52 C8
Sevenoaks TN13 153 E5
Homefield Row CT14 215 B6
Homefleet Ho [13] CT11 117 F2
Home Gdns DA1 15 E1
Home Hill BR8 32 C5
Homelands CI TN25 303 D1
Home Lea BR6 86 F5
Homeleigh Rd CT12 83 B3
Homemead
[7] Gravesend DA12 37 B8
Swanscombe DA9 17 B1
Home Mead CI [6] DA12 37 B8
Homemead Rd BR2 52 F4
Homepeak Ho [12] CT21 333 B2
Homepine Ho [5] CT20 335 C4
Home Pk RH8 183 A4
Homer CI DA7 14 C6
Homersham CT1 174 D6
Homesdale Bsns Ctr
BR1 52 D6
Homesdale Rd
Bromley BR1, BR2 52 C6
Orpington BR5 53 E2
Homeside Farm CT4 240 F6
Homespire Ho [18] CT1 143 A1
Homestall CT2 142 C4
Homestall La ME13 139 B5
Homestall Rd ME9 136 D3
Homestead TN23 299 D8
Homestead CI [7] CT9 50 J1
Homestead La CT15 246 C7
Homestead Rd
Marlpit Hill TN8 217 B5
Orpington BR6 87 B4
Homestead The
Crayford DA1 14 E2
Dartford DA1 15 C1
Groombridge TN3 312 C2
Homestead View ME9 101 B2
Homestead Village
CT11 117 C5
Homevale Cotts TN14 120 E4
Homevale Ho [3] CT20 334 E3
Homeview [3] ME10 102 B4
Homeview Terr [2]
ME10 102 B4
Homewards Rd ME3 9 B2
Homewood Ave ME10 101 D3
Homewood Cotts DA12 37 B3
Homewood Cres BR7 30 C2
Homewood Rd
Langton Green TN3 284 F3
Sturry CT2 144 A6
Tenterden TN30 324 B1
Homewood Sch TN30 324 B1
Homlesdale Bsns Ctr
TN15 157 C8
Honduras Terr [8]
ME14 162 A7
Hone St ME2 63 B8
Honesty CI ME9/ME10 101 F1
Honeyball Wlk ME5 103 C2
Honeybourne Way BR5 53 D1
Honey CI ME7 98 A5
Honeycombe Lodge [7]
DA11 18 D1
Honeycrest Ind Pk
TN12 260 E5
Honeycrock Hill ME9 132 F8
Honeyden Rd DA14 31 E2
Honeyfield TN23 267 E1
HONEY HILL 141 E8
Honey Hill CT2, CT5 141 F8
Honey La ME15 196 B6
Honeypot CI ME2 63 D8
Honeypot La
Hodsoll Street TN15 92 D2
Kemsing TN15 155 C8
Limpsfield TN8 216 D4

Honeysuckle CI
[3] Chatham ME5 96 A5
Gillingham ME7 97 F4
Margate CT9 82 C8
Honeysuckle Ct
[4] Lewisham SE12 29 A8
Sittingbourne ME10 102 B5
Honeysuckle Rd CT11 117 F8
Honeysuckle Way CT6 77 D2
Honeywood CI
Canterbury CT1 143 F5
Dover CT16 278 A6
Lympne CT21 332 A4
Honeywood Ho CT16 278 A6
Honeywood Parkway
CT16 278 B5
Honeywood Rd CT16 278 A5
Honfleur Rd CT13 180 F8
Honiton Rd DA16 12 F5
Honner CI CT18 306 F3
Honywood Rd ME17 199 C4
HOO 114 F6
Hoo Comm ME3 41 A4
Hood Ave BR5 54 B4
Hoo Farm CT12 114 F6
Hook CI Chatham ME5 96 E5
Folkestone CT20 334 F5
Hook Farm Rd BR2 52 D4
Hookfields DA11 36 E5
HOOK GREEN Dartford 33 A4
Lamberhurst 316 C4
Meopham Station 60 A3
Northfleet 36 A2
Hook Green Ct DA13 60 A4
Hook Green La DA2 32 F5
Hook Green Rd DA13 35 F1
Hook Hill TN5 338 A6
Hook La Bexley DA16 13 A4
Brookland TN29 370 C6
Charing TN27 234 A7
Harrietsham ME17 198 C6
Hook Lane Prim Sch
DA16 13 A4
Hook Place Cotts DA13 36 A2
Hook Rd ME6 127 F8
Hookstead TN26 324 C7
Hook Wall TN29 370 E5
Hookwood Bglws RH8 183 B7
Hookwood Cnr RH8 183 B7
Hookwood Cotts TN14 120 C8
Hookwood Rd BR6,
TN14 120 C7
Hooper Rd E16 1 A7
Hoopers La
Herne Bay CT6 77 D3
St Mary Hoo ME3 24 F5
Hooper's PI ME1 63 C4
Hooper's Rd ME1 63 C4
Hoopers Yd TN13 154 C1
Hoo Rd ME2, ME3 40 D3
HOO ST WERBURGH 41 D5
Hoo St Werburgh Prim Sch
ME3 41 D5
Hop Bine CI TN12 225 A7
Hope Ave TN11 190 E1
Hope CI SE12 29 B5
Hope Cotts DA2 35 B6
Hopedale Rd SE7 11 B8
Hopehouse La TN17,
TN18 356 E7
Hope La
New Romney TN28 373 A8
St Mary in the Marsh
TN29 364 F2
Hope Rd Deal CT14 215 D5
Swanscombe DA10 17 F1
Hopes Gr TN26 324 D7
Hope's La CT12 83 C3
Hope St Chatham ME4 64 A3
Maidstone ME14 161 F6
Sheerness ME12 28 B2
Hope Terr ME3 9 B2
Hope View Sch CT4 205 D8
Hope Villas CT1 174 D6
Hope Way ME12 102 A4
Hopeville Ave CT10 83 E6
Hopewell Bsns Ctr ME5 97 C8
Hopewell Dr
Chatham ME5 97 C8
Gravesend DA12 37 F3
Hop Farm Family Pk *
TN12 225 A3
Hopgarden CI
Lamberhurst TN3 317 A5
[12] Marlpit Hill TN8 217 B3
Hopgarden La TN13 187 A8
Hopgarden Oast ME18 192 F1
Hopgarden Rd TN10 222 D6
Hop Garden Way CT1 174 E6
Hop Gdn TN26 347 C1
Hoppers Cnr ME15 193 D7
Hoppers Way TN9 299 D8
Hop Pocket CI TN17 321 A8
Hop Pocket La TN12 256 F7
Hopsons PI ME12 47 C5
Hopton CI BR2 52 A1
Hopton Rd SE18 2 B3
Hopwood Gdns TN4 286 A6
Horace Rd ME2 62 E5
Horatio PI ME1 63 B4
Horizon CI TN4 286 B8
Horizon Prim Sch BR8 55 E7
Horley CI DA6 14 A2
Horley Rd SE9 29 E4
Hornash La TN26 327 D8
Hornbeam Ave
Chatham ME5 97 B2
Royal Tunbridge Wells
TN4 254 D1
Hornbeam CI
Ashford TN23 267 F3
Larkfield ME20 128 B2
Paddock Wood TN12 256 F5
Hornbeam Ho [6] DA15 31 A5

Hornbeam La DA7......14 C5
Hornbeam Prim Sch
  CT14......214 F4
Hornbeams DA13...126 B8
Hornbeam Way BR2...53 A3
Hornbrook La TN26...347 C7
Horncastle CI SE12....29 A8
Horncastle Rd SE12...29 A8
Horne Ho SE18......11 E6
Horne's Place Chapel★
  TN26......347 D2
Hornet CI CT10......83 D3
Hornfair Rd SE7......11 D7
Hornfield Cotts DA13...93 C3
Horn Hill ME9......134 E2
Horning CI SE9......29 E4
Horn La SE10......1 A2
Horn Link Way SE10...1 A2
Horn Park CI SE12......11 B2
Horn Park La SE12......11 B1
Horn Park Prim Sch
  SE12......29 B8
HORNS GREEN......119 E2
Horns La ME18......158 C1
Horns Lodge Farm
  TN11......222 C8
Horns Lodge La TN11. 222 A8
Horn's Oak Rd DA13...93 B6
Horns Rd TN18......354 E8
Horn St CT19, CT20,
  CT21......334 B4
HORN STREET Ditton . 127 D6
  Folkestone......334 B4
Horn Yd [7] DA11......19 B1
Horsa Rd Birchington CT7 80 D7
  Deal CT14......215 D8
  Eltham SE12......29 C8
  Erith DA8......14 C7
Horsebridge Rd CT5...74 D2
Horsecroft CI BR6......54 B1
Horsegrove Ave TN5..338 F1
Horse Leaze E6......2 A7
HORSELEES......140 A2
Horselees Rd ME13...140 A2
Horsell Rd BR5......54 B8
Horseshoe CI
  Gillingham ME7......97 F5
  Maidstone ME14......162 E5
HORSESHOE GREEN..250 E1
Horseshoes La ME17 196 E8
Horse Wash La ME1...63 C6
Horsfeld Gdns SE9...11 E2
Horsfeld Rd SE9......11 D2
Horsfield CI DA2......34 C8
Horsford Wlk ME13...138 A8
Horsham Hill ME9......66 E4
Horsham Rd DA6......14 A2
Horshams The CT6......77 D5
Horsley CI CT18......307 B4
Horsley Ho SE18......12 A7
Horsley Rd Bromley BR1. 52 B8
  Rochester ME1......63 B4
HORSMONDEN......290 A5
Horsmonden CI BR6...53 F2
Horsmonden Prim Sch
  TN12......290 A6
Horsmonden Rd TN12 289 D6
Horsted Ave ME4......63 E1
Horsted Inf Sch ME4...96 B5
Horsted Jun Sch ME5..96 B5
Horsted Ret Pk ME5...96 D5
Horsted Way ME1......96 D7
HORTON......173 F3
Horton Cotts CT4......173 E4
Horton Downs ME15..162 F1
Horton Gdns CT4......173 E4
HORTON KIRBY......57 D7
Horton Kirby CE Prim Sch
  DA4......57 C6
Horton PI TN16......151 D1
Horton Rd DA4......57 C6
Hortons CI TN17......342 D7
Hortons Way [1] TN16. 151 D1
Horton Tower [2] BR5..54 C5
Horton Way DA4......56 F2
Horwood CI ME1......96 B8
Hoselands View DA3...58 E8
Hoser Ave SE12......29 A6
Hoser Gdns CT7......81 A7
Hosey Common La
  TN16......184 F5
Hosey Common Rd TN8,
  TN16......184 D5
Hosey Hill TN16......184 E8
Hoskin's CI E16......1 C7
Hospital Hill CT20,
  CT21......334 C4
Hospital La
  Canterbury CT1......174 F8
  [3] Chatham ME1......63 E4
Hospital Meadow Cotts
  CT3......178 D2
Hospital Rd
  Hollingbourne ME17... 197 C8
  Sevenoaks TN13......154 C6
Hostier CI ME2......95 B4
Hotel Rd Gillingham ME8 .65 A2
  St Margaret's at Cliffe
  CT15......280 B6
Hotham CI
  Sutton at Hone DA4...34 B1
  Swanley Village BR8...56 B8
HOTHFIELD......267 A4
Hothfield Common Nature
  Reserve★ TN26...266 F8
Hothfield Rd ME8......65 F1
Hottsfield DA3......58 E6
Hougham Court La
  CT15......309 A3
Hougham Ho [11] BR5..54 D1
Houghton Ave ME7......98 B3
HOUGHTON GREEN.. 368 D2

Houghton Green La
  TN31......368 C2
Houghton Ho CT19...335 C5
Houghton La TN31...368 C3
Housefield TN24......268 C7
Housefield Rd ME13.. 202 C6
Houselands Rd TN9...222 B2
House Mdw TN23......299 C7
Hove CI RM17......18 A8
Hovenden CI CT1......143 A4
Hovendens TN17......321 A4
Hoveton Rd SE28......3 C7
Howard Ave
  Sidcup DA5......31 C8
  Sittingbourne ME10..101 D6
Howard CI ME12......47 C7
Howard Dr ME16......161 B5
Howard Gdns TN2......286 A1
Howard Rd
  Broadstairs CT10......84 A3
  Bromley BR1......29 A1
  Dartford DA1......16 A1
  East Malling ME19...159 E5
Howard Sch The ME8..98 D8
Howarth Rd SE2......3 A2
Howbury Ctr PRU The
  DA8......15 A7
Howbury La DA8......15 B7
Howbury Wlk ME8......98 D4
Howells CI CT15......90 E4
Howerd Way SE18......11 E6
Howes Cotts TN18....354 F8
Howfield La CT4......173 E5
HOW GREEN......218 C1
How Green La TN8...218 C2
Howick CI ME20......160 F8
Howick Mans SE18......1 E3
Howland Mews CT1...174 E6
Howland Rd TN12...259 E6
Howlands TN15......124 F4
Howlands CI TN15...124 F4
Howletts Oast CT4...176 C5
Howletts Wild Animal Pk★
  CT4......176 D6
Howlsmere CI ME2......95 B3
Hoxton CI TN23......299 D8
Hoystings CI The CT1. 175 A7
Hubbards Cotts.......66 C2
Hubbards Hill ME17... 200 B6
Hubbard's Hill TN13,
  TN14......187 B4
Hubbard's La ME15...195 C3
Hubble Dr ME15......195 E7
Hubert Way CT10......83 E6
Huckleberry CI ME5...97 B3
Hudson CI
  [7] Dover CT16......278 B3
  Gillingham ME8......65 C1
  Sturry CT2......143 F6
Hudson Ho DA4......57 D7
Hudson PI SE18......2 C1
Hudson Rd Bexley DA7..13 F6
  Canterbury CT1......143 B2
Huggen's College
  Almshouses DA11....18 B2
Hugh Christie Tech Coll
  TN10......222 D6
Hughes Dr ME2......40 D2
Hugh PI [5] ME13......138 D7
Hugh Price CI ME10.. 102 C5
Hugin Ave CT10......83 E7
Hulberry Farm DA4....89 B8
Hulkes La ME1......63 E4
Hull PI Deal CT14......214 F6
  Newham E16......2 C5
Hull Rd TN29......377 E6
Hulsewood CI DA2......33 B5
Hulsons CI [1] TN18...341 A2
Humber Ave ME4......75 F4
Humber Cres ME2......62 F7
Humber Rd Dartford DA1 15 D2
  Greenwich SE3......11 A8
Humboldt CI TN2......286 D5
Hume Ave RM18......19 B5
Hume CI RM18......19 A4
Hume Ct CT21......333 D1
Hume Terr E16......1 B7
Humphreys TN12......288 F6
Humphrey Terr CT18..306 F4
Hundred of Hoo Sch The
  ME3......41 C5
Hundreds CI CT8......81 D7
Hunger Hatch La TN27 233 F4
HUNGERSHALL PARK 285 E2
Hungershall Park CI
  TN4......285 E1
Hungershall Pk TN4.. 285 E2
Hunsdon Dr TN13....154 B4
Hunstanton CI ME8...98 E3
Hunt CI CT18......307 A4
Hunter Ave TN24......300 E8
Hunter CI TN24......300 E8
Hunter Rd TN24......268 E1
Hunters Bank CT4....273 F4
Hunters Chase
  Herne Bay CT6......77 C2
  Whitstable CT5......108 E7
Hunters CI DA3......32 E5
Hunters Ct [5] ME7......64 C7
Hunter Seal TN11......221 E2
Huntersfield CI ME5...97 C1
HUNTERS FORSTAL...77 C2
Hunters Forstal Rd CT6 77 C2
Hunter's Gr BR6......51 D8
Hunters Lodge [10] DA15 31 A5
Hunters Way
  Gillingham ME7......64 E1
  Marlpit Hill TN8......217 B2
  Royal Tunbridge Wells
  TN2......285 F1

Hunters Way continued
  Sheldwich ME13......170 C5
Hunters Way W ME5...64 E1
Hunters Wlk Deal CT14 215 B6
  Knockholt TN14......120 E5
Huntingdon Wlk [2]
  ME15......195 E7
Huntingfield Rd DA13..60 A2
Hunting Gate CT7......80 F8
Huntington CI TN17...320 D4
Huntington Rd ME17. 194 B3
Huntley Ave DA11......18 C1
Huntley Mill Rd TN5. 338 E3
Huntleys Pk TN4......285 F5
HUNTON......226 D8
Hunton CE Prim Sch
  ME15......226 D7
Hunton Gdns CT2......143 A4
Hunton Hill
  Coxheath ME15......194 A2
  Hunton ME15......193 F1
Hunton Ho [4] BR5......54 C4
Hunton Rd TN12......227 A3
Hunt Rd Northfleet DA11. 36 F5
  Tonbridge TN10......222 E6
Hunts CI SE3......11 A5
Hunts Farm CI TN15...157 A7
Huntsfield Ind Est
  CT20......334 D4
Hunts La TN17......318 E8
Huntsman Rd [3] DA11 36 F8
Huntsman La
  Maidstone ME14......162 B4
  Wrotham Heath TN15. 125 E1
Huntsmans CI ME1......63 E3
Huntsman's Cnr ME4... 96 E8
Hunts Mede CI BR7......22 F7
Huntsmoor House BR5 54 B5
Hunt St
  Nettlestead ME15,
  ME18......192 F5
  West Farleigh ME15... 193 B5
Huntswood TN23......267 E1
Hurlfield DA12......33 C5
Hurlingham CI TN10.. 222 E7
Hurlingham Rd DA7...13 F7
Huron CI [5] BR6......86 F4
Hurricane Rd ME19... 158 F3
Hurstbourne Cotts 32 B8
Hurst CI Chatham ME5...96 E6
  Staplehurst TN12......260 F4
  Tenterden TN30......344 F7
Hurst Ct Newham E6,......1 D8
  Sidcup DA15......31 A6
Hurst Farm Rd TN14. 187 B3
Hurstfield BR2......52 A4
Hurstford La TN26,
  TN27......234 C2
Hurst Gr CT12......83 C1
HURST GREEN......354 B3
Hurst Green CE Prim Sch
  TN19......354 A2
Hurst Green Rd RH8...183 A3
Hurst Green Sch RH8. 183 A3
Hurst Hill ME5......96 C3
Hurst Ho SE2......3 D1
Hurstings The ME15..161 D2
Hurst La
  Capel-le-Ferne CT18..308 B4
  Charing Heath TN27.. 233 C6
  Erith SE2......3 D1
  Sevenoaks Weald TN14 187 B2
  Sittingbourne ME10...68 F1
Hurst PI Gillingham ME8..98 F8
  Woolwich SE2......3 C1
Hurst Prim Sch DA5....31 F7
Hurst Rd Ashford TN24. 268 C1
  Erith DA8......14 C7
  Sidcup DA5......31 D7
Hurst Springs DA5......31 F7
Hurst Way
  Maidstone ME16......160 F2
  Sevenoaks TN13......187 C8
Hurstwood ME5......96 E4
Hurstwood Ave
  Bexley DA7, DA8......14 C6
  Sidcup DA5......31 E7
Hurstwood Dr BR1......52 F6
Hurstwood La TN4...285 F3
Hurstwood Pk TN4...285 F3
Hurstwood Rd
  Bredhurst ME7......98 B1
  Warren Street ME17...200 E8
Husheath Hill TN17...291 F6
Hussar Ho ME1......63 D4
Husseywell Cres BR2...52 A1
Hustlings Dr ME17......16 D8
Hutson Terr RM19......16 D8
Huxley CI [3] ME1......63 D4
Huxley Ho SE2......3 D1
Huxley Rd DA16......12 F4
Hyacinth Rd ME2......62 E6
Hybrid CI ME1......63 D1
Hyde Ct CT17......310 C7
Hyde Dr BR5......54 B5
Hyde Grove DA1......16 A5
Hyde PI CT3......210 F5
Hyde Rd Bexley DA7...13 F5
  Maidstone ME16......161 D6
Hyders Forge TN15...190 A8
Hyde's Orch TN27......262 E5
Hyde The CT4......173 B2
Hylands Cotts TN26.. 326 A4

Hylton St SE18......2 F2
Hyndford Cres DA9...17 C2
Hyperion Dr ME2......39 F1
HYTHE......333 D1
Hythe Ave DA7......13 F7
Hythe Bay CE Prim Sch
  CT21......333 B1
Hythe CI
  Folkestone CT20......334 F1
  Orpington BR5......54 C5
  Royal Tunbridge Wells
  TN4......254 A1
Hythe House Sch ME12 .46 E7
Hythe PI CT13......334 E1
Hythe Rd Ashford TN24. 268 E1
  Dymchurch TN29......352 E1
  Lympne CT21......332 D4
  Sittingbourne ME10...101 D5
  Smeeth TN25, TN24...302 C3
Hythe St Leonard's CE Jun
  Sch CT21......333 B2
Hythe St DA1......15 E1
Hythe Sta★ CT21......333 D1
Hyton Dr CT14......215 B6

I

Ian's Wlk CT21......334 A3
Ibis CI CT5......108 A3
Ice Bowl The★ ME8...65 A1
ICKHAM......145 C1
Ickham Court Farm
  CT3......145 C1
Ickleton Rd SE9......29 E4
Icough CI SE3......11 B7
Iddenden Cotts TN18. 340 D2
IDE HILL......185 F4
Ide Hill CE Prim Sch
  TN14......185 F4
Ide Hill Rd
  Bough Beech TN8,
  TN14......218 F5
  Ide Hill TN14......185 F2
IDEN......368 B4
Iden Cres TN12......260 F2
IDEN GREEN
  Goudhurst......319 C8
  Hawkhurst......342 C8
Iden Green Cotts TN17 319 C8
Iden La TN27......233 B4
Iden Rd Iden TN31......368 B3
  Rochester ME2......40 C1
Idenwood CI ME8......98 D6
Idleigh Court Rd DA3,
  DA13......92 C8
Iffin La CT1......174 E4
Ifield CI ME15......195 F7
Ifield Sch The DA12...37 C3
Ifield Way DA12......37 C3
IGHTHAM......156 C7
Ightham By-Pass
  TN15......156 C6
Ightham Cotts DA2...35 B6
Ightham Mote★ TN15 189 A7
Ightham Prim Sch
  TN15......156 C6
Ightham Rd Bexley DA8..14 A7
  Shipbourne TN11, TN15 189 C5
IGTHAM COMMON.. 156 A3
Ilex Ct CT19......334 F6
Ilkley Rd E16......1 C8
Illustrious CI ME5......97 A6
Imber Ct [4] SE9......30 A5
Imbert CI TN28......373 C6
Impala Gdns TN4......286 B6
Imperial Ave ME12......47 D7
Imperial Bsns Pk DA11. 18 F1
Imperial CI ME19......159 B3
Imperial Coll London (Wye
  Campus) TN25......237 D2
Imperial Ct BR7......30 B2
Imperial Dr
  Gravesend DA12......37 F3
  Warden ME12......49 E4
Imperial PI BR7......53 A8
Imperial Rd ME7......64 C3
Imperial Ret Pk DA11..19 A1
Imperial Way
  Ashford TN23......299 C8
  Chislehurst BR7......30 C5
Impton La ME5......97 A1
Inca Dr SE9......30 B8
Ince Rd CT2......143 F7
Indus Rd ME1......63 D1
Industrial Est The TN8 .217 B3
Ingleborough La TN15 157 C8
Ingleby Way BR7......30 A3
Ingle CI CT7......81 B7
Ingleden CI ME10......101 F8
Ingleden Park Rd
  TN30......324 C1
Ingledew Rd SE18......2 D1
Ingle PI ME18......159 A2
Ingle Rd ME4......63 F2
Ingleside Gr [3] SE3...11 A8
Ingles La [8] CT20......335 D5
Ingles Mews [4] CT20 335 D4
Ingles Rd CT20......335 C4
Ingleton Ave DA16......13 A2
Inglewood
  Chislehurst BR7......30 D2
  Swanley BR8......55 E7
Inglewood Copse BR1..52 F7
Inglewood Rd DA7......14 D3
Ingoldsby Rd
  Birchington CT7......80 E7
  Canterbury CT1......174 D6
  Folkestone CT19......335 E4
  Gravesend DA12......37 F7

Ingram CI
  Hawkinge CT18......306 F3
  New Hythe ME20......128 B4
Ingram Rd Dartford DA1. 33 E7
  Gillingham ME7......64 E6
Ingress Gdns DA9......17 C3
Ingress Park Ave DA9..17 C3
Ingress Terr DA13......35 E4
Inigo Jones Rd SE7......11 E7
Inner Lines ME7......64 A6
Institute Rd
  Chatham ME4......64 A4
  Faversham ME13......138 D7
Instone Rd DA1......33 D8
Intelligence Wlk TN25 267 F4
International University of
  America (London
  Campus) [12] SE18......2 B2
Inverary Ct CT11......83 E1
Inverary PI SE18......12 D8
Inverine Rd SE7......1 B1
Invermore PI SE18......2 C2
Inverness Ho [7] ME15 .195 E7
Inverness Mews E16....2 C5
Inverness Terr CT10...84 A3
Invicta Bsns Pk TN15.. 125 C2
Invicta Ct BR7......30 A3
Invicta Gram Sch for Girls
  ME14......162 C4
Invicta Ho
  Canterbury CT1......174 F7
  Margate CT9......51 C1
Invicta Par [3] DA14...31 B4
Invicta Prim Sch SE3...11 A7
Invicta Rd Dartford DA2.16 B1
  Folkestone CT19......335 D7
  Greenwich SE3......11 A8
  Lydd TN29......378 E6
  Margate CT9......83 B8
  Sheerness ME12......28 C2
  Whitstable CT5......108 F8
Invicta Villas ME14...163 C4
Inward Car Lanes
  CT16......310 G8
Inward Freight Lanes
  CT16......310 G8
Iona CI ME5......97 D1
Iona Rd ME15......195 A7
Ionia Wlk DA12......37 F5
Irchester St [11] CT11...117 F7
Ireland CI E6......1 F8
Ireland Ct TN24......268 D2
Irene Astor Ct [7] CT20 335 D5
Irene Rd BR6......53 F2
Iris Ave DA5......13 E1
Iris CI ME5......130 A8
Iris Cres DA7......13 F8
Iron Bar La [4] CT1...175 A8
Iron Mill La DA1......14 F3
Iron Mill PI DA1......14 F3
Ironside CI ME5......97 A8
Ironstones TN3......285 B3
Irvine Dr CT9......83 C8
Irvine Mews [6] CT9...83 C8
Irvine Rd ME3......39 B3
Irvine Way BR6......53 F2
Irving Ho TN1......286 B5
Irving Rd BR8......55 D7
Irving Wlk DA10......35 E8
Irwin Ave SE18......12 E7
Isabella Dr BR6......86 C6
Isis CI CT21......332 A3
Island Rd
  Upstreet CT3, CT7......112 C2
  Westbere CT2, CT3...144 C7
Island Wall CT5......74 C1
Island Way E ME4......41 C1
Island Way W ME4......41 B2
Isla Rd SE18......12 C8
Islehurst CI BR7......53 A8
Islington Farm Rd
  ME3......40 D4
Ismays Rd TN15......156 C3
ISP The [2] ME10...101 E4
ISTEAD RISE......59 E8
Istead Rise DA13......36 F1
Istead Rise Prim Sch
  DA13......59 E8
Italianate Greenhouse★
  CT11......84 A1
Itchingwood Common Rd
  RH8......183 E2
Ito Way ME8......65 A3
Ivanhoe Rd
  Herne Bay CT6......77 A4
  Westgate on Sea CT8...50 C1
Ivans Field ME17......196 B1
Ivedon Rd DA16......13 C5
Ivens Way ME17......198 D6
Iverhurst CI DA6......13 D2
Iversgate Ct ME8......65 F2
Ives Rd TN9......221 F1
Ivor Gr SE9......30 B7
Ivor Ho DA14......31 C3
Ivory CI ME13......105 A1
Ivorydown BR1......29 A4
Ivy Bower CI DA9......17 B2
Ivybridge Ct [1] BR7...53 A8
Ivy Cotts TN13......299 C8
Ivy Ct CT2......142 C6
IVY HATCH......156 A1
Ivy House La TN13,
  TN14......121 F2
Ivy House Rd CT5......74 F1

Ivy La
  Bells Yew Green TN3...315 A5
  Canterbury CT1......175 A8
  Knockholt TN14......120 E3
Ivy Mews ME7......197 E2
Ivy PI Canterbury CT1..174 E7
  Deal CT14......215 D7
  Rochester ME1......63 A2
Ivy Rd E16......1 A7
Ivyside CT8......50 C1
Ivy St ME8......98 F8
Ivy Villas DA9......17 A2
Ivy Way CT19......335 E7
IWADE......68 D4
Iwade Prim Sch ME9...68 D4
Izane Rd DA6......13 F3

J

Jaarlen Rd TN29......376 B6
Jacinth Dr ME10......101 C6
Jackass La BR2......85 C4
Jacklin CI ME5......96 F2
Jackson Ave ME1......96 E8
Jackson CI
  Gillingham ME8......65 C1
  [1] Stone DA9......17 A2
Jackson Ho [4] SE7......11 B8
Jackson Rd
  Canterbury CT1......174 E7
  Orpington BR2......85 F8
Jackson's Cnr ME3......24 A3
Jacksons Stables CT8...50 D1
Jackson St SE18......12 A5
Jackson Way TN17...322 C3
Jacob CI CT9......82 E7
Jacob Ho [5] DA18......3 D4
Jacobs Ho ME12......28 C2
Jacob's La ME13......42 B6
Jacobs Oak TN14......300 D6
Jacob Yd [8] ME13...138 D7
Jade CI Newham E16......1 D7
  Sittingbourne ME10..101 C7
Jade Hill ME2......95 A6
Jaffa Ct [1] CT5......108 D8
Jaffray Rd BR2......52 D5
Jaggard Way TN12...260 E3
Jagger CI DA2......34 C8
Jago CI SE18......12 C8
Jail La Biggin Hill TN16. 118 E7
  Cudham TN16......119 A3
Jamaica Terr ME14...162 A7
James Allchin Gdns
  TN24......268 F4
James Ave TN15......90 D3
James CI Ash CT3......147 D2
  Hadlow TN11......190 F1
  Lyminge CT18......305 C7
James Ct
  Folkestone CT20......335 A4
  [2] Margate CT9......51 B2
James Hall Gdns CT14 215 C3
James Haney Dr TN24 268 F5
James Morris Ct [3]
  CT20......335 D6
James Newman Ct SE9 30 A5
James Rd Ashford TN23 268 A2
  [5] Chatham ME4......63 F4
  Folkestone CT20......335 D6
  Gillingham ME7......64 C6
  Maidstone ME14......162 A5
  [1] Ramsgate CT11...117 D6
  Rochester ME1......63 C4
  Sheerness ME12......28 C2
James Watt Way DA8...14 F8
James Whatman Way
  ME14......161 F5
Jane Seymour Ct DA15 30 D8
Janet Ct [4] DA7......14 A3
Janson Ct [1] DA14...31 B4
Japonica CI ME5......97 C2
Jaquets Ct DA3......58 A7
Jardines CI [9] CT11...117 D7
Jarman's Field TN25.. 237 F2
Jarrah Cotts RM19......16 D8
Jarrett Ave ME2......40 C2
Jarrett Ho [10] CT20...335 C4
Jarrett's Ct [1] ME10.. 102 B4
Jarvis Dr TN24......301 A7
Jarvis La TN17......291 B3
Jarvis PI TN30......324 B3
Jarvist PI CT14......248 D6
Jasmine CI
  Chartham CT4......173 E1
  [2] Chatham ME5......96 F3
  [4] East Malling ME19 .159 F8
  Orpington BR6......86 B8
Jasmine Cotts
  Borough Green TN15...156 F7
  Groombridge TN3......312 C7
Jasmine Ct SE12......11 A1
Jasmine Rd ME19......159 F8
Jason Wlk SE9......30 A4
Jasper Ave ME1......63 D2
Jasper Rd E16......1 D7
Javelin Ent Pk TN25...268 E3
Javelin Rd ME19......158 F3
Javelin Way TN24......268 E3
Jay Gdns BR7......29 F4
Jayne Wlk CT5......108 B6
Jefferson CI TN23......267 F1
Jefferson Dr ME8......65 C3
Jefferson Rd ME12......28 D2
Jefferson Wlk SE18...12 A8
Jefferstone Gdns
  TN29......365 E4

Jefferstone La TN29...365 E4
Jeffery St ME7.........64 C6
Jeffery Cl TN12......260 E4
Jeffrey Cl DA8........14 C7
Jeffrey Row SE12......11 B2
Jeffrey St ME14......162 A5
Jeken Rd SE9..........11 C3
Jellicoe Ave DA12.....37 C5
Jellicoe Avenue W
DA12.................37 C5
Jellicoe Cl TN24.....301 A7
Jemmett Rd TN23......300 A8
Jenkins Cl DA11.......36 F5
Jenkins' Dale ME4.....63 F3
Jenkins Dr ME15.....195 E5
Jenner Cl DA14........31 A4
Jenner Ho 4 DA17......4 A3
Jenner Rd ME1........63 C4
Jenner's Way TN29...365 E4
Jenner Way ME20.....128 F6
Jennifer Cl ME3.......41 F5
Jennifer Gdns CT9....83 C8
Jenningtree Rd DA8...15 B7
Jenningtree Way DA17..4 C4
Jenton Ave DA7.......13 C5
Jerome Rd ME20......127 F4
Jersey Cl TN24.......268 C8
Jersey Dr BR5.........53 D3
Jersey La CT4........207 C6
Jersey Rd Newham E16..1 C8
Rochester ME2........63 A8
Jeskyns Ctry Pk★ DA12 60 E8
Jeskyns Rd DA12.......60 E6
Jesmond St 3 TN19...335 D6
Jessamine Pl DA2......34 C8
Jessamine Terr BR8....55 C8
Jesse's Hill CT4.....209 B1
Jessett Cl DA8.........4 D2
Jessica Mews
2 Canterbury CT1...143 B3
Sittingbourne ME10...101 E7
Jesson Cl TN29.......366 A4
Jesson Court Cvn Pk
TN29................365 F4
Jessup Cl SE18.........2 C2
Jesuit Cl CT2........143 A4
Jesus Hospl CT1.....143 A1
Jetty Rd Kingsnorth ME3 .42 D7
Sheerness ME12......27 F3
Warden ME12..........49 E4
Jetty Wlk 3 RM17.....18 A8
Jevington Way SE12...29 B7
Jewell Gr TN12......259 D5
Jewels Hill TN16....118 A6
Jewry La CT1.........174 F8
Jeyes Rd ME7.........64 D3
Jezreels Rd ME7......63 D3
Jillian Way TN23....299 F7
Jim Bradley Cl 10 SE18..2 A2
Jiniwin Rd ME1.......96 D7
Joan Cres SE9.........29 D8
Jo-Ann's Ct 5 CT10...84 A4
Jockey La TN17......320 D5
Johannesburg Ho 2
ME15................138 C5
Johannesburg Rd
CT16................278 C4
John Anderson Ct 11
ME13................138 D7
John Badger Cl TN24..268 E5
John Bowley Ho CT19.334 F6
John Brunt Ct TN12..257 A7
John Burns Cotts RH8 183 E5
John Coopper Ho ME3 .25 C5
John Dutton Way
TN24................268 E4
John F Kennedy Sch E16 1 D8
John Graham Ct CT1..175 A6
John Hall Cl ME13....105 B2
John Hunt Ct SE9.....29 E6
John Mayne CE Prim Sch
The TN27............294 F1
John Nash Cl ME9....136 B8
John Newington Cl
TN24................268 F5
John Newton Ct DA16 .13 B4
Johns Cl DA3..........58 F4
John's Gn CT13......180 E6
Johnson Ave ME7......64 C7
Johnson Cl
Ashford TN24........301 A7
Northfleet DA11......36 D5
Johnson Ct ME13.....105 B1
Johnson Ho ME10.....101 D4
Johnson Rd
Bromley BR2..........52 D4
Sittingbourne ME10...101 D4
Johnsons Ave TN14....88 B1
Johnson's Cnr TN26..349 A4
Johnsons Ct TN15....154 F6
Johnsons Way DA9....17 C1
Johnson Way ME12....47 A7
John Spare Ct TN4...286 A6
Johns Rd TN16......119 B3
John's Rd
Meopham Station DA13 .59 F4
Tatsfield TN16......107 D6
John St Broadstairs CT10 84 B4
Grays RM17..........18 C8
Maidstone ME14.....162 A6
Rochester ME1........63 C4
Royal Tunbridge Wells
TN4................286 A6
John Tapping Cl CT14 .215 B1
John Wesley CE/
Methodist Prim Sch The
TN23................299 D7
John Wesley Ct SE9...12 A3
John Wilson Bsns Pk
CT5..................75 B1
John Wilson St SE18...2 A2

Joiners Ct ME4........64 B2
Jointon Rd CT20.....335 B4
Jonas Dr TN5.........336 E5
Jonas La TN5.........336 E5
Jordan Cl ME15.......195 E5
Joseph Conrad Dr
TN25................329 F4
Joseph Conrad Ho
CT2..................142 D1
Joseph Wilson Ind Est
CT5..................109 A7
Josling Cl RM17......17 F8
Joss Gap Rd CT10.....51 H1
Joy Cl TN17..........320 C5
Joyce Dawson Way SE28 3 A6
Joyce Green Rd DA1...15 F4
Joyce Green La DA1...15 F4
Joyce Green Wlk DA1..15 F3
Joyce Page Cl SE7.....11 D8
Joyden's Park TN15...90 E3
JOYDEN'S WOOD.......32 F4
Joydens Wood Cty Inf Sch
DA5..................32 E4
Joyden's Wood Jun Sch
DA2..................32 E4
Joyden's Wood Rd DA5 32 E5
Joyes Cl
Folkestone CT19.....335 E7
Whitfield CT16......278 B7
Joyes Rd
Folkestone CT19.....335 E7
Whitfield CT16......278 B7
Joy La CT5...........108 B8
Joy Rd DA12...........37 C7
Joy Wood ME17.......195 D5
Jubilee Cl Hythe CT21.353 D8
Swanscombe DA9......17 C1
Jubilee Cnr ME17....230 E3
Jubilee Cotts
Sevenoaks TN14.....154 B7
Staple CT3...........179 B6
Sutton Valence ME17..229 E7
Throwley ME13......169 D1
Worth CT14..........181 B4
Jubilee Cres
Gravesend DA12.......37 C6
Ightham TN15........156 C6
Queenborough ME11...45 F5
Jubilee Ct
19 Broadstairs CT10..84 B4
Dartford DA1.........33 D8
17 Ramsgate CT11...117 F7
Whitstable CT5.......75 A3
Jubilee Ctry Pk★ BR1,
BR5..................53 B5
Jubilee Dr CT14.....215 D3
Jubilee Field TN30..359 E4
Jubilee Fields ME8...66 D2
Jubilee Ho CT20......335 B4
Jubilee Prim Sch SE28..3 C1
Jubilee Rd
Chelsfield BR6........88 A4
Littlebourne CT3.....176 F8
Sandwich CT13......180 F8
West Thurrock RM20...17 B8
Worth CT14..........181 B4
Jubilee Rise TN15...154 F6
Jubilee St ME10......101 E5
Jubilee Terr
Gillingham ME7.......64 C6
Knockholt TN14......120 E4
Jubilee Way
Dover CT15, CT16....279 A2
Faversham ME13.....138 E6
Sidcup DA14..........31 A6
Judd Rd
Faversham ME13.....138 A7
Tonbridge TN9.......254 B7
Judd Sch The TN9....254 A8
Judeth Gdns DA12.....37 E3
Judkins Cl ME5........97 C6
Juglans Rd BR6........54 A1
Julia Garfield Mews E16. 1 B5
Julian Ct
Folkestone CT19.....335 B5
3 Sidcup DA14........31 A4
Julian Rd
Folkestone CT19.....335 B6
Orpington BR6........87 A4
Julians Cl TN13......187 A8
Julians Way TN13....187 A8
Julie Cl CT10.........84 A7
Julien Pl TN24.......301 A8
Julie Rose Athletic
Stadium TN24........268 F4
Junction Rd
Bodiam TN18, TN32...355 A3
Dartford DA1.........15 D1
Gillingham ME7.......64 D4
Herne Bay CT6........76 C2
Junior Kings Sch CT2 .143 E5
Juniper Cl
Ashford TN23........267 C2
Biggin Hill TN16....118 E2
Canterbury CT1......175 A6
Chatham ME5.........97 A4
Hurst Green RH8....183 B2
Maidstone ME16.....161 B6
Royal Tunbridge Wells
TN4................254 D1
Whitstable CT5.......74 F1
Juniper La E6..........1 E8
Juniper Wlk BR8......55 D7
Jupiter La TN23......299 E5
Jupp Court ME3.......39 C6
JURY'S GAP..........374 D1
Jury's Gap Coastguard
Cotts TN31..........374 E1
Jury's Gap Rd TN29..376 A5
Jury St 12 TN31......19 B1
Jutland Cl ME3........9 D1
Jutland Ho SE18.......1 E2

K9 Est RM13...........4 E7
Kain Ct 6 CT12.......83 B1
Kake St CT4.........239 E7
Kale Rd DA18..........3 E4
Karloff Way ME2.....40 B2
Kashgar Rd SE18.......2 F2
Kashmir Rd SE7.......11 D7
Katherine Ct ME5.....97 B2
Katherine Gdns SE9...11 D3
Katherine Rd TN8...249 C8
Katherine Villas TN8 249 C8
Kaysland Park TN15...90 E3
KEARSNEY............277 D3
Kearsney Abbey★
CT16................277 D3
Kearsney Ave CT16...277 E4
Kearsney Ct CT16....277 D4
Kearsney Sta CT16...277 D4
Keary Rd DA10........35 F8
Keat Farm Cl CT6.....77 F5
Keating Cl ME1........63 A3
Keats Ave E16.........1 B5
Keats Gdns RM18.....19 B5
Keats Ho DA1.........14 E2
Keats Rd Bexley DA16 .12 F6
Erith DA17............4 C3
Lunsford ME20......127 F3
Kechill Gdns BR2......52 A2
Keddow's Cl CT21....353 D8
Kedleston Dr BR5.....53 F4
Kedleston Rd CT16...278 C5
Keeble Cl SE18........12 B8
Keedonwood Rd BR1...29 A3
Keefe Cl ME5..........96 D1
Keel Ct ME2...........63 D8
Keeley Mews ME7......64 E3
Keel Gdns TN4.......285 E8
Keeling Rd SE9........11 D2
Keemor Cl SE18.......12 A7
Keeper's Hill CT4....176 D2
Keep The SE3.........11 A5
Keightley Dr SE9......30 C7
Kell Ave CT12........117 A8
Sutton at Hone DA4...34 B2
Keith Park Cres TN16..118 C7
Keith Sutton House SE9 30 C6
Kelbrook Rd SE3......11 E4
Kelham Ho 10 SE18...12 B8
Kellaway Rd
Chatham ME5..........97 A2
Greenwich SE3........11 D5
Kellner Rd SE28.......2 F3
Kelly Dr ME7..........64 C7
Kelly Ho
15 Greenwich SE7....11 C8
Rochester ME1........96 C7
Kelsall Cl SE3.........11 B5
Kelsey Rd BR5.........54 B7
Kelso Dr DA12.........37 F4
Kelvedon Rd CT14....215 C2
Kelvin Cl TN10.......222 D7
Kelvin Ho 3 DA17......4 A3
Kelvin Par BR6.........53 E1
Kelvin Rd Bexley DA16..13 A4
Tilbury RM18.........19 A5
Kemble Cl TN2.......286 E7
Kemble Dr BR2........85 C7
Kembleside Rd TN16..118 C1
Kemnal Rd BR7........30 D3
Kemnal Tech Coll BR5 .31 B1
Kemnal Warren BR7...30 D2
Kemp Alley 2 TN5....74 D1
Kemp Cl ME5..........96 E4
KEMPE'S CORNER....237 A2
Kempes Pl TN25.....237 E2
Kempley Ct 2 RM17..18 D8
Kemp Rd CT5..........75 C2
Kempton Cl
Chatham ME5..........97 C2
Erith DA8............14 C8
Kempt St SE18.........12 A8
Kemsdale Rd ME13...139 F6
Kemnal Rd BR7........30 D3
KEMSING............123 B2
Kemsing Cl DA5.......31 B8
Kemsing Gdns CT2...143 B4
Kemsing Prim Sch
TN15................123 A2
Kemsing Rd
Greenwich SE10.......1 A1
Wrotham TN15......124 C3
Kemsing Sta TN15...155 D8
KEMSLEY.............68 E1
Kemsley Ct
Northfleet DA11......36 F4
Swanscombe DA9......17 B1
Kemsley Ct BR5.......54 B8
Kemsley Down Sta★
ME10..................69 C1
Kemsley Prim Sch
ME10..................68 F1
Kemsley Rd TN16....150 D8
Kemsley Sta ME10....68 E1
KEMSLEY STREET....98 C2
Kemsley Street Rd ME7 98 C1
KENARDINGTON......348 A6
Kenardington Rd TN26 347 E3
Kenbrook TN24......268 C7
Kencot Cl DA18........3 F4
Kendal Cl
Ramsgate CT11......117 B6
Tonbridge TN9.......222 C2
Kendal Dr TN9.......222 C2
Kendal Ave ME19....159 C3
Kendall Ct DA15......31 A5

Kendall Gdns DA11....36 F8
Kendall Lodge 9 BR1.52 B8
Kendall Pl 1 ME15...195 D8
Kendall Rd SE18.......11 C6
Kendal Mdw CT5.......75 E1
Kendal Pk TN4......285 E5
Kendal Rise CT10.....84 A5
Kendal Way ME8......98 D8
Kendon Bsns Pk ME2..63 D8
Kenfield Ct CT4......207 A6
Kengate Ind Est CT21 .332 F1
Kenia Wlk DA12.......37 F5
Kenilworth Cl CT15...280 A6
Kenilworth Ct
10 Dartford DA2......16 B1
Sittingbourne ME10...101 C5
Kenilworth Dr ME8....98 D6
Kenilworth Gdns
Gillingham ME8.......98 D7
Woolwich SE18........12 B5
Kenilworth Ho ME16..161 B2
Kenilworth Rd BR5....53 C3
Kenley Cl Sidcup DA5...32 A8
St Paul's Cray BR7....53 E6
Kenley Ho 6 BR5......54 B7
Kenmare Rd DA16.....13 C5
Kennacraig Cl E16......1 A5
Kennard Cl ME1.......62 F2
Kennard St E16........1 F5
Kennedy Ho
Faversham ME13.....138 D8
Orpington BR5.........53 D1
Kennedy Dr CT14.....215 B2
Kennedy Gdns TN13..154 D5
Kennedy Ho
Benenden TN17......342 C6
Northfleet DA11......36 D5
8 Ramsgate CT11...117 F7
Kennel Barn Rd ME9 .133 C5
Kennel Hill CT15.....245 E6
Kennelling Rd ME13,
TN27................201 D5
Kennels The CT15....245 E6
Kennet Ct 2 BR2......85 A7
Kennet Rd Crayford DA1 .15 A4
Tonbridge TN10......222 C5
Kennett Ct 15 BR5....54 D1
Kennett Dr CT14.....215 A2
Kennett La TN25.....332 B8
Kennett Lane Cotts
TN25................332 B8
KENNINGTON........268 E6
Kennington CE Jun Sch
TN24................268 E7
Kennington Cl
Gillingham ME8.......65 B4
Maidstone ME15.....195 F7
KENNINGTON LEES..268 C6
Kennington Pl TN24..268 E7
Kennington Rd TN24.269 A1
Kensington Ct 5 RM17 18 C8
Kensington Ho ME16..161 A2
Kensington Rd CT1...143 C4
Kent Ave Ashford TN24 .268 B3
Bexley DA16..........12 F2
Canterbury CT1......175 D8
Maidstone ME15.....162 C7
Minster (Sheppey) ME12 .47 B6
Sittingbourne ME10...101 D3
Kent Battle of Britain
Mus★ CT18...........306 F4
Kent & Canterbury Hospl
CT1.................175 A5
Kent Cl Orpington BR6..86 E4
Paddock Wood TN12..257 A6
Rochester ME1........96 C8
Kent Coll TN2.......255 D3
Kent College Canterbury
CT2.................142 D3
Kent College Canterbury
Inf & Jun Sch CT2...142 A1
Kent & East Sussex Rly★
Rolvenden TN30.....344 D5
Tenterden TN30......345 A8
Kent Gdns CT7........80 F7
KENT HATCH........184 B3
Kent Hatch Rd
Crockham Hill RH8,
TN8................184 B4
The Chart RH8, TN8..183 D4
Kent Ho
4 Broadstairs CT10..84 A4
Folkestone CT20.....335 B4
10 Hawkhurst TN18..341 A2
Royal Tunbridge Wells
TN1................286 C6
Sutton at Hone DA4...57 D7
Kent International Airport
CT12.................82 B1
Kentish Ct 8 ME16...161 E4
Kentish Gdns TN2...313 E8
Kentish Mans 15 TN1..286 A2
Kentish Rd DA17......4 A2
Kentish Way BR1, BR2..52 B6
Kent Kraft Ind Est DA11 17 F2
Kentlea Rd SE28........2 F3
Kentmere Ave CT11..116 F7
Kentmere Rd SE18......2 E2
Kent Music Sch 21
CT1.................142 F1
Kenton Gdns CT12...115 B6
Kent Pl CT11.........117 F6
Kent Rd Dartford DA1...15 E1
Folkestone CT19.....334 E7
Gravesend DA11......37 A7
4 Grays RM17........18 C8
Halling ME2...........95 A6
Longfield DA3.........58 D7
Margate CT9..........83 B8
Orpington BR5........54 C1

Kent Rd continued
Royal Tunbridge Wells
TN4................286 A6
Sheerness ME12......28 B1
Snodland ME6........128 C8
Kent Science Pk ME9 .134 D6
Kent Showground
ME14................131 C3
Kent St
Herne Pound ME18...158 E2
Whitstable CT5......108 D8
Kentstone Ct ME4.....64 A4
KENT STREET.......158 C2
Kent & Sussex Hospl
TN4................286 A4
Kent Terr Gillingham ME8 65 F1
Lower Higham ME3...39 D7
Meopham DA13.......93 A7
Ramsgate CT11......117 F6
Kent View Dr ME12....48 D1
Kenward Ct TN11....223 E8
Kenward Rd Eltham SE9 .11 D2
Maidstone ME6......161 C5
Yalding ME18........192 E2
Kenwood Ave
Chatham ME5..........97 A4
New Barn DA3.........59 C6
Kenwyn Rd DA1.......15 C2
Kenya Rd SE7..........11 D5
Kenya Terr 7 ME14...162 A7
Kenyon Wlk ME8......98 B3
Kerry Cl E16...........1 B7
Kerry Hill Way ME14..161 A6
Kersey Gdns SE9......29 A4
Kerton Rd TN29......380 D7
Kesteven Cl ME2......95 B5
Kestlake Rd DA5......13 C1
KESTON.............85 D6
Keston Ave BR2........85 C5
Keston CE Prim Sch
BR2.................85 D5
Keston Cl DA16.......13 C7
Keston Ct
Gillingham ME8.......65 A2
Sidcup DA5...........31 F8
Keston Gdns BR2......85 C5
KESTON MARK......85 D8
Keston Park Cl BR2...85 F7
Kestrel Ave E6.........1 E8
Kestrel Cl
Kingsnorth ME23.....300 C3
Marlpit Hill TN8......217 D3
Sittingbourne ME10...102 A2
Kestrel Ct
4 Sittingbourne
ME10................102 A4
Whitstable CT5.......75 A3
Kestrel Ho ME7.......64 B6
Kestrel Rd ME5........97 C2
Keswick Ave ME10...102 C3
Keswick Cl TN9.......222 C2
Keswick Ct ME7.......65 A5
Keswick Dr ME16.....161 B5
Keswick Gdns RM19..16 C8
Keswick Rd Bexley DA7..14 A6
Orpington BR6........54 A2
Ketridge La ME18....159 D2
Kettle Dr CT18.......307 B5
Kettle Hill ME18......168 F4
Kettle Hill Rd
Eastling ME13.......168 F5
Throwley ME13......169 A4
Kettle La ME15.......193 E6
Kettlewell Ct BR8.....55 F7
Kevin Dr CT11........117 B6
Kevington Cl BR5......53 F3
Kevington Dr BR7......53 F5
KEVINGTOWN.........54 E3
Kewlands ME14......162 C6
KEYCOL.............100 E6
Keycol Hill ME9......100 F5
Keyes Ave ME4........63 F2
Keyes Cl CT16.......278 A5
Keyes Gdns TN9.....253 F7
Keyes Pl CT19.......335 E7
Keyes Rd DA1..........16 A3
Keymer Cl TN16......118 D3
Keynes Coll CT2.....142 D4
Keynes Ct 3 SE28......3 B6
Keynsham Gdns SE9...11 E2
Keynsham Rd SE9.....11 C1
Keyworth Cl TN12...256 F6
Keyworth Mews 7
CT1.................143 B2
Khalsa Ave DA12......37 C8
Khartoum Pl DA12...19 C1
Khartoum Rd ME7....64 A6
Khartoum Sq CT16...278 A6
Khyber Rd ME4, ME7...64 A7
Kibbles La TN4.......285 E8
KIDBROOKE.........11 C5
Kidbrooke Gdns SE3..11 A4
Kidbrooke Gr SE3.....11 B4
Kidbrooke La SE9.....11 E3
Kidbrooke Park Cl SE3 .11 B4
Kidbrooke Park Prim Sch
SE3.................11 C4
Kidbrooke Park Rd SE12,
SE3.................11 D4
Kidbrooke Sta SE3....11 D3
Kidbrooke Way SE3...11 B4
Kiddens BR8...........55 B7
Kidd Pl SE7............1 F1
Kidds Cotts BR8......55 D3
Kierbeck Bsns Complex
E16...................1 D4
Kilbride Ct CT11......83 F1
Kilburn Ho 6 ME14..162 A5
Kildare Rd E16.........1 A8

Killewarren Way BR5..54 C3
Killick Cl TN13.......153 C1
Killick Rd ME9........41 D5
Killicks Cotts ME18..225 F4
Killigarth Ct 22 DA14 .31 A4
Kiln Barn Rd ME19, ME
20...................160 C7
Kilnbank CT1.........286 C7
Kiln Barn Rd ME19, ME
Kilnbridge Cl ME15...194 B7
Kilnbridge Wks ME15.194 B7
Kiln Cl Challock TN25..203 B3
Sittingbourne ME10...102 A3
Kiln Cnr CT21.......333 B4
KILNDOWN.........317 F3
Kilndown DA12........37 C8
Kilndown Cl
Ashford TN23.......299 D3
Maidstone ME16.....161 C7
Kilnstone Gdns
Canterbury CT2......143 A4
Margate CT9..........51 C2
Kiln Field TN30......345 C4
Kilnfields BR6.........88 A4
Kiln La Bethersden TN26 297 F2
Leigh TN11..........220 F1
Kiln Way TN12.......257 A5
Kilnwood TN14......120 F6
Kimball Pl SE3........11 C3
Kimber Ho 11 SE18...12 B8
Kimberley Cl CT16...278 C3
Kimberley Cnr CT11..83 F8
Kimberley Ct CT8.....50 C1
Kimberley Dr DA14...31 D6
Kimberley Gr CT5....107 F6
Kimberley Rd
Gillingham ME7.......64 D3
Ramsgate CT12......83 A1
Kimberley Way TN24..300 C5
Kimberly Ct DA17.....3 F2
Kimberly Terr CT18..305 C7
Kimmeridge Gdns SE9..29 A4
Kimmeridge Rd SE9...29 E4
Kincraig BR7..........53 A8
Kincraig Dr TN13....154 B4
Kinder Cl SE28.........3 D6
King Arthur Rd ME8..101 E3
King Arthur Rd CT12..116 D7
King Arthur's Dr ME2...40 A1
King Charles Ct CT14 .215 D2
King Edward Ave
Broadstairs CT10.....84 A4
Dartford DA1.........15 D1
Herne Bay CT6........77 B4
King Edward Ct CT6...77 B4
King Edward Rd
Birchington CT7......81 A5
Chatham ME4.........63 F2
Deal CT14..........215 D6
Gillingham ME7.......64 F6
Maidstone ME15.....161 D4
1 Ramsgate CT11...117 C6
Rochester ME1........63 C5
Stone DA9............17 A2
King Edward St CT5...74 D7
King Ethelbert Sch CT7 81 C7
Kingfisher Apartments 13
ME15................195 E5
Kingfisher Ave CT21..353 B8
Kingfisher Bsns Pk
TN24................268 D3
Kingfisher Cl
Ashford TN24........301 A7
Erith SE28.............3 C6
Iwade ME9............68 E4
Margate CT9..........82 B8
Orpington BR5........54 D5
Whitstable CT5.......108 C7
Kingfisher Ct
Herne Bay CT6........76 D3
11 Maidstone ME15..162 B4
West Kingsdown TN15..90 E3
Kingfisher Dr
Chatham ME5..........97 C7
Swanscombe DA9......17 A1
Kingfisher Gdns CT21 353 C8
Kingfisher Ho
Ashford TN23........267 F1
Orpington BR5........54 C8
Kingfisher Mdw ME16.161 F3
Kingfisher Pl DA4.....57 C7
Kingfisher Prim Sch
ME5...................97 B7
Kingfisher Rd ME20..128 A2
Kingfisher St E6.......1 E8
Kingfisher Wlk CT10..83 F5
King George Ave E16...1 D7
King George Rd ME5...96 E4
King George V Hill
TN1.................286 C5
King George VI Ave
TN16................118 D3
King George Villas
CT14................181 B3
King George V Meml
Houses ME8..........65 C2
King George V Sta E16..2 A5
King Harolds Way DA7 .13 E7
King Henry Mews 7
BR6...................86 F5
King Hill ME19.......159 A5
King John's Wlk SE9...11 C1
King Lear's Way CT17 .310 B5
Kingly Way CT17....310 A7
King & Queen Cl SE9...29 C4
Kings Acre ME15......163 A1
King's Ave BR1.........29 A2
King's Ave
Ashford TN23........268 A2
Birchington CT7......80 D7
Broadstairs CT10.....84 B6
Ramsgate CT12......83 B1
Rochester ME1........63 C3
Sandwich CT13......182 A8

King's Ave *continued*
Whitstable CT5 . . . . . . .74 E1
King's Bastion ME7 . . . .64 A5
Kingsbridge Ct **11**
CT20 . . . . .335 E5
Kingsbrook Pk CT1 . . . 143 A2
Kings Chase TN24 . . . 269 A2
Kings Cl DA1 . . . . .14 E3
King's Cl CT14 . . . . . . .248 D6
King's Cotts
Cranbrook TN17 . . . .320 D6
Leeds ME17 . . . . .196 F6
King's Cotts
Wateringbury ME18 . .192 D6
Yalding ME18 . . . . .11 D7
Kings Ct Deal CT14 . . .215 D3
Horsmonden TN12 . . . .290 A4
21 Sidcup DA14 . . . . .31 A5
Kingsdale Ct
Chatham ME5 . . . . . . .64 C1
Swanscombe DA10 . . .17 E1
Kingsdale Rd SE18 . . . .12 F8
KINGSDOWN Deal 248 D5
Lynsted 135 C4
Kingsdown Cl
Gillingham ME7 . . . . . .98 B4
5 Gravesend DA12 . . .37 F7
Maidstone ME16 . . . . .161 E4
Kingsdown Cotts ME9 .135 E4
Kingsdown Hill CT14 . .248 D6
Kingsdown Ind Est
ME20 . . . . .160 B8
KINGSDOWN PARK . . .74 F3
Kingsdown Pk CT5 . . . .74 F2
Kingsdown Rd
Kingsdown CT14 . . . . .248 D7
Lynsted ME9 . . . . .135 C4
St Margaret's at Cliffe
 . . . . .280 A7
Kingsdown & Ringwould
CE Prim SchCT14 . . . .248 C5
Kingsdown Way BR2 . .52 A3
Kings Dr DA12 . . . . . . .37 B5
KINGS FARM 37 C5
Kings Farm Prim Sch
DA11 . . . . .37 C4
Kingsfield Ho SE9 . . . .29 D5
Kingsfield Rd CT6 . . . . .77 B2
Kingsford Cl TN25 . . . .301 E4
Kingsford Com SchE6. . .1 F7
Kingsford Cotts TN17 .342 D6
Kingsford Ct CT17 . . . .278 B1
Kingsford St TN25 . . . .301 D5
Kingsford Way E6 . . . . . .1 F8
KINGSGATE 51 G1
Kingsgate Ave CT10 . . .51 F1
Kingsgate Bay Rd CT10 .51 F2
Kingsgate Castle CT10. .51 F2
Kingsgate Cl Bexley DA2 13 E6
Orpington BR5 . . . . . . .54 C6
Kingsgate ClCT10 . . . . .84 A8
Kingsgate La TN30 . . . .359 C5
Kingsground SE9 . . . . . .11 E1
Kings Hall The★ CT6 . .77 A5
King's Highway SE18,
SE2 . . . . .12 F8
KINGS HILL 159 A2
Kings Hill Ave ME19 . .159 A4
Kingshill Dr ME3 . . . . .41 D6
Kings Hill Prim Sch
ME19 . . . . .159 A3
Kingsholm Gdns SE9 . .11 B3
Kingshurst Rd SE12 . . .29 A8
Kingsingfield Rd TN15 .90 E3
Kingsingfield Rd TN15. .90 E2
Kings La TN12 . . . . . . .258 C7
KINGSLAND 265 C8
Kingsland Gdns CT14 .248 B8
Kingsland Gr TN27 . . . .262 D5
Kingsland Hollow
TN29 . . . . .366 A4
Kingsland La
Egerton Forstal TN27 .232 E1
Westwell TN25 . . . . . .235 F1
Kingsley Ave DA1 . . . . .16 A2
Kingsley Ct Bexley DA6 .14 A3
Wadhurst TN5 . . . . . . .337 A4
1 Woolwich SE28 . . . . .3 C5
Kingsley Mews BR7 . . .30 B2
Kingsley Rd
Maidstone ME15 . . . . .162 A3
Orpington BR6 . . . . . . .86 F3
Whitstable CT5 . . . . . .108 E8
Kingsley Wood Dr SE9. .29 F5
Kingsman Par SE18 . . . . .1 F3
Kingsman St SE18 . . . . .1 F2
Kingsmarsh La TN29 . .372 C5
Kings Mdw TN24 . . . . .268 E2
Kingsmead
Biggin Hill TN16 . . . . .118 D3
Folkestone TN19 . . . . .335 B8
Westgate on Sea CT8 . .50 C1
Kingsmead Cl DA15 . . .31 A6
Kingsmead Cotts BR2 . .52 E1
Kingsmead L CtrCT2 . .143 A2
Kingsmead Pk
Allhallows-on-Sea ME3 . .9 E3
Paddock Wood TN12 . .257 A6
Kingsmead Prim Sch **22**
CT1 . . . . .143 A1
Kingsmead Rd CT1,
CT2 . . . . .143 A2
Kingsmere BR7 . . . . . . .52 E8
Kings Mews
7 Canterbury CT1 . . .143 A1
Margate CT9 . . . . .50 J3
Kings Mill Cl ME10 . . .101 E6
KINGSNORTH Ashford .300 A4
Kingsnorth 42 D5
Kingsnorth CE Prim Sch
TN23 . . . . .300 B3
Kingsnorth Cl ME3 . . . .41 E6

Kingsnorth Ct
Crockenhill BR8 . . . . . .55 C3
2 Folkestone CT20 . . .335 B5
Kingsnorth Gdns CT20 335 C5
Kingsnorth Ind Est
Ashford TN23 . . . . . . .300 B6
Kingsnorth ME3 . . . . . .42 D7
Kingsnorth Rd
Ashford TN23 . . . . . . .300 A6
Faversham ME13 . . . . .138 C6
Gillingham ME8 . . . . . .65 C4
Kings Oak Mews ME5. .96 F4
King's Orch Eltham SE9. .11 E1
Rochester ME1 . . . . . . .63 C5
Kings Par **7** TN24 . . .268 B2
Kings Pk TN2 . . . . .286 D3
King's Pk CT1 . . . . .143 B1
Kingsdale Rd CT14 . . . .63 C5
Kings Prep SchCT1 . . . .63 C5
Kings Prospect TN24 . .300 E6
Kings Rd Aylesham CT3 .210 F6
Biggin Hill TN16 . . . . .118 C2
Dover CT17 . . . . .310 A7
Folkestone CT20 . . . . .334 D6
Headcorn TN27 . . . . . .262 C5
Minster (Sheppey) ME12 .47 D7
Orpington BR6 . . . . . . .86 F6
Ramsgate CT11 . . . . . .117 D8
King's Rd Birchington CT781 A6
Chatham ME5 . . . . . . .64 A4
Faversham ME13 . . . . .138 C7
Herne Bay CT6 . . . . . . .76 F5
Tonbridge TN9 . . . . . . .254 D7
Kings Reach ME15 . . . .195 C8
Kingsridge Gdns DA1. . .15 D1
Kings Ropewalk CT7 .310 B5
Kings Row
1 Maidstone ME15 . .162 A1
Rochester ME1 . . . . . . .63 B4
King's SchME1 . . . . . . .63 C5
King's Sch Canterbury The
CT1 . . . . .142 F2
King's Sch Recn Ctr The
CT1 . . . . .142 F2
Kings Sch The **16**CT1. 175 A8
King's Standing Ind Est
TN2 . . . . .254 F2
Kings Standing Way
TN2 . . . . .254 F1
King St Brookland TN29 362 C2
Canterbury CT1 . . . . . .142 F1
Chatham ME4 . . . . . . .64 A4
Deal CT14 . . . . .215 D6
Deal, Walmer CT14 . . .215 D3
Dover CT16 . . . . .310 D7
Fordwich CT2 . . . . . . .144 A4
Gillingham ME7 . . . . . .64 C6
Gravesend DA12 . . . . . .19 B1
Maidstone ME14 . . . . .162 A4
Margate CT9 . . . . .50 J3
Ramsgate CT11 . . . . . .117 E7
Rochester ME1 . . . . . . .63 C4
Sandwich CT13 . . . . . .149 A1
Sheerness ME12 . . . . . .28 A2
Sittingbourne ME10 . .101 E5
West Malling ME19 . . .159 C8
Kings Toll Rd TN2 . . . .288 A6
KINGSTON 209 D3
Kingston Ave CT9 . . . . .82 C7
Kingston Cl
Crabble CT17 . . . . .277 F3
Herne Bay CT6 . . . . . . .77 F5
Ramsgate CT12 . . . . . .83 B2
Kingston Cres ME5 . . . .97 C4
Kingston Ct DA11 . . . . .18 B1
Kingston Dr ME15 . . . .195 A8
Kingstone Ct **3** CT20. 335 B5
Kingsway Chatham ME5. .64 D1
Dymchurch TN29 . . . .352 E2
Gillingham ME7 . . . . . .64 E1
Orpington BR5 . . . . . . .53 D4
Kingswear Gdns ME2. .63 C7
Kings Wlk Grays RM17. .18 A8
Maidstone ME14 . . . . .162 B5
KINGSWOOD 197 E3
Kingswood Ave
Chatham ME4 . . . . . . .63 F2
Erith DA17 . . . . .3 F2
Swanley BR8 . . . . .55 F6
Kingswood Cl
Ashford TN24 . . . . . . .268 D5
Dartford DA1 . . . . .15 C1
Orpington BR6 . . . . . . .86 F3
Royal Tunbridge Wells
TN2 . . . . .286 C3
Kingswood Ho
12 Maidstone ME16 . .161 A3
16 Sidcup DA14 . . . . .31 A4
Kingswood Prim Sch
ME17 . . . . .197 E2
Kingswood Rd
Gillingham ME7 . . . . . .64 D6
Kit's Coty ME20 . . . . . .129 D8
Royal Tunbridge Wells
TN2 . . . . .286 C3
Sevenoaks TN13 . . . . .153 E7
Kingswood Villas
CT17 . . . . .278 A2
King William Rd **6**
ME7 . . . . .64 C7
Kinlet Rd SE18 . . . . . . .12 C6
Kinnell Ct **13** DA14 . . .31 B4
Kinnings Row TN9 . . . .222 C2
Kinross Cl ME5 . . . . . . .97 B1
Kinson Way CT16 . . . . .278 A5
Kinveachy Gdns SE7. . . .1 E1
Kipling Ave RM18 . . . . .19 C6
Kipling Dr ME20 . . . . . .127 F4
Kipling Rd
Ashford TN23 . . . . . . .268 B2
Bexley DA7 . . . . .13 C6
Dartford DA1 . . . . .16 B2

Kipping Cl CT18 . . . . . .307 A4
KIPPING'S CROSS 288 B5
KIPPINGTON 154 A1
Kippington Cl TN13 . . .153 F3
Kippington Dr SE9 . . . .29 D7
Kippington Rd TN13. . .154 A2
Kirby Cl Chattenden ME3 40 F5
Kirby Cl CT14 . . . . .248 D6
Kirby's Hts **8** CT2 . . . .142 F1
Kirby's La CT1 . . . . . . .142 F1
Kirkcourt TN13 . . . . . . .154 A4
Kirkdale Cl ME5 . . . . . .97 D1
Kirkdale Cotts ME15 . .194 F6
Kirkdale Rd
TN1 . . . . .286 B4
Kirk Gdns CT14 . . . . . .215 B4
Kirkham Rd E6 . . . . .1 E7
Kirk St SE18 . . . . .12 B8
Kirkins Cl TN12 . . . . . .290 A6
Kirk La SE18 . . . . .12 A8
Kirkland Cl DA15 . . . . .12 E1
Kirkland Ct TN12 . . . . .260 E3
Kirklside SE3 . . . . .11 A8
Kirkstone Ave CT11. . . .116 F7
Kirkwood Ave TN26 . . .326 A1
Kirton Cl CT18 . . . . . . .306 F4
Kitchener Ave
Chatham ME4 . . . . . . .64 A1
Gravesend DA12 . . . . . .37 C5
Kitchener Cl CT4 . . . . .242 F8
Kitchener Cotts ME3 . .25 C4
Kitchener Rd
Chattenden ME3 . . . . .40 F4
Dover CT17 . . . . .310 A4
Herne Bay CT6 . . . . . . .76 F5
Kitchener Sq CT19 . . . .335 E8
Kite Farm CT5 . . . . .75 D3
Kite La TN12 . . . . .289 A6
Kitewell La TN29 . . . . .376 D8
Kither Rd TN23 . . . . . .300 A4
Kit Hill ME13 . . . . .171 D8
Kit Hill Ave ME5 . . . . . .96 E3
Kitsbridge La TN26 . . .349 F5
KIT'S COTY 129 C6
Kittiwake Cl CT6 . . . . . .77 F5
Klondyke Ind EstME11. .45 F4
Knatchbull Way TN25. .302 E5
Knatts La TN15 . . . . . . .123 A8
KNATTS VALLEY 90 D1
Knatts Valley Rd TN15. .90 D2
Knaves Acre TN27 . . . .262 C5
Knavesacre Ct ME8. . . .98 D5
KNAVE'S ASH 111 C5
Knave Wood Rd TN15. .122 C2
Knee Hill SE2 . . . . .3 C1
Knee Hill Cres SE2 . . . . .3 C2
Knell La CT3 . . . . .147 C3
Knight Ave
Canterbury CT2 . . . . . .174 D8
Gillingham ME7 . . . . . .64 D7
Knighton Rd TN14 . . . .121 F2
Knight Rd Rochester ME2 63 B4
Tonbridge TN10 . . . . . .222 E6
Knightrider Ct ME15. . .162 A3
Knightrider St
Maidstone ME15 . . . . .162 A3
Sandwich CT13 . . . . . .149 A1
Knights Alley **20** CT5 . .74 D2
Knight's Ave **4** 84 B6
Knightsbridge Ct TN4 .285 D1
Knightsbridge Ct TN1 .286 B6
Knightsbridge Mews
BR7 . . . . .29 F1
Knights Cl
Hoo St Werburgh ME3 . .41 E5
Pembury TN2 . . . . .287 D7
Knights Croft DA1 . . . .91 F7
Knight's Ct Dover CT17. .278 B1
Sittingbourne ME10 . .101 E3
Knights Field ME4 . . . .89 E7
Knightsfield Rd ME10. .101 D7
Knights Manor Way
DA1 . . . . .15 F1
Knights Park Ind Est
ME2 . . . . .63 A6
Knights Pk TN11 . . . . . .254 F1
Knights Rd
Hoo St Werburgh ME3 . .41 D5
Newham E16 . . . . .1 A4
Knight's Ridge TN2. . . .287 D7
Knights Templars
CT17 . . . . .310 C6
Knights Way
Dover CT16 . . . . .278 A3
Royal Tunbridge Wells TN2,
TN11 . . . . .254 F1
Knight's Way TN27 . . . .262 D6
KNOCKHALL 17 C1
Knockhall Chase DA11. .17 C2
Knockhall Com Prim Sch
DA9 . . . . .17 C2
Knockhall Rd DA9 . . . . .17 C2
Knock Hill TN30 . . . . . .361 A2
KNOCKHOLT 120 D7
KNOCKHOLT POUND 120 D4
Knockholt Rd
Eltham SE9 . . . . .11 D2
Halstead TN14 . . . . . .120 F6
Margate CT9 . . . . .51 F3
Knockholt StaTN14. . . .87 E2
Knockhurst Ct TN30 . .324 C1
KNOCKMILL 122 A5
Knock Mill La TN15 . . .124 A5
Knock Rd TN23 . . . . . .300 A4
Knockwood Rd TN30 . .324 C1

Knold Pk CT9 . . . . .82 E8
Knole★ TN15 . . . . .154 D1
Knole Ct TN14 . . . . . . .187 B2
Knole Gate DA15 . . . . .30 E5
Knole La TN13, TN15 . .154 C1
Knole Paddock & Raleys
 . . . . .154 C3
Knole Rd Chatham ME5 . .97 C3
Dartford DA1 . . . . .33 B8
Sevenoaks TN13 . . . . .154 D4
Knole The Eltham SE9. . .30 A4
Faversham ME13 . . . . .138 B7
Istead Rise DA13 . . . . .36 F2
Knole Way TN13. . . . . .154 C2
Knoll Cl
Folkestone CT20 . . . . .335 C4
Orpington BR6 . . . . . . .86 F8
Knoll Hill TN25 . . . . . .330 C3
Knoll La TN23 . . . . .299 E7
Knoll Pl CT14 . . . . .215 C2
Knoll Rd Sidcup DA14 . .31 B4
Sidcup, Old Bexley DA5. .14 A1
Knoll Rise BR6 . . . . . . .53 F1
St Margaret's at Cliffe
CT15 . . . . .280 A6
Knoll Way ME14 . . . . . .49 D4
Knotley Hall Cotts
TN11 . . . . .220 A2
Knott Cres TN24 . . . . .301 A7
Knott Ct ME14 . . . . . . .161 F6
Knotts La CT15 . . . . . .279 F6
Knotts Pl TN13 . . . . . . .154 A3
Knotts Sq **1** TN23 . . .268 C2
Knowle Cl TN3 . . . . . . .284 F3
Knowle Cott TN3 . . . . .314 E1
Knowle Cotts TN3 . . . .314 E1
Knowle La TN12 . . . . . .257 C3
Knowle Lodge BR7 . . . .29 F2
Knowle Rd
Maidstone ME14 . . . . .162 B6
Orpington BR2 . . . . . . .85 E8
Paddock Wood TN12 . .257 D3
Wouldham ME1 . . . . . .95 D4
Knowler Way CT6 . . . . .77 C5
Knowles Gdns TN27 . .262 D5
Knowles Wlk TN12 . . . .260 F4
KNOWLTON 212 C7
Knowlton Gdns ME16 .161 B2
Knowlton Gn BR2 . . . . .52 A4
Knowlton Wlk **1** CT1. 143 B1
Knowsley Way TN11 . .221 D6
KNOX BRIDGE 292 F6
Knox Ct TN15 . . . . .154 F6
Kohima Pl CT15 . . . . . .278 F2
Koonowla Cl TN16. . . .118 D4
Kydbrook Cl BR5 . . . . . .53 C2
Kyetop Wlk ME8. . . . . . .98 D6
Kynaston Rd
Bromley BR1 . . . . .29 A3
Orpington BR5 . . . . . . .54 B2

L

La Belle Alliance Sq **9**
CT11 . . . . .117 E7
LABOUR-IN-VAIN 124 F5
Labour-in-Vain Rd
TN15 . . . . .124 C5
Laburnham Pl SE9. . . . .12 A2
Laburnum Ave
Dartford DA1 . . . . .33 D7
Sandwich CT13 . . . . . .180 F8
Swanley BR8 . . . . .55 D6
Laburnum Cl CT16 . . . .277 E4
Laburnum Ct TN2 . . . . .286 C2
Laburnum Dr ME20 . . .128 A2
Laburnum Gr
Northfleet DA11 . . . . . .36 D8
Sheerness ME12 . . . . . .28 H1
Laburnum Ho ME12 . . .28 B2
Laburnum La CT12 . . . .144 B7
Laburnum Pl ME10 . . .101 E7
Laburnum Rd ME2 . . . .62 E5
Laburnum Way BR2 . . .53 B2
Labworth Cl ME12 . . . .46 E6
Lacebark Cl DA15 . . . . .30 F8
Lacey Cl ME17 . . . . . . .196 E4
Laceys La ME17 . . . . . .227 C7
Lachlan Way **2** CT20 .334 F3
Lackenden Cotts CT3 . .176 D6
Lacknut Cotts DA13 . . .92 E2
Lacock Gdns
Loose ME15 . . . . .195 A8
Maidstone ME15 . . . . .162 A1
Lacton Oast TN24 . . . .301 B8
Lacton Way TN24 . . . . .301 A8
Lacy Cl ME16 . . . . .161 D7
Ladbrooke Cres DA14 . .31 D5
Ladbrooke Ho **7**
ME14 . . . . .162 A5
Ladbrooke Rd E16 . . . . . .1 B7
LADDINGFORD 225 E5
Laddingford Farm Ind Est
ME18 . . . . .225 D4
Laddingford St Mary's CE
Prim SchME18 . . . . . . .225 E4
Ladds Cnr ME7 . . . . . . .65 B5
Ladds La ME6 . . . . .95 A4
Ladds Way BR8 . . . . . . .55 D5
LADE 377 E6
Lade Fort Cotts TN29. .377 E6
Lade Fort Cres TN29. . .377 E6
Ladham Rd TN17 . . . . .291 A4
Ladies Mile TN11 . . . . .311 D4
Ladies Wlk CT21, TN2. .333 C1
Lady Boswell's CE Prim
SchTN13 . . . . .154 C2
Ladyclose Ave ME3. . . .40 A7
Ladycroft Gdns **6** BR6 .86 C5

Ladycroft Way BR6 . . . .86 C5
Ladyfern Ct TN2 . . . . . .286 C4
Ladyfields
Herne Bay CT6 . . . . . . .77 D2
Northfleet DA11 . . . . . .36 F4
Ladyfields Cl ME9 . . . .100 F5
Lady Garne Rd CT15 . .308 D1
Lady Joanna Thornhill
(Endowed) Prim Sch
TN25 . . . . .237 E2
Lady Oak La TN5, TN17 339 C7
Lady's Gift Rd TN4 . . . .285 E8
Lady Shaw **18** ME15 . .195 E5
Ladyshaw Gr CT5 . . . . .107 F6
Ladysmith Rd SE9 . . . .12 A1
Lady Vane Cl TN11 . . . .189 C5
Ladywell **7** CT16 . . . . .310 D8
Ladywell Ho
2 Dover CT16 . . . . . .310 D8
7 Orpington BR5. . . . .54 B7
Ladywood Ave BR5 . . . .53 C4
Ladywood Rd
Cuxton ME2 . . . . .62 B2
Dartford DA2 . . . . .34 E3
Sturry CT2 . . . . .143 F7
Lady Wootton's Gn **6**
CT1 . . . . .175 A8
La Galamina TN28 . . . .377 E6
Lagonda Way DA1 . . . .15 C3
Lagoon Rd BR5 . . . . . . .54 B4
Lagos Ave CT12 . . . . . .83 A1
Lake Ave BR1 . . . . .29 A2
Lakedale Rd SE18 . . . . . .2 E1
Lake Dr ME3 . . . . .39 C6
Lakelands
Harrietsham ME17 . . . .198 C6
Loose ME15 . . . . .195 A7
Lakeman Way TN14 . . .286 B7
Lakemead TN23 . . . . . .299 E8
Lake Rd Ditton ME20. . .160 E8
Royal Tunbridge Wells
TN4 . . . . .285 E4
Laker Ho ME14 . . . . . . .162 A6
Laker Rd ME1 . . . . .96 C6
Lakeside Ashford TN23 .299 E8
Royal Tunbridge Wells
TN2 . . . . .286 E6
Lakeside Cl
Bexley DA5, DA15. . . . .13 C2
Bough Beech TN8 . . . .218 F4
Lakeside Dr BR2 . . . . . .85 C5
Lakeside Gdns ME26 . .234 F1
Lakeside PkME2 . . . . . .63 E7
Lakes Rd BR2 . . . . .85 C5
Lakes The ME20 . . . . . .128 A4
Lakesview International
Bsns PkCT3 . . . . .112 A1
Lakeswood Rd BR5 . . . .53 C2
Lakeview Cl ME6 . . . . .128 A6
Lakeview Cl ME6 . . . . .128 A6
Lake View Rd TN13 . . .154 A4
Lake Wlk ME20 . . . . . .128 A5
Lakewood Rd ME8. . . . .98 C6
Laking Ave CT10. . . . . .84 B7
Laleham Gap SchCT10. 84 B2
Laleham Gdns CT9 . . . .51 B2
Laleham Rd CT9 . . . . . .51 B1
Laleham Wlk CT9. . . . . .51 B1
Lamb Ave SE9 . . . . .30 A4
Lambarde Ave ME2 . . . .95 A4
Lambarde Dr TN13 . . . .154 A4
Lambarde Rd TN13 . . . .154 A4
Lambardes DA3 . . . . . . .59 F1
Lambarde Ho **8** ME14 .162 A5
Lambermere Rd TN27 .265 C6
Lambe Cl ME6. . . . . . . .95 A4
LAMBERHURST 317 B5
Lamberhurst Cl **13** BR5 54 D1
Lamberhurst Gn ME8 . .65 B3
LAMBERHURST
QUARTER 288 D2
Lamberhurst Rd
Horsmonden TN12,
TN3 . . . . .289 E3
Lamberhurst St Mary's CE
Prim SchTN3. . . . . . . .317 A4
Lamberhurst Vineyard★
TN3 . . . . .317 A4
Lamberhurst Way CT9. .51 F3
Lambersart Ct TN4 . . . .254 D1
Lambert Cl TN16 . . . . .118 D3
Lambert Ct DA8 . . . . . . .14 C4
Lambert Ho CT14. . . . .215 A4
Lambert Mews **4**
ME6 . . . . .128 A6
Lambert Rd E16 . . . . .1 B7
Lamberts Pl TN12 . . . .290 B5
Lamberts Rd TN2 . . . . .286 D5
Lambert's Yd TN9 . . . . .222 B1
Lambes Ct ME8. . . . . . .98 D5
Lambeth Cl ME5 . . . . . .97 B4
Lambeth Rd CT1 . . . . .143 C7
Lambourn Dr ME19 . . .159 A2
Lambourne Pl
Gillingham ME8. . . . . . .66 A2
Greenwich SE3 . . . . . .11 B6
Lambourne Rd ME15 . .162 F2
Lambourn Ho BR1 . . . .29 E1
Lambourn Way
Chatham ME5 . . . . . . .97 C2
Royal Tunbridge Wells
TN2 . . . . .286 D1
Lambs Bank TN9 . . . . .254 B7
Lambscroft Ave SE9 . . .29 D5

Lamb's Cross ME17. . . .319 A5
Lambsfrith Gr ME7 . . . .98 B3
Lamb's Mobile Home Pk
TN12 . . . . .257 A7
Lamb's Wlk CT5 . . . . . .108 C6
Lambton Ct CT17 . . . . .278 A1
Laming Rd CT7. . . . . . .81 B6
Lammas Dr ME10. . . . .101 E6
Lammas Gate ME13 . . .138 D8
Lamorbey Cl DA15. . . . .30 F6
Lamorna Ave CT12 . . . .83 A1
Lamorna Cl BR6 . . . . . .54 A2
Lampington Row TN3 .284 E4
Lamplighters Cl
2 Dartford DA1. . . . . .15 F1
Gillingham ME7 . . . . . .97 F5
Lamport Cl SE18 . . . . . . .1 F2
Lamson Rd RM13. . . . . . .4 F8
Lancashire Rd ME15 . .195 E12
Lancaster Ave CT18 . . .308 C2
Lancaster Cl
Hamstreet TN26 . . . . .349 A8
Ramsgate CT12 . . . . . .83 B1
Lancaster Ct
Gillingham ME8. . . . . . .98 C1
Gravesend DA12 . . . . . .37 C5
Lancaster Gdns
Birchington CT7 . . . . . .80 F6
Bromley BR1 . . . . .52 E4
Herne Bay CT6 . . . . . . .77 D5
Lancaster Ho
Deal CT14 . . . . .215 A5
3 Dover CT17 . . . . . .310 D7
Lancaster Rd
Canterbury CT1. . . . . . .174 F6
Dover CT17 . . . . .310 D7
Lancaster The CT10 . . .84 B3
Lancaster Way
Ashford TN23 . . . . . . .267 F4
Kings Hill ME19. . . . . .158 F3
Lance Cl ME10 . . . . . . .101 F8
Lance Croft DA3. . . . . . .91 F8
Lancelot Ave ME2 . . . . .62 E7
Lancelot Cl Deal CT14. .215 A3
Rochester ME2 . . . . . . .62 E6
Lancelot Ct BR6 . . . . . .87 B8
Lancer Ho ME1. . . . . . . .63 C3
Lances La ME15 . . . . . .195 A6
Lancet La ME15 . . . . . .195 A6
Lancey Cl SE7. . . . . .1 E2
Lanchester Cl CT6 . . . . .76 A3
Lancing Rd BR6 . . . . . . .87 B8
Landale Gdns DA1 . . . .33 C8
Landbury Wlk TN23 . . .267 F4
Landon Rd CT6 . . . . . . .77 C4
Landor Ct ME7 . . . . . . .98 A3
Landrail Rd ME9. . . . . . .67 B3
Landseer Ave DA11. . . .36 D5
Landseer Cl TN10 . . . . .222 E6
Landstead Rd SE18 . . . .12 D7
Landway TN15. . . . . . . .154 F7
Land Way ME3 . . . . .39 C6
Landway The
Borough Green TN15 . .156 F7
Kemsing TN15 . . . . . . .123 A2
Maidstone ME14 . . . . .163 A4
Orpington BR5 . . . . . . .54 C6
Lane The DA9 . . . . .17 C1
LANE END 34 D3
Lane End Bexley DA7 . . .14 B4
Herne Bay CT6 . . . . . . .76 D5
Lanes Ave DA11 . . . . . .37 A5
Lanes The CT12 . . . . . .115 D6
Lane's Wlk CT5. . . . . . . .74 E2
Lane The
Fordcombe TN3 . . . . . .284 C5
Greenwich SE3 . . . . . . .11 A4
Guston CT15 . . . . .278 F6
Lanfranc Gdns CT2 . . .142 C1
Lanfranc Ho **5** CT1 . . .143 A1
Lanfranc Rd CT14 . . . .215 C8
Langafel CE Prim Sch
DA3 . . . . .59 A6
Langafel Cl DA3. . . . . . .58 E7
Langbrook Rd SE3. . . . .11 D1
Lang Ct CT5 . . . . .75 C3
Langdale TN23 . . . . . . .299 E8
Langdale Ave CT11 . . . .117 A7
Langdale Cl
Gillingham ME8. . . . . . .65 D1
Orpington BR6 . . . . . . .86 B7
Langdale Cres DA7. . . .14 A6
Langdale Rise ME16. . .161 C5
Langdale Wlk **5** DA11. 36 E5
Langdon Cl CT15 . . . . .279 F5
Langdon Cross CT15 . .279 C7
Langdon Prim Sch
CT15 . . . . .247 A1
Langdon Rd
Bromley BR2 . . . . .52 B6
Folkestone CT19 . . . . .334 D2
Rochester ME1 . . . . . . .63 C4
Langdon Shaw DA14. . .30 F7
Langford Pl DA14 . . . . .31 A5
Langham Cl CT9 . . . . . .50 F1
Langham Gr ME16 . . . .161 C4
Langholm Rd
Ashford TN23 . . . . . . .300 A7
Langton Green TN3. . . .284 F3
Langhorne Gdns **9**
CT20 . . . . .335 C4
Langhorne Ho **6**SE7. . .11 C8
LANGHURST 216 E7
LANGLEY 196 C4
Langley Ct **13** SE9 . . . .12 A1
Langley Gdns
2 Bromley BR2 . . . . . .52 C5

Langley Gdns continued
Margate CT9 . . . . .51 E3
Orpington BR5 . . . . .53 B3
LANGLEY HEATH 196 F4
Langley Ho
6 Bromley BR1 . . . . .29 B1
11 Maidstone ME16 . . . .161 A3
Langley Rd Bexley DA16 .13 C8
Sittingbourne ME10 . . . .101 F7
Langmore Ct DA7 . . . . . . .13 D4
Langney Dr TN23 . . . . . . .299 E6
Langport Rd ME18 . . . . .373 C6
Langton Ct ME14 . . . . . .162 C5
Langton Cotts CT3 . . . . .146 B5
LANGTON GREEN 284 E3
Langton Green Prim Sch
TN3 . . . . .284 E4
Langton La CT4 . . . . . . .175 A4
Langton Rd
Rusthall TN3, TN4 . . . . . .285 C3
Speldhurst TN3 . . . . .285 A7
Langton Ridge TN3 . . . .285 B3
Langton Way
Greenwich SE3 . . . . .11 B7
Maidstone ME15 . . . . . .161 A2
Langworth Cl DA2 . . . . . .33 D5
Lankester Parker Rd
ME1 . . . . .96 C6
Lannoy Rd SE9 . . . . .30 C7
Lanridge Rd SE2 . . . . .3 D3
Lansbury Cres DA1 . . . . . .16 A2
Lansbury Ct 4 SE28 . . . .3 B6
Lansbury Gdns ME16 . . . .19 A6
Lansbury Ho 5 DA17 . . . .3 F1
Lansdowne Ave
Bexley DA7 . . . . .13 C7
Maidstone ME15 . . . . . .195 C6
Orpington BR6 . . . . .53 B1
Lansdowne Ct 9 ME4 . .63 F4
Lansdowne La SE7 . . . . . .1 D1
Lansdowne Mews SE7 . . .1 D1
Lansdowne Prim Sch
Sittingbourne ME10 . . . .102 C3
Tilbury RM18 . . . . .18 F5
Lansdowne Rd
Bromley BR1 . . . . .29 B1
Chatham ME4 . . . . .63 E2
Royal Tunbridge Wells
TN1 . . . . .286 B4
Sevenoaks TN13 . . . . . .154 D5
Tonbridge TN9 . . . . .222 B2
Lansdowne Sq
Northfleet DA11 . . . . .18 F1
8 Royal Tunbridge Wells
TN1 . . . . .286 B4
Lansdown Pl DA11 . . . . . .36 F7
Lansdown Rd
Canterbury CT1 . . . . . . .175 A7
Sidcup DA14 . . . . .31 B5
Sittingbourne ME10 . . . .102 C4
Tilbury RM18 . . . . .18 F5
Lantern Cl BR6 . . . . .86 B6
Lantern Ho SE18 . . . . .2 A1
Lanthorne Mews
Royal Tunbridge Wells,
Calverley Park TN1 . . . .286 B3
Royal Tunbridge Wells
TN1 . . . . .286 B5
Lanthorne Rd CT10 . . . . . .84 A6
Lapins La ME19 . . . . . . .158 F2
Lapis Cl DA12 . . . . .38 B7
La Providence ME1 . . . . . .63 C5
Lapwing Cl Erith DA8 . . . .15 B7
Hawkinge CT18 . . . . . . .307 A3
Minster (Sheppey) ME12 .47 B5
Lapwing Dr
Ashford TN23 . . . . .300 D3
Lower Halstow ME9 . . . . .67 B3
Lapwing Rd ME3 . . . . .27 B5
Lapwings DA3 . . . . .59 B6
Lapwings The DA12 . . . . .37 D6
Lapworth Cl BR6 . . . . . . .87 C8
Larch Cl
Broadstairs CT10 . . . . . .83 D4
Hersden CT3 . . . . .144 E8
Larkfield ME20 . . . . .128 B2
Larch Cres
Hoo St Werburgh ME3 . . .41 E3
Tonbridge TN10 . . . . . . .222 C6
Larchcroft ME5 . . . . .97 A4
Larch Dene BR6 . . . . .86 A8
Larches The
Faversham ME13 . . . . . .138 A8
Higham ME3 . . . . .39 C3
Whitstable CT5 . . . . .108 C3
Larch Gr
Paddock Wood TN12 . . . .256 F6
Sidcup DA15 . . . . .30 F7
Larch Rd Dartford DA1 . .33 D7
Elvington CT15 . . . . .212 B1
Larch Terr ME12 . . . . .46 A8
Larch Way BR2 . . . . .53 A2
Larch Wlk
Ashford TN24 . . . . .268 C6
Swanley BR8 . . . . .55 D7
Larch Wood Cl ME5 . . . . .97 D1
Larchwood Rd SE9 . . . . . .30 B6
Largo Wlk DA8 . . . . .14 E6
Larkey View CT4 . . . . . . .173 E1
LARKFIELD 128 A2
Larkfield TN12 . . . . .256 A7
Larkfield Ave
Gillingham ME7 . . . . .64 E4
Sittingbourne ME10 . . . .101 E6
Larkfield Cl Hayes BR2 . .85 A8
Larkfield ME20 . . . . .128 A1
Larkfield L Ctr ME20 . . .128 A3
Larkfield Rd
Larkfield ME20 . . . . .128 B1
Sevenoaks TN13 . . . . . .153 C4

Larkfield Rd continued
Sidcup DA14 . . . . .30 F5
Larkfields DA11 . . . . . . .36 E5
Larkfield Trad Est
ME20 . . . . .128 B5
Larkin Cl ME2 . . . . .40 B2
Larking Dr ME16 . . . . . . .161 D7
Larkscliff Ct CT7 . . . . .80 D8
Larks Field DA3 . . . . .58 F5
Larksfield Rd ME13 . . . . .105 C1
Larkspur Cl
2 East Malling ME19 . . .128 A1
1 Newham E6 . . . . .1 E8
Orpington BR6 . . . . .87 C7
Larkspur Lodge DA14 . . .31 B5
Larkspur Rd
Chatham ME5 . . . . .96 E4
West Malling ME19 . . . .127 F1
**Larkstore PktN12 . . . . . .260 E5
Larkswood Cl DA8 . . . . . .15 A6
Larkwood La DA8 . . . . . . .14 E7
La Rocco TN28 . . . . .377 E8
Lascelles Rd CT17 . . . . .310 A6
Laser Quay ME2 . . . . .63 D6
LASHENDEN 294 F6
**Lashenden Air Warfare
Mus** ★ TN27 . . . . .263 A2
Lassa Rd SE9 . . . . .11 F2
La Tausco TN28 . . . . .377 D8
Latchgate CT20 . . . . .334 C3
La-Tene CT14 . . . . .215 B2
Latham Cl
Biggin Hill TN16 . . . . . . .118 C3
Dartford DA2 . . . . .34 E6
Newham E6 . . . . .1 E7
Latham Ho DA6 . . . . .14 A2
Lathe Barn ★ TN29 . . . . .352 D5
Latimer Cl CT6 . . . . .76 B2
Latimer Pl 4 ME7 . . . . . .64 C7
Latona Dr DA2 . . . . .37 F3
La Tourne Gdns BR6 . . . . .86 C7
Latymers ME11 . . . . .252 B4
Launcelot Prim Sch
BR1 . . . . .29 A4
Launcelot Rd BR1 . . . . . . .29 A4
Launder Way ME15 . . . . .161 E2
Laundry Rd CT12 . . . . . .115 D7
Launton Dr DA6 . . . . .13 D3
Laura Dr BR8 . . . . .33 A1
Laura Pl ME1 . . . . .63 A2
Laura Villas CT6 . . . . .76 E5
Laureate Ct CT9 . . . . .51 B2
Laurel Ave
Gravesend DA12 . . . . . . .37 C6
St Mary's Bay TN29 . . . .365 F4
Laurel Bank
Royal Tunbridge Wells
TN4 . . . . .286 B8
Wadhurst TN5 . . . . .337 A4
Laurel Cl Dartford DA1 . .33 C7
Folkestone CT20 . . . . . .334 E6
Sidcup DA14 . . . . .31 A5
Laurel Gdns BR1 . . . . .52 E5
Laurel Gr ME17 . . . . .197 D2
Laurel Ho Greenwich SE7 11 C8
Sheerness ME12 . . . . .28 B2
Laurel Rd
Gillingham ME7 . . . . .64 C7
Royal Tunbridge Wells
TN2 . . . . .286 D7
Laurels The
12 Bromley BR1 . . . . . . .52 B8
Bromley BR2 . . . . .52 A5
19 Erith DA17 . . . . .4 A1
Maidstone ME16 . . . . . .161 C2
New Barn DA3 . . . . .59 D6
Wilmington DA2 . . . . .33 C5
Laurel Way
Chartham CT4 . . . . .173 E1
Royal Tunbridge Wells
TN2 . . . . .286 D7
Laurel Wlk ME8 . . . . .98 E6
Laurensfield CT12 . . . . .115 C7
Laureston Pl CT16 . . . . .310 E8
Laurice Ct 6 CT11 . . . . .117 C6
Laurie Gray Ave ME5 . . .96 D1
Lauriston Ct CT19 . . . . . .117 A5
Lauriston Mount CT10 . .84 A5
Lausanne Rd CT9 . . . . . . .50 J2
Lausanne Terr 11 CT9 . .50 J2
Lavenda Cl ME7 . . . . .64 C8
Lavender Cl Bromley BR2 52 E3
1 Chatham ME5 . . . . . . .96 E4
East Malling ME19 . . . . .159 F8
Margate CT9 . . . . .82 C8
Whitstable CT5 . . . . .75 C2
Lavender Gdns TN5 . . . .338 E1
Lavender Hill
Swanley BR8 . . . . .55 D6
Tonbridge TN9 . . . . .254 C8
Lavender Ho 3 ME15 . .195 D8
Lavender La CT12 . . . . . .116 C5
Lavender Mews 19
CT1 . . . . .174 F8
Lavender Rd ME19 . . . . .159 F8
Lavender Sq 6 TN18 . . .341 A2
Lavenders Rd ME19 . . . .159 C6
Lavender Wlk 5 ME19 159 F8
Lavernock Rd DA7 . . . . . .14 A5
Laverstoke Rd ME16 . . . .161 C8
Lavidge Rd SE9 . . . . .29 F6
Lavinia Rd 1 DA1 . . . . . .15 F1
Lavisham Ho BR1 . . . . . . .29 B3
Law Cl CT2 . . . . .174 C8
Lawford Gdns DA1 . . . . . .15 C2
Lawley Cl CT12 . . . . .83 C1
Lawn Cl Bromley BR1 . . . .29 B1
Chatham ME4 . . . . .64 B2
Swanley BR8 . . . . .55 C7
Tenterden TN30 . . . . . . .344 F7
Lawn Pk TN13 . . . . .187 B8
Lawn Prim Sch DA11 . . .18 C1

Lawn Rd
Broadstairs CT10 . . . . . .84 A4
Deal CT14 . . . . .215 C1
Northfleet DA11 . . . . .18 C1
Tonbridge TN9 . . . . .254 B8
Lawns Cres RM17 . . . . . . .18 D8
Lawns The
Brenchley TN12 . . . . . . .289 B8
15 Ramsgate CT11 . . . .117 F7
Sidcup DA14 . . . . .31 B4
Lawn Villas CT11 . . . . . .117 E6
Lawrance Sq 1 DA11 . .36 F5
Lawrence Cl
Folkestone CT19 . . . . . .334 F6
Loose ME15 . . . . .195 A7
Lawrence Ct CT19 . . . . . .335 E6
Lawrence Dr DA2 . . . . . . .61 A5
Lawrence Gdns
Herne Bay CT6 . . . . .77 C4
Tilbury RM18 . . . . .19 B7
Lawrence Hill Gdns
DA1 . . . . .15 C1
Lawrence Hill Rd DA1 . .15 C1
Lawrence Rd Erith DA8 . .14 B7
Hayes BR4 . . . . .85 A6
Tonbridge TN10 . . . . . . .222 E6
Lawrence St ME7 . . . . . . .64 C5
Lawrence Trad Est
RM17 . . . . .17 E8
Laws La TN25 . . . . .329 D7
Lawson Cl
Chartham CT4 . . . . .173 D2
Newham E16 . . . . .1 C8
Lawson Gdns DA1 . . . . . .15 D3
Lawson Ho 1 SE18 . . . .12 A8
Lawson Rd DA1 . . . . .15 D3
Lawsons Mews TN9 . . . .222 C2
Laxey Rd BR6 . . . . .86 F4
Laxey The ME15 . . . . . . .161 E1
Laxton Cl ME15 . . . . .162 F3
Laxton Dr ME17 . . . . .196 A1
Laxton Gdns TN12 . . . . .256 E7
Laxton Way
Canterbury CT1 . . . . . . .175 C7
Faversham ME13 . . . . . .138 E5
Sittingbourne ME10 . . . .101 D6
Whitstable CT5 . . . . .75 C1
Laxton Wlk ME19 . . . . . .159 B3
Layfield Cotts ME9 . . . . .68 D1
Layfield Ho 4 SE10 . . . . .1 A1
Layfield Rd ME7 . . . . .64 F7
Layhams Rd BR2 . . . . .85 A3
Lay La CT3 . . . . .147 D2
Laylam Cl CT10 . . . . .83 D5
Laymarsh Cl DA17 . . . . . . .3 F3
Layzell Wlk SE9 . . . . .29 D7
**Lazarus Trust Havens of
Rest The** 4 CT11 . . . .117 F8
Leach Ho ME13 . . . . .140 A3
Lea Cl CT21 . . . . .333 B4
Leacon Cotts TN27 . . . . .234 E4
Leacon Cotts The
TN27 . . . . .234 E4
Leacon Rd TN23 . . . . . . .267 F2
Lea Ct ME4 . . . . .63 E1
**LEADINGCROSS
GREEN** 199 C3
Leafield TN25 . . . . .303 D1
Leafield La DA14 . . . . . . .31 F5
Leafy Glade ME8 . . . . . . .98 B6
Leafy Gr BR2 . . . . .85 C5
Leafy La
Culverstone Green
DA13 . . . . .93 A3
Maidstone ME16 . . . . . .161 E5
Leafy Oak Rd SE12 . . . . . .29 C5
Leahurst Ct CT16 . . . . . . .277 E4
Leake Ho 2 ME1 . . . . . . .63 C1
Lealands Ave TN11 . . . . .221 A1
Lealands Cl TN3 . . . . . . .312 C6
Leaman Cl ME23 . . . . .23 E4
Leamington Ave
Bromley BR1 . . . . .29 C3
Orpington BR6 . . . . .86 E6
Leamington Cl BR1 . . . . .29 C3
Leamington Dr ME16 . . .161 B4
Leamouth Rd E6 . . . . .1 E8
Leander Cl CT14 . . . . . . .215 A3
Leander Dr DA12 . . . . .37 F4
Leander Rd ME1 . . . . .96 C7
Lea Rd TN13 . . . . .187 C8
Learoyd Gdns E6 . . . . .2 A6
Learoyd Rd TN28 . . . . . .373 C6
Leas Dale SE9 . . . . .30 A5
Leas Gn Broadstairs CT10 83 D4
Chislehurst BR7 . . . . .30 F2
Leaside Cotts CT21 . . . . .333 B3
Leas Lift The ★ CT20 . .335 D4
Leas Rd CT14 . . . . .215 B4
Leas The
Faversham ME13 . . . . . .138 B8
Folkestone CT20 . . . . . .335 C4
Kingsdown CT14 . . . . . .248 D3
Minster (Sheppey) ME12 .47 C8
Sheerness ME12 . . . . .28 H1
Turner's Green TN5 . . . .337 A6
Whitstable CT5 . . . . .75 D1
Woolwich SE18 . . . . .12 B6
Leatherbottle Gn DA18 . .3 F3
Leather Cl TN8 . . . . .249 C8
Leatt Cl CT10 . . . . .83 F4
Lea Vale DA1 . . . . .14 D3
LEAVELAND 170 B1
Leaveland Cl TN23 . . . . .299 E6
Leaveland Cotts ME13 .170 B2
Leaves Gn DA12 . . . . .37 D6
LEAVES GREEN 118 D8
Leaves Green Cres
BR2 . . . . .118 C8
Leaves Green Rd
Biggin Hill TN16 . . . . . . .118 D8
Keston BR2 . . . . .85 D1
Lebanon Gdns TN16 . . .118 D2

Lebrun Sq SE3 . . . . .11 B4
Leckwith Ave DA7 . . . . . .13 E8
Leclair Ho SE3 . . . . .11 B4
Leconfield Cl TN9 . . . . . .253 F7
Leda Cotts TN25 . . . . . . .234 F3
Leda Rd SE18 . . . . .1 F3
Leechcroft Ave
Sidcup DA15 . . . . .12 F2
Swanley BR8 . . . . .55 F6
Leech Cl ME1 . . . . .63 D5
LEEDS 197 A7
**Leeds & Broomfield CE
Prim Sch** ME17 . . . . . .197 A7
Leeds Castle ★ ME17 . .197 D7
Leeds Cl BR6 . . . . .87 D8
Leeds Ho ME2 . . . . .40 C1
Leeds Rd ME17 . . . . .196 E3
Leeds Sq ME17 . . . . .65 B3
Lee Gn BR5 . . . . .54 A4
LEE GREEN 40 A6
Lee Green Rd ME3 . . . . . .40 B6
Lee Ho CT14 . . . . .215 C1
Leelands Ho CT14 . . . . . .215 B1
Lee Rd ME6 . . . . .128 A8
Lees Cl The TN25 . . . . . .302 D5
Lees Court Rd ME13 . . . .170 C5
Leesons Hill BR5, BR7 . . .54 A6
Leesons Prim Sch BR5 . .54 B6
Lees Rd Ashford TN24 . .269 A1
Brabourne Lees TN25 . .302 E6
Congelow ME18 . . . . . . .225 E7
Lee Sta SE12 . . . . .11 A1
Lees Terr CT4 . . . . .172 C2
LEES THE 203 A1
Lees The CT6 . . . . .77 C5
Leeswood TN24 . . . . .269 B1
Leeswood Cl SE12 . . . . . .11 A1
Leeswood Pl BR8 . . . . . . .55 D5
Legatt Rd SE9 . . . . .11 D2
Legge La ME19 . . . . .127 D6
Leggett's La TN3 . . . . . .284 E5
Leghorn Rd SE18 . . . . .2 D1
Leicester Ave CT9 . . . . . . .51 C2
Leicester Cl CT9 . . . . .51 D3
Leicester Dr TN2 . . . . . .313 F8
Leicester Gdns ME12 . . . .49 E3
Leicester Rd
Maidstone ME15 . . . . . .195 D7
Tilbury RM18 . . . . .18 F6
Leicester Sq TN11 . . . . .252 B4
LEIGH 220 E1
Leigh Ave ME15 . . . . .195 B6
Leigh Ct ME12 . . . . .46 F5
LEIGH GREEN 345 C6
Leigh Green Ind Est
TN30 . . . . .345 C6
Leigh Pl DA16 . . . . .13 C5
Leigh Prim Sch TN11 . . .220 F1
Leigh Rd
Gravesend DA11 . . . . . . .37 B6
Ramsgate CT12 . . . . .82 F1
Rochester ME3 . . . . .40 C3
Tonbridge TN11 . . . . . . .221 D3
Leigh Sta TN11 . . . . .220 F1
Leigh Tech Acad DA1 . . .34 A7
Leigh Terr
2 Orpington BR5 . . . . . . .54 B6
Teston ME18 . . . . .160 A1
Leighton Cl ME1 . . . . . . .286 A7
Leighton Ct 3 CT16 . . . .278 C1
Leighton Gdns RM18 . . .19 A7
Leighton Rd CT16 . . . . . .278 C1
Leighville Dr CT6 . . . . . . .76 D4
Leila Parnell Pl 22 CT11 .118 C8
Leitch Row ME7 . . . . .64 A7
Leith Hill BR5 . . . . .54 A8
Leith Hill Gn BR5 . . . . . . .54 A8
Leith Park Rd DA12 . . . . .37 B7
Leivers Rd CT14 . . . . . . .215 A3
Le May Ave SE12 . . . . . . .29 B5
Lemonwell Cl SE9 . . . . . . .12 C2
Lemonwell Dr SE9 . . . . . .12 C2
Lenacre Ave CT16 . . . . . .277 F7
Lenacre La CT16 . . . . . . .277 F8
Lenacre St TN25 . . . . . . .236 B2
Len Clifton Ho 6 SE18 . .1 F2
Lenderyou Cl DA1 . . . . . . .33 E8
Lendon Rd TN15 . . . . . . .156 F6
Lendrim Cl 11 ME7 . . . . .64 A8
Leneda Dr TN2 . . . . .313 E8
Leney Rd ME18 . . . . .192 E7
Lenfield Ave ME14 . . . . .162 B4
Length The CT7 . . . . .79 F2
LENHAM 199 D5
Lenham Cl CT10 . . . . .84 A2
Lenham Ct 16 ME15 . . .162 B4
LENHAM FORSTAL 200 B1
Lenham Forstal Rd
ME17 . . . . .233 B8
Lenham Gdns CT9 . . . . . .82 B8
LENHAM HEATH 233 B8
Lenham Heath Rd
ME17 . . . . .199 C2
Lenham Ho ME17 . . . . . .199 C5
Lenham Prim Sch
ME17 . . . . .199 C5
Lenham Rd Bexley DA7 . .13 F8
Broadstone TN27,
ME17 . . . . .232 F5
Fairbourne Heath ME17 198 C1
Headcorn TN27 . . . . . . .262 E6
Lenham Sta TN27 . . . . .199 C4
Lenham Way ME8 . . . . . . .65 A3
Lenmead ME17 . . . . .199 C5
Lennard Ct 4 CT20 . . . .335 E5
Lennard Rd
Folkestone CT20 . . . . . .335 E5
Orpington BR2 . . . . .52 F1
Sevenoaks TN13 . . . . . .153 D7

Lennox Ave DA11 . . . . . . .19 A1
Lennox Ho 6 DA17 . . . . . .4 A3
Lennox Rd
Gravesend DA11 . . . . . . .37 A8
Northfleet DA11 . . . . .36 F8
Lennox Road E DA11 . . .37 A8
Lenor Cl DA6 . . . . .13 C3
Lensbury Way SE2 . . . . . . .3 D3
Lenside Dr ME15 . . . . . . .163 A2
Lenton St SE18 . . . . .2 E2
Leona Ct 8 CT9 . . . . .51 B2
Leonard Ave
Otford TN14 . . . . .122 B3
Swanscombe DA10 . . . . .35 C8
Leonard Cl ME16 . . . . . . .161 B6
Leonard Ct DA14 . . . . .31 B5
Leonard Rd ME17 . . . . . .196 E3
Leonard Sq ME6 . . . . .65 B3
Leonard Judge Ho DA2 34 E3
Leonard Pl BR2 . . . . .85 E7
Leonard Rd
7 Greatstone-on-Sea
TN28 . . . . .64 B3
Leonard Robbins Path 3
SE28 . . . . .3 B6
Leonard's Ave CT11 . . . . .83 E1
Leonard St E16 . . . . .1 E5
Leonie Ct CT6 . . . . .76 D4
Leopold Rd
2 Chatham ME4 . . . . . . .64 A3
Ramsgate CT11 . . . . . . .117 E8
Leopold St CT11 . . . . . . .117 E6
Le Roux Cl CT18 . . . . . . .306 F4
Lerryn Gdns CT10 . . . . . .83 F8
Lesley Ave CT1 . . . . .175 A6
Lesley Chalk Ho 7
TN23 . . . . .268 C2
Lesley Cl
Istead Rise DA13 . . . . . .59 F8
Sidcup DA5 . . . . .32 B8
Swanley BR8 . . . . .55 D6
Lesley Pl ME16 . . . . .161 E5
Lesley Tew CT TN10 . . . .222 C5
Leslie Ave CT9 . . . . .82 B8
Leslie Cres TN30 . . . . . . .324 B2
Leslie Rd Birchington CT7 81 A8
Gillingham ME7 . . . . .64 D7
Newham E16 . . . . .1 C8
Leslie Smith Dr ME13. 138 C7
Leslie Smith Sq 7
SE18 . . . . .12 A8
**Lesnes Abbey (remains
of)** ★ SE2 . . . . .3 D2
Lesney Park Rd DA8 . . . .14 D8
Lesney Pk DA8 . . . . .14 D8
Lessness Ave DA7 . . . . . .13 D7
LESSNESS HEATH 4 B1
Lessness Heath Prim Sch
17 DA17 . . . . .4 A1
Lessness Pk DA17 . . . . . . .4 A1
Lessness Rd 12 DA17 . . . .4 A1
Les Spickett ME13 . . . . .138 E6
Lested La ME17 . . . . .196 B1
Lester Rd ME4 . . . . .64 A3
Lestock Ho SE3 . . . . .11 D6
Letchworth Ave ME4 . . . .63 F1
Letchworth Cl BR2 . . . . . .52 A4
Letchworth Dr BR2 . . . . . .52 A4
Le Temple Rd TN12 . . . . .257 B6
Letter Box La TN13 . . . . .187 C6
LETTS GREEN 119 F3
Leverholme Gdns SE9 . .30 A4
Levett Cl ME3 . . . . .27 B6
Levetts La TN32 . . . . . . .355 D1
Leviathan Way
Chatham ME4 . . . . .64 A8
St Mary's Island ME4 . . .41 A1
Lewd La TN27 . . . . .264 A3
Lewes Cl RM17 . . . . .18 A8
Lewes Rd BR1 . . . . .52 D7
Lewin Ct SE18 . . . . .2 E2
Lewing Cl BR6 . . . . .53 E1
Lewin Rd DA6 . . . . .13 E3
Lewis Ave ME4 . . . . .65 B2
Lewis Cl ME13 . . . . .138 A7
Lewis Court Dr ME17 . . .195 C3
Lewis Cres CT9 . . . . .51 B3
Lewis Ct Ashford TN23 . .299 F7
Northfleet DA11 . . . . .36 F6
LEWISHAM 29 C6
Lewisham Rd CT17 . . . . .277 E3
Lewis King Ho 7 BR1 . . .29 B1
Lewis Mews ME6 . . . . . . .127 F6
Lewis Rd Bexley DA16 . . .13 C4
Hawkinge CT16 . . . . . . .306 F3
Istead Rise DA13 . . . . . .59 F8
Sidcup DA14 . . . . .31 C5
Swanscombe DA10 . . . . .17 E1
Lewis Row ME17 . . . . . . .228 E6
Lewson Street Rd ME9 136 E8
Leybank TN11 . . . . .221 F4
LEYBOURNE 127 D2
Leybourne Castle ★
ME19 . . . . .126 D2
Leybourne Cl
Chatham ME5 . . . . .97 A2
Hayes BR2 . . . . .52 A3
Leybourne Dell TN17 . . .342 C6
Leybourne Dr CT9 . . . . . .82 B8
Leybourne Lakes Ctry Pk ★
ME20 . . . . .128 A5
Leybourne Rd ME2 . . . . . .62 F8
**Leybourne Ss Peter & Paul
CE Prim Sch** ME19 . . .127 E2
Leybourne Way ME20 . .127 F4
Leybourn Rd CT10 . . . . . .84 B2
Leybridge Ct SE12 . . . . . .11 A2
Leyburn Cl TN9 . . . . .222 C3
Leyburne Rd CT16 . . . . . .310 D8
Leyburn Ho SE18 . . . . . . .11 E7
Leycroft Cl CT2 . . . . .142 E3
Leycroft Gdns BR6 . . . . . .51 B6
Leydenhatch La BR8 . . . . .55 D8

Leyes Rd E16 . . . . .1 D7
Leyhill Cl BR8 . . . . .55 E4
Leyland Rd SE12 . . . . .11 A2
Leys The CT12 . . . . .82 D1
LEYSDOWN-ON-SEA . .49 H2
Leysdown Rd
Eastchurch ME12 . . . . . .48 E3
Eltham SE9 . . . . .29 E3
Leysdown-on-Sea ME12 .49 C1
Leysdown View 1
CT5 . . . . .108 C6
Leyton Ave ME7 . . . . .64 E1
Leyton Cross DA2 . . . . . . .33 A6
Leyton Cross Rd DA2 . . . .32 F5
Leywood Rd DA13 . . . . . . .93 D3
Lezayre Rd BR6 . . . . .86 F4
Liberty Mews BR2 . . . . . .86 F8
Library Rd CT2 . . . . .142 D4
Libya Terr 6 ME1 . . . . . .162 A7
Lichdale Cl BR8 . . . . .86 F6
Lichfield Ave CT1 . . . . . .175 B6
Lichfield Cl ME8 . . . . .65 B2
Lichfield Ho 12 ME15 . .195 E7
Liddon Rd BR1 . . . . .52 D6
LIDSING 97 F1
Lidsing Rd ME14 . . . . . . .130 E6
Lidwells La TN17 . . . . . . .290 E1
Liege Cl ME10 . . . . .68 F1
Lieth Park Rd DA12 . . . . .37 C7
Liffler Rd SE18 . . . . .2 E1
Lighterman's Mews 2
DA11 . . . . .36 E8
Lightermans Way 6
DA9 . . . . .17 C3
Lightfoot Gn TN18 . . . . .340 E3
Lighthouse Rd CT15 . . . .280 A5
Lilac Cres ME2 . . . . .62 E6
Lilac Ct TN23 . . . . .267 E3
Lilac Gdns BR8 . . . . .55 D6
Lilac Gn 4 ME19 . . . . . .128 A1
Lilac Pl DA13 . . . . .60 B2
Lilac Rd
Minster (Sheppey)
ME12 . . . . .47 B5
Rochester ME2 . . . . .62 E5
Lila Pl BR8 . . . . .55 E5
Lilburne Gdns SE9 . . . . . .11 E2
Lilburne Rd SE9 . . . . .11 E2
Lilian Barker Cl SE12 . . .11 A2
Lilk Hill ME14 . . . . .163 C3
Lillechurch Rd ME3 . . . . .39 F7
Lillian Rd CT11 . . . . .117 F8
Lilliebum ME19 . . . . .127 D2
Lillie Rd TN16 . . . . .118 D1
Lily Nichols Ho E16. . . . . . .1 E5
LILYVALE 302 F4
Lilyvale Cotts TN25 . . . .302 F4
Lilyvale Rd TN25 . . . . . . .302 F4
Limavady Ho SE18 . . . . . .2 A2
Lime Ave
Benenden TN17 . . . . . . .342 C8
Northfleet DA11 . . . . .36 B8
Lime Cl Ashford TN23 . . .267 F3
Bromley BR1 . . . . .52 E5
Chartham CT4 . . . . .173 E1
Frant TN3 . . . . .314 B3
Marden TN12 . . . . .259 C6
Lime Cotts TN12 . . . . . . .260 F3
Lime Cres ME19 . . . . .160 A2
Lime Ct Eltham SE9 . . . . .30 B6
Gillingham ME8 . . . . .98 C3
Lime Gr
Biddenden TN27 . . . . . . .323 D7
Halfway Houses ME12 . .46 D5
Orpington BR6 . . . . .86 B8
Sidcup DA15 . . . . .12 F1
Sittingbourne ME10 . . . .102 A4
Lime Hill Rd TN1 . . . . . . .286 A4
Limehouse Ct ME10 . . . .102 D5
Lime Kiln Dr SE7 . . . . .11 B8
Lime Kiln Rd CT1 . . . . . . .174 F6
Lime Kiln Wharf ME11 . .46 A5
Lime Pit La TN13, TN14 121 C2
Limepits Cross ME9 . . . .100 F3
Lime Rd BR8 . . . . .55 D6
Lime Row DA18 . . . . .3 F3
Limes Cl TN30 . . . . .345 C8
Limes Gr TN18 . . . . .340 F5
Limes Pl 15 ME13 . . . . .138 D7
Limes Rd Dover CT16 . . .278 C1
Folkestone CT19 . . . . . .334 F6
Limes Row BR6 . . . . .86 B5
Limes The
Ashford TN23 . . . . .300 A5
Edenbridge TN8 . . . . . . .217 C1
Frittenden TN17 . . . . . . .293 E6
Lenham ME17 . . . . .199 D5
Old Romney TN29 . . . . . .372 A7
Orpington BR2 . . . . .85 E8
Lime Tree Ave DA9 . . . . . .35 A7
Limetree Cl ME5 . . . . .97 B8
Lime Tree Cl TN9 . . . . . .222 C2
Limetree Mews TN9 . . . .150 D7
Lime Trees TN12 . . . . . . .260 E4
Limetree Terr
5 Bexley DA16 . . . . .13 A4
Lenham ME17 . . . . .199 E6
Lime Tree Wlk TN13 . . . .154 B2
Lime Villas CT4 . . . . .273 F5
Limewood Rd DA8 . . . . . . .14 C7
LIMPSFIELD 183 A6
Limpsfield CE Inf Sch
RH8 . . . . .183 C6
Limpsfield Grange Sch
RH8 . . . . .183 A8
Linces The TN16 . . . . . . .278 B4
Linchmere Rd 7 SE12. .29 A4
Lincoln Ave CT1 . . . . .175 B7
Lincoln Cl Erith DA8 . . . . .14 F5
Rochester ME2 . . . . .62 D6
Whitstable CT5 . . . . .75 D3

Lincoln Ct **3** SE12 . . . . . .29 C5
Lincoln Gdns CT7 . . . . . .80 F7
Lincoln Green Rd BR5 . .53 F4
Lincoln Rd Erith DA8 . . . .14 F5
  Maidstone ME15 . . . . . 195 D8
  Sidcup DA14 . . . . .31 B3
Lincol n Rd ME7 . . . . .64 D7
Lincolnshire Terr DA7 . .34 D4
Lincolnshott DA13 . . . . . .36 B3
Lindale Flats CT14 . . . . 215 C2
Lindel Ct ME19 . . . . 159 B3
Linden Ave
  Broadstairs CT10 . . . . . . .84 B5
  Dartford DA1 . . . . .33 C7
  Herne Bay CT6 . . . . .76 E4
  Whitstable CT5 . . . . .74 F1
Linden Chase
  Canterbury CT2 . . . . . . 142 E1
  Sevenoaks TN13 . . . . . 154 B5
Linden Cl Orpington BR6 .87 A5
  Paddock Wood TN12 . . 257 A6
  Purfleet RM19 . . . . .16 C8
  Royal Tunbridge Wells
  TN4 . . . . 286 A2
  Sittingbourne ME10 . . . 101 D3
  Westgate on Sea CT8 . . .81 E7
Linden Cres CT19 . . . . . 335 D6
Linden Ct Sidcup DA14 . .30 E4
  Tonbridge TN10 . . . . . . 222 B7
Linden Dr Elham CT4 . . 273 F5
  West Minst ME12 . . . . . .46 A7
Lindenfield BR7 . . . . .53 B7
Linden Fields TN2 . . . . 286 A1
Linden Gdns CT2 . . . . . 285 F1
Linden Gr CT2 . . . . 142 E1
Linden Grove Prim Sch
TN23 . . . . 299 F6
Linden Ho
  4 Bromley BR1 . . . . . . .29 B1
  5 Chatham ME5 . . . . . .96 F4
Linden Park Rd TN2 . . . 286 A2
Linden Rd
  Ashford TN24 . . . . 268 D1
  Chartham CT4 . . . . 173 E1
  Coxheath ME17 . . . . . . 194 C4
  Gillingham ME7 . . . . .64 E5
  Westgate on Sea CT8 . . .81 F8
Lindens CT21 . . . . 333 D2
Linden Sq TN13 . . . . . . 153 E5
Lindens The
  Aylesford ME20 . . . . . . 128 E1
  Tenterden TN30 . . . . . . 324 B1
Lindenthorpe Rd CT10 . .84 A6
Lindfield Cotts ME13 . . 138 A6
Lindisfarne CI DA12 . . . .37 E6
Lindisfarne Gdns
ME16 . . . . 161 E3
Lindridge Cl CT6 . . . . . . 111 A8
Lindridge La TN12 . . . . 260 C5
Lindsay Ho **2** SE18 . . . . .2 A2
Lindsey Cl BR1 . . . . .52 E6
Lindwood Cl **8** E6 . . . . . .1 F8
Lineacre Cl ME8 . . . . . . .98 D6
Linen Ct CT1 . . . . 174 F8
Lines Terr ME4 . . . . .64 A4
Lingey Cl DA15 . . . . .30 F6
Lingfield Ave DA2 . . . . . .34 B8
Lingfield Cres SE9 . . . . . .12 D3
Lingfield Mews **4**
TN8 . . . . 217 C1
Lingfield Rd
  Borough Green TN15 . . 157 B7
  Edenbridge TN8 . . . . . . 249 A8
  Gravesend DA12 . . . . . . .37 B6
Lingley Dr ME2 . . . . .40 C2
Ling Rd Erith DA8 . . . . . .14 C8
  Newham E16 . . . . .1 A8
Lingwood DA7 . . . . .14 B5
Linington Rd CT7 . . . . . . .81 A6
LINK 20 Bsns Pk ME20 128 B3
Linkden Cotts TN18 . . . 356 E5
Link Field BR2 . . . . .52 A3
LINKHILL 356 E4
Link Hill La TN27 . . . . . 232 D3
Link La CT1 . . . . 175 A8
Link Rd Broadstairs CT10 .83 F7
  Tyler Hill CT2 . . . . 142 E6
Links Cl CT6 . . . . .77 A3
Links Cres TN29 . . . . . . 366 A4
Links Ct Deal CT14 . . . . 182 C1
  Eltham SE9 . . . . .30 B7
Linksfield Ct CT8 . . . . . . .81 D7
Linksfield Rd CT8 . . . . . .81 D7
Links Rd CT14 . . . . 215 C8
Links The
  Addington ME19 . . . . . 126 E2
  Chatham ME5 . . . . .97 B8
Links View Dartford DA1 .33 C7
  Woolwich SE18 . . . . .12 B6
Linksway CT19 . . . . 335 E8
Links Way TN28 . . . . . . 373 D6
Linksway Cl CT19 . . . . . 335 E8
Link The Ashford TN23 . 299 E7
  Eltham SE9 . . . . .30 A5
  New Ash Green DA3 . . . .91 F8
Linkway Ditton ME20 . . 128 C1
  Iwade ME9 . . . . .68 D2
Link Way Bromley BR2 . .52 E2
  Royal Tunbridge Wells
  TN2 . . . . 286 B8
Linley Cl RM18 . . . . .20 D7
Linley Rd CT10 . . . . .83 E7
Linnet Ave
  Paddock Wood TN12 . . 257 A5
  Whitstable CT5 . . . . . . 108 B6
Linnet Cl SE28 . . . . .3 C6
Linslade Rd BR6 . . . . . . .87 A4
Linsted Ct SE9 . . . . .12 E1
LINTON 194 F1
Linton Cl Bexley DA16 . .13 B6
  2 Greenwich SE7 . . . . . .1 C1
Linton Dann Cl ME3 . . . .41 D6
Linton Gdns E6 . . . . .1 E7
Linton Gore ME17 . . . . 194 D3

Linton Hill TN12 . . . . . . 227 F6
Linton Mead Prim Sch
SE28 . . . . .3 B6
Linton Park Sch ME17 195 A2
Linton Rd ME15 . . . . . . 194 F4
Lintorn Symonds Rd
ME3 . . . . .40 F5
Linwood Ave ME2 . . . . . .62 E8
Lionard Ho **3** CT2 . . . . . 142 E1
Lion Ct CT14 . . . . 215 C5
Lionel Gdns SE9 . . . . .11 D2
Lionel Oxley Ho **5**
RM17 . . . . .18 B8
Lionel Rd Eltham SE9 . . . .11 D2
  Tonbridge TN9 . . . . 254 A8
Lion Field ME13 . . . . . . 138 B7
Lion Rd Bexley DA6 . . . . .13 F3
  Newham E6 . . . . .1 F8
Lions CI SE9 . . . . .29 D5
Lion's Rd TN28 . . . . 373 A6
Lion Yd
  Faversham ME13 . . . . . 138 A6
  3 Sittingbourne ME10 . 101 F4
Liphook Way ME16 . . . . 161 C8
Lipscombe Rd TN2 . . . . 286 D6
Lipton Cl SE28 . . . . .3 C6
Liptraps La TN2 . . . . . . 286 D7
Lipwell Hill ME23 . . . . . .23 B4
Lisa Ct CT5 . . . . .75 A2
Liskeard Cl BR7 . . . . .30 C2
Liskeard Gdns SE3 . . . . .11 A6
Lisle Cl DA12 . . . . .38 B6
Lismore Cl ME15 . . . . . 195 A7
Lismore Rd
  Herne Bay CT6 . . . . .77 D5
  Whitstable CT5 . . . . . . 109 B8
Liss Rd CT13 . . . . 180 A1
Lister Cl Deal CT14 . . . . 215 C5
  Dover CT17 . . . . 278 B1
  East Malling ME19 . . . . 159 F8
Lister Dr DA11 . . . . .36 C7
Lister Ho Erith SE2 . . . . . .3 D1
  Margate CT9 . . . . .83 A8
Lister Rd Margate CT9 . . .83 A8
  Tilbury RM18 . . . . .19 A5
Lister Way CT20 . . . . . . 334 F3
Lister Wlk SE28 . . . . .3 D6
Listmas Rd ME4 . . . . . . .64 B3
List Mdws CT3 . . . . 176 F8
List The CT3 . . . . 145 C2
Listways Cotts CT3 . . . . 211 B6
Little Acorns Sch
TN30 . . . . 324 A5
Little Acres TN25 . . . . . 328 E2
Little Alley TN8 . . . . 249 B5
Little Ave CT14 . . . . 214 F3
LITTLE BAYHAM 315 F4
Little Bayham Cotts
TN3 . . . . 315 F4
LITTLE
  BETTESHANGER . . . 213 E5
Little Birches DA15 . . . . .30 E6
Little Boundes Cl TN4 . 253 F3
LITTLEBOURNE 176 E8
Littlebourne Ave ME8 . .65 B4
Littlebourne CE Prim Sch
CT3 . . . . 176 F8
Littlebourne Rd
  Canterbury CT1, CT3 . . 175 E8
  Maidstone ME14 . . . . . 162 C6
Littlebrook Cl TN23 . . . 268 A3
Little Brook Rd TN23 . . 268 A3
Littlebrook Manor Way
DA1 . . . . .16 A2
Little Brook Rd TN23 . . 268 A3
Little Browns La TN8 . . 216 F4
Little Buckland Ave
ME16 . . . . 161 D6
Little Charles St CT6 . . . .76 F5
LITTLE CHART 234 A1
LITTLE CHART
  FORSTAL 266 C8
Little Chequers TN25 . . 237 E2
Littlecombe SE7 . . . . .11 B8
Little Copse Cl CT4 . . . . 173 E1
Littlecourt Rd TN13 . . . 154 A3
Littlecroft Eltham SE9 . . .12 A4
  Istead Rise DA13 . . . . . .36 E1
Little Ct ME16 . . . . 161 D2
Littledale Dartford DA2 . .34 C5
  Woolwich SE2 . . . . .13 A8
Littlefield TN11 . . . . 223 E8
Little Field TN12 . . . . . . 260 E5
Littlefield Rd ME8 . . . . . .66 B2
Little Footway TN3 . . . . 284 F3
Little Glovers ME10 . . . 101 F3
Little Heath SE7 . . . . .1 E1
Little Heath Rd DA7 . . . . .13 F7
Little Hempen TN23 . . . 299 D8
Little Hill TN30 . . . . 324 B2
LITTLE HOUSES 232 D2
Little Job's Cross TN17343 F1
Little John Ave ME5 . . . .96 F2
Littlejohn Rd BR5 . . . . . .54 B4
Little Julians Hill
TN13 . . . . **1** 187 A8
Little Kit's Coty Ho *
ME20 . . . . 129 C5
Little Knoll TN23 . . . . . . 299 E8
Little Mallett TN3 . . . . . 284 F3
Little Market Row
ME19 . . . . 127 E2
Littlemead CT19 . . . . . . 335 A7
Littlemede SE9 . . . . .29 C5
LITTLE MILL 224 D5
Little Mill Farm Cotts
TN12 . . . . 259 C8
LITTLE MONGEHAM . . 214 A2
Littlemore Rd SE2 . . . . . .3 A4
Little Mount Sion TN1 . 286 C4
Little Oakham CT3 . . . . .25 C4
Little Orch ME17 . . . . . 194 D3
Little Oxley ME19 . . . . . 127 E2

Little Paddocks CT5 . . . 109 D7
Little Pk TN5 . . . . 336 E5
Little Queen St DA1 . . . . .33 F8
Little Redlands BR1 . . . . .52 E7
Little Robhurst TN26 . . 324 D8
Little Sheephurst Cotts
TN12 . . . . 258 E5
Littlestone Ct TN28 . . . 373 E5
Littlestone Ho TN28 . . . 373 F5
LITTLESTONE-ON-
  SEA 373 F5
Littlestone Rd TN28 . . . 373 D6
Little Stone Stile Cotts
ME13 . . . . 171 F4
Little Switzerland
TN19 . . . . 335 G8
Little Thrift BR5 . . . . .53 C5
Little Victory Mount
ME4 . . . . .41 B2
Little Walton CT13 . . . . 180 C3
Little Wood TN13 . . . . . 154 D6
Little Wood BR5 . . . . .54 A8
Little York Mdws ME7 . .65 C4
Liverpool Lawn **18**
CT11 . . . . 117 E6
Liverpool Rd CT14 . . . . 215 D2
LIVERTON STREET . . . 198 F1
Liveryman Wlk **12** CT7 .17 C3
Livesey Cl SE28 . . . . .2 C3
Livesey St ME18 . . . . . . 160 A1
Livingstone Bldgs ME7 .64 D5
Livingstone Circ ME7 . . .64 D5
Livingstone Cl TN29 . . . 353 B4
Livingstone Gdns DA12 .37 D3
Livingstone Hospl **3**
DA1 . . . . .33 F8
Livingstone Rd
  Broadstairs CT10 . . . . . .83 E6
  Gillingham ME7 . . . . .64 E5
  Gravesend DA12 . . . . . . .37 D3
Livingstone Wlk **6**
ME15 . . . . 195 F5
Lizban St SE3 . . . . .11 B7
Llanover Rd SE18 . . . . . .12 A7
Lloyd Ct CT14 . . . . 215 D1
Lloyd Dr ME10 . . . . .69 A1
Lloyd Ho BR1 . . . . .29 B3
Lloyd Rd CT10 . . . . .84 A5
Lloyds Gn TN30 . . . . . . 359 D4
Loading Bay App CT13 149 A8
Loaland Bsns Ctr ME2 . .63 D8
Loam Ct DA1 . . . . .33 E7
Loampits CI TN9 . . . . . . 222 D3
Lobelia Cl
  Gillingham ME7 . . . . .64 E6
  5 Newham E6 . . . . .1 E8
Locarno Ave ME8 . . . . . .65 A2
Lochat Rd ME3 . . . . .40 E4
Lochmere Cl DA8 . . . . . . .8 B7
Lockesley Dr BR5 . . . . . .54 A3
Lockham Farm Ave
ME17 . . . . 195 D5
Lockholt Cl TN23 . . . . . 267 E3
Lockington Ct TN9 . . . . 253 F7
Lockington Gr ME1 . . . . .63 A5
Lock La ME14 . . . . 129 D1
Lockmeadow
  Entertainment Ctr
ME14 . . . . 161 F3
LOCKSBOTTOM 86 B7
Lockside TN9 . . . . 222 C2
Locksley CI ME5 . . . . . . .96 E2
Lock St ME7 . . . . .64 C5
Lockswood ME16 . . . . . 161 D7
Lock's Yd TN13 . . . . 154 C2
Lockyer Rd RM19 . . . . . .16 C8
Lockyers Hill DA13 . . . . .93 F5
Lodden Ct **14** BR5 . . . . .54 D1
Loddington La
  Linton ME17 . . . . 228 A8
  Maidstone, Boughton
  Monchelsea ME17. . . . 195 A1
Loder Cl ME17 . . . . 199 B5
Lodge Ave DA1 . . . . .15 C1
Lodge Cl Orpington BR6 .54 B1
  Wateringbury ME18 . . . 192 D8
Lodge Cres BR6 . . . . .54 B1
Lodge Farmhouse
ME20 . . . . 128 E3
Lodge Field Rd CT5 . . . . .75 D1
Lodge Gdns ME17 . . . . 230 F6
Lodge Hill DA16 . . . . .13 B7
Lodge Hill La ME3 . . . . . .40 F7
Lodge La Cobham DA12 .61 B5
  Royal Tunbridge Wells
  TN3 . . . . 313 A8
  Sidcup DA5 . . . . .13 D8
  Westerham TN16 . . . . . 184 C8
LODGE LEES 242 F4
Lodge Oak La TN9 . . . . 254 D8
Lodge Rd Bromley BR1 . .29 C1
  Maidstone ME14 . . . . . 162 D5
  Staplehurst TN12 . . . . . 260 E5
  Tonbridge TN9 . . . . 222 B2
Lodgewood Cotts TN8 218 D2
Lodge Wood Dr TN25 . 267 E5
Logs Hill BR1, BR2 . . . . .52 E8
Logs Hill Cl BR7 . . . . . . .52 E8
Lolland Ho **9** SE18 . . . . . .1 E2
Lomaria Ct TN2 . . . . . . 286 C4
Lomas La TN18 . . . . 356 F5
Lomas Rd ME10, ME9 . 102 D4
Lombard St
  Horton Kirby DA4 . . . . . .57 C5
  Margate CT9 . . . . .50 I3
Lombard Trad Est SE7 . . .1 B2
Lombard Wall SE7 . . . . . . .1 B2
Lombardy Cl ME7 . . . . . .98 A6
Lombardy Dr ME14 . . . 162 C5
Lomer Farm DA13 . . . . . .93 A8
LONDON BEACH 324 B5
London City Airport E16 .1 E5
London City Airport Sta
E16 . . . . .1 E5

Londonderry Ho **15**
ME15 . . . . 195 E7
Londonderry Par DA8 . .14 D7
London Ind Pk E6 . . . . . . .2 B8
London La Bromley BR1 .29 A1
  Sissinghurst TN17. . . . . 293 A2
London Pl **24** CT20 . . . 335 E5
London Rd
  Addington ME19 . . . . . 126 D2
  Badgers Mount TN14 . . 121 C6
  Bidborough TN4 . . . . . . 253 F3
  Bromley BR1 . . . . .52 A8
  Canterbury CT2 . . . . . . 142 D1
  Chelsfield TN14 . . . . .87 F2
  Crayford DA1 . . . . .14 D2
  Deal CT14 . . . . 215 B5
  Ditton ME20 . . . . 128 C1
  Dover CT16, CT17 . . . . 278 B1
  Dunkirk ME13 . . . . 140 E2
  Farningham BR8, DA4 . . .56 D3
  Faversham ME13 . . . . . 138 B6
  Flimwell TN5 . . . . 339 D3
  Gillingham ME8 . . . . .65 C1
  Grays RM17, RM20. . . . .17 E8
  Hartlip ME8, ME9 . . . . . .99 D7
  Hildenborough TN11, TN13,
  TN15 . . . . 221 B7
  Hurst Green TN19 . . . . 354 A3
  Hythe CT21 . . . . 332 F3
  Maidstone ME16 . . . . . 161 C6
  Newington ME9 . . . . . . 100 A6
  Northfleet DA11 . . . . .18 E1
  Otford TN13 . . . . 121 D1
  Ramsgate CT11 . . . . . . 117 B6
  Rochester ME2 . . . . .63 A7
  Royal Tunbridge Wells, Mount
  Sion TN1 . . . . 286 A3
  3 Royal Tunbridge Wells
  TN4 . . . . 286 A4
  Royal Tunbridge Wells
  TN4 . . . . 286 A4
  Sevenoaks, Dunton Green
  TN13 . . . . 153 E7
  Sevenoaks TN13 . . . . . 154 B2
  Sittingbourne ME10 . . . 101 C4
  Stone DA2, DA9 . . . . . . .16 E1
  Swanley BR8 . . . . .55 D7
  Swanscombe DA9 . . . . .17 C2
  Temple Ewell CT15,
  CT16 . . . . 277 B6
  Teynham ME9 . . . . 103 C1
  Tilbury RM18 . . . . .19 B5
  Tonbridge TN10, TN11 . 222 B3
  West Kingsdown TN15 . . .91 A1
  Wrotham Heath TN15,
  ME19 . . . . 125 F1
  Wrotham TN15 . . . . . . 125 B3
London Road E ME20 . . 160 F8
London Road Purfleet
RM19 . . . . .16 C8
London Road Ret Pk
ME16 . . . . 161 E5
London Road (River) CT16,
CT17 . . . . 277 F4
London Road Temple
  Ewell CT16 . . . . 277 D5
London Road Trad Est
ME10 . . . . 101 D4
London Road West
  Thurrock RM20 . . . . . . .17 A8
London St CT20 . . . . . . 335 E5
Lone Barn Rd ME17 . . . 200 B8
Lonefield TN26 . . . . 299 B1
Lonewood Way TN11 . . 190 F2
Longacre CT5 . . . . .75 D1
Long Acre Orpington BR6 .87 D8
  Westgate on Sea CT7 . . .81 C5
Long Acre Cl CT2 . . . . . 142 E2
Longacre Rd TN23 . . . . 299 D7
Longage Hill CT18, CT4 273 A1
Long Barn Rd TN14 . . . 187 B2
Long Barrow The
  TN24 . . . . 300 E6
Long Beech TN23 . . . . . 267 E1
Longbridge TN24 . . . . . 269 B1
Longbridge Terr CT21 332 F1
Longbury CI BR5 . . . . . . .54 B6
Longbury Dr BR5 . . . . . . .54 B7
Long Catlis Rd ME8 . . . . .98 C4
Longdon Wood BR2 . . . . .86 E6
Longdown Ho ME5 . . . . .96 F6
Long Dr CT13 . . . . 180 C2
Longfellow Rd ME7 . . . . .64 C3
LONGFIELD 58 E7
Longfield TN30 . . . . 345 A6
Longfield Acad DA3 . . . .58 F6
Longfield Ave
  High Halstow ME23 . . . . .23 E4
  New Barn DA3, DA13 . . .59 D7
Longfield Cl CT15 . . . . . .75 D2
Longfield Cres CT5 . . . . .75 D2
LONGFIELD HILL 59 D6
Longfield Pl ME15 . . . . 195 C8
Longfield Rd
  Dover CT17 . . . . 310 B7
  Meopham Station DA3,
  DA13 . . . . .59 E3
  Royal Tunbridge Wells TN1,
  TN2, TN11 . . . . 286 C8
Longfields Dr ME14 . . . 163 A5
Longfield Sta DA3 . . . . . .58 E6
LONGFORD 153 D6
Longford Cl ME8 . . . . . . .99 A8
Longford Ct ME8 . . . . . . .99 A8
Longford Terr **9** CT20 335 D4
Longford Way **10** ST20 335 D4
Longham Copse ME15 162 F1
Long Hill CT4 . . . . 172 C1
Longhill Ave ME5 . . . . . . .64 B3
Longhurst Dr ME5 . . . . . .96 F2
Long La Bexley DA7 . . . . .13 D6
  Rabbit's Cross CT17 . . . 228 D5
  Shepherdswell CT15. . . 244 D7

LONGLANDS 30 D5
Longlands Ct DA15 . . . . .30 F5
Longlands Park Cres
DA15 . . . . .30 E5
Longlands Prim Sch
DA15 . . . . .30 F5
Longlands Rd DA15 . . . . .30 F5
Longleat Ct **3** DA6 . . . . .13 F3
Longleigh La SE2, DA7 . .13 C8
Long Length TN23 . . . . 299 D4
Longley Rd
  Gillingham ME8 . . . . .65 C1
  Rochester ME1 . . . . .63 C4
Long Market **2** CT1 . . 175 A8
Long Mark Rd **5** E16. . . .1 D8
Longmarsh CI CT6 . . . . . .76 C3
Longmarsh View DA4 . . .57 B8
Long Mdw CT12 . . . . . . 114 D6
Longmead BR7 . . . . .53 A7
Longmead Cl CT6 . . . . . .76 C3
Longmead Dr DA14 . . . . .31 D6
Longmeade DA12 . . . . . .37 F7
Longmeadow TN13 . . . . .53 D6
Longmeadow Rd DA15 . .30 E7
Long Meadow Way
CT2 . . . . 143 A4
Long Mead Prim Sch
TN10 . . . . 222 B5
Long Meads TN3 . . . . . 285 B4
Long Mead Way TN10 . 222 B4
Longmete Rd CT3 . . . . . 146 C5
Long Rock CT5 . . . . .75 D3
Long Row TN25 . . . . . . 301 D2
Long's Acre TN25 . . . . . 237 E1
Long Shaw Cl ME17 . . . 195 D4
Longshaw Rd ME15 . . . 195 F5
Long Slip TN3 . . . . 285 A3
Longtail Rise CT6 . . . . . .76 E2
Longtern's Cotts DA12 . .38 E6
Longtown Ct **10** DA2. . . .16 B1
Longtye Dr CT5 . . . . 109 C7
Longview Way TN2 . . . . 286 D7
Longwalk DA13 . . . . .59 E8
Long Wlk Ashford TN23 267 E4
  Woolwich SE18 . . . . .12 B8
Longwood ME5 . . . . .97 B1
Longworth CI SE28 . . . . . .3 D7
Lonsdale Ave CT19 . . . . .51 C3
Lonsdale CI SE9 . . . . .29 C5
Lonsdale Cres DA2 . . . . .34 C7
Lonsdale Ct CT16 . . . . . 278 C1
Lonsdale Dr
  Gillingham ME8 . . . . .98 E7
  Herne Bay CT6 . . . . .76 B5
  Sittingbourne ME10 . . . 101 C4
Lonsdale Gdns TN1 . . . 286 A3
Lonsdale Rd DA7 . . . . . . .13 F5
Lookers La CT21 . . . . . . 333 B3
Loop Court Mews **9**
CT13 . . . . 148 F1
Loop Rd BR7 . . . . .30 C1
Loop St CT13 . . . . 148 F1
LOOSE 194 F4
Loose Down Rd ME13. . 202 F7
LOOSE HILL 194 F3
Loose Inf & Jun Schs
ME15 . . . . 195 A6
Loose Rd ME15 . . . . . . 195 A7
Loraine Ct BR7 . . . . .30 B3
Lord Chatham's Ride
TN14 . . . . 120 C1
Lord Cornwallis Ct
ME14 . . . . 162 F3
Lord Romney's Hill
ME14 . . . . 162 F3
Lords Cl ME9 . . . . 102 E2
Lords Cotts ME13 . . . . . 170 C4
Lord St Gravesend DA12 .37 B8
  Newham E16 . . . . .1 E5
LORDS WOOD 97 C1
Lordswood Cl DA2 . . . . .34 E4
Lords Wood Cl ME5 . . . . .97 B2
Lordswood Ind Est
ME5 . . . . 130 C8
Lordswood Inf & Jun Sch
ME5 . . . . .97 B3
Lords Wood La ME5 . . . . .97 B3
Lords Wood L Ctr ME5 . .97 C3
Lord Warden Ave
CT14 . . . . 215 D2
Lord Warden Ho CT17 310 D5
Lord Warden Sq CT17 310 D5
Lord Warwick St SE18 . . .1 E3
Lorden Park * ME13 137 F3
Lorenden Prep Sch
ME13 . . . . 137 E3
Lorien Flats TN24 . . . . 268 D7
Lorimar Bsns Ctr RM13 . .4 E8
Lorimar Ct ME10 . . . . . 101 C7
Lorina Rd CT12 . . . . 117 C8
Lorne Cotts CT14 . . . . . 215 C2
Lorne Rd
  Dover CT16, CT17. . . . . 278 B2
  Ramsgate CT11 . . . . . . 117 C6
Lorraine Ct
  1 Folkestone CT19 . . . 335 E6
  Swanscombe DA9 . . . . .17 B1
Lorton Cl DA12 . . . . .37 E6
Lossenham La TN18 . . . 357 D3
Lotus Rd TN16 . . . . 118 F1
Loudon Ct TN23 . . . . . . 267 E3

Loudon Path TN23 . . . . 267 E3
Loudon Way TN23 . . . . 267 E3
Loughborough Ct **2**
CT11 . . . . 117 E7
Louise Ct **3** DA6 . . . . . .13 E3
Louis Gdns BR7 . . . . .29 F4
Louisville Ave ME7 . . . . .64 D4
Lourdes Cl TN25 . . . . . . 303 D1
Louvain Rd DA9 . . . . .34 E8
Lovage App E6 . . . . .1 E8
Love La Adisham CT3 . . 177 F2
  12 Canterbury CT1 . . . 175 A8
  East Tilbury RM18 . . . . .20 C8
  Faversham ME13 . . . . . 138 A6
  Margate CT9 . . . . .50 I3
  Minster (Sheppey) ME12 .47 D7
  Rochester ME1 . . . . .63 C5
  Sidcup DA5 . . . . .14 A1
  Swift's Green TN27 . . . . 263 B5
  Wateringbury ME18 . . . 192 D7
  Woolbury SE18 . . . . .2 B2
Lovelace Ave BR2 . . . . . .53 A3
Lovelace Cl
  Gillingham ME8 . . . . .98 C4
  West Kingsdown TN15 . . .90 E4
Lovelace Ct TN26 . . . . . 297 C5
Lovelace Gn SE9 . . . . . . .11 F4
Lovel Ave DA16 . . . . .13 A5
Lovell Rd
  Minster (Sheppey)
  ME12 . . . . .47 A5
  Rough Common CT2 . . . 142 B3
Lovers La TN17 . . . . 290 F1
Lover's La DA9 . . . . .17 D3
Love Street CT16 . . . . . . .76 C2
Lovibonds Ave BR6 . . . . .86 B7
Low Cl DA9 . . . . .17 A2
Lowe Ave E16 . . . . .1 A8
Lower Bannister Cotts
ME9 . . . . 101 B2
Lower Bell La ME20 . . . 128 B2
LOWER BITCHET 155 C1
Lower Blackhouse Hill
CT21 . . . . 333 D3
Lower Bloors La ME8 . . .65 E3
Lower Boxley Rd **10**
ME14 . . . . 162 A5
Lower Bridge St CT1 . . . 175 A8
LOWER BUSH 61 F3
Lower Buttermere Cl
ME7 . . . . .65 A5
Lower Camden BR7 . . . . .30 E5
Lower Chantry La CT1 175 A8
Lower Church Hill DA9 . .16 E2
LOWER COUSLEY
  WOOD 337 E8
LOWER COX STREET 131 D6
Lower Croft BR8 . . . . . . .55 F5
Lower Denmark Rd
TN23 . . . . 300 C8
LOWER ENSDEN Rd CT4 172 D4
LOWER EYTHORNE . . . 245 B8
Lower Fant Rd ME16 . . . 161 D2
Lower Farm Rd ME17 . . 228 D5
Lower Featherby Rd
ME7 . . . . .65 B5
LOWER GOLDSTONE . 147 F7
Lower Gore La CT13. . . . 180 B3
Lower Gravel Rd BR2 . . .52 F1
LOWER GREEN
  Pembury 287 D8
  Rusthall 285 C5
Lower Green Rd
  Pembury TN2 . . . . 287 D8
  Rusthall TN3, TN4 . . . . 285 C6
LOWER HALSTOW 67 C3
Lower Halstow Prim Sch
ME9 . . . . .67 B2
LOWER HARDRES 208 A6
LOWER HARTLIP 99 E4
Lower Hartlip Rd ME9 . . .99 E5
LOWER HAYSDEN 253 D8
Lower Haysden La TN11,
  TN9 . . . . 253 D8
Lower Hazelhurst TN5 338 A4
LOWER HEPPINGTON 207 F8
LOWER HERNE 76 F1
Lower Herne Rd CT6 . . . 110 E8
LOWER HIGHAM 39 D6
Lower Higham Rd DA12 .38 B7
Lower High St TN5 . . . . 337 A4
LOWER ISLAND 74 C1
Lower Lees Rd CT4 . . . . 172 D2
LOWER LUDDESDOWN 61 A2
Lower Mill La CT14 . . . . 215 C5
LOWER NEWLANDS . . 104 A2
Lower Northdown Ave
CT9 . . . . .51 B2
Lower Norton La ME9 . . 104 A1
Lower Park Rd DA17 . . . .4 A2
Lower Platts TN5 . . . . . 338 F1
Lower Queens Rd
TN24 . . . . 268 C3
LOWER RAINHAM 65 F3
Lower Rainham Rd
  Gillingham, Lower Rainham
  ME8 . . . . .66 A3
  Gillingham ME7 . . . . .65 E5
Lower Range Rd DA12 . .37 E8
Lower Rd
  Eastchurch ME12 . . . . . .48 B3
  East Farleigh ME15 . . . 194 B7
  Erith DA8 . . . . .4 D2
  Erith DA17 . . . . .4 B3
  Faversham ME13 . . . . . 137 C8
  Hextable BR8 . . . . .33 B1
  Higham DA12, ME3. . . . .39 B6
  Maidstone ME15 . . . . . 162 B3
  Minster (Sheppey) ME12 .46 E4

Lower Rd continued
Northfleet DA11 . . . . .18 A3
Orpington BR5 . . . . .54 B3
River CT17 . . . . .277 E3
Shorne DA12. . . . . .38 E6
Staple CT3. . . . . .179 B6
Stone in Oxney TN30 . .360 D5
Sutton Valence ME17 . .229 E7
Temple Ewell CT16 . . . .277 D5
Teynham, Lower Newlands
  ME9, ME13 . . . . .103 E2
Teynham ME9. . . . . . . .103 B3
West Farleigh ME15 . . .193 D7
Woodchurch TN26. . . . .326 B1
Lower Road E CT16 . . . .310 H8
Lower Road W CT16 . . .310 G8
Lower Rochester Rd
  ME3. . . . . .39 E6
Lower Rowling Cotts
  CT3 . . . . .179 B2
Lower St Mary's TN5 .338 E1
Lower Sandgate Rd
  CT20 . . . . .335 B3
Lower Sands ME3 . . . . .352 E2
Lower St Eastry CT13 . .180 B1
  Leeds ME17 . . . . .197 A7
  Tilmanstone CT13 . . . .213 A2
  Tonbridge TN11 . . . . . .220 F5
Lower Station Rd DA1 .14 E1
LOWER STOKE 25 C5
Lower Stone St ME15. .162 A3
Lower Tovil ME15 . . . . .161 E2
LOWER TWYDALL 65 C5
Lower Twydall La ME7,
  ME8. . . . . .65 C4
LOWER UPNOR 41 A3
Lower Vicarage Rd
  TN24 . . . . .268 D7
Lower Wall Rd
  Burmarsh CT21. . . . . . .352 D8
  Dymchurch CT21. . . . . .353 A7
LOWER WALMER 215 C4
Lower Warren Rd
  ME20. . . . . .129 E6
Lower Woodlands Rd
  ME7. . . . . .65 A6
Lowestoft Mews E16 . . .2 B4
Lowfield Rd ME12 . . . . .46 E6
Lowfield St DA1. . . . . . .33 E8
Low Meadow ME2. . . . .95 B5
Lownds Ct BR1. . . . . . . .52 A7
Lowry Cl DA8. . . . . .4 D2
Lowry The 4 TN9 . . . .254 B8
Lowslip Hill CT15. . . . .309 A5
LOW STREET 19 E8
Low Street La RM18 . . .19 F8
Lowther Rd CT17 . . . . .310 B8
Loxwood Cl
  Orpington BR5, BR6 . . . .87 D8
  Whitfield CT16 . . . . . . .278 B7
Lubbock Cl ME15 . . . . .195 E5
Lubbock Ct BR7. . . . . . .29 F1
Lubbock Ho BR6. . . . . . .86 E8
Lubbock Rd BR7. . . . . . .29 F1
Lubbock Wlk ME8 . . . . .98 D5
Lucas Cl TN2, TN4. . . .286 C7
Lucas Cres 9 DA9. . . . .17 C3
Lucas Rd ME15. . . . . . .127 C7
Lucerne Ct 8 Erith DA18 . .3 E3
  Whitstable CT5. . . . . . .107 F6
Lucerne Dr CT5 . . . . . .107 F6
Lucerne La CT15 . . . . .247 C2
Lucerne Rd BR6. . . . . . .53 F1
Lucerne St ME14 . . . . .162 A5
Lucilina Dr TN8 . . . . . .249 C8
Lucilla Ave TN15 . . . . .299 F4
Luckhurst Gdns CT9 . . .51 E3
Luckhurst Rd
  Ashford TN24 . . . . .301 A7
  Crabble CT17 . . . . .277 E3
Luckley Ho TN25 . . . . .237 E2
Lucknow Cl CT15. . . . . .278 F3
Lucknow Rd TN12 . . . .257 A8
Lucknow St SE18. . . . . .12 E7
Lucks Hill ME19 . . . . . .159 D8
Lucks La
  Paddock Wood TN12. . .257 B8
  Rabbit's Cross ME17 . . .228 F6
Lucks Way TN12. . . . . .259 B6
Lucy Ave CT19. . . . . . . .335 B2
Lucy's Hill CT21. . . . . .333 B2
Luddenham Cl
  Ashford TN23 . . . . .299 F6
  Maidstone ME14. . . . . .162 C6
Luddenham Prim Sch
  ME13 . . . . .104 E1
Luddesdon Rd DA8. . . . .14 A7
LUDDESDOWN 60 F1
Luddesdown Court *
  DA13 . . . . .60 F1
Luddesdown Ho 5 BR5 54 C4
Luddesdown Rd DA13 . .61 A2
Ludgate Rd ME9. . . . . .135 F5
Ludham CT28 . . . . .3 C7
Ludlow Cl BR2. . . . . .52 A6
Luffield Rd SE2. . . . . . . .3 B3
Luffman Rd SE12. . . . . .29 B5
Lughorse La ME15,
  ME18. . . . . .193 C1
Lukes Ct CT17 . . . . . . .278 B1
Lukin Ho CT21. . . . . . . .332 F1
Lullarook Cl TN15 . . . .118 C3
Lullingstone Ave BR8 . .55 F6
Lullingstone Castle *
  DA4 . . . . .89 B5
Lullingstone Cl
  Gillingham ME7. . . . . . . .98 B3
  Orpington BR5 . . . . .31 B1
Lullingstone Cres BR5 . .31 B1
Lullingstone Ct 14 CT1 174 F8

Lullingstone La DA4. . . .89 C8
Lullingstone Pk * DA4. .89 A6
Lullingstone Pk Visitor
  Ctr * DA4. . . . . .89 B4
Lullingstone Rd
  3 Bexley DA17 . . . . .13 F8
  Maidstone ME16. . . . . .161 C2
Lullingstone Roman Villa
  (rems of) * DA4. . . . . . .89 B7
Lulworth Rd Bexley DA16 12 D5
  Bromley SE9 . . . . .29 E6
Lumley Cl DA17 . . . . .4 A1
Lumsden Terr 8 ME4. . .63 E4
Lunar Cl TN16. . . . . . . .118 D3
Lunedale Rd DA2. . . . . .34 C7
LUNSFORD 127 E4
Lunsford District Ctr
  ME20 . . . . .128 A4
Lunsford La ME20 . . . .127 F2
Lunsford Prim Sch
  ME20 . . . . .128 A4
Lupton Cl SE12 . . . . . . .29 B4
Lurkins Rise TN17 . . . .318 D7
Lushington Rd ME14. . .161 E7
Lusted Hall La TN16 . .150 C7
Lusted Rd TN13 . . . . . .153 E7
LUTON 64 B2
Luton Ave CT10 . . . . . . .83 F3
Luton Ct CT10 . . . . .83 F3
Luton High St ME5 . . . . .64 C2
Luton Inf Sch ME5 . . . . .64 C2
Luton Jun Sch ME4. . . . .64 C2
Luton Rd
  Chatham ME4, ME5 . . . .64 B2
  Faversham ME13 . . . . .138 E7
  Sidcup DA14 . . . . .31 C5
Luxfield Rd SE9 . . . . . . .29 E7
Luxon Rd DA13 . . . . .93 E4
LUXTED 119 A5
Luxted Rd BR6 . . . . . . .119 A6
Lyall Way ME8. . . . . .98 A4
Lychfield Dr ME2. . . . . . .63 A8
Lych Gate Rd BR6. . . . . .54 A1
Lydbrook Cl ME10 . . . .101 D4
Lydbury Cl ME15. . . . . . .54 A1
LYDD 376 D6
LYDD CAMP 376 B5
Lydd Cl DA14 . . . . .30 E5
LYDDEN Broadstairs. . . .82 E4
  Dover 276 E8
Lydden Cl SE9. . . . . .12 E1
Lydden Hill CT15 . . . . .244 C1
Lydden Hill Race Circuit
  CT4. . . . . .243 F3
Lydden Prim Sch CT15 276 F8
Lydden Temple Ewell
  National Nature
  Reserve * CT15 . . . . .277 B7
Lydd (London Ashford)
  Airport TN29 . . . . . . .377 A7
LYDD-ON-SEA 380 D7
Lydd Prim Sch TN29 . .376 C6
Lydd Rd Bexley DA7 . . . .13 F7
  Chatham ME5. . . . . .97 B5
  New Romney TN28,
    TN29. . . . . .372 F6
Lydd Town Crossing
  TN29 . . . . .376 D8
Lydd Town Mus * 376 C6
Lydens La TN8 . . . . . . .249 F6
Lydford Ct 18 DA2 . . . . .16 B1
Lydia Cotts 2 DA11 . . . .37 B8
Lydia Rd Deal CT14. . . .215 A4
  Erith DA8. . . . . .14 F8
Lydos Cl TN29 . . . . . . .377 E5
Lydstep Rd BR7 . . . . . . .30 A4
Lyeat Ct CT2 . . . . .142 C4
LYE GREEN 311 D1
Lyell Cl CT21 . . . . .333 A1
Lyell Ct 5 CT7 . . . . .80 F8
Lyell Rd CT7 . . . . .80 F8
Lyford St SE18 . . . . .1 E2
Lyle Cl ME2 . . . . .63 B8
Lyle Ct ME16 . . . . .161 C5
Lyle Pk TN13 . . . . .154 B4
LYMBRIDGE GREEN . .272 B4
Lyme Farm Rd SE12 . . .11 B3
Lyme Rd DA16. . . . . .13 B6
LYMINGE 305 B6
Lyminge CE Prim Sch
  CT18. . . . . .305 C7
Lyminge Cl
  Gillingham ME8. . . . . . . .65 C2
  Sidcup DA14 . . . . .30 F4
Lyminge Way CT9 . . . . .51 C1
Lymington Cl ME15 . . .195 F4
Lymington Ct CT8. . . . . .81 E7
LYMPNE 332 A3
Lympne Castle * CT21 331 F1
Lympne CE Prim Sch
  CT21. . . . . .332 A3
Lympne Hill CT21. . . . .332 A2
Lympne Ind Est CT21 .331 E3
Lynacre CT2. . . . . .142 C1
Lyn Ct CT20 . . . . .335 A5
Lyndale Est RM20. . . . . .17 B8
Lyndean Ind Est SE2. . . .3 A3
Lynden Way BR8 . . . . . .55 D6
Lyndhurst BR7 . . . . .30 B2
Lyndhurst Ave
  Gillingham ME8. . . . . . . .98 C2
  Margate CT9. . . . . .51 B2
Lyndhurst Cl Bexley DA7 14 B4
  Canterbury CT2. . . . . . .142 E3
  Orpington BR6 . . . . .86 B6
Lyndhurst Dr TN13 . . . .153 E3
Lyndhurst Gr ME10 . . .101 E2
Lyndhurst Rd
  Bexley DA7 . . . . .14 B4
  Broadstairs CT10 . . . . . .84 A6
  Crabble CT17 . . . . .277 E2
  Dymchurch TN29 . . . . .366 C8
  Maidstone ME15. . . . . .195 C8

Lyndhurst Rd continued
  Ramsgate CT11 . . . . . .117 F7
Lyndhurst Way DA13 . . .59 F8
Lyndon Ave DA15 . . . . . .12 F2
Lyndon Rd DA17. . . . . . . .4 A2
Lyndon Way CT18 . . . .305 C7
Lynette Ave ME2 . . . . . .40 A1
Lyngate Ct CT9 . . . . .51 D2
Lyngs Cl ME18. . . . . . . .225 F8
Lynley Cl ME15 . . . . . . .195 D6
Lynmead TN8. . . . . .217 B4
Lynmere Rd DA16 . . . . .13 B5
Lynmouth Dr ME12 . . . .47 C7
Lynmouth Rise BR5. . . .54 B5
Lynne Cl 7 BR6. . . . . . . .86 F4
Lynors Ave ME2 . . . . . . .40 A1
LYNSORE BOTTOM . . .241 D8
Lynstead Cl BR1. . . . . . .52 C7
Lynstead Ho ME16. . . . .161 A1
LYNSTED 136 A6
Lynsted Cl
  Ashford TN23 . . . . .299 F6
  Bexley DA6 . . . . .14 B2
Lynsted Gdns SE9 . . . . .11 D4
Lynsted La ME9 . . . . . .136 B7
Lynsted & Norton Prim Sch
  ME9 . . . . .136 A7
Lynsted Rd
  Gillingham ME8. . . . . . . .65 B3
  Halfway Houses ME12 . . .46 E7
Lynton Ave BR5 . . . . . . .54 B5
Lynton Court Mans CT9 51 B3
Lynton Dr ME5 . . . . .97 B3
Lynton Pl CT4 . . . . .176 A1
Lynton Rd
  Gravesend DA11. . . . . . .37 A7
  Hythe CT21 . . . . .333 C1
Lynton Road S DA11. . . .37 A7
Lynwood
  Folkestone CT19. . . . . .335 C2
  Groombridge TN3 . . . . .312 C6
Lynwood Gr BR6 . . . . . .53 E1
Lynx Way E16. . . . . .1 D6
Lyons Cres TN9 . . . . . .222 C2
Lyons The TN9 . . . . . . .222 C2
Lyoth Rd BR5. . . . . .86 C8
Lysander Cl
  Broadstairs CT10 . . . . . .83 C3
  Littlebourne CT4. . . . . .176 E4
Lysander Rd ME19 . . . .158 F3
Lysander Way BR6 . . . . .86 C7
Lysander Wlk CT18 . . . .307 A4
Lytchet Rd BR1. . . . . . . .29 B1
Lytham Ave CT6. . . . . . .76 D1
Lytham Ct SE28 . . . . .3 E7
Lytton Strachey Path 8
  SE28 . . . . .3 B6
Lyveden Rd SE3 . . . . . . .11 B7

M

Mabbett Ho 2 SE18. . . . .12 A8
Mabel Cotts DA3 . . . . . .59 A6
Mabel Rd BR8. . . . . .33 A2
Mabledon Ave TN24. . . .268 C5
Mabledon Ct TN28. . . . .373 B6
Mabledon Rd TN9. . . . .254 A8
MacAllister Ho 8 SE18 12 B8
McAlpine Cres 8 SE18 .194 F3
McArthur Dr ME19 . . . .159 D3
MacAulay Cl ME20. . . . .128 A4
MacAulay Way SE28 . . . .3 B4
McAuley Cl SE9 . . . . .12 A2
Macbean St SE18. . . . . . .2 B3
McCabe Ct TN12. . . . . .260 E2
McCall Cres SE7. . . . . . . .1 E1
McCarthy Ave CT2 . . . .143 F7
McClean Wlk ME12. . . . .71 C8
McCudden Rd DA1 . . . . .15 F4
McCudden Row 8 ME7 64 A6
McDermott Rd TN15. . .156 F7
MacDonald Ct TN12 . . .257 A6
MacDonald Par CT5 . . .108 A6
MacDonald Rd
  Dover CT17 . . . . .278 A1
  Gillingham ME7. . . . . . . .64 D6
McDowall Cl 11 E16 . . . .1 A8
Mace Ct RM17 . . . . .18 E8
Mace Farm Cotts
  TN14. . . . . .119 C6
Mace Ind Est TN24. . . .268 C3
Mace La Ashford TN24. .268 C2
  Downe TN14 . . . . .119 D6
Mace Terr TN26 . . . . . .299 A1
MacGregor Rd E16. . . . . .1 E7
McIntyre Ct 6 SE18 . . . .1 E2
Mackenders Cl ME20 . .129 A6
Mackenders Gn ME20 .129 A6
Mackenders La ME20 . .129 A6
McKenzie Cl ME20. . . . .160 F8
McKenzie Ct ME14 . . . .161 F5
Mackenzie Dr CT20. . . .334 E5
McKenzie Rd ME5. . . . . .97 A3
Mackenzie Way DA12. . .37 D2
Mackeson Ct 8 CT1. . . .333 B2
McKillop Way DA14 . . . .31 C1
McKinlay Ct Bexley DA16 13 C4
  Birchington CT7 . . . . . . .80 D8
Mackintosh Cl ME23. . . .23 F3
MACKLANDS 66 A2
Macklands Ho ME8. . . . . .66 A2
Macklands Way ME8 . . . .66 A2
MacLeod Ho SE18 . . . . .11 E6
McLeod Rd SE2. . . . . .3 B2
McMichaels Way TN19 354 A3
McMillan Cl DA12 . . . . . .37 C4
Macmillan Gdns 2 DA16 13 A3
Macoma Rd SE18 . . . . . .12 D8
Macoma Terr SE18 . . . . .12 D8
Madan Cl TN16 . . . . . . .151 E2
Madan Rd TN16 . . . . . .151 E2

Mada Rd BR6. . . . . .86 B7
Madden Ave ME5. . . . . . .96 E5
Madden Cl DA10 . . . . . . .17 E1
Maddocks Cl CT20 . . . .335 B3
Madeira Ave ME2 . . . . . .40 A1
MADEIRA PARK 286 B2
Madeira Pk TN2. . . . . . .286 B2
Madeira Rd
  Littlestone-on-Sea
    TN28 . . . . .373 E6
  Margate CT9. . . . . .51 A2
Madeira Wlk CT11. . . . .117 E6
Madginford Cl ME15. . . .163 A2
Madginford Park Inf Sch
  ME15 . . . . .163 A2
Madginford Park Jun Sch
  ME15 . . . . .163 A2
Madginford Rd ME15 . .162 F2
Madhuran Ct ME2 . . . . . .63 A7
Madison Cres DA7. . . . . .13 C7
Madison Gdns DA7 . . . . .13 C7
Madison Way TN13. . . .153 F4
Madras Ho 2 ME15. . . .195 E5
Maesmaur Rd TN16. . . .150 C7
Mafeking Rd ME5 . . . . . .96 F3
Magazine Rd TN24. . . .268 B3
Magdala Rd
  Broadstairs CT10 . . . . . .83 E6
  Dover CT17 . . . . .278 B1
Magdalen Ct
  Broadstairs CT10 . . . . . .84 A6
  Canterbury CT1. . . . . . .175 B7
Magdalan Gr BR7. . . . . . .87 B6
Magdalen Rd SE18 . . . . .2 D1
Magnes Rd CT14 . . . . . .215 A2
Magnet Rd RM20. . . . . .17 C8
Magnolia Ave
  Gillingham ME8. . . . . . . .98 B5
  Margate CT9. . . . . .51 D2
Magnolia Cl TN9 . . . . . .254 C7
Magnolia Dr
  Biggin Hill TN16 . . . . . .118 E3
  Chartham CT4. . . . . . . .143 F4
Magnolia Ho 3 ME16 161 A3
Magnolia Rise CT6 . . . . .77 D2
Magpie Bottom TN15. .122 F6
  Herne Bay CT6 . . . . .76 E2
Magpie Cl ME12 . . . . . . .47 A6
Magpie Ct ME12 . . . . . . .47 A6
Magpie Gn 3 TN8. . . . .217 D3
Magpie Hall Cl BR2. . . . .52 F3
Magpie Hall La BR2. . . . .52 F3
Magpie Hall Rd
  Chatham ME4 . . . . .64 A2
  Stubb's Cross TN26 . . .299 C8
Magpie La
  Rhodes Minnis CT4. . . .273 B3
  Yelsted ME9, ME14. . . .98 F1
Magpie Lodge 4 CT16 278 B2
Magwitch Cl ME4 . . . . . .63 B4
Maida Rd Chatham ME4. .64 A2
  Erith DA17. . . . . .4 A3
Maida Vale Rd DA1 . . . . .15 A1
Maiden Erlegh Ave DA5 31 E7
Maiden La
  Canterbury CT1. . . . . . .174 D6
  Crayford DA1. . . . . .15 A3
MAIDSTONE 162 C3
Maidstone Barracks Sta
  ME16 . . . . .161 E6
Maidstone East Sta
  ME14 . . . . .161 F5
Maidstone Gram Sch
  ME15 . . . . .162 B2
Maidstone Gram Sch for
  Girls ME16 . . . . .161 E5
Maidstone Hospl
  ME16 . . . . .161 F5
Maidstone L Ctr ME15 162 C2
  1 ME14 . . . . .161 F5
Maidstone Mus & Gallery *
  1 ME14 . . . . .161 F5
Maidstone Rd
  Bredhurst ME7, ME8 . . .98 B3
  Charing TN25, TN26,
    TN27. . . . . .234 D6
  Chatham ME4 . . . . .63 F7
  Chatham, Walderslade
    ME5. . . . . .96 D4
  Colt's Hill TN12, TN2 . .256 B4
  Danaway ME9. . . . . . . .100 D4
  Five Wents ME17 . . . . .196 E2
  Gillingham ME8. . . . . . . .98 C6
  Goose Green ME18,
    TN11 . . . . .191 C3
  Grays RM17 . . . . .18 A8
  Headcorn TN27. . . . . . .262 B7
  Horsmonden, Claygate
    TN12 . . . . .258 C3
  Horsmonden TN12 . . . .290 A7
  Lenham ME17. . . . . . . .199 D5
  Matfield TN12 . . . . .288 C6
  Nettlestead Green
    ME18 . . . . .192 C3
  Pembury TN2 . . . . .255 E1
  Platt TN15 . . . . .157 C7
  Potters Corner TN25,
    TN26. . . . . .267 D7
  Rochester ME1. . . . . . . .63 C3
  Seal TN15 . . . . .155 C5
  Sevenoaks TN13. . . . . .153 E5
  Sidcup DA14 . . . . .31 F1
  Staplehurst TN12 . . . . .260 E7
  Swanley DA14, BR8. . . .55 B8
  Underling Green TN12 .227 F2
Maidstone West Sta
  ME16 . . . . .161 F3
Mailyns The ME8. . . . . . .98 D7
Maine Cl CT16. . . . . . . .278 B8
Main Gate Rd ME4. . . . . .63 F7
Main Rd
  Biggin Hill TN16 . . . . . .118 C5
  Chattenden ME3. . . . . . .40 F4
  Cooling ME3. . . . . .55 D3
  Crockenhill BR8. . . . . . .55 D3

Main Rd continued
  Crockham Hill TN8 . . . .184 C1
  Cudham TN16 . . . . .151 A7
  Farningham DA4. . . . . . .56 F3
  Halstead TN14 . . . . . . .120 C3
  Hoo St Werburgh ME3 . .41 C5
  Kingsnorth ME3 . . . . . . .42 D7
  Longfield DA3 . . . . .58 E7
  Marlpit Hill TN8. . . . . . .217 B6
  Orpington BR5 . . . . .54 C7
  Queenborough ME11,
    ME12. . . . . .46 B5
  Sellindge TN25 . . . . . . .303 C1
  Sheerness ME12. . . . . . .28 A3
  Sidcup DA14, DA15. . . . .30 E5
  Sundridge TN14 . . . . . .152 E3
  Sutton at Hone DA4. . . .34 B1
  Swanley BR8. . . . . .55 F8
Mainridge Rd BR7. . . . . .30 A4
Main Road Gorse Hill
  DA4. . . . . .90 D7
Main St Iden TN31. . . . .368 B4
  Peasmarsh TN31 . . . . .367 B2
  St Mary's Island ME4. . .41 B7
Maison Des Fleurs
  ME16. . . . . .161 C2
Maison Dieu *
  17 Dover CT17 . . . . . . .310 D8
  Faversham ME13 . . . . .138 A6
Maison Dieu Pl 4
  CT16 . . . . .310 D8
Maison Dieu Rd CT16. .310 D8
Maitland Ct ME13 . . . . .105 B1
Majendie Rd SE18 . . . . . .2 D1
Majestic Par CT20. . . . .335 C4
Major Cl CT5. . . . . .108 B6
Major Clark Ho TN17 . .320 C5
Major York's Rd TN4 . .285 F2
Makenade Ave ME13 . .138 E6
Malan Cl TN16 . . . . .118 E2
Malcolm Sargent Rd
  TN23 . . . . .300 B5
Malden Dr ME14. . . . . . .162 A8
Malham Dr CT9 . . . . .51 A1
Mallard Apartments 14
  ME15. . . . . .195 E5
Mallard Cl Dartford DA1 .15 F2
  Herne Bay CT6 . . . . .76 E2
Mallard Cres ME9. . . . . . .68 D4
Mallard Ct ME12. . . . . . . .47 A6
Mallard Path 5 SE28 . . . .3 D3
Mallards TN24. . . . . . . .300 D7
Mallards Way ME15 . . .163 A1
Mallard Way
  Lower Stoke ME3 . . . . . .25 C4
  Marlpit Hill TN8. . . . . . .217 C3
Mallard Wlk
  Larkfield ME20 . . . . . . .127 F2
  Sidcup DA14 . . . . .31 C2
Malling Cl ME19. . . . . . .159 F7
Mallingdene Cl ME3 . . . .40 B8
Malling Rd
  Kings Hill M18, ME19 . .158 F2
  Lunsford ME6, ME20 . .127 F2
  Snodland ME6. . . . . . . .128 A7
  Teston ME18 . . . . .160 A1
Malling Sch The ME19 159 F7
Mallings La ME14 . . . . .163 C4
Malling Terr ME16. . . . .161 C4
Mallory Cl CT12 . . . . .83 C2
Mallow Cl DA11. . . . . . . .36 E4
Mallow Ct RM17. . . . . . . .18 D8
Mallows The ME14 . . . .161 E7
Mallow Way 1 ME5 . . . . .96 F4
Mall St St Michael The 5** DA6 14 A3
  4 Bromley BR1. . . . . . . .52 A6
  Faversham ME13 . . . . .138 C6
Mallys Pl DA4. . . . . .57 C8
Malmains Rd CT17 . . . .310 A6
Malmaynes Hall Rd
  ME3. . . . . .24 D3
Malmedy Ct CT14. . . . . .215 A1
Malta Ave ME5 . . . . .97 A7
Malta Ho 17 CT1. . . . . . .143 B2
Malta Rd RM18 . . . . .18 F5
Malta Terr 5 ME14. . . . .162 A7
Maltby Cl BR6. . . . . .54 A5
Malthouse Cl ME17. . . .199 D5
Malthouse Cotts
  Boughton Lees TN25. . .236 F4
  New Romney TN28 . . . .373 A6
Malthouse Hill
  10 Hythe CT21 . . . . . . .333 B2
  Maidstone ME15. . . . . .194 F4
Malthouse La
  Hamstreet TN26 . . . . . .327 D1
  Peasmarsh TN31. . . . . .367 D2
  Shorne DA12. . . . . .38 E3
Malt House La TN30. . . .345 A7
Malthouse Rd
  Canterbury CT2. . . . . . .142 F2
  Stansted TN15 . . . . .91 F7
Malthouses The
  Birchington CT7 . . . . . . .80 F7
  Brabourne TN25 . . . . . .303 B8
Malthouse The ME6 . . .194 A8
Malthus Path 7 SE28 . . . .3 C5
Maltings Bsns Pk The
  TN31. . . . . .367 C2
Maltings Ent Ctr The
  DA12 . . . . .37 F7
Maltings Hall The
  CT11 . . . . .117 D7
Maltings The
  7 Canterbury, St Dunstan's
    CT2 . . . . .142 E1
  10 Canterbury, St Martin's
    CT1 . . . . .175 A8
  Deal CT14 . . . . .248 B8
  Faversham ME13 . . . . .138 D6
  Gillingham ME8. . . . . . . .99 A8

Maltings The continued
  3 Gravesend DA11. . . . .19 A1
  Hadlow TN11. . . . . .223 E8
  Lostbourne CT3 . . . . . .176 F7
  Loose ME17 . . . . .195 B4
  Maidstone, Grove Green
    ME14 . . . . .162 E5
  Peasmarsh TN31 . . . . . .53 F1
  Peasmarsh TN31. . . . . .367 C2
  Westerham TN16 . . . . .184 C8
MALTMAN'S HILL 264 F3
Malt Mews ME1. . . . . . . .47 A5
Malton St SE18. . . . . . . .12 E8
Malton Mews SE18. . . . .12 E8
Malton Way TN2 . . . . . .286 F7
Malt Shovel Cotts DA4. .89 D7
Malus Cl ME5 . . . . .97 B1
Malvern Ave DA7. . . . . . .13 E7
Malvern Ho 5 DA11. . . . .18 E1
Malvern Mdw CT16. . . .277 E5
Malvern Pk CT6 . . . . .77 D4
Malvern Rd
  Ashford TN24 . . . . .268 A4
  Dover CT17 . . . . .310 C7
  Gillingham ME7. . . . . . . .64 E3
  Orpington BR6 . . . . .87 B6
  Temple Ewell CT16. . . .277 E5
Malvina Ave DA12 . . . . . .37 C6
Malyons Rd BR8. . . . . . . .32 F1
Mamignot Cl ME14 . . . .163 A3
Manchester Cl ME5. . . . .97 C6
Manchester Ct E16. . . . . .1 B7
Manciple Cl CT2. . . . . . .174 C8
Mandarin La CT14. . . . . .76 E2
Mandela Ho SE18. . . . . .12 D8
Mandela Rd E16 . . . . .1 A7
Mandeville Cl 1 SE3 . . . .11 A7
Mandeville Ct 1
  ME14 . . . . .162 A5
Mandeville Rd CT12 . . . .83 B2
Manford Ind Est DA8 . . .15 B8
Mangers La CT16. . . . . .278 A2
Mangers Pl CT16 . . . . . .278 A3
Mangold Way 4 DA18 . . .3 E3
Mangravet Ave ME15. .195 C4
Manister Rd SE2 . . . . .3 A2
Manitoba Gdns 6 BR6 . .86 F4
Manktelow Ct CT10. . . . .83 A2
Manley Boulevard ME6 . 95 A2
Manley Cl CT2 . . . . .278 A7
Manley Ho CT16. . . . . . .278 A7
Mannering Cl CT17. . . . .277 F3
Manning Ct 3 SE28 . . . . .3 E5
Manningham Ho ME19 160 A6
Manning Rd BR5. . . . . . . .54 B5
Mannock Ho 6 CT1. . . .143 B1
Mannock Rd DA1. . . . . . .15 F4
Manns Hill CT4. . . . . . . .241 A6
Mann Sq TN9 . . . . .254 D7
Manor Ave CT14. . . . . . .215 B4
Manorbrook SE3 . . . . . . .11 A3
Manor Cl
  Canterbury CT1. . . . . . .174 C5
  Chalk DA12. . . . . .38 C6
  Crayford DA1 . . . . .14 E3
  Dartford DA2 . . . . .33 A5
  Deal CT14 . . . . .215 A4
  Erith SE28. . . . . .3 C7
  Herne Bay CT6 . . . . .77 F6
  Maidstone ME14. . . . . .163 B3
  Royal Tunbridge Wells
    TN4 . . . . .285 E3
  Rushenden ME11. . . . . .46 A3
Manor Com Prim Sch The
  DA10. . . . . .35 F8
Manor Cotts
  Hernhill ME13. . . . . . . .140 B6
  Lamberhurst TN3 . . . . .317 B5
  Langley ME17 . . . . .196 C5
Manor Ct
  Canterbury CT1. . . . . . .174 F7
  Gillingham ME7. . . . . . . .65 C4
  Maidstone ME14. . . . . .163 B3
  Sole Street DA13 . . . . . .60 D4
Manordene Rd SE28. . . . .3 D7
Manor Dr
  Birchington CT7 . . . . . . .80 F6
  Hartley DA3 . . . . .59 A3
Manor Farm Cl CT21. . .332 A4
Manor Farm Cotts
  TN15 . . . . .156 A6
Manorfield
  Ashford TN23 . . . . .299 E8
  Elham CT4. . . . . .273 F4
Manor Field DA12 . . . . . .38 E3
Manor Fields TN4 . . . . .253 F3
Manorfields Cl BR7. . . . .53 F6
Manor Forstal DA3. . . . . .91 F7
Manor Gdns
  Chatham ME5. . . . . .96 F4
  Whitfield CT16 . . . . . . .278 A8
Manor Gr
  Sittingbourne ME10 . . .101 D3
  Tonbridge TN10. . . . . . .222 C3
Manor Ho
  14 Chatham ME7. . . . . .64 A6
  Chislehurst BR7 . . . . . . .53 D8
Manor Ho The
  Canterbury CT2. . . . . . .142 F7
  5 Folkestone CT20 . . . .335 B3
  Limpsfield RH8 . . . . . . .183 B7
  Sarre CT7 . . . . .113 D6
  Sidcup DA15 . . . . .31 A7
  Sidcup, Old Bexley DA5 .32 B7
Manor House Dr
  Ashford TN23 . . . . .300 D3
  Maidstone ME16. . . . . .161 D3
Manor House Gdns
  TN8 . . . . .217 C1
Manor La
  Fawkham Green DA3 . . .58 C2
  Hartley DA3 . . . . .59 A3
  Rochester ME1. . . . . . . .62 F3
Manor Lea Rd CT7. . . . . .79 F1

Manor Leaze TN25 . . . .302 F5
Manor Mews
　Chatham ME4 . . . . .63 F4
　Ringwould CT14 . . . . . .247 F5
Manor Oak Prim Sch
　BR5. . . . . .54 D4
Manor Park Ctry Pk★
　ME19 . . . . .159 B7
Manor Park Rd BR7 . . . .53 D8
Manor Pk
　Chislehurst BR7 . . . . . . .53 D8
　Erith DA8. . . . . .15 A8
　Royal Tunbridge Wells
　TN4 . . . . .285 E3
Manor Pl Bromley BR1. . .52 E8
　Chislehurst BR7 . . . . . . .53 D7
Manor Pound La TN25 302 F7
Manor Rd
　3 Broadstairs CT10 . . .84 A4
　Chatham ME4 . . . . .63 F4
　Crayford DA1 . . . . .14 E3
　Deal CT14 . . . . .215 A4
　Dover CT17 . . . . .310 A6
　Edenbridge TN8 . . . . . .217 B1
　Erith DA8. . . . . .15 A8
　Folkestone CT20 . . . . .335 C4
　22 Gravesend DA12 . . .19 B1
　Grays RM17 . . . . .18 C8
　Herne Bay CT6 . . . . .77 F6
　Knockmill TN15 . . . . . .123 F8
　Lydd TN29 . . . . .376 C6
　Milstead ME9 . . . . .134 F2
　New Barn DA3 . . . . .59 C4
　Royal Tunbridge Wells
　TN4 . . . . .253 E1
　Rushenden ME11 . . . . . .46 A3
　Rusthall TN4 . . . . .285 C4
　Sidcup DA15 . . . . .31 A5
　Sidcup, Old Bexley DA5 . .32 B7
　Sole Street DA13 . . . . . .60 D4
　St Nicholas at Wade CT7 .79 F1
　Sundridge TN14 . . . . . .152 D3
　Swanscombe DA10. . . . .35 E8
　Tatsfield TN16 . . . . . . .150 E7
　Tilbury RM18. . . . . .19 A5
　West Thurrock RM20 . . .17 C8
　Whitstable CT5. . . . . . . .75 A2
Manor Rise Dover CT17 310 A6
　Maidstone ME14. . . . . .163 B3
Manorside CI SE2 . . . . . . .3 D2
Manor St ME7. . . . . .64 A6
Manor The TN2 . . . . . . .286 E6
Manor Way
　Ashford TN23 . . . . .267 F4
　Bexley DA7. . . . . .14 C4
　Bromley BR2. . . . . .52 E3
　Eltham SE3 . . . . .11 A3
　Grays RM17 . . . . .18 B7
　Leysdown-on-Sea ME12 .49 H2
　Northfleet DA11 . . . . . . .18 A3
　Orpington BR5 . . . . .53 C5
　Sidcup DA5. . . . . .32 A7
　Swanscombe DA10. . . . .17 E3
　Warden ME12 . . . . .49 D6
Manor Way Bsns Ctr
　RM13 . . . . .4 D8
Manor Way Business Park
　DA11 . . . . .18 A3
Manse Ct DA14 . . . . .31 C3
Manse Field TN25 . . . . .302 E5
Mansel Dr ME1. . . . . .63 A2
Manse Par BR8. . . . . .56 A5
Mansergh CI SE18 . . . . . .11 E7
Manse Way BR8. . . . . . . .56 A5
Mansfield CI BR5. . . . . . .54 D2
Mansfield Dr ME9 . . . . . .68 D3
Mansfield Rd BR8 . . . . . .32 F2
Mansfield Wlk ME16. . . .161 E2
Mansion Gdns CT16 . . . .278 A4
Mansion House CI
　TN27 . . . . .295 A2
Mansion Row ME7. . . . . .64 A6
Mansion St CT9 . . . . . . .50 I3
Mansions The CT10. . . . .83 E4
MANSTON. 82 E1
Manston Court Cotts
　CT12 . . . . .82 C2
Manston Court Rd CT12,
　CT9 . . . . .82 D3
Manston Pk CT12. . . . . . .81 D2
Manston Rd
　Acol CT12, CT7 . . . . .81 D4
　Margate CT12, CT9. . . . .82 C4
　Ramsgate CT11, CT12 . .118 A7
Mansum Ct CT7 . . . . .79 F2
Manthorpe Rd SE18 . . . . .2 C1
Mantles Hill CT14 . . . . . .214 D1
Manton Rd SE2. . . . . .3 A2
Manwarings The TN12 290 A6
Manwood Almshouse
　CT2. . . . . .142 F4
Manwood Ave CT2 . . . . .142 F3
Manwood CI ME10. . . . . .101 F2
Manwood Rd CT13 . . . . .181 A8
Manwood St E16 . . . . . . .1 F5
Maple Ave
　Gillingham ME7. . . . . . . .64 G6
　Maidstone ME16. . . . . .161 C6
Maple CI Ashford TN23. . .267 F4
　Broadstairs CT10 . . . . . .51 E1
　Larkfield ME20 . . . . . . .128 A2
　Orpington BR5 . . . . .53 D4
　Rough Common CT2 . . .142 B3
　Royal Tunbridge Wells
　TN2 . . . . .286 A1
　Swanley BR8. . . . . .55 E1
Maple Cres DA15 . . . . . . .13 A1
Maplecroft CI E6 . . . . .1 E7
Maple Ct Erith DA8. . . . . .14 F7
　Hersden CT3. . . . . .144 E8
　Newham E6. . . . . .2 A8
　Rodmersham ME9 . . . . .135 A7

Maple Ct continued
　Royal Tunbridge Wells
　TN4 . . . . .285 E4
　Sidcup DA14 . . . . .31 B3
　Stone DA9. . . . . .34 E8
Mapledene BR7 . . . . .30 C3
Maple Dr
　Hawkinge CT18. . . . . . .307 C5
　St Mary's Bay TN29 . . .365 F4
Maplefields Gdns
　CT18 . . . . .307 C5
Maple Gardens TN2 . . . .314 B8
Maple Gdns CT3. . . . . . .144 E8
Maplehurst CI DA2 . . . . . .14 E8
Maple Leaf CI TN16. . . . .118 D3
Maple Leaf Dr DA15 . . . . .30 F7
Maple Rd Dartford DA1 . .33 C7
　Gravesend DA12. . . . . . .37 C4
　Grays RM17 . . . . .18 C8
　Hoo St Werburgh ME3 . .41 E3
MAPLESCOMBE. 90 B5
Maplescombe Farm Cotts
　DA4. . . . . .90 B5
Maplescombe La DA4 . . .90 B6
Maplesden TN12 . . . . . . .259 D5
Maplesden CI ME16 . . . .160 F3
Maplesden Noakes Sch
　ME16 . . . . .161 E6
Maple St ME12 . . . . .28 C1
Maples The
　Broadstairs CT10 . . . . . .83 D4
　Minster (Sheppey) ME12 .47 B6
　New Barn DA3 . . . . .59 B6
Mapleton TN8. . . . . .218 A7
Mapleton CI BR2. . . . . . . .52 A3
Mapleton Rd
　Four Elms TN8. . . . . . . .218 A8
　Westerham TN8, TN16 .184 E3
Maple Tree PI SE3. . . . . . .11 E6
Maplin Ho SE2 . . . . .3 D4
Maplin Rd E16 . . . . .1 B7
Maplins CI ME8. . . . . .65 F1
Mara Ct ME4 . . . . .63 F1
Maran Way DA18 . . . . . . .3 D3
Marathon Paddock
　ME7. . . . . .64 D4
Marathon Way SE28 . . . . .2 F4
Marble CI ME7. . . . . .64 F6
Marble Ho 1 SE18 . . . . . . .2 F1
Marbrook Ct SE12 . . . . . .29 C5
Marc Brunel Way ME4 . . .64 A7
Marcellina Way BR6. . . . .86 F7
Marcet Rd DA1 . . . . .15 C2
Marconi Ho SE2 . . . . .3 C1
Marconi Rd DA11. . . . . . . .36 D5
Marconi Way ME1. . . . . . .96 D7
Marcroft CT10. . . . . .84 B7
Marcus Rd DA1. . . . . .33 A8
Mardale CI ME8 . . . . .66 A1
MARDEN 259 C5
Marden Ave Hayes BR2. .52 A3
　Ramsgate CT12 . . . . . .117 B8
MARDEN BEECH. 259 B3
Marden Cres DA5 . . . . . .14 C2
Marden Prim Sch
　TN12. . . . . .259 B5
Marden Rd
　Rochester ME2. . . . . . . .40 C1
　Staplehurst TN12 . . . . .260 C5
Marden Road TN17 . . . . .292 A1
Marden Sta TN12 . . . . . .259 C6
MARDEN THORN 259 F3
Mardol Rd TN24. . . . . . . .268 C5
Marechal Niel Ave
　DA15 . . . . .30 D5
Marechal Niel Par
　DA15 . . . . .30 D5
Maresfield CI CT16 . . . . .278 B2
Margaret Barr Row
　DA10. . . . . .35 E8
Margaret Ct CT6 . . . . .76 F4
Margaret Gardner Dr
　SE9 . . . . .29 F6
Margaret Rd DA5. . . . . . .13 D1
Margaret St 10 CT20. . . .335 E5
MARGATE. 50 H2
Margate CI ME7 . . . . .64 E6
Margate Hill CT7 . . . . . . .81 C4
Margate Language Ctr 13
　CT9. . . . . .50 J2
Margate Local History
Mus★ CT9 . . . . .50 I3
Margate Rd
　Herne Bay, Broomfield
　CT6 . . . . .77 D2
　Ramsgate CT10, CT12,
　CT11 . . . . .83 B3
Margate Sta CT9 . . . . . . .50 H2
Margetts La ME1 . . . . . . .95 D1
Margetts PI ME2 . . . . . . .41 A3
Mar Ho 5 SE7 . . . . .11 C8
Marian Ave ME1. . . . . . . .47 A7
Marian Sq TN12 . . . . . . .260 F4
Marigold Dr ME10. . . . . .101 F1
Marigold Way ME16 . . . .161 A3
Marilyn Cres CT7. . . . . . .81 B7
Marina Ct ME2. . . . . .52 A6
Marina Ct Deal CT14 . . .215 D8
　Hythe CT21. . . . . .333 C1
Marina Dr Bexley DA16 . .12 E5
　Dartford DA1 . . . . .34 A7
　Minster (Sheppey) ME12 .47 A7
　Northfleet DA11. . . . . . .18 F1
Marina Espl CT11 . . . . . .117 F7
Marina Rd CT11 . . . . . . .117 F7
Marina The CT14 . . . . . .215 D8
Marine Ave TN29 . . . . . .352 F3
Marine Cres
　7 Folkestone CT20 . . .335 D4
　Whitstable CT5. . . . . . . .75 B3
Marine Ct
　18 Dover CT16 . . . . . .310 E7
　Whitstable CT5. . . . . . . .74 F3

Marine Dr
　Broadstairs CT10 . . . . . .51 G3
　Hoo St Werburgh ME3 . .41 E3
　Margate CT9. . . . . .50 I2
　Woolwich SE18 . . . . .1 F7
Marine Dr E ME3 . . . . . . .41 E3
Marine Gap CT5. . . . . . . .74 C1
Marine Gdns CT9. . . . . . .50 I2
Marine Ho CT5 . . . . .74 F3
Marine Hts CT8 . . . . .50 D1
Marine Par Dover CT16 310 E7
　Folkestone CT20 . . . . .335 E4
　Hythe CT21. . . . . .333 C1
　Littlestone-on-Sea TN28 373 E5
　Sheerness ME12 . . . . . .28 C2
　Whitstable CT5 . . . . .75 A3
Marine Parade Mews 5
　CT20 . . . . .335 E4
Marine Point CT20 . . . . .335 A3
Marine Rd CT14 . . . . . . .215 D4
Mariners CI
　Swanscombe DA9. . . . . .17 B3
　2 Whitstable CT5 . . . .108 C8
Mariners Lea CT10 . . . . . .83 D4
Mariners Lee CT5 . . . . . . .74 E3
Mariners View ME1. . . . .63 B4
Mariners Way 5 DA11. .36 E8
Mariners Wlk DA8. . . . . . .14 F8
Marine Terr
　Folkestone CT20. . . . . .335 E4
　Margate CT9. . . . . .50 H2
　Whitstable CT5. . . . . . . .74 C1
MARINE TOWN. 28 C2
Marine View ME8 . . . . . . .41 B1
Marine Walk St CT21. . . .333 C2
Marion CI ME5 . . . . .97 A2
Marion Cotts TN15 . . . . .157 E8
Marion Cres
　Maidstone ME15. . . . . .195 B8
　Orpington BR5 . . . . .54 B4
Maritime Ave CT6 . . . . . .77 C4
Maritime CI
　Rochester ME2. . . . . . . .63 D8
　Swanscombe DA9. . . . . .17 B3
Maritime Est ME4 . . . . . .63 D8
Maritime Gate DA11. . . . .36 E8
Maritime Ind Est SE7 . . . .1 B2
Maritime PI CT14. . . . . . .215 D7
Maritime Way ME4 . . . . .64 A8
Marjan CI CT17. . . . . .278 A1
Marjoram Dr ME9. . . . . . .101 F2
Marjorie McClure Sch
　BR7. . . . . .53 C8
Marjory Pease Cotts
　RH8 . . . . .183 E5
Mark Ave CT11 . . . . .117 B5
MARKBEECH 250 D2
Mark CI Bexley DA7. . . . . .13 E6
　Orpington BR2 . . . . .85 E6
Markers Lodge CT12 . . . .37 E8
Market Alley 9 DA11. . . .19 B1
Market Bldgs 4 ME14 161 F4
Market Colonnade 3
　ME14. . . . . .161 F4
Market Hill CT21 . . . . . .333 C2
Market La 12 TN13. . . . .268 B2
Market Mdw BR5. . . . . . . .54 C5
Market Par Bromley BR1 52 A8
　5 Sidcup DA14 . . . . . . .31 B4
Market PI
　Aylesham CT3. . . . . . . .210 F5
　2 Bexley DA6 . . . . .14 A3
　Charing TN27 . . . . .234 C7
　Dartford DA1 . . . . .33 E8
　1 Faversham ME13 . .138 D7
　20 Folkestone CT20 . .335 D5
　Margate CT9. . . . . .50 I3
　16 Royal Tunbridge Wells
　TN2 . . . . .286 A2
　1 Tilbury RM18. . . . . .19 A5
Market Sq Bromley BR1. .52 A7
　12 Dover CT16, CT17. .310 D7
　Royal Tunbridge Wells
　TN1 . . . . .286 B4
　Westerham TN16 . . . . .151 D1
Market St Dartford DA1. .33 E8
　Deal CT14 . . . . .215 D6
　Faversham ME13 . . . . .138 D7
　Herne Bay CT6 . . . . .76 F5
　2 Maidstone ME14 . .161 F4
　Margate CT9. . . . . .50 I3
　17 Royal Tunbridge Wells
　TN2 . . . . .286 A2
　Sandwich CT13 . . . . . .149 A1
　Staplehurst TN12 . . . . .260 C5
　Woolwich SE18 . . . . .2 A2
Market View CT3. . . . . . .210 F5
Market Way
　Canterbury CT2. . . . . . .143 A2
　2 Westerham TN16 . .151 D1
Mark La DA12 . . . . .19 E1
Markland Rd CT17. . . . . .309 F7
Marks Sq DA11. . . . . .36 F4
Mark St ME4 . . . . .64 A2
Mark Way BR8 . . . . .56 A4
Marlborough CI
　Broadstairs CT10 . . . . . .83 E3
　Littlestone-on-Sea
　TN28 . . . . .373 D6
　Orpington BR6 . . . . .53 F3
　Royal Tunbridge Wells
　TN4 . . . . .285 E4
Marlborough Cres
　TN13 . . . . .153 E3
Marlborough Ct
　Folkestone CT20. . . . . .335 B4
　Hythe CT21. . . . . .333 D1
　Westerham TN16 . . . . .151 C1
Marlborough Ctr ME3 . . .41 D5
Marlborough Ho
　4 Gillingham ME8. . . . .98 F8
　Margate CT9. . . . . .51 C1

Marlborough House Sch
　TN18. . . . . .340 E2
Marlborough La SE7 . . . .11 C7
Marlborough Par
　ME16 . . . . .160 F2
Marlborough Park Ave
　DA15 . . . . .31 A7
Marlborough Rd
　Bexley DA7. . . . . .13 D4
　Bromley BR2. . . . . .52 C5
　Dartford DA1 . . . . .15 C1
　Deal CT14 . . . . .215 A2
　Dover CT17 . . . . .309 F7
　Gillingham ME7. . . . . . . .64 B5
　Margate CT9. . . . . .50 I1
　6 Ramsgate CT11 . . .117 D6
　Woolwich SE18 . . . . .2 C3
Marlborough Road Ind Est
　CT14. . . . . .215 A2
Marlborough Sch DA15 31 A8
Marlborough St CT5. . . .108 D5
Marlborough Way
　TN24 . . . . .268 F7
Marle Place Gdns★
　TN12. . . . . .289 C4
Marle Place Rd TN12. . .289 C4
Marler Ho DA8 . . . . .14 F5
Marler Rd CT19 . . . . . . .334 E6
MARLEY Barham. 209 B1
　Deal. 214 A8
Marley Ave DA7 . . . . .13 D8
Marley CI CT2. . . . . .142 C4
Marley La Chislet CT3. . .112 A5
　Finglesham CT14 . . . . .214 A8
　Kingston CT4. . . . . .209 B1
　Smarden Bell TN27. . . .263 C3
Marley Rd
　Harrietsham ME17. . . . .198 F6
　Hoo St Werburgh ME3 . .41 D6
Marley Way ME1 . . . . . . .63 C2
Marlfield TN12 . . . . .260 E4
Marlhurst TN8 . . . . .217 B4
Marlin CI 12 DA14 . . . . . . .31 A4
Marling Cross DA12 . . . . .37 E1
Marlings CI BR7. . . . . .53 E5
Marlings Park Ave BR7 53 E6
Marling Way DA12. . . . . . .37 E3
Marlow CI CT5 . . . . .75 B1
Marlow Copse ME5. . . . . .96 F1
Marlow Ct TN13 . . . . . . .154 B4
Marlowe Arc 11 CT1. . . .174 F8
Marlowe Ave CT1 . . . . . .174 F8
Marlowe Ct BR7. . . . . .30 D2
Marlowe Ct 12 CT1 . . . . .174 F8
Marlowe Gdns SE9 . . . . .12 A1
Marlowe Rd
　Ashford TN23 . . . . .268 B2
　Dover CT16. . . . . .278 B3
　Margate CT9. . . . . .83 C8
　New Hythe ME20 . . . . .128 A3
Marlowes The DA11 . . . . .14 D3
Marlow Ho CT7. . . . . .81 B7
Marlow Mdws CT2 . . . . .143 F5
MARLPIT 195 E2
Marlpit CI TN8 . . . . .217 C4
Marlpit Cotts TN17. . . . .195 E2
Marlpit CI ME5. . . . . .338 E1
MARLPIT HILL. 217 C4
Marlpit The TN5. . . . . . . .336 E5
Marlwood DA15 . . . . .30 E6
Marmadon Rd SE18 . . . . . .2 F2
Marmion Way TN23 . . . .299 C8
Marne Ave DA16. . . . . . . .13 A4
Marquis Dr ME7 . . . . .98 B3
Marrabon CI DA15. . . . . . .31 A7
Marram Ct RM17 . . . . . . .18 E8
Marr CI ME12. . . . . .46 F7
Marrians View 1 ME5. .64 C2
Marriott Rd DA1. . . . . .34 A7
Marriotts Wharf 2
　DA11. . . . . .19 B1
Marrose Ave CT12. . . . . . .83 B3
Marrowbone Hill ME12 .48 B5
Marsden Way 2 BR6. . . . .86 F6
Marsh Acad The TN28.373 B7
Marshall Cres
　Broadstairs CT10 . . . . . .83 E4
　Rushenden ME11 . . . . . .45 F3
Marshall Gdns TN11. . . .190 E1
Marshall Path 10 SE28. . .3 B6
Marshall Rd ME8 . . . . .98 C8
Marshalls Gr SE18 . . . . . .1 E2
Marshalls Land TN30 . . .324 A2
Marshall St CT19. . . . . . .335 E7
Marsham CI BR7. . . . . .30 B3
Marsham Cres ME17. . . .196 B1
Marsham St ME14 . . . . . .162 A4
Marsham Way ME5. . . . . .95 A5
MARSHBOROUGH 180 B7
Marshborough Rd
　CT13. . . . . .180 B7
Marshbrook CI SE3. . . . . .11 D4
Marsh Cres
　High Halstow ME23 . . . .23 E4
　New Romney TN28 . . . .373 B6
Marsh Farm Rd CT12 . . .115 B4
MARSH GREEN. 249 B5
Marsh Green Rd TN8 . . .249 C5
Marsh La Cliffe ME3. . . . . .22 B6
　Deal CT14 . . . . .215 A8
　Teynham Street ME9 . .104 A4
Marshlands TN29. . . . . . .366 B7
Marshlands CI TN29 . . . .366 B7
Marshland View ME25 . . .25 C5
Marsh Quarter La
　TN18 . . . . .356 C3
Marsh Rd Halling ME2 . . .95 B5
　Ruckinge TN26. . . . . . .349 F6
Marsh Rise ME10. . . . . . .69 A1
MARSHSIDE. 78 D1
Marsh St Dartford DA1. .195 D7
　Rochester ME2. . . . . . . .63 B7
Marsh View
　Gravesend DA12. . . . . . .37 F7

Marsh View continued
　Hythe CT21. . . . . .353 C8
　Sheerness ME12. . . . . . .28 G1
Marsh Way
　New Hythe ME20 . . . . .128 A4
　Rainham RM13 . . . . .4 D8
Marshwood CI CT1 . . . . .143 C3
Marstan CI ME9 . . . . .66 E2
Marston CI ME5 . . . . .96 E3
Marston Ct DA14 . . . . . . .30 F4
Marston Dr ME14 . . . . . .162 C5
Marston Ho RM17 . . . . . .18 A8
Marston Wlk ME5 . . . . . .96 E3
Martello Cotts CT21 . . . .353 E8
Martello Ct CT21. . . . . . .332 F1
Martello Ind Ctr CT19 .335 F6
Martello Rd
　Folkestone CT20 . . . . .335 E6
　Folkestone, Sandgate
　CT20 . . . . .334 E3
Martello Terr 1 CT20 .334 F3
Martello St CT5. . . . . . . .108 D5
Marten Rd CT20 . . . . . . .335 B5
Martens Ave DA7 . . . . . . .14 C3
Martens CI DA7 . . . . .14 C3
Martha CI CT19 . . . . .335 B7
Martham CI SE28 . . . . .3 D6
MARTIN 247 B3
Martin Bowes Rd SE9 . . .11 F4
Martin Ct Gillingham ME7 98 A3
　Sittingbourne ME10 . . . .68 F1
Martindale Ave
　Newham E16. . . . . .1 A6
　Orpington BR6 . . . . .87 A5
Martindale CI CT1. . . . . . .175 A7
Martin Dale Cres CT15 247 C2
Martin Dene DA6 . . . . . . .13 F2
Martindown Rd CT5 . . . .108 C7
Martin Dr DA2. . . . . .16 C1
Martin Hardie Way
　TN10 . . . . .222 E5
Martin Ho Dartford DA2 . .34 C8
　Gravesend DA11. . . . . . .37 A2
　Wye TN25 . . . . .237 E2
Martin House DA11. . . . . .36 F6
Martin Mill Sta CT15. . . .247 C2
MARTIN MILL 247 C2
Martin Mill Sta CT15. . . .247 C2
Martin Rd Dartford DA2. .33 C5
　Rochester ME2. . . . . . . .63 B8
Martin Rise DA6 . . . . .13 F2
Martins CI
　Lower Higham ME3 . . . .39 D6
　Orpington BR5 . . . . .54 D6
　Tenterden TN30 . . . . . .345 C8
Martin's CI CT12. . . . . . . .83 C2
Martins La TN12. . . . . . . .191 E2
Martins PI SE28 . . . . .2 E5
Martin Sq ME20 . . . . . . .128 A2
Martin's Shaw TN13. . . .153 C5
Martin St SE28 . . . . .2 E5
Martins The TN26 . . . . . .325 A8
Martin's Way CT21 . . . . .353 D8
Martins Wlk SE28 . . . . .2 E5
Martyn Ho SE2 . . . . .13 D8
MARTYR'S FIELD. 174 F7
Martyrs' Field Rd CT1 174 F7
Marvels CI SE12 . . . . .29 B6
Marvels La SE12 . . . . .29 C5
Marvels Lane Prim Sch
　SE12. . . . . .29 C4
Marvillion Ct TN12 . . . . .224 F6
Marvin Ho 5 SE18 . . . . . .12 B8
Marwell Ho TN16 . . . . . .151 B1
Marwood CI DA16 . . . . . .13 C4
Marybank SE18. . . . . .1 F2
Mary Burrows Gdns
　TN15 . . . . .123 B2
Mary Ct ME4 . . . . .64 A2
Mary Day's TN17 . . . . . .318 E7
Maryfield CI DA5 . . . . .32 E5
Mary Green Wlk 5
　CT1 . . . . .143 B2
Mary Hougham
　Almshouses CT14. . . .215 D7
Maryland Ct
　Gillingham ME8. . . . . . . .98 C5
　Hythe CT21. . . . . .333 D3
Maryland Dr ME16. . . . . .160 F2
Maryland Gr CT1 . . . . . . .175 C6
Maryland Rd TN2. . . . . . .286 D1
Mary Last CI ME6. . . . . . .127 E7
Mary Lawrenson PI 2
　SE3. . . . . .11 A7
Mary Macarthur Ho 5
　DA17. . . . . .4 A3
Mary Magdalene Ho 8
　TN9. . . . . .254 B8
Maryon Ct BR5 . . . . .54 B5
Maryon Gr SE7. . . . . .1 E2
Maryon Rd SE7, SE18. . . . . .1 E2
Mary Rd CT14 . . . . .215 A3
Mary Rose Mall E6 . . . . . .1 F8
Mary Slessor Ho 14 DA17 4 A3
Maryville SE18 . . . . .12 F5
Mascall's Court La
　TN12. . . . . .257 B4
Mascall's Court Rd
　TN12. . . . . .257 A4
Mascalls CI 23 SE18 . . . .11 C8
Mascalls Pk TN12 . . . . . .256 F5
Mascalls Rd SE7 . . . . . . .11 C8
Mascalls Sch TN12. . . . .257 A4
Masefield CI DA8. . . . . . .14 F6
Masefield Dr ME3 . . . . . .40 B8
Masefield Rd
　Dartford DA1 . . . . .16 B2
　Lunsford ME20 . . . . . . .127 F4
　Northfleet DA11. . . . . . .36 D5
Masefield View BR6. . . . .86 C2
Masefield Way TN9. . . . .253 F7
Masham Ho 6 DA18. . . . . .3 D4
Mason CI Bexley DA7. . . . .14 B4
　Newham E16. . . . . .1 A6
Masons Hill Bromley BR2 52 B5
　Woolwich SE18. . . . . .2 B2

Masons Rd CT17. . . . . . . .278 B1
Mason's Rise CT10 . . . . . .84 A5
Mason Way ME2. . . . . . . .40 B2
Master Gunner PI SE18 11 E6
Masters La ME19 . . . . . . .127 B5
Masterson Ho DA4 . . . . . .57 D7
Masthead CI DA2. . . . . . . .16 C3
Matchless Dr SE18 . . . . .12 A7
MATFIELD 288 D8
Matfield CI BR2. . . . . .52 A4
Matfield Cres ME14 . . . .162 C5
Matfield Rd DA17. . . . . . . .14 A8
Mathon Ct TN24 . . . . . . .268 C5
Matilda CI ME8 . . . . .98 B8
Matrix Bsns Ctr DA1. . . . .15 E2
Matterdale Gdns ME16 160 E2
Matthews CI CT14 . . . . . .215 C6
Matthews Ho 13 SE7. . . .11 C8
Matthews La TN11,
　ME18. . . . . .190 F4
Matthew's PI 9 CT16. . . .278 C1
Matthews Rd CT6 . . . . . . .76 C2
Mattison PI ME9. . . . . . . .165 F7
Matts Hill Rd ME9. . . . . . .98 E2
Maud Cashmore Way
　SE18 . . . . .1 F3
Maude Rd BR8. . . . . .33 A2
Maudslay Rd SE9 . . . . . . .11 F4
Maugham Ct CT5 . . . . . . .108 D8
Maundene Prim Sch
　ME5. . . . . .97 B5
Maunders CI ME5 . . . . . . .97 C8
Maunsell PI TN24. . . . . . .300 D7
Maurice Ct CT9 . . . . .51 B3
Mavelstone CI BR1. . . . . .52 E8
Mavelstone Rd BR1. . . . . .52 E8
Mavis Wlk 10 E6. . . . . .1 E8
Maxey Rd SE18. . . . . .2 C2
Maximfeldt Rd DA8. . . . . . .4 E1
Maximilian Dr ME2. . . . . .95 B4
Maxim Rd Crayford DA1. .14 E2
　Erith DA8. . . . . .4 E2
Maxine Gdns CT10. . . . . .83 F5
Maxted CI TN12 . . . . . . .260 E4
Maxted Ct CT6 . . . . .77 C4
MAXTED STREET. 272 B6
MAXTON. 310 A6
Maxton CI Dover CT17. . .310 A6
　Maidstone ME14. . . . . .162 F5
Maxton Ct CT17 . . . . .310 A6
Maxton Rd CT17. . . . . . . .310 A6
Maxwell Dr ME16 . . . . . .161 B6
Maxwell Gdns BR6 . . . . . .86 F7
Maxwell Ho 12 SE18 . . . .12 B8
Maxwell House BR7. . . . . .30 B1
Maxwell PI CT14. . . . . . . .215 C4
May Ave Northfleet DA11 .36 F7
　Orpington BR5 . . . . .54 B4
May Avenue Ind Est 1
　DA11. . . . . .36 F7
Maybrook Ind Est 143 D4
Maybury Ave DA2 . . . . . . .34 C7
Maybury CI BR5. . . . . .53 B4
Maycotts La TN12 . . . . . .256 D1
May CI RM17 . . . . .18 E8
Mayday Gdns SE3 . . . . . .11 E5
Maydowns Rd CT5. . . . . . .75 D2
Mayerne Rd SE9. . . . . . . .11 C7
Mayers Rd CT14 . . . . . . .215 A1
Mayes CI BR8. . . . . .56 A5
Mayeswood Rd SE12 . . . .29 C4
Mayfair 2 ME2. . . . . .63 C8
Mayfair Ave Bexley DA7 .13 D6
　Loose ME15 . . . . .195 A8
Mayfair Rd DA1 . . . . .15 D2
Mayfield
　Bexley DA7. . . . . .13 F4
　Sevenoaks TN13 . . . . .153 E7
　Swanscombe DA10. . . . .17 E1
Mayfield Ave
　Dover CT16 . . . . .278 C2
　Orpington BR6 . . . . .53 F2
Mayfield CI
　Chatham ME5 . . . . .97 A1
　Gillingham ME8. . . . . . . .65 E2
Mayfield Ct
　3 Dover CT16 . . . . . .278 B2
　Sidcup DA14 . . . . .31 B3
Mayfield Gdns CT16 . . . .298 C2
Mayfield La TN5. . . . . . . .336 D4
Mayfield Pk TN5 . . . . . . .336 E5
Mayfield Rd
　Bromley BR1. . . . . .52 E4
　Erith DA17. . . . . .4 C2
　Herne Bay CT6 . . . . .77 A3
　Lyminge CT18 . . . . .305 C6
　Northfleet DA11. . . . . . .36 F8
　Royal Tunbridge Wells
　TN4 . . . . .285 F4
　Whitfield CT16. . . . . . . .278 A7
Mayfield Villas DA14 . . . .31 C2
Mayflower Ho ME1. . . . . . .63 B4
Mayfly CI BR5. . . . . .54 D5
Mayfly Dr CT18. . . . . .307 A4
Mayford CI ME5 . . . . .97 D2
Mayforth Gdns CT17. . . .111 B8
Mayhew CI TN23 . . . . . . .300 A8
Mayhill Rd SE7 . . . . .11 B8
Maylam CI TN10. . . . . . . .222 C4
Maylam Gdns ME10. . . . .101 A4
Maylands Dr DA14. . . . . . .31 D5
May Lodge CT14 . . . . .215 B5
Maymills Cotts CT13. . . .180 B2
Maynard Ave CT9 . . . . . . .28 B8
Maynard CI DA8. . . . . .14 F7
Maynard Ho SE18 . . . . .2 C2
Maynard PI ME5. . . . . .97 B7
Maynard Rd CT1 . . . . . . .174 E7
Maynards TN2. . . . . .259 C5
Mayor's La DA2 . . . . .33 C3

Mayor's Pl **10** TN30 . . . 345 A7
Maypits TN23 . . . . .299 F8
May Pl DA12 . . . . .60 D4
Mayplace Ave DA1 . . . . . . .15 A3
Mayplace Cl DA7 . . . . .14 B4
Mayplace La SE18 . . . . . . .12 B7
Mayplace Prim Sch
  DA7 . . . . .14 D3
Mayplace Road E DA7 . .14 C4
Mayplace Road W DA7 . .14 A3
MAYPOLE Dartford 32 E7
  Herne Bay 111 F6
  Orpington 87 F4
Maypole Cl CT18 . . . . . .307 B6
Maypole Cotts BR6 . . . . . .88 A4
Maypole Cres DA8 . . . . . . .15 D8
Maypole Dr ME19 . . . . . .159 C3
Maypole La
  Goudhurst TN17 . . . . . . .318 F8
  Hoath CT3 . . . . .111 E6
Maypole Prim Sch DA5 .32 E5
Maypole Rd
  Chelsfield BR6 . . . . .87 F4
  Gravesend DA12 . . . . .37 F7
  Hoath CT3 . . . . .111 E6
May Rd Gillingham ME7 . .64 C4
  Hawley DA2 . . . . .33 F4
  Rochester ME1 . . . . .63 C3
Mays Rd **3** CT11 . . . . . .117 C6
May St Cuxton ME2 . . . . . .62 B2
  Herne Bay CT6 . . . . .77 F4
  Snodland ME6 . . . . .128 B8
Mayston Mews **6** SE10 . .1 A1
Maystreet Cross CT6 . . . . .77 F3
May Terr ME7 . . . . .64 A7
Maytham Bglws TN17 . . .344 A1
Maytham Rd TN17 . . . . . .358 C7
Mayton La CT2 . . . . .110 C1
Maytree Cotts CT14 . . . .247 D8
Mayview DA1 . . . . .33 E7
Mayville Rd CT10 . . . . .83 E6
Mayweed Ave ME5 . . . . . .96 E4
May Wynne Ho E16 . . . . . . .1 B7
Mead Cl BR8 . . . . .56 A4
Mead Cres DA1 . . . . .33 D7
Meades Cl TN12 . . . . .259 B6
Meadfield Rd DA13 . . . . . .93 A8
Mead Gn ME5 . . . . .97 C3
Mead Ho TN16 . . . . .118 D3
Meadow Bank
  Leigh TN11 . . . . .220 F1
  Painters Forstal ME13 . .137 F2
  West Malling ME19 . . . .159 C8
Meadow Bank Cl TN15 . .90 F7
Meadowbank Ct ME19 159 C8
Meadow Bank Mews
  ME19 . . . . .159 C8
Meadowbank Rd ME4 . .64 A4
Meadowbrook CT20 . . . .334 E4
Meadowbrook Cl
  CT20 . . . . .334 E4
Meadow Brook Ct
  CT20 . . . . .334 E4
Meadowbrook Rd
  TN24 . . . . .268 D6
Meadow Cl Bexley DA6 . .13 F2
  Bridge 176 A1
  Chatham ME5 . . . . .96 F5
  Chilham CT4 . . . . .205 C8
  Chislehurst BR7 . . . . .30 B3
  Hawkinge CT18 . . . . . . .307 B4
  Herne Bay CT6 . . . . .77 C4
  Iwade ME9 . . . . .68 D4
  Sevenoaks TN13 . . . . . .154 A4
  Upper Halling ME2 . . . . . .94 C4
Meadow Cotts
  East Studdal CT15 . . . . .246 D8
  Goodnestone CT3 . . . . . .179 A2
Meadow Cres ME2 . . . . . .94 E4
Meadow Croft BR1 . . . . . .52 F6
Meadow Ct Margate CT9 83 B8
  Westenhanger CT21 . . . .332 B6
Meadowdown ME14 . . . .162 E4
Meadowdown Cl ME7 . .98 A4
Meadow Dr CT5 . . . . .109 D8
Meadowfield Sch
  ME10 . . . . .102 C3
Meadowford Cl SE28 . . . .3 A6
Meadow Gr TN25 . . . . . . .331 D8
Meadow Hill Cotts
  CT15 . . . . .276 D1
Meadow Hill Rd **6**
  TN1 . . . . .286 B3
Meadow Ho ME9 . . . . . . .101 B2
Meadow La
  Culverstone Green
    DA13 . . . . .93 A1
  Lewisham SE12 . . . . .29 B5
  Marlpit Hill TN8 . . . . . . .217 B4
Meadowlands
  Oxted RH8 . . . . .183 A1
  Seal TN15 . . . . .154 F7
Meadow Rd
  Ashford TN23 . . . . .268 A4
  Canterbury CT2 . . . . . . .142 C2
  Gravesend DA11 . . . . . . .37 A6
  Groombridge TN3 . . . . . .312 C2
  Margate CT9 . . . . .50 F1
  Northfleet DA11 . . . . .36 C7
  Royal Tunbridge Wells,
    Southborough TN4 . . . .253 F1
  Royal Tunbridge Wells
    TN1 . . . . .286 A4
  Rusthall TN4 . . . . .285 C4
  Sturry CT2 . . . . .143 F6
  Tonbridge TN9 . . . . .254 B8
Meadow Rise ME9 . . . . . . .68 A4
Meadows ME17 . . . . .321 D1
Meadows Ct DA14 . . . . . . .31 B2

Meadowside
  Dartford DA1 . . . . .33 E7
  Eltham SE3, SE9 . . . . .11 C3
Meadowside Cotts
  TN5 . . . . .338 F1
Meadows Sch TN4 . . . . . .253 F2
Meadows The
  Biddenden TN27 . . . . . .294 F2
  Halstead TN14 . . . . .120 F6
  Herne Bay CT6 . . . . .77 D2
  3 Maidstone ME15 . . .161 E2
  New Romney TN28 . . . . .373 C6
  Orpington BR6 . . . . .87 C4
  Sittingbourne ME10 . . . .101 F2
  Wittersham TN30 . . . . . .359 D4
Meadowsweet Cl **3** E16 .1 D8
Meadowsweet Ho
  TN23 . . . . .267 F1
Meadowsweet View
  ME4 . . . . .41 B2
Meadow The
  Chislehurst BR7 . . . . .30 C2
  Pembury TN2 . . . . .287 E8
Meadow View
  Flimwell TN5 . . . . .339 A3
  Hothfield TN26 . . . . .267 A6
  Lydd TN29 . . . . .376 D7
  Monkton CT12 . . . . .114 D6
  Orpington BR5 . . . . .54 C6
  Sidcup DA15 . . . . .31 B8
Meadow View Cotts
  Hurst Green TN19 . . . . . .354 A3
  Laddingford ME18 . . . . .225 E5
Meadow View Ind Est
  TN26 . . . . .349 C7
Meadowview Rd DA5 . .13 F1
Meadow View Rd
  Maidstone ME17 . . . . . .195 B3
  Shepherdswell CT15 . . . .244 E5
Meadow Way
  Dartford DA2 . . . . .34 C8
  Eythorne CT15 . . . . .245 C8
  Hythe CT21 . . . . .353 D8
  Marden TN12 . . . . .259 E6
  Orpington BR6 . . . . .86 A7
  Wouldham ME1 . . . . .95 C5
Meadow Wlk
  Dartford DA2 . . . . .33 C4
  Maidstone ME15 . . . . . .162 B3
  Snodland ME6 . . . . .127 F7
  Whitstable CT5 . . . . .108 C6
Mead Rd Ashford TN24 . .300 E7
  Chislehurst BR7 . . . . .30 C2
  Dartford DA1 . . . . .33 D7
  Edenbridge TN8 . . . . . . .249 D7
  Folkestone CT19 . . . . . . .335 D6
  Gravesend DA11 . . . . .37 B6
Mead Road Inf Sch BR7 30 C1
Meads Ave The ME10 . .101 D7
Mead Sch The TN2 . . . . .286 A1
Meadside Wlk ME5 . . . . .96 F6
Meads The
  Hartley TN17 . . . . .319 E1
  Royal Tunbridge Wells
    TN2 . . . . .286 C2
Meads Way TN29 . . . . . .365 E3
Mead The
  Leybourne ME19 . . . . . .127 E2
  New Ash Green DA3 . . . . .91 E8
Mead Wall ME3 . . . . .5 F2
Meadway
  Halstead TN14 . . . . .120 F6
  River CT17 . . . . .277 E3
  Tonbridge TN11 . . . . . . .221 E5
Mead Way
  Canterbury CT2 . . . . . . .142 E1
  Hayes BR2 . . . . .52 A3
Meadway The
  Orpington BR6 . . . . .87 B4
  Sevenoaks TN13 . . . . . .153 F5
Meath Cl BR5 . . . . .54 B4
Medbury Rd DA12 . . . . . . .37 F7
Medbourne Cl SE3 . . . . . .11 A4
Mede Ho BR1 . . . . .29 B3
Medhurst Cres DA12 . . . . .37 F6
Medhurst Gdns DA12 . .37 F5
MEDHURST ROW 218 A2
Medick Ct RM17 . . . . .18 E8
Medina Ave CT5 . . . . . . .108 B7
Medina Ho **6** 14 E7
Medina Rd Ditton ME20 128 C1
  Tonbridge TN10 . . . . . . .222 C6
Medlar Cl ME9 . . . . .134 A6
Medlar Gr ME7 . . . . .98 A4
Medlar Rd **3** DA15 . . . . .31 A5
Medlar Rd RM17 . . . . .18 E8
Medlars The
  Maidstone ME14 . . . . . .162 D6
  Meopham Station DA13 . .60 A3
Medway Ave
  High Halstow ME23 . . . . .23 E4
  Yalding ME18 . . . . .192 F1
Medway City Est ME2 . .63 D7
Medway Com Coll ME4 .64 A1
Medway Cotts
  Iden Green TN17 . . . . . .342 D3
  Marden TN12 . . . . .259 C6
Medway Ct
  Aylesford ME20 . . . . .128 F2
  Forstal ME20 . . . . .129 A2
  19 Orpington BR5 . . . . . .54 C1
Medway Ent Ct ME2 . . . .63 D8
Medway Gdns ME4 . . . . .63 F7
Medway Ho **7** ME14 . . .161 F4
Medway Hts **5** ME4 . . . .63 E4
Medway Maritime Hospl
  ME7 . . . . .64 B4
Medway Mdws TN12 . .225 A6
Medway Rd
  Crayford DA1 . . . . .15 A4
  Gillingham ME7 . . . . .64 C7

Medway Rd continued
  Royal Tunbridge Wells
    TN1 . . . . .286 B5
  Sheerness ME12 . . . . .28 B1
Medway St Chatham ME4 63 F5
  Maidstone ME14 . . . . . .161 F4
Medway Trad Est
  ME16 . . . . .161 F2
Medway View
  Barnes Street TN11 . . . . .224 A5
  Middle Stoke ME3 . . . . . .25 C3
Medway Villas ME15 . .194 B7
Medway Wharf Rd
  TN9 . . . . .222 C1
Meehan Rd TN28 . . . . . .373 E4
Meehan Road S TN28 . .373 E3
Meerbrook Rd SE3 . . . . . .11 C4
Meeres Court La ME10 102 C5
Meeson's Cl SE3 . . . . . . .168 E6
Meeson's La RM17 . . . . . .17 F8
Meeting Ct CT9 . . . . .50 I3
Meeting Ho La **2**
  ME4 . . . . .63 F4
Meeting St CT11 . . . . . . .117 E7
Megan Cl TN29 . . . . .376 D7
Megby Cl ME8 . . . . .98 D6
Meggett La CT15 . . . . . . .308 C7
Megone Cl CT18 . . . . .307 A4
Megrims Hill TN18 . . . . .356 A6
Meirs Court Rd ME8 . . . .98 E6
Melanda Cl BR7 . . . . .29 F3
Melanie Cl DA7 . . . . .13 E6
Melba Cl ME19 . . . . .159 D4
Melba Gdns RM18 . . . . . .19 A7
Melbourne Ave
  Dover CT16 . . . . .278 C4
  Ramsgate CT12 . . . . .83 B1
Melbourne Cl **5** . . . .
  Melbourne Ct RM18 . . . .18 E6
Melbourne Quay **4**
  DA11 . . . . .19 B1
Melbourne Rd
  Chatham ME4 . . . . .64 A3
  Tilbury RM18 . . . . .18 E6
Melbury Rd **7** 29 F2
Melbury Grange BR1 . .52 E8
Melbury Mews TN28 . .373 C8
Meldrum Cl
  Orpington BR5 . . . . .54 C3
  Oxted RH8 . . . . .183 A3
Melford Dr ME16 . . . . . .161 C4
Mellanby Cl DA7 . . . . .81 A6
Melliker La DA13 . . . . .60 A3
Melling St SE18 . . . . .12 E8
Mellish Ind Est SE18 . . . .1 D3
Mellor Row ME10 . . . . . . .68 F1
Mells Cres SE9 . . . . .29 F4
Melody Cl
  Gillingham ME8 . . . . .98 C4
  Warden ME12 . . . . .49 C4
Melody Rd TN16 . . . . . . .118 C1
Melon La TN26, TN29 . .364 B6
Melrose Ave
  Dartford DA1 . . . . .32 E8
  Kings Hill ME19 . . . . . . .159 C3
Melrose Cl
  Lewisham SE12 . . . . .29 B7
  Loose ME15 . . . . .195 A7
Melrose Cres BR6 . . . . . . .86 D5
Melrose Rd TN16 . . . . . . .118 C3
Melsetter Cl CT7 . . . . .81 B7
Melthorpe Gdns SE3 . . . .11 E6
Melville Cl ME4 . . . . .63 F6
Melville Lea CT13 . . . . . . .180 C7
Melville Rd
  Maidstone ME15 . . . . . .162 A3
  Sidcup DA14 . . . . .31 C6
Memel Pl **12** CT1 . . . . . .117 D6
Memess Path **4** SE18 . .12 A8
Memorial Hospl SE18 . . .12 A5
Mendfield St **5** ME13 138 C7
Mendip TN24 . . . . .268 B4
Mendip Ho **1** DA11 . . . . .18 D1
Mendip Rd DA7 . . . . .14 E6
Mendip Rise TN24 . . . . . .268 B4
Mendip Wlk TN2 . . . . . . .286 D5
Mennie Ho ME10 . . . . . . .68 F1
Mentmore Ho CT12 . . . . . .83 C3
Mentmore Rd CT12 . . . . . .83 C3
Menzies Ave CT14 . . . . . .215 B1
Menzies Cl ME14 . . . . . . .47 A5
Menzies Rd TN16 . . . . . .278 A5
Meon Ct **20** BR5 . . . . . . .54 C1
MEOPHAM 93 B8
MEOPHAM GREEN 93 A7
Meopham L Ctr DA13 . .93 A8
Meopham Prim Sch
  DA13 . . . . .60 A4
Meopham Sch DA13 . . .93 A8
Meopham Sta DA13 . . . . .60 A4
MEOPHAM STATION 60 B4
Mera Dr DA7 . . . . .14 A3
Merbury Cl SE28 . . . . .2 D5
Merbury Rd SE28 . . . . .2 E4
Mercer Cl ME20 . . . . .128 B4
Mercer Ct ME5 . . . . .96 E1
Mercer Dr ME17 . . . . . . .198 F6
Mercers
  Hawkhurst TN18 . . . . . . .341 A1
  Langton Green TN3 . . . . .285 A3
Mercers Cl TN12 . . . . . . .256 E6
Mercers Pl ME19 . . . . . . .159 A2
Mercer St TN1 . . . . .286 B5
Mercer Way ME17 . . . . . .196 B5
Mercery La **5** CT1 . . . . .174 F8
Merchant Pl TN1 . . . . . . .286 B5
Merchant Store The **7**
  TN19 . . . . .142 F1
Merchants Way CT2 . . . .174 C8
Merchland Rd SE9 . . . . . . .30 C7
Mercury Cl ME1 . . . . .63 A3
Mere Cl BR6 . . . . .86 B8

Meredale Ind Prim Sch
  ME8 . . . . .66 A1
Meredith Cl ME17 . . . . . .196 F7
Mere Gate CT9 . . . . .50 I1
MERESBOROUGH 99 A5
Meresborough Cotts
  ME8 . . . . .98 F5
Meresborough La ME8,
  ME9 . . . . .99 B5
Meresborough Rd ME8 99 A4
Mereside BR6 . . . . .86 A8
Merevale Ho **3** TN1 . . . .286 A3
Merewood Rd DA7 . . . . . .14 C5
Merewood **1** BR1 . . . . . .53 A7
MEREWORTH 191 D8
Mereworth Cl ME8 . . . . . .65 A3
Mereworth Com Prim Sch
  ME18 . . . . .191 D8
Mereworth Dr SE18 . . . . . .12 C7
Mereworth Ho ME2 . . . . . .40 C1
Mereworth Rd
  Royal Tunbridge Wells
    TN4 . . . . .286 A6
  West Peckham ME18 . . . .191 C7
Merganser Gdns SE28 . .2 D3
Meriden Cl BR1 . . . . .29 D1
Meriden Wlk CT18 . . . . . .305 D3
Meridian Ct
  Ashford TN23 . . . . .299 E7
  Maidstone ME16 . . . . . .161 E4
Meridian Pk ME2 . . . . .63 E6
Meridian Rd SE7 . . . . .1 D7
Meridian Trad Est SE7 . . .1 B2
Meriel Wk DA9 . . . . .17 B3
Merifield Rd SE9 . . . . .11 C3
Merileys Cl DA3 . . . . .59 C6
Merino Pl DA15 . . . . .13 A2
Merino Way TN23 . . . . . . .299 E5
Merivale Gr ME5 . . . . .97 B4
Merleburgh Dr ME10 . . .101 F8
Merle Common Rd
  RH8 . . . . .216 B7
Merlewood TN13 . . . . . .154 B4
Merlewood Dr BR7 . . . . . .52 F8
Merlin Ave ME20 . . . . . .127 F2
Merlin Cl
  Sittingbourne ME10 . . . .102 A4
  Tonbridge TN10 . . . . . . .222 E4
Merlin Gdns BR1 . . . . .29 A5
Merlin Ho Chatham ME4 .64 B8
  2 Sittingbourne ME10 102 A4
Merlin Rd RM16 . . . . .13 A3
Merlin Road N DA16 . . . . .13 A3
Merlin Way
  Ashford TN23 . . . . .299 E7
  Gillingham ME7 . . . . .64 D5
Mermaid Cl
  Chatham ME5 . . . . .97 A6
  Northfleet DA11 . . . . .36 D8
Mermerus Gdns DA12 . .37 F4
Merrals Wood Rd ME2 . .62 D5
Merrilees Rd DA15 . . . . . .30 E8
Merriman Ho ME3 . . . . . .40 F6
Merriman Rd SE3 . . . . . .11 C4
Merriments Gdns ★
  TN19 . . . . .354 B5
Merriments La
  Hurst Green TN18,
    TN19 . . . . .354 D5
  Hurst Green TN19 . . . . .354 B5
Merrion Cl TN4 . . . . .286 B7
Merrion Way TN4 . . . . . .286 B7
Merritt Rd TN28 . . . . . . .373 E2
Merrivale Hts CT10 . . . . . .84 A2
Merry Boys Rd ME3 . . . . .40 B8
Merrydown Way BR7 . . . .52 B9
Merryfield SE3 . . . . .11 A5
Merryfield Ct **9** TN9 . . .254 B8
Merryfield Ho **4** SE9 . .29 C5
Merryfields ME2 . . . . .40 A1
Merryfields Cl DA3 . . . . . .58 F5
Merryhills Cl TN16 . . . . . .118 C3
MERRYMAN'S HILL 47 C8
Merryweather Cl DA1 . .15 F1
Merrywood Gr CT6 . . . . . .77 D2
Mersey Rd TN10 . . . . . . .222 B5
MERSHAM 301 E4
Mersham Prim Sch
  TN25 . . . . .301 E3
Merton Cl ME5 . . . . .97 C5
Merton Court Prep Sch
  DA14 . . . . .31 C4
Merton Ct DA16 . . . . .13 B5
Merton Gdns BR5 . . . . . . .53 B4
Merton La CT4 . . . . .174 F4
Merton Rd ME15 . . . . . . .162 F2
Mervyn Ave SE9 . . . . .30 C6
Mervyn Stockwood House
  SE9 . . . . .30 C6
Meryl Gdns CT14 . . . . . .215 C1
Mesne Way TN14 . . . . . .121 F7
Messent Rd SE9 . . . . .11 D2
Messeter Pl SE9 . . . . .12 A1
Metcalfe Mews **1** CT1 143 B2
Meteor Ave CT5 . . . . . . .108 B7
Meteor Cl ME10 . . . . . . .101 E8
Meteor Rd ME19 . . . . . . .158 F3
Methuen Rd Bexley DA6 .13 F3
  Erith DA17 . . . . .4 B2
Metro Ctr The BR5 . . . . . .54 B3
Metropole Rd E **2** CT20 335 B3
Metropole Road E
  CT20 . . . . .335 B3
Metropole Road W
  CT20 . . . . .335 B3
Metropole The **3**
  CT20 . . . . .335 B3
Meverall Ave CT12 . . . . .116 E5
Mewsend TN16 . . . . .118 D1
Mews The
  Gravesend DA12 . . . . . . .37 D7
  Headcorn ME17 . . . . . . .262 C5

Mews The continued
  Longfield DA3 . . . . .58 E6
  1 Maidstone ME16 . . .161 E5
  Pembury TN2 . . . . .287 C6
  Rochester ME2 . . . . .62 F7
  5 Royal Tunbridge Wells
    TN1 . . . . .286 B3
  Sevenoaks TN13 . . . . . .154 A3
  7 Sidcup DA14 . . . . . . .31 A4
  Sittingbourne ME10 . . . .101 F4
Meyer Rd DA8 . . . . .14 D8
Meyrick Rd ME2 . . . . .28 C2
Micawber Cl ME5 . . . . . . .97 A1
Michael Ave CT11 . . . . . .117 G8
Michael Gdns DA12 . . . . . .37 E3
Michael Marshall House
  SE9 . . . . .30 C6
Michaels La DA3, TN15 . .91 C8
Michele Cotts ME3 . . . . . .39 C6
Michelle Gdns CT9 . . . . . .82 A8
Micketts Gdns ME10 . . . .101 B4
Mickleburgh Ave CT6 . .77 B4
Mickleburgh Hill CT6 . . .77 B4
Mickleham Cl BR5 . . . . . .54 A7
Mickleham Rd BR5 . . . . . .54 A7
Mid Comp Cotts ME15 .157 E6
Middelburg Ho CT19 . . .334 D6
Middelburg Sq CT20 . . .335 D4
Middle Cl TN23 . . . . .267 C1
Middle Deal Rd CT14 . . .215 B5
Middle Field TN2 . . . . . .287 E8
Middlefields ME8 . . . . . . .99 A8
Middle Garth TN17 . . . . .320 D4
Middleham Ct **26** DA2 . .26 B1
Middle La TN15 . . . . .154 F6
Middle Mead CT19 . . . . .335 B7
Middle Mill Rd ME19 . . .159 C7
Middle Park Ave SE9 . . . .29 E8
Middle Park Prim Sch
  SE9 . . . . .29 D8
MIDDLE QUARTER 296 D1
Middle Rd TN30 . . . . .315 A5
Middle Row
  3 Ashford TN23 . . . . .268 C2
  2 Faversham ME13 . . .138 D7
Middlesex Rd ME15 . . . . .195 D1
Middle St Ashford TN23 268 B2
  4 Chatham ME7 . . . . . .64 A6
  Deal CT14 . . . . .215 D6
MIDDLE STOKE 25 B4
Middleton Cl DA14 . . . . . .31 C3
Middleton Cl ME8 . . . . . . .99 E4
Middleton Cotts TN25 .236 E3
Middleton Ct
  13 Bromley BR1 . . . . . .29 B1
  5 Sittingbourne ME10 .101 E4
Middletune Ave ME10 . .101 E4
Middle Wall CT5 . . . . .74 D2
Middle Way ME10 . . . . . .102 B3
Middle Wlk TN2 . . . . .286 B5
Middlings Rise TN13 . . . .153 F1
Middlings The TN13 . . . .153 F2
Middlings Wood TN13 154 F2
Midfield Ave Bexley DA7 14 C4
  Hextable BR8 . . . . .33 B2
Midfield Prim Sch BR5 .31 A1
Midfield Way BR5 . . . . . . .54 B8
Midhurst Ct ME15 . . . . . .162 A3
Midhurst Hill DA6 . . . . . . .14 A2
Mid Kent Bsns Pk ME6 128 B7
MidKent Coll (Chatham
  Maritime) ME4 . . . . .64 B8
MidKent Coll (City Way
  Ctr) ME1 . . . . .63 E4
MidKent Coll (Horsted Ctr)
  ME5 . . . . .96 C6
MidKent Coll (Oakwood
  Park Ctr) ME16 . . . . . . .161 C3
Mid Kent Sh Ctr The
  ME16 . . . . .161 C7
Midley Cl ME16 . . . . .161 C7
Midsummer Ct SE12 . . . .11 A3
Midsummer Hill TN24 268 D6
Midsummer Rd ME6 . . . .127 E8
Midway The TN4 . . . . . . .285 D2
Midwinter Cl **3** DA16 . .13 A4
Mierscourt Cl ME8 . . . . . .99 A8
Miers Court Prim Sch
  ME8 . . . . .98 F7
Mierscourt Rd ME8 . . . . . .98 E6
Mike Spring Ct DA12 . . . .37 D4
Mikyle Ct CT1 . . . . .175 A6
Milbourne Gr ME10 . . . .101 E7
Milburn Rd ME7 . . . . .64 C7
Mildmay Pl TN14 . . . . . .121 F8
Mildred Cl DA1 . . . . .16 A1
Mildred Cotts CT19 . . . .334 F7
Mildred Rd DA8 . . . . .4 E1
MILEBUSH 259 E8
Milebush La TN12 . . . . . .227 E1
MILE END GREEN 58 C8
Mile End Green Cotts
  DA3 . . . . .58 D7
Mile La TN17 . . . . .319 B8
MILE OAK 257 C4
Mile Oak Rd TN12 . . . . . .257 C3
Mile Rd CT12 . . . . .113 F6
Miles Ct CT3 . . . . .178 A8
Miles Dr SE28 . . . . .2 D5
Miles Pl ME1 . . . . .63 D3
Milestone Bldgs TN12 .260 F3
Milestone Cl CT19 . . . . . .335 A7
Milestone Rd CT14 . . . . .215 B5
Mile Stone Rd DA2 . . . . . .16 B1
Milestone Sch DA3 . . . . . .58 F1
Miles Way CT7 . . . . .80 F7
MILE TOWN 28 B1
Mile Town Ind Est
  ME12 . . . . .28 A1
Milford Cl Bexley SE2 . . .13 B8
  Maidstone ME16 . . . . . .161 D5
Military Rd
  Canterbury CT1 . . . . . . .143 A1

Military Rd continued
  Chatham ME4 . . . . .63 F5
  2 Dover CT17 . . . . . . .310 D7
  Folkestone CT20 . . . . . .334 E4
  Houghton Green TN31 . .368 E3
  Hythe CT21 . . . . .333 B2
  Ramsgate CT11 . . . . . . .117 E6
  Stone in Oxney TN26,
    TN30 . . . . .361 B4
Milk House Cotts
  TN17 . . . . .321 A8
Milking La
  Biggin Hill, Downe
    BR6 . . . . .118 E7
  Biggin Hill, Leaves Green
    BR2 . . . . .118 D8
Milk St Bromley BR1 . . . . .29 B2
  Newham E16 . . . . .2 B5
Millais Pl RM18 . . . . .19 A7
Millais Rd CT16 . . . . .278 C1
Millars Mdw SE12 . . . . . .11 A3
MILLBANK Headcorn . . .262 B6
  Herne Bay 111 F6
Mill Bank
  Headcorn TN27 . . . . . . .262 C6
  Lydd TN29 . . . . .376 B6
  Tonbridge TN9 . . . . .222 C2
Mill Bank Cotts CT13 . .180 A3
Millbank La TN29 . . . . . .371 E7
Millbank Rd TN23 . . . . . .299 F5
Millbank Way SE12 . . . . .11 A2
Mill Bay CT20 . . . . .335 E5
Millbro BR8 . . . . .56 A8
Millbrook Hythe CT21 . .333 D2
  Leybourne ME19 . . . . . .127 D1
Millbrook Ave DA16 . . . .12 D3
Millbrook Cl ME15 . . . . .161 F1
Millbrook Mdw TN23 . .267 C1
Mill Brook Rd BR5 . . . . . .54 C5
Mill Cl Crabble CT17 . . .277 F2
  Lenham ME17 . . . . .199 C4
  Rochester ME2 . . . . .40 B1
  Sandwich CT13 . . . . . . .148 E2
  Wickhambreaux CT3 . . .145 C2
Mill Cotts
  Queenborough ME11 . . .46 A5
  Ramsgate CT11 . . . . . . .117 D6
  West Farleigh ME15 . . . .193 B6
  Worth CT14 . . . . .181 A4
Mill Court Cl CT6 . . . . . . .77 B2
Mill Cres TN9 . . . . .222 C2
Millcroft Rd ME3 . . . . .22 B4
Mill Ct Ashford TN24 . . .268 D2
  Bidborough TN3 . . . . . . .253 C3
  Sittingbourne ME10 . . . .102 A3
  Sutton at Hone DA4 . . . . .57 C7
Milldale Cl CT14 . . . . . . .215 B4
Millen Ct DA4 . . . . .57 C5
Millenium Terr CT1 . . . .174 C6
Millennium Cl E16 . . . . . . .1 B7
Millennium Way
  Broadstairs CT10 . . . . . . .83 C4
  Sheerness ME12 . . . . . . .28 B2
Millen Rd ME10 . . . . .101 E5
Millen's Row ME13 . . . . .170 B3
Miller Ave CT2 . . . . .174 D8
Miller Cl Ashford TN24 .268 C2
  Bromley BR1 . . . . .29 B3
  Deal CT14 . . . . .215 C8
  Sittingbourne ME10 . . . .102 A8
  Wingham CT3 . . . . .178 B7
Miller Cotts TN24 . . . . . .268 D2
Miller Ct Bexley DA2 . . . . .14 B4
  Minster (Sheppey) ME12 .47 A5
Miller Rd DA12 . . . . .38 A6
Millers Cl DA1 . . . . .33 D8
Millers Cotts TN11 . . . . .255 C6
Millers Ct
  5 Ramsgate CT12 . . . . .83 B1
  Whitstable CT5 . . . . . . .108 D7
Millers La CT12 . . . . .114 C7
Millersthumb TN17 . . . .292 C4
Millers Wharf **1** ME15 161 E2
Millers Wlk DA3 . . . . .93 A7
Millers Yd CT1 . . . . .174 E7
Miller Way ME2 . . . . .40 D2
Millfield Ashford TN23 . .299 D8
  Folkestone CT20 . . . . . .335 D5
  Hawkinge CT18 . . . . . . .307 C5
  High Halden TN26 . . . . .324 D7
  New Ash Green DA3 . . . . .91 E8
  St Margaret's at Cliffe
    CT15 . . . . .279 F7
Mill Field Ash CT3 . . . . . .147 L1
  Broadstairs CT10 . . . . . . .83 F5
Millfield Cl CT18 . . . . . . .307 B5
Millfield Dr DA13 . . . . . . .36 E6
Millfield La DA3 . . . . .91 E8
Millfield Manor CT5 . . . . .74 E1
Millfield Rd
  Faversham ME13 . . . . . .138 E7
  Ramsgate CT12 . . . . .83 B3
  West Kingsdown TN15 . . .90 D4
Millfields Chatham ME5 .97 D2
  Shepherdswell CT15 . . . .244 E4
Millfields Cl BR5 . . . . . . .54 B5
Millfields Cotts BR5 . . . .54 B5
Mill Fields Rd CT21 . . . . .332 F2
Mill Gn CT13 . . . . .180 A2
Millhall ME20 . . . . .128 E2
Mill Hall Bsns Est
  ME20 . . . . .128 D2
Mill Hall Rd ME20 . . . . . .128 C3
Mill Hamlet CT3 . . . . . . .145 C2
MILL HILL 215 A3
  Edenbridge TN8 . . . . . . .249 D7
Mill Hill Deal CT14 . . . . .215 A3
Mill Hill La DA12 . . . . . . .38 D3
Mill Ho CT17 . . . . .277 F3
Mill House Cl DA4 . . . . . .56 E1
Millhouse La ME19 . . . . .126 D3

Mill La Ashford TN24.. 269 A1
Benover ME18 .... 226 A7
Birchington CT7 ...... 80 F6
Bonnington TN25 ..... 329 E5
Bridge CT4 .... 175 F1
Canterbury CT1...... 142 F1
Canterbury, Harbledown
CT2 .... 174 C8
Chatham, Bluebell Hill
ME5 .... 96 D1
Chatham, Luton ME5.. 64 C1
Chilham CT4 .... 205 D7
Coxheath ME17...... 194 D4
10 Dover CT16 ...... 310 E7
Eastry CT13 .... 180 B2
Eynsford DA4 .... 56 E1
Farthing Street BR6... 86 B1
Frittenden TN17 ..... 293 D8
Hartlip ME9 .... 99 E6
Hawkinge CT18...... 307 B5
Herne Bay CT6 ...... 77 B2
Hildenborough TN11,
TN15 .... 188 C2
Horsmonden TN12 ... 258 B1
Ightham TN15 ...... 156 E5
Lydd TN29 .... 376 D7
Lynsted ME9 .... 136 C5
Maidstone ME14..... 161 F6
Margate CT9........ 50 J2
Newchurch TN29..... 350 F3
Nonington CT15 ..... 211 F4
Northbourne CT14 ... 213 F4
Oxted RH8.......... 183 A1
Preston CT3 .... 146 D6
Sevenoaks TN14 .... 154 D6
Shepherdswell CT15.. 244 F5
Shoreham TN14 ..... 88 F1
Sissinghurst TN17.... 320 F8
Smarden TN27 ...... 264 A2
Snodland ME6....... 128 B8
Stelling Minnis CT4... 240 F2
Tenterden TN30 ..... 324 B1
The Chart RH8....... 183 F4
Tonbridge TN9....... 192 D7
Wateringbury ME18 .. 192 D7
Westerham TN16 .... 184 C8
West Thurrock RM20.. 17 D8
Whitfield CT16 ...... 278 A8
Woolwich SE18 ...... 2 A1
Worth CT14 .... 181 A4
Mill Lane Cotts CT14 214 A4
Millman Ct SE3....... 11 B7
Millmead Ave CT7..... 51 D1
Millmead Gdns CT9.... 51 D1
Millmead Rd CT9...... 51 C1
Mill Mews CT14 ...... 215 B4
Mill Pl Chislehurst BR7 . 53 B8
Crayford DA1 .... 15 A3
Faversham ME13 .... 138 D8
Millpond Cl ME2 ..... 63 B8
Mill Pond Cl TN14 .... 154 D6
Millpond La TN30 .... 323 D2
Mill Pond Rd DA1 .... 15 E1
Mill Race CT17 ...... 277 F3
Mill Rd
Bethersden TN26 .... 297 E5
Bramling CT3 .... 177 E6
Deal CT14 .... 215 C4
Dymchurch TN29..... 366 B7
Erith DA8.......... 14 C7
Gillingham ME7...... 64 C6
Hawley DA2 .... 33 F4
Hoath CT3.......... 111 F5
Hythe CT21......... 333 D2
Lydd TN29 .... 376 D7
Newham E16 .... 1 B5
Northfleet DA11..... 36 E8
Rochester ME2....... 63 B8
Sevenoaks TN13 .... 153 E6
Staple CT3.......... 179 B5
Sturry CT2.......... 143 F5
Mill Row Birchington CT7 80 F6
Sidcup DA5......... 32 B8
Mills Cl ME12....... 46 F6
Mills Cres TN15 ..... 154 F8
Millside Ind Est DA1...15 D3
Mills Rd ME20....... 160 E7
Mill St
East Malling ME19 ... 159 F7
Iden Green TN17, TN18 342 C3
Maidstone, Loose ME15 194 F5
Maidstone ME15..... 161 F4
Sittingbourne ME10 .. 101 E5
Snodland ME6....... 128 B8
Temple Ewell CT16 ... 277 D5
Westerham TN16 .... 184 D8
Mills Terr ME4 ...... 64 A3
Millstock Terr 2
ME15 .... 161 E2
Mill Stone Cl DA4 .... 57 C7
Millstone Mews DA4 .. 57 C8
Millstream Cl
Ashurst TN3 .... 283 D2
Faversham ME13 .... 138 C7
Whitstable CT5...... 74 E1
Millstream Cotts CT5 .108 E8
Millstream Gn TN24.. 300 F7
Mill Stream Pl TN9 ... 222 D3
MILL STREET........ 159 E7
Millstrood Rd CT5.... 108 E8
Mill Terr Bridge CT4... 175 F1
Chartham CT4 ...... 173 D3
Mill Vale BR2........ 52 A7
Mill View Ashford TN24 300 F8
Hadlow TN11........ 190 D1
Woodchurch TN26.... 326 A3
Mill View Rd CT6...... 77 A1
Mill Wall Pl CT13..... 181 A8
Mill Way ME10 ...... 101 F6
Mill Wlk ME16....... 161 A3
Millwood Ct 4 ME4... 63 F4
Millwood Ho 1 SE28...2 D3
Millwood Rd BR5..... 54 C6
Millyard Way CT15 ... 212 D1

Milne Gdns SE9........11 E2
Milne Ho 11 SE18.......1 F2
Milner Cl CT15 ...... 212 B1
Milner Cres CT3...... 210 E5
Milne Rd TN24 ...... 300 F8
Milner La CT2........ 143 F5
Milner Rd
Elvington CT15 ..... 212 B1
Gillingham ME7...... 64 D7
Whitstable CT5 ..... 108 A6
Milners ME17....... 196 F6
Milner Wlk SE9...... 30 D7
Milroy Ave DA11..... 36 C6
MILSTEAD.......... 134 E2
Milstead Cl
Maidstone ME14.... 162 C5
West Minst ME12.... 46 B7
Milstead & Frinstead CE
Prim Sch ME13..... 134 E1
Milsted Rd ME8..... 65 C3
MILTON........... 19 D1
Milton Ave
Badgers Mount TN14 . 88 B1
Cliffe Woods ME3.... 40 B8
Gravesend DA12..... 37 C7
Margate CT9........ 50 J1
Milton Cl
Canterbury CT1..... 175 D4
Dover CT16......... 278 B4
Milton Court Prim Sch
ME10 .... 101 E6
Milton Ct
Gravesend DA12..... 37 C6
Kings Hill ME19..... 159 A3
Milton Dr TN2....... 286 D7
Milton Gdns
Tilbury RM18........ 19 B6
Tonbridge TN9....... 253 F7
Milton Hall Rd DA12... 37 C7
Milton Ho DA1 ...... 14 E2
Milton La ME19...... 159 B3
Milton Lodge 9 DA14 ..31 A4
Milton Pl DA12 ...... 19 C1
Milton Rd Ashford TN23 268 B2
Bexley DA16........ 12 F6
Canterbury CT1..... 175 A6
Dover CT16......... 278 B4
Erith DA17......... 4 A2
Gillingham ME7..... 64 C3
Gravesend DA12..... 37 C8
Sevenoaks TN13 .... 153 E6
Sittingbourne ME10 .. 101 E4
Swanscombe DA10....17 E1
Milton Sq 4 CT9 ..... 50 J1
Milton St
Maidstone ME15.... 161 C2
Swanscombe DA10....17 D1
Milverton Way SE9.... 30 A4
Milward Wlk 14 SE18...12 A8
Mimosa CT BR6....... 87 C8
Mincers Cl ME5...... 97 C2
Mineral St SE18...... 2 E2
Miners Way
Aylesham CT3 ..... 211 A5
Hersden CT3........ 112 A1
Minerva Ave CT16 ... 278 C2
Minerva Cl DA14 .... 30 E4
Minerva Ho 4 CT11 .. 117 D7
Minerva Rd ME2..... 63 A8
Ministry Way SE9..... 29 F6
Minnis Field CT4 .... 240 E2
Minnis Gn CT4 ...... 240 E2
Minnis La CT15, CT17.. 277 C2
Minnis Rd CT7 ...... 80 E7
Minnis Terr CT17 .... 278 A2
Minnis Way CT14 .... 181 B5
Minshaw Ct 4 DA14...30 F4
MINSTER Sheppey 47 B7
Thanet............ 115 A4
Minster Abbey ★
Minster (Sheppey)
ME12 .... 47 D6
Minster CE Prim Sch
CT12 .... 115 B5
Minster Cl CT10 ..... 84 A2
Minster Coll ME12.... 46 F6
Minster Dr
Herne Bay CT6 ..... 76 D4
Minster (Sheppey) ME12 . 47 D6
Minster Gatehouse Mus ★
ME12 .... 47 D6
Minster Lodge 4
CT11 .... 117 C6
Minster Rd
Acol CT12, CT7...... 81 C2
Bromley BR1........ 29 B1
Faversham ME13 ... 138 E7
Gillingham ME8..... 65 E7
Minster (Sheppey) ME12 .47 B6
Ramsgate CT11 ..... 117 B5
Westgate on Sea CT8.. 81 F7
Minster Sheppey Prim Sch
ME12 .... 47 C6
Minster Sta CT12 .... 115 C5
Minstrels Cl TN8 .... 217 C2
Mint Bsns Pk E16......1 A8
Mintching Wood La
ME9............ 134 F2
Minter Ave CT18...... 306 F7
Minter Cl CT18 ...... 306 F7
Minterne Ave ME10... 101 D2
Minterne Jun Sch
ME10 .... 101 D1
Minters Ind Est CT14 . 215 B6
Minters Orch TN15 .. 157 B7
Mint The CT. 142 C1
Miranda Ct ME12 .... 28 B1
Miranda Ho 6 DA17....4 A1

Mirfield St SE7.........1 D3
Miriam Ct DA14 ...... 31 B4
Miriam Rd SE18....... 2 E1
Mirror Path SE9...... 29 C5
Miskin Cotts ME3...... 22 B6
Miskin Rd Dartford DA1..33 D8
Hoo St Werburgh ME3..41 E5
Miskin Way DA12..... 37 D2
Misling La CT4 ...... 272 C2
Missenden Ct 6 CT20 335 D5
Mitcham Rd ME29... 366 C8
Mitchell Ave
Chatham ME4 ...... 63 F2
Hawkinge CT18..... 307 B5
Northfleet DA11..... 36 D6
Mitchell Rd
Kings Hill ME19..... 158 F2
Orpington BR6...... 86 F6
Mitchell Way 5 BR1.. 52 A8
Mitchell Wlk Newham E6 . 1 F8
Swanscombe DA10....35 E8
Mitchem Ct TN15..... 90 E3
Mitre Ct 5 Erith DA17...4 A2
Tonbridge TN9....... 222 C2
Mitre Rd ME1........ 63 B4
Mittell Ct TN9....... 376 B6
Moatbridge Sch SE9....11 D1
Moat Cl Orpington BR6.. 86 F7
Sevenoaks TN13 .... 153 D5
Moat Croft DA16 .... 13 C4
Moat Ct Eltham SE9 ..11 A5
Sidcup DA15........ 30 F5
Moat Farm TN2 ..... 34 A2
Moat Farm Cl CT19 .. 335 C7
Moat Farm Rd
Folkestone CT19..... 335 C7
St Mary Hoo ME3... 23 C5
Moatfield Mdw TN23 .300 B4
Moat Ho
Canterbury CT1..... 174 F7
Charing TN27 ...... 234 C7
Moat La Ash CT3..... 147 E1
Cowden TN8 .... 282 E7
Erith DA8.......... 15 A6
Fordwich CT2 ...... 144 A3
Rough Common ME2 . 142 B4
Moat Pk TN27 ...... 234 C6
Moat Rd TN27 ...... 262 B5
Moat Sole CT13 ..... 148 F1
Moat The TN27 ..... 234 C7
Moat Way ME11...... 46 A5
MOCKBEGGAR 104 B1
Mockbeggar La TN17,
SE9............ 30 A4
Mockett Ct 4 ME10 .. 101 E4
Mockett Dr CT10 .... 83 F7
Mock La TN23....... 299 B6
Model Farm CT SE9... 29 E5
Modest Cnr TN4..... 253 E5
MODEST CORNER 253 E5
Moira Rd SE9 ...... 11 F3
Moland Cl TN3...... 285 A3
Monterey Ct DA5..... 32 C6
Montfort Cl
Ashford TN23...... 299 F7
Canterbury CT2..... 143 A4
Montfort Dr ME19 ... 159 A2
Montfort Rd
Chatham ME5 ..... 96 F2
Kemsing TN15...... 122 E2
Rochester ME2...... 63 A8
Montgomery Ave ME5.. 97 A7
Montgomery Cl
2 Gravesend DA12... 37 D4
Sidcup DA15........ 12 F1
Montgomery Rd
Gillingham ME7..... 64 C3
Royal Tunbridge Wells
TN4 .... 286 B7
Sutton at Hone DA4 .. 57 D8
Montgomery Way
CT19 .... 335 E8
Montpelier Ave
Sidcup DA5 .... 31 D8
Whitstable CT5..... 108 C8
Montpelier Bsns Pk
TN23............ 267 F1
Montpelier Gate ME16 161 B5
Montreal Cl 8 CT16 .. 278 B3
Montreal Rd
Sevenoaks TN13 .... 153 E4
Tilbury RM18........ 19 A5
Montrose Ave
Bexley DA16........ 12 E4
Gillingham ME8..... 64 E2
Sidcup DA15........ 31 A8
Montrose Cl DA16.... 12 F4
Mont St Aignan Way
TN8 .... 249 C8
Monument Way TN4.. 300 F5
Monypenny TN17.... 343 F3
Monypenny Ct TN11 . 223 D8
Moon Ct SE12....... 11 A3
Moonfleet Cl ME10 ... 69 A1
Moon Hill CT15...... 244 E4
MOON'S GREEN 359 A3
Moon's La RH7...... 249 A1
Moonstone Dr ME5... 97 B2
Moonstone Sq 1
ME10 .... 101 E6
Moorcroft Gdns BR2.. 52 E4
Moorden La TN11 ... 220 A1
Moordown SE18..... 12 B6
Moore Ave Grays RM20..17 E8
Tilbury RM18........ 19 B8
Moore Cl Brenzett TN29 363 A4
Dartford DA2 ...... 26 C5
Mooreland Rd 1 BR1.. 52 A8
Moore Rd DA10 ..... 17 E1
Moore Rd ME2....... 63 A8

Monks Cl continued
Erith SE2........... 3 D2
Faversham ME13 ... 138 B8
MONK'S HILL....... 295 C7
Monkshill Rd ME13....107 B2
Monks La
Limpsfield TN8 ..... 216 E6
Newbury's TN5 ..... 337 B8
Monks Orch DA1 .... 33 D6
Monk St SE18 ...... 2 A2
Monks Way Dover CT16 278 A3
Orpington BR5...... 53 D1
Monk's Way CT13 ... 148 F3
Monk's Well 13 DA9...17 C3
Monks Wlk
Charing TN27 ...... 234 C7
Northfleet DA13..... 36 A2
6 Tonbridge TN9 ... 254 B8
MONKTON.......... 114 D7
Monkton CE Prim Sch
CT12 .... 114 D7
Monkton Cl 2 TN23 .. 299 F6
Monkton Ct CT5..... 109 D8
Monkton Gdns CT9... 51 E3
Monkton Manor CT12 114 C7
CT12. .... 114 C8
Monkton Pl CT11..... 117 D7
Monkton Rd Bexley DA16 12 F5
Borough Green TN15 .. 156 F7
Minster (Thanet) CT12 . 115 A6
Monkton Rdbt CT12 .. 114 D8
Monkton St CT12 .... 114 D7
Monkwood Cl ME1 ... 96 B8
Monmouth Cl
Bexley DA16........ 13 A3
Gillingham ME8..... 65 D2
Monroe Way ME19 .. 159 D3
Mons CT ME10 ...... 68 F1
Monson Rd TN1..... 286 A4
Mons Way BR2...... 52 E3
Montacute Ct CT20... 335 B4
Montacute Gdns TN2 . 285 F2
Montacute Rd TN2 .. 286 A1
Montague Ct
Sheerness ME12..... 28 B1
13 Sidcup DA15..... 31 A5
Montague Pl BR8..... 55 F5
Montague Rd CT11... 117 E8
Montague St CT6.... 76 D5
Montague Terr 1 BR2..52 A5
Montbelle Prim Sch
SE9............ 30 A4
Montbelle Rd SE9.... 30 B5
Montbretia Cl BR5.... 54 C5
Montcalm Cl BR2..... 52 A5
Montcalm Rd SE7 .... 11 D7
Montefiore Ave
Broadstairs CT10 .... 84 A1
Ramsgate CT11 ..... 83 F1
Montefiore Cotts CT11 117 F8
Monteith D TN3...... 285 A3
Montfort Cl

Moorfield CT2........ 142 F4
Moorfield Rd BR6..... 54 A2
Moorhead Way SE3... 11 B4
Moorhen Cl DA8..... 15 B7
Moor Hill TN18....... 354 F8
Moorhouse Cotts
TN16 .... 184 A7
Moorhouse Rd RH8,
TN16 .... 184 A6
Mooring Rd ME1..... 63 D1
Moorings The
Conyer ME9........ 103 E6
Newham E16........ 1 C8
Moor La
Edenbridge TN8 .... 249 A4
Ivychurch TN29..... 363 D4
Woodchurch TN26... 346 E6
Moorland Rd CT15... 244 E4
Moorlands BR7...... 30 B1
Moorside Rd BR1.... 29 A4
Moor St ME8........ 99 B8
Moor La ★........... 245 D7
Moorstock La TN25... 303 C2
Moorstock La TN25 .. 303 C2
MOOR STREET...... 99 B7
MOOR THE 354 F8
Moor The TN18...... 354 F8
Moorwell Dr CT15.... 244 D5
Morants Court Cross
TN14 .... 121 C1
Morants Court Rd
TN13 .... 153 C8
Moray Ave CT7...... 80 F8
Mordaunt Ave CT8... 81 E8
Morden Road Mews
SE3............ 11 A5
Morden St ME1...... 63 C4
Morebreddis Cotts
TN17 .... 291 A1
MOREHALL......... 334 F6
Morehall Ave CT19... 334 F6
Morehall Prim Sch
CT19............ 334 F6
Morel Ct TN3....... 154 B5
Morella Wlk ME17.... 199 C5
Morello Cl Swanley BR8 .55 D5
Teynham ME9 ...... 103 C2
Morel St ME3....... 41 D6
More Park RC Prim Sch
ME19 .... 159 D8
Moreton Almhouses 3
TN16 .... 215 C2
Moreton Ct Crayford DA1 14 E4
Moreton Ind Est BR8.. 56 A4
Moreton Terr TN26... 299 A1
Morewood Cl TN13... 153 F4
Morgan Dr DA9...... 34 E8
Morgan Kirby's Gdn
ME13 .... 170 D5
Morgan Rd Bromley BR1 29 A1
Rochester ME2...... 63 A8
Morgan St E16 ...... 1 A8
Morhen Cl ME6...... 127 E7
Moriarty Cl BR1...... 53 B5
Morland Ave DA1 .... 15 B2
Morland Dr
Lamberhurst TN3 ... 317 B5
Rochester ME2...... 40 A1
Morland Ho 4 BR7....53 A8
Morley Bsns Ctr TN9 . 222 D1
Morley Dr TN12 ..... 290 A6
Morley Rd
Chislehurst BR7 .... 53 C8
Tonbridge TN9....... 222 D1
Morley's Rd TN14 ... 187 D2
Morne Cotts TN14 ... 121 F8
Morning Cross Cotts
ME3............ 22 B4
Mornington Ave BR1.. 52 C6
Mornington Cl TN16.. 118 D2
Mornington Cres DA5.. 32 D7
Morris Ave CT6...... 75 F4
Morris Cl
Maidstone ME17.... 195 D5
Orpington BR6...... 86 E7
West Malling ME19.. 127 F1
Morris Court Cl ME9.. 102 D2
Morris Gdns DA1 .... 15 A2
Morrison Rd CT20.... 335 E6
Morry La
Chartway Street
ME17 .... 197 D1
Ulcombe ME17...... 230 D7
Morston Gdns SE9 ... 29 F4
Mortgramit Sq SE18... 2 A3
Mortimer Cl TN23.... 300 B7
Mortimer Rd
Biggin Hill TN16 .... 118 C7
Dover CT16......... 310 F8
Erith DA8.......... 14 D8
Orpington BR6...... 54 A1
Mortimers Ave ME3... 40 A8
Mortimer St CT6 .... 76 F5
Mortlake Rd E16 .... 1 B7
Mortley Cl TN9...... 222 C2
Morton Cl
Maidstone ME15.... 195 D6
Swanley BR8........ 55 E7
Morvale Cl DA17 .... 3 F2
Mosquito Rd ME19 .. 158 F3
Mossbank ME5...... 97 A3
Mossdown Cl DA17... 4 A2
Mosselle Rd TN16.... 118 F1
Moss La CT20....... 335 D5
Moss Way DA2 ...... 34 D4
Mossy Glade ME8 ... 98 E6
Mostyn Rd ME14 .... 162 C4

Mosul Way BR2....... 52 E3
Mosyer Dr BR5....... 87 D8
Mote Ave ME5....... 162 B3
Mote Cotts TN15 .... 189 A7
Mote Hall Villas ME14 162 C4
Mote Pk ME15....... 162 D2
Mote Rd
Maidstone ME15.... 162 A3
Shipbourne TN11, TN11 189 A7
Mote The DA3........ 91 F8
Motherwell Way RM20.. 18 A2
Motney Hill Rd ME8... 66 A4
Motorway Ind Est
ME20 .... 129 C2
MOTTINGHAM....... 29 C6
Mottingham Ct SE9... 29 F7
Mottingham Gdns SE9.. 29 D7
Mottingham La
Bromley SE12, SE9... 29 C7
Eltham SE12 ...... 29 C7
Mottingham Prim Sch
SE9............ 29 F5
Mottingham Rd SE9... 29 F5
Mottingham Sta SE9.. 29 F7
Mottisfont Rd SE2.... 3 B2
MOTT'S HILL........ 312 A3
Mouat Ct ME5....... 97 A3
Mouchotte Cl TN16... 118 C7
Moultain Hill BR8..... 56 A5
Mound The SE9 ..... 30 A5
Mountain Cl 6 TN15 .124 F3
Mountain St CT4 .... 205 B6
MOUNTAIN STREET .. 205 B6
Mount Ave ME18 .... 193 A1
Mountbatten Ave
Chatham ME5....... 97 A7
Higham ME3........ 39 C4
Mountbatten Cl SE18.. 12 E8
Mountbatten Ho CT14 215 D3
Mountbatten Way
TN25 .... 302 E6
Mount Castle La ME17 199 F1
Mount Charles Wlk
CT4 .... 175 F1
Mount Cl Bromley BR1.. 52 E8
Sevenoaks TN13 .... 153 F4
Mount Culver Ave DA14 31 D2
Mount Dr Bexley DA6... 13 C2
Maidstone ME14..... 163 B4
Mount Edgcumbe Rd
TN4 .... 286 A3
MOUNT EPHRAIM ... 285 F4
Mount Ephraim TN4 .. 286 A4
Mount Ephraim Ct
TN4 .... 285 F4
Mount Ephraim Gdns ★
ME13 .... 140 A3
Mount Ephraim Rd
TN1 .... 286 A4
Mountfield TN15 .... 157 A7
Mountfield Ct
Faversham ME13 ... 138 B6
Queenborough ME11...46 A5
Mountfield Cl DA13... 92 F2
Mountfield Ct 4 TN1 . 286 B3
Mountfield Gdns TN1 . 286 B3
Mountfield Mews CT8.. 81 F8
Mountfield Pk TN9 ... 254 C8
Mountfield Rd
New Romney TN28... 373 C6
Royal Tunbridge Wells
TN1 .... 286 B3
Mountfield Way
1 Orpington BR5.... 54 C5
Westgate on Sea CT8.. 81 F8
Mount Green Ave
CT12 .... 116 D5
Mount Harry Rd TN13 154 F8
Mounthurst Rd BR2... 52 A2
Mountjoy Cl SE2 .... 3 B2
Mount La Hartlip ME9 .. 99 D4
Maidstone ME14..... 163 B4
Mount Lodge ME1.... 63 B2
Mount Pleasant
Aldington TN25 ..... 330 A6
Biggin Hill TN16 .... 118 D2
Blean CT2 .... 142 A6
Chatham ME5 ...... 64 B3
Durgates TN5 ...... 336 E5
Faversham ME13 ... 105 B2
Forstal ME20....... 129 A3
Ide Hill TN14....... 185 F4
Kingsdown CT14..... 248 D5
Lamberhurst TN3 ... 316 E6
Minster (Thanet) CT12 . 115 C8
Paddock Wood TN12.. 256 F7
Tenterden TN30 .... 345 C8
The Moor TN18..... 354 F8
Tonbridge TN11...... 221 D6
Mount Pleasant Ave 2
TN1 ....286 B3
Mount Pleasant Cl
CT18 .... 305 C7
Mount Pleasant Ct
TN11 .... 221 D6
Mount Pleasant Dr
ME14............ 163 B4
Mount Pleasant La
TN3 .... 317 A6
Mount Pleasant Pl SE18 . 2 D2
Mount Pleasant Rd
Dartford DA1 ...... 15 F1
4 Folkestone CT20... 335 D5
Royal Tunbridge Wells
TN1 .... 286 A3
Sevenoaks Weald TN14 187 B2
Mount Pleasant Terr
ME17 .... 198 E2
Mount Pleasant Wlk
DA5............ 14 C2
Mount Rd Bexley DA6... 13 E2

Mount Rd *continued*
Canterbury CT1........175 C6
Chatham ME4 ....63 F3
Crayford DA1 ....14 F1
Dover CT17 ....310 A6
Rochester ME1 ....63 B2
Mounts Cl CT14 ......215 A5
Mountsfield Cl ME16 ..161 D5
Mounts Hill TN17......342 B7
MOUNT SION 286 A2
Mount Sion TN1 ......286 A2
Mounts La TN17 ......344 A3
Mounts Rd DA9 ....17 B1
Mount St CT21 ....333 C2
Mounts View TN23 ...267 F4
Mount The Bexley DA6 ..14 B2
3 Chislehurst BR7 ....53 A8
Mountview ME9........101 B2
Mount View CT3 ......138 A5
Mount View ME4 .63 F3
Mountview Rd ME6....54 A2
Mount View CT6 ....77 A2
MOWSHURST 217 D5
Moyes Cl CT12 ....116 D5
Moyle Cl ME8 ....98 D4
Mozart Ct ME4 ....215 A5
Muddy Bush Cnr CT3..177 F2
Muddy La ME10 ....102 B2
Mudie Cl CT18 ....307 A5
Muir Rd
Maidstone ME15......162 A2
Ramsgate CT11 ......117 F8
Muir St E16 ....12 D5
Mulbarton Ct BR7 .....30 D2
Mulberry Cl
Gillingham ME7.......98 A4
Greenwich SE17 ....11 D8
Meopham Station DA13..60 B3
Ramsgate CT11 ......117 F8
Royal Tunbridge Wells
TN4 ....254 D1
St Mary's Bay TN29 ..365 F4
Mulberry Ct Bexley DA16 12 F5
Canterbury CT1.......174 F8
Hythe CT21 ....333 D3
Littlestone-on-Sea TN28 373 E5
Maidstone ME14......162 B5
Mulberry Field TN13...148 F1
Mulberry Gdns TN30...345 B8
Mulberry Hill CT4 ....172 D1
Mulberry Rd
Ashford TN23 ....267 D3
Northfleet DA11 ......36 A4
Sittingbourne ME10 ..102 C5
Mulberry Way DA17 .....4 C4
Mulgrave Rd **13** SE18 .....1 F2
Mulgrave Prim Sch **16**
SE18 ....2 A2
Mulgrave Rd SE18 .....2 A2
Mullein Ct **7** RM17......18 D8
Mullender Ct DA12 .....38 A7
Muller Ho SE18 ....2 A1
Multon Rd TN15.......90 E4
Mummery Ct ME13 ....137 E2
MUNDAY BOIS 264 F8
Munday Bois Cotts
TN27 ....264 F8
Munday Bois Rd TN27 .232 E1
Munday Ind Est TN9 ..222 D1
Munday Rd E16 ....1 A7
Munday Works Est
TN9...............222 C1
Mundella Prim Sch
CT19 ....335 D6
Munford Dr DA10......35 E8
Mungeam Ho ME1......63 C4
Mungo Park Rd DA7 ...47 D3
Mungo Park Way BR5 ..54 D2
Munnery Way ME4.....86 B8
Munnings Ho E16 ....1 B5
Munn's La ME9 ......100 E3
Munsgore La ME9 ....100 C3
Murchison Ave DA5 ...31 E7
Murrain Dr ME15 .....163 A1
Murray Ave BR1........52 B7
Murray Bsns Ctr BR5 ..54 B6
Murray Cl E28 ....2 E5
Murray Ho **9** SE18 .....1 F2
Murray Lodge TN2 ...286 D2
Murray Rd Orpington BR5 54 B6
Rochester ME2 ....63 C8
Murray Sq E16 ....1 B6
MURSTON 102 B5
Murston Inf Sch ME10 102 B4
Murston Jun Sch
ME10 ....102 B5
Murston Rd ME10 ....102 B4
Murthwaite Ct ME12...47 A5
Murton-Neale Cl **3**
TN18 ....341 A2
Murton Pl ME13 ......106 E1
Muscovy Ho DA18 ......3 E4
Muscovy Rd TN25 ....268 C7
Muscovy Way CT6 ....76 E3
Musgrave Cl CT12 ....81 F2
Musgrave Rd ME10 ...101 F6
Musgrove TN23 ....300 A8
Muskerry Ct TN4 .....285 B4
Musket La
Eyhorne Street ME17...164 C2
Leeds ME17 ....164 A2
Mus of Canterbury with
Rupert Bear Mus ★ **22**
CT1...............174 F8
Mussenden La DA3, DA4 57 E3
Mustang Rd ME1......158 F3
Mustards Rd ME12 ....49 D2
Mutrix Gdns CT9 ......50 E1
Mutrix Rd CT9..........82 E8
Mutton La ME13 ......138 A6
Mycenae Rd SE3 ......11 A6

Mymms Cl CT5 ......109 C8
Mynn Cres ME14 .....163 A4
Myra St SE2...........3 A2
Myrtle Alley SE18......2 A3
Myrtle Cl DA8 ....14 E6
Myrtle Cres ME5 ......96 F5
Myrtle Cl TN23 ......300 A3
Myrtledene Rd SE2......3 A1
Myrtle Gn TN23 ......267 D4
Myrtle Pl DA2 ....34 D8
Myrtle Rd Dartford DA1 ..33 D6
5 Folkestone CT19....335 E6
Mystole Ho CT4 ......206 B8
Mystole La CT4.......206 C8

N

NACCOLT 269 E6
Nacholt Cl CT5........75 A2
NACKINGTON 175 A2
Nackington Ct **2** CT1 175 B6
Nackington Pk CT4....175 A4
Nackington Rd CT1,
CT4 ....175 A3
Nadine St SE7..........1 C1
Nagpur Ho **4** ME15 ...195 E5
Nag's Head La
Bexley ME6 ....13 B4
Rochester ME1 ....63 D4
Nailbourne Cl CT4....209 D3
Nailbourne Ct CT18....305 C7
Naildown Cl CT21 ....334 A3
Naildown Rd CT21....334 A3
Nairn Ct RM18.........18 F5
Nairne Ct TN26 ......327 A8
Naldera CT10 ....84 C7
Namur Pl CT15 ....278 F3
NAPCHESTER 246 C3
Napchester Rd CT16...278 A8
Napier Cl ME10......101 C4
Napier Ct
2 Lewisham SE12......29 B5
Maidstone ME14......161 F7
Napier Gdns CT11 ....333 C1
Napier Prim Sch ME7...64 D4
Napier Rd
Broadstairs CT10 ......83 E6
Bromley BR2..........52 B5
Dover CT16 ....278 B2
Erith DA17 ....3 F2
Gillingham ME7.......64 D4
Northfleet DA11 ......36 F7
Royal Tunbridge Wells
TN2 ....286 D2
Napleton Ct **7** CT11 .117 C6
Napleton Rd
Faversham ME13 .....138 C7
Ramsgate CT11 ......117 C6
Napoleon Dr TN12....259 D5
Napoleon Wlk ME17...199 C5
Napwood Cl ME8......98 D6
Nares Rd ME8 ....98 D4
Nargate Cl CT3.......177 A8
Nargate St CT3.......177 A8
Narrabeen Rd CT19...334 E6
Narrow Boat Cl SE8 ....2 D4
Narrowbush La TN29 ..371 B7
Narrow Way BR2......52 E3
Naseby Ave CT20 ....334 D5
Naseby Ct DA14 ......30 F4
NASH Keston 85 A4
Preston 146 F2
Nash Bank DA13......59 F7
Nash Cl ME5 ....97 C2
Nash Cotts **16** DA14....31 A5
Nash Court Gdns CT9..82 F8
Nash Court Rd CT9....82 F8
Nash Croft CT11......36 E4
Nashenden Farm La
ME1 ....96 A8
Nashenden La ME1....62 F1
Nash Gdns CT10 ....84 B4
Nash La Margate CT9 ..82 F7
Wingham CT3 ....146 D2
Nash Rd DA13........60 A7
NASH STREET 60 A7
Nasmyth Rd CT7......81 A8
Nassau Path **6** SE28 ....3 C5
Natal Rd Chatham ME4...64 C3
Dover CT16 ....278 C4
Nathan Way SE28, SE18...2 E3
Nativity Cl ME10......101 E4
Nat's La TN25 ....270 A5
Nautilus Cl ME1......47 A6
Nautilus Dr ME12.....47 A6
Naval Terr ME12.......28 A3
Naylands CT9 ....50 H1
Naylor's Cotts ME7....98 B1
Neale St ME4.........63 F2
Neal Rd TN15.........90 E5
Neal's Place Rd CT2...142 C3
Neame Rd CT7 ....81 A7
NEAMES FORSTAL ...171 D7
Neason Way CT19....335 F6
Neath Rd SE20 ....375 A2
Neatscourt Cotts ME12 46 C4
Neatscourt Rd E6 ......1 D8
Neills Rd TN3 ....316 D2
Nellington Ct TN4....285 B4
Nellington Rd TN3, TN4 285 B4
Nelson Ave
Minster (Sheppey)
ME12 ....47 D5
Tonbridge TN9.......222 A1
Nelson Cl Ashford TN24 301 B8

Nelson Cl *continued*
Biggin Hill TN16 .....118 E2
West Minst ME12......46 A8
Nelson Cres CT11 ....117 E6
Nelson Ct
Birchington CT7 ......80 E8
Chatham ME5 ....64 C1
Nelson Gdns ME13 ...138 C6
Nelson Ho
8 Maidstone ME15...195 F5
Swanscombe DA9......17 C2
Nelson Mandela Rd
SE3 ....11 C4
Nelson Mews CT11 ...373 E5
Nelson Park Rd CT15 .279 E8
Nelson Pl CT10........84 B5
Nelson Rd Bromley BR2...52 C5
Dartford DA1 ....15 C1
Erith DA17 ....3 F1
Gillingham ME7.......64 D4
Northfleet DA11 ......36 F6
Royal Tunbridge Wells
TN4 ....286 D2
Sidcup DA14 ....31 A4
Whitstable CT5 ....74 D1
Wouldham ME1.......95 C5
Nelson St Deal CT14 ..215 D7
Faversham ME13 .....138 C6
Nelson Terr ME5 ......64 C1
Nelson Wlk ME10......101 B5
Nepicar Farm ★ TN15...125 D1
Nepicar La CT15 .....125 D3
Neptune Bsns Pk ME2..63 E7
Neptune Cl ME2.......63 E7
Neptune Terr ME12....28 D2
Neptune Way ME2.....63 E6
Neptune Wlk DA8 ......4 D2
Nesbit Rd Eltham SE9...11 D3
St Mary's Bay TN29 ..365 F4
Nesbitt Ho DA6........14 B2
Ness Rd Erith DA8......15 D8
Lydd TN29 ....376 C6
Ness The CT1 ....175 B5
Nestor Ct ME18.......193 A8
Nether Ave TN28 .....373 D6
Nethercombe Ho **4**
SE3 ....11 A8
NETHERCOURT 117 A6
Nethercourt Cir CT12 .117 A6
Nethercourt Farm Rd
CT11 ....117 B7
Nethercourt Gdns
CT11 ....117 B6
Nethercourt Hill CT11 .117 B6
Nethergong Ho CT3 ...112 D3
Netherhale Farm Rd
CT7 ....80 B3
Nethersole Cl ME7....143 A4
Nethersole Rd CT4 ...210 F1
Nethewode Ct DA17 ....4 B3
Netley Cl ME14 ......162 D6
Nettlefield TN24......268 E5
Nettlepole La TN27 ..233 D1
NETTLESTEAD 192 B6
Nettlestead Cotts
TN12 ....257 A7
Nettlestead Court
TN12 ....257 A8
Nettlestead Ct ME18...192 C5
NETTLESTEAD
GREEN 192 B2
Nettlestead La TN12 ..192 A6
Nettlestead Oast TN12 257 A8
Nevill Ct ME19........127 C1
Neville Cl
Maidstone ME14......162 B8
Sidcup DA15 ....30 F4
Neville Ho CT14 .....215 D6
Neville Rd Chatham ME4 63 C4
Herne Bay CT6 ....77 F4
Nevill Gate TN2 .....286 B1
Nevill Gdns CT14 ....215 B1
Nevill Ground The
(Tunbridge Wells CC)
TN1...............286 B1
Nevill Lodge TN2 ....286 C4
NEVILL PARK 285 D2
Nevill Pk TN4 ....285 E3
Nevill Pl ME4 ....128 A7
Nevill Ridge TN4.....285 D3
Nevill St TN2 ....286 A2
Nevill Terr TN2.......285 F2
New Acres Rd SE28.....2 E4
Newark Ct **1** ME4......63 B7
Newark Knok E6 ....2 A7
Newark Yd ME2........63 B7
NEW ASH GREEN 91 F8
New Ash Green Prim Sch
DA3 ....91 F8
NEWBARN 305 B4
NEW BARN 59 A7
Newbarn La TN14,
TN16 ....119 C2
New Barn Pk BR8 .....55 E8
New Barn Rd
Northfleet DA13......36 C3
Sutton Valence ME17,
TN12 ....229 E2
Swanley BR8 ....55 F8
New Barns Rd ME14 ..162 A8
New Barn St E13 ......1 B8
New Bassetts Cotts
TN12 ....290 B5
New Beacon Sch TN14 186 F8
Newbery Rd DA8 ......14 F6
New Beverley Rd CT2..142 F2
Newborough Ct TN10 .222 C6
New Bridge Cl CT10...310 E7
Newbridge Ave ME10..101 B5
Newbridge Pk TN12 ...25 A1
New Bridge Way TN29 365 E3
New Brompton Coll
ME7...............64 B4

NEWBURY.............135 D4
Newbury Ave ME16...161 C6
Newbury Cl
Birchington CT7 ......81 B6
Cliffe Woods ME3 .....40 B8
Dartford DA1 ....34 B8
Dover CT17 ....309 F7
Folkestone CT20.....334 D5
Newbury Cotts TN5...337 B8
Newbury Ct DA14......30 F4
Newbury La TN5......337 C8
Newbury Rd BR2 .....52 A6
NEWBURY'S...........337 B8
Newcastle Hill **8**
CT11 ....117 E7
NEW CHARLTON 1 C2
NEWCHURCH 350 E3
Newchurch La TN26 ..364 A7
Newchurch Rd ME15 .162 A1
Newcomen Rd
Royal Tunbridge Wells
TN4 ....286 A5
Sheerness ME12 ......28 C2
New Cotts Bean DA2 ...35 B5
Guston CT15 ....278 E6
Harbledown CT2 ....141 E1
Shipbourne TN11 ...189 D5
Teynham ME9 ....103 A4
Tilbury RM16..........19 B8
New Covenant Pl **4**
ME1 ....63 D4
New Creek Rd ME13...138 E8
New Cross St CT9 .....50 I2
New Ct **3** TN9 ....222 C2
New Cut ME15 ....194 D7
New Cut Rd
Chilham CT4, ME13....172 A3
Harbledown ME13....141 A1
Maidstone ME14......162 A1
New Delhi Ho **5** ME15 195 E5
New Dover Rd
Canterbury CT1, CT4 ..175 C6
Capel-le-Ferne CT18...308 C2
NEW ELTHAM 30 C6
New Eltham Sta SE9 ...30 C7
NEWENDEN 357 D3
Newenden Cl
Ashford TN23 ....299 F6
Maidstone ME14......162 D6
Newenden Rd ME4 ....40 C2
New England Rd TN4..286 A4
New Farm Ave BR2....52 A5
New Ferry App SE18....2 A3
New Forest La CT4 ...172 B3
New Gardens Rd ME9 103 C3
Newgate Gap CT9 ....51 A3
Newgate Lower Prom
CT9 ....51 A3
Newgate Prom CT9....51 A3
New Haine Rd CT12 ...83 A3
New Hall Cl TN29.....366 B3
New Hall Farm La ME3 .25 B6
NEWHAM..............1 C6
Newham College of FE
E16...............1 C7
Newham L Ctr E16......1 C8
Newham Way E13 ......1 B7
Newhaven Gdns SE9 ...11 D3
Newhaven **4** E16 .....1 A8
NEW HOUSE...........36 F6
New House Cl CT1....174 E4
Newhouse Cnr CT3....113 D1
Newhouse Farm Cotts
ME13 ....170 E7
Newhouse La ME13....170 D7
New House La
Canterbury CT4......174 C2
Gravesend DA11 ......37 A6
Hythe, Saltwood CT21 333 B4
Langley ME17 ....196 C5
Limpsfield RH8 .....183 B5
Meopham Station DA13 59 F4
Minster (Sheppey) ME12 47 C6
Orpington BR6 ....54 A2
Paddock Wood TN12...257 A6
Rochester ME1 ....63 D4
Rough Common CT2 ..142 B3
Sheerness ME12 ......28 A1
Sundridge TN14 .....152 E2
Sutton at Hone DA4...57 D7
Swanley BR8.........55 F6
New Rectory La TN23 .300 B4
New Rents **5** TN23 ..268 B2
New Road Ave ME4....63 E4
New Road Bsns Est
ME20 ....160 B8
New Road Hill
Bonnington TN25 ....329 F4
Farthing Street BR2, BR4 85 F2
New Road Ind Est ME12 28 A1
New Road Prim Sch **4**
ME4 ....64 A3
NEW ROMNEY 373 A5
New Romney Pl CT13...180 F8
New Romney Sta ★
TN28..............373 C6
New Ruttington La
CT1 ....143 A1
Newry Road ME14 .....41 B8
New Sch at West Heath
The TN15 ....187 B6
New St Ash CT3.......147 E1
Ashford TN24 ....268 B2
Canterbury CT1, St Dunstan's
CT2 ....142 C1
Chatham ME4 ....63 E3
Deal CT14 ....215 D7
12 Dover CT16, CT17...310 D8
Folkestone CT20.....335 D5
Herne Bay CT6 ....76 F5

NEWLANDS ME10......101 B5
Newlands Ct **8** SE9 ....12 A1
Newlands Dr CT14....248 B8
Newlands Farm Cotts
ME13 ....202 C4
Newlands Farm Rd ME3 24 B4
Newlands Ho CT11 .....83 E2
Newlands La
Culverstone Green
DA13 ....92 F1
Ramsgate CT12 ......83 D2
Newlands Lodge DA8...14 D8
Newlands Prim Sch
CT11 ....83 E1
Newlands Rd
Charing TN27 ....233 F5
Ramsgate CT12 ......83 D1
Royal Tunbridge Wells
TN4 ....286 B7
Newlands Rise TN4...286 A6
Newland St E16 ......1 F5
Newlands Way TN4...286 B7
New Lincoln Ho CT19 .335 D8
New Line Learning
Academy ME15.....195 B6
Newling Cl E6..........1 F7
New Lydenburg
Commercial Est SE7...1 C3
New Lydenburg St SE7 ..1 C3
Newlyn Cl BR6 ....87 A6
Newlyn Ct **1** ME14 ...162 A4
Newlyn Dr TN12......260 F5
Newlyn Rd DA16.......12 F5
Newlyn's Mdw CT15 .276 D1
Newman Ct
11 Bromley BR2.......52 A8
6 Hythe CT21 ....333 B1
Newman Dr ME10 ....102 A8
Newman Ho SE18 ....12 A7
Newman Rd
Aylesham CT3 ....210 E5
Bromley BR1.........52 A8
Newmans Cl
Broadstairs CT10 .....84 A6
7 Hythe CT21 ....333 B1
Newman's Rd ME11....36 F6
Newmarket Gn SE9....29 D8
Newmarsh Rd SE28 ....2 F5
Newmans Cl
Broadstairs CT10 .....84 A6
New Mill Rd BR5......54 D8
NEWNHAM............168 C7
Newnham Cl ME8 .....65 C2
Newnham La ME9,
ME13 ....168 D7
Newnham Lodge DA17 . .4 A1
Newnhams Cl BR1.....52 F6
Newnham St ME4 .....64 B3
New Pond Rd TN17 ...342 D6
Newport Ct CT1......175 B6
Newports BR8.........55 D2
New Pound La ME18 ..158 C1
New Rd Bexley DA16...13 B5
Burham ME1 ....95 F1
Chatham ME4 ....63 F4
Cliffe ME3 ....22 A4
Cranbrook TN17 ....320 B4
Ditton ME20 ....128 C1
East Malling ME19 ...160 A8
Egerton ME17.......232 F3
Egerton TN27 ....233 A2
Elham CT4 ....273 F4
Erith SE2 ....3 D1
Eythorne CT15 ......245 C7
Fordcombe TN11 ....252 A1
Gravesend DA11 ......19 B1
Grays RM17 ....18 B8
Harbledown CT2 ....141 D3
Headcorn ME17 .....262 D5
Herne CT2, CT6......110 C4
Hextable BR8 ....32 F1
Hythe CT21 ....333 B1
Langley ME17 ....196 C5
Limpsfield RH8 .....183 B5
Meopham Station DA13 59 F4

New St *continued*
Lydd TN29 ....376 C6
Margate CT9.........50 I2
New Street TN15......92 D4
Sandwich CT13 ......181 A8
Sheerness ME12.......28 B1
Westerham TN16 ....184 C8
2 Whitstable CT5 ....74 D2
Newstead Ave BR6 .....86 E8
Newstead Wood Sch for
Girls BR6 ....86 D7
NEW STREET 92 D5
New Street Hill BR1....29 C3
New Street Rd DA13,
TN15..............92 C6
New Strs ME4 ....63 F6
New Swan Yd **8** DA12...19 B1
New Tavern Fort ★
DA12..............19 C1
Newton Abbot Rd DA11 36 F6
Newton Ave TN10 ....222 C6
Newton Cl Chatham ME5 97 C2
1 Maidstone ME16....161 A3
Newton Ct **4** BR1.....52 E6
Newton Gdns TN12...256 F7
Newton Ho
Swanscombe DA9......17 D2
Woolwich SE2 ....3 C1
Newton Rd Bexley DA16 13 A4
Faversham ME13 .....138 D7
Royal Tunbridge Wells
TN1 ....286 B4
Tilbury RM18.........19 A5
Whitstable CT5.......75 B2
Newton's Ct DA9......16 D3
Newton Terr BR2......52 D3
Newton Willows TN3 .312 C7
NEWTOWN 250 D4
NEW TOWN Ashford ..300 D7
Dartford 16 A1
Halling 95 A6
West Malling.........109 F7
Newtown Cotts TN12 .260 E6
New Town Cotts TN11 220 A3
New Town Gn ★ 300 D8
New Town Rd TN23,
TN24..............300 D7
New Town St
Canterbury CT1......143 B2
Chartham CT4.......173 C5
New Villas ME15 .....194 C7
New Wharf Rd TN9 ...222 B1
New Wlk **4** TN15......114 A3
New Years La BR6,
TN14 ....120 A5
Niagara Cl ME19......159 B3
Nicholas Cl ME16.....161 A3
Nicholas Ct SE12 .....29 A7
Nicholas Dr CT12....116 D5
Nicholas Rd TN24 ....268 B6
Nicholas Stacey Ho **4**
SE7 ....1 B1
Nichol La ME1.........29 A1
Nicholls Ave CT10 ....83 F2
Nicholson Ho SE18 ....11 E7
Nicklaus Dr ME5 ......96 F3
Nicklebury Cl SE28 ....3 C7
Nickleby Ho ME1......63 C2
Nickleby Rd DA12 .....38 A7
Nickle Cotts CT4 .....173 A4
Nickley Wood Rd
TN26 ....327 C6
Nicola Terr DA7.......13 E6
Nicolson Rd BR5......54 D2
Nicolson Way TN13...154 D5
Nigeria Rd SE7 ....11 D7
Nightingale Ave
Hythe CT21 ....353 D6
Whitstable CT5 ......108 B6
Nightingale Cl
Ashford TN24 ....301 B8
Biggin Hill TN16 .....118 C4
Chartham CT4.......173 C6
Gillingham ME8 ......98 E6
Larkfield ME20 ......127 F2
Northfleet DA11 ......36 E4
Nightingale Cnr BR5....54 D5
Nightingale Ct ME2....62 C6
Nightingale Gr **3** DA1..16 A3
Nightingale Ho SE18 ...2 A1
Nightingale La
Bromley BR1.........52 D7
Goathurst Common
TN14 ....186 B5
Nonington CT15 ....211 C2
Nightingale Pl
Margate CT9.........51 A2
Woolwich SE18 ......12 B8
Nightingale Prim Sch
SE18 ....2 B1
Nightingale Rd
Dover CT16 ....278 C2
Faversham ME13 ....138 C7
Herne CT6 ....110 F7
Kemsing TN15.......122 F2
Orpington BR5 ....53 C3
Nightingales The
Margate CT9.........82 F8
Royal Tunbridge Wells
TN4 ....286 A5
Sissinghurst TN27...321 F8
Nightingale Vale SE18..12 A4
Nightingale Way
Newham E6 ....1 E8
Swanley BR8.........55 F6
Nile Path **6** SE18 .....12 A8
Nile Rd ME7 ....64 C4
Nine Acres CT17 .....268 C5
Nine Acres Rd ME2....62 B3
Nine Ash La ME13 ...139 D3
Nine Elms Gr DA11 ...37 A8
Nine Hams Rd TN16 ..150 D6
Nineveh La TN17, TN18 341 E6

Ninhams Wood BR6 . . . . .86 A6
Ninn La TN23. . . . . .267 B2
Nita Ct SE12. . . . . .29 A7
Nithdale Rd SE18. . . . . . . .12 C7
Niven Cl ME3. . . . . .40 C3
Niwrim Way ME12. . . . . . .28 G1
Nixon Ave CT12. . . . . .83 C1
Nizels La TN11. . . . . .220 F8
No 1 St SE18. . . . . .2 B3
NOAH'S ARK 155 A8
Noah's Ark TN15. . . . . . .123 B1
Noah's Ark Rd CT17 . . . .310 A8
Noah's Ark Terr TN17. .310 A8
Noakes Mdw TN23. . . . .300 A8
Nobel Cl ME9 . . . . .103 C2
Nobel Ct ME13 . . . . .138 C7
Noble Ct CT9. . . . . .82 A8
Noble Gdns CT9. . . . . . . .82 A8
Noble Tree Cross
  TN11. . . . . .221 B6
Noble Tree Rd TN11. . . .221 B6
Noel Terr 15 DA14. . . . . . .31 B4
NOKE STREET. 40 B4
No Man's Orch Nature
  Reserve★ CT4 . . . . . . .173 D7
No Name St 3 CT13. . . .149 A1
NONINGTON 211 D5
Nonington CE Prim Sch
  CT15. . . . . .211 C5
Nonington Ct CT15. . . . .211 E5
Nonsuch Cl CT1 . . . . . . .175 C8
Nook The ME18. . . . . . . .192 F2
Norah La ME3. . . . . .39 B3
Nore Cl Gillingham ME7 . .64 E1
  Sheerness ME12. . . . . . . .28 C1
Noreen Ave ME12. . . . . . .47 A6
Norfield Rd DA2. . . . . . . .32 D3
Norfolk Cl Chatham ME5 . .16 A2
  Gillingham ME8. . . . . . . .65 D2
Norfolk Cres DA15. . . . . . .30 E8
Norfolk Dr TN23. . . . . . .268 A2
Norfolk Gdns DA7. . . . . . .13 F6
Norfolk Pl DA16. . . . . . . .13 A5
Norfolk Rd
  Canterbury CT1. . . . . . .174 E6
  Gravesend DA12. . . . . . . .37 D8
  Maidstone ME15. . . . . . .195 C8
  Margate CT9. . . . . .51 B3
  Margate, Lydden CT9. . . .82 D5
  Royal Tunbridge Wells
  TN1. . . . . .286 B2
  Tonbridge TN9. . . . . . . .222 A1
Norfolk Sq CT12. . . . . . . .83 B2
Norfolk St 3 CT5. . . . . .108 D8
Norham Ct 25 DA2. . . . . .16 B1
Norheads La TN16. . . . . .118 B2
Norlands Cres BR7. . . . . .53 B8
Norlands Gate BR7 . . . . .53 B8
Norman Castle★ CT1. .174 F7
Norman Cl
  Gillingham ME8. . . . . . . .98 A5
  Kemsing TN15. . . . . . . .122 D2
  Maidstone ME14. . . . . . .162 B6
  Orpington BR6. . . . . .86 C7
  Rochester ME2. . . . . .62 C4
Norman Ct TN8. . . . . . . .217 B2
Normandy Prim Sch
  DA7. . . . . .14 D6
Normandy Terr E16 . . . . . .1 B7
Normandy Way DA8. . . . .14 E6
Normanhurst Ave DA7,
  DA16. . . . . .13 D6
Normanhurst Rd
  Borough Green TN15. . .157 A7
  Orpington BR5. . . . . .54 B7
Norman Par DA14. . . . . . .31 D6
Norman Rd
  Ashford TN23, TN24. . . .300 B7
  Broadstairs CT10 . . . . . . .83 F6
  Canterbury CT1. . . . . . .175 A7
  Dartford DA1. . . . . .33 E7
  Erith DA17. . . . . .4 B1
  Faversham ME13. . . . . . .138 C7
  Ramsgate CT11. . . . . . . .117 B6
  Royal Tunbridge Wells
  TN1. . . . . .286 B2
  Snodland ME6. . . . . .128 A6
  St Margaret's at Cliffe
  CT15. . . . . .280 B6
  Warden ME12. . . . . .49 A6
  Westgate on Sea CT8. . . .50 D1
  West Malling ME19. . . . .159 B8
  Whitstable CT5. . . . . . . .108 E8
Norman Rise TN17 . . . . .320 D4
Normans Cl DA11. . . . . . .37 A8
Norman St
  8 Dover CT17. . . . . . . .310 D8
  Ide Hill TN14. . . . . .185 F5
Norman Tailyour Ho
  CT14. . . . . .215 D5
Norman Villas 4 TN18 340 F2
Norreys Rd ME8. . . . . . . .98 E7
Norrie Rd CT7. . . . . .81 A6
Norrington Mead 3
  CT19. . . . . .335 A7
Norrington Rd ME15. . . .195 B6
Norris Cl 15 TN18. . . . . .341 A2
Norris Ho 8 SE7 . . . . . . .11 C8
Norris Way DA1. . . . . . . .14 F4
Norstead Gdns TN4. . . . .286 B8
Norsted La BR6. . . . . . . .120 B8
Northall Rd DA7. . . . . . . .14 C5
North Ash Rd DA3. . . . . . .91 F7
North Aux Boiler House Rd
  TN29 . . . . .380 C2
North Ave CT11 . . . . .117 D6
North Bank Cl ME2. . . . . .62 F5
North Barrack Rd
  CT14. . . . . .215 D4
North Beckton Prim Sch
  E6. . . . . .1 F8
North Borough Jun Sch
  ME14. . . . . .162 A6

NORTHBOURNE 214 A4
Northbourne BR2 . . . . . . .52 A2
Northbourne Ave CT17310 B8
Northbourne CE Prim Sch
  CT14. . . . . .213 F5
Northbourne Park Pre
  Prep Sch CT14 . . . . . . .213 D6
Northbourne Park Sch
  CT14. . . . . .213 C6
Northbourne Rd
  East Studdal CT15 . . . . .213 E1
  Gillingham ME8. . . . . . . .65 B4
  Great Mongeham CT14. .214 C4
Northbourne Way CT9. . .51 C2
Northbrooke TN24 . . . . .268 C3
Northbrooke La TN24. . .268 C3
North Camber Way
  CT16. . . . . .279 B1
North Ct Bexley DA6. . . .13 D7
  Folkestone CT20. . . . . . .334 D4
Northcliffe Gdns CT10. .84 A7
North Close Bsns Ctr
  CT20. . . . . .334 D4
North Contractor's Rd
  TN29. . . . . .380 B3
Northcote Rd
  Deal CT14. . . . . .215 D5
  Kingsdown CT14. . . . . . .248 A8
  Northfleet DA11. . . . . . . .36 F7
  Rochester ME2. . . . . .63 A7
  Sidcup DA14. . . . . .30 E4
  2 Tonbridge TN9. . . . . .222 B1
North Court Cl CT3. . . . .178 A8
North Court La CT14. . . .213 A4
North Court Rd CT3. . . . .178 A8
NORTH CRAY. 31 F5
North Cray Rd DA14. . . . .31 E4
North Cres ME17 . . . . . .194 D4
North Ct 4 Bromley BR1 52 B8
  Deal CT14. . . . . .215 C7
  North Ct 2 ME15. . . . . .162 A1
North Dane Way ME5. . . .97 C4
NORTHDOWN. 51 D1
Northdown
  Ashford TN24 . . . . .268 C4
  Doddington ME9. . . . . . .167 F7
  Stockbury ME9 . . . . .132 D8
North Down TN12. . . . . .260 E4
Northdown Ave CT9. . . . .51 B2
Northdown Bsns Pk
  ME17. . . . . .199 F6
Northdown Cl
  Lenham ME17. . . . . .199 F6
  Maidstone ME14. . . . . . .162 B7
  Paddock Wood TN12. . . .256 F6
Northdown Hill CT10,
  CT9. . . . . .83 D7
Northdown Park Rd
  CT9. . . . . .51 C1
Northdown Prim Sch
  CT9. . . . . .51 C1
Northdown Rd
  Bexley DA16. . . . . .13 C5
  Broadstairs CT10 . . . . . . .83 E6
  Kemsing TN15. . . . . . . .122 E2
  Longfield DA3. . . . . .58 E7
  Margate CT9. . . . . .51 B2
North Downs Bsns Pk
  TN13. . . . . .121 C3
Northdowns CI CT15. . .246 B6
North Downs Cl CT4. . . .172 C2
North Downs Terr
  ME19. . . . . .126 A5
Northdown Trad Est
  CT10. . . . . .83 E7
North Down View
  ME17. . . . . .198 F6
Northdown Way CT9. . . .51 C1
North Dr BR6. . . . . .86 E6
North Eastling Rd
  ME13. . . . . .168 F8
NORTH ELHAM 274 A6
NORTH END. 14 F6
North End Farm DA13 . . .35 F4
North End La BR6. . . . . . .86 B2
Northend Prim Sch DA8 14 F6
Northend Rd DA8. . . . . . .14 F6
North End Trad Est DA8 14 E6

NORTH HALLING. 95 A8
North Hill Rd TN18 340 C1
North Holmes Rd CT1 .175 B8
NORTHIAM. 357 C1
Northiam Sta★ TN31 . .357 C2
North Kent Ave DA11. . .18 C1
North La
  Canterbury CT1. . . . . . . .142 F1
  Faversham ME13 . . . . . . .138 C1
  7 Folkestone CT20. . . . .334 E3
  Selling ME13. . . . . .171 F8
Northlands 5 BR1. . . . . .52 C7
Northlands Ave BR6. . . . .86 E6
Northlands CT TN32355 C1
North Lea CT14. . . . . . . .215 C7
Northleigh Cl ME15. . . . .195 A8
North Lockside Rd ME4 64 D8
NORTH LYMINGE 305 C7
North Lyminge La
  CT18. . . . . .305 C7
North Meadow ME19 . . .158 D7
North Meadow Cotts
  ME19. . . . . .158 D7
North Military Rd
  CT17 . . . . .310 C7
Northolme Rise BR6. . . . .86 E8
Northover BR1. . . . . .29 A4
North Pends TN24. . . . . .268 E5
North Pk Pk SE9. . . . . . . .12 A1
Northpoint 12 BR1. . . . . .52 A8
Northpoint Bsns Est
  ME2. . . . . .63 D8
North Pole La BR2. . . . . .85 A4
North Pole Rd ME16,
  ME18. . . . . .160 C2
North Pondside Rd
  ME4. . . . . .64 A8
North Quay ME9. . . . . . .103 A6
North Quay La TN29. . . .105 D1
North Rd 4 Bromley BR1. .52 B8
  Chatham, Brompton ME4,
  ME7. . . . . .64 A7
  Chatham ME4. . . . . .64 B8
  Cliffe ME3. . . . . .22 B6
  Cliffs End CT13. . . . . . . .116 A1
  Dartford DA1. . . . . .15 A1
  Deal CT14. . . . . .248 D6
  Dover CT17. . . . . .310 C8
  Erith DA17. . . . . .4 B4
  Folkestone CT20. . . . . . .334 D4
  Goudhurst TN17. . . . . . .290 E1
  Hythe CT21. . . . . .333 B2
  Queenborough ME11. . . .45 F5
  Sandwich CT13. . . . . . . .182 A7
  Woolwich SE18. . . . . .2 E1
North Return Rd CT16 310 G8
Northridge Rd DA12. . . . .37 C5
North Riding DA3. . . . . . .59 D6
North Road W CT1. . . . .333 A3
North St The TN24. . . . .268 D1
Northside Rd BR1. . . . . .52 A8
North Side Three Rd
  ME4. . . . . .64 A8
North St Ashford TN23 .268 C2
  Bexley DA7. . . . . .14 A3
  Biddenden TN27 . . . . . . .295 A2
  Bromley BR1. . . . . .52 A8
  Cowden TN8. . . . . .282 A6
  Dartford DA1. . . . . .33 D8
  Deal CT14. . . . . .215 D7
  Dover CT17. . . . . .310 B7
  Folkestone CT20. . . . . . .335 E5
  Gravesend DA12. . . . . . . .37 B8
  Headcorn TN27 . . . . . . .262 C5
  Herne Bay CT6 . . . . .77 A5
  Maidstone ME16. . . . . . .160 F2
  New Romney TN28 . . . . .373 A6
  Rochester ME2. . . . . .63 B7
  Royal Tunbridge Wells
  TN2 . . . . .286 C3
  Sheldwich ME13 . . . . . . .170 C8
  Sittingbourne ME10. . . .101 F7
  Sutton Valence ME17 . . .229 E8
  Warmlake ME17. . . . . . .196 E1
North Terr ME3 . . . . .40 F6
Northumberland Ave
  Ashford TN24 . . . . .268 D5
  Bexley DA16. . . . . .12 E4
  Gillingham ME8. . . . . . . .65 C1
  Margate CT9. . . . . .51 C2
Northumberland Cl
  DA8. . . . . .14 C7
Northumberland Ct
  Bexley DA8. . . . . .14 C6
  Maidstone ME15. . . . . . .195 D7
  Margate CT9. . . . . .51 C3
Northumberland Gdns
  BR1. . . . . .53 A5
NORTHUMBERLAND
  HEATH. 14 C7
Northumberland Heath
  Prim Sch DA8. . . . . .14 B7
Northumberland Pk
  DA8. . . . . .14 C7
Northumberland Rd
  Istead Rise DA13. . . . . . .36 F1
  Maidstone ME15. . . . . . .195 D8
  Newham E6. . . . . .1 E7
Northumberland Way
  DA8. . . . . .14 C6
Northview BR8. . . . . .55 E7
North View
  Hersden CT3. . . . . .111 F1
  Maidstone ME15. . . . . . .195 C7
Northview Ave RM18 . . .19 A6
North View Cotts
  ME15. . . . . .194 C7

North View Rd TN13,
  TN14. . . . . .154 C6
Northwall Ct CT14. . . . .215 C7
Northwall Mews CT14 215 C7
Northwall Rd CT14. . . . .215 B8
Northward Hill Nature
  Reserve★ ME3. . . . . .7 B2
North Way
  Finglesham CT14. . . . . .214 A7
  Maidstone ME14. . . . . . .162 B7
North West Kent Coll
  (Dartford Campus)
  DA1. . . . . .33 C6
North West Kent Coll
  (Gravesend Campus)
  DA12. . . . . .37 F7
North West Kent Coll
  (Thameside Campus)
  DA12. . . . . .19 F1
NORTHWOOD 83 C3
Northwood Ave ME23. . . .23 E4
Northwood Dr
  Sittingbourne ME10 . . . .101 F1
  2 Swanscombe DA9. . . . .17 A1
Northwood Pl ME18. . . . . .3 F3
Northwood Prim Sch
  DA18. . . . . .3 F3
Northwood Rd
  Broadstairs, Ramsgate CT10,
  CT12. . . . . .83 D3
  Tonbridge TN10. . . . . . .222 C6
  Whitstable CT5. . . . . .74 F2
NORTH WOOLWICH 2 A4
North Woolwich Old Sta
  Mus★ E16. . . . . .2 A4
North Woolwich Rd E16 . .1 A5
North Woolwich Rdbt
  E16. . . . . .1 D5
NORTON ASH. 136 F8
Norton Ave CT6 . . . . . . .111 A8
Norton Cres TN10 . . . . .222 B7
Norton Dr CT12. . . . . . . .115 B6
Norton Gr ME5 . . . . .96 E3
Norton Knatchbull Sch The
  TN24. . . . . .268 A2
Norton La TN26 . . . . . . .297 D5
Norton Rd
  Five Wents ME17 . . . . . .196 D1
  Lewson Street ME13,
  ME9 . . . . .136 E5
  Nortons La TN30 . . . . . .323 E5
  Nortons Way TN12 . . . .256 B7
Norvic Ho DA4 . . . . .14 F7
Norview Rd CT5. . . . . . . .108 B7
Norway Dro CT15 . . . . . .280 A8
Norway Terr 4 ME14. . .162 A7
Norwich Cl ME2. . . . . .62 D6
Norwich Ave TN10. . . . . .222 D5
Norwood Cl ME3 . . . . . . .22 B4
Norwood Cl 5 DA1. . . . . .16 A3
Norwood Gdns TN23 .268 B2
Norwood La
  Meopham Station DA13 . .60 B3
  St Mary in the Marsh
  TN29. . . . . .364 E8
Norwood Rise ME17 . . . .47 C7
Norwood St TN23 . . . . .268 B2
Norwood Walk E
  ME10. . . . . .101 C5
Norwood Walk W
  ME10. . . . . .101 B5
Oak Dr
  Boughton Street
  ME13. . . . . .140 A3
  Hawkinge TN18. . . . . . . .307 B5
Notley Cl CT1. . . . . .143 A1
Notley Terr 3 CT1. . . . . .143 A1
Notre Dame RC Prim Sch
  SE18. . . . . .12 B8
Nottidge Rd TN4 . . . . . .285 D1
Nottingham Ave
  Maidstone ME15. . . . . . .195 D7
  Newham E16. . . . . .1 C7
Nottingham Rd CT1 . . . . .54 A2
Nottingham Wlk ME2. . .62 D6
Nouds La ME9. . . . . .136 D6
Nouds Rd ME9. . . . . .136 D7
Novar Cl BR6. . . . . .53 F2
Novar Rd SE9 . . . . .30 C7
Nower The TN14, TN16 .151 F8
Nuffield Rd BR8. . . . . .33 A2
Nugent Ind Pk BR5. . . . .54 C5
Nunappleton Way RH8 183 A3
Nunnery Fields CT1 . . .175 A7
Nunnery La TN11. . . . . .283 F8
Nunnery Rd CT1. . . . . . .174 F7
Nunnington Cl SE9 . . . . .29 E5
Nuralite Ind Ctr ME3. . .39 A8
Nursery Ave Bexley DA7 .13 F4
Nursery Cl Dartford DA2 .34 C8
  Densole CT18 . . . . .307 A7
  Flimwell TN5 . . . . .339 B3
  Orpington BR6 . . . . .54 A2
  Ramsgate CT11. . . . . . . .117 C7
  Sevenoaks TN13 . . . . . . .154 C5
  Sheerness ME12. . . . . . . .28 D1
  Swanley BR8. . . . . .55 C1
  Tonbridge TN10. . . . . . .222 E4
  Whitstable CT5. . . . . .75 A1
Nursery Fields Acol CT7 81 B3
  Hythe CT21. . . . . .333 A2
Nursery Gdns
  Broadstairs CT10 . . . . . . .51 E1
  Chislehurst BR7 . . . . .30 B2
  Hoo St Werburgh ME3 . . .41 E5
Nursery Grove DA11/
  DA12. . . . . .37 B3
Nursery Ho DA4 . . . . .57 C5
Nursery La
  Densole CT18 . . . . .307 A7
  Sheldwich ME13 . . . . . . .170 D5
  Whitfield CT16 . . . . .277 F7
Nurserylands CT6 . . . . . .76 F3

Nursery Pl TN13. . . . . . .153 D4
Nursery Rd
  Ditton ME20. . . . . .128 C1
  Gillingham ME8. . . . . . . .98 C8
  Meopham Station DA13 . .60 A4
  Paddock Wood TN12. . . .256 F8
  Royal Tunbridge Wells
  TN4. . . . . .286 B8
Nursery The DA8. . . . . . .14 F7
Nursery Wlk CT2 . . . . . .142 E2
Nurstead Ave DA3. . . . . .59 D6
Nurstead Church La
  DA13. . . . . .60 A5
Nurstead La DA3, DA13 .59 D5
Nurstead Rd DA8. . . . . . .14 A7
Nutberry Cl ME9. . . . . . .103 D2
Nutfield Cl ME5. . . . . .97 B8
Nutfield Ct 7 BR1. . . . . .52 A6
Nutfields Ightham TN15 156 B4
  Sittingbourne ME10 . . . .102 B3
Nutfield Way BR6 . . . . . .86 B8
Nuthatch DA3. . . . . .59 B7
Nuthatch Gdns SE28. . . .2 D4
Nutley Cl Ashford TN24 268 C3
  Swanley BR8. . . . . .55 F8
Nutmead Cl DA5. . . . . . . .32 C7
Nuttall Ct BR5. . . . . .54 B6
Nut Tree Cl BR6. . . . . . . .87 D7
Nutts Ave ME12 . . . . .49 G2
Nutwood Cl ME14 . . . . . .162 E4
Nuxley Rd DA17 . . . . .4 A1
Nyanza St SE18. . . . . . . .12 D8

O

OAD STREET 100 E1
Oak Apple Ct SE12. . . . . .29 A7
Oakapple Ho 10 ME16 161 A3
Oakapple La ME16. . . . . .161 A3
Oak Ave
  Biddenden ME27 . . . . . .323 D7
  Eythorne CT15. . . . . . . .245 D5
  Gillingham ME7. . . . . . . .64 E6
  Minster (Sheppey) ME12 .47 F6
  Sevenoaks TN13 . . . . . . .187 B7
Oak Bglws TN29. . . . . . .376 C6
Oakbrook Cl BR1. . . . . . .29 A4
Oak Cl Crayford DA1. . . . .14 F3
  Hoo St Werburgh ME3 . . .41 E3
Oak Cotts
  Barrowhill TN25 . . . . . . .331 D7
  East Studdal CT15 . . . . .246 E8
  Four Elms TN8. . . . . . . .218 B6
  Selling ME13 . . . . .171 D4
Oakcroft 3 SE12 . . . . . . .29 B5
Oak Croft ME14 . . . . . . .163 B4
Oak Cl BR1. . . . . .52 F7
Oakdale La TN8 . . . . . . .184 C2
Oakdale Rd
  Herne Bay CT6 . . . . .77 A4
  Royal Tunbridge Wells
  TN4. . . . . .285 F4
Oakdene Ave
  Chislehurst BR7 . . . . .30 A3
  Erith DA8. . . . . .14 C8
Oakdene Rd
  Orpington BR5. . . . . .54 A3
  Ramsgate CT12. . . . . .83 C1
  Sevenoaks TN13 . . . . . . .154 A5
Oakenden La TN8 . . . . . .251 C2
Oakenden Rd DA13. . . . .59 D7
Oakenholt Ho 1 SE2. . . . .3 D4
Oakenpole TN23. . . . . . .267 E1
Oakes Cl E6. . . . . .1 F7
Oak Farm Gdns CT7 . . . .262 D6
Oak Farm La TN15 . . . . . .92 E1
Oakfield
  Hawkinge TN18. . . . . . . .340 F1
  Rolvenden ME17 . . . . . . .344 A1
Oakfield Cotts TN17. . . .342 D4
Oakfield Court Rd TN2 286 C3
Oakfield Cl CT12. . . . . . .117 B8
Oakfield La
  Dartford DA1, DA2. . . . . .33 B6
  Orpington BR2. . . . . .85 D6
Oakfield Pl CT14. . . . . . . .33 B6
Oakfield Prim Sch DA1 33 D6
Oakfield Rd
  Ashford TN24 . . . . .268 D5
  Marlpit Hill TN8. . . . . . .217 B5
  Matfield TN12 . . . . .288 D8
Oakfields
  Sevenoaks TN13 . . . . . . .154 B1
  Sittingbourne ME10 . . . .101 C3
Oak Gr CT15. . . . . .212 B2
Oak Hall Pass CT21. . . .333 C2
Oakham Dr Bromley BR2 .52 A5
  Lydd TN29. . . . . .376 D7
Oak Hill CT13. . . . . .180 B6
Oakhill House BR5. . . . . .54 A8
Oakhill Rd BR6. . . . . .86 F8
Oak Hill Rd TN15 . . . . . .154 A2
Oak Ho 6 Chatham ME5 .96 F4
  3 Royal Tunbridge Wells
  TN2 . . . . .286 C3
  13 Sidcup DA15. . . . . . . .31 A5
Oakhouse Rd DA6. . . . . .14 A2
Oakhurst Ave DA7. . . . . .13 C6
Oakhurst Cl Bromley BR7 52 F8
  Chatham ME5. . . . . .96 F3
Oakhurst Gdns DA7 . . . .13 C6
Oak La Headcorn TN27 . .262 D6

Oak La continued
  Lydd TN29. . . . . .376 B6
  Minster (Sheppey) ME12 .47 F7
  Sevenoaks TN13 . . . . . . .187 A8
  Upchurch ME9. . . . . .66 D2
Oakland Cl ME5. . . . . .96 F3
Oakland Ct
  Cliffs End CT12. . . . . . . .116 C5
  Herne Bay CT6 . . . . .76 F6
Oaklands Ashford TN23 .267 F1
  Chislehurst BR7 . . . . .30 D2
  Cranbrook TN17 . . . . . . .320 D4
  Loose ME15 . . . . .195 A8
  Mersham TN25 . . . . . . .301 E4
  Sturry CT2. . . . . .144 B7
Oaklands Ave
  Broadstairs CT10 . . . . . . .83 E5
  Sidcup DA15. . . . . .29 F8
Oaklands Cl Bexley DA6. .13 F2
  Orpington BR5. . . . . .53 E3
  West Kingsdown TN15. . .90 E4
Oaklands Inf & Jun Sch
  ME5. . . . . .96 F3
Oaklands Inf Sch TN16 118 C3
Oaklands Jun Sch
  TN16. . . . . .118 C3
Oaklands La CT13. . . . . .118 C3
Oaklands Rd Bexley DA6 13 F2
  Dartford DA2. . . . . .34 C7
  Groombridge TN3 . . . . . .312 B6
  Hawkhurst TN18. . . . . . .341 A1
  Northfleet DA11. . . . . . . .36 F4
Oaklands Way
  Sturry CT2. . . . . .144 B7
  Tonbridge TN11. . . . . . .221 F4
Oakland Villas TN3 . . . .312 B7
Oaklea Rd TN12 . . . . . . .256 F6
Oakleigh Cl
  Chatham ME5. . . . . .96 E2
  Swanley BR8. . . . . .55 E6
Oakleigh Ct CT12. . . . . .289 F6
Oakleigh Gdns BR6. . . . . .86 E6
Oakleigh Ho TN3. . . . . . .299 E8
Oakleigh La CT7. . . . . . . .176 B5
Oakleigh Park Ave BR7 53 A8
Oakley Cl 8 Newham E6. .1 E7
  West Thurrock RM20 . . . .17 C8
Oakley Ct DA1. . . . . .34 B7
Oakley Dr Orpington BR2 85 E7
  Sidcup SE9. . . . . .30 D7
Oakley Lodge SE12. . . . . .29 A8
Oakley Pk DA5. . . . . .31 C8
Oakley Rd BR2. . . . . .85 E8
Oakley Sch
  Pembury TN2 . . . . .287 C5
  Tonbridge TN10. . . . . . .222 B5
Oakleys The CT15 . . . . .244 D5
Oak Lodge
  Royal Tunbridge Wells
  TN2 . . . . .286 D2
  Sevenoaks TN13 . . . . . . .154 A3
Oak Lodge La TN16. . . . .151 D2
Oak Lodge Rd TN28 . . . .373 B7
Oakmead
  Meopham DA13 . . . . .93 A8
  Tonbridge TN10. . . . . . .222 C6
Oakmead Ave BR2. . . . . .52 A3
Oakmere Rd SE2 . . . . . . .13 A8
Oakmont Pl 6 BR6. . . . . .53 D1
Oak Rd Erith DA8. . . . . . .15 A5
  Erith, Northumberland Heath
  DA8 . . . . .14 C7
  Five Oak Green TN12 . . .256 B7
  Gravesend DA12. . . . . . . .37 C4
  Grays RM17 . . . . .18 C8
  Hoo St Werburgh ME3 . . .41 E3
  Orpington BR6. . . . . .87 A3
  Rochester ME2. . . . . .62 E6
  Royal Tunbridge Wells
  TN2 . . . . .286 D2
  Sittingbourne ME10 . . . .102 C5
  Stone DA9. . . . . .16 E1
  Westerham TN16 . . . . . .151 D2
Oak Ridge TN26 . . . . . . .349 F8
Oaks Ave CT6 . . . . .76 D2
Oaks Bsns Village The
  ME5. . . . . .97 C1
Oaks Dene ME5 . . . . .96 F1
Oakside Rd CT3. . . . . . . .210 E5
Oaks Inf Sch The
  ME10. . . . . .101 D2
Oaks Pk CT2 . . . . .142 B3
Oaks Rd
  Folkestone CT20. . . . . . .334 D6
  Tenterden TN30 . . . . . . .345 B8
Oak St CT14. . . . . .215 D6
Oaks The
  Aylesford ME20. . . . . . . .128 L1
  Broadstairs CT10 . . . . . . .83 F7
  Dartford DA2. . . . . .16 B1
  Hawkinge TN18. . . . . . . .307 B3
  Hersden CT3. . . . . .111 F1
  Smarden TN27 . . . . .263 F2
  St Nicholas at Wade CT7 .79 F2
  Swanley BR8. . . . . .55 E7
  Whitstable CT5. . . . . . . .108 B6
  Woolwich SE18. . . . . .2 C1
Oaks View CT21 . . . . . . .353 C8
Oak Terr 3 TN18. . . . . .340 F2
Oak Tree Ave
  Maidstone ME15. . . . . . .195 C7
  Stone DA9. . . . . .34 F8
Oak Tree Cl
  Marden TN12 . . . . .259 D5
  Minster (Sheppey) ME12 .48 A5
  Royal Tunbridge Wells
  TN2 . . . . .286 A1
Oak Tree Gdns BR1. . . . .29 B3
Oak Tree Gr CT9 . . . . . . .82 A8

Oaktree Ho ME10. . . . . . .102 B3
Oak Tree Rd TN23 . . . . .299 F8
Oak Trees **19** ME15 . . . .195 E5
Oak Trees Com Sch
ME15. . . . . .195 C7
Oakum Ct ME4 . . . . .64 B2
Oakvale Cl CT17. . . . . . .310 B7
Oak View TN8 . . . . .217 B2
Oak Warren TN13 . . . . . .187 A6
Oakway Cl DA5. . . . . .13 C1
Oakways SE9 . . . . .12 B1
Oak Wlk CT21 . . . . .333 C2
Oakwood **2** CT9 . . . . . . .83 C8
Oakwood Ave BR2. . . . . .52 B6
Oakwood Cl
Chislehurst BR7 . . . . . . .30 A2
Dartford DA1. . . . . .34 B7
Oakwood Ct
Maidstone ME16. . . . .161 D3
Swanley BR8. . . . . .55 C7
Oakwood Dr Bexley DA7 14 C3
Sevenoaks TN13 . . . . . .154 B4
Whitstable CT5. . . . . .75 A1
Oakwood Gdns BR6 . . . .86 C8
Oakwood Ind Est
Broadstairs CT10 . . . . . .83 E6
Northfleet DA11 . . . . . . .18 A2
Oakwood Park Gram Sch
ME16 . . . . .161 C3
Oakwood Rd
Maidstone ME16. . . . .161 D3
Orpington BR6 . . . . .86 C8
Sturry CT2. . . . . .144 A7
Oakwood Rise
Longfield DA3. . . . . .58 E6
Royal Tunbridge Wells
TN2 . . . . .286 E7
Oakwood Sch
Bexley DA7 . . . . .14 E3
Folkestone CT19. . . . . .335 E7
Oakwood Terr ME10. . . .102 C4
Oakwood Villas CT11. . . .83 E1
OARE 105 A3
Oare Gunpowder Works
Ctry Pk★ ME13 . . . . . .105 A1
Oare Marshes Nature
Reserve★ ME13. . . . . .105 B6
Oare Rd ME13 . . . . .105 C1
Oasis The **7** BR1. . . . . . .52 C7
Oast Cl TN2 . . . . .286 D7
Oast Cotts
Dargate ME13. . . . . . . .140 D8
Sheldwich ME13. . . . . .170 C8
Wormshill ME9 . . . . . .166 C5
Oast Ct Margate CT9 . . . .82 F8
Sittingbourne ME10 . . .101 E2
Yalding ME18 . . . . .192 F1
Oastfield Close ME3 . . . .22 E1
Oastfield Ct TN15. . . . . .154 C2
Oast Ho CT4. . . . . .172 C2
Oast Ho The
Canterbury CT3. . . . . .175 F8
3 Gillingham ME8. . . . . .98 F8
Oasthouse Field TN29 .363 F4
Oast House Way BR5 . . .54 B5
Oast La
Throwley Forstal
ME13 . . . . .202 E6
Tonbridge TN10. . . . . .222 A4
Oast Mdw TN24 . . . . . . .268 F1
Oast Paddock The
CT3 . . . . .179 A6
Oasts The ME14 . . . . . . .163 C4
Oast The
Canterbury CT1. . . . . .175 B6
Staple CT3. . . . . .179 A6
Oastview ME8 . . . . .99 A8
Oast View TN12 . . . . . . .290 A6
Oast Way DA3. . . . . .58 E3
Oaten Hill CT1 . . . . .175 A7
Oaten Hill Pl CT1. . . . . .175 A7
Oatfield Cl TN17. . . . . . .320 C5
Oatfield Dr TN17 . . . . . .320 C5
Oatfield Rd BR6. . . . . . . .53 F1
Oaze The CT5 . . . . .108 C6
Occupation La SE18 . . . .12 B6
Occupation Rd TN25. . .237 F2
Ocean Cl CT7. . . . . .81 B8
Ocean View
Broadstairs CT10 . . . . .84 A1
Herne Bay CT6 . . . . .77 F6
Ocelot Ct **6** ME4. . . . . . .64 B3
Ockham Dr BR5 . . . . . . .31 A1
OCKLEY. 341 A3
Ockley Cl DA14. . . . . .30 E5
Ockley La TN18. . . . . . .341 A3
Ockley Rd TN18 . . . . . .341 A2
Octavia Ct ME5. . . . . .97 B3
Octavian Dr CT21. . . . . .332 A3
Octavian Way TN23. . . .299 E5
Octavia Way **12** SE28 . . . .3 B6
Odd Rise ME7 . . . . .65 A5
Odeon Ct **1** E16 . . . . .1 A8
Odeon Par SE9 . . . . .11 E3
Odiham Dr ME16 . . . . . .161 C7
Odo Rd CT17 . . . . .310 C8
Offenham Rd SE9 . . . . . .29 F4
Offen's Dr TN12 . . . . . . .260 E3
OFFHAM 158 D8
Offham Prim Sch
ME19 . . . . .158 D8
Offham Rd ME19 . . . . . .159 A2
Officers' Rd ME4 . . . . . . .64 B8
Officers Terr ME4 . . . . . .63 F7
Offley Cl CT9. . . . . .51 C1
Ogilby Ct SE18 . . . . .1 F2
Ogilvy Ct CT10. . . . . .83 E7
Okehampton Cl TN24. . .268 F7
Okehampton Cres DA16 13 C6
Okemore Gdns BR5 . . . .54 C5
Olantigh Ct CT7 . . . . .81 A7

Olantigh Rd TN25, CT4 .237 F3
Olave Rd CT9. . . . . .51 B1
Old Ash Cl TN24 . . . . . .268 C5
Old Ashford Rd
Charing TN27. . . . . . . .234 C7
Lenham ME17. . . . . . .199 E5
Old Badgins Rd ME13.170 B6
Old Bailey The ME17. . .198 E6
Old Bakery Cl TN29. . . .365 E4
Old Bakery Mews
ME13. . . . . .139 F4
Old Bakery The ME12. . .46 F5
Old Barn Cl
Gillingham ME7. . . . . . .97 F6
Kemsing ME7. . . . . . . .123 A2
Tonbridge TN9. . . . . . .253 F8
Old Barn Rd ME19 . . . .127 E2
Old Barn Way DA7. . . . . .14 D4
OLD BEXLEY 32 B8
Old Bexley Bsns Pk DA5 32 B8
Old Bexley CE Prim Sch
DA5 . . . . .31 F7
Old Bexley La DA5. . . . . .32 A8
Old Billet La ME12. . . . . .48 C6
Old Boundary Rd CT8. . .50 D1
Old Bridge Rd CT5 . . . . .74 E1
OLDBURY. 156 B6
Oldbury Cl
Oldbury TN15 . . . . . . .156 B5
Orpington BR5 . . . . .54 D5
Oldbury Cotts TN15. . . .156 B6
Oldbury La TN15 . . . . . .156 B6
Old Carriageway The
Gillingham ME7. . . . . . .97 F4
Sevenoaks TN13 . . . . .153 C5
Old Chapel Rd ME8. . . . .55 C2
Old Charlton Rd CT16 278 D2
Old Chatham Rd
Kit's Coty ME20. . . . . .129 D6
Sandling ME14 . . . . . .129 F1
Old Church Cl **3** BR6. . . .54 B1
Oldchurch Ct **3** ME8 161 E3
Old Church La TN12. . . .191 E4
Old Church Rd
Burham ME1. . . . . .95 C1
Chartham CT4. . . . . . .173 E1
Mereworth ME18, TN12 191 D5
Pembury TN2. . . . . . . .255 D2
Old Clem Sq **12** SE18 . . . .12 A8
Old Coach Rd TN15. . . .124 E5
Old Coachworks The **10**
CT13 . . . . .148 F1
Old Coal Yd The **7** CT5 74 D1
Old Coastgaurd Cotts
TN29 . . . . .380 D3
Old Corn Stores The
ME14. . . . . .163 C4
Old Court Hill CT15,
CT3 . . . . .211 C6
Old Court Ho The
TN13 . . . . .154 E5
Old Courtyard The BR1 52 B8
Old Crossing Rd **1** CT9 82 B8
Old Dairy Cl **4** CT11. . . .117 F7
Old Dairy The TN12. . . .224 E6
Old Dairy Yd CT12. . . . . .117 C7
Old Diary Mews The
ME12. . . . . .46 D7
Old Dover Rd
Barham CT4 . . . . .210 B1
5 Canterbury CT1 . . .175 B6
Capel-le-Ferne CT18. . .308 C1
Greenwich SE3 . . . . . . .11 B7
Old Downs DA3. . . . . . . .58 E4
Old Downs The DA3. . . .58 E4
Old Dr ME15. . . . . .194 F6
Old Dungeness
Lighthouse★
TN29 . . . . .380 D2
Old Farm Ave DA15. . . . .30 E6
Old Farm Cl CT5. . . . . . .108 C6
Old Farm Gdns BR8. . . . .55 F6
Old Farmhouse The
BR8. . . . . .32 E1
Old Farm Rd DA7. . . . . . .80 D7
Old Farm Road E DA15. .31 A6
Old Farm Road W DA15 30 F6
Old Ferry Rd ME9 . . . . . .68 E7
Oldfield Cl Bromley BR1. 52 F5
Gillingham ME8. . . . . . .98 D8
Maidstone ME15. . . . .162 E1
Oldfield Dr ME1. . . . . . . .95 C5
Oldfield Rd Bexley DA7 . .13 E5
Bromley BR1. . . . . .52 F5
Old Fire Sta The SE18 . .12 B7
Old Flour Mill The
CT17 . . . . .278 B2
Old Fold CT5. . . . . .109 C8
Old Folkestone Rd
CT17 . . . . .310 A4
Old Forge La ME9 . . . . .132 F3
Old Forge Way DA14 . . .31 B4
Old Garden Ct CT4 . . . .173 E1
Old Gardens Cl TN2 . . .314 B8
Old Gate Rd ME13 . . . . .138 B8
Old Gdn The TN13. . . . .153 D4
Old George Ct ME3. . . . .40 F4
Old Green Rd
Broadstairs CT10 . . . . .83 F7
Margate CT9. . . . . .51 C1
Old Hadlow Rd TN10 . .222 F4
Old Hall Dr CT12 . . . . . .116 C5
Old Halls The **8** CT5 . .74 D2
Old Ham La ME17. . . . . .199 A4
Oldhawe Hill CT3, CT6. 111 D7
Old High St The CT20. .335 E5
Old Hill Chislehurst BR7 . 53 A8
Orpington BR6 . . . . .86 E4
Old Hockley Rd ME13. . .40 B1
Old Homesdale Rd BR2 52 C5
Old Hook Rd ME12. . . . . .47 F2
Old Hop Gdn The
TN31 . . . . .367 C2

Old Ho The BR7. . . . . . . .53 D8
Oldhouse La TN29. . . . .362 E1
Old House La
Hartlip ME9. . . . . .99 E4
Langton Green TN3. . . .284 D4
Old Kent Rd TN12 . . . . .257 A6
Old Kingsdown Cl CT10 83 E3
Old La Ightham TN15. . .156 C4
Tatsfield TN16. . . . . . .150 D6
Old Lain ME17. . . . . . . .198 F6
Old Lenham Rd ME9. . .167 C4
Old London Rd
Badgers Mount TN14. . . .88 A1
Halstead TN14 . . . . . . .120 E4
Hythe CT21. . . . . .332 F2
Tonbridge TN10. . . . . .222 C3
Wrotham TN15. . . . . . .124 F4
Old Loose Cl ME15 . . . .194 E5
Old Loose Hill ME15. . .194 F4
Old Maidstone Rd
Keycol ME9. . . . . .100 F5
Sidcup DA14. . . . . .31 F1
Oldman Cl SE12 . . . . . . .29 B6
Old Manor Dr DA12. . . . .37 C7
Old Manor Way
Bexley DA7. . . . . .14 D5
Bromley BR7. . . . . .29 F3
Old Market The TN12. .259 D6
Old Mead CT19 . . . . . . .335 A7
Old Mill Cl DA4. . . . . . . .56 E1
Old Mill Court TN27. . .295 A1
Old Mill La ME20. . . . . .129 C3
Old Mill Mews CT19 . . .334 D7
Old Mill Rd
Maidstone ME17. . . . .163 F1
Woolwich SE18. . . . . . .12 D8
Old Oast Bsns Ctr The
ME20. . . . . .129 A1
Old Orch Ashford TN23 299 D8
Charcott TN11. . . . . . .220 A3
Old Orchard TN18. . . . .356 B5
Old Orchard La ME9. . .127 D1
Old Orchard The ME8 . .99 A8
Old Otford Rd TN14. . . .122 B1
Old Palace Rd CT4 . . . .176 C3
Old Park Ave
Canterbury CT1. . . . . .143 C2
Dover CT16. . . . . .278 A3
Old Park Cl CT15. . . . . .278 A4
Old Park Ct CT1 . . . . . . .143 C2
Old Park Hill CT16. . . . .278 B4
Old Park Rd
Dover CT16. . . . . .278 B2
Woolwich SE2. . . . . .3 A1
Old Parsonage Ct
ME19. . . . . .159 C7
Old Pattens La ME4 . . . .63 D2
Old Perry St
Chislehurst BR7 . . . . . . .30 E1
Northfleet DA11. . . . . . .36 E6
Old Pk Pl CT15. . . . . . . .278 A5
Old Polhill TN14. . . . . . .121 D4
Old Police Sta The **4**
CT5. . . . . .74 D2
Old Pond Rd TN23. . . . .299 F8
Old Post Office La SE3 .11 B4
Old Print Ho **4** CT16 .310 E7
Old Printworks Cl **5**
CT5 . . . . .108 D8
Old Priory Sch The
CT11. . . . . .117 D6
Old Railway Works (Ind
Est) TN24 . . . . .300 D8
Old Rd Chatham ME4. . . .63 F4
Crayford DA1, DA7. . . . .14 D3
East Peckham TN12 . . .225 A6
Elham CT4. . . . . .273 F4
Sarre CT7. . . . . .113 C6
Wateringbury ME18. . .192 C7
Old Rectory Cl
Hawkinge CT18. . . . . .307 B4
Mersham TN25. . . . . . .301 E5
Old Rectory The TN25 .236 E2
Old Regent Dr TN17 . . .343 E3
Old Riding School The
TN3 . . . . .312 B2
Old Road E DA12. . . . . . .37 D7
Old Road W DA11 . . . . . .37 A7
Old Roman Rd CT15. . .247 C1
Orchard Ave
Aylesford ME20. . . . . .128 E1
Bexley DA17. . . . . .13 F8
Dartford DA1. . . . . .33 B7
Deal CT14. . . . . .215 B5
Gravesend DA11. . . . . . .37 B3
Rochester ME2. . . . . . .39 F1
Orchard Bank ME17 . . .196 B1
Orchard Bsns Ctr
Maidstone ME16. . . . .161 C8
Paddock Wood TN12. .257 A8
Royal Tunbridge Wells
TN2 . . . . .286 D8
Tonbridge TN9. . . . . . .222 C1
Orchard Cl Bexley DA7 . .13 C8
Canterbury CT2. . . . . .142 F4
Coxheath ME17. . . . . .194 C3
Edenbridge TN8 . . . . . .217 B2
Horsmonden TN12. . . .289 F6
Langley Heath ME17. . .196 A4
Littlebourne CT3. . . . . .176 F7
Mersham TN25. . . . . . .301 E3
Minster (Thanet) CT12 .115 B7
New Barn DA3. . . . . . . .59 B7
Ramsgate CT12 . . . . . . .83 B3
Royal Tunbridge Wells
TN2 . . . . .286 D6
Sevenoaks TN14 . . . . .154 C7
Whitfield CT16. . . . . . .277 F8
Whitstable CT5. . . . . . . .74 F3
Wingham CT3. . . . . . . .178 A7

Old Station Rd TN5. . . .336 E6
Old Surrenden Manor
TN26 . . . . .298 C5
Old Surrenden Manor Rd
TN26 . . . . .298 C5
Old Tannery Cl TN30. . .344 F7
Old Terry's Lodge Rd
TN15 . . . . .124 A4
Old Timber Top Cotts The
TN13 . . . . .154 C4
Old Timber Yard E
CT12. . . . . .117 A8
Old Timber Yard Ind Est
CT11. . . . . .117 A7
Old Tovil Rd ME15. . . . .162 A2
Old Town Gaol Mus★ **18**
CT17 . . . . .310 D8
Old Trafford Cl ME16. . .161 B6
Old Tramyard **4** SE18 . . . 2 B7
Old Tree La ME17. . . . . .195 D3
Old Tree Rd CT3. . . . . . .112 B7
Old Tye Ave TN16. . . . . .118 E3
Old Valley Rd CT4 . . . . .242 F7
Old Vicarage Gdn **2** 143 F6
Old Vicarage Gdns
TN25. . . . . .237 E2
Old Vicarage Sch The
TN12. . . . . .259 E7
Old Vicarage The
Meopham DA13. . . . . . .60 A1
Woodnesborough CT13 180 C7
Old Walting St **21** CT1.174 F8
Old Wardsdown TN5 . .339 B3
Old Watling St
Gravesend DA11. . . . . . .37 A3
Rochester ME2. . . . . . .62 B8
Old Way TN26 . . . . .361 D7
Old Weavers Cotts
TN17. . . . . .342 D5
Old Whetsted Rd TN12 225 A2
Old White Hart Cotts
TN16. . . . . .152 C5
OLD WIVES LEES 172 C3
Old Wlk The TN1 . . . . . .122 C2
Old Yard The TN16. . . . .152 C3
Old Yews The DA3. . . . . .59 B6
Oleander Cl BR6. . . . . . .86 D5
Olive Gr **2** CT11. . . . . . .117 F7
Oliver Cl Chatham ME4. .64 B2
West Thurrock RM20. . .16 F7
Oliver Cres DA4. . . . . . . .56 F2
Oliver Ct SE18. . . . . .2 C2
Olive Rd DA1. . . . . .33 D7
Oliver Gdns E6. . . . . .1 E8
Oliver North Ho ME15 .193 E7
Oliver Rd
Staplehurst TN12 . . . . .260 E4
Swanley BR8. . . . . .55 D6
West Thurrock RM20 . . .16 F7
Oliver's Mill DA3. . . . . . .91 E8
Olivers Row ME14 . . . . .163 C4
Oliver Twist Cl ME1 . . . .63 B4
Olivier Dr ME1. . . . . .40 B2
Olivine Cl Chatham ME5 130 A8
Sittingbourne ME10 . . .101 C7
Olliffe Cl ME5. . . . . .96 F2
Olron Cres DA6. . . . . . . .13 E2
Olven Rd SE18. . . . . .12 C8
Olyffe Ave DA16. . . . . . . .13 A5
Omer Ave CT9. . . . . .51 C2
O'Neill Path **11** SE18. . . . .12 A8
Onslow Cres BR7 . . . . . .53 B8
Onslow Dr DA14. . . . . . . .31 D6
Onslow Rd ME1. . . . . . . .63 D3
Ontario Way CT16. . . . .278 B3
Onyx Dr ME10 . . . . .101 D6
Opal Cl E16. . . . . .1 D7
Opal Gn ME5. . . . . .97 B2
Openshaw Rd SE2. . . . . . 3 B2
Opie Wlk CT18 . . . . .306 F3
Orache Dr ME14. . . . . . .162 E5
Orange Court La BR6. . . .86 A2
Orangery La SE9 . . . . . . .11 F2
Orange St CT1. . . . . .174 F8
Orange Terr ME1. . . . . . . .63 D5
Orbital One DA1. . . . . . . .34 B6
Orbital Pk TN24. . . . . . .300 F6
Orbit Cl ME5 . . . . .130 A8
Orchard Ave
Aylesford ME20. . . . . .128 E1
Bexley DA17. . . . . .13 F8
Dartford DA1. . . . . .33 B7
Deal CT14. . . . . .215 B5
Gravesend DA11. . . . . . .37 B3
Rochester ME2. . . . . . .39 F1
Orchard Bank ME17 . . .196 B1

Old Surrenden Manor
Orchard Cotts
Nettlestead Green
ME18 . . . . .192 C1
Orchard Cres
Horsmonden TN12 . . . .290 A6
Wateringbury ME18 . . .192 D6
Orchard Ct
Ashford TN23 . . . . .300 B8
Benenden TN17. . . . . . .342 D6
Chillenden CT3 . . . . . . .211 F8
Herne Bay CT6 . . . . .76 F1
Sidcup DA15 . . . . .12 F2
Orchard Dr
Crabble CT17 . . . . .277 E3
Edenbridge TN8 . . . . . .217 B2
Hythe CT21 . . . . .333 B1
Littlestone-on-Sea TN28 373 E6
Maidstone ME14 . . . . . .162 E4
Meopham Station DA13 . 59 F4
Newington ME9 . . . . . .100 A5
Tonbridge TN10 . . . . . .222 C5
Wye TN25 . . . . .237 F1
Orchard End CT11 . . . . .117 A5
Orchard Field TN26 . . . .297 D4
Orchard Fields CT21. . .304 E2
Orchard Flats CT1 . . . . .175 D7
Orchard Gdns CT9 . . . . .82 A8
Orchard Glade TN27 . . .262 E5
Orchard Gn Bromley BR1 52 C8
Orpington BR6 . . . . .86 B8
Orchard Gr
Larkfield ME20 . . . . . . .128 B2
Minster (Sheppey) ME12 .47 C6
Orpington BR6 . . . . .53 F1
Royal Tunbridge Wells
TN1 . . . . .286 B5
Whitstable CT5 . . . . . . .108 D8
Orchard Hill ME14 . . . . . .14 E2
Orchard Ho Erith DA8 . .14 F6
9 Faversham ME13 . . .138 C7
Orchard Hts TN23 . . . . .267 F5
Orchard Ind Est ME15. .195 F3
Orchard La
Ashford TN24 . . . . .268 F6
Challock TN25 . . . . . . .203 B2
Monkton CT7, CT12 . . .114 A8
St Nicholas at Wade CT7 .79 F1
Orchardlea DA13 . . . . . . .35 F3
Orchard Lea TN11. . . . . .221 F5
Orchard Mews CT14. . . .215 D5
Orchard Pk CT6 . . . . .77 D4
Orchard Pl
Coxheath ME17 . . . . . .194 C3
Faversham ME13 . . . . .138 D7
Keston BR2. . . . . .85 D7
2 Maidstone ME16. . . .161 E3
Orpington BR5 . . . . .54 C6
Sittingbourne ME10 . . .102 A3
Sundridge TN14 . . . . . .152 D3
Orchard Prim Sch DA14 31 B3
Orchard Rd Bexley DA16 13 A4
Bromley BR1. . . . . .52 C8
East Peckham TN12 . . .225 A6
Eastry CT13 . . . . .180 B3
Erith DA17. . . . . .4 A2
Herne Bay CT6 . . . . .76 F3
Margate CT9. . . . . .82 A8
Northfleet DA11. . . . . . .36 C6
Orpington BR6 . . . . .86 B5
Otford TN14 . . . . .121 F3
Pratt's Bottom BR6. . . . .87 C1
Sevenoaks TN13 . . . . .153 E5
Sidcup DA14. . . . . .30 E4
St Mary's Bay TN29 . . .366 A5
Swanscombe DA10. . . . .17 E2
Tenterden TN30 . . . . . .324 A3
Orchard Residences The
CT1 . . . . .175 A5
Orchard Rise TN3 . . . . .312 B7
Orchard Rise E DA15. . .12 F2
Orchard Rise W DA15. . .12 E2
Orchard Row CT6 . . . . . .77 A1
Orchard Sch The CT1 . .174 F6
Orchard St Ctr **5** DA1. .15 C1
Orchard St
Canterbury CT2. . . . . .142 E1
Dartford DA1. . . . . .15 E1
Gillingham ME8. . . . . . .98 E8
Maidstone ME15. . . . .162 A3
Orchards The CT4. . . . .273 F4
Orchard Terr DA9 . . . . . .16 E2
Orchard The
Maidstone ME14. . . . .163 B4
Monkton CT12. . . . . . .114 D6
Sevenoaks TN13 . . . . .153 E6
Swanley BR8. . . . . .55 D7
ORCHARD VALLEY. . . .333 B3
Orchard Valley CT21. . .333 A2
Orchard View Ash CT3 .147 F1
Detling ME14 . . . . .163 A8
Tenterden TN30 . . . . . .345 C8
Teynham ME9 . . . . . . .103 C3
Orchard Villas
Chainhurst TN12. . . . . .227 A4
1 Chatham ME4 . . . . . .64 B3
Chislehurst BR7. . . . . . .30 E2
Kearsney CT17 . . . . . . .277 E4
Sidcup DA14. . . . . .31 C2
Orchard Way
Cranbrook TN17 . . . . . .320 B4
Dartford DA2. . . . . .33 D5
Eastchurch ME12. . . . . .48 D1
Horsmonden TN12. . . .290 A6
Kemsing TN15. . . . . . .123 A2
Oxted RH8. . . . . .183 A2
Peasmarsh TN31. . . . . .367 C1
Snodland ME6. . . . . . .127 F7
Orchid Cl
Minster (Sheppey)
ME12. . . . . .47 A4
1 Newham E6. . . . . .1 E8
Rochester ME2. . . . . . .62 C6
Orchid Ct TN23 . . . . . . .300 D2
Orchidhurst TN2 . . . . . .286 D7

Orchids The
Etchinghill CT18 . . . . . .305 D7
Mersham TN25 . . . . . . .301 E6
Ordinance Way TN23 . .267 F2
Ordnance Rd
Gravesend DA12. . . . . . .21 C1
Woolwich SE18. . . . . . . .12 A8
Ordnance St ME4. . . . . . .63 E4
Ordnance Terr **9** ME4. .63 E4
Oregon Sq ME6. . . . . . . .53 D1
Orford Ct **7** DA2. . . . . . . .16 B1
Orgarswick Ave TN29 .366 D2
Orgarswick Way TN29 366 C2
Oriental Rd E16 . . . . .1 D5
Orient Court ME19. . . . .159 B3
Orient Pl CT2. . . . . .142 F1
Oriole Way
Larkfield ME20. . . . . . .127 F2
Woolwich SE28. . . . . . . .3 B6
Orion Rd ME1. . . . . .96 C5
Orion Way TN24. . . . . . .300 E8
Orissa Rd SE18. . . . . .2 E1
Orlestone Gdns BR6. . . .87 E5
Orlestone View TN26 . .348 E5
Orlestone Villas TN26 349 A8
Orlick Rd DA12. . . . . .38 E7
Ormesby Cl SE28 . . . . . . .3 D6
Ormiston Rd SE10. . . . . .1 A1
Ormonde Ave BR6. . . . . .86 C8
Ormonde Ct CT21 . . . . .333 C1
Ormonde Rd
11 Folkestone CT20. . .335 E6
Hythe CT21. . . . . .333 C1
Ormsby Gn ME8 . . . . . . .98 E3
Ormsby Point **8** SE18. . . .2 B2
Orpines The ME18. . . . .192 F7
ORPINGTON. 54 C2
Orpington By-Pass
TN14. . . . . .88 A2
Orpington Coll of FE
BR6. . . . . .54 A1
Orpington Hospl BR6. . .86 F6
Orpington Sta BR6 . . . . .86 E8
Orpington Trad Est **10**
BR5. . . . . .54 C5
Orpins Cl TN25 . . . . . . .302 D6
Orr Cl CT18. . . . . .306 F4
Orwell Cl ME20. . . . . . . .127 F3
Orwell Cl RM13. . . . . .4 D8
Orwell Spike ME19. . . . .159 A5
Osberton Rd SE12. . . . . .11 A4
Osborne Gdns CT6 . . . . .77 D4
Osborne Rd
Ashford TN24. . . . . . . .300 F8
Bexley DA17. . . . . .13 F8
Gillingham ME7. . . . . . .64 C5
Kingsdown CT14. . . . . .248 C6
Osborne Terr CT9 . . . . . .50 J1
Osbourn Ave CT8. . . . . . .81 E8
Osbourne Rd
Broadstairs CT10 . . . . .83 F4
Dartford DA2. . . . . .16 B1
Oscar Rd CT10 . . . . .84 B4
Osgood Ave BR6. . . . . . .86 F5
Osgood Gdns **1** BR6. . . .86 F5
Osier Field TN24 . . . . . .268 E7
Osier Rd ME9 . . . . .103 E3
Oslin Wlk ME19. . . . . . .159 C2
OSMERS HILL. 336 F7
Osmers Hill TN5. . . . . . .336 F7
Osmunda Ct TN2 . . . . . .286 C4
Osney Ho **4** SE2 . . . . .3 D4
Osney Way DA12. . . . . . .37 F6
Osprey Ave ME5. . . . . . . .64 C2
Osprey Cl Newham E6 . . .1 E8
Orpington BR2 . . . . .52 E1
Whitstable CT5. . . . . . .108 C7
Osprey Ct
2 Dover CT16. . . . . . .278 B2
Hawkinge CT18. . . . . .306 F3
Sittingbourne ME10 . . .102 A3
Osprey Wlk ME20. . . . . .127 F1
OSPRINGE. 138 B6
Ospringe CE Prim Sch
ME13 . . . . .138 A6
Ospringe Ct SE9. . . . . . . .12 D1
Ospringe Pl
Faversham ME13 . . . . .138 B6
Royal Tunbridge Wells
TN2 . . . . .286 F6
Ospringe Rd ME13. . . . .138 B7
Ospringe St ME13 . . . . .138 A6
Ostend CT10 . . . . .68 F1
Osterberg Rd DA1. . . . . .15 F3
Osterley Cl BR5. . . . . . . .54 A8
Ostlers Ct **2** ME6 . . . . .128 A8
Ostlers La CT7 . . . . .113 C6
Oswald Drive ME2. . . . . .62 E5
Oswald Pl CT17. . . . . . .278 B2
Oswald Rd CT17 . . . . . .278 B2
OTFORD. 122 A3
Otford Cl Bromley BR1. . .53 A6
Sidcup DA5. . . . . .14 B1
Otford La TN14. . . . . . . .121 B6
Otford Prim Sch TN14 .122 B3
Otford Rd TN14. . . . . . .154 B7
Otford Sta TN14 . . . . . .122 C3
OTHAM. 196 B7
Otham Ct **1** TN12 . . . . .143 A4
OTHAM HOLE 196 B6
Otham La ME15 . . . . . . .163 C2
Otham St
Maidstone ME15. . . . .163 C2
Otham ME15. . . . . .196 B7
Otley Rd E6. . . . . .1 C7
Otlinge Rd BR5. . . . . . . .54 D5
Ottawa Cres CT9 . . . . . .278 C3
Ottawa Rd RM18. . . . . . .19 A5
Ottawa Way CT10. . . . . .278 B3
Otterbourne Pl ME15 .162 E1
Otterden Cl
Ashford TN23. . . . . . . .299 F6
Orpington BR6. . . . . . . .86 E6

Otterden Rd ME16.....168 D3
OTTERHAM QUAY.....66 C3
Otterham Quay La ME8 66 B2
Otteridge Rd ME14.....163 A3
Otterpool La CT21,
TN25.....331 D4
Otters Cl BR5.....54 C5
Ottershaw Ho BR5.....54 B8
OTTINGE.....273 D1
Otway St Chatham ME4...64 A3
Gillingham ME7.....64 D6
Otway Terr 1 ME4.....64 A3
Oulton Cl SE28.....3 C7
Our Lady of Grace RC Prim
Sch 7 SE7.....11 B8
Our Lady of Hartley RC
Prim Sch DA3.....58 F4
Our Lady of the Rosary RC
Prim Sch DA15.....12 E1
Our Lady's RC Prim Sch 11
DA1.....15 D1
OUT ELMSTEAD.....209 F2
Out Elmstead La CT4..209 F2
Outfall Ave TN29.....380 C2
Oval The
Dymchurch TN29.....352 D1
New Barn DA3.....59 C6
Sidcup DA15.....31 A8
Ovenden Rd
Sevenoaks TN14.....152 F1
Sundridge TN14.....152 D6
Overcliffe DA11.....19 A1
Overcourt Cl DA15.....13 B1
Overdale TN14.....187 B2
Overland La CT3.....147 A3
Overmead Eltham DA15..30 D8
Swanley BR8.....55 E4
Over Minnis DA3.....91 F7
OVERSLAND.....171 F7
Overton Ho ME12.....28 C2
Overton Rd SE2.....3 D3
Overy Liberty DA1.....33 E8
Overy St DA1.....15 E1
Owen Cl
2 East Malling ME19 .159 F8
Woolwich SE28.....3 C5
Owenite St SE2.....3 B2
Owen's Cl CT21.....334 B3
Owens Court Cotts
ME13.....170 F8
Owen Sq CT14.....215 B2
Owens Way ME7.....65 A6
Owletts * DA12.....60 F6
Owletts Cl ME15.....195 D8
Owl House Gdns *
TN3.....316 F2
Owl's Hatch Rd CT6.....76 C1
Oxenden Cnr CT3.....77 F1
Oxenden Cres CT3.....18 A8
Oxenden Park Dr CT6 ..76 E4
Oxenden Rd CT20.....334 E4
Oxenden St CT6.....76 E5
Oxenden Way CT4.....242 F8
Oxenden Wood Rd BR6 87 C4
Oxenhill Rd TN15.....122 E2
Oxenhoath Rd TN11 ..190 D4
Oxen Lease TN23.....299 E8
Oxenturn Rd TN25.....269 E8
Oxfield TN8.....217 D3
Oxford Cl
Gravesend DA12.....37 F6
5 Whitstable CT5.....74 D1
Oxford Ct
Canterbury CT1.....174 F7
6 Sidcup DA14.....30 F4
Oxford Mans 6 CT5.....74 D1
Oxford Mews DA5.....32 A8
Oxford Rd
Canterbury CT1.....174 F7
Gillingham ME7.....64 D3
Maidstone ME15.....195 D8
Sidcup DA14.....31 B3
Oxford St
6 Margate CT9.....50 J1
Snodland ME6.....128 A8
Whitstable CT5.....74 D1
Oxford Terr CT20.....335 D4
Oxhawth Cres BR2.....53 B3
Ox La TN30.....324 B2
Ox Lea TN3.....285 A3
Oxleas E6.....2 B7
Oxleas Cl DA16.....12 D5
Oxleas Wood Nature
Reserve * SE18.....12 C4
Oxley Shaw La ME19...127 E2
Oxney Cl CT7.....80 F7
Oxney Cotts TN30.....361 A4
Oyster Catchers Cl E16...1 B7
Oyster Cl Herne Bay CT6 .76 B3
Sittingbourne ME10 ..101 E6
Oyster Mews 4 CT5.....74 D1
Ozengell Pl CT12.....83 A2
Ozolins Way E16.....1 A7

P

Pacific Cl DA10.....17 E2
Pacific Rd E16.....1 A7
Packer Pl ME5.....97 A8
Packer's La 5 CT11 ..117 E7
Packham Cl BR6.....87 C7
Packham Rd DA11.....36 F5
Packhorse Rd TN13 ..153 C4
Packmores Rd SE9.....12 E2
Padbrook RH8.....183 A6
Padbrook Cl RH8.....183 B6
Padbrook La CT3.....146 D6
PADDLESWORTH.....306 C4
Paddlesworth Rd ME6..94 D1
Paddock.....202 E1
Paddock Cl Deal CT14 ..214 F5

Paddock Cl continued
Folkestone CT20.....334 F5
Fordcombe TN3.....284 B5
Greenwich SE3.....11 A5
Limpsfield RH8.....183 A4
Lydd TN29.....376 B6
Marlpit Hill TN8.....217 C3
Orpington BR6.....86 B6
Platt TN15.....157 C6
Sutton at Hone DA4.....57 C8
Paddock Rd
Ashford TN23.....299 E7
Bexley DA6.....13 E3
2 Birchington CT7.....81 A7
Paddocks Cl BR5.....87 D8
Paddocks The
Addington ME19.....126 D4
Ashford TN23.....267 C1
Broadstairs CT10.....83 F7
Cowden TN8.....282 B7
Densole CT18.....307 A8
Gillingham ME7.....98 A5
Herne Bay CT6.....77 F5
Margate CT9.....51 C1
Sevenoaks TN13.....154 D3
Paddock The
Ashurst TN3.....283 F5
Canterbury CT1.....175 B8
Chatham ME4.....63 F4
Dover CT16.....310 D8
Farthing Street Br.....85 E2
Hadlow TN11.....190 E1
Old Wives Lees CT4 ..172 C2
Pembury TN2.....287 C6
Vigo Village DA13.....125 F7
Westerham TN16.....151 C1
Woodchurch TN26.....326 A1
Paddock View CT5.....108 E7
Paddock Way BR7.....30 D1
PADDOCK WOOD.....256 F8
Paddock Wood Bsns Ctr
TN12.....257 A7
Paddock Wood Prim Sch
TN12.....257 A7
Paddock Wood Sta
TN12.....257 A7
Pad's Hill ME15.....162 A4
Padsole La ME15.....162 A4
Padstow Cl 3 BR6.....86 F6
Padstow Manor 1 ME7 64 C6
Padwell La TN23.....299 C8
Paffard Cl CT2.....143 F6
Paffard Ct CT2.....143 F6
Pageant Cl RM18.....19 C6
Page Cl DA2.....35 C5
Page Cres DA11.....36 D4
Page Heath La BR1.....52 D6
Page Heath Villas BR1 .52 D6
Pagehurst Rd TN12.....260 B3
Page Pl CT19.....335 D8
Page Rd CT18.....306 F3
Paget Gdns BR7.....53 B8
Paget Rise SE18.....12 A7
Paget Row ME7.....64 C5
Paget St ME7.....64 C5
Paget Terr SE18.....12 A7
Pagitt St ME4.....63 E3
Paiges Farm CT14 ..187 C2
Paine Ave TN29.....376 C6
Painesfield Cl TN29 ..352 C4
Pains Hill RH8.....183 C4
Painters Ash La DA11...36 D5
Painters Ash Prim Sch
DA11.....36 D5
PAINTER'S FORSTAL .137 E3
Painter's Forstal Rd
ME13.....137 E3
Palace Ave ME15.....162 A4
Palace Cl CT5.....75 B2
Palace Cotts ME9.....167 F8
Palace Ct
5 Bromley BR1.....52 B8
Eltham SE9.....11 F1
Gillingham ME5.....64 D2
Hythe CT21.....333 C2
Palace Gr BR1.....52 B8
Palace Ind Est ME15...195 F4
Palace Rd Bromley BR1 .52 B8
Hill Park TN16.....151 A6
Palace St 18 CT1.....143 A1
Palace View
Bromley BR1.....52 B8
Lewisham SE12.....29 A6
Palace Wood Prim Sch
ME16.....161 C6
Pal Cres CT7.....81 E5
Pale Park La DA12.....61 E8
Palewell Cl BR5.....54 B7
Palladian Circus 1
DA9.....17 C3
Pallant Way BR6.....86 A7
Pallet Way ME6.....11 E6
Palmar Cres DA7.....14 A5
Palmar Rd Bexley DA7 .14 A5
Maidstone ME16.....161 D6
Palmars Cross Hill
CT2.....142 A1
PALMARSH.....353 D7
Palmarsh Ave CT21...353 D7
Palmarsh Cres CT21 ..353 D7
Palmarsh Prim Sch
CT21.....353 D8
Palmarsh Rd BR5.....54 D5
Palm Ave DA14.....31 D2
Palm Bay Ave CT9.....51 D3
Palm Bay CP Sch CT9 .51 D3
Palm Bay Gdns CT9.....51 C3
Palmbeach Ave CT21..353 D8
Palm Ct CT8.....50 C1
Palmeira Rd DA7.....13 D4
Palmer Ave DA12.....37 D4
Palmer Cl CT6.....111 B8
Palmer Cres CT9.....83 C8

Palmer Rd CT3.....178 A8
Palmers Brook TN11 ..190 F2
PALMER'S GREEN.....289 D8
Palmers Green La
TN12.....257 D1
Palmers Orch TN14....121 F8
Palmerston Ave
Broadstairs CT10.....84 B3
Deal CT14.....215 C4
Palmerston Cres SE18 .12 C8
Palmerston Ct CT14 ..215 D2
Palmerston Rd
Chatham ME4.....63 F1
Dover CT16.....277 F4
Grays RM20.....17 D8
Orpington BR6.....86 C5
Palmerston St 4
CT19.....335 D6
Palmerston Wlk ME10 102 C4
Palmers Yd TN27.....262 E5
PALMSTEAD.....241 D5
Palm Tree Cl CT15.....245 D7
Palm Tree Way CT18 ..305 B7
Palting Way CT20.....335 B4
Pamela Ct ME4.....64 D5
Panbro Ho SE18.....11 F6
Panfield Rd SE2.....3 A3
Pankhurst Ave E16.....1 B5
Pankhurst Ho SE18.....12 A7
Pankhurst Rd ME3.....41 D6
Pannell Dr CT18.....306 F4
Pannell Rd ME3.....27 A6
Pantenry La ME9.....102 E2
Panter's BR8.....32 F1
Pantheon Gdns TN23 ..299 F5
Pantiles Sh Ctr The
TN1.....286 A2
Pantiles The Bexley DA7 .13 E5
Bromley BR1.....52 E6
20 Royal Tunbridge Wells
TN2.....286 A2
Panton Cl ME5.....97 C4
Pantyles The TN14.....186 B5
Paper La TN14.....300 F6
Papillons Wlk SE3.....11 A4
Papion Gr ME5.....96 E2
Papworth Ct 1 CT19 .335 A7
Parade CT1.....174 F8
Parade Rd CT20.....334 F3
Parade The
Ashford TN24.....300 F5
Birchington CT7.....80 D8
Crayford DA1.....14 F2
Eastry CT13.....180 B2
Folkestone CT20.....335 E5
Gravesend DA11.....37 D6
Greatstone-on-Sea TN28,
TN29.....377 E7
Kemsing TN15.....122 E2
Margate CT9.....51 C1
Meopham Station DA13 .60 A2
Rochester ME2.....62 E8
Sittingbourne ME10 ..101 F2
Staplehurst TN12.....260 F3
Swanscombe DA10.....17 F2
Paradise CT11.....117 D7
Paradise Cotts ME9.....99 E5
Paradise Path SE28.....3 A5
Paradise Pl 14 SE18.....1 E2
Paradise Row CT13.....148 F1
Paragon CT11.....117 E5
Paragon Cl E16.....1 A7
Paragon St CT11.....117 D5
Paragon The SE3.....11 A5
Paraker Way CT21.....334 B4
PARAMOUR STREET ..147 D7
Parbrook Rd ME3.....24 B2
Pardoner Cl CT2.....174 C7
Pardoners Way CT16 ..278 A3
Parfitt Way CT16.....278 B2
Parham Cl CT1.....143 B2
Parham Ct CT1.....143 B2
Parham Rd
Canterbury CT1.....143 B2
Chatham ME4.....63 F2
Paris Cnr TN26.....297 F6
Parish CE Prim Sch
BR1.....29 A1
Parish Cl CT10.....83 E6
Parish Gate Dr DA15...12 E1
Parish Rd
Chartham CT4.....173 C3
Minster (Sheppey) ME12 .47 A5
Parish Wharf 5 SE18.....1 E2
Park App DA16.....13 B3
Park Ave Birchington CT7 81 A6
Broadstairs CT10.....83 E2
Bromley BR1.....29 A2
Deal CT14.....215 C5
Dover CT16.....278 D1
Edenbridge TN8.....217 B2
Gillingham ME7.....64 D3
Gravesend DA12.....37 C7
Leysdown-on-Sea ME12 .49 G1
Maidstone ME17.....194 E2
Maidstone, Penenden Heath
ME14.....162 B6
Northfleet DA11.....36 C4
Orpington BR6.....86 A8
Queenborough ME11 ..46 B4
Sittingbourne ME10 ..101 E1
Tonbridge TN11.....221 F5
West Thurrock RM20.....17 D8
Whitstable CT5.....74 F3
Park Barn Rd ME17 ..197 C5
Park Chase CT10.....83 E2
Park Cl Hawkinge CT18 307 A4
Margate CT9.....51 D1
Park Cliff Rd DA9.....17 C3
Park Corner Rd DA13...35 F4
Park Cotts
8 Hawkhurst TN18.....341 A2
Preston CT3.....146 B6

Park Cotts continued
Ramsgate CT11.....83 E2
Sevenoaks TN13.....154 C2
Park Cres Chatham ME4 .14 D8
Erith DA8.....14 D8
Park Crescent Rd
Erith DA8.....14 D8
Margate CT9.....51 A1
Park Ct ME13.....138 E7
Parkdale Rd SE18.....2 E1
Park Dr Hothfield TN26 .267 A6
Longfield DA3.....58 E6
Sittingbourne ME10 ..101 D1
Woolwich SE7.....11 E8
Parker Ave RM18.....19 C6
Parker Cl Gillingham ME8 98 E5
Hamstreet TN26.....349 A7
Newham E16.....1 E5
Parker Ho 4 SE18.....2 B1
Parker Ind Ctr DA1.....34 C7
Parker Pl CT18.....307 C5
Parker Rd RM17.....17 F8
Parker's Cnr ME3.....9 C2
Parker St E16.....1 E5
Park Farm Cl
Folkestone CT19.....335 C8
Shadoxhurst TN26.....299 A1
Tyler Hill CT2.....142 E6
Park Farm Houses
ME20.....160 B8
Park Farm Prim Sch
CT19.....335 C8
Park Farm Rd
Bromley BR1.....52 D8
Folkestone CT19.....335 C7
Ryarsh ME19.....126 F6
Park Farm Ret Pk
CT19.....335 B8
Parkfield Hartley DA3 ..58 E3
Sevenoaks TN15.....154 F4
Parkfield Rd
Folkestone CT19.....335 C6
Gillingham ME8.....65 F1
Parkfields ME7.....62 C7
Parkfield Way BR2.....52 F4
Parkgate CT10.....83 F2
Parkgate Cotts BR6.....88 C6
Parkgate Rd BR6.....88 C6
Park Gdns DA8.....4 D2
Park Gr Bexley DA7.....14 C3
Bromley BR1.....52 E6
Park Hill Bromley BR1 .52 F5
Meopham Station DA13 .59 F5
Parkhill Rd Sidcup DA15 .31 E6
Sidcup, Old Bexley DA5 .31 F8
Park Hill Rd TN14.....122 E2
Park Ho Dover CT16 ..278 D1
Maidstone ME14.....162 B6
Sevenoaks TN13.....154 C5
Sidcup DA14.....31 A3
Park House Cotts DA4 254 A2
Park House Rd TN4 ..254 A2
Parkhurst Gdns 2 DA5 32 A8
Parkhurst Rd DA5.....32 A8
Park La
Bethersden TN26.....298 C8
Birchington CT7.....81 A6
Bishopsbourne CT4 ..209 C5
Elham CT4.....273 F5
Gill's Green TN17, TN18 340 D7
Godden Green TN15 ..155 A4
Kemsing TN15.....123 A1
Maidstone, Cock Stone
ME17.....195 D2
Maidstone, Ringleston
ME14.....161 F7
Margate CT9.....51 A2
Sevenoaks TN13.....154 C3
Swanley Village BR8.....56 C7
Parkland Cl TN13.....187 D6
Parkland Ct CT10.....83 F6
Parkland Mead BR1 ..53 B6
Parklands TN4.....285 E8
Park Lane TN17.....318 D3
Park Lea CT14.....215 C5
Park Mall Sh Ctr 2
TN24.....268 B2
Park Manor ME7.....64 B5
Park Mead DA15.....13 B1
Park Mews
Chislehurst BR7.....30 B2
6 Dover CT16.....310 D8
Parkmore BR7.....30 B1
Park Par TN29.....366 C7
Park Pl
Ashford, Beaver TN23 . 300 B7
Ashford, Willesborough
TN24.....300 F8
8 Bromley BR1.....52 B8
Dover CT16.....310 D8
Gravesend DA12.....37 C8
Herne CT6.....111 A8
Hever TN8.....250 D4
Margate CT9.....50 I1
Sevenoaks TN13.....153 D4
Park Rd
Addington ME19.....126 C3
Ashford TN24.....268 D6
Birchington CT7.....81 C7
Broadstairs CT10.....84 B6
Bromley BR1.....52 B8
Chislehurst BR7.....30 B2
Dartford DA1.....34 A8
Dover CT16.....278 D2
Dunk's Green TN11.....190 C5
Faversham ME13.....138 D7
Folkestone CT19.....334 E6
Gravesend DA11.....37 C7
Herne Bay CT6.....76 F4
Hythe CT21.....333 B1
Leybourne ME19.....127 D3
Littlestone TN28 373 E5

Park Rd continued
Maidstone ME15.....162 C1
Marden Thorn TN12 ..260 A4
Margate CT9.....51 A2
Mereworth ME18.....191 F5
Orpington BR5.....54 C4
Preston CT3.....146 D7
Queenborough ME11 ..45 F5
Ramsgate CT11.....117 C7
Royal Tunbridge Wells,
Southborough TN4 ..254 A2
Royal Tunbridge Wells
TN4.....286 B5
Sheerness ME12.....28 D1
Sittingbourne ME10 ..101 E3
Swanley BR8.....55 F5
Swanscombe DA10.....17 E1
Temple Ewell CT16 ..277 D5
Westgate on Sea CT7...81 D6
Park Road Ind Est BR8 .55 F6
Park Road N TN24.....268 B3
PARK SIDE.....275 D7
Parkside
Cliffe Woods ME3.....40 B7
Halstead TN14.....120 F6
Sidcup DA14.....31 B6
Park Side CT14.....215 C5
Parkside Ave
Bexley DA7, DA7.....14 E5
Bromley BR1.....52 E5
Tilbury RM18.....19 B5
Parkside Com Prim Sch
CT1.....143 D2
Parkside Cotts TN16...150 E6
Parkside Cross DA7.....14 E5
Parkside Ct
Herne Bay CT6.....76 F5
Ramsgate CT11.....117 D7
Parkside Lodge DA17...4 C1
Parkside Par BR1.....14 F5
Parkside Pl CT1.....143 D3
Parkside Rd DA17.....4 C2
Park St Ashford TN24 ..268 C2
Deal CT14.....215 C4
Dover CT16.....310 D8
Lydd TN29.....376 C6
Royal Tunbridge Wells
TN2.....286 B5
Park Terr
Sundridge TN14.....152 D3
Swanscombe DA9.....17 B2
Throwley ME13.....169 D1
Woodnesborough CT13 180 D7
PARK THE.....222 B3
Park The DA14.....31 A3
Park Vale CT14.....268 D6
Parkview TN2.....286 D4
Park View
Folkestone CT19.....335 E7
Hodsoll Street TN15 ..92 C2
Margate CT9.....51 A2
Peasmarsh TN31.....367 B2
Sevenoaks TN13.....154 C3
Sturry CT2.....143 F6
Park View Cl
Edenbridge TN8.....217 B2
Goodnestone CT3.....178 D2
Parkview Ct DA11.....37 A6
Park View Ct
2 Lewisham SE12.....29 C5
Maidstone ME15.....162 B1
Parkview Rd SE9.....30 B6
Park View Rd DA16.....13 C4
Park View Rise CT15 . 211 D4
Park View Terr 2
TN30.....345 A7
Park Villas ME14.....162 E4
Park Way Erith DA18.....3 E3
Tonbridge TN10.....222 D5
Parkway
Coxheath ME17.....194 D3
Joyden's Wood DA5.....32 E5
Maidstone ME15.....162 B1
Parkway Prim Sch DA18 .3 E4
Park Way Prim Sch
ME15.....162 B1
Parkway The CT7.....81 B7
PARK WOOD Gillingham .98 D4
Maidstone.....195 E4
Parkwood TN31.....368 B4
Parkwood Cl
Broadstairs CT10.....83 F2
Royal Tunbridge Wells
TN2.....286 C6
Park Wood Cl TN23.....300 B5
Park Wood Forest Wlks *
TN26.....347 C4
Park Wood Gn ME8.....98 D5
Parkwood Hall Sch BR8 56 B6
Park Wood Ind Est
ME15.....196 A4
Parkwood Inf Sch ME8 .98 D5
Parkwood Jun Sch ME8 98 D5
Park Wood La TN12 ..261 C1
Park Wood Par 13
ME15.....195 F5
Parkwood Rd
Biggin Hill TN16.....150 F6
Sidcup DA14.....31 F8
Park Wood Rd CT2.....142 C4
Park Wood Sh Ctr ME8 .98 D5
Park Wood Trad Est
ME15.....196 A4
Parnham Cl BR1.....53 B6
Paroma Rd DA17.....4 A3
Parr Ave ME7.....64 D6
Parr Ct CT10.....35 E8
Parrock Ave DA12.....37 C7
Parrock Ct DA12.....37 C7
PARROCK FARM.....37 D4
Parrock Rd DA12.....37 C7
Parrock St DA12.....37 C7
Parrock The DA12.....37 C7
Parrs Head Mews ME1 .63 C6

Parry Ave E6.....1 F7
Parry Pl SE18.....2 B2
Parsley Way ME16.....161 A3
Parsonage Bank DA4...89 E8
Parsonage Chase ME12 46 F5
Parsonage Cl CT4.....285 B5
Parsonage Cotts ME9..134 A5
Parsonage Farm ME13 169 F4
Parsonage Fields
CT12.....114 C2
Parsonage La
Lamberhurst TN3.....317 B6
Rochester ME2.....63 C8
Sidcup DA14.....31 F4
Sittingbourne ME9.....101 A8
Sutton at Hone DA4.....34 B2
Parsonage Manorway
DA17.....14 A8
Parsonage Oast CT12..114 C7
Parsonage Rd
Herne Bay CT6.....77 A3
Rusthall TN4.....285 B5
West Thurrock RM20...17 C8
Parsonage Stocks Rd
ME13.....169 F5
Parsonage Villas CT15 309 C5
Parson's Croft TN8.....250 C5
Parsons La Dartford DA2 33 B5
Stansted TN15.....91 E1
Parsons Way CT16.....278 A3
Partridge Ave ME20...127 F3
Partridge Cl
Herne Bay CT6.....77 C3
1 Newham E16.....1 D8
Partridge Dr
Orpington BR6.....86 C7
St Mary's Island ME4...41 B1
Partridge La SE9.....30 A5
Partridge La ME3.....138 D7
Partridge Rd DA14.....30 E4
Partridge Sq 8 E6.....1 E8
Pasadena Cvn Pk TN15 .90 B1
Pasley Rd SE18.....2 D2
Pasley Road E ME7.....64 A7
Pasley Road S ME4.....64 A7
Pasley Road W ME7.....64 A7
Passey Pl SE9.....11 F1
Passfield Ho SE18.....2 D2
Passfield Path 18 SE18 .3 B6
Passmore Way ME15 ..161 E4
Pastens Rd RH8.....183 C4
Pastime Cl ME10.....101 E8
Paston Cres SE12.....29 B8
Pasture The
Ashford TN24.....268 D6
Hawkinge CT18.....307 B4
Patagonia Ho TN2.....286 C3
Pat Bassant Row DA10 .35 E8
Patch The TN13.....153 E5
Patchways TN9.....350 E3
Pat Drew Ho BR1.....52 C8
Path Field Cotts CT15 308 E5
Pathway The 22 CT10...84 B4
Patience Cotts TN14 ..187 B2
Patricia Ct Bexley SE2 .13 B7
Chislehurst BR7.....53 D8
Patricia Way CT10.....83 D3
PATRIXBOURNE.....176 B3
Patrixbourne Ave ME8 .65 C7
Patrixbourne Rd CT4 ..176 B2
Pattenden Gdns TN12 225 A7
Pattenden La TN12.....259 C7
Pattens Gdns ME1.....63 E2
Pattens La ME1, ME4...63 E1
Pattens Pl ME1.....63 D2
Patterdale Rd DA2.....34 D7
Patterson Cl CT14.....215 A4
Patterson Ct DA1.....16 A2
Pattinson Point 14 E16...1 E8
Pattison Farm Cl TN25 329 F4
Pattison Wlk SE18.....2 C1
Paulinus Cl BR5.....54 C6
Paul's Pl 8 CT16.....278 C1
Pavement The TN30 ..324 B3
Pavilion Cl CT14.....215 C8
Pavilion Cl 4 CT20.....335 E4
Pavilion Dr ME10.....68 F1
Pavilion Gdns TN13.....154 C3
Pavilion La ME18.....192 A8
Pavilion L Ctr The BR1 ..52 A7
Pavilion Mdw CT17.....277 E4
Pavilion Rd TN13.....335 D6
Pavilion Shop Ctr The 7
TN9.....222 B1
Pavilion The 5 TN9.....222 B1
Paving The ME11.....164 C2
Paxton Ave CT18.....306 F3
Paxton Ct 5 SE12.....29 C5
Paxton Rd BR1.....29 A1
Payden St ME17.....200 D8
PAYDEN STREET.....167 B1
Payers Pk CT20.....335 D5
Paynes Cotts TN13.....121 D3
Paynesfield Rd TN16 ..150 D7
Payne's La ME15.....195 B7
Pay St CT18.....306 F7
Payton Cl CT3.....147 A8
Payton Mews 4 CT1 ..143 B1
Peace Cotts ME15.....226 D7
Peace St SE18.....12 A8
Peach Croft DA11.....36 E4
Peach Hall TN10.....222 C6
Peacock Mews 7
ME16.....161 E4
Peacock Pl ME13.....171 A6
Peacock Rise ME5.....97 A4
Peacock St DA12.....37 C8
Peacock Wlk E16.....1 B7
Peafield Wood Rd CT4 261 E4
Peak Dr E6.....180 B3
Peal Cl ME13.....41 E5

Pean Court Rd CT5 . . . . 108 D3
Pean Hill CT5 . . . . 108 D2
Peareswood Rd DA8 . . 14 F6
Pearl Cl E6 . . . . 2 A7
Pearl Way ME18 . . . . 159 C3
Pearmain Wlk CT1 . . 175 C7
Pearman Cl ME8 . . . . 66 A1
Pearse Pl TN3 . . . . 317 B5
PEARSON'S GREEN . 257 F3
Pearson's Green Rd
Paddock Wood, Mile Oak TN12 . . . . 257 D5
Paddock Wood, Pearson's Green TN12 . . . . 257 F3
Pearson's Way CT10 . . 83 E7
Pearson Way DA1 . . 33 F6
Pear Tree Alley 2 ME10 . . . . 101 E5
Pear Tree Ave ME20 . 128 C1
Peartree Cl Bexley DA8 . 14 F6
Bromley BR2 . . . . 52 D4
Pear Tree Cl
Broadstairs CT10 . . . 83 C4
Cranbrook TN17 . . . 320 D3
Swanley BR8 . . . . 55 D7
Peartree Cotts ME8 . . 99 B8
Peartree La DA12 . . 39 A2
Pear Tree La
Dymchurch TN29 . . 352 D1
Gillingham ME7 . . . 97 E7
Loose ME15 . . . . 195 B6
Pear Tree Pl ME3 . . . 39 B3
Peartree Rd CT6 . . . 77 C3
Pear Tree Row ME17 . 196 B5
Peartree Way ME10 . 1 A2
Pear Tree Wlk ME9 . . 100 A5
Pease Hill TN15 . . . 91 F4
Peasley La TN17 . . . 318 D6
PEASMARSH 367 A2
Peasmarsh CE Prim Sch TN31 . . . . 367 B1
Peatfield Cl DA15 . . . 30 E5
Peat Way ME8 . . . . 10 D1
Pebble Hill Cotts RH8 .183 B6
PECKHAM BUSH . . . 224 E8
Peckham Cl ME2 . . . 63 C8
Peckham Ct TN12 . . 224 F6
Peckham Ho 6 BR5 . . 54 D1
Peckham Hurst Rd TN11 . . . . 190 E7
Pedding Hill CT3 . . 147 A1
Pedding La CT3 . . . 179 A8
Pedham Place Est BR8 .56 A4
PEDLINGE 332 D4
Peel Dr ME10 . . . . 102 C4
Peelers Ct CT2 . . . 142 F1
Peel Rd BR6 . . . . 86 C5
Peel St ME14 . . . . 162 A6
Peel Yates Ho 12 ME8 . 1 E2
PEENE 334 B8
Peene Cotts CT18 . . 306 B1
PEENING QUARTER . 359 B6
Peens La ME17 . . . 228 C7
Pegasus Ct DA12 . . 37 C5
Peggoty Cl ME4 . . . 39 B3
Pegley Gdns SE12 . . 29 A6
PEGWELL 117 B5
Pegwell Ave CT11 . . 117 A5
Pegwell Bay Ctry Pk★ CT12 . . . . 116 C2
Pegwell Bay Nature Reserve★ CT12 . . 116 C3
Pegwell Cl CT11 . . . 117 A5
Pegwell Ct CT11 . . . 117 A5
Pegwell Rd CT11 . . . 117 B5
Pegwell St SE18 . . . 12 E1
Pelham Cotts ME3 . . 32 B7
Pelham Ct TN24 . . . 36 B3
Pelham Ct 19 DA14 . . 31 A5
Pelham Gdns CT20 . . 335 A4
Pelham Prim Sch DA7 .14 A4
Pelham Rd Bexley DA7 .14 A4
Gravesend DA11 . . 37 A8
Pelham Road S DA11 . 36 F7
Pelham Terr 4 . . . . 36 F8
Pelican Cl ME2 . . . 62 C6
Pelican Ct ME18 . . . 192 E7
PELL BRIDGE 337 A5
Pell Cl TN5 . . . . 337 A6
PELL GREEN 337 A7
Pellipar Gdns SE18 . . 1 F1
Pellipar Rd SE18 . . . 1 F1
Pells La TN15 . . . . 124 A7
Pelwood Rd TN31 . . 374 A2
Pemberton Ct CT21 . . 334 B3
Pemberton Gdns BR8 . 55 E7
Pemberton Rd TN24 . 268 D2
Pemberton Sq 4 ME2 . 63 C8
Pemble Cl TN12 . . . 256 A7
Pembroke ME4 . . . 64 B8
Pembroke Ave CT9 . . 50 F1
Pembroke Cl DA8 . . 4 D2
Pembroke Ct
Chatham ME4 . . . 64 A4
Folkestone CT19 . . 335 E6
1 Ramsgate CT11 . . 117 E7
Pembroke Gdns ME8 . 98 E4
Pembroke Ho TN26 . . 373 C8
Pembroke Mews TN28 373 C8
Pembroke Par DA8 . . 4 C1
Pembroke Pl CT7 . . . 57 B8
Pembroke Rd
Bromley BR1 . . . . 52 D7
Coxheath ME17 . . 194 C3
Erith DA8 . . . . 4 D2
Newham E6 . . . . 1 F8
Sevenoaks TN13 . . 154 B2
Tonbridge TN9 . . . 222 A1
Pembroke Rise ME4 . . 64 A2
PEMBURY 287 C6
Pembury Cl DA14 . . 287 D7
Pembury Cres DA14 . . 31 C6

Pembury Ct 6 ME10 . .101 E4
Pembury Gdns ME16 . 161 D3
Pembury Gr TN9 . . . 254 C8
Pembury Grange TN2 287 A6
Pembury Hall Rd TN11, TN2 . . . . 255 C3
Pembury Hosp TN2 . . 287 B7
Pembury Pl TN25 . . . 267 F4
Pembury Rd Bexley DA7 13 E8
Royal Tunbridge Wells TN2 . . . . 286 E4
Tonbridge TN11, TN9 . 254 D7
Pembury Sch TN2 . . . 287 D8
Pembury St ME10 . . . 101 E4
Pembury Way ME8 . . 65 E2
Pembury Wlks TN11, TN2 . . . . 255 C2
Penbury Ct CT5 . . . 215 C1
Pencester Ct 3 CT16 .310 E8
Pencester Rd CT16 . . 310 E8
Pencroft Dr DA1 . . . 33 C8
Pendant Ct BR6 . . . 87 A5
Penda Rd DA8 . . . . 14 B7
Pendennis Rd
Orpington BR6 . . . 87 C8
Sevenoaks TN13 . . 154 B4
Penderel Mews TN30 .345 E4
Pendlebury Gn SE18 . 11 E6
Pendragon Rd BR1, SE12 . . . . 29 A5
Pendragon Sch BR1 . . 29 A5
Pendrell St SE18 . . . 12 D8
Pendrill Dr TN5 . . . 336 F5
Penenden La DA3 . . 91 F8
Penenden Ct ME14 . . 162 B7
PENENDEN HEATH . 162 B7
Penenden Heath Rd ME14 . . . . 162 C7
Penfield La ME9 . . . 135 A4
Penfold Cl Chatham ME5 97 B7
Maidstone ME15 . . 195 E5
Penfold Gdns
Maidstone ME15 . . 195 E4
Shepherdswell CT15 . 244 E5
Penfold Hill ME17 . . 197 B8
Penfold Ho 14 SE18 . . 12 B8
Penfold La DA5 . . . 31 D7
Penfold Rd CT19 . . . 335 F6
Penfolds CT11 . . . . 222 C5
Penfold Way ME15 . . 194 F6
Penford Gdns SE9 . . 11 D4
Pengarth Rd DA5 . . . 13 D1
Pengelly Pl CT2 . . . 142 F2
Penguin Cl ME2 . . . 62 D6
Penhale Cl BR6 . . . 87 A6
Penhall Rd SE7 . . . 1 D2
Penhill Rd DA5 . . . 31 C8
Penhurst Cl ME14 . . 162 F5
Peninsular Park Rd SE7 .1 A2
Penlee Cl TN8 . . . . 217 C2
Penlee Point TN24 . . 268 D5
Penmon Rd SE2 . . . 3 A3
Pennant Rd ME1 . . . 96 C7
Penn Cl ME10 . . . . 102 B2
Penney Cl DA1 . . . 33 D8
Penn Gdns BR7 . . . 53 B7
Penn Hill TN23 . . . 299 E6
Pennine Way
Ashford TN24 . . . 268 B4
Bexley DA7 . . . . 14 E6
Maidstone ME15 . . 163 A1
Northfleet DA11 . . 36 E5
Pennine Wlk TN2 . . 286 D5
Pennington Ct CT12 . 144 C7
Pennington Manor 1 TN4 . . . . 253 F2
Pennington Pl TN4 . . 254 B1
Pennington Rd TN4 . . 254 A2
Pennington Way SE12 . 29 B6
Penn La Bexley DA5 . . 13 D1
Ide Hill TN14 . . . 185 E8
Penns Yd TN2 . . . . 287 C6
Penny Cress Gdns ME16 . . . . 161 C3
Penny Cress Rd ME12 . 47 A4
Penn Yd TN2 . . . . 287 C6
Pennyfields TN17 . . 320 D4
PENNYPOT 332 E1
Pennypot Ind Est CT21 332 F1
Penny Pot La CT4 . . 206 B4
Pennyroyal Ave E6 . . 2 A7
Penpool La DA16 . . . 13 B4
Penrith Ct ME7 . . . 65 A5
Penrose Ct CT21 . . . 333 C1
Penryn Manor 4 ME7 . 64 C6
Pensand Ho CT1 . . . 333 D1
PENSHURST 252 B4
Penshurst Ave DA15 . .13 A1
Penshurst CE Prim Sch TN11 . . . . 252 A4
Penshurst Cl
Canterbury CT2 . . 143 A3
Gillingham ME8 . . 65 E2
New Barn DA3 . . . 59 D7
West Kingsdown TN15 . 90 A4
Penshurst Enterprise Ctr TN11 . . . . 252 C4
Penshurst Pl & Gdns★ TN11 . . . . 252 B4
Penshurst Rd
Bexley DA7 . . . . 13 F6
Penshurst TN3, TN11 . 252 A5
Poundsbridge TN11, TN3 . . . . 284 D8
Ramsgate CT11 . . 117 F7
Penshurst Rise ME3 .138 B8
Penshurst Sta TN11 . .219 F1
Penshurst Way ME5 . 54 C5
Penstocks The ME15 . 161 D2
Pentagon Sh Ctr ME4 . .63 F4
Penton Ho 3 SE2 . . . 3 D4

Pentstemon Dr DA10 . .17 E2
Pent Vale Cl CT19 . . 335 A6
Pent Valley Tech Coll CT19 . . . . 334 F7
Penventon Ct 3 RM18 .19 A5
Pen Way TN10 . . . . 222 E5
Pepingstraw Cl ME19 .158 D7
Pepper Cl E6 . . . . 1 F8
Pepperhill ME19 . . . 36 C5
Pepperhill La DA11 . . 36 C5
Pepys Ave ME12 . . . 28 B2
Pepys Cl 4 Dartford DA1 16 A3
Northfleet DA11 . . 36 D5
Tilbury RM18 . . . 19 C6
Pepys Cres E16 . . . 1 A5
Pepys Rise BR6 . . . 53 F1
Pepy's Way ME2 . . . 62 F8
Perch Rd ME20 . . . 128 A4
Perch La TN3 . . . . 288 D1
Percival Rd BR6 . . . 86 B8
Percival Terr CT17 . . 310 B7
Percy Ave CT10 . . . 51 F2
Percy Rd Bexley DA7 . 13 E5
Broadstairs CT10 . . 83 F5
Margate CT9 . . . 51 A3
Ramsgate CT11 . . 117 D8
Percy St 13 RM17 . . . 18 C8
Percy Terr Bromley BR1 .53 B6
Royal Tunbridge Wells TN4 . . . . 286 A6
Peregrine Cl TN21 . . 353 D8
Peregrine Ct DA16 . . 12 F6
Peregrine Dr ME10 . . 102 A2
Peregrine Rd ME19 . . 159 A2
Peri Ct CT1 . . . . 174 E6
Peridot Ct ME15 . . . 195 E5
Peridot St E6 . . . . 1 B7
Perie Row 9 ME7 . . . 64 A6
Perimeter Rd
Dover CT16 . . . . 310 G8
New Hythe ME20 . . 128 C3
Periton Rd SE9 . . . 11 D3
Periwinkle Cl ME10 . . 101 E5
Periwinkle Ct 3 ME10 101 E5
Perkins Ave CT9 . . . 82 F8
Perkins Ct DA9 . . . 16 F2
Perpins Rd SE9 . . . 12 E1
Perran Cl DA3 . . . . 58 F5
Perries Mead CT19 . .335 B4
Perrot Way CT18 . . . 307 B5
PERRY 146 C3
Perryfield St ME14 . . 161 F6
Perry Gr ME13 . . . . 16 A3
Perry Hall Cl BR6 . . . 54 A2
Perry Hall Prim Sch BR6 . . . . 53 F3
Perry Hall Rd BR6 . . 54 A2
Perry La ME13 . . . . 22 C1
Perry Ho DA14 . . . . 31 A3
Perry La CT3 . . . . 146 C3
Perry's Cl ME13 . . . 138 D8
Perrys La BR6, TN14 . 120 C6
Perry St Chatham ME4 . 63 E3
Chislehurst BR7 . . 30 E2
Crayford DA1 . . . 14 E4
Maidstone ME14 . . 161 F6
Northfleet DA11 . . 36 F7
PERRY STREET . . . 36 F8
Perry Street Gdns BR7 .30 E2
PERRYWOOD 171 C4
Perth Gdns ME10 . . 101 C4
Perth Ho 4 RM18 . . . 19 A5
Perth Way CT16 . . . 278 C3
Pescot Ave DA3 . . . 59 B6
PESTED 203 C4
Pested Bars Rd ME17 . 195 D5
Pested La TN25 . . . 203 C4
Petchart Cl ME2 . . . 62 C3
Petchell Mews 11 CT1 143 B2
Peterborough Gdns ME2 . . . . 62 C6
Peter Candler Way TN24 . . . . 268 E4
Peters Cl DA16 . . . 12 E5
Petersfield Cl ME14 . . 287 E7
Petersfield Dr DA13 . . 92 F1
Petersham Dr BR5 . . 54 A6
Petersham Gdns BR5 . 53 F7
Peter St Deal CT14 . . 215 D1
Dover CT16 . . . . 310 C8
5 Folkestone CT20 . 335 E5
5 Gravesend DA12 . .37 B8
Peterstone Rd SE2 . . 3 B4
Petfield Cl ME12 . . . 47 C6
PETHAM 207 B3
Petham Court Cotts BR8 . . . . 55 F4
Petham Gn ME8 . . . 65 C2
Petham Prim Sch CT4 207 C3
Petlands ME17 . . . . 195 D5
Petrel Cl CT6 . . . . 77 F4
Petrel Way CT18 . . . 307 A3
Petrie Ho 3 SE18 . . . 12 A8
Pettacre Cl SE28 . . . 2 C3
PETT BOTTOM . . . 208 B5
Pett Bottom Rd CT4 . 208 C5
Petten Cl BR5 . . . . 54 D1
Petten Gr BR5 . . . . 54 D1
PETTERIDGE 288 F6
Petteridge La TN12 . . 288 F7
Pettfield Hill Rd ME13 169 B1
Pett Hill CT4 . . . . 175 F1
PETTINGS 92 B3
Pettings Row TN12 . . 258 D8
Petta La Charing TN27 . 234 D7
Silver Street ME9 . . 133 B7
Pettman Cl CT3 . . . 76 E3
Pettman Cres SE28, SE18 2 D3
Pettman Pl 5 CT10 . . 83 E5
Pettmans Mews CT5 . .74 C2
Pett's Cres CT15 . . 115 B5
Petts La CT3 . . . . 178 A8
Pett St CT15 . . . . 1 E2

PETTS WOOD 53 D5
Petts Wood Rd BR5 . . 53 D4
Petts Wood Sta BR5 . . 53 C4
Petworth Rd DA6 . . . 14 A2
Pevensel Ct ME16 . . 161 F4
Peverel E6 . . . . 2 A7
Peverel Dr ME14 . . . 163 A5
Peverel Gn ME8 . . . 98 D4
Peverell Rd CT16 . . . 278 B4
Peveril Ct 15 DA2 . . . 16 B1
Pewter Ct CT1 . . . 174 F7
Pfizer Monk's Wall Nature Reserve★ CT13 . . 148 E3
Phalarope Wlk ME4 . . 41 C2
Phalarop Way ME4 . . 41 C2
Pharos Dr CT16 . . . 278 C1
Pharos St CT16 . . . 278 C1
Pheasant Cl E16 . . . 1 B7
Pheasant La ME15 . . 195 B8
Pheasant Rd ME4 . . . 64 C2
Pheasants' Hall Rd CT4 . . . . 208 F2
Phelps Cl TN15 . . . 90 E4
Philimore Cl SE18 . . . 2 E5
Philip Ave BR8 . . . 55 D5
Philip Corby Cl CT9 . . 51 B2
Philip Almshouse SE9 11 F1
Philpot Path 2 SE9 . . 11 F1
Philippa Gdns SE9 . . 11 D2
Philippa Ho CT19 . . 335 F6
Phillippa Cl ME10 . . 101 E8
Phillippa St ME4 . . . 63 D2
Phillip Rd CT19 . . . 334 E6
Phillips Cl DA1 . . . 15 B1
Phillips Ct ME8 . . . 65 C3
Phillips Rd CT7 . . . 81 A6
Philpots La TN11 . . 220 E6
Philpott's Cross TN18 340 E2
Phineas Pett Rd SE9 . 11 E4
Phipps Ho 1 SE7 . . . 1 B1
Phoenix Com Prim Sch TN24 . . . . 268 D5
Phoenix Cotts ME18 . 192 D6
Phoenix Ct 11 ME7 . . 64 C6
Phoenix Dr
Orpington BR2 . . . 85 D7
Wateringbury ME18 . 192 E7
Phoenix Ind Est ME2 . 62 D7
Phoenix Pk ME15 . . 195 F4
Phoenix Pl DA1 . . . 33 C8
Phoenix Yard Cotts ME18 . . . . 159 F1
Picardy Manorway DA17 .4 B3
Picardy Rd DA17 . . . 4 A3
Picardy St DA17 . . . 4 A3
Piccadilly Apartments 4 ME5 . . . . 64 B3
Pickelden La CT4 . . 205 F8
Pickering Ct 20 DA2 . .16 B1
Pickering Ho 4 SE18 . . 2 A2
Pickering St ME15 . . 195 B6
Pickford Cl DA7 . . . 13 E5
Pickforde La TN5 . . . 338 D1
Pickford La DA7 . . . 13 E5
Pickford Rd DA7 . . . 13 E4
Pickhill Oast TN30 . .345 B6
Pickhurst La BR2 . . . 52 A1
Pickle's Way ME3 . . 22 A6
Pickmoss La TN14 . . 122 A3
Pickneybush La TN29 . 365 A7
Pickwick Cres ME1 . . 63 C3
Pickwick Ct SE9 . . . 29 F7
Pickwick Gdns DA11 . 36 D5
Pickwick House DA11 . 36 D5
Pickwick Way BR7 . . 30 C2
Picton Rd CT11 . . . 117 C7
Piedmont Rd SE18 . . 2 D1
Pie Factory Rd CT15 . 211 E2
Pier Approach Rd ME7 .64 D7
Pier Ave Herne Bay CT6 . 76 E4
Whitstable CT5 . . 75 A2
Pierce Mill La TN11 . . 224 C6
Piermont Pl BR1 . . . 52 E7
Pier Par 3 E16 . . . 2 A5
Pier Pl E16 . . . . 41 A3
Pierpoint Rd CT5 . . . 108 D7
Pier Rd Gillingham ME7 .64 E7
Newham E16 . . . . 2 A4
Northfleet DA11 . . 18 F1
Swanscombe DA9 . . 17 B3
Pier Road Ind Est ME7 .64 D7
Pier Sports Ctr The CT6 76 E5
Pier The CT16 . . . 277 F8
Pier Way SE28 . . . 2 D2
Pigdown La TN8 . . . 250 D4
Pigeon La CT6 . . . . 77 A2
Piggott's Cross TN8 . . 218 D7
Pigsdean Rd DA13 . . 61 B2
Pigtail Cnr ME12 . . . 47 E6
Pike Cl Bromley BR1 . . 29 B3
Folkestone CT19 . . 335 A7
New Hythe ME20 . . 128 A4
Pikefields ME8 . . . 65 C2
PIKEFISH 225 F3
Pikefish La TN12, ME18 225 F2
Pike Rd CT14, CT15 . . 212 D1
Pike Rd Ind Est CT15 . 212 D1
Pikey La ME19 . . . . 159 E5
Pilar Ct CT8 . . . . 50 D1
Pilckem Cl CT1 . . . 143 D1
Pile La TN12 . . . . 261 A5
Pilgrim Sch The ME1 . .62 F2
Pilgrims Cl ME7 . . . 166 A3
Pilgrims Ct
Charing TN27 . . . 234 C7
Dartford DA1 . . . 16 A2
Greenwich SE3 . . . 11 A6
Pilgrims La
Chilham CT4 . . . . 172 E1
Titsey RH8 . . . . 150 D3
Whitstable CT5 . . 108 B4
Pilgrims Lakes ME17 . 198 E6
Pilgrim Spring CT19 . 335 D8

Pilgrims Rd
Canterbury CT1 . . . 175 C7
Upper Halling ME2 . . 94 F6
Wouldham ME1 . . . 95 E5
Pilgrims View
Sandling ME14 . . . 129 E3
Swanscombe DA9 . . 17 C1
Pilgrims Way
Boughton Aluph TN25 . 237 A4
Boxley ME14 . . . 130 E3
Broad Street ME14, ME17 . . . . 164 C6
Canterbury CT1 . . . 175 C7
Charing TN27 . . . 234 E8
Cuxton ME2 . . . . 62 C3
Dartford DA1 . . . 34 B8
Detling ME14 . . . 131 B1
Dover CT16 . . . . 278 A3
Eccles ME20 . . . 129 B6
Hollingbourne ME17 . .164 F3
Lenham ME17 . . . 199 B7
Thurnham ME14 . . 163 E8
Upper Halling ME2, ME6, ME19 . . . . 94 D3
Vigo Village ME19 . . 126 B7
Westwell TN25 . . . 235 D5
Wrotham TN15 . . . 125 A3
Pilgrims' Way
Brabourne TN25 . . 303 E8
Hill Park TN16 . . . 151 B4
Kemsing TN14, TN15 . 123 C3
Pilgrim's Way Cotts TN15 . . . . 123 A2
Pilgrim's Way E TN14 . 122 D3
Pilgrims Way W TN14 .121 E3
Pilgrims Way Prim Sch CT1 . . . . 175 C7
Pilkington Rd BR6 . . 86 C8
Pillar Box La
Crouch TN15 . . . 190 D5
Oldbury TN15 . . . 155 E5
Pilot Rd ME1 . . . . 96 C8
Pilots Ave CT14 . . . 215 A4
Pilot's Farm Rd CT4 . 208 A4
Pilots Pl DA12 . . . . 171 C2
Pimpernel Cl ME14 . . 163 B4
Pimpernel Way ME5 . 96 C4
Pimp's Court Cotts ME15 . . . . 194 E6
Pinchbeck Rd BR6 . . 86 F4
Pincott Rd DA6 . . . 14 A3
Pincroft Wood DA3 . . 59 C6
Pincus Ho ME10 . . . 101 E5
PINDEN 58 C7
Pine Ave DA12 . . . . 37 D7
Pine Cl Larkfield ME20 . 128 A2
Swanley BR8 . . . 55 F5
Pine Cotts ME14 . . . 161 E8
Pinecrest Gdns BR6 . 86 B6
Pinecroft DA16 . . . 13 A7
Pine Glade BR6 . . . 85 F6
Pine Gr Edenbridge TN8 217 B2
Gillingham ME7 . . 98 A5
Maidstone ME14 . . 162 B6
PINEHAM 278 D8
Pineham Rd CT15 . . 278 C6
Pine Ho 3 Chatham ME5 96 F5
5 Maidstone ME14 . 162 B4
Pinehurst
Chislehurst BR7 . . 30 B2
Sevenoaks TN14 . . 154 C3
Pinehurst Wlk 4 BR6 . 53 D1
Pine Lodge ME16 . . 161 C3
Pine Lodge Ct CT14 . 215 B5
Pineneedle La TN13 . 154 B4
Pine Pl ME15 . . . . 161 E1
Pine Rd ME2 . . . . 62 F6
Pine Ridge TN10 . . . 222 B6
Pine Rise DA13 . . . 44 A4
Pinesfield La ME19 . .126 B6
Pines Garden The★ CT15 . . . . 280 B5
Pineside Rd CT3 . . . 176 E8
Pines Rd BR1 . . . . 52 E7
Pines The
Broadstairs CT10 . . 83 D4
Canterbury CT1 . . 175 A6
Pine Tree Ave CT2 . . 142 E2
Pinetree Cl CT5 . . . 74 F3
Pine Tree Cl CT7 . . . 81 B7
Pine Tree La TN15 . . 156 A2
Pine View TN15 . . . 157 C7
Pine Way TN19 . . . 334 D7
Pine Wlk CT6 . . . . 77 E5
Pinewood Ave
Sevenoaks TN13 . . 154 D6
Sidcup DA15 . . . 30 E7
Pinewood Cl
Orpington BR6 . . . 53 D1
Paddock Wood TN12 . 256 F6
Ramsgate CT12 . . 83 C1
Pinewood Dr CT4 . . . 254 E7
Chatham ME5 . . . 130 D8
Orpington BR6 . . . 86 E5
Pinewood Gdns TN4 . .254 A2
Pinewood Rd Bexley SE2 13 B8
Bromley BR2 . . . 52 A5
Royal Tunbridge Wells TN2 . . . . 286 D5
Pin Hill CT1 . . . . 174 F7
Pinkham Ct TN12 . . 225 A8
Pinkham Gdns TN12 . .225 A8
Pinks Cnr ME12 . . . 115 D6
Pinks Hill BR8 . . . 55 E4
Pinnacle Hill DA7 . . 14 B3
Pinnacle Hill N DA7 . .14 B3
Pinnacles The ME4 . . 41 C1
Pinnell Rd SE9 . . . 11 D3
Pinners Cl CT15, CT3 . 211 C6
Pinners La CT15 . . . 211 C5

Pinnock La TN12 . . . 260 E1
Pinnock's Ave DA11 . . 37 B3
Pinnock Wall CT14 . . 181 D5
Pintail Cl Grain ME3 . . 27 B6
Newham E6 . . . . 1 E8
Pintail Dr ME9 . . . . 68 E3
Pintails The ME4 . . . 41 B1
Pintail Way CT6 . . . 77 C2
Pinton Hill TN5 . . . 338 B3
Pinto Way SE3 . . . 11 B3
Pioneer Bsns Pk CT11 117 C8
Pioneer Cotts TN11 . . 252 A1
Pioneer Ct 5 DA11 . . 19 A1
Pioneer Rd CT16 . . . 278 A3
Pioneer Way BR8 . . . 55 F6
Pipers Cl TN5 . . . . 337 A4
Piper's Green Rd TN16 185 B8
Pipers La TN16 . . . 185 A8
Pippenhall SE9 . . . 12 B1
Pippin Ave CT4 . . . 209 B8
Pippin Cl Ash CT3 . . 147 C1
Coxheath ME17 . . 194 B2
8 Sittingbourne ME10 101 D6
Pippin Croft ME7 . . . 98 A6
Pippin Rd TN12 . . . 224 F6
Pippins Cl TN10 . . . 222 C5
Pippins The DA13 . . 60 A3
Pippin Way ME19 . . 159 A2
PIPSDEN 341 D1
Pip's View ME3 . . . 22 F5
Pirbright Cl ME5 . . . 97 C2
Pirie St E16 . . . . 1 B5
Pirrip Cl CT2 . . . . 37 F6
Pitchfont La RH8 . . .183 B8
Pitfield Cres SE28 . . 3 A5
Pitfield Dr CT13 . . . 92 F7
Pitfold Cl SE12 . . . 11 B1
Pitfold Rd SE12 . . . 11 A1
Pit La TN8 . . . . 217 C4
Pitstock Rd ME9 . . . 135 B5
Pittlesden TN30 . . . 345 A7
Pittlesden Pl 1 TN30 . 345 A7
Pittock Ho CT14 . . . 215 B3
Pitt Rd
Chartway Street ME17 . . . . 197 A2
Maidstone ME16 . . 161 B1
Orpington BR6 . . . 86 C6
Pittsmead Ave BR2 . . 52 A2
PITTSWOOD 223 B8
Pittswood Cotts TN11 223 A8
Pivington La TN27 . . 233 C2
Pivington Mill Ind Est TN27 . . . . 233 C2
Pixot Hill TN12 . . . 257 B2
Pix's La TN17 . . . . 344 A3
Pixwell La CT14 . . . 214 D3
Pizien Well Rd ME18 . 192 B7
Place Farm Ave BR6 . . 53 D1
Place La Hartlip ME9 . . 99 D4
Woodchurch TN26 . . 326 B3
Place The CT14 . . . 210 F1
Plain Cotts CT20 . . . 335 A4
Plain Rd
Brabourne Lees TN25 . 302 F5
Folkestone CT20 . . 335 B4
Marden TN12 . . . 259 C4
Plains Ave ME15 . . . 162 C1
Plains of Waterloo CT11 . . . . 117 F7
Plain The TN17 . . . 318 E8
PLAISTOW 29 A2
Plaistow Gr BR1 . . . 29 B1
Plaistow La BR1 . . . 52 C8
Plaistow Sq ME14 . . 162 C6
Plane Ave DA11 . . . 36 D8
Plane Tree Ho SE7 . . 1 D1
Plane Wlk TN10 . . . 222 C7
Plantagenet Ho SE18 . 1 F3
Plantation Cl
Hothfield TN26 . . . 267 A4
Stone DA9 . . . . 16 F1
Plantation Ct ME9 . . 68 E4
Plantation La BR5 . . 54 D1
Plantation La ME14 . . 163 A3
Plantation Rd Erith DA8 .15 A6
Faversham ME13 . . 138 C7
Gillingham ME7 . . 65 A6
Hextable BR8 . . . 33 A2
Whitstable CT5 . . 75 D2
Plantation The SE3 . . 11 A5
PLATT 157 C7
Platt CE Prim Sch TN15 . . . . 157 C7
Platt Comm TN15 . . 157 C7
Platters The ME8 . . . 98 C7
Plat The TN8 . . . . 217 D1
Platt House La TN15 . 125 C6
Platt Ind Est TN15 . . 157 C8
Platt Mill Cl TN15 . . 157 B7
Platt Mill Terr TN15 . . 157 B7
PLATT'S HEATH . . . 198 E1
Platts Heath Prim Sch ME17 . . . . 198 F2
Platt The Frant TN3 . . 314 E1
Sutton Valence ME17 . 229 E7
Plaxdale Green Rd TN15 . . . . 124 D7
PLAXTOL 189 E8
Plaxtol Cl BR1 . . . 52 C8
Plaxtol La TN15, TN11 . 189 D8
Plaxtol Prim Sch TN15 189 E7
Plaxtol Rd DA8 . . . 14 A2
PLAXTOL SPOUTE . . 190 A8
Playdell Ct 12 CT20 . 335 C8
Playden La TN31 . . . 368 C3
Playhouse Theatre★ 15 CT5 . . . . 74 D1
Playing Fields CT13 . .180 E7
Playstool Cl ME9 . . . 100 B6
Playstool Rd ME9 . . 100 A6
Plaza Ct 7 ME10 . . . 102 A4
Pleasance Rd BR5 . . 54 B6

Pleasance Road Central TN29 . . . . . 380 D7
Pleasance Road N TN29 . . . . 377 E5
Pleasant Row 10 ME7 . . . . 64 A6
Pleasant Valley La ME15 . . . . .194 B4
Pleasant View
15 Erith DA8 . . . . 4 E1
Orpington BR6 . . . . 86 C5
Pleasaunce Ct SE9 . . . . 11 F3
Pleasent Pl ME12 . . . . . . .46 E6
Pleasure House La ME17 . . . . 230 A8
Plenty Brook Dr CT6 . . . .76 F3
Plewis Ho ME7 . . . . .64 E7
Pleydell Cres CT2 . . . . . . .143 F7
Pleydell Gdns CT20 . . . . 335 D4
Plimsoll Ave CT19 . . . . . .335 E8
Plomley Cl ME8 . . . . .98 F2
Plough Cotts ME17 . . . . . .196 D2
Plough Ct CT6 . . . . .77 D2
Plough Hill
Basted TN15 . . . . .156 F4
Church Hougham CT15 . . 309 C4
Plough La CT5 . . . . .75 D3
Ploughmans Way
Ashford TN23 . . . . .299 D5
Chatham ME5 . . . . .97 A1
Gillingham ME8 . . . . .98 E6
Plough Rd ME12 . . . . .48 C5
Plough Wents Rd ME17 . . . . 196 B2
Plough Wlk TN8 . . . . .217 C3
Plover Cl Chatham ME5 . . .97 D1
Herne Bay CT6 . . . . .77 F5
Marlpit Hill TN8 . . . . .217 C3
Plover Rd
Hawkinge CT18 . . . . . . .306 F3
Larkfield ME20 . . . . .127 F2
Minster (Sheppey) ME12 .47 A5
Plowenders Cl ME19 . . . 126 D2
PLUCKLEY 265 D7
Pluckley CE Prim Sch TN27 . . . . 265 D7
Pluckley Cl ME8 . . . . .65 C3
Pluckley Gdns CT9 . . . . . .51 E2
Pluckley Rd
Bethersden TN26 . . . . . .297 D7
Charing TN27 . . . . .234 B5
Hothfield TN26, TN27 . . .266 E6
Smarden TN27 . . . . .264 D2
Pluckley Sta TN27 . . . . . .265 C7
PLUCKLEY THORNE 265 B6
PLUCKS GUTTER 113 F3
Plug La DA13 . . . . .93 D5
Plumcroft Prim Sch SE18 . . . . .12 C8
Plumey Feather Cotts TN6 . . . . 311 E3
Plumford Rd ME13 . . . . . 138 A2
Plum La SE18 . . . . .12 C7
Plummer La TN30 . . . . . .344 F6
Plummers Croft TN13 . . .153 E6
Plumpton Wlk
5 Canterbury CT1 . . . . . .143 B1
6 Maidstone ME15 . . . . 162 A6
Plumpudding La ME13 . . 107 E1
PLUMSTEAD 2 E2
PLUMSTEAD COMMON 12 F8
Plumstead Common Rd SE18 . . . . .12 C8
Plumstead High St SE18, SE2 . . . . .2 E2
Plumstead Manor Sch SE18 . . . . .12 D8
Plumstead Sta SE18 . . . . . .2 C2
Plumstead Rd SE18 . . . . . .2 C2
Plumstone Rd CT7 . . . . . .80 F1
Plum Tree Cotts TN18 . . .354 C8
Plum Tree Gdns TN26 . . .326 B1
Plumtree Gr ME7 . . . . .98 A4
PLUMTREE GREEN 262 A8
Plum Tree La ME9 . . . . . .132 B2
Plumtree Rd TN27 . . . . . .261 F7
Plumtrees ME16 . . . . .161 A2
Plurenden Manor Farm Cotts TN26 . . . . .325 D7
Plurenden Rd TN26 . . . . .325 F7
Plymouth Dr TN13 . . . . . .154 C3
Plymouth Pk TN13 . . . . . .154 C3
Plymouth Rd
Bromley BR1 . . . . .52 B8
Newham E16 . . . . .1 A8
Plympton Ct 8 DA17 . . . .3 E3
Plymstock Rd DA16 . . . . .13 C7
Poachers Cl ME4 . . . . .41 B1
Poachers End CT3 . . . . . .78 B1
Pochard Cl ME4 . . . . .41 B1
Pochard Cres CT6 . . . . . . .76 E3
Pocket Hill TN13 . . . . . . .187 A7
Pococks Bank TN8 . . . . . .218 C3
Podkin Wood ME5 . . . . . .129 F8
Poets Cnr CT9 . . . . .50 J1
Poets Wlk CT14 . . . . .215 C1
Pointer Cl SE28 . . . . .3 D7
Pointer Sch The SE3 . . . . .11 A7
Poison Cross CT13 . . . . . .180 B4
Poldark Ct 22 CT11 . . . . .117 F7
Polebrook Rd SE3 . . . . . . .11 C4
Polegate Cotts RM17 . . . . .17 E8
Polesden Rd TN2 . . . . . . .286 D2
Polesteeple Hill TN16 . . .118 D2
Poles The ME9 . . . . .66 E4
Polhill TN13, TN14 . . . . . .121 C4
Polhill Bank Nature Reserve ★ TN14 . . . . . .121 D6
Polhill Dr ME5 . . . . .96 F2
Police Station Rd ME19 . . . . 159 C8
Pollard Cl Ashford TN23 299 F8
Newham E16 . . . . .1 A6
Pollard Ct ME7 . . . . .64 C5
Pollard Pl 3 CT5 . . . . . . .108 C6

Pollards Oak Cres RH8 . . . . 183 A3
Pollards Oak Rd RH8 . . 183 A3
Pollards Wood Hill RH8 . . . . .183 B5
Pollards Wood Rd RH8 . . . . .183 B4
Pollard Wlk DA14 . . . . . . .31 C2
Polley Cl TN2 . . . . .287 D7
Pollyhaugh DA4 . . . . .89 E7
Polo Way CT5 . . . . .75 D1
Polperro Cl BR6 . . . . .53 F3
Polthorne Gr SE18 . . . . . . .2 D1
Polytechnic St 14 SE18 . . .2 A2
Pomfret Ho CT4 . . . . .173 D1
Pomfret Rd CT4 . . . . .173 D1
Pommeus La CT14 . . . . . .247 D7
Poncia Rd TN23 . . . . .300 A7
Pond Cl SE3 . . . . .11 A5
Pond Cotts
Herne Bay CT6 . . . . .77 D2
Sittingbourne ME10 . . . .134 D8
Pond Dr ME10 . . . . .102 A2
Pond Farm Rd
Hucking ME17 . . . . .132 D1
Oad Street ME9 . . . . . . .100 F1
Pondfield La DA12 . . . . . . .38 E1
Pondfield Rd BR6 . . . . . . .86 B7
Pond Hill Adisham CT3 . . 177 D1
Cliffe ME3 . . . . .22 B6
Pond Hill Rd CT20 . . . . . .334 C5
Pond La
St Margaret's at Cliffe CT15 . . . . 279 D7
Stone Strret TN15 . . . . . .155 E2
Womenswold CT4, CT3 . .210 D3
Pondmore Way TN25 . .267 F4
Pond Path BR7 . . . . .30 B2
Pontefract Rd BR1 . . . . . . .29 A3
Pontoise Cl TN13 . . . . . . .153 F5
Pontoon Dock Sta E16 . . . .1 C5
Ponycart La CT4 . . . . . . .240 E3
Pook La TN27 . . . . .295 D3
Poona Rd TN1 . . . . .286 B2
Poorhole La CT10 . . . . . . .83 B5
POOTINGS 217 E7
Pootings Rd TN8 . . . . . . .217 E7
Poot La ME9 . . . . .66 C5
Pope Dr TN12 . . . . .260 E4
Pope House La TN30 . . . .324 D4
Pope Rd BR2 . . . . .52 D4
Popes La
Limpsfield RH8 . . . . .216 A8
Sturry CT2 . . . . .143 F7
Pope St
Godmersham CT4 . . . . . .205 E4
Maidstone ME16 . . . . . . .161 C2
Pope Street Ct SE9 . . . . . .29 F7
Popes Wood ME14 . . . . .162 F6
Popjack Rd ME9 . . . . . . .134 E6
Poplar Ave
Gravesend DA12 . . . . . . .37 C4
Orpington BR6 . . . . .86 B8
Poplar Cl Ashford TN23 .267 F3
Hoo St Werburgh ME3 . . .41 E3
Rochester ME2 . . . . .62 F5
Poplar Dr
Elvington CT15 . . . . .212 B2
Herne Bay CT6 . . . . .76 D2
Poplar Field TN30 . . . . . .359 D4
Poplar Gr E16 . . . . .161 C5
Poplar La TN29 . . . . .376 D1
Poplar Mount DA17 . . . . . .4 C2
Poplar Pl SE28 . . . . .3 C6
Poplar Rd
Broadstairs CT10 . . . . . . .83 E6
Ramsgate CT11 . . . . .117 D7
Rochester ME2 . . . . .62 E5
Wittersham TN30 . . . . . .359 D4
Poplar Row CT7 . . . . .81 E5
Poplars TN26 . . . . .348 A4
Poplars Cl DA3 . . . . .59 C6
Poplars The
Ashford TN23 . . . . .300 A7
Bethersden TN26 . . . . . .297 E6
Gravesend DA12 . . . . . . .37 E8
Hersden CT3 . . . . .111 F1
Poplar View TN26 . . . . . .139 F2
Poplar Wlk DA13 . . . . . . .60 B3
Poplicans Rd ME2 . . . . . .62 B3
Poppy Cl Erith DA17 . . . . . .4 B4
Gillingham ME7 . . . . .64 C5
Maidstone ME16 . . . . . . .161 D3
Poppy Cres ME12 . . . . . . .47 A4
Poppyfield TN31 . . . . . . .368 C1
Poppy Mead TN23 . . . . . .300 C2
Popsal La CT3 . . . . .178 B6
Porchester Cl
Hartley DA3 . . . . .58 F5
Loose ME15 . . . . .195 A6
Porchfield Cl DA12 . . . . . . .37 C6
Porcupine Cl SE9 . . . . . . .29 C6
Porrington Cl BR7 . . . . . . .53 A8
Portal House Sch CT15 . . . . 280 A6
Port Ave DA9 . . . . .17 B1
Port Cl Chatham ME5 . . . . .97 B3
Maidstone ME14 . . . . . . .163 A5
Portebello Ct CT14 . . . . .215 D7
Porter Cl
Minster (Sheppey) ME12 . . . . .47 A6
West Thurrock RM20 . . . . .17 C8
Porter Rd E6 . . . . .1 F7
Porters Cl TN12 . . . . .288 F6
Porter's La ME18 . . . . . . .138 B2
Porters Wlk ME17 . . . . . .196 E4
Porters Wood TN12 . . . . .288 E6
Portery The CT14 . . . . . . .215 D6
Porteus Ct DA1 . . . . .33 D6
Porthallow Ct 11 BR6 . . . .86 F6
Port Hill BR6 . . . . .120 B7

Porthkerry Ave DA16 . . . .13 A3
Portland Ave
Gravesend DA12 . . . . . . .37 B6
Sidcup DA15 . . . . .13 A1
Sittingbourne ME10 . . . .102 C4
Portland Cl
Ashford TN24 . . . . .268 C7
Hythe CT21 . . . . .333 B2
Tonbridge TN10 . . . . . . .222 D2
Portland Cres SE9 . . . . . . .29 E6
Portland Ct
3 Chatham CT1 . . . . . . .333 B2
Ramsgate CT11 . . . . . . .117 E7
Portland Pl
1 Snodland ME6 . . . . . .128 A8
Swanscombe DA9 . . . . . .17 C3
Portland Rd
Bromley, Mottingham SE9 . . . . .29 E6
Bromley, Sundridge BR1 . .29 C3
Gillingham ME7 . . . . .64 E6
Gravesend DA12 . . . . . . .37 B7
Hythe CT21 . . . . .333 B2
Northfleet DA11 . . . . .18 D1
Wouldham ME1 . . . . .95 C4
Portland Sq CT1 . . . . .175 B7
Portland St 1 ME4 . . . . . . .64 A2
Portland Terr
Ripple CT14 . . . . .247 D8
Sheerness ME12 . . . . . . .28 C2
Portland Villas DA12 . . . .37 B7
Portlight Pl CT5 . . . . .108 A6
Port Lympne Wild Animal Pk ★ CT21 . . . . .331 D2
Portman Cl Bexley DA7 . . .13 E4
Maypole DA5 . . . . .32 E7
Portman Pk TN9 . . . . . . .222 C3
Portmeadow Wlk SE2 . . . .3 D4
Portobello Par TN15 . . . . .91 A4
Portree Mews ME7 . . . . . .64 E3
Port Richborough Bsns Pk CT13 . . . . .149 A7
Portsdown Cl ME16 . . . . . .161 B2
Portsea Rd RM18 . . . . . . .19 C6
Portsmouth Cl ME2 . . . . . .62 D6
Portsmouth Mews E16 . . .1 B5
Port Victoria Rd ME3 . . . .27 C4
Portway CT5 . . . . .108 C8
Portway Gdns SE18 . . . . . .11 D7
Portway Rd ME3 . . . . .40 B7
Post Barn Rd ME4 . . . . . . .63 F7
Postern Ind Est TN9 . . . . .222 D1
Postern La TN9, TN11 . . .222 E1
Postley Ind Ctr ME15 . . . .162 A2
Postley Rd ME15 . . . . . . .162 A1
POSTLING 304 F2
Postling CT23 . . . . .267 E1
Postling Rd CT19 . . . . . . .334 E7
Postling Wents CT21 . . . .332 F8
Postmill Dr ME15 . . . . . . .161 F1
Post Office Rd 12 TN18 . . . . 340 F2
Post Office Row CT4 . . . .171 D1
Post Office Sq TN1 . . . . . .286 A3
Potash La TN15 . . . . .157 C6
Pot Kiln La TN26 . . . . . . .296 E4
POTMAN'S HEATH 358 E4
POTTEN STREET 79 D3
Potten Street Rd CT7 . . . .79 E3
Potteries The ME9 . . . . . . .66 E1
Potters Cl TN24 . . . . .267 E6
Potters Cnr TN24 . . . . . . .267 E6
POTTERS CORNER 267 F6
POTTER'S FORSTAL 232 B2
Potter's La TN18 . . . . . . .341 A6
Potter St CT13 . . . . .149 A1
Pottery Cotts TN25 . . . . .269 E5
Pottery Rd Coldblow DA5 .32 C6
Hoo St Werburgh ME3 . . .41 D5
Potyn Ho ME1 . . . . .63 C4
Pouces Cl ME12 . . . . .81 F1
Poulders Gdns CT13 . . . .180 E8
Poulders Rd CT13 . . . . . .180 E8
Poulsen Ct 8 ME10 . . . . .102 B4
Poulters Wood BR2 . . . . . .85 D5
Poulton Cl CT17 . . . . . . .309 F8
Poulton Close Bsns Pk CT17 . . . . 277 E1
Poulton La CT3 . . . . .79 C8
Pound Bank Cl TN15 . . . .90 F2
Pound Cl BR6 . . . . .86 D8
Pound Court Dr BR6 . . . . .86 D8
Pound Ct TN23 . . . . .300 A3
Pound Farm Cotts CT18 . . . . 334 A7
Poundfield Rd TN18 . . . .336 B5
Pound Green Ct 4 DA5 . .32 A8
Pound Ho Ashford TN23 300 B8
Hadlow TN11 . . . . .223 D8
Poundhurst Rd TN26 . . . .297 D3
Pound La Ashford TN23 .299 F4
Brabourne Lees TN25 . . .302 F5
Canterbury CT1 . . . . . . .142 F1
Elham CT4 . . . . .144 F2
Halstead TN14 . . . . .120 D4
Molash CT4 . . . . .203 F4
Sevenoaks TN13 . . . . . .153 D5
Pound Park Rd SE7 . . . . . .1 D2
Pound Pl SE9 . . . . .12 A1
Pound Rd TN12 . . . . .224 F6
POUNDSBRIDGE 284 D8
Poundsbridge Hill TN11, TN3 . . . . 284 D7
Poundsbridge La TN11 . . . . 252 D2
Pound Way CT20 . . . . . . .335 D4
Pounsley Rd TN13 . . . . . .153 E6
Pout Rd ME6 . . . . .127 F7
POVEREST 54 A4
Poverest Prim Sch BR5 . . 54 A4
Poverest Rd BR5 . . . . .54 A4
Povey Ave ME2 . . . . .40 C2
Powdermill Cl TN4 . . . . . .286 C8

Powder Mill La
Dartford DA1 . . . . .33 F6
Leigh TN11 . . . . .221 B1
Royal Tunbridge Wells TN4 . . . . 286 B8
Tonbridge TN11 . . . . . . .221 E2
POWDER MILLS 221 E2
Powell Ave DA2 . . . . .34 E6
Powell Cl ME20 . . . . .129 A3
Powell Cotton Dr CT7 . .81 B6
Powell Cotton Mus ★ CT7 . . . . .81 B5
Powerhub Bsns Ctr ME16 . . . . .161 F5
Power Ind Est DA8 . . . . . . .15 A4
Powerscroft Rd DA14 . . . .31 C2
Power Station Rd
Grain ME3 . . . . .27 B4
Halfway Houses ME12 . . .46 E7
Powis St SE18 . . . . .2 A3
Powlett Rd ME2 . . . . .40 C1
Powster Rd BR1 . . . . .29 B3
Powys Cl DA7 . . . . .13 D8
Poynder Drive ME6 . . . . .95 A2
Poynder Rd RM18 . . . . . . .19 B6
Poynings Cl BR6 . . . . .87 C8
Poyntell Cres BR7 . . . . . . .53 D8
Poyntell Rd TN12 . . . . . . .260 F4
Pragnell Rd SE12 . . . . .29 B6
Prall's La TN12 . . . . .256 E2
Pratling St ME20 . . . . . . .129 C4
PRATLING STREET 129 C3
PRATT'S BOTTOM 87 D1
Precincts The CT1 . . . . . .175 A8
Premier Bsns Ctr ME4 . . . .64 C1
Premier Par ME20 . . . . . .128 E1
Premier Way ME10 . . . . . .68 F2
Prentis Cl ME10 . . . . .101 C5
Prentis Quay ME10 . . . . .101 F5
Prentiss Ct SE7 . . . . .1 D2
Prescott Ave BR5 . . . . .53 B3
Prescott Cl CT15 . . . . . . .278 E6
Prescott Ho TN28 . . . . . .373 A7
Presentation Ho 9 DA12 . . . . .37 B8
Prestbury Sq SE9 . . . . . . .29 F4
Prestedge Ave CT11 . . . . .83 E2
PRESTON Ash 146 B6
Faversham 138 D6
Preston Ave
Faversham ME13 . . . . . .138 D6
Gillingham ME7 . . . . .64 E1
Preston Ct
Faversham ME13 . . . . . .138 D6
Sidcup DA14 . . . . .30 F4
Preston Dr DA7 . . . . .13 D6
Preston Gr ME13 . . . . . . .138 D6
Preston Hall Gdns ME12 . . . . .49 E4
Preston Hall Hospl ME20 . . . . .128 F1
Preston Hill CT3 . . . . .146 B1
Preston Ho
Sutton at Hone DA4 . . . . .57 D7
1 Woolwich SE18 . . . . . . .2 A2
Preston La
Faversham ME13 . . . . . .138 D6
Preston CT3 . . . . .146 B5
Preston Malt Ho ME13 138 D6
Preston Par CT5 . . . . .107 F7
Preston Pk ME13 . . . . . . .138 D6
Preston Prim Sch CT3 146 C6
Preston Rd
Manston CT12 . . . . .82 E2
Northfleet DA11 . . . . .36 E7
Stourmouth CT3 . . . . . . .113 D1
Tonbridge TN9 . . . . .222 A1
Wingham CT3 . . . . .146 B3
Prestons Rd BR2 . . . . .85 A8
Preston St ME13 . . . . . . .138 D7
Preston Way ME8 . . . . . . .65 B2
Prestwood Cl SE18 . . . . . .13 A8
Pretoria Ho 4 Erith DA8 14 E7
8 Maidstone ME15 . . . . .195 E5
Pretoria Rd
Canterbury CT1 . . . . . . .175 B8
Chatham ME4 . . . . .63 F2
Gillingham ME7 . . . . .64 D3
Prettymans La TN8 . . . . .217 F4
Ramsgate CT11 . . . . .117 C6
Prices Ct 5 ME10 . . . . . .102 B4
Pridmore Rd ME6 . . . . . .127 F8
Priest Ave CT2 . . . . .174 C7
Priestdale Ct ME4 . . . . . . .63 E3
Priestfield Rd ME7 . . . . . .64 E5
Priestfields ME1 . . . . .63 B3
Priest Fields CT6 . . . . .77 F5
Priestfield Stad (Gillingham FC) ME7 . . .64 E5
Priest Hill RH8 . . . . .183 B6
Priestlands Park Rd DA15 . . . . .30 F5
Priestley Dr
Lunsford ME20 . . . . .127 F4
Tonbridge TN10 . . . . . . .222 E7
Priest & Sow Cnr CT5 . . . .75 B3
Priest's Wlk DA12 . . . . . . .38 A6
Priest Wlk CT5 . . . . .75 C3
PRIESTWOOD 93 B5
PRIESTWOOD GREEN 93 C5
Priestwood Rd DA13 . . . . .93 C5
PRIMMER'S GREEN 336 F5
Primmett Cl TN15 . . . . . . .90 E4
Primrose Ave ME8 . . . . . . .98 B5
Primrose Cl ME4 . . . . .26 E7
Primrose Dr
Aylesford ME20 . . . . . . .128 D1
Kingsnorth TN23 . . . . . .300 B4
Primrose Gr ME9 . . . . . . .134 A6
Primrose Hill CT4 . . . . . . .173 B7
Primrose Ho 10 ME15 . .195 E7

Primrose La ME9 . . . . . . .134 A6
Primrose Pl CT17 . . . . . . .278 B1
Primrose Rd
Dover CT17 . . . . .278 A1
Upper Halling ME2 . . . . . .94 E5
Primrose Terr DA12 . . . . .37 C7
Primrose Way
Cliffs End CT12 . . . . .116 C5
Whitstable CT5 . . . . .75 C1
Primrose Wlk TN12 . . . . .257 A5
Prince Andrew Rd CT10 83 E7
Prince Arthur Rd ME7 . . .64 B6
Prince Charles Ave
Chatham ME5 . . . . .79 B2
Minster (Sheppey) ME12 .47 C6
Sittingbourne ME10 . . . .102 C3
Sutton at Hone DA4 . . . . .57 D7
Prince Charles Rd CT10 83 E7
Prince Consort Dr BR7 .53 D8
Prince Henry Rd SE7 . . . . .11 C7
Prince Imperial Rd
Chislehurst BR7 . . . . .30 B1
Woolwich SE18 . . . . .11 F6
Prince John Rd SE9 . . . . . .11 E2
Prince Michael of Kent Ct DA1 . . . . .15 A5
Prince of Wales Rd SE3 11 A6
Prince of Wales Rdbt CT17 . . . . .310 D6
Prince of Wales Residential Pk CT21 .353 E8
Prince of Wales Terr CT14 . . . . .215 D5
Prince Phillip Lodge The ME20 . . . . .128 F1
Prince Regent La E16 . . . .1 C7
Prince Regent Sta E16 . . . .1 C6
Prince Rupert Rd SE9 . . .11 F3
Princes Ave
Chatham ME5 . . . . .97 B5
Dartford DA2 . . . . .34 B7
Minster (Sheppey) ME12 .47 D7
Orpington BR5 . . . . .53 E4
Prince's Ave CT12 . . . . . . .83 B1
Princes Cl
Birchington CT7 . . . . .80 D7
Sidcup DA14 . . . . .31 D5
Princes Cres 10 CT9 . . . .50 J2
Princes Dr CT3 . . . . .182 A8
Princes Gate 18 CT20 . . .335 E5
Prince's Gdns CT9 . . . . . . .51 C2
Princes Par CT21 . . . . . . .333 E2
Prince's Par CT5 . . . . .75 C5
Princes Plain BR2 . . . . . . .52 E1
Princes Plain Prim Sch BR2 . . . . .52 E2
Princes Rd Dartford DA1 33 D7
Dartford, Fleet-Downs DA1 . . . . .34 C7
Gravesend DA12 . . . . . . .37 C5
Hextable BR8 . . . . .33 A2
Ramsgate CT11 . . . . .117 D8
Princess Alice Way SE28 2 D4
Princess Anne Rd CT10 83 E7
Princess Cl Erith SE28 . . . .3 D7
Whitstable CT5 . . . . .75 C3
Princess Margaret Ave
Margate CT9 . . . . .51 E2
Ramsgate CT12 . . . . .83 A1
Princess Margaret Rd RM18 . . . . .20 D7
Princess Mary Ave ME4 64 B7
Princess Par BR6 . . . . .86 A7
Princess Rd CT5 . . . . .75 C3
Princess Royal University Hospl BR6 . . . . .86 A6
Princess St Bexley DA7 . . .13 F4
Folkestone CT19 . . . . . . .335 E6
Princes St Deal CT14 . . . .215 D7
11 Dover CT16 . . . . . . .310 D7
Gravesend DA11 . . . . . . .19 B1
Maidstone ME14 . . . . . . .195 E5
9 Ramsgate CT11 . . . . .117 E6
Rochester ME1 . . . . .63 C4
Prince's St Margate CT9 .50 J2
Princes Terr CT11 . . . . . . .332 F1
Princes View DA1 . . . . . . .34 A7
Princes Way
Canterbury CT2 . . . . .142 E1
Detling ME14 . . . . .131 A1
Prince's Wlk CT9 . . . . . . .51 D3
Prince William Ct CT14 . . . . 215 D7
PRINTSTILE 253 A3
Prinys Dr ME8 . . . . .98 C4
Priolo Rd SE7 . . . . .1 C1
Prioress Cres 11 DA9 . . . .17 C3
Prioress Rd CT2 . . . . .174 D8
Prioress Wlk CT16 . . . . . .278 A3
Prior Pl ME1 . . . . .63 B1
Prior Rd TN28 . . . . .377 E8
Priorsdean Cl ME16 . . . . .160 E1
Priorsford Ave BR5 . . . . . .54 B5
Priors Heath TN17 . . . . . .318 C2
Prior's Lees 8 CT20 . . . . .335 D4
Prior's Way TN18 . . . . . . .282 A6
Priory Ave BR5 . . . . .53 D3
Priory Ct
Broadstairs CT10 . . . . . . .83 F3
Bromley BR7 . . . . .52 F8
Dartford DA1 . . . . .15 D2
East Farleigh ME15 . . . .194 B8
New Romney TN28 . . . . .372 F6
Priory Ctyd CT11 . . . . .117 D6
Priory Dr SE2 . . . . .3 D1
Priory Fields DA4 . . . . . . .89 F8
Priory Fields Sch CT17 310 B8

Priory Gate 4 ME14 . . . .162 A5
Priory Gate Rd CT17 . . . .310 C8
Priory Gdns
Canterbury CT1 . . . . .175 A6
Dartford DA1 . . . . .15 D2
Folkestone CT20 . . . . . . .335 D4
Priory Gdns ★ BR6 . . . . . .54 B2
Priory Gr
Aylesford ME20 . . . . . . .128 D1
Dover CT17 . . . . .310 C8
Tonbridge TN9 . . . . .254 B8
Priory Hill Dartford DA1 . .15 D1
Dover CT17 . . . . .310 C8
Priory Ho Dover CT17 . . .310 C7
4 Greenwich SE7 . . . . . . .11 C8
Priory Hospl Hayes Grove The BR2 . . . . .85 A8
Priory Inf Sch CT11 . . . . .117 D7
Priory La Eynsford DA4 . . .56 F1
Herne Bay CT6 . . . . .77 A3
Sellindge TN25 . . . . .303 D3
Priory Leas SE9 . . . . .29 E7
Priory Mews DA2 . . . . . . .34 C8
Priory of St Jacob CT1 174 E6
Priory Pl Dartford DA1 . . .15 D1
Faversham ME13 . . . . . .105 C1
Priory Rd
Aldington Frith TN25 . . .329 C4
Dartford DA1 . . . . .15 D1
Dover CT16, CT17 . . . . .310 D8
Faversham ME13 . . . . . .138 C8
Gillingham ME8 . . . . .65 A2
Maidstone ME15 . . . . . .162 A3
Ramsgate CT11 . . . . .117 D6
Rochester ME2 . . . . .63 A6
Tonbridge TN9 . . . . .254 B8
Priory Retail Pk DA1 . . . . .15 D2
Priory Row 3 CT1 . . . . . .138 C8
Priory Sch The BR5 . . . . . .54 C1
Priory Sh Ctr The DA1 . . .33 E8
Priory Sports Ctr BR6 . . . .54 C1
Priory St
10 Dover CT16 . . . . .310 D8
Tonbridge TN9 . . . . .254 B8
Priory Station Approach Rd CT17 . . . . .310 C7
Priory The TN9 . . . . .376 C6
Priory Way TN30 . . . . . . .345 C2
Priory Wlk TN9 . . . . .254 B8
Pristling La TN12 . . . . . . .292 B8
Pritchard Ct ME7 . . . . . . .64 C3
Pritchard Dr CT18 . . . . . .307 A4
Probyn Mews CT18 . . . . .306 F3
Proctor Wlk CT18 . . . . . .306 F4
Progress Est The ME15 . . . . .196 A4
Promenade
Birchington CT7 . . . . .80 F8
Deal CT14 . . . . .215 D3
Promenade The 5 ME2 . . .49 G2
Prospect Ave 8 ME2 . . . .63 B8
Prospect Cl Erith DA7 . . . . .4 A2
Westgate on Sea CT8 . . . .81 F7
Prospect Cotts
Boughton Lees TN25 . . .236 E3
Harbledown CT2 . . . . . . .141 E1
Lamberhurst TN3 . . . . . .317 A3
Pratt's Bottom BR6 . . . . .87 C2
Shepherdswell CT15 . . . .244 D4
Prospect Ct 20 CT11 . . . .117 E6
Prospect Gdns CT12 . . . .115 B7
Prospect Gr DA12 . . . . . . .37 D8
Prospect Hill CT6 . . . . . . .77 A5
Prospect Mews CT21 . . .333 C2
Prospect Pk TN4 . . . . . . .253 F1
Prospect Pl
7 Broadstairs CT10 . . . . .84 B4
Bromley BR2 . . . . .52 B6
Canterbury CT1 . . . . .175 A7
Collier Street TN12 . . . . .226 C2
Prospect Pl DA1 . . . . .15 F1
Prospect Pl Dover CT17 278 B1
Eastling ME13 . . . . .168 A6
Gravesend DA12 . . . . . . .37 D8
Grays RM17 . . . . .18 B8
Hamstreet TN26 . . . . . . .348 F4
Maidstone ME16 . . . . . . .161 B3
St Nicholas at Wade CT7 .79 E1
Prospect Rd
Birchington CT7 . . . . .80 F7
Broadstairs CT10 . . . . . . .84 B4
Folkestone CT20 . . . . . . .334 D3
Hythe CT21 . . . . .333 C2
Minster (Thanet) CT12 . 115 B6
Royal Tunbridge Wells, Camden Park TN2 . . . . .286 C3
Royal Tunbridge Wells TN4 . . . . 285 F8
Sevenoaks TN13 . . . . . .154 C4
Prospect Row
Chatham, Brompton ME7 . . . . .64 A6
Chatham ME4 . . . . .64 A3
Prospect Terr
Elham CT4 . . . . .273 F4
21 Ramsgate CT11 . . . . .117 E6
Prospect Vale SE18 . . . . . .1 E2
Prospect Way TN25 . . . .302 E5
Prospero Ho 7 DA17 . . . .4 A1
Provender La ME13, ME9 . . . . .137 A6
Provender Way ME14 . . .162 E5
Providence Chapel TN12 . . . . .259 C6
Providence Cotts
Groombridge TN3 . . . . . .312 C7
Higham ME3 . . . . .39 B2
Providence Pl TN27 . . . . .262 A7
Providence St
Ashford TN23 . . . . .300 C8
Stone DA9 . . . . .17 A2

Prudhoe Ct 27 DA2 . . . . . 16 B1
Puckle La CT1 . . . . 175 A6
Pucknells Cl BR8 . . . . . . 55 C8
Puddingcake La TN17 344 C5
Pudding La Ash CT3 . . . 147 D1
Maidstone ME14 . . . . . . 161 F4
Seal TN15 . . . . 154 F6
Pudding Rd ME8 . . . . 98 F8
PUDDLEDOCK 32 E2
Puddledock La
Hextable BR8, DA2 . . . . . 32 F2
Toy's Hill TN16 . . . . 185 A3
Puffin Ct CT18 . . . . 307 A3
Puffin Rd Grain ME3 . . . . 27 B5
Herne Bay CT6 . . . . 77 F4
Pullington Cotts TN17 342 E6
Pullman Cl CT12 . . . . . . 117 C8
Pullman Mews SE12 . . . . 29 B5
Pullman Pl SE9 . . . . 11 E2
Pump Cl ME19 . . . . 127 D1
Pump La Chelsfield BR6 . . 88 B5
Gillingham ME7, ME8 . . . 65 D3
1 Margate CT9 . . . . 50 J2
Pump Terr TN1 . . . . 286 B4
Punch Croft DA3 . . . . 91 E7
Purbeck Rd ME4 . . . . 63 E2
Purcell Ave TN10 . . . . . . 222 F6
Purchas Ct CT2 . . . . 142 C4
Purchase La TN26 . . . . . 298 E8
PURFLEET 16 A8
Purfleet By-Pass RM19 16 D8
Purland Rd SE28 . . . . 2 F4
Purneys Rd SE9 . . . . 11 D3
Purrett Rd SE18 . . . . 2 F1
Purr Wood CT4 . . . . 205 B2
Purser Way ME7 . . . . 64 C7
Pursey Cl TN15 . . . . 90 E4
PUTLANDS 256 F5
Putlands Sp & L Ctr
TN12 . . . . 257 A5
Puttenden Rd TN11 . . . . 189 F3
Puttney Dr ME10 . . . . . . 102 A8
Pye Alley La CT5 . . . . . . 108 C3
PYE CORNER 231 A6
Pym Ho TN27 . . . . 234 D7
Pym Orch TN16 . . . . 152 C3
Pympes Court Farm Ctr★
ME15 . . . . 194 E6
Pynham Cl SE2 . . . . 3 B3
Pynson's Ind Est CT10 . . 83 D4
Pyott Mews 3 CT1 . . . . . 143 B1
Pyrus Cl ME5 . . . . 130 A8
Pyson's Rd CT10, CT12 . . 83 D3
Pyson's Road Ind Est
CT10 . . . . 83 D3

Q

Quadrant The DA7 . . . . . 13 D7
Quaggy Wlk SE3 . . . . 11 A3
Quain Ct CT20 . . . . 335 C4
Quaker Cl TN13 . . . . 154 D4
Quaker Dr TN17 . . . . . . 320 D6
Quaker La TN17 . . . . 320 D6
Quakers Cl DA3 . . . . 58 E6
Quaker's Hall La TN13 154 C5
Quantock Cl TN2 . . . . . . 286 D5
Quantock Dr TN24 . . . . . 268 B4
Quantock Gdns CT12 . . . 83 B3
Quantock Rd DA1 . . . . . . 14 E5
QUARRIES THE 195 C4
Quarries The ME17 . . . . 195 C4
Quarrington La TN25 . . 302 B8
Quarry Bank TN9 . . . . . . 254 A7
Quarry Cotts
Rockrobin TN5 . . . . 336 D7
Sevenoaks TN13 . . . . . . 154 A4
Stone in Oxney TN30 . . 360 C3
Quarry Hill TN15 . . . . . 154 D4
Quarry Hill Par 3 TN9 254 B8
Quarry Hill Rd
Borough Green TN15 . . . 156 F6
Tonbridge TN9 . . . . 254 B8
Quarry Rd Hythe CT21 . . 333 B3
Maidstone ME15 . . . . . . 162 A2
Royal Tunbridge Wells
TN1 . . . . 286 B5
Quarry Rise TN9 . . . . . . 254 A7
Quarry Sq ME14 . . . . . . 162 A5
Quarry View TN23 . . . . 299 D7
Quarry Wlk CT21 . . . . . . 334 A3
Quarry Wood TN25 . . . . 330 A6
Quarry Wood Ind Est
ME20 . . . . 160 E8
QUARTER THE
Headcorn 264 B5
Staplehurst 260 E1
Tenterden 345 A4
Quay Cotts ME9 . . . . 103 E6
Quay Ct CT5 . . . . 74 E2
Quay La
Faversham ME13 . . . . . 138 D8
Sandwich CT13 . . . . 149 A1
Swanscombe DA9 . . . . . 17 B3
Quayside ME4 . . . . 64 B8
Quay The ME9 . . . . 103 E6
Quebec Ave TN16 . . . . . 151 D1
Quebec Cotts 9 TN16 151 D1
Quebec Ho★ TN16 . . . 151 D1
Quebec Rd RM18 . . . . . . 19 A5
Quebec Sq 10 TN16 . . . 151 D1
Queen Anne Ave BR2 . . . 52 A6
Queen Anne Gate DA7 . . 13 D4
Queen Anne Rd ME14 . 162 B4
Queen Bertha Rd CT11 117 C6
Queen Bertha's Ave
CT7 . . . . 81 C8
QUEENBOROUGH 46 A5
Queenborough Dr ME12 47 B7
Queenborough Fst Sch
ME11 . . . . 46 B5
Queen Borough Gdns
BR7 . . . . 30 D2
Queenborough Rd
Halfway Houses ME12 . . . 46 C6
Queenborough ME12 . . . 46 C4
Queenborough Sta
ME11 . . . . 46 A5
Queenbridge Ind Pk
RM20 . . . . 17 A8
Queendown Ave ME8 . . . 98 D5
Queendown Rd CT7 . . . . 82 A3
Queendown Warren
Nature Reserve★ ME9 99 B3
Queen Elizabeth Ave
CT9 . . . . 51 D1
Queen Elizabeth Rd
CT16 . . . . 310 F8
Queen Elizabeth's Gram
Sch ME13 . . . . 138 D8
Queen Elizabeth Sq
ME15 . . . . 195 D6
Queen Elizabeth The
SE18 . . . . 11 E7
Queen Elizabeth the Queen
Mother Hospl CT9 . . . . 82 F8
Queen Mary's Hospl
DA14 . . . . 31 A2
Queen Mother Ct
CT14 . . . . 215 D2
Queen Mother Ct The
ME1 . . . . 63 B4
Queens Ave
Canterbury CT2 . . . . . . 142 E1
Dover CT17 . . . . 310 A7
Folkestone CT20 . . . . . 334 B6
Herne Bay CT6 . . . . 77 D5
Queen's Ave
Birchington CT7 . . . . 80 D7
Broadstairs CT10 . . . . . . 84 B6
Maidstone ME16 . . . . . . 161 D5
Margate CT9 . . . . 50 I1
Ramsgate CT12 . . . . 83 B1
Snodland ME6 . . . . 128 A8
Queensbridge Dr CT6 . . 76 C4
Queens Cotts TN5 . . . . . 336 E6
Queens Court TN12 . . . 257 C8
Queenscroft Rd SE9 . . . . 11 D1
Queens Ct
Ashford TN24 . . . . 268 C3
Edenbridge TN8 . . . . . . 217 D1
Gillingham ME8 . . . . 99 A8
11 Hawkhurst TN18 . . . . 341 A2
2 Hythe CT21 . . . . 333 B1
Margate CT9 . . . . 51 A3
1 Sidcup DA14 . . . . 31 A4
Queen's Ct CT6 . . . . 77 A4
Queensdown Rd CT14 248 D4
Queen's Dr TN14 . . . . . . 154 C7
Queen's Farm Rd DA12 38 E7
Queensgate ME16 . . . . . 161 D5
Queens Gate Gdns BR7 53 D8
Queens Gate Rd CT11 117 C8
Queens Gdns
Broadstairs CT10 . . . . . . 84 B3
Dartford DA2 . . . . 34 B7
Herne Bay CT6 . . . . 76 F5
Queen's Gdns
Dover CT16, CT17 . . . . . 310 D8
Royal Tunbridge Wells
TN4 . . . . 286 B6
Queens Ho ME16 . . . . . . 161 B3
Queensland Ct RM18 . . . 18 F5
Queensland Ho 2 E16 . . . 2 A5
Queen's Lea CT15 . . . . . 308 E5
Queens Lodge CT9 . . . . . 51 B3
Queens Mews CT14 . . . 215 D6
Queen's Mews 12
TN18 . . . . 341 A2
Queens Par
12 Faversham ME13 . . 138 D7
Margate CT9 . . . . 51 A3
Queen's Pas BR7 . . . . 30 B2
Queen's Prom CT9 . . . . . 51 B3
Queens Rd
Aylesham CT3 . . . . 210 F5
Erith DA8 . . . . 14 E8
Gravesend DA12 . . . . 37 C5
Minster (Sheppey) ME12 47 D7
Whitstable CT5 . . . . 75 A2
Queen's Rd Ash CT3 . . . 147 D2
Ashford TN24 . . . . 269 A1
Bexley DA16 . . . . 13 B5
Broadstairs CT10 . . . . . . 84 B4
Bromley BR1 . . . . 52 A7
Chatham ME5 . . . . 64 D1
Chislehurst BR7 . . . . 30 B2
Faversham ME13 . . . . . 138 B7
Gillingham ME7 . . . . 64 C4
Hawkhurst TN18 . . . . . . 341 A2
Littlestone-on-Sea
TN28 . . . . 373 D6
Lydd TN29 . . . . 376 C6
Maidstone ME16 . . . . . . 161 C4
Ramsgate CT11 . . . . 117 F7
Royal Tunbridge Wells
TN4 . . . . 286 B6
Snodland ME6 . . . . 128 A8
Westgate on Sea CT8 . . . 81 F8
Queen's Rise CT14 . . . . 247 F5
Queens St ME3 . . . . 41 B8
Queen St Ashford TN23 . 268 B2
Bexley DA7 . . . . 13 F4
Chatham ME4 . . . . 64 A4
Deal CT14 . . . . 215 D6
Dover CT16, CT17 . . . . . 310 D7
Erith DA8 . . . . 14 E8
Folkestone CT20 . . . . . 335 E5
Gravesend DA12 . . . . 19 B1
Herne Bay CT6 . . . . 76 F5
Kings Hill ME19 . . . . 159 B3
Margate CT9 . . . . 50 I2
Queen St *continued*
Paddock Wood TN12 . . . 257 D7
Ramsgate CT11 . . . . 117 E6
Rochester ME1 . . . . 63 C4
Sandhurst TN18 . . . . . . 356 B5
Queens The CT14 . . . . . 215 D5
QUEEN STREET 257 D7
Queensway
Allhallows-on-Sea ME3 . . . 9 D3
Dymchurch TN29 . . . . . 352 E2
Hayes BR2, BR4 . . . . 85 A6
Lydd TN29 . . . . 376 C6
Orpington BR5 . . . . 53 C3
Queens Way ME14 . . . . 131 A1
Queen's Way ME12 . . . . . 46 A8
Queenswood Rd
Kit's Coty ME20 . . . . . . 129 D7
Sidcup DA15 . . . . 12 F1
Queen Victoria Meml
Hospl CT6 . . . . 77 B4
Quentins Rd TN16 . . . . 119 B3
Quernmore Cl BR1 . . . . . 29 A2
Quernmore Rd BR1 . . . . 29 A2
Quern Rd CT14 . . . . 215 A2
Querns Pl CT1 . . . . 175 B8
Querns Rd CT1 . . . . 175 C8
Quern The ME15 . . . . . . 161 E1
Quested Rd CT19 . . . . . 334 E6
Quested Way ME17 . . . . 198 C6
Questor DA1 . . . . 33 F6
Quetta Rd CT12 . . . . 82 F1
Quex Ct CT7 . . . . 81 B6
Quex House & Gdns★
CT7 . . . . 81 B5
Quex Rd CT8 . . . . 81 F8
Quex View Rd CT7 . . . . . 81 A5
Quickrells Ave ME3 . . . . 22 B5
Quickstep Cl ME10 . . . . 101 F8
Quickthorn Cres ME5 . . . 96 E5
Quiet Nook BR2 . . . . 85 D7
Quilter Rd BR5 . . . . 54 D1
Quilters Place SE9 . . . . . 30 C7
Quilter St SE18 . . . . 2 F1
Quince Orch TN26 . . . . 349 A7
Quincewood Gdns
TN10 . . . . 222 B7
Quindell Place ME19 . . 159 C3
Quinion Cl ME5 . . . . 130 A8
Quinnel Cl SE18 . . . . 2 F1
Quinnell St ME8 . . . . 65 E1
Quinneys Pl CT5 . . . . 75 D2
Quinton Rd ME10 . . . . . 101 C7
Quixote Cres ME2 . . . . . . 40 B1

R

Rabbit Hole CT4 . . . . . . 243 A7
RABBIT'S CROSS 228 E3
Rabbits Rd DA4 . . . . 57 E7
Rablus Pl DA4 . . . . 56 F3
Racefield Cl DA12 . . . . . . 38 E1
Rackham Cl DA16 . . . . . . 13 B5
Radburn Pl DA10 . . . . 17 E2
Radcliffe Ct CT21 . . . . . 333 B2
RADFALL 109 C5
Radfall Cnr CT5 . . . . . . 109 C6
Radfall Gate CT5 . . . . . 109 C6
Radfall Hill CT5 . . . . . . 109 D5
Radfall Rd CT5 . . . . 109 D4
Radfall Ride CT5 . . . . . 109 C5
RADFIELD 103 A2
Radfield Dr 3 DA2 . . . . . 34 C8
Radfield Way DA15 . . . . . 30 D8
Radland Rd E16 . . . . 1 A7
Radleigh Gdns ME1 . . . . 63 E1
Radley Cl CT10 . . . . 84 A6
Radley Ho 13 SE2 . . . . 3 D4
Radnor Ave DA16 . . . . . . 13 B2
Radnor Bridge Rd CT19,
CT20 . . . . 335 E5
Radnor Chambers 13
CT20 . . . . 335 D4
Radnor Cl
Chislehurst BR7 . . . . 30 E2
Herne Bay CT6 . . . . 77 B1
Maidstone ME14 . . . . . . 161 E7
Radnor Cliff CT20 . . . . 335 A3
Radnor Cliff Cres
CT20 . . . . 335 A3
Radnor Cres SE18 . . . . . 13 A7
Radnor Park Ave CT19 335 C6
Radnor Park Cres
CT19 . . . . 335 C5
Radnor Park Gdns
CT19 . . . . 335 C6
Radnor Park Ho CT19 . 335 C6
Radnor Park Rd CT19 . 335 C6
Radnor Park W CT19 . . 335 B6
Radnor St 20 CT19 . . . . 335 E5
Radzan Cl DA2 . . . . 32 E6
Raeburn Ave DA1 . . . . . . 15 B2
Raeburn Cl TN10 . . . . . . 222 E6
Raeburn Rd DA15 . . . . . . 12 E1
Rafford Way BR1 . . . . 52 B6
RAF Manston Spitfire &
Hurricane Meml Mus★
CT12 . . . . 82 A2
Raggatt Pl ME15 . . . . . . 162 B2
Ragge Way TN15 . . . . . . 154 F7
Raggleswood BR7 . . . . . . 53 A8
Rag Hill TN16 . . . . 150 E6
Rag Hill Cl TN16 . . . . . . 150 E6
Rag Hill Rd TN16 . . . . . 150 E6
Raglan Ct SE12 . . . . 11 A2
Raglan Pl 10 CT10 . . . . . 84 B4
Raglan Prim Sch BR2 . . . 52 D5
Raglan Rd Bromley BR2 . . 52 C5
Erith DA17 . . . . 3 F2
Woolwich SE18 . . . . 2 C1
Ragstone Ct ME20 . . . . 160 C8
Ragstone Fields ME15 195 E4
Ragstone Hollow
TN25 . . . . 330 A6
Ragstone Rd ME15 . . . . 163 A2
Ragstones TN15 . . . . . . 154 F7
Railway Ave CT5 . . . . 74 E1
Railway Cotts
Cowden TN8 . . . . 282 D8
Marden TN12 . . . . 259 D6
Teynham ME9 . . . . 103 D3
Railway Hill CT4 . . . . . . 242 E8
Railway Pl Erith DA17 . . . . 4 A3
21 Gravesend DA12 . . . . . 19 B1
Railway Rd ME12 . . . . 28 B2
Railway Sidings The
DA13 . . . . 60 A4
Railway St Chatham ME4 63 F4
Gillingham ME7 . . . . 64 D6
Northfleet DA11 . . . . 18 A2
Railway Street Ind Pk
ME7 . . . . 64 D6
Railway Terr
Margate CT9 . . . . 50 H1
Queenborough ME11 . . . . 46 A5
Westerham TN16 . . . . . 151 D1
RAINHAM Chatham 98 E8
Essex 4 F8
Rainham Cl
Maidstone ME15 . . . . . . 162 A1
Sidcup SE9 . . . . 12 E1
Rainham Mark Gram Sch
ME8 . . . . 65 D2
Rainham Rd ME5 . . . . 64 C3
Rainham Sch for Girls
ME8 . . . . 98 C8
Rainham Sh Ctr 2 ME8 65 F1
Rainham Sta ME8 . . . . . . 65 F1
Rainton Rd SE7 . . . . 1 A1
Raite Gn 5 ME10 . . . . . 101 D6
Raleigh Cl
Ashford TN24 . . . . 301 A8
Chatham ME5 . . . . 97 A6
Erith DA8 . . . . 14 F8
Raleigh Ct 1 CT11 . . . . 117 F8
Raleigh Mews 6 BR6 . . . 86 F5
Raleigh Way ME12 . . . . . 46 E6
Ramac Ind Est SE7 . . . . . . 1 B1
Ramac Way SE7 . . . . 1 B1
Ramillies Cl ME5 . . . . 97 A6
Ramillies Rd DA15 . . . . . 13 B1
Ram La TN25, TN27 . . . . 266 C8
RAM LANE 234 E2
Rammell Mews TN17 . 320 D4
Ramp A CT16 . . . . 310 H8
Rampart Rd CT21 . . . . . 333 B2
Ramparts The CT13 . . . 181 A8
Ramp B CT16 . . . . 310 H8
Ramp C CT16 . . . . 310 G8
Ramp D CT16 . . . . 310 G8
Rampion Cl ME14 . . . . . 162 E5
RAMSDEN 54 C1
Ramsden Cl BR5 . . . . 54 C1
Ramsden La TN17 . . . . . 342 F4
Ramsden Rd Erith DA8 . . 14 D7
Orpington BR5 . . . . 54 B1
Ramsey Cl
Canterbury CT2 . . . . 142 E1
Maidstone ME15 . . . . . . 162 A2
Ramsey Ho
8 Canterbury CT1 . . . . . 174 F7
Deal CT14 . . . . 215 C3
RAMSGATE 117 C4
Ramsgate Cl E16 . . . . 1 B5
Ramsgate Holy Trinity
Prim Sch CT10 . . . . 84 A1
Ramsgate Maritime Mus★
CT12 . . . . 117 E6
Ramsgate Rd
Broadstairs CT10 . . . . . . 84 B4
Broadstairs, Dumpton CT10,
CT11 . . . . 83 F2
Margate CT10, CT9 . . . . . 83 A6
Sandwich CT13 . . . . 149 A7
Ramsgate Sports Ctr
CT11 . . . . 117 D7
Ramsgate Sta CT12 . . . 117 C8
RAMSLYE 285 D1
Ramslye Rd TN4 . . . . . . 313 E8
Ramstone Cl TN25 . . . . 302 E5
Ramus Wood Ave BR6 . . 86 E5
Rance Ho 11 SE18 . . . . . . 1 E2
Rancliffe Gdns SE9 . . . . . 11 E3
Rancorn Rd CT9 . . . . 50 G1
Randall Cl DA8 . . . . 14 C8
Randall Hill Rd TN15 . . 124 F3
Randall Rd ME4 . . . . 63 E1
Randalls Row ME15 . . . 194 F5
Randall St ME14 . . . . . . 161 F6
Randle's La TN14 . . . . . 120 D5
Randle Way ME9 . . . . . . 102 E2
Randolph App E16 . . . . . . 1 C7
Randolph Cl Bexley DA7 . 14 C4
Canterbury CT1 . . . . 175 A7
Randolph Cotts ME2 . . . . 40 B1
Randolph Ct CT8 . . . . 50 C1
Randolph Gdns TN24 . . 268 E5
Randolph Ho
15 Folkestone CT20 . . . 335 E5
Gillingham ME7 . . . . 64 C5
Randolph La TN31 . . . . 368 B3
Randolph Rd
Dover CT17 . . . . 278 B1
Gillingham ME7 . . . . 64 C5
Orpington BR2 . . . . 52 F1
Randolph Sq CT9 . . . . . . 50 J3
Ranelagh Gdns
1 Broadstairs CT10 . . . . 83 E5
Northfleet DA11 . . . . 36 F8
Ranelagh Gr CT10 . . . . . 83 E5
Ranelagh Rd
Deal CT14 . . . . 215 D5
Sheerness ME12 . . . . 28 C2
Rangefield Rd BR1 . . . . . 29 A3
Range Rd
Eastchurch ME12 . . . . . . 48 D1
Range Rd *continued*
Gravesend DA12 . . . . 37 E8
Hythe CT21 . . . . 333 B1
Range Road Ind Est
CT21 . . . . 333 B1
Rangeworth Pl DA15 . . . 30 F5
Rankine Rd TN2 . . . . . . 286 D7
Ranleigh Gdns DA7 . . . . . 13 F7
Ranmore Path BR5 . . . . . 54 A5
Ranscombe Cl ME2 . . . . . 62 D5
Ranscombe Farm Cotts
ME2 . . . . 62 C4
Ransley Gn TN26 . . . . . 349 F8
Ransome Way CT7 . . . . . 80 F6
Ransom Rd 1 SE7 . . . . . . 1 C1
Ranters La TN17 . . . . . . 318 C7
Ranworth Cl DA7, DA8 . . 14 E5
Raphael Ave RM18 . . . . . 19 B7
Raphael Ct TN11 . . . . . . 221 E7
Raphael Rd DA12 . . . . . . 37 D8
Rare Species Conservation
Area★ CT13 . . . . 180 E6
Rashleigh Way DA4 . . . . 57 C5
Raspberry Hill La ME9 . . 68 D6
Ratcliffe Cl SE12 . . . . . . 29 A8
Ratcliffe Highway
High Halstow ME3 . . . . . 24 D5
Hoo St Werburgh ME3 . . 41 C6
Rathmore Rd
Gravesend DA11 . . . . 37 B8
Greenwich SE7 . . . . 1 B1
RATLING 211 A8
Ratling Rd CT3 . . . . 210 F7
Rattington St CT4 . . . . 173 E2
Ravelin Ho ME12 . . . . . . 28 C2
Raven Cl ME20 . . . . 128 A1
Ravenlea Rd CT20 . . . . 335 A5
Ravensbourne Ave CT6 77 B3
Ravensbourne Coll of
Design &
Communication BR7 . . 29 F3
Ravensbourne Ct 22
BR5 . . . . 54 D1
Ravensbourne Rd
Bromley BR1 . . . . 52 A6
Crayford DA1 . . . . 15 A4
Ravensbourne Sch The
BR2 . . . . 52 B5
Ravensbury Rd BR5 . . . . 54 A5
Ravenscourt Rd
Deal CT14 . . . . 215 C5
Orpington BR5 . . . . 54 B7
Rough Common CT2 . . . 142 B3
Ravenscroft Cl 5 E16 . . . 1 A8
Ravenscroft Cres SE9 . . 29 F5
Ravenscroft Rd E16 . . . . . 1 A8
Ravens Dane Cl ME15 . 163 A1
Ravenshill BR7 . . . . 53 B8
Raven's Hoe DA14 . . . . . 31 A3
Ravens Knowle ME1 . . . . 95 D4
Ravensleigh Gdns BR1 . 29 B3
Ravensquay Bsns Ctr
BR5 . . . . 54 B4
Ravens Way SE12 . . . . . . 11 A2
Ravenswood DA5 . . . . . . 31 E7
Ravenswood Ave
Rochester ME2 . . . . 40 B1
7 Rochester ME2 . . . . . . 63 B8
Royal Tunbridge Wells
TN2 . . . . 286 D6
Ravens Wood Sch BR2 . 85 D7
Ravensworth Rd SE9 . . . 29 F4
Ravine Gr SE18 . . . . 12 E8
Rawdon Rd
Maidstone ME15 . . . . . . 162 A3
Ramsgate CT11 . . . . 117 C6
Rawlings Cl 3 BR6 . . . . . 86 F5
Rawling St ME9 . . . . . . 134 F3
Rawsthorne Cl E16 . . . . . . 1 F5
Rayfield Cl BR2 . . . . 52 E3
Rayfield Ct ME6 . . . . 95 B1
Rayford Cl DA1 . . . . 15 C2
Rayham Rd CT5 . . . . . . 109 A8
Ray Lamb Way DA8 . . . . 15 B7
Rayleas Cl SE18 . . . . 12 B6
Rayleigh Cl ME16 . . . . . 161 D7
Rayleigh Ho 2 ME15 . . 195 D8
Rayleigh Rd E16 . . . . 1 B5
Raymere Gdns SE18 . . . . 12 E7
Raymer Rd ME14 . . . . . 162 B8
Raymond Ave CT1 . . . . 175 A6
Raymond Fuller Way
TN24 . . . . 268 E4
Raymond Postgate Ct 5
SE28 . . . . 3 B6
Raymoor Ave TN29 . . . 366 A4
Raynehurst Com Prim Sch
DA12 . . . . 37 F5
Rayner Hill Cotts
ME17 . . . . 200 C5
Rayners Ct DA11 . . . . 18 B1
Rayners Hill ME17 . . . . 200 C5
Raynham Villas TN12 . 227 A4
Rays Hill DA4 . . . . 57 C4
Raywood Office Complex
TN27 . . . . 234 B4
Reach Cl CT15 . . . . 279 F5
Reachfields CT21 . . . . . 333 A1
Reach Mdw CT15 . . . . . 280 A6
Reach Rd Lympne CT21 331 D2
St Margaret's at Cliffe
CT15 . . . . 279 F5
Reactor One Rd TN29 . 380 C2
Reactor Two Rd TN29 380 C2
Reader's Bridge Rd
TN30 . . . . 323 E4
Readers Ct ME18 . . . . . 193 A8
Readers La TN31 . . . . . 367 F5
Reading Cl CT14 . . . . . 215 B1
Reading Ho 4 ME15 . . . 195 F5
Reading Rd CT17 . . . . . 309 F7
Reading St
Broadstairs CT10 . . . . . . 83 F8
Tenterden TN30 . . . . . . 346 C2
READING STREET
Broadstairs 83 F7
Tenterden 346 C2
Reading Street Rd CT10,
CT9 . . . . 83 E8
Readscroft Rd ME8 . . . . 98 D5
Read Way DA12 . . . . 37 E3
Realgar Ct 4 ME10 . . . . 101 D6
Reams Way ME10 . . . . . . 69 A1
Rebecca Ct
6 Margate CT9 . . . . 51 B2
Sidcup DA14 . . . . 31 B4
Recca La CT15, CT18 . . 275 A4
Recreation Ave ME6 . . . 128 A8
Recreation Cl ME14 . . . 162 B6
Recreation Ground Rd
TN30 . . . . 345 B7
Recreation Way ME10 . . 69 A1
Rectory Bglws TN26 . . . 326 F8
Rectory Bsns Ctr 2
DA14 . . . . 31 B4
Rectory Cl Crayford DA1 . 14 E3
Sidcup DA14 . . . . 31 B4
Snodland ME6 . . . . 128 A8
Woodchurch TN26 . . . . . 326 A2
Wouldham ME1 . . . . 95 C5
Rectory Ct 3 RM17 . . . . . 18 D8
Rectory Dr TN3 . . . . 253 D3
Rectory Field Cres SE7 . 11 C7
Rectory Fields TN17 . . 320 D5
Rectory Gdns CT5 . . . . . . 75 D2
Rectory Grange ME1 . . . 63 D3
Rectory La Barham CT4 210 A2
Brasted TN16 . . . . 152 C3
Harrietsham ME17 . . . . 198 E5
Hythe CT21 . . . . 333 B5
Ightham TN15 . . . . 156 C5
Lyminge CT18 . . . . 305 C6
Maidstone ME16 . . . . . . 161 A1
Sevenoaks TN13 . . . . . . 154 C1
Sidcup DA14 . . . . 31 C4
Sutton Valence ME17 . . 229 C6
Titsey TN16 . . . . 150 E4
Rectory Lane N ME19 . . 127 E2
Rectory Lane S ME19 . . 127 E1
Rectory Mdw DA13 . . . . . 36 A2
Rectory Park Rd TN12 290 A2
Rectory Pl SE18 . . . . 2 A2
Rectory Rd
Broadstairs CT10 . . . . . . 84 B5
Cliffe ME3 . . . . 22 A3
Deal CT14 . . . . 214 F4
4 Grays RM17 . . . . 18 D8
New Ash Green TN15 . . . 92 C5
Orpington BR2 . . . . 85 D3
Sittingbourne ME10 . . . 102 B3
St Mary in the Marsh
TN29 . . . . 365 B4
Swanscombe DA10 . . . . . 35 E8
West Tilbury RM18 . . . . . 19 D8
Rectory Way TN24 . . . . 268 C5
Rectory Wlk TN26 . . . . 349 A7
RECULVER 78 C7
Reculver Ave CT7 . . . . . . 80 E8
Reculver CE Prim Sch
CT6 . . . . 78 A4
Reculver Cl CT6 . . . . 77 F5
Reculver Ctry Pk★ CT6 78 B6
Reculver Dr CT6 . . . . 77 E5
Reculver La CT6 . . . . 78 B6
Reculver Rd CT6 . . . . 77 D5
Reculvers Rd CT8 . . . . . . 81 F7
Reculver Towers and
Roman Fort★ CT6 . . . . 78 D7
Reculver Wlk ME15 . . . 195 F7
Redan Pl ME12 . . . . 28 D2
Redbank ME19 . . . . 127 E2
Red Barn La CT15 . . . . 276 A4
Red Barracks Rd 4 SE18 1 F2
Redberry Rd TN23 . . . . 300 B5
Redbourne Dr SE28 . . . . . 3 D7
Red Brick Cotts ME13 172 A6
Redbridge Cl ME5 . . . . . . 97 C4
Redbrook St TN26 . . . . 325 D5
Redbrooks Way CT21 . . 332 F2
Red Cedars Rd BR6 . . . . 53 E2
Redcliffe La ME14 . . . . 162 B7
Redcot La CT2 . . . . 144 B7
Redding Cl DA2 . . . . 34 E6
Redding Ho SE18 . . . . 1 E3
Reddy Rd DA8 . . . . 14 F8
Rede Court Rd ME2 . . . . 62 E8
Rede Wood Rd ME16 . . 160 F3
Redfern Ave ME7 . . . . . . 64 E5
Redfern Ho ME2 . . . . 94 F5
Redgate Dr BR2 . . . . 85 B8
RED HILL 159 F1
Red Hill Chislehurst BR7 . 30 B3
Red Hill ME18 . . . . 159 F1
Red Hill Prim Sch BR7 . . 30 B3
Redhill Rd
New Ash Green DA3 . . . . 91 F6
Westgate on Sea CT8 . . . 81 E8
Redhill Wood DA3 . . . . . 92 A7
Redhill Wood Sch DA3 . . 58 F3
Red Ho The
Limpsfield RH8 . . . . 183 C5
Littlestone-on-Sea TN28 373 E6
Red House★ DA6 . . . . . . 13 E3
Redhouse Farm CT14 . 182 B1
Red House Gdns ME18 192 C7
Redhouse La CT4 . . . . . 207 D6
Red House La DA6 . . . . . 13 E3
Redhouse Rd TN16 . . . . 150 C6
Redhouse Wall CT14 . . 182 B1
Redington TN24 . . . . . . 268 C3
Red La Limpsfield RH8 . . 216 B7
Oxted RH8 . . . . 183 B2
Redlands Ct CT17 . . . . . 277 E4
Redland Shaw ME4 . . . . . 63 E1
Redlands Rd TN13 . . . . 153 F3
Redlane Cotts RH8 . . . . 183 B2
Redleaf Cl Erith DA17 . . . 14 A8

Red–ROL 423

Redleaf Cl *continued*
Royal Tunbridge Wells TN2 286 D6
Red Leaf Cl TN11 219 F2
Red Lion Cl BR5 54 C3
Red Lion Ct 6 CT21 333 B2
Red Lion La
11 Whitstable CT5 74 D2
Woolwich SE18 12 A6
Red Lion Pl SE18 12 A6
Red Lion Sq
7 Hythe CT21 333 B2
Plaxtol TN15 189 E8
Red Lodge Cres DA5 32 E5
Red Lodge Rd DA5 32 D5
Redmans Ind Est RM18 20 A8
Redmans La BR6, TN14 88 E4
Redmill Cl CT20 334 E5
Red Oak TN18 354 E8
Red Oak Cl BR6 86 B8
Red Oast Cotts TN5 339 C3
Redoubt Way TN29 353 B4
Redpoll Way DA18 3 D3
Redpoll Wlk TN12 257 A5
Red Rd CT2 140 D5
Red Robin Cotts ME9 100 B6
Redroses Cl TN12 224 F6
Redruth Manor 3 ME7 64 C6
Redsells Cl ME15 163 A1
Redshank Rd ME4 41 B1
Red St DA13 36 B2
Redstart Cl E6 1 E8
REDSTREET 36 B2
Redsull Ave CT14 215 A3
Red Tree Orch TN23 289 E7
Redvers Cotts CT16 277 E5
Redvers Rd ME4 64 A2
Redwall La
Bogden TN12 228 C4
Linton ME15, ME17 227 C6
Redwell Gr ME19 159 C2
Redwell La TN15 156 B4
Redwing Cl
Hawkinge CT18 307 A3
Larkfield ME20 128 A2
Redwing Path SE28 2 D4
Redwing Rd ME5 97 B7
Redwings La TN2 255 E2
Redwood Cl
Canterbury CT2 142 E2
Chartham CT4 173 E1
Chatham ME5 97 B2
Sidcup DA15 31 A7
Redwood Ct DA1 16 A1
Redwood Pk TN12 256 A5
Redyear Cotts TN24 269 A1
Redyear Ct TN24 269 A1
Reece Adams Ho CT18 308 B1
Reed Ave
Canterbury CT1 143 D3
Orpington BR6 86 E7
Reed Cl Eltham SE12 11 A2
Newham E16 1 A8
New Hythe ME20 128 A5
Reed Court DA9 17 C3
Reed Court Cotts
TN12 227 A5
Reed Court Farm★
TN12 227 A5
Reed Cres TN23 300 C3
Reedham Cres ME3 40 C7
Reedland Cres ME13 138 C8
Reedmace Cl TN23 299 D8
Reeds Cl CT6 77 C4
Reeds La TN11 189 E5
Reed St ME3 22 B6
Reeves Alley 1 CT5 74 D1
Reeves Cl
Canterbury, Harbledown CT2 174 C8
Staplehurst TN12 260 E4
Reeves Cres BR8 55 D6
Reeves Ct Ditton ME19 128 A1
Fordcombe TN3 284 B5
Reeves Pas 7 ME13 138 C7
Reeves Rd SE18 12 B8
Reeves Terr TN5 338 E1
Reeves Way CT5 75 C2
Reeves Yd CT5 74 D2
Reflection The E16 2 B4
Reform Rd ME4 64 B2
Regency Cl
Gillingham ME8 98 C3
Sheerness ME12 28 A3
West Kingsdown TN15 90 E4
Whitstable CT5 108 F7
Regency Ct ME10 101 D4
Regency Hall 21 TN2 286 A2
Regency Ho TN2 286 B2
Regency Pl CT1 143 B2
Regency Sch of English
CT11 117 D5
Regency Villas CT4 243 C5
Regency Way DA6 13 E4
Regent Dr ME15 195 A8
Regent Pl TN2 286 D3
Regent Rd ME7 64 C4
Regents Ct
14 Ashford TN23 268 B2
3 Gravesend DA11 19 B1
Regents Dr BR2 85 D5
Regents Pl TN23 268 B2
Regent's Pl SE3 11 A5
Regent Sq DA17 4 B2
Regent St
Rolvenden TN17 343 E4
Whitstable CT5 74 D2
Regents Wlk CT6 77 D5
Regent Way ME19 159 C3
Regina Ct TN4 285 F4
Reginald Ave ME2 62 C3
Reginald Rd ME16 161 E3
Regis Bsns Pk ME12 28 A1
Regis Cres ME10 101 F7
Regis Ind Est ME12 46 A8
Regis Manor Com Prim
Sch ME10 101 E7
Reidhaven Rd SE18 2 E2
Reigate Rd BR1, SE12 29 A5
Reinckendorf Ave SE9 12 D1
Reinden Gr ME15 162 F1
Rembrandt Cl TN10 222 E6
Rembrandt Dr DA11 36 E5
Remington Rd E6 1 E7
Remston Mews 12 CT1 143 B2
Remus Cl TN23 299 F4
Renault Cl CT6 76 A4
Rendezvous St CT20 335 D5
Rendezvous The CT9 50 I3
Rendlebury Ho 12 SE18 1 F2
Renfrew Cl E6 2 A6
Rennets Cl SE9 12 E2
Rennets Wood Ho SE9 12 D2
Rennets Wood Rd SE9 12 D2
Renovation The E16 2 B4
Renown Rd ME5 97 C2
Renshaw Cl 7 DA17 13 F8
Rentain Rd CT4 173 D2
Renton Dr BR5 54 D2
Repository Rd SE18 1 F1
Repton Cl CT10 83 F6
Repton Manor Rd
TN23 268 A3
Repton Rd BR6 87 A6
Repton Way ME5 96 F4
Reservoir Ave TN29 380 D2
Reservoir Cl DA9 17 C1
Reservoir Rd CT5 74 E2
Resolution Cl ME5 97 A6
Resolution Wlk SE18 1 F3
Restavon Pk TN16 119 B3
Rest Harrow ME13 170 C5
Restharrow Rd ME14 162 E4
Restharrow Way ME4 41 C1
Restons Cres SE9 12 E1
Retreat The
Birchington CT7 81 B8
Doddington ME9 167 D7
Grays RM17 18 B8
Orpington BR6 87 B4
Platt TN15 157 D8
Ramsgate CT12 117 B8
Rettendon Dr ME10 101 F8
Revell Rise SE18 12 F8
Revenge Rd ME5 130 C8
Reventlow Rd SE9 30 C7
Reynard Cl BR1 53 A6
Reynolah Gdns 3 SE7 1 B1
Reynolds Cl
Herne Bay CT6 77 B4
Tonbridge TN10 222 E6
Reynolds Fields ME3 39 C6
Reynolds La
Herne Bay CT3 78 D3
Royal Tunbridge Wells
TN4 285 F7
Reynolds Performing Arts
Academy DA5 32 E6
Reynolds Pl SE3 11 B7
Rhee Wall TN26 361 D7
Rheims Ct CT2 142 D1
Rheims Way CT1, CT2 174 E8
Rhodaus Cl CT1 174 F7
Rhodaus Ho CT1 174 F7
Rhodaus Town CT1 174 F7
RHODE COMMON 172 A6
Rhodes Gdns CT10 84 A6
Rhodes Ho 5 ME5 64 C2
RHODES MINNIS 273 A3
Rhode St ME4 64 A4
Rhodewood Cl ME15 163 A1
Rhododendron Ave
DA13 93 A2
Ribblesdale Rd DA2 34 C7
Ribston Cl BR2 52 F1
Ribston Gdns TN12 256 F7
Ribston Way TN23 299 B8
Ricardo Path 5 SE28 3 C5
Rice Par BR5 53 D4
Richard Beau Nash
Apartments 4 TN1 286 B4
Richard Cl SE18 1 E2
Richard Ct 7 CT9 51 B2
Richard House Dr E16 1 E7
Richard Neve Ho 1 SE18 2 E2
Richard's Cl TN11 219 F2
Richardson Cl 7 DA9 17 A2
Richardson Rd TN4 286 A5
Richardson Way CT12 116 D5
Richard St Chatham ME4 63 F4
Rochester ME1 63 C4
Richborough Cl BR5 54 D5
Richborough Dr ME2 40 A1
Richborough Rd CT8 81 F7
Richborough Roman Fort★
CT13 148 E5
Richborough Way
TN23 299 E5
Richbourgh Rd CT13 148 E3
Richdore Rd CT4 239 C6
Richings House BR5 54 A8
Richmer Rd DA8 15 A7
Richmond Ave
Kings Hill ME19 159 B3
Margate CT9 51 B1
Richmond Cl
Biggin Hill TN16 150 B8
Chatham ME5 97 B4
Rochester ME2 40 F1
Richmond Ct
Bromley BR1 29 B1
Dover CT16 278 D1
Sevenoaks TN13 154 B4
Richmond Dr
Gravesend DA12 37 E6
Herne Bay CT6 77 E5
New Romney TN28 373 C8
Richmond Dr *continued*
Sittingbourne ME10 101 E7
Richmond First Sch
ME12 28 D2
Richmond Gdns CT2 142 C2
Richmond Ho 26 CT20 335 E5
Richmond Meech Dr
TN24 268 E4
Richmond Pl
Royal Tunbridge Wells
TN2 286 B1
Woolwich SE18 2 C2
Richmond Rd
Gillingham ME7 64 C7
1 Grays RM17 18 C8
Ramsgate CT11 117 D6
Whitstable CT5 75 B1
Richmond St
Folkestone CT19 334 D6
Herne Bay CT6 76 F5
Sheerness ME12 28 D2
Richmond Way ME15 195 A8
Richmount Gdns SE3 11 A4
Ricketts Hill Rd TN16 150 E7
Rickyard Path SE9 11 E3
Riddlesdale Ave TN4 286 A6
Riddles Rd ME10, ME9 101 C3
Riddons Rd SE12 29 C4
Rideout St SE18 1 F2
Rider Cl DA15 12 E1
Ridge Ave DA1 14 F1
Ridgebrook Rd SE3 11 D4
Ridge Cl SE28 2 D4
Ridgecroft Cl DA5 32 C7
Ridge La DA13 93 A2
Ridgelands TN3 253 C4
Ridge Meadow Prim Sch
ME5 96 F6
RIDGE ROW 274 E1
Ridge The
Ashford TN24 268 E6
Groombridge TN3 312 A6
Orpington BR6 86 D8
Sidcup DA5 31 F8
Ridge View Sch TN10 222 D5
Ridgeway Dartford DA2 34 E3
Hayes BR2 85 A8
Hurst Green TN19 354 A3
Lympne CT21 332 A3
Pembury TN2 287 D7
The Moor TN18 354 E8
Ridge Way Crayford DA1 14 F1
Marlpit Hill TN8 217 D4
Ridgeway Ave DA12 37 B5
Ridgeway Bglws DA12 38 F1
Ridgeway Cliff CT6 76 C5
Ridgeway Cres
Orpington BR6 86 E7
Tonbridge TN10 222 D4
Ridgeway Crescent Gdns
BR6 86 E7
Ridgeway Dr BR1 29 B4
Ridgeway E DA15 12 F2
Ridgewaye The TN4 254 B1
Ridgeway Rd CT6 111 A7
Ridgeway Terr TN25 302 C5
Ridgeway The
Boughton Street
ME13 140 A3
Broadstairs CT10 83 F3
Chatham ME4 96 E7
Crabble CT17 277 E2
Gillingham ME7 64 C7
Margate CT9 51 B1
Shorne DA12 38 E1
Smeeth TN25 302 B5
Tonbridge TN10 222 D4
Whitstable CT5 75 B1
Ridgeway W DA15 12 E2
Ridgeway Wlk CT6 111 A7
Ridgewood DA3 59 C7
Ridgway ME16 161 B2
Ridgwell Rd E16 1 C8
Ridgy Field Cl TN15 125 A2
Ridham Ave ME10 69 A1
Ridham Dock ME9 69 B6
Riding Hill TN24 268 C6
Riding La TN11 188 D2
Riding Pk TN11 221 D7
Ridings The
Biggin Hill TN16 118 E2
7 Canterbury CT1 143 B1
Margate CT9 51 F3
Paddock Wood TN12 257 A7
Royal Tunbridge Wells
TN2 286 F6
Whitstable CT5 75 D1
Ridlands CT1 175 A5
Ridlands Gr RH8 183 E5
Ridlands La RH8 183 E5
Ridlands Rise RH8 183 E4
RIDLEY 92 B4
Ridley Cl CT6 111 A8
Ridley Ct BR6 86 C6
Ridley Rd Bexley DA16 13 B6
Bromley BR2 52 A6
Rochester ME1 63 B4
Riefield Rd SE9 12 C2
Rigden Rd TN23 300 B7
Rigden's Ct 6 ME10 101 E5
Riggall Ct ME2 62 A3
Riggs Way 5 TN15 124 F3
Rigshill Rd ME13 201 B6
Riley Ave CT6 75 F4
Rimpton Ct CT10 83 F7
Ring Cl BR1 29 B1
Ringden Ave TN12 256 F6
Ringer's Ct 5 BR1 52 A6
Ringer's Rd BR1 52 A6
Ringle Gn TN18 356 C5
Ringlemere La CT13 179 F6
RINGLESTONE
Harrietsham 165 F4
Maidstone 161 E7
Ringlestone Cres
ME14 161 F8
Ringlestone Rd ME17 165 D4
Ringlet Cl E16 1 B8
Ringlet Rd ME4 41 B2
Ringmer Way BR1 52 F4
Ringold Ave CT12 117 A8
Ringshall Rd BR5 54 A6
Rings Hill TN11 221 B4
Ringside TN8 217 C2
Ringsloe Ct CT7 80 D8
Ringwood Ave BR6 87 C1
Ringwood Cl
Canterbury CT2 142 E3
Gillingham ME8 98 D8
Ringwood Rd ME15 195 C8
RINGWOULD 247 F5
Ringwould Rd
Kingsdown CT14 248 B5
Ringwould CT14, CT15 247 D4
Ripley Arts Ctr★ BR1 52 D8
Ripley Cl BR1 52 F4
Ripley Rd Ashford TN24 301 A8
Erith DA17 4 A2
Newham E16 1 C7
Ripleys Market DA1 33 E8
Ripon Cl ME8 65 D3
Ripon Rd SE18 12 B8
Ripper's Cross TN26 266 D4
Rippersley Rd DA16 13 A6
RIPPLE 247 D8
Ripple Cross CT14 247 F6
Ripple Rd CT14 247 F7
Ripplevale Sch CT14 247 E8
Rippolson Rd SE18 2 F1
Risborough La CT19,
CT20 334 D5
Risborough Way CT20 334 E6
Risden La TN18 355 D7
Risdon Cl CT2 143 F6
Risedale Rd DA7 14 C4
RISEDEN Durgates 336 B1
Kilndown 318 A5
Riseden Rd TN5 336 C1
Rise The Ashford TN23 299 E7
Borden ME9 101 B2
Chatham ME4 64 A7
Crayford DA1 14 F3
Gillingham ME7 98 A3
Gravesend DA12 37 E4
Halfway Houses ME12 46 C5
Kingsdown CT14 248 D5
Rochester ME1 63 D3
Sevenoaks TN13 187 C7
Sidcup DA5 31 C8
St Margaret's at Cliffe
CT15 280 B6
Swanscombe DA9 17 A1
Rising Rd TN23 268 A1
Ritch Rd ME6 127 E8
Ritter St SE18 12 A8
Ritz Blgs TN1 286 A3
Rivendell Cl ME3 27 B5
Rivenhall Way ME3 41 F6
RIVER 277 E3
River Bank Cl 8 ME15 162 B4
Riverbank Rd BR1 29 A5
Riverbank Way TN24 300 D6
Riverbourne Ct 6
ME10 101 F4
River Cl ME15 194 A7
River Cotts BR5 54 C7
River Ct Chartham CT4 173 D3
Crabble CT17 277 F2
Sevenoaks TN13 153 E5
River Dale CT17 277 F3
Riverdale Est TN9 254 D8
Riverdale Rd
Canterbury CT1 143 B2
Erith DA8 4 C1
Sidcup DA5 13 F1
Woolwich SE18 2 F1
River Dr Crabble CT17 277 F2
Rochester ME2 62 E7
RIVERHEAD 153 E5
Riverhead Cl
Maidstone ME16 161 D6
Margate CT9 51 B1
Sittingbourne ME10 101 C3
Riverhead Ho TN13 153 E5
Riverhead Inf Sch
TN13 153 E4
Riverhead Mews TN13 153 E4
Riverhill TN15 187 E4
Riverhill Cotts TN15 187 E5
Riverhill House Gdns★
TN15 187 E5
Riverhope Mans SE18 1 E3
River Lawn Rd TN9 222 B1
River Mdw CT17 277 F3
Rivermead ME4 41 C2
Rivermead Sch ME7 64 E6
River Park View BR6 54 B2
River Prim Sch CT17 277 E3
River Rd Barking IG11 3 A8
Sandwich CT13 149 B4
Rivers Cl ME18 192 E7
Riversdale DA11 36 E5
Riversdale Rd
Ashford TN23 300 C8
Ramsgate CT12 83 B1
Riverside Chartham CT4 173 C3
Crabble CT17 277 F3
Edenbridge TN8 217 C1
Eynsford DA4 89 D8
Greenwich SE7 1 B3
Temple Ewell CT16 277 C5
Riverside Bsns Pk
TN24 268 D2
Riverside Business Park
ME20 128 C5
Riverside Cl Bridge CT4 176 A1
Kingsnorth TN23 300 A4
Orpington BR5 54 C7
Riverside Cotts TN14 88 F1
Riverside Ct
11 Canterbury CT2 142 F1
2 Orpington BR5 54 C4
Tonbridge TN9 222 C1
Riverside Ctry Pk & Visitor
Ctr★ ME7 65 D5
Riverside East Rd ME4 41 C1
Riverside Ind Est
Dartford DA1 15 E2
West Hythe CT21 332 B1
Riverside Mews CT4 176 A1
Riverside Pk ME16 194 A8
Riverside Prim Sch
ME8 66 A1
Riverside Rd
Cliffs End CT13 116 A1
Sidcup DA14 31 E6
Riverside Ret Pk
Canterbury CT1 174 D6
Sevenoaks TN14 154 C8
Riverside Sch BR5 54 C7
Riverside Way DA1 15 E2
Rivers Rd ME9 103 D2
River St 6 Chatham ME7 64 A6
River CT17 277 E3
Riverston Sch SE12 11 A2
Rivers Wlk ME17 199 C5
Riverview Ashford TN23 267 E1
6 Dartford DA1 16 A3
River View
Gillingham ME8 65 D3
Greenwich SE7 1 C3
Maidstone ME15 161 F2
Rushenden ME11 45 F3
Sturry CT2 143 F7
River View Cl 6 ME4 63 F3
Riverview Ct
16 Erith DA17 4 A1
Stone DA9 16 F1
Riverview Cty Inf Sch
DA12 37 E4
Riverview Hts SE18 12 B7
Riverview Jun Sch
DA12 37 E4
RIVERVIEW PARK 37 E4
Riverview Rd DA9 17 A2
River Way ME20 128 B4
River Wlk TN9 222 B1
Riverwood La BR7 53 D8
Riviera Ct 6 CT20 334 E3
Riviera Rd CT20 335 A3
Riviera The CT20 334 F3
Rixon Ho SE18 12 B8
Roach St ME2 63 A7
Road of Remembrance
CT20 335 D4
Roan Ct ME2 62 F8
Robert Brundett Cl
TN24 268 E5
Robert Napier Sch The
ME7 64 E3
Roberton Dr BR1 52 C8
Roberts Cl Eltham SE9 30 D7
8 Orpington BR5 54 C4
Sittingbourne ME10 101 D7
Roberts Ho SE18 11 E6
Roberts Mews BR6 54 A1
Robertson Ho SE18 11 F6
Roberts Orchard Rd
ME16 160 F3
Roberts Rd Erith DA17 4 A1
Gillingham ME8 98 E8
Greatstone-on-Sea
TN28 373 E1
Snodland ME6 127 F8
Whitstable CT5 107 F6
Robert St Deal CT14 215 D7
Newham E16 2 B5
Woolwich SE18 2 D2
Robeshaw ME9 134 E2
ROBHURST 325 C2
Robina Cl DA6 13 D3
Robina Ct Margate CT9 51 D3
Swanley BR8 56 A5
Robin Cres E6 1 D8
Robin Ct
6 Rochester ME1 63 D4
Whitstable CT5 75 A3
Robin Hill Dr BR7 29 E2
Robin Ho 5 ME16 161 E4
Robin Hood Gn BR5 54 A4
Robin Hood La
Bexley DA6 13 E2
Chatham ME5 96 D1
Lydd TN29 376 C5
Robin Hood Lane (Lower)
ME5 96 F2
Robin Hood Lane (Upper)
ME5 96 E1
Robinia Ave DA11 36 D8
Robin La TN29 376 C6
Robins Ave ME17 199 C5
Robins Cl ME17 199 C4
Robin's Cl CT21 353 C8
Robins Ct ME14 162 B7
Robins Gr BR4 85 A7
Robin Way BR5 54 B6
Robinwood Dr TN15 154 F8
Robson Cl E6 1 E7
Robson Dr
Aylesford ME20 128 D2
Hoo St Werburgh ME3 41 D6
Robson Ho SE18 12 A7
Robson's Yd CT17 310 C8
Robus Cl CT18 305 C7
Robus Terr CT18 305 C7
Robyn Cotts TN26 324 E8
Robyns Croft 6 DA11 36 E5
Robyns Way
Edenbridge TN8 249 D8
Sevenoaks TN13 153 F5
Rocfort Rd ME6 128 A8
Rochdale Ho TN1 286 C5
Rochdale Rd
Royal Tunbridge Wells
TN1 286 C6
Woolwich SE2 3 B2
ROCHESTER 63 B6
Rochester Airport ME1,
ME5 96 C6
Rochester Airport Ind Est
ME1 96 C5
Rochester Ave
Bromley BR1 52 B7
Canterbury CT1 175 B7
Rochester ME1 63 C4
Rochester Castle★ ME1 63 C6
Rochester Cath★ ME1 63 C6
Rochester Cl 1 DA15 13 B1
Rochester Cres ME3 41 D6
Rochester Ct
Canterbury CT1 175 B6
Rochester ME2 63 E8
Rochester Dr DA5 14 A1
Rochester Gate ME1 63 D5
Rochester Gram Sch for
Girls ME1 63 C2
Rochester Ho 1 ME15 195 D7
Rochester Ind Coll ME1 63 D4
Rochester Rd
Burham ME1 95 E2
Burham ME1 129 A8
Chalk DA12 38 B6
Chatham ME1, ME5 96 C4
Dartford DA1 34 A8
Pratling Street ME20 129 B4
Rochester ME2 62 D4
Tonbridge TN10 222 D4
Rochester St ME4 63 E3
Rochester Sta ME1 63 D5
Rochester Way
Dartford DA1 32 F8
Eltham, Kidbrooke SE3,
SE9 11 D4
Eltham SE9 12 B4
Rock Ave ME7 64 C3
Rock Cotts TN3 314 B1
Rockdale TN13 154 B2
Rockdale Rd TN13 154 C2
Rock Farm Oasthouse
ME18 192 C6
Rock Hill BR6 88 B4
Rock Hill Rd TN27 232 E2
Rockingham Pl CT6 77 B2
Rockliffe Manor Prim Sch
SE18 12 F8
Rockmount Rd SE18 2 F1
Rock Rd
Borough Green TN15 156 F7
Maidstone ME14 162 A6
Sittingbourne ME10 101 E4
ROCKROBIN 336 D6
Rocks Cl ME19 160 A6
Rocks Hill TN17 293 A4
Rocks Rd The ME19 160 B6
Rockstone Way CT12 83 A1
Rock Villa Rd TN1 286 A4
Rockwell Ct ME15 161 E1
Rocky Bourne Rd
TN25 329 D5
Rocky Hill ME16 161 E4
Rocky Hill Terr 2
ME16 161 E4
Rodeo Cl DA8 15 B6
Roding Rd E6 2 B8
Rodmell Rd TN2 286 A2
Rodmer Cl ME12 47 C8
RODMERSHAM 135 C8
Rodmersham Gn ME9 135 B7
RODMERSHAM
GREEN 135 B7
Rodmersham Prim Sch
ME9 135 B7
Rodney Ave TN10 222 E4
Rodney Gdns BR4 85 A6
Rodney St CT11 117 D6
Rodway Rd BR1 52 B8
Roebourne Way E16 2 A5
Roebuck Bsns Pk
ME17 198 D5
Roebuck Ho ME1 63 E5
Roebuck Rd
Faversham ME13 138 A7
Rochester ME1 63 C5
Roedean Cl BR6 87 B6
Roedean Rd TN2 286 A1
Roehampton Cl DA12 37 E8
Roehampton Dr BR7 30 C2
Roentgen Ho ME10 101 D5
Roethorne Gdns TN30 345 B8
Roffen Rd ME1 63 C2
Rogers Ct BR8 56 A5
Rogersmead 14 TN30 345 A7
Rogers Rough Rd
TN17 318 B2
Rogers Wood La DA3 91 B6
Rogley Hill TN27 322 B6
Rogues Hill TN11 252 C3
Rokesby Cl DA16 12 D5
Rokesley Rd CT16 278 B5
Rolfe La TN28 373 B7
Rolinsden Way BR2 85 D6
Rollesby Way SE28 3 C7
Rolleston Ave BR5 53 B3
Rolleston Cl BR5 53 B2
Rollo Rd BR8 32 F1
Roll's Ave ME12 48 C1
ROLVENDEN 343 F4
Rolvenden Ave ME8 65 C3
Rolvenden Dr ME10 101 B5
Rolvenden Gdns BR1 29 D1
Rolvenden Hill TN17 344 C5
ROLVENDEN LAYNE 344 B1

Rolvenden Prim Sch
TN17............343 E3
Rolvenden Rd
Rochester ME2.......40 C2
Tenterden TN30......344 E4
Rolvenden Sta★ TN17 344 D2
Roly Eckhoff Ho CT16 .278 B3
Roman Amphitheatre★
CT13.............148 E4
Roman Cl Chatham ME5..96 D1
Deal CT14........215 B6
Roman Hts ME4....162 C6
Roman Painted House★
CT17.............310 D8
Roman Rd
Canterbury CT4......175 D4
Dover CT16........278 D2
East Studdal CT15...246 C5
Edenbridge TN8......249 D5
Faversham ME13.....138 C7
Northfleet DA11......36 C5
Ramsgate CT12......83 C2
Snodland ME6.......127 F8
Whitfield CT15......278 D8
Roman Sq
Sittingbourne ME10...101 F3
Woolwich SE28.......3 A5
Roman Villa Rd DA2,
DA4.............34 C2
Roman Way
Crayford DA1.......14 E2
Elvington CT15.......212 B2
Folkestone CT19.....334 C6
Kingsnorth TN23.....300 C4
Maidstone ME15.....195 E4
Rochester ME2......62 F4
St Margaret's at Cliffe
CT15............279 F5
Romany Cl ME5.....64 D1
Romany Rd ME8.....65 C2
Romany Rise BR5....53 C1
ROMDEN..........264 C1
Romden Rd
Smarden, Haffenden
Quarter TN27......296 B8
Smarden, Romden
TN27............264 D1
Rome House Cnr TN28 373 A6
Rome Rd TN28......373 A6
Romero Sq SE3......11 C3
Rome Terr ME4......63 F4
ROMFORD.........287 F7
Romford Rd TN2.....287 F7
Romilly Gdns CT12...83 C2
Romney Ave CT20....334 F5
Romney Cl
▣ Birchington CT7.....81 A7
Maidstone ME14.....163 A3
Romney Ct ME10....101 E5
Romney Dr BR1......29 D1
Romney Gdns DA7....13 F6
Romney, Hythe &
Dymchurch Rly★
CT21............333 A2
Romney Marsh Ho
TN29............366 C7
Romney Marsh Rd TN23,
TN24............300 B6
Romney Marsh Visitor
Ctr★ TN28.........365 D1
Romney Pl ME15.....162 A4
Romney Point TN25...267 F4
Romney Rd
Ashford TN24.......268 E1
Chatham ME5.......97 B5
Hamstreet TN26.....349 A7
New Romney TN29...372 E3
Northfleet DA11......36 E5
Woolwich SE18........2 C3
Romney Sands Sta★
TN28............377 E8
Romney St TN15.....123 A4
Romney Warren Cntry Pk★
TN28............365 D1
Romney Way
Hythe CT21.........332 F1
Tonbridge TN10.....222 E5
Romsey Cl
Ashford TN24.......269 A2
Orpington BR6......86 C6
Rochester ME2......62 E8
Romulus Ct TN23....299 F4
Ronald Ho SE3......11 C3
Ronalds Ct ▣ ME10..102 A4
Ronalds Rd BR1......52 A8
Ronaldstone Rd DA15..12 E1
Ronfearn Ave BR5....54 D4
Ron Green Ct DA8....14 D8
Ronver Rd SE12......29 A7
Roodlands La TN8....218 D6
Rookdean TN13......153 C5
Rookery Cl
Ashford TN24.......268 D7
Bredgar ME9........134 A6
Rookery Cres ME3....22 B6
Rookery Ct RM20....17 A8
Rookery Dr BR7......53 A8
Rookery Gdns BR5....54 C4
Rookery Hill ME6.....127 E8
Rookery La BR2......52 D3
Rookery Lodge ME3...22 C5
Rookery Rd BR6......86 A1
Rookery The RM20....17 A8
Rookery View
Grays RM17........18 D8
Iwade ME9.........68 D4
Rookesley Rd BR5....54 D2
Rook La ME9........100 F6
Rookley Ct TN2......286 D2
Rooks Hill TN15.....188 D6

Rookston Cnr CT3....113 D1
Rooks View ME9....100 E6
Rook Wlk ▣ E6.......1 E7
Roonagh Ct ME10....101 E2
Roopers TN3........285 A7
Roosevelt Ave ME5....97 A8
Roosevelt Rd CT16...278 B3
Ropemakers Ct ME4...64 A1
Roper Cl
Canterbury CT2......142 E1
Gillingham ME8......98 C3
Roper Rd
Canterbury CT2......142 E1
Teynham ME9.......103 D3
Roper's Gate TN2....285 E1
Roper's Green La ME3..24 B2
Roper's La ME3......41 F8
Roper St ▣ SE9......12 A1
Ropery Bsns Pk SE7...1 C2
Rope Walk Mews CT13 180 F8
Rope Wlk Chatham ME4..63 F5
Cranbrook TN17.....320 C5
Rope Wlk The TN18...356 B5
Rope Yard Rails SE18...2 B3
Rosamund Ct CT19...335 C6
ROSEACRE.........163 A4
Roseacre Cl CT2.....142 E1
Roseacre Cl CT9......51 E2
Roseacre Gdns ME14.163 A3
Roseacre Jun Sch
ME14............163 A4
Roseacre La ME14....163 A4
Roseacre Rd DA16....13 B4
Rose Ave DA12......37 C7
Rosebank Gdns DA11..36 E7
Rosebank Wlk ▣ SE18..1 E2
Roseberry Gdns
Dartford DA1.......33 C8
Orpington BR6......86 E7
Rosebery Ave
Herne Bay CT6......77 E5
Ramsgate CT11......83 F1
Sidcup DA15........30 E8
Rosebery Gdns
Dartford DA1.......33 C8
Orpington BR6......86 E7
Rosebery Ct ME10...102 D4
Rosebery Ct DA11....36 F7
Rosebery Rd
Chatham ME4.......63 E2
Gillingham ME7.....64 D7
Grays RM17........17 E8
Rose Bruford Coll DA15 31 B4
Rose Cotts Hythe CT21 .333 B4
Lamberhurst TN3....317 A3
Lenham Heath ME17..233 B8
Ramsgate CT12......82 F2
Rochester ME2......62 B8
St Mary Hoo ME3....24 C1
Rosecroft Cl
Biggin Hill TN16.....118 F1
Orpington BR5......54 C3
Rose Ct ME17.......194 D1
Rose Dale BR6.......86 B8
Rosedale Cl
Dartford DA2.......34 B8
Woolwich SE2........3 B3
Rosedale Cnr BR7....52 F8
Rosedale Rd CT9.....51 A1
Rosedene Cl DA1.....33 C8
Rose Farm La TN27...265 A5
Rosefield
Sevenoaks TN13.....154 A3
▣ Sidcup DA14......31 A4
Rosegarth DA13......59 E8
Rose Gdns
Birchington CT7......80 F6
Eythorne CT15......245 D7
Herne Bay CT6......77 C4
Minster (Thanet) CT12.115 B6
Rose Hill
▣ Ramsgate CT11...117 E6
Wittersham TN30....360 B5
Rosehill Rd TN16....118 C2
Rosehill Wlk TN16....286 A3
Rose Hill Sch TN4....285 E5
Roseholme ME16....161 D2
Rose La
Bishopsbourne CT4..209 C6
Canterbury CT1......174 F8
Lenham Heath ME17..233 B8
Roselands CT14.....215 C1
Roselands Gdns CT2..142 D2
Roselare Cl TN16....151 D1
Roselawn Gdns ▣ CT9 .82 B8
Roselea Ave CT6.....76 F3
Roseleigh Ave ME16..161 C5
Roseleigh Rd ME10...101 D2
Rosemary Ave
Broadstairs CT10.....84 A3
Halfway Houses ME12..46 D6
Rosemary Cl
▣ Chatham ME5.....96 F4
Oxted RH8.........183 A4
Rosemary Ct ▣ ME1...63 D4
Rosemary Gdns
Broadstairs CT10.....83 F2
Whitstable CT5......109 A8
Rosemary La
▣ Canterbury CT1...174 F8
Flimwell TN5.......339 A5
Hodsoll Street TN15...92 D3
Swift's Green TN27..263 F5
Rosemary Rd
Bexley DA16.........12 F6
Maidstone ME15.....163 A3
West Malling ME19..127 F1
Rosemead Gdns TN27.262 B7
Rosemont Cl ME15...194 F4
Rosemount Cl ME2....40 A1
Rosemount Dr BR1....52 F5
Rosenheath ▣ BR6...87 C3
Rose St Northfleet DA11..18 B1
Rookston ME1.......63 D3

Rose St continued
Sheerness ME12.......28 B2
Tonbridge TN9.......254 C8
Rose Street Sch ME12..28 B2
Rose Terr
Faversham ME13.....138 D5
Offham ME19.......158 D7
Rosetower Ct CT10...83 F8
Rosetta Prim Sch E16...1 B8
Roseveare Rd SE12....29 C4
Rose Way SE12......11 A2
Rose Wlk CT18......307 A4
Rosewood DA2.......32 E4
Rosewood Cl DA14....31 C5
Rosewood Ct BR1.....52 D8
Rosewood Dr TN25...267 F4
Rosewood Way CT7...81 B7
Rose Yd ME14......162 A4
Rosebero Ho DA11....18 F1
ROSHERVILLE.......18 E1
Rosherville CE Prim Sch
DA11............18 E1
Rosherville Way DA11..18 E1
Rosiers Ct ▣ CT2....142 E1
Roslin Way BR1......29 A3
Ross Ct BR7.........29 F1
Rossdale TN2.......286 D5
Rosse Mews SE3.....11 B6
Rossendale Ct ▣ CT20 335 E6
Rossendale Gdns ▣
CT20............335 E6
Rossendale Rd CT20..335 E6
Rossetti Ct CT7......80 F7
Rossetti Rd CT7......80 F7
Ross Gdns CT2......142 B3
Ross House SE18.....11 E6
Rossland Cl DA6......14 B2
Rossland Rd CT12....117 A8
Rosslyn Gn ME16....161 B5
Rossmore DA14......31 A3
Ross Rd SE18........15 A1
Ross St ME1.........63 D4
Ross Way Eltham SE9..11 E4
Folkestone CT20....334 E5
Rotary Gdns ME7.....64 F2
Rothbrook Dr TN24...268 C7
Rother Ct ▣ BR5....54 C1
Rothermere Cl TN17..342 E6
Rother Rd TN10.....222 C5
Rother Vale ME5......97 C3
Rothesay Ct ▣ SE12..29 B5
Rothley Ct TN30.....345 B8
Rothsay Ct CT11......83 F1
Rouge La DA12......37 B7
Rougemont St E16....159 C2
ROUGH COMMON....142 B3
Rough Common Rd
CT2.............142 B3
Roughetts Rd ME19..126 F3
Roughway La TN11....190 C7
Round Ash Way DA3...58 E3
Roundel Cl ME9.....103 D3
Roundel The ME10...101 E2
Roundel Way TN12...259 D5
ROUND GREEN......291 F4
Round Green Cotts
TN17............291 F4
Roundhay ME19......127 E1
Roundhill Rd TN2....286 D1
Roundlyn Gdns BR5...54 B5
Round St DA12, DA13...60 E5
ROUND STREET......60 D5
Roundtable Rd BR1...29 A5
Roundway TN16.....118 D4
Roundwell ME14....163 D3
Roundwood BR7......53 B7
Round Wood Cl ME5..97 A1
Routh St E6..........1 F8
Rover Rd ME5.......97 B2
Rowan Cl Ashford TN23 269 E2
Aylesford ME20.....128 E1
Meopham Station DA13 ..60 B3
Paddock Wood TN12..256 F5
Staple CT3.........179 A6
Sturry CT2.........143 F6
Rowan Cres DA1......33 C7
Rowan Ct Ashford TN24 300 E8
Broadstairs CT10.....84 A5
▣ Lewisham SE12....29 A8
Rowan Ho
▣ Chatham ME5.....96 F5
▣ Maidstone ME1...161 A3
Royal Tunbridge Wells
TN4.............285 E4
Rowan House DA14...30 F5
Rowan Lea ME5.......64 B1
Rowan Mews TN9,
TN10............222 C4
Rowan Rd Bexley DA7..13 E4
Swanley BR8........55 D6
Rowans Cl DA3......58 D7
Rowan Shaw TN10....222 D6
Rowans The ME12....47 B7
Rowan Tree Pk CT5...108 B6
Rowan Tree Rd TN2...285 E1
Rowan Wlk
Chatham ME4.......63 E3
Orpington BR2......85 F7
Rowanwood Ave DA15..31 A7
Rowbrocke Cl ME8....98 D3
Rowdow La TN14, TN15 122 C5
Rowe Cl CT9.........82 F7
Rowena Rd CT8......50 C1
Rowenden Vineyard★
TN17............343 B2
Rowe Pl ME20.......128 F6
Rowetts Way ME17....48 D3
Rowfield ▣ TN8......217 D3
Rowhill Cotts DA2....32 E2
Rowhill Rd DA2......33 A3
Rowhill Sch DA2.....33 C4
Rowland Ave ME7.....64 E2
Rowland Cl
Gillingham ME7......64 E1

Rowland Cl continued
Maidstone ME16.....161 E3
Rowland Cotts CT21..331 F5
Rowland Cres TN5....77 E5
Rowland Dr CT6......76 C2
Rowlands Manor BR5..54 C3
Rowlatt Cl DA2......33 C4
Rowlatt Rd DA2......33 C5
Rowley Ave DA15.....31 B8
Rowley Hill TN2......255 D1
ROWLING..........179 A2
Rowling St TN25....328 E6
ROWLING STREET...328 E6
Rowmarsh Cl DA11....36 D4
Rowntree Path ▣ SE28..3 B5
Row The Ash CT3....147 E5
Chillenden CT3......211 F8
Elham CT4.........273 F5
New Ash Green DA3...91 F8
Ruckinge TN26......349 F8
Rowton Rd SE18......12 C7
Rowzill Rd BR8......32 F2
Roxburgh Rd CT8.....50 D1
Royal Albert Sta★....1 E6
Royal Albert Way
Newham, Cyprus E6...2 A6
Newham E16........1 E6
Royal Ave
Tonbridge TN9......254 D8
Whitstable CT5......108 C5
Royal Chase TN4....285 F4
Royal Cl Broadstairs CT10 83 F4
Orpington BR6......86 B6
Royal Connaught
Apartments E16......1 D5
Royal Cres Margate CT9 .50 H2
Ramsgate CT11......117 D5
Royal Ct Eltham SE9...29 F7
Whitstable CT5......75 A3
Royal Docks Com Sch The
E16.............1 C7
Royal Docks Heritage Rly★
E16.............1 E6
Royal Docks Rd E6....2 B7
Royal Eagle Cl ME2...63 E7
Royal Engineers Mus★
ME7.............64 B6
Royal Engineers' Rd
ME14............161 F7
Royal Espl Margate CT9..50 F1
Ramsgate CT11......117 C8
Royal Fountain Mews
ME12............28 A2
Royal Harbour App
CT11............117 C5
Royal Mews ▣ CT11..117 F7
Royal Military Ave
CT20............334 D5
Royal Military Canal (dis)
CT21............333 D2
Royal Military Rd CT21 332 E1
Royal Mus & Free Liby★ ▣
CT1.............174 F8
Royal Navy Way ▣...108 A6
Royal Oak Cotts TN8 .184 C2
Royal Oak Rd DA6....13 F3
Royal Oak Terr DA12..37 C7
Royal Par
Chislehurst BR7......30 C1
Ramsgate CT11......117 C6
Royal Parade Mews
BR7.............30 C1
Royal Park Prim Sch
DA14............31 E5
Royal Pier Rd DA12...19 C1
Royal Rd Newham E16...1 D7
Ramsgate CT11......117 D6
Sheerness ME12......28 C2
Sidcup DA14........31 D5
Sutton at Hone DA2...34 A3
Royal Rise TN9......254 C8
Royal St George's Golf
Links★ CT13......149 E2
Royal School for Deaf
Children The CT9....50 J2
Royal Sovereign Ave
ME4.............64 B7
Royal Star Arc ▣
ME14............161 F4
ROYAL TUNBRIDGE
WELLS..........286 D3
Royal Tunbridge Wells
Bsns Pk TN2.......254 D1
CT19............335 C6
Royal Victoria Hospl
CT19............335 C6
Royal Victoria Pl ▣
▣ Dover CT16......310 D8
Newham E16.........1 D7
Royal Victoria Place Sh Ctr
TN1.............286 B4
Royal Victoria Sq E16...1 B6
Royal Victoria Sta E16...1 A6
Royal Wells Coll ▣
TN4.............286 A4
Royal West Kent Ave
TN10............222 D4
Roydene Rd SE18.......2 E1
Roydon Hall Rd TN12..191 F4
Royds Rd TN24......300 D6
Royston Gdns CT15..279 F6
Royston Rd Crayford DA1 14 F1
Maidstone ME15.....163 A3
Roystons Cl ME8.....65 F2
Royton Ave ME17....199 D5
RSPCA Leybourne Animal
Ctr★ ME19.......127 E5
Rubery Dro CT3.....148 C6
Rubin Pl ME19......159 B3
Ruby Cl ▣ ME10.....101 D6
Ruby Walk ME19....159 F2
RUCKINGE........349 F8
Ruckinge Cnr TN26..349 F8
Ruckinge Rd TN26...349 A7

Ruckinge Way ME8....65 C3
Ruck La TN12.......289 E3
Ruddstreet Cl SE18....2 C2
Rudge ME5.........97 D2
Rudland Rd DA7......14 B4
Ruegg Ho ▣ SE18...12 A8
Ruffet Ct TN2.......285 E1
Ruffets Wood
Gravesend DA12.....37 C2
Kingsnorth ME23...300 C3
Rugby Cl
Broadstairs CT10.....83 F5
Chatham ME5.......96 F4
Rugby Gdns DA3....300 C8
Rugby Rd CT17.....310 A6
Ruggles Cl ME23.....23 E3
Ruglys Way TN27...234 B7
Ruins Barn Rd ME10,
ME9.............134 D6
Rule Ct ME12........46 B8
Rumania Wlk DA12...37 F5
Rumfields Rd CT10...83 C6
Rumstead La ME17,
ME9.............132 D4
Rumstead Rd ME9....132 E4
Rumwood Ct ME17...196 B5
Runcie Ho ▣ CT1...174 F7
Runcie Pl CT2......142 D1
Runciman Ct BR6....87 C1
Runham La ME17....198 E3
Running Foxes La
TN23............299 D7
Running Horse Rdbt The
ME14............129 E1
Runnymede Ct DA2...34 C7
Runnymede Gdns
ME15............195 A8
Runnymede Mews
ME13............138 C7
Rural Vale DA11......36 E8
Ruscombe Cl TN4....253 F2
Rusham Rd CT3.....146 C1
Rushbrook Rd SE9....30 C6
Rush Cl Chatham ME5..97 A3
Dymchurch TN29....366 B6
Rushdean Rd ME2....62 D5
Rushdene SE2........3 D3
Rushdene Wlk TN16..118 D2
RUSHENDEN.......45 F3
Rushenden Ct ME11...45 F3
Rushenden Rd ME11..46 A4
Rushes The ME20....128 B4
Rushet Rd BR5......54 A7
Rushett La ME13....136 F4
Rushetts TN3.......284 F4
Rushetts Rd TN15....90 E3
Rusheymead Ho ▣ SE18..2 F1
Rushford Ct TN27...262 D5
Rushgrove St SE18....1 F2
Rushley Cl BR2......85 E6
Rushlye Ct TN3......314 F5
Rushmead Cl CT2....142 D2
Rushmead Dr ME15...195 A7
Rushmere Ct TN15...156 D7
Rushmere Cl BR1.....52 E6
Rushmore Hill BR6,
TN14............120 D6
Rushymead TN15....123 A1
Ruskin Ave DA16.....13 A5
Ruskin Cl ME19......159 F8
Ruskin Ct SE9.......11 F1
Ruskin Dr Bexley DA16..13 A4
Dartford DA1.......16 A2
Orpington BR6......86 E7
Ruskin Gr Bexley DA16..13 A4
Ruskin Rd Dartford DA1..16 A2
Northfleet DA11......4 A2
Ruskins View CT6....77 A1
Ruskin Wlk BR2......52 F3
Rusland Ave BR6.....86 D7
Russell Cl Bexley DA7..15 A3
Crayford DA1.......15 A3
Greenwich SE7......11 C7
Sittingbourne ME10..101 C3
Russell Ct ME4......64 B3
Russell Dr CT5.......75 D3
Russell House Sch
TN14............122 C3
Russell Pl
Faversham ME13....105 B3
Sutton at Hone DA4...57 A8
Russell Quay ▣ DA11..19 A1
Russell Rd
▣ Folkestone CT19..335 D6
Gravesend DA12.....19 D1
Kit's Coty ME20.....129 D7
Newham E16.........1 D7
Tilbury RM18........18 F5
Russells Ave ME8.....99 A8
Russell Sq DA3......58 D6
Russell St Dover CT16.310 E7
Sheerness ME12......28 B2
Russells Yd TN17....320 D4
Russell Terr DA4.....57 C5
Russet Ave ME13....138 E5
Russet Cl ME2.......62 E8
Russet Ct
Coxheath ME17.....194 C3
▣ Erith DA17........4 A1
Russet Ho RM17.....18 C7
Russets The
Maidstone ME16.....161 D5
Meopham Station DA13 ..60 A3
Whitstable CT5......75 D5
Russett Cl Ash CT3...147 F1
Ditton ME20........160 E8
Orpington BR6......87 B5
Russett Rd
Canterbury CT1......175 C8
East Peckham TN12..224 F6
Russett Way BR8.....55 D8
Russet Way ME19...158 F2
RUSTHALL.........285 D4
Rusthall Grange TN4..285 D4
Rusthall Pk TN4....285 D4

Rusthall Rd TN4.....285 D4
Rustic Wlk E16........1 F7
Ruston Rd SE18.......1 E3
Rustwick TN4.......285 D4
Rutherford Coll CT2..142 E4
Rutherford Rd TN24..268 B5
Rutherford Way TN10 222 D7
Rutherglen Rd SE2....13 A8
Ruth Ho ▣ ME16....161 E5
Ruthin Rd SE3.......11 A8
Ruth St ME4.........64 A2
Rutland Ave
Margate CT9........51 C2
Sidcup DA15.......31 A8
Rutland Cl
Canterbury CT1......175 D7
Dartford DA1.......33 D8
Sidcup DA5.........31 D7
Rutland Ct
Chislehurst BR7......53 A8
Sidcup SE9.........30 C6
Rutland Gate DA17....4 B1
Rutland Gdns
Birchington CT7......80 F7
Margate CT9........51 C2
Rutland Ho
▣ Margate CT9......51 B2
▣ Woolwich SE18....1 F2
Rutland Pl ME8......98 C3
Rutland Rd CT16....278 B3
Rutland Sch of English
CT9.............50 G1
Rutland Way
Maidstone ME15.....195 A8
Orpington BR5......54 C3
RUXLEY..........31 E1
Ruxley Cl DA14......31 E2
Ruxley Cnr DA14.....31 E2
Ruxley Corner Ind Est
DA14............31 D2
Ruxley Ct ▣ BR1.....52 C7
Ruxton Cl BR8.......55 E6
Ruxton Ct ▣ BR8....55 E6
Ryan Cl SE3.........11 C3
Ryan Dr ME15.......163 A2
RYARSH..........126 F4
Ryarsh Cres BR6.....86 E6
Ryarsh La ME19.....127 B1
Ryarsh Pk ME19.....126 F4
Ryarsh Prim Sch ME19 127 B5
Rycault Cl ▣ ME16..161 E3
Rycaut Ct ME8.......98 D3
Rycroft La TN14.....186 E5
Rydal Ave CT11.....117 B7
Rydal Cl TN4.......285 E5
Rydal Dr Bexley DA7..14 A6
Royal Tunbridge Wells
TN4.............285 E5
Rydal Ho ME15.....195 E7
Ryde Cl ME5........97 B8
Rydens Ho SE9......29 C5
Ryder Cl BR1........29 B3
Ryders TN3........285 A3
Ryder's Ave CT8......81 D8
Ryde St CT2........142 E1
Rydons Ct SE9......11 E4
Rye Cl DA5.........14 B1
Rye Cres BR5.......54 D1
Ryecroft Gravesend DA12 37 E3
New Barn DA3......59 D5
Ryecroft Rd
Orpington BR5......53 D3
Otford TN14.......122 A2
Rye Ct TN23........299 D7
Ryedale Ct TN13....153 E6
Rye Field ▣ BR5.....54 D1
RYE FOREIGN.......367 E1
Ryegrass Cl ME5.....97 C6
Rye La Otford TN14...122 A2
Sevenoaks TN13, TN14..153 F7
Ryelands Cres SE12...11 C1
Rye Rd Brookland TN29 370 D8
Four Throws TN18....355 D8
Hawkhurst TN18.....341 B1
Peasmarsh TN31....367 E2
Wittersham TN30....360 A2
Rye Wlk CT6.........77 C2
Rye Wood Cotts TN14 153 F7
Ryland Ct ▣ CT20...335 E6
Ryland Pl ▣ CT20...335 E6
Rylands Rd TN24....268 D5
Rymers Cl TN2......286 D7
Rymill St E16.........2 A5
Rype Cl TN29.......376 C5
Rysted La TN16......151 D1
Ryswick Mews TN28..373 E4

S

Sabre Ct ME7.......65 A1
Sackett's Gap CT9....51 C3
Sacketts Hill CT10....83 C6
Sackville Ave BR2....52 A1
Sackville Cl
Hothfield TN26......267 A7
Sevenoaks TN13.....154 B5
Sackville Cres TN23..268 A2
Sackville Rd DA2.....33 C6
Sackville Sch TN11...221 C6
Sacred Heart Sch TN26 336 D5
Saddington St CT12...37 C8
Saddlers Cl ME14....162 E5
Saddlers Cl CT3.....178 D2
Saddlers Mews
Ramsgate CT12......82 F1
Whitstable CT5......75 D1
Saddler's Pk DA4.....89 D7
Saddler's Wall La
TN29............362 B1
Saddlers Way TN23...300 B5

Saddleton Gr 6 CT5 . 108 D8
Saddleton Rd CT5.... 108 D8
Sadlers Cl ME5.........96 D2
Saffron Cl ME5.........161 B3
Saffron's Pl 14 CT20..335 E5
Saffron Way
 1 Chatham ME5........96 F5
 Sittingbourne ME10 ...101 F7
Sage Cl 7 E6 ....1 F8
Sage Rd ME1..........63 B3
Saigasso Cl E16.......1 D7
Sailfield Cl ME4.......63 F7
Sailmakers Ct 5 ME4 .64 B2
St Agnes Gdns ME12...28 C1
St Aidan's Way DA12...37 E5
St Albans Cl ME7.....64 E7
St Alban's Cl DA12 ....37 D5
St Albans Gdns DA12 ..37 D5
St Albans Rd ME2.....62 D6
St Alban's Rd
 Dartford DA1........15 F1
 Hersden CT3.........111 F3
St Alban's Road Inf Sch
 DA1.................15 F1
St Alfege Rd SE7 .....11 D8
St Alphege CE Inf Sch 13
 CT5................74 D1
St Alphege Cl CT5....108 B7
St Alphege La 17 CT1..142 F1
St Alphege Rd 4
 CT16...............278 C1
St Ambrose Gn TN25 .237 E2
St Andrews CT19 .....335 E5
St Andrew's Art Ctr ★
 DA11...............19 B1
St Andrews Cl
 Canterbury CT1......174 E7
 Erith SE28...........3 D7
 Folkestone CT19.....335 E4
 Herne Bay CT6.......77 A4
 Margate CT9..........82 F7
 Paddock Wood TN12..257 A6
St Andrew's Cl
 Maidstone ME16.....161 A2
 Whitstable CT5......108 E7
St Andrews Ct
 26 Gravesend DA12....19 B1
 Royal Tunbridge Wells
 TN4...............254 A1
St Andrew's Ct 4 BR8..55 E6
St Andrews Dr BR5.....54 B2
St Andrews Gdns CT17 278 B2
St Andrew's Gdns
 CT15...............244 E5
St Andrews Ho BR1.....29 B2
St Andrew's Lees CT13181 A8
St Andrews Mews SE3 ..11 A7
St Andrews Park Rd
 TN4...............254 A1
St Andrews Pk ME16 .161 A3
St Andrews Rd
 Gillingham ME7........64 D7
 Paddock Wood TN12...257 A6
 Ramsgate CT11.......117 F8
 Sidcup DA14..........31 D5
St Andrew's Rd
 Deal CT14...........215 C6
 10 Gravesend DA12.....37 B8
 Littlestone-on-Sea TN28 373 E6
 Maidstone ME16......161 A3
 Tilbury RM18..........18 E5
St Andrews Sch ME1...63 C4
St Andrews Way
 The Chart RH8.......183 F4
 Tilmanstone CT14.....213 A3
St Andrew's Wlk ME3...9 D2
St Andrew Terr CT17 ..278 A4
St Angela's Jun Sch
 CT8................81 D7
St Annes Ct ME16....161 E4
St Anne's Ct
 1 Dover CT16.......278 B2
 Herne Bay CT6.......76 E5
St Anne's Dr CT6.......76 D4
St Anne's Gdns CT9 ...82 F8
St Anne's Rd
 Ashford TN23........299 F7
 Whitstable CT5.......74 F1
ST ANN'S GREEN.....259 F8
St Ann's Green La
 TN12...............259 F8
St Ann's Rd
 Dymchurch TN29.....366 B7
 Faversham ME13.....138 B7
St Anns Way TN16.....119 B3
St Anselm's RC Prim Sch
 DA1................16 A2
St Anselms RC Sch
 CT1................175 C5
St Anthonys Ct BR6....86 B8
St Anthonys Sch CT9...51 C1
St Anthony's Way CT9...51 C1
St Aubyns Cl BR6.......86 F7
St Aubyns Gdns BR6....86 F8
St Audrey Ave DA7.....14 A5
St Augustine Ho 1
 TN9................254 B8
St Augustine of Canterbury
 RC Prim Sch ME8.....98 D3
St Augustine's ★ CT8 ...81 E8
St Augustine's Abbey
 CT11...............117 D5
St Augustine's Abbey
 (rems of) ★ CT1.....175 A8
St Augustine's Ave
 Bromley BR2.........52 E4
 Margate CT9..........82 F8
St Augustines Bsns Pk
 CT5................75 E3
St Augustines Cath Prim
 Sch CT21...........333 A3
St Augustine's Cres
 CT5................75 D3
St Augustines Ct CT6 ..76 F2

St Augustine's Ct 3
 CT1................175 B8
St Augustines Pk CT8 ..81 E8
St Augustine's Pk
 CT11...............117 C6
St Augustine's Prim Sch
 DA17................3 F2
St Augustine's RC Prim
 Sch TN4............286 A7
St Augustine's Rd
 Canterbury CT1......175 B8
 Deal CT14..........214 F4
 Erith DA17...........3 F2
 Ramsgate CT11......117 D5
St Augustine's Sch CT8 81 E8
St Barnabas CE Prim Sch
 1 TN1..............286 B5
St Barnabas Cl
 Ashford TN23........299 F7
 Gillingham ME7........64 D3
 Maidstone ME16.....161 C8
St Barnabas' Cl TN1..286 B5
St Bartholemews Cl 4
 CT17...............310 C8
St Bartholomew's Hospl
 ME1................63 E4
St Bartholomew's Hospl
 CT13...............181 A7
St Bartholomew's La 4
 ME1................63 E4
St Bartholomews RC Prim
 Sch 7 BR8..........55 E6
St Bartholomew's Terr 2
 ME1................63 E4
St Bart's Cl 5 CT17 ...310 C8
St Bart's Rd CT13.....180 F8
St Benedict Rd ME6...127 E8
St Benedict's Ave CT2 37 E6
St Benedict's Lawn
 CT11...............117 D5
St Benedicts Prim Sch
 ME5................97 C2
St Benets Ct TN30....345 B8
St Benet's Rd CT8......81 E7
St Benets Way TN30...345 B8
St Benjamins Dr BR6...87 C2
St Bernards Rd TN10 .222 C6
St Blaise Ave BR1......52 B7
St Boltophs Cl TN13...154 B3
St Boltophs Rd DA11...36 D5
St Botolph's Ave TN13 154 A3
St Botolph's CE Prim Sch
 DA11...............36 D8
St Botolph's Rd TN13..154 B3
St Brelade's Ct TN8 ...217 A3
St Brides Cl DA18.......3 D4
St Catherines TN29....372 A7
St Catherines Ct
 Ramsgate CT11.......83 F1
 Rochester ME1.......63 D5
St Catherine's Dr
 ME13...............138 D6
St Catherine's Gr CT12 .82 D1
St Catherine's RC Sch for
 Girls DA6...........14 C2
St Cecelia Ho CT14...215 B1
St Chad's Dr DA12.....37 E5
St Chad's Rd RM18.....19 A7
St Christopher Cl CT9 .83 D8
St Christophers Gn
 CT10...............83 F5
St Christophers Mews
 CT11...............117 D8
St Christophers Sch 7
 CT1................175 B6
St Clare Rd CT14......215 C1
St Clements 8 CT13...149 A1
St Clement's Ave RM20 17 B8
St Clements Cl
 Leysdown-on-Sea
 ME12...............49 D2
 Northfleet DA11......36 F5
St Clements Ct
 Broadstairs CT10......83 E6
 Folkestone CT20.....335 F5
 Grays RM17..........17 E4
 Ramsgate CT11......117 D7
St Clement's Ct CT6...77 A3
St Clement's Ho ME1...63 D5
St Clements Rd ME12...49 E3
St Clement's Rd
 Westgate on Sea CT8...50 C1
 West Thurrock RM20 .16 F8
St Clements Road DA9 .17 C3
St Clement's Way RM20 16 F8
St Clere Hill Rd TN15..123 F7
St Columba's Cl DA12 ..37 E5
St Columba's RC Boys Sch
 DA6................14 B2
St Cosmus Ct TN25 ...203 B1
St Crispin's Inf Sch CT8 81 E7
St Crispin's Rd CT8.....81 E7
St Cuby CT10..........84 C7
St Davids Ave CT17....310 A5
St David's Bridge
 TN17...............320 D4
St David's Cl
 Birchington CT7.......51 A8
 Whitstable CT5......108 E8
St Davids Cres DA12 ..37 D4
St Davids Gate ME16 .161 A2
St Davids Rd 5 CT11 ..117 F8
St David's Rd
 Allhallows ME3........9 D2
 Deal CT14..........215 C6
 Hextable BR8.........32 F1
 Ramsgate CT11.......83 F1
 Royal Tunbridge Wells
 TN4...............286 B6
St Denys Rd CT18.....307 B5
St Domingo Ho SE18 ...1 F3
ST DUNSTAN'S.......142 D1
St Dunstan's Cl CT2 ..142 E1
St Dunstans Ct 4 CT2 142 E1

St Dunstan's Dr DA12...37 E5
St Dunstan's Rd CT9...51 A2
St Dunstan's St CT2 ..142 E1
St Dunstans Wlk TN17 320 D4
St Dunstans CE Prim
 Sch 6 CT20.........335 E4
St Eanswythe's Court
 TN9................254 C8
St Eanswythe Way 19
 CT20...............335 D5
St Edith's Rd TN15 ...123 A2
St Edmund Ho SE2.....13 A2
St Edmunds Cl DA18....3 D4
St Edmund's Cotts TN1591 A2
St Edmund's Cotts TN15..91 A2
St Edmund's Jun Sch
 CT2................142 C3
St Edmunds Rd CT5
 CT16...............278 D2
St Edmunds Rd
 20 Canterbury CT1...174 F8
 Dartford DA1........175 A8
St Edmund's Rd CT14..214 E4
St Edmund's Sch CT2...142 C3
St Edmunds Way ME8 ..66 B1
St Edward's RC Prim Sch
 ME12...............28 B2
St Elisabeth Ho CT1...143 A1
St Ethelberts RC Prim Sch
 CT11...............117 F8
St Faith's at Ash Sch
 CT3................147 C1
St Faiths Ct ME14.....163 B4
St Faith's La ME14....163 B4
St Faith St ME14.....161 F4
St Fidelis RC Prim Sch
 DA8................147 A8
St Fidelis' Rd DA8......4 D1
St Francis Ave CT2.....37 E6
St Francis Cl Deal CT14 214 F4
 Maidstone ME14.....162 B7
 Margate CT9..........83 D8
 Orpington BR6........53 E3
 Rochester ME2........62 E6
St Francis Ct
 3 Bromley BR2......52 A7
 Greenwich SE3.......11 B6
 Stone DA9...........16 F1
St Francis' RC Prim Sch
 ME15...............161 C4
St Francis Rd
 Folkestone CT19.....334 F6
 Harvel DA13..........93 B3
St Francis' Rd DA8......4 D2
St Gabriel's Ct 12 CT20335 E6
St Georges Ave ME12...48 D2
St Georges' Ave
 Herne Bay CT6.......76 D4
 Sheerness ME12.......28 B1
St George's Bickley CE
 Prim Sch BR1........52 D7
St George's Bsns Ctr
 TN23...............267 F2
St Georges Bsns Pk
 ME10...............102 B4
St Georges CE Foundation
 Sch CT10............83 C5
St George's CE Prim Sch
 Minster (Sheppey)
 ME12...............47 E6
 7 Wrotham TN15 ....124 F3
St George's CE Sch
 DA11...............37 A6
St Georges Cl CT5.....108 C7
St Georges Cres CT17 .310 B5
St George's Cres DA12 .37 D4
St Georges Ct
 Dover CT17..........278 A2
 3 Royal Tunbridge Wells
 TN4...............286 A5
St George's Ct
 West Minst ME12.....46 B8
 Wrotham TN15......124 F3
St Georges La CT1.....175 A8
St George's Lees CT13 181 A4
St Georges Mews 11
 TN9................254 B8
St George's Pas CT14. 215 D6
St George's Pk TN2 ...313 F4
St Georges Pl
 Sandwich CT13......181 B8
 St Margaret's at Cliffe
 CT15...............279 F6
St George's Pl
 Canterbury CT1......175 A8
 Hythe CT21.........353 D8
St George's RAF Chapel of
 Remembrance ★
 TN16...............118 C6
St Georges Rd
 Orpington BR5........53 D3
 Ramsgate CT11......117 F8
 Swanley BR8.........55 F5
St George's Rd
 Broadstairs CT10......84 A4
 Bromley BR1.........52 F4
 Deal CT14..........215 D6
 Folkestone CT19.....334 F6
 Gillingham ME7........64 C6
 Sandwich CT13......181 A8
 Sevenoaks TN13.....154 B5
 Sidcup DA14..........31 D2
St George's Rd W BR1..52 F7
St George's Sh Ctr
 DA11...............37 A6
St Georges Sq DA11....58 E6
St George's Sq
 3 Ashford TN24.....268 B2
 Maidstone ME16......161 E3
St Georges St CT1.....175 A8
St George's St CT1 ....175 A8
St George's Terr CT6...76 E5
St George's Wlk ME3...9 D2
St German's Pl SE3....11 A6
St Giles Cl Dover CT17..310 B5

St Giles Cl continued
 Orpington BR6.........86 D5
St Giles Rd CT17.......310 B5
St Giles Wlk CT17.....310 B5
St Gregory's Cl CT14 .214 F4
St Gregory's Cres CT12 37 E6
St Gregory's Ct
 Canterbury CT1......143 B1
 Gravesend DA12......37 E6
St Gregory's RC Comp Sch
 TN4...............286 A7
St Gregorys RC Prim Sch
 CT9.................82 E8
St Gregory's Rd CT1..143 B1
St Helens DA14.........31 B5
St Helens CE Prim Sch
 ME3................22 B5
St Helens Cotts ME15..193 E8
St Helens La ME15.....193 E8
St Helens Rd Cliffe ME3 ..3 D4
 7 Erith DA18..........3 D4
St Helen's Rd ME12....28 D1
St Helier's Cl ME16...161 B2
St Hilary Ho SE2........13 D8
St Hilda Rd CT19.......334 E6
St Hildas TN15........189 F8
St Hilda's Rd CT21.....333 B1
St Hilda's Way DA12...37 E5
St Jacob's Pl CT1.....174 D6
St James Ave CT12....117 C8
St James' Ave
 Broadstairs CT10......83 E5
 Ramsgate CT12.......83 B1
St James' CE Inf Sch
 TN2...............286 C4
St James' CE Jun Sch
 TN2...............286 C4
 ME3................27 B6
St James Cl
 6 East Malling ME19 .159 F8
 Grain ME3...........27 B6
 Tonbridge TN10.....222 D7
 Warden ME12........49 E4
St James Ct
 3 Bromley BR2......52 A7
 Greenwich SE3.......11 B6
 Stone DA9...........16 F1
St James' Cotts SE25 .108 D8
St James La 7 CT16...310 E7
St James' La DA9.......34 E8
St James Oaks DA11...37 A8
St James' Park Rd CT9 .82 A8
St James Pl DA11.......15 D1
St James RC Prim Sch
 BR5................53 B4
St James Rd Grain ME3..27 B5
 Kingsdown CT14.....248 D5
St James' Rd TN1.....286 C5
St James's Ave DA11...37 A8
St James's Cl SE18.....2 C1
St James's Ct SE TN1...286 B4
St James's Rd
 Gravesend DA11.......19 A1
 Sevenoaks TN13.....154 B5
St James's St SE11.....19 A1
St James St CT16......310 E7
St James's Terr CT7 ...81 B8
St James the Great Prim
 Sch ME19...........159 F8
St James Way DA14....31 E3
St Jean's Rd CT8........81 E7
St Joachim's RC Prim Sch
 E16.................1 C6
St John Fisher RC Prim
 Sch DA18............3 E3
St John Fisher RC Sch
 (Main Site) ME4......63 E3
St John RC Prim Sch
 (Sixth Form Site) ME4 63 F2
ST JOHN'S
 Royal Tunbridge
 Wells.............286 A5
 Seavenoaks.........154 B5
St Johns Ave CT12......82 F1
St John's Ave
 Ramsgate CT12.......83 A1
 Sittingbourne ME10 ..102 B3
St John's CE Inf Sch
 ME4................63 E3
St John's CE Prim Sch
 Maidstone ME14.....162 E4
 Royal Tunbridge Wells
 TN4...............286 B7
 Sevenoaks TN13.....154 D4
St John's Church Rd
 CT19...............335 C6
St John's Cl
 Densole CT18.........307 A7
 Higham ME3...........39 C4
St John's Commandery
 (rems of) ★ CT15....275 E4
St John's Cotts
 Bethersden TN26 .....297 D5
 12 Sandwich CT13...148 F1
St Johns Cres CT2....142 D6
St Johns Ct DA8........4 D1
St John's Ct
 Ashford TN24........301 A6
 Sevenoaks TN13.....154 C5
St John's Hill TN13,
 TN14...............154 C5
St John's Hospl 6
 CT1................143 A1
St John's Jerusalem ★
 DA4.................34 B1
St John's La
 Ashford TN23, TN24 .268 C2
 Canterbury CT1......174 F8
 Hartley DA3..........58 F3
St John's Par 4 DA14..31 B4

St John's Pk
 Greenwich SE3........11 A7
 Royal Tunbridge Wells
 TN4...............286 A8
St John's Pl CT1.......143 A1
St John's Prim Sch
 DA12...............37 D7
St John's RC Comp Sch
 DA12...............37 D7
St Johns Rd
 Elvington CT15......212 B2
 Hoo St Werburgh ME3 ..41 E6
 Hythe CT21.........333 A3
St John's Rd
 Bexley DA16..........13 B4
 Dartford DA2........34 C8
 Dover CT17..........310 C7
 Erith DA8............4 D1
 Faversham ME13.....138 D7
 Gillingham ME7........64 C3
 Gravesend DA12......37 D8
 Higham ME3..........39 C4
 Margate CT9..........50 J2
 Newham E16..........1 A7
 New Romney TN28 ...373 A6
 Orpington BR5........53 E3
 Royal Tunbridge Wells
 TN4...............286 A6
 Sevenoaks TN13.....154 C5
 Sidcup DA14..........31 B4
 Whitstable CT5.......75 D3
St John's St
 Folkestone CT20.....335 D5
 7 Margate CT9.......50 J2
St John's Terr SE18....12 D8
St Johns Way
 Edenbridge TN8......217 C3
 Rochester ME1........63 A2
St John's Way CT18...307 A7
St Josephs Cl BR6......86 F6
St Josephs Convent Prep
 Sch DA12............37 F6
St Josephs Ct 4 SE12..29 B5
St Joseph's RC Prim Sch
 Aylesham CT3........211 A5
 1 Broadstairs CT10...83 F5
 Bromley BR1.........29 C1
 Crayford DA1........14 D3
 Northfleet DA11......36 D8
St Julien Ave CT1.....143 D1
St Justin Cl BR5........54 D6
St Katharine's Knockholt
 CE Prim Sch TN14...120 B2
St Katherine Rd ME12..46 E7
St Katherines Cotts
 DA12...............38 E4
St Katherine's La ME6 127 F7
St Katherines Rd DA18 ..3 D4
St Katherine's Sch
 ME6................127 F7
St Keverne Rd SE9.....29 E4
St Keverne Road SE9...29 F8
St Kilda Rd BR6.......53 F1
St Laurence Ave ME16 161 C8
St Laurence CE Jun Sch
 CT11...............117 B8
St Laurence Cl
 Orpington BR5........54 D6
 Sittingbourne ME9 ...102 D2
St Laurence Coll CT11 117 D8
St Laurence Coll Jun Sch
 CT11...............117 B7
St Laurence Ct TN28 . 373 A6
St Lawrence Ave
 Bidborough TN4......253 D3
 Ramsgate CT11.......117 B5
St Lawrence CE Prim Sch
 TN15...............155 C3
St Lawrence Chase
 CT11...............117 B7
St Lawrence Cl CT11 ..175 B6
St Lawrence Coll CT11 117 D8
St Lawrence Ind Est
 CT11...............117 B7
St Lawrence Ct TN28 .373 A6
St Lawrence Forstal
 CT11...............175 B6
St Lawrence Gd The (Kent
 Cty Cricket Club)
 CT11...............175 B6
St Leonards Ave ME4...63 F2
St Leonards Cl
 4 Bexley DA16.......13 A4
 Grays RM17..........17 F8
St Leonards Ct 1
 CT21...............333 B1
St Leonards Mews 5
 CT21...............333 B1
St Leonards Rd CT14..215 A4
St Leonard's Rd CT14..215 A4
St Leonards Rise BR6 ..86 B7
St Leonard's St ME19 .159 B7
ST LEONARD'S
 STREET............159 B6
St Leonard's Tower ★
 ME19...............159 A7
St Louis Gr CT6........76 C4
St Lukes Ave CT11....117 E8
St Luke's Ave ME14...162 B5
St Lukes Cl Dartford DA2 34 E3
 Swanley BR8.........55 D7
 Whitstable CT5......108 E7
St Luke's Cl CT8........81 E8
St Lukes Cotts BR8.....55 D7
St Lukes Ct
 Ashford TN23........299 F7
 Maidstone ME14......162 A4
St Lukes RC Sixth Form
 Coll DA14............31 A3
St Luke's Rd
 Maidstone ME14.....162 B5

St Luke's Rd continued
 Ramsgate CT11......117 E8
 Royal Tunbridge Wells
 TN4...............286 B6
St Luke's Way ME3......9 D2
St Luke's Wlk CT18....306 C4
St Magnus Cl CT7......81 A8
St Magnus Ct CT7......81 A8
St Malo Ct 2 CT20....335 C4
St Margaret Clitherow
 RC Prim Sch
 Tonbridge TN10......222 B6
 Woolwich SE28.......3 B5
ST MARGARETS......34 D1
ST MARGARET'S AT
 CLIFFE............280 A6
 Prim Sch CT15......280 A6
St Margarets at Troy Town
 Prim SchME1.........63 C4
St Margarets Ave DA15 30 D5
St Margaret's Banks
 ME1................63 D5
St Margaret's CE Prim Sch
 SE18................2 C1
St Margarets Cl
 Maidstone ME16.....161 B2
 Orpington BR6........87 B6
St Margaret's Cl
 Dartford DA2........34 D6
 Whitstable CT5......108 A6
St Margarets Collier Street
 CE Prim SchTN12....226 D1
St Margarets Cres
 DA12...............37 E5
St Margarets Ct 1
 CT20...............335 B5
St Margaret's Ct
 6 Gillingham ME8....98 F8
 High Halstow ME23 ...23 E3
St Margarets Dr
 Deal CT14..........248 B8
 Gillingham ME8.......98 C5
St Margaret's Gr SE18 .12 C8
St Margarets Inf Sch
 ME8................98 E8
St Margaret's Jun Sch
 ME8................98 E8
St Margaret's Mews
 ME1................63 C5
St Margarets Rd
 St Margaret's at Cliffe
 CT15...............248 A1
 Westgate on Sea CT7...81 F3
St Margaret's Rd
 Dartford DA2, DA4 ....34 E2
 Northfleet DA11......36 E7
 St Margaret's at Cliffe
 CT15...............280 A5
 Westgate on Sea CT8...81 E7
St Margaret's St
 Canterbury CT1......174 F4
 Rochester ME1.......63 C5
St Margaret's Terr SE18 .2 C1
St Margarets Villas
 TN12...............258 D8
St Mark's Ave DA11....36 F8
St Marks CE Prim Sch
 ME20...............128 F6
St Mark's CE Prim Sch
 Bromley BR2.........52 A6
 Royal Tunbridge Wells
 TN4...............285 D1
St Marks Cl CT5.......108 B8
St Mark's Cl CT20.....334 D5
St Marks Cl ME20.....128 F6
St Marks Ho ME7.......64 C5
St Marks Ind Est E16 ...1 D5
St Mark's Rd
 Bromley BR2.........52 B6
 Royal Tunbridge Wells
 TN2...............313 F4
ST MARTIN'S.........175 B8
St Martins Ave CT1....175 B8
St Martin's Church ★
 CT1................175 B8
St Martins Cl
 Canterbury CT1......175 B8
 Erith DA18............3 D4
 Newington ME9......100 C7
St Martin's Cl
 Detling ME14........131 A1
 Dover CT17..........310 B5
St Martins Ct 4 CT1...175 B8
St Martin's Dr DA4......89 D7
St Martin's Hill CT1....175 C8
St Martins Ho CT17....310 D5
St Martins Hospl CT1..175 D8
St Martins Mdw TN16..152 C4
St Martin's Pl CT1.....175 B8
St Martins Rd
 Folkestone CT20.....334 D6
 New Romney TN28 ...373 D6
St Martin's Rd
 Canterbury CT1......143 B1
 Dartford DA1.........15 F1
 Deal CT14..........214 F4
 Dover CT15..........278 E4
St Martins Sch CT17...310 A7
St Martin's Terr CT1...175 B8
St Martin's View CT6...111 A8
ST MARY CRAY......54 B4
St Mary Cray Prim Sch
 BR5................54 C3
St Mary Cray Sta BR5...54 B5
St Mary Ct 13 ME13...138 D7
ST MARY HOO.......24 D6
ST MARY IN THE
 MARSH...........365 B4

St Mary Magdalene CE
   Prim Sch 15 SE18 . . . . 2 A2
St Mary of Charity CE Prim
   Sch ME13 . . . . 138 D7
St Mary's ME3 . . . . 24 D5
St Mary's Abbey ME19 159 C8
St Mary's Ave CT9 . . . . 51 D1
ST MARY'S BAY 366 A4
St Mary's Bay Sta★
   TN29 . . . . 365 F4
St Marys CE Prim Sch
   6 Dover CT16 . . . . 310 E8
   Folkestone CT19 . . . . . . 335 F6
St Mary's CE Prim Sch
   BR8 . . . . 55 E5
St Mary's Church★ CT6 78 C7
St Mary's Church Rd
   TN14 . . . . 152 F2
St Marys Cl CT18 . . . . . . 305 D3
St Mary's Cl
   Eastry CT13 . . . . 180 C2
   Gravesend DA12 . . . . . . 37 C6
   Grays RM17 . . . . 18 D8
   Hamstreet TN26 . . . . . . 349 A8
   Laddingford ME18 . . . . 225 E4
   Nonington CT15 . . . . . . 211 C5
   Orpington BR5 . . . . 54 C7
   Platt TN15 . . . . 157 C7
   Ticehurst TN5 . . . . 338 D1
   Woodnesborough CT13 180 B6
St Marys Ct SE7 . . . . 11 D7
St Mary's Ct
   16 Canterbury CT1 . . . .174 F8
   Erith DA17 . . . . 3 D2
   Herne Bay CT6 . . . . 76 E4
   5 Westerham TN16 . . . 151 D1
St Marys Dr CT18 . . . . . . 305 D3
St Mary's Dr TN13 . . . . . 153 E4
St Mary's Gdns
   Chatham ME4 . . . . 64 B7
   St Mary's Bay TN29 . . . 366 A5
   Upstreet CT3 . . . . 112 E3
St Marys Gn TN24 . . . . . 268 E7
St Mary's Gn TN16 . . . . . 118 C1
St Mary's Gr
   Biggin Hill TN16 . . . . . . 118 C1
   Tilmanstone CT14 . . . . 213 A4
   Whitstable CT5 . . . . 107 F7
ST MARY'S ISLAND 41 C1
St Mary's Island CE Prim
   Sch ME4 . . . . 41 B2
St Mary's La
   Speldhurst TN3 . . . . . . 285 A8
   Ticehurst TN5 . . . . 338 D1
St Mary's Mdw CT3 . . . . 178 A8
St Marys Mews TN24 . . . 300 F8
St Mary's Pl Eltham SE9 . .12 A1
   Newington ME9 . . . . . . 100 C7
St Mary's RC Prim Sch
   CT5 . . . . 74 F2
St Mary's RC Prim Sch
   Deal CT14 . . . . 214 F3
   Eltham SE9 . . . . 12 A2
   Gillingham ME7 . . . . 64 D6
   Tilbury RM18 . . . . 18 F5
St Mary's Rd
   5 Broadstairs CT10 . . . 84 B4
   Coldblow DA5 . . . . 32 C7
   Deal CT14 . . . . 215 C1
   Elham CT4 . . . . 273 F4
   Faversham ME13 . . . . . 138 D7
   Gillingham ME7 . . . . 64 C6
   Minster (Thanet) CT12 . 115 B6
   Patrixbourne CT4 . . . . . 176 B3
   Rochester ME2 . . . . 63 B7
   St Mary in the Marsh TN28,
   TN29 . . . . 365 C5
   Stone DA9 . . . . 16 E2
   Swanley BR8 . . . . 55 E5
   Tonbridge TN9 . . . . 254 B7
   West Hythe CT21 . . . . . 332 B1
   Wrotham TN15 . . . . 125 A2
St Mary's Row ME12 . . . . 47 A6
St Mary's St CT1 . . . . . . 174 F8
St Mary St SE18 . . . . 2 A1
St Mary's Terr 2 CT20 335 E5
St Mary's View ME9 . . . 100 C7
St Marys Way ME3 . . . . . 58 E6
St Mary's Wlk ME1 . . . . . 95 F1
St Matthew's Cl ME9 . 100 C7
St Matthews Dr
   Bromley BR1 . . . . 52 F6
   Rochester ME1 . . . . 63 A2
St Matthew's High Brooms
   CE Prim Sch TN4 . . . . . 286 B8
St Matthew's Way ME3 . .9 D2
St Mawes CT8 . . . . 50 C1
St Mellion Cl SE28 . . . . 3 D7
St Merryn Cl SE18 . . . . . .12 D7
St Michael & All Angels
   Church CT14 . . . . 215 C4
ST MICHAELS 324 B4
St Michaels RH8 . . . . . . 183 A5
St Michael's Alley 14
   CT11 . . . . 117 E6
St Michaels Ave CT9 . . . . 83 D8
St Michael's CE Inf Sch
   ME16 . . . . 161 E3
St Michael's CE Jun Sch
   ME16 . . . . 161 E3
St Michael's CE Prim Sch
   Bexley DA16 . . . . 13 C6
   Houghton Green TN31 . 368 C2
   Tenterden TN30 . . . . . . 324 A3
St Michaels Cl
   Bromley BR1 . . . . 52 E6
   Canterbury CT2 . . . . . . 142 A1
   4 Newham E16 . . . . 1 D8
   Pratling Street ME20 . . 129 C3
St Michael's Cl
   Chatham ME4 . . . . 63 F3

St Michael's Cl continued
   Erith DA18 . . . . 3 D4
   5 Sittingbourne ME10 . 101 F4
St Michaels Ct ME11 . . . 221 E7
St Michael's Ct
   8 Folkestone CT20 . . . 335 E5
   6 Rochester ME2 . . . . . 63 B8
St Michaels Dr TN14 . . . 122 E3
St Michael's Pl CT2 . . . . 142 E2
St Michael's Prim Sch
   TN7 . . . . 311 B5
St Michael's RC Prim Sch
   8 ME4 . . . . 63 F3
St Michael's Rd
   Bexley DA16 . . . . 13 B4
   Canterbury CT2 . . . . . . 142 E2
   Maidstone ME16 . . . . . 161 D3
   Royal Tunbridge Wells
   TN4 . . . . 286 B7
   Sittingbourne ME10 . . . 101 F4
St Michael's Rise DA16 . 13 B6
St Michael's Sch TN14 .122 E4
St Michael's St CT20 . . . 335 E5
St Michael's Terr TN30 324 A3
St Michael's Wlk CT18 306 F4
St Mildred's Ave
   Birchington CT7 . . . . 80 E8
   Broadstairs CT10 . . . . . . 84 A4
   Ramsgate CT11 . . . . . . 117 B5
St Mildred's Cl 4
   TN30 . . . . 345 A7
St Mildreds Ct
   Canterbury CT1 . . . . . . 174 E8
   Deal CT14 . . . . 215 C1
   Westgate on Sea CT8 . . 50 D1
St Mildred's Gdns CT8 . .50 D1
St Mildreds Pl CT1 . . . . 174 E7
St Mildreds Prim Inf Sch
   6 CT10 . . . . 84 A7
St Mildreds Rd 5 SE12 29 A4
St Mildred's Rd
   Margate CT9 . . . . 51 A2
   Minster (Thanet) CT12 . 115 B5
   Ramsgate CT11 . . . . . . 117 C6
   Westgate on Sea CT8 . . 50 C1
St Monicas Deal CT14 . . 248 D6
   Dover CT17 . . . . 310 C7
St Monicas Rd CT14 . . . 248 D6
ST NICHOLAS AT
   WADE 79 E1
St Nicholas at Wade CE
   Prim Sch CT7 . . . . 79 E2
St Nicholas CE Inf Sch
   ME2 . . . . 63 A7
St Nicholas CE Prim Sch
   TN28 . . . . 373 B7
St Nicholas Cl
   Deal CT14 . . . . 214 F4
   Sturry CT2 . . . . 143 F7
St Nicholas Cnr CT7 . . . . 79 F1
St Nicholas Ct TN13 . . . 154 B1
St Nicholas Dr TN3 . . . . 154 C1
St Nicholas Gdns ME2 . . 62 F7
St Nicholas Ho CT3 . . . . 147 D2
St Nicholas Hospl CT2 142 C1
St Nicholas Lodge CT10 83 F4
St Nicholas Rd
   Canterbury CT1 . . . . . . 174 D6
   Faversham ME13 . . . . . 138 A7
   Hythe CT21 . . . . 333 A2
   Littlestone-on-Sea TN28 373 E6
   Woolwich SE18 . . . . 2 F2
St Nicholas Rdbt CT7 . . . 80 B2
St Nicholas Sch CT1 . . . 174 F6
St Nicholas Terr 1
   CT21 . . . . 333 B2
St Nicolas La BR7 . . . . . . 52 E8
St Olaves Prep Sch SE9 . 30 B6
St Olave's & St Saviour's
   Gram Sch BR6 . . . . 87 B7
St Patrick's Cl
   Deal CT14 . . . . 215 C6
   Whitstable CT5 . . . . 108 E7
St Patrick's Gdns DA12 37 D5
St Patrick's RC Prim Sch
   SE18 . . . . 2 D2
St Patricks Rd
   Dover CT17 . . . . 310 A4
   Ramsgate CT11 . . . . . . 117 F8
St Patrick's Rd CT14 . . . 215 C6
St Patrick's Row ME9 . .135 B7
St Paulinus CE Prim Sch
   DA1 . . . . 14 E3
St Paulinus Ct DA1 . . . . . 14 E3
St Paul's Acad SE2 . . . . . 13 A8
St Paul's Ave ME13 . . . . 138 A7
St Pauls CE Prim Sch 6
   TN4 . . . . 285 B4
St Paul's Cl CT2 . . . . 142 E1
St Paul's Cl TN10 . . . . . 222 D5
St Paul's Cl
   Greenwich SE7 . . . . 1 D1
   Rochester ME2 . . . . 62 D5
   Swanscombe DA10 . . . . 35 E8
ST PAUL'S CRAY 54 A7
St Paul's Cray CE Prim Sch
   BR5 . . . . 54 D6
St Paul's Cray Rd BR5,
   BR7 . . . . 52 B8
St Pauls Cres ME13 . . . . 140 A3
St Pauls Ct ME9 . . . . . . 136 A6
St Paul's Ct
   Folkestone CT20 . . . . . . 334 E4
   Rusthall TN4 . . . . 285 B4
St Pauls Inf Sch ME14 . 162 A7
St Pauls Rd ME13 . . . . . 140 A3
St Paul's Rd Erith DA8 . . 14 C7
   Margate CT9 . . . . 51 A2
St Paul's Sq BR2 . . . . 52 A7
St Paul's St
   Rusthall TN4 . . . . 285 C4
   Sittingbourne ME10 . . . 101 E5
St Pauls Terr CT1 . . . . . 175 A8

St Paul's Way CT20 . . . . 334 F4
St Paul's Wood Hill BR5 53 F7
St Peter Ave TN16 . . . . . 119 B3
St Peter Chanel RC Prim
   Sch DA14 . . . . 31 C3
St Peter in Thanet CE Jun
   Sch CT10 . . . . 83 F7
St Peter & Paul RC Prim
   Sch BR5 . . . . 53 E7
ST PETER'S 83 E5
St Peter's Bridge ME14 161 F4
St Peters CE Prim Sch
   Folkestone CT19 . . . . . . 335 E5
   Forstal ME20 . . . . 129 A3
St Peter's CE Prim Sch
   TN2 . . . . 286 C3
St Peters Cl
   Chislehurst BR7 . . . . 30 D1
   Ditton ME20 . . . . 128 B1
St Peter's Cl
   Halfway Houses ME12 . . 46 D6
   Swanscombe DA10 . . . . 35 F8
St Peters Cotts 5 CT5 . 74 D2
St Peter's Ct
   Broadstairs CT10 . . . . . . 83 F5
   Ditton ME20 . . . . 128 C1
   Faversham ME13 . . . . . 138 A7
St Peters Footpath 2
   CT9 . . . . 51 A1
St Peter's Footpath
   Margate CT9 . . . . 50 J1
   Margate, Drapers Mill
   CT9 . . . . 83 A8
St Peter's Gr CT1 . . . . . 174 F8
St Peters Inf Sch ME1 . . 63 C3
St Peters La BR5 . . . . 54 A7
St Peter's La CT1 . . . . . . 142 F1
St Peters Meth Prim Sch
   CT2 . . . . 174 F8
St Peter's Park Rd CT10 83 F5
St Peter's Path ME1 . . . . 63 D5
St Peters Pl
   Eccles ME20 . . . . 128 F6
   Lynsted ME9 . . . . 136 A6
St Peter's Pl CT1, CT2 . 174 F8
St Peter's RC Prim Sch
   Sittingbourne ME10 . . 101 D2
   Woolwich SE18 . . . . 2 B2
St Peters Rd ME20 . . . . 128 B1
St Peter's Rd
   Boughton Street
   ME13 . . . . 140 A3
   Broadstairs CT10 . . . . . . 83 F5
   Margate CT10, CT9 . . . . 83 A7
   Whitstable CT5 . . . . 74 D2
St Peters Row TN3 . . . . 284 B5
St Peter's Row TN26 . . . 297 D5
St Peters Sch of English 20
   CT1 . . . . 142 F1
St Peter's St 15 CT1 . . 142 F1
St Peter's St
   Canterbury CT1, CT2 . . 174 F8
   Maidstone ME16 . . . . . 161 F4
   Royal Tunbridge Wells
   TN2 . . . . 286 C3
   Sandwich CT13 . . . . . . 149 A1
St Peter St ME1 . . . . 63 D4
St Peter's Way TN26 . . 297 D5
St Peters Wharf Ret Pk
   ME16 . . . . 161 F4
St Philip Howard RC Prim
   Sch CT6 . . . . 76 E5
St Philip's Ave ME15 . . 162 B2
St Philips Ct TN2 . . . . . . 286 D6
St Philomena's RC Prim
   Sch BR5 . . . . 54 C2
St Pierre Ct CT14 . . . . . 215 D5
St Quentin Rd DA16 . . . . 12 F4
ST RADIGUND'S 278 A2
St Radigund's Ct CT17 278 A2
St Radigund's Pl CT1 . . 143 A1
St Radigund's Rd CT17 278 A1
St Radigunds St CT1 . . 142 F1
St Richards RC Prim Sch
   CT16 . . . . 278 D1
St Richard's Rd CT14 . . 214 F3
St Richard's Wlk CT17 310 A4
St Ronan's Cl ME15 . . . . 195 C7
St Ronan's Sch TN18 . . 341 D2
St Rowans View 2 DA1 33 F8
St Saviour's CE Jun Sch
   CT8 . . . . 81 E8
St Saviours Cl CT19 . . . 335 D7
St Saviour's Cl ME13 . . 138 E7
St Saviours Ct CT8 . . . . . 81 E8
St Saviours Rd ME15 . . . 195 D6
SAINT'S HILL 284 A8
Saints Hill TN23 . . . . . . 300 A8
St Simon of England RC
   Prim Sch TN23 . . . . . . 300 A8
St Simon Stock RC Sch
   ME16 . . . . 161 C4
ST STEPHEN'S 142 F2
St Stephen's Cl
   Canterbury CT2 . . . . . . 142 F2
   Newington ME9 . . . . . . 100 C7
St Stephen's Cotts
   TN1 . . . . 286 B5
St Stephen's Ct
   Canterbury CT2 . . . . . . 142 F2
   Royal Tunbridge Wells
   TN1 . . . . 286 B5
St Stephens Fields 5
   CT2 . . . . 142 F1
St Stephen's Fields
   CT2 . . . . 142 F1
St Stephen's Gn CT2 . . 142 F2
St Stephen's Hill CT2 . . 142 F4
St Stephens Ho 7 CT2 142 F1
St Stephen's Inf & Jun Sch
   CT2 . . . . 142 F2
St Stephen's Lodge
   CT2 . . . . 142 F2

St Stephen's Manor
   CT10 . . . . 84 B7
St Stephens Mews ME1 96 E8
St Stephen's Mews
   TN23 . . . . 300 A6
St Stephens Pathway 4
   CT2 . . . . 142 F1
St Stephen's Prim Sch
   TN9 . . . . 254 D8
St Stephen's RC Prim Sch
   DA16 . . . . 13 A5
St Stephen's Rd CT2 . . 142 F2
St Stephen's Sq ME15 . 161 E2
St Stephen's St TN9 . . 254 B8
St Stephen's Way CT20 334 F4
St Stephen's Wlk TN23 299 F7
St Swithin's Rd CT5 . . . 75 B3
St Teresas RC Prim Sch
   TN24 . . . . 268 B4
St Theresas Cl TN24 . . 268 B3
St Thomas-a-Becket RC
   Prim Sch SE2 . . . . 3 A3
St Thomas' Cross
   TN26 . . . . 327 E3
St Thomas Ct CT5 . . . . . . 32 A8
St Thomas' Dr BR5 . . . . . 53 C1
St Thomas Hill CT2 . . . 142 D3
St Thomas More RC Prim
   Sch
   Bexley DA7 . . . . 13 F5
   Chatham ME5 . . . . 97 A5
   2 Eltham SE9 . . . . 11 E4
St Thomas More RC Sch 14
   SE9 . . . . 12 A1
St Thomas of Canterbury
   RC Prim Sch ME8 . . . . . 65 B2
St Thomas' RC Prim Sch
   20 Canterbury CT1 . . . . 143 A1
   Grays RM17 . . . . 18 C8
   Sevenoaks TN13 . . . . . 154 B2
St Thomas Rd Erith DA17 4 C4
   Newham E16 . . . . 1 A7
   Northfleet DA11 . . . . . . 36 E6
St Thomas's Almshouses
   DA1 . . . . 37 B7
St Thomas's Ave DA11 . . 37 B7
St Thomas's Hospl
   CT13 . . . . 148 F1
St Thomas's Pl 1 RM17 18 C8
St Timothy's Mews 3
   BR1 . . . . 52 B8
St Vincent Rd CT15 . . . 279 F7
St Vincents Ave DA1 . . . . 16 A2
St Vincent's Cl
   Littlebourne CT3 . . . . . 144 F1
   Whitstable CT5 . . . . 108 E7
St Vincents La TN19 . . 126 A2
St Vincents RC Prim Sch
   SE9 . . . . 29 C4
St Vincents Rd DA1 . . . . 16 A1
St Welcume's Way
   ME17 . . . . 198 E6
St Werburgh Cres ME3 . 41 D5
St Werburgh St ME3 . . . 41 D5
St William of Perth Prim
   Sch ME1 . . . . 63 B2
St William's Way ME1 . . 63 D2
St Winifred Rd CT19 . . . 334 F6
St Winifred's Rd TN16 . 118 F1
Sala Ho SE3 . . . . 11 B3
Salamons Way RM13 . . . . 4 E7
Salbris Ct TN29 . . . . 366 D8
Salcote Rd DA12 . . . . 37 E3
Salem Pl DA11 . . . . 36 D8
Salem St ME15 . . . . 162 A3
Salhouse Cl SE28 . . . . 3 C7
Salisbury Ave
   Broadstairs CT10 . . . . . . 83 F2
   Gillingham ME8 . . . . 98 D8
   Ramsgate CT11 . . . . . . 117 F8
   Swanley BR8 . . . . 56 A5
Salisbury Cl
   Sittingbourne ME10 . . . 102 C4
   Tonbridge TN10 . . . . . . 222 D5
Salisbury Ho
   Canterbury CT2 . . . . . . 142 D2
   4 Maidstone ME15 . . . 195 D7
Salisbury Mews BR2 . . . 52 E4
Salisbury Rd
   Bromley BR2 . . . . 52 E4
   Canterbury CT2 . . . . . . 142 E2
   Chatham ME4 . . . . 64 A3
   Dartford DA2 . . . . 34 C7
   Deal CT14 . . . . 215 B2
   Dover CT16 . . . . 278 D1
   Folkestone CT19 . . . . . 334 E7
   2 Grays RM17 . . . . 18 C8
   Herne Bay CT6 . . . . 77 C5
   Kit's Coty ME20 . . . . . . 129 D7
   Langton Green TN3 . . . 284 F7
   Maidstone ME14 . . . . . 162 A6
   Northfleet DA11 . . . . . . 36 F7
   Royal Tunbridge Wells
   TN4 . . . . 286 C8
   Sidcup DA5 . . . . 32 A7
St Margaret's at Cliffe
   CT15 . . . . 280 B6
   Tonbridge TN10 . . . . . . 222 D4
   Whitstable CT5 . . . . 108 D8
Salix Rd RM17 . . . . 18 D8
Sallow Cl ME4 . . . . 41 C1
Sallows Shaw DA13 . . . . 60 C4
Sally Port ME7 . . . . 64 B6
Sally Port Gdns ME7 . . . 64 B6
Salmestone Grange★
   CT9 . . . . 82 E8
Salmestone Prim Sch
   CT9 . . . . 82 E8
Salmestone Rd CT9 . . . . 82 F8
Salmestone Rise CT9 . . . 82 E8
Salmon Cres ME12 . . . . . 46 F6
Salmon Rd Dartford DA1 15 F4
   Erith DA17 . . . . 4 A1
Salomons Mus★ TN3 . 285 D8

Salomons Rd
   Newham E13 . . . . 1 C8
   Rusthall TN4 . . . . 285 C4
Saltash Rd DA16 . . . . . . 13 C6
Saltbox Hill TN16 . . . . . 118 B6
Saltcote Cl DA1 . . . . 14 E1
Salter's Cross ME18 . . . 193 A1
Salters La ME13 . . . . . . 138 D4
Salter's La TN29 . . . . . . 370 C8
Saltford Cl 2 DA8 . . . . . . 4 E1
Salthouse Cl TN29 . . . . 370 D8
Saltings Rd ME6 . . . . . . 128 A7
Saltings The Iwade ME9 68 B4
   Littlestone-on-Sea TN28 373 E5
   5 Swanscombe DA9 . . . 17 C3
   16 Whitstable CT5 . . . . 74 D2
Salt La ME3 . . . . 21 F4
Saltley Cl E6 . . . . 1 E7
Salt Marsh La 21 CT5 . .74 D2
Salt's Ave ME15 . . . . . . 194 F3
Salts Cl CT5 . . . . 74 D1
Salt's Dr CT10 . . . . 83 E5
Salts La ME15 . . . . 195 A4
SALTWOOD 333 C4
Saltwood CE Prim Sch
   CT21 . . . . 333 B4
Saltwood Cl BR6 . . . . 87 C6
Saltwood Gdns CT9 . . . . 51 E2
Saltwood Rd ME15 . . . . 161 F1
Salvadori Ct TN2 . . . . . 287 D6
Samara Cl ME5 . . . . 97 A1
Sam Bartram Cl SE7 . . . . 1 C1
Samian Cres CT19 . . . . 334 C6
Samphire Cl ME14 . . . . 162 E4
Samphire Ct
   Dover CT16 . . . . 310 E8
   Grays RM17 . . . . 18 E8
Samphire Hoe Ctry Pk★
   CT15 . . . . 309 E2
Samphire Way ME4 . . . . 41 A2
Sampson Cl DA17 . . . . . . 3 D3
Samson Ho SE18 . . . . 2 C2
Samuel Cl SE18 . . . . 1 E2
Samuel Ct CT9 . . . . 51 A3
Samuel Dr ME10 . . . . 69 A1
Samuel Mews TN29 . . . 376 D7
Samuel Palmer Ct BR6 . 54 A2
Samuel St SE18 . . . . 1 E2
Samuels Terr ME4 . . . . . 64 B4
Sancroft Ave CT2 . . . . . 142 C1
Sanctuary Cl
   Broadstairs CT10 . . . . . . 83 F2
   Dartford DA1 . . . . 15 D1
   Kearsney CT17 . . . . 277 D4
Sanctuary Rd ME8 . . . . . 65 A3
Sanctuary The
   Sandwich CT13 . . . . . . 182 A7
   Sidcup DA5 . . . . 13 D1
Sanctus Court ME3 . . . . 41 E6
Sandalwood Dr CT7 . . . . 79 F1
Sandalwood House
   DA15 . . . . 30 F5
Sandbach Ho CT9 . . . . . . 51 B3
Sandbach Pl SE18 . . . . . . 2 C1
Sandbanks Hill DA2 . . . . 35 B2
Sandbanks Rd ME13 . . 106 C2
Sandbourne Dr ME14 . . 129 F1
Sandby Gn SE9 . . . . 11 E4
Sandcliff Rd DA8 . . . . 4 D1
Sandcroft TN28 . . . . 373 F7
Sandcroft Way ME15 . . 162 A2
Sand Ct ME12 . . . . 49 G2
Sandeman Way TN27 . . 294 F2
Sand End CT5 . . . . 108 C6
Sanderling Ct SE28 . . . . . 3 C5
Sanderling Rd CT6 . . . . . 77 F5
Sanderling Way
   Iwade ME9 . . . . 68 C5
   Swanscombe DA9 . . . . . 17 A1
Sanders Ct ME12 . . . . . . 47 A5
Sandersons Ave TN14 . . 88 B1
Sanderson Way TN9 . . . 222 E1
Sanderstead Rd BR5 . . . 54 B3
Sandfield Rd TN11 . . . . 284 A7
Sandford Rd
   Bexley DA7, DA6 . . . . . . 13 E4
   Bromley BR2 . . . . 52 A5
   Sittingbourne ME10 . . . 101 B5
SANDGATE 334 E3
Sandgate Ct ME8 . . . . . . 98 F4
Sandgate Espl CT20,
   CT21 . . . . 334 D2
Sandgate High St
   CT20 . . . . 334 E3
Sandgate Hill CT20 . . . . 335 A4
Sandgate Prim Sch
   CT20 . . . . 334 F4
Sandgate Rd
   Bexley DA16 . . . . 13 C4
   Folkestone CT20 . . . . . . 335 C4
   Folkestone CT20 . . . . . . 335 D4
Sandgates CT4 . . . . 272 E2
Sandham Point SE18 . . . 2 B2
Sandhill La ME3 . . . . 39 D6
Sandhole Cotts TN12 . . 288 C4
SANDHURST 356 F6
Sandhurst Ave TN2 . . . 287 E5
Sandhurst Cl
   Canterbury CT2 . . . . . . 143 A4
   Gillingham ME8 . . . . 65 C3
   Royal Tunbridge Wells
   TN2 . . . . 286 C6
   Sandhurst Cross TN18 . 356 A4
Sandhurst Ho TN2 . . . . 286 D5
Sandhurst La TN17 . . . 343 B2
Sandhurst Pk TN2 . . . . . 286 C6
Sandhurst Prim Sch
   TN18 . . . . 356 F5
Sandhurst Rd
   Bexley DA5 . . . . 13 D2
   Margate CT9 . . . . 51 F2

Sandhurst Rd continued
   Orpington BR6 . . . . 87 A6
   Royal Tunbridge Wells
   TN2 . . . . 286 D6
   Sidcup DA15 . . . . 31 A5
   Tilbury RM18 . . . . 19 C5
Sandhurst Vineyards★
   TN18 . . . . 356 E5
Sandilands
   Ashford TN24 . . . . 268 E2
   Sevenoaks TN13 . . . . . 153 D5
Sand La TN17 . . . . 293 F4
Sandle's Rd CT7 . . . . 80 F7
SANDLING 129 F1
Sandling Cl TN23 . . . . . 299 F6
Sandling Ct ME14 . . . . . 162 B7
Sandling La ME14 . . . . . 162 A8
Sandling Park Woodland
   Gdn★ TN25 . . . . 332 E6
Sandling Prim Sch
   ME14 . . . . 162 B8
Sandling Rd
   Hythe CT21 . . . . 332 F6
   Maidstone ME14 . . . . . 161 F6
   Maidstone, Ringlestone
   ME14 . . . . 161 F7
Sandling Rise SE9 . . . . . 30 A5
Sandling Sta CT21 . . . . 332 F6
Sandling Way ME4 . . . . . 41 B1
Sandown Cl Deal CT14 182 D1
   Royal Tunbridge Wells
   TN2 . . . . 286 F6
Sandown Cotts
   Margate CT9 . . . . 51 A3
   Teynham ME9 . . . . 103 E1
Sandown Ct CT14 . . . . . 215 C7
Sandown Dr
   Gillingham ME8 . . . . 98 D7
   Herne Bay CT6 . . . . 76 D4
Sandown Gr TN2 . . . . . . 286 F6
Sandown Lees CT13 . . . 181 D8
Sandown Pk TN2 . . . . . . 286 F6
Sandown Pl CT14 . . . . . 215 C7
Sandown Prim Sch
   CT14 . . . . 215 C7
Sandown Rd Deal CT14 215 D8
   Gravesend DA12 . . . . . . 37 C2
   Sandwich CT13 . . . . . . 181 B8
   West Malling ME19 . . . . 159 D8
Sandow Pl ME19 . . . . . . 159 D4
Sandpiper Cl 3 CT7 . . . . 17 A1
Sandpiper Ct
   8 Gillingham ME8 . . . . . 98 D2
   Herne Bay CT6 . . . . 76 D4
Sandpiper Ct 3 CT7 . . . . 80 F8
Sandpiper Dr DA8 . . . . . . 15 B7
Sandpiper La ME9 . . . . . 68 E3
Sandpiper Rd
   Chatham ME5 . . . . 97 D2
   Hawkinge CT18 . . . . . . 307 A3
   Whitstable CT5 . . . . 108 B7
Sandpipers The DA12 . . . 37 D6
Sandpiper Way BR5 . . . . 54 D6
Sandpit Hill CT3 . . . . . . 112 C4
Sandpit Pl SE7 . . . . 1 E1
Sandpit Rd DA1 . . . . 15 C3
Sandra Cl 5 ME2 . . . . . . 63 B8
Sand Rd TN3 . . . . 317 A4
Sandringham Ct ME19 159 A1
Sandringham Dr
   Bexley DA16 . . . . 12 E5
   Maypole DA2 . . . . 32 E6
Sandringham Mews
   TN4 . . . . 286 A5
Sandringham Rd
   Bromley BR1 . . . . 29 A3
   Gillingham ME8 . . . . 98 E3
   Sandrock Ho TN2 . . . . . 286 D4
   Sandrock Rd TN2 . . . . . 286 C4
   Sandrook Villas TN18 . 340 F2
Sandshaw Ct DA3 . . . . . . 58 E4
Sandstone Ct CT20 . . . . 335 A3
Sandstone Dr ME10 . . . 101 E8
Sandstone La E16 . . . . 1 B6
Sandstone Rise ME5 . . . 130 C8
Sandtoft Rd SE7 . . . . 11 B8
SANDWAY 199 A3
Sandway Path 6 BR5 . . 54 C5
Sandway Rd
   Harrietsham ME17 . . . . 198 F4
   Orpington BR5 . . . . 54 C5
SANDWICH 149 B1
Sandwich Bay Bird Obsy★
   CT13 . . . . 181 E7
Sandwich Cl CT20 . . . . . 334 F5
Sandwich Guildhall Mus★
   CT13 . . . . 148 F1
Sandwich Ind Est CT13 149 B1
Sandwich Inf Sch
   CT13 . . . . 148 F1
Sandwich Jun Sch
   CT13 . . . . 180 F7
Sandwich Rd Ash CT3 . .147 F1
   Cliffs End CT12 . . . . . . 116 D4
   Eastry CT13 . . . . 180 C3
   Eythorne CT15 . . . . 245 C8
   Nonington CT15, CT3 . 211 F6
   Sandwich CT13, CT14 . 180 D5
   Whitfield CT15, CT16 . 278 A7
   Woodnesborough CT13 180 D7
Sandwich Sta CT13 . . . . 181 A8
Sandwich Tech Sch
   CT13 . . . . 180 F6
Sandwood Rd
   Ramsgate CT10 . . . . 83 D1
   Sandwich CT13 . . . . . . 180 F6
Sandy Bank Rd DA12 . . . 37 B7
Sandy Bury BR6 . . . . 86 D7
Sandy Cnr TN26 . . . . . . 298 F5
Sandycroft SE2 . . . . 13 A8
Sandycroft Rd ME2 . . . . 39 F1
Sandy Dell ME7 . . . . 98 A3
Sandy Hill Ave SE18 . . . . 2 B1
Sandy Hill La SE18 . . . . . 2 B1
Sandy Hill Rd SE18 . . . . . 2 B1

Sandyhurst La TN25 . . .268 B8
Sandy La Ashford TN24 .269 B1
  Bean DA13, DA2. . . . . . .35 D5
  Daniel's Water TN26. . . .298 E6
  Hythe CT20, CT21. . . . .334 B3
  Ightham TN15. . . . . . . .156 B3
  Limpsfield RH8 . . . . . . .183 B7
  Maidstone, Harbourland
    ME14. . . . . .162 C8
  Maidstone, Penenden Heath
    ME14. . . . . .162 C7
  Maidstone, Ware Street
    ME14. . . . . .163 B5
  New Town ME19 . . . . . .127 A1
  Orpington BR6. . . . . . . .54 A2
  Ruxley BR5 . . . . .54 D8
  Sevenoaks TN13 . . . . . .154 C4
  Snodland ME6, ME19 . . .127 E6
  Tenterden TN30 . . . . . .345 A4
  Tilbury RM16. . . . . .19 B8
  Westerham TN16 . . . . . .151 D2
  West Thurrock RM20 . . . .17 B8
  Wrotham Heath TN15,
    . . . . .125 F1
Sandy Mount ME14. . . .163 B5
Sandy Pl TN25 . . . . . . .302 D5
Sandy Ridge
  Borough Green TN15 . . .157 A7
  Chislehurst BR7 . . . . . . .30 A2
Sanger Cl CT9. . . . . .50 I1
Sangro Pl CT1. . . . . . . .143 D1
San Remo CT8 . . . . .50 C1
Sanspareil Ave ME12 . . .47 A6
Santana Ho SE18 . . . . . .12 B7
Santer Ho TN18 . . . . . .354 E8
Santers Court TN18 . . .340 E4
Santon La CT3 . . . . . . .146 E8
Sapho Pk DA12. . . . . . . .37 F4
Saphora Cl BR6 . . . . . . .86 D5
Sappers Wlk ME7 . . . . . .64 C5
Sapphire Cl Newham E6 . .2 A7
  Sittingbourne ME10 . . .161 C2
Saracen Cl ME7. . . . . . . .65 A1
Saracen Fields ME5 . . .130 C8
Sarafand Ho ME1. . . . . . .63 B4
Sarah Ct 7 DA6. . . . . . .13 E3
Sarah Gdns CT9 . . . . . . .83 D8
Sara Ho 1 DA8 . . . . .14 E7
Sara Pk DA12. . . . . .37 C4
Sara Turnbull Ho 3
  SE18 . . . . .1 F2
Sark Cl TN29 . . . . .366 C8
Sark Wlk E16. . . . . .1 B7
SARRE 113 D7
Sarre Ct CT7 . . . . .113 D6
Sarre Pl CT13 . . . . .180 F8
Sarre Road 9 BR5 . . . . .54 C4
Sarre Windmill★ CT7 113 D7
Sarsen Hts ME5 . . . . . . .96 F1
Sarsens Ct DA12. . . . . . .60 F6
Sassoon Cl
  Hawkinge CT18. . . . . . .307 A4
  New Hythe ME20 . . . . . .128 A4
Satanita Cl E16. . . . . . . .1 D7
Satis Ave ME10 . . . . . . .101 E7
SATMAR 308 D3
Satmar La CT15, CT18 . .308 E4
Satmore La CT18 . . . . .308 C4
Saunders Cl DA11. . . . . .36 E6
Saunder's Cross TN14 . .88 B2
Saunders La CT3 . . . . .147 F1
Saunders Rd
  Royal Tunbridge Wells
    TN4 . . . . .285 E1
  Woolwich SE18. . . . . .2 F1
Saunders St
  7 Chatham ME4 . . . . . . .63 F3
  Gillingham ME7. . . . . . . .64 C6
Saunders Way
  Camber TN31 . . . . .374 A2
  Dartford DA1 . . . . .33 F6
  Woolwich SE28. . . . . .3 B6
Savage Gdns E6. . . . . . . .1 F7
Savage Rd ME5. . . . . . . .97 B3
Savernake Dr CT6 . . . . . .77 B2
Saville Cl TN10 . . . . . . .222 D7
Saville Ho E16. . . . . .2 B5
Saville Rd E16. . . . . .1 E5
Savoy Rd DA1 . . . . .15 D2
Savoy The 8 CT11 . . . . .117 C6
Saw Lodge Field TN23 300 C4
Sawpit Rd ME9 . . . . . . .135 B2
Sawyers Ct ME4 . . . . . . .64 B2
Saxbys Rd TN15 . . . . . .155 D5
Saxby Wood TN11 . . . . .220 F1
Saxon Ave ME12 . . . . . . .47 B6
Saxon Cl Hythe CT21. . . .333 E2
  Kings Hill ME19. . . . . . .158 F2
  Northfleet DA11 . . . . . . .36 C5
  Otford TN14 . . . . .121 F2
  Rochester ME2 . . . . .39 F1
Saxon Pl
  Horton Kirby DA4 . . . . . .57 C4
  Rochester ME2 . . . . .62 F5
Saxon Rd Bridge CT4 . . .176 A1
  Bromley BR1. . . . . .29 A1
  Faversham ME13 . . . . . .138 C2
  Hawley DA2 . . . . .33 E4
  Ramsgate CT11 . . . . . . .117 B6
  Westgate on Sea CT8. . . .50 D1
Saxons Cl CT14. . . . . . .215 C8
Saxons Dr ME14. . . . . . .162 B7
Saxon Shore
  Sittingbourne ME10 . . . .69 A1
  Whitstable CT5. . . . . . .108 C8
Saxon Sq 9 CT17 . . . . .310 C8
Saxon Way Prim Sch
  . . . . .64 E6
Saxon Wlk Iwade ME9. . .68 D4
  Sidcup DA14 . . . . .31 C2
Saxton Rd TN29 . . . . . .377 E5
Saxton St ME7. . . . . .64 C5
Saxville Rd BR5 . . . . . . .54 B6

Sayer Cl DA9. . . . . .17 A2
Sayer Rd TN27 . . . . . . .234 C8
Sayers La 6 TN30 . . . . .345 A7
Sayes Court Rd BR5. . . . .54 B5
Scabharbour Rd TN14 187 C1
Scadbury Gdns BR5. . . . .54 A7
Scadbury Pk★ BR7. . . . . .30 E7
Scads Hill Cl BR6. . . . . . .53 F3
Scaffold St TN29 . . . . . .380 D2
Scanlons Bridge Rd
  Folkestone CT21. . . . . . .334 C2
  Hythe CT21. . . . . .333 A2
Scarborough Cl TN16. . .118 C1
Scarborough Dr ME12 . .47 C8
Scarborough La ME1 . . . .95 D2
Scarlet Cl BR5. . . . . .54 B5
Scarlett Cl ME5 . . . . . . .97 C5
Scarsbrook Rd SE3. . . . .11 D4
Sceales Dr CT12. . . . . . .116 D6
Sceptre Way CT5. . . . . .108 B7
Scholars Rise ME2 . . . . . .62 D7
Scholey Cl ME2. . . . . . . .95 B4
School App 3 TN15. . . .156 F7
School Ave ME7. . . . . . . .64 E4
School Cl DA13. . . . . .60 A2
School Cl The CT8. . . . . .50 C1
School Cotts
  Bromley BR1. . . . . .29 A1
  Crockenhill BR8 . . . . . . .55 D2
  Seal TN15 . . . . .154 F6
  Sidcup DA14 . . . . .31 C3
School Cres DA1 . . . . . . .14 F3
School Field TN8. . . . . .217 C2
Schoolfield Rd RM20 . . .17 A8
School Hill Chilham CT4 205 B8
  Lamberhurst TN3 . . . . . .317 B6
School Ho ME10. . . . . . .101 E3
School House La TN12 290 E7
School La Bean DA2. . . . .35 C5
  Bekesbourne CT4 . . . . . .176 C4
  Bexley DA16. . . . . .13 B4
  Blean CT2. . . . . .142 A6
  Borden ME9 . . . . .100 F4
  Boughton Street ME13 . .139 F3
  Culverstone Green DA13 .93 A2
  Fordwich CT2 . . . . .144 A4
  Goodnestone CT3 . . . . .178 D2
  Hadlow TN11. . . . . .223 E8
  Herne Bay CT6 . . . . .77 B1
  Hextable BR8 . . . . .33 B1
  Higham ME3 . . . . .39 C5
  Hoath CT3. . . . . .111 E6
  Horton Kirby DA3, DA4. . .57 E4
  Ickham CT3. . . . . .177 C8
  Iwade ME9 . . . . .68 C4
  Knockmill TN15 . . . . . . .123 F8
  Lower Halstow ME9 . . . . .67 B2
  Lower Hardres CT4 . . . . .208 B4
  Maidstone ME15. . . . . . .162 A4
  Newington ME9 . . . . . . .100 B7
  Peasmarsh TN31. . . . . . .367 B2
  Platt's Heath ME17 . . . . .198 F2
  Plaxtol TN11, TN15 . . . .189 E6
  Ramsgate CT11 . . . . . . .117 E7
  Seal TN15 . . . . .154 F6
  Sittingbourne ME9 . . . . .102 D2
  Stalisfield Green ME13 . .201 D6
  Staple CT3. . . . . .179 A6
  Stourmouth CT3 . . . . . .113 E2
  Sutton Valence ME17 . . .229 E7
  Trottiscliffe ME19 . . . . . .126 A5
  Wingham CT3 . . . . .178 A7
  Wouldham ME1. . . . . . . .95 D5
School Mews ME9. . . . . .68 E4
School Path CT3 . . . . . .176 F7
School Rd
  Appledore Heath
    TN26 . . . . .347 C1
  Ash CT3. . . . . .147 C2
  Bethersden TN26 . . . . . .297 D4
  Charing TN27 . . . . .234 C8
  Chislehurst BR7 . . . . . . .30 C1
  Densole CT18. . . . . .306 E7
  Faversham ME13 . . . . . .138 C6
  Gravesend DA12. . . . . . .37 C5
  Hothfield TN26 . . . . . . .267 A7
  Hythe CT21. . . . . .333 B4
  Sandwich CT13 . . . . . . .148 F1
  Sittingbourne ME10 . . . .102 B3
  Tilmanstone CT14. . . . . .212 F4
School Rise TN2. . . . . . .285 F1
Schools at Somerhill The
  TN11. . . . . .254 F7
School Terr 6 TN18. . . .340 F2
School View ME9. . . . . .134 C8
School Villas ME18 . . . .192 D5
Schooner Ct DA2. . . . . . .16 C3
Schooner Ho 1 DA8 . . . . .4 E1
Schooner Wlk ME2. . . . . .40 F3
Schrieber Mews ME7. . . .64 D5
Scilla Ct 11 RM17. . . . . .18 D8
Scimitar Cl ME7. . . . . . . .65 A1
Scocles Cotts ME12 . . . .47 C5
Scocles Rd ME12 . . . . . .47 C5
Scoggers Hill ME13. . . .172 A7
Scoones Cl ME9. . . . . . .102 E2
Scords La TN16 . . . . . . .185 C4
Scotby Ave ME5. . . . . . . .97 B4
Scotchmen Cl ME12 . . . .46 E7
Scotland Comm CT16. . .277 D4
Scotland La DA12 . . . . . .60 E7
Scotney Castle★ TN3. . .317 D3
Scotney Castle & Gdns★
  TN3. . . . . .317 D3
Scotney Cl BR6. . . . . . . .86 A6
Scotney Ho ME2. . . . . . . .40 C1
Scotsdale Cl BR5. . . . . . .53 E5
Scotsdale Rd SE12 . . . . .11 B2
Scot's La TN25 . . . . . . .303 F8
Scott Ave
  Canterbury CT1. . . . . . .174 E5
  Gillingham ME8. . . . . . . .66 A1
Scott Cl ME20 . . . . .160 C8

Scott Cres DA8. . . . . . . .14 F6
Scotteswood Ave ME4. . .63 F2
Scott Ho 4 DA17. . . . . . . .3 F1
Scotton St TN25 . . . . . .237 F2
Scott Rd
  Gravesend DA12. . . . . . .37 D3
  Tonbridge TN9. . . . . . . .253 F7
Scotts Ho ME13 . . . . . . .52 C8
Scotts Rd BR1. . . . . .29 A1
Scotts Passage 11 SE18. .2 B2
Scott St ME14 . . . . .161 F6
Scotts Terr SE9 . . . . .29 E6
Scott's Terr ME4 . . . . . . .63 F3
Scotts Way
  Royal Tunbridge Wells
    TN2 . . . . .313 E8
  Sevenoaks TN13 . . . . . .153 E5
Scott Wilkie Prim Sch
  E16. . . . . .1 C7
Scoulding Rd E16 . . . . . . .1 A7
Scragged Oak Rd
  Detling ME14 . . . . .131 C5
  Hucking ME14. . . . . . . .132 C1
Scrapsgate Rd ME12. . . .47 A7
Scraps Hill ME9 . . . . . . .102 F4
Scratchers La DA3. . . . . .90 E7
Scratton Fields DA12 . . .60 D4
Scrubbs La ME16 . . . . . .161 D4
Scudders Hill DA3. . . . . .58 C3
Sea App ME12. . . . . .49 E4
Seabourne Cl TN29. . . .366 B6
Seabourne Way TN29. . .366 B7
Seabrook CE Prim Sch
  CT21. . . . . .334 B2
Seabrook Ct CT21 . . . . .334 B2
Seabrooke Rise RM17. . .18 B8
Seabrook Gdns CT21 . . .334 B2
Seabrook Gr CT21 . . . . .334 A2
Seabrook Rd
  Hythe CT21. . . . . .333 E2
  Tonbridge TN10. . . . . . .222 A3
Seabrook Vale CT21 . . . .334 B4
Seacourt Rd SE2 . . . . . . .3 D4
Seacroft Rd CT10. . . . . . .84 A1
Seadown Cl CT21. . . . . .334 A4
Seafield Rd
  Broadstairs CT10 . . . . . .84 A4
  Ramsgate CT11 . . . . . . .117 C6
  Whitstable CT5. . . . . . . .75 B4
Seaford Ct ME1. . . . . . . .63 B5
Seagar Rd ME13. . . . . . .105 B1
Seager Rd ME12. . . . . . . .28 E2
Seagrave Cres CT19. . . .335 F6
Seagull La E16 . . . . .1 A6
Seagull Rd ME2. . . . . . . .62 D6
SEAL. 155 A6
Sealand Ct ME1. . . . . . . .63 B5
Seal CE Prim Sch
  TN15. . . . . .154 F7
Sealcroft Cotts TN15 . . .154 F8
Seal Dr TN15. . . . . .154 F6
Seal Ho TN15. . . . . .154 F6
Seal Hollow Rd TN13 . . .154 F6
Seal Rd TN13, TN14,
  . . . . .154 D6
Seamark Cl CT12. . . . . .114 D7
Seamark Rd CT12, CT7. .80 E2
Sea Meadows Sch CT10 83 E7
Seamew Ct ME12 . . . . . .62 C7
Seapoint Rd CT10 . . . . . .84 B3
Searchlight Heights
  ME3. . . . . .41 A4
Sea Rd Deal CT14 . . . . .248 D6
  Hythe CT21. . . . . .334 A2
  Westgate on Sea CT8. . . .50 C1
Searles Dr E6 . . . . .2 B8
SEASALTER. 108 A7
Seasalter Beach CT5 . . .108 B7
Seasalter Cl ME12 . . . . . .49 E4
Seasalter Cross CT5. . . .108 A6
Seasalter La CT5. . . . . . .108 A5
Sea Sch ME13 . . . . .106 C3
Seascape 10 CT20 . . . . .334 E3
Seaside Ave ME12 . . . . . .47 C8
Sea St Herne Bay CT6 . . .76 C3
  St Margaret's at Cliffe
    CT15 . . . . .280 A6
  Whitstable CT5. . . . . . . .74 D2
Seathorpe Ave ME12 . . . .47 C8
Seaths Cnr CT3. . . . . . . .178 A7
SEATON. 145 D2
Seaton Ave CT21 . . . . . .333 B3
Seaton Cotts TN25 . . . .236 E3
Seaton Rd Bexley DA16. .13 C7
  Dartford DA1 . . . . .33 A8
  Gillingham ME7. . . . . . . .64 C3
Seaview ME3 . . . . .27 B5
Seaview Ave ME12. . . . . .49 H1
Sea View Cl CT18 . . . . . .308 B1
Sea View Cl CT18. . . . . .308 B1
Seaview Cotts 6 CT10. .84 B4
Sea View Cotts ME9. . . .67 B3
Seaview Ct CT10 . . . . . . .84 B3
Sea View Gdns ME12 . . .49 E3
Seaview Ho CT19. . . . . .335 D8
Sea View Hts TN29 . . . .366 C7
Sea View Hts ME7. . . . . .80 D8
Seaview Rd
  Gillingham ME7. . . . . . . .64 C4
  Greatstone-on-Sea
    TN28 . . . . .373 E1
Sea View Rd
  Birchington CT7 . . . . . . .80 A6
  Broadstairs CT10 . . . . . .84 A6
  Cliffs End CT12 . . . . . . .116 D6
  Herne Bay CT6 . . . . .77 C5
  St Margaret's at Cliffe
    CT15 . . . . .279 F4
Sea View Sq CT6 . . . . . . .76 F5
Sea View Terr
  Folkestone CT20. . . . . . .334 D3

Sea View Terr continued
  Margate CT9. . . . . .50 G2
  Minster (Sheppey) ME12 .48 A5
Seaville Dr CT6. . . . . .77 E5
Sea Wall
  Dymchurch TN29. . . . . .366 D8
  Whitstable CT5. . . . . . . .74 D2
Seaway Cotts CT5 . . . . . .74 C1
Seaway Cres TN29. . . . .365 F4
Seaway Gdns TN29 . . . .365 F4
Seaway Rd TN29 . . . . . .366 A4
Second Ave
  Broadstairs CT10 . . . . . .51 G2
  Chatham ME4 . . . . .64 C1
  Eastchurch ME12 . . . . . .48 F5
  Gillingham ME7. . . . . . . .64 C3
  Margate CT9. . . . . .51 B3
  Rushenden ME11 . . . . . .45 F3
  Sheerness ME12. . . . . . .28 B1
  West Thurrock RM20 . . . .17 A8
Secretan Rd ME1. . . . . . .63 B1
Secret Gdns of Sandwich
  The★ CT13 . . . . .149 A1
Sedcombe Cl DA14. . . . . .31 C4
Sedgebrook Rd SE3 . . . .11 D4
Sedge Cres ME5. . . . . . . .96 E4
Sedge Ct RM17. . . . . . . .18 E7
Sedgemere Rd SE2 . . . . . .3 C3
Sedgemoor Ho ME1 . . . . .63 E5
Sedley Cl
  Aylesford ME20. . . . . . .128 F2
  Cliffe Woods ME3 . . . . . .40 C7
  Gillingham ME8. . . . . . . .98 C3
Sedley's CE Prim Sch
  DA13. . . . . .36 A3
Seesholt Cl CT5. . . . . . .108 E8
Sefton Cl BR5. . . . . .53 F5
Sefton Rd BR5. . . . . .53 F5
Segrave Rd CT19. . . . . .335 F5
Sejant Ho 4 RM17. . . . . .18 B8
Selah Dr ME2 . . . . .55 C8
Selbey Cl CT6 . . . . .77 C4
Selborne Ave DA5. . . . . .31 E7
Selborne Ho CT17 . . . . .310 C7
Selborne Rd
  Margate CT9. . . . . .83 B8
  Sidcup DA14 . . . . .31 B4
Selborne Terr CT17 . . . .310 C7
Selbourne Wlk ME15 . . .195 F6
Selby Cl Chislehurst BR7 .30 A4
  14 Newham E16. . . . . . . .1 B8
Selby Ct ME9 . . . . .103 D2
Selby Rd
  Maidstone ME15. . . . . . .195 F4
  Newham E13. . . . . .1 D1
Select Bsns Ctr TN12 . .260 E5
Selkirk Rd DA8 . . . . .14 E6
Selkirk Rd CT16 . . . . . . .278 E5
Sellbourne Pk TN3 . . . . .314 C4
SELLINDGE 303 D1
Sellindge Prim Sch
  TN25. . . . . .303 C1
SELLING 171 C6
Selling CE Prim Sch
  ME13 . . . . .171 B6
Selling Ct ME13 . . . . . . .171 C5
Sellinge Gn ME8 . . . . . . .65 C3
Selling Sch Chilham CT4 .172 B3
  Faversham ME13 . . . . . .138 F3
  Selling ME13. . . . . .171 B6
Selling St ME13 . . . . . . .171 B6
Selling Sta ME13 . . . . . .171 C7
Sellwood Dr ME15. . . . . .195 F4
Sellwood Cl ME12. . . . . . .46 E6
Selwood Ho BR7. . . . . . . .30 C7
Selwyn Cres DA16 . . . . . .13 B3
Selwyn Dr CT10. . . . . . . .83 F5
Selwyn Ho CT10. . . . . . . .83 F5
Selwyn Pl 1 BR5. . . . . . .54 E6
Selwyn Rd RM18 . . . . . . .18 F5
Semaphore Rd CT7. . . . . .80 F8
Semple Cl ME12 . . . . . . .115 C7
Semple Gdns ME4. . . . . .63 E3
Senacre La ME15. . . . . . .195 E6
Senacre Sq ME15 . . . . . .195 F7
Senacre Wood Prim Sch
  ME15 . . . . .195 F7
Senator Wlk 4 SE28 . . . . .2 D3
Sencler Ho Bexley SE2. . . .3 D1
  Erith SE2. . . . . .3 D1
Sene Pk CT21 . . . . .333 D3
Senlac Cl CT11 . . . . .117 B6
Senlac Pl TN3. . . . . .312 C7
Senlac Rd SE12. . . . . . . .29 B7
Sennen Wlk SE9. . . . . . . .29 E5
Sennocke Ct TN13. . . . .154 B2
Senoaks L Ctr TN13 154 C2
Senonoaks Mus & Gall
  TN13. . . . . .154 C2
SEPHAM HEATH. 121 B6
Sequoia Gdns BR6. . . . . .53 F2
Serene Ct 12 CT10 . . . . .84 B4
Serene Pl 9 CT10 . . . . . .84 B4
Sermon Dr BR8 . . . . .55 C6
Serpentine La TN13 . . . .154 D5
Serpentine Rd TN13 . . . .154 D4
Serviden Dr BR1 . . . . . . .52 D8
Sessions House Sq
  ME14. . . . . .161 F5
Setford Rd ME5. . . . . . . .97 C6
Setterfield Ho CT21. . . .333 D2
Setterfield Rd CT9. . . . . .50 J1

Settington Ave ME5. . . . .64 C1
Sevastopol Pl CT1. . . . .143 D1
Sevenacre ME13 . . . . . .138 C6
Seven Acres
  Crockenhill BR8 . . . . . . .55 D3
  New Ash Green DA3. . . . .91 E7
Seven Mile La
  Kings Hill TN15, ME18 . .158 A3
  Mereworth TN11, TN12. .191 E3
  Wrotham Heath TN15. . .157 F7
SEVENOAKS 154 D2
Sevenoaks Bsns Ctr
  TN14. . . . . .154 C2
Sevenoaks By-Pass TN13,
  TN14 . . . . .186 F7
Sevenoaks Cl DA7. . . . . .14 B3
SEVENOAKS
  COMMON 187 B6
Sevenoaks Hospl
  TN13. . . . . .154 C6
Sevenoaks Mus★
  TN13. . . . . .154 C2
Sevenoaks Prep Sch
  TN15. . . . . .155 A1
Sevenoaks Prim Sch
  TN13. . . . . .154 B5
Sevenoaks Sch
  Borough Green TN15 . . .156 F7
  Ightham TN15. . . . . . . .156 A4
  Orpington BR6. . . . . . . .86 F6
  Otford TN14 . . . . .122 B3
  Pratt's Bottom BR6, TN14 87 C2
Sevenoaks Sch
  Sevenoaks TN13. . . . . . .154 B1
  Sevenoaks TN13. . . . . . .154 C1
Sevenoaks Sta TN13 . . .154 C1
Sevenoaks Way ME5. . . .54 C7
Sevenoaks Way Ind Est 1
  BR5. . . . . .54 C7
SEVENOAKS WEALD . . .187 B2
Sevenoaks Wildfowl
  Reserve★ TN14 . . . . . .154 A7
Sevenscore CT12 . . . . . .116 A5
Sevenscore Farm Cotts
  CT12. . . . . .116 A5
Seven Stones Dr CT10 . .84 A1
Seven Wents TN15 . . . . .156 A4
Severn Cl TN10. . . . . . . .222 C5
Severn Rd ME5. . . . . .97 C5
SEVINGTON 301 B6
Sevington La TN24 . . . .301 A7
Sevington Pk ME15. . . . .194 F6
Sewell Cl CT7 . . . . .81 A6
Sewell Rd SE2 . . . . .3 B4
Sexburga Dr ME12. . . . . .47 B8
Sextant Pk ME2 . . . . .63 E6
Sexton Rd RM18 . . . . . . .18 F6
Seymour Ave
  Westgate on Sea CT9. . . .50 D1
  Whitstable CT5. . . . . . . .74 E1
Seymour Cl CT6 . . . . .77 B1
Seymour Dr BR2. . . . . . . .52 F1
Seymour Pl CT1. . . . . . .174 E7
Seymour Rd
  1 Chatham ME4 . . . . . . .64 B3
  Gillingham ME8. . . . . . . .66 C1
  Northfleet DA11 . . . . . . .36 F6
  St Margaret's at Cliffe
    CT15 . . . . .279 F8
  Tilbury RM18. . . . . .18 F8
Seymour Villas 10
  CT20 . . . . .334 F3
Seymour Wlk DA10. . . . . .35 E8
Shacklands Rd TN14. . . .88 D1
Shackleton Cl ME5. . . . . .97 B6
Shades The ME2 . . . . . . .62 C7
SHADOXHURST 327 A8
Shadoxhurst Rd TN26 . .326 C7
Shaftesbury Ave CT19 .334 E7
Shaftesbury Cl ME19 . . .127 F1
Shaftesbury Ct
  Deal CT14 . . . . .215 D2
  Erith DA8. . . . . .14 F6
  3 Woolwich SE28. . . . . . .3 C5
Shaftesbury Dr ME16 . . .161 C4
Shaftesbury La DA1 . . . .16 B3
Shaftesbury Rd
  Canterbury CT2. . . . . . .142 F3
  Hersden CT3. . . . . .111 E1
  Royal Tunbridge Wells
    TN4 . . . . .286 A5
  Whitstable CT5. . . . . . . .74 D1
Shaftsbury Ct E6. . . . . . . .2 A7
Shaftsbury St CT11 . . . .117 F7
Shah Pl CT11. . . . . .117 D7
Shakespeare Ave ME18 19 B6
Shakespeare Ct CT17. . .310 B9
Shakespeare Farm Rd
  ME3. . . . . .24 F7
Shakespeare Ho 1 DA17 3 F1
Shakespeare Pas CT9 . . .50 H2
Shakespeare Rd
  Bexley DA7. . . . . .13 E6
  Birchington CT7 . . . . . . .81 A8
  Dartford DA1 . . . . .16 A3
  Dover CT17 . . . . .310 B6
  Gillingham ME7. . . . . . . .64 C3
  Margate CT9. . . . . .50 J1
  Sittingbourne ME10 . . . .102 A4
  Tonbridge TN9. . . . . . . .253 F8
Shakespeare Terr 12
  CT20 . . . . .335 C4
Shalder Ho ME7 . . . . .64 D7
Shalfleet Cl 1 ME5. . . . . .97 A7
Shalford Cl BR6. . . . . . . .86 C6
Shalloak Rd CT2. . . . . . .143 D6
Shallows Rd ME9. . . . . . .30 B4
Shallows Rd CT10. . . . . . .83 D6
Shalmsford Ct CT4 . . . . .173 C2
Shalmsford St CT4 . . . . .172 C2
Shalmsford St CT4 . . . . .173 D2
SHALMSFORD
  STREET 173 B1

Shambles The TN13 . . . .154 C2
Shamel Bsns Ctr ME2. . . .63 C7
Shamley Rd ME5 . . . . . . .97 D2
Shamrock Ave CT5 . . . . .108 B7
Shamrock Rd DA12. . . . . .37 F8
Shandon Cl TN2. . . . . . .286 C6
Shanklin Cl ME5. . . . . . . .97 C8
Shannon Ct BR6. . . . . . . .54 A2
Shapland Cl CT6 . . . . . . .77 C3
Share & Coulter Rd
  CT5 . . . . .75 D1
Sharfleet Cres ME9. . . . . .45 C8
Sharfleet Dr ME2. . . . . . .62 B7
Sharland Rd DA12. . . . . .37 C6
Sharman Ct DA14 . . . . . .31 A4
Sharnal La ME6 . . . . . . .128 A7
Sharnal St ME3. . . . . .24 A2
SHARNAL STREET. 24 A1
Sharnbrooke Cl DA16. . . .13 C4
Sharon Cres ME5. . . . . . .96 F4
Sharon Ct 10 DA14. . . . . .31 B4
Sharp's Field TN27 . . . . .262 E5
Sharps Gn ME8. . . . . . . .65 D5
Sharp Way DA1 . . . . .15 F4
Sharsted Hill ME9 . . . . .168 C8
Sharsted Way
  Gillingham ME7. . . . . . . .98 A3
  Maidstone ME14. . . . . . .163 B5
SHATTERLING. 146 E1
Shatterlocks Inf Sch 7
  CT16. . . . . .278 B2
Shawbrooke Rd SE9. . . . .11 D3
Shaw Cl
  Cliffe Woods ME3 . . . . . .40 B8
  Maidstone ME14. . . . . . .162 C7
  Woolwich SE28. . . . . .3 B5
Shaw Cross TN24. . . . . .268 D5
Shawdon Ave CT13 . . . .182 A7
Shawfield Pk BR1. . . . . . .52 D7
Shawhill Ho ME9 . . . . . .126 B1
Shaw Ho 6 Erith DA17. . . .3 F1
  5 Newham E16. . . . . . . .2 A5
Shaw Rd TN16. . . . . . . .150 C2
Shawstead Rd ME7, ME7 97 D5
Shaws Way ME1. . . . . . . .63 C3
Shaw The TN2. . . . . . . .286 C2
Sheafe Dr TN17 . . . . . . .320 C5
Sheal's Cres ME15. . . . . .162 A2
Sheals Ct ME15. . . . . . . .162 A4
Shearers Cl ME14 . . . . .162 E4
Shears Cl DA2. . . . . .33 C6
Shears Green Ct DA11. . .37 A6
Shears Green Jun & Inf
  Schs 8 DA11. . . . . .36 F5
Shearwater
  Maidstone ME16. . . . . . .161 B5
  New Barn DA3 . . . . .59 B6
Shearwater Ave CT5. . . .108 C7
Shearwater Cl ME2. . . . . .62 C7
Shearwater Ct ME12. . . . .46 B8
Shearwater Ho TN29 . . .366 A3
Shear Way TN29. . . . . . .352 C5
Shearway Bsns Pk
  CT19. . . . . .334 F7
Shearway Rd CT19 . . . . .334 F7
Shearwood Cres DA1. . . .15 A4
Sheen Ct CT9 . . . . .50 C2
Sheen Rd BR5. . . . . .53 F5
Sheepcote La BR5, BR8. .54 F4
Sheep Ct La CT4. . . . . . .240 A3
Sheepfold La TN23 . . . . .300 C4
Sheephurst La TN12. . . .258 E5
SHEERNESS. 28 C3
Sheerness Harbour Est
  ME12. . . . . .27 F3
Sheerness Heritage Ctr★
  . . . . .28 C2
Sheerness Mews E16. . . . .2 B4
Sheerness-on-Sea Sta
  ME12. . . . . .28 B2
Sheerness Swim Pool
  ME12. . . . . .28 B3
Sheerstone ME9. . . . . . . .68 D4
SHEERWATER. 146 F6
Sheerways Rd
  Newham E16. . . . . .1 D8
  Preston CT3. . . . . .146 F5
Sheerways ME15 . . . . . .138 A6
Sheet Glass Rd ME11. . . .46 A3
Sheet Hill TN15. . . . . . . .156 D2
Sheffield Gdns CT14 . . .215 C4
Sheffield Rd 4 TN4 . . . .253 F2
Sheilings The TN15. . . . .154 F7
Shelbury Cl DA14. . . . . . .31 A5
Shelden Dr ME8. . . . . . . .98 F8
Sheldon Bsns Ctr ME2. .63 D8
Sheldon Cl
  Aylesham CT3. . . . . . . .211 A6
  Eltham SE12 . . . . .11 B2
Sheldon Ho DA7. . . . . . . .13 F6
Sheldon Way ME20 . . . .128 B3
Sheldrake Cl E16. . . . . . . .1 F5
Shelduck Cl ME9 . . . . . . .68 E4
SHELDWICH 170 C6
Sheldwich Cl 3 TN23 .299 F6
SHELDWICH LEES 170 C5
Sheldwich Prim Sch
  ME13 . . . . .170 C6
Sheldwich Terr BR2. . . . .52 E3
Shellbank La DA2. . . . . . .35 B4
Shellbeach Rd ME12. . . .73 D6
Shell Cl BR2. . . . . .52 E3
Shelldrake Cl ME3. . . . . .27 D6
Shelley Ave CT1. . . . . . .143 C2
Shelley Cl BR6 . . . . .86 E7
Shelley Dr DA16. . . . . . . .12 E6
Shelley Ho DA1. . . . . . . .14 E2
Shelley Pl RM18 . . . . . . .19 B6
Shelley Rd ME16 . . . . . .161 C2
Shelley Rise ME1. . . . . . .63 A3

Shelleys La TN14 .... 120 A3
Shell Grotto ★ 15 CT9 . .50 J2
Shellness Rd ME12 . . . .73 D7
Shellons St CT20 . . . . 335 D5
Shelton Cl TN10 . . . . . 222 C5
SHELVIN 243 C3
Shelvin La CT4 . . . . . . 243 C3
Shenden Cl TN13 . . . . 187 C7
Shenden Way TN13. . . 187 C7
Shenfield Ho SE18. . . . . . 11 D7
Shenley Gr ME14 . . . . 129 F2
Shenley Rd DA1 . . . . . . .34 A8
Shenstone Sch DA1 . . . . 14 D3
Shenstone Cl DA1 . . . . . 14 D3
Shepherd Cl BR6 . . . . . .86 F7
Shepherd Dr TN24 . . . 301 A8
Shepherd Neame
Brewery ★ 16
ME13 . . . . 138 D7
Shepherds Cl BR6 . . . . .86 F7
Shepherd's Close Rd
CT4 . . . . 176 E1
Shepherds Cl Rd CT4. 176 E1
Shepherd's Cross
CT15 . . . . 246 B1
Shepherdsgate CT2 . .142 F1
Shepherds Gate ME7 . .97 C5
Shepherdsgate Dr
CT6 . . . . 111 A8
Shepherds Gate Dr
ME14 . . . . 162 E6
Shepherds Gn BR7 . . . .30 D1
Shepherdsgrove La
RH19 . . . . 281 A4
SHEPHERDS HILL . . . 171 A4
Shepherds La
Dartford DA1 . . . . . . .33 B8
Woolwich SE28 . . . . 2 E5
Shepherds Leas SE9. . .12 D3
Shepherd St DA11. . . . .36 D1
Shepherds Way
Langley Heath ME17. . 196 E4
Lower Stoke ME3 . . . . .25 C4
Whitstable CT5 . . . . . 109 C8
SHEPHERDSWELL OR
SIBERTSWOLD 244 E5
Shepherdswell Rd
CT15 . . . . 245 A7
Shepherds Well Sta★
CT15 . . . . 244 D5
Shepherds Wlk
Hythe CT21 . . . . 332 E1
Royal Tunbridge Wells
TN2 . . . . 286 D6
Whitstable CT5 . . . . . 109 C8
Sheppards Coll 8 BR1 .52 A8
Shepperton Cl ME5. . . .97 C4
Shepperton Rd BR5. . . .53 C3
Sheppey Cl
3 Birchington CT7 . . . .81 A7
Erith DA8 . . . . 15 B7
Sheppey Coll ME12 . . . .28 B3
Sheppey Com Hospl
ME12 . . . . 47 A5
Sheppey Cotts ME12. . .28 C2
Sheppey L Complex The
ME12 . . . . .28 C3
Sheppey Little Theatre★
ME12 . . . . .28 B2
Sheppey Rd ME15 . . . . 195 A7
Sheppey St ME12. . . . . .28 A2
Sheppey Terr ME12. . . . .47 F5
Sheppey View CT5 . . . 108 C6
Sheppey Way
Iwade ME9 . . . . .68 F6
Queenborough ME12,
ME9 . . . . .46 D2
Sittingbourne ME9 . . . 101 B7
Sheppy Ho 1 BR1. . . . .29 B1
Sheppy Pl DA12. . . . . . .37 B8
SHEPWAY 195 D8
Shepway TN24 . . . . . . 268 E5
Shepway Cl CT19 . . . . 335 D6
Shepway Cross CT21 . .332 B3
Shepway St ME15 . . . . 195 C8
Sherard Mans SE9. . . . . 11 F2
Sherard Rd SE9 . . . . . . 11 E2
Sheraton Ct ME5 . . . . . .96 F1
Sherborne Gr TN15 . . 123 A2
Sherborne Rd BR5 . . . .53 F4
Sherbourne Cl
Royal Tunbridge Wells
TN2 . . . . 286 D2
West Kingsdown TN15 . .90 A4
Sherbourne Dr
Maidstone ME16. . . . 161 B2
Rochester ME2 . . . . . .40 A1
Sherbrooke Ct DA14 . .14 A3
Sherenden La TN12 . . 291 D8
Sherenden Pk TN11. . . 224 A5
Sherenden Rd TN11. . . 255 D7
Sherfield Rd RM17 . . . .11 B8
Sheridale Bsns Ctr ME2 63 A6
Sheridan Cl
Chatham ME5 . . . . . . .97 C7
Maidstone ME14. . . . 161 E8
Swanley BR8. . . . . 55 F6
Sheridan Cres BR7 . . . .53 B7
Sheridan Ct
Dartford DA1 . . . . 16 A3
Rochester ME1 . . . . . .63 A3
Sheridan Lodge 1 BR2 52 C5
Sheridan Pl BR1. . . . . .52 D7
Sheridan Rd Bexley DA7 13 E4
Dover CT16 . . . . 278 B3
Erith DA17. . . . . 4 A2
Sheriff Dr ME5 . . . . . . .97 A2
Sheringham Ct ME16. 161 D7
Sheringham Ho 5
ME15. . . . . 195 D8

Sherington Prim Sch 6
SE7 . . . . .11 B8
Sherington Rd SE7 . . . .11 B8
Sherlies Ave BR6 . . . . .86 E8
Sherman Cl ME7 . . . . . .65 B1
Sherman Rd BR1. . . . . .52 A8
Shernden La TN8 . . . . 249 C4
Shernolds ME15. . . . . 195 B7
Shernold Sch ME16. . . 161 D5
Sheron Cl CT14. . . . . . 215 A5
Sherriffs Court La
CT12 . . . . 114 E6
Sherway Cl TN27 . . . . 262 E5
Sherway Rd TN27 . . . . 263 D6
Sherwin Knight Inf Sch
ME2 . . . . .62 C5
Sherwin Knight Jun Sch
ME2 . . . . .62 C5
SHERWOOD 286 E6
Sherwood Ave ME5. . . .97 A2
Sherwood Avenue
ME20. . . . . 128 B4
Sherwood Cl
Ashford TN24 . . . . . 268 D7
Faversham ME13 . . . . 105 B1
Herne Bay CT6 . . . . . .77 C2
Sidcup DA5 . . . . 13 C1
Whitstable CT5 . . . . . 108 C6
Sherwood Ct CT8. . . . . .50 C1
Sherwood Dr CT5 . . . . 108 C6
Sherwood Gdns CT11. . .83 E1
Sherwood Ho
Chatham ME5 . . . . . . .97 A3
Erith DA8. . . . . 14 E8
Sherwood Park Ave
DA15 . . . . .13 B1
Sherwood Park Prim Sch
Royal Tunbridge Wells
TN2 . . . . 286 D6
Sidcup DA15. . . . . 13 B1
Sherwood Pl TN3. . . . . 284 E3
Sherwood Rd
Bexley DA16. . . . . 12 E4
Birchington CT7 . . . . .80 F5
Royal Tunbridge Wells
TN2 . . . . 286 D6
Sherwood Way TN2 . . 286 D6
Shieldhall St SE2. . . . . . .3 C2
Shillingheld Cl ME14 . 162 F5
Shimmin Rd ME9 . . . . 134 D5
Shinecroft TN14. . . . . 122 A3
Shingle Barn La ME15 193 C3
Shinglewell Rd DA8 . . .14 A7
SHIPBOURNE 189 C5
Shipbourne Prim Sch
TN11. . . . . 189 C4
Shipbourne Rd
Shipbourne TN11 . . . 189 D2
Tonbridge TN10. . . . . 222 C5
Ship Cl TN29 . . . . 366 C8
Ship Field Cl TN16. . . 150 C6
Ship Hill TN16. . . . . . 150 D6
Ship La Rochester ME1. .63 A8
Sutton at Hone BR8, DA4 56 E8
SHIPLAND 265 D8
Shipland Hos TN27. . . 265 D8
Shipley Ct ME14 . . . . . 162 A4
Shipley Hills Rd DA13 .59 E1
Shipley Mill Cl TN23 . 300 C4
Shipman Ave CT2 . . . . 174 C8
Shipman Rd ME14 . . . . . 1 C7
Shipmans Way CT16. . 278 A3
Ship St CT19 . . . . 335 D6
Shipway Ho CT21. . . . 333 D1
Shipwrights Ave ME4. . .64 B2
Shipwrights Lee CT5 . .74 C2
Shipyard Area ME13 . . 105 D1
Shirebrook Rd SE3 . . . .11 D4
Shire Ct DA18 . . . . 3 D3
Shirehall Rd DA2. . . . . .33 E4
Shire La
Farthing Street BR6 . . .86 C3
Orpington BR6 . . . . . .86 E5
Stalisfield Green ME13. 201 C6
Shires The TN12. . . . . 257 A7
Shireway Cl CT19. . . . 335 A7
SHIRKOAK 326 A5
Shirkoak Pk TN26 . . . 326 A5
Shirley Ave
Chatham ME5 . . . . . . .96 D5
Ramsgate CT11 . . . . . .83 E1
Sidcup DA5 . . . . 31 D7
Shirley Cl Chalk DA12. . .38 B6
Dartford DA1 . . . . 15 C3
Shirley Ct ME15 . . . . . 195 E5
Shirley Gdns TN4. . . . 285 C5
Shirley Gr TN4 . . . . . . 285 C5
Shirley House Dr SE7. . .11 C7
Shirley Hts 5 DA6 . . . .13 E3
Shirley Rd DA15. . . . . .30 E5
Shirley Way ME15 . . . 163 A3
Shoebury Terr ME12. . . .48 A5
Shoesmith Lane ME19 159 D3
SHOLDEN 214 F5
Sholden Bank CT14. . . 214 E4
Sholden CE Prim Sch
CT14. . . . . 214 F6
Sholden Gdns BR5 . . . .54 C4
Sholden New Rd CT14 214 F6
Sholden Rd ME2. . . . . .40 C1
Shooters Chase ME9 . . .68 D4
SHOOTERS HILL. 12 C6
Shooters Hill
Eythorne CT15 . . . . . 245 C8
Woolwich SE18. . . . . . 12 A6
Shooter's Hill Post 16
Campus SE18 . . . . . . 12 A6
Shooters Hill Rd SE18,
SE3 . . . . .11 D6
Shore Cl Birchington CT7 80 D8
Herne Bay CT6 . . . . . .76 B3
Shorefields ME8. . . . . .66 B2

Shoregate La ME9. . . . .66 F6
SHOREHAM 121 F8
Shoreham Aircraft Mus★
TN14. . . . . 121 F8
Shoreham Cl DA5. . . . . .31 D7
Shoreham Ho TN14. . . 122 A8
Shoreham La
Badgers Mount TN14 . 121 A7
Chelsfield BR6 . . . . . . .88 A3
Sevenoaks TN13 . . . . 153 F4
Tenterden TN30 . . . . 324 A3
Shoreham Pl TN14 . . . 122 A7
Shoreham Prim Sch
TN14. . . . . 121 F8
Shoreham Rd
Orpington BR5 . . . . . .54 B7
Otford TN14 . . . . 122 B5
Shoreham Sta TN14. . . 122 B8
Shoreham Way BR2. . . .52 A3
Shoreham Wlk ME15 . . 195 F7
Shorehill Cl TN15 . . . . 122 F2
Shorehill La TN15 . . . . 122 F2
Shore The
Northfleet DA11. . . . . .18 C2
Northfleet, Rosherville
DA11 . . . . .18 F1
Shorland Ct ME1 . . . . . .63 B5
Shorncliffe Cres CT20 .334 E5
Shorncliffe Ind Est
CT20. . . . . 334 D4
Shorncliffe Rd CT20 . .334 F5
SHORNE 38 E3
Shorne CE Prim Sch
DA12 . . . . .38 E3
Shorne Cl Orpington BR5 54 D5
3 Sidcup DA15. . . . . .13 B1
Shornefield Cl BR1. . . .53 A6
Shorne Ifield Rd DA12. .38 C2
Shornells Way SE2 . . . . .3 C1
Shorne Marshes Nature
Reserve★ ME3. . . . . .21 B4
SHORNE RIDGEWAY . .38 E2
Shorne Woods Ctry Pk★
DA12 . . . . .38 E4
Short La Alkham CT15 . 276 D1
Limpsfield RH8 . . . . . 183 B3
Snargate TN29 . . . . . 362 D6
Shortlands Cl DA17. . . . .3 F3
Shortlands Gn ME15 . . 195 F5
Shortlands Rd ME10. . . 102 B4
Short Path SE18. . . . . . .12 B8
Short's Prospect CT12 . .71 C8
Short St 3 Chatham ME4 64 B3
Chillenden CT3 . . . . . 212 A8
5 Sandwich CT13 . . . 149 A1
Sheerness ME12. . . . . .28 B2
Shorts Way ME1. . . . . .63 A3
Shortway SE9 . . . . .11 E4
Shotfield Cl CT3. . . . . 116 C6
Shottendane Rd CT9,
CT8 . . . . .82 C7
SHOTTENDEN 171 D1
Shottenden La CT4. . . 204 A7
Shottenden Rd
Gillingham ME7. . . . . .64 D7
Shottenden CT4, ME13. 203 D8
Shottery Cl SE9 . . . . . .29 E5
SHOVER'S GREEN. . . 337 C1
Showfields Rd TN2. . . 285 F1
Shrapnel Cl SE18. . . . . .11 E7
Shrapnel Rd SE9 . . . . . .11 F4
Shrewsbury La SE18. . . . 12 B6
Shrimpton Cl CT4 . . . . 172 B3
Shroffold Rd BR1. . . . . .29 A5
Shropshire Terr 1
ME15. . . . . 195 E7
Shrubbery Rd
Gravesend DA12. . . . . .37 C7
Sutton at Hone DA4 . . .57 D8
Shrubbery The CT14. . 215 C1
Shrubcote TN30. . . . . 345 C7
Shrub Hill Rd CT5 . . . 109 D7
Shrublands Ct
Royal Tunbridge Wells
TN2 . . . . 286 A4
1 Tonbridge TN9 . . . 222 C2
Shrubsall Cl SE9 . . . . . .29 E7
Shrubshall Mdw TN15 190 A8
Shrubsole Ave ME15. . . .28 C1
Shrubsole Dr ME14. . . 129 F3
Shuart La CT7. . . . . .79 F4
Shunters Cl ME13 . . . . 138 E6
Shurland Ave
Leysdown-on-Sea
ME12. . . . . .49 H1
Minster (Sheppey) ME12 .47 B6
Sittingbourne ME10 . . 101 F1
Shurlock Ave BR8. . . . . .55 D7
Shurlock Dr BR6 . . . . . .86 C6
Shutler Rd CT10. . . . . .84 B5
Shuttle Cl
Biddenden TN27 . . . . 295 A2
Sidcup DA14. . . . . . . .30 F8
Shuttlemead DA5 . . . . . .31 F8
Shuttle Rd DA1. . . . . . .15 A4
SHUTTLESFIELD 306 A6
Shuttlesfield La CT4. . 273 D1
Sibert's Cl CT15 . . . . . 244 F5
Sibertswold CE Prim Sch
CT15. . . . . 244 E4
SIBERTSWOLD OR
SHEPHERDSWELL. .244 E5
Sibley Cl Bexley DA6. . .13 C2
Bromley BR1. . . . . . . .52 E4
Sibthorpe Rd SE12 . . . .29 C8
SIDCUP 31 A3
Sidcup By-Pass DA14. .30 E4
Sidcup By Pass Rd BR5, BR7,
DA14. . . . . .31 B1
Sidcup Hill DA14 . . . . .31 B3
Sidcup Hill Gdns DA14. 31 C3
Sidcup Pl DA14. . . . . . .31 A3
Sidcup Rd SE12, SE9 . . .29 D7
Sidcup Sta DA15. . . . . .31 A6

Sidcup Tech Ctr DA14. .31 D2
Sidewood Rd SE9 . . . . .30 D7
Sidings Cl ME13 . . . . . 138 E6
Sidings The
Dymchurch TN29. . . . 366 B7
Lyminge CT18 . . . . . . 305 C7
Sevenoaks TN13 . . . . 153 E7
Whitstable CT5 . . . . . .74 E2
Sidmouth Ct DA1. . . . . .34 B7
Sidmouth Rd
Bexley DA16. . . . . 13 C7
Orpington BR5 . . . . . .54 B5
Sidney Cl TN2 . . . . . . 313 F8
Sidney Cooper Gall★
CT1. . . . . 142 F1
Sidney Gdns TN14. . . 122 C2
Sidney Rd SE18 . . . . . . 11 F6
Sidney Ho SE18. . . . . . 11 F6
Sidney Rd
Gillingham ME7. . . . . .64 C7
Rochester ME1 . . . . . .63 A2
Sidney St
Folkestone CT19 . . . . 335 E7
Maidstone ME16. . . . 161 C2
Siebert Rd SE3. . . . . . .11 A8
Siedle Ho 9 SE18 . . . . .12 A8
Siemens Rd SE18 . . . . . 1 D3
Signal Ct 6 ME8 . . . . . .65 F1
Silchester Ct ME14 . . 162 C7
Silcroft Ct TN23. . . . . 267 E1
Silcroft Rd DA7 . . . . . . 14 A6
Silk Cl SE12 . . . . .11 A6
Silk Mills Cl TN13 . . . 154 C6
Silvanus Ho 5 CT11. . 117 D7
Silver Ave CT7 . . . . . . .81 B6
Silver Bank ME5. . . . . .97 A6
Silver Birch Ave DA13. 92 F1
Silver Birch Cl
Joyden's Wood DA2 . . .32 E4
Woolwich SE28 . . . . . . 3 A5
Silverbirch Ct TN26. . 299 A1
Silver Birch Ct TN26 . 299 A1
Silver Birches
Chatham ME5 . . . . . . .97 A3
Sheerness ME12. . . . . .28 G1
Silver Birches Mobile
Homes Pk TN26 . . . 328 A4
Silver Birch Gr TN23. 300 B4
Silver Birch Wlk ME18 192 D6
Silver Cl TN9 . . . . 254 E6
Silverdale Hartley DA3. .58 F5
Maidstone ME16. . . . 161 A2
Silverdale Ave ME12. . . .47 A6
Silverdale Dr
Bromley SE9 . . . . .29 E6
Gillingham ME8. . . . . .98 F7
Herne Bay CT6 . . . . . .77 D2
Silverdale Gr ME10. . . 101 D3
Silverdale La
Royal Tunbridge Wells
TN4 . . . . 286 B6
Sandhurst Cross TN18 . 355 F5
Silverdale Rd
Bexley DA7. . . . . 14 B5
Orpington, Petts Wood
BR5 . . . . .53 C5
Orpington, St Paul's Cray
BR5 . . . . .54 A6
Ramsgate CT11 . . . . . 117 A5
Royal Tunbridge Wells
TN4 . . . . 286 B6
Silverden Cotts TN18 . 355 F4
Silver Hill Chatham ME4 63 F3
Hurst Green TN19. . . . 354 B1
Rochester ME1 . . . . . .62 F2
Tenterden TN30 . . . . 324 B1
Silver Hill Gdns
Ashford TN24 . . . . . . 269 A1
4 Chatham ME4 . . . . .63 F3
Silver Hill Rd TN24 . . 269 A1
Silverhurst Dr TN10 . . 222 C7
Silverlands Rd TN18 . . 305 C7
Silverland St E16. . . . . . 1 F5
Silverlocke Rd RM17 . . .18 D8
Silver Rd DA12 . . . . . . .37 E6
Silver Spring CT DA8. . .14 B8
Silver St Deal CT14. . . 215 D7
Silver Street ME9 . . . . 133 F5
Silversted La TN16 . . . 151 D6
Silvers The CT10 . . . . . .83 C4
Silverstone Ct 10 BR1 .52 C7
Silver Streak Way ME2 .62 E5
SILVER STREET 133 F5
SILVERTOWN 1 C4
Silvertown Way E16. . . . 1 A5
Silver Tree ME5 . . . . . .97 B1
Silverweed Rd ME5. . . .96 F4
Silwood Cl TN2. . . . . . 286 E7
Simmonds Ct 2 TN4 . 285 B6
Simmonds Dr DA3. . . . .59 A4
Simmonds La ME15. . . 196 B6
Simmons Rd SE18 . . . . .2 B1
Simmons Rd CT1. . . . . 174 E7
Simnel Rd SE12 . . . . . .29 B8
Simon Ave CT19. . . . . .51 D2
Simon Ct 5 SE28. . . . . . 3 B5
Simone Cl BR1. . . . . . .52 A7
Simone Weil Ave TN24 268 B4
Simon Langton Girls Gram
Sch CT1. . . . . 175 C5
Simon Langton Gram Sch
for Boys CT4 . . . . . . 175 A4
Simon's Ave TN23 . . . 299 F7
Simpson Rd
Sittingbourne ME10 . . 101 C5
Snodland ME6. . . . . . 127 C8
Simpson's Cotts BR2. . .85 C7
Simpsons Pl 8 BR1 . . . .52 A7
Simpson's Rd BR1, BR2. .52 A6
Sinclair Cl ME8. . . . . . .98 E5
Sinclair Way DA2. . . . . .34 D4
Sindal Shaw Ho ME5 . .96 E4
Singapore Dr ME7. . . . .64 B5
Singer Ave CT6. . . . . . .76 B4

Singledge Ave CT16 . . 277 F6
Singledge La CT15 . . . 245 C2
Single's Cross TN14 . . 120 D4
Single's Cross La TN14 120 C5
Single St TN16 . . . . . . 119 B4
SINGLE STREET 119 B4
SINGLETON 299 E7
Singleton Cl CT12 . . . 115 B6
Singleton Ctr The
TN23. . . . . 299 D8
Singleton Hill TN23 . . 299 D8
Singleton Rd TN23 . . . 267 C1
SINGLEWELL 37 C2
Singlewell Prim Sch
DA12 . . . . .37 D2
Singlewell Rd DA11. . . .37 B4
Sinkerweazel TN17. . . 320 C2
SINKHURST GREEN. . 261 C2
Sion Hill CT11. . . . . . . 117 C6
Sion Pass 12 CT11. . . 117 C6
Sion Wlk 8 TN1. . . . . 286 A2
Sirdar Strand DA12. . . .37 F3
Sir David's Pk TN4 . . . 253 E1
Sir Evelyn Rd ME1. . . . .63 B1
Sir John Fogge Ave
TN23. . . . . 267 F4
Sir John Hawkins Hospl
ME4. . . . . .63 C4
Sir John Hawkins Way
ME4. . . . . .63 C4
Sir John Moore Ave
CT21 . . . . 333 B2
Sir John Moore Ct 5
CT20 . . . . 334 C3
Sir Joseph Williamson's
Mathematical Sch
ME1 . . . . .63 C4
Sir Martin Bowes Ho 11
SE18 . . . . .11 F4
Sir Roger Manwoods Sch
CT13 . . . . 181 B8
Sir Thomas Longley Rd
ME2. . . . . .63 E6
Siscup Rd SE9 . . . . . . .30 B6
Siskin Cl Ashford TN25. 268 D7
Hawkinge CT18. . . . . 306 F4
Siskin Gdns TN12. . . . 257 A5
Siskin Wlk ME20. . . . . 127 F2
SISSINGHURST 321 E3
Sissinghurst Castle Gdn★
TN17. . . . . 293 D1
Sissinghurst CE Prim Sch
TN17. . . . . 321 E8
Sissinghurst Dr ME16. 161 B4
Sissinghurst Rd
Biddenden TN27 . . . . 294 C2
Sissinghurst TN17,
TN27 . . . . 321 D8
SITTINGBOURNE 101 D8
Sittingbourne Com Coll
ME10 . . . . 102 C2
Sittingbourne Ind Pk
ME10 . . . . 101 F5
Sittingbourne & Kemsley
Light Rly★ ME10 . . . 102 A7
Sittingbourne Meml Hospl
ME10 . . . . 101 F3
Sittingbourne Rd
Maidstone, Detling
ME14. . . . . 162 E8
Maidstone, Penenden Heath
ME14. . . . . 162 B6
Sittingbourne Retail Pk
ME10 . . . . 101 E5
Sittingbourne Sta★
ME10 . . . . 101 E5
Sittingbourne Sta
ME10 . . . . 101 F1
Siward Rd BR2. . . . . . .52 C6
Six Bells La TN13 . . . . 154 C1
Six Bells Pk TN26. . . . 326 A3
Six Fields Path TN30 . 345 A7
SIXMILE. 272 D5
Six Penny Cl TN8. . . . . 249 C8
SKEETE 304 D7
Skeete Rd CT18 . . . . . 304 D7
Skeet Hill La BR5, BR6. .87 E8
Skeffington St SE18 . . . .2 C3
Skene Cl ME8 . . . . .66 A1
Skeynes Rd TN8. . . . . 217 B1
Skibbs La BR5, BR6. . . .87 E7
Skinner Gdns TN17. . . 321 A8
Skinner Rd TN29 . . . . 376 C6
Skinner's Alley 3 CT5 .74 D1
Skinners Cl ME20. . . . 129 A6
Skinners La TN8. . . . . 217 D2
Skinner's Sch The TN4 286 A6
Skinner St Chatham ME4 63 F3
Gillingham ME7. . . . . .64 E4
Skinner's Terr 15 TN9 .254 B8
Skinner Street Prim Sch 2
ME7 . . . . .64 C6
Skinner's Way ME17. . 196 E4
Skinney La DA4 . . . . . .57 D6
Skippers Cl DA9. . . . . . 17 B2
Skua Ct ME2 . . . . .62 C7
Skye Cl ME15. . . . . . . 195 A7
Skylark Way TN23 . . . 300 D3
Sky Studios E16. . . . . . . 2 A4
SLADE. 167 E1
Sladebrook Rd SE3. . . .11 D4
Slade Cl ME5 . . . . .97 B2
Sladedale Rd SE18 . . . . 2 E1
Slade Gdns DA8 . . . . . .14 F6
SLADE GREEN 15 B6
Slade Green Inf Sch
DA8 . . . . .15 A7
Slade Green Jun Sch
DA8 . . . . .15 A7
Slade Green Rd DA8 . . .15 B7
Slade Green Sta DA8 . .15 A6
Slade Prim Sch TN9 . . 222 B2
Slade Rd ME17 . . . . . . 200 D8
Slades Cl CT5 . . . . 109 C8

Slades Dr BR7 . . . . .30 C4
Slade The
Lamberhurst TN3. . . . 317 A3
Tonbridge TN9. . . . . . 222 B2
Woolwich SE18. . . . . . 12 E8
Slaney Rd TN12 . . . . . 260 F4
Slater Cl 9 SE18 . . . . . . 2 A2
Slaters TN8 . . . . 218 F2
Slatin Rd ME2. . . . . . . .63 B8
Sleeches Cross TN3 . . 314 B2
Sleepers Stile Rd TN5 316 B1
Sleigh Rd CT2 . . . . . . 143 F6
Slicketts Hill ME4 . . . . .64 A4
Slip La CT15 . . . . 276 C2
Slip Mill Rd TN18. . . . 340 E4
Slip The TN16 . . . . . . 151 C1
Slipway Rd ME12. . . . . .27 F3
Sloane Gdns BR6. . . . . .86 C7
Sloane Sq DA3 . . . . . . .58 E6
Slocum Cl SE28 . . . . . . 3 C6
Sloe La CT10, CT9 . . . . .83 B6
Slough Rd ME9. . . . . . 135 A3
SLUTSHOLE 140 A5
SLY CORNER 347 F5
Small Bridge Cotts
TN17. . . . . 290 B2
Small Bridge Rd TN12,
TN17. . . . . 290 B2
Small Grains DA3 . . . . .91 B7
SMALL HYTHE 345 C1
Small Hythe Cl ME15 .163 B2
Smallhythe Place (Mus)★
TN30. . . . . 345 B4
Small Hythe Rd TN30 .345 B4
Small Profits ME15,
ME18. . . . . 193 A4
SMARDEN 264 A1
SMARDEN BELL 263 D2
Smarden Bsns Est
TN27. . . . . 295 D7
Smarden Cl 3 DA17. . . . 4 A1
Smarden Gr SE9. . . . . .29 F4
Smarden Prim Sch
TN27. . . . . 264 A1
Smarden Rd
Pluckley TN27 . . . . . 265 B6
Standen TN27 . . . . . . 295 B6
Swift's Green TN27. . . 263 B4
Smarts Cotts ME14 . . 163 C4
Smarts Hill TN11 . . . . 252 A1
Smarts Rd DA12 . . . . . .37 C6
Smeed Cl 4 ME10. . . . 102 A4
Smeed-Dean Ctr The
ME10 . . . . 102 A4
SMEETH 302 C1
Smeeth Prim Sch
TN25. . . . . 302 C1
Smetham Gdns ME2. . . .40 B1
Smithers Cl TN11. . . . 190 E1
Smithers Ct TN12. . . . 225 A7
Smithers La TN12 . . . . 225 A7
Smithfield Rd ME3 . . . .27 C5
Smithies Rd SE2. . . . . . 3 B2
Smith Rd ME5 . . . . . . .97 B3
Smith's Hill ME15 . . . 193 C5
Smiths La TN6 . . . . . . 184 C2
Smiths Orch ME9. . . . 133 F5
Smith St ME7 . . . . .63 A6
Smithy Dr TN23 . . . . . 300 C4
Smithy Field 7 TN8 . . 217 D1
Smithy The TN5 . . . . . 336 A3
Smugglers TN18. . . . . 341 A1
Smugglers Leap Cvn Pk
CT12 . . . . 115 C8
Smuggler's Way CT7. . .81 A8
Smugglers Wlk DA9 . . .17 B2
Smythe Cl TN4 . . . . . . 253 E3
Smythe Rd DA4 . . . . . .57 A8
Snag La TN14 . . . . 119 D7
Snakes Hill CT3 . . . . . 178 A5
Snape La TN5 . . . . . . 336 D1
Snape View TN5. . . . . 336 F4
SNARGATE 362 E6
Snargate La TN29 . . . 362 C5
Snargate St CT17 . . . . 310 D2
Snelgrove Ho 14 CT16 310 D8
Snell Gdns CT6. . . . . . .76 B2
Snelling Ave DA11. . . . .36 F6
Snipe Cl Ashford TN25. 268 C7
Erith DA8. . . . . 15 B7
Pembury TN2 . . . . . . 287 E8
Snipe Ct ME2. . . . . . . .62 C7
SNIPESHILL 102 D4
Snoad La TN12 . . . . . . 292 A8
Snodhurst Ave ME5 . . . .96 E5
Snodhurst Ho 2 ME5 . .97 A2
SNODLAND 128 B7
Snodland CE Prim Sch
ME6 . . . . 127 F8
Snodland Rd ME19 . . . 127 D7
Snodlands Rd BR6. . . . .86 A1
Snodland Sta ME6. . . . 128 B8
SNOLL HATCH 224 F5
Snoll Hatch Rd TN12 . 224 F5
Snowbell Rd TN23. . . . 300 B4
Snowdon Ave ME14 . . 162 B5
Snowdon Cl ME5 . . . . . .97 B7
Snowdon Par ME14. . . 162 C5
SNOWDOWN 211 A3
Snowdown Ct CT3. . . . 210 F5
Snowdown Sta CT15 . . 211 B3
Snowdrop Cl CT19. . . . 335 C8
Snow Ho ME7 . . . . .64 E7
Snughorne La TN27 . . 295 D8
Sobraon Villas TN15 . . 157 C7
Sobraon Way CT1. . . . 143 D1
Solar Ct CT12 . . . . 117 C7
Solefield Sch TN13 . . 187 C8
Solefields Rd TN13 . . 187 C8
Solent Gdns ME5. . . . . .97 B8
Soleoak Dr TN13 . . . . 187 B8
Soleshill Rd CT4. . . . . 171 E1
Sole St DA12, DA13. . . .60 D4

SOLE STREET Ashford .239 B7
Gravesend. 60 C4
Sole Street Cotts CT4 .239 B7
Sole Street Farm ME3 . .40 B3
Sole Street Sta DA13 . . . .60 D4
Solomon Ho CT14 . . . . . .215 B7
Solomon Rd ME4 . . . . . . .66 A1
Solomons La ME13 . . . . 138 D7
Solomons Rd ME4. . . . . . .63 F4
Somerden Rd BR5. . . . . . .54 D2
Somerfield Barn Ct
TN25 . . . . 331 C8
Somerfield Cl ME16 . . . 161 D5
Somerfield Hospl The
ME16 . . . . .161 E5
Somerfield La ME16 . . . 161 D4
Somerfield Rd ME16. . . 161 D4
Somerhill Ave DA15 . . . .31 B8
Somerhill Rd
Bexley DA5 . . . . .13 B5
Tonbridge TN9 . . . . . . 254 D5
Somerset Ave DA16 . . . .12 F3
Somerset Cl
Chatham ME5 . . . . .97 C8
Sittingbourne ME10 . . 101 C4
Whitstable CT5 . . . . . . 108 B7
Somerset Ct
2 Broadstairs CT10 . . . .84 A4
Deal CT14 . . . . 215 B3
Ramsgate CT12 . . . . . . .83 B2
Somerset Rd
Ashford TN24 . . . . 268 B3
Canterbury CT1. . . . . . 175 D8
Dartford DA1 . . . . .33 B8
Deal CT14 . . . . 215 C3
Folkestone CT19 . . . . . 334 E6
Maidstone ME15. . . . . 195 C8
Orpington BR6 . . . . .54 A2
Royal Tunbridge Wells
TN4 . . . . 286 A6
Somerset Villas TN3. . 312 C4
Somersham Rd DA7. . . .13 E5
Somertrees Ave SE12. . .29 B6
Somerville Gdns TN4.285 F4
Somerville Rd DA1 . . . . .15 F1
Somme Ct CT1 . . . . 142 D1
Sommerville Cl ME13.138 E7
Somner Cl CT2 . . . . 142 D1
Somner Wlk ME15. . . . .195 F4
Sondes Cl CT6 . . . . .77 A2
Sondes Rd CT14 . . . . . 215 D5
Sonnet Wlk TN16. . . . . 118 C3
Sonora Way ME10 . . . . 101 C7
Soper's La TN18. . . . . . 340 D4
Sophia Rd E16 . . . . .1 B7
Sophurst La TN12 . . . . 288 C5
Sopurst Wood TN12. . . 288 D5
Sopwith Cl TN16 . . . . . 118 D3
Sorrel Cl SE28. . . . . .3 A5
Sorrel Ct 8 RM17. . . . . .18 D8
Sorrel Gdns E6. . . . . .1 E8
Sorrell Cl 4 TN8. . . . . . 217 D3
Sorrell Rd ME6. . . . . . . .96 F4
Sorrell Way DA11. . . . . . .36 E4
Sortmill Rd ME6. . . . . . 128 B7
Sotherton TN24 . . . . . . 300 E7
Souberg Cl CT14 . . . . . 215 C8
Sounds Lodge BR8. . . . . .55 C3
SOUTH ALKHAM. 308 B8
Southall Ct CT12 . . . . . 115 C7
Southampton Mews E16.1 B8
South Ash Rd TN15. . . . .91 E4
South Ave
Aylesham CT15. . . . . . 211 A3
Gillingham ME8. . . . . . . .65 B2
Sittingbourne ME10 . . 102 A3
South Avenue Jun & Inf
Schs ME10 . . . . 102 A3
South Aylesford Ret Pk
ME20 . . . . .160 E8
Southbank BR8. . . . . .2 C7
South Bank Cliffe ME3. . .22 B2
Staplehurst TN12 . . . . 260 E2
Sutton Valence ME17 . . 229 E7
Westerham TN16 . . . . . 151 D1
South Bank of the Swale
Nature Reserve★
ME13 . . . . 106 A6
South Barham Rd CT4 242 E6
SOUTHBOROUGH
Bromley. 52 F3
Royal Tunbridge Wells. 254 B1
Southborough CE Prim
Sch TN4. . . . . .285 F8
Southborough Ct TN4 254 A2
Southborough La BR2. .52 F4
Southborough Prim Sch
BR2. . . . . .53 A4
South Borough Prim Sch
ME15 . . . . 162 A2
Southborough Rd BR1. .52 E5
Southbourne
Ashford TN23 . . . . 299 E5
Hayes BR2. . . . . .52 A2
Southbourne Gdns
SE12 . . . . .11 B2
Southbourne Gr ME5. . .97 A4
Southbourne Rd CT19 .335 E5
South Brook La TN8. . . 218 C7
South Brooks Rd TN29 378 H6
South Bush La ME8. . . . .99 B6
South Camber Way
CT16 . . . . .279 B1
South Canterbury Rd
CT1 . . . . 175 A6
South Cl Bexley DA6. . . .13 D3
Canterbury CT1. . . . . . 175 A8
South Cliff Par CT10. . .84 B1
South Court Dr CT3 . . 178 A7
South Cres ME17 . . . . . 194 C4
Southcroft Ave DA16 . .12 E4
Southcroft Rd BR6. . . . . .86 E7
South Ct Deal CT14. . . . 215 D6

South Ct continued
Ramsgate CT12 . . . . . . .83 B2
Royal Tunbridge Wells
TN4 . . . . 286 A6
SOUTH DARENTH 57 D8
Southdene TN14 . . . . . 120 F6
Southdown Rd ME12 . . .46 E6
SOUTHDOWNS 57 D7
South Dr BR6 . . . . .86 E5
South Eastern Rd
Ramsgate CT11 . . . . . . 117 D7
Rochester ME2. . . . . . . .63 C7
Southenay La TN25. . . 303 C4
Southend Cl SE9 . . . . . . .12 B1
Southend Cres SE9. . . . .12 B1
SOUTHENDEN 92 F4
Southenden Rd TN27 231 E1
Southern Pl BR8 . . . . . . .55 D5
Southern Way CT19 . . .335 E6
Southernwood Rise
CT20. . . . . 334 B8
South Exit Rd CT16 . . . 310 G8
Southey Mews E16. . . . . .1 A5
Southey Way 1 ME20 .127 F4
Southey Wlk RM18 . . . . .19 B6
Southfield Ct DA1 . . . . . .15 F4
Southfield Rd
Orpington BR7 . . . . .54 A6
Royal Tunbridge Wells
TN4 . . . . 286 A6
Southfields Hextable BR8 32 F1
Rochester ME1. . . . . . . .63 C3
Speldhurst TN3. . . . . . 285 A7
Turner's Green TN5 . . .336 F6
Southfields Green CT14 137 B3
Southfield Shaw DA13. .93 B1
Southfields Rd TN15. . . .90 F2
Southfields Way TN4 .286 B8
SOUTHFLEET. 36 A3
Southfleet Ave DA3 . . . .59 B7
Southfleet Rd Bean DA2 35 C4
8 Northfleet DA11 . . . .36 F7
Orpington BR6 . . . . .86 E6
Swanscombe DA10. . . . .36 A7
South Foreland
Lighthouse★
CT15 . . . . .279 F3
South Frith TN4 . . . . . . 254 A6
Southgate TN4 . . . . 285 F9
Southgate Rd TN30. . . 345 C7
South Gipsy Rd ME6.13 D4
South Glade The DA5. . .31 F7
South Goodwin Ct
CT14 . . . . 215 D8
South Gr TN1 . . . . 286 A2
SOUTH GREEN 133 A5
South Green La ME9. . 132 F6
South Hall Cl DA4 . . . . .56 F2
South Hill BR7 . . . . .29 F2
South Hill Rd DA12. . . . .37 C7
Southill Rd Bromley BR7 29 F1
Chatham ME4 . . . . .63 F3
South Kent Ave DA11. . .18 C1
South Kent Coll (Ashford
Campus) TN23 . . . . . 300 A8
South Kent Coll (Dover
Campus) 16 CT16 . . . 310 D8
South Kent Coll
(Folkestone Campus)
CT20. . . . . 335 B5
South Kent Coll (South
Ashford Campus)
TN23. . . . . 299 F6
South La ME17 . . . . . . 229 E6
Southland Rd SE18. . . . .12 F7
Southlands Ave BR6. . . .86 E5
Southlands Ct BR2. . . . .52 D5
Southlands Gr BR1. . . . .52 E6
Southlands Rd BR1, BR2 52 D5
South Lea TN3 . . . . 300 A3
Southlees La ME9 . . . . 132 F3
South Lodge CT5. . . . . . .74 E3
South Lodge Cl CT5. . . .74 E3
Southmead Cl CT19 . . . 335 A6
Southmont Rd
CT17 . . . . 310 C5
South Molton Rd E16. . . .1 A7
South Motto TN23. . . . 300 B5
South of England Rare
Breeds Ctr★ TN26. . . 326 D1
Southold Rise SE9. . . . . .29 F5
Southover BR1. . . . . .29 A3
Southover Ct 2 CT20.334 E3
South Park Bsns Village
ME15 . . . . 162 A1
South Pk TN13 . . . . . . .154 B2
South Pondside Rd
ME4. . . . . .64 A8
Southport Rd SE18 . . . . . .2 D2
South Quay ME13. . . . . 105 D1
South Rd
Chatham, Brompton ME4,
ME7. . . . . .64 A7
Chatham ME4 . . . . .64 B7
Dover CT17. . . . . 310 B8
Erith DA8. . . . . .14 F7
Faversham ME13 . . . . 138 C7
Herne Bay CT6 . . . . .77 A5
Hythe CT21. . . . . 333 D1
Kingsdown CT14. . . . . 248 D5
Marden TN12 . . . . 259 E5
Sandwich CT13. . . . . . 149 A8
South Ridge BR2. . . . . . .52 C5
South Rise Prim Sch
SE18. . . . . .2 D1
South Rise Way SE18 . . . .2 D2
South Row
Greenwich SE3 . . . . . . .11 A5
Penshurst TN8 . . . . . . 251 D5
Southsea Ave ME12 . . . .47 C8
Southsea Dr CT6 . . . . . . .76 D7
South Side Three Rd
ME4. . . . . .64 C8
Southspring DA15. . . . . .30 D8

South St Bromley BR1 . . .52 A7
Canterbury CT1. . . . . . 143 C2
Culverstone Green DA13 .92 F4
Deal CT14 . . . . 215 D6
3 Folkestone CT20. . . 335 E4
Gravesend DA12. . . . . . .37 B8
Lydd TN29 . . . . 376 C6
Maidstone ME16. . . . . 160 E1
Queenborough ME11. . . .45 F5
Selling ME13 . . . . 171 F8
Whitstable CT5 . . . . . . 109 A7
Southstone Ct CT21 . . 333 C1
South Stour Ave TN23 300 C8
SOUTH STREET
Biggin Hill 151 A8
Meopham. 92 F4
Selling 171 F8
Stockbury 132 C7
Whitstable. 109 A7
Southstreet Crossing
CT5. . . . . 109 A7
South Street Rd ME9. 132 C7
SOUTH TANKERTON. . .75 A1
South Terr
Chattenden ME3. . . . . . .40 F6
Farningham ME9. . . . . . .56 A4
South Turbine Hall Rd
TN29 . . . . 380 C2
South View Bromley BR1 52 C7
Hersden CT3. . . . . 111 F1
Oxted RH8. . . . . 183 A2
Southview Ave RM18 . . .19 A4
Southview Cl BR8 . . . . . .56 A5
South View Cl DA15 . . .13 F1
South View Ct 11 BR1 . .52 C7
Southview Gdns ME12. . .28 C1
Southview Hts RM20. . . .17 C8
South View Rd
Dartford DA2 . . . . .33 D5
Royal Tunbridge Wells
TN4 . . . . 286 B8
Turner's Green TN5 . . 336 F6
West Thurrock RM20. . . .17 C8
Whitstable CT5 . . . . . . 108 D6
South View Terr TN17 318 E8
South Wall CT14. . . . . . 215 B7
Southwall Ind Est
CT14. . . . . 215 B6
Southwall Rd CT14 . . . 215 B6
Southwark Rd ME2. . . . .62 D6
Southway BR2. . . . . .52 A2
Southways ME17 . . . . . 229 E7
Southwell Rd ME2. . . . . .62 D6
SOUTH
WILLESBOROUGH . . 300 E6
Southwold Pl CT8 . . . . . .81 E7
Southwold Rd DA5. . . . .14 B1
Southwood Ave ME16. .160 F2
Southwood Ave TN4. . 286 A6
Southwood Bldgs 5
TN4 . . . . .285 B4
Southwood CI CT3 . . . . 267 E3
Southwood Gdns CT11 117 B6
Southwood Ho SE9. . . . .30 B6
Southwood Hts CT11 . 117 C6
Southwood Rd
Eltham SE9 . . . . .30 B6
Ramsgate CT11 . . . . . . 117 C6
Rusthall TN4 . . . . 285 B5
Whitstable CT5. . . . . . . .75 B2
Woolwich SE28. . . . . .3 B5
Sovereign Bvd ME7, ME8 64 F2
Sovereign Cl
Bromley BR2. . . . . .52 A7
Sutton at Hone DA4 . . . .57 B8
Sovereign Ho SE18. . . . . .1 F3
Sovereigns The ME16 . 161 D4
Sovereigns Way TN12 259 C6
Sovereign Way TN9 . . 222 C1
Soverign Ho BR7 . . . . . . .30 D1
Sowell St CT10 . . . . .83 F5
Sowerby Cl SE9 . . . . .11 F2
Spade La ME9. . . . . .99 C6
Spa Ind Pk TN2. . . . . . .286 C8
Spanton Cres CT21 . . . 333 A3
Spar Cl TN11 . . . . .190 F1
Sparepenny La DA4 . . . .56 E1
Sparkes Cl BR2. . . . . . . .52 B5
Sparkeswood Ave
TN17. . . . . .343 F3
Sparkeswood Cl TN17 .343 F3
Sparrow Castle 3 CT9 .50 J1
Sparrow Dr BR5. . . . . . . .53 D1
SPARROW'S GREEN . .336 F5
Sparrows Green Rd
TN5 . . . . .336 F5
Sparrows La SE9 . . . . . . .30 C7
Sparrow Way CT3 . . . . 112 A1
Spartan Rd TN23 . . . . . 299 C8
Spa Valley Rly★ TN3. 312 D7
Speakman Cl 5 CT11 117 C6
Spearhead Rd ME14. . 161 F7
Spearman St 8 SE18. . .12 A8
Spearpoint Cnr TN24. .268 F5
Spectrum Bsns Ctr ME2 63 E8
Spectrum Bsns Est
ME15 . . . . .195 F4
SPEED GATE 90 F8
Speedgate Farm DA3. . .90 F8
Speedgate Hill DA3. . . .91 A8
Speedwell Ave ME5 . . . .96 F4
Speedwell Cl
Gillingham ME7. . . . . . . .64 F3
Maidstone ME14. . . . . 162 E5
5 Marlpit Hill TN8. . . 217 D3
Speedwell Ct RM17. . . .18 C7
Speedwell Rd CT5. . . . . 108 B6
Spekehill SE9 . . . . .29 F5
Speke Rd CT10 . . . . .83 E6
Spekes Rd ME7. . . . . . . .98 B6
Spelders Hill TN25 . . . 270 A5

SPELDHURST 285 B7
Speldhurst CE Prim Sch
TN3. . . . . 285 A7
Speldhurst Cl TN23. . . 299 E5
Speldhurst Ct ME16 . . 161 D4
Speldhurst Gdns CT9. . .51 F3
Speldhurst Hill TN3 . . 285 B8
Speldhurst Rd
Langton Green TN3. . . .284 F5
Royal Tunbridge Wells TN3,
TN4 . . . . 285 E8
Spelmonden Rd TN12 .289 F2
Spembley Ct ME4 . . . . . .63 E4
Spence Cl CT18 . . . . . . 307 A4
Spencer Cl Chatham ME5 97 A5
Orpington BR6 . . . . .86 F8
Spencer Ct 5 BR6 . . . . .86 C5
Spencer Flats ME5 . . . . .97 B8
Spencer Gdns SE9. . . . . .11 F2
Spencer Ho 3 CT20 . . .334 F5
Spencer Mews
6 Royal Tunbridge Wells,
Mount Sion TN1. . . . . 286 A2
10 Royal Tunbridge Wells
TN1 . . . . 286 B4
Spencer Rd CT7. . . . . . . .81 A8
Spencer Sq CT11 . . . . . 117 D6
Spencer St
Gravesend DA11. . . . . . .37 A8
9 Ramsgate CT11. . . . 117 D6
Spencer Way ME15 . . . 195 E7
Spencer Wlk RM18 . . . . .19 B5
Spenlow Dr ME5 . . . . . 130 A8
Spenny La TN12 . . . . . .258 B7
Spenser Rd CT6 . . . . . . .76 F4
Speranza St SE18 . . . . . . .2 F1
Speyside TN10 . . . . 222 B5
Spicer Homes ME10 . . 101 F2
Spicers Ct CT21 . . . . . 333 C1
Spicers Field CT6 . . . . . .77 D2
Spicer's Pl CT3. . . . . . . 145 C2
Spielman Rd DA1. . . . . . .15 F3
Spiers The ME7 . . . . .65 C5
Spillett Cl ME13 . . . . . 138 B6
Spillway The ME15 . . . 161 D2
Spindle Cl SE18 . . . . .1 E3
Spindle Glade ME14 . . 162 C5
Spindle Ho 8 DA15 . . . .31 A5
Spindles RM18 . . . . .19 A7
Spindlewood Cl ME5 . . .97 B3
Spindlewood End
TN23 . . . . 267 D4
Spinel Cl SE18. . . . . .2 F1
Spinnaker Ct 4 ME1 . . .63 C1
Spinners Acre Jun Sch
ME5 . . . . .97 C1
Spinners Cl TN27 . . . . 295 A2
Spinners Wents TN11. 190 D8
Spinney Oak BR1. . . . . . .52 E7
Spinneys The BR1. . . . . .52 F7
Spinney The
Ashford TN23 . . . . 267 E3
Chatham ME5 . . . . .97 B1
Crabble CT17 . . . . 277 E2
Maidstone ME15. . . . . 162 B2
Margate CT9. . . . . .51 E1
Sidcup DA14. . . . . .31 E3
Swanley BR8. . . . . .55 E7
Tonbridge TN9. . . . . . 254 D4
Spinney Way TN14 . . . 119 D8
Spire Alexandra Hospl
ME5 . . . . 130 A8
Spire Ave CT5 . . . . 109 A8
Spire Cl DA12 . . . . .37 B7
Spires Acad CT2. . . . . . 144 C8
Spire St Saviour's Hospl
CT21. . . . . .333 F2
Spires The
Canterbury CT2. . . . . . 142 F2
Dartford DA1 . . . . .33 D6
Maidstone ME16. . . . . 161 D4
Rochester ME2. . . . . . . .62 D5
Spire Tunbridge Wells
Hospl TN3. . . . . .284 B3
Spitalfield La TN28 . . . 372 F6
Spitalfield Terr TN28 . 372 F6
Spital St DA1. . . . . .15 D1
Spitfire Cl ME5 . . . . .97 B6
Spitfire Rd ME19 . . . . . 158 F3
Spitfire Way CT18 . . . . 307 B3
Splashes L Ctr ME8. . . . .65 D1
Split Ho CT17 . . . . 278 A1
Split La CT4. . . . . 241 A5
Spode La TN8 . . . . 282 A7
Sponden La TN18. . . . . 356 A7
Spongs La TN17 . . . . . . 293 A1
Spong Wood Nature
Reserve★ TN25 . . . . 272 A8
Sportsfield ME14 . . . . 162 B5
Sportsmans Cotts
ME19. . . . . .159 B5
Spot La ME15. . . . . 163 A2
Spout La
Brenchley TN12. . . . . . 289 C5
Crockham Hill TN8 . . . 184 C1
Spratling La CT12. . . . . .82 F1
Spratling St CT12. . . . . .82 E1
Spray Hill TN3. . . . . . . .317 B4
Spray St SE18 . . . . .2 B2
Sprig The ME14 . . . . . . 163 A4
Spring Cott DA1. . . . . . . .33 D8
Spring Cross DA3 . . . . . .59 A4
Spring Cl 17 DA15 . . . . .31 A5
Springdale Cotts ME3 . .40 A3
Springett Almshouses
TN18. . . . . .354 E8
Springett Cl ME20 . . . . 128 C6
Springett Way TN12. . 194 D3
Spring Farm TN29. . . . 363 D5
Springfarm Rd TN29. . 363 C5

Springfield Ave
Maidstone ME14. . . . . 161 F7
Swanley BR8. . . . . .55 F5
Tenterden TN30 . . . . . 324 C2
Springfield Cl TN11. . . .83 C2
Springfield Cotts TN12 289 F5
Springfield Gdns BR1 . .52 F5
Springfield Gr SE7 . . . . .11 C8
Springfield Ind Est
TN18. . . . . .340 F3
Springfield Pass CT21 333 F2
Springfield Rd
Bexley, Bexleyheath
DA7. . . . . .14 B3
Bexley, Welling DA16 . . .13 B4
Bromley BR1. . . . . .52 F5
Dover CT16 . . . . 278 B2
Edenbridge TN8 . . . . . 217 B1
Gillingham ME7. . . . . . . .64 E6
Groombridge TN3. . . . 312 C2
Gillingham ME7. . . . . . . .64 E6
Lunsford ME20 . . . . . . 127 F4
Margate CT9. . . . . .51 E3
Sittingbourne ME10 . . 101 D5
Springfields TN5 . . . . . 338 E1
Springfield Terr 7 ME4 63 F4
Springfield Sq CT11 . . 117 D6
Springfield Wlk 3 BR6 53 D1
Spring Gdns
Biggin Hill TN16 . . . . . 118 C1
Orpington BR6 . . . . .87 B4
4 Rusthall TN4 . . . . . 285 B4
Spring Gr DA12. . . . . . . .37 B7
Spring Grove Sch
TN25 . . . . 237 C2
Springhead TN2 . . . . . 286 D5
Springhead Ent Pk
DA11 . . . . .36 C7
Springhead Rd
Erith DA8. . . . . .14 F8
Faversham ME13 . . . . 105 D1
Northfleet DA11 . . . . . . .36 C7
Spring Head Rd TN15. 122 F2
Spring Hill TN11, TN3 . 284 A7
Spring Ho CT21 . . . . . . 333 C2
Spring Hollow TN29. . 366 A4
Springholm Cl TN16 . . 118 C1
Spring La
Bidborough TN3 . . . . . 253 D3
Canterbury CT1. . . . . . 175 C9
Fordwich CT2 . . . . 144 A4
Hythe CT21. . . . . 334 A4
Oldbury TN15. . . . . . . 156 B5
Spring Lodge 3 BR5. . .54 C4
Springrove Cotts TN12 259 F5
Springshaw Cl TN13. . 153 D4
Springside Terr CT18. 305 C6
Spring Terr 15 CT20 . . 335 D5
Springvale
Gillingham ME8. . . . . . .98 C6
Iwade ME9. . . . . .96 C6
Spring Vale Bexley DA7. .14 B3
Dartford DA1. . . . . .33 D8
Maidstone ME16. . . . . 161 E4
Swanscombe DA9. . . . .17 C1
Spring Vale Cl BR8. . . . .55 F8
Springvale Ct
Eltham SE12 . . . . .11 A3
Northfleet DA11 . . . . . . .36 C6
Spring Vale N DA1 . . . . .33 D8
Springvale Ret Pk 2
BR5. . . . . .54 C6
Spring Vale S DA1 . . . . .33 D8
Springvale Way BR5. . . .54 C6
Springview Apartments
TN2 . . . . 286 D6
Springwater Cl SE18. . . .12 A6
Springwell Rd TN9 . . . 254 B8
Spring Wlk CT5 . . . . . . 108 C7
Springwood Cl
1 Maidstone ME16. . . 161 A3
Springwood Ct TN28 . 373 B6
Springwood Dr TN23 . 267 E3
Springwood Hall TN11 189 D1
Springwood Rd TN16. . .87 A8
Sprivers Gdn★ TN12. 289 E4
Sprotlands Ave TN24 . 268 F1
Sprotshill Cl ME10. . . . 101 E6
Spruce Cl ME20 . . . . . . 128 B2
Sprucedale Cl BR8 . . . . .55 E7
Spruce Ho TN4 . . . . 285 E4
Spruce Rd TN16. . . . . . 118 D3
Spurgeon Cl RM17. . . . .18 C8
Spurgeons Cotts ME17 194 E2
Spur Rd BR6 . . . . .87 A8
Spurrell Ave DA5. . . . . . .32 D4
Spurway ME14 . . . . 163 A4
Square Hill ME15 . . . . . 162 B4
Square Hill Rd ME15. . 162 B4
Square The
Birchington CT7 . . . . . . .81 A7
Chilham CT4 . . . . 205 B8
Cowden TN8 . . . . 282 B6
Hadlow TN11. . . . . 223 E8
Hunton ME15 . . . . 226 D7
Leigh TN11 . . . . 220 F1
Lenham ME17. . . . . . . 199 D5
Selling ME13 . . . . 171 A6
Sevenoaks TN13 . . . . 153 E5
Sittingbourne ME10 . . .68 F1
Swanley BR8. . . . . .55 D6
Tatsfield TN16. . . . . . . 150 C7
Wadhurst TN5. . . . . . . 337 A4
Squeeze Gut Alley 14
CT5 . . . . .74 D2
Squerryes Court★
TN16. . . . . 184 C7
Squerryes Mede TN16 184 C8
Squire Ave CT2. . . . . . . 174 C8
Squires Cl ME12. . . . . . .62 B7
Squires Ct ME12. . . . . . .48 E3

Squires Field BR8. . . . . .55 F8
Squires Ho 3 SE18. . . . .12 B8
Squires Way
Dover CT16. . . . . 278 A3
Joyden's Wood DA2 . . . .32 D4
Squires Wood Dr BR7 . .29 F1
Squirrel La TN25 . . . . . 267 F5
Squirrel Way TN2 . . . . 286 E5
Stable Cl ME5. . . . . .97 C5
Faversham ME13 . . . . 138 D6
Stabledene Way 3 TN4 287 D6
Stable Lane CT4 . . . . . . .32 B6
Stablemead CT19. . . . . 335 A7
Stables End BR6. . . . . . .86 C7
Stables The TN18. . . . . 354 E8
Stace Cl TN30 . . . . 345 C8
Stacey Cl DA12. . . . . . . .37 E3
Stacey Rd TN10 . . . . . . 222 A4
Staceys St ME14 . . . . . 161 F5
Stackfield 1 TN8. . . . . 217 D3
Stack La DA3. . . . . .58 F8
Stacklands Cl TN15. . . . .90 E4
Stack Rd DA4 . . . . .57 D5
Stade St CT21 . . . . 333 C1
Stade The CT19 . . . . . . 335 E5
Stadium Rd SE18. . . . . . .11 F8
Stadium Way
Crayford DA1 . . . . .14 E2
Sittingbourne ME10 . . 102 C4
Stadler Rd ME16 . . . . . 161 D7
Staffa Rd ME15. . . . . . .195 A7
Staffhurst Wood Rd TN8,
RH8 . . . . 216 C6
Stafford Cl
Ashford TN23 . . . . 267 F2
Stone DA9. . . . . .16 F2
Stafford House Sch of
English 2 CT1 . . . . . . 175 A7
Stafford Rd
Royal Tunbridge Wells
TN2 . . . . 286 E4
Sidcup DA14. . . . . .30 E4
Tonbridge TN9. . . . . . 222 B2
Staffordshire St 11
CT11 . . . . .117 E7
Stafford St ME7 . . . . . . .64 C5
Stafford Way TN13 . . . 187 C8
Stag Rd Chatham ME5. .97 B5
Royal Tunbridge Wells
TN2 . . . . 286 E4
Stagshaw Cl ME15. . . 162 A2
Stag Theatre The★
TN13. . . . . 154 B2
Stainer House SE3 . . . . .11 C3
Stainer Rd TN10. . . . . . 222 F6
Staines Hill CT2. . . . . . 144 B7
Staines Pl CT10 . . . . . . .84 B5
Staines Wlk DA14. . . . . .31 C4
Stainmore Cl BR7 . . . . . .53 D8
Stainfoot La TN13. . . . 153 C5
Stair Rd TN10 . . . . 222 F4
Stake La ME2 . . . . .95 A6
Staleys Acre 7 TN15 . 156 F7
Staleys Rd TN15. . . . . . 156 F7
Stalham Bsns Ctr ME11 46 A3
Stalham St ME7. . . . . . . .98 B4
Stalin Ave ME5 . . . . .97 B8
STALISFIELD GREEN. 201 C6
Stalisfield Pl BR6. . . . . . .86 A1
Stalisfield Rd
Charing TN27 . . . . 201 E3
Stalisfield Green ME13,
TN27 . . . . 201 C5
Throwley ME13. . . . . . 169 C6
Stamford Villas ME12. . .48 C2
Stampers The ME15 . . 161 D2
Stanam Rd TN2 . . . . . . .287 E6
Stanbridge Rd TN8 . . . 217 B2
Stanbrook Rd
Northfleet DA11 . . . . . . .36 F8
Woolwich SE2. . . . . .3 B4
Stanbury Cres CT19 . . 335 F7
Stancomb Ave CT11 . . 117 C5
Standard Ave CT6. . . . . .76 A4
Standard Ind Est E16 . . . .1 F4
Standard Rd Bexley DA6 13 E3
Erith DA17. . . . . .4 A1
Farthing Street BR6. . . .86 A1
STANDEN. 295 B5
Standen Cl ME8 . . . . . . .98 C4
Standen La CT18 . . . . . 307 E5
Standen St
Benenden TN17,
TN18 . . . . 342 D2
Royal Tunbridge Wells
TN4 . . . . 286 A5
Standen Street TN17 . . 356 E8
Standings Cross TN12 256 E1
Standish Ho SE3 . . . . . . .11 B3
Staner Ct CT12 . . . . 117 A8
Staner Hill CT12 . . . . . 116 F8
Stane Way SE18 . . . . . . .11 E7
STANFORD. 304 B1
Stanford Dr ME16 . . . . 161 C3
Stanford La TN11. . . . . 191 C2
Stanford Way ME2 . . . . .62 C2
Stangate Dr ME9 . . . . . .68 D4
Stangate Rd
Birling ME19 . . . . 127 B8
Rochester ME2. . . . . . . .62 C7
Stangrove Rd TN8. . . . 217 C1
Stanham Pl DA1. . . . . . . .15 A3
Stanham Rd DA1. . . . . . .15 C2
Stanhill Cotts DA2. . . . .32 D6
STANHOPE. 299 F6
Stanhope Ave
Hayes BR2. . . . . .52 A1
Sittingbourne ME10 . . 102 A3
Stanhope Cl ME14. . . . 161 E7

Stanhope Rd
Ashford TN23 299 E6
Bexley DA7 13 E5
Deal CT14 215 D6
Dover CT16 278 C2
Rochester ME2 63 A7
Royal Tunbridge Wells TN1 286 C5
Sidcup DA15 31 A4
Swanscombe DA10 17 F1
Stanhopes RH8 183 B7
Stanhope Sq TN23 299 F6
Stanhope Way TN13 153 D5
Stan La ME18 191 A7
Stanley Ave
Minster (Sheppey) ME12 47 D7
Queenborough ME11 46 A4
Stanley Cl
Dymchurch TN29 353 B4
Eltham SE9 30 C7
Staplehurst TN12 260 E4
Stone DA9 16 E2
Stanley Cotts DA2 34 E3
Stanley Cres DA12 37 D3
Stanley Gdns CT6 76 F3
Stanley Glyn Ct BR7 30 A3
Stanley Holloway Ct E16 1 A7
Stanley Pl
Broadstairs CT10 84 A4
Ramsgate CT11 117 E7
Stanley Rd
Broadstairs CT10 84 A6
Bromley BR2 52 C5
Chatham ME5 97 C6
Deal CT14 215 D5
Folkestone CT19 334 E6
Gillingham ME7 64 C6
Grays RM17 18 B8
Herne Bay CT6 76 F4
Marden TN12 259 D5
Margate CT9 51 A3
Northfleet DA11 36 E7
Orpington BR6 53 F1
Ramsgate CT11 117 D8
Royal Tunbridge Wells TN1 286 B5
Sidcup DA14 31 A5
Swanscombe DA10 17 F1
Whitstable CT5 108 D7
Stanley Way BR5 54 B4
Stanmore Ct CT1 175 B7
Stanmore Ho SE12 29 B7
Stanmore Rd DA17 4 C2
Stansfeld Ave CT18 307 A4
Stansfeld Rd E16 1 D7
STANSTED 91 F1
Stansted CE Prim Sch TN15 91 F1
Stansted Cl ME16 161 D7
Stansted Cres DA5 31 D7
Stansted Hill TN15 92 A1
Stansted La TN15 91 C1
Stanton Cl BR5 54 C2
Stanton Ct
9 Bromley BR1 52 C7
5 Sidcup DA15 31 A5
STAPLE 179 A5
Staple Cl
Joyden's Wood DA5 32 D5
Sittingbourne ME10 101 E5
Staple Dr TN12 260 F4
Stapleford Ct TN13 153 F4
STAPLEHURST 260 D4
Staplehurst Ave CT10 84 A2
Staplehurst Gdns CT9 51 E2
Staplehurst Ho BR5 54 C4
Staplehurst Lodge Ind Est ME10 101 D5
Staplehurst Prim Sch TN12 260 E3
Staplehurst Rd
Bogden TN12 228 C2
Frittenden TN12, TN17 261 D1
Gillingham ME8 65 B3
Sittingbourne ME10 101 D5
Staplehurst Sta TN12 260 E5
Staple Rd CT3 178 C6
Staplers Ct ME14 162 B8
Staples Ho E6 2 A7
Staple St ME13 139 F5
Staples The BR8 56 B8
STAPLESTREET 140 A5
Staplestreet Rd ME13 140 A4
Stapleton Rd Bexley DA7 13 F8
Orpington BR6 86 F7
Stapley Rd DA17 4 A1
Starboard Ave DA9 17 B1
Star Bsns Ctr RM13 4 E8
Starbuck Cl SE9 30 A8
Star Hill Crayford DA1 14 E2
Rochester ME1 63 D5
Star Hill Rd TN14 121 A2
Star Ho TN3 317 B5
Star La Folkestone CT19 334 D7
Gillingham ME7 98 A7
Margate CT9 83 A5
Orpington BR5, BR8 54 E5
Starle Cl CT1 143 B1
Starling Cl DA3 59 B6
Star Mill Ct ME5 64 D2
Star Mill La ME5 64 D2
Starnes Ct 5 ME14 162 A5
Starr Cotts TN12 226 C2
Star Rd TN24 268 D2
Starts Cl BR6 86 A7
Starts Hill Ave BR6 86 B6
Starts Hill Rd BR6 86 B6
Starvation Cnr 1 CT5 74 D2
Starveacre La ME9 101 B1
Starve Goose La TN17 319 E4
State Farm Ave BR6 86 C6
Stately Pk ME18 192 C1
STATENBOROUGH 180 C4
Station App
Adisham CT3 210 E8
Bexley, Barnehurst DA7 14 C5
Bexley, Bexleyheath DA7 13 E5
Bexley, Welling DA16 13 A5
Birchington CT7 80 F7
2 Borough Green TN15 156 F7
Bromley BR7 29 E2
Chelsfield BR6 87 B5
Chislehurst BR7 53 A7
Dartford DA1 15 E1
Edenbridge TN8 217 C2
Grays RM17 18 A8
Greenwich SE3 11 B4
Halling ME2 95 A5
Hayes BR2 52 A1
Maidstone ME16 161 F3
Martin Mill CT15 247 C2
Minster (Thanet) CT12 115 C5
New Romney TN28 373 C6
Orpington BR6 86 F8
Orpington, St Mary Cray BR5 54 B5
Otford TN14 122 C3
Paddock Wood TN12 257 A7
Staplehurst TN12 260 E5
Swanley BR8 55 E5
Station App Rd CT11 117 C8
Station Approach Rd CT11 117 D8
Station Chine CT6 76 F5
Station Cotts
Gill's Green TN18 340 F5
Hartley TN17 319 E2
Horsmonden TN12 290 B5
Selling ME13 171 E7
Station Cres SE3 1 A1
Station Ct 1 TN15 156 F7
Station Dr CT14 215 A1
Station Hill
Chiddingstone Causeway TN11 252 A8
Hayes BR2 85 A8
Station Hill Cotts ME15 194 A7
Station Mews
Elham CT4 273 F4
2 Ramsgate CT12 83 C1
3 Tenterden TN30 345 A7
Station Par
Sevenoaks TN13 154 A3
Sidcup DA15 31 A6
Station Rd Adisham CT3 177 E1
Ashford TN23 268 C2
Aylesford ME20 128 E2
Bekesbourne CT4 176 C4
Betsham DA13 36 A4
Bexley DA7 13 E4
Birchington CT7 81 A7
Borough Green TN15 156 F7
Brasted TN16 152 B4
Bridge CT4 175 F2
Bromley BR1 52 A8
Charing TN27 234 C7
Chartham CT4 173 D3
Cliffe ME3 22 B3
Crayford DA1 14 F1
Cuxton ME2 62 C2
Deal CT14 215 B1
Dymchurch TN29 366 B7
East Farleigh ME15 194 A7
East Tilbury RM18 20 B7
Edenbridge TN8 217 C2
Erith DA17 4 A3
Eynsford DA4 89 D7
Faversham ME13 138 D6
Folkestone CT19 334 F5
Gillingham ME8 66 A2
Goudhurst TN17 318 C7
Groombridge TN3 312 C7
Halstead TN14 120 F8
Harrietsham ME17 198 D6
Headcorn TN27 262 D5
Herne Bay CT6 76 E4
Hurst Green TN19 354 A3
Hythe CT21 333 D3
Longfield DA3 58 E6
Lydd TN29 376 D7
Lyminge CT18 305 C6
Maidstone ME14 161 F5
Margate CT9 50 H2
Martin Mill CT15 247 D1
Meopham Station DA13 60 A4
Minster (Thanet) CT12 115 C5
Nettlestead Green ME18 192 C1
Newington ME9 100 B6
New Romney TN28 373 C6
Northfleet DA11 18 B1
Northiam TN31 357 C1
Orpington BR6 86 F8
Orpington, St Mary Cray BR5 54 C5
Otford TN14 122 C3
Paddock Wood TN12 256 F7
Pluckley TN27 265 C5
Rochester ME2 63 C7
Rockrobin TN5 336 C6
Sevenoaks TN13 153 E7
Shepherdswell CT15 244 D5
Shoreham TN14 122 A7
Sidcup DA14, DA15 31 A5
Smeeth TN25 302 B3
Snodland ME20 128 D2
Staplehurst TN12 260 F5
St Margaret's at Cliffe CT15 279 E8
Stone DA9 17 A2
Sutton at Hone DA4 57 B7
Swanley BR8 55 E5
Tenterden TN30 345 A7
Station Rd *continued*
Teynham ME9 103 D2
Westgate on Sea CT8 50 D1
Whitstable CT5 74 E2
Withyham TN7 311 B5
Station Road E CT1 174 F7
Station Road N DA17 4 B3
Station Road W CT2 142 F1
Station Row ME9 103 D3
Station Sq BR5 53 C4
Station St Newham E16 2 B5
Sittingbourne ME10 101 F4
Station Terr TN28 373 C6
Steadman Cl ME3 39 C6
Steddy Cl 4 TN23 299 F6
Stede Hill ME17 165 F3
STEDE QUARTER 295 E1
Stedley 17 DA14 31 A4
Stedman Cl DA5 32 E5
Steed Cl CT6 111 B8
Steeds Cl TN23 300 A1
Steeds La TN23, TN26 300 B1
Steele Ave DA9 17 A2
Steele's La DA13 93 A6
Steele St ME2 63 A8
Steele Wlk DA8 14 B7
Steellands Rise TN5 338 F1
Steep Cl BR6 86 F4
Steephill Sch DA3 58 D5
Steeple Heights Dr TN16 118 D2
Steerforth Cl ME1 63 C2
Steers Pl TN11 190 E2
Stella Cl TN12 259 D5
Stella Maris RC Prim Sch CT19 335 C6
STELLING MINNIS 240 F2
Stelling Minnis CE Prim Sch CT4 240 F6
Stelling Minnis Windmill & Mus★ CT4 240 F2
Stelling Rd DA8 14 D7
Stembrook CT16 310 D8
Stembrook Ct 4 CT16 310 D7
Stempe Cl CT18 307 B3
Stenning Ct TN10 222 C4
Stephen Cl
Broadstairs CT10 84 A4
Orpington BR6 86 F7
Stephen Ct 2 CT20 335 D5
Stephen Rd DA7 14 C4
Stephens Cl
Faversham ME13 138 B8
Ramsgate CT11 117 C8
Stephen's Cl CT9 82 B7
Stephenson Ave RM18 19 A6
Stephenson Ho SE2 3 D1
Stephenson Rd CT2 142 F3
Stephen's Rd TN4 286 B6
Stepneyford La TN17 343 C7
Steps Hill Rd ME9 132 D6
Step Style ME10 102 B2
Sterling Ave ME16 161 C5
Sterling Cl CT10 83 E5
Sterling Ct 12 CT1 142 F1
Sterling Ho SE3 11 B3
Sterling Rd
Queenborough ME11 46 A5
Sittingbourne ME10 101 D1
Sterndale Rd DA1 33 F8
Sterry Gdns ME15 195 E7
Stevanne Ct 1 DA17 4 A1
Stevedale Rd DA16 13 C5
Steven Cl ME4 64 A3
Stevens Cl Dartford DA2 34 E3
Egerton TN27 232 F3
Joyden's Wood DA5 32 D4
Snodland ME6 128 A8
Stevens Cotts TN30 345 A7
Stevens Ho CT17 310 C8
Stevenson Cl Erith DA8 15 B7
Maidstone ME15 161 F3
Stevenson Way ME20 127 F4
Stevens Rd ME20 128 F6
Stewart Cl BR7 30 B4
Stewart Ho ME3 40 F6
Stewart Rd TN4 286 C7
Steyning Gr SE9 29 F4
Steynton Ave DA5 31 D6
Stickens La ME19 159 E7
Stickfast La
Sittingbourne ME9 68 A1
Ulcombe ME17 230 D3
STICK HILL 250 A3
Stickland Rd 2 DA17 4 A2
STIFF STREET 133 E7
Stilebridge La ME17 228 A5
Stiles Cl Bromley BR2 52 F3
Erith DA8 4 B1
Folkestone CT19 335 A7
Minster (Sheppey) ME12 47 A6
Still La TN4 253 F2
Stillwater Mews ME4 41 B2
Stirling Cl
Gillingham ME8 98 E4
Rochester ME1 63 A3
Sidcup DA14 30 F4
Stirling Dr BR6 87 B5
Stirling Ho 5 SE18 2 B1
Stirling Rd ME19 158 F3
Stirling Way CT12 83 A2
Stirlng Rd TN24 300 D7
Stisted Way TN27 232 F3
STOCKBURY 132 E8
Stockbury Dr ME16 161 D7
Stockbury Gdns CT9 51 E2
Stockbury Hill Wood Nature Reserve★ ME9 132 D6
Stockbury Ho 7 BR5 54 D1
Stockdale Gdns CT14 215 C4
Stockenbury TN12 224 F6
Stockers Brow ME9 135 A7
STOCKER'S HEAD 201 F1
Stockers Hill ME9 135 A7
Stocker's Hill ME13 139 E4
Stockett La ME15 194 D6
Stockham Ct CT19 334 E7
Stock Hill TN16 118 D2
Stock La Dartford DA2 33 C4
Smeeth TN25 302 A4
STOCKLAND GREEN 253 C1
Stockland Green Rd
Royal Tunbridge Wells TN3 285 D8
Speldhurst TN3 285 B8
STOCKS GREEN 221 B4
Stocks Green Prim Sch TN11 221 E5
Stocks Green Rd TN11 221 C5
Stocks Mill Windmill★ TN30 360 A3
Stocks Rd TN30 359 F3
STOCKS THE 360 A3
Stocks The ME13 170 C6
Stockton Cl ME14 162 B8
Stockwell Cl BR1 52 B7
Stockwood Chase CT2 142 A2
Stoddart Rd CT19 334 E6
STODMARSH 145 B6
Stodmarsh National Nature Reserve★ CT3 145 D8
Stodmarsh Rd CT3 144 C3
Stofield Gdns SE9 29 D5
STOKE 25 A3
Stoke Com Sch ME3 25 C5
Stoke Rd Allhallows ME3 9 C1
Hoo St Werburgh ME3 41 F6
Kingsnorth ME3 42 C8
Lower Stoke ME3 24 E1
Stokesay Ct 14 DA2 16 B1
Stombers La CT18 307 C6
Stonar Cl Ramsgate CT11 83 E1
Sandwich CT13 149 A1
Stonar Gdns CT13 149 A2
STONE 16 F2
Stoneacre★ ME15 196 B7
Stoneacre Cl ME8 98 D5
Stoneacre Ct 7 ME15 162 A1
Stoneacre La ME15 196 B7
Stone Barn Ave CT7 81 A6
Stone Bay Sch CT10 84 B6
STONE BRIDGE 336 E6
Stonebridge TN25 270 A5
Stonebridge Cotts TN23 300 B8
STONEBRIDGE GREEN 233 A4
Stonebridge Green Rd TN27 232 F4
Stonebridge Rd
Canterbury CT2 143 A2
Northfleet DA11 18 B2
Stonebridge Way ME13 138 B7
Stone Castle Dr DA9 17 A1
Stonechat Sq 6 E6 1 E8
Stone Cnr TN30 360 A6
Stone Cotts TN3 316 F4
Stone Court La TN2 287 E8
Stonecroft DA13 126 A8
Stonecroft Rd DA8 14 C7
Stonecrop Cl ME4 41 C1
STONE CROSS
Aldington Frith 328 F6
Langton Green 284 A2
Sandwich 180 E7
Wadhurst 337 A3
Stone Crossing Sta DA9 16 E2
Stonecross Lea ME5 64 C1
Stone Cross Lees CT13 180 F7
Stone Cross Rd
Bromley Green TN25 328 E5
Wadhurst TN5 337 A4
STONECROUCH 338 F6
Stone Ct DA8 4 F1
Stonedane Ct ME13 138 C8
Stonefield Cl DA7 14 A4
Stonefield Way SE7 11 D7
Stonegate TN25 237 E2
Stonegate Cl BR5 54 C6
Stonegate Rd TN5 337 C1
Stone Gdns CT10 84 B5
Stone Gn TN30 360 F4
STONEHALL 276 F8
Stonehall Rd CT15 276 F8
Stoneheap Rd CT14, CT15 213 E1
STONE HILL 303 A2
Stone Hill TN25 303 A2
Stone Hill Rd TN27 232 F2
Stonehill Woods Pk DA14 32 B2
Stone Ho CT10 84 B7
Stonehorse Ct ME3 40 A3
Stonehorse La ME2 40 A2
Stonehouse Cnr RM19 16 E8
Stonehouse La
Halstead TN14 120 E8
Pratt's Bottom TN14 87 E1
Purfleet RM19 16 E8
Stone House Mews CT10 84 B7
Stonehouse Rd BR6, TN14 87 D1
Stoneings La TN14 151 F8
STONE-IN-OXNEY 360 F4
Stone Lake Ind Pk SE7 1 C2
Stone Lake Ret Pk SE7 1 C2
Stoneleigh Rd
Bromley BR1 53 B6
The Chart RH8 183 E5
Stonely Crescent 3 DA9 17 C3
Stoneness Rd RM20 17 C7
Stone Pit La TN18 356 E5
Stone Place Rd DA9 16 E2
Stone Rd
Broadstairs CT10 84 B5
Bromley BR2 52 A5
Stonerock Cl CT2 144 B7
Stone Row TN3 284 B5
Stone Row Cotts TN3 284 D1
Stone St Mary's CE Prim Sch DA9 34 E8
Stones Cross Rd BR8 55 C4
Stones Rdbt ME4 41 B1
Stone St
Cranbrook TN17 320 D5
Faversham ME13 138 C7
Gravesend DA11 19 B1
Lympne CT21 332 A4
Royal Tunbridge Wells TN1 286 B4
Stanford TN25 304 C3
Stelling Minnis CT4 240 D4
Westenhanger TN25, CT21 332 B6
Stonestile Bsns Pk TN27 262 A7
Stonestile Farm Rd TN27 201 A3
Stone Stile La CT4 171 D1
Stonestile Rd TN27 262 A7
STONE STREET 155 E2
STONESTREET GREEN 330 A7
Stone Street Rd TN15 155 E2
Stoneswood Rd RH8 183 B5
Stonewall E6 2 A8
Stonewall Park Rd TN3 284 F3
Stoneway Pk CT4 240 D7
Stone Wood DA2 35 C5
Stonewood Cl TN4 286 A8
Stonewood Rd DA8 4 E1
Stoney Alley SE18 12 A5
Stoney Bank ME7 64 F1
Stoney Rd ME13 140 B3
Stonyfield TN8 217 D3
Stony La ME1 96 C5
Stonyway La CT15 309 C5
Stopford Rd ME7 64 D4
Storehouse Wharf ME12 27 F3
Store Rd E16 2 A4
Stores Rd TN29 380 C2
Storey Cres CT18 307 A5
Storey St E16 2 A4
Stornaway Strand DA12 37 F4
Stotfold BR1 52 E8
Stour Cl Ashford TN23 267 E1
Chartham CT4 173 D2
Orpington BR2 85 C6
Rochester ME2 62 F7
Tonbridge TN10 222 B5
Stour Cres CT1 143 D3
Stour Ct
7 Canterbury CT1 174 F8
21 Orpington BR5 54 D1
8 Sandwich CT13 148 F1
Stour Ctr TN24 268 C1
Stourfields TN24 268 D4
Stourmouth Rd CT3 146 C8
Stour Rd Chartham CT4 173 D2
Crayford DA1 15 A4
Stour Retail Pk CT1 143 D3
Stourside Studios 13 CT1 142 F1
Stour St CT1 174 F8
Stour Valley Cl CT3 112 D3
Stour Valley Ind Est CT4 173 E4
Stourville 9 CT1 174 F8
Stow Ct DA2 34 C8
Stowell Cl TN23 299 C8
Stowe Rd BR6 87 B6
STOWTING 304 A8
Stowting CE Prim Sch TN25 304 B8
STOWTING COMMON 272 A4
Stowting Hill TN25 272 A1
Stowting Rd BR6 86 E6
Straight La TN29 362 F1
Strait Rd E6 1 F6
Strakers Hill
East Studdal CT15 246 D8
Tilmanstone CT15 213 C1
Strand Approach Rd ME7 64 E7
Strand Cl DA13 60 A3
Strand Ct SE18 2 E1
Strandfield Cl SE18 2 E1
Strand L Pool & Pk ME7 64 F7
Strand Rdbt The ME7 64 E7
Strand St CT13 148 F1
Strand The CT14 215 D4
Stranger's Cl CT1 174 C6
Stranger's La CT1 174 C6
Strangford Pl CT6 77 B2
Strangford Rd CT5 74 F2
Strasbourg St CT9 83 A6
Stratfield Ho SE12 29 A6
Stratford Ave ME8 98 D8
Stratford Dr ME15 195 D6
Stratford House Ave BR1 52 E6
Stratford La 2 ME8 98 F8
Stratford Rd ME19 159 A8
Stratford St TN1 286 C5
Strathaven Rd SE12 11 B1
Stratheden Par SE3 11 A7
Stratheden Rd SE3 11 A7
Stratton Cl DA7 13 E4
Stratton Rd DA7 13 E4
Stratton Terr TN16 184 C8
Strawberry Cl TN2 313 E7
Strawberry Fields
Orpington BR6 86 B5
Swanley BR8 55 E7
Strawberry Vale TN9 222 C1
Straw Mill Hill ME15 161 E1
Streamdale SE2 13 B8
Stream La TN18 355 A7
Stream Pit La TN18 356 B5
Streamside ME20 128 B1
Stream Side TN10 222 D6
Streamside Cl
Bromley BR2 52 A5
Hildenborough TN11 221 E5
Stream The ME20 128 C1
Stream Way DA17 14 A8
Stream Wlk CT5 74 D2
Streatfield TN8 217 D1
Streatfield Ho TN16 151 C1
Street E TN29 380 D2
Streete Court Rd CT8 81 F8
Streete Ct CT8 81 F8
STREET END 207 F7
Street End CT3 147 E1
Street End Rd ME5 64 B1
Street Farm Cotts ME3 41 F6
Streetfield Herne CT6 111 B8
Ulcombe ME17 230 F7
Streetfield Mews SE3 11 A4
Streetfield Rd ME8 65 F1
Street The Acol CT7 81 B3
Adisham CT3 210 C8
Appledore TN26 361 D8
Ash CT3 147 D1
Ashford, Great Chart TN23 267 C1
Ashford, Kennington TN24 268 E6
Ashford, Willesborough Lees TN24 301 B8
Ash TN15 91 E5
Barham CT4 209 F1
Benenden TN17 342 D6
Bethersden TN26 297 D5
Bishopsbourne CT4 209 C6
Borden ME9 101 B2
Bossingham CT4 241 A7
Boughton Street ME13 140 A3
Boxley ME14 130 C3
Brabourne TN25 303 C8
Bredgar ME9 134 A5
Bredhurst ME7 98 B1
Brook TN25 270 B6
Chilham CT4 205 B8
Cobham DA12 60 F6
Deal CT14 214 F6
Denton CT4 243 B3
Detling ME14 131 A1
Doddington ME9 167 E7
East Langdon CT15 247 A1
Eastling ME13 168 E6
Egerton TN27 232 F3
Eythorne CT15 245 D7
Faversham ME13 105 B2
Finglesham CT14 214 B8
Frittenden TN17 293 E7
Godmersham CT4 205 B2
Goodnestone CT3 178 D2
Guston CT15 278 E6
Hamstreet TN26 349 A7
Hartlip ME9 99 D5
Hastingleigh TN25 271 B6
Hawkinge CT18 307 B5
High Halstow ME23 23 E3
Horton Kirby DA4 57 C5
Hothfield TN26 267 A6
Ickham CT3 145 C1
Ightham TN15 156 D6
Iwade ME9 68 E4
Kingston CT4 209 D3
Lower Halstow ME9 67 B3
Lympne CT21 331 F2
Lynsted ME9 136 A6
Maidstone ME14 163 C4
Martin Mill CT15 247 B3
Meopham DA13 60 A1
Mereworth ME18 191 D8
Mersham TN25 301 E4
Molash CT4 203 F4
Newnham ME9 168 C8
Nonington CT15 211 D1
Northbourne CT14 214 A5
Patrixbourne CT4 176 B3
Peene CT18 334 A7
Petham CT4 207 B3
Plaxtol TN15 189 F7
Pluckley TN27 265 D7
Postling CT21 304 F2
Preston CT3 146 C6
Ryarsh ME19 126 F4
Selling ME13 171 B6
Shadoxhurst TN26 327 A8
Shorne DA12 38 E3
Sissinghurst TN17 321 B8
Sittingbourne ME9 102 E3
Smarden TN27 264 A1
Staple CT3 178 F6
St Nicholas at Wade CT7 79 F2
Stockbury ME9 132 E8
Stone in Oxney TN30 361 A5
Stourmouth CT3 113 E1
Teston ME18 193 A7
Trottiscliffe ME19 126 A5
Ulcombe ME17 230 F7
Upchurch ME9 66 F4
Upper Halling ME2 94 E5
West Hougham CT15 308 F5
Wickhambreaux CT3 145 C2
Wittersham TN30 359 D3
Womenswold CT4 210 D2
Woodnesborough CT13 180 C7
Wormshill ME9 166 A7
Worth CT14 181 B5
Street W TN29 380 C2
Strettit Gdns TN12 224 F5
Stretton Ct CT14 215 D5
Strickland Ave DA1 15 F4
Strickland Way 5 BR6 86 F6

Stringer Dr CT7 . . . . .81 A6
Strode Cres ME12 . . . . . . .28 C2
Strode Park Rd CT6 . . . .77 A2
Strond St CT17 . . . . .310 D6
Strongbow Cres SE9 . . . .11 F2
Strongbow Rd SE9 . . . . . .11 F2
STROOD Rochester 62 F7
Tenterden 344 B5
Strood Ret Pk ME2 . . . .63 B7
Strood Sports Ctr ME20 .62 F7
Strood Sta ME2 . . . . .63 C7
Strouts Rd TN3 . . . . . . .299 D7
Strover St ME7 . . . . .64 C7
Struttons Ave DA11 . . . .36 F6
Stuart Ave BR2 . . . . .52 A1
Stuart Cl Hextable BR8 . .3 A1
Maidstone ME14 . . . . .162 C6
Royal Tunbridge Wells
TN2 . . . . .313 F8
Stuart Ct
Canterbury CT1 . . . . . .175 A6
Dover CT17 . . . . .310 C8
Stuart Evans Cl DA16 . .13 C4
Stuart Ho CT14 . . . . . . .215 A5
Stuart Mantle Way DA8 14 E7
Stuart Rd Bexley DA16 . .13 B6
Folkestone CT19 . . . . . .335 E6
Gillingham ME7 . . . . . . .64 D3
Gravesend DA11 . . . . . .19 A1
STUBB'S CROSS 299 C2
Stubbs Hill BR6, TN14 .120 C6
STUDDAL 246 C7
STUDD HILL 76 A4
Studds Cotts CT6 . . . . . .76 A3
Studfall Cl CT21 . . . . . .353 D8
Studio Cl CT1 . . . . .268 E6
Studios The CT1 . . . . . . .91 F8
Studland Cl DA15 . . . . . .30 F5
Studley Cres DA3 . . . . . .59 C7
Studley Ct DA14 . . . . . . .31 B3
Stumble Hill TN11 . . . .189 C5
Stumble La TN23 . . . . .300 B1
Stuppington Court Farm
CT1 . . . . .174 E4
Stuppington La CT1 . . .174 F5
Sturdee Ave ME7 . . . . . .64 E4
Sturdee Cotts ME3 . . . . .42 A6
Sturdy Cl CT21 . . . . . . .333 D2
Sturges Field BR7 . . . . . .30 D2
Sturges Rd TN24 . . . . . .268 B3
Sturla Rd ME4 . . . . .64 A3
Sturmer Cl CT1 . . . . . . .175 C7
Sturmer Ct ME19 . . . . .159 A2
STURRY 143 E6
Sturry CE Prim Sch
CT2 . . . . .144 A7
Sturry Court Mews
CT2 . . . . .143 F5
Sturry Hill CT2 . . . . . . .143 F6
Sturry Rd CT1, CT2 . . .143 C3
Sturry Sta CT2 . . . . . . .143 F5
Sturry Way ME8 . . . . . . .65 C2
STYANTS BOTTOM . . .155 F5
Styants Bottom Rd
TN15 . . . . .155 F5
Style Cl ME8 . . . . .98 E4
Styles Cl TN8 . . . . .218 B5
Styles Cotts TN8 . . . . . .218 B5
Styles Ct TN12 . . . . . . .256 F7
Styles La ME14 . . . . . . .130 C3
Subdown Cotts TN25 .303 C8
Sudbury E6 . . . . .2 A7
Sudbury Cres BR1 . . . . . .29 A3
Sudbury Pl CT8 . . . . .81 E7
Suffolk Ave
Gillingham ME8 . . . . . . .65 F1
Westgate on Sea CT8 . .81 D7
Suffolk Cl ME8 . . . . .65 F1
Suffolk Dr TN23 . . . . . .268 A2
Suffolk Gdns CT17 . . . .309 F7
Suffolk Mews TN1 . . . .286 A4
Suffolk Rd
Canterbury CT1 . . . . . .175 D8
Dartford DA1 . . . . .15 E1
Gravesend DA12 . . . . . .19 D1
Maidstone ME15 . . . . .195 D8
Sidcup DA14 . . . . .31 C2
Suffolk St CT5 . . . . . . .108 C8
Suffolk Way TN13 . . . .154 C2
Sugarloaf Wlk CT19 . . .335 D8
Sullivan Ave E16 . . . . . . .1 D8
Sullivan Cl
Canterbury CT1 . . . . . .174 D6
Dartford DA1 . . . . .33 C8
Sullivan Rd Tilbury RM18 .19 F4
Tonbridge TN10 . . . . .222 E5
Sultan Mews ME5 . . . . . .97 C2
Sultan Rd ME5 . . . . .97 C2
Summer Cl Hythe CT21 .332 F2
Tenterden TN30 . . . . . .324 C1
Summer Ct
Canterbury CT2 . . . . . .142 C1
Whitstable CT5 . . . . . . .75 C2
SUMMERFIELD 179 B4
Summerfield
Bromley BR1 . . . . .52 B8
Marden TN17 . . . . .291 B6
Summerfield Ave CT5 . .74 F1
Summerfield Rd CT9 . . .51 D2
Summerfield St
SE12 . . . . .29 A8
Summerhill
Ashford TN23 . . . . . . .299 E6
Headcorn TN27 . . . . . .262 A6
Summer Hill
Canterbury CT2 . . . . . .142 C1
Chislehurst BR7 . . . . . .53 A7
Summerhill Ave TN4 . .253 F1
Summerhill Cl BR6 . . . . .86 E7
Summer Hill Pk TN24 .301 C7
Summerhill Rd
Bogden TN12 . . . . .228 C1
Dartford DA1 . . . . .33 D8
Summerhill Villas BR7 .53 B8

Summerhouse Dr DA2,
DA5 . . . . .32 D4
Summer La CT2 . . . . . .142 E6
Summerlands Lodge
BR6 . . . . .86 A6
Summer Leeze TN24 . .300 E8
Summer Leeze Gdns
TN24 . . . . .300 E8
Summer Rd CT7 . . . . . . .79 E1
Summerson Rd CT1 . . . .63 C1
Summerton Way SE28 . .3 D7
Summervale Rd TN4 . .285 E1
Summerville Ave ME12 .47 A5
Sumner Cl
Orpington BR6 . . . . .86 C6
Rolvenden TN17 . . . . .343 F3
Sumpter Way ME13 . . .137 F7
Sunbeam Ave CT6 . . . . .75 F4
Sunburst Cl TN12 . . . . .259 D5
Sunbury St SE18 . . . . . . .1 F3
Sun Ct DA8 . . . . .14 F5
Sunderland Cl ME1 . . . .63 A4
Sunderland Dr ME8 . . . .99 A8
Sunderland Ho ME7 .64 C7
Sunderland Point E16 . . .2 C5
Sundew Cl RM17 . . . . . .18 D8
Sundew Gr CT11 . . . . . .117 E8
Sundorne Rd SE7 . . . . . . .1 C1
SUNDRIDGE Lewisham .29 C2
Sevenoaks 152 F3
Sundridge Ave
Bexley DA16 . . . . .12 D4
Bromley BR1 . . . . .52 D8
Sundridge & Brasted CE
Prim Sch TN14 . . . . .152 E2
Sundridge Cl
Canterbury CT2 . . . . . .143 A4
Dartford DA1 . . . . .16 A1
Sundridge Ct BR1 . . . . .29 B1
Sundridge Dr ME5 . . . . .97 A4
Sundridge Hill
Cuxton ME2 . . . . .62 C3
Halstead TN14 . . . . . . .120 C1
Sundridge Ho BR1 . . . . .29 B3
Sundridge La TN14 . . . .120 C2
Sundridge Park Sta
BR1 . . . . .29 B1
Sundridge Rd TN14 . . .153 B8
Sunfields Pl SE3 . . . . . . .11 B7
Sun Hill ME3 . . . . .91 A8
Sunhill Ct TN2 . . . . . . .287 C6
Sun La Gravesend DA12 .37 C6
Greenwich SE3 . . . . . . .11 B7
Hythe CT21 . . . . .333 C2
St Nicholas at Wade CT7 .79 F2
Sunland Ave DA6 . . . . . .13 E3
Sunningdale Ave
CT19 . . . . .335 A7
Sunningdale Cl Erith SE28 3 E7
Gillingham ME8 . . . . . . .98 D6
Sunningdale Ct ME15 .162 B4
Sunningdale Dr ME8 . . .98 D6
Sunningdale Rd BR1 . . .52 E4
Sunningdale Wlk CT6 . .76 D1
Sunninghill E16 . . . . . . .36 E6
Sunninghill Ave
Biggin Hill TN16 . . . . .118 B2
Biggin Hill TN16 . . . . .118 B2
Sunninghill Cl TN16 . .118 D3
Sunnybank TN5 . . . . . .339 E3
Sunny Bank
Eythorne CT15 . . . . . .245 B8
Hythe CT21 . . . . .332 F2
Sittingbourne ME10 . .102 B5
Sunny Cnr CT17 . . . . . .310 B5
Sunnydale BR6 . . . . .86 A8
Sunnydale Rd SE12 . . . .11 B2
Sunnyfield Rd BR7 . . . . .54 A6
Sunnyfields Cl ME8 . . . .98 E8
Sunnyfields Dr ME12 . .46 C6
Sunnyhill Rd CT6 . . . . . .76 C4
Sunnymead Ct 142 D7
Sunnymead Ave ME7 . .64 E5
Sunnyside
Doddington ME9 . . . . .167 E7
Littlebourne-on-Sea
TN28 . . . . .373 D6
Lydd TN29 . . . . .376 B6
Marlpit Hill TN8 . . . . .217 B3
Sunnyside Ave ME12 . .47 A6
Sunnyside Cl CT14 . . . .214 D1
Sunnyside Cotts CT14 215 C6
Sunnyside Gdns CT13 .180 E8
Sunnyside Rd
Folkestone CT20 . . . . .334 D3
Rusthall TN4 . . . . .285 C4
Whitstable CT5 . . . . . .108 D5
Sunray Ave Bromley BR2 52 F3
Whitstable CT5 . . . . . .108 B7
Sun Rd DA10 . . . . .17 F1
Sun Rise TN25 . . . . . . .267 F5
Sunrise Way ME19 . . . .159 C3
Sunset Cl
Eastchurch ME12 . . . . . .48 F6
Erith DA8 . . . . .15 B7
Whitstable CT5 . . . . . .108 C6
Sunset Rd SE28 . . . . .3 A5
Sunshine Ct ME8 . . . .98 F8
Sun St CT1 . . . . .174 F8
Sunstone Dr ME10 . . . .101 C7
Sun Terr ME5 . . . . .97 B4
Sun Valley Way CT15 . .304 C8
Superabbey Est ME20 .129 B2
Superior Dr BR6 . . . .86 F4
Surf Cres 48 F6
Surlingham Cl SE28 . . . .3 D6
Surrenden Rd
Folkestone CT19 . . . . .334 F6
Staplehurst TN12 . . . .260 E3
Surrey Cl
Ramsgate CT12 . . . . . . .83 B1
Royal Tunbridge Wells
TN1 . . . . .313 F8
Surrey Gdns CT7 . . . . . .80 F7

Surrey Rd
Canterbury CT1 . . . . . .175 D7
Maidstone ME15 . . . . .195 D8
Margate CT9 . . . . .51 B3
Surtees Cl TN24 . . . . . .300 E6
Susan Rd SE3 . . . . .11 B5
Susan's Hill TN26 . . . . .325 D1
Susan Wood BR7 . . . . . .53 A8
Sussex Ave
Ashford TN24 . . . . . . .268 B3
Canterbury CT1 . . . . . .175 D7
Margate CT9 . . . . .51 B3
Sussex Cl Herne Bay CT6 76 B4
Royal Tunbridge Wells
TN2 . . . . .286 C1
West Kingsdown TN15 . .90 E3
Sussex Dr ME5 . . . . .97 A4
Sussex Gdns
Birchington CT7 . . . . . . .80 F7
Herne Bay CT6 . . . . . . .76 B4
Westgate on Sea CT8 . .50 D1
Sussex Mans CT8 . . . . . .50 D1
Sussex Mews TN2 . . .286 A2
Sussex Rd Dartford DA1 .34 A8
Erith DA8 . . . . .14 B7
Folkestone CT19 . . . . .335 D6
Maidstone ME15 . . . . .195 D8
New Romney TN28 . . .373 A6
Orpington BR5 . . . . .54 C3
Sidcup DA14 . . . . .31 B3
Tonbridge TN9 . . . . . . .254 A8
Sussex Road Prim Sch
TN9 . . . . .254 A8
Sussex St CT11 . . . . . . .117 E7
Sussex Wlk CT1 . . . . . .175 D7
Sutcliffe Pk Athletics
Track SE12 . . . . .11 B2
Sutcliffe Rd Bexley DA16 13 C5
Woolwich SE18 . . . . . .12 E8
Sutherland Ave
Bexley DA16 . . . . .12 E3
Biggin Hill TN16 . . . . .118 E1
Orpington BR5 . . . . .53 F4
Sutherland Cl
Chalk DA12 . . . . .38 B6
Hythe CT21 . . . . .333 A2
Stone DA9 . . . . .16 F2
Sutherland Dr ME7 . . . .81 B6
Sutherland Gdns ME8 . .98 E6
Sutherland Ho
Hythe CT21 . . . . .333 C4
Woolwich SE18 . . . . . .11 F6
Sutherland Rd
Deal CT14 . . . . .215 C6
Erith DA8 . . . . .14 A2
Royal Tunbridge Wells
TN1 . . . . .286 B3
Sutlej Rd SE7 . . . . .11 C7
SUTTON 247 A7
SUTTON AT HONE . . .34 A1
Sutton at Hone CE Prim
Sch DA4 . . . . .34 A1
Sutton Baron Rd ME9 .134 A8
Sutton Cl
Folkestone CT19 . . . . .335 A7
Gillingham ME8 . . . . . . .99 A8
Sutton Cotts ME13 . . . .171 C3
Sutton Ct TN12 . . . . . .259 C5
Sutton Forge TN12 . . .259 D5
Sutton Hts ME15 . . . . .195 F6
Sutton La
Ringwould CT14 . . . . .247 F5
Ripple CT14 . . . . .247 C8
Sutton Rd Hersden CT3 .111 E1
Langley ME17 . . . . . . .196 C5
Maidstone ME15 . . . . .195 D6
Sutton Row CT14 . . . . .215 B5
Sutton St ME14 . . . . . .163 D4
Suttons The TN31 . . . .374 A1
SUTTON VALENCE . . .229 E6
Sutton Valence Castle
(rems of) ME17 . . . . .229 F7
Sutton Valence Prep Sch
ME17 . . . . .229 E7
Sutton Valence Prim Sch
ME17 . . . . .229 E7
Sutton Valence Sch
ME17 . . . . .229 E7
Swadelands Cl ME17 . .199 C5
Swadelands Sch ME17 199 C5
Swaffer Way TN23 . . .299 C7
Swaffield Rd TN13 . . . .154 C5
Swain Cl ME2 . . . . .62 F4
Swain Rd Gillingham ME8 98 B6
Tenterden TN30 . . . . . .324 D3
Swaisland Rd DA1 . . . . .15 B1
Swaislands Dr DA1 . . . .14 F2
Swakeley Wlk CT5 . . . . .75 D3
Swale Ave
Rushenden ME11 . . . . . .45 F3
Sheerness ME12 . . . . . .28 B1
Swale Cl CT6 . . . . .77 A3
SWALECLIFFE 76 B4
Swalecliffe Ave CT6 . . . .76 B4
Swalecliffe Com Prim Sch
CT5 . . . . .75 B2
Swalecliffe Court Dr
CT5 . . . . .75 D3
Swalecliffe Rd CT5 . . . . .75 B2
Swaledale Rd DA2 . . . . .34 C7
Swale Ho ME11 . . . . . . .45 F5
Swale National Nature
Reserve ME12 . . . . . . .73 E4
Swale Rd Crayford DA1 .15 A3
Rochester ME2 . . . . . . .62 C7
Swale Sta ME9 . . . . .69 A7
Swale View ME13 . . . . .140 B6
Swallow Ave CT5 . . . . .108 B6
Swallow Cl Bexley DA8 .14 E6
Margate CT9 . . . . .82 C8
Stone DA9 . . . . .16 F2
Swallow St Herne CT6 .110 F7
Lewisham SE12 . . . . . .29 A8

Swallow Dr TN2 . . . . . .286 F6
Swallowfield TN24 . . . .300 E7
Swallowfield Rd SE7 . . . .1 B1
Swallowfields DA11 . . . .36 E5
Swallow Ho
Dover CT17 . . . . .310 A6
Maidstone ME16 . . . . .161 E4
Swallow Rd ME20 . . . .127 F2
Swallow Rise ME5 . . . . .97 A5
Swallows L Ctr ME10 . .101 F3
Swallows St CT13 . . . . .181 A8
Swallows The CT13 . . . .181 A8
Swallow St ME20 . . . . .127 F2
Swallowtail Cl BR5 . . . . .54 D5
Swamp Rd TN29 . . . . . .372 B4
Swan Apartments
ME15 . . . . .195 E5
Swan App E6 . . . . .1 E8
Swanbridge Rd DA7 . . . .14 B6
Swan Bsns Pk DA1 . . . . .15 C3
Swan Cl Orpington BR5 . .54 A6
Sittingbourne ME10 . .102 B4
Swan Cotts TN30 . . . . .359 D3
Swanfield Rd CT5 . . . . .108 D8
Swan Gn TN25 . . . . . . .303 D1
Swan La Brandfold TN17 290 F3
Dartford DA1 . . . . .32 F8
Marlpit Hill TN8 . . . . .217 C4
Sellindge TN25 . . . . . .303 C2
Swanland Dr TN9 . . . . .253 F7
SWANLEY 55 E5
Swanley Cr BR8 . . . . . . .55 E6
Swanley La BR8 . . . . . . .55 F6
Swanley New Barn
Railway ★ BR8 . . . . . . .55 E8
Swanley Sta BR8 . . . . . .55 D5
Swanley Tech Coll BR8 .55 E6
SWANLEY VILLAGE . . .56 B7
Swanley Village Rd BR8 56 B8
Swanmead Way TN9 . .222 D2
Swann Way CT18 . . . . .307 A4
Swan Rd SE18 . . . . .1 D3
Swan Ridge TN8 . . . . . .217 D4
SWANSCOMBE 17 D2
Swanscombe Bsns Ctr
DA10 . . . . .17 E2
Swanscombe Ho
BR5 . . . . .54 B7
Swanscombe St DA10 . .17 F1
Swanscombe Sta DA10 .17 F2
Swansea Ct E16 . . . . .2 B4
Swan St
West Malling ME19 . . .159 C8
Wittersham TN30 . . . .359 C3
Swanstree Ave ME10 . .102 B2
SWANTON 191 A8
Swanton La
Littlebourne CT3 . . . . .144 D2
Lydden CT15 . . . . .276 C6
Swanton Rd Erith DA8 . .14 A7
Mereworth ME18 . . . . .191 A8
SWANTON STREET . .133 F3
Swan Valley Com Sch
DA10 . . . . .35 F8
Swanzy Rd TN4 . . . . . .154 C7
Sward Rd BR5 . . . . .54 A3
Swarling Hill Rd CT4 . .207 C7
Swattenden La TN17 . .320 B1
Swaylands Rd DA17 . . .14 A8
Swaynesland Rd RH8 . .183 F1
Swaynes Way CT3 . . . .180 B2
Sweechbridge Rd CT6 . .77 F3
Sweechgate CT2 . . . . . .143 E7
Sweeps Hill CT2 . . . . . .287 D7
Sweeps La BR5 . . . . .54 D5
Sweet Bay Cres TN3 . . .267 D3
Sweet Briar CT16 . . . . .161 D5
Sweetbriar La CT15 . . .212 B2
Sweetings La TN3, TN5 316 D1
Sweet La ME19 . . . . . . .160 A4
Sweetlands La TN12 . . .261 A5
Sweetlove Pl CT3 . . . . .178 A8
Swetenham Wlk SE18 . .2 C1
Sweyne Rd DA10 . . . . . .17 E1
Sweyn Pl SE3 . . . . .11 A5
Sweyn Rd CT9 . . . . .51 A3
Swievelands Rd TN16 .118 C1
Swift Cl Larkfield ME20 .128 A2
Woolwich SE28 . . . . . . .3 B6
Swift Cres ME5 . . . . .97 C6
Swift Ho ME16 . . . . . . .161 E4
SWIFT'S GREEN 263 E6
Swifts View TN17 . . . . .320 D6
Swiller's La DA12 . . . . . .38 E3
Swinburne Ave CT10 . . .84 A3
Swinburne Gdns RM18 .19 B5
Swinford Gdns CT9 . . . .83 C8
Swingate Ave ME3 . . . . .22 B6
Swingate Cl ME5 . . . . . .97 B2
Swingate Inf Sch ME5 . .97 C1
Swingate La SE18 . . . . . .12 E7
Swingfield Cl BR2 . . . . . .52 D4
Swingfield Minnis .275 B3
SWINGFIELD STREET 275 E4
Swinton Ave ME3 . . . . . .40 F5
Swires Shaw BR2 . . . . . .85 D6
Swiss Way CT19 . . . . . .335 F7
Switch House Ave
TN29 . . . . .380 C2
Swithland Gdns SE9 . . . .30 A4
Syamore Mews SE28 . . .4 D1
Sycamore Ave
Aylesham CT3 . . . . . . .210 E5
Sidcup DA15 . . . . .12 F1
Sycamore Cl
Broadstairs CT10 . . . . . .83 C4
Chartham CT4 . . . . . . .173 F1
Dymchurch TN29 . . . . .366 C8
Gravesend DA12 . . . . . .37 D8
Herne Bay CT6 . . . . . . .77 C5
Hythe CT21 . . . . .332 E1
Lydd TN29 . . . . .376 D7
Margate CT9 . . . . .82 E7
Tilbury RM18 . . . . .19 A5

Sycamore Cl continued
Tilbury RM18 . . . . .19 E5
Sycamore Cotts
Bidborough TN3 . . . . .253 D3
Pembury TN2 . . . . . . .287 C6
Sycamore Cres ME10 . .101 E5
Sycamore Ct Erith DA8 . .4 D1
Stone DA9 . . . . .34 E8
Sycamore Dr
Aylesford ME20 . . . . . .128 E1
Deal CT14 . . . . .215 B4
Swanley BR8 . . . . .55 E7
Sycamore Gdns
Dymchurch TN29 . . . . .366 C8
Paddock Wood TN12 . .256 F5
Sycamore Grange CT11 83 F1
Sycamore La TN23 . . . .267 E4
Sycamore Lodge BR6 . .86 F8
Sycamore Rd
Dartford DA1 . . . . .33 D7
Rochester ME2 . . . . . . .62 E5
Sycamores The CT3 . . .144 E8
Sychem La TN12 . . . . . .256 A6
Sychem Pl TN12 . . . . . .256 A7
Sydcot Dr CT14 . . . . . .215 D8
Sydenham Cotts SE12 . .29 C6
Sydenham Rd CT14 . . .215 D7
Sydenham St CT5 . . . . . .74 D2
Sydney Ave ME10 . . . . . .96 B8
Sydney Cooper Cl CT2 142 A7
Sydney Cooper Gallery ★
CT1 . . . . .142 F1
Sydney Cotts BR5 . . . . .54 C5
Sydney Rd Bexley DA6 . .13 D3
Chatham ME4 . . . . .64 A3
Deal CT14 . . . . .215 A1
Erith SE2 . . . . .3 D3
Ramsgate CT11 . . . . . .117 F8
Sidcup DA14 . . . . .30 E4
Tilbury RM18 . . . . .19 A5
Whitstable CT5 . . . . . .108 E8
Sydney Terr TN18 . . . .340 F3
Sylewood Cl ME1 . . . . . .96 B8
Sylvan Cl RH8 . . . . .183 B6
Sylvan Glade ME5 . . . . .130 A8
Sylvan Mews DA9 . . . . .17 B3
Sylvan Rd ME8 . . . . .98 C8
Sylvester Ave BR7 . . . . .29 F2
Sylvestre Cl ME2 . . . . . .95 A4
Sylvestres TN13 . . . . . .153 E6
Symonds Dr ME10 . . . .102 A6
Symonds Cl TN15 . . . . . .90 E5
Symonds La ME18 . . . .225 F6
Symonds Rd ME3 . . . . . .22 A4
Symons Ave ME4 . . . . . .64 A2
Syndale Pl CT11 . . . . . .117 F7
Syon Lodge ME12 . . .29 A8
Syringa Ct RM17 . . . . . .18 D8

Tanners St ME13 . . . . . .138 C7
Tannery Ct ME10 . . . . .101 E5
Tannery La
Ashford TN23 . . . . . . .268 C2
Sandwich CT13 . . . . . .148 F1
Tannery Rd TN9 . . . . . .222 C1
Tansy Cl E6 . . . . .2 A7
Tanyard
Rolvenden TN17 . . . . .343 E4
Sandhurst TN18 . . . . .356 B5
Tanyard Cotts DA12 . . .38 E1
Tanyard Hill DA12 . . . . .38 E2
Tanyard La TN4 . . . . . .253 F1
Tanyard The TN17 . . . .320 D4
Tapleys Hill CT4 . . . . . .208 B5
Taplin Ct CT5 . . . . . . .81 A7
Tappan Dr ME4 . . . . . . .41 B2
Tapsell's La TN5 . . . . . .336 D5
Tarbutts TN17 . . . . . . .320 D4
Target Bsns Ctr ME15 .195 F4
Target Firs CT16 . . . . . .277 D5
Tariff Reform Cotts
ME13 . . . . .138 C5
Tarland Ho TN2 . . . . . .286 D3
Tarling Cl DA14 . . . . . . .31 B5
Tarnwood Pk SE9 . . . . . .29 F7
Tar Pot La TN25, TN26 .350 B6
Tarragon Rd ME16 . . . .161 B3
Tartane La TN29 . . . . . .366 C8
Taryes Ho CT11 . . . . . .117 C6
Tasker Cl ME15 . . . . . . .163 B3
Tasmania Ho RM18 . . . .19 A6
Tasman Wlk E16 . . . . . . .1 D7
Tassell Cl ME19 . . . . . . .128 A1
Tassell's Wlk CT5 . . . . . .75 D3
Taswell Cl CT16 . . . . . .310 E8
Taswell Rd ME8 . . . . . . .66 A1
Taswell St CT16 . . . . . .310 E8
Tatchell Dr TN27 . . . . .234 C7
Tate Rd E16 . . . . .1 F5
Tates TN18 . . . . .341 A1
Tates Orch DA3 . . . . . . .58 F3
Tatler Cl ME5 . . . . .97 D2
TATSFIELD 150 D7
Tatsfield Cl ME8 . . . . . . .65 A2
Tatsfield La
Biggin Hill TN16 . . . . .150 F6
Hill Park TN16 . . . . . . .151 A6
Tatsfield Prim Sch
TN16 . . . . .150 D6
Tattersall Cl SE9 . . . . . .11 E2
Tattershall Ct DA2 . . .16 B1
Tattershall Rd ME15 . .162 A1
Tattlebury La TN17 . . . .290 F1
Tattlebury Rd TN27 . . .262 C8
Taunton Cl Bexley DA7 .14 D5
Maidstone ME15 . . . . .195 F6
Taunton Rd DA11 . . . . . .18 A2
Taunton Vale DA12 . . . .37 D5
Tavern Cl TN15 . . . . . . .156 F7
Tavern Cotts TN15 . . . .155 A3
Taverners Rd ME8 . . . . .98 E7
Tavistock Cl
Chatham ME5 . . . . .96 F1
Gillingham ME8 . . . . . . .98 E7
Sittingbourne ME10 . .101 D4
Tavistock Rd
Bexley DA16 . . . . .13 C6
Bromley BR2 . . . . .52 A5
Ramsgate CT11 . . . . . . .83 E1
Tavy Bridge SE2 . . . . . . .3 C4
Tawney Rd SE28 . . . . . . .3 B6
Tay Cl ME5 . . . . .97 B5
Tayfields TN12 . . . . . . .261 C6
Taylers Yd TN25 . . . . . .237 E2
Taylor Cl
Harrietsham ME17 . . . .198 D6
Orpington BR6 . . . . .86 C7
Taylor Ct TN2 . . . . . . .286 C7
Taylor Rd
Folkestone CT19 . . . . .334 E6
Lydd-on-Sea TN29 . . . .377 E6
Minster (Thanet) CT12 . 115 B6
Snodland ME6 . . . . . . .127 F8
Taylor Row DA2 . . . . . . .33 C5
Taylor's Bldgs SE18 . . . .2 B2
Taylors Cl Sidcup DA14 . .30 F4
St Mary's Bay TN29 . . .365 F3
Taylors Hill CT4 . . . . . .205 B8
Taylors La
St Mary's Bay TN29 . . .365 F3
Vigo Village ME19 . . . .125 F6
Taylor's La Higham ME3 .39 B5
Rochester ME2 . . . . . . .63 B7
Taylors Pl ME19 . . . . . .125 E5
Taymouth Ho CT16 . . .310 E8
Taywood TN24 . . . . . . .268 F1
Tea Garden La TN3 . . . .285 C2
Teakcroft CT RM13 . . . .4 D7
Teal Ave BR5 . . . . .54 D5
Teal Cl Grain ME3 . . . . .27 B5
Hawkinge CT18 . . . . . .306 F3
Newham E16 . . . . .1 D8
Teal Dr Herne Bay CT6 . .76 E2
St Mary's Island ME4 . . .41 B2
Teal Way ME9 . . . . .68 E3
Teapot La ME20 . . . . . .128 E1
Teardrop Ctr BR8 . . . . . .56 C4
Teardrop Ind Pk BR8 . . .56 C4
Teasaucer Hill ME15 . .194 F8
Teasel Cl ME14 . . . . . . .162 F4
Teasel Cres SE28 . . . . . . .2 E5
Teasel Rd ME5 . . . . .96 F4
Teasels TN27 . . . . .295 A1
TEASLEY MEAD 283 C4
Teasley Mead TN3 . . . .283 C4
Tebbs Way TN15 . . . . . .156 C3
Teddars Leas Rd CT18 305 E4
Tedder Ave ME5 . . . . . . .97 A7

Tedder Rd TN4........286 B7
Teddington Cl CT1...143 B2
Teelin Cl TN29......366 A4
Teesdale Rd DA2......34 C7
Teeswater Ct DA18....3 D3
Teign Mews SE9......29 E6
Teignmouth Rd DA16..13 C5
Teise Cl TN2........286 D2
Tekram Cl TN8.......217 C1
Telegraph Hill ME3...39 C3
Telegraph Hill Ind Pk
  CT12..............115 D7
Telegraph Rd CT14...215 B3
Telemann Sq SE3......11 B4
Telescope Alley ME12..28 D2
Telford Ct
  Folkestone CT19....335 E6
  Herne Bay CT6......76 C2
Telford Ho 2 Erith DA17..4 A3
  1 Maidstone ME14..162 A6
Telford St SE9.......30 D6
Telford St CT6.......76 E5
Telham Ave CT12.....117 B8
Tellson Ave SE18.....11 E6
Telscombe Cl BR6.....86 E8
Telston La TN14.....121 F2
Temeraire Hts CT20..334 C3
Temeraire Manor 2
  ME7...............64 A6
Tempest Rd ME19.....158 F3
Templar Ct
  9 Canterbury CT2...142 F1
  11 Dover CT17......278 C1
Templar Dr Erith SE28..3 D7
  Gravesend DA11......37 A3
Templar Rd CT16.....277 D5
Templars Ct 11 TN8..217 C3
Templar St CT17.....310 C8
Temple Cl
  Ashford TN23.......299 F5
  Temple Ewell CT16..277 D6
  Woolwich SE28......2 C3
Temple Ct CT2.......142 D1
TEMPLE EWELL........277 D6
Temple Ewell CE Prim Sch
  CT16..............277 D6
Temple Gdns
  Rochester ME2......63 A6
  Sittingbourne ME10..102 B3
TEMPLE HILL.........16 A3
Temple Hill DA1......15 F2
Temple Hill Prim Sch
  DA1...............16 A2
Temple Hill Sq DA1...15 F2
Templeman Libr CT2..142 E4
Temple Manor ★ ME2..63 A6
Temple Mews 10 CT1..174 F8
Temple Mill Prim Sch
  ME2...............40 B1
Templemore DA14.....31 B3
Temple Rd
  Biggin Hill TN16...118 D2
  Canterbury CT2.....142 D1
  Temple Sch ME2.....40 B2
Temple Side CT16....277 D6
Temple Way
  Royal Tunbridge Wells
  TN2...............286 C7
  West Malling ME19..127 F1
  Worth CT14.........181 A4
Ten Acre Way ME8.....66 B1
Tenby Rd DA16........13 D6
Tenchley's La
  Limpsfield RH8.....183 D4
  The Chart RH8......183 E2
Tenney Ho RM17.......18 B7
Tennison Way ME15...195 D6
Tennyson Ave
  Canterbury CT1.....143 D3
  Cliffe Woods ME3....40 B7
Tennyson Cl DA16.....12 F6
Tennyson Gdns CT3...210 F6
Tennyson Ho
  Canterbury CT1.....143 D3
  2 Erith DA17.......3 F1
Tennyson Pl
  Canterbury CT1.....143 D3
  Folkestone CT19....335 E7
Tennyson Rd
  Ashford TN23.......300 A6
  Dartford DA1.......16 A2
  Gillingham ME7......64 C3
Tennyson Wlk
  Northfleet DA11.....36 D5
  Tilbury RM18.......19 B5
Tenor Dr ME3........41 E6
Ten Perch Rd CT14...174 D6
Tensing Ave DA11.....36 E5
TENTERDEN...........345 C8
Tenterden CE Jun Sch
  TN30..............345 B7
Tenterden Cl SE9.....29 F4
Tenterden & District Mus ★
  TN30..............345 A7
Tenterden Dr CT2....143 A4
Tenterden Inf Sch
  TN30..............345 B7
Tenterden L Ctr TN30..345 B7
Tenterden Rd
  Appledore Heath
  TN26..............347 B1
  Biddenden TN27.....323 B8
  Chatham ME5........97 B5
  Fosten Green TN27...322 F4
  Rolvenden TN17.....344 A1
Tenterden Station Est
  TN30..............345 A8
Tenterden Town Sta ★
  TN30..............345 A8
Tenterden Vineyard ★
  TN30..............345 C1

Tenterden Way CT9....51 C1
Tent Peg La BR5......53 C4
Tenzing Ct SE9.......29 E6
Terance Butler Ave
  ME2...............63 E8
Terence Ct Chatham ME4..64 A2
  Gravesend DA12......37 F6
Terence Ct 6 DA17....13 F8
Terminus Dr CT6......77 D5
Terminus Rd ME16....161 A2
Terminus Wlk 3 CT20..335 E5
Tern Cres ME2........62 C6
Terrace Apartments The
  CT21..............333 C1
Terrace Cotts CT4....241 A6
Terrace Rd
  Elvington CT15.....212 B1
  Maidstone ME16.....161 E3
  Sittingbourne ME10..102 B3
Terrace St
  Gravesend DA12......19 B1
  Gravesend DA12......19 C1
Terraces The DA2.....34 C8
Terrace The
  Canterbury CT2.....142 F3
  Chatham ME4........63 F7
  Faversham ME13.....138 A7
  25 Gravesend DA12...19 B1
  Pluckley TN26.......234 A1
  Rochester ME1......63 C5
  Sevenoaks TN13.....153 D5
  Shepherdswell CT15..244 D5
Terry's La CT5........74 D2
Terry's Lodge Rd TN15..124 C6
Terry Wlk TN9........127 E2
Testers Cl RH8......183 B3
TESTON.............193 A8
Teston Ho ME18.......193 A7
Teston La ME15, ME18..193 C7
Teston Rd
  Kings Hill ME19....159 B5
  Offham ME19........158 C7
  Red Hill ME18......159 E2
  West Malling ME19..159 A6
Tetley Mews TN2.....286 D4
Tetty Way BR1, BR2...52 A7
Teviot Cl DA16.......13 B6
Tewson Rd SE18.......2 E1
TEYNHAM............103 C3
Teynham Cl CT9.......51 F2
Teynham Dr CT5.......74 F2
Teynham Gn
  Gillingham ME8......65 A4
  Hayes BR2..........52 A4
Teynham Ho SE9......12 D1
Teynham Parochial CE
  Prim Sch ME9.......103 C2
Teynham Rd
  Gillingham ME8......65 A4
  Whitstable CT5......74 F2
Teynham St ME9......103 F4
Teynham Sta ME9.....103 D3
Thackeray Ave RM18...19 B6
Thackeray Rd ME20...127 F3
Thames Ave
  Gillingham ME8......98 E8
  High Halstow ME23..23 E4
  Sheerness ME12......28 B1
Thamesbank Pl SE28...3 C7
Thames Barrier Pk ★ E16..1 C4
Thames Barrier The ★
  E16...............1 C4
Thames Barrier Visitor
  Ctr ★ SE18.........1 D3
Thames College of
  Technology 17 SE18..2 A2
Thames Ct ME12.......49 G2
Thames Gate DA1......16 A3
Thamesgate Sh Ctr 20
  DA11..............19 B1
Thameside Ind Est E16..1 D1
Thameside Inf & Jun Schs
  RM17..............18 C8
THAMESMEAD..........3 A5
Thamesmead Sh Ctr
  SE28..............3 A6
Thamesmere Dr SE28...3 A6
Thamesmere L Ctr SE28..3 A6
Thames Rd Crayford DA1..15 A4
  Grays RM17.........18 B7
  Newham E16.........1 D1
  Tonbridge TN10.....222 C5
Thames Road Ind Est
  E16...............1 D4
Thames Terr ME3......22 B6
Thamesview DA9.......17 C2
Thames View ME3......40 C7
Thames View Cotts
  ME3...............39 D3
Thames View Inf Sch
  ME8...............65 D2
Thames View Jun Sch
  ME8...............65 D2
Thamesview Sch DA12..37 F5
Thames Way
  Gravesend DA11......19 A1
  Northfleet DA11.....36 E7
Thanet Cl CT10........84 B5
Thanet Coll
  Broadstairs CT10....84 A3
  Margate CT9........50 I2
Thanet Dr BR2.......85 D7
Thanet Ent Ctr CT10..83 D7
Thanet Gdns CT19....335 F6
Thanet Ho
  7 Maidstone ME15..195 F5
  8 Northfleet DA11..36 F7
Thanet Place Gdns
  CT10..............84 B6
Thanet Rd
  Broadstairs CT10....84 B5
  Erith DA8..........14 E7

Thanet Rd continued
  Gillingham ME8......98 C4
  Margate CT9........50 J2
  Ramsgate CT11.....117 F7
  Sidcup DA5.........32 A8
  Westgate on Sea CT8..81 D8
Thanet Reach Bsns Pk
  CT10..............83 C4
Thanet Stars Sch of Dance
  & Drama CT9........50 I1
Thanet Terr TN26....267 A6
Thanet View
  Eythorne CT15......245 B8
  St Nicholas at Wade CT7..79 F2
Thanet Way
  Boughton Street
  ME13..............139 D6
  Herne Bay CT6......77 C3
  Whitstable CT5......75 C2
  Yorkletts CT5, ME13..107 E2
THANINGTON.........174 B6
Thanington Court Farm
  CT1...............174 C6
Thanington Ct CT1....12 E1
Thanington Rd CT1...174 C6
Thatch Barn Rd TN27..262 D6
Thatcher Ct DA1......33 D8
Thatcher Rd TN12....260 E4
Thatchers La ME4.....22 B5
Thatchers The ME16..161 B5
Thaxted Rd SE9.......30 C6
Theaker Ho DA4......57 D7
Theatre Royal ★ CT9..50 I1
Theatre Sq 7 TN30...345 A7
Theatre St CT21......333 C2
The Cut ME4..........63 F4
The Davenport Ctr
  CT12..............117 A8
Thelma Cl DA12.......37 F3
Thelma Gdns SE3......11 E6
The Marlowe Acad
  CT12..............83 A2
Theobalds TN18......340 F2
Theobalds Cl TN15...123 A1
Theodore Cl TN2.....286 E7
Theodore Pl ME7......64 C5
Theresa Rd CT21.....333 B1
Thicketts TN13.......154 C4
Third Ave Chatham ME5..64 C1
  Eastchurch ME12....48 F6
  Gillingham ME7......64 F4
  Margate CT9........51 B3
  West Thurrock RM20..17 A8
Third St TN3.........284 F3
Thirlemere Cl ME16..161 D8
Thirlmere TN24......268 D6
Thirlmere Ave CT11...117 A7
Thirlmere Cl
  Gillingham ME7......65 A5
  Rochester ME2......40 C1
Thirlmere Gdns CT3..210 F6
Thirlmere Rd
  Bexley DA7.........14 C6
  Royal Tunbridge Wells
  TN4...............285 E5
Thirsk Ho 6 ME15....195 F5
Thirza Rd DA1........15 F1
Thistlebank ME5......97 A3
Thistlebrook SE2......3 C4
Thistlebrook Ind Est SE2..3 C4
Thistle Ct DA1.......34 B7
Thistledown Deal CT14..248 B8
  Gravesend DA12......37 D2
  Maidstone ME14.....162 F4
Thistledown Cl ME7...98 A4
Thistle Dr CT5.......108 B6
Thistlefield Cl DA5...31 D7
Thistle Hill Way ME12..47 A4
Thistlemead BR7......53 B7
Thistle Rd DA12......37 E8
Thistle Wlk ME10....102 B5
Thistlewell Rd
  ME1...............96 C8
Thomas Cl TN23......300 A6
Thomas Cotts DA13....36 B1
Thomas Cribb Mews E6..2 A7
Thomas Ct 9 ME10....102 B4
Thomas Dinwiddy Rd
  SE12..............29 B6
Thomas Dr DA12.......37 D6
Thomas Dunk Almshouses
  13 TN18...........341 A2
Thomas Harris Cl ME2..95 B4
Thomas Rd
  Faversham ME13.....138 D7
  Sittingbourne ME10..102 B4
Thomas Rider Way
  ME15..............195 E4
Thomas Seth Bsns Pk
  ME11..............46 A3
Thomas Shearley Ct
  DA5...............32 B8
Thomas St
  Rochester ME1......63 C3
  Royal Tunbridge Wells
  TN4...............286 A5
  Woolwich SE18......2 B2
Thomas Tallis Sch SE3..11 B4
Thomas Way CT3......112 A1
Thomas Wyatt Way 2
  TN15..............124 F3
Thompson Cl
  Deal CT14..........248 B8
  Folkestone CT19....335 B7
  Gillingham ME8......99 A8
Thomson Cl ME6......95 A1
Thomson Rd TN25....268 B5
THONG..............38 A2
Thong La Basted TN15..156 F5
  Gravesend DA12......38 A8
Thornbridge Rd CT14..215 B2
Thorn Cl Bromley BR2..53 A3
Thorndale BR7........29 F1

Thorndale Cl ME5......96 D4
Thornden Cl CT6......76 B2
Thornden Ct
  Canterbury CT2.....142 C4
  Rolvenden Layne TN17..358 A8
Thornden La
  Rolvenden Layne
  TN17..............358 A8
  Rolvenden TN17.....344 A1
Thornden Wood Rd
  Herne Bay CT6......76 B1
  Whitstable CT6.....109 E4
Thorndike Ho ME4.....96 F8
Thorndike Rd TN29...352 D4
Thorndon Cl BR5......53 F7
Thorndon Rd BR5......53 F7
Thorndyke Way 1
  TN15..............124 F3
Thorne Cl Erith DA8...14 B8
  Newham E16.........1 A7
Thorne Hill CT12.....116 A6
Thorne Rd CT12......115 B6
Thorn Est The TN27...265 B6
Thornet Wood Rd BR1..53 A6
Thorneycroft ME17...197 D2
Thorneycroft Rd ME13..201 D5
Thornfield Gdns TN2..286 F5
Thorn Gdns CT11......83 E1
Thornham Rd ME8......65 C3
Thornhill Ave SE18...12 E7
Thornhill Pl ME14....162 A6
Thorn Hill Rd ME12...49 D4
Thornhurst CT6.......77 D4
Thorn La CT4.........240 C2
Thornlea TN23........267 E2
Thorn Rd TN12.......259 E4
Thorn's Mdw TN16....152 C4
Thornton Cl TN24....269 A1
Thornton Dene DA4...31 A3
Thornton La CT13,
  CT14..............212 E7
Thornton Rd
  Bromley BR1........29 A3
  Erith DA17.........4 B2
Thornton's La 9 CT6..310 E7
Thorntree Prim Sch SE7..1 D1
Thorntree Rd SE7......1 D1
Thorn Wlk ME10......102 C5
Thorold Rd ME5.......64 B3
Thorpe Ave TN10.....222 C5
Thorpe Cl BR6........86 E8
Thorpe Wlk ME8......98 D3
Thrale Way ME8......98 E4
Thread La ME13.......140 B4
Three Acres Site CT19..335 B8
THREE CHIMNEYS......294 B2
Three Corners DA7....14 B5
Three Elm La TN11...223 D5
Three Gates Rd DA3...58 A2
Three King's Yd CT13..149 A1
THREE LEG CROSS....338 D3
Three Leg Cross Rd
  TN5...............338 D3
Three Oaks La TN5....336 D7
Thresher Field TN8...251 A6
Threshers Dr ME14....162 E5
Thrift La TN14.......119 E2
Thrift The DA2........35 C5
Throckmorten Rd E16..1 A5
THROWLEY...........169 E4
Throwley Cl SE2.......3 C3
Throwley Dr CT6.......76 C4
THROWLEY FORSTAL 169 D1
Throwley Rd ME13....169 D5
Thrupp Paddock CT10..51 G1
Thrush Cl ME5........97 B7
Thruxted La CT4.....173 B1
Thunderer Rd RM9.....3 F8
Thundersland Rd CT6..77 B4
Thurlow Ave CT6......77 C5
THURNHAM...........163 D8
Thurnham CE Inf Sch
  ME14..............163 A4
Thurnham Ho 5 BR5...54 D1
Thurnham La ME14....163 C7
Thurrock Bsns Ctr
  RM20..............16 F8
Thurrock Ent Ctr RM18..18 A8
Thurrock Park Way
  RM17..............18 D7
Thursland Rd DA14....31 E3
Thursley Rd SE9......29 F5
Thurston Dr ME2......62 D7
Thurstone Ct ME14...161 F6
Thurston Pk CT5......74 E1
Thwaite Cl DA8.......14 C8
Thyer Cl BR6.........86 C6
Thyme Cl SE3.........11 C4
Thyme Wlk ME14......161 C8
Tibbs Court La TN12..289 A6
Tiber Cl CT19.......334 C6
TICEHURST..........338 E2
Ticehurst Cl BR5......31 A1
Tichborne Cl ME16...161 C6
TICKENHURST........179 D1
Tickford Cl SE2.......3 C4
TICKHAM............136 D6
Tickham La ME9......136 D5
Tickner's La CT7.....363 B1
Tidal Basin Rd E16....1 A6
Tidebrook Ct 4 BR5..54 C5
Tidelock Ho SE28......2 D4
Tideside Ct SE18......1 E3
Tideway The ME1......96 C8
Tidford Rd DA16......12 F5
Tiger La BR2.........52 A4
Tilbrook Rd SE3......11 D4
TILBURY............19 B4
Tilbury Cl BR5.......54 B7
Tilbury Fort ★ RM18..19 C3
Tilbury L Ctr RM18...19 B5

Tilbury Manor Inf Sch
  RM18..............19 B7
Tilbury Manor Jun Sch
  RM18..............19 B7
Tilbury PRU RM18.....18 F6
Tilbury Rd ME8.......66 A2
Tilbury Town Sta RM18..18 F5
Tilden Cl TN26......324 D7
Tilden Ct TN26......324 E7
Tilden Gill Rd TN30..345 C7
Tilden La TN12......227 C3
Tilden Rd ME17, TN27..230 E2
Tilebarn Cnr TN10...222 E4
Tile Farm Rd BR6.....86 D7
Tile Fields ME17.....164 D2
Tile Fields Cl ME17..164 D2
Tile Ho The CT21.....333 C2
Tilehurst Point 2 SE2..3 C4
Tile Kiln Hill CT2....142 B5
Tile Kiln La
  Coldblow DA5.......32 C6
  Dartford DA2, DA5..32 F5
  Folkestone CT19....334 F7
Tile Kiln Rd TN24....268 C7
Tile Lodge Cotts TN27..233 E8
Tile Lodge Rd TN27...233 E8
Tilghman Way ME16...95 B1
Tillard Cl CT4.......207 B3
Till Ave DA4.........56 F2
Tillery La TN29......371 A8
Tilley Cl ME3........41 D5
Tillingbourne Gn BR5..54 A5
Tilmans ME5.........157 A7
Tilmans Mead DA4....57 A2
TILMANSTONE........213 A3
Tilsden La TN17......320 E3
Tilton Rd TN15......156 F7
Tilt Yard App SE9....11 F1
Timberbank ME5......97 A6
Timber Bank DA13...125 F8
Timber Cl BR7........53 A7
Timbercroft La SE18..12 E7
Timbercroft Prim Sch
  SE18..............12 E7
Timber Ct RM17......18 A8
TIMBERDEN BOTTOM..55 D1
Timbertop Rd TN16...118 C1
Timber Tops ME5 130 D8
Timeball Tower Mus ★
  CT14..............215 D5
Timms Ct BR1........52 F5
Timothy Cl DA6......13 E3
Timothy Ho DA18......3 E4
Timperley Cl CT14...215 B6
Tina Gdns CT10......84 A6
Tinbridge Pk ME13...139 A5
Tinker Pot La TN15..123 D6
Tinkerpot Rise TN15..123 C5
Tinker's Alley ME4...63 F7
Tinkers La TN5.......338 E3
Tintagel Gdns ME2....62 C1
Tintagel Manor 6 ME7 64 C6
Tintagel Rd BR5......54 C1
Tintern Rd ME16.....161 D7
Tippens Ct TN17.....320 D4
Titan Rd RM17.......18 B8
Titchfield Cl 5 ME15..195 F6
Titchfield Rd ME15...195 F6
Tithe Barn La TN23..299 D8
Tithe Yd ME17.......199 D5
Titmuss Ave SE28......3 C5
TITSEY.............150 B2
Titsey Cnr RH8......183 B7
Titsey Hill CR6, RH8..150 B4
Titsey Pl ★ RH8......150 B3
Titsey Rd
  Limpsfield RH8.....183 B8
  Titsey RH8.........150 B1
Tiverton Dr SE9......30 C4
Tivoli Brooks CT9.....50 I1
Tivoli Gdns
  Gravesend DA12......37 B7
  Woolwich SE18......1 E2
Tivoli Park Ave CT9..50 H1
Tivoli Rd CT9........82 E8
Toad Hall Cres ME3...41 A4
Tobruk Way ME5......96 F6
Toby Gdns TN11.....223 E8
Toby Rd TN29.......377 E6
Tockwith Ct TN13....154 D4
Todd Cres ME10......102 A8
Toddington Cres ME5..96 D1
Toke Cl TN23........267 C1
Toke Pl ME17........227 E8
Tolcairn Ct 2 DA17...4 A1
Tolgate Ct 2 ME2.....63 B7
Tolgate Way ME14....129 E4
Tolhurst Rd TN12....256 A7
Tollemache Cl CT12..81 F2
TOLLGATE...........157 A8
Toll Gate CT14.......215 A4
Tollgate Cl CT5......108 C3
Tollgate Mews TN15..157 A8
Tollgate Pl TN27.....262 E5
Tollgate Rd
  Dartford DA2........34 D8
  Newham E6.........1 E8
Toll La TN27.........234 E7
Tolputt Ct CT19.....335 C6
Tolsey Mead TN15....157 A8
Tolsford Cl
  Etchinghill CT18....305 D3
  Folkestone CT19....334 F6
Tomay Cotts CT6......78 A3
Tom Cribb Rd SE28....2 D3
Tom Jenkinson Rd E16..1 A5
Tom Joyce Cl ME6....127 F7
Tomlin Cl
  Snodland ME6......128 A8
  Staplehurst TN12...260 E4
Tomlin Dr CT9........83 C8
TONBRIDGE..........222 A2

Tonbridge By-Pass
  Tonbridge, Stocks Green
  TN11, TN9, TN4, TN14,
  TN15..............221 B5
  Tonbridge TN4, TN9,
  TN11..............254 C6
Tonbridge Castle ★
  TN9...............222 B2
Tonbridge Chambers 10
  TN9...............254 B8
Tonbridge Cottage Hospl
  TN11..............254 C6
Tonbridge Ct ME16...161 D3
Tonbridge Gram Sch
  TN9...............254 C7
Tonbridge Ho ME2.....40 C1
Tonbridge Rd
  Hadlow TN11........223 C7
  Ightham TN15......156 C3
  Little Mill TN11, TN12..224 D4
  Maidstone, East Barming
  ME16..............160 E1
  Maidstone, Upper Fant
  ME16..............161 C3
  Pembury TN2........287 A7
  Sevenoaks TN13, TN15..187 D7
  Tonbridge TN11.....221 E5
  Wateringbury ME18..192 C8
Tonbridge Sch TN10..222 C3
Tonbridge Sta TN9....222 B1
Tonbridge Swim Pool
  TN9...............222 B2
Tonford La
  Canterbury CT1.....174 B6
  Harbledown CT1.....174 A7
TONGE CORNER.......102 F7
Tonge Rd ME10......102 C4
TONG GREEN.........169 B1
Tong La TN12........289 B2
Tong Rd TN12, TN3...289 A4
Tongswood Dr TN18...341 C1
Tontine St CT20......335 E5
Tony Law Ho SE12....11 A2
Tookey Rd TN28......373 B6
Tooley St DA11.......36 D8
Topaz Dr ME10.......101 C6
Topcliffe Dr BR6......86 D6
Top Dartford Rd BR8,
  DA2...............33 A2
Topley Dr ME23......23 E3
Topley St SE9........11 D3
Top Rd TN30.........360 E3
Torbay Rd TN12......225 B6
Torbrook Cl DA5......13 E1
Tor Gr SE28..........2 E5
Tormore Mews CT14..215 A4
Tormore Pk CT14.....215 A4
Tormount Rd SE18....12 E8
Toronto Cl 6 CT16...278 B3
Toronto Rd
  Gillingham ME7......64 C4
  Tilbury RM18........19 A5
Tor Rd DA16.........13 C6
Torrens Wlk DA12.....37 E3
Torrington Cl ME15..191 D8
Torrington Cotts CT12 115 D7
Torrington Rd TN23..300 C8
Torver Way BR6.......86 D7
Tothill St CT12.......115 C7
Totnes Rd DA16......13 C7
Tourmaline Dr ME10..101 C6
Tournay Cl TN23.....299 F8
Tourney Cl CT21.....331 F3
Tourney Rd TN29.....376 C5
Tourtel Rd CT1......143 A1
Tovey Sq ME7........64 F6
TOVIL..............161 E1
Tovil Gn ME15.......161 E2
Tovil Green Bsns Pk
  ME15..............161 E1
Tovil Hill ME15......161 E1
Tovil Rd ME15.......161 F2
Tovil Sch ME15......161 D2
Tower Bglws CT7.....81 A8
Tower Ct
  Gravesend DA12......37 E3
  Orpington BR6......86 F7
Tower Croft DA4......89 E8
Tower Ct 4 CT20.....334 E3
Tower Est TN29......352 E2
Towerfields BR2......85 E6
Tower Gdns
  Hythe CT21.........333 C1
  Maidstone ME14.....163 B4
TOWER HAMLETS.....310 B8
Tower Hamlets Rd
  CT17..............310 C8
Tower Hamlets St 1
  CT17..............310 C8
Tower Hill Dover CT17..310 C8
  Offham ME19.......158 D7
  Whitstable CT5......74 E3
Tower Ind Est TN15..124 D5
Tower La ME14.......163 B4
Tower Par CT5........74 E3
Tower Park Rd DA1...14 F2
Tower Rd Bexley DA7..14 A3
  Dartford DA1.......15 C1
  Erith DA17.........4 C2
  Orpington BR6......86 F7
  Whitstable CT5......74 E2
Tower Ret Pk DA1....14 F2
Towers Point ME1.....63 B4
Towers Sch The TN24..268 B8
Tower St CT17.......310 C8
Towers The TN27.....201 E1
Towers View TN24....268 C7
Towers Wood DA4.....57 D8
Tower View
  Chartham CT4......173 F1
  Kings Hill ME19....159 B3
Tower Way 1 CT1....174 F8
Town Acres TN10.....222 C4

Towncourt Cres BR5 ...53 D5
Towncourt La BR5....53 D2
Townfield Cnr DA12 ....37 D7
Towngate Wood Park
Mobile Home Pk
TN10 ....222 E7
Town Hill Bridge CT4 ..175 F2
Lamberhurst TN3 ...317 A4
West Malling ME19...127 C1
Town Hill ME19 .....127 C1
Town La CT4 ....173 C6
Townland Cl TN27....295 A2
TOWNLAND GREEN. 326 A1
Townlands Rd TN5 ...336 F4
Townley Gram Sch for
Girls DA6 ....13 F2
Townley Rd DA6......13 F2
Townley St CT11 .....174 D6
Town Lock Ho 4 TN9 222 C2
Town Mdw TN17 .....320 D4
Town Pier Sq 5 DA11 .19 B1
Town Rd
Cliffe Woods ME3.....40 A6
Petham CT4 ....207 C5
Townsend Farm Rd
CT15 ....279 F6
Townsend Rd ME6....127 F8
Townsend Sq ME19...159 A2
Townsend Terr CT17 .310 B5
Townshend Ho 14 SE18.. 1 F2
Townshend Rd BR7....30 B3
Town Sq DA8.........14 C8
Town Square Cres DA9 34 F8
Town Station Cotts
TN8 ....217 D1
Townwall St CT16 ....310 E7
Town Wlk CT20......335 D4
Toynbec Cl BR7 ......30 B4
TOY'S HILL 185 C3
Toy's Hill TN16, TN8...185 C3
Tracies The ME9 .....100 C6
Trader Rd E6 ....2 B7
Tradescant Dr DA13 ...60 B8
Tradewinds CT5.......108 B6
Trafalgar Dr CT14 ....215 D4
Trafalgar Par ME12....47 B6
Trafalgar Rd
Dartford DA1 ....33 E6
Gravesend DA11.......37 A8
Westgate on Sea CT7...81 F3
Wouldham ME1........95 C5
Trafalgar St ME7 .....64 C5
Tram Rd The CT20....335 E5
Tramways ME5........64 C2
Tranquil Rise DA8 ......4 E1
Transfesa Rd TN12 ..257 A7
Transformer Ave TN29 380 C2
Transmere Cl BR5....53 C3
Transmere Rd BR5....53 C3
Transom Ho 3 ME1...63 C5
Trapfield Cl ME14 ...163 C4
Trapfield La ME14 ...163 C4
Trapham Rd ME16....161 D5
Trasa Ct 10 RM17 .....18 C8
Travers Gdns ME9...133 F5
Travers Rd CT14.....215 A5
Travertine Rd ME5....97 B1
Treasury View CT3 ..177 C8
Trebble Rd DA10 .....17 E1
Trebilco CT17 ....286 D7
Tredegar Rd DA2.....33 A5
Tredwell Cl BR1......52 E5
Treebourne Rd TN16 118 C1
Tree La TN15 ....189 E8
Tree Rd E16..........1 C7
Treetops
Gravesend DA12......37 B4
Kemsing TN15.......123 A2
Tonbridge TN9.......254 B7
Treetops Cl SE2 ......3 E1
Treewall Gdns BR1....29 B4
Trefoil Ho Erith DA18...3 E4
Grays RM17 ....18 B7
Trefoil The ME9, ME13 .136 E6
Trefor Jones Ct CT16 ..278 B2
Tregony Rd BR6......86 F6
Trelawn Cres ME5....97 B2
Trellyn Cl ME16 .....160 F2
Trench Rd TN10 .....222 C6
TRENCH WOOD 222 B6
Trenear Cl BR6.......87 A6
Trenley Dr CT3 ......143 F1
Trentham Dr BR5....54 A5
Trenton Cl ME16 ....161 B7
Trent Rd ME5........97 B5
Trevale Rd ME1 ......63 B1
Trevelyan Cl DA1.....15 F3
Trevereux Hill RH8...183 F4
Trevino Dr ME5 ......96 F2
Trevithick Dr DA1 ...15 F3
Trevor Cl BR2........52 A2
Trevor Dr ME16 .....161 C5
Trewin Cl ME20 .....128 D2
Trewsbury Ho 2 SE2....3 D4
Triangle Ct E16 ....1 C8
Triangle The DA15....31 A8
Tribune Ct ME12 .....46 B8
Tribune Dr ME10....101 F6
Tricorn Ho SE28 ......2 E7
Trident Cl ME2.......63 E7
Triggs Cotts ME9 ....103 D2
Trigg's Row ME9.....103 D2
Trilby Way CT5.......108 B8
Trimworth Rd CT19...334 F6
Trinity Cl Orpington BR2 .52 E1
Royal Tunbridge Wells
TN2 ....286 D4
Trinity Cres CT20....335 B4
Trinity Ct Dartford DA1 ..34 B7
Deal CT14 ....215 A4
Eltham SE9 ....12 B1
Forstal ME20........129 A3
Margate CT9..........50 J3

Trinity Gdns
Dartford DA1 ....15 D1
Folkestone CT20.....335 C4
Trinity Hill CT9.......50 J3
Trinity Homes CT14 .215 C1
Trinity Mews SE9....12 D1
Trinity Pl Bexley DA6...13 F3
Deal CT14 ....215 A4
Ramsgate CT11 .....117 F7
Trinity Rd Ashford TN24 268 B7
Folkestone CT20.....335 B4
Gillingham ME7......64 C6
Gravesend DA12......37 C8
Sheerness ME12......28 C2
Sittingbourne ME10...101 F7
Trinity Sch ME1......63 D4
Trinity Sch, Belvedere
DA17 ....4 C2
Trinity Sq
Broadstairs CT10 ....83 F7
Margate CT9..........50 J3
Trinity St 12 E16.....1 A8
Trinity Theatre & Arts Ctr★
5 TN1 ....286 A4
Trinity Trad Est ME10 .101 F6
Trinity Way ME12.....28 C2
Tristan Gdns TN4....285 F6
Tristram Way CT16...278 B5
Triton Lodge 9 DA8 ...4 E1
Tritton Fields TN24...268 F7
Tritton Gdns TN29...352 D1
Tritton La TN28......373 B6
Triumph Rd E6.......1 F7
Trivett Cl DA9........117 C2
Trolling Down Hill DA2 34 C6
Trona Ct 7 ME10....101 D6
Troodos Hill ME14...161 F8
Troon Cl SE28........3 D7
Trosley Ave DA11....37 B6
Trosley Ctry Pk★ ME19,
DA13 ....126 A7
Trosley Ctry Pk Visitor
Ctr★ DA13.........125 E7
Trosley Rd DA17.....14 A8
TROTTISCLIFFE 126 A5
Trottiscliffe CE Prim Sch
ME9 ....134 C8
Trottiscliffe Rd ME19 .126 D3
Trotts Hall Gdns ME10 101 F3
Trotts La TN16 ......184 C8
Trotwood Cl ME5.....130 A8
Trotwood Pl 14 CT10 ..84 B4
Troubridge Mews CT9..50 H1
Troughton Mews CT9...50 H1
Troughton Rd SE7.....1 B1
Troutbeck Ho ME20 .128 C1
Trove Ct 7 CT11 .....117 F7
Troy Ct 6 SE18 ......2 B2
Troy La TN8..........216 F4
Troy Mews ME1......63 C4
Troys Mead ME17 ...164 D2
TROY TOWN Brook ..270 B5
Edenbridge 216 F5
Rochester 63 C5
Troy Town La TN25...270 B5
Trubridge Rd ME3.....41 E5
Trueman Ct CT2.....142 A7
Trumpet Ho TN3......300 B8
Trunley Way CT18...306 F3
Truro Cl ME8.........65 D3
Truro Rd
Gravesend DA12......37 D5
Ramsgate CT11 .....117 F7
Truro Wlk TN10 .....222 D5
Trusedale Rd E6 ......1 F7
Trycewell La TN15...156 D6
Tuam Rd SE18 ....12 D8
Tubbenden Cl BR6....86 E7
Tubbenden Dr BR6....86 D6
Tubbenden Inf & Jun Sch
BR6................86 D6
Tubbenden La BR6....86 E7
Tubbenden Lane S BR6 86 D5
Tubs Hill TN13 ......154 B3
Tubs Hill Par TN13 ..154 A3
TUDELEY............255 B7
TUDELEY HALE 223 C1
Tudeley La
Tonbridge TN9.......254 D7
Tonbridge, Tudeley TN11,
TN9 ....255 B8
Tudeley Woods Nature
Reserve★ TN11 ....255 B4
Tudor Ave
Dymchurch TN29.....352 D1
Maidstone ME14......162 B6
Tudor Byway TN24 ..268 D6
Tudor Cl Birchington CT7 81 B8
Bromley BR7.........52 F8
Dartford DA1 ....15 B1
Northfleet DA11......36 E7
Tudor Cres TN14....122 D3
Tudor Ct
Biggin Hill TN16 ....118 E2
Canterbury CT2 .....142 C4
Crockenhill BR8......55 C2
Royal Tunbridge Wells
TN2 ....285 E1
Sidcup DA14 ....31 A5
Whitstable CT5......75 A3
Tudor Dr TN24 ......122 C3
Tudor End TN24.....268 D5
Tudor Farm Ct TN23...300 A3
Tudor Gr Chattenden ME3 40 F4
Gillingham ME8......98 F8
Tudor Ho CT14 .....215 A5
Tudor Ho★ CT9 .....50 J3
Tudor Mews CT14 ...215 B4
Tudor Par SE9 ....11 E3
Tudor Rd Ashford TN24 268 D5
Canterbury CT1 .....174 E7
Folkestone CT19.....334 D6
Tudor Way BR5......53 D3

Tudor Wlk DA5 ....13 E1
Tudway Rd SE3.......11 C3
Tufa Cl ME5..........97 B1
Tuffs Cotts ME3......25 C3
Tufnail Rd DA1.......15 F1
Tufton Rd
Ashford TN24 ....268 D2
Gillingham ME8......65 F1
Hothfield TN26......267 A7
Tufton St Ashford TN24 268 B7
Maidstone ME14......162 A4
Tufton Wlk 9 TN23 ..268 B2
Tugboat St SE28......2 E4
Tugmutton Cl BR6....86 B6
Tulip Cl 5 E6.........1 F8
Tulip Tree Cl TN9 ...254 E8
Tumblefield Hill TN25 235 F4
Tumblefield Est TN15..124 D7
Tumblefield Rd TN15..124 D7
Tumblers Hill ME3....35 A7
Tunbridge Way TN23 .299 C8
Tunbridge Wells Girls'
Gram Sch TN4......286 A6
Tunbridge Wells Gram Sch
for Boys TN4.......286 A7
Tunbridge Wells High Sch
TN2................286 A5
Tunbridge Wells Mus & Art
Gall★ TN1 ....286 B4
Tunbridge Wells Nuffield
Hospital The TN2....286 D3
Tunbridge Wells Sta
TN1................286 B3
Tunbridge Wells Trad Pk
TN2................286 D8
Tunbridge Wells West
Sta★ TN2 ....285 F1
Tunbury Ave ME5 ....96 F1
Tunbury Avenue S ME5 96 F1
Tunbury Prim Sch ME5 .96 F1
Tunis Ct CT1 ....143 D1
Tunis Row CT10 .....84 B5
Tunnan Leys E6 ......2 A7
Tunnel Ave 1 SE10....1 A1
Tunnel Cotts RM20 ...17 A8
Tunnel Est RM20.....16 F8
Tunnel Rd TN1.......286 B4
TUNSTALL 134 D8
Tunstall CE Prim Sch
ME9 ....134 C8
Tunstall Cl BR6.......86 C6
Tunstall Rd
Canterbury CT2.....143 A4
Sittingbourne ME10,
ME9 ....134 D8
Tunstock Way ME1 ....3 E3
Tupman Ct ME1......63 B4
Tuppy St SE28........2 F4
Turbine Hall Ave TN29 380 C2
Turgis Cl ME17 ......196 E4
Turketel Rd CT20 ....335 A4
Turks Hall Pl ME2....94 E5
Turley Cotts TN3 ....285 A8
Turmine Ct ME12.....47 A5
Turnagain La 3 CT1 .174 F8
Turnberry Way BR6 ...53 D1
Turnbull Cl DA9......34 E8
Turnbury Cl SE28......3 D7
TURNDEN............320 B4
Turnden Gdns CT9 ...51 E2
Turnden Rd TN17....320 A3
Turner Ave TN17....320 A3
Turner Cl Ashford TN24 268 D7
Biggin Hill TN16 ....118 C7
Sittingbourne ME10...102 A7
Turner Ct Dartford DA1 ..15 C2
5 Folkestone CT20...334 F5
Margate CT9..........51 A2
Turner Ho
Gravesend DA12......37 C6
5 Greenwich SE7....11 B8
Turner Rd Bean DA2 ..35 B5
Tonbridge TN10......222 E5
Turners Ave TN30 ...345 B8
Turners Cl ME12.....28 C1
Turners Gdns TN15 .187 C7
Turners Green La TN5 336 F6
Turners Green Rd TN5 336 F6
Turner's Oak DA3 ....91 E7
Turners Pl ME4......57 C8
Turner St Cliffe ME3....22 B5
Ramsgate CT11 .....117 E7
Turnpike Cl CT21 ....333 A2
Turnpike Ct DA6 ......13 D3
Turnpike Dr BR6 .....87 D2
Turnpike Hill CT21 ..333 A3
Turnpike La RM18.....19 D8
Turnstone DA3 ....59 A7
Turnstone Cl ME9 ....68 E4
Turnstone Ct TN29 ..365 F3
Turnstone Rd ME5....97 C1
Turnstones The DA12..37 B6
Turpington Cl BR2....52 E2
Turpington La BR2....52 E3
Turpin La DA8........15 A8
Turrets The Deal CT14..215 D6
9 Sittingbourne ME10 102 A4
Turton Ho 5 SE18....12 B8
Tuscan Dr ME5.......97 C1
Tuscan Rd SE18......2 D1
Tutsham Ct TN24 ...268 C5
Tutsham Way TN12..256 F6
TUTT HILL...........235 A1
Tuxford Rd TN4......285 B5
Tweed Rd TN10 .....222 C5
Tweed Terr CT21....333 A1
Tweedy Rd BR1......52 A8
Twelve Acres ME4...300 F8
Twigg Cl DA8........14 E7
Twin Tumps Way SE28...3 A6
Twisden Rd ME19 ...159 F8
Twiss Ave CT21......333 D1
Twiss Gr CT21.......333 D1

Twiss Ho 6 SE18......2 B1
Twiss Rd CT21.......333 D2
Twistleton Ct 7 DA1..15 D1
TWITHAM............178 E6
TWITTON............121 E4
Twitton La TN14.....121 E3
Twitton Mdws TN14..121 E3
Two Gates Hill ME3...39 F5
TWYDALL.............65 B2
Twydall Ent Ctr ME8 ..65 C4
Twydall Gn ME8......65 B2
Twydall Inf Sch ME8 ..65 B2
Twydall Jun Sch ME8..65 B2
Twyford Cl ME8......66 A2
Twyford Rd ME14 ...162 D6
Twyford Rd TN11....190 E1
Twymans Mill ME13 ..138 C7
Twysden Cotts TN18...356 A4
Twysden Ct TN25....237 E2
Tydeman Rd ME15...162 F2
Tydeman's Ave CT15..75 C1
Tye La Hawkinge CT18..307 A5
Orpington BR6.......86 C5
Tyeshurst Cl SE2......3 E1
Tyland Barn Wildlife
Park★ ME14 ....129 E3
Tyland La ME14......129 F3
TYLDEN.............295 E7
Tyler Cl Canterbury CT2 142 F3
1 East Malling ME19 .159 F8
Erith DA8...........14 B7
Tyler Dr ME8.........98 E4
Tyler Gr DA1.........15 F3
TYLER HILL..........142 E6
Tyler Hill Rd CT2 ....142 E6
Tylers Green Rd BR8..55 C2
Tyler Way CT5........75 E3
Tylney Rd BR1.......52 D7
Tyndale Pk CT6......77 B5
Tyndall Rd DA16......12 F4
Tyne Cl ME5..........97 C5
Tynedale Cl DA2 .....34 D7
Tynemouth Cl E6......2 B7
Tynemouth Rd SE18 ...2 E1
Tyne Rd TN10 ....222 B5
Typhoon Rd ME19 ...158 F8
Tyron Way DA14......30 F3
Tyrrell Ave DA16.....13 B2
Tyrrells Hall Cl 5
RM17..............18 D8
Tyrwhitt-Drake Mus of
Carriages★ 9 ME15 162 A3
Tysoe Ct TN22.......47 A5
Tyson Ave CT9.......50 E1
Tyson Rd CT19......335 E7

U

Uckfield La TN8 .....250 D4
Udall Cotts DA15.....30 E5
Uden Rd TN29.......353 B4
Uffington Ct CT3 ....178 A2
Ufton Cl ME15.......162 E1
Ufton La ME10.......101 E3
ULCOMBE...........230 F7
Ulcombe CE Prim Sch
ME17 ....230 F6
Ulcombe Gdns CT2 ..143 A3
Ulcombe Hill ME17 ..197 F1
Ulcombe Rd
Headcorn ME17.....262 C6
Langley Heath ME17...196 E3
Ulley Rd TN24.......268 E7
Ullswater Gdns CT3 .210 F6
Ullswater Ho ME15 .195 E7
Ulster Rd CT9........82 F8
Undercliff CT20 .....334 A3
Undercliffe Rd CT14..248 D5
UNDERDOWN........206 B8
Underdown Ave ME4...63 F1
Underdown La CT6....76 F2
Underdown Rd
Dover CT17..........310 B7
Herne Bay CT6.......76 F5
Underhill Cotts CT18 .334 B8
Underhill Rd CT20....334 B5
UNDERLING GREEN ..227 F2
Underlyn Ind Est TN12 227 F2
Underlyn La TN12 ...227 D1
UNDERRIVER........188 A5
Underriver House Rd
TN15 ....188 D5
Underwood
Hawkinge CT18......307 C6
Offham ME19 ....158 D7
Underwood Cl
Ashford TN24 ....268 D6
Canterbury CT4......175 B5
Maidstone ME15.....161 F2
Underwood Ct 11 TN5 336 F6
Underwood Rise TN27 285 F1
Underwood The SE9....29 F6
Unicorn Cotts CT4....176 B5
Unicorn Wlk DA9.....16 F2
Unicumes La ME16 ..161 C2
Union Cres CT9........50 J2
Union Mill The★ TN17 320 D4
Union Pk ME15......195 F4
Union Pl
4 Canterbury CT1...143 A1
Chatham ME4........64 A4
Union Rd Bridge CT4 .175 F1
Bromley BR2.........52 C8
Deal CT14 ....215 D6
Minster (Sheppey) ME12 .47 C7
Ramsgate CT11 .....117 F8
Union Row CT9.......50 J2
Union Sq
3 Broadstairs CT10 ..84 B4

Union Sq continued
22 Royal Tunbridge Wells
TN2 ....286 A2
Union St
Canterbury CT1......143 A1
Chatham ME4........64 A3
Dover CT17..........310 D6
Faversham ME13 ....138 C7
Flimwell TN5........339 B3
Maidstone ME14.....162 A5
Rochester ME1......63 C5
Sheerness ME12......28 A2
UNION STREET......339 B3
Unity Cl ME19........28 D2
Unity Pl 3 CT11.....117 F7
Unity St Sheerness ME12 28 D2
Sittingbourne ME10...101 E3
Unity Way SE18 ......1 D3
Univ Centre Folkestone 23
CT20...............335 D5
University Gdns DA5...31 F8
University Pl DA8......14 C7
University Rd CT2 ...142 D3
University Way
Dartford DA1 ....15 E4
Woolwich SE18......2 B6
Univ for the Creative Arts
at Canterbury CT1...175 B7
Univ for the Creative Arts
at Maidstone ME16..161 C3
Univ for the Creative Arts
at Rochester ME1....63 E4
Univ of East London E16 .2 A6
Univ of Greenwich Avery
Hill Campus (Mansion
Site) SE9...........12 C1
Univ of Greenwich Avery
Hill Campus (Southwood
Site) SE9...........30 D8
Univ of Greenwich The
ME4...............64 B8
Univ of Kent (Canterbury)
CT2................142 D4
Univ of Kent (Universities
at Medway Campus)
ME4...............64 B8
Unwin Cl ME20 .....129 A3
Upbury Way ME4.....64 A4
Upchat Rd ME2, ME3 ...40 F3
Upchurch Wlk CT9 ...51 E2
Updale Rd DA14......30 F4
Updown Way CT4 ...173 F1
Uphill CT18..........307 B4
Upland Prim Sch DA7...13 F4
Upland Rd DA7......13 F4
Uplands Canterbury CT2 142 F4
Woolwich SE18......2 B1
Uplands Cl
Rochester ME2......62 D6
Sevenoaks TN13 ....153 F4
Uplands Com Coll TN5 337 A4
Uplands Rd BR6......54 B1
Uplands Way
Halfway Houses ME12 .46 C5
Sevenoaks TN13 ....153 F4
Uplees Cotts ME13...104 F5
Uplees Rd ME13.....105 A3
Upnor Castle★ ME2...40 F2
Upnor Ho ME15......195 E8
Upnor Rd ME2.......40 E2
Upper Abbey Rd DA17...4 A2
Upper Approach Rd
CT10...............10 C1
Upper Austin Lodge Farm
Cotts DA4...........89 C3
Upper Austin Lodge Rd
DA4................89 D4
Upper Ave DA13......59 E8
Upper Balcom Mews 5
CT9................21 E3
Upper Barn Hill ME15 .193 E3
Upper Brents ME13...138 D8
Upper Bridge St
Canterbury CT1......175 A8
Wye TN25 ....237 C2
Upper Britton Pl ME7...64 B5
UPPER BUSH.........61 E7
Upper Bush Rd ME2...61 E7
Upper Chantry La CT1 175 A7
Upper Church Hill DA9 .16 E2
Upper Corniche CT20 334 C5
Upper Cumberland Wlk
TN1................286 B1
Upper Dane Ct CT9 ...51 E1
Upper Dane Rd CT9...51 E1
UPPER DEAL.........215 B6
Upper Denmark Rd
TN23 ....300 B8
Upper Dr TN16 ......118 C1
Upper Dumpton Park Rd
CT11...............117 E8
Upper Dunstan Rd
TN4................286 B6
Upper East Rd ME4...64 B8
UPPER EYTHORNE ..245 C7
Upper Fans La ME9...68 C4
Upper Fant Rd ME16..161 D2
Upper Field Rd ME10..102 B5
Upper Free Down CT6 .77 B2
UPPER GOLDSTONE .147 C6
Upper Gore La CT13..180 A2
Upper Gore Ct CT13..180 A2
Upper Green La TN11 189 D5
Upper Green Rd TN11 189 D5
Upper Grosvenor Rd TN1,
TN4................286 B6
Upper Grove Rd DA17 ..13 B8
UPPER HALLING 94 C5
UPPER
HARBLEDOWN......141 F1
UPPER HARVEL......93 C3

UPPER HAYESDEN ..253 C6
Upper Haysden La TN11,
TN9 ....253 E6
Upper Holly Hill Rd DA17 4 B1
Upper Hunton Hill
ME15 ....194 A3
Upper Luton Rd ME5...64 C2
Upper Malthouse Hill
CT21 ....333 B2
Upper Maltings Pl CT7 .80 F7
Upper Mill
East Malling ME19 ...159 F7
Wateringbury ME18 ..192 D8
Upper Nellington TN3..285 B4
Upper Park Rd
Bromley BR1.........52 C8
Erith DA17..........4 B2
Upper Platts TN5.....338 F1
Upper Profit TN3 ....285 A3
Upper Queens Rd
TN24 ....268 B3
Upper Rd
Dover CT15, CT16...279 C2
Dover, Eastern Docks
CT16 ....310 G8
Maidstone ME15.....162 B2
UPPER
RODMERSHAM......135 C6
UPPER RUXLEY 32 A1
Upper Ruxley Cotts
DA14...............32 A1
Upper St Ann's Rd
ME13...............138 B6
Upper Sheridan Rd DA17 4 A2
Upper Spring La TN15 156 B5
Upper St
Hollingbourne ME17 .164 E3
Kingsdown CT14 ....248 D5
Leeds ME17 ....196 F5
Rusthall TN4 ....285 D4
Tilmanstone CT14....213 A3
Upper Stephens TN3 .285 A4
Upper Stone St ME15..162 A4
Upper Strand St CT13 149 A1
Upper Street S DA3 ...91 F8
Upper Tickham Cotts
ME9................136 D6
UPPER TOLHURST ..338 A2
Upperton Rd DA14....30 F3
UPPER UPNOR.......40 F1
Upper Vicarage Rd
TN24 ....268 D7
UPPER WALMER.....215 B3
Upper Wickham La
DA16...............13 B6
UPSTREET..........112 D3
Upstreet CT18........305 D3
UPTON...............83 F4
Upton Cl Bexley DA5...13 F1
Folkestone CT19.....335 A7
Upton Day Hospl DA6...13 E3
Upton Jun Sch CT10...83 F4
Upton Prim Sch DA6...13 F1
Upton Quarry TN3...284 F3
Upton Rd
Bexley DA5, DA6.....13 F2
Broadstairs CT10 ....83 F5
Woolwich SE18......12 C8
Upton Road S DA5....13 F1
Uptons TN27 ....262 C6
Upton Villas 4 DA6...13 E3
UPTON WOOD 244 E2
Upwood Rd SE12 ....11 A1
Uridge Cres TN10 ...222 C4
Uridge Rd TN10 ....222 C4
Urquhart Cl ME5.....97 A5
Ursula Lodges DA14...31 B3
Ursuline Coll CT8.....81 D8
Ursuline Dr CT8.....81 D7
Usborne Cl TN12 ....260 C3

V

Vaizeys Wharf SE7 ...1 B3
Vale Ave
Royal Tunbridge Wells,
Mount Sion TN1.....286 A3
Royal Tunbridge Wells,
Southborough TN4...253 F1
Valebrook Cl CT20....334 C5
Vale Cl BR6..........86 A6
Vale Cotts ME9.......133 A8
Vale Ct
10 Ramsgate CT11...117 D6
Royal Tunbridge Wells
TN4................254 A2
Vale Dr ME5.........96 E6
Valence Ho ME15....195 C7
Valence Rd DA8......14 D7
Valence Sch TN16...151 F1
Valence View TN17..293 E7
Valenciennes Ho ME4..64 A4
Valenciennes Rd ME10 101 C3
Valentine Ave DA5 ...31 E7
Valentine Cl ME7.....65 A1
Valentine Dr ME23 ...2 B8
Valentine Rd ME15...195 E7
Valentine Pl CT11 ...117 D6
Vale Rd Broadstairs CT10 83 F4
Bromley BR1.........53 A7
Dartford DA1 ....33 B7
Hawkhurst TN18.....340 F3
Maidstone ME15.....194 E4
Northfleet DA11......36 E7
Ramsgate CT11 .....117 D6
Ripple CT14, CT15 ...247 B8
Royal Tunbridge Wells, Mount
Sion TN1 ....286 A3

Vale Rd continued
Royal Tunbridge Wells, Southborough TN4.......253 F1
Tonbridge TN9.......222 C1
Whitstable CT5.......108 D8
Valerian Cl ME5.......96 E4
Vale Rise TN9.......254 E8
Vale Sq CT11.......117 D6
Valestone Cl CT21.......334 B4
Vale The CT10.......84 A4
Valetta Way ME1.......63 B4
Vale View Com Sch CT17.......310 B7
Vale View Rd
Aylesham CT3.......210 E5
Dover CT17.......310 B7
Valiant Ho 5 SE7.......1 C1
Valiant Rd ME5.......97 C2
Valiant Way E6.......1 F8
Valkyrie Ave CT5.......108 C7
Vallance Cl ME9.......136 A6
Valley Cl DA1.......14 F1
Valley Cotts
Alkham CT15.......276 C1
Stalisfield Green ME13.......201 D8
Valley Dr
Gravesend, Riverview Park DA12.......37 D4
Gravesend, Singlewell DA12.......37 E1
Maidstone ME15.......194 F6
Sevenoaks TN13.......154 B1
Valley Forge Cl TN10.......222 F4
Valley Gdns DA9.......17 B1
Valley Gr SE7.......1 C1
Valley Hts DA1.......15 F3
Valley Industries TN11.......223 B7
Valley La DA13.......93 B2
Valley L Ctr CT19.......334 F7
Valley Mushroom Farm TN16.......118 D1
Valley Park Com Sch ME14.......162 C4
Valley Rd Barham CT4.......209 E2
Canterbury CT1.......174 E6
Crabble CT17.......277 E3
Crayford DA1.......14 F1
Erith DA8.......4 D2
Fawkham Green DA3.......58 C2
Folkestone CT20.......334 E4
Gillingham ME7.......64 E4
Margate CT9.......82 E4
Orpington BR5.......54 B8
Rusthall TN4.......285 D4
Valley Rise ME5.......96 F1
Valleyside SE7.......1 D8
VALLEY THE.......201 D8
Valley The ME17.......194 D3
Valley The (Charlton Athletic FC) SE7.......1 C1
Valley View
Biggin Hill TN16.......118 D1
Eythorne CT15.......245 E6
Royal Tunbridge Wells TN4.......254 A2
Swanscombe DA9.......17 B1
Valley View Rd ME1.......63 B1
Valley View Terr DA4.......56 F1
Valley Wlk CT21.......334 B3
Valliers Wood Rd DA15.......30 E7
Vambery Rd SE18.......12 C8
Vanbrugh Cl 2 E16.......1 D8
Vanbrugh Pk SE3.......11 A7
Vanburgh Cl BR6.......53 E1
Vancouver Cl BR6.......87 A6
Vancouver Dr ME8.......65 C1
Vancouver Rd CT16.......278 C3
Vandome Cl E16.......1 B7
Vandyke Cross SE9.......11 E2
Vanessa Cl DA17.......4 A1
Vanessa Way DA5.......32 D5
Vanessa Wlk DA12.......37 F3
Vange Cottage Mews ME1.......63 B4
Vanguard Cl E16.......1 A8
Vanguard Way ME2.......63 E8
Vanity La ME17.......194 D1
Vanity Rd ME12.......49 F2
Vanoc Gdns BR1.......29 A4
Vanquisher Wlk DA12.......37 F5
Varley Rd E16.......1 B7
Varne Cl 6 CT20.......334 F3
Varne Lodge 5 CT20.......334 F3
Varne Mews TN28.......373 E4
Varne Pl CT19.......335 F5
Varne Rd CT19.......335 F5
Varnes St ME20.......128 F6
Vaughan Ave TN10.......222 C4
Vaughan Cl DA1.......33 D8
Vaughan Dr ME10.......101 F8
Vaughan Rd DA16.......12 F5
Vauxhall Ave
Canterbury CT1.......143 C3
Herne Bay CT6.......76 A3
Vauxhall Cl DA11.......36 F8
Vauxhall Cres
Canterbury CT1.......143 C3
Snodland ME6.......128 A6
Vauxhall Gdns TN9.......254 C7
Vauxhall Industrial Rd CT1.......143 D4
Vauxhall La
Bidborough TN11, TN4.......254 B4
Tonbridge TN11.......254 D6
Vauxhall Pl DA1.......33 E8
Vauxhall Rd CT1, CT2.......143 C4
Vectis Dr ME10.......101 F8
Veitchil Barn BR8.......55 F8
Veles Rd ME6.......127 F8
Venmead Rd 4 DA17.......4 A2

Venners Cl DA7.......14 E5
Ventnor Cl ME5.......97 C8
Ventnor La 12 CT9.......50 J2
Venture Cl
Dymchurch TN29.......352 D1
Sidcup DA5.......31 E8
Venture Ct SE12.......29 A8
Venus Rd SE18.......1 F3
Verdun Rd SE18, SE2.......13 A8
Vere Rd CT10.......84 A4
Vereth Rd 2 CT11.......117 D6
Vermont Rd TN4.......285 C4
Vernham Rd SE18.......12 C8
Vernon Cl Orpington BR5.......54 B6
West Kingsdown TN15.......90 F2
Vernon Pl
Canterbury CT1.......175 A7
Deal CT14.......215 D8
Vernon Rd
Royal Tunbridge Wells TN1.......286 C6
Swanscombe DA10.......17 F1
Vern Pl TN16.......150 C6
Veroan Rd DA7.......13 E5
Verona Gdns DA12.......37 E4
Verona Ho DA8.......14 F7
Vert Ho RM17.......18 C7
Verwood Cl CT2.......142 E2
Veryan Cl BR5.......54 C5
Vespasian Way TN23.......299 F4
Vesper Ct TN27.......264 A1
Vestey Ct CT8.......50 C1
Vestry Cotts
New Barn DA3.......59 C5
Sevenoaks TN14.......154 C8
Vestry Rd TN14.......154 C8
Viaduct Cl CT12.......117 C8
Viaduct Terr
Hamstreet TN26.......348 F7
Sutton at Hone DA4.......57 C7
Viaduct The CT17.......310 D5
Via Romana DA2.......38 B7
Viburnum Cl TN23.......267 E2
Vicarage Ave SE3.......11 A7
Vicarage Cl
Aylesford ME20.......128 F3
Erith DA8.......14 C8
Halling ME2.......95 A5
Stoke ME3.......25 A3
Vicarage Cotts ME9.......67 C3
Vicarage Cres 8 CT5.......50 J1
Vicarage Ct Chalk DA12.......38 A7
Newington ME9.......100 B7
Vicarage Dr DA11.......18 C1
Vicarage Gdn CT12.......114 C7
Vicarage Gdns CT3.......178 A7
VICARAGE GREEN.......337 A5
Vicarage Hill
Petham CT4.......207 B4
Westerham TN16.......151 D1
Vicarage La
Ashford TN23.......268 C2
Blean CT2.......142 A6
Chalk DA12.......38 A6
Charing Heath TN27.......233 C7
Deal CT14.......214 F5
East Farleigh ME15.......194 B6
Elham CT4.......273 F4
Faversham ME13.......138 A4
Hoo St Werburgh ME3.......41 E4
Lower Halstow ME9.......67 C3
Nonington CT15.......211 C5
Rochester ME1.......63 B7
Rochester, Strood ME2.......63 B7
Selling ME13.......171 C6
Sevenoaks TN13.......153 D8
St Margaret's at Cliffe CT15.......279 F6
Stoke ME3.......25 A3
Tilmanstone CT14.......213 A3
Vicarage Pk SE18.......2 C1
Vicarage Pl CT9.......50 J1
Vicarage Rd
Coldblow DA5.......32 B7
Gillingham ME7.......64 C5
Halling ME2.......94 F5
Minster (Sheppey) ME12.......47 D7
Rochester ME2.......63 B8
Royal Tunbridge Wells TN4.......253 F2
Sittingbourne ME10.......101 E6
Woolwich SE18.......2 C1
Yalding ME18.......193 A1
Vicarage Row ME1.......39 C4
Vicarage Sq RM17.......18 A8
Vicarage St
Broadstairs CT10.......83 C5
Faversham ME13.......138 D8
Vicarage Way TN19.......354 A3
Vicary Way ME16.......161 D5
Vickers Cl CT18.......307 A4
Vickers Rd DA8.......4 D1
Victor Ave CT9.......51 D2
Victoria Ave
Broadstairs CT10.......83 B8
3 Gravesend DA12.......37 B8
Hythe CT21.......333 B2
Margate CT9.......51 B1
St Margaret's at Cliffe CT15.......280 B6
Westgate on Sea CT8.......81 F8
Victoria Bglws DA14.......31 F1
Victoria Bsns Ctr DA16..13 B5
Victoria Cl Chatham ME6.......96 D2
Edenbridge TN8.......249 C8
Victoria Cotts
Cranbrook TN17.......320 D5
Edenbridge TN8.......249 C8
Victoria Cres
Ashford TN23.......268 B1
Dover CT16.......310 D8
Victoria Ct Hythe CT21.......333 C1
6 Maidstone ME16.......161 E3
Victoria Dock Rd E16.......1 B6

Victoria Dr
Herne Bay CT6.......76 C5
Kings Hill ME19.......158 F1
Sutton at Hone DA4.......57 D7
Victoria Gdns TN16.......118 C4
Victoria Gr
12 Folkestone CT20.......335 D5
Hythe CT21.......334 B2
Victoria Hill Rd BR8.......56 A8
Victoria Ho 7 CT5.......74 D2
Victoria Hospl CT14.......215 B5
Victoria Ind Pk DA1.......15 C2
Victoria Mews
Deal CT14.......215 C6
Westgate on Sea CT8.......50 D1
Victoria Orch ME16.......161 B3
Victoria Par
Broadstairs CT10.......84 B4
Ramsgate CT11.......117 D8
Victoria Park Mews 2 CT16.......310 E8
Victoria Pk Dover CT16 310 E8
Herne Bay CT6.......77 A5
Victoria Pl
Faversham ME13.......138 C7
Hythe CT21.......333 B4
Victoria Rd
Ashford TN23.......268 B1
Bexley DA6.......14 A3
Broadstairs CT10.......83 E6
Bromley BR2.......52 D4
Canterbury CT1.......174 E7
Capel-le-Ferne CT18.......308 B2
Chatham, Kit Hill ME5.......96 E3
Chatham, Luton ME4.......64 B2
Chislehurst BR7.......30 A3
Dartford DA1.......15 E2
Deal CT14.......215 D5
Edenbridge TN8.......249 C8
Erith DA8.......14 E8
Folkestone CT19.......335 C5
Golden Green TN11.......223 F6
Hythe CT21.......333 C1
Kingsdown CT14.......248 C4
Littlestone-on-Sea TN28 373 E5
Margate CT9.......50 J2
Margate, Lydden CT9.......82 D4
Northfleet DA11.......36 F7
Ramsgate CT11.......117 F7
Royal Tunbridge Wells, Southborough TN4.......253 E1
Royal Tunbridge Wells TN1.......286 B4
Sevenoaks TN13.......154 B2
Sidcup DA15.......31 A5
Sittingbourne ME10.......101 D4
Victoria Road Ind Pk TN23.......268 B1
Victoria Road Prim Sch TN23.......268 B1
Victoria Road W TN28.373 E5
Victoria Row
Canterbury CT1.......143 A1
Ramsgate CT11.......117 C5
Victoria Scott Ct DA1.......14 F4
Victoria St Dover CT17..278 B1
Eccles ME20.......128 F6
Erith DA17.......3 F1
Gillingham ME7.......64 D6
Maidstone ME16.......161 E3
New Romney TN28.......373 A6
Rochester ME1.......63 A8
Rochester, Strood ME2...63 B7
Sheerness ME12.......28 C1
Whitstable CT5.......74 D2
Victoria Terr
Hythe CT21.......334 B2
Minster (Sheppey) ME12.48 A5
Rochester ME1.......63 A2
Sittingbourne ME10.......101 D4
Victoria Way SE7.......1 B1
Victoria Wharf DA1.......15 E2
Victoria Yd 21 CT1.......143 A1
Victor Mills Cotts DA14 32 A1
Victory Cotts TN14.......187 C2
Victory Dr ME19.......159 D3
Victory Lodge 10 DA8.......4 E1
Victory Manor 1 ME7...64 A6
Victory Pk ME2.......63 E7
Victory Rd CT15.......247 F1
Victory St ME12.......28 B2
Victory Terr ME17.......229 E8
Victory Way DA2.......16 C3
Vidal Manor ME7.......64 C5
Vidgeon Ave ME3.......41 D6
View Cl TN16.......118 C3
Viewfield Rd DA5.......31 C7
Viewland Rd SE18.......2 F1
Viewlands ME5.......64 C3
Viewlands Ave TN16.......151 E7
Viewpoint ME14.......162 C8
Viewpoint Ct DA3.......58 F5
View Rd ME3.......40 B7
View The SE2.......3 E1
Vigilant Way DA12.......37 F3
Vigo Hill ME19, TN15.......125 E6
Vigo Rd TN15.......125 C7
Vigo Terr ME9.......103 C1
VIGO VILLAGE.......126 B8
Vigo Village Sch DA13 126 B4
Viking Cl Birchington CT7 80 D8
Rochester ME2.......62 F4
Viking Ct
Broadstairs CT10.......84 B3
Canterbury CT2.......142 F2
Margate CT9.......51 A2
Viking Ho 3 SE18.......1 E2
Viking Rd DA11.......36 C5
Viking Ship 'Hugin' ★ CT12.......116 E5
Viking Way Erith DA8.......4 C3
West Kingsdown TN15.......90 A5
Villa Cl DA12.......38 B6
Villacourt Rd SE18, SE2..13 A8

Villa Ct DA1.......33 E6
Village Green Ave TN16.......118 E2
Village Green Rd DA1.......15 A4
Village Green Way TN16.......118 E2
Village The SE7.......11 D8
Village View ME5.......64 C2
Village Way TN26.......349 A7
Villa Rd ME3.......39 B3
Villas Rd SE18.......2 C2
Villas The CT13.......112 A1
Villiers Ct CT13.......310 C7
Villiers Ho CT10.......84 B7
Villiers Rd CT1.......143 D1
Vincent Cl
Broadstairs CT10.......83 C3
Bromley BR2.......52 B5
Folkestone CT20.......334 E5
Sidcup DA15.......30 E7
Vincent Ct ME20.......128 C1
Vincent Gdns ME12.......28 C1
Vincent Pl TN24.......268 F4
Vincent Rd
Kit's Coty ME20.......129 C7
Margate CT9.......82 C4
Sittingbourne ME10.......102 C3
Woolwich SE18.......2 B2
Vincent Sq TN16.......118 C6
Vincent St 13 E16.......1 A8
Vine Ave TN13.......154 B3
Vine Cl CT11.......83 E2
Vine Court Rd TN13.......154 C4
Vine Ct
16 Gravesend DA11.......19 B1
Staplehurst TN12.......260 F3
Wateringbury ME18.......192 D8
Vine End CT11.......83 E2
Vine Lands TN29.......376 B6
Vine Lo CT11.......83 E2
Vine Lodge TN13.......154 C3
Vine Pavilion The (Sevenoaks Vine CC) TN13.......154 C3
Vine Rd BR6.......86 F4
Vineries The ME7.......64 E5
Viners Cl ME10.......101 F1
Vines La
Hildenborough TN11.......188 C1
Rochester ME1.......63 C5
Vine The TN13.......154 C3
Vine Wlk TN12.......260 C3
Vineyard Cres ME8.......66 B1
Vineyard La TN5.......338 C2
Viney's Gdns TN30.......324 C1
Vinson Cl
Culmers ME13.......106 D1
Orpington BR6.......54 A1
Vinson Ct DA15.......31 A6
Vinten Cl CT6.......111 B8
Vinters Rd ME14.......162 B4
Vinters Valley Nature Reserve ★ ME14.......162 D5
Vintners Way ME14.......162 E4
Viola Ave SE2.......3 B1
Violet Ave CT12.......83 C2
Violet Cl ME5.......130 A8
Violet Ct ME10.......101 F2
Violets The TN12.......257 A5
Violet Way TN23.......300 C5
VIP Trad Est SE7.......1 C1
Virginia Rd
Gillingham ME7.......64 C7
Whitstable CT5.......109 A8
Virginia Wlk DA12.......37 E2
Viscount Dr E16.......1 F8
Vista The Eltham SE9.......29 E8
Sidcup DA14.......30 F3
Vixen Cl ME5.......97 C6
Vlissingen Dr CT14.......215 C8
Voce Rd SE18.......12 D7
Vogue Ct 11 BR1.......52 B8
Volante Rd ME10.......101 E7
Vostry Ind Est TN4.......154 C8
Voyagers Ct SE28.......3 C7
Vulcan Cl Chatham ME5..97 B7
Newham E6.......2 A1
Whitstable CT5.......108 C7
Vyne The DA7.......14 B4
Vyvyan Cotts TN17.......342 C3
Vyvyan Ho SE18.......12 A6

W

Wacher Cl CT2.......142 F2
Wadard Terr BR8.......56 C4
Waddenhall Barns CT4.......240 B5
Waddington Dr CT18.......307 A4
Waddle Cnr TN30.......360 D3
Wade Ave BR5.......54 D2
Wades Cl TN29.......365 B4
Wadeville Cl DA17.......4 A1
Wadham Pl ME10.......102 B2
WADHURST.......337 A4
Wadhurst Bsns Pk TN5.......336 B7
Wadhurst CE Prim Sch TN5.......336 F5
Wadhurst Rd TN3.......314 D1
Wadhurst Sta TN5.......336 C6
Wadlands Rd ME3.......22 B5
Waghorn Rd ME6.......128 A8
Waghorn St ME4.......64 B2
Wagoners ME14.......162 E4
Wagon La TN12.......225 C1
Waid Cl DA1.......15 F1
Wain Ct ME12.......47 A5
Wainhouse Cl TN8.......217 D3
WAINSCOTT.......40 D3

Wainscott Prim Sch ME2.......40 D2
Wainscott Rd ME2.......40 D2
Wainscott Wlk ME2.......40 D2
Wainwright Ct CT10.......84 B6
Wainwright Rd TN24.......300 D8
Waite Davies Rd 8 SE12.......29 A8
Wakefield Cl ME2.......62 D6
Wakefield Rd DA9.......17 C2
Wakefield Way CT21.......333 B1
Wakeford Cl DA5.......31 D7
Wakehurst Ct ME17.......194 F3
Wakeley Rd ME8.......66 A1
Wakeleys Cotts ME8.......99 B8
Wake Rd ME1.......96 C8
Wakerley Cl 6 E6.......1 F7
Walcheren Cl CT14.......215 C8
Walcot Pl CT6.......77 B3
Waldeck Rd DA1.......16 A1
Waldegrave Rd BR1.......52 F5
Walden Ave BR7.......29 A4
Walden Cl DA17.......3 F1
Walden Ct CT2.......143 A4
Waldenhurst Rd BR5.......54 D2
Walden Par BR7.......29 F2
Walden Rd BR7.......29 F2
Waldens Cl BR5.......54 E3
Waldens Rd BR5.......54 E3
Waldens The ME17.......197 E2
Waldershare Ave CT13 182 A4
Waldershare Ho CT15 245 D5
Waldershare La CT15..246 E2
Waldershare Rd CT15..246 E3
WALDERSLADE.......96 F1
WALDERSLADE BOTTOM.......97 A2
Walderslade Ctr ME5.......97 A3
Walderslade Girls Sch 7 ME5.......96 F5
Walderslade Prim Sch ME5.......96 F6
Walderslade Rd ME5.......96 F6
Walderslade Village Bypass ME5.......96 F3
Walderslade Woods ME5.......96 E2
Waldo Ind Est BR1.......52 D6
Waldo Rd BR1.......52 D6
Waldrist Way DA18.......3 F4
Waldron Dr ME15.......194 F6
Waldron Rd CT10.......84 B2
Waldstock Rd SE28.......3 A6
Walkden Rd BR7.......30 A3
Walker Cl Crayford DA1...14 F4
Woolwich SE18.......2 C2
Walker La CT7.......80 D8
Walker Pl TN15.......156 D6
Walkhurst Cotts TN17 342 F7
Walkhurst Rd TN17.......342 F7
Walkley Rd DA1.......15 B2
Walks The ME17.......197 E2
Walk The ME17.......197 E2
Wallace Cl Erith SE28.......3 D6
Royal Tunbridge Wells TN2.......314 A8
Wallace Gdns DA10.......17 E1
Wallace Mews CT19.......335 D7
Wallace Rd ME1.......96 E8
Wallace Terr TN15.......91 E4
Wallace Way CT10.......83 E4
Wallbridge La ME8.......66 D3
Wall Cl ME3.......41 D7
WALLCROUCH.......337 F1
WALL END.......112 F4
Waller Hill TN17.......293 B5
Waller Rd TN28.......377 E2
Wallers TN3.......285 A8
Wallhouse Rd DA8.......15 C7
Wallis Ave ME15.......195 E5
Wallis Cl DA2.......32 F5
Wallis Ct CT6.......77 F5
Wallis Field TN3.......312 B6
Wallis Oak Ave 12 ME15.......195 F5
Wallis Pk DA11.......18 B2
Wallis Rd TN24.......268 D2
Wall Rd TN24.......268 B3
Wall The ME10.......101 E5
Wallwood Rd CT11.......117 F8
WALMER.......215 C2
Walmer Castle ★ CT14 215 D1
Walmer Castle Rd CT14.......215 C1
Walmer Cl BR6.......86 D6
Walmer Ct 3 ME14.......162 A5
Walmer Gdns
Cliffs End CT12.......116 D5
Deal CT14.......215 A2
Sittingbourne ME10.......101 D5
Walmer Ho ME2.......40 C1
Walmer Rd CT5.......108 E8
Walmers Ave ME3.......39 A4
Walmer Science Coll CT14.......215 B2
Walmer Sta CT14.......215 A1
Walmer Terr SE18.......2 D2
Walmer Way Deal CT14 215 A2
1 Folkestone CT20.......334 F5
WALMESTONE.......146 D3
Walmsley Ho 4 CT19.......335 F6
Walmsley Rd CT10.......83 F5
Walner Gdns TN28.......373 B7
Walner La TN28.......373 B7
Walnut Cl
Ashford TN24.......268 D6
Broadstairs CT10.......83 F2
Chatham ME5.......97 B8
Eynsford DA4.......89 D7
Paddock Wood TN12.......257 A6
Yalding ME18.......192 F1

Walnut Hill Rd DA13.......59 E6
Walnut Mews CT7.......80 F7
Walnut Ridge TN25.......330 A6
Walnuts L Ctr BR6.......54 A1
Walnuts Rd BR6.......54 B1
Walnuts Sh Ctr The BR6.......54 A1
Walnut Tree Ave
Dartford DA1.......33 E6
Loose ME15.......195 A5
Walnut Tree Cl
6 Birchington CT7.......81 A7
Chislehurst BR7.......53 C8
Westerham TN16.......151 D1
Walnut Tree Cotts ME13.......171 E8
Walnut Tree Ct ME20..128 B3
Walnut Tree Dr ME10..101 D4
Walnut Tree La
Loose ME15.......195 A5
Westbere CT2.......144 D7
Walnut Tree Rd DA8.......4 E1
Walnut Tree Way DA13 60 B3
Walnut Way
Royal Tunbridge Wells TN4.......286 D8
Swanley BR8.......55 D7
Walpole Cl ME19.......127 F1
Walpole Ho 4 BR7.......53 D8
Walpole Pl.......2 B2
Walpole Rd Bromley BR2 52 D4
Margate CT9.......50 J3
Walsby Dr ME10.......102 A8
Walsham Cl SE28.......3 D6
Walsham Rd ME5.......96 F1
Walshaw Ho 2 ME14.......162 A6
Walsingham Cl ME8.......98 D3
Walsingham Ho 3 ME14.......162 A6
Walsingham Pk BR7.......53 D7
Walsingham Rd BR5.......54 B8
Walsingham Wlk DA17..14 A8
Walter Burke Ave ME1..95 C5
Walter Burke Way ME4..64 A8
WALTER'S GREEN.......283 E6
Walters Green Rd TN11.......283 F6
Walters Ho SE18.......12 A7
Walters Rd ME3.......41 E6
Walterstown Ct DA1.......33 D8
Walters Yd BR1.......52 A7
WALTHAM.......239 E6
Waltham Cl
Ashford TN24.......269 A2
Dartford DA1.......15 A1
Margate CT9.......51 E2
26 Orpington BR5.......54 D1
Waltham Rd
Gillingham ME8.......65 C3
Petham CT4.......207 B3
Waltham CT4.......206 F1
Walthamstow Hall Jun Sch TN13.......154 B5
Walthamstow Hall Senior Sch TN13.......154 B5
Walton Gdns CT19.......335 D6
Walton Manor Cl CT19 335 D7
Walton Rd
Folkestone CT19.......335 D6
Sidcup DA14.......31 C5
Tonbridge TN10.......222 F6
Waltons The CT19.......335 C8
Walwyn Ave BR1.......52 D6
WANDEN.......264 B7
Wanden La TN27.......264 C8
Wansbury Way BR8.......56 A5
WANSHURST GREEN 260 A7
Wanstall Ct CT7.......81 A7
Wanstead Cl BR1.......52 C7
Wanstead Rd BR1.......52 C7
Wansunt Rd DA5.......32 C7
Wantsum Cl CT6.......77 F5
Wantsum Lees CT13..148 E2
Wantsum Mews 7 CT13.......148 F1
Wantsum Way CT7.......79 E3
Warberry Park Gdns TN4.......285 E4
Warblers Cl 3 ME2.......63 A7
Ward Cl Durgates TN5..336 E5
Erith DA8.......14 D8
WARDEN.......49 D4
Warden Bay Rd ME12...49 E3
Warden Cl ME16.......161 C4
Warden Ct 10 CT17.......278 C1
Warden House Mews CT14.......215 A4
Warden House Prim Sch CT14.......215 A5
Warden Mill Cl ME18..192 E7
Warden Point Way 2 CT5.......108 C6
Warden Rd
Rochester ME1.......63 C2
Sheerness ME12.......49 B5
Wardens Field Cl 2 BR6.......54 A6
Warden Terr ME12.......48 A6
Warden View Gdns ME12.......49 D1
Warden Way ME12.......49 B5
Warde's ME18.......192 F2
Wardona Ct DA10.......17 F1
Wardour Cl CT10.......84 B4
Wardour Ct 11 DA2.......16 B1
Wards Hill Rd ME12.......47 C8
Ward's La TN5.......337 E4
Wards Wharf App E16.......1 D4
Wardwell La ME9.......67 C1
WARE.......147 B6
WAREHORNE.......348 D6
Warehorne Rd TN26.......349 A7
Warepoint Dr SE28.......2 D4

Ware St ME14 . . . . 163 A5
WARE STREET 163 B5
Warham Rd TN14 . . . . . 122 B3
Waring Cl BR6 . . . . 87 A4
Waring Dr BR6 . . . . 87 A4
Waring Rd DA14 . . . . 31 C2
Warland Rd
  West Kingsdown TN15 . . . 90 F2
  Woolwich SE18 . . . . 12 E1
Warlingham Cl ME8 . . . . 66 A1
WARMLAKE 196 E1
Warmlake ME17 . . . . . . 196 F1
Warmlake Bsns Est
  ME17 . . . . 196 E1
Warmlake Rd ME15 . . . 196 C1
Warne Pl **4** DA15 . . . . . 13 B1
Warner St 63 F3
Warnett Ct ME6 . . . . 95 A1
Warnford Gdns ME15 . . 195 A8
Warnford Pl ME15 . . . . 195 A8
Warnford Rd BR6 . . . . . . 86 F5
Warre Ave CT11 . . . . . . 117 C5
Warren Ave BR6 . . . . 86 F5
Warren Cl Bexley DA6 . . . 14 A2
  Folkestone CT19 . . . . . 335 F6
  Sittingbourne ME10 . . . 102 B2
Warren Cotts TN11 . . . . 252 A3
Warren Ct TN15 . . . . . . 154 C3
Warren Dr
  Broadstairs CT10 . . . . . . 83 E5
  Orpington BR6 . . . . 87 B5
Warren Dr The CT8 . . . . . 81 D7
Warren Farm La TN3 . . 313 B4
Warren Gdns BR6 . . . . . . 87 A5
Warren Hastings Ct
  DA11 . . . . 18 F1
Warren Hos TN27 . . . . . 233 E8
Warren Hts TN25 . . . . . 302 E5
Warren La
  Ashford TN24 . . . . 268 A4
  Lydden CT15 . . . . 276 D6
  Oxted RH8 . . . . 183 A1
  Woolwich SE18 . . . . 2 B3
  Yelsted ME9 . . . . 99 C3
Warren Lo CT1 . . . . 174 B6
Warren Rd Bexley DA6 . . 14 C4
  Dartford DA1 . . . . 33 E5
  Folkestone CT19 . . . . . 335 F6
  Hayes BR2 . . . . 85 A8
  Kit's Coty ME5 . . . . 129 D7
  Littlestone-on-Sea
   TN28 . . . . 373 D6
  Luddesdown ME2 . . . . . . 61 D3
  Northfleet DA13 . . . . 36 B3
  Orpington BR6 . . . . 87 C5
  Sidcup DA14 . . . . 24 A3
Warren Ret Pk TN24 . . 268 B4
Warren Ridge TN3 . . . . 314 C3
Warren Road Prim Sch
  BR6 . . . . 86 F6
Warren St
  Stalisfield Green
   TN27 . . . . 201 A3
  Warren Street ME17 . . 200 D7
Warrens The DA3 . . . . . . 58 F3
WARREN STREET 200 D7
Warren The
  Brabourne Lees TN25 . . 302 E5
  Gravesend DA12 . . . . 37 D4
  2 Greenwich SE7 . . . . . 11 C8
  Penshurst TN11 . . . . . . 252 A4
  Selling ME13 . . . . 171 E7
  Ticehurst TN5 . . . . 338 E1
  Whitstable CT5 . . . . . . 108 C6
Warren View
  Ashford TN23 . . . . 267 F4
  Shorne DA12 . . . . 38 E2
Warren Way CT19 . . . . 335 F6
Warren Wlk **1** SE7 . . . . 11 C8
Warren Wood BR2 . . . . . 85 C8
Warren Wood Com Prim
  Sch ME1 . . . . 96 C4
Warren Wood Rd ME1 . . 96 C7
Warrington Rd TN12 . . 257 A6
Warrior Cl SE28 . . . . 2 D5
Warrior Ave DA12 . . . . . 37 C4
Warsop Trad Est TN8 . . 249 D8
Warspite Rd SE18 . . . . . . 1 E2
Warten Rd CT11 . . . . 83 F1
Warwall E6 . . . . 2 B7
Warwick Cl
  Orpington BR6 . . . . 87 A7
  Sidcup DA5 . . . . 31 F8
Warwick Cres
  Rochester ME1 . . . . 62 F2
  Sittingbourne ME10 . . . 101 C5
Warwick Ct **8** DA8 . . . . 14 F7
Warwick Dr CT11 . . . . . 117 B5
Warwick Gdns DA13 . . . 93 A8
Warwick Pk TN2 . . . . . . 286 B1
Warwick Pl
  Maidstone ME16 . . . . . 161 E3
  Northfleet DA11 . . . . 18 B2
Warwick Rd
  Ashford TN24 . . . . 268 E5
  Bexley DA16 . . . . 13 C4
  Canterbury CT1 . . . . . . 175 C8
  Deal CT14 . . . . 215 D2
  Margate CT9 . . . . 51 B2
  4 Royal Tunbridge Wells
   TN1 . . . . 286 A2
  Sidcup DA14 . . . . 31 B3
  Whitstable CT5 . . . . 74 D2
Warwick Terr SE18 . . . . 12 D8
Warwick Way DA11 . . . . 33 E6
Washford Farm Rd
  TN23 . . . . 299 E5
Washington Cl **4**
  CT16 . . . . 278 B3
Washington Ho ME15 . . 195 E5
Washington La TN29 . . 371 C6
Washneys Rd BR6 . . . . . 120 B6
Washwell La TN5 . . . . . 336 F3

Wassall La TN17 . . . . . . 357 E7
Wass Dro CT3 . . . . 147 B7
Watchester Ave CT11 . . 117 C5
Watchester La CT12 . . . 115 B5
Watchgate DA2 . . . . 34 E3
Watchmans Terr **6**
  ME5 . . . . 64 C2
Waterbrook Ave TN24 . 301 A4
Watercress Cl TN14 . . . 154 C4
Watercress Dr TN14 . . . 154 C7
Watercress Ho TN23 . . 267 F1
Watercress La
  Ashford TN23 . . . . 299 F8
  Wingham CT3 . . . . 177 F6
Watercroft Rd TN14 . . . . 87 F1
Waterdale Rd SE2 . . . . . 13 A8
Waterdales DA11 . . . . . . 36 D7
Waterditch La TN17,
  TN27 . . . . 200 C5
Waterdown Rd TN4 . . . 285 E1
Waterfall Rd TN26 . . . . 267 B6
Water Farm CT4 . . . . . . 273 F4
Waterfield TN2 . . . . 314 A7
Waterfield Cl Erith DA17 . 4 A3
  Woolwich SE28 . . . . 3 B5
Waterfrets Cotts TN3 . . 284 F5
Waterfront L Ctr SE18 . . 2 A3
Waterfront Studios Bsns
  Ctr E16 . . . . 1 A5
Watergate Ho **5** SE18 . . 2 A2
Waterglade Ind Pk
  RM20 . . . . 16 F8
WATERHAM 107 C2
Waterham Rd ME13 . . . 107 C1
Waterhead Cl DA8 . . . . . 14 E7
Waterhouse Cl E16 . . . . . 1 D8
WATERINGBURY 192 D7
Wateringbury CE Prim Sch
  ME18 . . . . 192 E6
Wateringbury Rd BR5 . . 54 B7
Wateringbury Rd
  ME19 . . . . 159 F3
Wateringbury Sta
  ME18 . . . . 192 E6
Water La
  Canterbury CT1 . . . . . . 174 F8
  6 Faversham ME13 . . 138 C7
  Harrietsham ME17 . . . . 198 A5
  Hawkhurst TN18 . . . . . 341 B4
  Headcorn TN17, TN27 . . 262 A4
  Hunton ME15 . . . . 226 D6
  Kingswood ME17 . . . . . 197 F3
  Limpsfield RH8 . . . . . . 183 A8
  Maidstone, Bearsted
   ME14 . . . . 163 E6
  6 Maidstone ME15 . . 162 A4
  Painters Forstal ME13 . . 137 A4
  Shoreham TN14 . . . . . . 121 F6
  Sidcup DA14 . . . . 31 F6
  Smarden TN27 . . . . 263 F2
  Sturry CT2 . . . . 143 F5
  West Malling ME19 . . . 159 C8
Waterlakes TN8 . . . . . . 249 C8
Waterlock Cotts CT3 . . 178 A7
Waterloo Cres CT16,
  CT17 . . . . 310 E7
Waterloo Hill ME12 . . . . 47 D6
Waterloo Mans **14**
  CT17 . . . . 310 E7
Waterloo Pl
  Cranbrook TN17 . . . . . 320 D5
  High Halston ME3 . . . . . 41 B8
  10 Ramsgate CT11 . . . 117 F7
  Tonbridge TN9 . . . . 254 B8
Waterloo Rd
  Cranbrook TN17 . . . . . 320 D6
  Folkestone CT20 . . . . . 334 D5
  Gillingham ME7 . . . . 64 C4
  Sittingbourne ME10 . . . 101 D5
  Tonbridge TN9 . . . . 254 B8
  Whitstable CT5 . . . . 74 D2
Waterloo St
  1 Gravesend DA12 . . . 37 C8
  Maidstone ME15 . . . . . 162 A3
Waterloo Terr ME12 . . . . 48 A5
Waterlow Rd
  Maidstone ME14 . . . . . 162 A6
  Vigo Village DA13 . . . . 125 F7
Waterman Ho TN23 . . . 300 B8
WATERMAN
  QUARTER 262 D2
Waterman's La TN12 . . 257 B3
Watermans Way DA9 . . . 17 B3
Water Mdws CT2 . . . . . 143 F4
Watermead Cl TN23 . . . 299 F7
Watermeadow Cl
  Erith DA8 . . . . 15 B6
  Gillingham ME7 . . . . 97 F6
Watermill Cl
  Maidstone ME16 . . . . . 161 B5
  Rochester ME2 . . . . 63 C8
Water Mill Way DA4 . . . 57 B7
Watermint Cl BR5 . . . . . 54 D5
Waters Cotts TN5 . . . . . 337 A4
Waters Edge ME15 . . . . 161 F2
Waters Edge Ct DA8 . . . . 4 F1
Watersend CT16 . . . . . . 277 D5
Waterside
  Ashford TN24 . . . . 268 C4
  Crayford DA1 . . . . 14 F2
  8 Maidstone ME14 . . 161 F4
Waterside Cl
  Faversham ME13 . . . . . 105 D1
  Woolwich SE28 . . . . 3 A6
Waterside Ct
  5 Hythe CT21 . . . . . 333 B2
  Leybourne ME19 . . . . . 127 F2
Waterside Ct ME2 . . . . . . 63 E6
Waterside Dr CT8 . . . . . . 50 D1
Waterside Gate ME16 . . 161 F5
Waterside La ME7 . . . . . 64 F7
Waterside Mews
  ME18 . . . . 192 D6

Waterside Prim Sch **4**
  SE18 . . . . 2 D1
Waterside Terr TN23 . . 267 C1
Waterside View ME12 . . 49 E4
Water Slippe TN11 . . . . 190 D1
Watersmeet Cl ME15 . . 194 F2
Watersmeet Way SE28 . . 3 D7
Waters Pl ME7 . . . . 98 A6
Water St CT14 . . . . 215 D7
Waterstone Pl ME13 . . 138 A6
Waterstone Way DA9 . . . 17 A1
Waterton BR8 . . . . 55 D5
Waterton Ave DA12 . . . . 37 E8
Waterworks Cotts
  TN14 . . . . 154 B6
Waterworks Hill CT15 . 247 B8
Waterworks La CT15 . . 247 B3
Watery La
  Heaverham TN15 . . . . . 155 D7
  Petham CT4 . . . . 207 C5
  Sidcup BR5, DA14 . . . . . 31 B2
Watford Rd E16 . . . . 1 A8
Watkin Rd CT19 . . . . . . 335 C6
Watkins Cl TN12 . . . . . . 260 E5
Watling Ave ME5 . . . . . . 64 D2
Watling Ho **10** SE18 . . . 12 A8
Watling Pl ME10 . . . . . . 102 A3
Watling St Bean DA2 . . . 35 D4
  Bexley DA6, DA7 . . . . . . 14 C3
  Canterbury CT1 . . . . . . 174 F8
  Dartford DA1, DA2 . . . . . 34 C8
  Gillingham ME5 . . . . 64 D2
  Gravesend DA11, DA12 . . 37 C2
  Northfleet DA11, DA13 . . 36 D4
  Rochester ME2 . . . . 62 D7
Watson Ave ME5 . . . . . . 96 D5
Watson Cl RM20 . . . . . . 17 A6
Watsons Cl TN25 . . . . . 268 C8
Watsons Hill ME10 . . . . 101 E5
Watt Ho SE2 . . . . 3 C1
Wattle Cnr TN30 . . . . . 360 D3
Watts' Ave ME1 . . . . 63 C4
Watts Cl Snodland ME6 . 128 B8
  Wadhurst TN5 . . . . 336 F4
Watts Cotts TN24 . . . . . 268 D7
WATT'S CROSS 221 B7
Watt's Cross Rd TN11 . 221 B6
Watt's La BR7 . . . . 53 C8
Watts' St ME4 . . . . 63 E3
Watts Yd **13** CT13 . . . 148 F1
Wat Tyler Way ME5 . . . 162 A4
Wauchope Rd **1** CT5 . 108 A6
Wave Crest CT5 . . . . 74 C1
Wavell Dr DA15 . . . . 12 E1
Waveney Rd TN10 . . . . 222 B5
Waverley Ave ME12 . . . . 47 B7
Waverley Cl
  Bromley BR2 . . . . 52 D4
  Chatham ME5 . . . . 97 D2
  Coxheath ME17 . . . . . . 194 C3
Waverley Cres SE18 . . . 12 D8
Waverley Dr TN2 . . . . . 286 F6
Waverley Gdns E6 . . . . . 1 E8
Waverley Rd
  Margate CT9 . . . . 82 C8
  Woolwich SE18 . . . . 2 D1
WAY 115 D7
Wayborough Hill CT12 115 D7
Way Farm Cotts CT12 . 115 E7
WAYFIELD 97 A8
Wayfield Com Prim Sch
  ME5 . . . . 97 A7
Wayfield Link SE9 . . . . . 12 D1
Wayfield Rd ME5 . . . . . . 97 A7
Way Hill CT12 . . . . 115 E7
Waylands BR8 . . . . 55 F5
Waylands Cl TN14 . . . . 120 E4
Wayne Cl
  Broadstairs CT10 . . . . . . 83 E5
  Orpington BR6 . . . . 86 F7
Wayne Ct ME2 . . . . 40 D2
Wayside
  3 Chislehurst BR7 . . . . 53 D8
  Tenterden TN30 . . . . . . 324 B2
Wayside Ave TN30 . . . . 324 B3
Wayside Dr TN8 . . . . . . 217 D3
Wayside Flats TN30 . . . 324 B2
Wayside Gr SE9 . . . . 29 F4
Waystrode Manor★
  TN8 . . . . 281 F6
Wayville Rd DA1 . . . . . . 34 B8
Way Volante DA12 . . . . . 37 E4
Weald Cl
  Istead Rise DA13 . . . . . . 36 E1
  Maidstone ME15 . . . . . 195 C6
  Orpington BR2 . . . . 85 E8
  Sevenoaks Weald TN14 187 C2
Weald Com Prim Sch
  TN14 . . . . 187 B2
Weald Ct Charing TN27 . 201 E1
  Sittingbourne ME10 . . . 101 D2
  Tonbridge TN11 . . . . . . 221 D6
Wealden Ave TN30 . . . . 324 B1
Wealden Ct **5** ME5 . . . 64 B3
Wealden Pl TN13 . . . . . 154 D6
Wealden View TN17 . . . 318 E8
Wealden Way ME20 . . . 160 E7
Wealdhurst Pk CT10 . . . 83 D5
Weald of Kent Gram Sch
  TN9 . . . . 254 C7
Weald Rd TN13 . . . . . . 187 B7
Weald Sports Ctr The
  TN17 . . . . 320 C6
Weald The
  Ashford TN24 . . . . 268 C3
  Bromley BR7 . . . . 29 F2
Weald View
  Frittenden TN17 . . . . . . 293 E6
  Paddock Wood TN12 . . 257 E1
  Turner's Green TN5 . . . 336 F6
Weald View Rd TN9 . . . 254 B7
Wear Bay Cres CT19 . . 335 F6
Wear Bay Rd CT19 . . . 335 F5

Weardale 185 B5
Weardale Rd DA2 . . . . . . 34 C7
Weare Rd TN4 . . . . 286 C8
Weatherall Cl ME1 . . . . . 63 C4
Weatherly Cl ME1 . . . . . . 63 C4
Weatherly Dr CT10 . . . . 83 F2
Weaver Cl E6 . . . . 2 B6
Weaverdown ME4 . . . . . 40 B2
Weavering Cotts ME14 162 E3
Weavering St ME14 . . . 162 E5
WEAVERING STREET . 162 F5
Weavers Cl
  Gravesend DA11 . . . . . . 37 A7
  Staplehurst TN12 . . . . 260 F4
Weavers Cotts TN17 . . 318 E8
Weavers La TN14 . . . . . 154 C6
Weaver's Orch DA13 . . . 36 A2
Weavers The
  Biddenden TN27 . . . . . 295 A1
  Maidstone ME16 . . . . . 161 B5
Weavers Way
  Ashford TN23 . . . . 299 E7
  Dover CT16 . . . . 278 A3
Webb Cl
  Folkestone CT19 . . . . . 335 A7
  Hoo St Werburgh ME3 . . 41 D6
Webb Ct **6** SE28 . . . . . . 3 B6
Webber Cl DA8 . . . . 15 B7
Webb's Mdw TN15 . . . . 154 F6
Webbs Orchard TN12 . . 288 E8
Webster Rd ME8 . . . . . . 65 F1
Webster Way CT18 . . . 307 B4
WEDDINGTON 147 E3
Weddington La CT3 . . . 147 E2
Wedgewood Cl ME16 . . 161 B5
Wedgewood Ct DA3 . . . . 57 A8
Wedgewood Dr ME5 . . . 97 A7
Wedgwoods TN16 . . . . 150 C6
Weeds Wood Rd ME5 . . 96 F4
Weekes Ct ME11 . . . . . . 46 A5
Weeks La TN27 . . . . . . 295 A5
Week St ME14 . . . . 162 A4
Weigall Pl CT11 . . . . . . 117 C7
Weigall Rd SE12, SE3 . . 11 A3
Weighbridge Way
  CT16 . . . . 310 H8
Weird Wood DA3 . . . . . . 59 C6
Weir Mill ME19 . . . . 159 F7
Weir Rd DA5 . . . . 32 B8
Welbeck Ave
  Bromley BR1 . . . . 29 A4
  Royal Tunbridge Wells
   TN4 . . . . 286 C8
Welcombe Ct ME8 . . . . . 98 D8
Weld Cl TN12 . . . . 260 F4
Weldstock Ho **2** SE28 . . 2 D3
Wellan Cl DA16 . . . . 13 B2
Welland Rd TN10 . . . . . 222 B4
Wellands Cl BR1 . . . . . . 52 F7
Wellbrook Rd BR6 . . . . . 86 A6
Well Cl Leigh TN11 . . . . 220 F1
  Sturry CT2 . . . . 144 A6
Wellcome Ave DA1 . . . . 15 E3
Weller Ave ME1 . . . . 63 D2
Weller Pl BR6 . . . . 119 A8
Weller Rd TN4 . . . . 285 C4
Wellers Cl TN16 . . . . . . 184 C8
WELLER'S TOWN 251 D5
Wellesley Ave CT14 . . . 215 C3
Wellesley Cl
  Broadstairs CT10 . . . . . . 83 E3
  7 Greenwich SE7 . . . . . 1 C1
  Westgate on Sea CT8 . . . 81 E7
Wellesley Ct **13** CT11 . 117 F7
Wellesley Ho CT14 . . . . 215 C1
Wellesley House Sch
  CT10 . . . . 83 F3
Wellesley Rd
  Ashford TN23 . . . . 268 C2
  Dover CT16 . . . . 310 E7
  Margate CT9 . . . . 51 B1
  Sheerness ME12 . . . . . . 28 D2
  Westgate on Sea CT8 . . . 81 E7
Wellesley Terr CT13 . . . 181 A8
Wellesley Villas TN24 . 268 C3
Well Field CT20 . . . . . . 335 A5
Wellfield Rd CT20 . . . . 335 A5
Well Hall Par SE9 . . . . . 11 F1
Well Hall Pleasaunce★
  SE9 . . . . 11 E2
Well Hall Rd SE18, SE9 . 11 F5
WELL HILL 88 A4
Well Hill BR6 . . . . 88 B5
Well Hill La BR6 . . . . . . 88 A4
Well Hill Nursery BR6 . . 88 C4
Wellhurst Cl BR6 . . . . . 86 F3
WELLING 13 B4
Wellingfield Ct **1** DA16 13 A4
Welling High St DA16 . . 13 B4
Welling Sch DA16 . . . . . 13 B6
Welling Sta DA16 . . . . . 13 A5
Wellington Ave
  Sidcup DA15 . . . . 13 A1
  Woolwich SE18 . . . . 2 B3
Wellington Cl CT8 . . . . . 50 C1
Wellington Cotts
  Gill's Green TN18 . . . . . 340 E4
  Meopham DA13 . . . . . . 93 A7
Wellington Cres CT11 . 117 F6
Wellington Ct CT14 . . . 215 D3
Wellington Gdns
  2 Dover CT16 . . . . . . 278 B3
  Greenwich SE7 . . . . 1 C1
  Margate CT9 . . . . 50 J3
Wellington Ho
  6 Maidstone ME15 . . 195 E6
  Margate CT9 . . . . 51 C3
Wellingtonia Way TN8 217 C2
Wellington Mews SE7 . . 11 C8
Wellington Par
  Bexley DA15 . . . . 13 A2

Wellington Par continued
  Deal CT14 . . . . 248 D1
  Kingsdown CT14 . . . . . 248 D1
Wellington Pl
  Folkestone CT20 . . . . . 334 D3
  Maidstone ME14 . . . . . 161 F6
  Sparrow's Green TN5 . . 336 F5
Wellington Rd
  Bexley DA5 . . . . 13 D2
  Bromley BR2 . . . . 52 C5
  Dartford DA1 . . . . 15 C1
  Deal CT14 . . . . 215 D5
  Erith DA17 . . . . 3 F1
  Folkestone CT20 . . . . . 334 D5
  Gillingham ME7 . . . . 64 C4
  Margate CT9 . . . . 82 D4
  Orpington BR5 . . . . 54 C3
  Sittingbourne ME10 . . . 101 B6
  Temple Ewell CT16 . . . 277 D5
  Tilbury RM18 . . . . 19 A5
Wellington St
  Gravesend DA12 . . . . . . 37 C8
  Woolwich SE18 . . . . 2 A2
  Yorkletts CT5 . . . . 108 D5
Wellington Terr CT20 . 334 D3
Wellington Way ME19 158 F3
Welling Way DA16 . . . . . 12 D4
Wellis Gdns CT9 . . . . . . 50 G1
Well La
  Fordwich CT2, CT3 . . . 144 A3
  Painters Forstal ME13 . 137 B3
  St Margaret's at Cliffe
   CT15 . . . . 279 F6
Wellmeade Dr TN13 . . . 187 B8
Well Penn Rd ME3 . . . . . 22 C3
Well Rd Lyminge CT18 . 305 C6
  Maidstone ME14 . . . . . 162 A5
  Otford TN14 . . . . 122 C3
  Queenborough ME11 . . . 46 A5
  Rushenden ME11 . . . . . 45 F3
Wells Ave CT1 . . . . 175 B7
Wells Cl
  New Romney TN28 . . . 373 C6
  Royal Tunbridge Wells
   TN1 . . . . 286 A3
  Tenterden TN30 . . . . . 345 B8
  Tonbridge TN10 . . . . . . 222 D4
  Westerham TN16 . . . . . 184 C8
Wells Cotts SE18 . . . . . 192 C2
Wells Ct ME2 . . . . 62 D5
Wells Ho Bromley BR1 . . 29 B3
  Royal Tunbridge Wells
   TN4 . . . . 285 E7
  Sittingbourne ME10 . . . 102 B4
Wellsmoor Gdns BR1 . . 53 A6
Wells Rd Bromley BR1 . . 52 F7
  Folkestone CT19 . . . . . 334 C4
  Rochester ME2 . . . . 62 D5
Well St
  East Malling ME19 . . . 159 E6
  Maidstone ME15, ME17 194 A4
WELL STREET 159 E6
Wells Way ME13 . . . . . 105 B3
Well Winch Rd ME10 . . 101 D5
Welsdene Rd CT9 . . . . . . 82 B8
Welson Rd CT20 . . . . . . 335 A5
Welton Cl TN9 . . . . 253 F7
Welton Rd TN4 . . . . 285 C4
Wemmick Cl ME1 . . . . . . 96 C7
Wemyss Ct **13** CT1 . . . 143 B2
Wemyss Ho **14** CT1 . . 143 B2
Wemyss Way CT1 . . . . . 143 C1
Wenderton La CT3 . . . . 146 A2
Wendover Cl ME2 . . . . . . 95 B5
Wendover Ct BR2 . . . . . . 52 B6
Wendover Rd
  Bromley BR1, BR2 . . . . 52 B6
  Eltham SE9 . . . . 11 D4
Wendover Way
  Bexley DA16 . . . . 13 A3
  Orpington BR6 . . . . 54 A3
Wenham's La TN29 . . . 363 E2
Wensley Cl SE9 . . . . 11 F1
Wents Wood ME14 . . . . 162 F5
Wentworth Ave CT19 . . 50 E1
Wentworth Cl Erith SE28 3 D7
  Gravesend DA11 . . . . . . 37 A3
  Hayes BR2 . . . . 85 A8
  Lyminge CT18 . . . . 305 C6
  Orpington BR6 . . . . 86 E5
Wentworth Dr
  Cliffe Woods ME3 . . . . . 40 B8
  Dartford DA1 . . . . 15 A1
  Gillingham ME8 . . . . 98 E2
  Ramsgate CT12 . . . . 83 A1
  Sittingbourne ME10 . . . 101 C5
Wentworth Gdns CT6 . . 76 D2
Wentworth Ho
  3 Greenwich SE3 . . . . 11 A7
  Sittingbourne ME10 . . . 101 C5
Wentworth Prim Sch
  DA1 . . . . 33 A8
Wenvoe Ave DA7 . . . . . . 14 B5
Wernbrook St SE18 . . . . 12 C1
Wesley Ave E16 . . . . 1 B5
Wesley Cl
  Maidstone ME16 . . . . . 160 F3
  Orpington BR5 . . . . 54 C6
Wesley Ho BR1 . . . . 52 D6
Wesley Sch Rd TN23 . . 299 D7
Wesley Terr CT18 . . . . . 305 C7
Wessex Dr DA8 . . . . 14 E6
Wessex Wlk DA2 . . . . . . 32 E6
West App BR5 . . . . 53 C4
West Beach CT5 . . . . 74 C1
WESTBERE 144 C7
Westbere Ho BR5 . . . . . 54 C4
Westbere La CT2 . . . . . 144 B7
West Blean Wood Nature
  Reserve★ CT6 . . . . . . 110 D2
West Borough Prim Sch
  ME16 . . . . 161 B3
Westbourne TN23 . . . . 299 D6

Westbourne Gdns
  CT20 . . . . 335 B4
Westbourne Rd DA7 . . . 13 E7
Westbourne St ME10 . . 101 E4
WESTBROOK 50 F1
Westbrook Ave CT9 . . . . 50 F1
Westbrook Cotts CT9 . . 50 G1
Westbrook Ct SE3 . . . . . 11 B6
Westbrook Dr BR5 . . . . 54 D1
Westbrook Gdns ME4 . . 64 A2
Westbrook Cres DA16 . 13 C4
Westbrooke Rd
  Bexley DA16 . . . . 13 C4
  Sidcup DA15 . . . . 30 D6
Westbrooke Sch DA16 . 13 D4
Westbrook Gdns CT9 . . 50 G1
Westbrook La CT6 . . . . . 76 B3
Westbrook Prom CT9 . . 50 G2
Westbrook Rd
  Greenwich SE3 . . . . 11 B6
  Margate CT9 . . . . 50 G2
Westbrook Terr TN2 . . . 286 D3
West Brow BR7 . . . . 30 B3
Westbury Cres CT17 . . 310 B6
Westbury Ct **5** DA14 . . 31 A4
Westbury Hts CT17 . . . 310 B6
Westbury Rd
  Bromley BR1 . . . . 52 D8
  Dover CT17 . . . . 310 B6
  Westgate on Sea CT8 . . . 81 E7
Westbury Terr TN16 . . . 184 C8
West Cliff CT5 . . . . 74 D1
West Cliff Arc **10** CT11 117 E6
West Cliff Ave CT10 . . . 84 B3
West Cliff Ct CT10 . . . . 84 B3
West Cliff Dr ME12 . . . . 47 D8
West Cliff Dr CT6 . . . . . 76 B4
WEST CLIFFE 279 D6
Westcliff Gdns CT9 . . . . 50 F1
West Cliff Gdns
  Folkestone CT20 . . . . . 335 D4
  Herne Bay CT6 . . . . 76 B4
Westcliff Ho **4** CT20 . . 335 D4
West Cliff Prom CT11 . . 117 C5
Westcliff Rd CT9 . . . . . . 50 G1
West Cliff Rd
  Broadstairs CT10 . . . . . 84 B3
  Ramsgate CT11 . . . . . . 117 D6
West Cliff Terr CT11 . . . 117 B5
Westcombe Hill SE3 . . . 11 A8
Westcombe Park Rd
  SE3 . . . . 11 A7
Westcombe Park Sta
  SE3 . . . . 1 A1
West Common Rd BR2 . 85 B7
Westcott Ave DA11 . . . . 37 A5
Westcott Cl BR1 . . . . . . 52 F4
WESTCOURT 37 E6
Westcourt La CT15 . . . 244 C5
Westcourt Prim Sch
  DA12 . . . . 37 E6
Westcourt St ME7 . . . . . 64 A6
West Crescent Rd DA12 19 C1
WEST CROSS 343 D4
West Cross TN30 . . . . . 344 F7
West Cross Gdns TN30 344 F7
West Ct **3** ME5 . . . . . 162 A1
Westdale Rd SE18 . . . . . 12 B8
Westdean Ave SE12 . . . 29 C7
Westdean Cl CT17 . . . . 277 E2
West Dr Chatham ME5 . . 96 D5
  Sutton Valence ME17 . . 230 B7
WEST DUMPTON 83 D1
West Dumpton La CT11 83 E1
Wested Farm Cotts BR8 55 F2
Wested La BR8 . . . . 56 A3
WEST END Doddington 167 D7
  Herne Bay 110 B8
West End Brasted TN16 152 B2
  High Halden TN26 . . . . 325 F3
  Kemsing TN15 . . . . 123 A2
  Marden TN12 . . . . 259 C6
West End Cotts Mews . . 167 D7
Westenhanger Castle★
  CT21 . . . . 332 A7
WESTENHANGER 332 B6
Westenhanger Sta
  TN25 . . . . 332 B7
Westerdale Rd **5** SE10 . 1 A1
Westergate Rd
  Bexley SE2 . . . . 13 E8
  Rochester ME2 . . . . 39 F1
WESTERHAM 151 C1
Westerham Cl
  Canterbury CT2 . . . . . . 143 A4
  Gillingham ME8 . . . . 65 B3
  Margate CT9 . . . . 51 F1
Westerham Dr DA15 . . . 13 E7
Westerham Hill TN16 . 151 B5
Westerham Rd
  Brasted TN16 . . . . 152 A2
  Limpsfield RH8, TN16 . 183 C6
  Orpington BR2 . . . . 85 B7
  Sevenoaks TN13 . . . . . 153 C4
  Sittingbourne ME10 . . . 101 C3
  Westerham TN16 . . . . . 184 A8
Westerhill Rd ME17 . . . 194 C1
Westerhout Cl CT14 . . . 215 C4
Westerly Mews **5** CT2 142 E1
Western Ave
  Ashford TN23 . . . . 268 A3
  Bridge CT4 . . . . 176 A1
  Chatham ME4 . . . . 64 A8
  Halfway Houses ME12 . . 46 D6
  7 Herne Bay TN18 . . 340 F2
  Herne Bay CT6 . . . . 76 E4
Western Beach
  Apartments E16 . . . . . 1 A5
Western Cl CT17 . . . . . . 310 C6
Western Cross Cl DA9 . 17 C1

Western Espl
　Broadstairs CT10 . . . . .84 B2
　Herne Bay CT6 . . . . .76 C5
Western Gateway E16 . . . . .1 A6
Western Gdns TN24 . . . . .300 E8
WESTERN HEIGHTS . 310 C6
Western Heights Rdbt
　CT17 . . . . .310 C5
Western Ho CT14 . . . . . . .215 C7
Western Hts★ CT17 . 310 C6
Western Link ME13 . . . . .138 A8
Western Rd
　Borough Green TN15 . . .156 F7
　Deal CT14 . . . . .215 C7
　Hawkhurst TN18 . . . . . .340 F2
　Maidstone ME16 . . . . . .161 C2
　Margate CT9 . . . . .83 C8
　Royal Tunbridge Wells,
　　Southborough TN4 . . . 254 A1
　Royal Tunbridge Wells
　　TN1 . . . . .286 C5
　Turner's Green TN5 . . . .336 F6
Western Service Rd
　CT16 . . . . .310 G8
Western Undercliff
　CT11 . . . . .117 C5
Western Way SE28 . . . . .2 E4
WEST FARLEIGH 193 D6
Westfield Blean CT2 . . . . .142 A6
　■ Orpington BR6 . . . . .86 C5
　Sevenoaks TN13 . . . . . .154 C5
Westfield Bsns Ctr ME2 63 C7
Westfield Cl DA12 . . . . . . .37 C2
Westfield Cotts
　Cudham TN14 . . . . .119 D3
　Lower Halstow ME9 . . . . .67 A2
　West Kingsdown TN15 . . .90 F4
Westfield Gdns ME9 . . . . .100 C3
Westfield Ho TN30 . . . . . .344 F7
Westfield La CT18 . . . . . . .305 C3
Westfield Rd Bexley DA7 14 C4
　Birchington CT7 . . . . .81 A7
　Margate CT9 . . . . .82 C8
Westfields TN27 . . . . .265 D8
WESTFIELD SOLE . . . 130 C2
Westfield Sole Rd ME5,
　ME14 . . . . .130 D8
Westfield St SE18 . . . . .1 D3
Westfield Terr TN17 . . . . .319 F1
Westfield Villas TN12 . . . .259 B5
Westgate Ave CT7 . . . . . . .82 A4
Westgate Bay Ave CT8 . .50 C1
Westgate Cl CT7 . . . . .82 A4
Westgate College for Deaf
　People CT9 . . . . .50 J2
Westgate Court Ave
　CT2 . . . . .142 D1
Westgate Ct
　■ Canterbury CT2 . . . . .142 E1
　Lewisham SE12 . . . . .29 A7
Westgate Garden Flats
　CT2 . . . . .174 E8
Westgate Gr CT2 . . . . . . .142 F1
Westgate Hall Rd ■
　CT1 . . . . .142 F1
Westgate Ho ■ DA1 . . . . .15 D1
WESTGATE ON SEA . .81 E7
Westgate-on-Sea Sta
　CT8 . . . . .81 E8
Westgate Prim Sch
　DA1 . . . . .33 D8
Westgate Rd
　Dartford DA1 . . . . .15 D1
　Faversham ME13 . . . . . .138 E7
Westgate Terr CT5 . . . . . . .74 E2
Westgate Tower Mus★
　CT1 . . . . .142 F1
West Gn ME10 . . . . .68 F1
West Hallowes SE9 . . . . . .29 C7
Westharold BR8 . . . . .55 D6
WEST HEATH 13 D8
West Heath Cl DA1 . . . . . .14 F1
West Heath La TN13 . . . . .187 B7
West Heath Rd
　Bexley SE2 . . . . .13 D8
　Crayford DA1 . . . . .14 F1
West Hill Biggin Hill BR6 118 F7
　Dartford DA1 . . . . .15 D1
Westhill CL DA12 . . . . .37 B7
West Hill Dr DA1 . . . . .15 C1
West Hill Prim Sch DA1 15 C1
West Hill Rd CT6 . . . . .76 C5
West Hill Rise DA1 . . . . . .15 D1
Westholme BR6 . . . . .53 F2
West Holme DA8 . . . . .14 C6
Westhorne Ave SE12,
　SE9 . . . . .11 C2
WEST HOUGHAM . . . 308 F5
Westhurst Dr BR7 . . . . . . .30 A3
WEST HYTHE 332 B1
West Hythe Rd CT21 . . . .353 A8
West Kent Ave TN11 . . . . .18 C1
WEST KINGSDOWN . . .90 F2
West Kingsdown CE Prim
　Sch TN15 . . . . .90 F2
West Kingsdown Ind Est
　TN15 . . . . .90 F2
West La Grain ME3 . . . . . .26 F6
　Sheerness ME12 . . . . .28 A2
　Sittingbourne ME10 . . .102 A4
Westland Ho ■ E16 . . . . . .2 A5
Westland Lodge ■ BR1 52 C7
Westlands Ave ME10 .101 B4
Westlands Rd CT6 . . . . . . .76 C3
Westlands Sch The
　ME10 . . . . .101 B4
Westland Way CT18 . . . .307 B3
West Lane Trad Est
　ME10 . . . . .102 A4

WEST LANGDON 246 D3
West Lawn Gdns CT20 334 D3
West Lea CT14 . . . . .215 C7
Westlea Ct CT20 . . . . .335 A3
Westleigh Dr BR1 . . . . .52 E8
Westleigh Rd CT8 . . . . .81 D8
West Lodge Prep Sch ■
　DA14 . . . . .31 A5
WEST MALLING 159 C7
West Malling CE Prim Sch
　ME19 . . . . .159 B8
West Malling Ind Pk
　ME19 . . . . .126 E2
West Malling Sta
　ME19 . . . . .159 D8
WESTMARSH 147 B7
Westmarsh Cl ME15 . . . .195 F7
Westmarsh Dr CT9 . . . . . .51 E2
Westmarsh Dro CT3 . . . . .147 A8
Westmead ME20 . . . . . . .128 C4
Westmeads Com Inf Sch ■
　CT5 . . . . .74 D1
Westmeads Rd CT5 . . . . . .74 E2
West Mersea Cl E16 . . . . . .1 B5
West Mill DA11 . . . . .18 F1
WEST MINSTER 46 A7
Westminster Ind Est
　SE18 . . . . .1 D3
West Minster Prim Sch
　ME12 . . . . .46 B8
Westminster Rd CT1 . . . .143 C4
Westminster Sq ME16 .161 B4
Westminster Wlk CT12 .83 C1
Westmoors TN23 . . . . . . .299 E6
Westmoor St SE7 . . . . .1 D3
Westmoreland Ave
　DA16 . . . . .12 E3
Westmoreland Dr ME9 42 C3
Westmoreland Pl ■
　BR1 . . . . .52 A6
Westmoreland Rd BR2 .52 A5
Westmore Rd TN16 . . . . .150 C7
Westmorland CT Prim Sch
　ME15 . . . . .195 E7
Westmorland Gn
　ME15 . . . . .195 E7
Westmorland Rd ME15 195 E7
West Motney Way ME8 .66 A3
Westmount Ave ME4 . . . .63 F3
Westmount Ho ■ ME9 . .51 B2
Westmount Rd SE9 . . . . . .12 A3
West Norman Rd CT16 310 E8
Weston Ave RM20 . . . . . .16 F8
Weston Rd ME2 . . . . .63 A8
Westonville Ave CT9 . . . . .50 F1
Westover Gdns CT10 . . . . .83 E7
Westover Rd CT10 . . . . . . .83 E6
West Par CT21 . . . . .333 B1
West Park Ave
　Margate CT9 . . . . .51 D1
　Royal Tunbridge Wells
　TN4 . . . . .253 F1
West Park Rd ME15 . . . . .162 B2
West Parkside SE10 . . . . . . .1 A2
West Pas ME12 . . . . .28 A2
WEST PECKHAM 191 A6
West Pk SE9 . . . . .29 C7
West Pl TN29 . . . . .370 D8
West Ramp CT16 . . . . . . .310 G8
West Rd Chatham ME4 . .64 A7
　Cliffs End CT13 . . . . . . .116 A1
　Folkestone CT20 . . . . . .334 C4
　Goudhurst TN17 . . . . . .318 E8
　Kilndown TN17 . . . . . . .317 F3
Westree Ct ■ ME16 . . . . .161 E3
Westree Rd ME16 . . . . . . .161 E3
West Ridge ME10 . . . . . . .101 D3
Westrise TN9 . . . . .254 A7
West Shaw DA3 . . . . .58 D7
West Side CT15 . . . . .247 A1
Westside Apartments ■
　CT2 . . . . .142 F1
West Silvertown Sta E16 1 A5
West St Ashford TN23 . . .268 B2
　Bexley DA7 . . . . .13 F4
　Bromley BR1 . . . . .52 A7
　Deal CT14 . . . . .215 D6
　Dover CT17 . . . . .310 C8
　Erith DA8 . . . . .4 E1
　Faversham ME13 . . . . . .138 C7
　Gillingham ME7 . . . . .64 D6
　Gravesend DA11 . . . . . . .19 B1
　Grays RM17 . . . . .18 A8
　Harrietsham ME17 . . . . .198 C6
　Hunton ME15 . . . . .226 D7
　Lenham ME17 . . . . .166 E1
　New Romney TN28 . . . .373 A6
　Queenborough ME11 . . .45 F5
　Rochester ME2 . . . . .40 B1
　Sheerness ME12 . . . . . . .28 A2
　Sittingbourne ME10 . . .101 E4
　West Malling ME19 . . . .159 B8
　Woodside Green ME17 .199 E8
　Wrotham TN15 . . . . . . .124 F3
WEST STOURMOUTH 113 D2
WEST STREET Eastry .180 F1
　Lenham ME17 . . . . .166 E1
West Street Cotts
　CT14 . . . . .181 A1
West Tank Farm Rd
　TN29 . . . . .380 C2
West Terr
　Folkestone CT20 . . . . . .335 D4
　Sidcup DA14 . . . . .30 E7
WEST THURROCK 17 B8
West Thurrock Prim Sch
　RM20 . . . . .17 A8
West Thurrock Way
　RM20 . . . . .17 B8
WEST TILBURY 19 E8
Westview ME4 . . . . .41 B2
West View
　Folkestone CT20 . . . . . .335 D8
　Sutton Valence ME17 . .229 E8

West View Cl CT6 . . . . . . .76 C2
West View Hospl TN30 .344 E6
West View Rd
　Crockenhill BR8 . . . . . . .55 D3
　Dartford DA1 . . . . .33 F1
　Swanley BR8 . . . . .56 A5
Westway
　Coxheath ME17 . . . . . . .194 C3
　Pembury TN2 . . . . .287 D7
West Way BR5 . . . . .53 D4
Westways
　Edenbridge TN8 . . . . . . .217 C2
　Westerham TN16 . . . . . .151 C1
WESTWELL 235 E3
Westwell Cl BR5 . . . . .54 D1
Westwell Ct
　Tenterden TN30 . . . . . . .344 F7
　Westwell TN25 . . . . .235 E3
Westwell Ho TN30 . . . . . .344 F7
Westwell La
　Charing TN25, TN27 . . .234 F7
　Potters Corner TN24,
　TN25 . . . . .267 E7
Westwell TN25, TN26 . . .235 B4
West Wlk ME16 . . . . .161 B3
WESTWOOD Barham . .241 E8
　Broadstairs 83 B5
　Swanscombe 35 D1
Westwood Cl BR1 . . . . . . .52 D6
West Wood Cott BR6 . . . .88 B4
Westwood Dr ME15 . . . . .138 E3
Westwood Farm DA1 . . . .35 D2
Westwood Ind Est CT9 . .83 A6
Westwood La
　Betsham DA13 . . . . .35 E2
　Broadstairs CT10 . . . . . . .83 C4
　East Peckham TN12 . . . .224 E6
　Kingston CT4 . . . . .208 T1
　Loose ME15 . . . . .195 A7
　Rusthall TN4 . . . . .285 C5
West Wood Rd ME9 . . . .132 B8
West Woodside DA5 . . . . .31 E7
Westwood Way TN13 . . . .153 F5
Westwood Wlk ME9 . . . .100 B7
WEST YOKE 91 D7
West Yoke TN15 . . . . .91 D7
WETHAM GREEN 66 F5
Wetheral Dr ME5 . . . . .97 B4
Wexford Pl ME15 . . . . . . .195 D6
Weybridge Cl ME5 . . . . . . .97 C4
Weyburn Dr CT12 . . . . . . .83 A1
Wey Cl ME5 . . . . .97 C5
Weyhill Cl ME14 . . . . .162 C6
Weyman Rd SE3 . . . . .11 C6
Weymouth Cl
　Folkestone CT19 . . . . . .334 D7
　Newham E6 . . . . .2 B7
Weymouth Rd CT19 . . . . .334 D7
Weymouth Terr CT19 . . .334 D7
Wey St TN26 . . . . .349 D3
Wharfdale Sq ME15 . . . . .161 E1
Wharfedale Rd
　Dartford DA2 . . . . .34 C7
　Margate CT9 . . . . .51 A1
Wharf La ME3 . . . . .22 B6
Wharf Rd Gillingham ME7 64 C7
　Gravesend DA12 . . . . . . .19 E1
　Grays RM17 . . . . .17 F8
　Maidstone ME15 . . . . . .161 B2
　Sandwich CT13 . . . . . . .149 B4
Wharf Road S RM17 . . . . .17 F8
Wharfside Cl DA8 . . . . .4 F1
Wharncliffe Ho ■ BR1 . . .7 B1
Wharton Gdns TN24 . . . .300 E8
Wharton Rd BR1 . . . . .52 B8
Whatcote Cotts TN15 . . .157 C7
Whatman Cl ME14 . . . . . .162 C6
Whatman Ho ME13 . . . . .139 F4
Whatmer Cl CT2 . . . . .144 A5
WHATSOLE STREET . 271 F5
Wheatcroft Cl 37 C7
Wheatcroft ME14 . . . . . . .102 B4
Wheatcroft Gr ME8 . . . . . .98 F7
Wheatear Way ME5 . . . . .97 B7
Wheatfield ME19 . . . . . . .127 E1
Wheatfield Cl TN17 . . . . .320 C5
Wheatfield Dr TN17 . . . . .320 C5
Wheatfield Lea TN17 . . . .320 C5
Wheatfields
　Chatham ME5 . . . . .97 D2
　Maidstone ME14 . . . . . .162 D4
　Newham E6 . . . . .2 B7
Wheatfield Way TN17 320 C5
Wheatley Cl DA9 . . . . .17 A2
Wheatley Rd
　Ramsgate CT12 . . . . .83 C1
　Whitstable CT5 . . . . .74 D2
Wheatley Terrace Rd
　DA8 . . . . .14 F8
Wheatsheaf Cl
　Boughton Street
　ME13 . . . . .140 A3
　Loose ME15 . . . . .195 B8
Wheatsheafe La CT5 .247 B2
Wheatsheaf Gdns ME12 28 B1
Wheatsheaf Hill
　Chelsfield TN14 . . . . .87 F2
　Ide Hill TN14 . . . . .185 F4
Wheatsheaf Way TN10 222 D6
Wheatstone Rd DA8 . . . . . .4 D1
Wheelbarrow Park Est
　TN12 . . . . .259 B4
WHEELBARROW
　TOWN 272 F8
Wheeler Pl Bromley BR2 52 B5
　Kings Hill ME18 . . . . . . .159 A2
Wheeler's La ME17 . . . . .227 E7
Wheeler St
　Headcorn TN27 . . . . . . .262 E5
　Maidstone ME14 . . . . . .162 A5

Wheelers The ME8 . . . . . .98 B6
Wheelock Cl DA8 . . . . .14 B7
Wheelwrights The
　ME17 . . . . .198 D6
Wheelwrights Way
　CT13 . . . . .180 B2
Wheelwrites TN15 . . . . . .189 E7
Wheler Ct ME13 . . . . .138 A7
Wheler Rd TN27 . . . . .234 C8
Whenman Ave CT4 . . . . . .32 C5
Whernside Cl SE28 . . . . . . .3 C6
Wherry Cl CT9 . . . . .83 A5
WHETSTED 224 E1
Whetsted Rd
　Five Oak Green TN12 . .256 C8
　Whetsted TN12 . . . . . . .224 F1
Whetstone Rd SE3 . . . . . .11 D6
Whewell Terr ■ CT20 . . .335 E5
Whiffen's Ave ME4 . . . . . .63 F5
Whiffen's Ave W ME4 . . .63 F5
Whiffen Wlk ME15 . . . . . .128 B1
Whigham Cl TN23 . . . . . .299 D7
Whimbrel Cl
　Sittingbourne ME10 . . .101 E4
　Woolwich SE28 . . . . .3 C6
Whimbrel Gn ME20 . . . . .127 F2
Whimbrels The ME4 . . . . .41 B1
Whimbrel Wlk ME5 . . . . . .97 C1
Whinchat Rd SE28 . . . . . . .2 D3
Whinfell Ave CT11 . . . . . .116 F7
Whinfell Way DA12 . . . . . .37 F4
Whinless Rd CT17 . . . . . .310 A8
Whinyates Rd SE9 . . . . . . .11 E4
Whippendell Cl BR5 . . . . .54 B8
Whippendell Way BR5 . .54 B8
Whistler Rd TN10 . . . . . . .222 D6
Whiston Ave TN26 . . . . . .297 C4
Whitbourne Ct ■ CT5 108 D8
Whitby Cl
　Biggin Hill TN16 . . . . . .118 B1
　Stone DA9 . . . . .17 A2
Whitby Rd
　Folkestone CT20 . . . . . .334 D4
　Woolwich SE18 . . . . .1 F2
Whitchurch Cl ME16 . . . .161 E4
Whitcombe Cl ME5 . . . . . .97 C3
White Acre Dr CT14 . . . . .248 B8
Whiteacre La CT4 . . . . . . .239 E4
White Ave DA11 . . . . .36 F5
Whitebeam Ave BR2 . . . .53 A3
Whitebeam Cl
　Ashford TN23 . . . . .267 D4
　Kemsing TN15 . . . . .123 A2
Whitebeam Dr ME17 . . . .194 B3
White Bear Pas ■
　TN1 . . . . .286 A2
Whitebine Gdns TN10 225 A6
Whitebread La TN31 . . . .357 D1
White Cl CT16 . . . . .278 B5
White Cliffs ■ CT20 . . . .335 D4
White Cliffs Bsns Ctr
　CT16 . . . . .278 A4
White Cliffs Bsns Pk
　CT16 . . . . .278 B6
White Cliffs of Dover
　Visitor Ctr★ CT16 . . .279 A1
White Cliffs Prim Coll for
　the Arts CT17 . . . . . . .278 A1
Whitecliff Way CT19 . . . .335 F6
White Cottage Rd
　TN10 . . . . .222 D6
Whitecroft BR8 . . . . .55 E7
White Ct ■ CT20 . . . . . . .334 E3
Whitefield Cl BR5 . . . . . . .54 C6
Whitefield Rd TN4 . . . . . .286 A6
Whitefriars TN13 . . . . . . .187 A8
Whitefriars Mdw ■
　CT13 . . . . .148 F1
Whitefriars Way ■
　CT13 . . . . .148 F1
Whitefriars Wharf
　TN9 . . . . .222 C1
White Gate ME2 . . . . .62 F8
Whitegate Cl TN4 . . . . . . .286 A8
Whitegate ME8 . . . . .98 D5
White Gates DA14 . . . . . . .31 A3
Whitegates Ave TN15 . . . .90 E4
Whitegates La TN5 . . . . . .336 D8
WHITEHALL 83 C1
Whitehall
　Brookland TN29 . . . . . . .370 E8
　Sandwich CT13 . . . . . . .182 A7
Whitehall Bridge Rd
　CT2 . . . . .174 E8
Whitehall Cl CT2 . . . . . . .174 E8
Whitehall Dr ME17 . . . . .197 D3
Whitehall Gdns CT2 . . . .142 E1
Whitehall La Erith DA8 . .14 F5
　■ Grays RM17 . . . . .18 C8
Whitehall Rd
　Broad Street ME14 . . . .164 A6
　Bromley BR2 . . . . .52 D5
　Canterbury CT2 . . . . . . .174 E8
　Canterbury, Harbledown
　CT2 . . . . .174 D7
　Ramsgate CT12 . . . . .83 C1
　Sittingbourne ME10 . . .101 E2
Whitehall Way TN25 . . . .303 D1
White Hart Ave 2 E3
White Hart Cl TN13 . . . . .187 C7
White Hart Mans CT9 . . . .50 I3
White Hart Par TN13 . . . .153 E5
White Hart Rd
　Orpington BR6 . . . . .54 A2
　Woolwich SE18 . . . . .2 E2
White Hart Wood
　TN13 . . . . .187 C6
White Hart Yd ■ DA11 .19 B1
Whitehaven Cl BR2 . . . . . .52 A5
Whitehaven Ct ■ DA6 . .13 C3
Whitehead Cl DA2 . . . . . . .26 B6
Whiteheads La ME14 . . . .163 B4
WHITEHILL Faversham .137 F3
　Hartley 58 D7

Whitehill TN15 . . . . .125 B3
White Hill
　Boughton Aluph TN25 . .237 B6
　Challock TN25 . . . . .203 E1
　Chilham CT4 . . . . .172 E1
White Hill Cl CT14 . . . . . .208 A8
White Hill La DA12 . . . . . .37 D5
White Hill Par CT12 . . . . .37 C5
Whitehill Prim Sch
　CT12 . . . . .37 C5
Whitehill Rd
　Dartford DA1 . . . . .15 A2
　Gravesend DA12 . . . . . . .37 C6
　Longfield, Whitehill DA13 58 D8
　Meopham DA13 . . . . .93 B7
White Hill Rd ME9,
　ME14 . . . . .98 D1
Whitehorse Hill ME5 . . . .64 B3
White Horse Hill
　Eltham BR7, SE9 . . . . . . .30 A4
　Hawkinge CT18 . . . . . . .307 C3
White Horse La
　■ Canterbury CT1 . . . .174 F8
　Harvel DA13 . . . . .93 C2
　Otham Hole ME15 . . . . .196 A6
　Rhodes Minnis CT4 . . . .273 A3
White Horse Rd DA13 . . .93 E1
White Horse Wood Cntry
　Park★ ME14 . . . . .131 D2
White House Cl ME3 . . . . .41 E4
Whitehouse Cres ME1 129 A8
Whitehouse Dro CT13,
　CT3 . . . . .148 D7
White House Farm Ct
　CT15 . . . . .211 E5
White House La TN13 . . .186 F5
White House Rd TN14 . . .186 F5
White La RH8, TN16 . . . .150 B3
Whitelake Rd TN10 . . . . .222 C5
Whiteleaves Rise ME2 . .62 B3
Whitelimes ME18 . . . . . . .340 D8
Whitelocks CT4 . . . . .209 D3
White Lodge TN1 . . . . . . .286 C4
White Lodge Cl TN13 . . .154 B4
White Marsh Ct CT5 . . . . .74 E2
White Mill Rural Her Ctr★
　CT13 . . . . .148 D2
Whitenbrook CT21 . . . . .334 A3
Whitenbrook Dell
　CT21 . . . . .334 A3
Whiteness Gn CT10 . . . . .51 F1
Whiteness Rd CT10 . . . . . .51 G1
WHITE OAK 55 F7
White Oak Cl CT15 . . . . .254 E6
Whiteoak Ct ■ BR8 . . . . .55 E6
White Oak Gdns DA15 . .30 F8
White Oak Sq ■ BR8 . . . .55 E6
WHITE POST 283 D7
Whitepost ■ CT5 . . . . .74 D2
White Post
　Four Elms TN8 . . . . .218 A6
　Hollingbourne ME17 . . .165 B5
White Post Cnr TN11 . . . .189 F5
White Post Gdns CT13 . .147 E1
White Post Hill DA4 . . . . . .57 A2
Whitepost La DA13 . . . . .126 A8
White Post La
　Culverstone Green
　DA13 . . . . .92 F2
　Sole Street DA13 . . . . . . .60 B5
White Rd ME4 . . . . .64 F3
White Rock Ct ME16 . . . .161 E3
White Rock Pl ■
　ME16 . . . . .161 E3
Whites Cl DA9 . . . . .17 C1
Whites Hill CT14 . . . . . . .213 B2
White's La TN18 . . . . .341 B2
White's Mdw BR1 . . . . . . .53 A5
Whitewall CT Ind Est
　ME2 . . . . .63 D8
Whitewall Rd ME2 . . . . . . .63 D7
Whitewall Way ME2 . . . . .63 D7
Whiteway Rd ME11,
　ME12 . . . . .45 F6
Whitewebbs Way BR5 . .53 F8
Whitewell La TN17 . . . . .320 D7
White Willow Cl TN24 300 D6
Whitewood Cotts
　TN16 . . . . .150 C7
Whitewood Post La
　ME20 . . . . .160 F7
White Wood Rd TN13 . . .180 B1
Whitfeld Rd TN23 . . . . . .300 B8
WHITFIELD 278 A7
Whitfield Ave
　Broadstairs CT10 . . . . . . .83 E7
　Dover CT16 . . . . .278 C7
Whitfield Cotts TN23 . . .300 B8
Whitfield Cres ■ DA2 . .34 C8
Whitfield Ct CT16 . . . . . .278 A6
Whitfield Hill
　Dover CT16 . . . . .277 F4
　Temple Ewell CT16 . . . .277 E4
Whitfield Lodge CT16 . .278 A6
Whitfield Rd DA7 . . . . .13 F7
Whitfield Rdbt CT16 . . . .278 A6
Whitfold Sch & Aspen
　Prim Sch CT16 . . . . . .278 A7
Whitgift Ct CT2 . . . . .142 D1
Whiting Cres ME13 . . . . .138 A8
Whiting Ho TN29 . . . . . . .376 C5
Whitings Way E6 . . . . .2 A8
Whitmore St ME16 . . . . . .161 D2
Whitney Wlk DA14 . . . . . .31 E2
WHITSTABLE 74 C3
Whitstable Jun Sch ■
　CT5 . . . . .74 D1
Whitstable Mus & Art
　Gallery★ ■ CT5 . . . . . .74 D1
Whitstable Rd
　Canterbury CT2 . . . . . . .142 D2
　Faversham, Goodnestone
　ME13 . . . . .139 B6
　Faversham ME13 . . . . . .138 E7

Whitstable Rd continued
　Herne Bay CT5, CT6 . . .76 B3
　Rough Common CT2 . . .142 B4
Whitstable & Seasalter
　Endowed CE Jun Sch ■
　CT5 . . . . .74 D1
Whitstable Sports Ctr
　CT5 . . . . .108 F8
Whitstable Sta CT5 . . . . . .74 E1
Whitstable & Tankerton
　Hospl CT5 . . . . .75 A2
Whittaker St ME4 . . . . . . .64 B4
Whittington Terr CT15 244 E4
Whitworth Rd SE18 . . . . . .12 A7
Whybornes Chase
　ME12 . . . . .47 C7
Whybourne Crest TN2 286 D1
Whyman Ave ME4 . . . . . . .64 A1
Whytecliffs CT10 . . . . .84 A2
WICHLING 167 C5
Wichling Cl
　Canterbury CT2 . . . . . . .143 D3
　Orpington BR5 . . . . .54 C5
Wickenden Cres TN24 301 A6
Wickenden Rd TN13 . . . .154 C5
Wicken Ho ME16 . . . . . . .161 E4
Wicken La TN25, TN27 . .234 E6
Wickens Pl ME19 . . . . . . .159 C8
Wickets The
　Ashford TN24 . . . . .300 E8
　Sevenoaks Weald TN14 187 C2
Wicketts End ■ CT5 . . . . .74 D1
Wickham Ave CT11 . . . . .117 G8
WICKHAMBREAUX . . 145 B3
Wickhambreaux CE Prim
　Sch CT3 . . . . .145 C2
Wickham Cl ME9 . . . . . . .100 B5
Wickham Common Prim
　Sch BR4 . . . . .85 A6
Wickham Court La
　CT3 . . . . .145 B3
Wickham Ct DA16 . . . . . . .12 E5
Wickham Field TN14 . . . .121 F3
Wickham Gdns TN4 . . . .285 D5
Wickham La
　Ickham CT3 . . . . .145 B1
　Woolwich SE2, SE18 . . . .13 A8
Wickham Mill CT3 . . . . . .145 C2
Wickham Pl ME17 . . . . . .199 D5
Wickham Rd CT3 . . . . . . .145 B2
Wickham St Bexley DA16 13 A6
　Rochester ME1 . . . . .63 D3
Wickhams Way DA3 . . . . .58 F4
Wickham Terr ME11 . . . . .45 F5
WICK HILL 294 F8
Wickhurst Rd TN14 . . . . .186 F3
Wick La CT4 . . . . .243 E7
Wicks Cl SE9 . . . . .29 C4
Wicksteed Cl DA5 . . . . . . .32 D5
Widbury TN3 . . . . .284 F3
Widecombe Rd SE9 . . . . .29 E5
Widgeon Cl E16 . . . . .1 B7
Widgeon Path SE28 . . . . . .2 D3
Widgeon Rd Erith DA8 . . .15 B7
　Rochester ME2 . . . . .62 D6
Widgeon Wlk CT18 . . . . .307 B3
WIDMORE 52 E7
Widmore Lodge Rd
　BR1 . . . . .52 D7
Widmore Rd BR1 . . . . .52 C7
Widred Rd CT17 . . . . .310 C8
WIERTON 228 F8
Wierton Hill ME17 . . . . . .228 D7
Wierton La ME17 . . . . . . .195 E1
Wierton Rd ME17 . . . . . . .228 E8
Wife of Bath Hill CT2 . .174 C8
Wigeon Rd ME9 . . . . .68 E3
WIGMORE 98 B4
Wigmore Cotts CT15 . . . .245 C8
Wigmore Glade ME8 . . . .98 B4
Wigmore La CT15 . . . . . .245 C8
Wigmore Rd ME8 . . . . . . .98 B4
Wigmore Wood CT15 . . .245 C8
Wigwam Paddocks CT7 81 A8
Wihtred Rd ME9 . . . . . . .102 D2
Wilberforce Ct ■ SE28 . . .3 C5
Wilberforce Rd
　Coxheath ME17 . . . . . . .194 D3
　Folkestone CT20 . . . . . .334 E3
Wilberforce Way DA12 .37 D3
Wilbrough Rd CT7 . . . . . . .81 A7
Wilcox Cl CT3 . . . . .210 D5
Wild Air CT7 . . . . .80 F8
Wilde Cl RM18 . . . . .19 C5
Wilden Park Rd TN12 . . .291 E7
Wilde Rd DA8 . . . . .14 B7
WILDERNESSE 154 E4
Wildernesse Ave TN15 154 F5
Wildernesse Mount
　TN13 . . . . .154 D5
Wildernesse Sch The
　TN13 . . . . .154 E6
Wilderness Hill CT9 . . . . .51 A2
Wilderness Mews TN2 286 C4
Wilderness Rd BR7 . . . . . .30 B1
Wildfell Cl ME5 . . . . .130 C8
Wildish Rd ME13 . . . . . . .138 A8
Wildman Cl ME8 . . . . .98 D3
Wildwood Cl
　Kingswood ME17 . . . . .197 E2
　■ Lewisham SE12 . . . . .29 A8
Wildwood Glade ME7 . . .98 B4
Wildwood Rd CT2 . . . . . .143 F6
Wildwood Wealden Forest
　Pk★ CT2, CT6 . . . . . . .110 E4
Wiles Ave TN28 . . . . .373 B6
Wiles Ho TN28 . . . . .373 B6
Wilford Ho ■ SE18 . . . . . .2 B1
Wilfred Rd CT1 . . . . .117 C8
Wilfred St ■ DA12 . . . . . .19 B1
WILGATE GREEN 169 F6
Wilgate Green Rd
　ME13 . . . . .169 F6
Wilkes Rd CT10 . . . . .83 E4

Wilkie Rd CT7 . . . . .81 A8
Wilkinson Cl 1 DA1. . .16 A3
Wilkinson Dr CT14 . . 215 D3
Wilkinson Pl ME18 . . 159 A2
Wilkins Way TN16 . . . . .152 B3
Wilks Cl ME8 . . . . .66 B2
Will Adams Ct 9 ME7 . .64 C6
Will Adams Rdbt ME8 . .64 F2
Will Adams Way ME8. . .64 F1
Will Crooks Gdns SE9 . .11 D3
Willement Rd SE18 . . . . .2 B1
Willenhall Rd SE18 . . . . .2 B1
Willersley Ave
  Orpington BR6 . . . . . . .86 D7
  Sidcup DA15 . . . . .30 F7
Willersley Cl DA15. . . . .30 F7
WILLESBOROUGH 300 F8
Willesborough Ct
  TN24 . . . . 269 A2
Willesborough Ind Pk
  TN24. . . . . .269 A1
Willesborough Inf & Jun
  Schs TN24. . . . . 301 A8
WILLESBOROUGH
  LEES 269 B1
Willesborough Rd
  TN24. . . . . .268 F4
Willesborough Windmill★
  TN24. . . . . .268 F4
Willesley Gdns TN17. .320 D6
Willett Cl BR5. . . . . .53 E3
Willetts Cotts TN3. . . .283 C4
Willetts Hill CT12. . . . .114 D7
Willetts La TN3. . . . . . .283 C4
Willett Way BR5, BR6. . .53 E3
William Ave
  Folkestone CT19. . . . .335 B7
  Margate CT9. . . . . .83 C8
William Baker Ho
  ME20 . . . . .160 F8
William Barefoot Dr
  SE9 . . . . .30 A5
William Foster La DA16 13 A5
William Gibbs Ct 14
  ME13 . . . . .138 D7
William Harvey Hospl
  TN24. . . . . .269 C1
William Ho 4 DA12 . .37 B8
William Judge Cl
  TN30 . . . . .345 D7
William Luck Cl TN12. .224 E6
William Muge Ho 15
  CT16 . . . . .310 D8
William Petty Way BR5 54 C1
William Pitt Ave CT14 .215 B6
William Pitt Cl CT21 . .333 D2
William Rd
  Ashford TN23 . . . . . . .300 B8
  Cuxton ME2. . . . . .62 C2
William Rigby Dr ME12 46 E7
Williams Cl ME9. . . . . .134 E5
William Smith Ho 10
  DA17 . . . . .4 A3
Williamson Rd TN29. .377 E5
William St
  Faversham ME13 . . . .138 D7
  Gillingham ME8. . . . . .66 A1
  Gravesend DA12. . . . . .37 B8
  Grays RM17 . . . . .18 C8
  Herne Bay CT6 . . . . . . .76 F5
  Royal Tunbridge Wells
   TN4 . . . . .286 A5
  Sittingbourne ME10 . .101 E4
  Whitstable CT5 . . . . . . .74 D2
Williams Way DA2. . . . .32 D6
Willicombe Ho TN2. . .286 D4
Willicombe Pk TN2. . .286 D4
Willingdon TN23 . . . . .299 E5
Willingdon Pl CT14. . .215 C1
Willingdon Rd CT16 . . .37 E6
WILLINGTON 162 E1
Willington Gn ME15 . .162 E7
Willington St ME15. . .162 E7
Willis Cl ME12. . . . . . . .46 F5
Willis Ho ME1 . . . . .63 C4
Willis Rd DA8 . . . . .4 D2
Willop Cl TN29. . . . . . .352 E2
Willop Way TN29. . . . .352 E2
Willoughby Ct 13 CT1. .174 F8
Willoughby Way SE7 . .1 B2
Willow Ave
  Broadstairs CT10 . . . . .83 D4
  Faversham ME13 . . . .138 A7
  Hoo St Werburgh ME3 . .41 C8
  Sidcup DA15 . . . . .13 A1
  Swanley BR8. . . . . .55 F5
Willow Bank TN24 . . . .269 C4
Willowbank Cl TN29. .366 A4
Willowbank Ct 12
  ME15. . . . . .162 B4
Willowbank Dr ME23 . .23 E4
Willow Bank Ind Est
  ME9 . . . . .68 E6
Willowby Gdns ME8 . .98 E4
Willow Cl Bromley BR2 . .52 F4
  Canterbury CT1 . . . . .143 A2
  Harrietsham ME17. . . .198 D6
  Hythe CT21. . . . . .332 E1
  Margate CT9. . . . . .51 C2
  Orpington BR5 . . . . . . .54 B2
  Sidcup DA5 . . . . .13 F1
Willow Cres
  Five Oak Green TN12 . .256 B7
  Staplehurst TN12 . . . .260 F5
Willow Ct
  Broadstairs CT10 . . . . .84 A5
  Dartford DA1 . . . . .33 C7
  Folkestone CT20. . . . .334 E4
  Loose ME15 . . . . .195 A6
  Whitstable CT5 . . . . . .108 E8
Willow Dene Sch SE18. .12 E6

Willow Dr
  Hamstreet TN26 . . . . .349 A7
  St Mary's Bay TN29 . .365 F3
Willow Farm Way CT6. .77 C2
Willowfields Cl 1 SE18. .2 E1
Willow Gr BR7 . . . . .30 B2
Willow Grange DA14 . .31 B5
Willowherb Cl ME4. . . .41 C1
Willow Ho
  Ashford TN23 . . . . . . .267 F1
  2 Chatham ME5 . . . .96 F5
  8 Maidstone ME16. . .161 A3
  Sheerness ME12. . . . . .28 B2
  Sittingbourne ME10 . .102 B3
Willow La
  Paddock Wood TN12. . .257 E6
  Woolwich SE18 . . . . . . .2 A2
Willow Lea TN10 . . . . .222 C7
Willow Lodge
  Folkestone CT19. . . . .335 D7
  Royal Tunbridge Wells
   TN4 . . . . .285 E4
Willowmead ME19. . . .127 E2
Willow Pk TN14 . . . . . .121 F2
Willow Rd Dartford DA1. .33 C7
  Erith DA8. . . . . .15 A6
  Great Mongeham CT14. .214 C3
  Larkfield ME20 . . . . . .127 F3
  Rochester ME2 . . . . . . .62 E6
  Whitstable CT5 . . . . . .108 C5
Willow Rise ME15 . . . .162 F1
Willows Cl CT2 . . . . . .142 C4
Willowside ME6 . . . . . .95 A1
Willows Prim Sch The
  CT6. . . . . .77 B4
Willows The
  Ashford TN24 . . . . . . .268 D6
  Gillingham ME8. . . . . .65 E2
  Grays RM17 . . . . .18 D8
  Newington ME9 . . . . . .100 B6
  Sheerness ME12. . . . . .28 H1
  Sittingbourne ME10 . . .68 F1
Willow Terr DA4 . . . . . .89 E8
Willow Tree Cl
  Ashford TN24 . . . . . . .268 F1
  Herne Bay CT6 . . . . . . .77 D5
Willow Tree Ct DA14 . .30 F1
Willow Tree Rd TN2 . .285 F1
Willow Tree Wlk BR1. .52 E8
Willow Vale BR7 . . . . . .30 B2
Willow Way
  Biddenden TN27 . . . . .323 D7
  Maidstone ME15. . . . . .162 B3
  Margate CT9. . . . . .82 C8
  Whitstable CT5 . . . . . .109 C8
Willow Waye CT15. . . .245 D7
Willow Wents ME18 . .158 D1
Willow Wlk
  Culverstone Green
   DA13 . . . . .92 F3
  Orpington BR6 . . . . . . .86 B7
  Royal Tunbridge Wells
   TN2 . . . . .286 E8
Willowwood 20 ME15. .195 E5
Willow Wood Rd DA13. .92 F2
Willrose Cres SE2 . . . . .3 B1
Wills La TN29 . . . . .350 C4
Willson's Rd CT11. . . . .117 D6
Will Thorne Pav E16 . . .1 E7
Wilman Rd TN4 . . . . . .286 B7
Wilmar Way TN15 . . . .154 F7
Wilmecote Ct ME8 . . . .98 D8
WILMINGTON 33 C4
Wilmington Ave BR6 . .37 F1
Wilmington Court Rd
  DA2. . . . . .33 A6
Wilmington Enterprise Coll
  DA2 . . . . .33 B5
Wilmington Gram Sch for
  Boys DA2. . . . . .33 B5
Wilmington Ho DA2. . .33 D6
Wilmington Prim Sch
  DA2. . . . . .33 B5
Wilmington Way ME8 . .65 B2
Wilmot Rd DA1. . . . . . .15 B2
Wilmott Pl CT13 . . . . . .180 B2
Wilmount St SE18 . . . . .2 B2
WILSLEY GREEN 320 D7
WILSLEY POUND 320 E8
Wilson Ave Deal CT14 .214 F4
  Rochester ME1. . . . . . .96 E7
Wilson Cl Ashford TN24 269 A1
  Maidstone ME15. . . . . .195 E7
  Tonbridge TN11. . . . . .221 E5
Wilson Cl ME18 . . . . . .193 A1
Wilson Ho 3 SE7 . . . . .11 C8
Wilson La DA4 . . . . .57 F7
Wilson Rd TN10 . . . . . .222 E5
Wilsons La ME15 . . . . .194 A5
Wilsons Way DA13 . . . .92 F3
Wiltie Cl CT19. . . . . . . .335 C5
Wiltie Gdns CT19. . . . .335 C5
Wilton Cl CT14 . . . . . . .215 C5
Wilton Row ME17 . . . .196 D2
Wilton Ho 2 BR7 . . . . .53 D8
Wilton Rd
  Folkestone CT19. . . . .335 B6
  Ramsgate CT12 . . . . . .82 F1
  Woolwich SE2. . . . . . . .3 C2
Wilton Terr ME10. . . . .101 B5
Wiltshire Cl
  Chatham ME5 . . . . .97 C8
  Dartford DA2 . . . . .34 D8
Wiltshire Rd BR6. . . . . .54 A2
Wiltshire Way
  4 Maidstone ME15. . .195 E6
  Royal Tunbridge Wells
   TN2 . . . . .286 D7
Wimborne 6 DA14 . .31 B4
Wimborne Ave BR7. . . .53 F4
Wimborne Ho DA12 . . .37 D5
Wimborne Pl CT12. . . .117 B8
Wimborne Dr ME8 . . . .98 D6
Wimpole Cl BR2. . . . . . .52 C5

Winant Way CT16 . . . .278 B3
Winch Cl TN17 . . . . . . .320 D3
Winchcomb Gdns SE9. .11 D4
Winch Dr ME9. . . . . . . .134 C6
Wincheap CT1 . . . . .174 E7
Wincheap Gr 4 CT1. .174 F7
Wincheap Ind Est CT1 174 D7
Wincheap Prim Sch
  CT1. . . . . .174 E6
Winchelsea Ave DA7 . .7 D8
Winchelsea Ct CT17 . .310 C7
Winchelsea Rd
  Chatham ME5 . . . . .97 B5
  Dover CT17. . . . . .310 B7
  Rye TN31. . . . . .310 B7
Winchelsea St CT17 . .310 B7
Winchelsea Terr CT17 310 A7
Winchester Ave ME5 . .96 F4
Winchester Cl 11 E6. . .1 F7
Winchester Cres CT1. .37 D5
Winchester Ct 14 DA17. .4 A1
Winchester Gdns CT1 175 A6
Winchester Gr TN13 . .154 B4
Winchester Ho
  3 Maidstone ME15. . .195 D7
  Woolwich SE18. . . . . .11 D7
Winchester Mews
  CT14 . . . . .215 B3
Winchester Pl 9
  ME14. . . . . .162 A5
Winchester Rd
  Bexley DA7 . . . . .13 D5
  Hawkhurst TN18. . . . .341 A2
  Orpington BR6 . . . . . . .87 C6
  Tonbridge TN10. . . . . .222 D5
Winchester Way ME8. . .99 A8
WINCHET HILL 291 B6
Winch Rd ME9 . . . . . . .134 D6
Winch's Garth TN12 . .260 F5
Wincliff Rd TN9 . . . . . .254 B8
Wincrofts Dr SE9. . . . .12 D3
Windermere ME13. . . .138 E6
Windermere Ave CT11 117 A7
Windermere Cl
  Dartford DA1 . . . . .33 B7
  Orpington BR6 . . . . . . .86 B7
Windermere Ct TN24 .268 C4
Windermere Dr ME8 . .98 D7
Windermere Gdns CT3 210 F6
Windermere Gr ME10. 101 D3
Windermere Ho 4
  ME15. . . . . .195 E7
Windermere Rd DA7 . .14 C5
Wind Hill ME17 . . . . . .233 E7
Wind Hill La TN27 . . . .233 E7
Windhover Way DA12 . .37 E4
Winding Hill ME13. . . .170 F6
Windmill Ave CT12 . . . .83 B3
Windmill Cl
  Ashford TN24 . . . . . . .269 A1
  Bridge CT4 . . . . .176 A1
  Canterbury CT1. . . . . .175 C8
  Herne Bay CT6 . . . . . . .77 A2
  Rochester ME2 . . . . . . .40 B1
Windmill Cotts
  Cranbrook TN17 . . . . .320 D6
  Lower Stoke ME3 . . . . .25 C5
Windmill Ct
  Maidstone ME17. . . . . .195 B3
  Royal Tunbridge Wells
   TN2 . . . . .286 C3
Windmill Dr BR2 . . . . . .85 C6
Windmill Grange TN15 .90 F3
Windmill Hill
  Brenchley TN12. . . . . .257 B1
  Fairbourne Heath ME17 198 B1
  Platt TN15. . . . . .157 D7
  Pye Corner ME17 . . . .231 B7
Windmill Hts ME14 . . .163 B4
Windmill La
  Cousley Wood TN5 . . . .337 C8
  Durgates TN5 . . . . . . .336 E4
  Faversham ME13 . . . .105 B1
  Keston BR2. . . . . .85 C6
  Wrotham Heath TN15. .187 B2
Windmill Lane E ME19 159 C6
Windmill Lane W
  ME19. . . . . .159 A6
Windmill Manor ME7. . .64 C4
Windmill Pk TN15 . . . .157 E7
Windmill Quay Rd ME12 47 F2
Windmill Rd
  Canterbury CT1. . . . . .175 C8
  Gillingham ME7. . . . . .64 C4
  Herne Bay CT6 . . . . . . .77 A2
  Sevenoaks TN13 . . . . . .187 B6
  Sevenoaks Weald TN14 187 B2
  Sittingbourne ME10 . .101 D6
  Whitstable CT5 . . . . . .108 D7
Windmill Rise ME15 . .47 E6
Windmill St
  Gravesend DA12. . . . . .37 B7
  12 Gravesend DA12. . .37 B8
  Hythe CT21. . . . . .333 B1
  Rochester ME2 . . . . . . .40 B1
  Royal Tunbridge Wells
   TN2 . . . . .286 C3
Windmill View CT9 . . . .83 A8
Windmill Wlk CT12. . . .83 B1
Windrush Ct 8 DA8. . . .4 E1
Windrush Prim Sch SE28 3 B5
Windsor Ave
  Chatham ME4 . . . . .63 F2
  Margate CT9. . . . . .51 B1
Windsor Ct
  Broadstairs CT10 . . . . .83 E5
  Chislehurst BR7 . . . . . .30 B3
  Maidstone ME14. . . . . .162 B6
Windsor Ct continued
  Gillingham ME7. . . . . .64 D5
  Margate CT9. . . . . .51 B1
  18 Sidcup DA14 . . . . .31 A5
Windsor Dr Dartford DA1 15 A1
  Orpington BR6 . . . . . . .87 A5
  Sittingbourne ME10 . .101 D2
Windsor Gdns
  Herne Bay CT6 . . . . . . .76 B3
  Warden ME12. . . . . . . .49 D4
Windsor Hall E16. . . . . .1 B5
Windsor Ho Deal CT14 215 A5
  6 Dover CT17. . . . . .310 D7
  Whitstable CT5 . . . . . . .74 D1
Windsor Mews
  9 Margate CT9. . . . . .50 J2
  New Romney TN28 . . .373 C8
Windsor Rd Bexley DA6. .13 E3
  Canterbury CT1. . . . . .174 C6
  Cliffs End CT12 . . . . . .116 D7
  Gillingham ME7. . . . . .64 D5
  Gravesend DA12. . . . . .37 B4
Windward Rd ME1. . . . .63 C1
Windy Ridge ME7. . . . . .64 E1
Windy Ridge BR1. . . . . .36 C3
Winehouse La CT18 . . .308 D3
Wineycock ME9 . . . . . .168 C8
Winfield TN15 . . . . . . .156 E3
Winford Mews ME1. . . .63 A2
Win'freds Cl TN17. . . . .343 E3
Wingate Ct 7 ME10. .101 C2
Wingate Rd
  Folkestone CT19. . . . .335 D7
  Sidcup DA14 . . . . .31 C2
Wingfield Ct DA15. . . . .30 F7
Wingfield Prim Sch SE3 11 B4
Wingfield Rd DA12 . . . .37 B8
WINGHAM. 178 B7
Wingham Cl
  Gillingham ME8. . . . . .65 C3
  Maidstone ME15. . . . . .195 F7
WINGHAM GREEN 177 F7
Wingham Ind Est CT3. .178 B6
Wingham Prim Sch
  CT3. . . . . .178 A7
Wingham Rd CT3. . . . .177 D8
Wingham WELL 177 E6
Wingham Well La CT3 177 F5
Wingham Wildlife Pk★
  CT3. . . . . .146 C1
Wing Ho ME12 . . . . . . .49 H1
WINGMORE 242 B2
Wing Rd ME12. . . . . . . .49 H1
Wingrove Dr
  Maidstone ME14. . . . . .162 E5
  Rochester ME2 . . . . . . .63 C7
Wingrove Hill CT17. . . .277 E2
Wings Cl CT10. . . . . . . .84 B5
Winifred Ave CT12 . . . .83 C2
Winifred Rd
  Dartford DA1 . . . . .15 B2
  Erith DA8. . . . . .4 E1
  Maidstone ME15. . . . . .162 F3
Winifred St E16 . . . . . . .1 F5
Winkle Cl CT6. . . . . .76 B8
Winn Common Rd SE18 12 E8
Winnipeg Cl CT16 . . . .278 C3
Winnipeg Dr 3 BR6. . .84 F4
Winn Rd SE12, SE9 . . . .29 B7
Win Pine Ho CT21. . . .333 A1
Winser Rd TN17 . . . . . .344 A1
Winsor Prim Sch E6 . . .2 A7
Winsor Terr E6. . . . . . . .2 A8
Winstanley Cres CT11 117 D8
Winstanley Rd ME12. . .28 C2
Winston Ave ME19. . . .159 B3
Winston Cl
  Canterbury CT1. . . . . .175 C7
  Stone DA9. . . . . .16 F1
Winston Ct
  Birchington CT7 . . . . . .81 A8
  10 Bromley BR1. . . . .52 B8
Winston Dr
  Biggin Hill TN16 . . . . .118 D2
  Rochester ME2 . . . . . . .40 D2
Winston Scott Ave
  TN3 . . . . .284 E4
Winston Gdns CT6. . . . .77 D4
Winston Ho 4 CT20. . .334 F5
Winston Rd ME2. . . . . . .62 D5
Winterage La CT18 . . .306 C7
Winterborne Ave BR6 . .86 D7
WINTERBOURNE 172 A8
Winter Dr CT18. . . . . . .307 B5
Winterfield La ME14. . .163 B4
Wintergarden Cres DA9 35 A8
Winter Gdns & Queens
  Hall CT9 . . . . .50 J3
Wintergreen Cl
  8 Newham E16. . . . . .1 E8
  St Mary's Island ME4. .41 C1
Winters Croft DA12. . . .37 D2
Winterstoke Cres
  CT11 . . . . .117 G8
Winterstoke Way CT11 117 F8
Winterton Ct 8 TN16. 151 D1
Winton Ct BR8 . . . . .55 E5
Winton Rd BR6. . . . . . . .86 B6
Winton Way TN9 . . . . .366 A5
Wireless Rd TN16 . . . .118 D4
Wirrals The ME5 . . . . . .97 A4
Wirral Wood Cl BR7. . . .30 A2
Wise Ho SE18 . . . . .12 A7
Wise La ME10, ME9. . . .101 A4
Wise's La TN15 . . . . . . .91 E2
Wishart Rd SE3 . . . . . . .11 D5
Wish The TN26. . . . . . .347 F6
Wish Valley Mews
  TN18 . . . . .354 F8
Wisley Rd BR5. . . . . . . .31 B1
WISSENDEN. 296 F7
Wissenden La
  Bethersden TN26 . . . . .297 B6

Wissenden La continued
  Smarden, Romden
   TN27 . . . . .264 D1
Wistaria Cl BR6. . . . . . .86 B8
Wisteria Gdns BR8. . . . .55 D5
Wisteria Ho 11 ME15 . .195 E7
Witches La TN13 . . . . .153 D4
Witham Way ME2 . . . . .62 F7
Withens Cl BR5. . . . . . .54 C5
WITHERSDANE 269 F8
Withersdane Cotts
  TN25 . . . . .238 A2
Witherston Way SE9. . .30 A5
WITHYHAM 311 A3
Withyham Rd TN3. . . .312 B9
Witley Wlk CT16. . . . . .278 B7
WITTERSHAM 359 D3
Wittersham CE Prim Sch
  TN30. . . . . .359 D2
Wittersham Cl ME5. . . .97 B5
Wittersham Ho 2 BR5 .54 D1
Wittersham Rd TN31. .368 B5
Wittersham Rd
  Iden TN31. . . . . .368 D7
  Stone in Oxney TN30 . .360 C3
  Wittersham, Potman's Heath
   TN17, TN30. . . . . . . .358 D4
  Wittersham TN30 . . . .359 C5
Wittersham Road Sta★
  TN17. . . . . .358 D6
Wivenhoe TN23 . . . . . .299 E5
Wivenhoe Cl ME8 . . . . .66 A2
Wixom Ho SE3 . . . . . . .11 C3
Wodehouse Cl ME20. .127 F4
Wodehouse Rd DA1. . . .16 A3
Woldham Pl BR2 . . . . . .52 C5
Woldham Rd BR2. . . . . .52 C5
Wolds Dr BR6 . . . . .86 A6
Wolfe Cl BR2. . . . . .52 A3
Wolfe Cres SE7. . . . . . . .1 D1
Wolfe Cl CT14. . . . . . . .215 D3
Wolfe Rd ME16. . . . . . .161 B2
Wolf Ho ME4 . . . . .64 B8
Wolf's Cnr RH8. . . . . . .183 B6
Wolf's Hill RH8. . . . . . .183 A4
Wolf's Rd RH8. . . . . . . .183 B5
Wolf's Row RH8. . . . . .183 B5
Wolfs Wood RH8 . . . . .183 A3
Wollaston Cl ME8 . . . . .98 D3
Wollaston Rd CT14 . . .215 D4
Wolseley Ave CT5 . . . . .76 A4
Wolseley Pl 4 TN24. .268 B3
Wolseley Rd TN4 . . . . .286 C7
Wolseley Terr TN29 . . .376 C5
Wolsey Cres 3 DA9 . . .17 A1
Wolsey Ct SE9. . . . . . . .11 C1
Wolsey Mews BR6. . . . .86 F5
Wolsley Cl DA1. . . . . . .14 E2
Wolsley Ho DA1 . . . . . .14 E2
Wolvercote Rd SE2. . . . .3 D4
WOLVERTON 29 F2
Wombell Gdns DA11. . .36 E6
WOMBWELL PARK. 36 D6
Women's Land Army Mus
  The★ CT15 . . . . .309 E5
WOMENSWOLD 210 D2
Wood Ave CT19 . . . . . .335 E7
Woodberry Dr ME10. . .102 C3
Woodberry Flats CT10. .84 A3
Woodberry Gr DA5 . . . .32 D5
Woodbine Cotts ME2 . .94 E5
Woodbine La DA15. . . . .30 E7
Woodbridge Dr ME15. .161 F1
Woodbrook TN27. . . . .234 D7
Woodbrook Rd SE2. . . .13 B8
Woodbury Cl
  Biggin Hill TN16 . . . . .118 D2
  2 Royal Tunbridge Wells
   TN4 . . . . .286 A5
Woodbury Gdns SE12. . .29 B4
Woodbury La TN30 . . .345 A7
Woodbury Park Gdns
  TN4 . . . . .286 B5
Woodbury Park Rd
  TN4 . . . . .286 B5
Woodbury Rd
  Chatham ME5 . . . . .96 F1
  Hawkhurst TN18. . . . .341 A2
WOODCHURCH Margate 81 F3
  Tenterden 326 A2
Woodchurch CE Prim Sch
  TN26. . . . . .326 A2
Woodchurch Cl
  Chatham ME5 . . . . .97 B5
  Sidcup DA14 . . . . .31 A5
Woodchurch Cotts CT7 81 F4
Woodchurch Cres ME8 .65 C2
Woodchurch Ct 11 BR5 54 C4
Woodchurch Dr BR1 . . .29 D2
Woodchurch Ho ME8. . .65 C2
Woodchurch Rd
  Appledore Heath
   TN26 . . . . .347 C4
  Margate CT7, CT9. . . . .82 A5
  Shadoxhurst TN26. . . .299 A1
  Tenterden TN30 . . . . . .345 D8
  Westgate on Sea CT7. . .81 F4
Woodchurch Windmill★
  TN26. . . . . .326 A3
Wood Cl Ditton ME20. .160 E8
  Joyden's Wood DA5. . . .32 E5
Woodclyffe Dr BR7. . . .53 A7
Woodcock Gdns CT18 307 A4
Woodcock La
  Grafty Green ME17. . . .231 E5
  Iden Green TN17 . . . . .342 E3
Woodcocks
  Headcorn TN27. . . . . .262 D5
  Newham E16. . . . . .1 D8
Woodcote CT5 . . . . .75 D1
Woodcote Dr BR6. . . . . .53 D7

Wood Cottage La
  CT19 . . . . .334 D7
Woodcourt CT10 . . . . .101 E2
Woodcroft SE9. . . . . . . .29 F5
Woodcut ME14. . . . . . .162 B8
Wood Dr Bromley BR7. . .29 E2
  Sevenoaks TN13 . . . . . .153 F1
Wood End BR8. . . . . . . .55 C5
Woodend Rd DA1 . . . . .14 F3
Woodfield Ave
  Folkestone CT19. . . . .334 E7
  Gravesend DA11. . . . . .37 B6
  Tonbridge TN11. . . . . .221 E5
Woodfield Ct CT19 . . .334 E7
Woodfield Rd TN9. . . .254 B8
Woodfields TN13 . . . . .153 E4
Woodfield Way ME3. . . .40 E4
Woodford Ave CT11,
  . . . . .83 D1
Woodford Cl CT7. . . . . .81 A7
Woodford Gr 9 ME9. .159 B3
Woodford Ho 13 SE18. .12 B8
Woodford Rd ME16. . . .161 B2
Woodgate CT4 . . . . . . .208 E3
Woodgate Cl ME13 . . .138 C8
Woodgate Cl ME13 . . .171 E7
Woodgate La ME9. . . . .100 C2
Woodgate Rd ME19. . .126 D4
Woodgates Cl TN26 . .324 D7
Woodgate Way TN9,
  . . . . .254 E7
Woodgers Gr BR8. . . . . .55 F7
Woodget Cl E1 . . . . . . .1 E7
Woodgrove Prim Sch
  ME10 . . . . .101 D3
Woodhall Terr ME11. . .46 A5
Woodhatch Cl E6 . . . . .1 E8
Woodhayes BR7. . . . . . .30 B2
Woodhead Dr BR6. . . . .86 E8
Woodhill SE18 . . . . . . .1 E2
Wood Hill CT7. . . . . . . .142 E6
Woodhill Pk TN2 . . . . .287 C6
Woodhill Prim Sch SE18 .1 E2
Woodhurst ME5 . . . . . .96 D4
Woodhurst Ave BR5. . . .53 C3
Woodhurst Cl ME2 . . . .62 B2
Woodhurst Rd SE2 . . . . .3 A2
Woodington Cl SE9. . . .12 A1
Woodknoll Dr BR7 . . . . .52 F8
Wood La Dartford DA2. . .34 F4
  East End TN17. . . . . . .322 C3
  Kingsnorth TN23. . . . .300 D3
  Woodland. 304 F8
Woodland Ave
  Aylesham CT3 . . . . . . .210 E5
  Birchington CT7. . . . . .81 B6
  Hartley DA3. . . . . .58 F5
Woodland Cl
  Crabble CT17 . . . . . . .277 E2
  New Barn DA3 . . . . . . .59 C6
  Royal Tunbridge Wells
   TN4 . . . . .286 C7
  West Malling ME19. . . .159 A8
Woodland Cotts CT18 .305 B7
Woodland Dr
  Marlpit Hill TN8. . . . . .217 D3
  Minster (Sheppey) ME12 .47 B7
Woodland Rd
  Herne Bay CT6 . . . . . . .76 B2
  Lyminge CT18 . . . . . . .304 E8
  Royal Tunbridge Wells
   TN4 . . . . .286 C7
Woodland Rise TN15 . .154 E4
WOODLANDS 123 C6
Woodlands Bexley DA6 . .14 B2
  Blean CT2. . . . . .141 F7
  Chatham ME5 . . . . .97 A2
  Coxheath ME17. . . . . .194 B3
  Cranbrook TN17 . . . . .320 D6
  Hernhill ME13 . . . . . . .140 C7
  Hurst Green TN19. . . .354 A2
  Paddock Wood TN12. .256 F7
  Pembury TN2 . . . . . . .287 F7
  Royal Tunbridge Wells
   TN4 . . . . .254 A2
Woodlands Ave
  Sidcup DA15. . . . . .30 E7
  Snodland ME6. . . . . . .127 F8
Woodlands Cl
  Bromley BR1. . . . . .52 F7
  Maidstone ME14. . . . . .162 B7
  Peasmarsh TN31. . . . .367 C2
  Swanley BR8. . . . . .55 F7
  Teston ME18. . . . . . . .193 B8
Woodlands Ct ME5 . . . .96 F3
Woodlands Dr CT21 . . .334 A4
Woodlands Farm DA16 .12 C5
Woodlands Inf & Jun Schs
  TN10. . . . . .222 C6
Woodlands La CT12. . . .38 E1
Woodlands Par ME20. .160 D8
Woodlands Pk CT3. . . . .32 D4
Woodlands Prim Sch
  ME7 . . . . .64 F4
Woodlands Rd
  Adisham CT3 . . . . .210 C8
  Ashford TN24 . . . . . . .268 F2
  Bexley DA7 . . . . .13 E4
  Bromley BR1. . . . . .52 F7
  Ditton ME20 . . . . .160 D8
  Gillingham ME7. . . . . .64 F4
  Orpington BR6 . . . . . . .87 A4
  Sittingbourne ME10 . .102 B3
  Tonbridge TN9. . . . . . .254 A7
Woodlands Rise BR8 . .55 F7
Woodlands Terr
  Crockenhill ME6 . . . . . .55 B3
  Gillingham ME7. . . . . .64 F3
Woodlands The BR6. . . .87 B4

Woodlands View TN14. .88 A1
Woodland Terr SE7 ..... 1 E2
Woodland View TN30. .359 E4
Woodland Way
Bidborough TN4 ...... 253 D3
Broadstairs CT10 ..... 51 G1
Canterbury CT1 ...... 142 C2
Dymchurch TN29. ..... 353 A5
Erith SE2 .... 3 D2
Maidstone ME14 ...... 162 B7
Orpington BR5 .... 53 C4
Swanscombe DA9. ..... 17 A3
Woodnesborough CT13 180 C6
Woodlark Rd ME4 .... 41 B1
Woodlawn St CT5 .... 74 D2
Woodlea Ashford TN24 268 C3
Leybourne ME19 ...... 127 F2
New Barn DA3 .... 59 C6
Woodleas ME16 ...... 160 F2
Woodley Rd BR6 ...... 87 C8
Wood Lodge Gdns BR1 .29 E1
Wood Lodge Grange
TN13 .... 154 C5
Woodman Ave CT5 .... 75 E3
Woodman Par 4 E16 . .2 A5
Woodman St E16. ..... 2 A5
Woodmere SE9 .... 29 F7
Woodmount BR8. ..... 55 D2
WOODNESBOROUGH 180 C6
Woodnesborough La
CT13 .... 180 B3
Woodnesborough Rd
CT13 .... 180 E7
Woodpecker Cl 2
TN8 .... 217 D3
Woodpecker Dr ME9 ..68 E4
Woodpecker Glade
ME8 .... 98 D6
Woodpecker Rd
Larkfield ME20 ...... 127 F1
Woolwich SE28 .... 3 C6
Wood Pl DA14 ...... 31 A3
Wood Point 10 E16 ... 1 A8
Wood Rd
Biggin Hill TN16 ..... 118 C1
Hythe CT21 .... 333 B1
Wood Retreat SE18. ..12 D7
Wood Ride BR5 ...... 53 E5
Woodrow SE18 .... 1 F2
Woodrow Chase CT6 .. 77 A1
Woodruff Cl ME8 ..... 66 D4
Woodrush Pl ME4 .... 41 B1
Woodsgate Way TN2 .287 B6
WOOD'S GREEN 336 F8
Woods Green Cotts
TN5 ....336 F7
Woods Hill CT4. ..... 239 C5
Woodshole Cotts ME9. .68 D1
Woodside Ashford TN23 299 E6
Boughton Street ME13 . 140 B2
Gillingham ME8. ...... 98 C6
Kilndown TN17 .... 317 F2
Orpington BR6 .... 87 B5
Vigo Village DA13 .... 125 F8
Woodside Ave
Chartham CT4 .... 173 D2
Chislehurst BR7 ..... 30 C3
Woodside Cl
Crayford DA7 .... 14 D3
Pembury TN2 .... 287 E6
Temple Ewell CT16 ... 277 E4
Woodside Cotts ME13 .140 B2
Woodside Cres DA15 ...30 E5
Woodside Dr DA2 .....32 E4
Woodside Gdns ME10 101 D2
Woodside Gn ME3. ....40 B7
WOODSIDE GREEN ..199 F8
Woodside La DA5 .....13 D1
Woodside Par DA15 ...30 E5
Woodside Rd
Bromley BR1 ....52 E4
Crayford DA7 .... 14 D3
Maidstone ME15 ..... 195 C7
Pembury TN2 .... 287 E6
Rusthall TN4 .... 285 D4
Sevenoaks TN13 .... 154 B4
Sidcup DA15 ....30 E5
Sturry CT2 ....143 F7

Sundridge TN14 ...... 152 E3
Tonbridge TN9. ...... 254 B7
Woodside Sch DA17 .... 4 B2
Woods Ley CT3. ...... 147 D2
Wood's Pl CT17 .....278 B2
Wood St Chatham ME7. ..64 A6
Cuxton ME2 ....62 B2
Dover CT16. .... 310 D8
9 Grays RM17. ......18 C3
Lynsted ME9 .... 135 F8
Royal Tunbridge Wells
TN1 .... 286 B4
Sheerness ME12. ......28 C2
Swanley Village BR8. ..56 D8
Woods Terr DA12. .....37 C5
WOODSTOCK 134 E6
Woodstock Cl DA5 ....31 F7
Woodstock Ct SE12. ...11 A1
Woodstock Rd
Deal CT14 .... 215 C4
Rochester ME2 ....63 A7
Sittingbourne ME10 .. 101 E1
Woodstock Way TN24 268 C6
Woodvale Ave CT5 ... 109 C8
Woodvale Ct BR1. .....52 B8
Wood View CT3 ...... 111 E5
Woodview Cl BR6 .....86 C8
Wood View Cl TN15 ...90 E3
Woodview Cres TN11. .221 F5
Woodview Rd BR8. ....55 D7
Woodview Rise ME2 ..39 F1
Woodville SE3 ....11 B6
Woodville Cl
Canterbury CT1. ..... 174 D6
Eltham SE12 ....11 A2
Woodville Gr 2 DA16 . .13 A4
Woodville Halls 14
DA12 ....37 B8
Woodville Pl DA12. ....37 B8
Woodville Rd
Maidstone ME15. .... 162 A2
Ramsgate CT12 ....83 C1
Woodville St 15 SE18. ..1 E2
Woodward Terr DA9 ..16 E1
Wood Way BR6. ......86 A8
Woodyates Rd
Eltham SE12 ....29 B8
Lewisham SE12. ......11 A1
Wood Yd CT14 ...... 215 D6
Woolacombe Rd SE3 ..11 C5
Woolage Green CT4. .243 F8
WOOLAGE VILLAGE. .210 F1
Woolaston CT14 ..... 161 F1
Woolbrook Cl ME8 ....66 B2
Woolbrook Rd DA11. ...14 E1
Woolcomber St CT16 .310 E7
Wooldeys Rd ME8 .....65 F2
Woolett Rd ME10 .... 101 C5
Woolf Cl SE28 ....3 B5
Woolf Coll CT2 ....142 E5
Woolf Wlk RM18 .....19 C5
Woollets Cl CT6 ......76 C3
Woollett Cl DA1 ......15 A3
Woollett St ME14 .... 162 A5
Woolley Cl TN4 ...... 253 F1
Woolley Rd
Maidstone ME15 ..... 195 F7
Royal Tunbridge Wells
TN4 ....253 F1
Woolmer Dr TN24 ... 301 A7
Woolpack Cnr TN27 .. 323 A7
Woolpack Cotts TN27. 323 A7
Woolpack Hill TN25 .. 302 D5
Woolreeds Rd TN23 .. 300 A7
WOOLWICH 2 B3
Woolwich Arsenal Sta
SE18. ....2 B2
Woolwich Church St
SE18 ....1 E3
Woolwich High St ME5 ..97 A7
Woolwich Comm SE18. .12 A8
Woolwich Dockyard Ind
Est SE18 ....1 E3
Woolwich Dockyard Sta
SE18. ....1 F2
Woolwich High St SE18. .2 A3
Woolwich Manorway
E16 ....2 B4
Woolwich Manor Way
E6 ....2 A7
Woolwich New Rd SE18 . 2 B2

Woolwich Polytechnic Sch
SE28. ....3 A5
Woolwich Rd
Bexley DA7 ....14 A4
Erith SE2 ....3 E1
Greenwich SE10, SE7 . . .1 C2
Woolwich Tramshed The ★
13 SE18 ....2 B2
WOOTON 243 C1
Wootton Cl CT4 ..... 207 A4
Wootton Dr CT4 .... 207 A4
Wootton Gn ME8 .....65 D3
Wootton Ho SE9 ......12 D1
Wootton La CT15, CT4 . 275 C7
Wopsle Cl ME1 ....96 D7
Worcester Ave ME19 . 159 A2
Worcester Cl
Faversham ME13 .... 138 E6
Istead Rise DA13 .....36 F1
Minster (Sheppey) ME12 . .47 C6
Rochester ME2 ....17 B3
Swanscombe DA9. ....17 B3
Worcester Dr ME14. . 162 A4
Worcester Gr CT10 ...83 F6
Worcester La CT3 .... 175 F7
Worcester Rd ME15 . 195 D7
Wordsworth Cl
Chatham ME5 ....97 C7
Tilbury RM18. ....19 C5
Wordsworth Gdns CT3 210 F6
Wordsworth Ho 15
SE18 ....12 A8
Wordsworth Rd
Bexley DA16 ....12 E6
Maidstone ME14 .... 162 B7
Wordsworth Way
Dartford DA1 ....16 A3
New Hythe ME20 ... 128 A4
Workhouse La
Chartway Street
ME17 ....197 A1
Coxheath ME15. ..... 194 C4
Sutton Valence ME17 . . 230 A8
Workhouse Rd
Ryarsh ME19. ....126 F4
Throwley ME13. ...... 169 F1
World's End ME9. .... 136 E7
Worlds End La BR6 ....87 B3
Worleys Dr BR6 ......86 D6
Wormdale Hill ME9. .100 B3
Wormdale Rd ME9 .. 100 B4
WORMSHILL 166 A7
WORMS HILL 291 B5
Worsenden TN27. ... 294 E1
WORSENDEN GREEN 294 D2
Worsfold Ct 5 ME15 . 162 A1
Worships Hill TN13 .. 153 E4
WORTEN 266 F3
WORTH 181 B4
Worth Cl BR6 ....86 E6
Worthgate Pl 2 CT1 . 174 F7
Worthing Cl RM17 ....17 E8
Worthington St 11 CT16,
CT17 ....310 D8
Worth La CT20 ...... 334 E3
Worth Prim Sch CT14 . 181 B5
Wotton Cl ME15 ..... 195 E5
Wotton Gn BR5. ......54 D5
Wotton Rd TN23. .....19 C5
Wotton Trad Est TN23 . 300 B6
WOULDHAM 95 D5
Wouldham CE Prim Sch
ME1 ....95 C5
Wouldham Ct ME1 ....95 C5
Wouldham Rd
Grays RM17, RM20. ...17 E8
Rochester ME1 ....62 E1
Wouldham Terr 3 BR5 54 B6
Wraightsfield Ave
TN29 ....366 D8
Wraik Hill CT5. ...... 108 C5
Wrangleden Cl ME15 . 195 E5
Wrangleden Rd ME15. 195 E5
Wrangling La DA13. ...93 F3
Wreight Ct ME13 .... 105 B1
Wrekin Rd SE18. .....12 C7
Wren Cl Larkfield ME20 .127 F1
Orpington BR5 ....54 D6
Wren Ind Est ME15 .. 195 F4
Wren Path SE28 ....2 D4
Wren Rd DA14. ....31 C5

Wrens Croft DA11 ....36 E4
Wren's Cross ME15 .. 162 A3
Wrens Ct ME9 ...... 134 A8
Wrens Rd ME9 ...... 134 A7
Wrentham Ave CT6. ..76 B2
Wren Way ME5. ......97 B6
Wren Wlk RM18 ......19 B7
Wricklemarsh Rd SE3 . .11 B6
Wright Cl Gillingham ME8 65 C2
Swanscombe DA10. ...17 D1
Wrights Cl TN30 .... 345 A4
Wright's Way ME12. ..71 C8
WROTHAM 124 F7
Wrotham Ave 20 CT10 . .84 B4
WROTHAM HEATH . 126 A1
Wrotham Hill Rd TN15 125 A6
Wrotham Rd
Bexley DA16 ....13 C6
Borough Green TN15 .. 157 A8
Broadstairs CT10 .....84 B4
Gravesend DA11, DA13 . .37 A4
Meopham Station DA13 . .60 A3
Wrotham Road Prim Sch
13 DA11 ....37 B8
Wrotham Sch TN15 ...25 E5
Wrotham Water La ME19,
TN15 ....125 E5
Wrotham Water Rd TN15,
ME19 ....125 C4
Wrottesley Rd SE18 ..12 C8
Wrott & Hill Ct DA4. ..57 B8
Wroxham Rd SE28. ....3 D6
Wulfred Way TN15 .. 123 B5
Wyatt Cl TN15 ...... 156 F7
Wyatt Ho 1 ME2 .....63 A7
Wyatt Pl ME2. ....63 A7
Wyatt Rd DA1 ....14 F4
Wyatt St ME14. ..... 162 A4
Wyborne Prim Sch SE9 30 B7
Wybourne Rise TN2 . 314 B8
Wybournes La ME23. ..23 C3
Wych Elm Way CT21. 353 E8
Wycherley Cres CT16. 278 B4
Wycliffe Cl DA16 .....12 F6
Wycliffe Ho 6 DA11 . .36 F7
Wycliffe Row DA11. ..36 F7
Wycombe Cl SE3 .....11 A7
Wydeville Manor Rd
SE12 ....29 B4
WYE 237 F1
Wye Bsns Pk TN25 .. 237 E3
Wye Cl BR6 ....53 F2
Wye Gdns CT9. ....51 F2
Wye Gn CT6 ....76 F3
Wye National Nature
Reserve ★ TN25 ... 270 D7
Wye Rd
Borough Green TN15 . 157 A8
Boughton Lees TN25. 236 F3
Gravesend DA12. .....37 D6
Tonbridge TN10. .... 222 C5
Wye Sta TN25 ...... 237 D2
Wyfold Ho 10 SE2 .....3 D4
Wykeham Cl
Gravesend DA12 .....37 E2
Rushenden ME11 .....45 F3
Wykeham Cotts ME17 194 F2
Wykeham Ct BR7. ....30 E2
Wykeham Gr ME17 .. 197 A7
Wykeham Rd ME10 .. 102 B4
Wykeham St ME2 .....63 B8
Wyke Manor Rd ME14 162 A4
Wyles Rd ME4 ....63 E2
Wyles St ME7 ....64 C7
Wylie Ho ME3 ....40 F6
Wylie Rd ME3 ....41 D6
Wyllie Ct ME10 ...... 101 E7
Wyncham Ave DA15 ..30 E7
Wyncroft Cl BR1 .....52 F6
Wyndcliff Rd SE3, SE7. .11 B8
Wyndham Ave
Leigh TN11 .... 220 F1
Margate CT9. ....51 B2
Wyndham Cl
Leigh TN11 .... 220 F1
Orpington BR6 ....53 C1
Wyndham Rd
Chatham ME4 ....63 E2
Dover CT17. .... 310 B8
Sevenoaks TN13 .... 153 D4
Stanford TN25. ...... 304 B1
Wynd The TN27 ..... 201 D1
Wyndy La TN25. .... 267 F4

Wynford Gr BR5. .....54 B6
Wynford Pl DA17 .....14 A8
Wynford Way SE9 ....29 F5
Wynn Ellis Ho CT5. ...74 E3
Wynn Rd CT5. ....75 A2
Wynn's Ave DA15. ....13 A2
Wytchlings The ME17. 197 D2
Wytherling Cl ME14 . 162 F5
Wythes Cl BR1 ....52 F7
Wythes Rd E16. ....1 E5
Wythfield Rd SE9. .....11 F1
Wyvern Cl Dartford DA1. .33 C8
Orpington BR6 ....87 B7
Sittingbourne ME10 .. 101 E7
Snodland ME6. ...... 128 A7
Wyvern Ho 3 RM17 ..18 B8
Wyvern Sch The TN23. 267 E1
Wyvern Way TN24 .. 268 E3
Wyvill Cl ME8 ....98 E5

Y

YALDING 192 F1
Yalding Cl ME2. ....40 B1
Yalding Gr BR5. ......54 D5
Yalding Hill ME18 ... 193 A3
Yalding Organic Ctr ★
ME18 ....225 F7
Yalding St Peter & St Paul
CE Prim Sch ME18 .. 193 A1
Yalding Sta ME18 ... 192 D1
Yantlet Dr ME2. ......62 C7
Yardhurst Gdns CT9. .51 F3
Yardley Cl TN9 ...... 222 D3
Yardley Ho CT10 .....84 B7
Yardley Park Rd TN9 . 222 D3
Yard The Barham CT4 . 209 F1
Chatham ME5 ....97 B3
Yarnton Way SE2, DA18 . .3 E4
Yarrow Cl CT10. ......84 A3
Yarrow Cres E6 ....1 E8
Yarrow Ct ME14 .... 162 F5
Yarrow Dr ME12 .....47 A5
Yarrow Rd ME5 ....96 F4
Yateley St SE18 ....1 D3
Yates Cl TN31 ...... 374 A2
Yaugher La ME9 ......99 C3
Yeates Dr ME10 .... 102 A8
Yellow Sands ME12. ..73 E5
YELSTED 99 A1
Yelsted La
Chatham ME14 ..... 130 D7
Yelsted ME9 ....99 A1
Yelsted Rd ME9 .... 132 A7
Yeoman Cl E6. ....2 B6
Yeoman Ct ME14 .... 163 B3
Yeoman Dr ME7 ......64 F1
Yeoman Gdns
Ashford TN24 ...... 301 B8
Paddock Wood TN12 . 256 F6
Yeoman Ho ME1 ......63 D4
Yeoman La ME14 .... 163 B4
Yeoman Pk ME15 ... 163 A2
Yeoman's Mdws TN13 154 A1
Yeomans Sq TN23 ... 299 D8
Yeoman Way ME15 .. 163 A2
Yeovil Cl BR6 ....86 E8
Yester Dr BR7. ....29 E1
Yester Pk BR7. ....29 F2
Yester Rd BR7. ....29 F1
Yevele Cl ME11. ......46 A5
Yew Cl TN23 .... 267 E2
Yew Hedges ME13. .. 168 E4
Yew Rd ME3. ....41 E3
Yews The DA12. ......37 D7
Yew Tree Cl
Aylesford ME20. .... 128 E1
Bexley DA16 ....13 A6
Broadstairs CT10 .....83 D4
Chatham ME5 ....97 C1
Deal CT14 .... 215 A4
New Barn DA3 ....59 D7
Sevenoaks TN13 .... 153 D4

Yew Tree Cotts
Groombridge TN3 ...312 F8
Halstead TN14 ...... 120 F1
Sandling ME14 ...... 129 F1
Yewtree Cross CT18. 305 C8
Yew Tree Farm CT3 . 212 A8
Yew Tree Gdns
Birchington CT7 ......81 A7
Fordwich CT2 .... 144 A4
YEWTREE GREEN .. 258 B1
Yew Tree Green Rd
TN12 ....258 A1
Yewtree Ho 2 ME1 ..63 D4
Yewtree Ind Est ME20. 128 D2
Yew Tree Mews
Deal CT14 .... 215 A3
Westerham TN16 ... 184 D8
Yew Tree Pk ME17 .. 200 F1
Yew Tree Pl ME7. .....98 B1
Yew Tree Rd
Royal Tunbridge Wells
TN4 ....286 B8
St Mary's Bay TN29 . 365 F3
Yoakes La TN29 .... 363 F1
Yoakley Sq CT9 ......82 F8
Yoke Cl ME2 ....63 B8
Yokosuka Way ME7 ..65 A7
Yolande Gdns SE9. ...11 E2
Yopps Gn TN15 ..... 156 E1
YOPPS GREEN 156 E1
York & Albany Cl CT14 215 B1
York Ave
18 Broadstairs CT10 ...84 B4
Chatham ME5 ....96 F3
Gillingham ME7. ......64 C4
Sidcup DA15 ....30 F6
York Cl Herne Bay CT6 ..76 D4
Newham E6. ....1 F7
York Hill ME5 ....64 C2
York Ho 10 CT17. ... 310 D7
Yorkland Ave DA16 ..12 F3
YORKLETTS 107 F2
York Mews CT19 .... 334 E2
York Par CT10. ....222 C6
York Pl RM17. ....18 A8
York Rd Ashford TN24 . 268 D5
Biggin Hill TN16 .... 150 B8
Canterbury CT1. .... 174 E7
Dartford DA1 ....33 F8
Deal CT14 .... 215 D4
Gravesend DA12. .....37 C5
Herne Bay CT6 ....76 D5
Maidstone ME15. .... 162 C2
Northfleet DA11. .....36 D8
Rochester ME1 ....63 C3
Royal Tunbridge Wells
TN1 ....286 A4
Tonbridge TN10. .... 222 D5
**York Rise BR6. ....86 A8
York Road Jun Sch** 4
DA1 ....33 F8
York St Broadstairs CT10 84 B4
Dover CT16, CT17. .. 310 D7
Ramsgate CT11 ..... 117 E6
York Street Rdbt CT16,
CT17 ....310 D7
York Terr Bexley DA8. .14 C6
Birchington CT7 ......81 B7
Youens Pl ME3 ....39 B3
Young Cl CT14 ...... 215 B6
Young Rd E16. ....1 C7
Young's Pl CT15. .... 308 F5
Ypres Ct CT1. .... 143 D1
Ypres Dr ME10 ......68 F1

Z

Zambra Way TN15 .. 154 F7
Zangwill Rd SE18, SE3. .11 D6
Zarena Ct 8 CT20. .. 334 F3
Zealand Ho SE18 .....1 E2
Zealand Rd CT1 ..... 174 F6
Zelah Rd BR5 ....54 C2
Zetland Ave ME7 .....64 C2
Zillah Gdns ME8. .....98 C6
Zion Pl Gravesend DA12. .37 B8
Margate CT9. ....50 J3
Zion St TN15 .... 154 F6